H Volume 9

The World Book Encyclopedia

World Book, Inc.

a Scott Fetzer company

Chicago London Sydney Toronto

The World Book Encyclopedia

Copyright © 1988, U.S.A.
by
World Book, Inc.

Hh

H is the eighth letter of our alphabet. It was also a letter in the alphabet used by the Semites, who once lived in Syria and Palestine. The Semites named the letter *cheth,* and adapted an Egyptian *hieroglyphic,* or picture symbol, for a twisted hank of rope to represent the letter. The ancient Greeks later took the letter into their alphabet and named it *eta.* They gave it the sound of long *e.* The Romans borrowed the letter from the Greeks, and gave it its final capital form. They also gave it its present sound of *h.* See **Alphabet.**

Uses. *H* or *h* ranks as about the ninth most frequently used letter in books, newspapers, and other printed material in English. In abbreviations, *H* may stand for *Hawaii* and *Hindustan* in geography. *H* also represents *His* or *Her* in the abbreviation *H. M., His* or *Her Majesty.* In chemistry, *H* stands for the element *hydrogen,* and in physics it represents the intensity of the magnetic field. *H* means *henry,* the unit of induction, in electricity. The abbreviation for *harbor* is *h; h.c.l.* means *high cost of living;* and *h.p.* means *horsepower.*

Pronunciation. In English, people pronounce *h* by shaping their lips for the sound of the vowel that follows it. Their vocal cords are apart. In words such as *hail, hat,* and *haste,* a slight impulse of breath normally crosses the vocal cords. But when the *h* sound occurs between two vowels, as in the words *behind* or *ahead,* the *h* sound may be voiced. *H* is silent in words such as *hour* and *honest.* See **Pronunciation.**   Marianne Cooley

Development of the letter H

The ancient Egyptians, about 3000 B.C., wrote a symbol that represented a twisted length of rope.

The Semites modified the Egyptian symbol about 1500 B.C. They called it *cheth.*

The Phoenicians, about 1000 B.C., made the letter with three crossbars.

The Greeks added the letter to their alphabet about 600 B.C. They named the letter *eta.*

The Romans borrowed the letter from the Greeks about A.D. 114. They gave the H the shape and sound we use today.

The small letter h first appeared during the A.D. 300's as a rounded letter. By about 1500, the letter had developed its present shape.

A.D. 300   1500   Today

Special ways of expressing the letter H

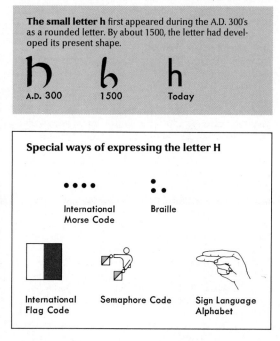

International Morse Code

Braille

International Flag Code

Semaphore Code

Sign Language Alphabet

Common forms of the letter H

Handwritten letters vary from person to person. *Manuscript* (printed) letters, *left,* have simple curves and straight lines. Cursive letters, *right,* have flowing lines.

Roman letters have small finishing strokes called *serifs* that extend from the main strokes. The type face shown above is Baskerville. The italic form appears at the right.

Sans-serif letters are also called *gothic letters.* They have no serifs. The type face shown above is called Futura. The italic form of Futura appears at the right.

Computer letters have special shapes. Computers can "read" these letters either optically or by means of the magnetic ink with which the letters may be printed.

How habeas corpus protects our liberty

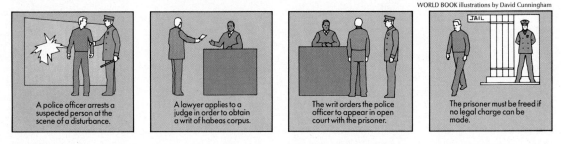

A police officer arrests a suspected person at the scene of a disturbance.

A lawyer applies to a judge in order to obtain a writ of habeas corpus.

The writ orders the police officer to appear in open court with the prisoner.

The prisoner must be freed if no legal charge can be made.

H-bomb. See Nuclear weapon.

Habakkuk, *HAB uh kuhk* or *huh BAK uhk,* **Book of,** is a book of the Old Testament, or Hebrew Bible. The book is named for Habakkuk, an Israelite prophet. A reference to the Chaldeans in the book indicates that Habakkuk lived about 600 B.C.

The Book of Habakkuk is only 56 verses long. It consists of two parts. The prophecies appear in the form of laments and responses in Chapters 1 and 2. Chapter 3 is a hymn. In one of his prophecies, Habakkuk asks why the innocent and good should suffer with the wicked. God answers, "The just shall live by his faith" (Hab. 2:4). Habakkuk closes with a hymn on God's victory over His enemies. Some scholars think the last chapter was composed for use in temple worship. The book formed the basis of an important ancient Biblical commentary found in the Dead Sea Scrolls (see **Dead Sea Scrolls**).

Eric M. Meyers

Habana, La. See Havana.

Habeas corpus, *HAY bee uhs KAWR puhs,* is a legal term which, in its original Latin, means *you are ordered to have the body.* If a person has been arrested or is held by police, a lawyer or friend can obtain a *writ of habeas corpus.* This writ orders the police to produce the arrested person in court. The court then decides if the police have sufficient reason to hold the prisoner.

The writ is one of the basic guarantees of personal freedom in English and American law. It prevents unjust or wrongful imprisonment or detention by legal authorities. No person can be denied the writ except in times of public danger or when martial law is in force.

In 1679, the Habeas Corpus Amendment Act was passed in England. The act strengthened the use of habeas corpus by stating that the Crown could not detain a prisoner against the wishes of Parliament and the courts. This concept of personal freedom has been carried over into the legal systems of the United States and Canada.

Besides its common use, the writ of habeas corpus has been used to free a wife who is held captive and mistreated by her husband. It has also been used when a child of divorced parents is held by one parent longer than the time allowed by the court.   Erwin N. Griswold

Haber-Bosch process. See Haber process.

Haber process, *HAH buhr,* is a commercial method of producing ammonia from nitrogen and hydrogen. Fritz Haber, a German chemist, developed the process and demonstrated it in 1909. He patented it in 1910. Another German chemist, Carl Bosch, later adapted the process for industrial use. It is also called the *Haber-Bosch process.*

In the Haber process, three parts of hydrogen unite with one part of nitrogen to form ammonia (NH_3). The process takes place at about 550° C and at 200 to 250 times atmospheric pressure. The nitrogen and hydrogen combine at the surface of a solid *catalyst,* a substance that speeds up the reaction. It consists mainly of iron, with small amounts of alumina and potassium oxide. All the hydrogen and nitrogen do not combine. The uncombined gases are recirculated through the process.

Almost all modern ammonia plants use the Haber process or variations of it. Most early ammonia plants that used the Haber method obtained hydrogen from *water gas* and nitrogen from *producer gas.* Water gas and producer gas are made from hot coke (see **Gas** [How gas is manufactured]). Today, many ammonia plants obtain hydrogen and nitrogen from other sources. Hydrogen may be obtained from natural gas, and nitrogen may come from the distillation of liquid air (see **Liquid air**). Other modifications of the process include changes in the composition of the catalyst and the temperature and pressure used.   Kathleen C. Taylor

Habit is something a person learns to do over and over again without thinking about how to do it. Many everyday actions are habits. Imagine how difficult it would be to walk down the street if you had to think of every action needed to take every step. A habit is different from an *instinct.* An instinct is behavior that is inborn, instead of learned (see **Instinct**).

How we learn habits. Most habits begin as actions that a person is aware of. The more the person performs an action, the easier it becomes. Strong habits become automatic, and require little or no thought.

Psychologists generally agree that a *stimulus* (something that starts an action) must be present each time the habit is carried out. For example, a red traffic light is a stimulus to an experienced automobile driver. It triggers the habit of pressing the brake pedal. To learn this habit, each new driver must practice under actual traffic conditions, learning to press the brake pedal when the light is red.

Many psychologists believe that people will learn a habit only if it benefits them. Psychologists call this satisfaction a *reward* or a *reinforcement.* If the habit satisfies people, they tend to keep it. When a habit offers no reward or becomes unpleasant, they may *break* (discard) it. For example, some people get pleasure from smoking. Because of the pleasure (reward), smoking becomes a habit. If the habit becomes unpleasant (no longer brings a reward), a person may stop smoking.

Psychologists who support the reward idea of habit formation disagree with an older idea. The older idea said that "paths" were made in the nervous system when an act was repeated. However, psychologists have taught rats habits and then cut their nervous systems at many points. Despite the cuts, the rats continued to perform the habits. This result suggests that the learning of habits does not depend on specific nerve connections and does not occur only in particular parts of the brain.

Kinds of habits. Some habits are simple and require only movements of the muscles. When approaching a door, a person grasps the doorknob. This action is called a *simple motor act.* The movement seems quite natural, but the person once had to learn this habit. A doorknob is a strange thing to a child when first encountered. The child may toy with the knob many times before learning to open the door by turning the knob.

Some habits are more than simple motor acts. They are thoughts and attitudes we have about things and people. Psychologists call them *habits of adjustment.* Some of these habits are "good" and others are "bad," depending on how they affect other people. We learn "good" habits to act as others expect us to act. Neat appearance and pleasant manners are considered good habits. A person may learn "bad" habits, thinking something can be gained from them. But such habits may be annoying to others.   Richard S. Lazarus

See also **Learning; Behavior.**

Habitat, *HAB uh tat,* is the kind of place in which a plant or animal usually lives in nature. Water lilies and desert cactus plants have different habitats. The habitat of deep-sea fishes is quite different from that of mountain goats. Various animals and plants can be kept alive outside their natural habitats if given special care in aquariums, zoos, or botanical gardens.

Plants and animals live where they can satisfy their needs. Every habitat limits the kinds of things that live there, and their numbers. Goldfish and pond plants require fresh water. On the other hand, the barnacles that cling to a ship must live in salt water. In some cases, creatures can adapt themselves to a changing habitat.

A single area may satisfy the needs of many kinds of plants and animals. These organisms that associate together in a common habitat form communities. Communities exist in various places, including (1) on the seashore, (2) in deserts, (3) in freshwater lakes, and (4) in tropical forests.   Lawrence C. Wit

See also **Animal** (Where animals live); **Plant** (Where plants live); **Ecology.**

Habsburg, *HAPS burg,* **House of,** was one of Europe's most famous royal families. The Habsburgs (also spelled *Hapsburg*) ruled the Holy Roman Empire for nearly 400 years. Members of the family occupied thrones in Europe from the 1200's to the early 1900's, except for a few years.

The name *Habsburg* comes from one of the family's first castles, the *Habichtsburg (Hawk's Castle),* built about 1020 in Switzerland. In 1273, Rudolf became the first member of the Habsburg family to be elected Holy Roman emperor. Three years later, he conquered Austria, which became the Habsburgs' new home. Beginning in 1438, family members were elected Holy Roman emperor almost without interruption until 1806.

In the late 1400's, Maximilian I greatly increased the family's power by arranging a number of marriages between Habsburgs and members of other royal houses. By 1519, his grandson Charles V had inherited many

kingdoms, including Spain and the Spanish empire in America. In 1522, Charles gave Austria to his younger brother Ferdinand. Through marriage, Ferdinand acquired Hungary and Bohemia four years later. Thus, after 1526, the Habsburgs consisted of two branches—a Spanish line headed by Charles's descendants, and an Austrian line descended from Ferdinand.

The Spanish branch lasted until 1700. Charles VI, the last male heir of the Austrian Habsburgs, died in 1740. In 1736, Charles's daughter Maria Theresa married Francis Stephen, Duke of Lorraine. As Francis I, he regained the throne of the Holy Roman Empire for the family in 1745. The descendants of Francis and Maria Theresa were Holy Roman emperors until 1806 and emperors of Austria from 1804 to 1918.   Charles W. Ingrao

Related articles in *World Book.* For information on Habsburg rule, see the *History* section in the articles **Austria; Belgium; Czechoslovakia; Germany; Hungary; Prague; Switzerland;** and **Vienna.** See also:

Charles (Holy Roman emperors)	Francis Joseph
Ferdinand II	Holy Roman Empire
Ferdinand III	Maria Theresa
Francis II (Holy Roman emperor)	Maximilian I

Hacienda, *hah see EHN duh* or *ah SYEHN dah,* is a large farm or country estate in Spanish America. In such countries as Mexico, most farms are called haciendas. The word *hacienda* may also refer to the main building on the estate. Many haciendas have adobe walls (see **Adobe**). Large wooden beams fastened with rawhide strips support a low, sloping tile roof. Haciendas are built for inside coolness and outdoor living. Shady verandas may surround three sides of a *patio* (open court). See also **Mexico** (Agriculture).   Bernard Lemann

Hackberry, also called *nettle tree,* is one of a group of trees related to the elms. The *hackberry* of the Eastern United States and the *sugarberry* of the Southeast are medium to large trees. *Netleaf hackberry* grows as a shrub or small tree in the Western States. Hackberries have smooth gray bark that often has corky warts or ridges. Their long-pointed leaves grow in two rows. They bear small round berries that can be eaten. Hackberry wood is yellowish and can be used for furniture. See also **Tree** (Familiar broadleaf and needleleaf trees [picture]).

Scientific classification. Hackberries are in the elm family, Ulmaceae. The eastern hackberry is genus *Celtis,* species *C. occidentalis.* Sugarberry is *C. laevigata.* Netleaf hackberry is *C. reticulata.*   Elbert L. Little, Jr.

Hackmatack. See **Larch.**

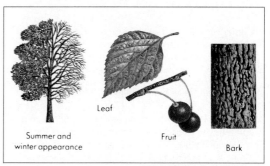

Leaf

Fruit

Summer and winter appearance

Bark

WORLD BOOK illustration by John D. Dawson
The hackberry bears small, round, edible berries.

Hackney. See **Horse** (table: Some types and breeds).

Hadassah, *huh DAH suh,* is an organization of Jewish women in the United States. It helps strengthen links with Israel, provides information about contemporary issues, and conducts educational programs for members and Jewish youth. Its official name is *Hadassah, The Women's Zionist Organization of America, Inc.*

Hadassah supports two medical facilities in Jerusalem. It also sponsors a high school and a community college in Israel and participates in land reclamation and development there. In addition, Hadassah contributes to *Youth Aliyah,* a program that provides day-care centers and other facilities for disadvantaged youth from Israel and for youngsters from other countries.

Hadassah is the Hebrew name of Queen Esther, whose story is told in the Old Testament. The organization was founded in New York City in 1912 by the social worker Henrietta Szold. It has about 370,000 members. Headquarters of Hadassah are at 50 West 58th Street, New York, NY 10019.   Critically reviewed by Hadassah

See also **Szold, Henrietta.**

Haddock, *HAD uhk,* is an important food fish that belongs to the codfish family. A black line along each of its sides and a black spot just back of its head distinguishes the haddock from other codfish. The front fin on the haddock's back is more pointed than that of other codfish. Haddock live in the western North Atlantic Ocean off New England, Newfoundland, and Nova Scotia. In the eastern North Atlantic, they are found off northern Europe, Great Britain, and Iceland. They are abundant in the North Sea. Haddock weigh about 3 pounds (1.4 kilograms) and are about 2 feet (61 centimeters) long.

The worldwide commercial catch of haddock is approximately 480,000 short tons (435,000 metric tons) each year. Most of the United States catch is taken with large, funnel-shaped nets called *otter trawls.* Haddock

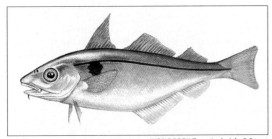

WORLD BOOK illustration by John F. Eggert
The haddock is an important food fish.

are sold fresh and frozen and are made into fillets, fish sticks, and smoked fish products.

Haddock travel in schools and live along the ocean floor. They feed on crabs, shrimp, worms, and small fish.

Scientific classification. Haddock belong to the codfish family, Gadidae. The common haddock is *Melanogrammus aeglefinus.*   Robert R. Rofen

Hades, *HAY deez,* was the god of the dead in Greek mythology. He ruled the kingdom of the dead, which had the same name. The ancient Romans preserved without change almost all the myths about Hades and his kingdom, but they called the god Pluto.

Hades was the son of Cronus and Rhea, and the older brother of Zeus, the king of the gods. In spite of Hades' importance to the Greeks, they did not devote any rituals to him. Few myths involve Hades directly.

The kingdom of Hades was a neutral region reserved for the souls of people who deserved neither punishment nor reward upon death. The Greeks believed that Hades was drab and dull, but not necessarily painful. The souls of those who had led virtuous lives dwelled happily in Elysium. The souls of those who had sinned greatly went to Tartarus, a land far below the earth. There, they suffered eternal torment.

The Greeks believed Hades was beneath the earth. It had five rivers—the Acheron, the Kokytos, the Lethe, the Phlegethon, and the Styx. Each served as a boundary between the land of the living and the land of the dead.

The Styx was the best-known river in Hades. To cross it, a soul had to be ferried by Charon, a boatman. He demanded payment, so the Greeks placed coins in the mouths of their dead before burying them. Hades' house stood on the shore of the Styx. Cerberus, a monstrous three-headed dog, guarded the house. After crossing the river, each soul was assigned to its proper eternal home by one of three judges—Aeacus, Minos, or Rhadamanthys. Those guilty of serious offenses were tormented by three goddesses called *Furies* or *Erinyes.*

C. Scott Littleton

Related articles in *World Book* include:

Cerberus	Furies	Persephone	Sisyphus
Charon	Hell	Pluto (god)	Tartarus
Elysium	Lethe		

Hadj. See **Hajj.**

Hadrian (popes). See **Adrian.**

Hadrian, *HAY dree uhn* (A.D. 76-138), a Roman emperor, stabilized Roman law into a single, uniform code, and made government more efficient. The law code served as a basis for the Justinian Code, established in the 500's by the Byzantine emperor Justinian I (see **Justinian Code**). Hadrian started an empire-wide communications system similar to the pony express. He fortified parts of the frontier, and built a stone wall in northern Britain (see **Roman walls**). He founded two new cities—Antinoopolis in Egypt and Hadrianople in Thrace (now Edirne, Turkey). He also completed the huge temple of Zeus in Athens, which had been begun in the 500's B.C.

Hadrian's official name was Publius Aelius Hadrian. He was born in Spain. His father died during Hadrian's youth, and Trajan, Hadrian's cousin, became his guardian. Trajan became emperor in 98. Hadrian held military and civilian government posts and traveled to the northern and eastern frontiers of the empire. He became emperor after Trajan's death in 117.

Hadrian was a poet, an amateur architect, and a student of Greek culture. His reign was generally peaceful. He rejected Trajan's aggressive policies, ending a war with Parthia, a land beyond Rome's eastern frontiers. To avoid further wars, he returned Parthian territory that Rome had won. The only major conflict occurred in 132, when Jews in Palestine revolted. Hadrian crushed the revolt in 135. He made Jerusalem a Roman city and forbade Jews to worship there. In 138, Hadrian picked Titus Aurelius Antoninus (Antoninus Pius) to succeed him.

Ramsay MacMullen

Hadron, *HAD rahn,* is a major group of subatomic particles. Hadrons include protons and neutrons, which are found in an atom's nucleus. Hadrons are readily affected by the *strong interaction,* a force that holds the nucleus together.

Hadrons consist of smaller particles called *quarks* and *antiquarks.* These smaller particles occur in two combinations, which form the chief types of hadrons—*mesons* and *baryons.* A quark linked to an antiquark makes up a meson. Three quarks combined comprise a baryon. The baryon has an antimatter counterpart called an *antibaryon,* which consists of three antiquarks. See **Antimatter.**

All hadrons except protons and neutrons are extremely unstable. They disintegrate spontaneously in a few hundred millionths of a second or less. For this reason, only protons and neutrons are found in ordinary matter. However, physicists can readily produce unstable hadrons by causing a beam of high-energy particles to collide with matter. They have discovered nearly 300 kinds of hadrons by this means.

All hadrons are nearly the same size, ranging from about 0.7 to 1.7 *femtometers* (quadrillionths of a meter) in diameter. But hadrons vary widely in mass. The lightest, the *pions,* have only about $\frac{1}{7}$ of an *atomic mass unit* (see **Atom** [Atomic weight]). The heaviest, the *upsilons,* carry more than 10 atomic mass units.   Robert H. March

See also **Baryon; Gluon; Meson; Quark; Upsilon particle.**

Haeckel, *HEHK uhl,* **Ernst Heinrich,** *HYN rihk* (1834-1919), a German zoologist, became known for his theory of *recapitulation.* This theory states that each animal during its growth as an embryo repeats the changes its ancestors underwent (see **Embryo**). For example, if a land animal had ancestors which lived in water and used gills, then each embryo of that animal continues to develop gills as did its ancestors, even though the gills may be lost during later embryonic development. Haeckel studied embryos of many animals and made drawings, which are still seen in biology books. He also used his findings to support Charles Darwin's theory of evolution (see **Darwin, Charles R.**). Haeckel's widely read book, *The Riddle of the Universe* (1899), explained many of his theories. He was the first to draw a "family tree" of animal life, showing the supposed relationships of the various animal groups. His early work included a study of one-celled sea animals.

Haeckel was born in Potsdam. As a young boy, he became interested in nature. He liked botany, but studied medicine at his father's insistence. He was educated at Würzburg and Berlin universities. He served as a professor of zoology at the University of Jena from 1862 to 1909.   A. M. Winchester

Haema or **Haemo.** For words beginning with these syllables, see *hema* or *hemo,* as in **Hemolysis.**

Hafiz, *hah FIHZ* (?-1389?), is the poetic name of the Persian poet *Shams ud-Din Mohammed.* His chief work was a *divan,* a collection of about 700 poems. He wrote odes and quatrains (four-line rhymes). The people of Persia (now Iran) called Hafiz "the Tongue of the Hidden" because of the sweetness and beauty of his lyrics. They looked on his poems as love songs. His name in Arabic means "one who knows the Koran by heart." He was born in Shiraz.   Walter J. Fischel

Hafnium, *HAF nee uhm,* a chemical element, is a silver-colored metal. It absorbs neutrons better than most metals and is resistant to corrosion. For these reasons,

rods made of hafnium are used to control the rate of reactions in nuclear reactors of nuclear submarines. When the reaction rate is too high, the rods are pushed into the reactor to absorb some of the neutrons. When the rate is low, the rods are withdrawn. Hafnium is also used in some gas-filled and incandescent lamps.

The highest concentrations of hafnium occur in the minerals zircon and baddeleyite. Hafnium is always found in combination with the more common element zirconium, which it resembles in its chemical and physical properties. Hafnium is a common by-product of the production of this element.

Hafnium has the chemical symbol Hf. Its atomic number is 72 and its atomic weight is 178.49. It melts at about 2227° C and boils at 4602° C. Its specific gravity is 13.31 grams per cubic centimeter. Dirk Coster, a Dutch physicist, and Georg von Hevesy, a Hungarian chemist, discovered hafnium in 1923 in Copenhagen, Denmark. The word *hafnium* comes from *Hafnia,* the Latin name for Copenhagen.   R. Craig Taylor

See also **Zirconium.**

Hagar. See Ishmael.

Hagen, *HAY guhn,* **Walter** (1892-1969), was a great golfer and the player most responsible for elevating professional golf into a major sport. Hagen's insistence on first-class treatment at tournaments raised the stature of professional golfers during a time when amateur players dominated the game. His popularity greatly contributed to making golf a spectator sport.

Hagen's skill as a player combined with his showmanship and colorful lifestyle to make him golf's first celebrity. Hagen sometimes arrived for a match in a chauffeur-driven limousine and wearing a tuxedo. He was the first golfer to earn more than a million dollars in tournaments and exhibitions and the first player to market golf equipment bearing his name.

Walter Charles Hagen was born in Rochester, N.Y. Between 1914 and 1929, he won 11 major tournaments. He won the United States Open in 1914 and 1919; the British Open in 1922, 1924, 1928, and 1929; and the Professional Golfers' Association (PGA) tournament in 1921, 1924, 1925, 1926, and 1927.   Marino A. Parascenzo

Hagenbeck, *HAH guhn behk,* **Karl** (1844-1913), originated the type of trained wild animal acts that are presented today. He operated a zoo near Hamburg, Germany. Animals are still obtained from his zoo by circuses and zoos all over the world.

Hagenbeck was born in Hamburg. His father made a hobby of collecting and training a few animals. Hagenbeck decided when he was 12 to collect and train animals as a career. One of his first orders came from the American showman, P. T. Barnum, who ordered wild beasts worth $15,000. In 1905, Hagenbeck sold 1,000 camels to the German government for use in Africa.

Hagenbeck came to the United States for the first time in 1886. His trained wild animals were a sensation at the World's Columbian Exposition in Chicago in 1893. The spectacle of a lion riding a horse and a tiger riding an elephant appealed to the imagination of the public and forward-looking circus people.   F. B. Kelley

Hagfish is a slimy eellike creature that is related to the lampreys. Hagfishes live in the sea. Some kinds live in deep water and others in muddy bays. The largest hagfishes grow 3 feet (91 centimeters) long. A hagfish has a round mouth surrounded by eight *barbels* (tentacles). Its tongue has sharp, horny teeth. It uses them to bore into dead or dying fish and eat their flesh.

Scientific classification. Hagfishes make up the hagfish family, Myxinidae. A common hagfish is *Myxine glutinosa.*

Leonard P. Schultz

See also **Fish** (Lampreys and hagfish; picture: The chief kinds of fish); **Lamprey.**

Haggai, *HAG ee eye* or *HAG eye,* **Book of,** is a book of the Hebrew Bible, or Old Testament, named for an ancient Hebrew prophet. Haggai lived in Jerusalem about 520 B.C. The Jews had just returned from exile in Babylon, and Haggai convinced them to take up the task of rebuilding the holy temple in Jerusalem. Haggai preached that the rebuilt temple would signify the return of God's favor to the Jewish people and would bring them better times. He called upon the priests to purify certain religious activities. He addressed Zerubbabel, the Persian-appointed governor of Judah, about a glorious future age when God would destroy foreign kingdoms. Then a king, a descendant of the great King David, would reign.   Eric M. Meyers

Haggard, Sir Henry Rider (1856-1925), was one of the most successful English writers of popular fiction in the late 1800's. He wrote 58 volumes of fiction, and 7 volumes of economic, political, and social history. Haggard's best novels are based on his experiences in Africa. *King Solomon's Mines* (1885) became a young people's classic. It is the story of a search for the legendary lost treasure of King Solomon. *She* (1887) is the story of Ayesha, a white goddess of Africa who is 2,000 years old but still appears young and beautiful.

Haggard was born in Norfolk, England. After studying law, he moved to South Africa in 1875 to serve as secretary to the governor of Natal, a South African province. Haggard was knighted in 1912.   Philip Durham

Hagia Sophia, *HAY ee uh soh FEE uh,* is the finest and most famous example of Byzantine architecture in the world. It was built as a Christian cathedral by the emperor Justinian I between A.D. 532 and 537 in Constantinople (now Istanbul). After an earthquake damaged the original dome, a higher one was built between 558 and 563. The building was used as a *mosque* (Muslim temple) after 1453 when the Turks conquered the city. Since 1935, Hagia Sophia has served as a museum. Hagia Sophia is a Greek phrase that means Holy Wisdom. It is sometimes called Saint Sophia.

The inside appearance is one of great space, height, and richness. The rare and costly building materials were brought from many parts of the Roman Empire. The marble-lined walls have many colors and designs. Mosaics decorate some of the walls and vaults. These were covered over by the Turks. After the building became a museum, the mosaics were uncovered. Many beautiful pictures were found. Among these are figures of Christ and the Virgin Mary and portraits of rulers.

The floor plan of Hagia Sophia is oblong. The building is 250 feet (76 meters) from east to west and 235 feet (72 meters) from north to south. Over the center is the great dome, 185 feet (56 meters) above the floor and measuring 107 feet (33 meters) across.   Spiro Kostof

See also **Architecture** (pictures).

Hague, *hayg,* **Frank** (1876-1956), served as the mayor of the Jersey City, N.J., area from 1917 to 1947. He be-

came famous for his remark, "I am the law." He made the remark in an attempt to avoid delay in the issuance of work permits to two boys. Through his firm control of Democratic politics in his home area, Hague became important in national politics. He was a member of the Democratic National Committee for more than 20 years. Hague was born in Jersey City. He was elected to the city's first Board of Commissioners in 1913.

Richard P. McCormick

Hague, *hayg,* **The** (pop. 449,338; met. area pop. 677,962), is the seat of the Netherlands government and the official residence of the queen. It is officially called 's Gravenhage (*SKRAH vun HAH kuh*), which means *the count's hedge.* Many important European treaties have been signed at The Hague. However, Amsterdam is the capital of the Netherlands, and by law, the inauguration of the king or queen takes place there.

In the early 1900's, the world's eyes hopefully turned toward this little spot on the map. Peace-loving peoples dreamed that The Hague might become the neutral capital of the world, where representatives of all nations could meet to settle international quarrels and prevent war. A magnificent Palace of Peace was built as a monument to that dream. Andrew Carnegie furnished funds for the Palace, which still serves as headquarters for the Permanent Court of Arbitration.

The Hague lies on the southwest coast of the Netherlands, about 3 miles (5 kilometers) inland from the North Sea. It is a handsome city which has been described as half Dutch, half French in its architecture. Broad streets are crossed by picturesque canals, lined with shops and dwellings and shaded by beautiful trees. The city has many parks, as well as fine old buildings which include the royal palace, the government buildings, a Gothic church, and a famous art gallery. Half the city is 25 feet (8 meters) above sea level and half is 4 feet (1.2 meters) below sea level. For location, see **Netherlands** (map).

Buildings and monuments of great historic interest also stand in The Hague. In the center of Willems Park stands a national monument erected to celebrate the regaining of Dutch independence in 1813. The Huis ten Bosch, or House in the Wood, is a beautiful suburban villa where the first Hague peace conference took place.

The prosperity of the city depends chiefly on its importance as a center of international affairs and as a resort. Nearby on the North Sea coast lies Scheveningen, the most important seaside resort in the Netherlands. The Hague is not an important trading or manufacturing center. However, its factories produce some gold and silver ware, porcelain, hats, and furniture.

History. The Hague was originally a hunting lodge belonging to the counts of Holland. In 1250, it became a royal residence. The city was chosen as the seat of the States-General in the 1500's and thus became the capital of Holland. The Triple Alliance of England, Sweden, and Holland was signed here in 1668, and the Triple Alliance of England, France, and Holland was signed at The Hague in 1717. At the suggestion of the Russian czar, a peace conference took place in the city in 1899. By then The Hague had become a permanent site for international conferences. In 1907, representatives of European nations met here in an unsuccessful effort to solve the problems which later led to World War I. Geneva was chosen as the world capital of the League of Nations,

The Hague Peace Palace stands in formal gardens on the southwest coast of the Netherlands. Andrew Carnegie, an American industrialist, donated funds to build the structure.

D. Bartruff, FPG

but The Hague became the seat of the "World Court," now the International Court of Justice.

The city was occupied by German forces in 1940 and was freed by the Allies in 1945. The people then began to clear away the ruins. Scheveningen had formed part of Germany's West Wall. The Germans had launched V-2 rockets from The Hague, and some of them had destroyed part of the city. Benjamin Hunningher

Hahn, Otto (1879-1968), was a German chemist who won the 1944 Nobel Prize in chemistry for splitting the atom. This splitting process is called *nuclear fission.* Scientists working in the United States used Hahn's discovery in developing the atomic bomb in the early 1940's, during World War II. Peaceful uses of nuclear fission have also been developed.

Hahn first split the uranium atom in 1938. He and his associate, Fritz Strassmann, were studying the effects of bombarding uranium with neutrons. They found that the bombardment changed some of the uranium to barium, an element with about half the atomic weight of uranium. In 1939, Austrian-born physicists Lise Meitner and Otto Frisch explained that barium resulted from a splitting of the uranium atom.

Hahn studied many radioactive substances, including actinium and thorium. In 1917, he and Meitner shared the credit for the discovery of a radioactive metal called *protactinium* (see **Protactinium**).

Hahn was born in Frankfurt in what is now West Germany. He received a Ph.D. degree from the University of Marburg in 1901. In 1912, he joined the faculty of the Kaiser Wilhelm Institute for Chemistry (now the Max Planck Institute in Göttingen). He became president of the institute in 1946. Daniel J. Kevles

See also **Nuclear energy** (Development).

Hahnemann, *HAH nuh muhn,* **Samuel** (1755-1843), a German physician, founded the homeopathic method of treating disease. He believed that a drug which produces symptoms in a healthy person will cure those symptoms in a sick person (see **Homeopathy**). Hahnemann published his major work, the *Organon der rationellen Heilkunst (Principles of Rational Medicine),* in

1810. The book contains his chief ideas: to let like cure like, that medicines become more potent as they are diluted and shaken, and that only one remedy should be given at a time. Hahnemann was born in Meissen, Germany. His full name was Christian Friedrich Samuel Hahnemann. He practiced in Leipzig. George Rosen

Haida Indians, *HY duh,* once occupied the Queen Charlotte Islands of British Columbia and part of Prince of Wales Island, Alaska. They lived by fishing, hunting, and collecting wild plants. Haida communities included highly organized clans, social classes, secret societies, and a hereditary nobility. The upper classes owned much wealth in the form of slaves and fishing grounds. The Haida excelled in such crafts as canoe and house building, and wood carving. They were the only Pacific Northwest Indians to carve soft black slate, but they probably did not begin to do this until white settlers brought cutting tools in the 1800's. Many Haida have moved to the mainland of British Columbia and to southern Alaska. A few hundred Indians still speak the Haida language. Melville Jacobs

Haifa, *HY fuh* (pop. 266,100; met. area pop. 374,950), is Israel's chief port and an important manufacturing and cultural center. It lies on and around Mount Carmel in northern Israel. The city borders the Bay of Haifa at the eastern end of the Mediterranean Sea. For location, see **Israel** (map). Haifa has three sections. The lower section, which spreads around the bottom of Mount Carmel, includes port facilities, warehouses, apartment buildings, and scattered slums. The main business district covers most of the mountain slopes. The upper part of Haifa consists mostly of large houses, apartment buildings, and gardens and parks on top of the mountain.

Many religious landmarks are in Haifa, including the Bahai Temple, the Monastery of Our Lady of Mount Carmel, and Elijah's Cave. The prophet Elijah hid in the cave to escape from his enemies. Haifa has two universities.

The city's industries include oil refining and the manufacture of cement, chemicals, electronic equipment, glass, steel, and textiles. Haifa is also a shipping and railroad center.

People lived in what is now the Haifa area about 3,000 years ago. Haifa was a small town until the mid-1850's, when it was first used as a port. Saul B. Cohen

Haig, *hayg,* **Alexander Meigs, Jr.** (1924-), became secretary of state under President Ronald Reagan in 1981 and resigned the position in 1982. Haig, a retired four-star general, was the second military leader to serve as head of the Department of State. General George C. Marshall was the first. In 1987, Haig announced that he was a candidate for the 1988 Republican presidential nomination.

Haig was born in Philadelphia. He graduated from the U.S. Military Academy at West Point in 1947 and served in the Army in Japan, Korea, and other countries. Haig held a series of posts in the De-

UPI

Alexander M. Haig, Jr.

partment of Defense from 1962 to 1965. In 1966 and 1967, he served in combat in the Vietnam War.

In 1969, Haig became senior military adviser to Henry A. Kissinger, then assistant to the President for national security affairs. Haig was promoted to four-star general in 1972. He was named Army vice chief of staff, the second highest Army post, in 1973. That same year, he left the Army to serve as White House chief of staff under President Richard M. Nixon.

From 1974 to 1979, Haig served as supreme commander of the North Atlantic Treaty Organization forces in Europe. He retired from military service in 1979 and became president and chief operating officer of United Technologies Corporation, a major manufacturer of aircraft and other products.   Lee Thornton

Haig, *hayg,* **Earl** (1861-1928), commanded the British forces in France during most of World War I. In 1918, he directed the attack that broke Germany's defensive Siegfried Line (see **Siegfried Line**). After the war, he was made an earl. Douglas Haig was born in Edinburgh. He took command of the British Expeditionary Force in 1915.   Alfred F. Havighurst

Haiku. See **Japanese literature.**

Hail is a precipitation in the form of round or irregularly shaped lumps of ice. These lumps of ice are called *hailstones.* Hailstones range from the size of peas to the size of oranges or larger. Most hailstones are smaller than 1 inch (2.5 centimeters) in diameter. Large hailstones can have bumps on their surfaces where they have grown more.

Hail can break windows, damage roofs, and dent cars and airplanes. It causes hundreds of millions of dollars of damage to crops each year. Damage from hail is greater when the wind is strong. Occasionally, people caught in the open in severe hailstorms have been killed.

Hail is often observed from central Texas through the Great Plains states into Alberta. In the United States, it falls most frequently in southeastern Wyoming, western Nebraska, and eastern Colorado. Elsewhere in the world, hail often falls in Argentina, northern Italy, Kenya, South Africa, and the Caucasus region of the Soviet Union.

Hailstones form in thunderstorm clouds and begin as frozen raindrops or snow pellets called *hail embryos.* Embryos originate in one part of the hailstorm and are then carried by air currents to the main region of hail growth. Hailstones develop as the embryos come into

National Severe Storms Laboratory (NOAA)

The largest hailstone on record, *above,* fell at Coffeyville, Kans., on Sept. 3, 1970. It weighed 1 $\frac{2}{3}$ pounds (0.76 kilogram) and measured 17 $\frac{1}{2}$ inches (44.5 centimeters) around.

contact with *supercooled water droplets,* droplets that remain liquid at temperatures below freezing. As an embryo moves through the droplets, they strike its surface and freeze. An embryo grows into a hailstone as this freezing water accumulates on its surface.

Hailstones become large if they remain for a long time in parts of the hailstorm where there is a large amount of supercooled liquid water. Hailstones grow large if they are supported in the same cloud updraft for a long time. They also grow if they repeatedly fall out of an updraft but are then carried upward by other air currents. Hailstones fall to the ground when they leave the region of updrafts or become too heavy for the air currents to support. They fall at a speed of about 22 miles (35 kilometers) per hour or more.   Alexis B. Long

See also **Sleet; Storm.**

Hail to the Chief is a song that has often been played at public appearances of the President of the United States. It first came into use around 1828. James Sanderson wrote the music. The words are those of the "Boat Song" in Sir Walter Scott's *Lady of the Lake.*

Haile Selassie I, *HY lee suh LAS ee* (1892-1975), became emperor of Ethiopia in 1930. His reign ended in 1974, when military leaders overthrew him.

Haile Selassie worked for economic and social reforms, such as making slavery punishable by law. He gave Ethiopia its first written constitution in 1931. Ethiopia was attacked by Fascist Italy in 1935, and Haile Selassie lived in exile in England until 1941. British forces liberated Ethiopia during World War II and restored him to the throne. Rebels seized the government on Dec. 13, 1960, while he was in South America, but he regained his throne four

United Press Int.

Haile Selassie I

days later. Haile Selassie was born in Harer. His given and family name was Tafari Makonnen. He became Ras (Duke) Tafari in 1916. He belonged to a *dynasty* (series of rulers) that claimed to be descended from King Solomon and the Queen of Sheba. He took the title Haile Selassie I when he became emperor. *Haile Selassie* means *Power of the Trinity.*   T. Walter Wallbank

See also **Ethiopia** (History); **Jamaica** (People).

Haiphong, *hy fawng* (pop. 1,190,900), is a manufacturing center and seaport in northern Vietnam. The city lies near the Gulf of Tonkin, about 55 miles (89 kilometers) east of Hanoi (see **Vietnam** [map]). Factories in Haiphong produce cement, china, glass, phosphates, and textiles. Other industries include electric power production, food processing, and shipbuilding. The city is a deepwater port for Hanoi. Products shipped to Haiphong are carried by railroad to Hanoi. During the Vietnam War, Haiphong became Communist North Vietnam's major port for importing military supplies. The city was heavily bombed by U.S. planes during the war. North Vietnam defeated South Vietnam in the war in 1975 and unified the two countries into the single nation of Vietnam in 1976. See also **Vietnam War.**   David P. Chandler

Hair is a threadlike structure that grows from the skin of mammals. Most kinds of mammals have a thick coat of hair that serves chiefly to provide warmth. Many species also have certain hairs for special uses, such as for protection or for sense functions. Among human beings, however, hair has primarily a cosmetic value.

Most of the human body is covered by tiny, light-colored hairs that are barely visible. Thick hair grows from the scalp and some other parts of the body. However, certain areas, such as the palms of the hands and the soles of the feet, have no hair at all. In human beings, as in other mammals, hairs around the eyes and ears, and in the nose, serve a protective function. They prevent dust, insects, and other matter from entering these organs. In addition, the eyebrows decrease the amount of light reflected into the eyes.

Among mammals other than human beings, a number of species have special hairs that respond to touch. Many nerves lie around these *tactile hairs,* which are commonly called *whiskers.* Whiskers grow on the lips and cheeks of most mammals, but they also occur on other parts of the body. These hairs help the animals feel their way through narrow or dark places.

Hair also provides various kinds of protection for animals. The hair color of many species of mammals blends with their surroundings and helps them hide from their enemies and prey. The quills of porcupines, which also furnish protection against enemies, are a special type of hair. Hair acts as padding against blows and falling objects as well.

Manufacturers use animal hair in making a variety of products. The thick, soft fur that covers some mammals is used for coats and other warm clothing. The woolly fleece of sheep is spun into thread and into cloth for such products as blankets, clothing, and rugs. Felt is manufactured by pressing and matting animal hair. Bristles, the short, stiff hair of hogs, are used in making various kinds of brushes.

The structure and growth of hair

The root and shaft. The part of a hair below the surface of the skin rests in a baglike structure called the *follicle.* The *root,* which is the lowest section of a hair, enlarges at the end into a soft, light-colored structure called the *hair bulb.* Hair develops from the cells of the bulb, which divide rapidly. A structure called the *papilla* projects into the hair bulb at the base of the follicle. It contains an artery that supplies the blood necessary for the rapidly growing cells.

The cells of the hair bulb move upward as new cells begin to form beneath them. As these cells move higher, they are cut off from their supply of nourishment and start to form a hard protein called *keratin.* This protein is found in the nails, claws, and hoofs of mammals; the scales of reptiles; and the feathers of birds. The formation of keratin is called *keratinization,* and the hair cells die as it occurs.

The keratinization process is completed by the time the hair has risen about a third of the way to the surface of the skin. The part of the hair above where keratinization has occurred is called the *shaft.*

Three layers of dead cells compose the shaft of a hair. The outer layer, called the *cuticle,* consists of flattened cells that are known as *cuticular scales.* Beneath the cuti-

The parts of a hair

The top diagram shows the parts of a human hair. A hair develops from the cells of the hair bulb. These cells move up to form the root and then the shaft of the hair. The bottom diagram shows the three layers of dead cells that make up a hair shaft.

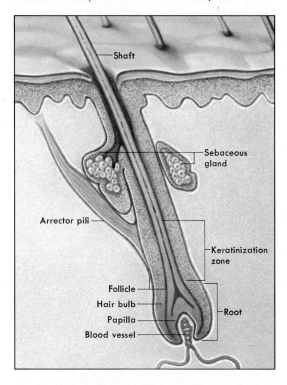

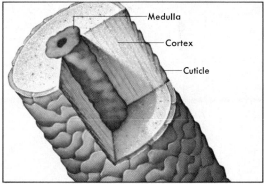

WORLD BOOK illustrations by Lou Bory

cle lies the *cortex,* a layer of tightly packed, cigar-shaped cells. The cortex contains the *pigment* (coloring matter) that determines the color of hair. The core of the shaft, called the *medulla,* is made up of loosely packed, box-like cells.

Glands and muscles. Most hair follicles contain an oil gland called the *sebaceous gland.* This gland secretes oil into the follicle. The oil flows over the hair, lubricating it and keeping it soft.

A muscle known as the *arrector pili* is attached to most hair follicles. When this muscle contracts, it causes a hair to "stand on end." In mammals with heavy coats, hair in this position traps air close to the animal's body, providing extra insulation against the cold. Hair standing on end also makes an animal look larger and more dangerous. When a human being is cold or frightened, the muscles contract and produce little bumps around the hair. These bumps are commonly known as "goose bumps."

Color and texture. The color of hair is determined largely by the amount and distribution of a brown-black pigment called *melanin.* Hair also contains a yellow-red pigment that is most visible in people whose hair has little melanin. Most people's hair gradually becomes gray or white as they grow older, because pigment no longer forms.

The texture of hair depends largely on the shape of the hair, which can be seen in cross section under a microscope. Straight hairs have a round shape, and wavy and curly hairs are flat. The flattest hairs are the waviest or curliest.

Cycles of hair growth. The growth of hair in the follicles occurs in cycles. In each cycle, a follicle goes through a growth phase and a resting phase. A hair stops growing during every resting phase, when it is known as a *club hair.* The club hair remains in the resting follicle until the next growing phase. During the growing phase, the club hair is shed as a new hair grows and pushes it out of the follicle.

The length of hair depends on the length of the growing phase of the follicle. The follicles in the human scalp are active for two to six years, and then they rest for about three months. Scalp hairs grow less than half an inch (13 millimeters) per month. Shorter hairs, such as those in the eyebrows and eyelashes, grow for about 10 weeks and then rest for 9 months.

The human scalp contains an average of about 100,000 hairs. From 5 to 15 per cent of the hairs in the scalp are in the resting stage at any time. A person sheds from 70 to 100 hairs a day from follicles that are in the resting stage.

Many factors affect the growth of hair. They include age, diet, general health, and changes in the seasons. For example, hair grows faster in children than in adults, and it grows faster in summer than during any other season. Cutting or shaving hair on any part of the body does not have any effect on the future growth or texture of the hair.

Disorders of the hair and scalp

Baldness occurs if the follicles on the scalp die and no longer produce new hair. Heredity is the most common cause of baldness. However, other factors, including scalp infections and reactions to drugs or radiation, can also cause it. Baldness caused by heredity is more common in men than in women. Such baldness cannot be cured.

Various factors, including illness and pregnancy, can affect the growth cycles of the hair follicles. The growing phases of the follicles are shorter in such cases, and a large number of club hairs occur. These club hairs may be shed at one time, causing thinning of the hair or even baldness. This type of hair loss is not permanent because new hairs grow after the growing cycles start again.

Excess hair on the face or elsewhere can also be caused by heredity or by certain medical problems. Such hair can be removed by a process called *electrolysis.* This process, in which the papillae are destroyed by an electric needle, prevents new hair from growing. Unwanted hair above the surface of the skin can be removed by the application of a liquid or paste that is called a *depilatory.* However, the root of the hair stays alive, and so the hair grows out again.

Other disorders of the scalp include *dandruff, ringworm,* and *head lice.* Dandruff consists of scales of skin that fall from the scalp. It does not cause a loss of hair unless accompanied by an infection severe enough to damage the follicles. Ringworm is an infection caused by tiny plants called *fungi,* which feed on the keratin in the hair. The hairs break off, leaving bare areas on the scalp. Head lice are insects that suck blood from the scalp and attach their eggs to hairs. Orville J. Stone

Related articles. For information on the care of the hair, see Hairdressing. Other related articles in *World Book* include:

Baldness
Beard
Dandruff
Felt
Fur
Louse
Mammal (Skin and hair)

Races, Human (table: Geographical races)
Ringworm
Skin (Hair, nails, and glands)
Wool

Hair hygrometer. See Hygrometer (The hair hygrometer).

Hair snake. See Horsehair worm.

Hair transplanting. See Baldness.

Hairball. See Cat (Grooming).

Hairbell. See Bluebell.

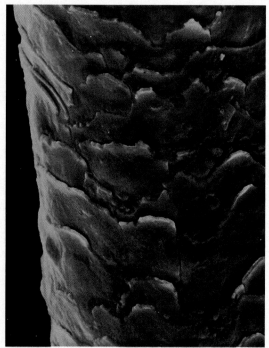

Tony Brain, Science Photo Library

The shaft of a hair, shown highly magnified, consists of three layers of dead cells. The outer layer, *above,* called the *cuticle,* is made up of flattened cells known as *cuticular scales.*

Detail of an Egyptian limestone relief of *Amenmes and His Wife* (about 1300 B.C.); The Louvre, Paris

Ancient Egyptians wore long wigs of spiral curls, such as those worn by this nobleman, *left,* and his wife, *right.* The curls were made of human hair, palm-leaf fibers, or wool.

Hairdressing is the art of cutting, setting, arranging, and otherwise caring for the hair. Women and men style their hair to improve their appearance and for comfort. A different hairstyle can alter a person's appearance more than almost any other physical change. Hairdressing can accent good features and hide bad ones, or draw attention away from undesirable characteristics. It provides attractive, easy-to-manage hairstyles that meet the needs and desires of the people who wear them.

Hair is the most easily changed physical feature of the human body. Since prehistoric times, people have cut, braided, and dyed their hair and changed it in other ways as well. Professional hairdressers first became

---

Vidal Sassoon, the contributor of this article, is one of the world's leading hairdressers. He is Chairman of the Board of Vidal Sassoon, Inc.; author of Sorry I Kept You Waiting, Madam; *and coauthor of* A Year of Beauty and Health.

---

common during the 1700's. Today, most women and men depend on hairdressers for such services as cutting, coloring, straightening, and permanent waving. Hairdressers are also known as *beauticians, beauty operators, cosmetologists,* and *hairstylists.* Those hairdressers who work mainly with men's hair are usually called *barbers.*

Hairdressing through the ages

People painted and tattooed their bodies during prehistoric times, and they probably also arranged their hair in various ways. Archaeologists have discovered hairpins and hair ornaments from the New Stone Age, which began about 8000 B.C.

Ancient times. In ancient Egypt, both men and women shaved their heads for cleanliness and relief from the heat. However, they frequently wore long wigs made of braids or spiral curls stitched to a woven foundation. These wig styles lasted for centuries.

In ancient Greece and Rome, most people wore a narrow band called a *fillet* around their heads to hold their hair in place. Fashionable men frizzed their hair and powdered it with gold dust. Women braided, curled, or tied their hair into fancy styles. Many women bleached their hair blond.

Two early Germanic peoples, the Angles and the Saxons, dyed their hair blue, green, or orange. The ancient Gauls, who lived in France, colored theirs red.

The Middle Ages began in the late 400's and lasted until about the 1400's. Hairstyles changed little during this period. Most men wore medium-length hair that reached no lower than their shoulders. Priests and monks had a shaved patch called a *tonsure* on the crown of the head. Girls and unmarried women wore their hair loose. Married women covered theirs with a veil or a hoodlike covering. Sometimes they plucked or shaved the hair at the hairline to make the forehead seem higher.

The Renaissance. Women wore many hairstyles during the Renaissance, which began in Italy about 1300 and spread throughout Europe during the 1400's and 1500's. Some had long braids that fell to their knees.

Marble sculpture (about 100 B.C.); Museo Civico, Bologna, Italy (Raymond V. Schoder, S.J.)

A fillet was a band worn by ancient Greeks and Romans to hold their hair in place. This sculpture is probably of the Greek goddess Athena.

Detail of *Lady in Yellow* (about 1465) by Alesso Baldovinetti; National Gallery, London

A woman of the 1400's plucked or shaved her hair at the hairline to make her forehead seem higher. Blond hair was extremely fashionable.

Detail of a painting (about 1700); Musée des Beaux-Arts, Orleans, France (Lauros-Giraudon)

A periwig was a huge, curly wig worn by men of the 1600's and 1700's. The wig might be unpowdered, like this one, or covered with white powder.

Detail of *Marie-Thérèse of Savoy* (1700's) attributed to Antoine Callet; Versailles, France

A towering hairdo of the mid-1700's was supported by a wire frame. Such hairstyles were decorated with flowers, jewels, or other ornaments.

Others drew their hair back into a large roll called a *chignon* at the back of the head. A hairstyle called *Venus' hair* featured thick strands, stiffened with gold lacquer, that seemed to flow from the head. Blond hair was extremely fashionable, and women spent long hours in the sun to bleach their hair.

Most men wore short or shoulder-length hair, and many had bangs covering the forehead. King Henry VIII of England ordered Englishmen to wear short hair in imitation of French noblemen.

The 1600's. Most men of the 1600's had long, flowing curls. Many wore a side curl called a *lovelock,* which was longer than the other curls and tied with a ribbon. During the Civil War in England (1642-1649), the chief opponents of King Charles I were the Puritans. They were called *Roundheads* because they had their hair cut close to their heads. Their short haircuts distinguished them from the king's supporters, a group called the *Cavaliers,* who had long hair. King Louis XIII of France started a fashion for men's wigs after he lost his own hair. Many men wore huge, curled wigs called *periwigs.*

During much of this period, women wore their hair piled high on their heads. However, curls that fell to the shoulders were fashionable in the mid-1600's.

The 1700's. Fancy hairstyles became popular with both women and men during the 1700's. Women's hairdos were extremely high and had to be supported by small cushions and wire frames. Many styles measured more than 2 feet (60 centimeters) high and had floral, operatic, or poetic themes. Women covered their hair with white or pastel powder and decorated their hairdos with feathers, jewels, tassels, or other ornaments. Sometimes they did not wash or comb their hair for several weeks because the styles were so complicated. Professional hairdressers became common to help create and care for such hairdos.

Men covered their hair with powdered wigs. The most popular wig styles were smaller than those of the 1600's. A style called a *tie wig* was pulled back and tied with a short ribbon. The ends of a *bag wig* were covered with a silk bag.

The 1800's brought simpler hairstyles. Fashionable styles for women included braids, topknots, and heavy coils of hair over each ear or at the nape of the neck. Long, smooth curls shaped like sausages were stylish during the 1840's. In the 1870's, a French hairdresser named Marcel Grateau invented the *marcel wave,* a series of deep, soft waves made with heated tongs. Another French hairdresser, Alexandre F. Godefroy, invented a hairdrier about 1890. Godefroy's clients wore a bonnetlike covering that was attached to the chimney pipe of a gas stove. Beginning in the 1890's, fashionable women wore their hair up in a soft style called the *Gibson girl look.* This style was made popular by the American artist Charles Dana Gibson.

Men wore their hair short during the 1800's and dressed it with hair oil, particularly *Macassar oil.* This type of oil became so popular that protective coverings called *antimacassars* were made for chairs and sofas.

The 1900's. Hairdressers of the 1900's developed new processes for curling the hair. Charles L. Nessler, a German-born hairdresser, invented the permanent wave about 1905. Nessler first applied a borax paste and then wound the hair on electrically heated curlers. The permanent-wave treatment took up to 12 hours and cost hundreds of dollars.

During the 1940's, many women cut their hair in a short style called the *bob* and had it permanent-waved. The *cold wave,* a permanent wave that did not require heat, was developed in the 1930's. A cold wave took about two hours and cost only a few dollars.

During the 1940's, many women wore the *sheepdog,* or *Veronica Lake,* style. This hairstyle was made popular by Veronica Lake, a motion-picture star who had long hair that covered one eye. In the 1950's, large numbers of women began to color their hair or *frost* their hair— that is, bleach a few strands. The puffy appearance of *bouffant* hairdos was stylish in the late 1950's and early 1960's. To give their hair the necessary fullness, women combed it from the ends toward the scalp in a process called *backcombing* or *teasing.*

Men wore their hair short throughout the early and

From *The Best of Charles Dana Gibson* © 1969, by Crown Publishers, Inc.

The Gibson girl look, a soft, puffy hairstyle of the 1890's, was created by the American artist Charles Dana Gibson.

Artstreet

The crew cut, in which a man's or boy's hair is cut very short and brushed upward, was popular during the 1950's.

© Paul Fusco, Magnum

The Afro, a hairdo popular in the 1960's and 1970's, resembles bushy hairstyles worn by many African men and women.

Vidal Sassoon Salons, Inc. (WORLD BOOK photo)

Modern hairdressers create many styles by cutting the hair so that it falls into place and needs no setting. Such styles can be blown dry with a hand drier or allowed to dry naturally.

mid-1900's. During the 1920's, many young men wore *patent leather hair,* which they slicked down with oil in the manner of the movie star Rudolph Valentino. During the 1950's, some men wore a *crew cut,* in which the hair was cut extremely short and combed upward to resemble a brush. Other men of the same period wore a *duck-tail.* This style left the hair long on the sides and swept it back, so that it looked somewhat like a duck's tail. During the 1960's, young men copied the haircuts of the Beatles, a British rock music group, who wore long bangs that covered the forehead.

A number of *unisex* styles, which were fashionable for both sexes, appeared during the 1960's and 1970's. Many men and women wore their hair long, either straight or curly; or in a bushy style called the *Afro.* Partly as a result of such styles, more men visited hairdressers for permanent waves and other services. Many hairdressers began to style men's and women's hair.

Caring for the hair

Clean, healthy hair results from regular brushing and shampooing, and a well-balanced diet. Brushing removes dirt and tangles and spreads the natural scalp oils through the hair. Dry hair should be washed about once a week. Oily hair may need a daily washing.

Most people handle the daily care of their hair at home. They visit a hairdresser only for haircuts, coloring, straightening, or permanent-waving. Many styles need no setting and can be blown dry with a hand drier or allowed to dry naturally.

Careers in hairdressing

A high school student who wishes to become a hairdresser should study a broad range of subjects, includ-

ing the arts, biology, and psychology. Courses in the arts help develop creativity and artistic ability. Biology courses aid in understanding the structure and growth of the hair. A knowledge of psychology helps in dealing with people.

A student may attend a professional hairdressing school or serve an apprenticeship under an established hairdresser. Most European hairdressers serve an apprenticeship. In the United States, most students take a 6- or 12-month course at a state-licensed cosmetology school. They learn to shampoo, cut, color, style, and straighten and permanent-wave hair. They also learn to give manicures, scalp and facial treatments, and advice on makeup. Many hairdressing programs also include courses in *trichology,* the treatment of disorders of the hair and scalp.

All the states require hairdressers to have a license. State boards of cosmetology establish the requirements for licensing. These requirements vary from state to state.

The chief professional associations for hairdressers in the United States are the Associated Master Barbers and Beauticians of America, the National Beauty Culturists' League, and the National Hairdressers and Cosmetologists Association. Major professional publications for hairdressers include *American Hairdresser/Salon Owner, Beauty World, The Hairstylist, Journeyman Barber and Beauty Culture,* and *Modern Salon Magazine.*

Vidal Sassoon

Related articles in *World Book* include:

Barber

Beard

Careers (picture: A hairdresser)

Clothing (Clothing through the ages; pictures)

Colonial life in America (Clothing)

Cosmetics

Dandruff

Hair

Wig

Hairstylist. See Hairdressing.

Hairworm. See Horsehair worm.

Haise, Fred Wallace, Jr. (1933-   ), served as lunar module pilot of the United States Apollo 13 space flight in April 1970. About 56 hours after the flight began, the command module became crippled. An explosion caused by a short circuit destroyed the systems that supplied electricity and oxygen to the module. Haise and his fellow astronauts, James A. Lovell, Jr., and John L. Swigert, Jr., retreated into the lunar module and used it as a space "lifeboat." This module had enough oxygen to keep the men alive during their return trip to the earth. The astronauts landed safely on earth nearly four days later.

Haise was born in Biloxi, Miss. He became a naval aviation cadet in 1952. Haise also served with the U.S. Marine Corps, the Air National Guard, and the Air Force. He graduated from the University of Oklahoma in 1959. He was a test pilot from 1959 until he became an astronaut in 1966. He resigned from the space program in 1979.

William J. Cromie

NASA

Fred W. Haise, Jr.

Arnold H. Crane from Marilyn Gartman

The National Palace in Port-au-Prince is the official home of the president of Haiti. It also houses some of Haiti's governmental offices. Haiti is the oldest black republic in the world and the second oldest independent nation in the Western Hemisphere.

Haiti, *HAY tee,* is a country in the West Indies. It covers the western third of the island of Hispaniola, which lies between Cuba and Puerto Rico in the Caribbean Sea. The Dominican Republic covers the eastern part of the island. Most of Haiti is covered with rugged mountains, and the name *Haiti* comes from an Indian word meaning *high ground.*

Haiti is one of the most densely populated countries in the Western Hemisphere. It is also one of the hemisphere's least developed countries. About four-fifths of its people cannot read and write. Most Haitians are farmers who raise barely enough food to feed their families. Haiti has a shortage of hospitals and doctors. Because of poor diet and medical care—especially in rural areas—the average Haitian lives only about 50 years.

Haiti is the oldest black republic in the world and the second oldest independent nation in the Western Hemisphere. It has been independent since 1804, but most of the time it has been ruled by dictators who have not been interested in the welfare of the people.

Christopher Columbus arrived at the island of Hispaniola in 1492. He established a Spanish base in what is now Haiti. Later, the French developed Haiti into what was then the richest colony in the Caribbean.

Haiti's official name in French, the official language, is République D'Haiti (Republic of Haiti). Port-au-Prince is Haiti's capital and largest city.

Government. In 1986, Haitians overthrew the government of the dictator Jean-Claude Duvalier. A new government made up of military and civilian leaders was formed. It consisted of a three-member National Governing Council, assisted by a Cabinet. The head of the country's armed forces became head of state, the president of the National Governing Council. In 1988, Haitians elected a parliament and a civilian president to head the government.

People. Most of the people are descendants of black Africans who were brought to Haiti as slaves. Most of them are jammed into the country's overcrowded coastal plains and mountain valleys, where the soil is most productive. A typical Haitian family farms a tiny plot of land less than 2 acres (0.8 hectare) in size that was once part of a plantation where the family's ancestors worked as slaves. The members of the family raise beans, corn, rice, and yams for their own food. If they are fortunate, they may have some chickens, a pig, or a goat. The family lives in a small, one-room hut that has a thatched roof and walls made of sticks covered with dried mud.

Most Haitians still follow some of the customs their ancestors brought with them from Africa. Much of the work on the small farms of Haiti is done by groups of neighbors who move from field to field planting or harvesting crops to the sound of music and singing. This combination of work and play is called a *combite* (also spelled *coumbite*).

Most Haitians practice a religion called *voodoo.* Voodoo is a blend of Christian and African beliefs. Haitians believe that by performing certain ceremonies they can be possessed by gods. For example, a *houngan* (voodoo priest) draws designs on the ground with flour. Then, the people dance until they believe a god has possessed one or more of them. The followers of voodoo believe in many gods, such as gods of rain, love, war, and farming. A small minority of the people practice other religions, chiefly Roman Catholicism.

About 5 per cent of the people of Haiti are *mulattoes* (people of mixed black and white ancestry). Most of the mulattoes belong to the middle or upper class, and many have been educated in France. Most of them live comfortably in modern houses, and are prosperous merchants, doctors, or lawyers. A few Americans, Europeans, and Syrians also live in Haiti.

Most Haitians speak a language called Haitian Creole, which is partly based on French. The middle and upper classes also speak French.

Facts in brief

Capital: Port-au-Prince.
Official language: French.
Area: 10,714 sq. mi. (27,750 km²). *Greatest distances*—east-west, 180 mi. (290 km); north-south, 135 mi. (217 km). *Coastline*—672 mi. (1,081 km), including offshore islands.
Elevation: *Highest*—Pic La Selle, 8,783 ft. (2,677 m) above sea level. *Lowest*—sea level.
Population: *Estimated 1988 population*—5,697,000; distribution, 72 per cent rural, 28 per cent urban; density, 532 persons per sq. mi. (205 per km²). *1982 census*—5,053,792. *Estimated 1993 population*—6,260,000.
Chief products: *Agriculture*—coffee, sisal, sugar cane. *Mining*—copper, bauxite.
National anthem: "La Dessalienne" ("Song of Dessalines").
Flag: The dark blue top half of the *national flag,* flown by the people, stands for the blacks of Haiti; the red bottom half represents its mulattoes. In the center of the *state flag,* used by the government, is the Haitian coat of arms. See **Flag** (picture: Flags of the Americas).
Money: *Basic unit*—gourde. See **Money** (table).

Land. Two chains of rugged mountains run across the northern and southern parts of Haiti, and form two peninsulas at the west end of the island. The northern peninsula juts about 100 miles (160 kilometers) into the Atlantic Ocean, and the southern peninsula extends about 200 miles (320 kilometers) into the Caribbean Sea. A gulf, Golfe de la Gonâve, and an island, Île de la Gonâve, lie between the two peninsulas.

The wide Artibonite Valley of the Artibonite River lies between the mountains in the eastern part of the country. Tortuga Island lies off the northern coast. Cedar and mahogany forests cover some mountains, and tropical fruit trees grow on others.

The people farm as much of the land as they can. In some areas, they raise crops on slopes so steep that the farmers anchor themselves with rope to keep from sliding down the hillside. The people grow coffee and *cacao* (seeds used to make cocoa and chocolate) in the mountains. Sugar cane is the main crop in the black, fertile soil of the Artibonite Valley.

Haiti has a tropical climate with mild temperatures. Temperatures range from 70° to 95° F. (21° to 35° C) along the coasts and from 50° to 75° F. (10° to 24° C) in the mountains. The tropical forests in the northern mountains receive about 80 inches (200 centimeters) of rain a year. The southern coast of the country receives less than 40 inches (100 centimeters) of rain yearly. Destructive hurricanes sometimes strike Haiti between June and October.

Economy. About 7 out of 10 Haitians live in rural areas. Most of these people are farmers who own less than 2 acres (0.8 hectare) of land, barely enough to grow food for their families. Some people who live in the mountains raise fruits and coffee beans that they sell in the market places. A few mulattoes own large plantations, where laborers raise coffee, sugar cane, or *sisal* (a plant used to make twine). Many Haitians work on plantations in the Dominican Republic and Cuba.

Haiti has few industries. Coffee and sugar cane are processed there, and sold to the United States, France, and other countries. Haiti also has a few cotton mills. Craftworkers in the cities sell handicrafts that they have woven from sisal or carved out of mahogany to tourists. Haiti buys small amounts of cotton goods, grain, and machinery, mainly from the United States.

Several international airlines make stops in Port-au-Prince. The cities of Cap-Haïtien, Les Cayes, and Saint-Marc are important seaports. Cruise ships stop at Cap-Haïtien, and many of the passengers visit the city. Haiti has only about 50 miles (80 kilometers) of railroads.

Haiti

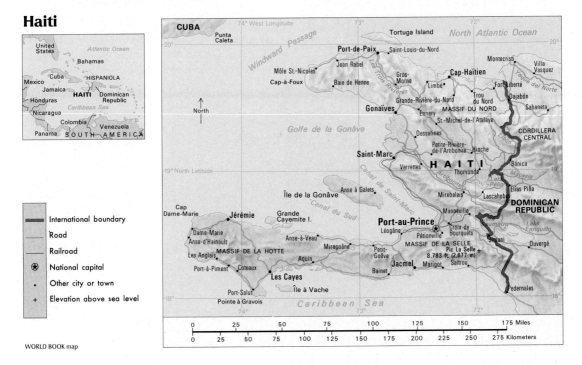

International boundary
Road
Railroad
⊛ National capital
• Other city or town
+ Elevation above sea level

WORLD BOOK map

Gerald S. Adams, Shostal

The gateway to the Iron Market in Port-au-Prince is framed by Moorish-style turrets. In the market, merchants sell food, clothing, and many other items in indoor and outdoor stalls.

Most of the track is on the sugar plantations. Only about 375 miles (600 kilometers) of the country's 2,500 miles (4,000 kilometers) of roads can be used in all kinds of weather.

History. Christopher Columbus arrived at Hispaniola in 1492. One of his ships, the *Santa Maria,* ran aground on reefs near the present-day city of Cap-Haïtien on Christmas. Columbus' crew used the ship's timber to build a fort which Columbus named Fort Navidad. Some of the crew stayed to hold the fort when Columbus sailed on. But the Arawak Indians who lived on the island destroyed the fort and killed the men.

Columbus discovered gold in what is now the Dominican Republic, and other Spanish settlers then rushed to Hispaniola. These settlers forced the Indians to mine gold and raise food for them. They treated the Indians so harshly that by 1530 only a few hundred Indians were still alive. The settlers then brought in slaves from Africa to work for them.

Spanish settlers began leaving Hispaniola for more prosperous Spanish settlements in Peru and Mexico. By 1606, there were so few Spaniards left on Hispaniola that the king of Spain ordered all of them to move closer to the city of Santo Domingo (in what is now the Dominican Republic). French, English, and Dutch pirates then took over the abandoned northern and western coasts of Hispaniola. The pirates used the small island of Tortuga as a base and attacked ships carrying gold and silver to Spain. The Spanish tried to drive out the pirates, but failed. In 1697, Spain recognized French control of the western third of the island.

France named its new colony Saint Domingue. French colonists brought in African slaves, and developed big coffee and spice plantations. By 1788, there were eight times as many slaves (almost 500,000) as there were French colonists. The colony of Saint Dominigue prospered, and became more important to France than its colony in Canada.

In 1791, during the French Revolution, the slaves in Saint Domingue rebelled against their French masters. The slaves destroyed plantations and towns. Toussaint L'Ouverture, a former slave, took control of the government and restored some order to the country. But after Napoleon I came to power in France in 1799, he sent an army to restore colonial rule. The army sent by Napoleon captured Toussaint and imprisoned him in France. However, many of the French soldiers caught yellow fever and died, and the rebels defeated the weakened French army in 1803. On Jan. 1, 1804, General Jean Jacques Dessalines, the leader of the rebels, proclaimed the colony an independent country named Haiti.

Dessalines became the nation's first president. When

© Carl Frank, Photo Researchers

Sugar cane is one of Haiti's major crops. These rural laborers are loading the cane onto trucks for shipment to a mill, where it will be refined. Haiti exports refined sugar to the United States, France, and other countries.

he was killed in 1806, two other generals, Alexander Pétion and Henri Christophe, struggled for power. Pétion took control of southern Haiti and Christophe took control of the northern part of the country. Jean-Pierre Boyer replaced Pétion in 1818 and reunited the country after Christophe committed suicide in 1820. In 1821, Boyer took control of the Spanish colony in eastern Hispaniola. Haiti ruled it until the colony revolted in 1844. During the next 70 years, 32 different men ruled Haiti. Unrest spread throughout the country.

In 1915, President Woodrow Wilson of the United States sent marines to Haiti to restore order. He feared other nations might try to take Haiti if unrest continued. Haitians resented this interference. The U.S. occupation force made Haiti pay on its large debts to other countries. It strengthened the government, built highways, schools, and hospitals, and set up a sanitation program that eliminated yellow fever in Haiti.

The U.S. force withdrew in 1934, and Haiti regained control of its own affairs. The next two Haitian presidents encouraged foreign companies to invest money in Haiti. But the upper-class mulattoes gained most of the benefits from these investments.

There has been much unrest in Haiti since 1946. Army officers took control of the government in 1946, and again in 1949 after riots broke out. An army officer, Paul Magloire, was elected president of Haiti in 1950, and he encouraged some agricultural and industrial development. But he resigned in 1956 when rioting broke out, and the army took control of the government again.

François Duvalier, a country doctor, was elected president of Haiti in 1957. In 1964, he declared himself president for life. Duvalier ruled as a dictator. In 1971, Haiti's Constitution was amended to allow the president to choose his successor. Duvalier chose his son, Jean-Claude. François Duvalier died in April 1971. Jean-Claude, then only 19 years old, succeeded him. He also declared himself president for life and ruled as a dictator. Both François and Jean-Claude Duvalier controlled Haiti's armed forces and a secret police force. The secret police enforced the policies of the Duvaliers, and they often used violence. The people called secret police members *Tontons Macoutes* (bogeymen).

In the early 1970's, large numbers of Haitians began leaving their country because of poor economic conditions there and severe treatment by the secret police. Many sought refuge in the United States.

In 1986, Haitians staged a revolt against Jean-Claude Duvalier. Jean-Claude fled from Haiti. Lieutenant General Henri Namphy, the commander of Haiti's armed forces, became head of the government. He disbanded the Tontons Macoutes.

In March 1987, Haitian voters adopted a new constitution. The constitution provided for a new government headed by a president and a national assembly elected by the people. The government tried to shift control of the elections from a civilian electoral council to the army. Large numbers of Haitians staged demonstrations against the attempt, and violence broke out between the demonstrators and the army. The presidential election was to be held on Nov. 29, 1987. But terrorists attacked many voters at polling places, and killed more than 30 of them. Observers claimed the terrorists included former Tontons Macoutes and active members of the army. The election was canceled. In January 1988, new elections were held. The voters elected a parliament and a civilian president. But many Haitians charged that the elections were fixed by the government, and they boycotted the elections.   Gary Brana-Shute

Related articles in *World Book* include:

Cap-Haïtien	Duvalier, François
Christophe, Henri	Port-au-Prince
Columbus, Christopher	Toussaint L'Ouverture
Dessalines, Jean J.	Voodoo (with picture)
Dominican Republic	West Indies

Additional resources

Area Handbook for Haiti. Ed. by Thomas E. Weil and others. U.S. Government Printing Office, 1973.

Courlander, Harold. *The Drum and the Hoe: Life and Lore of the Haitian People.* Univ. of California Press, 1973. First published in 1960.

Rodman, Selden. *Haiti: The Black Republic.* 6th ed. Devin-Adair, 1984.

Hajj, *haj,* also spelled *hadj,* is a holy pilgrimage to Mecca, the holy city of the Islamic religion. The Kaaba, the most sacred shrine of Islam, is in Mecca and is the chief goal of the pilgrimage. The Islamic religion requires every Muslim to make this journey at least once, if possible. The hajj includes a number of ceremonies that last several days. Muslims believe a person who makes the hajj secures great religious merit. Such a person is called a *hajji* and is held in esteem. See also **Kaaba; Mecca; Muslims.**   Ali Hassan Abdel-Kader

Hake, *hayk,* is an ocean fish related to the cod. Two different kinds of fishes are called hakes. The *silver hake,* or *whiting,* of New England belongs to the true hakes. So do the *European hake* and the *Pacific hake.*

The other kind of hake, called *squirrel hake,* lives on

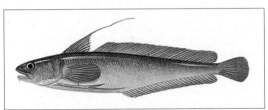

WORLD BOOK illustration by Colin Newman, Linden Artists Ltd.

The squirrel hake grows about 1 foot (30 centimeters) long. The back fin extends into a long, narrow feeler.

the ocean bottom from Cape Hatteras to Labrador. It is sometimes sold as boneless cod or as corned hake. Manufacturers use its air bladder in making glue.

Scientific classification. True hakes are in the codfish family, Gadidae. The silver hake is *Merluccius bilinearis.* The squirrel hake is *Urophycis tenuis.*   Leonard P. Schultz

Halas, *HAL uhs,* **George Stanley** (1895-1983), was a pioneer of professional football. He organized, owned, and coached the Chicago Bears, one of the original teams in the National Football League (NFL).

Halas was born in Chicago. He formed the Decatur (Ill.) Staleys professional team in 1920. He moved the team to Chicago in 1921, and renamed it the Chicago Bears in 1922. Halas played end for the team until 1929. He coached the Bears from 1920 to 1929, from 1933 to 1942, from 1946 to 1955, and from 1958 to 1968. Halas' Bears won six NFL championships. In the late 1930's, Halas and Clark Shaughnessy helped set the stage for modern, wide-open football by adding the man-in-motion to the T-formation. Halas was elected to the NFL Hall of Fame in 1963.   Herman Weiskopf

Halcyon days, *HAL see uhn,* according to sea tradition, is the two-week period of calm weather before and after the shortest day of the year, about December 21. People often use the term to refer to a time of peace or prosperity. The phrase is taken from *halcyon,* the name the ancient Greeks gave to the kingfisher. According to folklore, the halcyon built its nest on the surface of the ocean, and was able to quiet the winds while its eggs were hatching.   Sharron G. Uhler

Haldeman, H. R. See Watergate.

Hale, Edward Everett (1822-1909), was a Unitarian clergyman, editor, and humanitarian. He wrote many books, but only the short story "The Man Without a Country" (1863) has remained well known. It is the story of a young Army officer, Philip Nolan, who exclaimed during his trial by court-martial that he wished he would never hear of the United States again. Nolan was put on a ship with instructions that no one was ever again to give him any news of his own land. But before he died, he redeemed himself and begged for reconciliation with his country. Hale's story caused such a sensation that many people failed to realize that it was fiction. It has been said that Hale's formula in his stories was to take an impossible situation and make it appear probable by simplicity and directness.

Hale was born in Boston, son of Nathan Hale, first editor of the *Boston Daily Advertiser,* and grandnephew of Nathan Hale, the Revolutionary War hero (see **Hale, Nathan**). As a youngster, he wrote stories and printed them. He also published a small newspaper which he circulated among his relatives and neighbors.

Hale graduated from Harvard College when he was 17. After graduation, he studied theology and taught in the Boston Latin School. He became pastor of the Church of the Unity, in Worcester, Mass., in 1846. He moved 10 years later to the South Congregational Church in Boston, and stayed there for 43 years.

His works include *A New England Boyhood* (1893), and the story "My Double, and How He Undid Me" (1859). He himself thought his best book was the novel *In His Name* (1873). Hale edited a monthly magazine, *Old and New,* for five years, and worked for the New England Emigrant Aid Society. He was a leader in the Lend-a-Hand charity movement, whose motto was "Look up and not down, look forward and not back, look out and not in, lend a hand."   Edward Wagenknecht

Hale, George Ellery (1868-1938), was an American astronomer who pioneered in the development of instruments for studying the sun. He also planned the construction of several giant telescopes, including the Hale Reflecting Telescope at the Palomar Observatory near San Diego. This instrument has a diameter of 200 inches (508 centimeters).

Hale was born in Chicago and graduated from the Massachusetts Institute of Technology. In 1891, he introduced the *spectroheliograph,* an instrument that enables astronomers to photograph the surface of the sun with light of a single wavelength. Photographs made with a spectroheliograph reveal the distribution on the sun's surface of such elements as calcium, hydrogen, and iron. Hale also made important discoveries about

sunspots. For example, he proved that these dark areas on the sun have strong magnetic fields. In 1895, Hale founded the *Astrophysical Journal,* which became the leading journal for astronomers. Hale founded and served as first director of the Yerkes Observatory in Wisconsin and, later, the Mount Wilson Observatory in California.   Raymond E. White

Hale, John Parker (1806-1873), of New Hampshire, was a leading opponent of slavery before the Civil War. Hale served in the United States House of Representatives from 1843 to 1845. In 1845, the Democratic Party refused to renominate him because he opposed the admission of new slave states into the Union. Hale served in the U.S. Senate from 1847 to 1853, and again from 1855 to 1865. He was nominated for President by the Liberty Party in 1848, but he withdrew when the party merged with the Free Soil Party. In 1852, he was unsuccessful in his bid for the presidency on the Free Soil ticket. He served as Minister to Spain from 1865 until 1869. Hale was born in Rochester, N.H.   J. Duane Squires

Hale, Nathan (1755-1776), was an American patriot of the Revolutionary War. He was hanged by the British as an American spy when he was only 21 years old. His conduct and his courage have made him one of America's most-remembered heroes.

Hale, one of 12 children, was born in Coventry, Conn., on June 6, 1755. He had a strong, athletic body, and a relatively calm, rather pious temperament. As a boy, he took part in sports. A friend later recalled how high Hale could kick a ball, and how much he enjoyed sports competition.

Hale also took advantage of opportunities for education. He prepared for college and learned the classics under the tutorship of the Reverend Joseph Huntington. In 1769, Hale entered Yale College, where he was a diligent student. After graduation in 1773, he taught school for a year at East Haddam, Conn. He then moved to New London, Conn.

The American Revolution. Although Hale was highly successful in his teaching, he was also deeply concerned about American rights. In July 1775, he received a lieutenant's commission from the Connecticut assembly, and helped in the siege of Boston. When the British forces evacuated Boston and entered the New York area, Hale, along with other patriot soldiers, went there to meet the new threat. By this time he had become a captain in the Continental Army. Hale's resourceful leadership, especially in capturing a supply-loaded vessel from under the guns of a British warship, won him a place in a select fighting group called the Rangers. The Rangers were known for their daring leadership and fighting qualities in dangerous missions.

The fateful mission. Unknown to Hale or anyone else, the time had come for a dramatic moment of the Revolutionary War. General George Washington asked the Rangers' commander to select a man to pass through the British lines to obtain information on the British position. The commander called for a volunteer. Hale agreed to undertake the mission.

Disguising himself in civilian clothes as a Dutch schoolmaster, Hale succeeded in crossing the British lines. He obtained the information that Washington requested. But as Hale returned to the American lines on Sept. 21, 1776, he was captured by the British. Many

Chicago Historical Society

Captain Nathan Hale was executed in New York City near what is now 66th Street and Third Avenue. Major Cunningham, who stands facing Hale, denied his last request for a Bible and destroyed a letter Hale had written.

believe that Hale's cousin, an ardent British loyalist, betrayed him.

Hale was taken before General William Howe, the British commander. Howe saw that Hale was out of uniform and condemned him to hang the next day as a spy. With remarkable calmness of mind and spirit, Hale prepared for his execution. Before the hanging he made a speech. Historians are not sure what Hale really said. According to tradition, he ended his speech with the inspiring words, "I only regret that I have but one life to lose for my country."

There are several Hale monuments. A boulder marks *Halesite* near Huntington, N.Y., where it is believed Hale was captured. A Nathan Hale Homestead stands in South Coventry, Conn.   James Kirby Martin

Additional resources

Brown, Marion. *Young Nathan.* Westminster, 1949. For younger readers.
Darrow, Jane. *Nathan Hale: A Story of Loyalties.* Century Co., 1932. Suitable for younger readers.
Johnston, Henry P. *Nathan Hale, 1776: Biography and Memorials.* Rev. ed. Yale, 1914. A standard work.

Hale, Sarah Josepha, *joh SEE fuh* (1788-1879), became one of the most famous magazine editors in the United States during the 1800's. As editor of the *Ladies' Magazine* and, later, of *Godey's Lady's Book,* she helped shape the taste and thought of thousands of women. She received credit for persuading President Abraham Lincoln to make Thanksgiving a national holiday. She did much writing. Her major surviving work is the children's poem, "Mary Had a Little Lamb." Sarah Hale was born in Newport, N.H.   John Tebbel

Hale, William. See Rocket (History).

Hale Observatories. See Mount Wilson Observatory; Palomar Observatory.

Haleakala National Park, *HAH leh AH kah LA,* became a separate park in 1960. It had been part of Hawaii Volcanoes National Park since 1916. Haleakala National Park lies on the island of Maui, in Hawaii. Its chief attraction, the inactive volcano Haleakala (*house of the sun*), has colorful rock formations in its crater. For the park's area, see **National Park System** (table: National parks).
Critically reviewed by the National Park Service

Halevi, *hah LAY vee,* **Judah** (1085-1141?), was one of the greatest Hebrew poets of the Middle Ages. His poetry included both national and religious songs, and dealt with the suffering and hopes of the Jewish people.

Werner Stoy, Camera Hawaii

Haleakala National Park lies on the island of Maui in Hawaii. It features the crater of Haleakala, an inactive volcano, *above*.

Many of his hymns to Zion (the land of Israel), called "Zionids," are still read in Jewish religious services. He was also a physician and a religious philosopher, His most important philosophical work was *Sefer ha-Kuzari,* or *al-Khazari,* an eloquent defense and profound explanation of Judaism. Halevi was born in Toledo, Spain.

Gary G. Porton

Haley, Alex (1921-   ), is an American author who became famous for his book *Roots: The Saga of an American Family* (1976). In the book, Haley combined fact and fiction as he described the history of his family, beginning in the mid-1700's in Africa. *Roots* tells how Haley's ancestor Kunta Kinte was kidnapped in Gambia in 1767 and taken to America as a slave. It follows the struggles of Haley's family in America as slaves and later as free people.

Warner Bros. Television Distribution, Inc.

Alex Haley

Haley spent 12 years researching *Roots.* His fame grew after an eight-part dramatization of *Roots* appeared on television in the United States in 1977. The final episode attracted one of the largest audiences in television history. That same year, Haley received the Spingarn Medal and a special citation from the Pulitzer Prize Board for his book.

Alex Palmer Haley was born in Ithaca, N.Y., and grew up in Henning, Tenn., and other Southern communities. He served in the Coast Guard from 1939 to 1959 and began to write articles and short stories during that period. Haley edited *The Autobiography of Malcolm X* (1965).   Edgar Allan Toppin

Half dollar is a United States coin worth 50 cents. The half dollar featuring President John F. Kennedy has been minted since February 1964. It has the presidential seal on the reverse side. This half dollar replaced the Franklin half dollar, which was first issued in 1948. In 1975 and 1976, the government issued special bicentennial half dollars. These coins featured Kennedy on one side and Independence Hall on the other.

The first half dollars were minted in 1794, along with the first silver dollars. Both coins had a portrait or figure of Liberty on one side and an eagle on the reverse.

Until 1965, half dollars contained 90 per cent silver and 10 per cent copper. The Coinage Act of 1965

WORLD BOOK photo by James Simek

The U.S. half dollar pictures President John F. Kennedy. The presidential seal appears on the coin's reverse side.

changed the ratio to 40 per cent silver and 60 per cent copper. A 1970 act eliminated all silver from the half dollar.   Burton Hobson

Half-life. See **Radioactivity** (Half-life).

Halfway house. See **Prison** (Reforms in the 1900's).

Haliburton, Thomas Chandler. See **Canadian literature** (The early 1800's).

Halibut is one of the largest and most important of the flatfishes. Its name comes from the word *holy,* and refers to the fact that it was once widely used as food on Christian holy days. A cold-water fish, the halibut belongs to the flounder group, and has the characteristic flat body, with both eyes on the same side of the head. Its eyes lie on the right side, which is dark brown. The

WORLD BOOK illustration by Colin Newman, Linden Artists Ltd.

The halibut is an important food fish that lives in northern waters. It has a flat body with both eyes on its right side.

left side is white. Halibut can be found in all northern seas. They are among the largest of the world's true bony fishes. Some female halibut weigh as much as 400 pounds (180 kilograms).

Halibut are caught with strong hooks tied a short distance apart on long lines. The hooks are baited and then dropped to the ocean bottom. The most important fishing grounds in North America are the waters from Puget Sound to Alaska, the Grand Banks off Newfoundland, and the waters of Greenland.

Halibut flesh has a mild, pleasant flavor. The landings of halibut in United States ports total about 11,000 short tons (10,000 metric tons) a year.

Scientific classification. Halibut make up the family Hippoglossidae. The Atlantic halibut is *Hippoglossus hippoglossus.* The Greenland halibut is *Reinhardtius hippoglossoides.*

Robert R. Rofen

See also **Fish** (picture: Fish of coastal waters and the open ocean); **Fishing industry** (Fishery conservation); **Flatfish; Flounder.**

Halifax (pop. 113,577; met. area pop. 295,990) is the capital of Nova Scotia and the largest city in Canada's four Atlantic Provinces. Halifax has a large harbor that ranks as Canada's main naval base and busiest east coast port. The harbor remains open in winter when ice closes most other eastern Canadian ports. Halifax lies on the east coast of Nova Scotia. For location, see **Nova Scotia** (political map).

British settlers founded Halifax in 1749. Great Britain built a military base there because of its growing struggle with France for control of North America. France had forces stationed at nearby Louisbourg (see **Louisbourg**). Halifax was named for George Dunk, the Earl of Halifax, who headed the government board that super-

Halifax City Hall, completed in 1887, is a famous city landmark. It stands in downtown Halifax. The modern office buildings in the background are part of the Scotia Square commercial center.

vised the colony. Halifax is one of Canada's most historic cities. Canada's first representative government, the General Assembly of Nova Scotia, was established in Halifax in 1758. The first Protestant church in Canada was built there in 1749, and Canada's first newspaper appeared there in 1752.

Description. Most of Halifax lies on a peninsula between the harbor and an inlet called the North West Arm. Halifax covers about 24 square miles (62 square kilometers), including 1 square mile (3 square kilometers) of inland water. The Halifax metropolitan area spreads over about 968 square miles (2,508 square kilometers) and includes Dartmouth, the "sister city" of Halifax. Two bridges across the harbor connect the cities.

Province House, Canada's oldest parliament building, stands in downtown Halifax. This building, the home of the Nova Scotia legislature, was completed in 1818. The Citadel, a stone fortress built in 1828, overlooks the downtown area from a hilltop. York Redoubt, a defense post on the North West Arm, dates from 1793. The Prince of Wales Martello Tower, a fortification built in 1796, stands in Point Pleasant Park.

The economy of Halifax depends heavily on six military bases in the area. About 5,000 civilians and 10,000 men and women of the armed forces work at these bases. The Port of Halifax handles about 12 million short tons (11 million metric tons) of cargo annually. Halifax International Airport lies about 25 miles (40 kilometers) northwest of the city.

Over 100 manufacturing plants operate in the Halifax area. Food processing and oil refining are the city's leading industries. Hospitals in Halifax form the largest Canadian medical center east of Quebec City.

Halifax has more than 50 public schools. Institutions of higher education include Dalhousie University,

Mount St. Vincent University, Nova Scotia College of Art and Design, St. Mary's University, and the Technical University of Nova Scotia. The Bedford Institute and other research organizations in the area make up one of the world's largest centers of ocean study.

The Dalhousie University Arts Centre offers art exhibits, concerts, and plays. Halifax has a resident theater group and about 10 art galleries. Museums in the city include the Public Archives of Nova Scotia and five branches of the Nova Scotia Museum.

Government and history. Halifax has a council-manager form of government. The voters elect a mayor and 10 aldermen to three-year terms on the city council. The council appoints a city manager, who serves as administrative head of the government. The city gets most of its revenue from property taxes.

Micmac Indians lived in what is now the Halifax area before white explorers arrived there. In 1749, the British government sent Governor Edward Cornwallis and about 2,500 settlers to establish a fort and town. The town became the capital of Nova Scotia that year.

Halifax served as a major British naval base during the Revolutionary War in America (1775-1783) and the War of 1812. Military officers governed the city until 1841. That year, Joseph Howe, a newspaper editor and statesman, led a campaign that brought the city incorporation and self-government. Halifax had 20,749 people in 1851. By 1901, its population had reached 40,832.

In 1917, during World War I, a French ammunition ship exploded in the city's harbor. This disaster killed about 2,000 people and wrecked much of Halifax. The population grew to 58,372 by 1921, largely as a result of wartime military activities. During World War II (1939-1945), Halifax became the chief North American base for Allied ships carrying food and war supplies to Europe.

In the 1960's, private businesses developed the Scotia Square commercial center in downtown Halifax. The center includes more than 100 stores, a trade mart, office and apartment buildings, restaurants, and a hotel. Port operations boomed after the Halifax Container Terminal opened in 1970. Cranes at the terminal quickly transfer large containers of cargo between ships and trains. This procedure made shipment via Halifax one of the fastest freight routes between Europe and central Canada. A second container terminal, Fairview Cove, was completed in 1981.

In 1971, drillers struck oil off Sable Island near the Nova Scotia coast. Halifax became a center of oil industry activity. Optimism about an oil-based economic boom led to the construction of office buildings, condominiums, and hotels in downtown Halifax and the harbor area. When the international price of oil dropped sharply in the mid-1980's, drilling activity off Sable Island was reduced.   Basil W. Deakin

For the monthly weather in Halifax, see **Nova Scotia** (Climate). See also **Nova Scotia** (pictures).

Halifax Citadel National Historic Park. See Canada (National historic parks and sites).

Halite. See Salt.

Hall, Charles Martin. See Aluminum (How aluminum is made; History).

Hall, G. Stanley (1844-1924), an American educator and psychologist, became an authority on the study of children. Hall was the first educator to apply results of child psychology experiments to teaching.

In 1889, Hall became the first president of Clark University in Worcester, Mass. There he stimulated research in psychology. His writings include *The Contents of Children's Minds on Entering School* (1894), *The Story of a Sand Pile* (1897), *Adolescence* (1904), *Youth* (1907), *Educational Problems* (1911), and *Founders of Modern Psychology* (1912). He also founded and edited the *American Journal of Psychology.*

Granville Stanley Hall was born in Ashfield, Mass. He graduated from Williams College in 1867, and then studied abroad for several years. He was professor of psychology at Antioch College from 1872 to 1876. He lectured on psychology at Harvard University and Williams for a year. Hall served as a professor and lecturer at Johns Hopkins University from 1881 to 1888, and then went to Clark University.   Claude A. Eggertsen

Hall, James N. See Nordhoff and Hall.

Hall, Lyman (1724-1790), an American Revolutionary War statesman, urged independence from Great Britain and influenced Georgia's decision to join the other colonies. He was a delegate to the Continental Congress and signed the Declaration of Independence.

Hall was born in Wallingford, Conn., and studied for the ministry at Yale College. Later, he became a doctor and settled in Georgia. He was elected governor of Georgia in 1783.   Clarence L. Ver Steeg

Hall, Prince (1748-1807), founded the first all-black Masonic lodge in America. Hall's lodge and other all-black lodges founded later made up the first major organization created by blacks in America.

Hall was born in the West Indies, and moved to the area around Boston in 1765. He educated himself and became a property owner and a pastor of a Methodist congregation in Cambridge, Mass. In 1775, Hall and 14 other free blacks joined an all-white British Army Masonic lodge in Boston. The blacks formed a separate "African Lodge" after the Revolutionary War started. Hall's group could not get an American Masonic charter, but was chartered by English Masons in 1787.   Richard Bardolph

Hall effect is an electrical phenomenon that occurs when a current flows through a material in a magnetic field. For example, if a material has a current flowing through it perpendicular to a magnetic field around the material, the Hall effect is observed as a voltage across the material. The Hall voltage is perpendicular to both the direction of the current and the direction of the magnetic field.

For any given material, the Hall voltage is proportional to the current and the magnetic field. Different materials produce different Hall voltages. Therefore, scientists can use the Hall effect as an experimental tool to describe the electrical properties of materials. For example, the Hall voltage produced in metals is much smaller than that produced in semiconductor materials. The Hall effect was discovered in 1879 by the American physicist Edwin H. Hall.   Robert M. Burger

Hall of fame is a museum honoring people who have gained fame in a particular field. One of the best-known halls of fame is the Hall of Fame for Great Americans in New York City. The National Baseball Hall of Fame and Museum, the Pro Football Hall of Fame, and other institutions pay tribute to great athletes. Halls of fame also honor achievements in a number of other fields.

The Hall of Fame for Great Americans is a memorial to Americans who have gained lasting fame for their great achievements. The building is a semicircular, covered, outdoor corridor, 630 feet (192 meters) long and a little over 10 feet (3 meters) wide. Between granite columns there are 102 spaces for bronze busts of persons elected to the Hall of Fame. Beneath each bust is a bronze tablet bearing the name, dates of birth and death, and a quotation from the honored person. The structure was designed by the American architect Stanford White about 1900.

The Hall of Fame for Great Americans was founded in

Hall of Fame for Great Americans

Busts of honored U.S. citizens stand in the colonnade of the Hall of Fame for Great Americans in New York City.

Members of the Hall of Fame for Great Americans

1900		
George Washington	Henry Wadsworth Longfellow	Robert E. Lee
Abraham Lincoln	Washington Irving	Eli Whitney
Daniel Webster	Jonathan Edwards	John James Audubon
Benjamin Franklin	Samuel F. B. Morse	Horace Mann
Ulysses S. Grant	David G. Farragut	Henry Ward Beecher
John Marshall	Henry Clay	James Kent
Thomas Jefferson	Nathaniel Hawthorne	Joseph Story
Ralph Waldo Emerson	George Peabody	John Adams
Robert Fulton	Peter Cooper	William Ellery Channing
		Gilbert Stuart
		Asa Gray

1905		
John Quincy Adams	William T. Sherman	James Madison
James Russell Lowell	Emma Willard	John Greenleaf Whittier
	Mary Lyon	Maria Mitchell

1910		
Harriet Beecher Stowe	James Fenimore Cooper	Frances E. Willard
Oliver Wendell Holmes	Phillips Brooks	Andrew Jackson
Edgar Allan Poe	William Cullen Bryant	George Bancroft
		John Lothrop Motley

1915		
Mark Hopkins	Joseph Henry	Rufus Choate
Francis Parkman	Louis Agassiz	Daniel Boone
Elias Howe	Charlotte Cushman	Alexander Hamilton

1920		
Mark Twain	Augustus Saint-Gaudens	Roger Williams
James B. Eads	Patrick Henry	Alice Freeman Palmer
William T. G. Morton		

1925		
Edwin Booth		John Paul Jones

1930		
Walt Whitman	James A. McNeill Whistler	James Monroe
Matthew F. Maury		

1935		
William Penn	Simon Newcomb	Grover Cleveland

1940		
Stephen Foster		

1945		
Booker T. Washington	Sidney Lanier	Walter Reed
	Thomas Paine	

1950		
Woodrow Wilson	Susan B. Anthony	Theodore Roosevelt
Alexander Graham Bell	William C. Gorgas	Josiah W. Gibbs

1955		
Wilbur Wright	Stonewall Jackson	George Westinghouse

1960		
Thomas Alva Edison	Henry David Thoreau	Edward MacDowell

1965		
Jane Addams	Oliver Wendell Holmes, Jr.	Sylvanus Thayer
		Orville Wright

1970		
Albert Abraham Michelson		Lillian D. Wald

1973		
George Washington Carver	Franklin D. Roosevelt	John Philip Sousa
Louis D. Brandeis		

1976		
Clara Barton	Luther Burbank	Andrew Carnegie

1900 by New York University. In 1974, the university transferred responsibility for the hall to a newly organized board of trustees. Elections were suspended indefinitely in 1977 because of a lack of money. But the Hall of Fame remained open to visitors. It is on the campus of Bronx Community College of the City University of New York in New York City.

Sports halls of fame honor great athletes of the past. The National Baseball Hall of Fame and Museum in Cooperstown, N.Y., pays tribute to great baseball players from the major and Negro leagues. The museum displays bats, gloves, and other equipment of the players. See the **Baseball** article for a list of players in the baseball hall of fame. The College Football Hall of Fame in King's Island, Ohio, honors outstanding college players and coaches. The Pro Football Hall of Fame in Canton, Ohio, is dedicated to athletes, coaches, and others who helped develop and promote professional football. The Hockey Hall of Fame in Toronto honors players and other individuals who made important contributions to the sport. Bowling, boxing, golf, skiing, and tennis organizations also elect top-ranking players to their halls of fame.

Other halls of fame honor men and women in professional and other groups. The Hall of Immortals in the International College of Surgeons in Chicago honors great surgeons and scientists. The Agricultural Hall of Fame in Bonner Springs, Kans., honors those who have contributed significantly to farming. The National Hall of Fame for Famous American Indians is in Anadarko, Okla. The National Cowboy Hall of Fame and Western Heritage Center is in Oklahoma City, Okla. The Songwriters' Hall of Fame in New York City honors composers of popular songs. The National Women's Hall of Fame in Seneca Falls, N.Y., honors great American women. The International Space Hall of Fame in Alamogordo, N.M., honors pioneers in space travel.

See also **Cowboy** (Cowboy Hall of Fame); **Michigan** (Places to visit [National Ski Hall of Fame]).

Halleck, *HAL ihk,* **Henry Wager,** *WAY juhr* (1815-1872), was a military scholar and a Union general in the Civil War. He wrote and translated several books on war. In the Civil War, he first commanded the Western department. From 1862 to 1864, he acted as general in chief of all armies. He became chief of staff, a secretarial office, in 1864. After the war, he was a major general and department commander. Born in Westernville, N.Y., Halleck was graduated from the United States Military Academy in 1840.   T. Harry Williams

See also **Civil War** (The war in the West).

Halley, *HAL ee,* **Edmond** (1656-1742), also spelled Edmund, was an English astronomer noted for his work on comets. He calculated the orbit of a comet he observed in 1682 and proved that the comet was the same one astronomers had seen in 1531 and in 1607. He predicted its return in 1758. It was seen on Christmas Day of that year and reached its nearest point to the sun in 1759. This comet became known as Halley's Comet. See **Halley's Comet.**

Brown Bros.

Edmond Halley

Halley produced the first accurate map of the stars visible from the Southern Hemisphere. He proved that stars have *proper motion*—that is, they change position in relation to each other. Halley studied the orbit of the moon and the effect of the moon on ocean tides. He also determined an accurate way to measure the distance of the sun from the earth. This measurement was needed for determining the size of the solar system and the distances of other stars from the earth.

Halley was born in London. He attended Oxford University and served as England's astronomer royal from 1720 until his death. C. R. O'Dell

See also Insurance (History).

Halley's Comet, *HAL eez,* is a brilliant comet named for the English astronomer Edmond Halley. Before Halley made his investigations, most people believed that comets appeared by chance and traveled through space in no set path. But Halley believed that comets belonged to the solar system and took definite paths around the sun at regular intervals.

Halley found that the paths of certain comets seen in 1531 and 1607 were identical with the path of a comet observed in 1682. He concluded that all the observations were of a single comet traveling in a set orbit around the sun. Halley predicted that the comet would reappear in 1758 and at fairly regular intervals thereafter. The comet was indeed seen in 1758. Halley's Comet appears an average of every 77 years. The first reported sightings were made by Chinese astronomers about 240 B.C.

Halley's Comet can be seen in its orbit only as it nears the sun. In August 1909, scientists at Helwan Observatory in Egypt photographed the comet when it was about 300 million miles (480 million kilometers) from the sun. On April 24, 1910, it came as close as 55 million miles (89 million kilometers) to the sun. On May 21, 1910, the earth is believed to have passed through the comet's tail. The comet was last observed during that appearance on July 1, 1911.

On Oct. 16, 1982, astronomers at the Palomar Observatory in California made the next sighting of Halley's Comet. They photographed the comet when it was about 1 billion miles (1.6 billion kilometers) from the sun. The comet made its closest approach to the sun on Feb. 9, 1986. In March of that year, several unmanned spacecraft drew near the comet, collecting information about its composition and the size of its *nucleus* (center). The *Giotto,* launched by the European Space Agency, made

the closest approach, coming within 338 miles (544 kilometers) of the comet's nucleus.

The earth passes through the orbit of Halley's Comet each May and October. Pieces of dust left behind by the comet enter the earth's atmosphere and burn, producing meteor showers during these months.

Lee J. Rickard

See also **Comet; Halley, Edmond.**

Additional resources

Asimov, Isaac. *Asimov's Guide to Halley's Comet.* Walker, 1985. Suitable for younger readers.
Tattersfield, Donald. *Halley's Comet.* Basil Blackwell, 1985.

Halliburton, Richard (1900-1939), was an American adventurer, author, and lecturer. He visited many parts of the world and wrote excitedly about his trips. Halliburton's daring got him into dangerous situations that give suspense to his books. His deep knowledge of history helped him relive the lives of leading historical figures in many countries.

Halliburton's writings include *The Glorious Adventure* (1927), *New Worlds to Conquer* (1929), *The Flying Carpet* (1932), *Seven League Boots* (1935), and *Richard Halliburton's Complete Book of Marvels* (1937).

Halliburton was born in Brownsville, Tenn. He graduated from Princeton University. In 1939, he tried to cross the Pacific Ocean in a specially built Chinese junk. The junk was caught in a storm, and everyone on board was lost. Frank Goodwyn

Hallmark is a mark stamped on manufactured objects. It guarantees their quality. The word comes from the practice of jewelers in Goldsmiths' Hall in London, who put the mark of their hall on gold and silver objects to certify their value. It now refers to stamps placed on metal by assayers and mints. It has come to mean good quality in almost any product.

Halloween is a festival that takes place on October 31. In the United States, children wear costumes on Halloween and go trick-or-treating. Many carve jack-o'-lanterns out of pumpkins. Halloween parties feature such activities as fortunetelling, storytelling about ghosts and witches, and bobbing for apples.

Halloween developed from ancient new year festivals and festivals of the dead. In the A.D. 800's, the church established All Saints' Day on November 1 so that people could continue a festival they had celebrated before becoming Christians. The Mass that was said on this day was called *Allhallowmas.* The evening before All Saints' Day became known as *All Hallow e'en,* or *Halloween.*

Halloween customs

Trick-or-treating is the main Halloween activity for most children in the United States. The youngsters dress in costumes and masks and go from door to door saying "trick or treat." The neighbors, to avoid having tricks played on them, give the children such treats as candy, fruit, and pennies.

Some children trick or treat for UNICEF, the United Nations Children's Fund. They collect money for the agency in official orange and black cartons. UNICEF uses the money to provide food, medical care, and other services for poor children throughout the world.

Certain safety measures can help prevent accidents on Halloween. A child who goes trick-or-treating should

A jack-o'-lantern for Halloween is made by carving a pumpkin. Most jack-o'-lanterns are hollowed-out pumpkins with funny faces cut into them. Candles or other lights are placed inside.

© Larry Day

wear a light-colored costume or one with reflecting tape sewn on. Such a costume can be easily seen by motorists. The costume should be made of a material that does not burn easily. Because some masks can block vision, many parents use makeup to paint a mask on the child's face.

Younger trick-or-treaters should be accompanied by an adult. Children should visit only homes in their own neighborhood. Many parents allow their children to eat only packaged candy. Some communities set aside certain hours for trick-or-treating so that people can prepare for the children, and so motorists can be especially alert.

Jack-o'-lanterns are hollowed-out pumpkins with a face cut into one side. Most jack-o'-lanterns contain a candle or some other light. People in England and Ireland once carved out beets, potatoes, and turnips to use as lanterns on Halloween. After this custom reached America, pumpkins began to be used. Today, jack-o'-lanterns are used as decorations.

According to an Irish legend, jack-o'-lanterns were named for a man called Jack, who could not enter heaven because he was a miser. He could not enter hell either, because he had played jokes on the devil. As a result, Jack had to walk the earth with his lantern until Judgment Day.

Fortunetelling. Certain fortunetelling methods began in Europe hundreds of years ago and became an important part of Halloween. For example, such objects as a coin, a ring, and a thimble were baked into a cake or other food. It was believed that the person who found the coin in the cake would become wealthy. The one who found the ring would marry soon, but the person who got the thimble would never get married. Today, some people use such fortunetelling techniques as cardreading or palmistry in addition to the traditional Halloween methods.

Other Halloween traditions. Bobbing for apples in a tub of water probably began in England. Today, some people stick a coin into each apple as an extra reward.

People once believed that ghosts roamed the earth on Halloween. They also thought that all witches met on October 31 to worship the devil. Today, most people do not believe in ghosts or witches, but these supernatural beings remain symbols of Halloween.

History

The Celtic festival of Samhain is probably the source of the present-day Halloween celebration. The Celts lived more than 2,000 years ago in what is now Great Britain, Ireland, and northern France. Their new year began on November 1. A festival that began the previous evening honored Samhain, the Celtic lord of death. The celebration marked the beginning of the season of cold, darkness, and decay. It naturally became associated with human death. The Celts believed that Samhain allowed the souls of the dead to return to their earthly homes for this evening.

On the evening of the festival, the Druids, who were the priests and teachers of the Celts, ordered the people to put out their hearth fires. The Druids built a huge new year's bonfire of oak branches, which they considered sacred. They burned animals, crops, and possibly even human beings as sacrifices. Then each family relit its hearth fire from the new year's fire. During the celebration, people sometimes wore costumes made of animal heads and skins. They told fortunes about the coming year by examining the remains of the animals that had been sacrificed.

The Romans conquered the Celts in A.D. 43 and ruled what is now Great Britain for about 400 years. During this period, two Roman autumn festivals were combined with the Celtic festival of Samhain. One of them, called *Feralia,* was held in late October to honor the dead. The other festival honored Pomona, the Roman goddess of fruit and trees. Apples probably became associated with Halloween because of this festival.

All Saints' Day. Many of the customs of the Celts survived even after the people became Christians. During the 800's, the church established All Saints' Day on November 1 (see **All Saints' Day**). The people made the old pagan customs part of this Christian holy day. The church later began to honor the dead on November 2. This day became known as All Souls' Day.

Regional Halloween customs developed among various groups of Celts. In Ireland, for example, people begged for food in a parade that honored Muck Olla, a god. The leader of the parade wore a white robe and a mask made from the head of an animal. In Scotland, people paraded through fields and villages carrying torches. They lit huge bonfires on hillsides to drive away witches and other evil spirits. In Wales, every person marked a stone and put it into a bonfire. The people believed that if a person's stone was missing the next morning, he or she would die within a year.

In England, Halloween was sometimes called *Nutcrack Night* or *Snap Apple Night.* Families sat by the fire and told stories while they ate apples and nuts. On All Souls' Day, poor people went *a-souling* (begging). They received pastries called *soulcakes* in exchange for promising to say prayers for the dead.

Halloween in the United States. Many early American settlers came from England and other Celtic regions, and they brought various customs with them. But because of the strict religious beliefs of other settlers,

Halloween celebrations did not become popular until the 1800's. During that period, large numbers of immigrants arrived from Ireland and Scotland and introduced their Halloween customs.

During the mid-1900's, trick-or-treating became less popular in large cities, where many neighbors did not know one another. Halloween pranks, which had once been harmless, sometimes became rowdy and destructive. Traffic accidents also became a major problem on Halloween. As a result, family parties and large community celebrations gained popularity. Today, many communities sponsor bonfires, costume parades, dances, skits, and other forms of entertainment to celebrate Halloween.   Carol Bain

Additional resources

Barth, Edna. *Witches, Pumpkins, and Grinning Ghosts: The Story of the Halloween Symbols.* Seabury, 1972.
Corwin, Judith H. *Halloween Fun.* Messner, 1983.
Dobrin, Arnold. *Make a Witch, Make a Goblin: A Book of Halloween Crafts.* Four Winds, 1977.
Herda, D. J. *Halloween.* Watts, 1983.
Kessel, Joyce K. *Halloween.* Carolrhoda, 1980.
Linton, Ralph and A. S. *Halloween Through Twenty Centuries.* Schuman, 1950. For older readers.

Hallucination, *huh LOO suh NAY shuhn,* is a mental state in which a person sees, hears, tastes, smells, or feels something that is not present. Hallucinations may indicate the presence of a mental or physical disorder. But normal people also may hear voices or see visions when deprived of stimuli, such as in solitary confinement or when under the influence of drugs. See also **Mental illness** (Schizophrenia).   Allen Frances

Hallucinogenic drug, *huh LOO suh nuh JEHN ihk,* is any of several substances that distort a person's understanding of himself and his surroundings. These drugs temporarily change the chemistry of the brain. They affect the senses, emotions, reasoning, and the brain's control of muscles and certain body functions. The changes may be extremely pleasant or highly unpleasant and frightening. In the United States, laws prohibit the manufacture, distribution, and possession of these drugs except for government-approved research.

Hallucinogenic drugs are also called *psychedelic* (mind revealing) drugs. The most powerful such drug is *LSD* (see **LSD**). This drug and three others, *STP, DMT,* and *PCP,* are chemically manufactured. PCP, also known as "angel dust," "crystal," or "peacepill," is an especially dangerous drug. It was developed in the 1950's and originally used as an anesthetic for animals. PCP later was discovered to produce an intensely euphoric state of mind in human beings when sprinkled on marijuana or tobacco or taken in other ways. However, the drug also may cause violent and impulsive behavior in some users.

The effects of hallucinogenic drugs are sometimes called *trips.* During a trip, a drug user may see bright, moving colors. The size, arrangement, and shape of objects may appear to change constantly. The user may *hallucinate* (see or hear things that are not present). The person may step out of a window, not realizing the danger of being hurt or even killed. Drug users may vividly recall past experiences. They may have a sense of overwhelming fear, sadness, and horror, or feel intense love and joy. During a trip, drug users may feel that they have gained a new understanding of God, the universe, and themselves.

The effects of hallucinogenic drugs last from one hour to several days. But these effects may appear again months later as a *flashback.* People may feel unusually happy or upset for weeks after using hallucinogenic drugs. Some users become mentally ill. A trip and its effects vary from person to person and from trip to trip. The experience and its effects are influenced by (1) the type and amount of drug taken, (2) the circumstances in which the drug is used, and (3) the user's personality and mood. Hallucinogenic drugs are not addicting. Some scientists believe that hallucinogenic drugs cause birth defects.

Hallucinogenic drugs may someday prove useful to science. Scientists have used them to study the chemistry of the brain. Physicians have used the drugs experimentally to treat emotional disorders.   Donald J. Wolk

See also **Drug abuse.**

Additional resources

Grinspoon, Lester, and Bakalar, J. B. *Psychedelic Drugs Reconsidered.* Harper, 1979.
Mind Drugs. Ed. by Margaret O. Hyde. 4th ed. McGraw, 1981.
Schultes, Richard E., and Hofmann, Albert. *Plants of the Gods: Origins of Hallucinogenic Use.* McGraw, 1979.

Halo is a luminous ring or a disk of light that surrounds an object. Halos commonly appear in Christian religious art as a symbol of saintliness or divinity. In many religious paintings created since the 400's, Jesus Christ and the Virgin Mary, as well as the angels and saints, have been portrayed with a shining circle around the head. The golden or jeweled crowns worn by royalty were originally modeled after the sacred halo. Such a crown was meant to signify the wearer's "divine right" to rule.

The term *halo* is also used in connection with various natural phenomena. The pale ring of light that occasionally appears around the sun or moon is called a halo. Such rings are most often seen during winter. They appear when light rays are *refracted* (bent) by ice crystals in the earth's upper atmosphere.

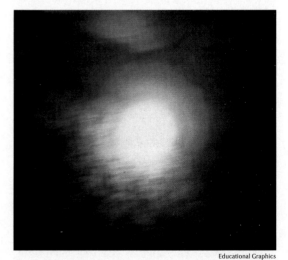

Educational Graphics

A lunar halo appears as a ring of light around the moon. It is seen when light rays reflected from the moon are bent as they pass through ice crystals in the earth's upper atmosphere.

Another type of halo is the luminous ring of stars that surrounds a spiral or elliptical galaxy (see **Galaxy**). This *galactic halo* consists of older stars containing few elements heavier than hydrogen and helium. It may extend hundreds of thousands of light-years from the center of a galaxy. Astronomers also speak of a halo of comets surrounding the solar system. The comets in this ring all orbit the sun at a distance of about 100,000 *astronomical* units (see **Astronomy** [Astronomy terms]). Many of the comets themselves are enveloped by a halo composed of hydrogen gas. This halo forms when a comet travels close enough to the sun for the frozen methane and ammonia in the comet's head to change directly into gas.

Raymond E. White

Halogen, *HAL uh juhn.* The halogens are the chemical elements astatine (chemical symbol, At), fluorine (F), chlorine (Cl), bromine (Br), and iodine (I). They are nonmetals, and make up part of the seventh main group in the periodic system of the elements. *Halogen* means *salt producer.* The salts in the sea are compounds of halogens with metals. Common table salt, the best known such compound, is *sodium chloride.*

The halogens all have a strong, unpleasant odor, and will burn the flesh. They do not dissolve well in water. At ordinary temperatures, fluorine is a yellow gas, chlorine a yellowish-green gas, bromine a red liquid, and iodine a black solid. Fluorine is the lightest halogen; astatine is the heaviest. The atomic weight of fluorine is 18.9984; of chlorine, 35.453; of bromine, 79.909; of iodine, 126.9044; and of astatine, 210.

The five elements of the halogen group are electronegative. This means that the atoms of halogens tend to take up electrons from other chemicals and become charged with negative electricity. They are then called *ions.* The salts, called the *halides,* are compounds formed by these ions. The halogens are oxidizing agents, but the heavier the halogen, the weaker is its oxidizing power. Fluorine is the strongest of all oxidizing agents. It is also extremely reactive.

The halogens react with most metals and many nonmetals. Their reactions with hydrogen give the halogen acids. The most important of these is hydrochloric acid, a solution of hydrogen chloride in water.

The halogens have many uses. Chlorine is a bleach and a water disinfectant. Bromine is used to make antiknock gasoline. The antiseptic, tincture of iodine, is a solution of iodine in alcohol. Many useful compounds are formed from the halogens. For example, fluorides are used in small quantities to halt tooth decay, and hydrofluoric acid is used to etch glass. Bromides and iodides are valuable medicines.

George L. Bush

See also **Astatine; Bromine; Chlorine; Fluorine; Iodine.**

Halophyte, *HAL uh fyt,* is a plant that grows in salty soil where most plants would die. Many halophytes have fleshy or hairy stems and leaves. Examples of halophytes are asparagus, saltwort, and mangrove.

Halothane, *HAL uh thayn,* is a drug doctors use to make patients insensitive to pain during surgery. Halothane is a *general anesthetic*—that is, it produces unconsciousness and loss of feeling throughout the entire body.

Halothane is a clear, colorless liquid that gives off pleasant-smelling, nonirritating vapors. In contrast to

ether and other earlier inhaled anesthetics, halothane vapor is nonflammable. Halothane therefore poses no risk of fire or explosion when used in the presence of electrical medical equipment. Patients who have received halothane regain consciousness rapidly.

Halothane is usually administered along with other drugs. Doctors often bring about anesthesia with an injection of thiopental, a barbiturate. Halothane is then administered to maintain anesthesia during surgery. Patients inhale the halothane vapor, usually in combination either with oxygen or with a mixture of oxygen and nitrous oxide. In many cases, drugs that provide additional muscle relaxation are also administered.

Halothane was discovered in England in 1951 and was first used in surgery in 1956 in the United States. Since then, halothane has become extremely popular. It has replaced ether as the standard by which other inhaled anesthetics are judged. Halothane's chemical formula is $F_3C-CHBrCl$. Its trade name is *Fluothane.*

The discovery of halothane led to the search for other safe and effective anesthetics that contain halogens (see **Halogen**). Of the hundreds of such compounds that have been found and studied, only two—enflurane and isoflurane—have emerged as useful agents for producing anesthesia.

Edwin S. Munson

See also **Ether; Nitrous oxide.**

Hals, *hahls,* **Frans,** *frahns* (1580?-1666), was one of the finest Dutch portrait painters of the 1600's. His portraits are known for showing lively expressions and poses. In his group portraits, the expressions and poses are coor-

Oil painting on canvas (1623); The Metropolitan Museum of Art, New York City; bequest of Benjamin Altman

Frans Hals' *Yonker Ramp and His Sweetheart* shows the smiling, healthy people who made the Dutch painter famous. Hals was known for his ability to portray lively expressions.

dinated to maintain the balance of the composition. He painted with bold, broad brushstrokes.

Hals used several kinds of subjects for his portraits, including individuals and married couples. He painted group portraits of *civic guards* (social organizations for men) and leaders of social welfare organizations. One of these paintings, *Banquet of Officers of the Civic Guard of Saint George at Haarlem, 1616,* appears in the **Painting** article. Before 1640, along with formal portraits, Hals often painted half-lengths of children and the colorful types of people he may have met at inns. These paintings probably have symbolic or allegorical meanings.

Hals was born in Antwerp, Belgium. He spent most of his life in Haarlem, the Netherlands, where his parents moved to escape Spanish rule. See also **Descartes, René** (picture).   Linda Stone-Ferrier

Halsey, *HAWL zee,* **William Frederick, Jr.** (1882-1959), was one of the leading United States naval commanders in World War II. General Douglas MacArthur called him "the greatest fighting admiral" of the war.

Halsey became vice-admiral in command of a Pacific carrier division in 1940. He commanded this division in attacks on the Gilbert and Marshall islands and on Wake Island and Marcus Island in February 1942. Later in 1942, he took command of U.S. naval forces in the South Pacific. In a series of bloody battles, his forces defeated the Japanese in the Solomon Islands. This victory enabled American land forces to occupy the entire island chain. During this period, Halsey also supported the opening offensives of General MacArthur in the Southwest Pacific. Halsey took command of the Third Fleet on June 15, 1944. In the Battle of Leyte Gulf in October 1944, Halsey's fleet and Admiral Thomas Kincaid's Seventh Fleet smashed the Japanese Navy and virtually eliminated it from the war.

The Japanese later signed the surrender on Halsey's flagship, the battleship *Missouri.* Halsey was born in Elizabeth, N.J., and was graduated from the U.S. Naval Academy in 1904.   Donald W. Mitchell

See also **World War** II (The South Pacific; The liberation of the Philippines).

Ham, son of Noah. See **Noah.**

Ham. See **Radio, Amateur.**

Ham is the meat taken from the hind leg of a hog. Ham is an important food product. It is an excellent source of protein. It is also high in thiamine, iron, and other vitamins and minerals.

People serve ham in a wide variety of ways, including as a main dish, mixed into salads, on sandwiches, and in spreads. The ways to prepare ham include broiling, roasting, and frying. Some ham comes fully cooked and can be sliced and eaten without reheating.

Kinds of ham. Ham is sold as a whole leg or cut into smaller portions. The chief types of cuts are called *rump cuts, shank cuts,* and *center cuts.* The names refer to the part of the leg from which a cut is taken. Rump cuts come from the upper leg; shank cuts, from the lower leg; and center cuts, from the center of the leg.

Ham is sold also in unprocessed and processed forms. The processed form is the kind most commonly referred to as ham. Fresh ham, usually called *pork leg,* is an unprocessed, lean meat that has a delicious pork flavor when cooked. It spoils quickly and must be cooked or stored in a freezer soon after purchase.

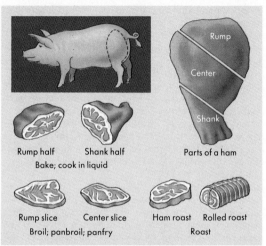

Rump half   Shank half   Parts of a ham
      Bake; cook in liquid

Rump slice   Center slice   Ham roast   Rolled roast
      Broil; panbroil; panfry   Roast

WORLD BOOK illustrations by Oxford Illustrators Limited.

Cuts of ham include those shown above. There are many ways to prepare the various cuts of ham, including baking, broiling, frying, and roasting. Some ham is sold cooked and ready to eat.

Ham producers process ham by curing and smoking it. Ham prepared using either or both of these methods may be stored for several weeks or months without spoiling. Cured and smoked ham generally has a salty or sweet flavor and a smoky aroma.

Curing and smoking. Ham is cured using such ingredients as salt, sodium ascorbate, sodium nitrite, sodium phosphate, and sugar. Producers usually dissolve these ingredients in water to form a *curing brine.* They pump some of the brine into the ham. They then soak the ham in the remaining brine for three to seven days. Ham cured in this manner includes canned ham and Scotch-style ham. Producers cure some types of ham by rubbing them on the outside with dry curing ingredients. Such ham includes dry-cured ham, country ham, and country-style ham. These kinds of ham do not require refrigeration for storage, but must be soaked in water before they can be cooked and eaten.

Most cured ham is also smoked. Producers begin the smoking process by placing the ham in a large, walk-in oven called a *smokehouse* for cooking. They then create smoke by burning sawdust in a separate stove called a *smoke generator.* While the ham is cooking, fans blow the smoke from the smoke generator into the smokehouse. The smoke adds flavor to the ham. It also turns the ham a golden brown on the outside. Cooking causes chemical reactions to occur in the curing ingredients. These reactions make the meat turn pink.

Donald H. Beermann

See also **Meat; Meat packing; Pork.**

Hamadryas. See **Baboon.**

Haman, *HAY muhn,* in the Old Testament, is the villain of the book of Esther. A favorite of the Persian king, Ahasuerus, he won a high rank. Everyone bowed to him. However, Mordecai, who was a Jew, refused to bow. Haman became enraged and plotted to have all the Jews in the empire killed.

Queen Esther, a Jew, was Mordecai's cousin. The king did not know that she was Jewish. Risking her life, Esther told the king she was a Jew and pleaded for her people Esther succeeded, and Haman was hanged instead of Mordecai. See also **Esther, Book of.**

J. Maxwell Miller

Hamburg (pop. 1,579,884) is West Germany's second largest city and its most important industrial center. It is one of the largest seaports on the European continent.

Hamburg is located on the Elbe River, about 68 miles (110 kilometers) from the river's mouth at Cuxhaven, on the North Sea. The Alster River flows through Hamburg and forms two large lakes in the city. These lakes are called the Binnen-alster and the Aussen-alster. Many narrow canals crisscross the city. Hamburg covers 289 square miles (748 square kilometers). For location, see **Germany** (political map).

The city today. Hamburg was one of the most heavily bombed German cities during World War II. Large parts of the city's port and commercial areas were wiped out and many old churches and fine homes were badly damaged or destroyed. But the port and commercial areas have been rebuilt since the war. The old *Rathaus* (town hall), the new opera house, and many modern buildings give Hamburg an attractive appearance. The Hagenbeck zoo, the University of Hamburg (founded in 1919), and many museums are located there.

Hamburg's industries include chemical plants, iron and steel works, and saw mills. They process many raw materials such as farm products, ores and metals, wood, and wood pulp. Shipbuilding has been an important industry for many years. The city's food industry processes cereals, coffee, meat, fish, and tobacco.

The harbor, stretching along the Elbe, is the hub of Hamburg's economic life. It is a center for foreign and inland shipping. Many of West Germany's industrial products, including automobiles, machinery, and optical goods, are exported from Hamburg. Imports include

Dan Porges, Bruce Coleman Inc.

Hamburg is located on the Elbe River in northern West Germany. Over half of Hamburg's buildings were destroyed during World War II. Since then, the city has been extensively rebuilt. Hamburg is now a center of modern architecture.

such products as fruit, coffee, paper, and tobacco.

Hamburg is also one of West Germany's leading railroad centers. There is heavy rail traffic between the city and every part of Europe. Airlines connect Hamburg with all parts of the world.

In the 1200's, Hamburg was a leading member of the Hanseatic League, a confederation of North German cities. In the late 1800's and early 1900's, it was a state in the German Empire and the Weimar Republic.

Hamburg State is a *land* (state) in the Federal Republic of Germany and is represented in the parliament in Bonn. Hamburg State has its own constitution, passed in 1952. It has a *Bürgerschaft* (parliament). The people elect the 120 Bürgerschaft members to four-year terms. Bürgerschaft members choose a 15-member senate to administer the laws. The *first bürgermeister* (chief official) heads the senate. Hamburg is divided into seven administrative districts.   James K. Pollock

Hamelin, now Hameln. See **Pied Piper of Hamelin.**

Hamilcar Barca, *huh MIHL kahr* or *HAM uhl kahr* (? -229 B.C.), was a great general of Carthage and the father of Hannibal, Carthage's most famous general. In 247 B.C., during the First Punic War, Hamilcar took command of the Carthaginian forces in western Sicily. His forces fought the Romans valiantly, but the Carthaginians suffered a disastrous naval defeat. Carthage was forced to sue for peace in 241 B.C. After the war, Hamilcar put down a rebellion in Africa of *mercenaries* (hired troops) who had not been paid. He moved against other rebellious mercenaries on the island of Sardinia, but Rome stepped in and demanded and got Sardinia and money from Carthage.

Hamilcar governed Carthage's holdings in Spain from about 237 B.C. until his death. He expanded Carthaginian power and territory. His work helped bring the economic strength that Carthage and Hannibal needed to fight the Second Punic War.   Henry C. Boren

See also **Carthage; Hannibal; Barcelona.**

Hamilton (pop. 2,500) is the capital and chief port of the Bermuda Islands. The town has wide, clean, palm-shaded streets, and attractive stone tropical-style houses. Bermuda is a popular vacation resort, and Hamilton's chief industry is tourism. The city has many fine hotels and shops. For location, see **Bermuda** (map).

Hamilton, Ohio (pop. 63,189), is an important manufacturing center in the industrial valley of the Great and Little Miami rivers. It lies about 20 miles (32 kilometers) north of Cincinnati, on the Great Miami River. Hamilton and the nearby city of Middletown form part of a metropolitan area with a population of 258,787. For Hamilton's location, see **Ohio** (political map).

Hamilton is one of the nation's leading producers of coated papers and safes. Other products include automobile parts, fuel-injection units for aircraft and missiles, hydraulic and mechanical presses, industrial textiles, laminated wood products, machine tools, papermaking and sugar-refining machinery, and prefabricated houses.

Hamilton serves as the seat of Butler County. It has a council-manager form of government. It was named for Fort Hamilton, an army post built on the present site of the city in 1791. In 1986, the Hamilton City Council altered the city's official name to *Hamilton!,* adding an exclamation point.   James L. Blount

© Derek Trask, The Stock Market

Hamilton, Ont., is a leading Canadian industrial center. Most of the city lies on a plain between Hamilton Harbour and a high ridge called the Niagara Escarpment.

Hamilton, Ont., is the center of the Canadian steel industry. Plants in the Hamilton area produce about half the nation's steel. Hamilton's location on Hamilton Harbour on the west end of Lake Ontario makes the city an important link in the St. Lawrence Seaway route. Among Canada's inland ports, only Montreal and Thunder Bay handle more trade than Hamilton.

George Hamilton, a pioneer farmer, laid out a town on the site in 1813. The town's position in the center of Ontario's most populated area helped it grow as a manufacturing and marketing center. Today, Hamilton ranks behind only Toronto and Montreal among Canadian manufacturing cities. But Hamilton's nearness to Toronto, which lies less than 50 miles (80 kilometers) away, has limited the city's growth. Many business companies have their headquarters in Toronto, with only smaller offices in Hamilton. Hamilton ranks as Ontario's second largest city in population. Only Toronto has more people.

The city covers 54 square miles (141 square kilometers) in the Regional Municipality of Hamilton-Wentworth. Suburbs of Hamilton include Ancaster, Dundas, Flamborough, Glanbrook, Grimsby, and Stoney Creek.

Most of Hamilton lies on a plain between Hamilton Harbour and the Niagara Escarpment, a high ridge that the people of the area call "the Mountain." Hamilton Harbour is a landlocked triangular harbor. A long sand bar called Burlington Beach separates the harbor from Lake Ontario. Ships traveling from the lake enter the harbor through a short canal. Motor vehicles cross the canal via the James N. Allan Burlington Bay Skyway.

The intersection of James and King streets is the center of the Hamilton business district. City Hall stands a few blocks away at Main and Bay streets. The Canadian Football Hall of Fame and Museum is next to City Hall. A modern shopping mall and several office buildings occupy Lloyd D. Jackson Square across the street from City Hall. Nearby is Hamilton Place, a theater-auditorium complex. The Art Gallery of Hamilton and the Hamilton Trade and Convention Centre adjoin Hamilton Place. Two blocks away is the Copps Coliseum, which seats 18,000 people.

Hamilton's steel mills and factories stand along the waterfront. The Royal Botanical Gardens, including Cootes Paradise Marsh, occupy about 2,000 acres (810 hectares) at the west end of the harbor.

People. Almost 70 per cent of Hamilton's people were born in Canada. About 60 per cent of the people have British ancestors. Italians make up about 8 per cent of the population. Many people of Italian ancestry work in the city's factories. Hamilton also has large German and Polish communities.

Economy. Steel companies in the Hamilton area produce about 9 million short tons (8.2 million metric tons) of steel yearly. Ships bring iron ore to the steel plants from northern Quebec via the St. Lawrence Seaway.

Industry employs almost 75 per cent of the workers of metropolitan Hamilton. More than 750 Hamilton factories produce a total of over $2 billion worth of goods annually. The city makes many steel products, including

Facts in brief

Population: 306,728. *Metropolitan area population*—557,029.

Area: 54 sq. mi. (141 km²). *Metropolitan area*—525 sq. mi. (1,359 km²).

Climate: *Average temperature*—January, 23° F. (−5° C); July, 71° F. (22° C). *Average annual precipitation* (rainfall, melted snow, and other forms of moisture)—32 in. (81 cm).

Government: Mayor-council. *Terms*—3 years for the mayor and 16 aldermen.

Founded: 1813. Incorporated as a city in 1846.

automotive parts, electrical goods, farm and machine tools, and wire.

Hamilton plants also process beef, dairy products, fruits, tobacco, and vegetables from the rich farming region south of the city. Farmers sell fresh produce at Hamilton's Central Market.

Three Canadian railroads run through Hamilton and connect with several major U.S. lines. Seven major highways serve the city, and two bus lines provide both local and long-distance service. Hamilton's Civic Airport furnishes service to a number of Canadian and U.S. cities. Lester B. Pearson International Airport, just outside Toronto, lies an hour's drive from Hamilton. Hamilton's port handles about 14 million short tons (13 million metric tons) of cargo annually.

Hamilton has one daily newspaper, *The Hamilton Spectator,* and five radio stations and one television station. Hamilton's CKOC, which began broadcasting in 1922, is Ontario's oldest radio station.

Education. About 55,000 children attend more than 90 public elementary schools and over 12 public high schools in Hamilton. The city has about 45 Roman Catholic elementary schools and high schools.

McMaster University has about 15,000 students. It owns the only nuclear reactor on a Canadian university campus. In 1971, McMaster opened its $65-million Health Sciences Centre, a combination hospital and medical school. Hamilton is also the home of Mohawk College of Applied Arts and Technology.

Two public library systems, the Hamilton Public Library and the Wentworth Library, serve the city and the surrounding region. The Hamilton library owns more than 700,000 books and has 14 branches. The Wentworth Library, with 10 branches, has over 130,000 volumes.

Cultural life. The Hamilton Philharmonic Orchestra performs in Hamilton Place. The city's other musical organizations include Opera Hamilton and the Bach Elgar Choir. The Art Gallery of Hamilton features drawings, paintings, prints, and sculptures from Canada, France, Great Britain, and the United States. Dundurn Castle, in Dundurn Park, includes a museum with exhibits of coins, costumes, and furniture from the middle 1800's. Sir Allan MacNab, a Canadian statesman, built the mansion and modeled it after a Scottish castle. The Cockpit Theatre and a children's theater are also in the park.

Hamilton has about 80 parks. They cover about 2,500 acres (1,010 hectares). The Royal Botanical Gardens account for most of this space. Parts of the gardens, including the Rock Garden, have been formally developed, but other sections remain in their natural state. The gardens offer educational programs and tours.

Hamilton has more than 80 summer playgrounds, 9 recreation centers with indoor swimming pools, and 9 outdoor pools. Other recreational facilities include golf courses, ice skating rinks, and tennis courts. The Hamilton Tiger-Cats of the Canadian Football League play their home games in Ivor Wynne Stadium.

Government. Hamilton has a mayor-council form of government. The voters elect a mayor and 16 aldermen to three-year terms. The city gets most of its revenue from local property taxes and from provincial and federal grants.

History. Huron Indians lived in what is now the Hamilton area before whites settled there. French fur traders and explorers charted the region during the 1660's, but no whites settled in the area until 1778. That year, two American colonists who supported the British moved there to escape the Revolutionary War in America (1775-1783).

City of Hamilton

Hamilton, on the shore of Lake Ontario, is the center of Canada's steel industry. The map shows points of interest in the Hamilton area.

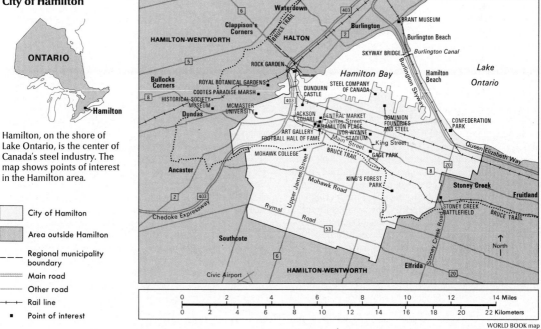

WORLD BOOK map

In 1813, George Hamilton, a member of a leading Canadian family, bought the land at the head of Lake Ontario and had it surveyed for a town. The town grew slowly until 1832, when the completion of a ship channel increased trade. Hamilton had 6,832 people when it was incorporated in 1846.

During the construction of the Great Western Railroad, from 1849 through 1855, Hamilton's population increased from 7,000 to 28,000. This railroad, promoted by Sir Allan MacNab, ran from the Niagara River via Hamilton, along Lake Erie to Windsor and Sarnia, Ont. Hamilton's first foundry was established during this period to meet the railroad's need for steel. By 1910, Hamilton mills had joined with others in Ontario and Montreal to form the Steel Company of Canada, Limited (Stelco Inc.), Canada's largest steel producer. The city's population grew from 52,000 in 1901 to 82,000 in 1911. Hamilton's second steel firm, Dominion Foundries and Steel, Limited (Dofasco Inc.), started operations in 1912, when new railroads produced the need for more steel. By 1921, the population of the city had passed 100,000, and by 1951 it had gone over 200,000.

During the 1960's, Hamilton began major air and water improvement programs, including construction of a $20-million water purification system. City leaders hoped to give Hamilton a new look with the construction of residential and commercial developments in the 1960's and early 1970's. But developers had difficulties finding tenants for high-rise apartment and office buildings. Businesses preferred to have their main offices in Toronto, and many families chose to live in houses rather than apartments. The city government took over one vacant structure and converted it into an apartment building for the elderly. One developer would have stopped construction of an office tower if the city had not agreed to rent part of it as a magistrates' court.

Hamilton entered the 1970's with a metropolitan population of almost 500,000. The city's chief renewal plans for the downtown area centered on Lloyd D. Jackson Square. The first buildings constructed on the square included a 24-story office tower and a banking pavilion. Fifty new stores and an office building opened in the complex in 1977. Another office tower, with ground-level stores, was completed in 1984. A hotel opened in 1985. The buildings in Jackson Square are connected to the Convention Centre and Hamilton Place Theatre by enclosed aboveground walkways.   Gerry Nott

Hamilton, Alexander (1755 or 1757-1804), was a noted statesman and political leader during the early years of the United States. He served in President George Washington's Cabinet as the nation's first secretary of the treasury. He also was a leader of the Federalist Party, one of the first political parties in the nation.

Hamilton was one of the boldest and most creative thinkers of his time. He supported the establishment of a strong federal government and believed that the U.S. Constitution should be interpreted loosely to give the government greater powers. Hamilton also favored the development of manufacturing to achieve an economic balance between agriculture and industry. He worked to protect the interests of merchants and other business leaders and believed the nation could best be governed by people from these groups.

Many of Hamilton's policies were strongly opposed

by Thomas Jefferson and other political leaders of the time. But today, scholars agree that Hamilton's ideas have had lasting importance.

Portrait by John Trumbull, Metropolitan Museum of Art
Alexander Hamilton

Early life. Hamilton claimed he was born on Jan. 11, 1757, but scholars have found evidence that shows the year of his birth to have been 1755. Hamilton was born on the island of Nevis in the West Indies. He was the second child of James Hamilton, a Scottish merchant, and Mrs. Rachael Lavien, who was separated from her husband. In 1765, James Hamilton left her and their two children.

As a boy, Alexander Hamilton worked for a trading firm on St. Croix, an island in what is now the Virgin Islands of the United States. His talents so impressed his employers that they helped send him to school in North America in 1772. He attended a school in Elizabethtown (now Elizabeth), N.J., and then entered King's College (now Columbia University).

In 1776, during the Revolutionary War, Hamilton was appointed captain of a New York artillery company. From 1777 to 1781, he served as a secretary and close assistant of General George Washington.

In 1780, Hamilton married Elizabeth Schuyler, the daughter of a wealthy New York family. Hamilton and his wife had eight children.

Early political career. Hamilton was admitted to the bar in New York in 1782 and soon began to practice law there. Also in 1782, he became a delegate from New York to the Congress of the Confederation. The Congress had been established by the Articles of Confederation in 1781, but it had little power (see **Articles of Confederation**). In 1786, Hamilton wrote a proposal calling for a convention of the states for the purpose of strengthening the federal government.

The Constitutional Convention met in Philadelphia in 1787. Few of Hamilton's ideas were included in the U.S. Constitution, but he worked hard for its ratification by the states. Hamilton and two other statesmen, John Jay and James Madison, wrote letters to newspapers urging approval of the Constitution. These letters were later republished in an influential book called *The Federalist* (see **Federalist, The**).

Secretary of the treasury. Hamilton became secretary of the treasury in 1789. He proposed that Congress establish a national bank to handle the government's financial operations. This measure was opposed by Secretary of State Thomas Jefferson, who did not believe that Congress had the power to establish such an institution. Hamilton then developed the *doctrine of implied powers.* This doctrine states that the government has *implied powers* (those reasonably suggested by the Constitution). The Supreme Court later upheld this doctrine.

Hamilton wanted the government to encourage manufacturing, and he recommended measures for that purpose. Jefferson and Madison opposed such a program because they thought that it would hurt farming interests. Congress partly followed Hamilton's suggestions.

In the early 1790's, the conflicts between Hamilton and a group led by Jefferson and Madison resulted in the development of the nation's first two political parties. Hamilton led the Federalist Party, which favored a strong federal government. The Democratic-Republican Party, headed by Jefferson and Madison, wanted a weak national government.

Political disputes. In 1795, Hamilton resigned as treasury secretary because of personal financial problems and increased opposition in Congress. But he remained active in public life and in 1796 helped President Washington write his Farewell Address.

John Adams, a Federalist, became President in 1797. Adams and Hamilton had many personal disputes, and they also disagreed about foreign policy and other issues. Shortly before the election of 1800, Hamilton wrote a pamphlet attacking the President. The pamphlet widened a split among the Federalists. As a result, the Democratic-Republican candidates, Thomas Jefferson and Aaron Burr, won the election. Jefferson and Burr received an equal number of electoral votes. Under the voting procedure of the time, both men were eligible for the presidency. See **Jefferson, Thomas** (National statesman).

The House of Representatives had to decide the winner of the election. Hamilton, who distrusted Burr even more than he did Jefferson, supported Jefferson for President. Jefferson finally won, and Burr became Vice President.

Burr ran for governor of New York in 1804. Hamilton criticized Burr's character and worked to defeat him. Burr lost and then challenged Hamilton to a duel with pistols. The two men fought on July 11, 1804. Hamilton was shot and died the next day.   Jacob E. Cooke

See also **Burr, Aaron.**

Additional resources

Cooke, Jacob E. *Alexander Hamilton.* Scribner, 1982.
Hecht, Marie B. *Odd Destiny: The Life of Alexander Hamilton.* Macmillan, 1982.
McDonald, Forrest. *Alexander Hamilton: A Biography.* Norton, 1979.
Stourzh, Gerald. *Alexander Hamilton and the Idea of Republican Government.* Stanford, 1970.

Hamilton, Alice (1869-1970), was an American physician who pioneered in industrial medicine. Her efforts led to greatly improved health conditions in industry and to the introduction of workers' compensation laws in the United States (see **Workers' compensation**).

From 1911 to 1921, Hamilton worked as a consultant to the United States Department of Labor. She inspected mines, mills, and smelting plants throughout the country and investigated the poisoning of factory workers by dangerous substances.

Hamilton was born in New York City but was raised in Fort Wayne, Ind. She graduated from the University of Michigan

Jane Addams Memorial Collection,
University of Illinois, Chicago

Alice Hamilton

Medical School in 1893. From 1897 to 1919, Hamilton lived and worked at Hull House, the famous Chicago settlement house founded by her friend Jane Addams (see **Hull House**). In 1919, Hamilton became the first woman faculty member of Harvard University.
                                                          Miriam Schneir

Hamilton, Virginia (1936-   ), is an American author of children's books. Her fiction imaginatively explores the heritage of black Americans. Hamilton won the 1975 Newbery medal and the 1975 National Book Award in children's literature for her novel *M.C. Higgins, the Great,* a story about a mountain family.

Hamilton's other children's books include *Zeely* (1967), *The House of Dies Drear* (1968), *The Time-Ago Tales of Jahdu* (1969), *The Planet of Junior Brown* (1971), *W. E. B. Du Bois* (1972), *Time-Ago Lost: More Tales of Jahdu* (1973), and *Paul Robeson* (1974). Hamilton was born in Yellow Springs, Ohio.   Zena Sutherland

Hamilton-Gordon, John Campbell. See Aberdeen and Temair, Marquess of.

Hamites are African peoples who are members of the *European* geographical race. They are sometimes called *Afro-Mediterranean* people because of their physical characteristics and the region where they live. Most Hamites are tall and have a narrow nose and brown skin. They live mainly in eastern, northern, and northeastern Africa, including parts of Ethiopia, the Sahara, and the Sudan. Because much of this vast region cannot be farmed, most Hamites tend herds of camels, cattle, goats, and sheep.

The ancient Egyptians were Hamites. Present-day Hamitic peoples include the Beja, Berbers, Fulani, Oromo, and Somali. The languages of Hamites have been called *Hamitic,* but this term correctly refers only to race. The languages used by the Hamites belong to the Cushitic group of Afro-Asiatic languages.
                                                          William A. Shack

See also **Berbers; Fulani; Hottentot; Somalia.**

Hamlet. See Shakespeare, William (Shakespeare's plays).

Hamlin, Hannibal (1809-1891), was Vice President of the United States from 1861 to 1865 during President Abraham Lincoln's first term. He also served as governor of Maine in 1857, and in the U.S. House of Representatives and the U.S. Senate.

Hamlin strongly opposed slavery. He left the Democratic Party in 1856, and helped organize the Republican Party as an antislavery group. He was not considered for a second vice presidential term because President Lincoln wanted a Democrat on the 1864 Republican ticket. It was a fateful decision, because the new Vice President, Andrew Johnson, became President shortly after Lincoln's second term began.

Hamlin was born in Paris, Me. The state of Maine placed his statue in Statuary Hall in Washington, D.C., in 1935.   Irving G. Williams

See also **Vice President of the United States** (picture).

Hammarskjöld, *HAH muhr SHOHLD,* **Dag,** *dahg* (1905-1961), served as secretary-general of the United Nations from 1953 until his death in a plane crash in Africa. After his death, Hammarskjöld was awarded the 1961 Nobel Peace Prize for his efforts to bring peace to the Congo.

Hammarskjöld worked to ease tension between the

The hammer throw requires strength and skill. The thrower whirls around in a circle, swinging the hammer in a lopsided plane. When he gains sufficient momentum, he lets the hammer fly.

Larry Day

United States and the Soviet Union. In 1955, he secured the release from China of American prisoners captured during the Korean War. In 1956, he helped solve the Suez crisis between Egypt and Israel and Israel's allies, France and Great Britain.

Markings, a book of poetry, prayers, and prose sayings written by Hammarskjöld, was published in 1964.

Hammarskjöld was born in Jönköping, Sweden. His father was once Sweden's prime minister. In 1941, Hammarskjöld became the youngest chairman of the Bank of Sweden in the bank's history. Hammarskjöld was deputy foreign minister of Sweden from 1951 to 1953.   Raymond E. Lindgren

See also **United Nations** (The secretary-general; picture).

Hammer is a tool used to drive nails and to work metals and other materials. Carpenters use a *claw hammer,*

Types of hammers

Hammers are made in many different shapes and sizes to do a variety of jobs. A comfortable grip on the handle and good balance are important factors in choosing a hammer.

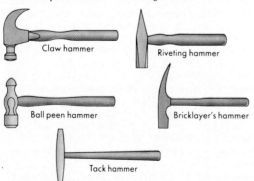

Claw hammer

Riveting hammer

Ball peen hammer

Bricklayer's hammer

Tack hammer

which has a *face* (striking surface) at one end, and a *claw* for pulling nails at the other end. Other types of hammers include the *stone hammer,* the *mason's hammer,* the *tack hammer,* and the *machinist's hammer,* which is also called the *ball peen hammer.*   Alva H. Jared

Hammer throw is a sports contest in which an athlete throws a *hammer* (metal ball) as far as he can. The hammer weighs 16 pounds (7.257 kilograms). The thrower holds it with a metal grip that is connected to the ball by a steel wire up to 4 feet (1.2 meters) long. He throws the hammer from a circle 7 feet (2.1 meters) in diameter.

At the beginning of his throw, the athlete faces the back of the circle and places his feet wide apart. He grips the metal handle with both hands, then swings the hammer around his head. When the hammer has gained enough momentum, the thrower takes three or four spins across the circle.

The thrower spins on his left foot to increase the speed of the hammer. At the end of the last spin, he has developed great momentum in the whirling hammer, which he then releases. The length of the throw is measured from the edge of the circle to the nearest mark made by the hammer.   Bert Nelson

For hammer throw championship figures, see **Track and field** (table: World track and field records); **Olympic Games** (table: Track and field).

Hammerhead. See **Shark** (Kinds of sharks; picture: Some kinds of sharks).

Hammerstein, Oscar, II (1895-1960), wrote the lyrics and scripts for many of the most famous shows in the history of American musical theater. He worked with such great composers of musical comedies as Jerome Kern and Richard Rodgers. Hammerstein maintained an optimistic attitude that was reflected in his songs. These included "Oh, What a Beautiful Mornin' "; "You'll Never Walk Alone"; and "My Favorite Things."

Hammerstein helped revolutionize musical comedies. When he began his career, most musicals consisted of a series of unrelated songs and dances that were held together by a weak plot. Hammerstein integrated the dialogue, songs, and dances into a unified work.

Oscar Greeley Clendenning Hammerstein was born in New York City and graduated from Columbia University. He wrote his first musical, *Always You* (1920), with the composer Herbert Stothart. He worked with Stothart and Rudolph Friml on *Rose-Marie* (1924). His other early musicals included *The Desert Song* (1926) and *The New Moon* (1928), which he wrote with Sigmund Romberg. Hammerstein wrote his first masterpiece, *Show Boat* (1927), with Kern. This show was also Hammerstein's first musical in which the songs and dances helped tell the story.

Hammerstein and Rodgers teamed up for the first time in *Oklahoma!* (1943), which won a Pulitzer Prize in 1944. They wrote eight other musicals—*Carousel* (1945), *Allegro* (1947), *South Pacific* (1949), *The King and I* (1951), *Me and Juliet* (1953), *Pipe Dream* (1955), *Flower Drum Song* (1958), and *The Sound of Music* (1959). In 1950, the two men shared a Pulitzer Prize for *South Pacific* with Joshua Logan, who helped write the dialogue for that musical. Ethan Mordden

See also **Kern, Jerome; Rodgers, Richard.**

Hammett, *HAM iht,* **Dashiell,** *DASH eel* (1894-1961), was the leader of the "hard-boiled" school of detective fiction. His stories feature "tough guys," realism, brutality, and violence. All his novels center around a *private eye* (private investigator). In *Red Harvest* (1929) and *The Dain Curse* (1929), Hammett introduced the "Op" (operator), an agent for the Continental Detective Agency. Sam Spade appears in *The Maltese Falcon* (1930) and Ned Beaumont in *The Glass Key* (1931). Hammett created the witty amateur detectives Nick and Nora Charles in *The Thin Man* (1934). Several of Hammett's short stories were collected in *The Big Knockover* (1966).

Samuel Dashiell Hammett was born in St. Mary's County, Maryland. Many of his stories reflect his personal experiences as a private detective. In the 1920's, Hammett began writing for *Black Mask,* a magazine that specialized in publishing "hard-boiled" detective stories. Philip Durham

Hammock is a hanging bed made of cloth or net with ropes attached to each end. These ropes are tied to hooks in the walls, to posts, or to trees. Some hammocks swing from metal supports.

Peruvian and Brazilian Indians made the first hammocks. They made them from the bark of the hamack tree and called them *hamacas.* Christopher Columbus' sailors learned to use hammocks from Indians who lived in the West Indies. Sailors on board ship used hammocks for years. They made them from heavy canvas 3 feet (0.9 meter) wide and 6 feet (1.8 meters) long. The ends of the canvas had cords attached to them. Sailors

Culver Pictures

Oscar Hammerstein

tied the cords to hooks fastened in the ship's *bulkheads* (walls) or posts. When a sailor died on a voyage, the body was wrapped in the sailor's hammock for burial at sea.

During World War II, most warships were equipped with bunks instead of hammocks. Merchant vessels also are usually equipped with bunks. People often hang hammocks on porches and in yards. Effa Brown

Hammond, Ind. (pop. 93,714), is one of the cities in the Calumet region. The region also includes the cities of Gary, East Chicago, and Whiting. The region is one of the world's greatest industrial centers and the steel-producing capital of the United States. Hammond extends 2 miles (3 kilometers) along Lake Michigan and 5 miles (8 kilometers) along the Illinois-Indiana state line. Gary, Hammond, and East Chicago form part of a metropolitan area with a population of 642,781. For Hammond's location, see **Indiana** (political map). The Hammond business section is 18 miles (29 kilometers) southeast of downtown Chicago.

Hammond factories produce a variety of goods. Products include soap, corn products, railway cars, tile roofing, chains, steel products, lead and iron oxides, shears and presses, cement blocks and tin cans. The city has one of the largest bookbinding firms in the country. Hammond is the home of the Calumet Campus of Purdue University.

All railway lines that approach Chicago from the east go through Hammond. Bus lines and the Indiana Toll Road connect Hammond with Chicago and with other cities in northern Indiana. The Indiana Harbor Ship Canal also serves Hammond.

Hammond was founded in 1868. It was named for G. H. Hammond, who started a meat-packing company there in 1869. In 1883, Hammond was organized as a town. It received its city charter the next year. The city was a meat-packing center until 1901, when fire destroyed the chief meat-packing plant. Hammond has a mayor-council government. Carole Leigh Hutton

Hammond, John Hays, Jr. (1888-1965), was an American inventor. He obtained hundreds of patents for his developments in radar, radio, television, and other electronic devices.

Hammond pioneered in the development of remote control. His devices for the remote control of ships, airplanes, and torpedoes aided the U. S. Army and Navy during World Wars I and II. Hammond also invented electronic circuits that stabilized and guided remote control vehicles. These circuits played an important role in the development of rocketry. Hammond also improved tuning systems for frequency modulation (FM) radio. Hammond was born in San Francisco. He graduated from Yale University in 1910. Michael M. Sokal

Hammurabi, *HAH mu RAH bee,* also spelled *Hammurapi,* was one of the greatest kings of Babylon. He developed the famous *Code of Hammurabi,* one of the first law codes in history. He strengthened and expanded his kingdom by diplomacy and military conquest.

Hammurabi was an efficient king who carefully planned every move, often years in advance. He was an outstanding administrator. His reign is known as *the golden age of Babylon.* Hammurabi ruled Babylon for 43 years, from 1792 to 1750 B.C.

Hammurabi changed the legal system of the country

The Louvre, Paris (Raymond V. Schoder, S. J.)

Hammurabi, King of Babylon, stands before the sun god Shamash, patron of justice. This relief is at the top of the text of the Code of Hammurabi. It shows Shamash commanding the king to establish just laws. The slab with code and relief, known as the stele of Hammurabi, was found in Susa.

by revising older legal codes, including one 300 years old. He compiled the great new code that bears his name. He also set up maximum prices and minimum wages, and gave his kingdom a fair, flexible, and efficient system of taxation. Hammurabi found time even for delicate language reforms. His handling of the Akkadian language, in which the Code of Hammurabi was composed, became a model for all of the future writers of ancient Mesopotamia.

The Code of Hammurabi was based on older collections of Sumerian and Akkadian laws, which Hammurabi revised, adjusted, and expanded. The code greatly influenced the civilization of all Near Eastern countries. It contained nearly 300 legal provisions. The code covered such matters as false accusation, witchcraft, military service, land and business regulations, family laws, tariffs, wages, trade, loans, and debts. The main principle of the code was that "the strong shall not injure the weak." The code set up a social order based on the rights of the individual and backed by the authority of Babylonian gods and the state.

The stone slab on which the code was carved was discovered in Susa, Iran, in 1901. An Elamite king had carried it off as a war trophy.   John W. Snyder

Hampton, Va. (pop. 122,617), lies at the south end of Chesapeake Bay, across from Norfolk (see **Virginia** [political map]). It is surrounded by military installations. Its industries produce building materials and metal products. Fishing is also a major industry. Hampton University was founded there in 1868 as Hampton Institute. Hampton, Norfolk, and Virginia Beach make up a metro-

politan area that has a population of 1,160,311.

Settled in 1610, Hampton is the oldest town founded by the English still in existence in the United States. It has a council-manager government.   David A. Parsons

See also **Hampton Roads; Hampton University.**

Hampton, Lionel (1913-   ), an American jazz musician, became the first major jazz stylist on the vibraphone. Hampton established the vibraphone, often called the *vibraharp* or simply the *vibes,* as an accepted jazz instrument.

Hampton gained fame playing with clarinetist Benny Goodman from 1936 to 1940. Hampton's rhythmic drive on the vibraphone, plus his enthusiastic showmanship, made him a major attraction. He occasionally played drums and piano as well. From 1937 to 1940, Hampton led small groups of musicians from various famous bands in a number of recording sessions. Many records by these Hampton groups rank as jazz classics.

Hampton formed his own band in 1940 and has led bands almost continually ever since. His 1942 record of "Flyin' Home" was a great success, and all of Hampton's bands have featured this tune. Hampton was born in Louisville, Ky.   John Norris

See also **Jazz** (picture: Benny Goodman).

Hampton, Wade (1818-1902), a Confederate general, served first in the infantry but later gained fame as a cavalry leader. After Jeb Stuart's death in 1864, Hampton commanded all of General Robert E. Lee's cavalry (see **Stuart, James E. B.**). He was transferred to South Carolina, where he tried to prevent General Sherman's march northward from Savannah, Ga.

Hampton was born in Charleston, S.C. He was the grandson of General Wade Hampton, who fought in both the Revolutionary War and the War of 1812. Hampton was graduated from South Carolina College. After the war, he entered politics, and worked for peaceful reconstruction. He was elected governor of South Carolina in 1876 and a U.S. Senator in 1878. He then served as commissioner of Pacific railroads. South Carolina placed a statue of Hampton in the U.S. Capitol in Washington, D.C., in 1929.   Frank E. Vandiver

Hampton Court Conference was a meeting called in 1604 by King James I of England. Its purpose was to settle the disputes between the Puritan and High Church parties of the Church of England.

The conference lasted for three days and resulted in a few trifling changes in the ritual. But it failed entirely to bring about the reforms desired by the Puritans, and actually made their position more difficult. An important indirect result of the conference was the revision of the Bible called the *King James,* or *Authorized, Version.* It first appeared in 1611. See **Bible** (The King James Version); **James** (I).   Howard R. Burkle

Hampton Roads is a natural channel and harbor formed at the place where the Nansemond, James, and Elizabeth rivers meet in Virginia. These rivers flow through Hampton Roads into Chesapeake Bay. The channel lies between Old Point Comfort and Sewall's Point. Newport News and Hampton lie on the north shore of the channel, and Norfolk and Portsmouth on the south shore. The famous Civil War battle between the *Monitor* and the *Merrimack* occurred at Hampton Roads. The Hampton Roads Conference, an attempt to end the war, was held in 1865.   Raus M. Hanson

Hampton Roads, Battle of. See **Warship** (Warships of the 1800's); **Monitor and Merrimack; Civil War** (First battle between ironclads).

Hampton Roads Conference was an attempt to end the Civil War. On February 3, 1865, representatives of the North and South met on the *River Queen,* a ship in Chesapeake Bay. The ship was anchored at Hampton Roads, near Fort Monroe. President Abraham Lincoln and Secretary of State William Henry Seward represented the North. The Confederacy's vice president, Alexander H. Stephens, Senator Robert M. T. Hunter, and Assistant Secretary of War John A. Campbell represented the South. President Lincoln refused to change any terms of the Emancipation Proclamation, or to consider any peace proposal that did not involve immediate restoration of the Union and the laying down of Confederate arms. The representatives failed to reach an agreement.   John Donald Hicks

Hampton University is a private coeducational university in Hampton, Va. It has played a historic role in the education of blacks and American Indians. It has schools of business, education, arts and letters, nursing, and pure and applied sciences. It also has a graduate college and a college of continuing education. The university grants bachelor's and master's degrees.

The school was founded in 1868 to help educate slaves freed after the Civil War. In 1870, it was chartered as Hampton Normal and Agricultural Institute. From 1878 to 1912, the school received federal aid for the education of American Indians. It began a college curriculum in 1923 and, in 1930, the name was changed to Hampton Institute. The present name was adopted in 1984. For enrollment, see **Universities and colleges** (table).   Critically reviewed by Hampton University

Hamster is any of several kinds of small, chunky, furry rodents that live in Asia and Europe. Most kinds of hamsters have a short tail and large cheek pouches in which they can carry a great amount of food. There are about 15 kinds of hamsters. The best-known species are the *golden hamster* and the *common hamster.*

The golden hamster, also called the *Syrian hamster,* has light reddish-brown fur on its back and white fur on its underside. Golden hamsters measure about 7 inches (18 centimeters) long and have a tail that is $\frac{1}{2}$ inch (13 millimeters) long. They weigh about 4 ounces (112 grams).

The common hamster is also called the *black-bellied hamster* because it has black fur on its underside. It has light brown fur on its back and white spots on its face, neck, and sides. Common hamsters measure about 11 inches (28 centimeters) long and weigh up to 32 ounces (908 grams). They are trapped for their fur.

Golden and common hamsters live alone and are active mostly at night. They dig burrows that have separate compartments for nesting, food storage, and body wastes. Hamsters eat many kinds of food, including fruits, seeds, green vegetation, and some small animals.

A female golden hamster carries her young in her body for 16 days, and the common hamster carries hers for 16 to 20 days. Both species generally give birth to six or seven young. Wild females usually have two litters a year, but they may give birth as often as once a month in captivity. Newborn hamsters are completely helpless and are cared for by their mother for about three weeks.

WORLD BOOK photo

A pet hamster eats many kinds of food, including fruit, raw vegetables, and grains. Fresh water should always be available, and the floor of the cage should have an absorbent lining.

Golden hamsters are frequently used as experimental animals in scientific research. They are also popular pets because they are easy to care for and seldom bite.

Pet hamsters should be kept in metal cages or in glass or plastic enclosures. Wood shavings, dried grass, or some other absorbent material should line the cage floor. Hamsters may be given many kinds of food, including fruits, greens, raw vegetables, small grains, whole or rolled oats, and some meat. Fresh water should be available at all times. Pet hamsters live three to four years.

Scientific classification. Hamsters belong to the family Cricetidae. The golden hamster is *Mesocricetus auratus,* and the common hamster is *Cricetus cricetus.*   James N. Layne

Additional resources

Roberts, Mervin F. *The T. F. H. Book of Hamsters.* T. F. H., 1981.
Silverstein, Alvin and V. B. *Hamsters: All About Them.* Morrow, 1974.
Zim, Herbert S. *Golden Hamsters.* Morrow, 1951.

Hamstring. See **Leg** (The thigh).

Hamsun, *HAHM sun,* **Knut,** *knoot* (1859-1952), was a Norwegian author who wrote with deep feeling about nature and the land. He won the 1920 Nobel Prize for literature for his novels. His best-known novel, *The Growth of the Soil* (1917), realistically describes the life of peasants in rural Norway. His early novels, *Hunger* (1890), *Mysteries* (1892), and *Pan* (1894), study those who have been rejected by society.

Hamsun was born in Lom, Norway. He had little formal education and spent most of his early adult life wandering from job to job. He made two trips to the United States in the 1880's. Hamsun favored a strong central government that would control society. He supported the World War II German occupation of Norway, and was later fined for pro-German activities. However, his powerful novels transcend the limitations of his political views.   Richard B. Vowles

Han dynasty, *hahn,* was a series of emperors of the same family who ruled ancient China for over 400 years. Under Han rule, arts and sciences thrived and China became as large and as powerful as the Roman Empire.

The Chinese still call themselves Han people in recognition of China's achievements during this period.

Liu Bang (also spelled Liu Pang) founded the Han dynasty in 202 B.C., after the fall of the Qin (Ch'in) dynasty (see **Liu Bang**). The Han rule was divided into two periods. The *Former* Han dynasty lasted from 202 B.C. to A.D. 8. Its capital was Chang'an (now Xian). The *Later* Han dynasty lasted from A.D. 25 to 220, and its capital was Luoyang. Because Chang'an lay west of Luoyang, the two periods are also called the *Western* and *Eastern* Han dynasties. From A.D. 8 to 23, China was ruled by Wang Mang, a revolutionary who set up the Xin (Hsin) dynasty. After the Xin fell, the Han soon regained control.

Han emperors after Liu had a strong centralized government. They used a civil service examination to select officials. This examination stressed knowledge of the teachings of Confucius. As a result, Confucian scholars held important government positions. Emperor Wudi, who ruled from 140 to 87 B.C., made Confucianism the state philosophy (see **Confucianism**).

During the Han rule, education gained in importance and a central university was built in Chang'an. Han poets and prose writers developed a clear style that is still famous in Chinese literature. Scholars wrote long histories of China. Artists produced glazed pottery and large stone carvings. The greatest invention of the Han period was paper.

Han China expanded southwest to what is now Tibet. Han warriors also conquered what are now North Korea and northern Vietnam and overcame nomadic tribes in the north and west. Overland trade routes linked China with Europe for the first time. Along the most famous route, the Great Silk Road, Chinese silk and other products flowed into the Roman Empire.

The Han dynasty collapsed because of rivalries among the scholar-officials, imperial relatives, advisers, and generals. For the next 400 years, China was divided into warring states.   Eugene Boardman

See also **China** (The early empire).

Han Kao-tsu. See Liu Bang.
Hancock, George W. See Softball (History).
Hancock, John (1737-1793), was an American revolutionary leader who became the first person to sign the Declaration of Independence in 1776. His bold signature

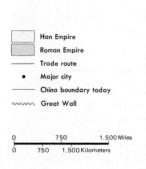

Ayer Collection, Newberry Library

The signature of John Hancock was the first signature placed on the historic Declaration of Independence at Philadelphia.

is still famous. Today, when people sign their names, they are said to have written their *John Hancock.*

Hancock was born in Braintree, Mass., where his father was a minister. His father died when John was a boy, and his uncle, Thomas Hancock, one of the wealthiest merchants in Boston, adopted him. After his graduation from Harvard College in 1754, John joined his uncle in business. He inherited the company after his uncle's death in 1764.

Hancock became known as a revolutionary after an incident called the Liberty Affair in 1768. One of his vessels, the *Liberty,* arrived in Boston Harbor to unload a shipment of wine and take on new cargo. British customs officials seized the *Liberty,* charging that Hancock had disobeyed regulations. This action enraged the citizens of Boston. Mobs rioted, and the British government sent troops to restore order. The Liberty Affair became one of the events that led to the Revolutionary War.

In 1769, Hancock had won election to the Massachu-

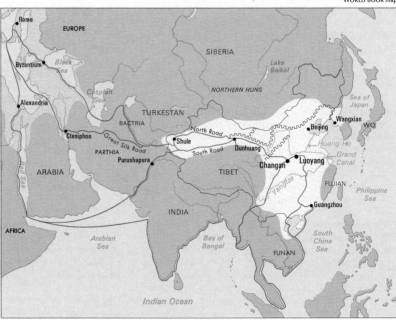

WORLD BOOK map

The Han Empire about A.D. 100

This map shows the Han Empire at its greatest size. A major expansion occurred about 100 B.C., when the empire was extended west into central Asia. Then, for the first time in history, overland trade routes linked China with Europe. About A.D. 100, Han armies conquered land north of the Great Wall.

Han Empire
Roman Empire
Trade route
• Major city
China boundary today
Great Wall

The Museum of Fine Arts, Boston

John Hancock was an American revolutionary leader. The American artist John Singleton Copley painted Hancock's portrait in 1765.

setts General Court, the lower house of the colonial legislature. The General Court became the Massachusetts Provincial Congress in 1774, and Hancock served as its president in 1774 and 1775.

As tensions between the Americans and the British grew, Hancock used his wealth and influence in the movement for independence. His activities caused the British to regard him as one of the most dangerous revolutionaries. He and Samuel Adams, another Massachusetts leader, were nearly arrested by the British in 1775. But the famous ride by their fellow patriot Paul Revere gave them warning and enabled them to escape.

Hancock served as president of the Continental Congress from 1775 to 1777. As president, he was the first to sign the Declaration of Independence adopted by the Congress. Hancock hoped to command the Continental Army that fought for independence during the Revolutionary War. He was disappointed that the Congress chose George Washington. In 1778, however, Hancock led about 5,000 Massachusetts soldiers in an unsuccessful attempt to free Rhode Island from the British.

Hancock presided over the convention that adopted the Massachusetts Constitution in 1780, and he became the first governor under the new charter. He served nine terms as governor, from 1780 to 1785, and from 1787 until his death in 1793.   William Morgan Fowler, Jr.

Additional resources

Fowler, William Morgan, Jr. *The Baron of Beacon Hill: A Biography of John Hancock.* Houghton, 1979.
Fritz, Jean. *Will You Sign Here, John Hancock?* Coward, 1976. For younger readers.

Hancock, Winfield Scott (1824-1886), was a general of the Union Army in the Civil War (1861-1865). He also ran as the Democratic Party candidate for President of the United States in 1880, but James A. Garfield defeated him.

Hancock was born in Montgomery Square, Pa., and was graduated from the U.S. Military Academy in 1844. He served in the Mexican War and remained in the regular army.

When the Civil War started, Hancock became a brigadier general of volunteers. He fought in the battles of the Peninsula, Antietam, Fredericksburg, and Chancellorsville. Promoted to major general, he helped select the battlefield at Gettysburg, and he commanded a corps there. He also served in the Wilderness campaign.
T. Harry Williams

Hancock Park. See La Brea pits.

Hand is the end of a *forelimb,* or arm. Hands are specially constructed for taking hold of objects. True hands have *opposable thumbs,* or thumbs that can be moved against the fingers. This action makes it possible to grasp things in the hand and make many delicate motions. Human progress would have been hampered without the use of opposable thumbs. To help understand the work that thumbs do, try to pick up a pen while keeping your thumb motionless alongside your hand.

Hands are also used to touch and feel things. The human hand contains at least four types of nerve endings that make the fingers and thumbs highly sensitive. Blind persons rely entirely on their sense of touch when reading. They run their fingers over the raised letters of Braille books.

The human hand also helps people communicate with each other—as in the sign language of the North American Indians or that of deaf persons. In these sign languages, gestures and positions of the hand and fingers represent words or phrases. Hands convey familiar expressions and ideas. Well-known examples include the clenched fist of anger, the raised palm of peace, the "V" for victory or for peace, the "thumbs down" for disapproval, and the gesture for hitchhiking.

Parts of the hand. The human hand consists of the *carpus,* or wrist; the *metacarpus,* or palm proper; and the *digits,* the four fingers and the thumb. There are 27 bones in the hand. Eight carpal bones make up the carpus. They are arranged across the wrist roughly in two rows. In the row nearest the forearm, starting from the thumb side, are the *navicular, lunate, triangular,* and *pisiform* bones. In the second row are the *greater multangular, lesser multangular, capitate,* and *hamate* bones. Five long metacarpal bones make up the palm. They connect the wrist with the fingers and thumb. Each of the four fingers contains three slender bones called *phalanges.* But the thumb has only two.

Thirty-five powerful muscles move the human hand. Fifteen are in the forearm rather than in the hand itself. This arrangement gives great strength to the hand without making the fingers so thick with muscles that they would be difficult to move. Near the wrist, the muscles become strong, slender cords called *tendons.* The tendons run along the palm and back of the hand to the joints of the fingers. When the muscles on the palm side of the forearm contract, the fingers close.

Anatomy of the hand

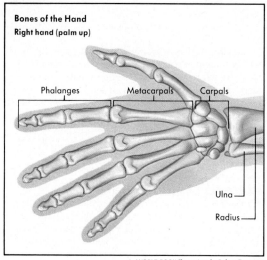

Bones of the Hand
Right hand (palm up)

Phalanges   Metacarpals   Carpals

Ulna

Radius

WORLD BOOK illustrations by Robert Demarest

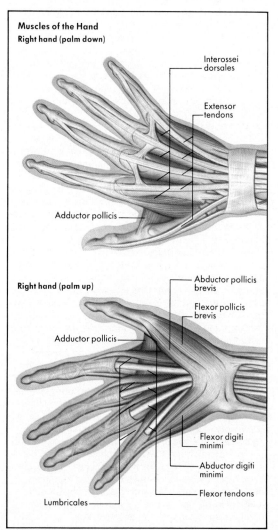

Muscles of the Hand
Right hand (palm down)

Interossei dorsales

Extensor tendons

Adductor pollicis

Right hand (palm up)

Abductor pollicis brevis

Flexor pollicis brevis

Adductor pollicis

Flexor digiti minimi

Abductor digiti minimi

Flexor tendons

Lumbricales

When the muscles on the back of the forearm contract, the fingers open. Twenty muscles within the hand itself are arranged so that the hand and fingers can make a variety of precise movements.

Animal hands. In many animals, part of the forelimb corresponds to the human hand. These parts have the same basic arrangement of bones and muscles whether the animal uses them to dig, fly, swim, or run. No animal "hand" has more than five digits. Animals have many kinds of "hands." The mole's short, chunky "hand" is ideally suited to act like a shovel in digging tunnels. The bat's forelimb is a wing, with a web of skin spread between the fingers. The bird's "hand" is also a wing. Phalanges and metacarpals support the wing. The seal's "hand" is its flipper. The bones have *fused,* or grown together, and form a broad, flat paddle useful for swimming. The "hand" of the horse is constructed so that the animal stands on its middle finger. Through millions of years of development, the middle finger has become stronger and longer. It is well adapted to running. The horse's other fingers have become quite small or have disappeared.   William V. Mayer

See also **Painting** (picture: *The Creation of Adam*); **Wrist.**

Hand, Learned (1872-1961), an American lawyer and judge, served from 1924 to 1951 as judge of the United States Court of Appeals (see **Court of appeals**). He became known as one of the most able American judges. In his legal opinions, he preserved respect for legal institutions. But at the same time, he helped mold the law to fit changing times. Hand's opinions won respect because of their insights and also because of their careful construction.

Hand was born in Albany, N.Y., and graduated from Harvard University. He practiced law in Albany and New York City from 1897 to 1909. He was appointed to the United States District Court, for the southern district of New York, in 1909, and to the United States Court of Appeals in 1924.   H. G. Reuschlein

Hand grenade. See Grenade.

Hand organ is the general name given to several kinds of musical instruments that produce music when the player cranks a handle. The most common kind is the *barrel organ,* or *piano organ,* played by street musicians. The instrument consists of a box that contains pipes or metal reeds and a cylinder, called a *barrel,* on which pegs are arranged. When the barrel is turned by a crank, the pegs open the valves of various pipes. The cranking action forces air into the open pipes to produce music.

The *hurdy-gurdy* is a kind of hand organ with strings that is seldom played today. Most hurdy-gurdies have from four to six strings. The instrument is played with keys and a rosin-covered wooden wheel. The keys determine the notes that are played. The wheel, turned by hand, rubs the strings to create the music. The hurdy-gurdy was popular in Europe during the 1000's and again during the 1700's. The Austrian composer Joseph Haydn wrote several works for the hurdy-gurdy.

Melvin Berger

Handball is a game in which players hit a rubber ball against a wall with their hands. Each side tries to hit the ball in such a way that the other side cannot return the ball to the wall. A handball game in which two people

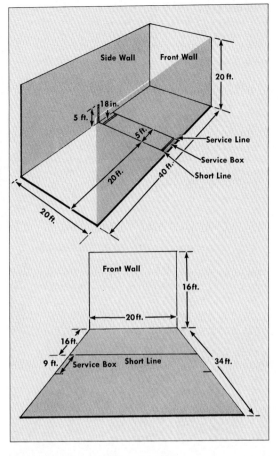

A **handball court** with glass walls, *above,* allows spectators to watch. The drawings at the right give the dimensions for three- and four-wall courts, *top,* and for a one-wall court, *bottom.*

oppose each other is called *singles.* Four people can form two teams and play *doubles.* Handball players use a hard, hollow ball that is $1\frac{7}{8}$ inches (4.8 centimeters) in diameter. The ball weighs 2.3 ounces (65.2 grams).

Handball is played on courts with four walls, three walls, or one wall. *Four-wall handball* is the most popular form. A standard four-wall court is 20 feet (6 meters) high, 20 feet wide, and 40 feet (12 meters) long. Its back wall must be at least 12 feet (3.7 meters) high.

One player starts a four-wall handball game as the *server.* The server stands in the *service box* (a zone 5 feet, or 1.5 meters, wide near the middle of the handball court). The server drops the ball on the floor and strikes it with one hand on the first bounce, driving the ball against the front wall. The ball must strike the front wall of the court before hitting the floor or ceiling or another wall. After hitting the front wall, the ball must bounce back over the *short line* (center line across the width of the court). The serve may hit one side wall after hitting the front wall, but must go over the short line before it hits the ground. A serve that falls in front of the short line is a *short,* and the server serves again. If the server hits another short, it is considered an *out,* and the other

A **hand organ** produces music when a player cranks a handle. Street musicians played a type of hand organ called a *barrel organ,* such as the one shown below in London about 1905.

team takes over the serve.

After a serve comes over the short line properly, the server's opponent hits the ball if possible. The players or teams then take turns hitting the ball against the front wall until one of them fails to return the ball before it bounces twice on the floor. Players cannot *hinder* (block) each other from hitting the ball. In returning a ball, a player can use a combination of side walls or ceiling with the front wall, or can hit the ball directly into the front wall. If the server misses a returned ball, the serve is lost. If the opponent misses, the server scores 1 point and serves again. The first side to score 21 points wins the game. A *match* usually consists of the best two out of three games.

Three-wall handball has the same playing area and rules as four-wall, but there is no back wall. Some three-wall courts have ceilings.

One-wall handball is played chiefly in the New York City area, usually outdoors. It is the only type of handball in which players can take a stationary block position against the opponent. A standard court is 20 by 34 feet (6 by 10 meters). Its wall is 20 feet (6 meters) high.

Team handball is played by two teams of seven players each. The court has no walls and is much larger than the court used in singles and doubles. The ball is inflated with air and is about the size of a small soccer ball. See **Team handball.**

Drawings made by Egyptians thousands of years ago

show people playing a game similar to handball. The type of handball that is played today probably originated among the Basque people of Spain. The U.S. Handball Association was set up in 1950 to help promote the game. Its headquarters are in Tucson, Ariz.

Critically reviewed by the United States Handball Association

Additional resources

The Handball Book. Ed. by Pete Tyson and Jim Turman. Leisure Press, 1983.
Zafferano, George J. *Handball Basics.* Sterling, 1977.

Handcuffs are used by law enforcement officers to prevent a suspect or prisoner from having full use of the hands. Most handcuffs consist of a pair of steel rings connected by a short chain. The rings fit over a person's wrists and can be adjusted to fit wrists of different sizes. One end of each ring has jagged edges that slip into the other end and lock automatically. Such handcuffs are opened with a key.

Another kind of handcuff is a 22-inch (56-centimeter) strip of inexpensive flexible plastic. One end is slipped through a slit at the other end. A small steel hook near the slit locks the ends together. These handcuffs are removed by cutting them off.

E. R. Degginger

Handcuffs commonly consist of two metal rings connected by a chain. They are designed to limit a person's hand movement.

In ancient times, handcuffs were called *shackles* or *manacles.* They were used either as a form of punishment or as a method of fastening both the hands and feet of a suspect or prisoner.   Marvin E. Wolfgang

Handel, George Frideric (1685-1759), was a German-born composer who is known today mainly through his musical compositions called *oratorios.* His famous oratorio *Messiah* is one of the most popular works in music. In the mid-1900's, Handel's operas, neglected for 200 years, gained recognition as at least equal in quality to his oratorios. Handel also composed much orchestral music, *chamber music* (music for small groups of instruments), and solo music for harpsichord.

His life. Handel was born on Feb. 23, 1685, in Halle, Germany. He began taking music lessons at the age of 7. By the time he was 12, he was assistant organist at the Halle cathedral. As a youth, he had a typical Lutheran education and studied law at the University of Halle for a year. His earliest activity as a composer began in 1703 in Hamburg, at that time a center of French, Italian, and German operatic styles.

Between 1706 and 1710, Handel worked in Italy, becoming one of the most popular composers of Italian opera. In 1710 and 1711, he served briefly as Director of Music in Hanover, Germany. He moved to England in 1712 and lived in London until his death. He is buried in Westminster Abbey.

Italian opera was still quite new to England when Handel arrived and it gained its greatest popularity among the nobility during his early years there. Then the flourishing middle class flocked to the English ballad operas, and the nobility turned to the lighter and often comic operas of the younger Italians.

In 1741, Handel abandoned opera and dedicated himself to composing oratorios. *Messiah* was the first of the oratorios that followed. In 1751, after completing *Jephtha,* Handel gave up composing because of blindness. But he remained active. He conducted a Holy Week performance of *Messiah* the day before he died.

His work. The oratorio developed in Italy as a music drama to be played without staging in the *oratory* (meeting room) of a religious association. Singers represented characters in a Biblical story or in the life of a saint. In addition to the dialogue and songs of the singers, a narrator often filled in necessary details in the story. A chorus usually represented groups of people or crowds and reacted to the events.

Handel based almost all of his oratorios on Biblical stories, favoring the Old Testament. *Messiah* is an exception. The text is a collection of quotations gathered by Handel's friend Charles Jennens from the Bible. *Messiah* contains no dramatic action. It illustrates the foundations of Christianity in a series of musical numbers that parallel the prophecy of Christ's coming, His birth, life, death, and resurrection.

The music of the solo singers in the oratorios was written in the manner of Italian opera of that time. The choruses often use the style of the sacred anthem. Most of Handel's oratorios were first performed in theaters. Audiences paid admission as they would to an opera. *Messiah* was first heard in a theater in Dublin in 1742.

The main reason for the popularity of *Messiah* lies in its glorious choruses. There are more inspired choruses in *Messiah* than in any of Handel's other oratorios, and they use a remarkable variety of mood and technique. "And the glory of the Lord" is a happy dancelike chorus in triple time. The voices come in and out casually and also join in resounding exclamations. In "And He shall purify," the four voice parts take turns singing the theme. "O thou that tellest good tidings" recalls earlier English music, particularly that of Henry Purcell, in its melody, lightness, and good cheer. In "Surely he hath borne our griefs," Handel portrayed grief with solemn rhythms and thick harmony. The thrilling "Hallelujah" chorus shows Handel as a master of choral effects, particularly in dividing a chorus into two groups singing different themes.
Saul (1739), Handel's

National Portrait Gallery, London

George Frideric Handel

most dramatic oratorio, is more typical of Handel's approach to the oratorio. Jennens' words represent the conflict between Saul, King of Israel, and David, the youthful warrior who slew Goliath. The action develops during the sections of speechlike song called *recitative.* These sections are usually accompanied only by a harpsichord and violoncello. The characters express their anger, hope, love, delight, joy, and other emotions in lengthy *arias* (solos) accompanied by orchestra. The reasons for these emotional outbursts are brought out in the recitative. The two types of music alternate unless a chorus or symphony breaks in. The arias often rely on the *da capo* formula. In this formula, the first section, based on one theme, returns after a middle section based on a similar or contrasting theme.

Few of the choruses of *Saul* are of the meditative, anthemlike variety of *Messiah.* They tend to be shorter and more direct. Like the chorus of Greek tragedy, they provide emotional reactions to dramatic events. Sometimes they point out a moral.

Handel's more than 40 operas were mostly written before *Saul.* Modern productions of his operas *Julius Caesar* (1724) and *Alcina* (1735) demonstrate that they are still stageworthy and appealing, filled with melodic invention and emotional variety. They have earned Handel a place among the world's great dramatic composers.

Handel wrote more than 150 instrumental compositions. The best known of these include two orchestra suites, *Water Music* (about 1717) and *Fireworks Music* (1749). Handel composed many harpsichord suites, organ concertos, and sonatas for chamber groups. He also wrote a number of *concerti grossi,* compositions that feature a small group of soloists against the background of a string orchestra.   Claude V. Palisca

Additional resources

Cudworth, Charles. *Handel: A Biography, with a Survey of Books, Editions, and Recordings.* Shoe String, 1972.
Dean, Winton. *The New Grove Handel.* Norton, 1983.
Handel: A Symposium. Ed. by Gerald Abraham. Greenwood, 1980. Reprint of 1954 edition.
Lang, Paul H. *George Frideric Handel.* Norton, 1966.

Handgun is a firearm that is operated with one hand. Other types of guns, such as rifles and machine guns, require the use of both hands, a *tripod* (three-legged stand), or a shooting rest.

Handguns are carried primarily by the police and by the armed forces. However, in the United States, private citizens own more than 55 million handguns, and over 750,000 handguns are owned by private citizens in Canada. These citizens use handguns for such lawful purposes as target shooting, hunting, and protection. Some people also collect antique or classic handguns. Nevertheless, about 15,000 to 20,000 handgun-related deaths occur in the United States annually, and about 350 to 400 in Canada. They include suicides, homicides and self-defense killings, and accidents.

Parts of a handgun

Handguns vary in appearance, size, type of ammunition used, and method of operation, but they all include the same basic parts. These parts are the *frame,* the *grip,* the *barrel,* the *sights,* and the *action.*

The frame is the main body of the gun that connects the other parts. The grip is the handle of the gun, and

the barrel is the metal tube through which the bullet is fired. The *lands* and *grooves* are alternating raised surfaces and channels inside the barrel. They cause the bullet to spin and thus make it travel in a direct path.

The shooter uses the sights to line up the handgun with the target. Some sights can be adjusted to help aim the gun more easily. All handguns made for target shooting have adjustable sights.

The action includes the main working parts of the handgun. It consists of such parts as the trigger, the hammer, and the cartridge chamber. The type of action a handgun has determines how it is loaded and fired.

Types of handguns

There are five main types of handguns: (1) single-action revolvers, (2) double-action revolvers, (3) single-action semiautomatic pistols, (4) double-action semiautomatic pistols, and (5) single-shot pistols. Revolvers carry ammunition in chambers in a rotating cylinder. Most pistols are loaded with *clips* of ammunition. Clips are metal holders inserted in the gun's *butt* (thicker end).

Single-action revolvers hold six cartridges. An arm near the hammer rotates the cylinder one-sixth of a turn when the hammer is cocked. This movement puts a cartridge into line with the barrel and the *firing pin* (part that strikes the primer to fire the cartridge). After cocking the hammer, the shooter pulls the trigger. The hammer unlocks and falls, exploding the cartridge. The Colt single-action Army revolver, produced during the mid-1800's, is the most famous weapon of this type.

Double-action revolvers, like single-action revolvers, hold six cartridges. But, unlike single-action revolvers, double-action revolvers do not require the user to manually cock the hammer before firing. Instead, the gun is fired by only pulling the trigger. When the trigger is pulled, a lock that holds the cylinder in place is released and the hammer revolves the cylinder. When the next chamber is lined up with the barrel, the cylinder locking bolt is raised into the locking notch, securing the cylinder. The hammer then falls and fires the cartridge. The cycle is repeated for the next shot.

The main advantage of the double-action revolver over the single-action revolver is that it can be fired rapidly. The Smith & Wesson military and police revolver is one of the most popular double-action revolvers. This weapon was first introduced in 1905.

Single-action semiautomatic pistols are fired by first pulling back a device called a *slide* to cock the ham-

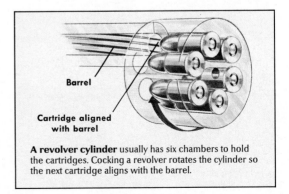

Barrel

Cartridge aligned
with barrel

A revolver cylinder usually has six chambers to hold the cartridges. Cocking a revolver rotates the cylinder so the next cartridge aligns with the barrel.

How an automatic handgun works

The Colt .45 automatic pistol is used primarily for personal defense. This weapon is fired by first pulling the slide and barrel to the rear to cock the hammer. Releasing the slide feeds the cartridge into the chamber, and returns the barrel to the firing position. When the trigger is squeezed, it presses against the sear, which in turn releases the hammer. As the hammer falls, it strikes the firing pin. The firing pin flies forward, striking the primer of the cartridge and exploding it. Recoil drives the barrel and slide to the rear, automatically cocking and loading the pistol for the next shot.

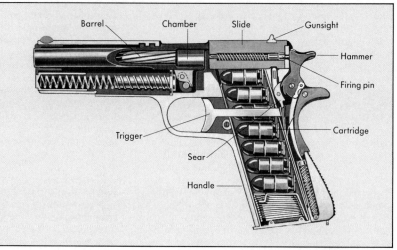

WORLD BOOK diagram

mer. When the slide is released, it moves forward and feeds a round from the clip into the cartridge chamber. When the shooter pulls the trigger, the hammer falls, striking the primer and exploding the gunpowder in the cartridge. The explosion causes the slide to move backward. This *recoil* automatically removes the empty cartridge and recocks the gun. When the slide moves forward again, it reloads the chamber. The most famous single-action semiautomatic is the Colt .45 automatic pistol. It has been the standard sidearm of the U.S. armed forces since it was first produced in 1911.

Double-action semiautomatic pistols operate somewhat like double-action revolvers. When the trigger is pulled, the hammer goes through the firing cycle and fires the cartridge. After the initial shot, the pistol begins to operate like a single-action semiautomatic pistol. The recoil of the first shot forces out the empty cartridge case, cocks the hammer, and inserts a new cartridge from the clip into the cartridge chamber. Double-action semiautomatics are widely used by sports enthusiasts and police officers. Popular models include the Smith & Wesson Model 39 and the Walther PPK.

Single-shot pistols are used chiefly in international target-shooting competitions. To load a single-shot pistol, the user moves the *operating lever* (part that opens and closes the action) forward and down to lower the *breech block* and to cock the firing pin. The breech block closes the *breech* of the gun—that is, the part behind the barrel. After the breech block has been lowered, the cartridge chamber is exposed. The user then inserts a cartridge into the chamber. Next, the operating lever is pulled up and back to close the chamber and move the cartridge into the closed position. The pistol is then ready to fire. When the trigger is pulled, the firing pin drops, exploding the cartridge. The procedure is then repeated to remove the cartridge and reload the

Some historic handguns Since handguns first appeared in the 1400's, certain models have become well known because of their special features, wide use, or both. Some of these handguns are shown below.

Roger Roland Fuhr, ROLANDesign, Los Angeles

English wheel lock (1640)

English belt flintlock (1800)

First Colt (1835)

Colt Walker (1847)

Derringer (1855)

Single-action Army revolver (1873-1940)

German Luger (1914)

Military and police semiautomatic used today

pistol. Famous single-shot pistols include the Hammerli Free Pistol, the Walther, and the Martini.

History

Early handguns. The first gun that could be operated with one hand was the matchlock gun, which appeared in the 1500's. It was fired by attaching a burning cord or match to the end of an S-shaped holder called a *serpentine.* About 1515, the wheel-lock gun was invented. Its metal wheel struck a spark when it revolved against a flint. With the wheel lock, soldiers no longer had to carry flames to ignite the powder in their guns.

During the mid-1500's, snaphance pistols, which were easier to operate than the wheel lock, came into widespread use. In the 1600's and 1700's, many kinds of gunlocks were developed, including the flintlock (see **Flintlock**). In 1807, Alexander Forsyth, a Scottish inventor, introduced the percussion cap. Percussion-cap pistols were loaded from the muzzle, with a sliding can of priming powder on the breech. Small handguns called derringers are descended from percussion-cap pistols, but are breech loaded. They are named for Henry Deringer, Jr., a U.S. pistol maker of the 1800's.

Rapid-fire handguns. One of the first practical revolvers was the Colt Paterson, patented in England in 1835 by Samuel Colt, a U.S. inventor. Breech loading became popular in 1856, when the U.S. inventors Horace Smith and Daniel Wesson developed a metallic cartridge that made cartridge shooting more convenient.

The Borchardt, the first self-loading semiautomatic pistol, appeared in 1895. It was loaded with an eight-cartridge clip placed in the hollow of the grip. George Luger, an Austrian-born inventor, improved the Borchardt in the early 1900's. In 1902, John M. Browning, a U.S. inventor, developed the Browning automatic pistol. It served as the basis for other semiautomatics.

Gun control

In the United States, more than 20,000 federal, state, and local laws restrict the use of firearms. Thousands of these laws pertain to handguns. Some laws prohibit the ownership of handguns. Others require investigations of the background of anyone wishing to buy a handgun.

In Canada, people seeking to buy a handgun must have a specific reason for owning one. Few Canadians are allowed to own handguns only for protection. Most European countries require handguns to be licensed or registered. But enforcement of these laws varies widely.

People who favor handgun control laws believe these laws reduce crime and handgun-related deaths. Many of them say there are no legitimate reasons for private ownership of handguns. Opponents of handgun control say handguns have many legitimate uses. They argue that laws against owning handguns affect only law-abiding citizens and not criminals. They also believe that the Second Amendment to the U.S. Constitution guarantees individuals the right to own firearms.   Ronald A. Ogan

Related articles in *World Book* include:

Ammunition	Colt, Samuel
Browning, John M.	Firearm
Bullet	Gun
Cartridge	Gun control

Handicap is a way to equalize sports competition between opponents who are unequal in ability. Handicaps include scoring bonuses and weight allowances.

Handicapped is a term used to describe people who have a physical or mental disability that interferes with their leading a happy, productive life. Physical disabilities include blindness, deafness, deformity, muscular and nervous disorders, paralysis, and loss of limbs. There are two general kinds of mental disabilities, mental illness and mental retardation.

A disability may or may not be a handicap. It becomes a handicap if it interferes with the person's expectations, job performance, or relationships with his or her family, friends, and society in general. People with a similar disability may not be equally handicapped. For example, a history professor may not be greatly handicapped by the loss of a finger. But the same disability would be a terrible handicap to a concert pianist.

WORLD BOOK photo

WORLD BOOK photo by Paul S. Conklin

Handicapped people can lead complete lives in spite of their disabilities. A woman confined to a wheelchair, *left,* holds a responsible office job. Football players at a college for the deaf, *above,* practice to the low-frequency beat of a drum. Before each play, the members of the offensive team agree that the play will begin on a certain beat of the drum.

There are about 35 million handicapped persons in the United States. Many common handicaps result from diseases. Heart disease may permanently decrease the victim's strength and endurance. Strokes may produce paralysis and loss of speech. Arthritis and many bone diseases can lead to deformity. Certain nerve diseases may result in blindness, deafness, and lack of coordination. Cerebral palsy is a disorder that damages the brain before, during, or after birth. Depending on what part of the brain is damaged, cerebral palsy can cause speech problems, mental retardation, muscular weakness, or involuntary movements of the arms and legs. Accidents cause a wide range of handicaps, including spinal damage and loss of limbs.

With proper motivation and special training, even severely handicapped persons can lead productive, fulfilling lives. Many famous people have overcome handicaps to make important contributions to mankind. The English poet John Milton was blind when he wrote his epic masterpiece, *Paradise Lost.* The great German composer Ludwig van Beethoven wrote much of his finest music after he became deaf. Franklin D. Roosevelt, paralyzed in both legs by polio at the age of 39, became President of the United States. Helen Keller became blind, deaf, and mute before she was 2 years old, but she learned to read, write, and speak. She devoted her life to helping the deaf and the blind.

Problems of the handicapped

A handicapped person faces special problems that may affect his or her personal life, family life, and community life.

In personal life. A major problem of many handicapped people is their limited ability to perform ordi-

Aids for the handicapped   Handicapped individuals may require special aids to perform everyday activities. Many public buildings provide structural aids that give the handicapped access to certain places and facilities. Various aids also enable the handicapped to enjoy television and other conveniences.

© Larry Day

The wheelchair symbol, *above,* appears on signs marking special facilities for the handicapped. Such facilities include ramps that enable wheelchair users to enter and leave a building alone.

© Larry Day

Braille numbers in elevators make it easy for a blind person to quickly locate the button for a certain floor.

HE WENT WITHOUT US?

© Peter Gonzalez

Captioned television programs enable the deaf to enjoy TV as completely as possible. Printed dialogue appears on the screen during such programs.

© L. Perkins

A low telephone enables people in wheelchairs to make calls easily. Other aids for wheelchair users include low drinking fountains and toilets in wide stalls.

nary daily activities. For example, a person with only one arm may have trouble getting dressed and undressed. An individual who has a hearing disability may have difficulty using the telephone. Some handicapped persons lack the ability or energy to get around without assistance.

Handicapped individuals also may experience special psychological problems. They may become depressed because their disability makes them different from most people. However, some handicapped persons consider their disability as a challenge, and this attitude helps them overcome the handicap.

Social relationships can be difficult for the handicapped. Many nonhandicapped people do not like to be reminded that disabilities exist. As a result, they may feel uncomfortable in the presence of a handicapped individual. One of the most important things a disabled person must learn is how to put others at ease.

In family life. A family's home life may change considerably if some member becomes handicapped. Previously, various members of the family had filled certain roles in the household, and difficulties can arise if these roles change. For example, adjustment problems may occur if the parent who provides the family's income suffers a stroke and no longer can do so. Severe depression could result if the other parent must get a job and take over that responsibility as head of the family. In addition, the children may have trouble accepting the new roles of their parents.

Other members of a family should not try to do too much for the disabled member. Handicapped people need to feel independent and should be allowed to solve their own problems whenever possible. If a handicapped person is overprotected or given extra attention, other family members may feel jealous and resentful. The other family members should let the handicapped member know they realize he or she has hopes, goals, and ambitions, just as they have.

In community life, the ignorance of most individuals creates problems for the handicapped. The majority of people do not realize how much a disabled person can achieve. As a result, they may exclude the handicapped from community activities, such as athletic events and theatrical productions. Some employers hesitate to hire a handicapped person because they believe the handicapped are poor workers. Actually, work records show that handicapped men and women produce as well or better than other people in the same job. The handicapped also hold their jobs longer.

Because of their limited ability to move around, many disabled persons may lack access to certain places and facilities. At school, for example, a student or teacher in a wheelchair needs ramps instead of stairs, toilets with wide stalls, and other structural aids. During the 1970's, such aids for the disabled were provided in increasing numbers of public buildings. However, accessibility in housing and public transportation remained a serious problem.

Overcoming handicaps

Few disabilities can be cured, and so most disabled persons must learn to live with their handicap. To overcome a disability, an individual must desire to be independent. Without this desire, the help of others has little

value and the degree of disability remains high.

Many types of professional assistance are available to help the handicapped conquer their disability. There are three vital areas in which experts can provide help: (1) rehabilitation medicine, (2) special education, and (3) vocational training.

Rehabilitation medicine is a branch of medicine that helps improve the condition of disabled people. In most cases, rehabilitation is carried out in a hospital by a team of specialists headed by a physician. These specialists may include nurses, psychologists, social workers, speech pathologists, and various other therapists.

The treatment used in rehabilitation depends on the patient's disability. Surgery can help certain kinds of blindness, deafness, and deformities. Drugs may be used to treat severe depression and other mental illnesses. Many handicapped people benefit from *physical therapy,* which involves treatment by such means as heat, light, and water. Physical therapy may also include special exercises that restore the patient's endurance and muscle strength.

A form of treatment called *occupational therapy* helps overcome or reduce handicaps by teaching patients various skills. These skills help disabled people gain confidence in their ability to live a full and normal life. For example, a person who has lost both legs may learn how to drive a specially equipped car.

Various mechanical devices also help the handicapped lead more complete lives. Paralyzed people can move around in electric wheelchairs. Artificial arms and legs replace lost limbs. Hearing aids greatly improve

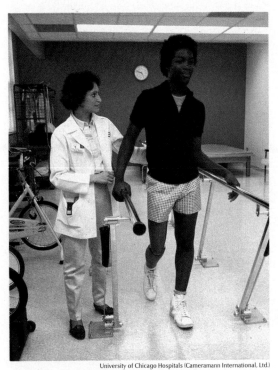

University of Chicago Hospitals (Cameramann International, Ltd.)

Rehabilitation of the handicapped includes therapy that helps them learn or regain various skills. The young man shown above is learning to walk with an artificial leg.

© Dan McCoy, Rainbow

Special education helps handicapped children use their full learning ability. In the picture above, mentally retarded children are working with computerized learning devices.

the hearing of people afflicted by certain types of deafness.

Special education is instruction designed to help handicapped children use their full learning ability. It includes instruction in the classroom, at home, and in hospitals and specialized institutions.

Teaching handicapped children requires special skills and materials. A specially trained teacher may be needed to teach mentally retarded children to care for themselves and to instruct them in basic school subjects. Partially sighted children may require books with large print. Blind children learn through braille books and *talking books* (recordings on records or tapes).

The United States government requires the states to make special education services available to all handicapped children of school age. Whenever possible, these services must be offered in regular classrooms so that handicapped children and nonhandicapped children can be educated together. This process of integrating handicapped children into regular school programs is called *mainstreaming.* Special classrooms or separate schools are provided only if the severity of a child's handicap makes the mainstreaming process impossible.

Vocational training prepares the handicapped to hold a job. Specialists called *vocational counselors* know what type of skills a person needs to succeed in a particular job. These experts conduct tests to determine a disabled person's abilities and interests. After a vocational counselor decides what kind of work might be best for a handicapped individual, the patient can be trained for that work. A blind person may be taught to devise programs for computers. A person confined to a wheelchair may be trained to hold an administrative position with a business company.

Attitudes toward the handicapped

In ancient times, hardly anyone helped the handicapped. The welfare of a group depended on the ability of each member to fight and to work. Handicapped persons who could not fulfill their responsibilities threatened the safety of all, and many were driven away and left to die. Most ancient peoples believed that evil spirits caused injury or disease. The Spartans let deformed newborn children die of exposure. In Rome, a disfigured infant could be legally drowned by its parents.

During the Middle Ages, from about the A.D. 400's to the late 1400's, people ridiculed the handicapped and regarded them with suspicion. Some nobles used the physically disabled as court jesters. Many handicapped persons were burned as witches.

Attitudes toward the handicapped began to change

© Larry Day

Vocational training prepares handicapped people for an occupation. The man shown above in the wheelchair is learning computer skills designed to help him find employment.

© Bernard Pierre Wolff, Photo Researchers

Speech therapy helps many handicapped people improve their ability to talk. An audio-therapy unit amplifies the voice of a therapist working with children who have a severe hearing loss.

Some organizations that help the handicapped

Organization	Address	Services
U.S. government agencies		
Library of Congress	Washington, DC 20542	Coordinates distribution of books for the blind.
President's Committee on Employment of the Handicapped	Washington, DC 20036	Encourages employers to hire handicapped workers.
U.S. Department of Education	Washington, DC 20202	Administers the Education for All Handicapped Children Act and the Rehabilitation Act of 1973.
U.S. Employment Service	Washington, DC 20213	Helps handicapped people search for jobs.
U.S. Health Resources and Services Administration	Rockville, MD 20857	Administers the block grant that provides funds for state services to disabled children.
U.S. Social Security Administration	Baltimore, MD 21235	Administers Supplemental Security Income programs.
U.S. Veterans Administration	Washington, DC 20420	Administers vocational programs for disabled veterans.
Nongovernment organizations		
Alexander Graham Bell Association for the Deaf	3417 Volta Place NW Washington, DC 20007	Promotes the teaching of speech and lip reading to deaf people.
American Association of Psychiatric Services for Children	1001 Connecticut Ave. N.W. Washington, DC 20036	Supports research on child mental health, promotes application of clinical knowledge, and serves as an information center.
American Foundation for the Blind	15 W. 16th St. New York, NY 10011	Serves as a national resource and information center for agencies that help the blind.
Association for Retarded Citizens	2501 Avenue J Arlington, TX 76006	Promotes research on mental retardation and works for improved treatment and social acceptance of the retarded.
Braille Institute	741 N. Vermont Ave. Los Angeles, CA 90029	Lends free braille books; provides education, counseling, and job placement for blind people.
March of Dimes Birth Defects Foundation	1275 Mamaroneck Ave. White Plains, NY 10605	Supports research on prevention of birth defects and offers programs to improve maternal and newborn health.
National Association of the Deaf	814 Thayer Ave. Silver Spring, MD 20910	Works to improve educational programs and job opportunities for the deaf. Promotes legislation to benefit deaf people.
National Easter Seal Society	2023 W. Ogden Ave. Chicago, IL 60612	Provides services to people with disabilities.
National Federation of the Blind	1800 Johnson St. Baltimore, MD 21230	Works to improve social conditions for the blind.
United Cerebral Palsy Associations	66 E. 34th St. New York, NY 10016	Supports research and provides vocational training for people with cerebral palsy, and sponsors professional and public education about the disease.

during the 1800's. Many people began to pity the disabled and treated them with special care. Nevertheless, individuals with handicaps were thought to bring shame on themselves and their families. As a result, most handicapped people were kept hidden away at home or in special institutions.

During the mid-1900's, important advances were made in the treatment of the handicapped. Until that time, many people who became paralyzed below the waist died as a result of urinary problems. But in the 1940's, the discovery of certain antibiotics enabled physicians to keep these patients alive. Modern rehabilitation techniques were developed to help such victims lead full, productive lives. During World War II, and after the war ended in 1945, extensive efforts were made to rehabilitate disabled veterans. Military hospitals established rehabilitation centers, and soon many other hospitals also set up these facilities.

During the 1970's, the United States Congress passed two important laws to help handicapped people. The Rehabilitation Act of 1973 prohibits unfair treatment of handicapped individuals in programs or activities that receive government funds. The act also requires many federally funded businesses to make an effort to hire qualified handicapped people. The Education for All Handicapped Children Act of 1975 orders the states to provide a free education for any handicapped child who is of school age. Canada has a similar law.

Henry B. Betts

Related articles in *World Book* include:

Famous handicapped persons

Beethoven, Ludwig van	Hogan, Ben
Braille, Louis	Keller, Helen A.
Browning, Elizabeth Barrett	Milton, John
Edison, Thomas A.	Roosevelt, Franklin D.
Goya, Francisco	Toulouse-Lautrec, Henri de

Other related articles

Artificial limb	Goodwill Industries	Occupational
Audiology	Guide dog	therapy
Bell, Alexander Graham	Hearing aid	Physical therapy
	Heart Association,	Poliomyelitis
Blindness	American	Psychiatry
Braille	Lip reading	Spastic paralysis
Cerebral palsy	March of Dimes	Special education
Deafness	Birth Defects	Speech therapy
Ear (Disorders of the ear)	Foundation	Vocational rehabilitation
Eye (Diseases of the eye)	Mental illness	
	Mental retardation	
	Multiple sclerosis	

Additional resources

Coombs, Jan. *Living with the Disabled: You Can Help: A Family Guide.* Sterling Publishing, 1984.
Harries, Joan. *They Triumphed over Their Handicaps.* Watts, 1981.
Haskins, James S. *Who Are the Handicapped?* Doubleday, 1978.

Handicraft, also called *handcraft,* refers to the creation of objects by hand. The range of handicrafts is limited only by an individual's imagination and ability. Handcrafted objects include boxes, bowls, lamps, wall hangings, toys, rugs, picture frames, leaded glass windows, baskets, moccasins, and boats.

Handicraft materials include wood, leather, cork, plaster, metal, fabric, yarns, beads, reeds, and shells. Most handicrafts require the use of such tools as hammers, needles, sewing machines, weaving looms, glass cutters, knives, or scissors. Traditional handicrafts, including basket weaving and pottery making, use natural materials and simple tools. Modern handicrafts, such as plastic sculpturing or model making, use industrial materials and techniques.

People create handicrafts for a number of reasons. Many people learn craft skills as a challenging and entertaining hobby. They may also enjoy expressing themselves artistically as they create objects. Other people get satisfaction from making the things they need in everyday life. Often craftworkers design and make original objects to exhibit and sell. Doctors sometimes recommend handicrafts as therapy for people with emotional problems or physical disabilities (see **Occupational therapy**).

The earliest handcrafted objects may have been items that people cut from wood with sharpened stones. Prehistoric people had to rely on handicrafts to make the things they needed, because they had no machines. Handcrafting served as the only method of creating objects for thousands of years.

The Industrial Revolution of the 1700's and early 1800's brought about great changes in the way objects were made. People using machines could make items much faster and cheaper than could individuals working by hand. The mass production of goods reduced the demand for homemade items and handicrafts became a hobby rather than a necessary activity.

After World War II (1939-1945), a new interest in handicrafts emerged. By the late 1950's, many people had become disenchanted with mass-produced goods. They disliked the sameness and lack of artistic design they saw in many mass-produced objects. In response to this dissatisfaction, manufacturers produced handicraft kits that provided precut parts and instructions showing people how to make various items.

As public interest increased, schools and colleges began to teach crafts. Educators came to recognize that creating a crafted object requires many of the same artistic skills and design knowledge as the fine arts. The popularity of handicrafts continued to grow during the 1960's, 1970's, and 1980's.   Dona Z. Meilach

See also the articles on *Handicraft hobbies* listed in the *Related articles* of the **Hobby** article.

Handkerchief, *HANG kuhr chihf,* is a small piece of cloth people carry to wipe their face, nose, or eyes. It is usually made of cotton or linen, but it may be of lace or silk. The people of ancient Greece and Rome used the first handkerchiefs we know about. During the Middle Ages (from the A.D. 400's to 1500), the handkerchief became a showy decoration. In France during the 1000's, wealthy men and women wore their handkerchiefs hanging from their belts.

As the use of the handkerchief spread, each nation developed its favorite materials. The French used silk and linen. The Italians used lace, and the English, silk or cotton. Today, some types are made only in certain countries. The best linen handkerchiefs are made in Ireland, Scotland, Belgium, France, and Switzerland. The best cotton handkerchiefs come from France and Italy, and the best silk handkerchiefs are made in China and Japan.   Lois M. Gurel

Hands. See Hand.

Bob Hahn, Taurus

Woodcarving is one of the world's oldest crafts. This craftworker is using a knife to carve decorative objects.

Frank Siteman, Taurus

Weaving colorful fabrics is a popular handicraft throughout the world. This woman is weaving a place mat on a hand loom.

Mary Heitner, Taurus

A potter uses the fingers to shape wet clay as it is spun around on a mechanical device called a *potter's wheel.*

© Jim Cronk

Learning to write is one of the most important parts of education. This teacher is showing a student how to write correctly.

Handwriting is one of the most useful skills. A person who has learned to write can put thoughts on paper for others to read. Handwriting plays a vital part in communication, and is one of the most important ways of keeping ideas ready for use. People can forget. But handwriting helps them remember. They can use pen or pencil to mark down letters, numbers, and other signs. People can move to another town, city, or country, but handwriting lets them "talk" to one another. The art and practice of attractive handwriting is called *penmanship,* or *calligraphy* (see **Calligraphy**).

The importance of handwriting

Some people believe that typewriters, computers, and printing presses have made handwriting unimportant. But it is still a necessary skill for everyone. When people write letters, they may want to write about their own ideas and feelings, or about their friends and families. A handwritten letter has a personal touch, because no two people have exactly the same handwriting.

Handwriting has other important uses. Students use handwriting to record and organize ideas they hear in lectures and classrooms. Later, they can use their notes for study and discussion. Secretaries of clubs usually write down important happenings at meetings. In school, students often write reports and tests by hand. Business executives, doctors, teachers, and many other adults keep records and make notes by hand. Later, they may have these ideas typewritten or printed.

Just being able to write is not enough. A person must also write *legibly,* so the words can be read. Handwriting that no one can read is useless and can create serious problems. For example, a student may write the cor-

rect answer to a question on a test. But if the teacher cannot read the answer, it may be marked wrong. An unclearly written check may result in serious financial loss. If a clerk writes a sales ticket so that the person delivering the package cannot read the ticket, it may delay the delivery and produce a dissatisfied customer.

Kinds of handwriting

In most schools, students are taught two kinds of handwriting—*manuscript writing* and *cursive writing.* Some writing systems combine manuscript and cursive letter forms for beginning writers. For details, see the *Handwriting Systems* section in this article.

Manuscript writing is a kind of handwriting most often learned by schoolchildren who are just beginning to write. It looks much like printing in a book. Each letter is straight up-and-down, and not joined to the next. Here is an example of manuscript writing:

Handwriting is an important skill in modern living.

Teachers find that learning to write is not always easy for young children. Most teachers prefer a way of writing that places as little strain as possible on a child's first efforts to put ideas down on paper.

Young children find manuscript easier to learn than cursive writing, the more difficult method used by adults. Manuscript writing is easier, chiefly because it makes only limited demands on the ability to use arm, hand, and eyes together effectively. Young children can easily make the simple curves and straight lines of manuscript letters. They can learn clear, easy-to-read handwriting quickly. Even a poorly made manuscript letter written by a beginner is likely to be more readable than anything attempted in cursive writing.

Manuscript also comes naturally from a young child's experiences with printed words. A youngster usually begins to do some reading before learning to write. Children read their teacher's manuscript writing on the chalkboard. In books, they read printed words that look much like manuscript words. So they know the letters with which they begin their own manuscript. At the same time, learning manuscript helps them learn to read and to spell. By the time children begin cursive writing, usually they can write fairly well in manuscript.

Cursive writing is used by most adults. Boys and girls usually learn cursive writing after they have mastered manuscript writing. The word *cursive* means *running.* In cursive writing, the letters join, or run together, instead of being separated as in manuscript. Also, the letters are slanted. Here is an example of cursive writing:

Handwriting is an important skill in modern living.

Some people use both manuscript and cursive writing. They may use manuscript to make signs, labels, and charts. They use cursive writing for their personal letters and notes.

Learning to write

Beginners should aim for easy-to-read handwriting. At the same time, they should try to attain a fair degree of speed. But teachers advise caution in trying to gain speed. Too much pressure to increase speed may hamper both clear writing and careful thinking.

Writing readiness. Children usually begin to learn to write in kindergarten or first grade. Sometimes children learn some handwriting even before entering school. If so, parents or teachers should make sure that children learn in the same way they will learn later in school. Also, they should be sure that the child is ready to learn.

A strong interest in writing is one of the most important signs of a child's readiness to learn to write. This interest often results from seeing adults and other children write at home and in school. But interest is not enough. Eye, hand, and arm control must be developed so that the child can manage paper and pencil. Coloring, drawing, and many kinds of play help build control. Puzzles, nesting toys, lacing frames, and similar playthings can help. A child also needs a strong sense of left and right. Otherwise, reverse writing or other problems may occur. Games and simple dances help develop a sense

of left and right. Most of all, the child must want to say something on paper and must be able to read what was written down. A child's readiness to read is usually an important clue that readiness to write will soon appear (see **Reading**).

Learning manuscript writing. When handwriting instruction begins, teachers usually encourage boys and girls to express their own ideas in writing. This kind of learning is called *functional,* because it puts handwriting to work at once. Teachers hold practice periods on letters only as long as necessary. These practice periods help students learn the different shapes and strokes required for letters.

In this kind of learning, children sometimes use oversize pencils. But many handwriting experts believe that ordinary pencils serve just as well. The writing paper has lines 1 inch (2.5 centimeters) apart. Halfway between these lines, there may be lines of another color, or dotted lines, that help in writing both capital and *lower case* (small) letters. Often, the teacher writes model letters on the chalkboard for the children to practice. The

Handwriting

There are two chief kinds of handwriting, manuscript and cursive. Several systems have been developed to teach each kind to beginning writers. A traditional system appears below. A newer system, called D'Nealian, is shown on the opposite page.

Traditional manuscript

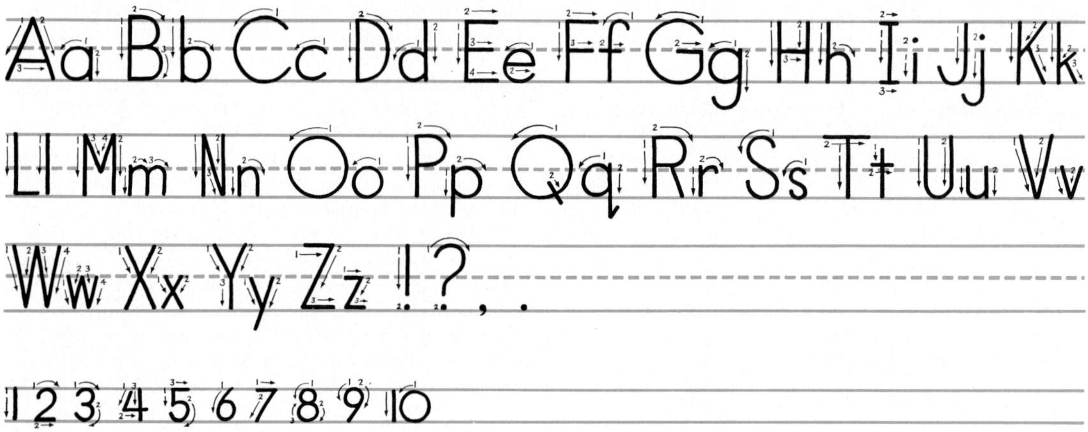

Traditional cursive

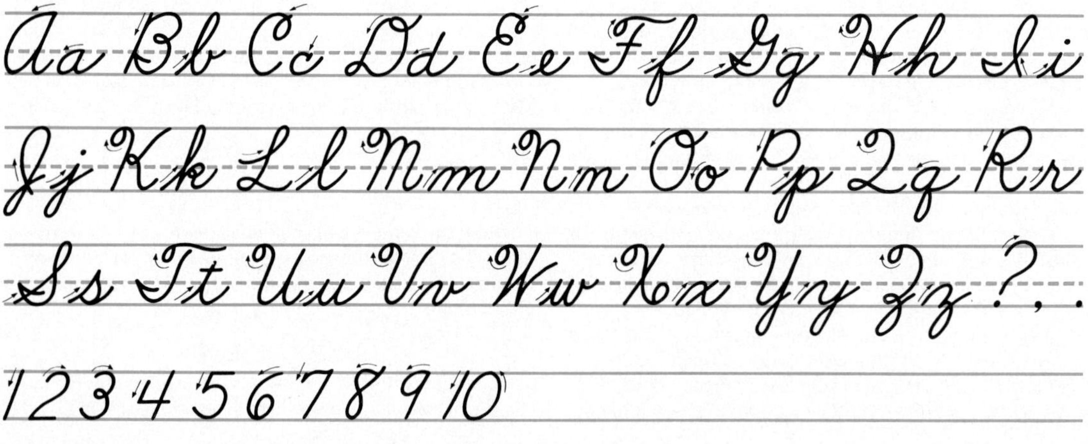

students may practice new letter shapes and words on the chalkboard before trying them on paper.

The opportunity to watch the teacher write is important in learning manuscript writing. The teacher shows in clear, easy-to-follow strokes just how to write. Each letter is made with exactly the same strokes in the same order every time it is written. The teacher may use the same words each time to name the strokes for the students. For example, when making the letter "a", the teacher may say, "Around, straight down." In general, the curves and straight lines that make up the letters are made from the top of the letter downward. The children learn to check the shape, the size, and the spacing of the letters.

The child should hold the chalk or pencil in a way that fits the hand naturally. No two children can hold pencil or chalk exactly alike. Some have hands that are long and thin. Others have short, wide hands. The paper is placed straight up-and-down for manuscript writing. For cursive writing, the paper slants to the left for people who are right-handed. For left-handed people, the paper slants to the right. The child should sit up straight, squarely in front of the table or desk, with both feet flat on the floor.

Learning cursive writing. Children should make the shift from manuscript to cursive writing only after they have gained a fair mastery of manuscript. The change usually occurs in the late second or third grade. In some cases, a later time makes the shift less difficult. At any grade level, the shift should be made gradually. It may require an average of four to six weeks. But children with varying abilities should be permitted considerable difference in the required time.

Learning cursive writing once consisted of practicing individual letters. Children practiced until they could make an exact copy of the letter from the chart, manual, or chalkboard. Today, the goal is still the development of clear, well-formed letters. But the child begins writing stories and reports soon after learning the letters. In this way, the child makes practical use of writing skills as soon as possible instead of delaying while striving for perfect letter shapes.

D'Nealian manuscript

From *D'Nealian ™ Handwriting* by Donald Thurber. © 1981 by Scott, Foresman and Company. Reprinted by permission.

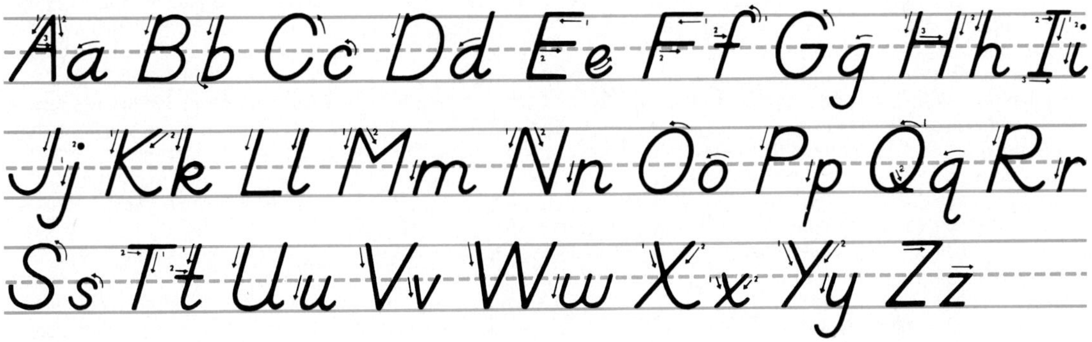

D'Nealian cursive

As in manuscript writing, students learn the most about cursive writing by watching a teacher write well. They can see how the paper is slanted to give slant to the writing. They learn which letters are made differently in cursive writing than in manuscript. The students also learn how to make the joining strokes between letters. They are taught not to raise the pencil from the paper until an entire word is finished. Then, they dot the "i's" and cross the "t's."

Handwriting systems. Teachers can use one of several systems to teach handwriting. Materials for these systems are prepared by various companies.

Since the mid-1900's, some companies have developed writing systems that combine manuscript and cursive letter forms for beginning writers. One of the best-known systems combining letter forms is *D'Nealian handwriting,* which was introduced in 1978. D'Nealian manuscript letters are oval and slanted. They more closely resemble cursive writing than conventional manuscript. This resemblance is intended to make cursive writing easier for children to learn. D'Nealian cursive letters look like those of other writing systems.

Research concerning handwriting techniques has shown no evidence that one particular system of handwriting is better than any other. Researchers have concluded that the individual instructor's skill plays the most important role in teaching a child to write.

Left-handedness. About 10 per cent of all people are left-handed. When left-handed children begin to learn to write manuscript, they may need some special help from the teacher. A left-handed child should hold the pencil so that the fingers are at least 1 inch (2.5 centimeters) from the point. This grip gives the child a better view of the paper while writing. Sitting at a desk or table that is slightly lower than normal height also may help. Left-handed children should be encouraged to keep the left arm close to the body when writing.

A left-handed child learning cursive writing may place the writing paper toward the left side of the desk, turned in a clockwise direction. Because it is difficult for left-handed children to slant their writing to the right, they should be allowed to write without a slant or to slant their writing to the left.

Teaching methods for left-handed children may include group lessons with a left-handed person demonstrating the writing technique. Practicing at the chalkboard also may be useful.

Common handwriting problems

The main goal for easy-to-read handwriting consists of good letter formation. The letters *a, e, r,* and *t* seem to cause difficulty. But in all letter forms, a few strokes determine whether or not a letter will be clear.

Too much spacing between letters and irregular slanting of letters may also result in poor handwriting.

In general, a person who wants improved handwriting should correct these common problems. But someone may have to help the person find the difficulties and correct them in the right way.

History

Early forms of writing. Prehistoric people invented the first crude "writing." They drew pictures of wild animals on the walls of caves and rock shelters. Their pic-

tures tell the story of how they hunted for food (see **Prehistoric people**). Later peoples made their pictures simpler and simpler. The pictures gradually became signs called *pictographs* (see **Pictograph**). Each pictograph stood for a word or an idea. This kind of picture writing probably reached its highest point about 3000 B.C. in Egypt. The Egyptians used a kind of picture writing called *hieroglyphics* (see **Hieroglyphics**). At about the same time, the Sumerians invented a system of writing that used wedge-shaped symbols called *cuneiform* (see **Cuneiform**).

About 1500 B.C., Semitic people in the Middle East invented the alphabet. In the alphabet, a written sign stands for a sound in the spoken language. For example, the letter *b* represents a certain sound. The Phoenicians developed the alphabet further. The Greeks took it over from the Phoenicians, and the Romans borrowed it from the Greeks. For more information, see **Alphabet** and the separate articles on each letter of the alphabet.

In ancient times, few persons knew how to write. Most of the people who wanted to send letters dictated them to people called *scribes,* who made their living writing for the public (see **Scribe**).

Both manuscript and cursive writing come from the Roman alphabet. In fact, we write a number of letters almost exactly as the Romans wrote them. In printing, the term *roman* refers to straight up-and-down letters similar to those used in manuscript writing. The Romans used letters like these for inscriptions on monuments and public buildings. Printers use the term *italic* for letters that slant to the right, similar to those used in cursive writing. Printing in italic letters began in Venice, Italy, during the 1500's. Several styles of cursive writing developed at this time.

Later writing styles. During the Middle Ages, monks in monasteries produced beautiful books written entirely by hand. They decorated the pages with fancy letters, borders, and pictures. Many museums treasure these books as masterpieces of writing. The monks often used a kind of writing called *Gothic* or *black-letter.* We sometimes use this kind of writing on diplomas.

During the 1700's and 1800's, schoolchildren in Europe and the United States learned beautiful, but complicated, styles of cursive writing. *English Round Hand,* or *Copperplate,* became popular in the 1700's.

During the 1800's, schools in the United States taught a fancy style of writing with many loops and curves. This *Spencerian* style took its name from Platt Rogers Spencer (1800-1864), an American teacher who published many textbooks on penmanship. Children in the 1800's worked long and hard to perfect a "fine Spencerian hand" in their writing.

The 1900's. Schools in the United States and Great Britain began to use simpler styles of writing, particularly manuscript writing for beginners. Cursive was also treated less as an art and more as a practical tool. As a result, the term *penmanship* dropped out of common usage because it carried the outdated idea of writing as an exercise in beauty for its own sake. Teachers began to aim more at developing ideas in clear form. Practice methods shifted from depending heavily on separate exercises to developing good handwriting through the writing of letters and reports. Today, the purpose of learning to write is communication. Teachers help individual children check their own writing and make it more legible and fluent. Lee M. Little Soldier

Related articles in *World Book* include:

Alphabet	Japanese language	Pictograph
Autograph	(picture)	Punctuation
Chinese language	Language	Reading
(picture)	Letter writing	Shorthand
Communication	Manuscript	Speedwriting
Cuneiform	Paleography	Spelling
Graphology	Pen	Writing
Hieroglyphics	Pencil	

Handwriting on the wall. According to a Bible story (Dan. 5:1-31), the Babylonian ruler Belshazzar, during a banquet, saw the fingers of a man's hand writing the Aramaic words *mene, mene, tekel, upharsin* on his palace wall. None of his wise men could interpret the meaning. Daniel, the Hebrew prophet, said they meant that God had weighed Belshazzar and his kingdom and had found them wanting, and would destroy them. The phrase *handwriting on the wall* now means impending disaster or misfortune. H. Darrell Lance

Handy, W. C. (1873-1958), an American composer and bandleader, became known as the father of the blues. He wrote some of the earliest and best blues songs, including "St. Louis Blues," "Beale Street Blues," "Memphis Blues," and "Joe Turner Blues."

William Christopher Handy, a black, was born in Florence, Ala. His father was a Methodist preacher who believed that nonreligious music was the work of the devil. Nevertheless, Handy learned *stomps* (dance tunes that feature spirited rhythm and feet stomping) from an old country fiddler. Handy and his friends used homemade instruments to play these "sinful tunes." Handy moved to Memphis, Tenn., in 1905.
He formed his own band, which toured the South for many years. In the early 1920's, Handy settled in New York City, where he started his own music publishing company. Gilbert Chase

Courtesy of W. C. Handy, Jr.
W. C. Handy

Additional resources

Handy, W. C. *Father of the Blues.* Macmillan, 1970. Reprint of 1941 ed.
Schuller, Gunther. *Early Jazz: Its Roots and Musical Development.* Oxford, 1968.
Wayne, Bennett, ed. *Three Jazz Greats.* Garrard, 1973.

Hang gliding. See Glider (Hang gliding).
Hangbird. See Baltimore oriole.
Hang-chou. See Hangzhou.
Hanging is a legal means of execution in some states of the United States. The condemned person stands on a platform with a noose of rope around his or her neck. A trap door opens under the person, and the person falls until jerked to a stop by the rope. The sudden jolt breaks or dislocates the bones of the neck, causing almost immediate loss of consciousness. Death occurs within a few minutes. For a list of the states that use hanging as a method of execution, see **Capital punishment** (table). Marvin E. Wolfgang

Hanging Gardens of Babylon. See Seven Wonders of the Ancient World.
Hanging valley. Glaciers or river waters often deepen the main valley of a stream more rapidly than its tributaries deepen their valleys. When the valleys of tributaries are not deepened at the same rate as the main valley, they are left high on the main valley's rim. Geologists call these valleys *hanging valleys.* Streams usually plunge from hanging valleys into the main stream in a series of waterfalls or cascades. Hanging valleys are common where small streams are dry most of the year, and along sea cliffs. Samuel N. Dicken
Hangzhou, *hahng joh* (pop. 1,191,582), is a Chinese tourist center and the capital of Zhejiang Province. The city's name is also spelled *Hang-chou.* The city lies on a bay about 100 miles (160 kilometers) southwest of Shanghai. For location, see **China** (political map). Industries in the area produce chemical and electronics products, iron and steel, and silk. Many tourists visit Hangzhou's famous Xi (West) Lake. Along the shore, and on four islands in the lake, are many gardens, statues, and temples.

Hangzhou began as a small fishing village. During the A.D. 500's, it became a trading center and grew rapidly. In the 1100's, the Song emperors made Hangzhou their capital. By the 1200's, Hangzhou had become one of the largest cities in the world. The city was badly damaged during the Taiping Rebellion (1850-1864), but was later rebuilt. The Japanese occupied Hangzhou from 1937 until the end of World War II in 1945. Most of Hangzhou's industries were developed after the Chinese Communists conquered the country in 1949. Richard H. Solomon

Hankou. See Wuhan.
Hanks, Nancy. See Lincoln, Abraham (Early life).
Hanna, Mark (1837-1904), an American politician and businessman, became famous by helping to make William McKinley President of the United States in 1896. He persuaded business leaders to contribute heavily to the Republican campaign, and emerged as the national boss of the Republican Party.

After McKinley's election, Hanna's prestige was enormous, and in 1897 he was elected a U.S. senator from Ohio. He helped settle the 1902 coal strike by persuading the coal-mine owners to come to terms with the strikers. Hanna believed that industry could deal more effectively with unions than with unorganized workers.

Hanna was a leader of the conservatives in the party. Theodore Roosevelt, who succeeded McKinley in 1901, worked to reduce conservative influence. When Hanna died, his influence was declining.

Marcus Alonzo Hanna was born in Ohio. He made a fortune in the grocery, coal, and iron businesses before he went into politics. John A. Garraty
Hannibal (247-183 B.C.) was the greatest general and statesman of Carthage, an ancient North African city. His excellent military strategy and leadership ability helped him overcome great handicaps and defeat armies much larger than his own. He united people of varied backgrounds under his command. Even under poor conditions, his army followed him with confidence.

His early life. Hannibal was born in Carthage. His father, Hamilcar Barca, was also a military leader. Hamilcar Barca hated the Romans, his city's chief enemy. Accord-

Hannibal fought the Romans in the Second Punic War. This scene shows the Roman general Scipio, *left,* meeting Hannibal, *right,* in an effort to negotiate peace. Scipio's forces defeated Hannibal at Zama in northern Africa in 202 B.C.

Detail of a Flemish tapestry; Palazzo del Quirinale, Rome (SCALA/Art Resource)

ing to tradition, Hamilcar made young Hannibal take an oath always to be an enemy of Rome. As a boy, Hannibal went with his father to Spain, a land partly ruled by Carthage. As a young man, Hannibal led troops against Spanish tribes, and helped increase Carthaginian power in Spain. Hannibal became the Carthaginian commander in Spain when he was 25 years old.

In the 220's B.C., trouble developed between Carthage and Rome over Hannibal's expansion. Hannibal attacked Saguntum, a Spanish ally of Rome, in 219 B.C. Rome declared war on Carthage—the Second Punic War—in 218 B.C.

His military campaigns. Early in the war, Hannibal astonished the Romans with a daring maneuver. Starting from Spain with about 60,000 troops, he crossed the Pyrenees, France, and the Alps, and entered Roman Italy. Snow and cold, and fierce mountain tribes killed many Carthaginians in the Alps. Hannibal reached the Po Valley in northern Italy with only about 26,000 troops and 6,000 horses. He also brought a few elephants because they could sometimes shatter enemy lines, like tanks in modern battles. He then recruited 10,000 to 15,000 Gauls into his army. The Gauls, a tribe from the Po Valley, were enemies of Rome.

A Roman army brought up from Sicily tried to stop Hannibal's advance. But Hannibal maneuvered the Romans into an ambush and defeated them in the Battle of the Trebia River. Hannibal moved on to central Italy in 217 B.C. There, he tricked a Roman army into following his army, and then destroyed the Romans in an ambush on the shores of Lake Trasimeno.

In 216 B.C., Hannibal found himself far outnumbered by the Romans at Cannae, in southern Italy. Hannibal arranged his troops in an arc. When the Romans attacked, the center of the formation retreated, and the two sides, with the help of Hannibal's superior cavalry, encircled and crushed the Romans. The Carthaginians killed about 50,000 enemy troops in one day in the worst defeat ever suffered by a Roman army.

The turning point. After Cannae, Hannibal's future looked good. But the tide soon turned against him and

Carthage. Hannibal had gained allies in southern Italy, Macedonia, and Syracuse, Sicily. But some of his allies became too busy with their own affairs to help him. The Romans still had allies and many troops of their own in central Italy, and were able to prevent reinforcements from reaching Hannibal. Meanwhile, the Roman general Publius Cornelius Scipio drove the Carthaginians out of Spain, and in 204 B.C. invaded Africa. Hannibal was called home to Africa in 203 B.C. He was finally defeated by Scipio at Zama, in northern Africa, in 202 B.C. The war ended in 201 B.C. with Rome the winner in spite of Hannibal's great effort.

After the war. Rome allowed Carthage to govern itself. Hannibal headed the government, and Carthage made a rapid recovery under his leadership. But he fled eastward in 195 B.C., after he heard that the Romans were going to demand his surrender. He found protection with King Antiochus III of Syria, who was about to go to war with Rome. Antiochus made little use of Hannibal's genius and lost the war in 189 B.C. Hannibal then fled to Bithynia, an ancient country in what is now Turkey. When the Romans demanded his surrender, Hannibal committed suicide.   Henry C. Boren

See also **Carthage; Hamilcar Barca; Punic Wars.**

Additional resources

Bradford, Ernle. *Hannibal.* McGraw, 1981.
Lamb, Harold. *Hannibal: One Man Against Rome.* Doubleday, 1958.
Webb, Robert N. *Hannibal: Invader from Carthage.* Watts, 1968. For younger readers.

Hannibal, Mo. (pop. 18,811), is the boyhood home of the writer Mark Twain. It lies about 100 miles (160 kilometers) north and west of St. Louis in a rich farming region along the Mississippi River. For location, see **Missouri** (political map). Hannibal's industries include printing, tourism, woodworking, and the production of canned food products, cement, cereals, chemicals, dairy and farm products, electrical heating elements, optical supplies, precision tools, and shoes. Chief points of interest are Mark Twain's home and Mark Twain Cave, the cave referred to in his novel, *The Adventures of Tom*

Sawyer. The city is the site of Hannibal-La Grange College. Hannibal was founded in 1819. It has a mayor-council form of government.   Gilbert J. Stuenkel

See also **Twain, Mark.**

Hannover, *HAN oh vuhr* (pop. 508,298), sometimes called Hanover, is one of the largest cities in West Germany. It is the capital of the German state of Lower Saxony. Until 1866, it was the capital of the Kingdom of Hannover. It lies in what was once the state of Prussia, about 60 miles (97 kilometers) from Bremen (see **Germany** [political map]). Hannover is a railway center and is served also by the Mittelland Canal. Hannover is also a trading and manufacturing city, with iron foundries, machine works, chemical plants, and tobacco and cigar factories. The city holds an industrial fair each year. It is famed for the pure German spoken by its citizens. Hannover was heavily bombed during World War II.

James K. Pollock

Hanoi, *hah NOY* (pop. 1,443,500), is the capital and second largest city of Vietnam. Only Ho Chi Minh City has more people. Hanoi lies at the head of the fertile Red River delta. For location, see **Vietnam** (map).

Hanoi served as the capital of Vietnam from the 1000's until 1802, when Hue became the capital. After an international agreement divided Vietnam in 1954, Hanoi became the capital of Communist North Vietnam. In the mid-1960's—during the Vietnam War—Hanoi relocated much industry to the countryside to escape bombing by the United States. The bombing damaged industrial suburbs but left the city almost untouched. North Vietnam took control of South Vietnam in 1975 at the end of the war. It unified North and South Vietnam into the single nation of Vietnam. Hanoi became the capital of the unified nation.

Hanoi is an important commercial center and river port. Haiphong, located about 55 miles (89 kilometers) from Hanoi near the Gulf of Tonkin, serves as a deepwater port for Hanoi. Hanoi's most important industry is food processing. The city also produces bicycles, cigarettes, and farm machinery.

Administrative offices, shops, and private houses line many of the broad streets of Hanoi. Bicycles, streetcars, and trucks crowd the streets day and night. Government officials drive the only cars. The University of Hanoi is the principal center of higher learning in northern Vietnam.   David P. Chandler

Hanover, *HAN oh vuhr,* spelled *Hannover* in German, is a historic area in what is now northern West Germany. In 1692, Hanover became an *electorate,* a territory whose ruler—called the *elector*—could help elect the emperor of the Holy Roman Empire. In 1714, the Elector of Hanover became King George I of England. Hanover and England remained associated until 1837, when George's last male heir died. Prussia gained control of Hanover in 1866, and Hanover became a province of the new German Empire in 1871. In 1946, Hanover became part of the West German state of Lower Saxony.

The Hanover region includes the cities of Göttingen, Emden, Hannover, and Oldenburg. Farming is Hanover's chief industry. But the region is also a manufacturing center. The Harz Mountains area yields timber and minerals.   J. A. Hellen

Hansard, *HAN suhrd,* is the family name of five English printers who published reports of Parliament's sessions. The government classed the Hansard reports as official records after 1855. The British government prints the official reports today, but the reports are still called *Hansard.*

Luke Hansard (1752-1828) published the *Journals of the House of Commons* from 1774 until his death. He began printing the *Journals* as the partner of London publisher John Hughs. Hansard bought the printing firm in 1800. He was born in Norwich, England.

Thomas Curson Hansard (1776-1833), the eldest son of Luke Hansard, printed the unofficial *Parliamentary Debates* for a time.

James Hansard (1781-1849) and **Luke Graves Hansard** (1783-1841), the younger sons, succeeded their father. **Henry Hansard** (1829-1904), son of Luke Graves Hansard, managed the firm after 1847.   Vernon F. Snow

Hubertus Kanus, Shostal

Hannover's city hall is located on beautifully landscaped grounds. Hannover lies about 60 miles (97 kilometers) southeast of Bremen. It was once the capital of the Kingdom of Hannover. It is now a trading and manufacturing city.

Hansberry, Lorraine (1930-1965), was a black American playwright. She became famous for *A Raisin in the Sun* (1959), a drama about the attempt of a black family to escape from the Chicago ghetto. This play provides a study of human weaknesses and prejudices.

Hansberry was born in Chicago and moved to New York City in 1950. *A Raisin in the Sun,* her first completed play, won the New York Drama Critics Circle Award in 1959. Hansberry later wrote *The Sign in Sidney Brustein's Window* (1964). This drama portrays a Jewish liberal whose involvement in various social causes almost ruins his marriage. Before her death from cancer at the age of 34, Hansberry began a play about race relations in Africa. The unfinished work was published as *Les Blancs* (1970). Selections from Hansberry's letters and works appeared in *To Be Young, Gifted and Black* (1969).   Thomas A. Erhard

Hanseatic League, *HAN see AT ihk,* was a confederation of north German cities, founded in the late 1200's. The decline of the imperial power in Germany made it necessary for these cities to band together for common protection of their interests. The Hanseatic League, or *Hansa,* seems to have resulted from two earlier confederations which were grouped around the cities of Cologne and Lübeck. By the middle 1300's, the members of the Hansa included almost all the larger German towns along the North and Baltic seas.

The League had no formal constitution. Its only governing body was a congress made up of merchants from the various cities. The main weapons of the League were commercial boycott and commercial monopoly (see **Boycott; Monopoly and competition**). If a town refused to join the League, its merchants would be unable to sell their goods in profitable markets. One of the greatest contributions of the Hanseatic League was the system of maritime and commercial laws it developed.

The Hanseatic League gained control of the fur trade with Russia, the fish trade with Norway and Sweden, and the wool trade with Flanders. In 1370, the Danish king tried to break the League's power by closing the Sound. A Hanseatic fleet seized Copenhagen and imposed severe peace terms on Denmark. The Hanseatic League had passed out of existence by the end of the Middle Ages.   William F. McDonald

See also **Flag** (picture: Historical flags).

Hansen's disease. See Leprosy.

Hanson, Howard (1896-1981), was an American composer, conductor, and educator. His works reflect the influence of the romantic movement and of such northern European composers as Jean Sibelius of Finland. Hanson's most important compositions are his orchestral works, notably his six symphonies and five symphonic poems. Hanson won the 1944 Pulitzer Prize in music for his Symphony No. 4 (1943).

Hanson served as director of the Eastman School of Music from 1924 to 1964. Through this position, he helped shape the musical style of several generations of American composers and musicians. He also introduced the works of American composers to a large audience by conducting programs of American music throughout the United States and Europe. Hanson served as director of the Institute of American Music at the University of Rochester from 1964 until his death. Howard Harold Hanson was born in Wahoo, Nebr.   Leonard W. Van Camp

Hanson, John (1721-1783), was a Maryland statesman at the time of the Revolutionary War in America (1775-1783). In 1781, he served as president of the Congress of the Confederation, which operated the first government of the United States.

Hanson was born in Charles County, Maryland. He served in the Maryland Assembly almost every year from 1757 to 1779. Hanson helped lead resistance to various British attempts to tax the American Colonies, including the Stamp Act of 1765 and the Townshend Acts of 1767. He also helped organize and arm troops to fight the British during the Revolutionary War.

In 1779, Hanson was elected to the Continental Congress. He signed the Articles of Confederation, the agreement by which the original 13 English colonies formed the United States in 1781. Maryland placed a statue of Hanson in the U.S. Capitol in 1903.

Pauline Maier

Hanukkah, *HAH nu kah,* is the Jewish festival of lights or Feast of Dedication. The Hebrew word *hanukkah* (also written *Hannuka* or *Chanukah*) means *dedication.* The Hanukkah holiday begins on the eve of the 25th day of the Hebrew month of Kislev (approximately December) and lasts eight days.

Cameramann International, Ltd.
Children light candles in a menorah during Hanukkah.

During Hanukkah, gifts are exchanged and contributions made to the poor. Each evening, one candle is lighted in a special eight-branched candelabrum called a *menorah* or *hanukkiyah.* Beginning on the second night, one candle is added every night until the total reaches eight on the last night. The candles are lighted by a separate candle called a *shamash.*

The two books of Maccabees in the Apocrypha tell the story of Hanukkah. In 165 B.C., after a three-year struggle led by Judah Maccabee, the Jews in Judea defeated the Syrian tyrant Antiochus IV. They held festivities in the Temple in Jerusalem, and dedicated it to God. According to the Talmud, written many centuries after the event, when the Jews cleaned the Temple of Syrian idols, they found only one small cruse of oil with which to light their holy lamps. But miraculously, the cruse provided them with oil for eight days. Other sources tell of a torchlight parade in the Temple, which may also have contributed to the tradition of lighting candles on Hanukkah.   B. Barry Levy

Additional resources

Chaikin, Miriam. *Light Another Candle: The Story and Meaning of Hanukkah.* Houghton, 1981. For younger readers.
Drucker, Malka. *Hanukkah: Eight Nights, Eight Lights.* Holiday, 1980.
Rockland, Mae Shafter. *The Hanukkah Book.* Schocken, 1975.

Hanyang. See Wuhan.

Hapsburg, House of. See Habsburg, House of.

Hara-kiri, *HAR uh KIHR ee* or *HAH ruh KIHR ee,* is a method of suicide used by members of the Japanese warrior class, or *samurai.* In hara-kiri, the warrior cuts a gash in his abdomen according to a prescribed manner. An assistant then cuts off the warrior's head from behind. The Japanese term this ceremonial rite *seppuku.*

During the feudal period in Japan, the samurai considered it a duty to sacrifice themselves through hara-kiri, rather than to submit to public disgrace (see **Samurai**). They performed the act as an ultimate gesture of loyalty to the lord or to a noble cause. Later, defeated commanders sometimes commited hara-kiri. Today, the custom is generally discredited and is viewed as a feudal relic.   Tetsuo Najita

Harald. See Harold.

Harappa. See Indus Valley civilization.

Harare, *hah RAH ray* (pop. 627,000), is the capital and largest city of Zimbabwe. The city—formerly called Salisbury—is located on a plain near the Hunyani River, in an area that produces tobacco and corn. Harare is a modern city. Cecil Square, which lies in the center of the city, was named for Cecil Rhodes, the British financier who founded Rhodesia (now Zimbabwe and Zambia).
Hibberd V. B. Kline, Jr.

Harbin, *hahr bihn* (pop. 2,590,000), is one of the large cities of China. It is the capital city of Heilongjiang, the northernmost province in the region of Manchuria. For location, see **China** (political map).

Harbin serves as an important railway center. The east-west and north-south lines of the Manchurian railways intersect there. Chinese rail lines extend from Harbin to the Soviet border in the northwest and east, and to Lüshun-Lüda and the Korean border in the south. Har-

bin's location on the Sungari River makes it an important port. The fertile soil in the area produces maize, soybeans, and wheat. Harbin's chief exports are soybean products and wheat flour. Manufactured products include agricultural implements, chemicals, and leather.

Russia established Harbin in 1895 as a railroad administration center. After Japan defeated Russia in the Russo-Japanese War (1904-1905), China and Japan controlled Harbin jointly. Japan governed Harbin from 1932 until 1945, when China gained control. The Chinese, fearing a Soviet attack, have built many underground factories and stores in Harbin.   Richard H. Solomon

Harbor is any sheltered body of water where ships may moor or anchor. Natural or landlocked harbors are found in bays and inlets where arms of land form a natural protection from waves and winds. Artificial harbors are made by erecting stone or steel *breakwaters.*

A harbor should be at least 35 feet (11 meters) deep, so the keels of large ships will not touch bottom. Ships also should have enough room to pass and to turn around. The bottom of the harbor should not be too rocky, too sandy, or too muddy, or else anchors will not be able to hold ships securely.

Large harbors are lined with quays, piers, and docks at which ships can be loaded and unloaded. A *quay* (wharf) is a stone or wood platform built along the shoreline, a *pier* is a platform which extends well out into the water, and a *dock* is the space between piers.

Some of the most beautiful harbors are at Rio de Janeiro, Brazil; Naples, Italy; and San Francisco. The world's busiest harbors include those at Khark, Iran; Kobe, Japan; New York City; Ras Tanura, Saudi Arabia; and Rotterdam, the Netherlands.   John J. Floherty

Related articles in *World Book* include:

Pictures of harbors

The following articles have pictures of harbors:

Los Angeles	Oslo	San Francisco
Madeira Islands	Rio de Janeiro	Ship
Naples	Saint John's	Singapore
New York City	San Diego	Sydney
Norway		

Other related articles

Breakwater	Dredging	Pier
Buoy	Free trade zone	Port
Dock		

Hardening of the arteries. See Arteriosclerosis.
Hardhack. See Spiraea.

Cameramann International, Ltd.

Artificial harbors, such as Belmont Harbor in Chicago, *above,* have been built at many points on Lake Michigan.

© David R. Frazier

Natural harbors, such as the one in Sydney, Australia, *above,* are the sites of some of the most important cities in the world.

**29th President
of the United States 1921-1923**

Wilson
28th President
1913-1921
Democrat

Harding
29th President
1921-1923
Republican

Coolidge
30th President
1923-1929
Republican

Calvin Coolidge
Vice President
1921-1923

Oil painting on canvas (1923) by Margaret Lindsay Williams; National Portrait Gallery, Smithsonian Institution, Washington, D.C.

Harding, Warren Gamaliel (1865-1923), was elected President by a people weary of wartime restraints and world problems. His supporters expected him to turn back the clock and restore the more carefree atmosphere of pre-World War I days. Harding, an easygoing newspaper publisher and Senator, encouraged this belief by campaigning on the slogan of "Back to Normalcy." Actually, Americans would probably have elected any Republican candidate to the White House in 1920 in protest against the policies of Democratic President Woodrow Wilson. They opposed particularly Wilson's definition of American ideals, and his unwillingness to accept any changes in his plan for a League of Nations. They wished to reduce their responsibilities in world affairs and to resume their normal activities with as little bother as possible.

It was easier to praise "normalcy" than to produce it during the Roaring Twenties. The word meant so many different things to different people. Some were rebels. They danced in cabarets, drank bootleg gin, and poked fun at "normal" American life in novels and plays. Others, reacting against the rebels, wanted to standardize thought and behavior. This group persecuted radicals, tried to enforce Prohibition, and fought to ban the teaching of evolution in the public schools. With so many crosscurrents at work in American society, Harding was bound to annoy somebody as soon as he did anything.

The popularity of Harding's administration was damaged by the short but severe depression of 1921. Within two years, the Teapot Dome oil scandal and other graft in governmental agencies destroyed faith in his administration. Harding probably became aware of this widespread corruption in the summer of 1923. His anxiety about it may have hastened his death. Historians almost unanimously rank Harding as one of the weakest Presidents. But these historians have recognized that the very qualities that made him weak also made him appealing in 1920. He failed because he was weak-willed and a

poor judge of character. Harding was the sixth President to die in office and was succeeded by Vice President Calvin Coolidge.

Early life

Childhood. Harding was born on Nov. 2, 1865, on a farm near Corsica (now Blooming Grove), Ohio, about 5 miles (8 kilometers) east of Galion. He was the eldest of the eight children of George Tryon Harding and Phoebe Dickerson Harding. George Harding supplemented his small income as a farmer by becoming a homeopathic doctor. He was descended from an English family that landed at Plymouth in 1624. The Hardings moved to Ohio in 1820.

Warren attended grammar schools at Corsica and Caledonia. He learned to set type on the *Caledonia Argus,* a weekly newspaper in which his father had a half ownership. Warren attended Ohio Central College, a high school in Iberia. He disliked the study of chemistry, and once put a bottle of ill-smelling hydrogen sulfide in his teacher's desk drawer. While in high school, Harding edited the school newspaper.

Newspaper career. In 1882, Harding passed an examination that allowed him to teach school. He taught for a term in a one-room schoolhouse near Marion, Ohio. Later he called teaching "the hardest job I ever had." Harding also read law and sold insurance before turning to journalism. He first worked for the *Marion Democratic Mirror.* But he was fired in 1884 for supporting James G. Blaine, the Republican candidate for President. Harding and two friends then bought the *Marion Star,* a bankrupt newspaper, for $300.

Marriage. In 1891, Harding married Florence Kling DeWolfe (Aug. 15, 1860-Nov. 21, 1924), the daughter of a prominent Marion banker. She was a divorcee, five years his senior. Florence, nicknamed "Duchess" by Harding, had a dominating personality, and great ambitions for her husband. She helped him build the *Star* into a prosperous newspaper. He became a director of several

The world of President Harding

The Unknown Soldier of World War I was buried at Arlington National Cemetery in 1921.
Separate peace treaties with Germany, Austria, and Hungary were signed by the United States in 1921, after the U.S. Senate refused to ratify the Treaty of Versailles.
The Irish Free State became a self-governing country in 1921.
William Lyon Mackenzie King became prime minister of Canada for the first time in 1921. He held the office for a total of 21 years, longer than any other prime minister in a country with a parliamentary form of government.
A naval limitation treaty was signed in 1922. The United States, Great Britain, Italy, France, and Japan agreed to limit the size, number, and guns of their battleships.
The Lincoln Memorial was dedicated in Washington in 1922.
The Union of Soviet Socialist Republics was established in 1922 by the Communist government.
Literature published in 1922 included *Babbitt,* Sinclair Lewis' novel about the limitations of American culture, and "The Waste Land," T. S. Eliot's controversial poem.
A fascist party, led by Benito Musolini, came to power in Italy in 1922.

Prohibition played an important role in American life during Harding's presidency. Government agents, such as the one shown above, destroyed huge amounts of beer and liquor.

Bettmann Archive

corporations, and a trustee of the Trinity Baptist Church. The Hardings had no children.

Political and public activities

Entry into politics. Harding soon became known as both an editor and a skillful orator. He was elected Republican state senator in 1898 and lieutenant governor in 1903, but lost the 1910 election for governor.

While in state politics, Harding gained the devoted friendship of Harry M. Daugherty, a shrewd Ohio political strategist. Years later, Daugherty worked as hard to make Harding President as Mark Hanna had worked to put William McKinley in the White House in the election of 1896.

In 1912, Harding was chosen to nominate President William Howard Taft for a second term at the Republican National Convention. This honor, he said, gave him a greater thrill than his own nomination. At the 1916 national convention, Harding gave the keynote speech and also served as permanent chairman.

U.S. senator. Urged on by Daugherty and by his wife, Harding ran successfully for the United States Senate in 1914. Genial and popular, he enjoyed the good fellowship and prestige of the Senate, but introduced no major bills during his six-year term. He missed almost half of the roll calls and spent more time hunting jobs for his friends than in studying legislation. Harding usually voted with the Republican leadership. He favored high tariffs, and opposed the League of Nations and federal regulation of industry. He voted for woman suf-

Important dates in Harding's life

1865   (Nov. 2) Born near Corsica, Ohio.
1891   (July 8) Married Florence Kling DeWolfe.
1898   Elected to the Ohio Senate.
1903   Elected lieutenant governor of Ohio.
1914   Elected to the United States Senate.
1920   Elected President of the United States.
1923   (Aug. 2) Died in San Francisco.

frage, but admitted to a group of suffragists that he was "utterly indifferent" to it.

The smoke-filled room. Early in 1919, some newspapers began to mention Harding as a compromise candidate for President. Harding insisted that the Senate was "far more to my liking than the presidency possibly could be." But Daugherty, aided by Mrs. Harding, persuaded him to run for President, and became his campaign manager.

The 1920 Republican National Convention opened in Chicago on a sweltering June day. Most of the delegates supported Governor Frank O. Lowden of Illinois; Major General Leonard Wood, former army chief of staff; or Senator Hiram W. Johnson of California. But the ever-present Daugherty was busy behind the scenes. His welcomers greeted every delegate, urging them to support Harding as a second- or even third-choice candidate.

On the first day of voting, the convention adjourned in deadlock after four ballots. That night, a small group of powerful senators and political bosses met at the Blackstone Hotel in what Daugherty called a "smoke-filled room." At about 2 a.m., they agreed upon Harding as a compromise candidate. The delegates nominated Harding the next day and chose Governor Calvin Coolidge of Massachusetts as his running mate.

The Democrats nominated Governor James M. Cox of Ohio for President and Assistant Secretary of the Navy Franklin D. Roosevelt for Vice President.

The front porch campaign. Harding conducted a front porch campaign from his home in Marion. He made speeches there and met visiting delegations. He told his secretary that handshaking "is the most pleasant thing I do." Harding avoided a clear-cut stand on the League of Nations by denouncing it but promising to work for an "association of nations." He also evaded specific domestic issues by promising "normalcy."

Harding won an overwhelming victory and became the first man to be elected to the presidency while serv-

Detail of an oil portrait (1921) by Philip de Laszlo'; © White House Historical Association (photography by the National Geographic Society)

Florence Harding had a dominating personality and great ambitions for her husband. She helped persuade Harding to run for the Senate and then the presidency.

ing in the Senate. It was the first presidential election in which all women could vote, and in which the returns were broadcast by radio.

Harding's Administration (1921-1923)

From the beginning of his administration, Harding depended on Congress and on his Cabinet to provide leadership. He took a narrow view of his constitutional powers. Like most Republicans, he felt that during World War I President Wilson had taken powers that properly belonged to Congress.

Return to normalcy. Harding moved quickly to end the deadlock on the League of Nations. He signed peace treaties that did not include the League covenant with Germany and the other Central Powers. Congress took the leadership in domestic legislation. In 1921, it placed quotas on immigration for the first time, and reduced taxes. In 1922, it raised tariffs to record heights.

Under the leadership of Secretary of State Charles Evans Hughes, the Washington Disarmament Conference was held in 1921 and 1922 (see **Washington Conference**).

Government scandals. Harding brought so many friends to Washington that they became known as "the Ohio gang." Some were untrustworthy, but he enjoyed them socially and gave them important jobs. A tide of corruption soon began to rise. The Teapot Dome scan-

Harding's election

Place of nominating convention	......Chicago
Ballot on which nominated	............10th
Democratic opponent	................James M. Cox
Electoral vote[*]	.........................404 (Harding) to 127 (Cox)
Popular vote	..........................16,133,314 (Harding) to 9,140,884 (Cox)
Age at inauguration	55

[*]For votes by states, see **Electoral College** (table).

dal was the most shocking case. It involved Secretary of the Interior Albert B. Fall, who accepted a bribe for leasing government-owned oil reserves to private companies. He was sentenced to prison in 1929 and began serving his term in 1931. See **Coolidge, Calvin** (Corruption in government); **Teapot Dome.**

Attorney General Harry M. Daugherty was tried in 1926 on charges concerning his administration of the Alien Property Custodian's Office. Two juries failed to agree on a verdict, and Daugherty was freed.

Jesse W. Smith, a friend of Daugherty, committed suicide in May 1923. It had been revealed that Smith was arranging settlements between the Department of Justice and law violators. Misuse of funds in the Veterans' Bureau resulted in the suicide of Charles F. Cramer, legal adviser of the agency, and the imprisonment of Charles R. Forbes, the director.

Death. A depression in the farm region caused the Republicans to slip badly in the 1922 Congressional elections. In June 1923, Harding sought to revive confidence in his Administration by making a speaking tour. With his wife and a large official party, he crossed the country and made the first presidential visit to Canada and Alaska. A long message in code from Washington reached Harding en route. It brought disturbing news about a Senate investigation of oil leases. Reporters later said that the depressed Harding asked them what a President could do when his friends betrayed him.

As his train passed through Seattle, Harding fell ill, presumably of food poisoning. The trip was halted in San Francisco, where doctors reported that Harding had pneumonia. After what seemed to be a short rally, the President died on August 2. No autopsy was performed, and the exact cause of Harding's death is not known.

The scandals had not yet become public, and sorrowing crowds gathered along the route as Harding's body was returned to Washington. In an effort to protect his

Vice President and Cabinet

Vice President	.....................* Calvin Coolidge
Secretary of state	................* Charles Evans Hughes
Secretary of the treasury	..........* Andrew W. Mellon
Secretary of war	...................John W. Weeks
Attorney general	...................Harry M. Daugherty
Postmaster general	................Will Hays
	Hubert Work (1922)
	Harry S. New (1923)
Secretary of the navy	...............Edwin Denby
Secretary of the interior	............Albert B. Fall
	Hubert Work (1923)
Secretary of agriculture	............Henry C. Wallace
Secretary of commerce	............* Herbert Hoover
Secretary of labor	..................James J. Davis

*Has a separate biography in *World Book.*

JUGGERNAUT.

Library of Congress

A stinging cartoon blamed Harding for the Teapot Dome scandal, a notorious case of corruption during his Administration. It involved accepting bribes for federal oil leases.

memory, Mrs. Harding burned as much of his correspondence as she could. She died the following year, and was buried beside Harding in Marion.

George H. Mayer

Related articles in *World Book* include:

Coolidge, Calvin
League of Nations
Mellon, Andrew W.
President of the United States
Roaring Twenties
Teapot Dome

Outline

I. Early life
  A. Childhood
  B. Newspaper career
  C. Marriage
II. Political and public activities
  A. Entry into politics
  B. U.S. senator
  C. The smoke-filled room
  D. The front porch campaign
III. Harding's Administration (1921-1923)
  A. Return to normalcy   C. Death
  B. Government scandals

Questions

Why was Harding's election to the presidency almost certain following his nomination?
What was an important achievement of the Harding administration in foreign affairs?
Which groups did Harding favor as President?
What was the Teapot Dome scandal?
What did Harding consider "the most pleasant thing" he did?
What member of Harding's Cabinet became President?
What was "the Ohio gang"?
What were Harding's weaknesses as President?
How did he avoid a positive stand on the League of Nations?
What was normalcy?

Additional resources

Downes, Randolph C. *The Rise of Warren Gamaliel Harding: 1865-1920.* Ohio State Univ. Press, 1970.
Mee, Charles L., Jr. *The Ohio Gang: The World of Warren G. Harding.* Evans & Co., 1981.
Murray, Robert K. *The Harding Era: Warren G. Harding and His Administration.* Univ. of Minnesota Press, 1969.
Russell, Francis. *The Shadow of Blooming Grove: Warren G. Harding in His Times.* McGraw, 1968.
Trani, Eugene P., and Wilson, D. L. *The Presidency of Warren G. Harding.* Univ. Press of Kansas, 1977.

Hardness is the ability of a material to scratch a mark on other substances, or to resist being scratched by them. Scientists measure the hardness of a material by comparing it with a table of 10 well-known minerals. The minerals are arranged in order from 1 to 10. Each mineral in the table scratches the ones with lower numbers, and can be scratched by all those with higher numbers. The standard "scale of hardness" follows:

1.	Talc	6.	Feldspar
2.	Gypsum	7.	Quartz
3.	Calcite	8.	Topaz
4.	Fluorite	9.	Corundum
5.	Apatite	10.	Diamond

To test another substance, you match it against the minerals of the hardness scale. You can get an approximate idea of the hardness of a mineral by using your fingernail, a copper coin, a knife blade, or a piece of window glass. The hardness of these materials is as follows: fingernail, about 2; copper coin, $2\frac{1}{2}$ to 3; knife blade and window glass, $5\frac{1}{2}$.

When materials must be accurately tested, as in the manufacture of tools and gears, machinists use an instrument called a *sclerometer*. This device registers the force required to dent or scratch the material with a diamond or borazon, the hardest substances known.

Ernest E. Wahlstrom

See also **Diamond; Borazon.**

Hardtack. See Scurvy.

Hardwood. See Lumber (Kinds of lumber); **Tree** (Broadleaf trees; Broadleaf forests; picture); **Wood.**

Hardy, Oliver. See Laurel and Hardy.

Hardy, Thomas (1840-1928), was an English novelist and poet. Fate is the "villain" in most of Hardy's books, and his characters fight a losing battle against this impersonal force. Hardy summed up his anger at the unfairness of life in the novel *Tess of the d'Urbervilles.* He wrote that, with the heroine's death, " 'Justice' was done, and the President of the Immortals, . . . had ended his sport with Tess."

Recent criticism has tended to view Hardy's characters as people with psychological weaknesses. But it seems fair to say that Hardy saw human downfall not primarily as personal weakness, but rather as the result of an unwilling conflict with a hostile, meaningless universe.

Most of Hardy's stories take place in the fictional county of Wessex, a place of gloomy landscapes well suited to stories of tragedy. Hardy modeled Wessex on the county of Dorset, his birthplace.

Hardy's first successful novel, *Far from the Madding Crowd* (1874), contrasts selfish love with selfless love. *The Return of the Native* (1878) is a somber story of the tragic results of a man's illicit love for a woman. *The Mayor of Casterbridge* (1886) traces the spiritual and physical deterioration of a respected man. Hardy's last great novels, *Tess of the d'Urbervilles* (1891) and *Jude the Obscure* (1895), treat the theme of sexual attraction with a frankness that shocked the people of his time. The public outcry against *Jude the Obscure* was so great that Hardy stopped writing novels and turned to poetry.

He wrote lyric poetry of high quality, but he is best known for a three-part epic drama in verse, *The Dynasts* (1903-1908). The poem centers around Napoleon. Hardy used abstract figures to symbolize "Immanent Will," the blind force that he felt moves the world.

Hardy was born in Upper (or Higher) Bockhampton in Dorset. He studied architecture and worked as an architect. In the early 1870's, he abandoned architecture for a full-time career as a writer.   Frank W. Wadsworth

Additional resources

Millgate, Michael. *Thomas Hardy: His Career as a Novelist.* Random House, 1971. *Thomas Hardy: A Biography.* 1982.
Pinion, F. B. *A Hardy Companion: A Guide to the Works of Thomas Hardy and Their Background.* Humanities Press, 1984. First published in 1968.

Hare is a long-eared mammal with powerful hind legs and a short, fluffy tail. Hares are related to rabbits and are often confused with them. But hares differ from rabbits in several ways. Hares give birth on the ground or in a scratched-out depression called a *form.* The young are born covered with fur and with their eyes open. Rabbits are born naked and blind in a fur-lined nest. Hares never dig burrows as do many rabbits. Also, hares usually try to escape from their enemies by leaping away rapidly. Rabbits usually try to hide from enemies. The *Belgian hare* is really a type of rabbit. The *snowshoe rabbit* and the *jack rabbit* are, in fact, hares.

Most hares are brownish-gray with a pure white belly. Some kinds of hares that live in cold climates turn completely white during the winter. The largest hares grow to nearly 27 inches (69 centimeters) long and can

Joe Van Wormet, Bruce Coleman Ltd.

The jack rabbit is a hare, and not a true rabbit. The black-tailed jack rabbit, *above,* is usually found in the southwestern parts of the United States. The white-tailed jack rabbit usually lives in the northern parts of the country.

reach a weight of more than 8 pounds (3.6 kilograms).

Hares court and mate in spring. During courtship, they often jump and twist in the air. This behavior may explain the phrase "mad as a March hare." Young hares are called *leverets.* There are usually fewer than five in a litter, but there may be as many as seven litters a year.

Hares rest during the day and generally look for food during the night and at dawn. Hares eat plants and can become pests by eating and destroying alfalfa and other farm crops. Hares *thump* (tap the ground) with their hind legs, which may warn other hares of danger. Their enemies include coyotes, eagles, bobcats, and foxes.

Scientific classification. Hares are in the rabbit and hare family, Leporidae. They belong to the genus *Lepus.*

Charles A. Long

See also **Animal** (picture: Animals of the polar regions); **Jack rabbit; Rabbit; Snowshoe hare.**

Hare Krishna. See **Cult.**

Hare system. See **Proportional representation.**

Harebell. See **Bluebell.**

Harelip. See **Cleft palate.**

Harem is the women's section of a household in some Middle Eastern and Asian countries. The word may also refer to the women who live there. The term comes from the Arabic word *haram,* meaning *forbidden.*

Traditionally, a harem was secluded and was open only to family members. The women cooked, raised children, and did other work in privacy, away from men except for their husband, sons, brothers, and fathers. Many harems housed the four wives permitted by Islam, the religion of the Muslims. A number of Turkish sultans and other wealthy rulers had large harems, which included their wives plus many mistresses, servants, and female relatives of the men. But such harems were rare because they were expensive.

Today, the practice of marrying more than one wife is forbidden by law in most nations. Middle Eastern women have become less secluded. Many attend coeducational schools and work outside the home. As a result, harems have nearly disappeared, though they exist among a few ruling families.   Elizabeth W. Fernea

Hargreaves, James (1722?-1778), invented the spinning jenny, the first machine to spin many threads at a time. He turned the spindles of several spinning wheels upright and placed them in a row. He then added a frame which alternately held and pulled the *rovings* (crude twists of cotton) from which threads were made. Hargreaves patented the jenny in 1770, shortly after he invented it. John Kay's flying shuttle had doubled the amount of cloth that weavers could produce, and Hargreaves' invention supplied the weavers with enough thread to make the cloth. No one really knows the origin of the term *jenny.*

Hargreaves was a weaver in Standhill, England, and first used the jenny at home. He then sold some machines. The sales made his patent invalid, and he was never rewarded for his invention. Local spinners worried that the increased amount of yarn the jenny spun might cost them their jobs. They burned Hargreaves' machine and drove him from the town. He moved to Nottingham in 1768, and helped found a prosperous spinning mill. His machine was used in the mill. Other manufacturers used the jenny without paying him. Hargreaves lived comfortably during the last years of

The spinning jenny invented by James Hargreaves was operated by a large wheel. When a worker turned the wheel, spools or spindles pulled and twisted the fibers. The spinning jenny replaced the slower one-thread spinning wheel, and made it possible for spinners to keep up with the weavers' demand for yarn.

Bettmann Archive

his life. But he never profited from his invention as much as he might have.   Robert E. Schofield

See also Crompton, Samuel; Spinning.

Hari, Mata. See Mata Hari.

Hari-kari. See Hara-kiri.

Harkins, William Draper (1873-1951), an American chemist, helped to clarify thinking on the nature of the atom. In 1927, he described a particle of matter, now called the *neutron,* which he reasoned must exist within the atom. He believed that the neutron could be formed from a positively charged proton and a negatively charged electron which combined in a way that neutralized their charges. James Chadwick's discovery of the neutron in 1932 confirmed this theory. Harkins was born in Titusville, Pa.   Herbert S. Rhinesmith

Harlan is the family name of two jurists who served as associate justices of the Supreme Court of the United States. They were grandfather and grandson.

John Marshall Harlan (1833-1911) served on the Supreme Court from 1877 until his death. An independent, he often dissented from the Court's majority opinions. He opposed the Court's gradual narrowing of the civil rights guaranteed by the 14th Amendment. He also opposed the Court's tendency to declare governmental regulation of business unconstitutional. During his term, many state legislatures tried to deal with problems created by the immense growth of industry across the United States. Harlan believed the Court should respect laws enacted by these legislatures.

Harlan was born in Boyle County, Kentucky. He attended Centre College and Transylvania University, and later practiced law. Although he owned slaves, he served in the Union Army during the Civil War. He served as Kentucky's attorney general from 1863 to 1867, and became a state Republican leader after the Civil War.   Jerre S. Williams

John Marshall Harlan (1899-1971) was an associate justice of the Supreme Court from 1955 to 1971. He served as an assistant United States attorney from 1925 to 1927, and as chief counsel to the New York State Crime Commission from 1951 to 1953. He was a member of the United States Circuit Court of Appeals in 1954 and 1955.

Harlan was born in Chicago, Ill. He studied at Prince-

ton and Oxford universities and New York Law School. He practiced law in New York City.   Merlo J. Pusey

Harlan, James (1820-1899), an American statesman, was a Republican United States senator from Iowa from 1855 until he became secretary of the interior in 1865. He resigned in 1866 because he opposed President Andrew Johnson's Reconstruction policies. He reentered the Senate in 1867 and voted for Johnson's impeachment. He served in the Senate until 1873. Born in Clark County, Ill., he graduated from Indiana Asbury University in 1845. He was president of Iowa Wesleyan College from 1853 to 1855 and from 1869 to 1870. A statue of Harlan represents Iowa in the U.S. Capitol in Washington, D.C.   Arthur A. Ekirch, Jr.

Harlem. See New York City (Manhattan; picture: Crowded tenements in Harlem).

Harlem Globetrotters. See Basketball (The history of professional basketball; picture).

Harlequin snake. See Coral snake.

Harlow, Harry Frederick (1905-1981), was an American psychologist. He provided new understanding of human behavior and development through studies of the social behavior of monkeys.

Harlow's research showed that maternal love and close social contacts are necessary at an early age for the normal development of behavior. He studied the behavior of monkeys that had been taken from their mothers at birth and given dummy mothers made of wire or cloth. The female infant monkeys responded to the dummy mothers as though they were real monkeys. However, these infant females, deprived of the care and affection of their natural mothers, did not develop maternal instincts. Harlow also found that monkeys raised in isolation did not get along well with other monkeys.

Harlow was born in Fairfield, Iowa, and graduated from Stanford University in 1927. He received a Ph.D. degree in psychology from Stanford in 1930. He served on the faculty of the University of Wisconsin from 1930 until he retired in 1974.   John F. Henahan

Harmattan, *HAHR muh TAN,* is a cool, extremely dry wind that forms over the Sahara and blows westward or southwestward to the African coast. It blows during the dry season from December through February. The harmattan is relatively cool because the Sahara is cool at that time of year. Many harmattans carry great quantities of fine dust from the Sahara. The turbulence in well-developed harmattans can be dangerous to airplanes. George F. Taylor

Harmonica, *hahr MAHN uh kuh,* is the name given to two simple musical instruments. The best known of these is the *mouth organ.* In this instrument, metal reeds are inside a case. The edge of the case has separate blowholes for each reed. The instrument is played either by blowing or sucking the air through these holes. The mouth organ is easy to play and is popular in the home. Such experts as Larry Adler have played the mouth organ in concerts and with orchestras.

The mouth organ dates back to two instruments developed in the 1820's. The first was the *aura,* which was patented by Friedrich Buschmann of Germany in 1821. The other, called the *symphonium,* was patented by Charles Wheatstone of England in 1829.

The second type of harmonica, called the *glass harmonica,* was invented in 1763 by Benjamin Franklin. He is said to have used the idea of an Irishman named Rich-

Caryle Calvin

The harmonica is a small wind instrument with reeds that produce tones when the player exhales or inhales.

© Pamella McReynolds

The chromatic harmonica, *top,* produces more tones and a more harmonious melody than the diatonic harmonica, *bottom.*

ard Pockrich. Franklin's instrument was a series of bowl-shaped glasses arranged in order of size on a spindle. The spindle was turned, and the rims of the glasses were moistened in a water-filled trough below. Music was made by holding the finger against the wet rim as the rim rotated. Wolfgang Amadeus Mozart composed a quintet for the glass harmonica, flute, oboe, viola, and violoncello. Melvin Berger

Harmonics, *hahr MAHN ihks,* are the components of a musical tone. A tone is actually a blend of several sep-

Elements of a musical tone

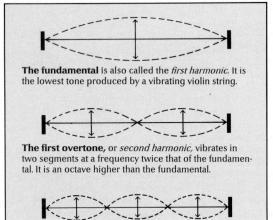

The fundamental is also called the *first harmonic.* It is the lowest tone produced by a vibrating violin string.

The first overtone, or *second harmonic,* vibrates in two segments at a frequency twice that of the fundamental. It is an octave higher than the fundamental.

Other overtones have vibrations three or more times that of the fundamental. The *second overtone* vibrates in three segments a fifth higher than the first overtone.

arate tones. This blend, called a *composite tone,* is caused by a set of vibrations, such as those made by a musical instrument or the human voice. For example, a violin string vibrates over its entire length. But it also vibrates in segments, called *partials,* which are shorter than the total length of the string. The string vibrates in segments such as one-half, one-third, or one-fourth, of the string. Each vibrating segment produces a separate tone, called an *overtone.*

The *first harmonic,* called a *fundamental,* is the lowest tone. It results from the vibration of the whole violin string. Other harmonics, called *overtones,* come from the various vibrating segments. The *second harmonic,* also called the *first overtone,* vibrates in two segments at a frequency twice that of the fundamental, and is an octave higher. Other overtones have vibration frequencies three or more times that of the fundamental. In most cases, the higher overtones are produced with less *intensity* (loudness) than the lower ones. The fundamental and overtones combine to produce one complete tone that is the same pitch as the fundamental.

The number and intensity of a tone's harmonics determine the *timbre* (quality) of the tone. The timbre is largely responsible for the different sounds produced by various musical instruments, even when they play the same note. In the human voice, harmonics create vowel sounds and the different tone qualities that separate the sound of one voice from another. Sounds with strong high harmonics are often called *resonant* or *rich* in quality, and sounds with relatively low weak harmonics are called *soft* or *muted*.   Thomas W. Tunks

See also **Sound** (Sound quality); **Tone.**

Harmonium, *hahr MOH nee uhm,* is a reed organ. Its keys control the flow of air across metal reeds. Air pressure is provided by bellows operated by the player's feet. Below the keyboard are levers which may be pressed by the knees of the player to make the tone louder or softer. Above the keyboard are "stops" by which the quality of tone may be changed. The harmonium was developed in France early in the 1800's. It is sometimes called a *parlor organ.*   F. E. Kirby

Harmony, *HAHR muh nee,* is the study of musical chords and their relationships. Most chords consist of three or four notes sounding at the same time. A melody is *harmonized* when chords are added to it.

Composers used traditional harmony from about 1680 to 1900. In traditional harmony, chords are built in *thirds* (two steps apart in the scale). The bottom note is called the *root* of the chord. Chords consisting of two thirds are *triads.* Those with three thirds are *sevenths.*

One form of traditional harmony is called *functional* harmony. In functional harmony, all chords are related to one of three basic chords of a key. The main chord is the *tonic,* which is based on the first note of the scale. The others are the *dominant,* based on the fifth note, and the *subdominant,* based on the fourth note. All other chords in a key are related to one of these three chords.

A major or minor triad is called a *consonant* chord. All other chords are called *dissonant* and, in traditional harmony, must be smoothly *resolved* (connected) to a consonant chord.

The history of harmony is the development of *chromatic* chords and *modulations.* Chromatic chords include tones outside the key. Modulation is changing from one key to another. Many composers use chromatic chords and modulations to add expression and harmonic variety to a composition.

After 1900, many composers abandoned traditional and functional harmony. Some have used streams of triads or sevenths in parallel motion. Some have built their chords out of intervals other than thirds. Many modern composers have also used triads in two or more keys sounded at the same time, or mixtures of notes sounded as chords.   R. M. Longyear

See also **Rameau, Jean Philippe.**

Harmsworth, Alfred Charles William. See Northcliffe, Viscount.

Harness is the equipment placed on a horse or other animal that enables it to pull a vehicle with its shoulders. The basic parts of a harness are the bridle, reins, collar, hames, and traces. A harness may also include other parts that are added for special situations. Most parts of a harness are made of leather and are held in place by metal buckles and clasps.

The bridle is used to control the animal's movements. It consists of straps that fit securely on the animal's head and a metal bit that fits in its mouth. The reins are attached to the bit and must be long enough to reach the vehicle's driver. The collar goes around the animal's neck at the shoulders. The hames are two curved pieces attached to each side of the collar. The traces are two long straps, ropes, or chains that connect the harness to

Parts of the harness

All parts of the harness work together to enable the driver to control and guide the horse and to help the horse pull the load. Different types of harnesses are used for different purposes. The light harness shown below is used to pull a buggy. Horses must wear stronger harnesses when they pull heavier loads.

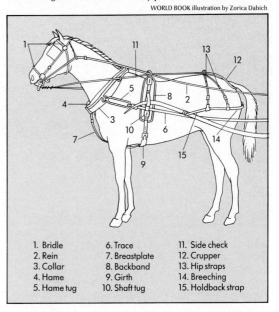

WORLD BOOK illustration by Zorica Dabich

1. Bridle	6. Trace	11. Side check
2. Rein	7. Breastplate	12. Crupper
3. Collar	8. Backband	13. Hip straps
4. Hame	9. Girth	14. Breeching
5. Hame tug	10. Shaft tug	15. Holdback strap

the vehicle. One end is attached to the hames and the other is hooked to the vehicle. Sometimes an animal is harnessed between two long wooden poles called shafts that are attached to the vehicle.   James H. Blackwell

Harness racing is a popular form of horse racing. In a harness race, each horse pulls a driver in a light, two-wheeled vehicle called a *sulky.* Millions of Americans attend harness races yearly. Many races are held at major race tracks, where people can bet on the horses. Others are held at county fairs, where betting is often allowed. Harness racing is also popular in Australia, Canada, New Zealand, and most European countries.

There are two kinds of harness horses—*trotters* and *pacers.* A trotter moves the front leg on one side of its body and the hind leg on the other side at the same time. A pacer moves the legs on the same side of its body together. About 80 per cent of the harness horses in the United States are pacers. In most European countries, only trotters race. The two types rarely race together because pacers generally go faster than trotters.

Harness horses are *standardbreds,* a breed that developed from thoroughbreds. The first thoroughbred to produce great trotters was Messenger. This horse was brought to the United States from England in 1788. One of Messenger's descendants, Hambletonian, is known as the "great father" of harness horses. Hambletonian was born in 1849 and sired 1,331 horses before his death in 1876. Almost all standardbreds in the United States can be traced back to him. The annual Hambletonian Stakes, the most famous harness racing event, is named after Hambletonian.

Drivers. In the United States, both amateur drivers and professional drivers may compete in harness races.

A harness race begins after the drivers line up their horses behind a specially designed automobile called a *mobile starting gate*. The gate has two arms that keep the horses in line. After the horses reach the starting line, the arms fold up and the automobile moves off the track.

United States Trotting Association

All drivers must be licensed by their state racing commission. The United States has more than 12,000 licensed harness drivers.

The race. Harness races are held on an oval track. The track ranges from $\frac{1}{2}$ mile (0.8 kilometer) to 1 mile (1.6 kilometers) long. The standard distance of a harness race is 1 mile. In some races, a horse must finish first in two out of three *heats* (parts of a race) to win the race.

Before a harness race begins, the horses and drivers line up behind a specially designed automobile called a *mobile starting gate.* This vehicle has two collapsible arms that keep the horses in line. The horses follow the starting gate as it moves around the track. The gate—and the horses—gradually gain speed. The race starts one or two seconds after the gate pulls away, when the horses pass the starting line and break an electronic beam. The arms of the gate fold inward. The starting gate then speeds ahead of the horses and moves to one side of the track. The horses race around the track to the finish line. Any horse that changes from the pace or trot to another gait must be moved to the outside of the track. It must regain the correct gait before rejoining the field.

Betting. People bet on horses to finish first, second, or third in a harness race. U.S. tracks use the *parimutuel system* of betting (see **Horse racing** [Betting]).

Regulation. The United States Trotting Association (USTA) regulates harness racing. In states where betting is legal, a state racing commission controls the races. Most commissions follow USTA rules. All drivers, harness horse owners, and most race officials must belong to the USTA.

History. Various forms of harness races have been held since ancient times. Modern harness racing developed in the United States. It probably began in the 1700's. In 1806, people in New York started to record harness racing speeds. That year, a trotter named Yankee became the first harness horse to race 1 mile in less than 3 minutes.

During the 1800's, harness racing became extremely popular in the United States. Only trotters competed in races until the 1860's, when pacers were introduced. Perhaps the most popular American harness horse was Dan Patch, a pacer. In 1905, he broke a record by pacing 1 mile in 1 minute $55\frac{1}{4}$ seconds.

Interest in harness racing declined in the United States in the early 1900's after cars began to replace horses as the most common means of transportation. But the sport again grew popular in the 1940's, after parimutuel betting and night races were introduced. The mobile starting gate was adopted for racing in 1946.

The top American harness drivers of the 1900's have included Stanley F. Dancer, William R. Haughton, and Joseph C. O'Brien. Herve Filion, a Canadian, has won more races than any other harness driver. Between 1961 and 1980, he won over 7,000 races.

In 1980, the pacer Niatross became the fastest horse in harness-racing history by pacing a mile in 1 minute $49\frac{1}{5}$ seconds during a time trial and 1 minute $52\frac{1}{5}$ seconds during a race. Niatross raced two seasons, 1979 and 1980, winning 36 of 38 races.

Critically reviewed by the U.S. Trotting Association

Harnett, William Michael (1848-1892), is often called the leading American still-life painter of the late 1800's. His style was hard and precise, well suited to such subjects as groups of objects on tabletops and minutely realistic paintings of currency.

Harnett was born in Ireland, and was brought to Philadelphia as a baby. He studied painting at the National Academy of Design in New York City. In 1875, he began painting still lifes that show the influence of the painting style of the Peale family. By 1880, he had saved enough money to travel to Europe, spending much time in Munich where his realistic style received much praise. Although at the height of his career, Harnett was prevented by illness from doing much painting after 1886. His work was largely forgotten after his death, but rediscovered about 1935.   Frederick A. Sweet

Harold was the name of two early English kings.

Harold I (?-1040), called Harefoot, was the son of Canute and Aelfgifu of Northampton. Harold was made king when Canute died in 1035, although his half-brother, Hardecanute, had a better claim to England. Harold's mother dominated his reign, which was marked by acts of cruelty.

Harold II (1022?-1066) succeeded Edward the Confessor and was the last Anglo-Saxon king of England. In 1053, Harold succeeded his father, Godwin, as the Earl of Wessex. This made him the most powerful man in England. He continued his father's resistance to Norman influence, which had become strong in England under King Edward's patronage.

When Harold was shipwrecked in 1064, he fell into the hands of Duke William of Normandy, later known as William the Conqueror. William forced Harold to swear that he would support William's claim to the English throne. But when Edward the Confessor died, the English nobles chose Harold king. When Harold accepted, William invaded England to fight for the throne. Harold was defeated and killed at the Battle of Hastings, in October 1066 (see **Hastings, Battle of**). England then came under Norman rule.   Robert S. Hoyt

See also **Norman Conquest.**

Harold I (860?-940?), also spelled Harald, was the first king of Norway. He formed the Kingdom of Norway about 900, after defeating a number of local rulers.

Harold Halfdansson succeeded his father as ruler of Vestfold, a small kingdom in what is now southeastern Norway. Harold later extended his authority to other areas of the country, especially the southern and western coastal regions. However, he had little control over local rulers in the north and east. Harold failed to establish a line of rulers acceptable to all parts of Norway. As a result, some of his successors had to reconquer most of the country.   H. Peter Krosby

Harold III (1015-1066) was king of Norway. He gained fame as a military leader and adventurer.

Harold Sigurdsson, also spelled Harald, was the son of the king of Ringerike, a small kingdom in what is now southeastern Norway. In 1030, Harold fled Norway to escape his enemies, traveling to Sweden and Russia. In 1034, he joined the military forces of the Byzantine Empire, a powerful empire in southern and eastern Europe. With the Byzantine forces, Harold achieved great suc-

cess as a commander in Sicily and the Middle East.

In 1046, Harold returned to Norway to share the rule of the country with his nephew King Magnus I. Magnus was the heir of Hardecanute (also called Hardeknud), who had been king of both Denmark and England. Magnus died in 1047, and Harold became the sole ruler of Norway. Then Harold, as Magnus' heir, claimed the Danish throne and later the English throne. Harold fought for 17 years to gain control of Denmark, but finally acknowledged its independence in 1064. He invaded England in 1066, but was killed in the Battle of Stamford Bridge, near the city of York. Harold founded the city of Oslo about 1050.   H. Peter Krosby

Harp is one of the oldest known stringed instruments. The chief instrument in the harp family is the large concert harp. Smaller harps are often used in folk music.

The modern concert harp is a large, triangular wooden instrument about 70 inches (178 centimeters) tall. The wood is often gilded and decoratively carved. The harp rests on a base called the *pedestal.* A perpendicular column called the *pillar* rises from the front of the pedestal. A hollow *soundbox,* which amplifies the sound, projects at an angle from the rear of the pedestal. The pillar and the soundbox are joined at the top by a gracefully curved *neck.*

Forty-seven strings of different lengths and thicknesses are stretched between the neck and the soundbox. Tuning pins in the neck set the strings to the notes of the scale over a range of $6\frac{1}{2}$ octaves. Seven foot-pedals extend from the pedestal. When a pedal is depressed, it raises the pitch of its corresponding strings a half-tone or whole-tone, depending on the distance the pedal is depressed. This mechanism, called *double action,* enables the performer to play in any key or sequence of keys.

The performer sits with the harp between the knees, tilting it so it rests against the right shoulder. The player plucks the strings with the thumb and first three fingers of each hand and operates the pedals with the feet.

Early forms of the harp existed in several ancient Near Eastern civilizations. In Europe, the first harps appeared in the 700's in Ireland, where the harp is now a national symbol.   Abram Loft

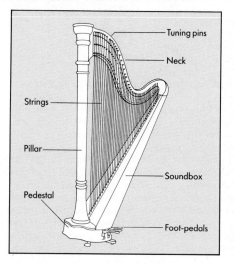

The harp is a large stringed instrument. The performer plays the harp sitting down, holding it between the knees. While playing, the performer tilts the harp so it rests against the right shoulder. The harp is played by plucking the strings with the fingers. The performer controls the pitch of the strings by depressing any of seven foot-pedals.

Tuning pins

Neck

Strings

Pillar

Soundbox

Pedestal

Foot-pedals

Harper, Frances Ellen Watkins (1825-1911), was
an American author and
lecturer. She was the leading black poet of her time.
Most of Harper's poems
concerned antislavery and
racial themes, but she also
wrote about a variety of
other subjects.

The Newberry Library, Chicago

Frances Harper

Frances Ellen Watkins
was born of free parents in
Baltimore. Her parents
died when she was 2 years
old, and an uncle reared
and educated her. She began to write poetry as a teen-
ager and started to lecture in 1854. She spoke forcefully
against slavery throughout the Northeastern United
States and Canada. She married Fenton Harper, a
farmer, in 1860. She then gave up lecturing until after his
death in 1864.

Harper often added variety to her lectures by reading
some of her poems to the audience. Her books included
Poems on Miscellaneous Subjects (1854); *Moses: A
Story of the Nile* (1869); and *Iola Leroy, or Shadows Up-
lifted* (1892), which is a novel.

During her later years, Harper became known for her
lectures supporting women's right to vote and opposing
the use of alcoholic beverages. From 1883 to 1890, Harper served as superintendent of activities among blacks
for the Woman's Christian Temperance Union (W.C.T.U.).

Otey M. Scruggs

Harper, William Rainey (1856-1906), an American
educator, became the first president of the University of
Chicago in 1891. His work as president contributed to
the school's rapid growth. He selected great professors
and backed them with a strong belief in academic freedom. He introduced the quarter system, the university
press, and an extension division.

Harper was born at New Concord, Ohio. He earned a
Ph.D. degree at Yale University when he was 18 years
old. Later, he taught Semitic languages at Yale.

Claude A. Eggertsen

Harpers Ferry, W. Va. (pop. 361), is a village situated
on the Potomac River, 55 miles (89 kilometers) northwest
of Washington, D.C. At Harpers Ferry, the Potomac
breaks through the Blue Ridge Mountains and meets
the Shenandoah River in a wide, sweeping curve between tree-covered hills. For the location of Harpers
Ferry, see **West Virginia** (political map). The village was
named for Robert Harper, a man who purchased the site
in 1747.

Harpers Ferry was made famous by John Brown's raid
in 1859, a critical event preceding the Civil War (see
Brown, John). At the outbreak of the war, the Virginia
government prepared to seize the United States arsenal
and armory at Harpers Ferry. The small Union garrison
withdrew before the approaching Virginia forces, after
destroying buildings and supplies that had military
value. Confederate troops under General Joseph E. Johnston occupied Harpers Ferry from April to June 1861.
Then they abandoned it.

Union soldiers occupied the town until Sept. 15, 1862,
when General Stonewall Jackson captured it during

General Robert E. Lee's invasion of Maryland. Jackson
took 12,520 prisoners and much valuable booty. Once
more the Confederate occupation was short. After Lee's
defeat at Antietam, a Union garrison again took charge.
During Lee's Gettysburg campaign in July 1863, Harpers
Ferry experienced another capture and recapture. It remained in Union hands during most of the rest of the
war.   Festus Paul Summers

Harpoon is an arrow-shaped weapon that is used to
spear large fish and whales. Whaling harpoons are fired
from powerful guns. A long, coiled line is tied to the
harpoon. When the harpoon strikes the whale, the
weapon's barbed point becomes firmly anchored in the
skin of the whale. Famous harpooners of the 1800's
hurled harpoons by hand from the bow of small boats.
Today, hand harpooning is practiced by Eskimos.

William W. Robinson

See also **Whale** (The Basque people; Hunting techniques; picture: Harpoon guns).

Harpsichord is a musical instrument that resembles a
small piano. A harpsichord can be played as a solo instrument, in a chamber-music ensemble, or with an orchestra.

A harpsichord is smaller and lighter than a piano and
has from one to three keyboards, usually called *manuals.* Like a piano, it produces sounds by causing metal

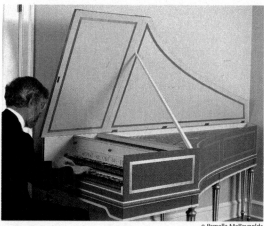

© Pamella McReynolds

A harpsichord is a musical instrument that looks somewhat
like a small piano. It has from one to three keyboards, usually
called *manuals.* The instrument shown above has two manuals.

strings to vibrate. But the strings of a harpsichord are
plucked, not struck like those of a piano. As a result of
these differences in size and mechanical action, a harpsichord produces a tone that is clearer and livelier than
that of a piano.

The strings of a harpsichord are stretched over two
strips of wood called the *bridge* and the *nut.* The bridge
is glued to a thin sheet of wood called the *soundboard.*
The nut is glued to a block of wood that runs parallel to
the keyboard and holds the tuning pins. When a string is
plucked, its vibrations are transmitted by the bridge to
the soundboard. The soundboard then transmits the vibrations to the sides and bottom of the instrument,
called the *case,* and into the air.

A note is produced by the plucking of the strings. Usually two or three strings are plucked. Each string is plucked by a small piece of quill or leather called a *plectrum*. The plectrum sticks out from a piece of wood called a *jack*. When a player strikes a key, the jack rises and the plectrum plucks a string. When the player releases the key, the jack drops. Then, when the plectrum touches the string, it swings back on a wooden pivot called a *tongue,* and passes the string without plucking it a second time. A *damper* (felt pad) on the jack then stops the string from vibrating.

Most harpsichords have two or three strips of wood called *registers* that are used to move the sets of jacks into or out of contact with their sets of strings. Often one set of strings sounds an octave higher than the other, and can be used to add brilliance to the sound.

The harpsichord first appeared in the 1300's, but no one knows who invented it. By the late 1500's, the instrument had become popular. During the 1600's, Italian and Flemish craftworkers built simple harpsichords to accompany solo performers. Musicians of the 1700's played richly decorated two-manual harpsichords. Famous composers of harpsichord music include Johann Sebastian Bach, François and Louis Couperin, Girolamo Frescobaldi, and Domenico Scarlatti.

By the late 1700's, the piano began to replace the harpsichord. But the harpsichord has regained some musical importance since the 1940's.   Dale C. Carr

See also **Bach** (family); **Couperin, François; Scarlatti, Domenico; Music** (picture: Keyboard instruments); **Piano** (History).

Harpy, in Greek and Roman mythology, was a frightful monster that was half woman and half bird. *Harpy* comes from a Greek word meaning *to snatch.* Harpies stole food from their victims and left a dreadful smell behind them. They tormented the blind king Phineus until the sons of the north wind, who were traveling with the Argonauts, drove the Harpies away. Phineus then told the Argonauts how to pass through the Clashing Rocks (see **Argonauts**). According to Virgil, Aeneas also met the Harpies in his wanderings.

Mary R. Lefkowitz

Harpy eagle is a large bird of prey that lives in lowland tropical forests. Harpy eagles inhabit southern

WORLD BOOK illustration by John F. Eggert

The harpy eagle is a South American bird of prey.

Mexico, eastern Bolivia, southern Brazil, and northern Argentina. Harpies weigh more than 10 pounds (4.5 kilograms) and stand 3 feet (91 centimeters) tall. Their wingspread reaches 7 feet (2 meters). The harpy eagle's head and neck are gray, its chest is black, and its underparts are white. A long black crest covers the back of the head. A large black beak and massive yellow feet distinguish the bird.

This powerful eagle uses its strength to capture monkeys, sloths, opossums, and porcupines. Harpies build large stick nests in tall trees. Mating pairs only breed every other year and the female lays one or two eggs. Harpy eagles are named after the "flying monsters" in ancient Greek and Roman mythology (see **Harpy** [in mythology]).

Scientific classification. Harpy eagles belong to the hawk family, Accipitridae. They are *Harpia harpyja.*

Thomas G. Balgooyen

Harquebus, *HAHR kwuh buhs,* also called *arquebus,* was an early handgun. The weapon consisted of a short metal tube attached to a wooden *stock* (handle). A soldier loaded the weapon through the muzzle with black

Roger Fuhr, ROLANDesign

The harquebus was an early type of handgun loaded through the muzzle. It had a matchlock firing mechanism operated by a trigger. Infantry soldiers first used harquebuses in the 1400's.

powder and a round bullet. A *touchhole*—a vent for carrying fire to the bullet and powder—led through the barrel to an open *pan.* The pan contained a small amount of powder. The gunner lit a slow-burning wick, called a match, held by an S-shaped *serpentine.* To fire the weapon, the gunner pulled a trigger attached to the lower end of the serpentine. This action applied the lighted match to the powder in the pan. This type of firing mechanism was the *matchlock.*

During the 1500's, gunsmiths developed another device, called the *wheel lock.* A *cock* held a pebble against a toothed wheel. The trigger spun the wheel, and set off sparks which ignited the powder. Wheel locks were safer to use than matchlocks, but they were much more expensive.

The harquebus developed from the small hand cannon first used during the 1300's. The hand cannon was a heavy weapon and required supports. Foot soldiers in the 1500's preferred to use muskets. But the harquebus survived for use by mounted troops in the early 1600's.

James B. Hodgson, Jr.

See also **Flintlock; Musket.**

Harrier is a breed of dog that was developed for the sport of hunting hares. It has a keen sense of smell and can move quickly. The harrier is sturdy and heavy-boned, with catlike feet. Most harriers have a short, white coat with black and tan patches, and floppy ears. They look like small foxhounds or large beagles. Harriers stand from 19 to 21 inches (48 to 53 centimeters) high at the shoulder and weigh 35 to 55 pounds (16 to 25 kilograms).

The breed probably originated as early as the 1000's.

Walter Chandoha

The harrier has been used to hunt hares.

Its ancestry is unclear, but many breeders believe that the harrier was developed in France from a type of fox-hound. Americans have raised harriers for rabbit hunting since colonial times.

Critically reviewed by the American Kennel Club

Harriman, W. Averell (1891-1986), an American statesman and businessman, was one of the leading diplomats of the mid-1900's. During World War II (1939-1945), Harriman arranged the sending of weapons and other supplies to Great Britain and the Soviet Union under the Lend-Lease program. He later served as U.S. ambassador to each of those countries.

Still later, Harriman became secretary of commerce from 1946 to 1948 under President Harry S. Truman. From 1948 to 1952, Harriman administered the European operations of the European Recovery Program, popularly known as the Marshall Plan. He served as governor of New York from 1955 to 1958.

Harriman was assistant secretary of state for Far Eastern affairs from 1961 to 1963, when he became undersecretary of state for political affairs. In that post, he negotiated a 1963 treaty with Britain and the Soviet Union banning many kinds of nuclear tests. Harriman resigned as undersecretary in 1965 but remained in the State Department as ambassador at large. He served as chief U.S. negotiator at the Paris peace talks on the Vietnam War in 1968 and 1969.

William Averell Harriman was born in New York City. He inherited a fortune from his father, the railroad executive E. H. Harriman. The younger Harriman served as chairman of the board of Union Pacific Railroad from 1932 to 1946.   V. E. Cangelosi

Harris, Benjamin (1660?-1720), published the first newspaper in America. As a bookseller in his native London, he was punished for circulating "false" pamphlets about Roman Catholics and Quakers. He fled to America in 1686. On Sept. 25, 1690, he published *Publick Occurrences Both Forreign and Domestick* in Boston. He planned to issue his "newes-paper" at least once a month, but its scandalous stories about the French antagonized colonial authorities, and no other issues were printed. See also **Literature for children** (The Puritans; picture).   Kenneth N. Stewart

Harris, Fred Roy (1930-   ), an Oklahoma Democrat, served in the U. S. Senate from 1964 to 1973. In 1969, he was elected chairman of the Democratic National Committee. He resigned from that post in 1970.

Harris was born in Walters, Okla. After eight years in the Oklahoma Senate, he was elected to the U.S. Senate to complete the term of the late Robert S. Kerr. He was reelected to a full term in 1966.

In 1967, President Lyndon B. Johnson appointed Harris to the National Advisory Commission on Civil Disorders, also known as the Kerner Commission. He served as cochairman of Hubert H. Humphrey's presidential campaign in 1968. Harris was an unsuccessful candidate for the Democratic presidential nomination in 1972 and in 1976.   David S. Broder

Harris, Joel Chandler (1848-1908), an American author and journalist, became famous for his Uncle Remus stories. Uncle Remus is a former slave who has become a beloved servant of a Southern family. He entertains the young son of the family by telling him traditional black stories, using Southern black speech of the 1800's. The stories include tales about animals that act like human beings. Among the best-known characters of the stories are Brer (Brother) Rabbit, Brer Fox, Brer Bear, and Brer Wolf.

Harris was born in Eatonton, Ga. From 1862 to 1866, he worked as a printer on a plantation near his home. The plantation owner, Joseph Addison Turner, published a newspaper called *The Countryman.* Turner introduced Harris to literature and encouraged him to write essays and poems. Harris became acquainted with the slaves on the plantation. He learned their customs and language and listened to their stories. This material formed the basis of his most successful writings.

From 1876 to 1900, Harris wrote for the *Atlanta Constitution.* His first Uncle Remus stories appeared in that newspaper. They became so popular that he collected them in book form as *Uncle Remus: His Songs and His Sayings* (1880). The book won immediate praise as a valuable contribution to American folklore. Readers enjoyed its humor, and critics praised it as an important record of the folk tales and manners of rural Southern blacks. The book's popularity led Harris to publish more collections of Uncle Remus stories. These collections include *Uncle Remus and His Friends* (1892) and *Uncle Remus and Brer Rabbit* (1906).

Harris also wrote many stories and novels about life in the South during and after the Civil War (1861-1865). In *On the Wing of Occasions* (1900), a collection of stories, Harris introduced a character called Billy Sanders, the Sage of Shady Dale. Through Sanders, Harris expressed the opinions of many middle-class Georgians.

Dean Doner

Additional resources

Bickley, Robert B., Jr. *Joel Chandler Harris.* Twayne, 1978.
Cousins, Paul M. *Joel Chandler Harris: A Biography.* Louisiana State Univ. Press, 1968.
Critical Essays on Joel Chandler Harris. Ed. by Robert B. Bickley, Jr. G. K. Hall, 1981.
Harris, Julia F. *The Life and Letters of Joel Chandler Harris.* AMS, 1973. First published in 1918.

Harris, Lawren. See **Group of Seven.**

Harris, Patricia Roberts (1924-1985), served as secretary of housing and urban development under President Jimmy Carter from 1977 to 1979. In 1979, Carter appointed her secretary of health, education, and welfare. Later that year, Congress established a separate Department of Education, and Harris' department became the Department of Health and Human Services. She headed the agency until 1981. Harris was the first black woman to hold a Cabinet post in the United States. She was also the nation's first black woman ambassador. President Lyndon B. Johnson appointed her ambassador to Luxembourg in 1965. She was an alternate delegate to the United Nations General Assembly in 1966 and 1967. Her activities in civil rights and Democratic Party politics brought her to Johnson's attention.

U.S. Dept. of State
Patricia Harris

Patricia Harris was born in Mattoon, Ill. She graduated from Howard University in 1945 and earned a law degree at George Washington University in 1960. She joined the faculty of the Howard University School of Law in 1961 and became dean of the school in 1969.

Harris left Howard University in 1970 and joined a Washington, D.C., law firm as a partner. In 1971, International Business Machines Corporation (IBM) appointed her a director. She was the first black woman to serve as a director of a major United States company.

Cynthia Fuchs Epstein

A Meeting of the School Trustees (1886), an oil painting on canvas; National Gallery of Canada, Ottawa

A Harris painting shows school trustees on Prince Edward Island interviewing a young teacher. The vivid, realistic character studies reflect Harris' skill as a portrait painter.

Harris, Robert (1849-1919), was one of the most popular and respected Canadian painters of the late 1800's and early 1900's. He became best known for his large dark-toned and richly textured portraits of influential Canadians and their families. Harris also painted landscapes, historical events, and scenes from everyday life. Harris' traditional realistic style was greatly influenced by his study of major European painters, especially the

Spanish baroque painter Diego Velázquez.

Harris was born in Conway, Wales, and immigrated to Canada with his parents in 1856. He received his first professional art training in Boston and later studied painting in London and Paris. Harris helped found the Royal Canadian Academy, an association of professional artists, in 1880 and served as the organization's president from 1893 to 1906.   Jeremy Adamson

Harris, Roy (1898-1979), was an American composer. He became famous for creating and promoting a distinctly American style of classical music. Harris greatly influenced a number of other American composers, including Aaron Copland and Walter Piston.

Harris wrote 16 symphonies, 14 for orchestra and 1 each for band and for chorus. His Symphony No. 3 (1939) is one of the most frequently performed of all symphonies written by American composers. Harris often used themes from American folk music in his compositions. For example, the themes of a number of American folk songs appear in his Symphony No. 4 (1940), also known as the *Folk Song Symphony*. He based his symphonic overture *When Johnny Comes Marching Home* (1935) on the American folk song of the same name. Harris also composed music for bands and chamber groups as well as choral music and works for solo piano.

Harris was born in a log cabin in Lincoln County, Oklahoma. He began his musical studies in California. From 1926 to 1929, Harris studied in Paris under the famous music teacher Nadia Boulanger.

Leonard Van Camp

Harrisburg (pop. 53,264; met. area pop. 555,158) has been the capital of Pennsylvania since 1812. The city lies along the Susquehanna River, in the south-central part of the state. For location, see **Pennsylvania** (political map).

Products of the Harrisburg area include candy, clothing, shoes, and steel products. The Pennsylvania Turnpike skirts the city, and other modern highways surround Harrisburg. Airlines, passenger trains, and rail freight lines serve the city. A large agricultural exhibition is held in Harrisburg each January.

The Pennsylvania State Capitol dome rises 272 feet (83 meters) above the city. Statues by sculptor George Grey Barnard flank the Capitol's central entrance.

John Harris, Sr., operated a ferry at Harrisburg in colonial days. His son John laid out the town of Harrisburg in 1785, and gave land to the Pennsylvania commonwealth which was later used for the Capitol grounds. Harrisburg has been a transportation center since the days of river boat traffic. It also became a leader in the iron industry. The city was a defense center during World War II. The seat of Dauphin County, Harrisburg has a mayor-council type of government.

Dale A. Davenport

Harrison, Benjamin (1726?-1791), was a Virginia delegate to the Continental Congress from 1774 to 1778. As chairman of the committee of the whole, he presided over the debates that resulted in the Declaration of Independence (see **Committee of the whole**). He also signed the Declaration. Harrison was born in Charles City County, and served as governor of Virginia from 1781 to 1784. His son, William Henry Harrison, and his great-grandson, Benjamin Harrison, became Presidents of the United States.   Richard B. Morris

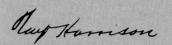

**23rd President of
the United States 1889-1893**

Cleveland
22nd President
1885-1889
Democrat

Harrison
23rd President
1889-1893
Republican

Cleveland
24th President
1893-1897
Democrat

Levi P. Morton
Vice President
1889-1893

Oil portrait (1895) by Eastman Johnson; © White House
Historical Association (photography by the National Geographic Society)

Harrison, Benjamin (1833-1901), was the only grandson of a President who also became President. He defeated President Grover Cleveland in 1888, but Cleveland regained the presidency by beating Harrison in 1892.

Harrison's grandfather was William Henry Harrison, the hero of the Battle of Tippecanoe. Both Harrisons ran for the presidency two times, winning once and losing once. Before being elected President, both had been successful army commanders and had served in the United States Senate. Benjamin Harrison won the presidency with the help of a Republican campaign song called "Grandfather's Hat Fits Ben."

Harrison did more than any other President to increase respect for the flag of the United States. By his order, the flag waved above the White House and other government buildings. Harrison also urged that the flag be flown over every school in the land.

Congress passed the Sherman Antitrust Act during Harrison's Administration, and provided for the building of a two-ocean navy of steel ships. The American frontier disappeared as pioneers took over the last unsettled areas of the West. Six new states joined the Union. Women squeezed into whalebone corsets so they could wear the new "hourglass" fashions. James A. Naismith originated basketball, and a lively tune called "Ta-ra-ra-boom-de-ay" helped usher in the period of the Gay Nineties.

Early life

Childhood. Benjamin Harrison was born on Aug. 20, 1833, on his grandfather's farm in North Bend, Ohio. He was named for his great-grandfather, a signer of the Declaration of Independence. Ben was the second of the 10 children of John Scott Harrison and Elizabeth Irwin Harrison. His father, a farmer, served two terms in Congress. Ben, a short, stocky boy, spent his youth on the farm.

Education. Harrison attended Farmers' College in a Cincinnati suburb for three years. While a freshman, he met his future wife, Caroline Lavinia Scott (Oct. 1, 1832-Oct. 25, 1892). She was the daughter of John W. Scott, the president of a women's college in the town. In 1849, Scott moved his college to Oxford, Ohio. The next year Harrison followed the Scotts to Oxford, where he graduated from Miami University in 1852.

Harrison's family. Harrison and "Carrie" Scott were married in 1853. They had two children, Russell Benjamin (1854-1936) and Mary (1858-1930).

Lawyer. After reading law with a Cincinnati firm, Harrison was admitted to the bar in 1854. He moved to Indianapolis that same year. In his first big court case, a single candle stood on the table where Harrison had his notes. He vainly shifted the candle back and forth to get more light, but finally threw the notes away. Harrison not only discovered that he was a good speaker, but he also won the case. Harrison bolstered his income by earning $2.50 a day as court crier, proclaiming the orders of the court.

Political and public activities

Political beginnings. As the son of a Whig congressman and the grandson of a Whig President, Harrison's name was familiar to many voters. Although his father wrote him that "none but knaves should ever enter the political arena," Harrison ran successfully for city attorney of Indianapolis in 1857. He became secretary of the Republican state central committee in 1858, and was

Six states—North Dakota, South Dakota, Montana, Washington, Idaho, and Wyoming—joined the Union during Harrison's term. The Oklahoma Territory was also formed.

The United States flag had 38 stars when Harrison took office in 1889. Five stars were added to the flag in 1890. Another was added in 1891, making a total of 44 stars, *left.*

The world of President Harrison

The Eiffel Tower was dedicated in Paris in 1889.
The Johnstown flood in Pennsylvania in 1889 killed more than 2,000 people and caused over $10 million in damage.
Mark Twain's satire on the King Arthur legend, *A Connecticut Yankee in King Arthur's Court*, was published in 1889.
A land rush into what had been Indian Territory in Oklahoma opened about 2 million acres (810,000 hectares) to white settlement in 1889.
Nellie Bly, a newspaper reporter, set a record by traveling around the world in 72 days 6 hours 11 minutes, beginning in November 1889.
The first Carnegie public library in the United States was established in 1890 in Allegheny City, Pa.
The Battle of Wounded Knee took place in South Dakota in 1890. It was the last major fight on the northern plains between Indians and U.S. troops. The soldiers massacred about 200 Indians.
Yosemite National Park was created by Congress in 1890.
Wyoming entered the Union in 1890 as the first state with women's voting rights.
Basketball was invented in 1891 by James A. Naismith, a physical education instructor in Springfield, Mass.
Ellis Island, an island in New York Harbor, became a reception center for immigrants in 1892.
Inventions included the diesel engine, patented in 1892 by a German engineer named Rudolf Diesel, and the zipper, patented in 1893 by Whitcomb L. Judson of Chicago.

WORLD BOOK map

elected reporter of the state supreme court in 1860. He was reelected twice.

A deeply religious man, Harrison taught Sunday school. He became a deacon of the Presbyterian Church in 1857, and was elected an elder of the church in 1861.

Army commander. In 1862, Governor Oliver P. Morton asked Harrison to recruit and command the 70th Regiment of Indiana Volunteers in the Civil War. As he and Morton walked down the steps of the state Capitol, Harrison recruited his first soldier—his former law partner, William Wallace.

Colonel Harrison molded his regiment into a well-disciplined unit that fought in many battles. His soldiers called him "Little Ben" because he was only 5 feet 6 inches (168 centimeters) tall. A fearless commander, Harrison rose to the rank of brigadier general.

National politics. After the war, Harrison won national prestige as a lawyer. In 1876, he ran unsuccessfully for the governorship of Indiana. President Rutherford B. Hayes appointed him to the Mississippi River Commission in 1879, and he held this post until 1881.

Important dates in Harrison's life

1833	(Aug. 20) Born in North Bend, Ohio.
1853	(Oct. 20) Married Caroline Lavinia Scott.
1862-1864	Commanded a regiment of the Union Army.
1881	Elected to the United States Senate.
1888	Elected President of the United States.
1892	Mrs. Caroline Harrison died. Defeated for reelection.
1896	(April 6) Married Mrs. Mary Dimmick.
1901	(March 13) Died in Indianapolis.

Harrison turned down a post in the Cabinet of President James A. Garfield because he had been elected to the U.S. Senate in January 1881.

During his term in the Senate, Harrison supported civil service reform, a protective tariff, a strong navy, and regulation of railroads. He criticized President Grover Cleveland's vetoes of veterans' pension bills.

President Benjamin Harrison Foundation

Harrison's birthplace was a red brick home on his grandfather's farm in North Bend, Ohio, near the Ohio River.

Library of Congress

Caroline Scott Harrison worked hard as First Lady despite poor health. She died in 1892, two weeks before the election in which her husband lost his bid for a second term as President.

Harrison's election

Place of nominating convention . .	Chicago
Ballot on which nominated	8th
Democratic opponent	Grover Cleveland
Electoral vote*	233 (Harrison) to
	168 (Cleveland)
Popular vote	5,534,488 (Cleveland) to
	5,443,892 (Harrison)
Age at inauguration	55

*For votes by states, see **Electoral College** (table).

Vice President and Cabinet

Vice President	* Levi P. Morton
Secretary of state	* James G. Blaine
	John W. Foster (1892)
Secretary of the treasury	William Windom
	Charles Foster (1891)
Secretary of war	Redfield Proctor
	Stephen B. Elkins (1891)
Attorney general	William H. H. Miller
Postmaster general	John Wanamaker
Secretary of the Navy	Benjamin F. Tracy
Secretary of the interior	John W. Noble
Secretary of agriculture	Jeremiah M. Rusk

*Has a separate biography in *World Book.*

Indiana's Democratic legislature defeated Harrison's bid for a second term by one vote.

Election of 1888. James G. Blaine, who had lost the 1884 presidential election to Cleveland, refused to run in 1888. The Republicans nominated Harrison, partly because of his war record and his popularity with veterans. Levi P. Morton, a New York City banker, was nominated for Vice President. The Democrats renominated Cleveland and named Allen G. Thurman, a former Ohio senator, as his running mate.

Harrison, in a "front porch" campaign from his home, supported high tariffs. Cleveland called for lower tariffs, but did not campaign actively because he felt it was beneath the dignity of the presidency.

In the election, Harrison trailed Cleveland by more than 90,000 popular votes. But, by carrying Indiana, New York, and several "doubtful states," Harrison won the election in the Electoral College.

Harrison's Administration (1889-1893)

The Republicans held a majority in both houses of Congress during the first half of Harrison's term. As a result, the President won enactment of his legislative program. In the congressional elections of 1890, the Democrats won control of the House of Representatives and the Republican majority in the Senate was reduced to six. The change partly reflected public disapproval of vast congressional appropriations, which reached al-

most a billion dollars. When Democrats accused the Republicans of wastefulness, Thomas B. Reed, Speaker of the House, replied by saying: "This is a billion-dollar country!"

Domestic affairs. During the campaign, Harrison had promised to extend the civil service law to cover more jobs. He kept his promise by increasing the number of classified positions from 27,000 to 38,000.

The four most important laws of Harrison's Administration were all passed in 1890.

The Sherman Antitrust Act. During the period of rapid industrialization in the late 1880's, many corporations formed *trusts* that controlled market prices and destroyed competition (see **Antitrust laws**). Farmers and owners of small businesses demanded government protection from these trusts. The Sherman Antitrust Act, fulfilling one of Harrison's campaign pledges, outlawed trusts or any other monopolies that hindered trade.

The Sherman Silver Purchase Act met another demand of farm voters. Farm prices were falling, and farmers asked the government to put more money into circulation, either paper money or silver coins. Farmers felt that this action would increase farm prices and thus make it easier for farmers to pay their debts. The owners of the silver mines naturally favored a demand that would boost their own profits. The Sherman Silver Purchase Act increased the amount of silver that could be coined. The government purchased this silver, and paid for it with treasury notes that could be redeemed either in silver or gold. Because most people chose to redeem their notes in gold, the fear of a resulting drain on the Treasury's gold reserves helped cause a financial panic in 1893.

The McKinley Tariff Act was designed mainly to protect U.S. industries and their workers. Its sponsors tried to make the law attractive to farmers by raising tariffs on imported farm products. But the McKinley Tariff Act set tariffs at record highs, and farmers regarded it chiefly as a benefit to business.

The Dependent Pension Bill broadened pension qualifications to include all Civil War veterans who could not perform manual labor. The cost of pensions soared from $88 million in 1889 to $159 million in 1893.

Foreign affairs. Harrison launched a program to build a two-ocean navy and expand the merchant marine. Both actions helped shape the new and vigorous foreign policy developed by Harrison and Secretary of State James G. Blaine.

Latin America. In 1889, the first Pan-American Conference met in Washington. The delegates began expanding the meaning of the Monroe Doctrine by promoting cooperation among the nations. The Pan American Union was created at this conference.

Trade with other nations was being threatened by U.S. tariffs that constantly grew higher. Harrison began to negotiate reciprocal trade agreements (see **Reciprocal trade agreement**). This was a constructive attempt to compromise between manufacturers who wanted free competitive markets and those who favored protective tariffs.

Hawaii. Early in 1893, Queen Liliuokalani had lost her throne in a revolution led by American planters. The new Hawaiian government asked the United States to make Hawaii a territory. Harrison had been defeated for reelection the previous November, but he rushed a treaty of annexation to the Senate before his term ended. Cleveland returned to the presidency before the Senate could act on the treaty, and withdrew it. He declared that the whole affair was dishonorable to the United States.

Other developments. The Harrison Administration also settled a number of old quarrels. The government agreed to arbitrate the long-standing dispute with Great Britain over fur seals in the Bering Sea (see **Bering Sea controversy**). In 1889, a quarrel seemed likely over the ownership of Samoa, and the United States joined Germany and England in establishing a protectorate over the islands. In 1892, Congress passed the Oriental Exclusion Act, which long remained a sore spot in America's relations with China and Japan (see **Oriental Exclusion Acts**).

Life in the White House was thoroughly photographed for the first time during Harrison's term. Electric lights and bells were installed in the mansion in 1891. But the Harrisons, fearing shocks, often used the old-style gas lights, or asked the White House electrician to turn the switches on and off.

Despite poor health, Mrs. Harrison worked hard as official hostess. She once told a reporter that "there are only five sleeping rooms and there is no feeling of privacy." Members of the Harrison family usually occupied these rooms. Mrs. Harrison's father lived in the White House, as did Mrs. Mary Dimmick, a widowed niece who served as her secretary. The Harrisons' daughter, Mrs. Mary McKee, and her husband and two children lived there most of the time.

Bid for reelection. The Republicans renominated Harrison in 1892, and chose Whitelaw Reid, editor of the *New York Tribune,* as his running mate. The Democrats again nominated Cleveland for President, and named Adlai E. Stevenson, a former Illinois congressman, for Vice President.

Discontented farmers turned from the Republicans to the new Populist Party, which had been formed in protest against falling farm prices (see **Populism**). Angry factory workers deserted the Republicans, charging hostile interference by the federal and state governments in the bloody Homestead strike and other labor disputes (see **Homestead Strike**). Opposition to the McKinley Tariff Act also helped defeat Harrison, who received 5,182,690 popular votes to Cleveland's 5,555,426. The Populist candidate, James B. Weaver, received more than a million votes. This gave Cleveland 277 electoral votes to Harrison's 145. Weaver received 22 electoral votes.

Personal tragedy struck Harrison just two weeks before the national elections of 1892, when his wife died on October 25.

Later years

Harrison returned to Indianapolis and the practice of law. In 1896, he married Mrs. Dimmick (April 30, 1858-Jan. 5, 1948), who had nursed his wife during her last illness. They had one child, Elizabeth (1897-1955).

In 1897, Harrison wrote *This Country of Ours,* a book about the federal government. In 1899, he represented Venezuela in the arbitration of a dispute with Great Britain over the British Guiana boundary. Harrison died in his home on March 13, 1901, and was buried in Indianapolis.   H. Wayne Morgan

Related articles in *World Book* include:

Cleveland, Grover
McKinley, William
Morton, Levi P.
Pan-American Conferences
President of the United States
Tariff

Outline

I. **Early life**
   A. Childhood
   B. Education
   C. Harrison's family
   D. Lawyer
II. **Political and public activities**
   A. Political beginnings
   B. Army commander
   C. National politics
   D. Election of 1888
III. **Harrison's Administration (1889-1893)**
   A. Domestic affairs
   B. Foreign affairs
   C. Life in the White House
   D. Bid for reelection
IV. **Later years**

Questions

Who was the only man whose father and son both became President?

What was unusual about the results of the 1888 presidential election?

How did Harrison please Civil War veterans?

Why did he decline a post in Garfield's Cabinet?

What reforms did farmers and persons who owned small businesses seek? Why?

How did the United States show its interest in Latin America during Harrison's Administration?

What factors led to Harrison's defeat in 1892?

How was the White House modernized during Harrison's Administration?

Additional resources

Benjamin Harrison, 1833-1901. Ed. by Harry J. Sievers. Oceana, 1969.

Garraty, John A. *The New Commonwealth, 1877-1890.* Harper, 1968.

Sievers, Harry J. *Benjamin Harrison.* 3 vols. Vol. 1, 2nd ed., University Publishers, 1960; Vol. 2, 1959; Vol. 3, Bobbs, 1968.

Harrison, George. See Beatles.

*9th President of
the United States 1841*

Van Buren
8th President
1837-1841
Democrat

Harrison
9th President
1841
Whig

Tyler
10th President
1841-1845
Whig

John Tyler
Vice President
1841

Detail of an oil portrait on canvas (1840) by Albert Gallatin Hoit; National
Portrait Gallery, Smithsonian Institution, Washington, D.C.

Harrison, William Henry (1773-1841), served the
shortest time in office of any President in American history. He caught cold the day he was inaugurated President, and he died 30 days later. Harrison was the first
President to die in office.

Harrison is best remembered as the first half of the
catchy political campaign slogan "Tippecanoe and Tyler
too." He had received the nickname "Tippecanoe" after
defeating the Shawnee Indians in 1811 at the Battle of
Tippecanoe. The Whig Party first ran Harrison for President against Democrat Martin Van Buren in 1836. He
lost. Then they ran him again in 1840. Using his colorful
military career as their theme, the Whigs turned the
campaign of 1840 into a circus. This time, Harrison defeated President Van Buren. Harrison was the first Whig
President, and the only chief executive whose grandson
(Benjamin Harrison) also became President.

During his brief term, Harrison showed an interest in
running the government efficiently. He made surprise
visits to government offices to check on the workers.
Upon Harrison's death, his office fell to Vice President
John Tyler, a former Virginia Democrat. The Whigs had
nominated Tyler to attract Southern votes. But when
Tyler became President, the Whigs unhappily learned
that he still believed in many of the ideas of the Democratic party. He vetoed bill after bill, and destroyed the
Whig program in Congress.

Early life

William Henry Harrison was born on Feb. 9, 1773, at
Berkeley, his father's plantation in Charles City County,
Virginia. He was the youngest of seven children, four
girls and three boys. His parents, Benjamin and Elizabeth Bassett Harrison, came from prominent Virginia

families. The elder Harrison had served in both Continental Congresses, and signed the Declaration of Independence.

William received his early education at home. He entered Hampden-Sydney College in 1787 and later enrolled at the University of Pennsylvania to study medicine. After his father died in 1791, Harrison dropped
medicine and joined the Army. George Washington, a
friend of his father, approved this decision.

Military and political career

Soldier. Harrison served in early American wars
against the Indians, and rose to the rank of lieutenant. In
1794, he developed a plan which led to an American victory on the Great Miami River. He was promoted to captain and given command of Fort Washington, Ohio.

Harrison's family. While at Fort Washington, Harrison met and married Anna Symmes (July 25, 1775-Feb.
25, 1864). She was the daughter of John C. Symmes, a
judge and wealthy land investor. The Harrisons had six
sons and four daughters. Six of the children died before
Harrison became President.

Entry into politics. Harrison resigned his Army commission in June 1798, and President John Adams appointed him secretary of the Northwest Territory. In
1799, Harrison was elected the first delegate to Congress from the Northwest Territory. In Congress, Harrison convinced the lawmakers to pass a bill that divided
western lands into sections small enough for even a
poor person to buy.

In 1800, Adams named Harrison governor of the Indiana Territory, a post he held for 12 years. As governor,
Harrison sought to protect the welfare of American Indians living in the territory. He banned the sale of liquor to

electoral votes. Democrat Martin Van Buren won the presidency with 170 electoral votes.

In 1840, the still-divided Whigs tried to broaden their appeal, which had been confined mainly to big eastern cities. They nominated Harrison again and, for Vice President, chose John Tyler, a Virginia Democrat.

The Whigs made no attempt to agree on issues or even to adopt a platform. They simply hoped to hang together until they won the presidency. They did this by emphasizing antics rather than issues. Party leaders told Harrison to say "not one single word about his principles or creed." A Democratic newspaper charged that all Harrison wanted for the rest of his life was a pension, a log cabin, and plenty of hard cider. The Whigs turned this sneer to their advantage by proudly presenting Har-

Important dates in Harrison's life

1773	(Feb. 9) Born in Charles City County, Virginia.
1795	(Nov. 25) Married Anna Symmes.
1800	Appointed governor of Indiana Territory.
1811	Defeated Indians in the Battle of Tippecanoe.
1812-1814	Served in the War of 1812.
1816	Elected to the U.S. House of Representatives.
1825	Elected to the United States Senate.
1828	Appointed U.S. Minister to Colombia.
1836	Defeated for presidency by Martin Van Buren.
1840	Elected President of the United States.
1841	(April 4) Died in the White House.

Harrison's birthplace, Berkeley, was his father's plantation in Charles City County. It stands on the James River, about 20 miles (32 kilometers) from Richmond, Va.

Berkeley Plantation

them, and ordered that they be inoculated against smallpox. In 1809, Harrison negotiated a treaty with Indian leaders which transferred about 2,900,000 acres (1,170,000 hectares) of land on the Wabash and White rivers to settlers. Many Indians denounced the treaty. They united under the Shawnee chief Tecumseh and his brother, known as the Shawnee Prophet. Harrison took command of the territorial militia and set out to drive the Indians from treaty lands. On Nov. 7, 1811, Harrison's outnumbered troops shattered the Indian forces in the Battle of Tippecanoe.

Army commander. When the War of 1812 began, President James Madison made Harrison a brigadier general in command of the Army of the Northwest. Harrison was promoted to major general early in 1813. In October 1813, his troops won a brilliant victory over combined Indian and British forces in the Battle of the Thames in southern Ontario.

Return to politics. Harrison again resigned from the army in 1814 after a quarrel with the secretary of war. He settled on a farm in North Bend, Ohio. In 1816, he was elected to the United States House of Representatives. He was accused of misusing public money while in the Army, but a House investigating committee held the charge false. His name cleared, Harrison returned to Ohio. In 1819, he was elected a state senator. The legislature elected him to the United States Senate in 1825. He resigned in 1828 to accept an appointment from President John Quincy Adams as the U.S. minister to Colombia. But the blunt-spoken Harrison lasted about a year in diplomacy. President Andrew Jackson appointed one of his supporters to replace Harrison in 1829.

Elections of 1836 and 1840. Harrison was one of three Whig Party candidates for the presidency in 1836. The party was a mixture of people with conflicting ideas of government, and Harrison's supporters felt he could unify the party. He ran surprisingly well, winning 73

Granger Collection

The 1840 campaign focused on slogans rather than issues. The cartoon, *above,* showed Harrison as a simple frontiersman, even though he came from a prominent Virginia family.

Harrison's election

Place of nominating convention	Baltimore
Ballot on which nominated	2nd
Democratic opponent	Martin Van Buren
Electoral vote*	234 (Harrison) to 60 (Van Buren)
Popular vote	1,275,390 (Harrison) to 1,128,854 (Van Buren)
Age at inauguration	68

*For votes by states, see **Electoral College** (table).

Vice President and Cabinet

Vice President	* John Tyler
Secretary of state	* Daniel Webster
Secretary of the treasury	Thomas Ewing
Secretary of war	* John Bell
Attorney general	John J. Crittenden
Postmaster general	Francis Granger
Secretary of the Navy	George E. Badger

*Has a separate biography in *World Book*.

rison as "the log cabin, hard cider" candidate. Torchlight parades with cider barrels and log cabins on wagons rolled down streets all over the nation. The Whigs blamed President Van Buren, the Democratic candidate, for the hard times in the country. They contrasted the hungry workers with the aristocratic Van Buren, who they said wore "corsets and silk stockings." Harrison won by about 147,000 votes, but had a huge electoral majority.

Harrison's Administration (1841)

Harrison's wife became too ill to travel just before he left for Washington, so he was accompanied by his widowed daughter-in-law, Jane Irwin Harrison. She served as White House hostess during his term. It was a cold, rainy day when Harrison gave his inaugural address. He caught a cold which a month later proved fatal.

Harrison spent his energy deciding political appointments. He left the development of a legislative program to Henry Clay, the Whig leader in Congress.

The *Caroline* affair. Just one week after Harrison took office, the United States faced a serious crisis with Great Britain. Over three years earlier, a member of the American crew of the steamboat *Caroline* had been killed while carrying supplies to Canadian rebels. Much later, police in Buffalo, N.Y., arrested a visiting Canadian who had been one of the party that attacked the *Caroline*. The British waited until Van Buren had left office, then demanded the prisoner's release on threat of war. Harrison turned the problem over to Daniel Webster, who apologized. But tension was not eased until Webster negotiated the Webster-Ashburton Treaty in 1842 (see **Webster-Ashburton Treaty**).

Death. Harrison sought relief from the pressures of his office by attending to minor details of running the White House. One raw March morning, he went out to

buy vegetables, and suffered a severe chill. The cold he had caught on inauguration day now developed into pneumonia. Harrison died on April 4, 1841, $12\frac{1}{2}$ hours short of 31 full days in office. He was buried in North Bend, Ohio.   Steven Mintz

Related articles in *World Book* include:
Indian wars (Other Midwestern conflicts)
President of the United States
Tecumseh
Tyler, John
Van Buren, Martin
War of 1812
Whig Party

Outline

I. **Early life**
II. **Military and political career**
   A. Soldier
   B. Harrison's family
   C. Entry into politics
   D. Army commander
   E. Return to politics
   F. Elections of 1836 and 1840
III. **Harrison's Administration (1841)**
   A. The *Caroline* affair   B. Death

Questions

What "firsts" mark Harrison's presidency?
What causes led to Harrison's death?
Why was "Tippecanoe and Tyler too" a good slogan?
Why did the Whigs nominate Tyler for Vice President?
How did the Whigs develop the idea of their "log cabin, hard cider" campaign in 1840?

Additional resources

Cleaves, Freeman. *Old Tippecanoe: William Henry Harrison and His Time.* Scribner, 1939.
Goebel, Dorothy B. *William Henry Harrison: A Political Biography.* Porcupine, 1974. First published in 1926.
Green, James A. *William Henry Harrison: His Life and Times.* Garrett & Mossie, 1941.
Gunderson, Robert G. *The Log-Cabin Campaign.* Greenwood, 1977. First published in 1957.

Harrow, *HAR oh.* After farmers plow the ground, they must break the clods of earth into smaller pieces with a harrow before they plant seeds. Otherwise, the delicate shoots could not break upward through the heavy clods left by the plow. The first harrow used by primitive people was a tree limb with many smaller branches which was pulled over the soil. Later, wooden frames with teeth set in them were used. Today there are three general types: (1) the disk harrow, (2) the smoothing, or drag, harrow, and (3) the spring-tooth harrow.

The *disk harrow,* sometimes called a *disk,* is a set of sharp disks, from 16 to 32 inches (41 to 81 centimeters) in diameter, mounted on a shaft from 5 to 10 feet (1.5 to 3 meters) long. As the harrow is pulled forward the disks revolve, cutting the soil as they go. Disk harrows are sometimes made with two or three sets of disks mounted on shafts. If the soil is not very hard, a disk harrow can be used instead of a plow. This means that the farmer can plow and break the soil into pieces at the

Courtesy Stefan Lorant; from his book *The Presidency*

The campaign of 1840 emphasized antics instead of issues. Harrison's supporters held parades like the one shown above, which featured a giant paper ball covered with election slogans.

same time. When used in this way, a disk harrow is usually weighted to make the disks cut more deeply.

The *smoothing,* or *drag, harrow* is a set of two to four iron frames. Each frame is about 5 feet (1.5 meters) square and has rods running across it. Each rod has iron teeth which "comb" the soil as the harrow is pulled.

The *spring-tooth harrow* is an iron frame which may be up to 10 feet (3 meters) wide. Teeth made of springs shaped in a half circle are bolted into the frame. The teeth are sharpened to a spoon shape, and they tear the soil when the harrow moves.   Melvin E. Long

Harrow School, *HAR oh,* is a leading public school in England. It was founded in 1571 by John Lyon, a wealthy landowner. Harrow School was at first intended to educate the poor boys of Harrow parish, which is about 12 miles (19 kilometers) from London. Most of its pupils are now admitted on payment of fees. Harrow taught only classical subjects until the 1800's.   P. A. McGinley

Harsha, *HUHR shuh* (A.D. 590?-647), was an Indian king who ruled most of northern India from A.D. 606 to 647. He was also called Harsha-vardhana (pronounced *HUHR shuh VUHR duh nuh*). Harsha was the first Indian monarch to establish a unified empire after the Huns from central Asia invaded India during the 400's and 500's. Harsha, the son of a king in the Ganges River Valley, had inherited the combined throne of two small kingdoms. He then conquered most of the neighboring area. Harsha supported the development of philosophy and literature and wrote three well-known plays—*Nagananda, Ratnavali,* and *Priyadarsika.* After Harsha died, the empire soon broke up.   J. F. Richards

Hart. See Red deer.

Hart, Gary Warren (1936-   ), a Colorado Democrat, served as a United States senator from 1975 to 1987. He was an unsuccessful candidate for the 1984 Democratic presidential nomination. Hart became a candidate for the 1988 Democratic presidential nomination. He withdrew from the race in May 1987 after newspaper accounts of his personal life suggested marital infidelity. Hart reentered the race in December 1987.

Hart was born in Ottawa, Kans. He changed his family name from Hartpence to Hart in 1961. Hart graduated from Bethany Nazarene College (now Southern Nazarene University) and from the divinity and law schools of Yale University. Hart first attracted national attention when he directed the 1972 presidential campaign of Senator George S. McGovern of South Dakota.

Dennis Whitehead, Sygma

Gary Hart

In the Senate, Hart supported programs to limit the development of nuclear weapons. He was the author of Strategic Talks on Prevention (STOP), a proposal urging the United States and the Soviet Union to work together to prevent the use of nuclear weapons. Hart also proposed a tax system that would aid small businesses and favor companies using advanced electronics. He opposed several costly military programs and proposed

federal programs to modernize factories and to retrain workers with outdated skills.   Lee Thornton

Hart, John (1711?-1779), was a signer of the Declaration of Independence. He was a prosperous farmer, and served in the colonial New Jersey Assembly from 1761 to 1771 and as speaker of the state's General Assembly in 1776. Hart was an early supporter of the American cause and opposed the Stamp Act (see **Stamp Act**). He was born in Stonington, Conn.   Robert J. Taylor

Hart, Lorenz (1895-1943), was an American writer of lyrics of popular songs. He became famous for the songs that he and the composer Richard Rodgers created for many musical comedies. This team produced its best work in the late 1920's and the 1930's. During that period, only Cole Porter rivaled Hart for satirical wit and freshness of rhymes. Hart's best-known songs include "Falling in Love with Love," "My Funny Valentine," and "Thou Swell."

Hart was born in New York City. He and Rodgers began to work together in 1919 and achieved their first success with *The Garrick Gaieties* (1925). They then created the songs for *Peggy-Ann* (1926), *A Connecticut Yankee* (1927), and other musicals.

Hart and Rodgers moved to Hollywood, Calif., in 1930 and composed songs for several motion pictures. After returning to New York City in 1934, they wrote songs for a number of musical comedies, including *On Your Toes* (1936), *Babes in Arms* (1937), *I'd Rather Be Right* (1937), and *Pal Joey* (1940).   Ethan Mordden

See also **Rodgers, Richard.**

Hart, Moss (1904-1961), was an American playwright and director. He became famous for a series of witty comedies on American life that he wrote with George S. Kaufman. Their first success was *Once in a Lifetime* (1930), a satire about the motion-picture industry. Hart and Kaufman won the 1937 Pulitzer Prize for drama for *You Can't Take It With You,* a comedy about a family of lovable eccentrics. Their other works included *Merrily We Roll Along* (1934), *The Man Who Came to Dinner* (1939), and *George Washington Slept Here* (1940).

Hart wrote several plays by himself, including *Winged Victory* (1943), *Light Up the Sky* (1948), and *The Climate of Eden* (1952). He also wrote the stories for several musical comedies. *Face the Music* (1932) and *As Thousands Cheer* (1933) had music by Irving Berlin, and *Lady in the Dark* (1941) had music by Kurt Weill.

Hart wrote the scripts for several motion pictures, including *Gentleman's Agreement,* which won the 1947 Academy Award as the best movie of the year. He directed many plays and musicals, including the hit musical comedy *My Fair Lady* (1956). His autobiography, *Act One* (1959), is an informative book about theater life. Hart was born in New York City.   Thomas A. Erhard

See also **Kaufman, George S.**

Harte, Bret (1836-1902), was an American author who became famous for his colorful stories about the West. His best-known works describe the California gold rush days of the mid-1800's. Harte portrayed a variety of people, such as gamblers, miners, and prostitutes. He described their personal characteristics, including their natural form of speech. Harte's descriptions helped shape a movement in American fiction called *local color writing.* This literary style tries to capture the feeling of some particular place and its people.

Harte was born in Albany, N.Y. His real name was Francis Brett Hart. He moved to California at the age of 18 and spent several years working at various jobs. After publishing several poems in 1857, he decided to be a writer. Two years later, Harte joined the staff of the *Northern Californian,* a newspaper in Union (now Arcata), Calif. In 1860, he wrote an editorial that criticized white Californians for their part in an Indian massacre. The angry townspeople forced him to resign.

From 1868 until early 1871, Harte served as editor of the *Overland Monthly,* a magazine published in San Francisco. The August 1868 issue included his story "The Luck of Roaring Camp." Californians disliked the story at first because it showed California life as rough and unsophisticated and was sympathetic to the tough gold rush miners. But the merit of the story soon gained Harte a nationwide reputation.

Harte's work in the *Overland* continued to gain popularity. His best-known writings from the magazine include two short stories, "The Outcasts of Poker Flat" (1869) and "Tennessee's Partner" (1869), and a humorous poem, "Plain Language from Truthful James" (1870), later published as "The Heathen Chinee." *The Luck of Roaring Camp and Other Sketches* (1870) was a collection of stories about life in California.

Harte became increasingly famous in the East, and in 1871 he moved to Boston. There, he failed to fulfill the terms of a contract with the *Atlantic Monthly* magazine. He handed in several stories after their deadlines, and the *Atlantic* was generally unhappy with his work. Harte's popularity soon declined. His only novel, *Gabriel Conroy* (1876), received harsh criticism, and he became discouraged by his lack of success. Harte left the United States in 1878 and spent seven years as a diplomatic representative of the U.S. government in Germany and Scotland. He lived in London from 1885 until his death.

Dean Doner

Additional resources

O'Connor, Richard. *Bret Harte: A Biography.* Little, Brown, 1966.
Stewart, George R. *Bret Harte, Argonaut and Exile: Being an Account of the Life of the Celebrated American Humorist.* AMS, 1979. First published in 1931.

Hartebeest, *HAHR tuh BEEST,* is a large African antelope. Its shoulders are much higher than its hindquarters, so the animal's back slopes to the rear. A hartebeest has a long, sad-looking face. Its ears are quite large. Its horns curve backward or outward, then forward and upward, and finally bend sharply backward and upward. Its tail looks like a cow's.

Many kinds of hartebeests are known. The *red hartebeest* grows from 4 to 5 feet (1.2 to 1.5 meters) high and has a reddish-brown coat with a white rump patch. It runs rapidly, despite its awkward appearance, and can easily outdistance a horse. It travels in herds of 15 to 50. Hartebeests were once found throughout the grassy plains of Africa, but some kinds have now become scarce. At least two kinds, Swayne's hartebeest of Ethiopia and the Tora hartebeest, which lives in Egypt, Ethiopia, and the Sudan, are considered to be endangered species.

Scientific classification. Hartebeests are in the bovid family, Bovidae. The red hartebeest is *Alcelaphus buselaphus.*

Victor H. Cahalane

Hartford (pop. 136,392; met. area pop. 715,923), is the capital and second largest city of Connecticut. Only Bridgeport has more people. About 50 insurance companies have their headquarters in Hartford, which is known as the *Insurance City.* It is also an important manufacturing center. Hartford lies on the west bank of the Connecticut River, in the north-central part of the state. For the location of Hartford, see **Connecticut** (political map).

In 1633, the Netherlands established a trading post in what is now the Hartford area. English settlers from Massachusetts, led by Thomas Hooker, a Congregationalist minister, founded Hartford in 1636. They named the town for the English town of Hertford.

Description. Hartford covers about 18 square miles (47 square kilometers). Constitution Plaza, a modern business center, lies in the heart of the downtown area. Nearby is the Hartford Civic Center, which includes an assembly hall, an exhibition hall, and a sports arena. The Hartford Whalers of the National Hockey League play in the center. State House Square in downtown Hartford includes the Pavillion, an indoor and outdoor shopping mall. The Capitol is located in Bushnell Park in the center of the city (see **Connecticut** [picture: City Place in Hartford]).

Hartford is the home of Trinity College, the Hartford Seminary, and the Hartford Graduate Center. The University of Hartford and St. Joseph College are in nearby West Hartford.

Hartford's landmarks include the Old State House; a home of the author Mark Twain; the Connecticut Historical Society; and the Wadsworth Atheneum, one of the first public art museums in the United States. The atheneum was established in 1842. *The Hartford Courant,* founded in 1764, is the oldest continuously published daily newspaper in the country.

Economy. Hartford's insurance companies employ about a fourth of the city's workers. The Hartford area has about 1,400 manufacturing firms. Leading industries

Philippa Scott, Photo Researchers

The hartebeest is a large African antelope with curved horns. The red hartebeest, *above,* has a reddish-brown coat and a white rump patch. They graze in herds on the African plains.

are, in order of importance, the manufacture of aircraft equipment, machinery, electrical equipment, chemicals, precision tools and instruments, and rubber. The area has about 5,000 stores and ranks second to Boston as the largest retail center in New England.

Government and history. Hartford has a council-manager government. The voters elect a mayor and nine city council members to two-year terms. The council appoints a city manager to run the city government.

Saukiog Indians lived in what is now the Hartford area before the Dutch founded a trading post there called the *House of Hope.* In 1639, English settlers of the Connecticut Colony met in Hartford and adopted the *Fundamental Orders,* sometimes called the first written constitution. The Fundamental Orders later served as a model for the United States Constitution.

Hartford was incorporated in 1784. New Haven and Hartford were twin capitals of Connecticut from 1701 to 1875, when Hartford became the only capital. In 1835, after a fire in New York City, the Hartford Fire Insurance Company was one of the few insurance firms that was able to pay its claims. As a result, Hartford became known for reliable insurance companies.

The city's population increased from 79,850 in 1900 to 138,036 in 1920 largely because of immigration from Europe. The population reached a high of 177,397 in 1950 but has declined since then as thousands of people moved to suburban areas.   Irving Kravsow

For the monthly weather in Hartford, see **Connecticut** (Climate). See also **Charter Oak; Twain, Mark** (picture).

Hartford, George Huntington (1833-1917), an American merchant, helped develop the retail chain-store industry. He and George F. Gilman founded the Great Atlantic and Pacific Tea Company (A&P).

Hartford was born in Augusta, Me. He worked in a Boston dry-goods house and then went to St. Louis, Mo. In 1858, he began working as a salesman in a St. Louis store owned by Gilman. The two men later became partners in New York City and operated stores first under the name of the Great American Tea Company.

After Gilman retired in 1878, Hartford headed the company. It became the largest in its industry. In 1913, he began developing cash-and-carry stores that set the pattern for today's supermarkets.   John B. McFerrin

Hartford Convention was a meeting of New England delegates during the War of 1812 to discuss their opposition to the war and to other United States government policies. The meeting took place in Hartford, Conn., from Dec. 15, 1814, to Jan. 5, 1815.

The main opposition to the war came from members of the Federalist Party in New England. They objected to the ruin of New England's shipping trade by the war, and they did not want to help France by fighting Great Britain. The Federalists generally opposed France in international disputes.

In 1814, the Massachusetts legislature called a meeting of New England states to discuss their problems. Most of the 26 delegates came from Massachusetts, Connecticut, and Rhode Island. Some people feared that New England would withdraw from the Union and make a separate peace with Britain. Their fears increased because the Hartford Convention met in secret, but the delegates decided on less drastic action.

The delegates issued a report urging that each New England state be given more control over its own military defense. The report also proposed amendments to the United States Constitution to make it harder for the government to make war or restrict trade. In addition, the delegates recommended amendments to reduce the influence of the South in the government.

The Treaty of Ghent, which ended the War of 1812, was signed while the Hartford Convention met. Nevertheless, Federalist opposition to the war, as shown by the convention, helped destroy the party.

Reginald Horsman

Hartley, Marsden (1877-1943), was one of the first American painters to experiment with cubism and abstract art. By about 1920 he had returned to a representational style, often using landscape or seashore themes. However, his representational paintings show the influ-

Oil painting on canvas (1941); The Metropolitan Museum of Art, Arthur H. Hearn Fund, New York City

Lobster Fishermen, Corea, Maine is Marsden Hartley's simple but powerful impression of life on the coast of Maine.

ence of his earlier abstract work in their emphasis on pattern and simplification of shapes. Hartley's reputation as a painter came first with his later works. A typical example of this representational style is *Lobster Fishermen, Corea, Maine* (1940-1941).

Hartley was born in Lewiston, Me. He studied with artist William Merritt Chase in New York and exhibited in the gallery of photographer Alfred Stieglitz, a supporter of pioneering modern artists.   George Ehrlich

Hartmann Von Aue (1170?-1210?) was a German poet. He introduced the legends of King Arthur into German literature by adapting *Erec* and *Yvain,* two romances by the French poet Chrétien de Troyes.

In *Erec,* Hartmann retold the story of an Arthurian hero who gave up knighthood for love. *Yvain* is the story of an Arthurian hero who gave up love for knighthood. *Poor Henry* and *Gregorius* are two original verse epics by Hartmann. They deal with sin and redemption. Hartmann also wrote love poetry and crusade songs.

Hartmann was born in Swabia. He was a knight in the service of a Swabian lord.   James F. Poag

See also **German literature** (Epic poetry).

Harun al-Rashid, *hah ROON ahl rah SHEED* (766-806), was an important ruler of the Abbasid Dynasty, which governed the Islamic empire during the Middle Ages. In A.D. 786, Harun became *caliph* (ruler) of the empire of the Muslims. At that time, the Muslim empire included northern Africa, part of Spain, most of the Middle East, and part of India. Harun was a patron of learning, music, and the arts. The empire prospered under his rule, and the capital, Baghdad, was a center of culture as well as wealth. Harun was a leading character in the *Arabian Nights,* a famous collection of Arabic folk tales (see **Arabian Nights**).

Early in Harun's reign, his tutor, Yahya ibn Khalid, and Yahya's sons, controlled the government, but Harun later seized control. He fought many wars against the Christian Byzantine Empire, sometimes leading the Muslim army. Harun died in battle.   Wilferd Madelung

Harunobu (1725-1770) was a Japanese printmaker. In 1765, he perfected a new technique for making Japanese wood-block prints in many colors. Before then, Japanese artists had made prints in black ink alone, or in black ink with at most two other colors, red and green. Harunobu's prints, called *nishiki-e* (brocade pictures), included as many as 10 colors.

Harunobu's art has been praised for its great refinement and beauty. Most of his wood-block prints portray delicate, doll-like girls in scenes from everyday life. These scenes reflect an atmosphere of serenity and intimacy. The charm of Harunobu's prints was enhanced by the multicolor printing process. Harunobu's birthplace is unknown, but he spent most of his life in Edo (now Tokyo).   Robert A. Rorex

See also **Japanese print** (picture: A tranquil night-time scene).

Harvard, John (1607-1638), was a minister and philanthropist. He left a library of 400 volumes, and about 780 pounds sterling, to the college at Cambridge, Mass., which was later named after him. He was not the founder of Harvard University, but he gave the college its first large gift.

Harvard was born in London. He attended Cambridge University, and received B.A. and M.A. degrees. In 1636, he married Anne Sadler. The following year, he and his wife sailed to Massachusetts. They settled in Charlestown, where he became a minister of the Charlestown church.   Robert H. Bremner

Harvard University is the oldest institution of higher learning in the United States. It was founded in 1636, just 16 years after the Pilgrims landed at Plymouth. Harvard is also one of the richest private universities in the United States, with an endowment of over $2 billion. The main campus is in Cambridge, Mass. The university also has several schools in Boston.

Harvard has played an important role in American life. Presidents John Adams, John Quincy Adams, Theodore Roosevelt, Franklin D. Roosevelt, and John F. Kennedy graduated from Harvard. President Rutherford B. Hayes attended Harvard law school.

Educational program. Harvard University has two major undergraduate divisions—Harvard College and Radcliffe College—with a joint admissions office. Men undergraduates are admitted to Harvard College and women to Radcliffe. All classes are coeducational and the students receive Harvard University degrees.

Harvard's 10 graduate and professional schools are open to both men and women. These schools have over half the university's enrollment. The schools of arts and sciences, design, divinity, education, law, and public ad-

ministration are on the Cambridge campus. The schools of business administration, dental medicine, medicine, and public health are in Boston.

Many Harvard departments use a tutorial plan. Under the plan, individual students or small groups meet periodically with faculty tutors for instruction in the students' major area of study. Most students who participate in tutorials do not do so until their sophomore year. Most honors candidates in departments with a tutorial plan receive tutorial instruction.

General examinations test the students' grasp of their major field. Students in most fields must pass general examinations to graduate, no matter how high their grades might be. Harvard awards about $85 million in financial aid to its students each year. Undergraduates receive about $24 million of this aid.

The Harvard campus. The Harvard Yard is the center of the original college. Dormitories, libraries, and class buildings in a variety of architectural styles stand near this grassy, shaded area. During the Revolutionary War, General George Washington's troops used Massachusetts Hall as barracks, and the provincial legislature met in Harvard Hall.

Freshmen live in dormitories in and near the Yard, but most other students live in the 12 residential houses. These houses are modeled after the residential colleges of Oxford and Cambridge universities. Harvard's residential houses are more than places where students eat and sleep. They are also centers for social and educational activities. Each house has its own dining hall, library, and athletic facilities. Faculty members live or eat at the house, permitting students to mix informally with instructors. The 12 residential houses are Adams, Cabot, Currier, Dunster, Eliot, Kirkland, Leverett, Lowell, Mather, North, Quincy, and Winthrop. Dudley House has facilities for students who live at home. All university housing is coeducational.

Harvard has the world's largest university library system. Its collection includes more than 11 million books and pamphlets and many manuscripts, maps, microfilms, slides, and other materials. Museums on the campus include the Peabody Museum of Archaeology and Ethnology; the Botanical Museum; the Geological Museum; the Mineralogical Museum; the Museum of Comparative Zoology; the Busch-Reisinger Museum of Central and Northern European Art; the University Herbarium; the Fogg Art Museum; and the Arthur M. Sackler Museum. The Arnold Arboretum has a famous collection of trees and shrubs in Boston.

The university supervises several research facilities outside the Cambridge-Boston area. They include a center for the study of Italian Renaissance culture at Villa I Tatti in Florence, Italy; a center for Byzantine studies in Washington, D.C.; and a center for Hellenic studies, also in Washington. The Harvard and Harvard Black Rock experimental forests are located in Massachusetts and New York. The Harvard-Smithsonian Center for Astrophysics in Cambridge is a joint enterprise of Harvard University and the Smithsonian Institution. It is a center for basic research in astronomy, astrophysics, and the space sciences.

History. Harvard College was founded at Newtowne on Oct. 28, 1636. In 1638, Newtowne was renamed Cambridge after Cambridge University in England, where

Harvard University

The Harvard College Yard, center of the original college, still keeps much of its Old World charm and dignity today. This picture comes from an engraving made in the 1770's by Paul Revere, the colonial patriot and silversmith. The small Holden Chapel, *left,* was built in 1744. The other four buildings, built in the Georgian Colonial style of architecture, are, *left to right,* Hollis Hall, Harvard Hall, Stoughton Hall, and Massachusetts Hall.

many of the colonists studied. The college opened in 1638. In 1639, it was named after John Harvard, a Puritan minister. Harvard left the college half his estate, including a collection of over 400 books, when he died in 1638. The first class graduated in 1642.

Harvard is the oldest collegiate foundation in North America. It still operates under a charter granted in 1650. A corporation of five fellows, together with the president and treasurer *ex officio,* manage the university. A board of 30 overseers, elected periodically by alumni, must approve the acts of the corporation.

Harvard's present educational system was shaped by Charles William Eliot, president of the school from 1869 to 1909. When Eliot came to Harvard, it was a small New England college. When he left, it was a national institution. Under Eliot's leadership, Harvard established the elective studies system, replacing the prescribed classical curriculum, and raised scholarly and professional standards in the graduate branches.

Abbott Lawrence Lowell, president of Harvard from 1909 to 1933, refined the elective system to include a tutorial system, specialized fields of study, and general examinations. Under James B. Conant, president from 1933 to 1953, Harvard reorganized professional training in the fields of engineering, architecture, and dental medicine. Conant developed the general education program for undergraduates.

Under Nathan M. Pusey, who served as president of the university from 1953 to 1971, Harvard placed strong emphasis on international and area studies. The university also strengthened its departments of divinity, education, humanities, social sciences, natural sciences, medicine, and public health.

Derek Bok became president in 1971. During his administration, the number of women students enrolled at Harvard increased greatly, and Harvard and Radcliffe merged their admissions and financial aid offices. In

1979, Harvard introduced a revised general education program for undergraduates. The new program, called the *core curriculum,* makes up about a fourth of each student's course work. Courses in the core curriculum teach students how to approach the study of the major areas of knowledge. For the enrollment of Harvard University, see **Universities and colleges** (table).

Critically reviewed by Harvard University

See also **Colonial life in America** (picture: The first college); **Conant, James B.; Eliot, Charles W.; Harvard, John; Radcliffe College.**

Harvest mite. See Chigger.

Harvest moon is the name given to the full moon that occurs nearest the autumnal equinox of the sun, about September 23. The moon rises at about the same time for several nights. It shines with such brightness that farmers in northern Europe and Canada can work until late at night to take in the fall harvest. In the Southern Hemisphere, the harvest moon occurs in March, at the vernal equinox.   C. R. O'Dell

Harvester. See Reaper; McCormick, Cyrus Hall.

Harvesting. See Farm and farming.

Harvestman. See Daddy longlegs.

Harvey, William (1578-1657), was an English physician who discovered how blood circulates in the human body. His discovery became an important foundation of medicine. Harvey's book, *An Anatomical Treatise on the Motion of the Heart and Blood in Animals,* appeared in 1628. It is considered the most important single volume in the history of physiology. Harvey showed that the heart, by repeated contractions, produces a continuous stream of blood that circulates throughout the body and continually returns to its source (see **Circulatory system; Heart**).

Although his theories were attacked by followers of the ancient Greek physician Galen, they were based on firsthand observation and experiment. Harvey lived to see his discovery widely accepted, although full credit for it came only after his death.

Harvey was born on April 1, 1578, in Folkestone, England. After graduation from Caius College, Cambridge, he studied medicine at the University of Padua in Italy. He returned to London in 1602 and practiced medicine. Harvey became a member of the Royal College of Physicians, and served as physician to James I and Charles I. In 1651, he published his second great work, *Exercitationes de Generatione,* considered the basis for modern embryology. This work deals with reproduction, particularly the part that the egg plays in fertilization.   Caroline A. Chandler

John Crerar Library
William Harvey

Hashish, *HASH eesh,* is a drug that affects the mind. It is obtained from the hemp plant. Hashish usually produces feelings of contentment and relaxation, but it may make a person sad, nervous, or worried. To a person who takes a strong dose of hashish, colors may appear extremely bright and flowing. Sound and music may seem alive and touchable. Near objects may appear distant, and minutes may seem like hours. In the United States, Canada, and many other countries, laws prohibit the possession, sale, or distribution of hashish, except for approved medical research.

Most hashish users smoke the drug in a pipe, but some mix it with food or drink. The drug is most powerful when smoked. The effects also depend on the size and purity of the dose, the mood of the user, and the circumstances in which it is used. Hashish loses strength if it has been stored for a long time. *Tetrahydrocannabinol* (THC), a chemical in hashish, affects the brain and nervous system. Large amounts of THC may produce *hallucinations,* during which the user sees or hears things that do not exist. A hashish user also may experience *delusions* (false beliefs about reality). In addition, THC decreases muscle coordination. The effects last for several hours.

Hashish does not lead to physical dependence, as do heroin, alcohol, and some other drugs. But some hashish users may become used to taking the drug and find it hard to stop. They may become more interested in taking hashish than in their work, family, or friends.

Hashish and marijuana both come from the hemp plant, but hashish contains from five to eight times as much THC as does marijuana (see **Marijuana**). Hashish is a sticky substance, called a *resin,* that is obtained from the top of the plant. Marijuana is made by drying the leaves and flowering stalks of the plant. Hemp grows in most parts of the world. But most hashish comes from the Near East and other parts of southern Asia, where it has been used for thousands of years.   Donald J. Wolk

See also **Assassination.**

Hasidism, *HAS ih dihz uhm,* is a movement in modern Judaism. Followers believe that God is everywhere and that divine light and power touch everything. Therefore, there is no cause for despair or unhappiness. They believe they can best serve God by expressing joy. Hasidism emphasizes joyous prayer. In their religious services, followers sing and dance a great deal. They also express their beliefs through storytelling. Hasidism is organized around spiritual leaders. Each leader heads a local center. Each has his own way of teaching and living and his own interpretation of the Hasidic tradition.

Baal Shem Tov, a Jewish teacher, and his followers founded Hasidism in Poland and Lithuania about 1760. The movement spread rapidly throughout eastern Europe. By the late 1700's, Hasidic settlements had been established in Palestine. Today, the most important Hasidic center is Habad Hasidism, located in the borough of Brooklyn in New York City.   Jacob Neusner

See also **Ba'al Shem Tov; Jews** (Changes in traditional beliefs).

Haskalah, *hah SKAW luh* or *HAH skuh LAH,* was a religious cultural movement that tried to modernize traditional Jewish beliefs and practices. *Haskalah* is the Hebrew word for *enlightenment.* The movement began among German and Polish Jews during the late 1700's and spread to other Jewish communities in Europe.

The Haskalah encouraged Jews to dress like non-Jews rather than in traditional Jewish clothing. It called for Jews to adopt the language of the country in which they lived instead of relying on Yiddish, a Jewish language. The Haskalah also urged Jews to enter such fields as agriculture, the arts, and science. The movement believed that Jews should seek a nonreligious education as well as a Jewish education. By following these goals, leaders of the movement hoped to draw Jews into the mainstream of western European culture.

The Haskalah greatly affected Jewish life. The movement revived a spirit of independent learning and creative activity among Jews. It was responsible for starting modern Hebrew literature and Jewish newspapers. In addition, the Haskalah helped develop a rational and critical approach to the study of Judaism and its holy books. Finally, many attitudes of the Haskalah were adopted by the Jewish nationalist movement known as Zionism and greatly influenced the founders of the state of Israel.   Jacob Neusner

Hassam, *HAS uhm,* **Childe** (1859-1935), was an American painter. His most important paintings show the influence of the French impressionist movement of the late 1800's. Like many French impressionists, Hassam used patchy brushstrokes to try to capture the effects of sunlight and atmospheric conditions, such as mist. But Hassam's pictures have more details, firmer outlines, more realistic colors, and a greater use of perspective than the works of the impressionists.

Frederick Childe Hassam was born in Dorchester, Mass. He met the French impressionists while studying painting in Paris in 1886. During the early 1900's, Hassam painted scenes of the New England seashore and countryside. Many of these pictures portray New England towns, with white churches outlined against dark pine trees and blue skies. Hassam also painted the fishing boats and surf of Gloucester, Mass.   Robert F. Reiff

Hassan II, *HAH sahn* (1929-   ), became king of Morocco in 1961. He succeeded his father, King Muhammad V. Under Hassan's leadership, Morocco expanded mining and other industries, irrigated desert land, and built hundreds of schools.

Hassan was born in Rabat. He wrote Morocco's first constitution, which was adopted in 1962. The constitution made the nation a constitutional monarchy governed by the king and a parliament. The parliament blocked Hassan's economic program, and, in 1965, he took full control of the government's lawmaking and executive powers. Another parliament was elected in 1970. Hassan took full control of the government again in 1972 after Moroccan military leaders tried to assassinate him, but another parliament was elected in 1977. In 1976, Spain gave up its control of Spanish Sahara, an area that borders Morocco on the south. Hassan claimed the area, now called Western Sahara, as Moroccan territory. But the Polisario Front, made up of people who live in Western Sahara, opposed him. Fighting broke out between Moroccan and Polisario Front forces. The fighting continued into the 1980's.   Keith G. Mather

See also **Morocco** (Constitutional monarchy).

Hastie, William Henry (1904-1976), was the first black to become a judge of the U.S. Circuit Court of Appeals. He was appointed in 1949 by President Harry S. Truman and served from 1950 until he retired in 1971. From 1937 to 1957, Hastie served on the board of directors of the National Association for the Advancement of Colored People (NAACP). He was dean of the Howard University School of Law from 1939 to 1946. From 1946 to 1949, he served as governor of the Virgin Islands. Hastie was awarded the Spingarn Medal in 1943. He was born in Knoxville, Tenn.   H. G. Reuschlein

Hastings, *HAY stihngz,* **Battle of** (October 1066), resulted in the conquest of England by William, Duke of Normandy. Historians rank it among the major battles that changed the course of history.

Harold Godwin became the king of England in 1066, after Edward the Confessor died. But William of Normandy claimed that Edward, his cousin, had promised him the English throne. Harold prepared to defend the coast against an attack, as William enlisted knights from Normandy and northern France. But the king of Norway suddenly invaded northern England to assert his claim to the throne. Harold took his best troops north on a forced march. His Anglo-Saxon forces soundly defeated the Norse.

During Harold's absence from the southern coast of England, William landed his army without opposition. Harold hastened south with his weary forces, and gathered such militiamen as he could from the southern shires. He met William's invading troops at the hill of Senlac, near the town of Hastings. Harold almost won a second major victory in three weeks in the day-long battle. His men held the top of the hill. Then the Normans pretended to retreat in disorder, causing the English militia on the flanks to rush down the hill in pursuit. The Norman knights split the English formation, cutting the separate elements of the enemy army to pieces. A Norman arrow killed Harold. But it took William five more years to complete the Norman conquest and end the last resistance to his rule.   Robert S. Hoyt

See also **Harold** (II); **William** (I, The Conqueror).

Hastings, *HAY stihngz,* **Warren** (1732-1818), was the first governor general of India. He extended British rule in India and improved the courts and tax systems. He also encouraged the study of Indian culture.

Hastings was born in Oxfordshire, England. In 1750,

he went to India as a clerk with the East India Company, a British trading company. In 1774, he was appointed governor general. He resigned in 1785 and returned to England. There, political enemies led by dramatist Richard Brinsley Sheridan and statesmen Edmund Burke and Charles James Fox accused him of betraying British ideals of justice and fair play. They impeached him on charges of corruption and misuse of power. After a trial that lasted from 1788 to 1795, Hastings was *acquitted* (declared innocent). But the trial used up all his money and he lived the rest of his life on a pension from the East India Company.   Brijen K. Gupta

Hat is the name of any of several kinds of coverings for the head. A hat consists of a *crown,* the part that fits on the head; and, in most cases, a circular *brim.* Hats differ from other head coverings, such as bonnets, caps, helmets, and hoods, most of which have a small brim or no brim at all. But the word *hat,* as used in this article, refers to such brimless headgear as well.

Hats vary widely in material and style, depending largely on the climate and people's customs. For example, a Soviet farmer wears a snug fur hat to protect himself from the cold. A South American cowboy wears a felt gaucho hat as part of his traditional costume, and the American cowboy wears a wide-brimmed hat for protection from the sun. The members of each branch of a nation's armed services wear a different type of hat as part of their uniform. People also wear hats as an accessory to their clothing. As a result, fashion often determines the styles of hats.

Throughout the centuries, the desire of people to be fashionable has resulted in many kinds of unusual hats. During the 1400's, many European women wore a tall, cone-shaped hat called a *hennin.* This hat measured from 3 to 4 feet (0.9 to 1.2 meters) high and had a long, floating veil. The *Gainsborough hat* became popular with both men and women in the late 1700's. It had a wide brim and was decorated with feathers and ribbons.

Why people wear hats. People wear hats for (1) protection, (2) communication, and (3) decoration.

People first began to wear hats to protect themselves from the climate. In hot, sunny climates, wide-brimmed hats provide shade from the sun. Many Mexicans wear such hats, called *sombreros,* which are made of felt or straw. In cold climates, people often wear fur or wool hats. The Lapps of far northern Europe wear tight-fitting wool hats that have earflaps. In some regions, people wear a variety of protective hats, depending on the season. They may wear a fur hat in winter, a rain hat in spring or fall, and a wide-brimmed hat in summer. Hats also provide protection. For example, construction workers, football players, and military personnel wear metal or plastic helmets for protection from injury.

Hats can communicate various things about the people who wear them. The hats of coal miners, fire fighters, and matadors indicate the wearer's occupation. Students may wear a *mortarboard*—a stiff, flat hat with a tassel—to show they are graduating from high school or college. Many clowns wear colorful, ridiculous hats to express fun and happiness. Among members of the religious group known as the *Amish,* the width of the hat brim and the height of the crown can communicate whether the wearer is married.

Most people wear a hat that they believe makes them

look attractive, though the hat's main purpose may be protection or communication. Much protective headgear, such as fur hoods and rain hats, is both attractive and stylish. Even the caps of police officers and military personnel are designed to improve the wearer's appearance. Certain decorative hats are worn in some countries as a tradition. In Scotland, for example, people wear a cap called a *tam-o'-shanter* that is part of their national costume.

History. No one knows when people first wore hats. The first coverings for the head were probably worn for protection from the climate. People in cold climates may have worn fur hoods 100,000 years ago.

Through the centuries, people also wore hats to indicate social status. In ancient Egypt, the nobility wore crowns as early as 3100 B.C. The ancient Greeks and Romans also wore hats to designate status. Some ancient Greeks wore hats called *pelos,* which were usually made from wool fibers. Pelos can still be found in parts of southern Siberia today. They are similar to the brimless, tasseled hat known as a *fez* (see **Fez**).

By the A.D. 1300's, people wore hats increasingly for

Some kinds of hats worn today People wear hats for several reasons. Hats may be worn for protection from the climate or from injury. People also wear hats that communicate information about their occupation. Some hats are worn for decoration. The reasons for wearing hats cause much variety in hat styles.

Hats worn for protection

Robert W. Young, DPI

Farmers in Indonesia

Paul Robert Perry

Construction worker in the U.S.

Howard Sochurek, Woodfin Camp Inc.

Herdsman in Siberia

Hats worn for communication

H. Taylor, De Wys, Inc.

Bishops in Greece

George Nelson, Artstreet

Bullfighter in Mexico

Paul Robert Perry

Policewoman in the United States

Hats worn for decoration

Woodfin Camp Inc.

Woman in Africa

SHE/Mike Laye, Camera Press

British woman

Werner Stoy, DPI

Girls in Taiwan

decoration, resulting in the development of a large variety of hats and frequent changes in styles. People in one area often adopted the hat styles worn in another. During the 1300's and 1400's, for example, women in western Europe wore a type of hat that resembled a turban. They adopted this style from the headgear worn by people who lived in the Middle East and the Orient.

Zadoc Benedict, a craftworker, established the first hat factory in the United States in 1780 in Danbury, Conn. In 1851, John Nicholas Genin, a New York City manufacturer, made the first soft felt hats for women.

During the 1900's, hat styles varied more widely than ever before. In the 1920's, women wore a drooping, bell-shaped hat called the *cloche*. In the 1930's, they wore the *harlequin hat,* which had a wide, upturned brim. A variety of hats were worn in the 1940's and

1950's. Since the 1960's, hats have been less popular among both women and men.   Lois M. Gurel

See also **Clothing** (Traditional costumes); **Derby; Fez; Helmet; Stetson, John B.**

Hatch Political Activities Act is a law that limits the political activities of United States government employees. The act, passed by Congress in 1939, was named for its sponsor, Senator Carl Hatch of New Mexico. It prohibits most federal employees from taking an active part in political campaigns. It also prohibits the promise of employment, payment, or other benefits for any political activities or support in any election. A 1940 amendment extended these provisions to include most state and local employees in federally funded projects. It also limits campaign contributions by individuals.

The Federal Election Campaign Act of 1971 removed

Some hats of the past   Hat styles have varied widely throughout history for several reasons, including changes in fashion and the use of different materials in making headwear. Most hats of the past have gone out of style. But varieties of some hats, such as the beret and the turban, are still worn.

WORLD BOOK illustrations by Anthony Saris

Greek Petasos
About 400 B.C.

German Headdress
and Cap
About A.D. 1200

Persian Turban
About 1400

European Hennin
1400's

European Beret
About 1500

European Cavalier Hat
1600's

European Tricorne Hat
1700's

English
Gainsborough Hat
Late 1700's

American Top Hat
1800's

American Poke Bonnet
1800's

French Cloche Hat
1920's

overall ceilings on campaign contributions. This act expanded the Hatch Act to prohibit any special favors offered in return for political support. It also applied conditions of the Hatch Act to caucuses and conventions and to primary, general, and special elections. In 1972, a U.S. district court held that the Hatch Act was too vague and too broad and that it violated the First Amendment. But in 1973, the Supreme Court of the United States upheld the constitutionality of the act. The Federal Election Campaign Act of 1974 repealed parts of the Hatch Act that barred state employees from participating in party politics.   Kenneth Janda

Hatcher, Richard Gordon (1933-   ), became one of the first blacks to win election as mayor of a major United States city. Hatcher, a Democrat, was first elected mayor of Gary, Ind., in 1967. He served as mayor until 1987, when he was defeated in a bid for reelection.

Hatcher was born in Michigan City, Ind. He worked his way through college and graduated from Indiana University and the Valparaiso University School of Law. In 1959, Hatcher moved to Gary and began practicing law in

John Mitchell, *Gary Post-Tribune*
Richard Hatcher

nearby East Chicago, Ind. He worked for civil rights causes in Gary and helped found Muigwithania, a local black political organization. From 1961 to 1963, Hatcher served as a deputy prosecutor for Lake County, Indiana. He was elected to the Gary city council in 1963.

Hatcher ran for mayor of Gary in 1967 in spite of opposition from local Democratic Party leaders. He waged an uphill fight to win the Democratic primary election and then won an unexpected victory in the general mayoral election. Blacks cast most of the votes that Hatcher received, but many white voters also supported him. Hatcher won reelection in 1971, 1975, 1979, and 1983.
          Charles V. Hamilton

Hathaway, Anne. See Shakespeare, William (Marriage).

Hathor, *HATH awr,* sometimes called Athor, was the ancient Egyptian goddess of heaven. She was also goddess of joy, music, and love. She helped at childbirth and protected children. Sometimes she was described as *The Lady of Terror,* who destroyed the enemies of the Sun God. Hathor was often represented as a cow. See also **Mythology** (Egyptian [picture]).   I. J. Gelb

Hatshepsut. See Egypt, Ancient (The New Kingdom).

Hatteras, Cape. See Cape Hatteras.

Hauptmann, *HOWPT mahn,* **Gerhart,** *GAYR hahrt* (1862-1946), a German author, won the Nobel Prize for literature in 1912. His plays are outstanding examples of naturalistic literature. They portray human beings as suffering creatures who act according to their basic drives.

Hauptmann was born in Silesia, a former province in eastern Germany. He first gained fame for his plays *Before Sunrise* (1889) and *The Weavers* (1892). *The Weavers,* perhaps his most famous play, describes the plight and revolt of exploited workers in Silesia. Hauptmann

used naturalistic language even in his comedies *The Beaver Coat* (1893) and *The Rats* (1910). His other works include the poem *The Assumption of Hannele* (1894), mythological and historical plays, and prose works. His best prose works include *Flagman Thiel* (1888) and *Till Eulenspiegel* (1928).   Walther L. Hahn

Hausa, *HOW sah,* are a black people of West Africa. The approximately 7 million Hausa make up an important cultural and political group in northern Nigeria and southern Niger. Most of them are Muslims.

The first Hausa settlements were probably built during the 1000's or 1100's. By the 1300's, many Hausa city-states had developed, including Kano, Katsina, Sokoto, and Zaria (see **Nigeria** [political map]). These city-states

Edward S. Ross
The Hausa have lived in West Africa for more than a thousand years. Most of them live in Niger or Nigeria.

became important trade centers.

The Songhai Empire controlled the Hausa states throughout much of the 1500's (see **Songhai Empire**). The states then became independent again and, during the 1600's and 1700's, engaged heavily in gold and slave trading. In the early 1800's, local Fulani people who were Muslims led a revolt against the traditional leaders of the city-states. The Fulani and Muslim Hausa rebels, conquered many of the city-states and established a Hausa-Fulani empire (see **Fulani**). The British colonized Nigeria in the late 1800's, but the Hausa-Fulani areas remained largely self-governing. Nigeria gained independence in 1960, and the Hausa have since played a major role in Nigerian politics.   Leo Spitzer

See also **Niger** (People; picture); **Nigeria** (Population and ancestry; Early kingdoms).

Havana, *huh VAN uh* (pop. 1,924,886), is the capital, chief port, and largest city of Cuba. It lies on the island's northwest coast, about 100 miles (160 kilometers) south of Key West, Fla. For location, see **Cuba** (political map). About 20 per cent of Cuba's people live in Havana. Havana's name in Spanish, the language of Cuba, is *La Habana.*

During the first half of the 1900's, Havana was a popular vacation center. Its lively night life and magnificent beaches attracted many tourists, especially from the United States. But tourism declined after Fidel Castro became prime minister in 1959. He soon made the country a socialist state, and Cuba's relations with the United

© John Dominis, Wheeler Pictures

Havana is the commercial and industrial center of Cuba. The city lies on a natural harbor on the country's northwest coast. Downtown Havana, *above,* has many modern office buildings.

States became strained. In 1961, the United States broke diplomatic relations with Cuba. The United States government severely restricted travel to the country by American citizens, and the number of visitors to Havana dropped sharply. In 1977, the U.S. government ended its restrictions on travel to Cuba. Americans began visiting Havana again, but tourism in the city remains far below its earlier level.

The city of Havana covers about 286 square miles (740 square kilometers). Spanish colonists built Havana in 1519 next to a large natural harbor. Morro Castle, a Spanish fort dating from the late 1500's, guards the entrance to the harbor.

Old Havana, the colonial part of the city, lies west of the harbor. Tile-roofed houses, built during the 1500's and 1600's, line the narrow streets. This historic area also includes the famous Havana Cathedral, built in the early 1700's, and the Spanish governor's palace. The former Capitol and many government buildings are located in downtown Havana, west of the old city.

Newer residential areas and suburbs lie west of downtown Havana. The Malecón, a beautiful boulevard, runs along the coast and connects the western residential districts with downtown Havana.

Education and cultural life. The government controls Havana's schools, and education is free. Many adults attend night school and job-training classes. The University of Havana has about 54,000 students.

Havana's cultural attractions include the government-sponsored National Ballet and the Havana Symphony. Museums include the Museum of Fine Arts, which features classical and modern art. The Museum of the Revolution, the Colonial Museum, and the Municipal Museum are historical museums.

Economy. Havana is the commercial and industrial center of Cuba. The government owns all the nation's businesses and industries. Most of Havana's workers are employed by government agencies or small factories.

Havana's most important manufacturing activity is the processing of tobacco. Other industries produce beer, chemicals, food products, shoes, and textiles.

About a fifth of Cuba's exports and over half its imports pass through Havana. Exports include canned fruits, fish, and sugar and tobacco products. The main imports include food, machinery, petroleum, and motor vehicles. Cuba trades mostly with Communist countries, but has steadily increased trade with other nations.

An international airport serves Havana. Buses provide most of the transportation within the city.

Government. A Municipal Committee governs Havana. Local workers' groups, made up of members of the Cuban Communist Party, elect committee members.

History. Diego Velázquez, the first Spanish governor of Cuba, founded Havana on the island's south coast in 1515. But the city failed to flourish, probably because of pirate attacks, and was rebuilt on its present site in 1519. Havana's location and its harbor attracted many trading ships. The city soon developed into an important commercial center. Havana became the capital of Cuba in 1552. By 1600, 4,000 persons lived there.

British troops captured the city in 1762 and held it for nearly a year. The British occupation opened up trade between Havana and the British colonies of North America. The increased trade helped the city's population grow to more than 50,000 by the late 1700's.

In 1898, the United States battleship *Maine* exploded mysteriously in Havana harbor. This event helped bring about the Spanish-American War.

During the first half of the 1900's, the Cuban government spent much money to make Havana a resort center. American companies invested heavily in Havana businesses. Thousands of visitors from the U.S. and other countries poured into Havana. In spite of Havana's prosperity, many of its people lived in poverty.

Since Castro became prime minister, the Cuban government has invested much of its economic resources in the development of the rural areas rather than Havana and other large cities. As a result, Havana has several serious problems. One of the city's most critical problems is a housing shortage. During the 1960's, the government nationalized many hotels and seized the mansions of people who left Cuba, and converted these dwellings into public housing. The government has also built some new housing.   Ivan A. Schulman

See also **Cuba; Spanish-American War.**

Haversian canals form a network of channels through compact bone tissue, the hard, outer layers of bone. Each canal contains blood vessels and *lymph* (tissue fluid) vessels, connective tissue, and nerves. The blood vessels carry nourishment from vessels in the *periosteum* (membrane covering the bone) to the spongy inner bone tissue. Layers of tissue called *osteons,* or *Haversian systems,* surround Haversian canals. The canals and osteons make up the structure of compact bone. Haversian canals are named for their discoverer, Clopton Havers (1650-1702) of England.

Marshall R. Urist

Haw. See Hawthorn.

Camera Hawaii

Hawaii's tropical splendor includes colorful plant life and beautiful beaches along the Pacific Ocean. Diamond Head, *above,* an extinct volcano, is a famous Hawaiian landmark. It lies on the island of Oahu, the most thickly populated of the eight main Hawaiian islands.

Hawaii   *The Aloha State*

Hawaii, *huh WY ee* or *huh WAH ee,* is the only state in the United States that does not lie on the mainland of North America. It is made up of islands near the middle of the North Pacific Ocean. Honolulu, the capital and largest city, is about 2,400 miles (3,860 kilometers) southwest of the U.S. mainland. Hawaii is also the southernmost state. Oahu, the island on which Honolulu is located, is as far south as central Mexico. Hawaii, the youngest state, joined the Union on Aug. 21, 1959.

Hawaii is world famous for its beauty and pleasant climate. It has deep-blue seas, brilliantly colored flowers, graceful palm trees, and magnificent waterfalls. These attractions provide some of the most thrilling scenery in the United States. Cool Pacific winds keep Hawaii pleasantly mild all year around.

Hawaii has many colorful ways of life. Some of these customs come from Pacific Islanders called *Polynesians,*

who were the original settlers of Hawaii. Many of the people of Hawaii are of Polynesian descent. The people's great friendliness toward tourists gives Hawaii its nickname of the *Aloha State. Aloha* means *love* in the Hawaiian language.

When vacationers arrive in Hawaii, they often receive *leis* (wreaths of flowers strung together). The visitors enjoy feasts, folk dancing, parades, and many special events. The hula has become a symbol of Hawaii. Hula dancers sway their hips and move their arms and hands to the music of Hawaiian guitars and other instruments.

The state has many nationality and racial groups. In addition to the people of Polynesian descent and whites and blacks from the mainland, Hawaii's population includes many citizens of Japanese, Filipino, Chinese, Korean, and Samoan ancestry. All these people have contributed customs to a colorful life.

Hawaii consists of a chain of 132 islands. The chain extends for 1,523 miles (2,451 kilometers). The eight main islands are at the southeastern end of the chain. Almost all the people of Hawaii live on seven of these eight islands. About 80 of every 100 people live on Oahu.

The contributors of this article are Pauline N. King, Associate Professor of History, and Lyndon Wester, Associate Professor of Geography, both at the University of Hawaii.

Camera Hawaii

The streets of downtown Honolulu are lined with palm trees and modern office buildings. Honolulu, which lies on the island of Oahu, is Hawaii's capital and largest city.

The state's location in the Pacific Ocean gives it a major role in U.S. military planning. The U.S. Army, Navy, Air Force, and Marine Corps units in the Pacific area are under a single command located in Hawaii. The salaries of military personnel and civilian employees at these bases provide an important source of income in Hawaii. Food processing is Hawaii's leading manufacturing activity. Hawaii is one of the world's leading producers of pineapples.

Most of the world did not know of the islands until 1778. Captain James Cook of the British Navy reached them that year. Local chiefs ruled the islands until about 1800, when the area was united under a Hawaiian king. The islands became a republic in 1894. Hawaii became a U.S. possession in 1898, and a U.S. territory in 1900. It is the only state that was once an independent monarchy. Hawaii was the first part of U.S. territory to be attacked in World War II. On Dec. 7, 1941, planes of the Japanese navy bombed the naval base at Pearl Harbor and other military installations.

For the relationship of Hawaii to other Pacific Island groups, see the article on the **Pacific Islands.**

Interesting facts about Hawaii

WORLD BOOK illustrations by Kevin Chadwick

Haleakala Crater

Haleakala is the world's largest inactive volcanic crater. The crater, which lies on the island of Maui, measures about 20 miles (32 kilometers) around and is about 3,000 feet (914 meters) deep.

The southernmost point of the United States is Ka Lea— which means *South Point*—on the island of Hawaii.

Hawaiian alphabet

The Hawaiian alphabet has only 12 letters—*a, e, h, i, k, l, m, n, o, p, u,* and *w.*

Hawaii was an independent monarchy. Polynesian monarchs ruled the islands from about 1800 to 1894 when they became a republic. No other U.S. state ever had this form of government.

The wettest place on earth is Mount Waialeale, on the island of Kauai. The average annual rainfall on the mountain is 460 inches (1,168 centimeters).

Camera Hawaii

Volcanoes formed the Hawaiian islands. Many of the volcanoes are no longer active. But Hawaii, the largest Hawaiian island, has active volcanoes, including Kilauea, *above.*

Hawaii in brief

Symbols of Hawaii

Both the state flag and the state seal were adopted in 1959. The flag has eight stripes of alternating red, white, and blue that represent the eight major islands of Hawaii. The state seal bears, in Hawaiian, the state motto, which translates: "The life of the land is perpetuated in righteousness." The state coat of arms is in the center, with a figure of King Kamehameha I to the left and the Goddess of Liberty to the right.

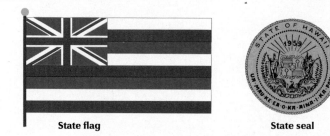

State flag

State seal

Hawaii ranks 47th in size among the 50 states.

The State Capitol has been in Honolulu since Hawaii became a state in 1959.

General information

Statehood: Aug. 21, 1959, the 50th state.
State abbreviation: HI (postal).
State motto: *Ua mau ke ea o ka aina i ka pono* (The Life of the Land Is Perpetuated in Righteousness).
State song: "Hawaii Ponoi" ("Hawaii's Own"), words by Kalakaua; music by Henry Berger.

Land and climate

Area: 6,471 sq. mi. (16,759 km²) including 46 sq. mi. (118 km²) of inland water.
Elevation: *Highest*—Mauna Kea, 13,796 ft. (4,205 m) above sea level. *Lowest*—sea level along coast.
Coastline: 750 mi. (1,207 km).
Record high temperature: 100° F. (38° C) at Pahala on April 27, 1931.
Record low temperature: 14° F. (−10° C) at Haleakala Crater on Jan. 2, 1961.
Average July temperature: 75° F. (24° C).
Average January temperature: 68° F. (20° C).
Average yearly precipitation: 110 in. (279 cm).

Greatest east-west distance 350 mi.(565 km)

Greatest north-south distance 230 mi. (370 km)

Lowest elevation along coasts

Highest elevation

Important dates

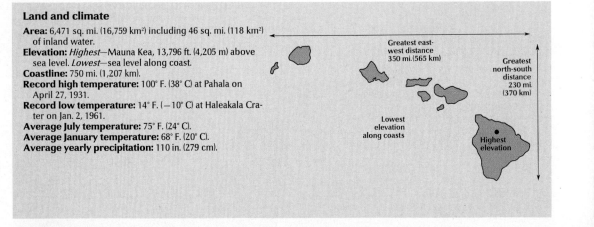

1778

Captain James Cook of the British navy reached Hawaii.

The first permanent sugar plantation in Hawaii was started on Kauai Island.

1835

c. 1885

The pineapple industry began with the importation of Jamaican pineapple plants.

State bird
Nene (Hawaiian goose)

State flower
Hibiscus

State tree
Kukui

People

Population: 964,691 (1980 census)
Rank among the states: 39th
Density: 149 persons per sq. mi. (58 per km²), U.S. average 67 per sq. mi. (26 per km²)
Distribution: 87 per cent urban, 13 per cent rural

Largest cities in Hawaii

Honolulu	365,048
Pearl City	42,575
Kailua*	35,812
Hilo*	35,269
Aiea*	32,879
Kaneohe*	29,919

*Unincorporated place.
Source: U.S. Bureau of the Census.

Population trend

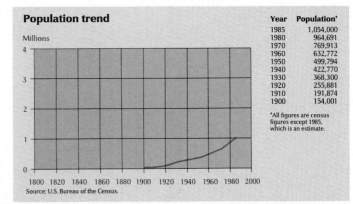

Millions

Source: U.S. Bureau of the Census.

Year	Population*
1985	1,054,000
1980	964,691
1970	769,913
1960	632,772
1950	499,794
1940	422,770
1930	368,300
1920	255,881
1910	191,874
1900	154,001

*All figures are census figures except 1985, which is an estimate.

Economy

Chief products

Agriculture: sugar cane, pineapples, beef cattle.
Fishing industry: tuna, snapper.
Manufacturing: food products, printed materials, clothing, transportation equipment, chemicals, fabricated metal products.
Mining: stone, sand and gravel.

Gross state product

Value of goods and services produced in 1985: $17,079,000,000. *Services* include community, business, and personal services; finance; government; trade; and transportation, communication, and utilities. *Industry* includes construction, manufacturing, and mining. *Agriculture* includes agriculture, fishing, and forestry.

Sources: U.S. Department of Agriculture and U.S. Department of Commerce.

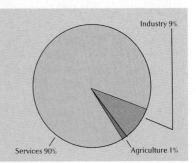

Industry 9%

Services 90%

Agriculture 1%

Government

State government

Governor: 4-year term
State senators: 25; 4-year terms
State representatives: 51; 2-year terms
Counties: 5

Federal government

United States senators: 2
United States representatives: 2
Electoral votes: 4

Sources of information

Tourism: Hawaii Visitors Bureau, P.O. Box 8527, Honolulu, HI 96815
Economy: Hawaii Department of Planning and Economic Development, P.O. Box 2359, Honolulu, HI 96804
Government: Hawaii Department of Planning and Economic Development, P.O. Box 2359, Honolulu, HI 96804
History: Hawaii State Library, Hawaii and Pacific Room, 478 South King Street, Honolulu, HI 96813

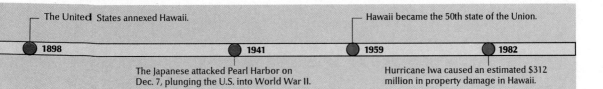

The United States annexed Hawaii.

Hawaii became the 50th state of the Union.

1898   **1941**   **1959**   **1982**

The Japanese attacked Pearl Harbor on Dec. 7, plunging the U.S. into World War II.

Hurricane Iwa caused an estimated $312 million in property damage in Hawaii.

Population. The 1980 United States census reported that Hawaii had 964,691 people. The population had increased 25 per cent over the 1970 figure, 769,913. The U.S. Bureau of the Census estimated that by 1985 the state's population had reached about 1,054,000.

More than four-fifths of the people live in urban areas. The Honolulu area is Hawaii's only metropolitan area (see **Metropolitan area**). This area, which consists of the entire island of Oahu, has a population of 762,565. Officially, Honolulu covers all of Oahu. But only the large urban area on the island's southeastern coast is commonly called Honolulu. This urban area has a population of 365,048. Pearl City, which is part of the Honolulu metropolitan area, has a population of 42,575 and is the state's second largest urban area. Hilo, on the island of Hawaii, is the state's largest urban area outside the Honolulu metropolitan area. It has a population of 35,269. Seventeen other urban areas on Oahu and four on the island of Maui have populations over 5,000. See **Hilo; Honolulu.**

Honolulu resembles large seaport cities in other parts of the United States. The other urban areas of Hawaii

Artstreet

Modern housing developments, such as the one near Honolulu pictured here, reflect the widespread urban growth in Hawaii. More than four-fifths of the state's people live in urban areas.

Population density

Hawaii consists of a chain of 132 islands in the Pacific Ocean. However, nearly all the state's people live on seven islands at the southeastern end of the chain—those shown below, excepting Kaula and Kahoolawe. About 80 per cent of the people live on the island of Oahu.

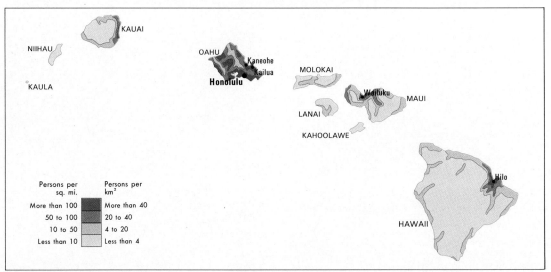

Persons per sq. mi.	Persons per km²
More than 100	More than 40
50 to 100	20 to 40
10 to 50	4 to 20
Less than 10	Less than 4

WORLD BOOK map; based on U.S. Bureau of the Census data.

Water sports are a favorite outdoor activity in Hawaii. The people shown on the left are preparing for the start of a canoe race. Other popular water sports on the islands include sailing, scuba diving, and surfing.

Camera Hawaii

serve as trade centers for sugar and pineapple plantations, or as ports for shipping farm products.

The people of Hawaii are proud that their state is a community of people with many different backgrounds. Many persons are mixtures of several nationalities and races. The descendants of the Polynesians who first settled in the Hawaiian Islands are called *Hawaiians*. They have bronze-colored skin, large dark eyes, and dark brown or black hair. Only about 15 per cent of the people are of chiefly Hawaiian ancestry. Nearly 50 per cent are of European ancestry, and about 25 per cent are of Japanese ancestry. Other groups include Filipinos, Chinese, Koreans, and Samoans.

People of almost every religious group live in Hawaii. Roman Catholics form the state's largest religious group, followed by Shintoist and Buddhist denominations and Mormons. The early Hawaiians practiced a religion that included numerous gods and centered around the worship of various aspects of nature. American and French missionaries converted most of the Hawaiians to Christianity during the 1820's and 1830's.

Language. Almost all the people of Hawaii speak English. But they frequently use some musical words of the Hawaiian language in their speech. For example, they often refer to a tourist as a *malihini* (newcomer). The Hawaiian alphabet has only 12 letters: A E H I K L M N O P U W. Every Hawaiian word and syllable ends with a vowel. Two consonants never occur without a vowel between them. The accent of most words falls on the next to last syllable.

Some frequently used words in the Hawaiian language include:

ae, *eye,* yes
ai, *AH ee,* eat
akamai, *ah kah MAH ee* or *ah kah MY,* wise; clever
ala, *AH lah,* path; road
aloha, *ah LOH hah,* love; greetings; welcome; farewell
aole, *ah OH lay,* no
hale, *HAH lay,* house
hana, *HAH nah,* work
haole, *HOW lay,* foreigner,

especially of Anglo-Saxon ancestry; applied generally to Caucasians
heiau, *HAY ow,* pre-Christian place of worship
hele mai, *HAY lay MY,* come here
hiamoe, *HEE ah MOY,* sleep
hoomalimali, *HO oh MAH lee MAH lee,* flattery
huhu, *hoo HOO,* angry
hula, *HOO lah,* dance

kai, *KAH ee,* the sea
kamaaina, *KAH mah EYE nah,* "child of the land"; old-timer; people long resident in Hawaii
kane, *KAH neh,* man
kapu, *KAH poo,* forbidden
kaukau, *KOW kow,* food
keiki, *KAY kee,* child
ko, *koh,* sugar cane
kokua, *koh KOO uh,* help; cooperation
lani, *LAH nee,* sky; heavenly
lei, *lay,* wreath or garland
luau, *LOO ow,* a feast
mahalo, *mah HAH loh,* thanks
mahimahi, *MAH hee MAH hee,* a delicious fish

maikai, *MY kah ee,* good; handsome; useful
makai, *MAH kah ee* or *mah KY,* at or toward the sea
malihini, *MAH lee HEE nee,* newcomer
manu, *MAH noo,* bird
mauka, *MAH oo kah* or *MOW kuh,* toward the mountains
mauna, *MOW nah,* mountain
mele, *MEH lay* or *MEHL eh,* song; chant
moana, *moh AH nah,* ocean
moopuna, *moh oh POO nah,* grandchild
nani, *NAH nee,* beautiful
nui, *NOO ee,* great; large
oe, *OH ee,* you

Camera Hawaii

A Buddhist monk sits in front of an altar in a Buddhist temple in Honolulu. Many Hawaiians of Asian ancestry are Buddhists who carry on their traditional ways of worship.

ohana, *oh HAH nah,* family
pali, *PAH lee,* cliff
pau, *POW,* finished; done
pehea oe, *pay HAY ah OY,* How are you?
pilikia, *PEE lee KEE ah,* trouble
poi, *POH ee* or *poy,* a food made of taro

pua, *POO ah,* flower
puka, *POO kah,* hole
punee, *POO nay ay,* couch
pupule, *poo POO lay,* crazy
wahine, *wah HEE nay,* woman
wai, *WAH ee,* fresh water
wikiwiki, *WEE kee WEE kee,* to hurry

Clothing. The people of Hawaii wear a great deal of loose, brightly colored clothing. Some of their garments are based on the clothing worn by early Hawaiians. Many Hawaiian fashions spread throughout the United States. For example, the Hawaiian *muumuu* became fashionable during the 1950's. A muumuu is a loose, floor-length dress that was introduced in Hawaii by early missionaries. The missionaries objected to the short skirts that were the only clothing worn by Hawaiian women. The *holomuu* is a fitted version of the muumuu. On formal occasions, women in Hawaii sometimes wear the *holoku,* a holomuu with a train. Another Hawaiian fashion that has become widespread is the *aloha shirt,* a sport shirt with brightly colored tropical or oriental designs.

The islanders often wear *leis* on festive occasions. A lei is a wreath, usually made of flowers strung together. Some leis are made by stringing together coral, feathers, nuts, seeds, shells, or pieces of ivory. People usually wear leis as necklaces, but sometimes wrap them around their heads or wear them as hatbands. Favorite flowers for leis include carnations, jasmine, orchids, plumeria (frangipani), tuberoses, and white and yellow ginger.

Food. Rice and fresh fruits such as bananas and papayas are basic parts of the islanders' diet. The people enjoy foods from many parts of the world. Restaurants and supermarkets offer many foods eaten by people of various countries. In addition to typical American food, Oriental and European foods are popular.

Some people in Hawaii eat *poi,* a starchy food made by pounding the cooked underground stem of the taro plant until it becomes a paste. Islanders also enjoy *laulau,* a package of spinachlike chopped taro leaf, fish, pork, and sometimes chicken, wrapped in ti plant leaves and steamed.

A *luau* (feast) is a popular tourist attraction. It features *kalua pig*—a whole young pig wrapped in leaves and roasted in a pit called an *imu.* Luaus also feature dancing and singing.

Dancing and music. Dancing is the most famous art of the islands. *Hula* means *dance* in Hawaiian. Hula dancers sway their hips and wave their arms gracefully to the rhythm of the music. The dances tell stories and describe the beautiful scenery of the islands. Hawaiians perform other traditional dances accompanied by chants and drums.

Hawaiian music features the ukulele and the Hawaiian steel guitar. The ukulele was developed from a small guitar brought to the islands by Portuguese laborers in the late 1800's. The word *ukulele* means *leaping flea.* The Hawaiian steel guitar was invented by Joseph Kekuku, a Hawaiian musician, about 1895.

Schools. American missionaries set up Hawaii's educational system in the 1820's. The Hawaiians had no writ-

Artstreet

Public elementary schools in Hawaii are attended by children aged 6 to 18. The state board of education runs the schools.

ten language before the missionaries came. In 1840, King Kamehameha III established the public school system of Hawaii.

Today, a 13-member state board of education controls the public school system. The voters elect the board members to four-year terms. The board members select a superintendent of education to administer the system. Hawaii is the only state in which local school boards do not control the public schools. The children of Hawaii must attend school between the ages of 6 and 18. For the number of students and teacherers in Hawaii, see **Education** (table). Hawaii has five universities and colleges accredited by the Western Association of Schools and Colleges.

Libraries. The Library of Hawaii (now the Hawaii State Library) in Honolulu was the first free public library on the islands. It opened in 1913. Today, a statewide public library system serves the islands of Hawaii, Kauai, Lanai, Maui, Molokai, and Oahu.

The Hamilton Library of the University of Hawaii

James P. Rowan

Polynesian dancers perform at festivals and other events in Hawaii. Polynesians were the original settlers of the islands.

Honfed and Bishop Museum from Camera Hawaii

The Bernice P. Bishop Museum, in Honolulu, Hawaii's oldest museum, is a major center for the study of the Pacific islands.

has fine collections of books on the Pacific area and Asia. Important collections of books on Hawaii are also in the Bishop Museum, the Hawaiian Historical Society Library, and the Hawaii State Library.

Museums. The Bernice P. Bishop Museum in Honolulu, which opened in 1889, is the oldest museum in Hawaii. Scholars at the Bishop Museum do research on the Pacific islands, mainly in anthropology, archaeology, botany, entomology, and zoology. The Bishop Museum has many collections and exhibits. Its displays include animals, archaeological discoveries, fish, plants, and shells from many Pacific islands. The Honolulu Academy of Arts has excellent exhibits of Western and Oriental art. The Mission Houses Museum in Honolulu includes the oldest house in Hawaii, built in 1821. Other museums include the Kauai Museum in Lihue, the Lyman House Memorial Museum in Hilo, and the Baldwin Home Missionary Museum in Lahaina.

Universities and colleges

Hawaii has five universities and colleges accredited by the Western Association of Schools and Colleges. Locations shown below refer to the schools' mailing addresses, and some schools may lie outside the listed community. For enrollments and further information, see **Universities and colleges** (table).

Name	Location
Brigham Young University— Hawaii Campus	Laie, Oahu
Chaminade University of Honolulu	Honolulu
Hawaii, University of	*
Hawaii Loa College	Kaneohe, Oahu
Hawaii Pacific College	Honolulu

*For campuses and founding dates, see **Universities and colleges** (table).

Camera Hawaii

The University of Hawaii at Manoa, in Honolulu, excels in the fields of marine biology, Pacific and Asian studies, and tropical agriculture. It is also noted for its courses in geophysics.

Hawaii map index

Metropolitan area

Honolulu 762,565

Counties

Hawaii ....92,053..J 13
Honolulu ....762,565..I 4
Kalawao ....144..F 10
Kauai ....39,082..D 4
Maui ....70,847..F 10

Islands

Hawaii ....92,053..J 13
Kahoolawe .... (no pop.)..G 10
Kauai ....38,856..D 4
Lanai ....2,119..G 9
Maui ....62,823..G 10
Molokai ....6,049..F 10
Niihau ....226..D 3
Oahu
(including outlying
islands) ....762,565..G 4

Cities, towns, and villages

Ahuimanu* ....6,238..F 8
Aiea ....32,879..I 5
Anahola ....915..D 5
Barbers Point
Housing ....1,373..J 3
Captain Cook ....2,008..J 12
Eleele ....580..D 4
Ewa ....2,637..J 3
Ewa Beach ......14,369..J 4
Haiku ....619..F 11
Haina ....H 13
Hakalau ....249..I 13
Haleiwa ....2,412..G 3
Haliimaile ....741..G 11

°County seat.
*Does not appear on map; key shows general location.

Hana ....643..G 12
Hanalei ....483..D 4
Hanamaulu ....3,227..D 4
Hanapepe ....1,417..D 4
Hauula ....2,997..G 5
Hawaii Kai ....J 7
Hawi ....795..H 12
Heeia* ....5,432..E ,8
Hickam
Housing ....4,425..J 4
Hilea ....J 13
Hilo ....35,269.°I 14
Holualoa ....1,243..I 12
Honaunau ....J 12
Honokaa ....1,936..H 13
Honokahua ....309..F 10
Honokowai, see
Napili-Honokowai .....F 10
Honolulu ...365,048.°F 8
Honomu ....559..I 13
Honouliuli ....F 4
Hoolehua ....F 9
Iroquois Point .....3,915..J 4
Kaaawa ....959..H 5
Kaanapali* ....541..G 10
Kahakuloa ....F 10
Kahaluu ....2,925..I 6
Kahana ....H 5
Kahana ....F 10
Kahua ....H 12
Kahuku ....935..E 7
Kahului ....12,978..F 11
Kailua ....4,751..I 12
Kailua ....35,812..E 8
Kailua ....F 11
Kainaliu ....512..J 12
Kalae ....F 9
Kalaheo ....2,500..D 4
Kalaupapa ....°F 10
Kalihiwai ....D 4
Kaluaaha ....F 10
Kaneohe ....29,919..E 8
Kapaa ....4,467..D 5

Kapaau ....612..H 12
Kaumakani ....888..D 4
Kaunakakai ......2,231..F 9
Kawaihae ....I 12
Kawailoa ....G 3
Kawailoa Beach ....G 3
Kawainui ....I 14
Keaau* ....775..I 14
Kealakekua ......1,033..J 12
Kealia ....D 5
Kealia ....I 12
Keaukaha ....I 14
Keei ....J 12
Kekaha ....3,260..D 4
Kelawea ....G 10
Keokea ....I 12
Keokea ....G 11
Keolu Hills ....J 7
Kihei ....5,644..G 11
Kilauea ....895..D 4
Koa Mill ....J 12
Koele ....G 10
Koloa ....1,457..D 4
Koloa Landing ....D 4
Kualapuu ....502..F 9
Kukui ....I 14
Kukuihaele ....332..H 13
Kukuiula ....D 4
Kuliouou ....K 7
Kumukumu ....D 5
Kunia ....I 3
Kurtistown ....I 14
Lahaina ....6,095..G 10
Laie ....4,643..G 5
Lanai City ....2,092..G 10
Lanikai ....I 7
Laupahoehoe ....500..I 13
Lawai ....D 4
Lihue ....4,000.°D 4
Lower Paia ......1,500..F 11
Lower Village ....J 4
Maili ....5,026..I 2
Makaha ....6,582..I 2

Makakilo City .....7,691..J 3
Makapala ....191..H 12
Makawao ....2,900..G 11
Makuu ....I 14
Maunaloa ....633..F 9
Maunalua ....K 7
Maunawai ....G 3
Maunawili ....5,239..J 6
Mililani
Town ....21,365..I 4
Mokapu ....11,615..I 7
Mokuleia ....G 2
Mountain View ......540..I 13
Naalehu ....1,168..K 13
Nanakuli ....8,185..I 2
Napili-
Honokowai* ....2,446..F 10
Napoopoo ....J 12
Nawiliwili ....D 4
Niulii ....H 12
Niumalu ....D 4
Numila ....D 4
Ohia Mill ....I 12
Olowalu ....G 10
Ookala ....401..H 13
Opihikao ....J 14
Paauhau ....H 13
Paauilo ....755..H 13
Pahala ....1,619..J 13
Pahoa ....923..J 14
Paia ....193..F 11
Paihaaloa ....J 14
Papaaloa ....267..I 13
Papaikou ....1,567..I 14
Paukaa ....544..I 14
Pauwela* ....468..F 11
Pearl City ....42,575..I 4
Pepeekeo ....I 14
Poamoho Camp ....H 3
Pohakapu ....J 6
Poipu ....685..D 4
Port Allen ....D 4
Princeville* ....500..D 4

Puhi ....991..D 4
Pukalani ....3,950..G 11
Punaluu ....J 13
Punaluu ....G 5
Pupukea ....F 3
Puuanahulu ....I 12
Puuiki ....G 3
Puuiki ....G 12
Puukolii ....F 10
Puunene ....572..G 11
Schofield
Barracks ....18,851..H 3
Spreckelsville ....F 11
Sunset Beach ....F 3
Umikoa ....I 13
Volcano ....J 13
Wahiawa ....16,911..E 7
Waiahukini ....K 12
Waiakoa ....G 11
Waialua ....4,051..E 7
Waianae ....7,941..I 2
Waihee ....413..F 11
Waikane ....H 5
Waikapu ....698..G 10
Wailea ....1,124..I 13
Wailua ....1,587..D 4
Wailuku ......10,260.°F 11
Waimanalo ....3,562..J 7
Waimanalo
Beach ....4,161..J 7
Waimea ....1,179..H 12
Waimea ....G 4
Waimea ....1,569..D 4
Waimea Camp ....G 3
Wainaku* ....1,045..I 13
Wainee ....G 10
Wainiha ....D 4
Waiohinu ....K 12
Waipahu ....29,139..I 4
Waipio
Acres ....4,091..I 4
Whitmore
Village ....2,318..H 4

Source: 1980 census. Places without population figures are smaller communities.

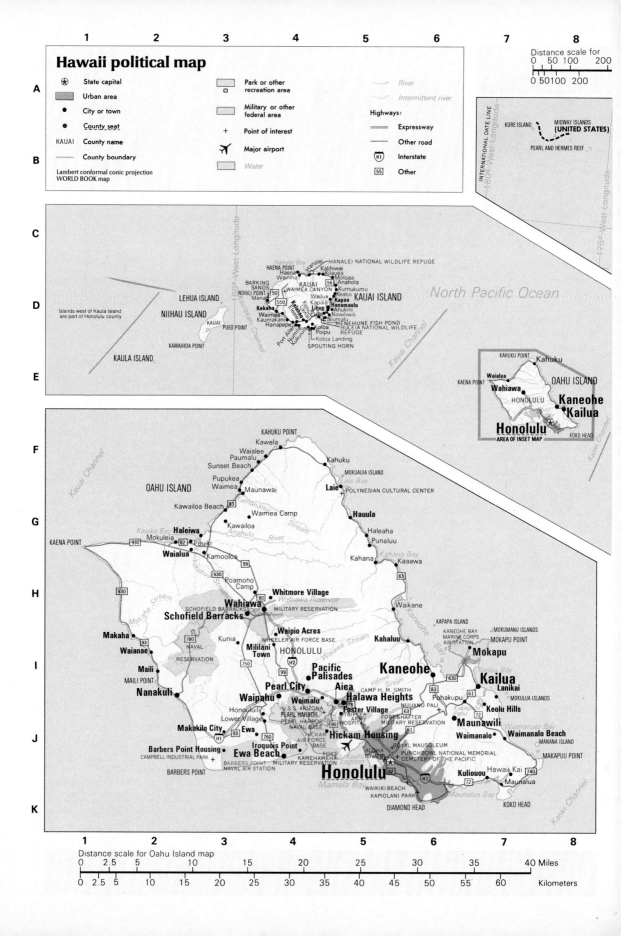

Hawaii political map

Legend:
- ⊛ State capital
- Urban area
- • City or town
- ● County seat
- KAUAI County name
- County boundary

- Park or other recreation area
- ▫
- Military or other federal area
- + Point of interest
- ✈ Major airport
- Water

- River
- Intermittent river
- Highways:
  - Expressway
  - Other road
  - H1 Interstate
  - 55 Other

Lambert conformal conic projection
WORLD BOOK map

Distance scale for
0 50 100 200
0 50100 200

INTERNATIONAL DATE LINE
180° West Longitude
175° West Longitude

KURE ISLAND
MIDWAY ISLANDS
(UNITED STATES)
PEARL AND HERMES REEF

North Pacific Ocean

160° West Longitude

LEHUA ISLAND
NIIHAU ISLAND
Islands west of Kaula Island are part of Honolulu county
KAUAI
PUEO POINT
KAWAIHOA POINT
KAULA ISLAND

KAUAI ISLAND
HANALEI NATIONAL WILDLIFE REFUGE
Hanalei Bay
Hanalei
Haena Point
Haena
Wainiha
Kalihiwai
Kilauea
Moloaa
Anahola
BARKING SANDS
NOHILI POINT 50
Mana
WAIMEA CANYON
KAUAI
Wailua
Kumukumu
Knalia
56
Kapaa
Kekaha 550
Waimea
Kaumakani
Hanapepe
Port Allen
Numulu
Koloa
Poipu
Koloa Landing
SPOUTING HORN
Hanamaulu
Lihue
Ahukini
Nawiliwili
Niumalu
MENEHUNE FISH POND
HULEIA NATIONAL WILDLIFE REFUGE
Kauai Channel

Kaulakahi Channel

KAHUKU POINT
Kahuku
Waialua
KAENA POINT
Wahiawa
HONOLULU
OAHU ISLAND
Kaneohe
Kailua
Honolulu
AREA OF INSET MAP
KOKO HEAD
Kaiwi Channel

OAHU ISLAND
KAHUKU POINT
Kawela
Waialee
Paumalu
Sunset Beach
Pupukea
Waimea
OAHU ISLAND
Maunawai
Kahuku
MOKUAUIA ISLAND
Laie Bay
Laie
POLYNESIAN CULTURAL CENTER
Kawailoa Beach
83
Waimea Camp
Kawailoa
Hauula
Haleiwa
Mokuleia
82 Puuiki
Haleaha
Punaluu
Waialua
Kamooloa
99
Kahana
Kaaawa
Kahana Bay
930
Poamoho Camp
83
Whitmore Village
Wahiawa Reservoir
Waikane
930
Wahiawa
80
SCHOFIELD BARRACKS
Schofield Barracks
MILITARY RESERVATION
Kaneohe Bay
KAPAPA ISLAND
Makaha
93
Kunia
Waipio Acres
WHEELER AIR FORCE BASE
Kahaluu
KANEOHE BAY MARINE CORPS AIR STATION
MOKUMANU ISLANDS
MOKAPU POINT
Waianae
780
NAVAL
Mililani Town
HONOLULU
Mokapu
Maili
RESERVATION
750
H2
Kaneohe
630
Kailua
MAILI POINT
99
Pacific Palisades
Lanikai
Nanakuli
Aiea
CAMP H. M. SMITH
83 Pohakupu
61
MOKULUA ISLANDS
Pearl City
Waipahu
Waimalu
78
Halawa Heights
Foster Village
FORT SHAFTER MILITARY RESERVATION
63
NUUANU PALI
Keolu Hills
Makakilo City
Honouliuli Lower Village
U.S.S. ARIZONA PEARL HARBOR
PEARL HARBOR NAVAL BASE
90
TRIPLER ARMY HOSPITAL
61
Maunawili
Ewa
760
HICKAM AIR FORCE BASE
Hickam Housing
ROYAL MAUSOLEUM
Waimanalo
Waimanalo Beach
MANANA ISLAND
Barbers Point Housing
CAMPBELL INDUSTRIAL PARK
Iroquois Point
Ewa Beach
KAMEHAMEHA
FORT
PUNCHBOWL NATIONAL MEMORIAL CEMETERY OF THE PACIFIC
MAKAPUU POINT
BARBERS POINT MILITARY RESERVATION
BARBERS POINT NAVAL AIR STATION
ALOHA TOWER
Keehi Lagoon
H1
Kuliouou
72
Hawaii Kai
740
BARBERS POINT
Honolulu
92
Maunalua
Mamala Bay
WAIKIKI BEACH
KAPIOLANI PARK
Maunalua Bay
KOKO HEAD
DIAMOND HEAD
Kaiwi Channel

Kauai Channel
Kaiaka Bay
Kamananui Stream
Anahulu River
Koolau Stream
Makaha Stream
Waiawa Stream
Halawa Stream
Waikele Stream

Distance scale for Oahu Island map
0 2.5 5 10 15 20 25 30 35 40 Miles
0 2.5 5 10 15 20 25 30 35 40 45 50 55 60 Kilometers

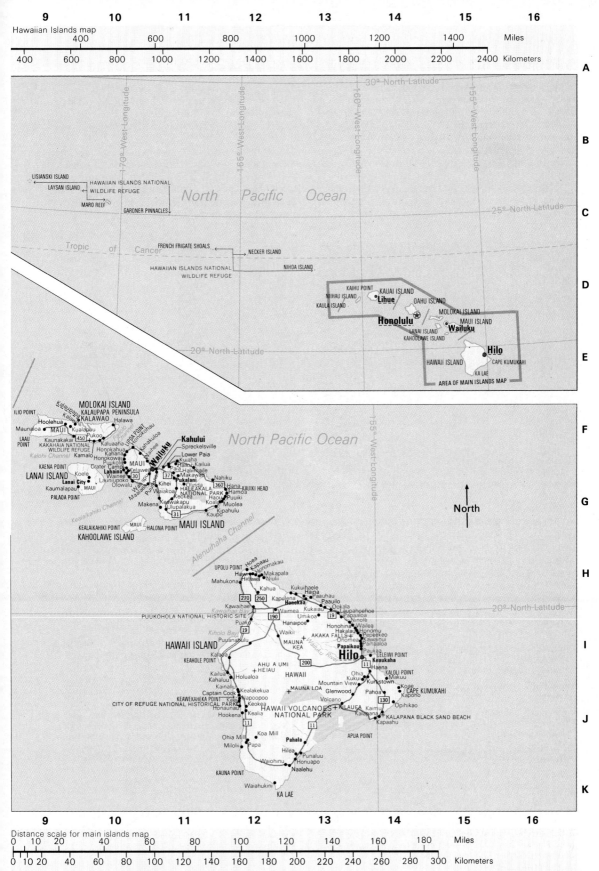

Hawaii's mild climate and beautiful scenery make the state one of the favorite year-round playgrounds of the world. Several million vacationers arrive in the islands each year by ship or by airplane. Many visitors remain in Honolulu to enjoy Waikiki Beach and other attractions on Oahu. Others prefer the less populated islands. Tourists find excellent hotels on Hawaii, Kauai, Maui, Molokai, and Oahu. Wherever they go, vacationers are likely to attend a luau, featuring delicious Hawaiian food and the hula.

Temperatures of the air and water seldom differ more than a few degrees in Hawaii. The state's mild temperatures add to the enjoyment of swimming and boating.

Water temperatures at Waikiki Beach average 75° to 77° F. (24° to 25° C) in March and 77° to 82° F. (25° to 28° C) in August. Swimmers at Waikiki Beach ride the long, rolling waves on surfboards. Many vacationers catch game fish in the deep waters between the islands. In winter, a few skiers race down Mauna Kea on Hawaii Island.

Hawaii's many celebrations and festivals attract thousands of tourists every year. One of the major events is Aloha Week Festivals, held from mid-September through mid-October on the islands of Hawaii, Kauai, Maui, Molokai, and Oahu. The islands offer feasts, folk and street dancing, and parades.

**Parade during an
Aloha Week festival**

Joe Solem, Camera Hawaii

Places to visit

Akaka Falls, near Hilo on Hawaii Island, is a long, slender waterfall on Kolekole stream. The falls plunge over a 442-foot (135-meter) cliff into a wooded gorge.

Aloha Tower, in Honolulu, rises above the piers where passenger ships dock. From the top, visitors have a fine view of Honolulu and its harbor.

Barking Sands, on Kauai, is a beach that is sometimes quite dry. At these times, the sand, when walked on, makes a sound like a barking dog.

Hamakua Coast lies between Hilo and Honokaa on Hawaii Island. A highway winds through sugar cane plantations and around the base of Mauna Kea, Hawaii's highest mountain.

Kaimu Black Sand Beach, on Hawaii Island, is a beach of glistening black sand that consists of grains of lava.

Kapiolani Park extends from Waikiki to Diamond Head, an extinct volcano in Honolulu. The park offers concerts and pageants and has a zoo.

Kealakekua Bay, on the west coast of Hawaii Island, is the site where Captain James Cook was killed in 1779. A monument at the bay honors Cook.

Menehune Fish Pond, near Lihue, Kauai, was supposedly built by the first Polynesian settlers. It has walls of cut stone.

Nuuanu Pali, at the upper end of Nuuanu Valley on Oahu, offers a magnificent view of the northeastern coast from a cliff 1,188 feet (362 meters) high. A highway leads to the top of the cliff. King Kamehameha I drove some of Oahu's defenders over this cliff when he conquered the island in 1795.

Pearl Harbor, on Oahu, is a huge natural harbor used as a U.S. naval base. The battleship *Arizona,* sunk in the Japanese attack of Dec. 7, 1941, rests on the harbor bottom. See **Pearl Harbor Naval Base.**

Polynesian Cultural Center, near Laie on Oahu, includes six Polynesian villages inhabited by people from Fiji, Tonga, Hawaii, New Zealand, Samoa, and Tahiti.

Royal Mausoleum, in Honolulu, has the remains of five Hawaiian kings and the only queen who ever ruled Hawaii.

Sea Life Park, at Makapuu Point on Oahu, is a scientific and recreational oceanarium with performing porpoises and whales.

Waimea Canyon, on Kauai, has a beautifully colored gorge 2,000 feet (610 meters) deep. It can be viewed from several lookouts along a highway.

National parks. Hawaii has two national parks—Haleakala National Park on Maui, and Hawaii Volcanoes National Park on Hawaii Island. The Puuhonua o Honaunau National Historical Park on Hawaii Island shows the history of the Polynesian people. Other places of interest include the Puukohola Heiau National Historic Site and the Kaloko-Honokohau National Historic Park, both on Hawaii Island. The Kalaupapa National Historical Park is on Molokai. See **Haleakala National Park; Hawaii Volcanoes National Park.**

State parks. Hawaii established its park system in 1949, 10 years before achieving statehood. The state now has 74 state park and historic site areas. For information, write to Director, Department of Land and Natural Resources, State of Hawaii, 1151 Punchbowl Street, Honolulu, HI 96813.

Annual events

January-March
Hula Bowl college all-star football game on Oahu (January); Narcissus Festival in Honolulu (January or February); Hawaiian Open International Golf Tournament on Oahu (January or February); Cherry Blossom Festival in Honolulu (February-March).

April-June
Merrie Monarch Festival in Hilo (April); Lei Day, statewide (May 1); Miss Hawaii Scholarship Pageant in Honolulu (May); 50th State Fair on Oahu (May-June); King Kamehameha celebration, statewide (June).

July-September
Makawao Rodeo on Maui (July); Japanese Bon Dances at Buddhist centers (weekends during July and August); Hawaiian International Billfish Tournament on Hawaii Island (August); Hula Festival in Honolulu (August); Macadamia Nut Harvest Festival on Hawaii (August); Hawaii County Fair in Hilo (September).

October-December
Orchid Plant and Flower Show in Honolulu (October); Kona Coffee Festival on Hawaii Island (November); Hawaiian Pro Surfing on the North Shore of Oahu (November or December).

Werner Stoy, Camera Hawaii
Colorful Waimea Canyon, on Kauai

Camera Hawaii
Kalapana Black Sand Beach, on Hawaii Island

Artstreet

Camera Hawaii
Performing whales at Sea Life Park

Reconstructed Polynesian village at the Polynesian Cultural Center, Oahu

Hawaii is made up of 132 islands. The islands extend northwest for 1,523 miles (2,451 kilometers), about the distance between New York City and Denver. Geographers divide the islands into three groups: (1) eight main islands in the southeast, (2) islets of rock in the middle, and (3) coral and sand islands in the northwest. All the islands were formed by volcanoes built up from the ocean floor. The volcanoes northwest of the eight main islands are submerged, having been worn away by waves and ocean currents. Only atolls and pieces of volcanic rock still remain above the water (see **Atoll**). These 124 minor islands have a combined area of only 3 square miles (8 square kilometers).

The total general coastline of the eight main islands is 750 miles (1,207 kilometers) long. The tidal shoreline, including bays, islets, and river mouths, is 1,052 miles (1,693 kilometers) long. Rough, black rocks of lava jut out of the water along some of the coasts. In many places, tall cliffs rise almost straight up from the water's edge. Most of the islands have white sand beaches. Black sand of powdered lava covers other beaches.

Thick growths of tropical plants and trees thrive in the areas of rich soil where rainfall is heavy. Many of the native plants are found nowhere else in the world. Many types are rare and in danger of extinction. Most of Hawaii's beautiful shrubs and trees have been imported, including bougainvillea, oleanders, and orchids. Hawaii has little wildlife. But most of the animals are rare and can be found only on the islands. Scientists take special interest in the brightly colored forest birds and tiny land snails. A wide variety of seabirds live along the island shores. Many kinds of fish, including tropical fish, are found in the waters around the islands.

People live on seven of the eight main islands. Kahoolawe has no permanent residents. The 124 minor islands are too infertile and small to support human life. Midway Island, in the far northwestern part of the Hawaiian group of islands, is not a part of the state of Hawaii. It is controlled by the U.S. Navy. The eight main islands, from east to west, are Hawaii, Maui, Kahoolawe, Molokai, Lanai, Oahu, Kauai, and Niihau.

Hawaii, often called the *Big Island,* is the largest island in the state. It covers 4,038 square miles (10,458 square kilometers). The island was formed by five volcanoes: Kohala in the north, Hualalai in the west, Mauna Kea and Mauna Loa near the center, and Kilauea on the southeastern slope of Mauna Loa. Mauna Kea (13,796 feet, or 4,205 meters) and Mauna Loa (13,677 feet, or 4,169 meters) are the highest points in the state.

Mauna Loa and Kilauea are Hawaii's only active volcanoes. Mauna Loa erupts at irregular times, and sometimes sends streams of fiery lava flowing down to the ocean. Kilauea erupts more frequently. A highway passes near the crater's edge, and people often refer to the mountain as a "drive-in volcano." The sight of bubbling lava and fire fountains dancing in the crater attracts thousands of visitors. They watch the fiery spectacle from roped-off ledges around the edge of the crater. In 1960, lava from Kilauea swept over farmland and destroyed the village of Kapoho. Scientists of the U.S. Geological Survey study volcanic activity at the Hawaiian Volcano Observatory on the rim of Kilauea.

The northeastern and southeastern coasts of the island are rimmed by cliffs. Here and there, silvery waterfalls plunge over the cliffs to the ocean below. Sugar cane is the major crop. On the western side of the island are coffee farms and cattle ranches. Hilo, the largest city on the island, lies in the northeast. It is the island's chief port and the seat of Hawaii County.

Maui (*MOW ee*) is often called the *Valley Island.* Many canyons cut into the two volcanic mountains that form the island. Between the mountains is a broad, low isthmus with sugar cane plantations. The highest point on Maui is 10,023-foot (3,055-meter) Haleakala, which has the largest inactive volcanic crater in the world. The crater measures about 20 miles (32 kilometers) around and is 3,000 feet (914 meters) deep. The largest city on Maui is Kahului. Wailuku is the seat of Maui County.

Kahoolawe (*KAH hoo LAH wee*) is the smallest of the main islands. It is dry and windswept, and no one lives there. The U.S. Army, Navy, and Air Force have created controversy by using the island for target practice.

Molokai (*MOH loh KAH ee*) is called the *Friendly Island* because of the courtesy its people show to visitors.

Werner Stoy, Camera Hawaii

Rugged cliffs and deep valleys cover most of the eastern part of Molokai. Crops are raised on the fertile plain that covers the western and central parts of the island.

Map index

Alenuihaha Channel .....C 5	Kaena Pt. ....B 3	Kawaihoa Pt. ....B 1	Maili Pt. ....G 9
Anahulu R. ....F 9	Kahoolawe (I.) ....C 5	Kawaikini Peak ....A 2	Makahuena Pt. ....B 2
Apua Pt. ....D 6	Kahuku Pt. ....B 4	Keahole Pt. ....D 5	Makapuu Pt. ....B 4
Auau Channel ....C 5	Kaiwi Channel ....B 4	Kealaikahiki	Mamala Bay ....G 9
Barbers Pt. ....B 3	Kaka Pt. ....C 5	Channel ....C 5	Manana (I.) ....G 11
Cape Kumukahi ....D 7	Kalaupapa	Kealaikahiki Pt. ....C 5	Maui (I.) ....C 5
Diamond Head ....G 10	Peninsula ....B 5	Kealakekua Bay ....D 6	Mauna Kea (Volcano—
Ewa Beach ....G 9	Kalohi Channel ....C 4	Keanapapa Pt. ....C 4	Highest Point
Haleakala, Crater of ....C 5	Kaloli Pt. ....D 7	Keawekaheka Pt. ....D 6	in Hawaii) ....D 6
Haleakala Nat. Park .....C 5	Kamananui R. ....F 9	Kiholo Bay ....D 6	Mauna Loa
Hawaii (I.) ....D 6	Kanapou Bay ....C 5	Kilauea Crater ....D 6	(Volcano) ....D 6
Hawaii Volcanoes	Kaneohe Bay ....G 10	Koko Head ....B 4	Maunalua Bay ....G 10
Nat. Park ....D 6	Kapapa (I.) ....G 10	Koolau Range ....F 10	Mokapu Pt. ....G 11
Hilo Bay ....D 6	Kauai (I.) ....A 2	Laau Pt. ....B 4	Mokapu Pt. ....G 11
Hualalai (Mt.) ....D 6	Kauai Channel ....B 3	Lanai (I.) ....C 4	Moku Manu (I.) ....G 11
Ilio Pt. ....C 4	Kaulakahi Channel .....A 1	Lehua (I.) ....A 1	Mokuaweoweo Crater ...D 6
Ka Lae (South Cape) ....E 6	Kauna Pt. ....D 6	Leleiwi Pt. ....D 7	Molokai (I.) ....B 4
Kaala Peak ....F 9	Kawaihae Bay ....C 6	Maalaea Bay ....C 5	N. Halawa R. ....G 10
			N. Poamoho R. ....F 9

Niihau (I.) ....B 1	
Nohili Pt. ....A 2	
Nuuanu Pali Pass ....G 10	
Oahu (I.) ....B 4	
Pailolo Channel ....B 5	
Palaoa Pt. ....C 5	
Palikea (Mt.) ....G 9	
Pearl Harbor ....B 3	
Pueo Pt. ....B 1	
Puu Konahuanui	
(Mt.) ....G 10	
Salt Lake ....G 10	
Sand I. ....G 10	
Upolu Pt. ....C 6	
Waianae Mts. ....G 9	
Waiawa R. ....G 10	
Wailuku R. ....D 6	
Waimanalo Bay ....G 11	

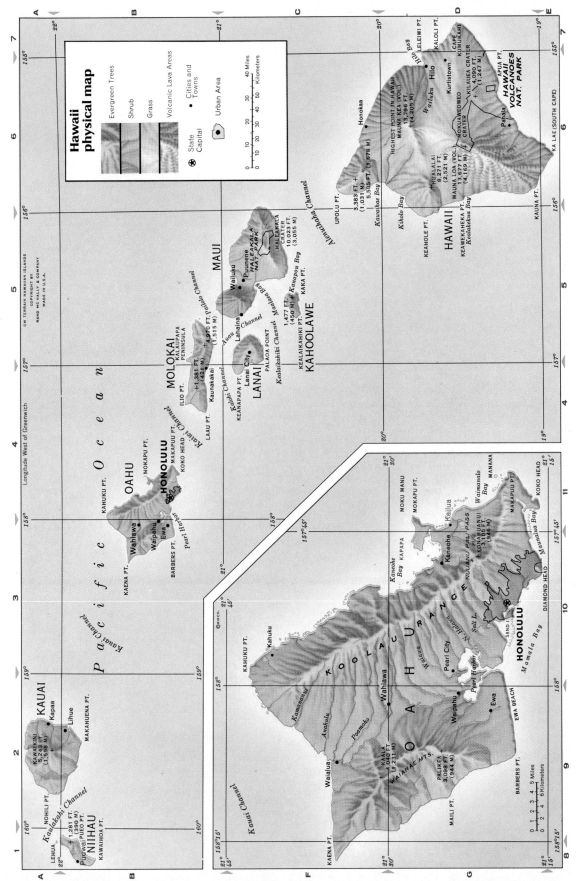

Hawaii physical map

Evergreen Trees
Shrub
Grass
Volcanic Lava Areas

⊛ State Capital
• Cities and Towns
Urban Area

0 10 20 30 40 Miles
0 10 20 30 40 50 Kilometers

CM TERRAIN HAWAIIAN ISLANDS
COPYRIGHT BY
RAND MCNALLY & COMPANY
MADE IN U.S.A.

Longitude West of Greenwich

P a c i f i c   O c e a n

Kauai Channel

KAUAI
KAWAIKINI
5,243 FT.
(1,598 M)
Kapaa
Lihue
MAKAHUENA PT.

Kaulakahi Channel

NIIHAU
1,281 FT.
(390 M)
LEHUA
NOHILI PT.
Puuwai PUEO PT.
KAWAIHOA PT.
MAKAHUENA PT.

OAHU
Kaiwi Channel
KAHUKU PT.
MOKAPU PT.
MAKAPUU PT.
KOKO HEAD
HONOLULU
Wahiawa
Waipahu
Ewa
KAENA PT.
BARBERS PT.
Pearl Harbor

MOLOKAI
KALAUPAPA PENINSULA
4,970 FT.
(1,515 M)
ILIO PT.
1,381 FT.
(421 M)
Kaunakakai
LAAU PT.
Kalohi Channel
KEANAPAPA PT.
Pailolo Channel

MAUI
Wailuku
Puunene
HALEAKALA NAT. PARK
HALEAKALA CRATER
10,023 FT.
(3,055 M)
Lahaina
Auau Channel
PALAOA POINT
Kealaikahiki Channel
KEALAIKAHIKI PT.
Maalaea Bay
Kanapou Bay
1,477 FT.
(450 M)
KAKA PT.

LANAI
Lanai City

KAHOOLAWE

Alenuihaha Channel

UPOLU PT.
3,383 FT.
(1,031 M)
5,505 FT.
(1,678 M)
Kawaihae Bay
Kiholo Bay
KEAHOLE PT.
KEAHOLE PT.
Kailua
Keawekaheka PT.
Kealakekua Bay

HAWAII
HUALALAI
8,271 FT.
(2,521 M)
MAUNA LOA (VOL.)
13,677 FT.
(4,169 M)
HIGHEST POINT IN HAWAII
MAUNA KEA (VOL.)
13,796 FT.
(4,205 M)
Honokaa
Hilo Bay
Hilo
Waiakea
LELEIWI PT.
KALOLI PT.
CAPE KUMUKAHI
KILAUEA CRATER
4,090 FT.
(1,247 M)
MOKUAWEOWEO CRATER
APUA PT.
HAWAII VOLCANOES NAT. PARK
Pahala
KA LAE (SOUTH CAPE)
KAUNA PT.

OAHU
KAHUKU PT.
Kahuku
MOKU MANU
MOKAPU PT.
MANANA
Kaneohe Bay
KAPAPA
Kaneohe
Kailua
Waimanalo Bay
MAKAPUU PT.
KOKO HEAD
NUUANU PALI PASS
PUU KONAHUANUI
3,105 FT.
(946 M)
KOOLAU RANGE
Waialua
Kamananui
Anahulu
Poamoho
Wahiawa
Pearl City
Kanenana
Waikele
N. FK. Halawa
Halawa
Pearl Harbor
Waipahu
Salt L.
HONOLULU
DIAMOND HEAD
SAND I.
Ewa
Ewa Beach
BARBERS PT.
WAIANAE MTS.
KAALA
4,040 FT.
(1,231 M)
PALIKEA
3,098 FT.
(944 M)
MAILI PT.
Waianae
KAENA PT.
Kauai Channel
Mamala Bay

Specially created for *The World Book Encyclopedia* by Rand McNally and World Book editors

The island has three regions. Western Molokai is a broad, dry plateau covered mostly by cattle ranches. The eastern region consists of rugged mountains and deep canyons. The central region is a fertile plain where pineapple and other crops are grown. Molokai is the site of a famous colony for victims of leprosy (Hansen's disease). Located on Makanalua, or Kalaupapa, Peninsula is the colony where Father Joseph Damien de Veuster worked (see **Damien de Veuster, Joseph**). Kaunakakai is the port on Molokai. Kalaupapa is the seat of Kalawao county.

Lanai (*lah NAH ee*), the *Pineapple Island,* has all its cultivated land on one pineapple plantation. Castle & Cooke, Inc., the maker of Dole pineapple products, owns 98 per cent of the island. The rest is owned by the state of Hawaii.

Oahu (*oh AH hoo*) is the center of life in Hawaii. Known as the *Gathering Place,* it is the home of about 80 per cent of the state's people. The island consists of two mountain ranges separated by a wide valley. The Koolau Range forms the island's eastern side, and the Waianae Range forms the western side. The valley between these ranges is a rolling, fertile plain with pineapple and sugar cane plantations.

Average monthly weather

	Honolulu					Hilo				
	Temperatures				Days of rain or snow		Temperatures				Days of rain or snow
	F° High Low		C° High Low				F° High Low		C° High Low		
Jan.	77	67	25	19	12	Jan.	78	62	26	17	20
Feb.	77	67	25	19	12	Feb.	79	62	26	17	19
Mar.	77	68	25	20	13	Mar.	79	63	26	17	24
Apr.	78	69	26	21	12	Apr.	79	64	26	18	25
May	80	71	27	22	11	May	81	65	27	18	25
June	81	72	27	22	11	June	83	66	28	19	24
July	82	74	28	23	13	July	83	67	28	19	27
Aug.	83	74	28	23	13	Aug.	83	68	28	20	27
Sept.	83	74	28	23	12	Sept.	83	68	28	20	23
Oct.	82	73	28	23	13	Oct.	82	67	28	19	24
Nov.	80	71	27	22	13	Nov.	80	66	27	19	23
Dec.	78	69	26	21	14	Dec.	79	64	26	18	24

Average yearly precipitation

Precipitation varies enormously throughout Hawaii. Rainfall on the mountaintops may exceed 200 inches (508 centimeters). The lowlands may receive less than 25 inches (64 centimeters).

WORLD BOOK map

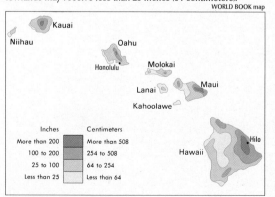

Inches	Centimeters
More than 200	More than 508
100 to 200	254 to 508
25 to 100	64 to 254
Less than 25	Less than 64

Pearl Harbor, one of the largest natural harbors in the Pacific Ocean, is on Oahu's southern coast. This coral-free harbor has about 10 square miles (26 square kilometers) of navigable water behind a narrow entrance. The U.S. Pacific Fleet has headquarters there. On Dec. 7, 1941, a surprise attack on the naval base by Japanese warplanes forced the United States into World War II. Honolulu, the state capital and largest urban area, lies east of Pearl Harbor.

Kauai (*KAH oo AH ee*) is called the *Garden Island* because of its rich greenery and beautiful gardens. The island looks like a circle, with 5,170-foot (1,576-meter) Kawaikini Peak in the center. Nearby is 5,080-foot (1,548-meter) Mount Waialeale, one of the world's rainiest spots. It has an average annual rainfall of 460 inches (1,170 centimeters). Dozens of streams flow from this rainy area to the sea through deep canyons, which have been worn into the volcanic rock that forms the island. One of these canyons, Waimea, has colorful rock walls 2,857 feet (871 meters) high. They look much like the rock formations in the Grand Canyon of Arizona. The rugged Na Pali (cliffs) on the northwestern coast make it impossible to build a road entirely around the island. Kapaa is the largest city on Kauai. Lihue is the seat of Kauai County.

Niihau (*NEE ee HAH oo*) is known as the *Forbidden Island.* No one can visit it without the owners' permission. Mrs. Elizabeth Sinclair bought most of the island from King Kamehameha V in 1864 for $10,000. She had been returning to New Zealand from British Columbia, but Kamehameha persuaded her to remain in Hawaii. The Robinson family, descendants of Mrs. Sinclair, still owns the island. The family runs a cattle ranch that almost covers the island.

Niihau is one of the few places where the people still usually speak the Hawaiian language. Low plains at each end of the island rise to a plateau in the center. Puuwai is the largest village.

Climate. Cool trade winds keep the climate of Hawaii mild all year. There is little difference in temperature between night and day, or between summer and winter. Temperatures in the lowlands average about 77° F. (25° C) in July and 71° F. (22° C) in January.

The highest temperature in Hawaii, 100° F. (38° C), was recorded at Pahala on April 27, 1931. The lowest temperature was 14° F. (−10° C), at Haleakala Crater on Jan. 2, 1961.

Rainfall varies from over 400 inches (1,020 centimeters) a year on the mountaintops to less than 10 inches (25 centimeters) in the lowlands. The heaviest rains generally fall on the northeastern sides of the islands. Snow sometimes covers the highest points on Hawaii and Maui.

Major islands

Island	Length In mi.	In km	Width In mi.	In km	Area In sq. mi.	In km²
Hawaii	93	(150)	76	(122)	4,038	(10,458)
Kahoolawe	11	(18)	6	(10)	45	(117)
Kauai	33	(53)	25	(40)	553	(1,432)
Lanai	18	(29)	13	(21)	140	(363)
Maui	48	(77)	26	(42)	729	(1,888)
Molokai	38	(61)	10	(16)	261	(676)
Niihau	18	(29)	6	(10)	73	(189)
Oahu	44	(71)	30	(48)	608	(1,575)

Hawaii's economy once relied chiefly on sugar and pineapple. Since the 1950's, Hawaii's service industries have grown in importance. These industries, including tourism and government activities, now make up most of Hawaii's *gross state product*—the total value of goods and services produced in a state in a year. Government services are the single most important economic activity. They account for about 25 per cent of the gross state product.

Natural resources. Hawaii has little soil that is extremely fertile. The deepest deposits of topsoil lie in the valleys between mountains. Rain seeps into the upland rocks and provides large reserves of underground water. Crops grow on only about 8 per cent of the land.

Hawaii has few minerals. Kauai and Maui have soils rich in titanium oxide, a paint pigment. Quarries provide building stone.

Service industries together account for 90 per cent of Hawaii's gross state product. No other state depends so heavily on income from the service industries.

Government activities account for more of Hawaii's gross state product than does any other industry. The U.S. Army, Air Force, Navy, and Marines all operate bases on Oahu. These installations employ both military and civilian workers. Other government employees in Hawaii work in local, state, and federal agencies.

Community, social, and personal services form Hawaii's second most important service industry, providing 19 per cent of the gross state product. This industry includes such economic activities as the operation of hotels and motels, private schools and hospitals, and ad-

Production and workers by economic activities

Economic activities	Per cent of GSP produced	Employed workers Number of persons	Per cent of total
Government	25	93,300	21
Community, social, & personal services	19	110,200	25
Wholesale & retail trade	17	115,500	26
Finance, insurance, & real estate	17	32,000	7
Transportation, communication, & utilities	12	33,300	8
Construction	5	17,000	4
Manufacturing	4	21,800	5
Agriculture	1	16,900	4
Mining	*	200	*
Total	100	440,000	100

*Less than one-half of 1 per cent.
Figures are for 1985.
Source: *World Book* estimates based on data from U.S. Bureau of Economic Analysis, U.S. Bureau of Labor Statistics, and U.S. Department of Agriculture.

vertising and data processing firms. About a fourth of the state's workers are employed in community, social, and personal services.

Two service industries each supply 17 per cent of the gross state product. They are: (1) wholesale and retail trade, and (2) finance, insurance, and real estate.

Tourist spending contributes greatly to the income from the service industries. Each year, several million tourists enjoy vacations in Hawaii. They spend about $4 billion. The busiest months are July, August, and December. In 1903, business people on the islands established an agency that later became the Hawaii Visitors Bureau. The bureau, with state assistance, conducts advertising campaigns to attract tourists.

Wholesale and retail trade employs more people than any other industry in Hawaii. Retail trade, especially in restaurants and small shops, receives much income from tourists. The most important wholesaling activity is the sugar trade.

Real estate is the most important part of the finance, insurance, and real estate industry. Property values in the state increase steadily because of Hawaii's rapidly growing population and small land area.

Transportation, communication, and utilities provide 12 per cent of the gross state product. Much of this income comes from airline and telephone companies.

Manufacturing in Hawaii provides 4 per cent of the gross state product. Goods manufactured there have a *value added by manufacture* of about $1 billion a year. Value added by manufacture is the increase in value of raw materials after they become finished products.

Food processing, Hawaii's leading manufacturing activity, has an annual value added of about $400 million. Hawaiian sugar processors produce about 1 million short tons (910,000 metric tons) of raw sugar yearly, about 18 per cent of the total U.S. sugar production. Each year, canneries produce about $13\frac{1}{2}$ million cases of pineapple fruit, juice, and frozen concentrate. Other industries in Hawaii, in order of importance, produce printed materials; clothing; stone, clay, and glass products; chemicals; and fabricated metal products.

Camera Hawaii

Food processing is Hawaii's leading manufacturing activity. The workers shown above are canning pineapples, one of the state's leading agricultural products.

Agriculture accounts for 1 per cent of the gross state product in Hawaii. The annual farm production has a net value of about $170 million. All the main islands except Kahoolawe have some kind of agriculture. Most of the farmland is occupied by ranches and by plantations owned by large corporations.

Sugar cane ranks as the most important crop. It is grown on more than three-fifths of Hawaii's cropland, or about 217,000 acres (87,800 hectares). Hawaii has about 15 sugar-plantation companies and about 300 independent sugar planters. They produce about 9 million short tons (8 million metric tons) of sugar cane yearly, or about a third of all sugar cane grown on United States soil. Pineapples are the second largest crop in the state. They grow on about 43,000 acres (17,400 hectares). Farmers in Hawaii also raise cattle, hogs, horses, and poultry.

Hawaii exports large quantities of flowers and leis. Hilo is the center of the orchid-growing and flower-packaging industry. Coffee grows on small farms on Hawaii Island. Several islands grow macadamia nuts and package them for sale. Avocados, bananas, guavas, papayas, and other fruits thrive in Hawaii. Small truck farms raise many vegetables for local use, including beans, Chinese cabbage, corn, potatoes, and taro.

Mining supplies less than 1 per cent of Hawaii's gross state product. Mineral products bring in an income of about $55 million yearly. Stone accounts for much of this total. Sand, gravel, and pumice are also mined.

Fishing industry in Hawaii produces an annual fish catch valued at about $25 million. The state's most im-

Transportation is one of Hawaii's chief problems. Because the state has little industry, most goods must be shipped by air or sea from the mainland. This makes many items more expensive than on the mainland. Travel within the state is expensive because the islands are widely separated. Airlines provide the quickest and easiest way to travel in Hawaii. Three airlines provide many daily flights among the main islands. Other airlines link Hawaii with other parts of the world. The main islands have about 55 airports.

Ships bring most of the food, manufactured products, and raw materials used in Hawaii. The chief ports of the islands include Honolulu on Oahu, Hilo and Kawaihae on Hawaii, Nawiliwili and Port Allen on Kauai, and Kahului on Maui. The main islands have more than 4,300 miles (6,900 kilometers) of surfaced highways. Many roads are in the coastal regions, except in areas of mountains or cliffs or in undeveloped regions. Highways run across some of the islands. Trucks haul most of the sugar cane and freight in Hawaii.

Communication. Hawaii's first English-language newspaper, the *Sandwich Island Gazette,* began publication in Honolulu in 1836. The islands have about 15 newspapers today. The *Honolulu Star-Bulletin* and *The Honolulu Advertiser* have the greatest daily circulations. Most of the newspapers are printed in English, but four dailies are in Chinese, Japanese, or Korean.

The state's first two radio stations, KDYX and KGU, began broadcasting in Honolulu in 1922. KGMB-TV, the first television station, opened in Honolulu in 1952. Hawaii has about 40 radio stations and 14 TV stations.

Farm products

This map shows where the state's leading farm products are produced. The major urban areas are shown on the map in red.

WORLD BOOK map

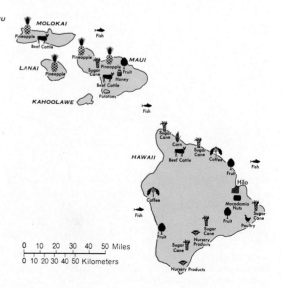

portant commercial fish are the yellowfin and the skipjack, two types of tuna. Honolulu is Hawaii's chief fishing port.

Aquaculture, the commercial raising of animals and plants that live in water, is a growing industry in Hawaii. Prawns are the leading product.

Electric power. Hawaii has no oil deposits, so most of its generating plants use petroleum shipped from Asia and the Near East. A small amount of the state's power is supplied by generating plants that use agricultural waste products as fuel. In 1981, a geothermal power plant on Hawaii Island began operating. Windmills called *wind turbines* take advantage of the trade winds to produce electricity.

Constitution. The Constitution of Hawaii went into effect in 1959, when Hawaii became the 50th state. The Constitution had been approved in 1950, when the islands were still a territory.

Amendments to the Constitution may be proposed by the legislature or by a constitutional convention. To be approved by the legislature, an amendment must receive a two-thirds vote in one session, or a majority vote in two successive sessions. Voters must approve a constitutional convention before it can meet. They must vote on holding a constitutional convention at least every 10 years.

All amendments to the Constitution must be approved by the voters during elections. In a general election, at least 50 per cent of those voting in the election must approve the amendment. In a special election, an amendment must be approved by at least 30 per cent of the registered voters.

Executive. The governor and lieutenant governor of Hawaii are the only elected top state officials. They are elected to four-year terms. The governor receives a yearly salary of $80,000.

The governor appoints the heads of state departments, including the attorney general, comptroller, and finance director. The governor also appoints judges of high courts and other officials. The state Senate must approve these selections. The governor can also veto legislation, but the legislature can reject the veto by a two-thirds majority vote in both houses.

Legislature consists of a 25-member Senate and a 51member House of Representatives. Senators are elected from 25 senatorial districts, and serve four-year terms. Representatives are elected from 51 districts, and serve two-year terms.

Hawaii's Constitution specifies the number of senators and representatives. It also provides for a commission to *reapportion* (redivide) legislative districts if necessary. The commission meets every 10 years to determine if the state's legislative districts, and also its congressional districts, must be changed.

In 1965, a federal court ordered Hawaii to redraw its senatorial districts to provide equal representation. The legislature set up senatorial districts based on the number of registered voters. But in 1982, a federal court ordered Hawaii to redraw the senatorial districts based on resident population.

The Hawaii legislature meets annually on the third Wednesday in January. Legislative sessions last 60 working days. Sessions may be extended 15 days if necessary.

Courts. The Supreme Court is the highest appeals court in Hawaii. It has a chief justice and four associate justices. Hawaii also has an intermediate court of appeals, which has a chief judge and two associate judges. Hawaii's highest trial courts are four circuit courts. The governor appoints members of the Supreme Court, the intermediate court of appeals, and the circuit courts to 10-year terms. The appointed judges are selected from lists of names provided by a judicial selection commission. Other courts include four district courts, a tax appeals court, a land registration court, a family court, and four small-claims courts.

Local government. All of Hawaii's populated places are governed as part of the county in which they are located. There are no self-governing, incorporated cities,

The governors of Hawaii

	Party	Term
William F. Quinn	Republican	1959-1962
John A. Burns	Democratic	1962-1974
George R. Ariyoshi	Democratic	1974-1986
John Waihee	Democratic	1986-

towns, or villages in the state. For example, Honolulu is officially known as the City and County of Honolulu. It is one governmental unit, and it consists of Oahu and all other islands in the state that are not in any other county. Honolulu is governed by a mayor and nine council members. All of these officials are elected to four-year terms.

Hawaii has five counties—Hawaii, Honolulu, Kalawao, Kauai, and Maui. Kalawao consists of the part of Molokai Island that is occupied by a settlement of present and former leprosy patients. The state department of health governs this area. Hawaii, Kauai, and Maui counties are governed by mayors and county councils elected by the voters.

Revenue. Taxation provides about three-fifths of the state government's *general revenue* (income). Most of the rest comes from federal grants and from charges for government services. The largest single source of state government revenue is a 4 per cent general excise tax. The state imposes the tax on nearly all businesses. Unlike most states, Hawaii does not require retail business people to collect the tax from their customers. However, most business people in Hawaii include the tax in their sales prices. The state also taxes personal income, public utilities, and financial institutions.

Politics. Until the mid-1950's, Republican candidates usually won office in Hawaii elections. The Democrats then began gaining strength. After Hawaii became a state in 1959, the voters elected Governor William F. Quinn, a Republican. Republicans controlled the Senate, and Democrats the House. In 1962, Democrat John A. Burns became governor and his party won control of both houses of the legislature. Since then, Democrats have held the governorship and have usually controlled Hawaii's legislature. For Hawaii's electoral votes and voting record in presidential elections, see **Electoral College** (table).

Werner Stoy, Camera Hawaii

Hawaii's House of Representatives, in the State Capitol in Honolulu, is the meeting place of the state's representatives.

Early days. The first people to live in what is now Hawaii were the Polynesians. They sailed there in giant canoes from other Pacific islands about 2,000 years ago. Hawaiian legends describe these settlers as dwarfish, playful, and shy. Another Polynesian people moved to the island from Tahiti about A.D. 1200. This group won control over the earlier settlers.

According to one legend, Polynesian settlers named the group of islands *Hawaii* in honor of a chief named *Hawaii-loa.* This chief supposedly led the Polynesians to the islands. But the name *Hawaii* is also a form of *Hawaiki,* the legendary name of the Polynesian homeland to the west.

European exploration. Spanish, Dutch, or Japanese explorers may have stopped at the Hawaiian Islands as early as the 1500's. The rest of the world did not know about the islands until after Captain James Cook of the British navy landed there on Jan. 18, 1778. Cook traded with the Hawaiians, who treated him well. They considered him a great chief with divine powers. Cook named the islands the *Sandwich Islands* in honor of the Earl of Sandwich, first lord of the British admiralty. Cook left after two weeks. He returned in November 1778 and was killed the next year in a quarrel between his men and the Hawaiians. See **Cook, James.**

Many other traders and explorers sailed to the islands after Cook's landing. They brought livestock, manufactured goods, and plants of other countries.

As many as 300,000 Hawaiians may have lived on the islands when the first Europeans arrived. The first trading ships known to have stopped at Hawaii arrived in 1786. They were bringing furs from Oregon to China. During the 1800's, many Hawaiians died of diseases brought from other parts of the world.

The kingdom of Hawaii. Local chiefs ruled the islands during the period of Cook's visits. One chief, Kamehameha, gained control of Hawaii Island in a bloody 10-year war that began in 1782. With the aid of firearms

The Great Seafarers, a 1951 oil painting on plywood, by
Paul Rockwood (Hawaii Volcanoes National Park)

Polynesians from various Pacific islands were the first people to inhabit the Hawaiian islands. They reached Hawaii in large double canoes some 2,000 years ago. Later, Polynesians arriving from Tahiti gained control of the islands.

obtained from white traders, he captured and united the other main islands in 1795, except for Kauai and Niihau. The local chiefs served as governors of their islands under King Kamehameha I of the Kingdom of Hawaii. In 1810, Kaumualii, ruler of Kauai and Niihau, accepted Kamehameha's rule.

Between 1811 and 1830, Hawaii shipped great quantities of sandalwood to China. Money from the sandalwood trade provided a major source of income for Kamehameha I and two later kings of Hawaii. The kings used the money to buy arms, clothing, ships, and other goods.

In 1813, Francisco de Paula Marín, a Spanish settler, wrote of planting pineapples. But commercial development of the pineapple did not begin until the 1880's. The first permanent sugar plantation in Hawaii began operating in 1835, at Koloa on Kauai. It was owned by Ladd & Company, an American firm. During the 1800's, hundreds of whaling ships, mostly from the United States, visited Hawaii each year. The sale of fresh water and other supplies to these ships provided the largest income for Hawaiians until the 1860's.

Kamehameha's son, Liholiho, became Kamehameha II after his father died in 1819. As one of his first acts, Kamehameha II abolished the local Hawaiian religion. This religion included the use of large temples, many orders of priests, and the belief in many gods and goddesses. In 1820, The American Board of Commissioners for Foreign Missions sent a group of Protestant missionaries and teachers to Hawaii aboard the brig *Thaddeus.* The missionaries converted most of the Hawaiians to Christianity.

The first Roman Catholic missionaries arrived in 1827. But the Hawaiian chiefs considered Protestantism the official religion. The Hawaiians forced the Roman Catholic priests to leave in 1831. They tried to prevent more priests from arriving and imprisoned many Hawaiians who had become Catholics. In July 1839 the French frigate *L'Artémise* blockaded Honolulu. The captain, C. P. T. Laplace, threatened to destroy the town if all the imprisoned Catholics were not freed. He also demanded that the Hawaiians grant religious freedom to Roman Catholics. The Hawaiians gave in to the captain's demands.

Growth of constitutional government. Hawaii adopted its first constitution in 1840. The constitution provided for a legislature and a supreme court. The legislature consisted of a council of chiefs and an elected house of representatives. In 1842, the United States recognized the Kingdom of Hawaii as an independent government.

The Hawaiian population declined from about 108,000 in 1836 to about 73,000 in 1853. The decrease was caused by disease and other factors.

Until 1848, the king owned all the islands. He granted or leased various areas to chiefs or people of other countries. A system of private property went into effect in 1848. A law called the *Great Mahele* (division) divided the land among King Kamehameha III and the chiefs. Each of these men gave most of his land to the government. Then the Hawaiian people claimed land or were allowed to buy *homesteads* (small farms). Some Hawaiians sold their land to residents from other countries.

From 1854 to 1872, during the reigns of Kame-

Historic Hawaii

Captain James Cook, a British naval explorer, reached Hawaii in 1778. His discovery led European traders to the islands.

King Kamehameha I gained control of Hawaii Island after a bloody 10-year war. In 1795 he became the ruler of most of the main islands.

Protestant missionaries from New England converted many native Hawaiians to Christianity in the early 1800's. They founded schools and churches.

Hawaii achieved statehood in 1959, after it had been a territory of the United States for 59 years. Hawaii is the nation's youngest state.

The U.S.S. *Arizona* Memorial honors those who died in the Japanese attack on Pearl Harbor on Dec. 7, 1941. The *Arizona* sank in the attack.

Important dates in Hawaii

WORLD BOOK illustrations by Kevin Chadwick

1778 Captain James Cook of the British navy reached Hawaii.

1795 King Kamehameha I unified Hawaii.

1820 Protestant missionaries from New England arrived to teach islanders Christianity.

1827 Roman Catholic missionaries arrived, but the Hawaiians forced them to leave in 1831.

1835 Ladd & Company started the first permanent sugar plantation in Hawaii on Kauai Island.

1839 The French blockaded Honolulu until the government agreed to give religious freedom to Roman Catholics.

1840 The Kingdom of Hawaii adopted its first Constitution.

c. 1885 The pineapple industry began in Hawaii with the importation of sweet pineapple plants from Jamaica.

1887 King Kalakaua gave the United States exclusive rights to use Pearl Harbor as a naval station.

1893 A revolution led by nine Americans and four Europeans removed Queen Liliuokalani from the throne.

1894 The Republic of Hawaii was established.

1898 The United States annexed Hawaii.

1900 The United States established the Territory of Hawaii.

1903 The legislature first petitioned Congress for statehood.

1927 A. F. Hegenberger and L. J. Maitland made the first airplane flight from the U.S. mainland to Hawaii.

1934 President Franklin D. Roosevelt became the first U.S. President to visit Hawaii.

1941 The Japanese attacked Pearl Harbor on December 7, plunging the United States into World War II.

1950 The territorial legislature approved a state Constitution, which went into effect in 1959—when Hawaii became a state.

1957 The first telephone cable from the U.S. mainland to Hawaii began operation.

1959 Hawaii became the 50th state of the Union.

1960 Hawaiians voted for a President for the first time. Congress established the East-West Center at the University of Hawaii.

1962 The jet-aircraft terminal at Honolulu International Airport was completed.

1965-1969 A new state capitol was built in Honolulu.

1982 Hurricane Iwa caused an estimated $312 million in property damage in Hawaii.

hameha IV and Kamehameha V, the islands began to be a melting pot of people from various countries. There were not enough Hawaiian workers for the plantations, so owners of the great sugar cane fields brought in laborers from other countries. Many Chinese came to work in Hawaii during the 1850's. Polynesians from the South Pacific first arrived in 1859, and Japanese in 1868. Other immigrants included the Portuguese during the 1870's, and Filipinos, Koreans, and Puerto Ricans in the early 1900's.

King Kalakaua, called the *Merry Monarch,* came to the throne in 1874. During his reign, Hawaiian music, the hula, and many other old Hawaiian customs became popular again. These customs had been prohibited by earlier rulers at the demand of Christian missionaries. The custom of wearing grass skirts began during this period. The first grass skirts were brought then to Hawaii from Samoa.

During Kalakaua's reign, sugar-cane planting became a large industry. Sugar planters shipped most of their crop to the United States, especially to San Francisco. The pineapple industry of Hawaii began after a thousand pineapple plants were shipped there from Jamaica about 1885. The plants were imported by Captain John Kidwell, a British *horticulturist* (an expert in growing flowers or fruits). In 1887, Kalakaua gave the United States exclusive rights to use Pearl Harbor as a naval base in exchange for certain trading privileges.

The republic of Hawaii. King Kalakaua died in 1891, and his sister, Liliuokalani, followed him to the throne. Queen Liliuokalani tried to increase her power beyond the limits set by the constitution. But in 1893, a bloodless revolution removed her from office. The revolution was led by nine Americans, two Britons, and two Germans. They received the help of American marines and sailors who landed to keep the peace.

The men who led the revolution wanted a more sympathetic government than that of Queen Liliuokalani. They and their followers formed the Republic of Hawaii in 1894. Sanford B. Dole, a judge, became the first and only president of the republic.

The territory of Hawaii. American business executives controlled the government of the new republic. The sugar planters wanted the islands to become a territory of the United States. Then they would receive a special payment when shipping sugar to the mainland. In 1898, the sugar planters succeeded in getting the United States to annex Hawaii as a possession in spite of some Hawaiian opposition. On August 12, the formal ceremony of annexation took place. For the next two years, the laws and government of the republic remained in force, except where they differed from the United States Constitution. The islands became a U.S. territory on June 14, 1900, and all islanders became American citizens. President William McKinley appointed Dole the first governor of Hawaii. Hawaii had a population of about 154,000 at this time.

As territorial citizens, the people could not vote in presidential elections. They elected one delegate to Congress. The delegate could introduce bills and debate but could not vote. The voters elected a senate and a house of representatives, but Congress could veto any bill passed by the Hawaiian legislature.

Shortly before World War I (1914-1918), the U.S. Navy started to build a great naval base at Pearl Harbor. The U.S. Army also established camps on Oahu. After the United States entered the war in 1917, two regiments of the Hawaii National Guard were called into federal service. These regiments were not sent overseas, but many Hawaiians fought in Europe as volunteers.

After the war, the statehood movement grew rapidly. The territorial government completed such improvements as draining swampland at Waikiki, now a world-famous beach. In 1927, two U.S. Army lieutenants, A. F. Hegenberger and L. J. Maitland, made the first airplane flight from the U.S. mainland to Hawaii. In 1934, President Franklin D. Roosevelt became the first U.S. President to visit Hawaii.

World War II. On Dec. 7, 1941, planes of the Japanese navy attacked Pearl Harbor and airfields on Oahu. The United States suffered heavy losses in lives, ships, and aircraft. The attack plunged the country into World

AP/Wide World

The attack on Pearl Harbor by Japanese bombers was a key event in U.S. history. Following the Dec. 7, 1941, attack on the U.S. naval base, the United States declared war on Japan and formally entered World War II (1939-1945).

War II. Many damaged or sunken warships were salvaged from Pearl Harbor. The armed forces repaired the damage to the naval base and to the airfields. These bases became the headquarters for the victorious United States campaign against the Japanese. Hawaii was under martial law from 1941 to 1944, though little further fighting took place in the region. See **World War II** (Japan attacks).

Some Americans feared that persons of Japanese ancestry in Hawaii might try to sabotage the war effort. But investigators found no more than one case of disloyalty among islanders of Japanese descent. Many of these islanders fought bravely in Italy and France as members of the famous 100th Infantry Battalion and the 442nd Regimental Combat Team.

The National Memorial Cemetery of the Pacific, in Honolulu, was dedicated in 1949. Thousands of American military personnel killed during World War II and the Korean War (1950-1953) are buried there.

Statehood. In 1919, Jonah Kuhio Kalanianaole, Hawaii's delegate to Congress, introduced the first bill for Hawaiian statehood. Many more statehood bills followed, but most were not even voted on. Several congressional committees wanted the islands to become a state. But many members of Congress feared that the thousands of Orientals in Hawaii might not support the United States in a war. The bravery of these Orientals in World War II and the Korean War (1950-1953) proved their loyalty.

In 1950, Hawaii adopted a constitution to go into effect when the territory became a state. Finally, in March 1959, Congress approved legislation to admit Hawaii as a state. President Dwight D. Eisenhower signed the bill on March 18. In June, the people of Hawaii voted almost 17 to 1 for statehood. Hawaii became the 50th state on Aug. 21, 1959. In 1960, Hawaiians voted in their first presidential election.

The 1960's. During the 1960's, Hawaii's population increased more than 20 per cent. Hawaii's economy also boomed. The Hawaii Visitors Bureau expanded its campaign on the U.S. mainland to promote tourism. To house the growing number of tourists, hotel construction valued at $80 million was started. A $15 million jet-aircraft terminal at Honolulu was completed in 1962. Jet airliners reduced the flying time between the mainland and Hawaii from nine hours to about five hours. Airfares also were lowered. By the late 1960's, about 1 million tourists were visiting Hawaii every year.

Large companies from the mainland purchased Hawaiian companies in several fields, including baking, insurance, and telephone service. Major Hawaiian corporations expanded their activities into more than 30 countries. Heavy industry also made a start in the state with an oil refinery, a steel mill, and two cement plants.

In 1960, Congress established the Center for Cultural and Technical Interchange Between East and West on the Manoa campus of the University of Hawaii. This institution, known as the East-West Center, provides a place where Americans, Asians, and Pacific Islanders can meet and study together.

In 1965, construction began on a new state capitol in Honolulu. The building was completed in 1969.

Recent developments. Hawaii's economy continues to rely heavily on tourism, with visitors spending about $4 billion annually. During the 1970's, new resort areas were developed on the islands of Hawaii, Kauai, Maui, and Molokai. However, increased fuel prices during the 1970's and early 1980's led to higher airfares, which slowed the growth of tourism in the state.

One of Hawaii's major problems is finding new ways to increase its tourist business and, at the same time, preserving its scenic beauty and recreational attractions. Another problem is the cost of living, which is higher in Hawaii than in most mainland areas. High costs of clothing, food, and housing all contribute to this problem.

Manufacturing gained strength in Hawaii during the late 1970's and early 1980's. Food processing, especially sugar refining and pineapple processing, ranks as the state's leading manufacturing activity. Hawaii's *aquaculture* industry gained strength during the late 1970's and early 1980's. Aquaculture is the commercial raising of animals and plants that live in water. The state's aquaculturists raise such animals as fish, oysters, and shrimp.

In order to reduce its dependence on oil, Hawaii is developing alternative sources of energy. These sources include *gasohol* (fuel made from gasoline and alcohol), solar energy, and wind power. Hawaii's goal is to be able to produce all its own energy by the year 2000.

In 1982, Hurricane Iwa struck Hawaii and caused an estimated $312 million in property damage. Kauai and Oahu were hardest hit by the hurricane.

Pauline N. King and Lyndon Wester

Study aids

Related articles in *World Book* include:

Biographies

Cook, James	Kamehameha I
Damien de Veuster, Joseph	Liliuokalani, Lydia K.
Dole, Sanford Ballard	

History

Cleveland, Grover	Pacific	World War II
(Foreign affairs)	Islands	(Japan attacks)

Military installations

Camp H. M. Smith	Hickam Air Force Base
Fort Shafter	Pearl Harbor Naval Base

Physical features

Kilauea	Mauna Loa	Volcano
Mauna Kea	Pacific Ocean	

Other related articles

Flower (picture:	Honolulu
Colorful leis)	Nene
Haleakala National Park	Ohia
Hawaii, University of	Races, Human
Hawaii Volcanoes	(picture: Polynesian)
National Park	Surfing
Hawaiian honeycreeper	United States (picture:
Hilo	Waimea Canyon)

Outline

I. People
  A. Population   D. Food   F. Schools
  B. Language   E. Dancing   G. Libraries
  C. Clothing   and music   H. Museums
II. Visitor's guide
  A. Places to visit   B. Annual events

III. Land and climate
A. Hawaii	D. Molokai	G. Kauai
B. Maui	E. Lanai	H. Niihau
C. Kahoolawe	F. Oahu	I. Climate

IV. Economy
A. Natural resources	F. Fishing industry
B. Service industries	G. Electric power
C. Manufacturing	H. Transportation
D. Agriculture	I. Communication
E. Mining	

V. Government
A. Constitution	D. Courts	F. Revenue
B. Executive	E. Local government	G. Politics
C. Legislature		

VI. History

Questions

What are the eight main islands of Hawaii?
How and when were the islands first united?
Why are airplanes so important in Hawaii?
When did Hawaii become a state?
What is the chief crop of Hawaii?
What are the main features of the Hawaiian language?
What has contributed to the growth of Hawaii's service industries since the 1950's?
Why is Pearl Harbor important in U.S. history?
Who were the first people in Hawaii?
Why is Hawaii called the *Aloha State*?

Additional resources

Level I

Carpenter, Allan. *Hawaii.* Rev. ed. Childrens Press, 1979.
Fradin, Dennis B. *Hawaii in Words and Pictures.* Childrens Press, 1980.
Rayson, Ann. *Modern Hawaiian History.* Peanut Butter, 1984.
Rublowsky, John. *Born in Fire: A Geological History of Hawaii.* Harper, 1981.

Level II

Carlquist, Sherwin J. *Hawaii: A Natural History.* Doubleday, 1970.
Daws, Gavan. *Shoal of Time: A History of the Hawaiian Islands.* Univ. of Hawaii Press, 1974. First published in 1968.
A Day in the Life of Hawaii. Produced by Rick Smolan and David Cohen. Workman, 1984. A collection of photographs.
Department of Geography, University of Hawaii. *Atlas of Hawaii.* Univ. of Hawaii Press, 1973.

Fuchs, Lawrence H. *Hawaii Pono: A Social History.* Harcourt, 1983. First published in 1961.
Kuykendall, Ralph S. *The Hawaiian Kingdom.* 3 vols. Univ. of Hawaii Press, 1938-1967.
Lind, Andrew W. *Hawaii's People.* 4th ed. Univ. of Hawaii Press, 1980.

Hawaii, University of, is a coeducational, state-supported institution. Its main campus, called the University of Hawaii at Manoa, is in Honolulu. It also operates campuses in Hilo and Aiea, and six community colleges. The Manoa campus has colleges of arts and sciences, business administration, continuing education and community service, education, engineering, and tropical agriculture and human resources; schools of accountancy, architecture, law, library studies, medicine, nursing, public health, social work, and travel industry management; and a graduate division. Courses lead to bachelor's, master's, and doctor's degrees. The community colleges offer certificates and associate degrees. The university was founded in 1907. For enrollment, see **Universities and colleges** (table). See also **Hawaii** (picture).

Critically reviewed by the University of Hawaii

Hawaii Volcanoes National Park is located on the island of Hawaii. The park includes two volcanoes, Mauna Loa and Kilauea. Mauna Loa stands 13,677 feet (4,169 meters) above sea level. It is often called the *Great Builder,* because it pours forth rock to enlarge the mountain. Kilauea lies about 30 miles (48 kilometers) from Mauna Loa. Kilauea's crater looks like a saucer hollowed out in a broad plain. Visitors can stand on its rim and watch geysers of molten lava. For area, see **National Park System** (table: National parks). The park was established in 1916. In 1961, a section on the island of Maui was designated as Haleakala National Park. See also **Haleakala National Park; Hawaii; Kilauea; Mauna Loa.**

Critically reviewed by the National Park Service

Hawaiian goose. See Nene.

Hawaiian honeycreeper is any member of a family of about 20 species of sparrow-sized birds that live only

The Hawaiian honeycreeper   Hawaiian honeycreepers live only in Hawaii. The apapane, *left,* is one of the most common species. Honeycreepers have three basic kinds of bills, *right,* each suited to a different type of food.

Apapane
Himatione sanguinea
Found in Hawaii
Body length 5¼ inches (13.3 centimeters)

The **long, curved bill** of the akialoa helps this bird feed on nectar from flowers.

The **heavy, parrotlike bill** of the Laysan finch is used to crush seeds and insects.

The **fairly straight bill** of the creeper enables this bird to probe tree bark for insects.

WORLD BOOK illustration by Harry McNaught

WORLD BOOK illustrations by Marion Pahl

in Hawaii. They get their name from the way honey-creepers *creep* (flutter) about when searching in flowers for insects and nectar.

Originally, there was one species of honeycreeper. The birds wandered to Hawaii or were blown there by a storm. Over time, this species evolved into many species, each with its own feeding habits. Some honeycreepers have a long, curved bill that helps them find food in flowers. Others have a heavy bill for crushing seeds. A third type feeds like a woodpecker, using its strong bill to chisel away tree bark in search of insects.

When Europeans settled in Hawaii in the late 1700's and early 1800's, they brought cats, rats, mosquitoes, and other animals. Some of these animals hunted honeycreepers, and others destroyed much of the forested areas where honeycreepers lived. The mosquitoes carried bird malaria that killed many honeycreepers. About a third of the species of honeycreepers became extinct.

In 1973, two students from the University of Hawaii found a previously unknown species of honeycreeper. This small brown and beige bird was the first bird species discovered in the Hawaiian Islands since 1893.

Scientific classification. Hawaiian honeycreepers make up the subfamily Drepanididae in the finch family, Fringillidae.

James J. Dinsmore

Hawk. A number of birds of prey living in many parts of the world are called hawks. The true hawks belong to the same family as the eagles, kites, Old World vultures, harriers, and ospreys. There are about 260 different kinds of birds in this large family.

The bodies of hawks. Male hawks range from 10 to 22 inches (25 to 56 centimeters) in length, and the females from 12 to 26 inches (30 to 66 centimeters). The female hawk is usually larger, stronger, and bolder than the male. The male and female of most species have the same coloring. However, there are a few species in which the male and female are colored differently. Their wings are slightly rounded and broader than the falcon's wings. Their heads and necks are more thickly feathered than those of the vultures of North America. Most hawks have light-colored eyes which give them a fierce look. They do not sing, but when disturbed they utter piercing whistles, screams, and chattering calls.

Food. Hawks capture living animals and kill them instantly for food. They have sharp eyesight—about eight times as sharp as a human being's. They are swift fliers, and they pounce on their prey with lightning speed. Their sharp curved claws, or talons, and powerful feet have a viselike grip to catch, crush, and carry off their prey. With their strong hooked beaks, they tear off fragments of flesh to eat. Hawks eat bones, feathers, and fur as well as flesh. They swallow them all whole. Material which cannot be digested is thrown up in the form of spindle-shaped masses called *pellets*.

Hawks kill almost every type of small mammal and bird. Different hawks eat different things, and there is probably no aquatic or land animal smaller than a rabbit that some kind of hawk will not attack. The *serpent eagle,* a tropical hawk of southern Asia, lives chiefly on snakes. The *broad-winged hawk* of eastern North America eats snakes and frogs. The *Swainson's hawk* of western North America eats grasshoppers. Both the broad-winged and Swainson's hawks are medium-sized, even though they eat such small prey. The *Malacca pern* of

the East Indies hunts at dusk and catches bats on the wing. Several kinds of *honey buzzards* of the Old World eat wild bees, honey, and larval insects.

Home life. Hawks seldom gather in groups of three or more except during migration periods. The male and female usually prefer to make their nest alone, and they defend their privacy from other hawks, as well as from large birds, animals, and people. Some of the larger hawks have attacked people who came close to their nests, causing painful cuts with their sharp talons.

The male and female usually make the nest together. The male helps hatch the eggs and care for the young. Hawks sometimes mate for life, and often use the same nest year after year. Most hawks build rough nests high in trees. Others nest in bushes, on cliffs, or on the ground. The female lays from two to six eggs, depending on the kind of hawk. The eggs hatch after three or four weeks. Larger hawks take the longest to hatch.

At first the young hawks are covered with a whitish down and are quite helpless. The parents bring food to the edge of the nest, where they tear it to pieces and drop it in the eager, open mouths. As the young grow older, they lose their down and grow feathers a little duller in color than those of their parents. They fly from the nest after a month or six weeks.

North American hawks. Seventeen kinds of hawks live in the part of North America north of Mexico. They are divided into three groups. The smallest group, the *harrier,* contains only the *marsh hawk.* The two main groups are the *bird hawks* and *buzzard hawks.*

Bird hawks have slim bodies and long pointed wings. These swift-flying hawks catch both birds and mice. They have also been called *chicken hawks* because they sometimes raid poultry yards. The largest bird hawk is the *goshawk.* The females are sometimes 25 inches (64 centimeters) long with a wingspread of 44 to 47 inches (112 to 119 centimeters). The *sharp-shinned hawk* is the smallest of the bird hawks. The males may be only 10 inches (25 centimeters) long with a wingspread of about 21 inches (53 centimeters). The third bird hawk is called *Cooper's hawk.* This type of hawk is between the goshawk and sharp-shinned hawks in size. The goshawk is rare and is found mainly in the deep woods of Canada and Alaska. The sharp-shinned and Cooper's hawks live in most parts of North America north of Mexico.

Buzzard hawks are large, heavy-bodied birds, with long, broad wings, and wide, rounded tails. They soar in the sky in wide circles, or sit quietly on some high perch and wait for their prey. Then they swoop down with great speed. They usually eat insects, frogs, snakes, lizards, and various harmful rodents. The largest buzzard hawks are about the size of the goshawk. They include the *red-tailed, red-shouldered,* and *rough-legged* hawks. The broad-winged hawk is the smallest, from 14 to 18 inches (36 to 46 centimeters) long. It lives only east of the Rocky Mountains, but the other species live in many parts of the United States.

Hawks play an important role in the balance of nature by preying on such small animals as mice and rats. In the United States, the federal government and most states have laws that prohibit the killing of hawks.

Scientific classification. Hawks are in the hawk family, Accipitridae. Bird hawks make up the genus *Accipiter.* The goshawk is *A. gentilis;* Cooper's hawk, *A. cooperii;* and the sharp-

Red-tailed hawk
Buteo jamaicensis
Found in North and Central America
and West Indies
Body length 25 inches (64 centimeters)

Marsh hawk
Circus cyaneus
Found in temperate Northern
Hemisphere
Body length 24 inches (61 centimeters)

WORLD BOOK diagram by Marion Pahl

Goshawk
Accipiter gentilis
Found in temperate Northern
Hemisphere
Body length 26 inches (66 centimeters)

The hawk's vision is sharper than a human being's. Its eyes have more light-sensitive cells, and most kinds of hawks have more than one *fovea* (an area of the retina). At a great distance, a person sees a rabbit as a blur, but a hawk sees it clearly.

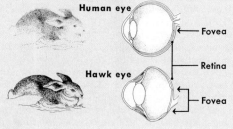

Human eye

Hawk eye

Fovea

Retina

Fovea

WORLD BOOK illustrations by Albert Gilbert

shinned hawk, *A. striatus.* Most buzzard hawks are in the genus *Buteo.* The red-tailed hawk is *B. jamaicensis;* the red-shouldered hawk, *B. lineatus;* the rough-legged hawk, *B. lagopus;* the broad-winged hawk, *B. platypterus;* and Swainson's hawk, *B. swainsoni.* The marsh hawk is *Circus cyaneus.* The serpent hawk is *Spilornis cheela.* The Malacca pern is *Machaerhamphus alcinus.* One common honey buzzard is *Pernis apivorus.*

Olin Sewall Pettingill, Jr.

Related articles in *World Book* include:

Bird (picture: How birds feed)	Harpy eagle
Buzzard	Kite (bird)
Falcon	Marsh hawk
Falconry	Vulture

Hawk moth is a member of a world-wide family of large, brightly colored moths that are also called *sphinx moths.* These moths have powerful, streamlined bodies; long, slender front wings; and small hind wings. They fly quickly and skillfully, hovering in front of flowers and sucking nectar, much like hummingbirds. For this reason they are sometimes called *hummingbird moths.* A hawk moth sips nectar through its *proboscis,* a coiled tube extending from the mouth. The proboscis of one species of hawk moth reaches 10 inches (25 centimeters) in length.

The caterpillars often have a sharp horn at the rear end, and are called *hornworms.* When these creatures rest, they raise the front part of the body. In profile, they look like the Egyptian sphinx. They spend their pupal stage in the soil, and do not spin cocoons.

Scientific classification. Hawk moths make up the sphinx moth family, Sphingidae.   Alexander B. Klots

See also **Death's-head moth; Moth** (pictures).

Hawke, Robert James Lee (1929-   ), became prime minister of Australia in 1983. He took office after the Labor Party, which he heads, defeated the Liberal Party-National Party coalition in parliamentary general elections. Hawke succeeded Liberal Party leader John Malcolm Fraser as prime minister. His party won elections held in 1984 and in 1987, and he remained prime minister. Hawke favors increased power for the federal government. As prime minister, he worked to create jobs through government spending and to improve relations between business and labor. He called for continued close ties between Australia and the United States, Western Europe, Japan, and Southeast Asia.

Hawke was born in Bordertown, South Australia. He received a law degree from the University of Western Australia and attended Oxford University in England on a Rhodes scholarship. He became a research officer for the Australian Council of Trade Unions in 1958 and served as its president from 1970

Australian Picture Library
Robert Hawke

to 1980. He became well known for settling disputes between labor unions and businesses. He was elected to Australia's House of Representatives in 1980. He became leader of the Australian Labor Party in February 1983.

J. D. B. Miller

Hawking. See Falconry.

Hawkins, Coleman (1904-1969), was the first important tenor saxophonist in jazz. His full rich tone and superb fluency made him one of the most widely imitated instrumentalists of the 1930's and 1940's.

Hawkins was born in St. Joseph, Mo. While a teenager, he went to New York City with a jazz group that accompanied blues singer Mamie Smith. From 1923 to 1934, while playing in Fletcher Henderson's orchestra, he gained an international reputation. He was extremely popular in other countries and he moved to Europe in 1934, returning to the United States in 1939. He recorded an improvised solo based on the song "Body and Soul" in 1939. It became a best seller and his most memorable performance. After 1940, Hawkins led small groups and toured with the "Jazz at the Philharmonic" concert series.   Leonard Feather

Hawkins, Sir John (1532-1595), also spelled *Hawkyns,* was one of the most famous Elizabethan sea captains. He was a fearless adventurer and ruthless slave trader. Hawkins became treasurer of the English navy in 1573. He commanded a squadron in the fleet that defeated the Spanish Armada in 1588, and was knighted aboard ship. Hawkins was born in Plymouth. See also **Drake, Sir Francis.**   Paul M. Kendall

Hawks, Howard (1896-1977), was an American motion-picture director known for his action films. Hawks also helped create a fast-paced style of comedy called *screwball comedy,* which ridiculed the eccentric or silly behavior of wealthy characters.

Two of Hawks's finest films deal with World War I (1914-1918). One of them, *The Dawn Patrol* (1930), describes the adventures of fighter pilots in the war. The other, *Sergeant York* (1941), tells the true story of the American soldier Alvin C. York, who became one of the war's most famous heroes. Hawks directed several Westerns, including *Red River* (1948) and *Rio Bravo* (1959). His violent melodrama *Scarface* (1932) became one of Hollywood's most famous gangster movies. His film *The Big Sleep* (1946) ranks among the best private detective movies ever made. Hawks's most successful comedies were *Twentieth Century* (1934), *Bringing Up Baby* (1938), and *His Girl Friday* (1940).

Hawks was born in Goshen, Ind. He entered the film industry in 1918 as a writer and editor. After making a number of short films, he directed his first feature film, *The Road to Glory* (1926). Hawks directed about 40 films.

John F. Mariani

Hawthorn, also called *thorn apple,* is a thorny shrub or tree with fragrant white, pink, or red flowers. The common English hawthorn is a favorite plant for hedges. It is noted for its beauty in May, when it blooms. The English countryside then becomes white with hawthorn blossoms. The hawthorn is one of the flowers for the month of May, and is sometimes even called the *mayhaw.* The hawthorn is a low, dense tree. Its leaves change to scarlet or yellow in autumn. Its fruit, called a *haw,* is a fleshy pome. It looks much like a small apple. For this reason, the hawthorn sometimes is called the red haw or scarlet haw.

Many species of hawthorn grow in America. One of these species is the *downy hawthorn.* This small tree has crooked, spreading branches. Its blossoms are white. The orange-scarlet haws ripen late in the summer, but fall soon after they mature. Another American hawthorn

© A-Z Collection from Photo Researchers

The hawthorn tree produces fragrant flowers. The English hawthorn, *above*, blooms in May. In autumn, its leaves change to scarlet or yellow.

is the *cockspur,* or *cockspur thorn.* It sometimes grows 25 feet (8 meters) tall, and has long, straight thorns. Some people cultivate the cockspur as an ornamental tree.

Scientific classification. The hawthorn belongs to the rose family, Rosaceae. The English hawthorn is classified as *Crataegus oxyacantha.* The downy hawthorn is *C. mollis* and the cockspur hawthorn is *C. crus-galli.*   Theodore W. Bretz

See also **Missouri** (picture: The state flower); **Tree** (Familiar broadleaf and needleleaf trees [picture]).

Hawthorne, Nathaniel (1804-1864), ranks among America's major authors. Between about 1825 and 1850, he developed his talent by writing short fiction and the novel *Fanshawe* (1828). Then he gained international fame for his novel *The Scarlet Letter,* a masterpiece of American literature.

Hawthorne's works are noted for their psychological probing into human nature, especially its darker side. Hawthorne set many stories against the somber background of Puritan New England, the world of his ancestors. Unlike most fiction writers of his time, he was not primarily interested in stirring the reader by sensational or sentimental effects. Hawthorne called his writing *romance,* and defined romance as a method of showing "the depths of our common nature." To Hawthorne, romance meant confronting reality, rather than evading it. Hawthorne often dealt with the themes of morality, sin, and redemption. Among his early influences were the parables and allegories of John Bunyan and Edmund Spenser.

Life. Nathaniel Hathorne was born in Salem, Mass. He added the "w" to his name when he began publishing. Hawthorne graduated from Bowdoin College in 1825. While attending Bowdoin, he became a friend of future U.S. President Franklin Pierce. After college, he settled in Salem and continued writing. Hawthorne worked in the Boston Custom House

Nathaniel Hawthorne by Charles Osgood. Essex Institute, Salem, Mass.

Nathaniel Hawthorne

in 1839 and 1840 and was a member of the idealistic Brook Farm community near Boston briefly in 1841 (see **Brook Farm**).

Hawthorne married Sophia Peabody in 1842. They moved to the now-famous *Old Manse* in Concord, Mass., where Hawthorne continued writing. See **Concord**.

Hawthorne was surveyor of customs in the port of Salem from 1846 to 1849. In 1853, President Pierce appointed Hawthorne to a four-year term as United States consul in Liverpool, England. After 1857, Hawthorne lived in Italy and again in England before returning to Concord in 1860. He died on May 18 or 19, 1864, while visiting New Hampshire with Pierce.

His stories and sketches. Between 1825 and 1850, Hawthorne wrote more than 100 tales and sketches for periodicals. Most of these works were collected in *Twice-Told Tales* (1837, 1842, 1851), *Mosses from an Old Manse* (1846), and *The Snow Image and Other Twice-Told Tales* (1851).

The stories and sketches reveal themes central to Hawthorne's imagination. He was haunted by the Puritan society of Massachusetts during the 1600's. To him, the society was represented by his stern forefathers, especially John Hathorne, who was a judge during the Salem witchcraft trials. Hawthorne painted a grim picture of the Puritan past in "Young Goodman Brown," "The Maypole of Merrymount," and other short stories. He was one of the first writers in the United States to re-create the past of his native region. Hawthorne showed the effects of secret guilt in "The Minister's Black Veil" and other stories. In "Wakefield," he described the effects of voluntary isolation from society.

In "The Birthmark," "Ethan Brand," and "Rappaccini's Daughter," three of Hawthorne's finest stories, the central characters suffer from intellectual pride. Hawthorne called such pride "the Unpardonable Sin," describing it as the "sin of an intellect that triumphed over the sense of brotherhood with man and reverence with God." Other stories, such as "The Artist of the Beautiful," show Hawthorne's concern for the artist's role in society. In "My Kinsman, Major Molineux," Hawthorne treated the conflict between youth and established authority.

Hawthorne's sketches deal chiefly with New England scenes of his time. They range in tone from the light whimsy of "A Rill from the Town Pump" to the satire of "The Celestial Railroad" and the dark fantasy of "The Haunted Mind." Hawthorne also wrote two popular children's books, *A Wonder Book for Boys and Girls* (1852) and *Tanglewood Tales* (1853).

His novels. *The Scarlet Letter* (1850) is introduced by "The Custom House," an essay in which Hawthorne sketched the novel's background and his experiences as a customs official while writing the book.

The novel itself is controlled by a single idea—the suffering that results from sin. Hawthorne believed that sin—adultery in *The Scarlet Letter*—results in the isolation of the sinners. Isolation leads to suffering, and suffering leads to further sinning and further suffering. The spiral continues until the sinners either destroy themselves or seek forgiveness and rejoin the community.

The Scarlet Letter is set in Puritan Boston. The plot is formed by the interactions of the adulteress Hester Prynne, the adulterer Arthur Dimmesdale, and Hester's husband, Roger Chillingworth. Hester symbolizes the force of love. Dimmesdale, a minister, represents the spirit, and Chillingworth symbolizes the mind.

Hawthorne shaped his tale in four parts, each dominated by a single force. The force in the first section (chapters 1-8) is the Puritan community; in the second (chapters 9-12) it is Chillingworth; in the third (chapters 13-20) it is Hester; and in the closing part, Dimmesdale. Each section centers on one great dramatic scene in a symbolic setting. The symbolic setting in the first, second, and fourth sections is the scaffold in the Boston market place, on which sinners were exhibited and shamed. The forest with its darkness is the symbol in the third section. Hawthorne expanded and intensified the meaning of the action by pictures of light and dark colors he created verbally and by his quiet, ironic tone.

The House of the Seven Gables (1851) tells the story of a curse placed on the House of Pyncheon by Matthew Maule, a victim of the Salem witchcraft trials. Hawthorne traces the curse's effect on the Pyncheon descendants and describes their final reconciliation to their past.

The Blithedale Romance (1852), a tragic love story, is Hawthorne's closest approach to a novel of observed life. He drew his characters in part from the men and women he had known in the Brook Farm community.

The Marble Faun (1860) is a psychological study of two young American artists in Italy and their relationship with a mysterious woman painter and a young nobleman.   John Clendenning

Additional resources

Gaeddert, LouAnn B. *A New England Love Story: Nathaniel Hawthorne and Sophia Peabody.* Dial, 1980. Suitable for younger readers.

Martin, Terence. *Nathaniel Hawthorne.* Rev. ed. Twayne, 1983.

Mellow, James R. *Nathaniel Hawthorne in His Times.* Houghton, 1980.

Turner, Arlin. *Nathaniel Hawthorne: A Biography.* Oxford, 1980.

Hay is a horse and cattle feed made up of the dried stems and leaves of plants. Hay may be made from cultivated grasses such as timothy, bluegrass, and redtop. Or it may be made from some of the wild, or prairie, grasses. Alfalfa, clover, velvet beans, rye, barley, and oats are also used. The use of this dried-plant food dates almost as far back as the taming of the horse.

After farmers cut the hay, they allow it to lie on the ground to dry. It is then raked into long rows, called *windrows,* and allowed to dry still further. To speed drying, some farmers use a *hay conditioner,* which cuts and crushes the hay and rakes it into windrows in one continuous operation. When the hay is dry enough, farmers either bale, stack, or chop it.

Baling machines tie the bales with string or wire. Conventional baling machines press the hay into rectangular bales that weigh from 50 to 100 pounds (23 to 45 kilograms). *Round balers* roll hay into round bales weighing as much as $1\frac{1}{2}$ short tons (1.4 metric tons). Some baling machines drop the bales on the ground to be picked up later. Others load the bales directly on a wagon. The bales are stored in barns or kept outdoors. Rectangular bales must be covered with loose hay or canvas for protection from the rain when stacked outside. Round bales shed water because of their shape, and so they may be kept uncovered. Machines called *hay stackers* compress or pile hay into large mounds.

© David R. Frazier

Hay is harvested with a baler. The baler shown above presses the cut hay into rectangular bales and then ties them with twine.

If a farmer chooses to chop the hay before storing it, a forage harvester is used. This machine cuts the hay into short pieces and blows it onto a wagon or truck. Some machines form the hay into wafers or *pellets* (tiny balls). The farmer then hauls the hay to the barn. A conveyor moves the hay from the wagon into another blower, which blows it into the barn's *haymow.*

Many farmers use artificial means for curing hay to speed up the harvest and to decrease the hazard of getting the hay wet with rain. After cutting the hay, farmers allow it to lie in the field until it is about half dry. Then they harvest the hay and haul it to a drier. There, large fans blow air through the hay until the moisture has been reduced to about 20 per cent.

Hay that contains too much moisture will spoil. Hay will *sweat* (heat) after it is stored in the barn. Sometimes it creates so much heat that it sets itself on fire. For this reason, farmers take great care to dry their hay adequately before they store it.   Wayne W. Huffine

See also **Alfalfa; Clover; Grass; Rake.**

Hay, John Milton (1838-1905), was an American diplomat and statesman. He is best remembered for his Open-Door Policy in China.

In 1899, powerful European nations and Japan were trying to extend their influence over the weak and backward Chinese Empire. Hay was U.S. secretary of state at that time, and he feared that partition of China would hurt American trade. He asked England, Russia, Germany, France, Italy, and Japan to respect the rights of all nations to trade in China on an equal basis. This he called the *Open-Door Policy* (see **Open-Door Policy**). The next year, because of European reaction to the Boxer Rebellion, Hay went beyond the Open Door to ask the other countries to keep China intact and independent (see **Boxer Rebellion**). The nations did not give the strict promises Hay wanted, but American policy did help prevent partition of China.

Hay was born in Salem, Ind. He graduated from Brown University and began practicing law in Springfield, Ill., in 1861. When Abraham Lincoln became President, he made Hay his assistant private secretary. After Lincoln's death, Hay entered the diplomatic service and became secretary of the legations in Paris, Vienna, and Madrid.

In 1870, Hay became an editorial writer on the *New*

York Tribune. For several years, he spent most of his time writing. In 1897, Hay was appointed United States ambassador to Great Britain. From 1898 until his death in 1905, he served as secretary of state under President William McKinley and President Theodore Roosevelt.

Hay based his foreign policy on close cooperation between the United States and Great Britain. He worked closely with the British in his policy toward China, in the peaceful settlement of a dispute over the boundary between Alaska and Canada, and in the diplomacy that prepared the way for building the Panama Canal (see **Hay-Pauncefote Treaty**).

Hay's books include the 10-volume *Abraham Lincoln: A History* (1886-1890), *Pike County Ballads* (1871), and several volumes of poems and essays.   Nelson M. Blake

Hay fever is an allergy that occurs most frequently during the spring, summer, and fall. Grasses, trees, and weeds produce pollen during those seasons, and hay fever sufferers are allergic to pollen. About 6 per cent of the people in the United States have hay fever. Like most allergies, hay fever runs in families. A person can develop the allergy at any age. The medical name for hay fever is *pollinosis.* See **Allergy.**

Symptoms of hay fever include runny, red, and itching eyes and a runny, stopped-up nose. The nose may also itch and swell. Hay fever victims have repeated periods of sneezing and may temporarily lose their sense of smell. A victim's ears may be stopped up as well.

About a third of those who suffer from hay fever develop seasonal asthma. Hay fever also may result in *sinusitis,* a sinus infection. In addition, it may cause the development of infection or of growths called *polyps* in the mucous membrane. See **Asthma; Sinus.**

Causes and prevention. The most common cause of hay fever in the United States is the pollen of the ragweed plant. In most areas, ragweed produces pollen in the late summer or fall. See **Ragweed.**

The pollen of other plants also causes hay fever. For example, Russian thistle is a major cause of hay fever in New Mexico and Utah. Airborne fungi and molds can also cause the allergy in some persons or even increase the seriousness of its symptoms.

Hay fever can be prevented or made less severe by avoiding the offending pollens. Some communities have tried to eliminate ragweed. But wind carries pollen considerable distances, and elimination programs have not generally been successful.

Many newspapers and radio and television stations in the United States announce the daily local *pollen index* during the summer months. This figure is based on the number of ragweed pollen grains in 1 cubic yard (0.8 cubic meter) of air. The Midwestern States have the greatest concentration of pollen in the country. Areas with little ragweed pollen include the Pacific Coast and the southern tip of Florida.

Treatment. Hay fever has the same symptoms as a year-round condition called *perennial allergic rhinitis.* A physician performs tests to identify the causes of a patient's allergy. If the person has hay fever, the doctor performs tests to discover which pollen, fungus, or mold caused it. Most persons with allergic rhinitis are sensitive to any kind of dust—especially house dust—and to some foods and even to animal dandruff.

Most doctors prescribe drugs called *antihistamines,*

which provide quick relief for some hay fever sufferers. These drugs should be taken only under a physician's supervision because they cause dangerous side effects in some persons. Other drugs lessen the swelling of the membranes lining the nose and reduce the running of the nose.

If a patient is extremely sensitive to pollen, the doctor may prescribe *hyposensitization.* This treatment involves injecting pollen extract into the patient's body at regular intervals, slowly increasing the strength of the concentration of the extract. The injections cause the body to form antibodies to help fight the allergic reaction. In most cases, this therapy helps provide relief from hay fever symptoms.   Joan S. Gallagher

Additional resources

Dehejia, Harsha V. *The Allergy Book.* Van Nostrand, 1981.
Knight, Allan. *Asthma & Hay Fever: How to Relieve Wheezing and Sneezing.* Arco, 1981.
Silverstein, Alvin and V. B. *Itch, Sniffle & Sneeze: All About Asthma, Hay Fever and Other Allergies.* Four Winds, 1978. For younger readers.

Hay-Pauncefote Treaty, *HAY PAWNS fut,* enabled the United States to build the Panama Canal. It was signed by the United States and Great Britain in 1901. The treaty gave the United States the sole right to build or supervise the construction of a canal across the Central American isthmus, as well as the right to manage it. All nations were to pay fair and equal traffic charges and enjoy equal rights during peacetime. In wartime, the U.S. could close the canal to any nation. Great Britain admitted that the United States also had the right to fortify and defend the canal. The treaty was named for its negotiators—U.S. Secretary of State John Milton Hay and British ambassador to the United States Sir Julian Pauncefote. See also **Panama Canal; Clayton-Bulwer Treaty; Treaty** (picture).   Richard Hofstadter

Hayakawa, *HAH yah KAH wah,* **S. I.** (1906-   ), is an American expert on *semantics* (the meaning of words). Hayakawa, a Republican, represented California in the United States Senate from 1977 to 1983. He was president of San Francisco State College (now San Francisco State University) from 1969 to 1973. In 1968, as acting president, he had gained fame for taking firm measures to end student disturbances.

Samuel Ichiye Hayakawa was born in Vancouver, B.C., the son of Japanese immigrants. He became a U.S. citizen in 1954. Hayakawa graduated from the University of Manitoba and earned graduate degrees at McGill University and the University of Wisconsin. He taught English at the University of Chicago before joining the San Francisco State faculty in 1955 as a professor of English. Hayakawa has written or edited several books on word meaning and usage. His works include *Language in Thought and Action* (1941) and *Symbol, Status and Personality* (1963).   Richard E. Gross

Hayden, Carl Trumbull (1877-1972), an Arizona Democrat, served in the United States Congress from 1912 until 1969—longer than any other person. He served in the House of Representatives from 1912, when his state was admitted to the Union, until 1927, when he entered the U.S. Senate. Hayden became chairman of the Senate Committee on Appropriations in 1955. He served as president *pro tempore* of the Senate from 1957 to 1969, when he retired. Hayden advocated legislation to advance forest preservation, federal highway construction, and irrigation of dry regions. Hayden was born in Hayden's Ferry (now Tempe), Ariz. He attended Stanford University. Paul Hubbard

Hayden, *HAYD uhn,* **Melissa** (1923-), is a Canadian ballerina. She danced in the Radio City Music Hall in New York City, then joined the Ballet Theatre in 1945. She danced with the New York City Ballet from 1950 to 1973, where she starred in several ballets created by George Balanchine. These include *Agon* (1957) and *A Midsummer Night's Dream* (1962). She won special praise for her interpretation of the title role in Birgit Cullberg's ballet *Medea* (1958).

Melissa Hayden was born in Toronto, and moved to New York City when she was 17. She won the *Dance Magazine* Award in 1961 for "her versatility, craftsmanship, and temperament." Selma Jeanne Cohen

See also **Ballet** (pictures).

Haydn, *HYD uhn,* **Joseph** (1732-1809), an Austrian composer, ranks among the most important persons in the development of instrumental music. He has been called the father of the symphony. Haydn did not write the first symphonies. However, he developed the symphony from a short, simple form of musical composition to a long form for large orchestra. The combination of instruments that he used in his symphonies became the basis of today's symphony orchestra.

Haydn composed more than 100 symphonies. Most of his later ones consist of four *movements* (sections)—fast, slow, minuet, fast. The first movement may have a slow, noble-sounding introduction.

Haydn wrote more than 80 *string quartets* (compositions for two violins, a viola, and a cello). The first violin dominates most of his early quartets, and the other instruments accompany. In his later quartets, Haydn gave the instruments greater equality, and the music suggests a lively conversation among four people. Many of Haydn's quartets are still popular and have acquired nicknames. These quartets include "The Bird" (1781), "Sunrise" (1799?), and "Emperor" (1799?).

Haydn wrote operas and other works for voices. Two *oratorios* (compositions for soloists, large chorus, and orchestra) rank among his greatest works. They are *The Creation* (1798) and *The Seasons* (1801).

Haydn was born Franz Joseph Haydn in Rohrau, an Austrian village near Vienna. A family friend noticed Haydn's pleasant voice and helped him gain admission to the boarding school at the emperor's court in Vienna in 1740. Singers were trained for the Court Chapel at the school. However, Haydn was dismissed from the choir school in 1749 after his voice changed.

Many difficult years followed for the young musician. Finally, in 1761, Haydn went to work at the court of Prince Esterhazy in eastern Austria. He was soon put in charge of all music at the court and remained there for about 30 years. The prince was fond of music, and Haydn was kept busy composing works for him.

Haydn met the composer Wolfgang Mozart in 1781. The two remained close friends until Mozart's death in 1791. Haydn acknowledged Mozart's superiority as a writer of operas, and Mozart admitted he learned much from Haydn about composing instrumental music.

Haydn visited England in 1791 and 1794. He wrote his last 12 symphonies (numbers 93 to 104) there. Generally called the "London" Symphonies, they include the famous "Surprise" Symphony (number 94). Haydn spent his last years in Vienna. Reinhard G. Pauly

Additional resources

Hodgson, Antony, ed. *The Music of Joseph Haydn: The Symphonies.* Fairleigh Dickinson, 1976.
Landon, H. C. Robbins. *Haydn: Chronicle and Works.* 5 vols. Indiana Univ. Press, 1976-1981. *Haydn: A Documentary Study.* Rizzoli, 1981.
Larsen, Jens P. *The New Grove Haydn.* Norton, 1983. First pub. in 1980 ed. of *The New Grove Dictionary of Music and Musicians.*

Hayek, *HY uhk,* **Friedrich August von** (1899-), an Austrian-born economist, won the 1974 Nobel Prize in economic science. He shared the award with Gunnar Myrdal, a Swedish economist.

Hayek is the leading speaker for the so-called Austrian school of economics, which favors a free-market economy. He believes no one will ever be able to understand all the complexities of economics. Therefore, he opposes government attempts to manage a nation's economic policies. For example, he opposes deficit spending—that is, a government's spending more than it receives in taxes—and unemployment compensation.

Hayek has written several books on the role of money in a nation's economy. They include *Prices and Production* (1931), *The Pure Theory of Capital* (1941), and *The Road to Serfdom* (1944).

Hayek was born in Vienna in 1899. He became a British citizen in 1938. Hayek has taught at the University of London, the University of Chicago, the University of Frieburg in West Germany, and Salzburg University in Austria. Roger LeRoy Miller

Hayes, Helen (1900-), is an American actress. Many critics consider the role of Queen Victoria in the play *Victoria Regina* (1935) her greatest success. Hayes won the 1931-1932 Academy Award as best actress for her performance in *The Sin of Madelon Claudet,* which was her first film. She received the 1970 Academy Award as best supporting actress for her performance in *Airport.*

Friedman-Abeles
Helen Hayes

Hayes made her stage debut in 1905 and played juvenile roles for years. Her performance in Sir James Barrie's play *Dear Brutus* in 1918 made her a star.

She was born Helen Hayes Brown in Washington, D.C. In 1928, she married playwright Charles MacArthur. Her autobiography, *On Reflection,* was published in 1968. Mary Virginia Heinlein

Hayes, Roland (1887-1977), was a famous black American lyric tenor. His recitals of classical songs and black folk melodies gained him an international reputation. He was born in Curryville, Ga., and attended Fisk University. Hayes gave his first concert in 1916. He appeared as soloist with leading orchestras in Europe and America. He won the 1924 Spingarn Medal (see **Spingarn Medal**). Martial Singher

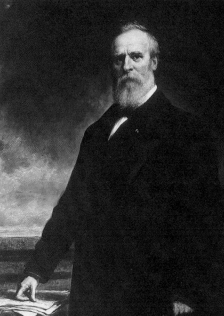

**19th President of
the United States 1877-1881**

Grant
18th President
1869-1877
Republican

Hayes
19th President
1877-1881
Republican

Garfield
20th President
1881
Republican

**William A.
Wheeler**
Vice President
1877-1881

Detail of an oil portrait (1884) by Daniel Huntington;
© White House Historical Association (photography by the National Geographic Society)

Hayes, Rutherford Birchard (1822-1893), was elected President by a margin of only one electoral vote. His victory over Samuel J. Tilden in 1876 climaxed the most disputed presidential election in United States history. Congress had to create a special Electoral Commission to decide the winner.

Hayes was a studious, good-natured man who enjoyed books more than politics. Ohio Republicans nominated him for Congress while he was fighting in the Civil War. Hayes refused to campaign. He declared that any officer who "would abandon his post to electioneer for a seat in Congress, ought to be scalped." Hayes won the election. He later served three terms as governor of Ohio.

When Hayes became President, the nation was suffering from a business depression and the political scandals of the previous Administration of Ulysses S. Grant. The unsolved problem of Reconstruction in the South still divided the American people, even though the Civil War had ended 12 years before. Hayes was not popular at first. Democrats charged he had "stolen" the election. His fellow Republicans were bitter because he refused to give special favors to party politicians.

However, by the time Hayes left office, most Americans respected him for his sincerity and honesty. He had promised to end Reconstruction, and he did. Within two months after he took office, the last federal troops marched from the South. Hayes also put the government on the path toward civil service reform. Throughout his career, Hayes tried to live by his motto: "He serves his party best who serves his country best."

During Hayes's Administration, the United States continued its remarkable growth. The nation became more industrialized than ever before, and labor unions gained

thousands of new members. The population of New York City soared above a million. Civil War General Lew Wallace won nationwide fame for his novel *Ben-Hur.* And Thomas A. Edison visited the White House to demonstrate his favorite invention, the phonograph.

Early life

Rutherford Birchard Hayes was born on Oct. 4, 1822, in Delaware, Ohio. He was the fifth child of Rutherford Hayes, Jr., and Sophia Birchard Hayes. The family had migrated to Ohio from Dummerston, Vt., in 1817. Hayes had two brothers and two sisters, but only he and his sister Fanny grew to adulthood. Hayes's father, a successful store owner, died two months before Rutherford, or "Rud," was born. A bachelor uncle, Sardis Birchard, became the children's guardian.

Education. Hayes was a champion speller in elementary school. He later boasted that "not one in a thousand could spell me down!" Hayes prepared for college at private schools in Norwalk, Ohio; and Middletown, Conn. In 1838, he entered Kenyon College in Gambier, Ohio. He graduated in 1842 at the head of his class. Hayes entered Harvard Law School the next year. He graduated and was admitted to the bar in 1845.

Lawyer. Hayes began practicing law in Lower Sandusky (later Fremont), Ohio, where his uncle lived. In 1850, he opened a law office in Cincinnati. At first, Hayes had so few clients and was so poor that he slept in his office to save money. He enjoyed studying literature, and joined the recently formed Literary Club of Cincinnati.

Hayes's law practice gradually increased. In 1852, he won statewide attention as a criminal lawyer in two widely publicized murder trials. His brilliant defense ar-

Railroad workers rioted during a nationwide strike in 1877. Hayes called out federal troops to restore order.

The electric light was invented by Thomas Edison in 1879. In 1877, Edison had invented a phonograph.

The U.S. flag gained a 38th star in 1877, marking Colorado's entry into the Union in 1876 as the 38th state.

The world of President Hayes

Reconstruction ended in 1877, when the last federal occupation troops were withdrawn from the South.
Flag Day was first officially celebrated on June 14, 1877.
The first black cadet to graduate from the United States Military Academy at West Point was H. O. Flipper, in 1877.
Henry M. Stanley, a Welsh explorer, reached the mouth of the Congo River in 1877, after a nearly three-year journey across Africa. He became the first white person to trace the river from Central Africa to its mouth on the Atlantic coast.
Famous books published during Hayes's presidency included *Black Beauty* (1877), a novel by Anna Sewell protesting cruel treatment of horses; *Ben-Hur: A Tale of the Christ* (1880), a novel by Lew Wallace; and *Uncle Remus: His Songs and His Sayings* (1880), a collection of Southern black folk tales by Joel Chandler Harris.
The Russo-Turkish War of 1877-1878 gave Russia control of important areas in the Caucasus region, near the Black Sea.
The first commercial telephone exchange opened in New Haven, Conn., in 1878. It had 21 subscribers.
The woman suffrage amendment was proposed in the United States Congress for the first time in 1878.
The first journalism course was given at the University of Missouri in 1879.
The first woman lawyer to practice before the Supreme Court of the United States was Belva Ann Lockwood, in 1879.
Wilhelm Wundt, a German philosopher, established one of the first laboratories of experimental psychology in 1879.

The Rutherford B. Hayes Presidential Center; Consolidated Edison Company of New York, Inc.

guments saved his clients from receiving the death penalty. In 1858, the Cincinnati City Council elected Hayes to fill a vacancy as city solicitor. He held this influential political and legal post until shortly before the Civil War began three years later.

Hayes's family. On Dec. 30, 1852, Hayes married Lucy Ware Webb (Aug. 28, 1831-June 25, 1889). They had eight children, but three died in infancy.

Lucy Hayes was the daughter of a Chillicothe, Ohio, physician. She had graduated in 1850 from the Wesleyan Female College in Cincinnati, and was the first President's wife to have a college degree. Her intelligence and social grace helped Hayes throughout his career. Mrs. Hayes championed many of the leading moral causes of the day. She became active in supporting the abolition of slavery, prohibition of alcohol, and aid to the poor.

Soldier. When the Civil War began in 1861, the Literary Club of Cincinnati formed a military drilling company, and elected Hayes captain. He was later appointed a major of a regiment of Ohio Volunteers. Hayes distinguished himself in several battles, and earned rapid promotion during his four years in the Army. He was wounded four times and had four horses shot from under him. On June 8, 1865, two months after the war

Important dates in Hayes's life

1822	(Oct. 4) Born in Delaware, Ohio.
1852	(Dec. 30) Married Lucy Ware Webb.
1864	Elected to the U.S. House of Representatives.
1867	Elected governor of Ohio.
1876	Elected President of the United States.
1893	(Jan. 17) Died in Fremont, Ohio.

ended, Hayes resigned from the Army with the rank of brevet major general.

Political career

Congressman. Hayes was nominated for the U.S. House of Representatives in 1864. He received the news while fighting in the Shenandoah Valley under General Philip H. Sheridan. He refused to campaign for the office because the outcome of the war was still in doubt. Hayes won the election, but did not take his seat in Congress until December 1865. He won reelection in 1866,

Brown Bros.

Hayes's birthplace, a brick house in Delaware, Ohio, *above,* was later used as a store. The building was torn down in 1928, and a bronze tablet now marks the site.

Detail of an oil portrait (1881) by Daniel Huntington;
© White House Historical Association (photography by the
National Geographic Society)

Lucy Webb Hayes was the first President's wife to have a college degree. She often was called "Lemonade Lucy" because she refused to serve alcoholic beverages at the White House.

but resigned in July 1867, a month after he was nominated for governor of Ohio.

While in Congress, Hayes did outstanding work as chairman of the Joint Committee on the Library of Congress. Under his leadership, Congress transferred the scientific library of the Smithsonian Institution to the Library of Congress.

Governor. In 1867, Hayes won election to the first of three terms as governor of Ohio. His election was a personal triumph because he campaigned in favor of an unpopular black suffrage amendment to the state constitution. Hayes planned to retire from politics at the end of his second term in 1872. But Republican leaders persuaded him to run for Congress. He was defeated, and spent the next three years at his home near Fremont, Ohio, where he lived quietly and dealt in real estate. In 1875, he won a third term as governor.

Hayes gained nationwide attention as a courageous administrator. He worked hard for economy in government and for a strong civil service program based on

merit rather than political influence. He also helped establish the college that became Ohio State University.

Campaign of 1876. As President Grant's second term drew to a close, the corruption-torn Republican Party split into two main factions. The *Stalwarts,* led by Senator Roscoe Conkling of New York, favored a third term for Grant. The *Half-Breeds,* led by Representative James G. Blaine of Maine, opposed the Stalwarts. Grant refused to run for a third term, but neither the Stalwarts nor the Half-Breeds had enough votes to nominate a presidential candidate. Many party leaders supported Hayes as a compromise candidate. At the Republican National Convention in June 1876, Hayes won the presidential nomination on the seventh ballot. The delegates nominated Representative William A. Wheeler of New York for Vice President.

Samuel J. Tilden, who had gained fame as a reform governor of New York, was Hayes's Democratic opponent. The Democrats chose Governor Thomas A. Hendricks of Indiana for Vice President. The new Greenback Party nominated Peter Cooper for President (see **Greenback Party**).

The Republicans seemed to have little chance for victory. The Democrats had increased their voting strength since 1874, when they gained control of the U.S. House of Representatives. As election day approached, however, President Grant sent federal troops to South Carolina and Louisiana to protect the rights of black voters, and gain support for the Republicans. Tilden received 4,288,546 popular votes to 4,034,311 for Hayes.

The election dispute. Four states—Louisiana, South Carolina, Florida, and Oregon—submitted two sets of electoral returns, one by the Democrats and one by the Republicans. As a result, both parties claimed victory. On December 6, the Electoral College met and voted. Hayes received 165 unquestioned votes. Tilden got 184 votes, one short of a majority. Twenty electoral votes, from the four states that submitted conflicting returns, were disputed. In January 1877, Congress appointed a 15-member Electoral Commission to settle the matter (see **Electoral Commission**). Its decisions were to be final, unless both houses of Congress voted otherwise. During the debate in Congress, members of both parties threatened to seize the government by force.

As Inauguration Day approached, leaders of both parties feared that the country might be left without a President. In a private meeting, Southern Democrats in Congress agreed not to oppose the decision of the Electoral Commission. This agreement gave Hayes the presidency because the Commission had a Republican majority. In exchange, the Republicans promised to end Reconstruction and withdraw federal troops from the

Hayes's election

Place of nominating convention	Cincinnati
Ballot on which nominated	7th
Democratic opponent	Samuel J. Tilden
Electoral vote*	185 (Hayes) to 184 (Tilden)
Popular vote	4,288,546 (Tilden) to 4,034,311 (Hayes)
Age at inauguration	54

*For votes by states, see **Electoral College** (table).

South (see **Reconstruction**). Southerners thus regained complete political control over their state and local governments for the first time since the Civil War. On March 2, 1877, just 56 hours before Inauguration Day, Hayes was formally announced as the winner.

Hayes's Administration (1877-1881)

The end of Reconstruction. One of Hayes's first acts as President was to withdraw federal occupation forces from the South, as promised. On April 10, 1877, the soldiers left South Carolina, and on April 24, the last federal troops marched from Louisiana. Hayes hoped that the end of Reconstruction would restore the two-party system in the South. But the Democrats won back their solid hold on the South.

Civil service reform. Hayes had announced that he intended to serve only one term as President so he could strive for civil service reform. Hayes based his appointments on merit rather than on the spoils system (see **Spoils system**). He even appointed a Southern Democrat, David M. Key, to his Cabinet. This and other Cabinet appointments angered members of his own party. Hayes also forced the removal of three fellow Republicans from their jobs in the New York Custom House. One of the men was Chester A. Arthur, who became the 21st President (See **Arthur, Chester Alan** [Custom house collector]).

Congress refused to act on the civil service legislation that Hayes proposed, but Hayes was the first President to fight Congress on this issue. His struggle gained wide public support and opened the way for later Presidents to make civil service reforms.

Money problems. Because of the depression of the 1870's, many people demanded *cheap money.* Farmers and business owners, for example, believed that putting more money into circulation would raise the prices of their products and thus help them pay off their debts. They wanted the government to issue more paper and silver money even though the money could not be backed by gold in the Treasury. Hayes favored a conservative money policy, and resisted their demands.

In 1878, Hayes vetoed the Bland-Allison Act, which required the Treasury to buy and coin between $2 million and $4 million worth of silver a month. Congress passed the bill over his veto. But the Treasury coined only the minimum amount required in an attempt to limit the inflationary effect of putting more money into circulation.

In 1879, the Hayes Administration resumed payment of *specie* (metal coin) for *greenbacks* (paper money issued to finance the Civil War). Secretary of the Treasury

Vice President and Cabinet

Vice President	*William A. Wheeler
Secretary of state	*William M. Evarts
Secretary of the treasury	*John Sherman
Secretary of war	George W. McCrary
	Alexander Ramsey (1879)
Attorney general	Charles Devens
Postmaster general	David M. Key
	Horace Maynard (1880)
Secretary of the Navy	Richard W. Thompson
	Alexander Ramsey (1880)
	Nathan Goff, Jr. (1881)
Secretary of the interior	*Carl Schurz

*Has a separate biography in *World Book*.

John Sherman gathered enough gold in the Treasury to redeem all of the greenbacks that were likely to be brought in. As soon as this became known, no one was anxious to exchange notes for gold. This policy helped to restore financial confidence, and business gradually improved.

Life in the White House. Rutherford and Lucy Hayes tried to set a good example for every American family. They quickly gained respect for their hospitality, simplicity, and modesty. Mrs. Hayes set the moral tone of the White House. She did not serve alcoholic drinks, even at formal dinners and receptions. Mrs. Hayes won high praise for her standards.

A typical day in the White House began with morning prayers. Early in the evening the family often gathered for music and singing. Mrs. Hayes held public receptions almost every evening, and welcomed everyone who wished to visit the White House. In 1878, she and President Hayes introduced the custom of Easter egg rolling by children on the White House lawn.

Later years

"Nobody ever left the Presidency with less regret . . . than I do," Hayes said when his term ended in 1881. No one seemed sorry that he did not run for a second term. But Hayes believed that the public showed its approval of his Administration by electing James A. Garfield, his friend and political supporter, as President.

Hayes returned to his home at Spiegel Grove, near Fremont, Ohio, and completely withdrew from politics. He devoted himself to philanthropic work in education, prison reform, Christianity, and veterans' affairs.

Mrs. Hayes died in June 1889. Hayes became ill while visiting friends in Cleveland in January 1893. His friends urged him to remain in bed. But Hayes insisted on returning home, saying: "I would rather die at Spiegel Grove than to live anywhere else." He died on Jan. 17, 1893, and was buried in Fremont. Spiegel Grove is now open to the public. It includes the Rutherford B. Hayes Library and Museum.   H. Wayne Morgan

Related articles in *World Book* include:

Arthur, Chester Alan	President of the United States
Civil service	Sherman (John)
Ohio (Places to visit)	Tilden, Samuel J.

Outline

I. Early life
  A. Education
  B. Lawyer
  C. Hayes's family
  D. Soldier

II. Political career
  A. Congressman   C. Campaign of 1876
  B. Governor   D. The election dispute

III. Hayes's Administration (1877-1881)
  A. The end of Reconstruction
  B. Civil service reform
  C. Money problems
  D. Life in the White House

IV. Later years

Questions

What were Hayes's outstanding personal qualities?
How did Hayes influence future civil service laws?
Why did the Republicans turn to Hayes as their presidential candidate in 1876?
How did Congress settle the dispute that resulted from the 1876 election?

What did Hayes expect to accomplish by ending Reconstruction? What actually happened?

Additional resources

Barnard, Harry. *Rutherford B. Hayes and His America.* Russell, 1967. Reprint of 1954 edition.

Davison, Kenneth E. *The Presidency of Rutherford B. Hayes.* Greenwood, 1972.

Geer, Emily A. *First Lady: The Life of Lucy Webb Hayes.* Kent State, 1984.

Morgan, H. Wayne. *From Hayes to McKinley: National Party Politics, 1877-1896.* Syracuse Univ. Press, 1969.

Haymarket Riot took place during a labor protest rally in Haymarket Square in Chicago on May 4, 1886. Many people were injured and eight policemen plus several spectators died after a bomb exploded during the rally. The Haymarket Riot increased antilabor feelings and weakened the radical element in American labor. It also strengthened the movement toward "pure and simple" unionism that condemned violence.

The riot occurred during a time when thousands of workers across the country were periodically on strike. It developed from a fight between strikers and strikebreakers on May 3, 1886, at an industrial plant in Chicago. Several workers were killed or wounded during the fight, leading some angry labor leaders to call for armed action by workers and a rally in Haymarket Square the next day. These leaders were *anarchists*—that is, people who wanted to abolish government authority. When police tried to break up the rally, an unknown person threw the bomb. A riot followed.

On Aug. 20, 1886, eight anarchists were convicted of conspiracy against the police. Although they were never found guilty of throwing the bomb or of causing the deaths, seven were sentenced to death and the eighth to prison. In 1887, four of the seven men hanged, one committed suicide, and the remaining two were resentenced to prison. In 1893, the three survivors were pardoned by Governor John P. Altgeld of Illinois, who declared that the evidence had been insufficient to support the charges.   James G. Scoville

Hayne, Robert Young (1791-1839), was an American statesman and champion of states' rights. In a famous Senate debate with Daniel Webster, held from Jan. 19 to 27, 1830, Hayne said that a state had the right to nullify a federal law. See **Nullification; States' rights.**

Hayne argued that the states had created the Constitution, and therefore they could limit the powers of the federal government. When South Carolina nullified the U.S. tariff laws in 1832, he resigned from the Senate to become governor. He opposed President Andrew Jackson in the nullification crisis. Hayne was born in Colleton County, South Carolina.   W. B. Hesseltine

Haynes, Elwood (1857-1925), a pioneer American automobile inventor and manufacturer, designed one of the first successful automobiles. The vehicle was built for him by Elmer and Edgar Apperson in Kokomo, Ind., and was first driven on July 4, 1894. It is now on exhibition in the Smithsonian Institution.

His inventions included carburetors and mufflers, which improved early automobiles. As a metallurgist, he created various alloys. His best-known alloy is a cobalt alloy called *Stellite.* It is used in metalworking tools because it retains a good cutting edge. Haynes was born in Portland, Ind.   Smith Hempstone Oliver

Haywood, William Dudley (1869-1928), was a leader of the Industrial Workers of the World (IWW), which advocated socialism through industrial unionism. He was an officer of the Western Federation of Miners, the leading union in the IWW. He was acquitted of murdering a former governor of Idaho in a famous trial in 1907. Because of his activities in opposing World War I, Haywood was sentenced to 20 years' imprisonment in 1919. He jumped bail and fled to Russia. Haywood was born in Utah.   Jack Barbash

Hazardous wastes are chemicals and chemical by-products that may endanger human health or pollute the environment if managed or disposed of improperly. Each year, billions of tons of wastes are produced in the United States by factories and other sources. Of this amount, a little more than 1 per cent is hazardous.

The Resource Conservation and Recovery Act of 1976 and its 1984 amendments list the properties that make a waste hazardous. The law declares a waste to be hazardous if it *corrodes* (wears away) other materials; explodes; is easily ignited; reacts strongly with water; is unstable to heat or shock; or is poisonous. Poisonous wastes are commonly called *toxic wastes.* The law also covers radioactive wastes that occur as by-products of mining operations or as a result of the use of radioactive substances in medical procedures. Radioactive wastes from nuclear power plants and other sources are controlled by the Nuclear Regulatory Commission (see **Nuclear energy** [Wastes and waste disposal]).

Producers of hazardous wastes. About 750,000 U.S. industries, hospitals, laboratories, and other establishments produce some wastes that may be hazardous. Factories, particularly chemical plants, account for most of these wastes. The manufacture of nearly all goods results in wastes, a small fraction of which may be hazardous. For example, the production of plastics yields harmful *organic compounds* (substances containing carbon). Oil and gasoline refining produces harmful oils, acids, ammonia, and *sludge* (muddy chemical deposits). Even the production of some medicines creates hazardous wastes, called *waste solvents.*

Effects of hazardous wastes. Harmful chemicals can pollute *ground water*—that is, water beneath the land's surface. Most rural areas and many cities depend on ground water for their drinking supplies.

Some hazardous wastes have polluted rivers or lakes, killing fish and water plants and endangering city and industrial water supplies. Certain wastes could contaminate food and so poison people or animals. Other substances could poison people or animals through touch or smell. Certain harmful wastes may pollute the air or create a fire hazard.

Disposal of hazardous wastes. The Resource Conservation and Recovery Act concerns the safe management and disposal of hazardous wastes. It particularly encourages recycling such wastes, if possible, to recover useful materials in them. The Comprehensive Environmental Response, Compensation, and Liability Act of 1980, also called "Superfund," provided $1.6 billion to clean up unsafe dump sites. A 1986 act reauthorized Superfund and provided an additional $9 billion.

Many industries have developed methods to deal with the problem of hazardous waste disposal. One method, called *landfilling,* involves storing harmful sub-

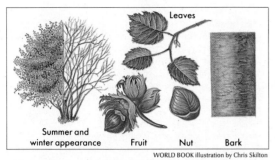

Leaves

Summer and
winter appearance   Fruit   Nut   Bark

WORLD BOOK illustration by Chris Skilton

The hazel tree produces light-brown nuts that are good to eat. Hazels have large, oval leaves with toothed edges. Their strong, flexible branches are used to make baskets and similar objects.

People also plant them as ornamentals or to shelter other plants. However, in some forests, particularly those around the Great Lakes, hazels form such dense thickets that tree seedlings cannot grow.

Although hazels are small, their branches are strong and flexible. People use them to make baskets, whip handles, hoops, and many similar articles.

In ancient times many persons believed that a forked hazel twig had supernatural powers. Stories tell how *divining rods* of hazel can be used to find water or minerals underground. *Witch* hazel does not belong to the group of true hazels. But it, too, was supposed by the ancients to have many magic powers. See **Witch hazel.**

Scientific classification. Hazels belong to the birch family, Betulaceae. The American hazel is *Corylus americana.* The common hazel of Europe is *C. avellana.*   Richard A. Jaynes

stances underground. A landfill must be lined with a nonporous substance, such as clay, to prevent the wastes from contaminating surrounding areas. Another method involves pumping wastes into deep wells designed to prevent contamination of ground water.

Some industries recycle their hazardous wastes or use the wastes of other industries as raw materials. Another disposal method involves the use of particular types of bacteria. The bacteria break down certain wastes, producing harmless substances. Some hazardous organic compounds are made harmless by burning them at high temperatures.   Gary F. Bennett

Hazel is any one of about 15 trees and shrubs that grow in the temperate climates of Asia, Europe, and North America. Two hazels are native to the United States—the beaked hazel and the American hazel. Hazel is often called *filbert* or *cobnut,* as are the edible nuts it produces. Most hazels cultivated for nuts grow in southern Europe and the northwestern United States.

Hazels have large, oval leaves with toothed edges. They turn yellow in the autumn. The plants bear both male and female flowers. The male flowers are naked catkins (see **Catkin**). The female blossoms, borne on separate twigs, are so small that they are hard to see.

Hazels furnish valuable cover and food for wildlife.

Hazlitt, William (1778-1830), was one of the best essayists and critics in English literature. His brilliant critical essays were sensitive and analytical. They were marked by enthusiasm and the pure enjoyment that Hazlitt felt in describing the effect of a literary work. His critical essays covered poets, dramatists, essayists, and novelists of earlier times. They were collected in *Characters of Shakespeare's Plays* (1817), *English Poets* (1818-1819), *English Comic Writers* (1819), and *A View of the English Stage* (1818-1821).

Hazlitt's personal essays appeared in two volumes called *Table Talk* (1821-1822). Their tone was straightforward and vigorous—and sounded like good talk. In "My First Acquaintance with Poets," Hazlitt described his first meeting with Samuel Taylor Coleridge. His "On the Feeling of Immortality in Youth" includes the famous line "No young man believes he shall ever die." Hazlitt was born in Maidstone.   John W. Dodds

Head is the part of the body that contains the brain, the mouth, and the chief sense organs—the eyes, ears, and nose. Its location depends on where the sense organs can best pick up messages from the environment.

In human beings and animals that walk on two legs, the head is at the top of the body. In four-legged animals, the head is at the front. Some animals, such as

Anatomy of the head   The bony frame of the head, *left,* is called the skull. Skull bones form a protective case around the brain and serve as a point of attachment for the muscles of the head. These muscles, *right,* play an important role in chewing and swallowing, and they are responsible for facial expressions.

WORLD BOOK illustrations by Leonard Morgan

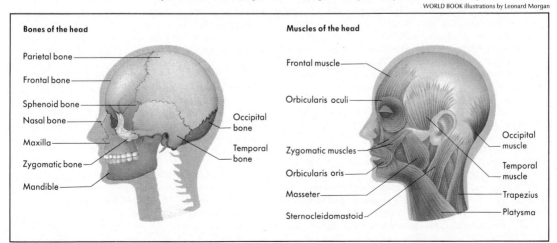

Bones of the head

Parietal bone
Frontal bone
Sphenoid bone
Nasal bone
Maxilla
Zygomatic bone
Mandible
Occipital bone
Temporal bone

Muscles of the head

Frontal muscle
Orbicularis oculi
Zygomatic muscles
Orbicularis oris
Masseter
Sternocleidomastoid
Occipital muscle
Temporal muscle
Trapezius
Platysma

the ameba and the starfish, have no head. These animals are sensitive to stimuli in various parts of the body.

The skeleton of the head is called the *skull.* It consists of the *facial area* and the *cranium,* a protective covering of the brain. The skull is usually composed of bone. In some animals, such as the shark, it is made of cartilage (see **Cartilage**). The skin that covers the top and back of the head is called the *scalp.*

A system of muscles and tendons joins the head to the spinal column, the collarbone, and the shoulder blades. These muscles and tendons control the movement of the head. The *occipital bone* forms the back of the skull. It rests on the spinal column and forms a joint on which the head moves. Most of the weight of the head is in front of the occipital bone, and the head is held in an erect position by muscles in the neck. When a person becomes sleepy, these muscles relax and the head falls forward. Other large bones of the head include the *parietal, frontal, sphenoid,* and *temporal.*

Muscles in the head play an important part in the processes of chewing and swallowing. They are also responsible for facial expressions such as smiling or frowning. Repeated activity of the facial muscles, the gradual loss of fat pads under the skin, and the loss of skin elasticity cause wrinkles to form in the faces of older people.

At birth, the head is extremely large in relation to the rest of the body. It measures about a fourth of the total body length. By adulthood, it is only about an eighth of the body length. The size and shape of the head vary from person to person. The normal cranial capacity is about 85 cubic inches (1,390 cubic centimeters). A larger cranium does not necessarily mean greater intelligence.

Charles W. Cummings

Related articles. See the Trans-Vision three-dimensional color picture with **Human body.** See also:

Brain	Face	Nose	Skull
Ear	Mandible	Phrenology	Tongue
Eye	Mouth	Sinus	

Head Start is a United States government program that provides educational, medical, and social service support to economically disadvantaged children and their families. The program focuses on the preparation of children for school and the improvement of family life. Local communities throughout the country operate Head Start centers. These centers work to provide activities to stimulate emotional, intellectual, physical, and social growth. The program is administered by the Office of Human Development Services of the U.S. Department of Health and Human Services.

The parents of children in the program play an important role in its operation. They serve on Parent Policy Committees with representatives of community groups and professional organizations. They also work in the centers as paid care-givers or as volunteers.

Head Start centers provide a preschool educational program; lunches and snacks; medical, dental, and mental health services; and social, vocational, and educational services for families. The youngsters take part in such activities as field trips, language development, music, and science. Programs vary according to neighborhood needs.

Between 1970 and 1974, the government supplemented Head Start with a number of related programs,

such as the Head Start Developmental Continuity Effort and the Child and Family Resource Program. These programs extend the benefits of Head Start to more family members in a wider variety of ways.

Head Start began in 1965 as part of the Community Action Program conducted by the Office of Economic Opportunity. It was delegated to the Department of Health, Education, and Welfare (now the Department of Health and Human Services) in 1969.   Edward Zigler

See also **Day-care center.**

Headache is one of the most common ailments among human beings. Headache pain varies from mild to severe and may last less than an hour or for days.

Headaches are caused by any of a number of conditions. A head injury, tense head muscles, or throbbing arteries in the scalp can cause a headache. Eye strain, fever, sinus infection, or an allergic reaction can also lead to a headache. In relatively few cases, headaches are related to a brain tumor or some other brain disease. Some headache victims may have additional symptoms during a headache. For example, they may suffer neck pain or upset stomach, or they may become extremely sensitive to noise or light.

There are two main kinds of headache, *acute* and *chronic.* Acute headaches occur infrequently and most of them last only a short time. Most people have acute headaches occasionally, but few seek a physician's advice because the pain does not persist. In most cases, rest and nonprescription drugs relieve the discomfort.

Chronic headaches occur frequently or may last several days. Two of the most common types of chronic headache are *tension headache* and *migraine.*

Tension headache, the most widespread kind of chronic headache, is related to increased tightening of the muscles in the head. When a person is tense or tired or is under extreme mental or physical strain, these muscles may contract, causing a tension headache. The victim has pain in the head or at the back of the head and neck. Physicians treat most tension headaches with pain-relieving drugs or with sedatives.

Migraine is one of the severest types of headache. It is also called *sick headache* because the pain may be accompanied by nausea and vomiting. Migraine is probably caused by increased stretching, swelling, and throbbing of the arteries in the head. Such foods as chocolate and nuts may trigger migraines in certain people.

Migraine recurs from time to time and is often so painful that the victim must stay in bed. Some people suffer migraines as frequently as two or three times a week. In other cases, attacks occur several months or even years apart. For many sufferers, each migraine attack follows the same pattern. Before the pain begins, they may see flashing lights or have a blind spot in their field of vision. The pain usually strikes on one side of the head, and nausea and vomiting may follow. Some victims also shed tears, experience blurred vision, or have numbness in an arm or leg.

Physicians prescribe various drugs to help lessen the swelling of the arteries in the head during a migraine attack. Some migraine patients practice *biofeedback,* a method of controlling normally involuntary body processes (see **Biofeedback**). Through biofeedback, they learn to raise the skin temperature in their hands. This technique can indirectly decrease the blood flow to the scalp, thus diminishing the throbbing of the arteries in the head.   Arthur H. Elkind

Additional resources

Diamond, Seymour, and Diamond-Falk, Judi. *Advice from the Diamond Headache Clinic.* International Universities Press, 1982.
Silverstein, Alvin and V. B. *Headaches: All About Them.* Harper, 1984.

Headdress. See Hairdressing; Hat; Indian, American.

Headhunter is a person who cuts off the head of a dead enemy to keep as a trophy. Headhunting was usually a part of intertribal warfare, and the heads were often used in rituals. Headhunters performed ceremonies after a hunt to prevent revenge by the spirits of the dead.

There is evidence that Neanderthal people, a prehistoric group, removed heads for ritual purposes. Headhunting was formerly practiced in many parts of the world, particularly in Malaysia, Melanesia, and South America. In South America, the Jívaro Indians of Ecuador removed the skull and used hot sand to shrink the skin of the head to a small size. The avenging soul of the dead person was then believed to be safely trapped inside. Today, headhunting is forbidden nearly everywhere.   Jennie Keith

Headphones are a device used for listening in private to various types of equipment that reproduce sound. Such equipment includes phonographs, radios, tape recorders, and telephones. High-fidelity headphones provide one headphone for each ear. These headphones can reproduce stereophonic sound (see **High-fidelity system** [Headphones]). Headphones are sometimes called *earphones.* One kind of earphone looks like a button and fits in the ear.

David R. Frazier

Headphones are devices used for listening in private to tape recorders and other electronic equipment that reproduce sound. Some headphones can reproduce stereophonic music.

All headphones receive electric waves from some type of sound-reproduction equipment and convert the waves into sound. Thus, headphones serve as miniature speakers (see **Speaker**). Various kinds of headphones work by means of different mechanisms. But nearly all such mechanisms function in much the same way as those in high-fidelity headphones.

Most high-fidelity headphones have three main parts: (1) a coil of wire called a *voice coil,* (2) a cone-shaped piece of paper or plastic called a *diaphragm,* and (3) a

permanent magnet. The voice coil is attached to the diaphragm. The permanent magnet is near the voice coil. When electric waves pass through the voice coil, they produce varying magnetic forces in the coil. These forces drive the coil alternately toward and away from the permanent magnet. The coil moves back and forth so rapidly that it vibrates. The vibrations of the coil create vibrations in the diaphragm. The diaphragm's vibrations, in turn, produce vibrations in the air, which the ear hears as sound.

The famous American inventor Alexander Graham Bell made the first earphone in 1876. It formed part of the first telephone.   Stanley R. Alten

See also **Telephone** (The receiver; illustration).

Health is a state of physical, mental, and social well-being. It involves more than just the absence of disease. A truly healthy person not only feels good physically but also has a realistic outlook on life and gets along well with other people. Good health enables people to enjoy life and have the opportunity to achieve the goals they have set for themselves.

To achieve and maintain good health, people must have basic knowledge about the human body and how it functions. Only then can they determine what will or what will not help or hurt their health. Therefore, learning about health should be a part of every person's education. Current knowledge about health, together with good living habits, can help almost everyone maintain good health and improve the quality of life.

Society as a whole benefits from people's good health just as individuals do. For that reason, many government and voluntary agencies strive to preserve and improve the health of all people. The World Health Organization (WHO), an agency of the United Nations, works to promote better health throughout the world.

Elements of physical health

All parts of the body must work together properly to maintain physical health. A person who is in good physi-

R. Laird, FPG

Jogging is a fine way to get the vigorous exercise necessary for physical fitness. Such exercise strengthens muscles and improves the function of the circulatory and respiratory systems.

cal condition has the strength and energy to enjoy an active life and withstand the stresses of daily life. The various practices that help maintain health are called *hygiene.* Proper nutrition, exercise, rest and sleep, cleanliness, and medical and dental care are all essential parts of hygiene.

Nutrition. A balanced diet provides all the food substances needed by the body for healthy growth and development. Nutritionists use the term *nutrients* for these substances and classify them into five main groups: (1) carbohydrates, (2) fats, (3) proteins, (4) vitamins, and (5) minerals. Water is also essential for life, but it is often considered separately from nutrients. The National Research Council has established a list of Recommended Daily Allowances (RDA), which provides information on how much of each nutrient a person needs each day.

A balanced diet consists of a wide variety of foods. Fruits and vegetables provide important vitamins and minerals. Meat, poultry, fish, eggs, dairy products, and nuts are rich sources of protein. Bread, cereals, and potatoes furnish carbohydrates in addition to vitamins and minerals.

Good nutrition also includes eating the proper amount of food each day. Overeating can lead to *obesity* (fatness). Excess weight puts extra strain on the heart and increases a person's chances of getting such diseases as diabetes and heart disease. Many people try to lose weight quickly and easily by following one of the many widely advertised fad diets. But these diets can be dangerous, especially if used over a long period of time. The safest way to lose weight is to consult a physician and follow the reducing program he or she prescribes. Most programs combine moderate daily exercise with a balanced diet that contains a limited number of calories.

Exercise helps keep the body healthy and fit. Vigorous exercise strengthens muscles and improves the function of the circulatory and respiratory systems. Physical fitness benefits both physical and mental health. It enables the body to withstand stresses that otherwise could cause physical and emotional problems.

To achieve fitness, a person should start an exercise program slowly and build it up gradually to a level that maintains a healthy heart and strong muscles. Daily exercise provides the greatest benefits, and so it is important to choose exercises that can be performed every day. Such popular activities as bicycling, jogging, and swimming—and even taking long, brisk walks—furnish the vigorous exercise necessary for fitness. Participating in golf, tennis, or some other sport only once or twice a week cannot develop and maintain fitness.

Rest and sleep help overcome fatigue and restore energy to the body. Everyone needs rest and sleep, but the amount required differs for each individual. Most adults sleep from 7 to $8\frac{1}{2}$ hours a night, though some need less sleep and others need more. Young children may need more sleep at night plus a daytime nap.

Nearly everyone has trouble falling asleep occasionally. However, frequent *insomnia* (inability to sleep naturally) can indicate various physical or emotional disorders. Therefore, it is best to consult a physician about any frequent sleep problem. Some people take sleeping pills to counteract insomnia, but such drugs should not be used without a doctor's prescription.

Rest and relaxation are as important as sleep. After strenuous work or exercise, a person may need a period of total rest. At other times, only relaxation or a change of pace is necessary. Any activity that differs from the normal routine of work or study can be relaxing. Pleasurable and relaxing activities help the body shed tension and remain robust. If rest and relaxation do not relieve fatigue and tension, the individual may have a physical or emotional problem.

Cleanliness controls the growth of bacteria and other germs that can cause disease. A daily bath or shower keeps the body free from dirt and odor. In addition, it helps prevent skin infections that may develop if bacteria grow and multiply on the skin. The hair should also be washed regularly.

Daily dental care is another important part of personal cleanliness. Brushing the teeth properly and using dental floss keep the teeth clean and help prevent decay and gum disease.

Medical and dental care. Regular checkups by a physician and dentist play an important role in safeguarding health. Doctors recommend that people have medical care at the first sign of any illness. Early care can result in quicker cure and lower medical costs. Treating oneself for more than a day or two is unwise unless the condition improves steadily. A physician or medical clinic has the knowledge, special instruments, and laboratory equipment to provide accurate diagnosis and treatment.

Prevention of disease is an important part of medical care. Parents should make sure that their children visit a doctor or clinic to receive immunization against diphtheria, German measles, measles, mumps, polio, tetanus, and whooping cough. See **Immunization.**

Elements of mental health

Physical health and mental health are closely connected. Mental health plays an important role in both the way people behave and the way they feel. Emotionally healthy individuals accept themselves as they are—with all their weaknesses as well as their strengths. They remain in contact with reality, and they are able to deal with stress and frustration. They also act independently of outside influences and show genuine concern for other people.

Emotional development. Experiences during childhood strongly influence a person's mental health throughout life. An infant is completely helpless at birth and must depend on its parents for all its needs. Children remain dependent for many years, but they slowly mature and learn to do things for themselves. They make many mistakes during this long period of growth and maturation. Through these errors, they learn certain guidelines for relating to other people. Children thus develop the knowledge necessary to deal with difficult situations in life. This knowledge helps them maintain good mental health throughout life.

Emotional development does not end when a person reaches adulthood. Similarly, an individual's mental health continues to change from time to time. These changes result from daily circumstances that cause either pleasure or pain for the person.

Handling stress is essential for avoiding both mental and physical illness. Feelings of stress are the body's response to any threatening or unfamiliar situation. Most severe stress results from such serious events as a divorce or loss of a job. However, stress can occur even in pleasant situations, such as watching a football game or waiting for a loved one to return from a trip. If not handled properly, stress can lead to physical or emotional illness. It may produce only mild symptoms, such as a cough, a headache, or a rash. But severe and prolonged stress can contribute to serious health problems, including high blood pressure and stomach ulcers.

No one can avoid stress, but a person can do certain things to help lessen the danger of becoming ill from it. Regular exercise and sufficient sleep strengthen the body's resistance to stress. Everyone should learn to relax by resting, taking a walk, meditating, working with a hobby, or by any other method that he or she finds successful. When serious stress occurs, a person should determine the source of the stress and try to eliminate or diminish it. Discussing a problem with a friend, relative, or some other person may also help relieve stress.

Social relationships have an important influence on mental health. Close personal relationships with friends and relatives provide opportunities for communication, sharing, and emotional growth. Such relationships also can provide strength and support for dealing with challenging situations or personal problems.

An individual's entire social environment also affects his or her mental health. Such social problems as poverty, racism, and overcrowding contribute to situations that influence emotional health. As a result, social and economic changes are needed to help reduce the rate of some types of mental illness.

Health hazards

The nature of health problems in the United States and Canada has changed dramatically during the 1900's. Until then, most people died from infectious diseases, such as diphtheria or pneumonia. Today, however, infectious diseases are no longer the main killers in the United States, Canada, and other industrialized nations. Improved sanitation, immunization programs, and the development of antibiotic drugs have brought these diseases under control. Today, health specialists are concerned chiefly with diseases related to the aging process, unhealthy lifestyles, and environmental hazards.

Tobacco, alcohol, and drug abuse. According to the U.S. Department of Health and Human Services (HHS), cigarette smoking is the principal cause of unnecessary and preventable illness and early death. Heart disease and lung cancer and other lung diseases occur at a much higher rate among smokers than among nonsmokers.

Many individuals use various drugs in an effort to solve their problems or to improve their alertness, mood, or self-confidence. However, the regular use of alcohol, narcotics, or sedatives can lead to addiction and also serious damage to the body. People may become psychologically dependent on a wide variety of other drugs, including amphetamines, cocaine, LSD, marijuana, and tranquilizers. These individuals may harm themselves further by neglecting their health and nutrition. In addition, drugs can distort a person's judgment and so increase the risk of accidents.

Alcohol is the most widely abused drug in the United States. The National Institute on Alcohol Abuse and Al-

coholism estimates that the nation has approximately 10 million alcoholics. About a tenth of all drinkers become alcoholics. There is no cure for alcoholism, but the condition can be treated. An alcoholic who gives up drinking can return to a healthy, productive life.

Environmental health hazards caused by modern technology can produce serious problems. Air pollution can worsen the condition of people who suffer such respiratory diseases as asthma and bronchitis. It may even help cause some diseases, including cancer and emphysema. In some areas, insecticides and industrial wastes contaminate food and water supplies. Excessive noise can also threaten people's health. Noise from airplanes, construction projects, and industrial plants can cause hearing loss as well as emotional damage.

Occupational health hazards threaten the health of many workers. In some cases, substances involved in a person's job may cause long-term damage that appears only after many years. For example, many coal miners develop a lung disease called *pneumoconiosis,* or *black lung,* from inhaling coal dust. Dust also causes lung diseases among workers in the asbestos and cotton industries. Some industrial chemicals, including arsenic and vinyl chloride, cause cancer. People who work with X rays and other forms of radiation also face a health hazard unless proper precautions are used.

Public health

Public health includes all actions taken to maintain and improve the general health of a community. Government health programs provide most public health services. In addition, many voluntary health agencies receive contributions to combat specific diseases, such as can-

Occupational health hazards threaten the health of many workers. This car refinisher is wearing safety glasses and a respirator to protect his eyes and lungs from harmful substances.

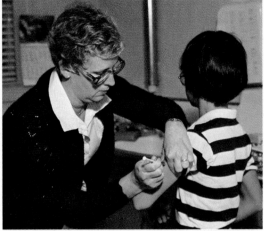

Pam Hasegawa, Taurus

Immunization programs are among the services provided by health departments and other public health agencies. These agencies work to improve the general health of communities.

cer and lung disease. These agencies provide medical services, campaign for health legislation, and make important contributions to health education.

In the United States, the Public Health Service administers the government's public health programs. State and local health departments also provide a wide range of services in most communities. For example, they work to prevent and control disease by providing proper sanitation, conducting immunization programs, and enforcing quarantines. These health departments also operate clinics that offer free laboratory tests and other medical services to the public. Another important function of public health agencies is to provide health education to individuals, groups, and organizations.

Vivian K. Harlin

Related articles in *World Book.* See **Public health** and its list of *Related articles.* See also the following articles:

Biographies

Barton, Clara	Hippocrates	Pasteur, Louis
Curie, Marie	Jenner, Edward	Reed, Walter
Sklodowska	Koch, Robert	Sabin, Albert B.
Dix, Dorothea L.	Lister, Sir Joseph	Salk, Jonas E.
Fleming, Sir	Metchnikoff, Élie	Servetus, Michael
Alexander	Nightingale,	Trudeau,
Galen	Florence	Edward L.
Gorgas (William C.)		

Personal health

Alcoholism	Drug abuse	Immunization	Smoking
Baby	Fat (Fats and	Nutrition	Stress
Bath	disease)	Physical	Teeth (Care
Child	Fatigue	fitness	of the teeth
Cigarette	Food	Posture	and gums)
Circumcision	Growth	Sauna	Weight con-
Diet	Human body	Sleep	trol
Disease	Immunity		

Organizations

Centers for Disease Control	Hope, Project
Health, Board of	National Institutes of Health
Health and Human Services, De-	Public Health Service
partment of	UNICEF
Health Council, National	World Health Organization

Other related articles

Careers (Health)	Holistic medicine	Pure food and
Environmental	Medicine	drug laws
pollution	Physical education	Recreation
Health care plans		Safety

Additional resources

Brody, Jane E. *Jane Brody's The New York Times Guide to Personal Health.* Times Books, 1982.
Corry, James M. *Consumer Health: Facts, Skills, and Decisions.* Wadsworth, 1983.
Louria, Donald B. *Stay Well.* Scribner, 1982.
Taylor, Ron. *Health 2000.* Facts on File, 1985.
Whaley, Russell F. *Health.* Prentice-Hall, 1982.

Health, Board of, is a policy-forming or advisory body that aids the executive branch of a state or local government in operating the health department.

Duties of a state board may be advisory or regulatory. Some state boards have executive and police powers to enforce public health laws. City and county boards may have similar duties and powers. Requirements for board membership vary. In some states, all members must be physicians. In others, members must represent all professions concerned with public health. Still others specify representation of the nonprofessional public. Members of state boards may be appointed by the governor or elected by the state medical society. Members of local boards may be appointed by the mayor or council, or elected by the citizens.

The United States does not have a federal board of health. In its place, Congress has authorized the appointment of advisory councils to the U.S. Public Health Service. The Public Health Service is part of the Department of Health and Human Services.   Thomas Parran

See also **Public Health Service; Sanitation.**

Health, National Institutes of. See **National Institutes of Health.**

Health, Public. See **Public health.**

Health and Human Services, Department of, is an executive department of the United States government. It deals with public health, social welfare, and income security. The department was created in 1953 as the Department of Health, Education, and Welfare (HEW). In 1979, Congress passed legislation transferring most education programs from HEW to a new Cabinet-level Department of Education. HEW was renamed the Department of Health and Human Services (HHS).

The secretary of health and human services directs the department and serves in the President's Cabinet. The secretary is appointed by the President with the consent of the Senate. The secretary's chief aides include an undersecretary, a chief of staff, an inspector general, a general counsel, and seven assistant secretaries. Some of these officials direct various departmental activities. Others oversee budget and legislative matters, planning and evaluation, public affairs, and administration. The secretary's office directs other activities, such as civil rights and consumer affairs.

Organization

The Department of Health and Human Services consists of the Office of the Secretary and five principal operating divisions: (1) the Public Health Service, (2) the Health Care Financing Administration, (3) the Office of Human Development Services, (4) the Social Security

The Department of Health and Human Services directs programs to improve public health and economic security throughout the United States. The department's headquarters, *right,* are in the Hubert H. Humphrey Building at 200 Independence Avenue SW, Washington, DC 20201.

Department of Health and Human Services

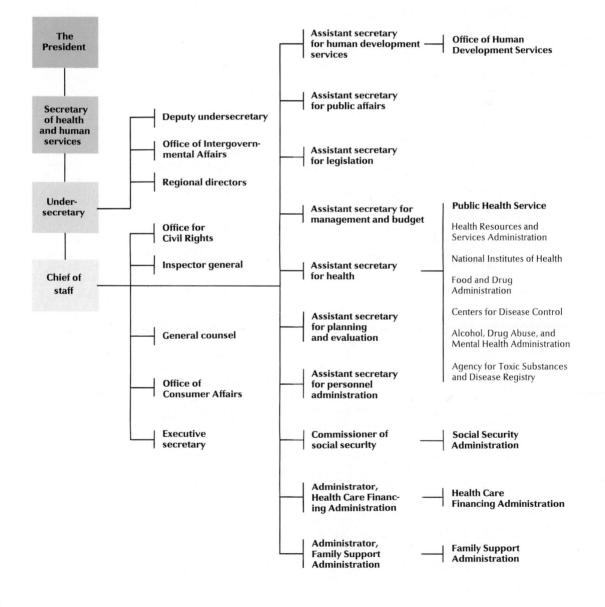

Administration, and (5) the Family Support Administration.

The Department of Health and Human Services has 10 regional offices. It administers about 250 programs, including health research, income maintenance, and drug addict rehabilitation.

The Public Health Service consists of the Office of the Assistant Secretary for Health and five agencies: (1) the National Institutes of Health, (2) the Health Resources and Services Administration, (3) the Food and Drug Administration, (4) the Centers for Disease Control, and (5) the Alcohol, Drug Abuse, and Mental Health Administration.

The Office of the Assistant Secretary for Health coordinates programs that deal with international health, adolescent pregnancy, smoking and health, disease prevention and health promotion, health services research, and health statistics.

The National Institutes of Health supports and conducts research into the causes and prevention of disease. It also publishes medical and health information.

The Health Resources and Services Administration administers community health and family planning services and maternal and child health programs. It also conducts health programs for American Indians and merchant sailors and supports health workers' education and training programs.

The Food and Drug Administration enforces laws designed to assure the purity, effectiveness, and truthful labeling of food, drugs, and cosmetics. It also inspects the production and shipment of these products.

The Centers for Disease Control conducts programs for preventing and controlling contagious diseases. It also establishes safety and health standards for workers.

The Alcohol, Drug Abuse, and Mental Health Administration administers programs for the prevention of alcoholism, drug addiction, and mental illness. It seeks improved treatment and rehabilitation methods.

Secretaries of health, education, and welfare

Name	Took office	Under President
* Oveta Culp Hobby	1953	Eisenhower
Marion B. Folsom	1955	Eisenhower
Arthur S. Flemming	1958	Eisenhower
* Abraham A. Ribicoff	1961	Kennedy
Anthony J. Celebrezze	1962	Kennedy, Johnson
* John W. Gardner	1965	Johnson
Wilbur J. Cohen	1968	Johnson
Robert H. Finch	1969	Nixon
* Elliot L. Richardson	1970	Nixon
* Caspar W. Weinberger	1973	Nixon, Ford
F. David Mathews	1975	Ford
* Joseph A. Califano, Jr.	1977	Carter
* Patricia R. Harris	1979	Carter

Secretaries of health and human services

Name	Took office	Under President
* Patricia R. Harris	1979	Carter
Richard S. Schweiker	1981	Reagan
* Margaret M. Heckler	1983	Reagan
Otis R. Bowen	1985	Reagan

*Has a separate biography in *World Book.*

The Health Care Financing Administration administers the Medicare and Medicaid programs. Medicare is the federal system of financing medical care for people 65 years old and older and for some disabled people. Medicaid provides health care for many people who could not otherwise afford it. An office of health maintenance organizations is part of this division.

The Office of Human Development Services administers programs for groups with special needs. These groups include children, youth, families, the aged, handicapped people, and American Indians.

The Social Security Administration administers the federal social insurance programs. The agency also administers the Supplemental Security Income program, a federal income maintenance project for the aged, blind, and disabled.

The Family Support Administration administers major income assistance and related programs for nonelderly families. Examples include Aid to Families with Dependent Children, Low Income Home Energy Assistance, and Child Support Enforcement.

History

In the 1800's, state and local governments provided most government welfare services. Federal activities began in this field in the 1900's. The Social Security Act of 1935 created many welfare agencies to carry out new federal programs. In 1939, the Federal Security Agency (FSA) was established to administer major programs in the fields of social and economic security, education, and public health. The Office of Education, the Public Health Service, and responsibility for the American Printing House for the Blind were transferred to the FSA from other departments. In 1940, the Food and Drug Administration was transferred to the FSA.

In the late 1940's, the Hoover Commission on Reorganization of the Executive Branch recommended that a new department be created for welfare and education. The Department of Health, Education, and Welfare was established in 1953. All FSA functions were transferred to it. The Social Security Administration's responsibilities increased with the creation of new programs and the expansion of old-age and survivors insurance. New programs included disability insurance, Medicare, and Supplemental Security Income. The Alcohol, Drug Abuse, and Mental Health Administration was established in 1973. The Health Care Financing Administration and the Office of Human Development Services were created in 1977. In 1979, Congress enacted a law that created a Department of Education and moved most education programs from HEW to the new department. HEW was renamed the Department of Health and Human Services. The Family Support Administration division of HHS was established in 1986.

Critically reviewed by the Department of Health and Human Services

Related articles in *World Book* include:

Children's Bureau
Food and Drug Administration
Head Start
Human Development Services, Office of
Medicare
National Institute for Occupational Safety and Health
National Institutes of Health
Public Health Service
Social Security Administration

Health Care Financing Administration. See Health and Human Services, Department of.

Health care plans are methods of paying and arranging for an individual's or family's medical care. They differ in these respects from public and private health insurance plans, which limit the types of medical service they cover and pay each time a service is rendered. Health care plans either pay a set fee covering nearly complete medical care or charge fees for services at a reduced rate. These plans are often called *competitive medical plans, managed care plans,* or *alternative delivery systems (ADS).* The most common types are *health maintenance organizations (HMO's)* and *preferred provider organizations (PPO's).*

HMO's provide their members with comprehensive health care for a fixed monthly or yearly fee. This care includes preventive care, checkups, emergency services, and hospitalization. Members may use only physicians and hospitals approved by the HMO. HMO's provide more benefits than do conventional health insurance plans. Another difference is that HMO's guarantee access to preventive care and treatment when needed.

HMO's control costs partly by selecting cost-effective physicians and hospitals and by emphasizing preventive care. They also reduce costs by substituting outpatient care for inpatient care when appropriate and by carefully reviewing the need for hospitalization. HMO's are organized either as group practices, in which participating physicians have offices in the same facility, or as individual practice associations (IPA's). An IPA contracts with doctors who provide care in their own offices.

PPO's consist of doctors and hospitals offering consumers effective, economical health care. PPO consumers pay lower than normal fees by using the "preferred" doctors and hospitals. Consumers are not restricted in their choice of physician, but they must pay the difference between the discounted fee of a "preferred" physician—that is, a doctor belonging to the PPO—and the generally higher fee of the nonpreferred doctor.

Another type of health care plan, called a *triple option plan,* gives consumers a choice of using an HMO, a PPO, or conventional health insurance. Users may select the most economical plan for their needs. For example, a person with a particular major health problem may be offered reduced payments in exchange for enrolling in a PPO specializing in that problem.

The first HMO's were set up in the 1930's. They grew slowly until the 1970's. Since then, health care costs have skyrocketed, and competition among the growing number of physicians has increased. As a result, HMO's have grown rapidly. Today, over 25 million people are enrolled in about 500 HMO's.

PPO's appeared during the early 1980's as a more flexible alternative to HMO's. In 1985, about 17 million people had access to PPO's.   Paul M. Ellwood, Jr.

See also **Insurance** (Private health insurance).

Health Council, National, founded in 1920, is a private, nonprofit association of leading voluntary, professional, business, and governmental health organizations in the United States. The council has about 70 member groups. Its chief programs aim (1) to encourage Americans to maintain and improve their health and (2) to educate Americans on how to use health resources wisely. The council provides a meeting ground between private and governmental health agencies. It sponsors the National Health Forum, produces publications on major

health issues, and works to promote awareness of health career opportunities. Council headquarters are at 622 Third Avenue, New York, NY 10017.

Critically reviewed by the National Health Council

Health, Education, and Welfare, Department of. See Health and Human Services, Department of.

Health insurance. See Insurance (Private health insurance); **Blue Cross and Blue Shield; Health insurance, National; Medicine** (Financing medical care; Financial problems).

Health insurance, National, is a government program that finances extensive health services for the majority of the people in a country. This type of program is sometimes called *socialized medicine.* Every industrial nation except the United States has some form of national health insurance, also called *NHI.*

More than a dozen NHI programs have been introduced in Congress since 1968. These programs may be divided into three groups. *Public-private plans* provide public assistance to the aged, the poor, and the unemployed. Other people must rely on benefits paid by private insurance companies. Most business firms, insurance companies, and medical organizations have supported such programs. *Wholly public plans* provide health care for the entire population and are financed through tax revenues. Supporters of this type of health insurance include consumer groups and labor unions. *Catastrophic plans* cover only unusually high medical expenses. These programs have received less support than the other two types of health insurance.

The opposition to NHI has been led by the American Medical Association (AMA). The AMA represents many of the nation's physicians and has great influence in Congress. The organization has argued that NHI would reduce the quality of medical care.

The first NHI plan was established in Germany in 1883. Since the early 1900's, various groups in the United States have supported NHI. In 1912, for example, the Progressive Party, led by Theodore Roosevelt, favored a national health care program. By the 1920's, several states were considering similar plans. In 1934, President Franklin D. Roosevelt set up the Committee on Economic Security to aid U.S. recovery from the Great Depression. The committee planned to include NHI as part of the social security system. But Roosevelt did not include it because of AMA opposition.

In 1965, Congress passed two programs—Medicaid and Medicare—that provide certain health benefits to individuals (see **Medicaid; Medicare; Social security**). These programs led to renewed consideration of NHI. Canada adopted an NHI program in 1968.

Since the early 1970's, most individuals and organizations, including the AMA, have favored some form of national health care. However, these groups have not agreed on the nature of the program or how to administer it.   Karen Davis

See also **Medicine** (Financing medical care).

Health maintenance organization. See Health care plans.

Health resort. See Bath (Medical bathing).

Healy, James Augustine (1830-1900), was the first black American bishop of the Roman Catholic Church. Pope Pius IX appointed him Bishop of Portland, Me., in 1875. Healy's diocese consisted of the entire state of

Maine. It also included New Hampshire until 1884, when that state became a separate diocese. In Maine, Healy served as religious leader of thousands of people, almost all of whom were whites.

Healy was born near Macon, Ga. His father was a white plantation owner and his mother was a slave. Healy graduated from the College of the Holy Cross in 1849 and then studied for the priesthood in Montreal and Paris. In 1854, he became the first black American to be ordained a Catholic priest. He served in Boston until 1875, first as the bishop's secretary, then as a parish priest.   Edgar Allan Toppin

Hearing. See Ear (The sense of hearing).

Hearing aid is a device that improves hearing. Many hearing-impaired persons depend on this device. It enables them to use the telephone, enjoy music, and more easily understand conversation.

Types of hearing aids. There are two types of hearing aids. The *air-conduction aid* amplifies sound and brings it directly to the ear. Not all people can use this type, because they cannot transmit sounds through their inner and outer ear. These people use *bone-conduction aids* that bring sound waves to the bony part of the head, usually directly behind the ear. The bone transmits the vibrations to the auditory nerves of the cochlea. Hearing is possible when these nerves are stimulated.

Electronic hearing aids are essentially small telephones. They consist of a microphone, an amplifier, and

a receiver. The receiver fits in the ear. In the case of bone conduction, it fits behind the ear. The first electronic hearing aid was developed about 1900. It was bulky and inconvenient to use.

People made only limited use of hearing aids until the development of the *vacuum-tube aid*. These used a crystal microphone, a vacuum-tube amplifier, and two batteries. They were much more compact, and easier to carry and conceal. These factors helped many persons overcome their reluctance to wear hearing aids.

Another important advance in hearing aids took place in 1953 with the introduction of an electronic *transistor hearing aid*. This device has completely replaced the vacuum-tube hearing aid, because it is much smaller and less expensive to operate.

Modern hearing aids may be adjusted to a wide range of frequencies and intensities. They can also be easily concealed because of their compactness. They are made in a wide range of styles and designs, so that they also serve an ornamental purpose. Many are worn in women's hair or are built into the frames of eyeglasses.

History. Air-conduction aids and bone-conduction aids have been used for hundreds of years. The principle of bone conduction was known in the early 1600's. The ear trumpet was used even earlier. In the late 1700's, the *audiphone,* or *dentiphone,* was invented. It was a cardboard or celluloid device shaped like a fan. Users held the edge between their teeth and bent the fan to-

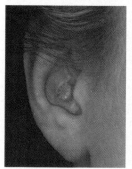

Phonic Ear Inc.

© Robert Rathe
Hearing Industries Association

Modern hearing aids serve the wearer's individual needs. An all-in-the-ear hearing aid, *left,* corrects moderate hearing loss. A behind-the-ear model, *right,* is for more serious hearing loss.

Kenneth W. Berger, School of Speech Pathology and Audiology, Kent State University

The ear trumpet, one of the earliest hearing aids used, gathered in sound from a large area and funneled it into the ear.

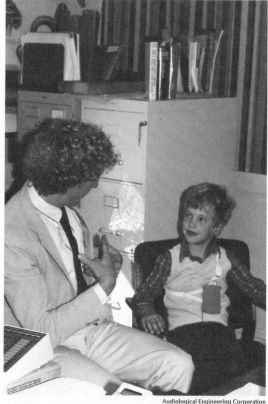

Audiological Engineering Corporation

A tactile aid can help people with severe hearing loss. The unit translates sounds into vibrations that the wearer can feel.

ward the sound. The sound vibrations traveled from the teeth to the jawbone, the skull, and to the auditory nerves.

In 1872, Alexander Graham Bell began to experiment on an electrical mechanism that would help deaf children to hear. His experiments led directly to the development of the telephone. Bell himself never invented a hearing aid. But his influence increased as a result of his invention, and he did much to call attention to the problems of the hard of hearing.   David P. Goldstein

Hearing loss. See Deafness.

Hearn, Lafcadio (1850-1904), was an American author. His best-known works display a weird imagination and a polished style. Hearn said, "I have pledged myself to the worship of the Odd, the Queer, the Strange, the Exotic, and the Monstrous."

Hearn was born in the Ionian Islands off the west coast of Greece. He moved to the United States at the age of 19 and eventually settled in New Orleans. There he wrote a series of eerie newspaper sketches called "Fantastics." After living for a time in the West Indies and New York City, he moved to Japan in 1890. Hearn became a Japanese citizen and a professor of English literature at the Imperial University of Tokyo.

Hearn wrote many fantastic and supernatural tales set in the West Indies and the Orient. They were collected in such works as *Some Chinese Ghosts* (1887), *Chita* (1889), and *Kwaidan* (1904). He also wrote several books about Japan.   Edward Wagenknecht

Hearne, Samuel (1745-1792), was an English explorer and fur trader. He was the first white person to journey overland from Hudson Bay to the Arctic Ocean. He reached the Arctic Ocean in July 1771, while exploring for the Hudson's Bay Company. He arrived at Great Slave Lake in northern Canada later that year. Hearne established the first Hudson's Bay Company inland post in Saskatchewan in 1774. He was in charge of Fort Prince of Wales in Manitoba from 1775 until the French captured it in 1782. In 1783, he set up a post at Churchill, Man. He returned to England in 1787. Hearne was born in London. He joined the Hudson's Bay Company about 1765.

Jean Bruchési

Hearst, Phoebe Apperson (1842-1919), an American philanthropist and educator, was a cofounder of the National Congress of Mothers. She and Alice J. M. Birney established the organization in 1897. In 1925, it became the National Congress of Parents and Teachers, the national organization of local parent-teacher associations (PTA's). Hearst was also the first woman regent of the University of California.

Phoebe Apperson was born on a farm near St. Clair, Mo. She taught school in St. James, Mo., until 1862, when she married George Hearst, a gold and silver miner who became a millionaire. Their son was the famous newspaper publisher William Randolph Hearst.

Phoebe Hearst was an early supporter of the kindergarten movement in the United States. In 1883, she financed a building in San Francisco that housed the Golden Gate Kindergarten Association and seven kindergartens. She helped set up the Columbia Free Kindergarten Association in Washington, D.C., in 1893 and served as its first president.   Kim O'Connor Kellogg

See also **Birney, Alice J. M.; National Congress of Parents and Teachers.**

Hearst, William Randolph (1863-1951), was a famous American publisher of newspapers and magazines. He developed a sensational journalistic style and spent millions of dollars to interest and attract readers. Critics described his style as *yellow journalism.*

Hearst had five sons, all of whom became executives in Hearst Newspapers, Inc. His second oldest son, William Randolph Hearst, Jr., won a Pulitzer Prize in 1956. One of Hearst's granddaughters, Patricia Hearst, was kidnapped in 1974 and became the object of one of the largest police searches in U.S. history.

Hearst was born in San Francisco. His father, George Hearst, was a mining magnate and U.S. senator. His mother was Phoebe Apperson Hearst, a philanthropist. Hearst attended Harvard University, where he served as business manager of the *Lampoon,* student comic magazine. In 1885, he was expelled from school because of a practical joke he played on his professors. His father then gave him the *San Francisco Examiner.* Hearst made this newspaper a remarkable financial success. In 1895, he bought the *New York Journal.* He matched the *Journal* against Joseph Pulitzer's *The* (New York) *World* in a circulation battle, which reached its height in 1898 during the Spanish-American War.

Hearst began buying other papers and magazines, and by 1937 owned 25 large dailies. In 1909, he founded the International News Service to serve them. His magazines included *Hearst's International-Cosmopolitan, Harper's Bazaar, House Beautiful,* and *Good Housekeeping.* Hearst pioneered in color comics, Sunday supplements, banner headlines, and editorial crusading. He had political ambitions and represented New York in the U.S. House of Representatives from 1903 to 1907. In 1904, he sought the Democratic nomination for President. He also ran unsuccessfully for governor of New York and mayor of New York City.

Hearst's estate at San Simeon, 175 miles (282 kilometers) south of San Francisco, was one of the most lavish private dwellings in the United States. It included 240,000 acres (97,100 hectares) of land, 50 miles (80 kilometers) of ocean frontage, four castles, and a priceless art collection. The main castle and part of the land became a California state park in 1958.

On Feb. 4, 1974, Patricia Hearst, the daughter of Hearst's son Randolph A. Hearst, was kidnapped by a revolutionary group called the Symbionese Liberation Army (SLA). After two months of captivity, Patricia Hearst announced in a tape-recorded message that she had joined the SLA. On April 15, 1974, she took part in a bank robbery with members of the group. The Federal Bureau of Investigation (FBI) arrested her on Sept. 18, 1975, and she was tried for robbery in 1976. At her trial, she testified that the SLA had threatened to kill her if she did not join the group. But she was found guilty and sentenced to seven years in prison. In January 1979, President Jimmy Carter *commuted* (lessened) her sentence and she was freed shortly afterwards. She had spent about 22 months in prison.   John Eldridge Drewry

Additional resources

Swanberg, William A. *Citizen Hearst: A Biography of William Randolph Hearst.* Scribner, 1984. First published in 1961.
Tebbel, John W. *The Life and Good Times of William Randolph Hearst.* Dutton, 1952.

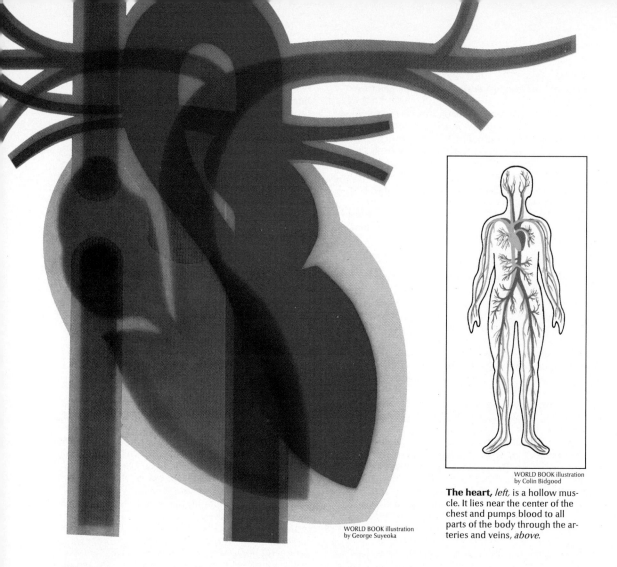

WORLD BOOK illustration
by Colin Bidgood

The heart, *left,* is a hollow muscle. It lies near the center of the chest and pumps blood to all parts of the body through the arteries and veins, *above.*

WORLD BOOK illustration
by George Suyeoka

Heart

Heart is a busy machine that pumps blood to all parts of the body. Blood carries oxygen to the brain and all other parts of your body. As long as your heart pumps blood, your body gets the oxygen it needs. If your heart stops, the oxygen is cut off and you will die unless a special device is used to circulate your blood.

The heart is a large hollow muscle. Tubes called *veins* bring blood to the heart. Other tubes called *arteries* carry blood away from the heart. Regulators called *valves* control the flow of blood through the heart itself.

Your heart is about the size of your fist, and the heart and fist grow at about the same rate. An adult's heart is about 5 inches (13 centimeters) long, $3\frac{1}{2}$ inches (9 centimeters) wide, and $2\frac{1}{2}$ inches (6.4 centimeters) thick. A man's heart weighs about 11 ounces (312 grams), and the heart of a woman weighs approximately 9 ounces (260 grams).

The heart lies in a slanting position near the middle of the chest toward the front. It is wider at the top than at the bottom. The wider end points toward the person's right shoulder. The narrower end points downward, to-

Your heart . . .

. . . is a busy pump linked by 100,000 miles (160,000 kilometers) of pipelines to all parts of your body.

. . . weighs less than 1 pound (0.5 kilogram).

. . . is as big as your fist.

. . . beats about 70 times a minute, and more than 100,000 times in a single day.

. . . pumps 5 quarts (4.7 liters) of blood through its chambers every 60 seconds.

. . . does enough work in one hour to lift a weight of $1\frac{1}{2}$ short tons (1.4 metric tons) more than 1 foot (30 centimeters) off the ground.

ward the front of the chest and to the left. The lower end is the part you can feel beating.

This article is about the human heart, but many kinds of animals have hearts. Earthworms, houseflies, snails, and some other *invertebrate animals* (animals without backbones) have hearts. Their hearts are not as well developed as human hearts. Often, they are just a thick-walled tube. All *vertebrate animals* (animals with backbones) have hearts. These animals include frogs, toads, lizards, snakes, and all birds and mammals.

Parts of the heart. The heart is completely enclosed by a thin sac called the *pericardium.* The pericardium is made of tough tissue. It protects the heart from rubbing against the lungs and the wall of the chest. The inside of the sac has a smooth lining that *secretes* (discharges) a slippery liquid. The heart beats smoothly and with little friction against the moistened lining of the pericardium.

A muscular wall called the *septum* divides the heart lengthwise. Two chambers, one above the other, are on each side of the septum. The upper chamber on each side is called an *atrium.* The thin-walled *atria* (plural of *atrium*) collect the blood flowing into the heart from the veins. Below each atrium is another chamber called a *ventricle.* The two ventricles pump the blood into the arteries. The walls of the ventricles are made of thick, strong muscles. The right ventricle pumps blood only to the lungs, but the left ventricle pumps blood to the entire body. The left ventricle has walls three times as thick as those of the right ventricle because it has to pump the blood so much farther.

Valves control the flow of blood through the heart. The *tricuspid valve* is between the right atrium and the right ventricle. The *mitral valve* is between the left atrium and the left ventricle. The *semilunar valves* control the flow of blood from the ventricles to the arteries. The semilunar valve that controls blood-flow from the left ventricle to the *aorta* (the main artery of the body) is also called the *aortic valve.*

Arteries carry blood from the heart to other parts of the body, but the heart itself also must receive nourishment. Blood flows to the heart muscle through *coronary arteries.* The coronary arteries lie over the walls of the heart in a complicated network, and carry oxygen to all parts of the hard-working heart muscle.

Development of the heart begins as soon as the embryo starts to develop inside the mother's body. The walls that divide the heart into chambers are forming when the embryo is only six weeks old.

At first, the human heart is a simple tube that soon begins to beat regularly. It grows so fast that there is no room for it to become longer inside the embryo. It doubles back on itself, twists around, and begins to look like the heart as we know it. A layer of tissue grows down the middle of the tube, dividing it into the right and left sides. A little later, the partitions between the atria and ventricles start to form.

The human heart goes through stages in which it resembles the hearts of various animals, before it is finally divided into four chambers. First, when it is a simple tube, it is like the heart of most fishes. Later, when the partitions begin to form, there is a time when the atria are partly separated but the ventricles have no wall between them. At this stage, the human heart looks like the heart of a frog. After the atria have divided, but the division between the ventricles is incomplete, the human heart resembles that of a snake or a turtle.

During the first weeks of growth, the human heart is nine times as large in proportion to the size of the whole body as it is in an adult. At this early stage, the heart is located high up in the chest. Later it moves into its permanent position in the middle of the chest.

The next striking change in the human heart occurs after birth. Before birth, there is no need for the blood to go through the lungs, because there is no air in them.

The blood flows from the right atrium directly to the left atrium through an opening in the septum called the *foramen ovale.* Another short circuit occurs through a blood vessel called the *ductus arteriosus.* The ductus arteriosus extends from the *pulmonary artery,* which connects the heart and lungs, to the aorta.

After the baby's supply of oxygen from its mother has been cut off following birth, the baby must use its own lungs. The openings through the ductus arteriosus and foramen ovale are no longer needed, and they gradually close. In most infants, the ductus arteriosus closes within three months. The foramen ovale usually closes before the end of the first year.

Three changes gradually take place in the heart as the baby grows into a child and then into an adult. First, the heart slowly increases in weight along with the rest of the body. At birth, the heart weighs only about $\frac{2}{3}$ of an ounce (19 grams). At two years, it weighs about $1\frac{1}{2}$ ounces (43 grams). At nine years, it weighs $3\frac{1}{3}$ ounces (94 grams), and at 15 or 16 years, about 7 ounces (200 grams). Second, the heart lies almost horizontal in small children. As the chest lengthens, the lower end of the heart shifts downward so that it lies in a more nearly vertical position. Third, the child's heart beats more slowly as the child grows older. An infant's heart beats about 120 times a minute. The heart of a 7-year-old child beats about 90 times a minute. An adult's heart beats about 70 times a minute.

How the heart works

Each side of the heart performs a different pumping job. The right side takes blood from the body and pumps it to the lungs. The left side collects blood from the lungs and pumps it to the body. Blood entering the right side of the heart contains *carbon dioxide,* a waste product of the body. All blood entering the right side of the heart goes to the lungs before it reaches the left side of the heart. In the lungs, the carbon dioxide is removed, and oxygen is added to the blood. Blood that flows to the body from the left side of the heart contains fresh oxygen. The oxygen is used in the body cells to produce energy. See **Circulatory system; Blood.**

Right side. Blood from the body flows into the right atrium through two large veins. One of these veins, the *superior vena cava,* carries blood from the head and arms. The other vein, the *inferior vena cava,* carries blood from the trunk and legs.

Blood from the body fills the right atrium. The atrium then contracts, squeezing blood through the tricuspid valve into the ventricle. The tricuspid valve is made of three little triangular flaps of thin, strong fibrous tissue. These flaps permit the blood to flow into the ventricle, but they prevent it from flowing back into the atrium. They are like doors that open only in one direction.

At first, the ventricle is relaxed, but it contracts when it is filled with blood. The resulting pressure closes the tricuspid valve and opens the semilunar valve between the ventricle and the *pulmonary artery.* Blood gushes through the semilunar valve into the pulmonary artery, which leads to the lungs. The valve is called *semilunar* because it is made up of three flaps that are shaped like half-moons. Blood squeezed from the ventricle pushes

Parts of the heart

The heart lies between the lungs at the center of the chest. The lower part of the heart points toward the left side of the body. Because the beating, or pumping, takes place in the lower part, many persons incorrectly think the heart is entirely on the left side of the body. This illustration shows the heart about two-thirds normal size.

The outer covering of the heart is a strong, thin membrane called the *pericardium*. The superior vena cava, aorta, and other large blood vessels lead in and out of the heart. Smaller blood vessels nourish the heart itself.

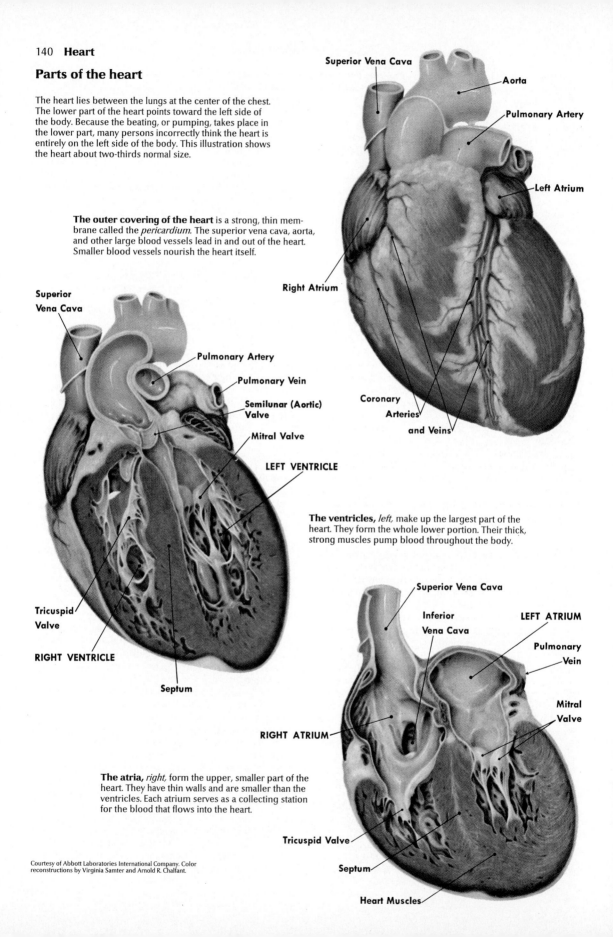

Superior Vena Cava

Aorta

Pulmonary Artery

Left Atrium

Right Atrium

Coronary Arteries and Veins

Superior Vena Cava

Pulmonary Artery

Pulmonary Vein

Semilunar (Aortic) Valve

Mitral Valve

LEFT VENTRICLE

Tricuspid Valve

RIGHT VENTRICLE

Septum

The ventricles, *left,* make up the largest part of the heart. They form the whole lower portion. Their thick, strong muscles pump blood throughout the body.

Superior Vena Cava

Inferior Vena Cava

LEFT ATRIUM

Pulmonary Vein

RIGHT ATRIUM

Mitral Valve

Tricuspid Valve

Septum

Heart Muscles

The atria, *right,* form the upper, smaller part of the heart. They have thin walls and are smaller than the ventricles. Each atrium serves as a collecting station for the blood that flows into the heart.

Courtesy of Abbott Laboratories International Company. Color reconstructions by Virginia Samter and Arnold R. Chalfant.

How your heart works

These drawings show how blood flows through the heart. Blood in the right chambers, shown in blue, flows to the lungs. Blood in the left chambers, shown in red, goes to the rest of the body.

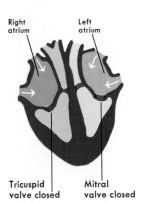

Right atrium | Left atrium

Tricuspid valve closed | Mitral valve closed

Right ventricle | Left ventricle

Tricuspid valve open | Mitral valve open

Semilunar valves open

Pulmonary artery | Aorta

Tricuspid valve closed | Mitral valve closed

Semilunar valves closed

Right atrium | Left atrium

Tricuspid valve closed | Mitral valve closed

WORLD BOOK diagrams

The heart relaxes between beats during the *diastolic* phase. Blood flows into the heart from the veins, filling both atria. The tricuspid and mitral valves are closed.

The atria contract, forcing blood through the mitral and tricuspid valves and into the ventricles. This action is called *atrial systole.* The ventricles are still in diastole.

The ventricles contract in *ventricular systole.* Blood forces the mitral and tricuspid valves shut and opens the semilunar valves. It enters the aorta and pulmonary artery.

The heart again relaxes. The semilunar valves close, and the atria expand and fill with blood. These steps mark the beginning of diastole, and the cycle is repeated.

the flaps against the walls of the pulmonary artery.

Left side. From the lungs, the blood flows back to the heart through the four *pulmonary veins.* It flows out of the pulmonary veins into the left atrium. The left atrium, like its neighbor on the right, then contracts, squeezing blood through the mitral valve into the left ventricle. The mitral valve is similar to the tricuspid valve, except that it has only two flaps. The left ventricle contracts, forcing blood through another semilunar valve into the aorta. The aorta, with its numerous branches, carries blood throughout the body.

Phases. The two sides of the heart relax and fill, and then contract and empty themselves at the same time. The atria contract only a split second before the ventricles do. The relaxing and filling phase is called the *diastole.* The contracting and pumping phase is called the *systole.* The action felt as a heartbeat is the systole.

Blood pressure. The blood in the circulatory system is always under pressure, as is the water in the pipes of a water system. Blood pressure depends upon the amount of blood in the system, the strength and rate of

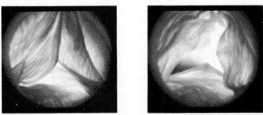

The aortic valve controls the flow of blood from the left ventricle to the aorta, the main artery in the body. These photographs show how the flaps of the aortic valve open to let out blood as the left ventricle contracts. The structure of the valve prevents blood from flowing back into the ventricle.

the heart's contraction, and the elasticity of the arteries. The heart regulates blood pressure by producing a hormone called *atrial natriuretic factor.* This hormone helps the kidneys get rid of salt. Excess salt in the body may contribute to *hypertension* (high blood pressure). Doctors measure two phases of blood pressure—the *systolic pressure* and the *diastolic pressure.* The systolic pressure is the blood pressure when the heart is contracted. The diastolic pressure is the pressure when the heart relaxes between beats. Doctors use a device called a *sphygmomanometer* to measure a patient's blood pressure. See **Blood pressure; Manometer.**

Beat of the heart. The walls of the heart are made of a special kind of muscle. The heart muscle contracts and relaxes regularly and automatically. A beat is one complete contraction and relaxation of the heart muscle.

A special system of muscles in the heart causes it to beat with a regular rhythm. One part of this system, the *sinoatrial (sinoauricular)* or *S-A node,* has the job of starting each heartbeat, setting the pace, and causing contraction of the heart muscle. It has been called the "pacemaker" of the heart. The impulse from this node spreads through the atria and reaches a second node, the *atrioventricular,* or *A-V node.* A part of this specialized system, called the *atrioventricular bundle* or the *bundle of His,* conducts the beating impulse from the atria and the A-V node to the rest of the heart. This system causes the heart to contract as a single unit.

Sometimes the heart may stop beating because of an accident, a heart attack, or surgical shock. Such an occurrence is called a *cardiac arrest.* If the heart stops during an operation, a doctor may open the patient's chest and massage the heart until it starts to beat again. In other emergency situations, doctors or other specially trained persons may give the victim *external heart massage.* They apply pressure to the chest in a certain way to restart the heartbeat.

A World Book science project

How exercise affects the heart

The purpose of this project is to determine how exercise affects the heartbeat by measuring the pulse of people performing various levels of activity.

Materials and subjects

For this project, you will need a notepad and a clock or watch with a second hand or a digital display. Select male and female subjects from various age groups; for example, under 25, from 25 to 40, and over 40 years old. CAUTION: Individuals with heart or respiratory problems should not be used as subjects in this project.

WORLD BOOK photo

Procedure

1. **Measuring heartbeat at rest.** Have the subject sit quietly for a few minutes, and then measure and record the subject's pulse.

   To take the pulse, place three middle fingers of one hand on the inside of the subject's wrist near the base of the thumb. Wait until you can clearly feel and count the heartbeats. Record the beats you count in one minute.

2. **Measuring heartbeat after mild activity.** Have the subject walk at a normal, relaxed pace for two minutes. As soon as the subject stops walking, measure and record the pulse.

3. **Measuring heartbeat after vigorous activity.** Have the subject walk or run up and down a flight of stairs for two minutes. Immediately afterward, measure and record the subject's pulse.

Organizing your information

1. Prepare a table, such as the one shown below, listing each subject's name, age group, and rate of heartbeat after each level of activity.

2. From the table, prepare a graph showing the heartbeat rate for each subject at each level of activity. Use a different color for each age group, as shown in the graph below.

   What conclusions might you draw from your information? How might you test these conclusions?

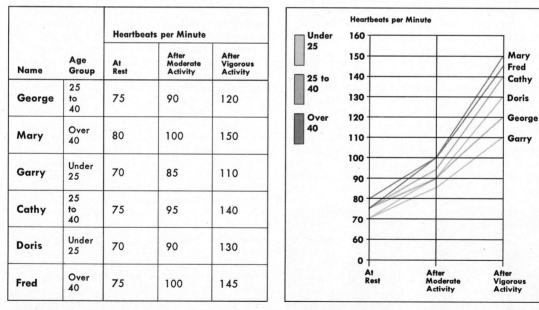

Name	Age Group	Heartbeats per Minute		
		At Rest	After Moderate Activity	After Vigorous Activity
George	25 to 40	75	90	120
Mary	Over 40	80	100	150
Garry	Under 25	70	85	110
Cathy	25 to 40	75	95	140
Doris	Under 25	70	90	130
Fred	Over 40	75	100	145

Additional activities and questions

Obtain additional information on each subject. Such information might include height, weight, average rate of activity (very active, moderately active, inactive), and whether the subject is a smoker or a nonsmoker. Prepare graphs that help answer such questions as: Is heartbeat affected more by the subject's age or by his or her body condition? Does exercise seem to have a greater effect on the heartbeat of males than that of females?

Rate of beating. Without oxygen, the body cells stop working. Sometimes the body needs much oxygen. At other times, it requires little. An adult's heart normally beats about 70 times a minute, but the rate changes automatically to provide as much or as little oxygen as the body needs. See **Pulse.**

The body needs a lot of fuel for such strenuous exercises as swimming or ice skating. For this reason, the heart beats rapidly when a person swims or skates. It is rushing more oxygen to the body by speeding the flow of blood. If the person stops exercising, the heart gradually slows down. It is regulating the flow of blood to the body's slower tempo.

There are many other examples of how the heart changes its rate of beating to meet a particular need. The heart beats faster when a person is angry, afraid, or excited. It is rushing more oxygen to the muscles to prepare the person for quick action, such as fighting or running away. During pregnancy, a woman's heart takes care not only of her own needs, but also the needs of the unborn baby. The woman's heart increases its output by half to three-fourths.

Heart diseases

Diseases of the heart and blood vessels are called *cardiovascular diseases.* The word *cardiovascular* comes from the word *cardiac,* meaning heart, and *vascular,* meaning blood vessel. Cardiovascular diseases cause about half of all deaths in the United States. The field of medicine that deals with the diagnosis and treatment of heart disease is called *cardiology.* Doctors who specialize in such medicine are called *cardiologists.*

The three most important kinds of heart disease are (1) *arteriosclerosis,* or hardening of the arteries; (2) *hypertension,* or high blood pressure; and (3) *rheumatic*

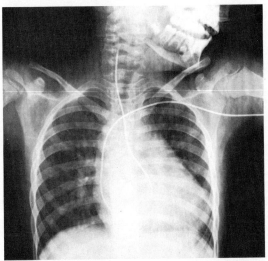

A. B. Shaffer, M.D.

Cardiac catheterization involves threading a *catheter* (thin tube) through the heart and tracing its route on an X-ray screen. The X ray above reveals the location of a hole between the ventricles. The tube was inserted into a vein in the arm and guided into the heart, through the hole, and up the carotid artery.

fever, which often leads to *rheumatic heart disease* later in life. Certain infections, such as diphtheria, and syphilis in its late stages, can produce heart disease. Some children are born with imperfectly formed hearts. They suffer from *congenital heart disease.*

Diagnosis. When examining the heart, a doctor first notes anything the patient reports that indicates the heart is not working properly. The doctor asks questions to help discover whether the patient may have a heart ailment. Next, the doctor examines the heart by trying to feel its tip pushing against the chest wall. The position of the heart tells its size. The doctor thumps on the chest over the heart to get an idea of its shape.

The doctor places a stethoscope on the chest over the heart to hear its beat. The heart makes two sounds each time it beats: first, a low-pitched, long sound, "lubb," and then a high-pitched, more snapping sound, "dup." The first sound is made by the closing of the tricuspid valve and the mitral valve. The second sound is caused by the snapping shut of the semilunar valves just as the heart begins to relax. If a valve is faulty, it may not close tightly when the heart relaxes or open completely when the heart contracts. The passage of blood around the valve causes a sound called a *heart murmur.* Heart murmurs can also be caused by other conditions. Sometimes they are present in normal hearts, but these murmurs sound different. See **Heart murmur.**

In some cases, a doctor uses an *electrocardiograph.* This instrument makes a record of the electrical changes that occur as the heart beats. To determine how the heart functions under heavy exertion, a doctor may check the heartbeat while the patient performs a strenuous activity. Such testing is called *stress electrocardiography.* In a kind of testing called *echocardiography,* a doctor uses ultrasonic equipment to reflect sound waves off the heart. Echocardiography can determine such things as the thickness of the heart walls and the size of the heart chambers.

The doctor may also use an X-ray machine. This machine gives off rays that pass through the body and make a shadow picture of the heart. With a *fluoroscope,* a kind of X-ray machine, a doctor can look directly at the heart shadow. The doctor can study the size and shape of the heart, and the way it beats.

Another method of examining the heart, called *cardiac catheterization,* consists of inserting a *catheter* (long tube) into a vein or artery—or both—in the arm. The catheter is then threaded into the heart, while a doctor observes with a fluoroscope. Cardiac catheterization is used especially when heart surgery is being considered. It enables a doctor to measure blood pressure and the oxygen content of the blood in the heart. Also, special materials may be injected through the catheter, making the blood flowing through the heart or the coronary arteries visible in X rays.

Arteriosclerosis is a condition in which the arteries harden. Deposits of fatty material and calcium narrow the arteries and roughen their normally smooth lining. These deposits, called *plaques,* cause cells in the artery walls to break down. Substances from the ruptured cells irritate nearby tissues, causing scars to form. As a result, the artery wall becomes hard, rough, and narrow.

The coronary arteries, which nourish the heart muscle itself, are more frequently affected by arteriosclesis than are any others. Hardening of these arteries reduces the heart's blood supply, and may cause a pain in the chest known as *angina pectoris* (see **Angina pectoris**).

The rough surface of the wall, together with the sluggish flow of blood through the narrowed channels, may cause a blood clot to form. A clot of this type is called a *thrombus*. A thrombus may break away from the place where it formed and be carried in the bloodstream. A moving clot is called an *embolus* (see **Embolism**). A thrombus or an embolus may block an artery altogether. A blocked artery in the brain causes a *stroke*. Blockage in a coronary artery causes a *heart attack*. See **Arteriosclerosis.**

Hypertension is continually high blood pressure. Uncontrolled hypertension strains the heart, damages arteries, and increases the risk of heart attack, stroke, and kidney problems. See **Hypertension.**

Rheumatic fever is caused by bacteria that belong to the *Streptococcus* group, the same group that causes blood poisoning and scarlet fever. It is usually, but not always, a disease of young persons. It ranks among the leading causes of heart disease among children. It is also responsible for much serious heart disease later in life. Rheumatic fever may damage the heart valves so that blood cannot flow through them normally. As a result, the heart must work harder to keep up with the needs of the body. See **Rheumatic fever.**

Congenital heart disease describes a heart disorder present at birth. A *blue baby* has a congenital heart disorder. Some of the baby's blood passes directly from the right side of the heart to the left side, without going to the lungs. Thus, the blood still contains carbon dioxide, and it has not picked up oxygen. Such blood gives the baby's skin a bluish tinge. See **Blue baby.**

Bacterial endocarditis is a serious infection of the *endocardium* (the lining of the chambers of the heart). It sometimes occurs when persons with congenital or rheumatic heart disease undergo an operation. Bacteria that enter the bloodstream during operations infect the heart and damage it even further. Most cases of endocarditis can be prevented by giving patients prone to infection adequate doses of antibiotics before and after operations, even minor ones such as tooth extractions.

Fibrillation is a condition in which the muscle fibers of the heart work without coordination, with an irregular rhythm, and usually at a far faster rate than normal. The result is a quivering or fluttering of the heart, instead of the strong, regular contractions that result when the muscle fibers work together properly. When fibrillation affects the ventricles, as in *ventricular fibrillation,* it usually is fatal, because the irregularly quivering ventricles cannot pump blood out of the heart. Doctors can correct ventricular fibrillation by giving the victim's heart a powerful electric shock. Fibrillation of the atria is not as serious as ventricular fibrillation.

Heart failure is a condition in which the heart does not pump efficiently. It does not mean the heart stops beating. Heart failure is usually an advanced stage of heart disease.

Heart attacks

Heart attacks are one of the leading causes of death in the United States. Every day they kill about 1,500 people and leave thousands of others crippled to some extent for the rest of their lives.

What happens to the heart? Almost all heart attacks result from the sudden blockage of a coronary artery. The blockage cuts off the blood supply to part of the heart, and so a portion of the heart muscle dies. Most blockages are caused by arteriosclerosis, which hardens and narrows the artery. After a heart attack, a blood clot also is found in the artery. It is not known if the clot causes the attack by blocking the artery, or if it is a result of the attack. Some heart attacks may result from a *vasospasm,* the constriction of muscles in an artery wall. A vasospasm narrows the artery and could shut off the blood flow. It can occur even in arteries that have not been narrowed by arteriosclerosis.

From 15 to 25 per cent of all people who suffer a heart attack die as a result. Chances of recovery are good if the blockage occurs in one of the smaller coronary arteries. But if one of the larger arteries is blocked, a large part of the heart may be damaged, and the attack is more likely to be fatal. Sudden death may occur from ventricular fibrillation, if the damaged area affects the system that regulates the heartbeat.

What causes a heart attack? A heart attack occurs suddenly, but the build-up of fatty deposits and calcium in the coronary arteries is a slow process. It may take years before an artery is narrow enough to be blocked. There is probably no single cause of arteriosclerosis or heart attacks. Several factors are involved, including diet, cigarette smoking, and hereditary traits.

Diet. People who eat too much and are overweight run a greater risk of a heart attack than those who eat sensibly. Furthermore, people who include large amounts of salt and salty foods in their diet increase their chances of developing hypertension. Hypertension, in turn, greatly increases the risk of a heart attack.

The fatty deposits that build up inside arteries contain large amounts of a substance called *cholesterol*. A diet that is rich in animal fats raises the levels of cholesterol in the blood. Many scientists maintain that such a diet increases the risk of arteriosclerosis and a heart attack. Foods high in animal fats include beef, pork, eggs, and whole milk products. Many doctors urge their patients to limit their intake of such foods. However, some experts question the value of such dietary changes in healthy people.

Cigarette smoking. People who smoke cigarettes are two to three times more likely to have a heart attack than nonsmokers, former smokers, or people who smoke pipes or cigars. Smoking does not cause heart attacks, but it increases the likelihood of an attack.

Hereditary traits may play a part in heart attacks by making a person more susceptible to arteriosclerosis. However, a person aware of a family history of arteriosclerosis is likely to take steps to reduce the risk of getting it. Many experts believe a person's habits and environment are far more important factors in heart attacks than any traits that may be inherited.

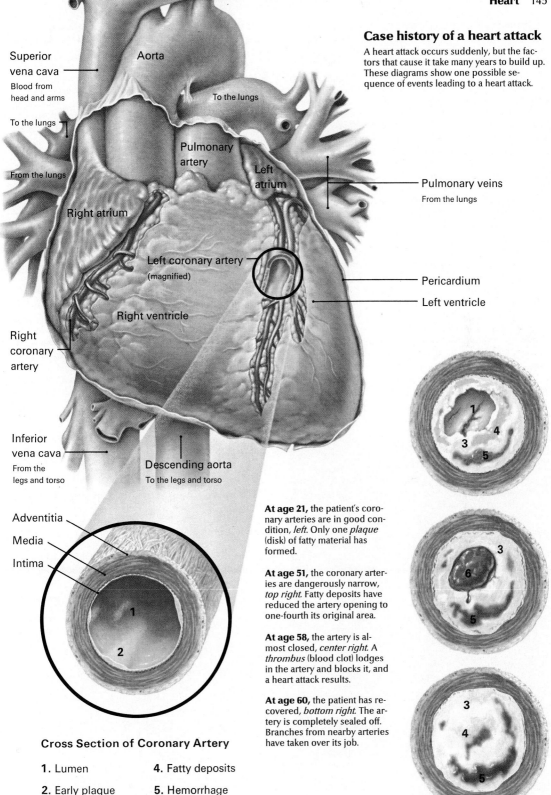

Superior
vena cava
Blood from
head and arms

Aorta

To the lungs

To the lungs

From the lungs

Right atrium

Pulmonary
artery

Left
atrium

Left coronary artery
(magnified)

Right
coronary
artery

Right ventricle

Inferior
vena cava
From the
legs and torso

Descending aorta
To the legs and torso

Pulmonary veins
From the lungs

Pericardium

Left ventricle

Case history of a heart attack

A heart attack occurs suddenly, but the factors that cause it take many years to build up. These diagrams show one possible sequence of events leading to a heart attack.

At age 21, the patient's coronary arteries are in good condition, *left*. Only one *plaque* (disk) of fatty material has formed.

At age 51, the coronary arteries are dangerously narrow, *top right*. Fatty deposits have reduced the artery opening to one-fourth its original area.

At age 58, the artery is almost closed, *center right*. A *thrombus* (blood clot) lodges in the artery and blocks it, and a heart attack results.

At age 60, the patient has recovered, *bottom right*. The artery is completely sealed off. Branches from nearby arteries have taken over its job.

Adventitia

Media

Intima

Cross Section of Coronary Artery

1. Lumen   **4.** Fatty deposits

2. Early plaque   **5.** Hemorrhage

3. Advanced plaque **6.** Thrombus

WORLD BOOK illustration by Paul Peck, M.D.

Treatment of heart problems

Some people suffer such serious heart conditions that they need medical treatment, perhaps including surgery, to have them corrected. Before the 1940's, there was little hope for many persons with serious heart problems. Since then, new kinds of drug therapy and spectacular advances in heart surgery have enabled physicians to treat many heart problems.

A number of advances in heart surgery have resulted from the development of the *heart-lung machine,* or *pump-oxygenator.* This machine has an electrically driven pump that takes over the job of the lungs. It removes carbon dioxide from the blood and replenishes it with oxygen. At the start of a heart operation, surgeons open the patient's chest and expose the heart. They then connect a heart-lung machine to the patient's circulatory system. They can now stop the heart, open it, examine it for defects, and repair it. Such surgery is called *open-heart surgery.*

Repairing holes in the heart. Normally, the two atria of the heart are separated by a membrane called the *atrial septum.* Before birth, babies have a small hole through this membrane. In most cases, the hole closes at birth or shortly thereafter, preventing the flow of blood from one atrium to the other. But in some babies the hole does not close. This kind of hole between the atria is one kind of *atrial septal defect.* Similarly, a *ventricular septal defect* is a hole between the two ventricles.

Unless it is repaired, a hole in the heart will strain the heart and lead to heart failure. In some cases, surgeons close the hole by *suturing* (sewing) the edges together. If the hole is very big, they mend it by sewing a patch of synthetic fabric over it.

Fixing defective heart valves. Defective heart valves may be present at birth or may develop later in life. Most persons who develop defective heart valves had rheumatic fever when they were young. A damaged valve may be *stenotic* (too tight) or *insufficient* (too loose). The two most frequently affected valves are the mitral valve and the aortic valve. Both valves may be faulty at the same time.

In a condition called *mitral stenosis,* the flaps of the mitral valve stick together, narrowing the valve opening. This narrowing interferes with the flow of blood from the left atrium to the left ventricle. A surgeon may separate the leaflets of the valve or replace the valve with an artificial one.

An insufficient valve leaks blood. *Mitral insufficiency* is caused by a leaking mitral valve. *Aortic insufficiency* involves a leaking aortic valve. To repair insufficient valves, a surgeon usually removes the faulty valve and replaces it with an artificial one. Several types of artificial valves may be used. One type, the *cage-ball valve,* consists of a tiny stainless-steel cage that encloses a ball made of *pyrolytic* (heat-treated) carbon. The cage has a soft ring of synthetic fabric attached to it so the valve can be sewn into the heart. The valve allows blood to pass in only one direction. Backflow is prevented because any reverse pressure forces the ball backward and closes the valve. Another kind of artificial valve is

Repairing a damaged heart

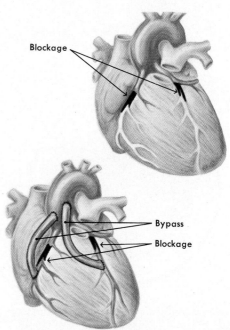

Baylor College of Medicine

Open-heart surgery, *above,* is a technique for repairing a damaged heart. The surgeon first opens the patient's chest, and then cuts through the pericardium and exposes the heart itself. Next, the surgeon connects a heart-lung machine to the patient's circulatory system and stops the heart by clamping the aorta.

WORLD BOOK illustrations by Virginia Samter

A coronary bypass enables blood to flow around blockages in coronary arteries. Such blockages, *top,* prevent blood from reaching the heart. The surgeon uses short segments of vein that have been taken from the patient's leg to construct bypasses around the blockages, *bottom.*

made from a valve of a pig's heart. It operates much like a normal human heart valve.

Treating coronary artery disease. In coronary artery disease, the coronary arteries become dangerously narrow. The narrowed arteries supply less blood to the heart, and the heart cannot do its job properly. The patient may suffer angina pectoris and may be stricken by a heart attack.

There is no cure for coronary artery disease. Many victims, however, can be treated with drugs or by surgical procedures to enable them to lead a normal life. Doctors evaluate each patient to determine which method of treatment would provide the greatest benefit.

Physicians use a variety of drugs to treat the symptoms and complications of coronary artery disease. Some patients who suffer a heart attack receive *anticoagulants* to reduce the risk of another attack. These drugs help prevent heart attacks by interfering with blood clotting in the arteries. Drugs called *beta-blockers* also reduce the risk of a second attack in some patients. See Beta-blocker.

Physicians prescribe beta-blockers and other drugs to reduce high blood pressure, a condition present in many heart attack victims. Doctors also use beta-blockers and another class of drugs, called *calcium blockers,* to relieve angina pectoris. *Nitroglycerin* also relieves angina pectoris, but it is effective for only a few minutes.

Surgical treatment helps many victims of coronary artery disease. One kind of operation, called a *coronary artery bypass,* may be performed if only a short section of a coronary artery is blocked. In this operation, the

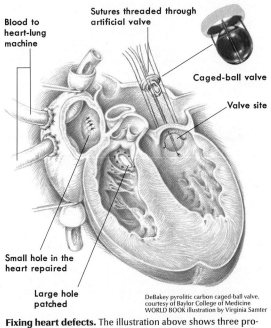

Blood to heart-lung machine

Sutures threaded through artificial valve

Caged-ball valve

Valve site

Small hole in the heart repaired

Large hole patched

DeBakey pyrolitic carbon caged-ball valve, courtesy of Baylor College of Medicine
WORLD BOOK illustration by Virginia Samter

Fixing heart defects. The illustration above shows three procedures for repairing heart defects. A surgeon mends a small hole in the heart by sewing the edges together, *left.* A larger hole is patched with synthetic fabric, *center.* A faulty valve is removed and replaced with a caged-ball valve, *right.* The surgeon threads sutures around the valve site and through the artificial valve, slips the valve into place, and sews it to the heart.

surgeon removes a short segment of vein from the patient's leg. One end of this segment is attached to the aorta. The other end is attached to the affected coronary artery at a point beyond the blockage. The vein thus provides a bypass around the blocked portion of the patient's artery. The surgeon may construct several bypasses, depending on the number of blocked arteries.

During the early 1980's, a new technique for clearing blocked arteries became available. In this technique, called *coronary angioplasty,* a balloon device attached to a catheter is inserted into the blocked artery. The balloon is then inflated. The inflated balloon reopens the artery by pushing the blockage into the artery wall. This technique provides an alternative to by-pass surgery for certain types of patients.

Also during the early 1980's, researchers began investigating the use of a clot-dissolving serum called *tissue plasminogen activator,* or *t-PA,* to aid heart attack victims. This serum is made from a protein that occurs naturally in the body. It is injected into a blood vessel during the early stages of the heart attack. The serum dissolves the clot, and thus the blood flow to the heart muscle is restored. Studies were also underway to determine the usefulness of two other clot-dissolving substances, *streptokinase* and *urokinase,* in treating heart attacks.

Correcting abnormal heart rhythms. Many people, including some who have coronary artery disease, suffer various types of *arrhythmias* (abnormal heart rhythms). Their heartbeat may be irregular, too rapid, or too slow. Some arrhythmias can be treated with beta-blockers, calcium blockers, digitalis, and other drugs. Ventricular arrhythmias can be treated with an electronic device called a *defibrillator.* The device, which is implanted in the body, continuously monitors the heart and delivers electric shocks to restore normal rhythm. In some cases, a surgical procedure can be performed to treat ventricular arrythmias.

In a condition called *heart block,* the normal impulse from the atrium to the ventricle is interrupted. Some cases of heart block can be treated with drugs. But in many cases, a small electronic device called a *pacemaker* is implanted in the body to correct the condition. A pacemaker transmits an electric impulse to the heart, stimulating the organ to beat in a regular manner. Most pacemakers are powered by a lithium battery that must be replaced from time to time. The battery usually lasts from 5 to 15 years. Some pacemakers have a rechargeable battery and others are nuclear-powered. See **Medicine** (picture: A pacemaker).

Helping the heart pump blood. A heart that is seriously weakened by disease cannot pump blood properly. This condition is called *heart failure.* In some cases, doctors prescribe digitalis to treat heart failure. Digitalis strengthens the ventricular contractions and corrects some types of arrhythmias. Doctors may also prescribe a drug called *amrinone* to patients suffering from congestive heart failure. This drug is taken through injection and stimulates the heart's ability to pump blood. Patients also may be treated with drugs called *diuretics.* These drugs improve the ability of the kidneys to eliminate the excess fluids that build up in body tissues as a result of heart failure.

In some cases, surgeons must help a failing heart by

Heart-lung machine

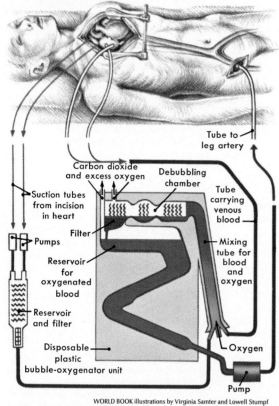

Tube to leg artery

Carbon dioxide and excess oxygen

Debubbling chamber

Suction tubes from incision in heart

Tube carrying venous blood

Filter

Pumps

Mixing tube for blood and oxygen

Reservoir for oxygenated blood

Reservoir and filter

Disposable plastic bubble-oxygenator unit

Oxygen

Pump

WORLD BOOK illustrations by Virginia Samter and Lowell Stumpf

A heart-lung machine can perform the jobs of the heart and lungs for several hours. It removes venous blood from the heart, adds oxygen to the blood, and pumps it into a leg artery.

Ventricular bypass pump

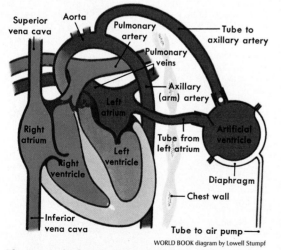

Superior vena cava

Aorta

Pulmonary artery

Tube to axillary artery

Pulmonary veins

Axillary (arm) artery

Left atrium

Right atrium

Artificial ventricle

Left ventricle

Tube from left atrium

Right ventricle

Diaphragm

Chest wall

Inferior vena cava

Tube to air pump

WORLD BOOK diagram by Lowell Stumpf

The ventricular bypass pump, *above,* helps a failing left ventricle. It takes blood from the left atrium and then forces it into the arm artery. As a result, the left ventricle has to pump less hard and the strain on the heart is relieved. Tubes connect the device to the arm artery and left atrium. Another tube goes to a pump, which controls the rate of "beating."

using a mechanical pump called an *assisting heart* or *artificial heart.* An assisting heart helps a failing left ventricle until it recovers and can pump an adequate amount of blood. If only several hours of assistance are needed, a heart-lung machine may be used. For periods of 24 to 36 hours, a balloon type of pumping device may be installed in the aorta. For periods of up to about a week, a *ventricular bypass pump* may be used. This device removes some of the blood entering the left atrium and pumps it back into the bloodstream through an artery in the patient's arm.

Replacing diseased hearts. In 1967, a human heart was transplanted for the first time. The operation was performed by a team of surgeons headed by Christiaan N. Barnard of the Groote Schuur Hospital in Cape Town, South Africa. During the next several years, many heart transplants were performed in human beings. But most of the patients died within a year, mainly because their bodies rejected the transplanted organ. The low survival rate, along with difficulties in obtaining suitable donor

Milestones in the study of the heart

1628   Circulation of the blood through the body was described by William Harvey, an English physician.

1706   The structure of the left ventricle and distribution of coronary vessels were described by Raymond de Vieussens, a French anatomy professor.

1733   Blood pressure was measured by Stephen Hales, an English clergyman and scientist.

1785   Digitalis, in the form of foxglove leaves, was introduced by William Withering, English physician.

1816   The stethoscope was invented by René T. H. Laënnec, a French physician.

1893   The atrioventricular bundle, a muscle bundle connecting the right atrium with the ventricles of the heart, was discovered by Wilhelm His, Jr., a Swiss anatomist. It is also called the *bundle of His.*

1903   The electrocardiograph, for showing the heart's electrical activity, was developed by Willem Einthoven, a Dutch physiologist.

1912   First diagnosis of coronary thrombosis and description of heart disease resulting from hardening of the arteries were made by James B. Herrick, an American cardiologist.

1938   First surgery for congenital heart disease was performed by Robert E. Gross, an American surgeon.

1951   Plastic ball valve for a leaky aortic valve was developed by Charles Hufnagel, an American surgeon.

1952   Open-heart surgery was first successfully performed by F. John Lewis, an American surgeon.

1953   Mechanical heart and blood purifier was used successfully for the first time by John H. Gibbon, an American surgeon.

1961   External cardiac massage, to restart a stopped heart without surgery, was introduced by J. R. Jude, American cardiologist, and his associates.

1965   Assisting hearts, mechanical devices to help a diseased or overworked left ventricle, were first successfully implanted by Michael E. DeBakey, and by Adrian Kantrowitz, American surgeons.

1967   First transplant of a whole heart from one person to another was performed by a surgical team headed by Christiaan Barnard of South Africa.

1982   First implantation of a permanent artificial heart was performed by a team headed by American surgeon William DeVries. The mechanical heart was designed by American physician Robert Jarvik.

hearts, has severely limited the value of heart transplants. By the early 1980's, however, the Stanford University Medical Center had achieved a survival rate of 70 per cent after the first year for heart-transplant patients.

The first implantation of a permanent—rather than temporary—artificial heart took place in 1982. The operation was performed at the University of Utah by a team headed by William DeVries. The patient, Barney Clark, survived for 112 days. See **Artificial heart.**

In 1984, the heart of an animal was transplanted into the body of a human infant. A surgical team led by Leonard L. Bailey of Loma Linda University in California performed the operation. The patient, a 12-day-old girl known as Baby Fae, received the heart of a 7-month-old baboon. The infant died 21 days later, but survived longer than any of the four persons who had previously received an animal heart.   Michael E. DeBakey

Study aids

Related articles in *World Book* include:

Aneurysm	Coronary thrombosis	Human body (Trans-Vision)
Angina pectoris	Debakey, Michael E.	Laënnec, René T. H.
Aorta	Disease (graph)	Myocarditis
Arteriosclerosis	Drug (Drugs that affect the heart and blood vessels)	Pulse
Artery		Rheumatic fever
Barnard, Christiaan N.	Electrocardiograph	Smoking
Blood	Embolism	Stroke
Blood pressure	First aid (Heart attack)	Tachycardia
Blue baby	Fluoroscopy	Taussig, Helen B.
Calcium blocker	Harvey, William	Vein
Capillary	Heart Association, American	Williams, Daniel H.
Cerebral hemorrhage	Heart murmur	
Circulatory system		

Outline

I. Its parts and development
  A. Parts of the heart   B. Development of the heart

II. How the heart works
  A. Right side   C. Phases   E. Beat of the heart
  B. Left side   D. Blood pressure   F. Rate of beating

III. Heart diseases
  A. Diagnosis   E. Congenital heart disease
  B. Arteriosclerosis   F. Bacterial endocarditis
  C. Hypertension   G. Fibrillation
  D. Rheumatic fever   H. Heart failure

IV. Heart attacks
  A. What happens to the heart?
  B. What causes a heart attack?

V. Treatment of heart problems
  A. Repairing holes in the heart
  B. Fixing defective heart valves
  C. Treating coronary artery disease
  D. Correcting abnormal heart rhythms
  E. Helping the heart pump blood
  F. Replacing diseased hearts

Questions

How large is your heart?
How does heart muscle differ from other muscles?
Why is blood pumped to the lungs?
Who first described the circulation of human blood?
How does a pacemaker correct abnormal heart rhythm?
What are three kinds of heart disease?
When and why does the heart change its rate of beating?
What is the normal heartbeat of an adult?
How widespread is heart disease in the United States?

Additional resources

Level I
Limburg, Peter. *The Story of Your Heart.* Coward, 1979.
Silverstein, Alvin and Virginia B. *Heart Disease.* Follett, 1976.
  Heartbeats: Your Body, Your Heart. Lippincott, 1983.
Zim, Herbert S. *Your Heart and How It Works.* Morrow, 1959.

Level II
American Heart Association. *Heartbook: A Guide to Prevention and Treatment of Cardiovascular Diseases.* Dutton, 1980.
Davis, Goode P., and Park, Edwards. *The Heart: The Living Pump.* Scribner, 1981.
DeBakey, Michael, and Gotto, Antonio. *The Living Heart.* McKay, 1977.
Riedman, Sarah R. *Heart.* Western Publishing, 1974.
Wertenbaker, Lael. *To Mend the Heart: The Dramatic Story of Cardiac Surgery and Its Pioneers.* Viking, 1980.

Heart Association, American, is a national voluntary health agency organized to fight diseases of the heart and blood vessels. It sponsors research, community services, and professional and public education on heart disease. The association has 55 affiliates, and nearly 2,000 local subdivisions. It has about 105,000 active members. About 40,000 of these members are physicians.

The American Heart Association gains financial support for its program from the general public through contributions made to the association or to its Heart Fund. The association has its headquarters at 7320 Greenville Avenue, Dallas, TX 75231.
  Critically reviewed by The American Heart Association, Inc.

Heart attack. See Heart (Heart attacks); **First aid** (Heart attack).

Heart diseases. See Heart (Heart diseases).

Heart murmur is an abnormal sound in a person's heartbeat. An *organic murmur* is a symptom of heart disease. It is produced by the blood flowing through defective heart valves or across defects between chambers of the heart. A diseased heart valve may not close tightly or open completely when the heart contracts, and the forceful passage of blood around the valve causes a murmur. Causes of organic murmur include (1) rheumatic fever, (2) heart deformities present at birth, and (3) *arteriosclerosis* (hardening of the arteries). A *functional murmur,* also called an *innocent murmur* occurs in the absence of heart disease. It may appear after a person exercises strenuously.   Bruce A. Reitz

Heartburn, also known as *pyrosis,* is a painful, burning sensation in the esophagus. Heartburn results when acidic stomach contents surge upward into the esophagus or when the esophagus undergoes intense spasms. Heartburn usually begins just below the tip of the breastbone, near the heart, and rises toward the throat. In some cases, the mouth suddenly fills with a large amount of clear, watery saliva called *water brash.* The pain of heartburn may last several hours.

Heartburn accompanies many types of indigestion. It most frequently occurs after a person drinks a hot or cold liquid. People who are tense or tired may suffer from heartburn, especially after eating. Pregnant women and people who have ulcers or gall bladder disease may also experience heartburn. Antacid medications can temporarily relieve heartburn pain.   Roberta L. Bondar
  See also **Indigestion; Ulcer.**

Heartwood. See Sap.

Heartworm. See Dog (Medical care).

Heat

People use heat in many ways to do work and to make life more comfortable. In this foundry furnace, for example, heat is used to soften steel so that it can be shaped into the desired form. The steel becomes so hot it gives off light.

Heat. When we think of heat, we usually think of how heat makes us feel. On a hot summer day, for example, heat may make us feel uncomfortable. But heat is far more important in our lives than simply how it may make us feel.

We must have a carefully controlled amount of heat to live. Our bodies use the food we eat to produce the heat that keeps our temperature at about 98.6° F. (37° C). If our temperature rises too far above normal—or falls too far below—we can die. In cold weather, we wear heavy clothes to hold in our body heat. During warm weather, we wear light clothes to let the unneeded heat escape.

No one knows how high temperatures may climb, but the temperature inside the hottest stars is many millions of degrees. The lowest possible temperature, called *absolute zero,* is −459.67° F. (−273.15° C).

Charles F. Squire, the contributor of this article, is Director of Research at the Squire Research Laboratory.

In our homes, we use heat in many ways. Heat warms our homes and cooks our food. It also provides hot water, dries the laundry, and makes electric light bulbs give off light.

In industry, the uses for heat are almost endless. Heat is used to separate metals from their ores and to refine crude oil. It is used to shape, cut, coat, and harden metals and to join metals together. Heat is also used to make or process foods, glass, paper, textiles, and many other products.

Heat also runs our machinery. The heat from burning fuels in engines provides the power to move airplanes, automobiles, and ships. Heat spins the wheels of giant turbines, which drive generators that produce electricity. Electricity provides light and furnishes power to run all kinds of equipment—from electric pencil sharpeners to electric railroads.

This article discusses where heat comes from and what heat is, how it travels, and what it does. The article also describes how we have put heat to work and the discoveries we have made about heat.

Anything that gives off heat is a source of heat. The heat that we use or that affects life on the earth comes from six main sources. They are (1) the sun, (2) fire, (3) the earth, (4) chemical reactions, (5) friction, and (6) nuclear energy.

We control some of these sources of heat, and others we do not. We use the sources we control, such as fire and nuclear energy, to heat buildings and to do other work. But the sources we do not control also benefit us. For example, the sun provides the heat and light that make life possible.

All sources of heat, even those that we normally control, can do great damage if they get out of control. Every year, for example, fires take many lives and destroy much property.

The sun is our most important source of heat. If the sun should ever cool, the earth would become cold and lifeless. Only a tiny fraction of the heat produced in the sun strikes the earth. Yet it is enough to keep us—and all other things—alive.

The sun's heat can be collected in large *solar furnaces,* producing a high temperature and a great amount of heat. These furnaces have mirrors that reflect the sun's heat from a wide area onto one spot. Such solar furnaces can collect enough solar heat to melt steel. Smaller solar furnaces can gather enough heat to cook food. See **Solar energy; Sun.**

Fire is one of the most useful and easily controlled sources of heat. When wood, natural gas, oil, or any other fuel burns, substances in the fuel combine with oxygen gas in the air. As these substances and oxygen combine, they form other compounds. This chemical reaction produces heat.

People use fire in many ways. Fire in a gas stove produces heat to cook food. Coal, oil, or gas fires in furnaces and boilers heat homes and other buildings. Fire also has many industrial uses. It heats metals red-hot so that they can be shaped into a variety of forms. Fire heats mixtures of sand and other materials until they melt and form glass. Special cutting torches can produce a flame that is hot enough to cut through metal. See **Fire.**

The earth itself contains much heat deep inside. When a volcano erupts, some of the earth's heat escapes to the surface. The lava flowing from a volcano is rock melted by the heat within the earth. Some of the earth's heat also escapes in *geysers.* These springs shoot forth boiling water, which has been heated by hot rocks deep within the earth. People have begun to make limited use of the earth's heat to generate electricity and do other work. See **Earth** (Inside the earth); **Geyser; Volcano.**

Chemical reactions can produce heat in a number of ways. A chemical reaction in which a substance combines with oxygen is called *oxidation.* Rapid oxidation produces heat fast enough to cause a flame. The rusting of iron is another example of oxidation. But unlike fire, rusting occurs so slowly that little heat and no flames are produced. See **Oxidation.**

When certain chemicals are mixed together, heat is produced. A good example is sulfuric acid and water. When these two substances are combined, the mixture becomes boiling hot.

In all living things, food is changed into heat—as well as energy and living tissue—by a process called *metabolism.* Metabolism consists of a complicated series of chemical reactions carried out by living cells. See **Metabolism.**

Friction. When one object rubs against another, heat is produced. Friction is usually an unwanted source of heat because it may damage an object. In a machine, for example, the heat created as the moving parts rub against one another may cause those parts to wear down. For this reason, oil is used between moving machinery parts. The oil reduces the friction and so decreases the heat. See **Friction.**

Nuclear energy can produce great quantities of heat. Atomic and hydrogen bombs release heat so quickly—in a fraction of a second—that they destroy everything around them. Their heat cannot be put to useful work. But in a device called a *reactor,* heat can be produced from nuclear energy slowly enough to generate electricity and to do other jobs. See **Nuclear energy; Nuclear reactor.**

Sources of heat

WORLD BOOK illustrations

The sun produces heat from nuclear reactions deep inside it. All life on the earth depends on this heat.

Friction—the rubbing of one object against another—produces heat. Scouts learn to start a fire with friction.

Chemical reactions produce heat by causing a chemical change in substances. Fire is a chemical reaction.

The earth contains much heat deep inside. Some of this heat escapes to the surface when a volcano erupts.

Heat is a form of energy. Heat and energy cannot be seen, but the work they do can. For example, the burning of fuel in the engines of a jet airplane creates hot gases. These gases expand and provide the power that moves the plane. See **Energy.**

Temperature and heat. All things are made up of atoms or molecules, which are always moving. The motion of the atoms or molecules gives every object *internal energy.* The *level* of the internal energy in an object depends on how rapidly its atoms or molecules move. If they move slowly, the object has a low level of internal energy. If they move violently, it has a high level. Hot objects have higher internal energy levels than cold objects have. The words *hot* and *cold* refer to the temperature of an object.

Temperature is an indication of an object's internal energy level. A thermometer is used to measure temperature. Thermometers have a numbered scale so that temperature can be expressed in degrees. The two most common scales are the *Fahrenheit* and the *Celsius,* or *centigrade,* scales. See **Temperature.**

The temperature of an object determines whether that object will take on more internal energy or lose some when it comes into contact with another object. If a hot rock and a cold rock touch each other, some of the internal energy in the hot rock will pass into the cold rock as heat. If a thermometer were placed on the hot rock, it would show that the rock's temperature falls steadily. A thermometer on the cold rock would show a steadily rising temperature.

Just as water flows only downhill, so heat flows only down a "temperature hill," passing from an object at a higher temperature to an object at a lower one. The greater the difference in temperature between two objects, the steeper the temperature hill will be and the faster the heat will flow between the objects. The thermometers on the two rocks would soon show the same

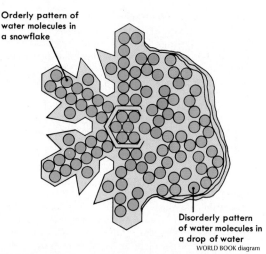

Orderly pattern of water molecules in a snowflake

Disorderly pattern of water molecules in a drop of water
WORLD BOOK diagram

Heat decreases the orderly arrangement of the atoms or molecules in an object. For example, the molecules of water in a snowflake are frozen in an orderly pattern. But as heat flows into the flake, its molecules move more rapidly. They become so disorderly that the snowflake begins to melt.

temperature. Then, no further flow of heat would occur between the rocks.

It is important to recognize that temperature and heat are not the same thing. Temperature is simply an indication of the level of internal energy that an object has. Heat, on the other hand, is the passage of energy from one object to another.

Heat is measured in two kinds of units—*British thermal units* (B.T.U.'s) and *calories.* One B.T.U. is the quantity of heat needed to raise the temperature of one pound of water one degree Fahrenheit. One calorie is the quantity of heat needed to raise the temperature of one gram of water one degree Celsius. The calorie used to measure energy in food is 1,000 times as large as this calorie. See **Calorie.**

Disorder. Temperature and internal energy tell only part of the story about heat. To tell the whole story, we need to see what happens to the atoms or molecules of an object when heat flows into it.

As heat raises the internal energy of an object, that object's atoms or molecules move around more. The more heat that flows into an object, the more its atoms or molecules move around and the more disorderly they become. For example, the water molecules in a snowflake have an orderly pattern. But if a snowflake is taken into a warm room, the flake will melt and become a drop of water. Heat has changed the orderly pattern of the snowflake into disorder. Scientists use the term *entropy* to describe the amount of disorder in an object. See **Entropy.**

Heat flowing into an object will always increase the internal energy and disorder in that object. Usually, the added heat also raises the temperature of the object. On the other hand, heat flowing out of an object will always decrease the internal energy and disorder in that object. Usually, the heat loss also lowers the temperature of the object.

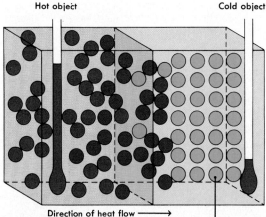

Hot object   Cold object

Direction of heat flow ⟶

Atoms or molecules
WORLD BOOK diagram

Heat energy flows from a hot to a cold object when they are in contact. The rapidly moving atoms or molecules in the hot object strike the less energetic atoms or molecules in the cold object and speed them up. In this way, internal energy in the form of heat passes from a hot object to a cold object.

Heat passes from one object or place to another by three methods: (1) conduction, (2) convection, and (3) radiation.

Conduction is the movement of heat through a material. When heat travels by conduction, it moves through a material without carrying any of the material with it. For example, the end of a copper rod placed in a fire quickly becomes hot. The atoms in the hot end begin to vibrate faster and strike neighboring atoms. These atoms then vibrate faster and strike adjoining atoms. In this way, the heat travels from atom to atom until it reaches the other end of the rod. But during the process, the atoms themselves do not move from one end to the other.

Convection is the transfer of heat by the movement of a heated material. For example, a hot stove in a room heats the air around it by conduction. This heated air expands and so is lighter than the colder air surrounding it. The heated air rises, and cooler air replaces it. Then the cooler air near the stove becomes warm and rises. This movement of heated air away from a hot object and the flow of cooler air toward that object is called a *convection current*. The current of air carries heat to all parts of the room.

Convection occurs in liquids as well as in gases. For example, convection currents will form in a pan of cold water on a hot stove. As the water near the bottom of the pan warms up and expands, it becomes lighter than the cold water near the top of the pan. This cold water sinks and forces the heated water to the top. The convection current continues until all the water reaches the same temperature.

Radiation. In conduction and convection, moving particles transmit heat. But heat can also travel through empty space, which has no particles. In any object, the moving atoms or molecules create waves of radiant energy. These waves are also called *infrared rays.* Hot objects give off more infrared rays than do cold objects. Infrared rays travel through space in much the same way as water waves travel on the surface of a pond. When the radiant energy strikes an object, it speeds up the atoms or molecules in that object. Much energy from the sun travels through space to the earth. These rays warm the earth's surface. See **Infrared rays.**

Insulation is a way to control the movement of heat by keeping it in or out of a place. For example, houses are insulated to keep the heat inside in winter and outside in summer. People use three methods of insulation because heat can travel in any one of three ways.

Certain materials, such as plastic and wood, make good insulators against the movement of heat by conduction. This is why many pots and pans have plastic or wood handles. The metal utensil itself heats rapidly by conduction, but the handle stays cool.

The movement of heat through the air by convection can be controlled by blocking the space between a hot and cold area with "dead air." For example, the layer of air between a storm window and the inner window acts as an insulator.

Surfaces that reflect infrared rays can insulate heat traveling by radiation. For example, shiny metal roofs reflect the sun's rays. See **Insulation.**

How heat travels

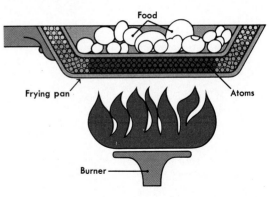

Conduction carries heat through an object. For example, heat from a burner makes the atoms on the underside of a frying pan vibrate faster. These atoms then strike atoms above them. In this way, heat passes through the pan to the food inside it.

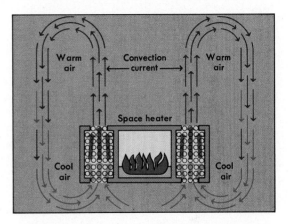

Convection carries heat by circulating a heated material. A space heater, for example, warms the air around it. This heated air rises and is replaced by cooler air. The movement of air creates a *convection current* that carries hot air through a room.

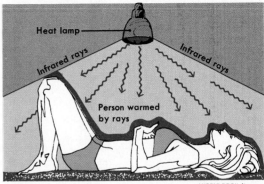

WORLD BOOK diagrams

Radiation carries heat in the form of waves through space. Heat causes a wire in a heat lamp to give off waves of radiant energy called *infrared rays.* When these rays strike someone, their energy warms that person.

When heat passes into or out of a substance, it may change that substance in three ways. Heat may cause (1) changes in temperature, (2) changes in size, and (3) changes in state.

Changes in temperature are one of the most common results when heat flows into or out of an object. The amount of heat needed to raise the temperature of one gram of a substance one degree Celsius is called the *specific heat capacity* of the substance. Specific heat capacity is often called simply *specific heat.* Scientists use the specific heat of water, which is given a value of 1, as the standard for figuring the specific heat of all other substances.

You can find out how much the temperature of a substance will rise when heat flows into it if you know how much *mass* (amount of matter) the substance has and what the specific heat of the substance is. First, multiply the mass by the specific heat of the substance. Then, divide the result into the amount of heat added. For example, if 10 calories of heat flow into one gram of water, how much will the temperature of the water rise? One gram times a specific heat of 1 equals 1. One divided into 10 calories equals a rise of 10 degrees Celsius.

Two substances with the same mass but different specific heats require different amounts of heat to reach the same temperature. The temperature of a substance with a low specific heat will increase more than that of a substance with a high specific heat if both substances receive the same amount of heat. For example, it takes 10 calories of heat to raise one gram of water 10 degrees Celsius. But 10 calories will raise the temperature of one gram of copper 111 degrees. Copper has a low specific heat of 0.09, compared with water's high specific heat of 1.

Changes in size. As we have seen, when heat flows into a substance, the motion of the atoms or molecules in the substance increases. As a result of their increased

motion, the atoms or molecules take up more space and the substance expands. The opposite occurs when heat flows out of a substance. The atoms or molecules move more slowly. They therefore take up less space, and the substance contracts.

All gases and most liquids and solids expand when heated. But they do not expand equally. If a gas, a liquid, and a solid receive enough heat to raise their temperatures the same amount, the gas will expand most, the liquid much less, and the solid the least.

Thermometers, thermostats, and many other devices work on the principle of expansion and contraction. Many thermometers contain a liquid, such as alcohol or mercury, that expands and contracts evenly as the temperature changes. A rise or fall in temperature causes the volume of the liquid to expand or contract only slightly. But by making the liquid occupy a narrow glass tube, the liquid column moves enough so the temperature change can be seen.

The expansion and contraction of the materials that are used in bridges, buildings, and other structures can cause serious problems unless the builders allow for it. For example, the steel beams used in a building will bend or break if they do not have room to expand. For this reason, structures have *expansion joints,* which allow extra space for the materials in a structure to expand and contract without damage when the temperature changes.

Engineers can determine how much the length of any material will be increased by a rise in temperature if they know the *coefficient of linear expansion* of the material. The coefficient of linear expansion indicates how much longer each meter of the material will become if its temperature increases by one degree. For aluminum, it is 0.000023. In an aluminum bar, each meter becomes 0.000023 of a meter longer with each degree Celsius increase in its temperature.

The specific heats of different metals can be compared by heating samples of equal weight to the same temperature and then setting them on a block of wax, *top.* The samples with high specific heats sink deepest in the wax, *bottom.*

WORLD BOOK photo

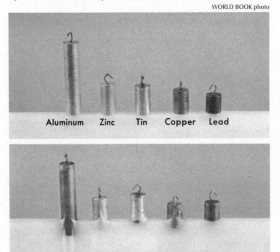

Aluminum   Zinc   Tin   Copper   Lead

An expansion joint allows the materials in bridges, buildings, and other structures to contract and expand without damaging the structure. The joint opens in winter, when the materials contract, and closes in summer, when they expand.

WORLD BOOK diagram

Winter   **Summer**

Expansion area

└── Two halves of joint ──┘   └── Two halves of joint ──┘

In winter, the fingers of the joint pull apart as the materials contract.

In summer, the fingers of the joint move closer together as the materials expand.

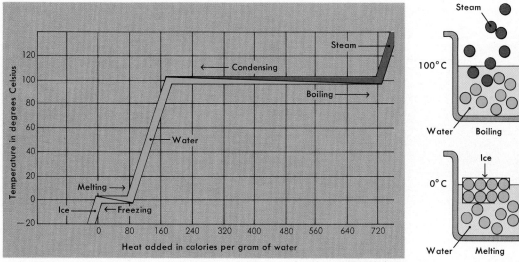

WORLD BOOK diagram

Heat causes solids to melt and liquids to boil. The heat added to a solid, such as ice, raises its temperature to its melting point. Then the temperature stops rising until enough additional heat flows in and melts all the ice. More heat raises the temperature of the water to the boiling point. The temperature again stops rising until enough heat is added to turn all the water to steam.

Changes in state. Ordinarily, the temperature of an object rises when heat flows into it. But under certain circumstances, the addition of heat causes no increase in an object's temperature. Instead, the disorder of the atoms or molecules in the object increases and causes the material to change state.

If heat is added to a block of ice that is colder than 0° C, the temperature of the ice will increase until it reaches 0° C, its melting point. Then the temperature will stop increasing for a time, even though more heat flows into the ice. The additional heat will increase the disorder of the molecules in the ice and cause the ice to melt. But until all the ice has melted, the water will remain at 0° C. The heat needed to change ice to water is called the *heat of fusion*. Each gram of ice at 0° C requires 80 calories of heat to melt it to water at 0° C.

As more heat flows into the water at 0° C, the temperature of the water will again rise until it reaches 100° C, its boiling point. Under normal atmospheric pressure, additional heat will not raise the temperature any further. Instead, some of the water will change into steam. Not until all the water has become steam will additional heat cause the temperature to increase again. The heat

required to change water at 100° C into steam at the same temperature is called the *heat of vaporization*. Each gram of water at 100° C requires 540 calories of heat to become steam. More heat added to the steam will raise its temperature above 100° C.

The heat needed to change a material from a solid to a liquid or from a liquid to a gas is called *latent heat*. It must be removed to change a gas back to a liquid or a liquid back to a solid. That is, 540 calories of heat must be removed from each gram of steam at 100° C to produce water, and 80 calories must be removed from each gram of water at 0° C to produce ice. The boiling and condensation points of a substance are at the same temperature, as are the melting and freezing points. The amount of heat that has entered or left a substance determines the substance's state.

A liquid can also become a gas at a temperature below its boiling point through evaporation. Evaporation occurs at the surface of a liquid. The molecules at the surface break free from those below and enter the air as a gas. The speed at which evaporation occurs depends on the kind of liquid, the temperature of the liquid, and the amount of liquid vapor above the liquid.

Putting heat to work

Changing heat into motion. Mechanical energy and heat energy are related. For example, mechanical energy is changed into heat by friction between the moving parts of a machine. Heat energy, in turn, can be changed into mechanical energy by *heat engines*.

Heat engines can be divided into two groups: (1) *external-combustion engines* and (2) *internal-combustion engines*. External-combustion engines use heat produced outside the engine. Such engines include gas and

steam turbines and reciprocating steam engines. Internal-combustion engines produce heat inside the engine from burning fuels. Such engines include diesel and gasoline engines, jet aircraft engines, and rocket engines.

A steam turbine is a good example of an external combustion engine. Heat from burning fuel or from a nuclear reactor changes water in a boiler to steam. Pipes carry the steam into the turbine, which has a series of

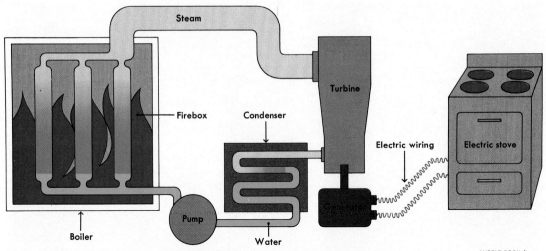

Heat energy can be changed into other forms of energy. This diagram shows how heat is changed into electricity. Heat in a boiler creates steam that turns a turbine. The turbine drives an electric generator. A condenser changes the steam back to water, and the cycle is repeated.

WORLD BOOK diagram

bladed wheels attached to a shaft. The high-temperature steam expands as it rushes through the turbine and so pushes on the blades and causes them to turn the shaft. Steam leaving the turbine has a much lower temperature. The spinning shaft can drive an electric generator, move a ship's propeller, or do other useful work. See **Turbine** (Steam turbines).

An automobile gasoline engine is a good example of an internal-combustion engine. The burning of gasoline in the cylinders of the engine produces hot gases. The gases expand and push down the pistons in the cylinders. The motion of the pistons moves other parts of the car that turn the car's wheels. See **Gasoline engine.**

Refrigeration. The temperature of an object can be lowered by bringing it in contact with another object that is colder. The temperature difference causes heat to flow from the warmer object into the colder one. For example, ice that is placed in an insulated chest will keep a picnic lunch cold by removing heat from it. However, in order to remove heat from an object without using a

colder object, *mechanical refrigeration* must be used.

Mechanical refrigeration works by changing a substance called a *refrigerant* from a gas to a liquid and back to a gas again. In a refrigerator, for example, a compressor squeezes a gaseous refrigerant into a small space. The compression reduces the refrigerant's disorder so much that it becomes a liquid. The compressed liquid refrigerant then expands at a valve leading to pipes in the insulated part of the refrigerator. As the pressure falls, so does the temperature, and the refrigerant absorbs heat from the foods in the refrigerator. As heat flows out of the foods, their temperature falls. The warmed refrigerant becomes a gas and then flows through pipes back to the compressor. There, the refrigeration cycle begins again. See **Refrigeration** (Mechanical refrigeration).

The lowest temperature a substance can have is *absolute zero,* which is $-459.67°$ F., or $-273.15°$ C. At this temperature, matter has the least possible internal energy, and it has almost no disorder. See **Absolute zero.**

Learning about heat

The caloric theory of heat. Until the late 1700's, many scientists believed that heat was an invisible fluid called *caloric.* They thought an object became warm when caloric flowed into it and grew cold when caloric flowed out of it. Because objects weighed the same whether hot or cold, the scientists reasoned that caloric had no weight and therefore could not be matter.

Near the end of the 1700's, the work of two men raised questions about heat that the caloric theory could not answer. In 1798, the American-born scientist Benjamin Thompson, also known as Count Rumford, observed the manufacture of cannons in Munich, Germany. He noted that the drills used to bore the cannons produced frictional heat even after the drills became

dull and no longer cut out metal. The caloric theory could not account for the release of heat unless a drill actually cut metal. Yet an unlimited quantity of heat resulted as long as a drill turned against metal.

In 1799, the British chemist Sir Humphry Davy melted two pieces of ice by rubbing them together in a container at a temperature below the freezing point of water. Again, the caloric theory could not account for the heat produced. Thompson's and Davy's observations raised doubts about the caloric theory. But no one proposed another explanation of heat.

Heat and energy. The idea that heat is a form of energy was proved during the mid-1800's. The proof was developed largely by three men—Julius Robert von

Mayer, a German physician and physicist; Hermann von Helmholtz, a German physicist; and James Prescott Joule, a British physicist.

Mayer observed that people in warm and cold climates needed different amounts of food energy to maintain their normal body temperature. He published his findings in 1842, but they did not receive scientific recognition for many years. In 1847, Helmholtz published a work on heat and energy. He stated that heat is a form of energy, and the idea won rapid acceptance.

During the 1840's, Joule measured the amount of mechanical energy needed to raise the temperature of a certain quantity of water. The relationship between mechanical energy and heat energy is called the *mechanical equivalent of heat.* Joule's early experiments showed that 838 foot-pounds of mechanical energy produced 1 B.T.U. of heat. Later scientists made more precise measurements. They found that the mechanical equivalent of heat was 778 foot-pounds per B.T.U., or, in the metric system, 4.186 newton-meters per calorie.

Thermodynamics is the study of the relationship between heat and energy. It is based on certain *laws* (principles).

The first law of thermodynamics is the law of conservation of energy. It states that energy is never created or destroyed. Energy may change form—for example, from internal energy to mechanical motion—but the total quantity of energy in any *system* (group of things) remains the same.

The second law states that all *spontaneous* (natural) events act to increase the entropy within a system. Until a system reaches its maximum entropy, it can do useful work. But as a system does work, its entropy increases until the system can no longer perform work.

The third law of thermodynamics describes matter at absolute zero. For example, when solid argon is at absolute zero, it has no disorder.   Charles F. Squire

Study aids

Related articles in *World Book* include:

Biographies

Clausius, Rudolf J. E.   Joule, James P.
Davy, Sir Humphrey   Kelvin, Lord
Gibbs, Josiah W.   Mayer, Julius R. von
Helmholtz, Hermann L. F. von   Thompson, Benjamin

Other related articles

Absolute zero   Evaporation   Nuclear energy
Boiling point   Expansion   Perpetual motion
British thermal unit   Fire   machine
Calorie   Friction   Petroleum
Celsius scale   Fuel   Solar energy
Coal   Gas (fuel)   Steam
Combustion   Heating   Sun
Cryogenics   Infrared rays   Temperature
Electricity   Insulation   Thermocouple
Energy   Metabolism   Thermodynamics
Entropy   Molecule   Thermometer

Outline

I. Sources of heat
  A. The sun   B. Fire   C. The earth

  D. Chemical   E. Friction   F. Nuclear energy
    reactions
II. What heat is
  A. Temperature and heat   B. Disorder
III. How heat travels
  A. Conduction
  B. Convection
  C. Radiation
  D. Insulation
IV. What heat does
  A. Changes in temperature
  B. Changes in size
  C. Changes in state
V. Putting heat to work
  A. Changing heat into motion
  B. Refrigeration
VI. Learning about heat
  A. The caloric theory of heat
  B. Heat and energy
  C. Thermodynamics

Questions

What was the *caloric* theory of heat?
Why do bridges, buildings, and other structures have *expansion joints*?
How does heat create disorder in an object?
In what three ways does heat travel?
What is our most important source of heat?
What is specific heat?
What is the basic difference between temperature and heat?
How does insulation stop heat from traveling by convection?
What do *heat engines* do?
In what three ways may the addition or removal of heat change a substance?

Additional resources

Adler, Irving. *Hot and Cold.* Rev. ed. Harper, 1975. For younger readers.
Adler, Irving and Ruth. *Heat and Its Uses.* Rev. ed. John Day, 1973. For younger readers.
Haines, Gail Kay. *Super Cold, Super Hot: Cryogenics and Controlled Thermonuclear Fusion.* Watts, 1976.
Mott-Smith, Morton C. *Concept of Heat and Its Workings.* Dover, 1933. Originally titled: *Heat and Its Workings.*
Stone, A. Harris, and Siegel, B. M. *The Heat's On!* Prentice-Hall, 1970. For younger readers.
Zemansky, M.W., and Dittman, R. H. *Heat and Thermodynamics.* 6th ed. McGraw, 1981.

Heat exhaustion. See Sunstroke; First aid (Heatstroke and heat exhaustion).

Heat pipe is a device that transfers large amounts of heat from one place to another at a fairly constant temperature. Heat pipes can transport much more heat per unit area than the best metal conductors, including copper and silver. Also, unlike most heat transfer devices, they require no external power source. This feature makes them more energy-efficient and more economical.

Heat pipes are used to remove waste heat from certain types of electronic equipment and industrial machinery. In many cases, they carry this heat to another place where it can be used. Some air-conditioning and heating systems employ heat pipes to regulate temperature. Heat pipes also have been used for such purposes as controlling the temperature in spacecraft and transporting heat from solar energy collectors.

A heat pipe consists of a metal tube that is sealed at both ends and lined with a porous material. The lining, called the *wick,* holds a liquid, such as water, methanol, or molten lithium. This liquid is known as the *working fluid.* It absorbs heat from a heat source at one end of the tube and vaporizes. The vapor flows out of the wick and builds up pressure at the hot end of the tube. This pressure, in turn, causes some of the vapor to travel to the cooler end of the tube. There the vapor condenses as it cools, transferring its heat through the wall of the tube. The liquid returns to the warmer end of the tube through the wick as a result of *capillarity* (see **Capillarity**).

The temperature of the heat delivered by a heat pipe is roughly equal to the working fluid's *boiling point,* the temperature at which the liquid vaporizes. The boiling point of a liquid remains constant as long as the atmospheric pressure does not change. For this reason, heat pipes provide precise temperature control.

Thomas T. Liao

Heat pump is a device that takes heat from one area and delivers it to another area at a higher temperature. In heating a building, a heat pump absorbs heat from outside the building and delivers it inside. In the summer, the same heat pump can be reversed so that it cools the building and discharges heat outside. A household refrigerator is a type of heat pump. A refrigerator absorbs heat from the food inside it and discharges the heat to the surrounding room air.

The fluid that circulates through a heat pump is called a *refrigerant.* Common refrigerants are Freon and ammonia. For heating, a cold refrigerant first flows through coils of pipe that are exposed to an outside heat source. The heat source may be outside air, well water, or even the ground. The refrigerant absorbs heat from these sources, then goes to a compressor which increases its temperature and pressure. The refrigerant then flows to a heat exchanger, which resembles an automobile radiator, and gives up its heat to room air which is circulating through the exchanger. The refrigerant then passes through a valve that lowers its pressure. This results in a drop in temperature. The cycle is repeated as the refrigerant circulates again through the coils of pipe and picks up heat from the low temperature source.

For cooling purposes, valves reverse the direction of the refrigerant flow. The refrigerant vapor flows at high temperature and pressure through the outside coils. At this point, water, earth, or outside air absorbs heat from the hotter refrigerant. This takes place even if the outside source is warm, because it is cooler than the refrigerant. The refrigerant then passes through a valve that lowers its pressure, thus decreasing the temperature. In the heat exchanger, the refrigerant absorbs heat from the room air. The refrigerant then returns to a compressor and the cycle is repeated. Heat pumps are controlled by thermostats that sense the temperature of the room and regulate the pump.   James B. Jones

See also **Air conditioning; Heating** (diagram: Heat pump); **Refrigeration.**

Heat rash. See Prickly heat.

Heat shield is a covering on a spacecraft or a rocket nose cone. It protects astronauts and instruments from the intense heat produced during high-speed flights through the atmosphere. Such heating occurs when a spacecraft descends from an earth orbit. Atoms and molecules of air generate heat by friction against the surface of the craft. The greater the craft's velocity, the more intense the heat. Common types of heat shields are heat sinks and ablation shields. *Heat sinks* absorb great amounts of heat, thus preventing heat from reaching delicate parts of the spacecraft. *Ablation shields* use up heat by melting and vaporizing. The air stream carries the molten particles and hot gas vapor away from the craft. Commonly used heat shield materials include graphite, graphite composites, and porous ceramics.

Ared Cezairliyan

Heath, *heeth,* also called *heather,* is a low evergreen shrub that grows on moors in Great Britain, other parts of Europe, and Africa. *Heath* also means an open area where few plants except these shrubs grow.

Most of the nearly 400 kinds of heather are native to Africa. *Scotch heather* is common on moors in Europe. It is also called *ling.* This plant has a low, grayish, hairy stalk, broomlike branches, and leaves like needles. Its tiny purple-rose blossoms are shaped like bells, and grow in long clusters called spikes.

Heather bells are often mentioned in Scotch songs and stories. They are the flowers of either the *cross-leaved* or *twisted* heath of the British Isles. Many African heathers have remarkably colorful blossoms.

In European countries, heather is used to make brooms and brushes. The trailing shoots are woven into baskets. Briarwood, used for pipes, comes from the roots of a heather common in France. Some people in Scotland build the thatched roofs of their houses from heather. In some places, a liquid made from heather is used in tanning leather. Domestic animals are fed on young heather shoots. Heather is also valuable because it makes up a large part of the material that fills peat bogs. Peat makes an important low-grade fuel in some European countries. In addition, many birds eat heather seeds.

John Markham, Bruce Coleman Ltd.

Cross-leaved heath has clusters of pinkish flowers.

True heather is not common in the United States, but many plants of the United States belong to the heath family. Among them are the blueberry, cranberry, huckleberry, manzanita, rhododendron, azalea, and trailing arbutus.

Scientific classification. Heath belongs to the heath family, Ericaceae. The cross-leaved heath is *Erica tetralix,* and the twisted heath is *E. cinerea.* Heather is classified as *Calluna vulgaris.*

J. J. Levison

Related articles in *World Book* include:

Arbutus	Huckleberry	Manzanita
Azalea	Indian pipe	Mountain laurel
Blueberry	Labrador tea	Rhododendron
Brier	Lingonberry	Sorrel tree
Cranberry	Madroña	Wintergreen

Heath, *heeth,* **Edward Richard George** (1916-   ), a member of the Conservative Party, served as prime minister of Great Britain from 1970 to 1974. Under Heath's leadership, Britain joined the European Community, an economic union also known as the European Common Market. Various economic problems in Britain led Heath to call for elections in 1974. After the Conservatives failed to win a parliamentary majority, Heath resigned.

Heath was first elected to the House of Commons in 1950 and rapidly advanced to political leadership. By 1955, he had become chief party whip, responsible for party conduct in the House of Commons. Heath became minister of labour in 1959.

From 1961 to 1963, he served as chief negotiator of Britain's first unsuccessful attempt to join the Common Market. He was president of the Board of Trade in 1963 and 1964.

Heath became head of the Conservative Party in 1965. He was the first Conservative leader ever elected by party members in the House of Commons. Previous leaders had been chosen by small groups of

Wide World

Edward Heath

influential party members. Heath served as party leader until 1975, when he ran for reelection but lost. But he has remained a member of the House of Commons.

Unlike most Conservative Party leaders, Heath inherited neither social position nor wealth. He was born in Broadstairs, Kent, England, where his father was a carpenter. Heath attended a state-supported secondary school and won a scholarship to Oxford University. During World War II (1939-1945), Heath rose from private to lieutenant colonel in the British Army.   Richard Rose

Heath hen. See Prairie chicken.

Heather. See Heath (with picture).

Heating. The development of efficient indoor heating systems has made it possible for people to live and work in places far from the warm parts of the world. Without such heating systems, people must spend too much of their time and energy combating winter cold in the temperate and frigid zones of the earth.

The first heating systems were open fires in crude caves. When human beings discovered a way to dig a hole in the side or top of a cave to let out the smoke, the first fireplace was developed. Later on, these fireplaces were provided with separate chimneys. After such fireplaces came stoves made of brick and tile, and then of cast iron. Finally, central heating systems were developed. These systems are used in many homes, office and industrial buildings, and schools today. Special

heating systems for automobiles, trains, ships, and airplanes enable people to travel comfortably in cold weather.

Principles of heating

Comfort. Human beings are warm-blooded animals. Their body has the relatively high average temperature of 98.6° F. (37° C). Food provides fuel for this body heat. When the temperature surrounding the body is extremely cold, the body loses too much heat. Clothing reduces the loss of heat. But for comfort in regions that are cold during the winter, indoor heating must be provided.

Most people feel comfortable in a room with a temperature of from 70° F. (21° C) to 78° F. (26° C). The humidity in a room also affects comfort. If two rooms have the same temperature but different humidity, most people will feel warmer in the room with the higher humidity. An indoor *relative humidity* of from 30 per cent to 60 per cent is the most comfortable for most people (see **Humidity**). The temperature in a home can be lower without sacrificing comfort for some people if moisture is added to the air with a device called a *humidifier.* However, adding the moisture may require more energy than simply raising the temperature.

Heat transfer. Heat is transferred in three important ways: *conduction, convection,* and *radiation.* Conduction is the heating of matter by bringing it in contact with a hot object. The heat passes directly from the hot object to the adjacent matter. This is much like the heat passing along an iron rod, one end of which is held in the hand while the other end is in a fire.

In natural convection, the hot object heats the surrounding air. This heated air rises because of its lighter weight. The hot air, in turn, is replaced by cool air which, in turn, is heated and rises. In this way, a continuous current of warm air rises from near a hot object, just as hot air rises over a bonfire or a hot stove.

A hot object radiates heat in the form of waves much like radio and light waves. These waves can go through a vacuum or through dry air without heating it. The earth receives radiant heat from the sun.

Central heating systems

Central heating systems generate heat for an entire building at one central place. The heat is then delivered where it is needed. Most systems serve only one building. But some heat a group of buildings, such as those at a college, a military base, or an apartment complex.

Central heating systems have automatic controls, with a thermostat to regulate the temperature of the rooms heated by the system. The thermostat turns on the system when the temperature drops below the setting of the thermostat. Most thermostats include a device called an *anticipator* to help the thermostat keep the room at an even temperature.

Another automatic control turns off the central heating system if any part of it becomes dangerously overheated. Still another control prevents the system from starting unless it can start safely.

There are two main kinds of central heating systems: (1) direct and (2) indirect. They differ in the way they distribute heat. A direct system circulates the warm air throughout the area being heated. An indirect system

Basic heating systems

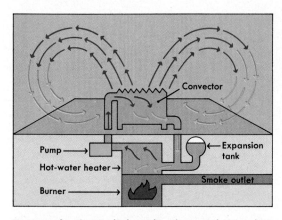

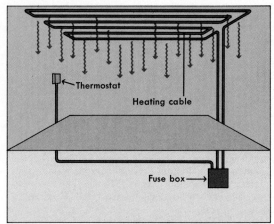

Hot-water heating. Fuel is burned in a hot-water heater to heat water. A pump forces the hot water through pipes to a convector in each room being heated. The water gives up its heat to the room and returns to the boiler through another pipe.

Radiant electric heating uses a cable that produces heat from electricity. The cable radiates heat to the room and may be installed in the ceiling or floor or along the baseboard. A thermostat controls the amount of heat produced by the cable.

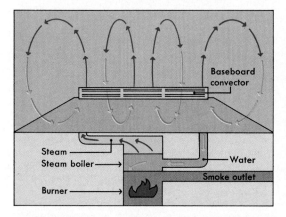

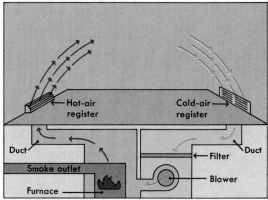

Steam heating works much like hot-water heating, except that water changes to steam in a boiler. The steam passes through pipes to convectors, where it gives up its heat to the room and becomes liquid again. The water then flows back to the boiler.

Warm-air heating. A furnace heats the air, and a blower forces it through a duct to a register that opens into the room being heated. Cool air returns to the furnace through another duct. A filter removes dust from the air as it circulates.

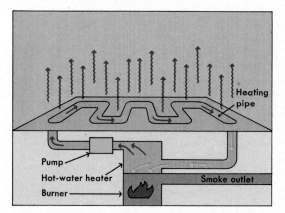

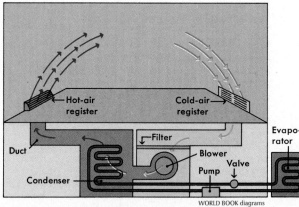

WORLD BOOK diagrams

Radiant hot-water heating. Water is heated in a boiler and pumped through a continuous coil of pipe in the floor of the room being heated. Heat radiates from these pipes and keeps the room temperature nearly the same from floor to ceiling.

Heat pump. A heating system that uses a heat pump operates much like a warm-air system. But the heat pump uses a condenser, evaporator, pump, and other equipment to get heat from outside air or the ground and "pump" it into the building.

circulates steam or hot water through pipes to *convectors* or *radiators,* which give off heat. Both direct and indirect heating systems use electricity or some kind of fuel, such as gas or oil, as their source of heat.

Warm-air heating. A warm-air heating system warms the air in a furnace and then forces it through a system of *ducts* (pipes) to each room. Another system of ducts carries cool air from the rooms back to the furnace. An electrically driven blower in the furnace moves the air through the ducts, and filters remove dust particles from the air.

Many private homes have warm-air systems. These systems can do more than just heat the air. With a humidifier, for example, a forced warm-air system adds moisture to the air and increases the humidity throughout the home. The ducts and blower can be used as part of a central air-conditioning unit.

Steam and hot-water heating systems. Steam or hot-water heating systems are used in many large buildings. These systems cost more than warm-air systems, but they have certain advantages over them. The pipes carrying steam or hot water are smaller than warm-air ducts and thus take up less space. Automatic valves can control the amount of hot water or steam flowing to convectors more easily than they can control warm air. Thus, it is easier to control the temperature in different rooms with these systems than with warm-air heating.

A steam heating system requires a boiler, and a hot-water heating system has a hot-water heater. Fuel burning in the boiler or heater produces heat for the system. The system also has a network of pipes and convectors. In steam heating, a condensate pump forces the condensed steam back to the boiler. In hot-water heating, a pump circulates the water through the system.

The convectors of a steam or hot-water system give off most of their heat by convection and radiation. The amount of heat given off by radiation depends on the temperature of the convector and its surface area. With lower temperatures typical of hot-water heating, a greater part of the heat is delivered by convection and less by radiation. The amount of heat given off by a convector depends upon its shape and the amount of exposed metal surface. The more metal that is exposed, the more heat is given off.

One difficulty in heating with high temperature convectors is that the air near the ceiling becomes warmer than the air in other parts of the room. For example, the air at knee height may be 60° F. (16° C), the air at the breathing level may be 68° F. (20° C), and the air at the ceiling may be 76° F. (24° C). The air at the floor level may be only 53° F. (12° C). Such a low floor temperature is too cold for comfort. If an attempt is made to raise the temperature of the floor, the average room temperature increases and the upper parts of the room become uncomfortably warm.

Radiant heating is a method of equalizing temperature within a room. A continuous loop of hot-water pipe or electric cable is installed in the ceiling or floor. Heat leaves the pipe or cable by radiation, which does not directly raise the temperature of the air within a room. Radiation affects only the objects it strikes, and so it produces more uniform heating than convection does. Radiant heat provides comfort at a lower room temperature than other heating systems.

Radiant heating may also be installed along the baseboards of a room. One system uses a metal shield about 6 inches (15 centimeters) high to cover a hot-water pipe that runs close to the floor. Such a system distributes heat evenly. All radiant heating systems limit the temperature difference between the floor and the ceiling to only a few degrees.

Electric heating differs from other central systems because it requires no combustion of fuel in the building being heated. The fuel used to make electricity is burned at an electric power plant that may be far away. Nuclear plants produce electricity from nuclear energy.

Electric heat is produced by electric heating units. Such units produce heat by passing electricity through a material that resists the flow of current. This type of heating, called *resistance heating,* produces much radiant heat. Such heat warms the surface of the skin and clothing and makes people feel comfortable even in a cool room. An electric heating unit can be placed in the ceiling, baseboards, floor, or wall. The temperature can be controlled by thermostats in each room, or area.

Heat pumps. Even in cold weather, the earth or outside air contains heat that can be used to heat a building. A mechanical system called a heat pump takes heat from the outside air and brings it inside. In winter, a heat pump circulates a liquid refrigerant through a coil outside the building. As the cold liquid passes through the coil, it picks up heat from the outside air or earth and becomes a vapor. The vapor then passes into a compressor. The compressor increases the temperature and pressure of the vapor. Then the hot vapor passes through an inside coil, where it heats the air. In the process, the vapor condenses into a hot liquid. The hot liquid then goes through a pressure-reducing valve and becomes cold again. Finally, the refrigerant is forced back to the outside coil and the cycle begins again.

In cold regions, a heat pump may not be able to supply all the necessary heat economically. In such places, electric resistance heating units provide additional heat on the coldest days. During the summer, a heat pump reverses its operation. It cools the building by pumping heat from the inside to the outside.

Sources of heat

Most homeowners heat with electricity, gas, or oil. At one time, many private homes were heated with coal. But gas, oil, and other fuels have largely replaced coal in homes because they are more convenient and produce less pollution.

In the 1970's, the United States faced shortages of petroleum fuels and some other energy sources. People termed this situation an "energy crisis." To conserve energy, scientists and engineers stepped up their efforts to develop more efficient heating systems and better insulation. They also attempted to develop efficient ways to harness energy from the sun.

Electricity provides convenient, comfortable heating. Resistance electric heating offers such major advantages as cleanliness, safety, and low maintenance expense. But it usually costs more than other heating methods. To help reduce costs, manufacturers of electric heating units have designed *electric storage heaters.* Such heaters use electricity to generate large amounts of heat during the late-night hours when rates are generally lower. These units store the heat until daytime, when it can be used to maintain comfortable room temperatures without the use of additional electricity.

Electric heat is clean for the homeowner. But the power plants that generate the electricity must burn about three units of energy for every one unit that is delivered to the home. In addition, the increased use of electricity for heating and other uses requires the construction of more power plants.

Many engineers believe it is more efficient for homes to burn fuel for heat than to produce electricity for heating. These experts point out that the best power plants change only about 30 to 40 per cent of the energy they use into electricity. A gas or oil heating system can deliver more than 60 per cent of the energy it consumes as heat. A heat pump driven by gas or oil can collect enough additional heat energy from external sources so that it delivers $1\frac{1}{2}$ times the energy it uses.

Gas produces heat with little air pollution. Nearly all the gas used for heating homes in the United States and Canada is natural gas or *LPG* (liquefied petroleum gas). Natural gas comes from underground rock formations as does oil. Most natural gas reaches homes through pipelines. Gas is simple to burn. A gas furnace pipes the fuel to burners that ignite it.

Since the early 1970's, certain areas of the United States have experienced occasional shortages of natural gas. Such shortages have resulted from an increased demand for gas and decreased domestic reserves of the fuel. Unequal distribution of gas to different parts of the country has contributed greatly to the problem.

Oil. Fuel oil used for home heating comes from the refining of petroleum. Local trucks deliver the oil to homes, where it is stored in tanks until used. A home oil furnace has either a *pot type* or a *gun type* burner. In a pot type burner, the fuel oil flows into a shallow depression in the bottom of the furnace. In a gun type burner, the oil is sprayed through a nozzle under air pressure. The burner uses an air pump to vaporize the fuel. The added air makes the oil burn more efficiently.

Heating oil has been widely used in the United States since the 1940's. However, U.S. petroleum reserves have become too scarce to meet the continued high demand, resulting in a dependence on imported oil. Because of this situation, shortages of heating oil have occurred whenever political disturbances in oil-producing countries reduced the availability of foreign oil. For example, the revolution in Iran in 1979 disrupted the flow of oil from that country and caused a temporary shortage of heating fuel in the United States.

Coal for heating is available in several grades, depending on its heating capability and sulfur content. The two most common types of coal burned in the United States are *anthracite* (hard coal) and *bituminous* (soft coal). Anthracite produces less smoke and sulfur dioxide when burned than does bituminous coal. As a result, anthracite causes less pollution. But most of the coal deposits in the United States are bituminous.

Local heating systems

Central heating is more common in the United States than in most other countries. Local heating is still in common use in many countries. Such heating comes from fireplaces, wood-burning stoves, or room heaters.

Fireplaces. The earliest type of local heating system was the open fire within an enclosure, such as a cave or a tent. Such a fire is not satisfactory because the area soon becomes filled with smoke. Also, an open fire without a chimney lacks enough draft to burn brightly.

If a fireplace is put at one side of a room and provided with a chimney, the smoke and combustion gases will pass up the chimney. The chimney provides a draft by which the air enters the front of the fireplace and passes up the chimney to aid the burning of the fuel. However, this draft reduces the energy efficiency of a fireplace. A typical fireplace allows enough warm air to escape through the chimney to empty an average room every few minutes. This air leak may waste almost as much heat produced by the house's central heating system as is provided by a fireplace.

Wood-burning stoves were widely used in the United States for cooking and heating before the development of gas and electric ranges and central heating systems. In the 1970's, such stoves again became popular due to the energy crisis. They were used most in rural areas of the Western and Northeastern states. In these areas, where wood is plentiful, wood-burning stoves may provide a cheaper source of heat than heating oil. But air pollution caused by smoke from wood-burning stoves has become a problem in some places.

Most wood-burning stoves are made of heavy cast iron or steel. *Combination stoves,* which resemble the stove invented by the American inventor and statesman Benjamin Franklin in the 1740's, fit into a fireplace. They have doors in the front that are used to control the draft. Such draft control enables the stove to burn wood more efficiently than an open fireplace can. In addition, when the stove becomes hot, it holds the heat better than a fireplace does. *Free-standing stoves* operate in basically the same manner as combination stoves. But they are not attached to a fireplace.

Room heaters. Some room heaters burn gas to produce heat. These can be placed in a corner of the room and used with a fan to circulate the heated air. Such heaters should not be used without adequate venting to the outside because combustion gases can be harmful to the occupants of the room. Other room heaters burn kerosene and must also be vented.

Electric room heaters pass an electric current through a series of wires. These wires resist the electricity and become red hot. Such electric heaters give off heat by radiation and convection. Many electric heaters are in such places as bathrooms, bedrooms, and workshops.

Most local sources of heat are relatively hot, compared with steam and hot-water radiators. For this reason they produce a larger proportion of radiant heat. When such large amounts of radiant heat are used, the temperature of the air in the room need not become so hot. For example, a resistance-type electric heater called a *quartz heater* warms anyone in the path of its heat rays. But the heat rays do not significantly warm the air through which they travel.   Merl Baker

Related articles in *World Book* include:

Air conditioning	Fuel	Heat pipe	Radiator
Coal	Furnace	Heat pump	Solar energy
Electricity	Gas	Insulation	Thermostat
	Heat	Petroleum	

Heatstroke. See Sunstroke.

Heaven, in the teachings of many religions, is the place or spiritual state in which God, gods, or spirits abide. According to most of these religions, the souls of people who have been faithful to their religion and performed good deeds go to heaven as a reward. Many scriptures describe heaven as a place of dazzling beauty that fulfills every idea of perfection.

The major Western religions—Christianity, Islam, and Judaism—teach that heaven is eternal and dominated by the presence of God. Most Christians believe the supreme reward of heaven is the happiness of being close to God. For followers of Islam, heaven is a refreshing garden where the face of God is seen. Jewish scriptures refer to heaven as the upper part of the universe, but they mention few details. Many Jews believe a future *Messianic Kingdom* will establish a kind of heaven on the earth (see **Judaism** [The Messiah]).

According to two Eastern religions, Buddhism and Hinduism, heaven has many levels. These levels represent degrees of spiritual purity. Buddhists and Hindus believe that if they perform good deeds, their souls will ascend to such levels. But heaven is not eternal. The most advanced believers pass beyond heaven to the eternal states of nirvana and buddhahood. The rest return and are reborn.   Robert S. Ellwood, Jr.

See also **Religion** (A doctrine of salvation); **Elysium; Nirvana; Paradise; Valhalla.**

Heaves, also known as *broken wind,* is a lung disease of horses. Horses suffering from heaves have difficulty exhaling and may develop a chronic cough. Their nostrils dilate and their sides heave as they struggle to breathe.

Heaves may result from any of a number of disorders that affect exhalation. The most common causes are allergies, prolonged inflammation of the lung airways by dust or mold, ballooning and rupturing of the tiny air sacs in the lungs, and viral or bacterial infections of the airways. Dietary factors also may be involved. Heaves may be mild and cause minor problems, or it may disable the horse completely. Important preventive measures include providing horses with clean, high-quality feed and well-ventilated shelters free of dust and mold. To relieve symptoms of heaves, veterinarians prescribe rest, corticosteroids and other drugs, and control of the horse's feed and surroundings.   Lawrence D. McGill

Heavy hydrogen. See Deuterium.

Heavy water (chemical formula D_2O or ^2H_2O) is water that contains the heavy isotope of hydrogen called *deuterium* (chemical symbol D) in place of ordinary hydrogen. The deuterium atom has a mass about twice as great as an ordinary hydrogen atom. Heavy water is also called *deuterium oxide.*

Because of the difference between the masses of the two kinds of hydrogen atoms, the physical properties of heavy water differ from those of ordinary water. Heavy water freezes at 3.82° C (38.88° F.), rather than at 0° C (32° F.). It boils at 101.42° C (214.56° F.), rather than at 100° C (212° F.). Seeds will not germinate in it, and animals cannot live in it.

Heavy water is useful in some kinds of nuclear reactors called *heavy water reactors.* It acts as a *moderator,* to control the energy of the neutrons released in a chain reaction. It also acts as a *coolant,* removing the heat produced in the reactor core. This prevents the tempera-

ture in the core from becoming too high, and carries off the heat so it can be used to produce steam and power. Large amounts of heavy water are produced by a catalytic exchange of deuterium between water and hydrogen sulfide gas. The resulting deuterium-enriched water is then distilled.

Heavy water was first separated from ordinary water in 1932 by Gilbert N. Lewis, a chemist at the University of California.   Peter A. Rock

See also **Deuterium** (Properties); **Nuclear energy** (Power reactors); **Nuclear weapon; Urey, Harold C.**

Hebe, *HEE bee,* was a goddess in Greek mythology who served nectar to the gods and goddesses on Mount Olympus. She was the daughter of Zeus, the king of the gods, and of the goddess Hera. The name Hebe comes from a Greek word meaning *youth* or *prime of life.* The nectar Hebe served was believed to keep the gods and goddesses youthful. After the hero Heracles (Hercules in Latin) was made a god, Hebe became his wife. See also **Nectar; Hercules.**   Jon D. Mikalson

Hebrew Bible. See Bible.

Hebrew calendar. See Calendar (Hebrew).

Hebrew language and literature. Hebrew is one of the world's oldest living languages. The ancient Israelites who lived in Palestine during Biblical times spoke and wrote in Hebrew. The Bible itself is the greatest product of Hebrew literature. Today, Hebrew still serves as the language of Judaism, the religion of the Jews, and is also one of the official languages of Israel. Many Jewish authors also write in a language called Yiddish. For information about these writers, see **Yiddish language and literature.**

The Hebrew language

Hebrew is a dialect of Canaanite, a branch of the Northwest Semitic languages (see **Semitic languages**). In sound, it has characteristics of Arabic and Aramaic. Hebrew may be pronounced in different ways. The most widespread systems of pronunciation are the *Ashkenazic* (European) and the *Sephardic* (Israeli). The main differences between the two occur in the pronunciation of certain vowels and in the accent of various words.

Words in Hebrew are written from right to left. The alphabet consists of 26 consonants, plus marks called *vowel points* that indicate vowels. Most Hebrew words are formed from roots consisting of three letters. The words are built from the roots by adding prefixes and suffixes and by changing the vowel sounds.

Hebrew literature

Beginnings. Spoken Hebrew existed by the 1300's B.C. The first known work of literature written in Hebrew was the Biblical poem "The Song of Deborah" (Judg. 5), which dates from about 1100 B.C. Along with the Bible, the other major product of early Hebrew literature was the *Talmud,* a collection of Jewish oral laws plus the interpretations of scholars (see **Talmud**). The Talmud was written from about A.D. 70 to 500. By the 500's, great verse prayers called *piyyutim* were being composed for religious services.

Medieval works. During the Middle Ages, such travelers as Eldad the Danite and Benjamin of Tudela wrote Hebrew accounts of their journeys. *Yosippon* (900's) and other anonymous works combined Jewish history with

Khaph   Kaph   Yod   Teth   Heth   Zayin   Vav   He   Daleth   Gimel   Veth   Beth   Aleph

Tav   Sin   Shin   Resh   Koph   Tsadi   Feh   Peh   Ayin   Samekh   Nun   Mem   Lamed

The Hebrew alphabet has 26 consonants. Five of them—Kaph, Mem, Nun, Peh, and Tsadi—are formed differently when they come at the ends of words. The illustration above shows the consonants in alphabetical order from right to left, which is the way Hebrew is read and written.

thrilling legends. Other Hebrew works of the 1100's and 1200's included the *Book of Delight* by Ibn Zabara and *Tahkemoni* by Judah Alharizi. Such writings reflect the migrations of the Jews to many countries. For example, the *Book of Delight* consists of rhymed prose narratives that contain elements of *Aesop's Fables* of Greece and of tales of Arabic, Indian, and Persian origin.

A number of works of Jewish philosophy were written during the Middle Ages. The greatest of them included Judah Halevi's *Kuzari* and Maimonides' *Guide for the Perplexed,* both from the 1100's. Both of these works were originally written in Arabic and later translated into Hebrew. The *Kuzari* is a defense of Judaism in dialogue form. *Guide for the Perplexed* tries to harmonize philosophy with Jewish tradition.

The period in Spain from the 900's to the 1400's was considered a golden age of Hebrew literature, especially poetry. Hebrew poets wrote about friendship, humor, love, and war, as well as religious themes. This great poetry included the war poems of Samuel Ibn Nagrela from the 1000's and Judah Halevi's *Songs of Zion* from the 1100's.

During the Middle Ages, the Jews suffered much persecution. In 1492, for example, they were expelled from Spain. Some Hebrew authors tried to understand such Jewish suffering by examining the relationship between God and human beings. Much of the literature of these writers formed part of the Jewish mystical tradition called the *Cabala* (see **Mysticism**). The *Zohar* (*Book of Splendor*), written chiefly in the Aramaic language with some Hebrew sections, is the greatest work of Cabalist

Dih   Dee   Deh   Day   Dah   Daw

Duh   Doh   Doh   Doo   Doo

Hebrew vowels are indicated by vowel points placed with a consonant. Some vowel points are shown above with Daleth.

literature. Scholars believe that most of the *Zohar* was written by Moses de Leon of Spain in the late 1200's.

Modern Hebrew literature, according to some scholars, began as early as the 1500's. The first important modern Hebrew cultural and literary movement was the *Haskalah* (Enlightenment), which started in the late 1700's. The Haskalah developed among the Jews of Western Europe and later spread east. Followers believed that Jews should abandon some of their traditional ways and adopt aspects of modern Western culture. Haskalah writings praised the beauty of nature and the glory of wisdom but also promoted equal rights for Jews in the non-Jewish world. See **Haskalah.**

The first Hebrew novel, *Love of Zion* (1853), was written by a Lithuanian-born author, Abraham Mapu. During the 1860's and 1870's, three writers—Yehudah Leib Gordon, Moshe Leib Lilienblum, and Peretz Smolenskin—dominated Hebrew literature. Gordon wrote poetry on historical themes and on women's rights and other issues of the time. Lilienblum was the author of a widely read autobiography, *Sins of Youth* (1876). Smolenskin was one of the first Hebrew writers to promote the idea that the Jews were a nation, not just a religious group.

Another great author of the late 1800's was Shalom Jacob Abramovich, who wrote under the name of Mendele the Bookseller. Abramovich helped develop a modern Hebrew literary style that was both precise and natural. Eliezer ben Yehudah, a journalist and dictionary writer, was the leader in reviving spoken Hebrew.

Starting in the 1880's, *Zionism,* the idea of establishing a national Jewish state, became an important force in Hebrew literature. The journalist Asher Ginsberg, also known as Ahad Haam, wrote philosophical essays on the proposed Jewish homeland. Many poems by Chaim Nachman Bialik show the excitement of the awakening of Jewish national feeling. Some of the novels and short stories of Shmuel Yosef Agnon describe the Jewish settlement in Palestine during the early 1900's. In 1966, Agnon became the first Hebrew writer to receive the Nobel Prize for literature. Other important Hebrew authors of the 1900's include the poets Yehudah Amichai, Uri Tzvi Greenberg, and Saul Tchernichovsky; and the prose writers Micha Yosef Berdyczewski, Yosef Haim Brenner, Haim Hazaz, Aharon Meged, and S. Yizhar.

A new generation of Hebrew writers began with the birth of Israel in 1948. Such works as the novels of

Moshe Shamir and the poetry of Haim Guri describe life in the new nation.

Hebrew literature today deals with a variety of subjects, among them the conflict between parents and children and the rejection of some once-sacred ideas of Judaism and Zionism. Novels on such topics include Amos Oz's *My Michael* (1968) and A. B. Yehoshua's *The Lover* (1976). Other modern themes of Hebrew literature include hostility between Israelis and Arabs, and memories of the Nazi mass murder of Jews during the 1930's and 1940's.   Stanley L. Nash

Related articles in *World Book* include:

Agnon, Shmuel	Halevi, Judah	Mendelssohn,
Aramaic language	Jews	Moses
Bialik, Chaim	Judaism	Yiddish language
Bible	Maimonides	and literature

Additional resources

Encyclopedia Judaica, 17 vols. Keter, 1972. Volume 8 includes articles on "Hebrew Grammar" and "Hebrew Literature, Modern."

Halkin, Simon. *Modern Hebrew Literature: Trends and Values.* Rev. ed. Schocken, 1970.

Horowitz, Edward. *How the Hebrew Language Grew.* Rev. ed. Ktav, 1967.

Kravitz, Nathaniel. *3,000 Years of Hebrew Literature, from the Earliest Time Through the 20th Century.* Swallow, 1972.

Hebrews. See Jews.

Hebrews, Epistle to the, is the 19th book of the New Testament. Although it is called an *epistle* (letter), it is really a type of religious essay. Its author is unknown. It was probably written during the persecution of Christians by Rome under the Emperor Domitian sometime between A.D. 81 and 96.

The author tries to help his readers to remain faithful as Christians, despite persecution, in three ways. First, he praises the greatness of Christian faith, mainly by showing that it is superior, in his view, to Judaism. Second, he presents Jesus to his readers as an example of being perfected through suffering. Third, he warns them of the spiritual consequences of abandoning their faith.

Terrance D. Callan

See also **Bible** (Books of the New Testament).

Hebrides, *HEHB rih DEEZ,* are a group of Scottish islands that lie northwest of the country's mainland. The Hebrides consist of about 500 islands and have an area of about 2,600 square miles (6,730 square kilometers). The largest islands are (1) Lewis with Harris and (2) Skye. Many of the islands are tiny and uninhabited.

The Hebrides are divided into two groups of islands, the Inner Hebrides and the Outer Hebrides, also called the Western Isles. The Inner Hebrides, which lie closest to the mainland, feature spectacular mountain scenery. The Cuillin Hills, on Skye, are especially noted for their rugged beauty. The islands of the Outer Hebrides have large areas of barren, rolling wasteland called *moors.* The Hebrides have a windy, humid climate.

About 15,000 people live in the Inner Hebrides and 31,000 in the Outer Hebrides. Many of the people rent small farms called *crofts* and grow such crops as barley, oats, and potatoes. Other economic activities include fishing, tourism, weaving, and the distilling of Scotch whisky. Harris Tweed, a famous brand of wool cloth, is made exclusively in the Outer Hebrides.

People have lived in the Hebrides since prehistoric times. Norway took control of the Hebrides in the late

800's and ruled them until 1266, when Scotland gained possession of the islands. Many songs and legends have been written about the Hebrides.   H. R. Jones

Hebron, *HEE bruhn* (pop. 50,000), is a city in the West Bank region of Jordan (see **Jordan** [map]). Israel has occupied the West Bank since 1967.

Mentioned in the Book of Genesis, Hebron is one of the world's oldest cities. It has religious importance to Jews, Muslims, and Christians. It was built on the site of the Cave of Machpelah, which is believed to house the tombs of Abraham and his wife, Sarah. Abraham was the founder of Judaism and the ancestor of both the Arabs—most of whom are Muslims—and the Jews. He is also an important figure in Christianity. Today, a *mosque* (Islamic house of worship) stands above the cave. Formerly part of Palestine, Hebron became part of Jordan in 1950. Israel gained control of the West Bank during the Arab-Israeli War of 1967.

Hebron is a major marketing and administrative center for the southern West Bank. It has glass-making, tanning, and food-processing plants, large marble and stone quarries, and an Islamic university called Hebron University.   Nicolas E. Gavrielides

Hecate, *HEHK uh tee,* was a goddess of witchcraft and black magic in Greek mythology. Hecate became best known as a torch-bearing goddess accompanied by hellhounds. At night, she presided at crossroads, which the ancient Greeks associated with evil.

Hecate originated as a beneficial power that influenced many areas of life. Farmers, fishermen, athletes, statesmen, and soldiers prayed to her for wealth and good fortune. She was also a nurse of young children and a patron of women. Occasionally, Hecate was represented as the daughter of Demeter, the goddess of the earth and agriculture.

According to the ancient Greek writer Hesiod, Hecate's parents were *Titans,* the first divinities in Greek my-

The Hebrides Islands are part of Scotland. They lie off the west coast of the Scottish mainland. The islands are divided into two groups—the Outer Hebrides and the Inner Hebrides.

WORLD BOOK map

thology. Hesiod described a 10-year battle in which the Olympian gods and goddesses led by Zeus defeated the Titans. Hecate alone of the Titans was allowed to retain her powers. Nancy Felson Rubin

Hecht, *hehkt,* **Ben** (1894-1964), was an American playwright, novelist, and screenwriter. Hecht wrote in a colorful style that may have been influenced by his years as a newspaperman in Chicago.

Hecht became best known for plays he wrote with Charles MacArthur. Their most famous collaboration, *The Front Page* (1928), is a comic melodrama about hard-boiled newspaper life in Chicago. Hecht and MacArthur also wrote *Twentieth Century* (1932), a fast-paced comedy about movie stars. Hecht's first and best-known novel, *Erik Dorn* (1921), deals with a brilliant, cynical journalist.

Hecht was born in New York City but was raised in Racine, Wis. After graduating from high school, he moved to Chicago and began working on the Chicago *Journal* as a reporter. After 1933, Hecht spent most of his time as a motion-picture screenwriter, director, and producer. He wrote scripts for such films as *Design for Living* (1933), *Nothing Sacred* (1937), *Spellbound* (1945), and *Notorious* (1946). He wrote the screenplay for *Wuthering Heights* (1939) with MacArthur. During his later years, Hecht worked hard for the establishment of the state of Israel. Hecht wrote an autobiography called *A Child of the Century* (1954). Samuel Chase Coale

Heckler, Margaret Mary (1931-   ), served as secretary of health and human services from 1983 to 1985. She was appointed to the position by President Ronald Reagan. She had previously served 16 years in the United States House of Representatives as a Republican from Massachusetts. In 1985, Reagan named Heckler U.S. ambassador to Ireland.

Department of Health and Human Services
Margaret M. Heckler

In Congress, Heckler strongly supported women's rights, and she worked for the adoption of the proposed Equal Rights Amendment to the U.S. Constitution. In 1977, Heckler and Representative Elizabeth Holtzman, a Democrat from New York, founded a group that became known as the Congressional Caucus for Women's Issues. As secretary of health and human services, Heckler introduced a system of set rates for Medicare payments to hospitals. She also helped win Congress's approval of a law that helps ensure payment of court-ordered child support.

Margaret Mary O'Shaughnessy was born in Flushing, N.Y. She was married to John M. Heckler from 1953 to 1985. She graduated from Albertus Magnus College and Boston College Law School. Lee Thornton

Hectare. See Metric system (Surface measurements).

Hector, in Greek mythology, was the greatest hero of the ancient city of Troy. He played a major part in the Trojan War, in which Greece defeated Troy. The famous epic poem the *Iliad* tells of important events during the last year of the war.

Hector was the son of Priam, the king of Troy, and Hecuba. According to some myths, the Greek god Apollo was Hector's father. The *Iliad* described Hector as brave, handsome, and patriotic.

During the Trojan War, Achilles, the greatest Greek warrior, refused to fight after quarreling with Agamemnon, the commander of the Greek forces. As a result, Hector's soldiers drove the Greeks from the walls of Troy. Achilles agreed to the request of his friend Patroclus, who wanted to wear Achilles' armor and fight in his place. Hector, aided by Apollo, killed Patroclus during the battle.

Achilles returned to the battlefield to seek revenge for the death of Patroclus. The sight of Achilles terrified Hector, who tried to flee. But Hector realized that he must fight Achilles, even though he knew he would die. Achilles killed Hector and tied the corpse behind his chariot. He dragged Hector's body around the walls of Troy for several days. King Priam secretly went to Achilles and begged him for his son's corpse. Achilles pitied Priam and gave him Hector's body so that the Trojans could bury it properly. Robert J. Lenardon

See also **Iliad; Priam; Trojan War.**

Hecuba, *HEHK yu buh,* was the second wife of Priam, the king of Troy, in Greek mythology. Hecuba and Priam had many children, including the Trojan heroes Hector and Paris. The deaths of her husband and several of their children during the Trojan War caused Hecuba great suffering.

When the city of Troy fell to the Greeks, Hecuba was awarded to the Greek leader Odysseus (Ulysses in Latin) as a slave. Odysseus sailed to Thrace, where Hecuba discovered that King Polymestor had murdered Polydorus, her youngest son. Polydorus had been sent to Polymestor for safety during the war but Polymestor killed him for the treasure the young man brought with him. Hecuba lured Polymestor and his two sons into her tent. There, Hecuba and her handmaidens killed the children and blinded Polymestor. Hecuba was later transformed into a fiery-eyed dog. Robert J. Lenardon

See also **Paris** (mythology); **Cassandra.**

Hedge apple. See Osage orange.

Hedgehog, *HEHJ hahg* or *HEHJ hawg,* is a small animal that looks somewhat like a porcupine. The *common*

© Giuseppe Mazza
The hedgehog has short, sharp spines on its back.

hedgehog lives in northern Europe and Asia, Asia Minor, southern and eastern Africa, and New Zealand. It is about 9 inches (23 centimeters) long. It has short ears and legs, a short tail, and a long nose. Stiff, needlelike growths called *spines* cover its back and protect the animal from its enemies. When it is in danger, the hedgehog rolls itself into a spiny ball.

Hedgehogs hunt for food at night. They eat insects, snakes, small mammals, birds, and birds' eggs. When cold weather comes, hedgehogs settle down to hibernate. Hedgehogs are easily tamed. Some people keep them as pets to get rid of insects and other house pests.

Scientific classification. Hedgehogs belong to the hedgehog family, Erinaceidae. The common hedgehog is *Erinaceus europaeus.*   Charles M. Kirkpatrick

Hedging. See Commodity exchange.

Hedonism, *HEE duh nihz uhm,* is the belief that pleasure is the highest good of life. The term *hedonism* comes from a Greek word meaning *pleasure.* In ancient Greece, the Epicureans and Cyrenaics based their ethical philosophies on the idea that pleasure is the highest good. But the Epicureans believed that people should seek pleasures of the mind rather than pleasures of the body. The wise person, they thought, avoids pleasures which may later cause pain. In modern philosophy, hedonism has taken a different form. The hedonistic utilitarians believe that people should seek not their own individual pleasure alone, but the greatest good for the greatest number of people. They think of good in terms of pleasure (see Utilitarianism).   S. Marc Cohen

Heel fly. See Warble fly; Bot fly.

Hegel, *HAY guhl,* **G. W. F.** (1770-1831), was one of the most influential German philosophers. Hegel argued that in order to understand any aspect of human culture, we must retrace and understand its history.

Hegel's emphasis on the importance of historical understanding has greatly promoted the development of the historical study of philosophy, art, religion, science, and politics. The historical approach to human culture inspired by Hegel eventually spread far beyond the borders of Germany.

Hegel's dialectic. Hegel developed a theory of history that became known as his *dialectic.* Hegel believed that all historical developments have three basic characteristics. First, they follow a course that is necessary— that is, they could not have happened in any other way. To understand a historical development in any area of human thought or activity, we must see why it necessarily happened as it did. Second, each historical development represents not only change but progress. Third, Hegel argued that one phase of any historical development tends to be confronted and replaced by its opposite. This opposite, in turn, tends to be replaced by a phase that is somehow a resolution of the two opposed phases. These three phases of a typical dialectical development have often been called *thesis, antithesis,* and *synthesis.* But Hegel did not use those terms.

Hegel applied his dialectic to all areas of human life. For example, he argued that the attempt to achieve satisfaction through the *external* pursuit of power and property tends to be rejected in favor of the attempt to achieve an *inner* state of harmony and tranquility. This opposition between external activity and an inner nonactive state of mind can be resolved by having one's ex-

ternal activity emerge from a harmonious inner state. Or to take a political example, a period marked by the concentration of political power in one person tends to be followed by a period of widely distributed power. This opposition might be resolved by a period in which there is both some distribution and some concentration of power. Thus, an absolute monarchy might be replaced by an absolute democracy and, in turn, by a representative form of government.

Hegel's writings. In most of his writings, Hegel tried to demonstrate the presence of dialectical developments. In his first published book, *Phenomenology of Spirit* (1807), he dealt with the development of "forms of consciousness." These forms of consciousness include a rich and bewildering variety of states of mind, views of the world, ethical positions, religious outlooks, types of physical activity, and forms of social organization. Hegel tried to demonstrate how they progressed in what he claimed was a necessary and historical sequence that moved through contradiction and resolution to ever greater levels of maturity.

In his second book, *Science of Logic* (1812-1816), Hegel tried to show the same sort of dialectic in the development of philosophical theories about reality. His *Encyclopedia of the Philosophical Sciences* (1817) contains his philosophic system in a condensed form. It has three sections: a shorter version of his book on logic, a "Philosophy of Nature," and a "Philosophy of Spirit." His last book, *Philosophy of Right* (1821), analyzes the dialectical development of social, ethical, and legal systems. After Hegel's death, his students published his lectures on the philosophy of history, religion, and art and on the history of philosophy. They reconstructed the lectures mainly from their notes.

Life. Georg Wilhelm Friedrich Hegel was born in Stuttgart. He attended the University of Tübingen, near Stuttgart. His university teaching career began in 1801 in Jena. He was professor of philosophy at the University of Berlin from 1818 until his death.   Ivan Soll

See also Marx, Karl (Marx's writings).

Additional resources

Cullen, Bernard. *Hegel's Social and Political Thought: An Introduction.* St. Martin's, 1979.
Singer, Peter. *Hegel.* Oxford, 1983.
Taylor, Charles. *Hegel.* Cambridge, 1975.

Hegira, *hih JY ruh* or *HEHJ uhr uh,* also spelled *Hejira* or *Hijra,* is the name of Muhammad's journey from Mecca to Medina on Friday, July 16, 622. *Hegira* comes from an Arabic word that means *to abandon* or *to desert.* During Muhammad's 10 years of preaching in Mecca, he had aroused opposition by proclaiming himself a prophet and criticizing aspects of life in the city. Finally, he decided to move to Yathrib, about 200 miles (320 kilometers) to the north, where he had friends. Yathrib thereafter was called *Madinatu-n-Nabi* (*City of the Prophet*), or *Medina.*

Muhammad's emigration to Medina was the turning point in his rise to power in Arabia and in his effort to establish his teaching and community. Because of this, the Muslim calendar is dated from the year of the Hegira.   Ali Hassan Abdel Kader

See also **Calendar** (The Islamic calendar); **Mecca; Medina; Muhammad.**

Heidegger, *HY dehg uhr,* **Martin** (1889-1976), was a German philosopher who exercised a tremendous influence on the philosophers of continental Europe, South America, and Japan. His work is an attempt to understand the nature of *Being* (*Sein* in German). To study Being, Heidegger analyzed human existence (*Dasein*) because it is the form of Being that can be known best. In his attempt to understand Being, he often sought philosophical enlightenment in the *etymologies* (origins) of words. Heidegger also sought enlightenment in the insights of poets, especially his favorite poet, Friedrich Hölderlin.

Heidegger's extensive discussion of human existence, which emphasizes anxiety, alienation, and death, has led many people to call him an existentialist (see **Existentialism**). However, he denied being an existentialist, claiming that he was interested in human existence only to better understand Being. He held that the most important philosophical question is: "Why is there something rather than nothing at all?"

Heidegger was born in Baden-Württemberg. He studied philosophy at the University of Freiburg under Edmund Husserl. Heidegger succeeded Husserl in 1928, and became rector of the university in 1933. His best-known book is *Being and Time* (1927). He also wrote *What Is Metaphysics?* (1929), *Introduction to Metaphysics* (1953), and *What Is Thinking?* (1954).   Ivan Soll

Heidelberg, *HYD uhl burg* (pop. 134,724), is a city in southern West Germany (see **Germany** [political map]). Heidelberg lies in a scenic setting along the Neckar River. The ruins of beautiful Heidelberg Castle, which dates from the Middle Ages, stand high on a steep bank of the river and overlook the city. Concerts and an annual summer drama festival are held at the ruins. The picturesque old section of the city is the home of the University of Heidelberg, which was founded in 1386 and is Germany's oldest university. Heidelberg's quaint features have inspired romantic works about the city. Sigmund Romberg's operetta *The Student Prince* is perhaps the most famous of these works. Many tourists visit Heidelberg and contribute greatly to the economy. Products of the city include leather goods, precision instruments, and machinery.

Heidelberg was developed in the Middle Ages on the site of two monasteries. In the late 1600's, French armies destroyed most of the city and left the castle in ruins.

Peter H. Merkl

See also **Germany** (picture: Lively German rathskellers).

Heidelberg, *HY duhl burg,* **University of,** is the oldest university in Germany. It was established in Heidelberg in 1386. The university has divisions of biology, classical and Oriental studies, economics, history, law, mathematics, modern philology, medicine, natural sciences, philosophy, social sciences, and theology. Its library, founded in the 1500's, consists of more than a million books, including a collection of old German manuscripts. Many of the university's 26,000 students come from countries other than Germany.

The University of Heidelberg, which was modeled after the University of Paris, originally had four departments—arts, law, medicine, and theology. During the 1500's, it became the center of Protestant learning.

The university was reorganized in 1803 and became a center for the study of German folklore and medieval literature. The Nazis seized control of the institution in 1933 and dictated what could be taught. The university was reorganized in 1945, following Germany's defeat in World War II. It is supported by the West German state of Baden-Württemberg.   P. A. McGinley

Heidelberg man, *HY duhl burg,* was a prehistoric human being who lived in Europe about 650,000 years ago. The only evidence of this creature's existence is a huge chinless jawbone with large teeth. Workers found the jaw in 1907 while digging in a sandpit in the village of Mauer, Germany, near Heidelberg. Heidelberg man belonged to an early type of prehistoric human being called *Homo erectus* (erect human being). Homo erectus appeared about 1,500,000 B.C. Scientists believe that Heidelberg man hunted now-extinct forms of buffalo, deer, elephants, moose, and rhinoceroses. Heidelberg man also probably made stone tools. See also **Prehistoric people.**   Karl W. Butzer

Heiden, Eric. See **Olympic Games** (History).

Heifer. See **Cattle** (introduction; Breeding).

Heifetz, *HY fehts,* **Jascha,** *YAH shuh* (1901-   ), a Lithuanian-born violinist, became famous for his international tours as well as his recordings. He appeared as soloist with virtually all the world's great orchestras, and made frequent broadcasts to large audiences. In the opinion of qualified critics, Heifetz raised the level of violin virtuosity to new heights. He often was the first performer to play the works of contemporary composers.

Heifetz was born in Vilna (now Vilnius), in Lithuania. His career began almost as soon as he could hold a violin and bow. When he was three years of age, his father, a good violinist, began to teach him. At five, Heifetz entered the Imperial School of Music in Vilna. He later studied with the famous teacher, Leopold Auer, in Saint Petersburg (now Leningrad), Russia.

Heifetz began to play in public when he was six. At 13, he made his debut in Berlin and won international fame. During the Russian Revolution, Heifetz escaped to the United States. He became an American citizen in 1925.

Dorothy DeLay

Height and weight tables, for boys and girls. See **Baby; Child; Adolescent.**

Heimlich maneuver. See **First aid** (Choking).

Heine, *HY nuh,* **Heinrich,** *HYN rihkh* (1797-1856), ranks among the most popular writers in German literature. Several of Heine's poems are so well known they are considered part of German folklore. Heine's poetry has been set to music by such composers as Schubert, Mendelssohn, and Brahms.

Heine was born in Düsseldorf. Much of his early poetry was collected in the *Book of Songs* (1827). This collection of love poetry is Heine's best-known work and the most famous book of poetry in German literature. The poems are described as "bittersweet" because they combine simplicity and beauty with an irony that gives them a cynical tone. The most famous of the poems is "The Lorelei."

Heine's early prose is a unique combination of fiction and essay that was often imitated. Much of it was published in four volumes of *Travel Pictures* (1826-1831). Like most of Heine's writings, these are characterized by wit, irony, clarity, and intelligence.

Heine was one of the "Young Germans," a group of

writers who were political radicals (see **German litera-ture** [The young Germans]). He was attracted to the atmosphere of liberalism in France and moved to Paris in 1831. He lived there for the rest of his life. In Paris, Heine tried to bring about understanding between France and Germany, traditional enemies. He wrote a series of essays and newspaper articles to explain to the Germans the newly organized French constitutional monarchy. He described German culture to the French in *The Romantic School* (1833), *On the History of Religion and Philosophy in Germany* (1835), and other books.

Heine grew increasingly bitter about the lack of freedom in Germany and his books were banned there in 1835. He satirized the German political situation in two long mock-epic poems, *Atta Troll, A Midsummer Night's Dream* (1843) and *Germany: A Winter Tale* (1844).

Heine became paralyzed in 1848 and was confined to a "mattress-grave," as he called his bed, for the rest of his life. But his sufferings did not destroy his wit, intelligence, or literary talent. He continued to write on cultural, political, and religious topics. He also produced two collections of poetry—*Romancero* (1851) and *Poems 1853-1854.*   Jeffrey L. Sammons

Heinlein, *HYN lyn,* **Robert A.** (1907-   ), is an American author of science fiction. He writes in a simple, matter-of-fact style for both adults and children. His stories include adventure tales and serious ideas. He makes the stories believable by describing in detail the customs and scientific advances of future societies.

Heinlein's most popular novel, *Stranger in a Strange Land* (1961), disputes many traditional ideas on morals, religion, and sex. *The Past Through Tomorrow* (1967) consists of a series of stories and novels that together describe a future history of the human race. Major characters and events from early episodes in the series become important in later stories. Heinlein's other adult novels include *Time Enough for Love* (1973), *The Number of the Beast* (1980), *Friday* (1982), and *Job: A Comedy of Justice* (1984). Heinlein's novels for young readers have become models for other authors. His children's novels include *Space Cadet* (1948) and *The Star Beast* (1954).

Robert Anson Heinlein was born in Butler, Mo., and graduated from the U.S. Naval Academy. He served as a naval officer for five years and then worked in other fields before becoming a writer.   Judy-Lynn del Rey

Heir, *air.* Technically, an heir is a person who receives money or property left by someone who died *intestate* (without making a will). *Legatee* is the legal term for the beneficiary of a will. However, the word *heir* is commonly used for any person who is awarded an estate, whether or not the deceased person left a will.

The word *heir* comes from the Latin *heres,* which means *one entitled to inherit.* But the right to inherit is given only by law. Widely varying laws in each state specify which surviving relatives qualify as heirs. A close friend also may qualify as an heir. If there are no surviving heirs, the property goes to the state. This transfer is called *escheat.*   William Tucker Dean

Related articles in *World Book* include:

Escheat	Personal property
Estate	Primogeniture
Fee	Real estate
Next of kin	Will

Heisenberg, *HY zuhn BURG,* **Werner,** *VEHR nuhr* (1901-1976), a German physicist, is best known for his contributions to atomic theory. Heisenberg developed the *uncertainty principle,* which states that both the position and the momentum of a subatomic particle cannot be accurately determined simultaneously. He won the 1932 Nobel Prize in physics for founding one version of the field of physics called *quantum mechanics* (see **Quantum mechanics**).

Heisenberg based his theories about atomic structure on the frequencies of light given off by atoms. In 1913, the Danish physicist Niels Bohr had suggested that electrons in an atom could travel only in a certain set of orbits around the nucleus. Bohr had also shown that atoms radiate light due to changes in the arrangement of their electrons. During the early 1920's, Heisenberg used studies of atomic spectra to develop *matrix mechanics,* a form of quantum mechanics that provides a mathematical description of electron orbits.

Heisenberg discovered the uncertainty principle in 1927. This principle holds true because even the best methods used to measure the position and momentum of a moving particle disturb the particle. For example, physicists might scatter *photons* (particles of light) off a moving electron to "see" its position. But, in a collision, a photon transfers momentum to the electron. In addition, the more uncertain is the momentum transferred to it. As a result, physicists cannot verify precisely both the position and momentum of the electron at the same time.

Heisenberg was born in Würzburg (now in West Germany). He studied at the University of Munich.   Richard L. Hilt

Heisman Memorial Trophy is awarded annually to the outstanding college football player in the United States. A group of sportswriters and sportscasters selects the winner of the trophy, which is sponsored by the Downtown Athletic Club of New York City.

The trophy was first awarded in 1935. The next year it was named for John W. Heisman, a leading football coach at a number of colleges from 1892 to 1927. Heisman helped revolutionize the rules and strategy of football. For example, he introduced the center snap and led the campaign to legalize the forward pass. A table of Heisman trophy winners appears in the *World Book* article on **Football.**   Bob Wolf

Hejira. See Hegira.

Hekla, *HEHK luh,* is a volcanic mountain in southwestern Iceland. The mountain lies about 20 miles (32 kilometers) from the coast, and rises 4,892 feet (1,491 meters) above sea level. Since the 1100's, there have been about 18 eruptions on or close to Hekla. The main crater of the mountain had been quiet for over 100 years when it erupted on March 29, 1947. That eruption lasted 13 months. Lava spread over an area of 15 square miles (39 square kilometers), and ash fell as far away as Finland.   Gordon A. Macdonald

Held, John, Jr. (1889-1958), was an American cartoonist. He was best known for his delightful pictures of the manners and pastimes of the period in America known as the Roaring Twenties. Held's drawing style was elegant and sophisticated, like the fashionable, fun-loving people he portrayed. His humor was sympathetic rather than harsh, and he dealt with his subjects affectionately.

Teaching Old Dogs New Tricks (1926); New York Historical Society

A magazine cover by John Held, Jr., portrays a stylish but frivolous woman of the 1920's called a *flapper.* Held became famous for his pictures of the period called the Roaring Twenties.

Held popularized the image of the stylish but frivolous young women of the 1920's called *flappers.* See **Roaring Twenties** (picture).

John Held, Jr., was born in Salt Lake City, Utah, and moved to New York City in 1910. He drew cartoons and covers for *Harper's Bazaar, Vanity Fair, Life, The New Yorker,* and other magazines. By the late 1920's, his cartoons were being distributed to newspapers across the United States. Elizabeth Broun

Heldentenor. See **Opera** (The singers).

Helen of Troy, in Greek mythology, was the most beautiful woman in the world. She was the major cause of the Trojan War, in which Greece defeated the city of Troy.

Helen was the daughter of Zeus, the king of the gods, and Leda, a human being. According to one myth, Zeus appeared in the form of a swan when he visited Leda. Helen later hatched from a swan's egg. Another myth tells that Zeus mated with Nemesis, the goddess of fate, who gave Leda the egg from which Helen was born.

When Helen was a child, an Athenian hero named Theseus fell in love with her and kidnapped her. Helen's brothers, Castor and Pollux, rescued her. Many Greek heroes courted Helen, but she married Menelaus, the king of Sparta.

A Trojan prince named Paris visited Sparta and persuaded Helen to return to Troy with him. Menelaus' brother, Agamemnon, led a Greek army against Troy to win Helen back. Paris was killed during the war. Helen then married Paris' brother, Deiphobus, who was also killed. After the Greeks captured Troy, Helen and Menelaus were happily reunited.

According to a legend told by the poet Stesichorus, Helen never reached Troy with Paris. She and Paris traveled as far as Egypt, where she remained as the guest of King Proteus. A phantom of Helen went to Troy in her place. After the war ended, Menelaus and Helen were reunited in Egypt.

Helen's personality has fascinated writers for centuries. Some authors have portrayed her as a deceitful woman driven by passion to betray her country and family. However, other writers have regarded Helen as an innocent victim of her own great beauty.

Robert J. Lenardon

See also **Menelaus; Trojan War.**

Helena, *HEHL uh nuh* (pop. 23,938), is the capital of Montana. It serves as the trading and supply center for a mining and agricultural region. Helena lies about 95 miles (153 kilometers) southwest of Great Falls. For location, see **Montana** (political map).

The town of East Helena, 3 miles (5 kilometers) east of Helena, is a center for refining lead and zinc ores. Products of Helena include beverages, bricks and tiles, foods, paints, and steel products. Many federal agencies have offices in Helena. The city is the home of Carroll College and the Montana Historical Society. The capitol is topped by a statue representing Liberty.

Helena sprang up after 1864, when gold was discovered in Last Chance Gulch. The gulch is now the main street of Helena. The territorial capital moved from Virginia City to Helena in 1875. According to one theory, Helena was named for Helena, Minn., by a former resident of the Minnesota community. In 1935, Helena was shaken by a series of earthquakes which began on October 12. A total of 1,200 shocks were recorded in an 80-day period. A severe series of shocks on October 18 caused two deaths and resulted in $3\frac{1}{2}$ million worth of damage to property in the city.

Helena is the seat of Lewis and Clark County. It has a commission form of government. Bill Skidmore

See also **Montana** (picture: The State Capitol).

Helgoland is an island in the North Sea. It belongs to West Germany, and covers about $\frac{3}{4}$ square mile (2 square kilometers). It has a population of about 2,200. Great Britain ceded Helgoland to Germany in 1890 in exchange for Zanzibar in Africa. Before World War I it was a summer resort and the home of people who fished for a living. At the beginning of the war, in 1914, the people were taken to the German mainland, and the island became a naval base. The peace treaty in 1919 ordered Helgoland's fortifications and sea wall torn down. It later became apparent that, unless the sea walls were restored, the

WORLD BOOK map

Location of Helgoland

entire island might disappear, for one third of it had already washed away. After Hitler's rise to power, the walls were rebuilt, and Helgoland became strategically important in World War II. In 1947, the island's population was removed, and the British Navy set off 3,500 short tons (3,180 metric tons) of high explosives. All the German submarine pens, underground fortifications, and all other military installations were destroyed. In 1952, Helgoland was returned to West Germany. The Germans resettled the island and built it into a resort area. Frank Ahnert

Hughes Helicopters, Inc.

A heavily armed attack helicopter on a mission

Doug Wilson, Black Star

A helicopter hovering over a logging site

Aerospatiale Helicopter Corp.

A transport helicopter flying supplies to an oil rig

Bell Helicopter Textron

A business helicopter landing on a downtown rooftop

The tasks of helicopters include jobs that airplanes cannot do. Unlike planes, military *attack helicopters* can turn instantly to fire weapons in almost any direction. Helicopters can hover in midair and take off and land in small areas, such as forest clearings, drilling platforms, and rooftops.

Helicopter

Helicopter is an aircraft that is lifted into the air and kept aloft by one or two powerful whirling rotors. A helicopter rotor resembles a huge propeller that is parallel to the ground. However, the rotor is actually a rotating wing. The name *helicopter* refers to the rotor. It comes from the Greek words *helix*, meaning *spiral*, and *pteron*, meaning *wing*. Nicknames for the helicopter include "chopper," "eggbeater," and "whirlybird."

A helicopter can fly straight up or straight down, forward, backward, or sideways. It can even *hover* (stay in one spot in the air). Unlike most airplanes, helicopters need no runway. They can take off and land in very small space. In addition, helicopters can fly safely at much slower speeds and lower altitudes than airplanes. However, they cannot fly as fast as most planes. Most helicopters cannot exceed 200 miles (320 kilometers) per hour. At faster speeds, strong vibrations develop that could damage the rotor blades. Helicopters also use more fuel than airplanes to travel the same distance. In general, helicopters can fly only two to three hours—or less than 600 miles (970 kilometers)—without refueling.

Helicopters range in size from tiny, single-seat models to huge transports that can carry two trucks in their

Floyd D. Kennedy, Jr., the contributor of this article, is coauthor of World Combat Aircraft Directory *and* Military Helicopters of the World: Military Rotary-Wing Aircraft Since 1917.

cargo hold. The heaviest helicopter ever manufactured is the Soviet Union's Mil Mi-26. It weighs 31 short tons (28 metric tons) and can carry 22 short tons (20 metric tons) of cargo.

Uses of helicopters

Helicopters can be used for many tasks because they are able to hover in midair and take off and land in small areas. They are particularly useful (1) for rescue missions, (2) for aerial observation, (3) for transportation and construction work, (4) for agricultural and forestry operations, and (5) for military missions.

For rescue missions. Many early developers of helicopters intended them to be used for saving lives. Over the years, many thousands of people have been rescued by these "angels of mercy." A helicopter can hover above the scene of a disaster. A sling or harness can then be lowered from the craft to endangered people below. They are then pulled up and flown to safety. Helicopters have been used to pluck people from burning skyscrapers, sinking ships, and rising floodwaters. They have flown stranded mountain climbers and injured skiers to safety. Serving as flying ambulances, helicopters can land near automobile or airplane crashes and rush the injured to hospitals. Helicopters can also deliver food and medicine to areas that other vehicles cannot reach because of earthquakes, floods, or storms.

For aerial observation. In many cities, police use helicopters to trail fleeing suspects and direct squad cars on the ground. Law enforcement agents in helicopters look for lost people and escaped convicts. They also patrol national borders on the lookout for smugglers and illegal immigrants.

Many radio and television stations use helicopters to cover news events from the air. In large cities, helicopter pilots observe the flow of traffic and broadcast radio reports warning drivers of traffic jams. Motion-picture companies often film from helicopters to give audiences a bird's-eye view of a scene. Helicopter pilots fly low along pipelines, railroad tracks, and power lines to inspect them for damage.

Helicopters are used to explore wilderness areas, to survey land, and to help locate oil and other resources. From helicopters, scientists count wildlife populations and chart the migration routes of wild animals. Some fishing fleets use helicopters to spot schools of tuna.

For transportation and construction work. Helicopter transportation is expensive. However, the convenience of helicopter flight makes "choppers" ideal transport vehicles for certain uses. The flexibility, security, and speed of helicopter travel have made it a major method of transportation for political leaders in many countries. Helicopter travel saves business executives time that they otherwise might waste in using slow-moving ground transportation. From *heliports* (airports for helicopters) atop downtown office buildings, business executives may fly directly to nearby cities for meetings.

Helicopter service is essential to many offshore oil-drilling operations. Numerous offshore wells are in rough ocean waters that make it hazardous to bring in replacement crews and supplies by ship. However, helicopters can land on the drilling platforms and so provide much faster and safer delivery than ships.

Helicopters are often used to transport cargo that is too large or awkward for other vehicles to haul. The cargo is carried in a sling hanging below the craft.

Powerful helicopters are used in construction work as "flying cranes." Workers in helicopters install antennas and huge air conditioners atop tall buildings and erect preassembled electric power transmission towers. Workers also use helicopters to pour concrete in hard-to-reach places and to put long bridge sections in position.

For agricultural and forestry operations. Farmers use helicopters to spread seeds, fertilizers, weedkillers,

U.S. Coast Guard

Helicopter rescue missions have saved the lives of thousands of people. The United States Coast Guard helicopter above has picked up the crew members from a sinking ship.

and insecticides over large areas. Instead of building roads, some companies that manufacture forest products depend on helicopters to transport logging crews into and out of forests and to carry out logs.

For military missions. In the armed forces, helicopters serve as flying ambulances and as troop transports. Powerful military helicopters carry artillery to key battle positions and fly jeeps, tanks, and other equipment wherever they are needed. Helicopters equipped with electronic gear pick up and disrupt enemy communications signals. The armed forces also use helicopters to observe the movements of enemy troops and ships. Many naval helicopters have devices to locate and track submarines. They may also be armed with depth charges, missiles, or torpedoes. Army *attack helicopters* may carry bombs, cannons, machine guns, or missiles. Their main targets are enemy tanks.

Types of helicopters

Single-rotor helicopters are the most common type of helicopters. A single-rotor helicopter has one main rotor mounted above its body. Although such an aircraft is called a single-rotor helicopter, it also has a second, smaller rotor mounted on its tail. The main rotor may have from 2 to 8 blades. It provides the helicopter's lift-

Fred Ward, Black Star

Crop-dusting by helicopter enables farmers to spray agricultural chemicals exactly where they are needed. This specially equipped helicopter is spraying a field with insecticide.

Sikorsky Aircraft

An antisubmarine helicopter, armed with torpedoes, takes off from the deck of a U.S. Navy ship. Such helicopters carry electronic devices to locate and track submarines.

ing power. The tail rotor has from 2 to 13 blades. It is mounted vertically on either side of the tail and so spins at a right angle to the main rotor. The tail rotor is used to control direction. It also overcomes the tendency of the helicopter to spin around in the direction opposite to that of the main rotor.

Twin-rotor helicopters have two main rotors. The rotors turn in opposite directions and so eliminate the need for a tail rotor. Two basic types of twin-rotor helicopters are widely used: *tandem-rotor helicopters* and *coaxial-rotor helicopters*. A tandem-rotor helicopter has a main rotor mounted above each end of its body. A coaxial-rotor helicopter has one rotor above the other. The rotors are mounted above the middle of the helicopter's body. The shaft of the upper rotor turns inside the shaft of the lower rotor.

How helicopters fly

Lift is the force that causes an aircraft to overcome gravity, climb into the air, and stay aloft. Most aircraft rely on wings to produce lift. An airplane has *fixed* (immovable) wings that create lift as the airplane moves forward. Helicopter rotor blades are *rotary wings*. An engine turns the rotor, and the blades generate lift as they whirl through the air.

The special shape of wings helps them create lift. A wing's upper surface is curved, and its lower surface is less curved or flat. As a wing moves or whirls through the air, air flows over and under the wing. In the same amount of time, the air flowing over the curved upper surface travels farther than the air flowing under the wing. The air thus flows faster over the wing than under it. This difference in air speed creates a difference in air pressure above and below the wing. There is less pressure on the upper surface than on the lower surface. Because air is pushing more strongly against the bottom of the wing than against the top, lift is created. For additional information, see the article **Aerodynamics** (Principles of aerodynamics).

Helicopter pilots, like airplane pilots, can control the amount of lift by changing the angle that the wings make with the airflow. This angle is called the *angle of attack*. You can demonstrate the relation between lift and the angle of attack by using a kite to serve as a simple wing. Hold the kite flat and point it into the wind. If you then slightly raise the front of the kite, you increase

Types of helicopters

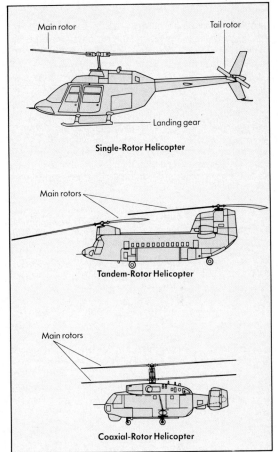
WORLD BOOK illustrations by Zorica Dabich

Single-Rotor Helicopter

Tandem-Rotor Helicopter

Coaxial-Rotor Helicopter

the angle of attack. You will feel a force trying to push the kite upward. This force is the lift created by the wind as it pushes against the bottom surface. If you decrease the angle of attack, the force becomes weaker.

Piloting a helicopter. The pilot of a single-rotor helicopter operates three basic controls inside the cockpit. (1) The *collective pitch lever* makes the helicopter climb,

How a helicopter rotor produces lift

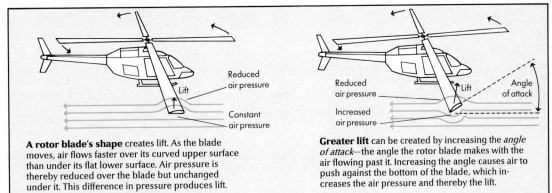
WORLD BOOK illustrations by Zorica Dabich

A rotor blade's shape creates lift. As the blade moves, air flows faster over its curved upper surface than under its flat lower surface. Air pressure is thereby reduced over the blade but unchanged under it. This difference in pressure produces lift.

Greater lift can be created by increasing the *angle of attack*—the angle the rotor blade makes with the air flowing past it. Increasing the angle causes air to push against the bottom of the blade, which increases the air pressure and thereby the lift.

hover, or descend. (2) The *control column*, also called the *cyclic pitch control,* causes it to fly forward, backward, or sideways. (3) The *rudder pedals* swing the tail around so that the helicopter can turn. Each control varies the *pitch* (angle) of the main rotor or tail rotor blades. A system of cables, rods, and other devices leads from the controls in the cockpit to the rotor blades.

Climbing, hovering, and descending. The pilot's left hand moves the collective pitch lever up and down. By raising the lever, the pilot increases the pitch of all main rotor blades equally. The increased pitch, in turn, increases the lift generated by the spinning rotor. When lift exceeds the force of gravity, the helicopter goes straight up. After reaching a particular altitude, the pilot may want to hover. The pilot then lowers the lever to decrease the pitch of the rotor blades and so reduce

Collective pitch lever

Control column

Rudder pedals

Helicopter controls. Moving the *collective pitch lever* makes the helicopter climb, hover, or descend. Tilting the *control column* causes forward, backward, or sideways flight. Pushing the *rudder pedals* controls the direction the helicopter points. This photo shows a craft with dual controls for the pilot and copilot.

Piloting a helicopter   A pilot flies a helicopter by varying the *pitch* (angle) of the rotor blades. The lift of the main rotor counteracts gravity. The force of the tail rotor counteracts *torque*, a force that tends to spin the aircraft in the direction opposite that of the main rotor. In the diagrams below, the pitch of the blades is indicated by the thickness of the circles showing the area swept by the rotor.

WORLD BOOK illustrations by Zorica Dabich

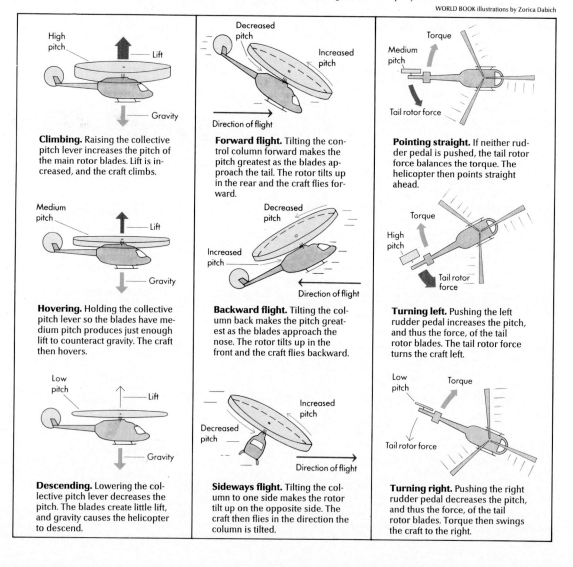

Climbing. Raising the collective pitch lever increases the pitch of the main rotor blades. Lift is increased, and the craft climbs.

Hovering. Holding the collective pitch lever so the blades have medium pitch produces just enough lift to counteract gravity. The craft then hovers.

Descending. Lowering the collective pitch lever decreases the pitch. The blades create little lift, and gravity causes the helicopter to descend.

Forward flight. Tilting the control column forward makes the pitch greatest as the blades approach the tail. The rotor tilts up in the rear and the craft flies forward.

Backward flight. Tilting the column back makes the pitch greatest as the blades approach the nose. The rotor tilts up in the front and the craft flies backward.

Sideways flight. Tilting the column to one side makes the rotor tilt up on the opposite side. The craft then flies in the direction the column is tilted.

Pointing straight. If neither rudder pedal is pushed, the tail rotor force balances the torque. The helicopter then points straight ahead.

Turning left. Pushing the left rudder pedal increases the pitch, and thus the force, of the tail rotor blades. The tail rotor force turns the craft left.

Turning right. Pushing the right rudder pedal decreases the pitch, and thus the force, of the tail rotor blades. Torque then swings the craft to the right.

the amount of lift. When the rotor's lifting force has been reduced just enough to counteract the pull of gravity, the craft will maintain a constant altitude. To descend, the pilot lowers the collective pitch lever farther, thereby decreasing the lift. When lift becomes weaker than the force of gravity, the craft descends.

Flying forward, backward, and sideways. The pilot's right hand operates the control column. The control column is a stick between the pilot's knees. It can be tilted in any direction. The helicopter moves in whatever direction the pilot tilts the column.

When the control column is tilted, the pitch of the main rotor blades alternately increases and decreases as they sweep through opposite sections of their circular path. To fly forward, the pilot pushes the column ahead. This causes the pitch to be greatest just before the blades pass over the tail. The blades have the least pitch just before they reach the nose. These changes in pitch cause the rotor blades to rise slightly in the rear. The rotor then tries to pull the helicopter both upward and ahead. Gravity counteracts the upward pull, however, and so the aircraft moves forward in level flight.

To fly backward, the pilot pulls back on the control column. This gives the blades the most pitch as they approach the nose and the least pitch as they approach the tail. The nose rises, the tail dips, and the helicopter flies backward. The aircraft can be made to fly sideways in a similar manner.

Turning. As a helicopter's main rotor spins in one direction, it creates a force that pushes against the body of the craft in the opposite direction. This twisting force is called *torque*. It must be overcome or the helicopter will be out of control and simply turn in circles.

The main rotor of a single-rotor helicopter spins in a counterclockwise direction, and so the push of the torque is clockwise. The pilot of a single-rotor craft uses the tail rotor to counteract torque and to change direction. The pilot controls the tail rotor by stepping on two rudder pedals. If neither pedal is depressed, the tail rotor blades spin at just the right pitch to produce exactly enough sideways force to counteract the torque. The helicopter then points straight ahead. To swing left, the pilot steps on the left rudder pedal, thereby increasing the pitch of the tail rotor blades. The increased force of the rotor pushes the tail in the direction opposite to the clockwise push of the torque. The helicopter then turns to the left. To turn right, the pilot depresses the right rudder pedal and so decreases the pitch—and thus the force—of the tail rotor blades. The torque itself then swings the tail in a clockwise direction, which turns the helicopter to the right.

On a twin-rotor helicopter, one main rotor turns clockwise and the other turns counterclockwise. As a result, the torque generated by one rotor cancels out that generated by the other. The pilot turns the craft by changing the pitch of the main rotors.

Development of the helicopter

Early designs and experiments. The earliest known mention of a rotor-powered flying machine appears in a Chinese text written about A.D. 320. The design of this machine may have been based on a Chinese toy called the *flying top*. Such toys flew by means of feather rotors. In 1483, the great Italian artist and scientist Leonardo da

Early helicopters

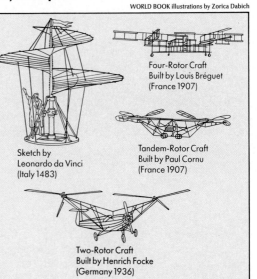

Sketch by
Leonardo da Vinci
(Italy 1483)

Four-Rotor Craft
Built by Louis Bréguet
(France 1907)

Tandem-Rotor Craft
Built by Paul Cornu
(France 1907)

Two-Rotor Craft
Built by Henrich Focke
(Germany 1936)

Vinci sketched a design for a helicopter. It had a large screwlike wing made of starched linen. In 1784, two Frenchmen named Launoy and Bienvenu built the first model helicopter in Europe that could fly. Based on the Chinese flying top, it had two rotors made of feathers. Throughout the 1800's, inventors in Europe and the United States experimented with model helicopters. The steam engines and electric motors of that time were too weak or too heavy to power a full-sized helicopter.

By the early 1900's, small, powerful gasoline engines had been developed that made manned helicopter flight possible. The first manned flight took place in 1907. The craft was a four-rotor helicopter built by Louis Bréguet, a French inventor. The helicopter lifted one of Bréguet's assistants 2 feet (61 centimeters) into the air for a minute. Assistants on the ground steadied the helicopter during the flight. Later in 1907, a French mechanic named Paul Cornu made the first free flight in a helicopter. He flew his tandem-rotor aircraft to a height of about 6 feet (1.8 meters) for about 20 seconds.

The first practical helicopters. Early helicopters were difficult to control, and their flight was wobbly. In 1935, Bréguet and another Frenchman, René Dorand, built a coaxial-rotor helicopter that was easier to control and flew far more steadily. In 1936, Henrich Focke, a German inventor, built a twin-rotor helicopter that was even further advanced. The following year, it reached a speed of 76 miles (122 kilometers) per hour and an altitude of about 8,000 feet (2,400 meters). It could stay aloft for 1 hour and 20 minutes.

The first flight of a practical single-rotor helicopter took place in the United States in 1939. The craft was built and flown by Igor I. Sikorsky, a Russian engineer who had moved to the United States in 1919. The British and the U.S. armed forces used an improved version of Sikorsky's helicopter during World War II (1939-1945).

Further improvements. During the mid-1900's, the military use of helicopters began to increase greatly, which led to major improvements in their design. Heli-

Sikorsky Aircraft

The first practical single-rotor helicopter was built and flown by Igor Sikorsky. Its first flight, *above*, was in 1939.

James Pickerell, Black Star

Helicopters in combat were first used on a massive scale by United States armed forces during the Vietnam War (1957-1975).

Sikorsky Aircraft

An experimental compound helicopter has coaxial rotors to provide lift. However, it uses jet engines for forward movement. Such aircraft can fly much faster than regular helicopters.

copters had been used mainly for patrol and rescue missions in World War II. New tasks for the helicopter during the Korean War (1950-1953) included armed observation of enemy positions and strength and transporting troops and supplies to hard-to-reach areas. During the Vietnam War (1957-1975), thousands of armed U.S. attack helicopters flew combat missions.

The ever-expanding military use of helicopters encouraged the development of faster, larger, and more powerful craft. In the 1940's and 1950's, engineers adapted the jet engine for use in helicopters. Jet engines were lighter and more powerful than the previous engines used to turn the rotor shafts. They enabled helicopters to fly faster and higher and to carry heavier loads. In addition, the use of new construction materials

made helicopters lighter, safer, and stronger. For example, metal or wooden rotor blades were replaced by longer-lasting plastic blades. Such improvements also made helicopters suitable for more civilian uses.

Recent developments include efforts by manufacturers to simplify the complicated operation of helicopters and to increase their speed. One manufacturer has developed a single-rotor helicopter that needs no tail rotor. Instead of a tail rotor, the craft uses jets of air to counteract torque and to change direction. Attempts to increase the speed of helicopters have led to the development of experimental *compound helicopters*. These vehicles do not depend entirely on rotors to provide forward movement as well as lift. Instead, they also have jet or propeller systems to help push or pull them ahead. One compound helicopter has reached the speed of 345 miles (555 kilometers) per hour.

Floyd D. Kennedy, Jr.

Related articles in *World Book* include:

Aerodynamics
Aircraft, Military (Helicopters; picture)
Autogiro

Cayley, Sir George
Sikorsky, Igor I.
V/STOL

Outline

I. Uses of helicopters
    A. For rescue missions
    B. For aerial observation
    C. For transportation and construction work
    D. For agricultural and forestry operations
    E. For military missions

II. Types of helicopters
    A. Single-rotor helicopters
    B. Twin-rotor helicopters

III. How helicopters fly
    A. Lift
    B. Piloting a helicopter

IV. Development of the helicopter

Questions

What kind of wings does a helicopter have?
How are helicopters used in the construction industry?
What is a *tandem-rotor helicopter*? A *coaxial-rotor helicopter*?
Who built and flew the first practical single-rotor helicopter?
What are some military uses of the helicopter?
Why does a single-rotor helicopter have a tail rotor?
What is a *compound helicopter*?
In what ways can a helicopter fly that an airplane cannot?
What happens when a helicopter pilot raises the collective pitch lever?
Why is helicopter service essential to many offshore oil-drilling operations?

Additional resources

Berliner, Don. *Helicopters.* Lerner, 1983. For younger readers.
Fay, John. *The Helicopter: History, Piloting and How It Flies.* 3rd ed. David & Charles, 1977.
Gablehouse, Charles. *Helicopters and Autogiros.* Rev. ed. Lippincott, 1969.
McDonald, John J. *Flying the Helicopter.* TAB, 1981.
Polmar, Norman, and Kennedy, Floyd D., Jr. *Military Helicopters of the World: Military Rotary-Wing Aircraft Since 1917.* Naval Institute Press, 1981.

Heliograph, *HEE lee uh graf,* was an instrument used to send signals by reflecting sunlight with a mirror or mirrors. Heliographs were used by the armies of several countries during the late 1800's.

Heliograph equipment varied somewhat from country to country. The heliograph used by the U.S. Army had a mirror with a sighting rod—or else two mirrors—mounted on a tripod. A screen or shutter for interrupting the flashes was mounted on another tripod. If the sun was in front of the sender, its rays were reflected directly from a mirror to the receiving station. The sender used the sighting rod to line the flash up with the receiver. If the sun was behind the sender, its rays were reflected from one mirror to another, and from the second mirror to the receiver. The flash was lined up with the receiver by adjusting the two mirrors. Messages were sent as short and long flashes by opening and closing the shutter. The flashes represented the dots and dashes of the Morse code.

The distance that heliograph signals could be seen depended on the clearness of the sky, the length of uninterrupted sight, and the size of the mirrors used. Under ordinary conditions, a flash could be seen 30 miles (48 kilometers) with the naked eye and much farther with a telescope.   Paul J. Scheips

See also **Morse code.**

Helios, *HEE lee ahs,* was the sun and god of the sun in Greek mythology. His sisters were Selene (the moon) and Eos (dawn). The Greeks believed Helios, accompanied by Eos, drove a four-horse chariot across the sky each day. Each evening, a huge golden cup brought him back to his palace in the east on the river Oceanus. His daily journeys made him an all-seeing god, and Greeks often called upon him to witness their oaths. The island of Rhodes was sacred to Helios and a famous statue of him stood there.   Nancy Felson Rubin

See also **Seven Wonders of the Ancient World** (The Colossus of Rhodes); **Phaëthon.**

Heliotrope, *HEE lee uh trohp,* is a popular plant with beautiful, fragrant flowers. These flowers always face toward the sun. Another name for heliotrope is *turnsole.* Both names mean *turning to the sun.*

WORLD BOOK illustration by Christabel King

The heliotrope produces beautiful, fragrant flowers. The tiny star-shaped blossoms form large, colorful clusters on the plant.

The species of heliotrope grown in most places is native to Peru. It grows easily from cuttings or from seed. The plant is shrubby, has many branches, and grows from 1 to 2 feet (30 to 61 centimeters) high. The oval leaves have veins and wrinkles. The tiny, sweet heliotrope blossoms form huge clusters that range from lilac to dark blue in color. Each flower is shaped like a slender tube that broadens into a five-pointed star. The fragrance of the Peruvian heliotrope is like vanilla. Another kind smells like narcissus. Heliotrope perfumes imitate this scent.

Scientific classification. All heliotropes are members of the borage family, Boraginaceae. They make up the genus *Heliotropium.*   Marcus Maxon

Helium, *HEE lee uhm,* is a lightweight gas and chemical element. Hydrogen is the only element that weighs less than helium. Helium is called an *inert gas* or *noble gas.* These terms are used because helium does not combine with other elements.

Helium makes up only a small fraction of the earth's matter. But it is one of the most common elements in the universe. The sun and other stars are made mostly of helium and hydrogen. The energy of these stars is produced when hydrogen atoms *fuse* (join together) to form helium atoms. This process is also what gives the hydrogen bomb its energy (see **Nuclear weapon**).

On the earth, helium occurs in natural gas deposits and in the atmosphere. The atmosphere contains about 5 parts of helium per million parts of air. Because helium is so light, it constantly escapes from the atmosphere and drifts into space. But the lost helium is replaced by radioactive minerals that shoot out *alpha particles* (helium nuclei). Each alpha particle captures two electrons to form a complete helium atom. See **Radioactivity.**

Helium was discovered in the sun by the French astronomer Pierre J. Janssen in 1868. Janssen found evidence of helium while studying a solar eclipse. Sir Joseph Lockyer, an English astronomer, and Sir Edward Frankland, an English chemist, suggested the name helium for the element. The name comes from the Greek word *helios,* meaning sun. In 1895, helium was first found on the earth. The Scottish chemist Sir William Ramsay and the Swedish chemists Nils Langlet and Per Theodor Cleve discovered it in the mineral clevite.

Uses. About 700 million cubic feet (20 million cubic meters) of helium are used in the United States yearly. Federal agencies use about three-fourths of this amount and private industries use the rest.

The government's chief use of helium is in maintaining the proper pressures in rockets. Pressure must be maintained in rocket fuel tanks during flight, or the thin walls of the large tanks might collapse as the fuel drains from them. Helium also produces the pressure that forces fuel into rocket pumping systems.

The largest industrial use of helium is in *heliarc welding* (a type of electric arc welding). The inert helium keeps oxygen in the air from reaching the metal. If oxygen reaches the metal, it may cause the metal either to burn or to corrode. Helium is used to prevent chemicals from reacting with other elements during storage, handling, and transportation.

Helium is also used to fill scientific balloons. The balloons rise to high altitudes, because helium is lighter than air. In air, helium has 92 per cent of the lifting ability of hydrogen. It is safer than hydrogen because it will not burn, as hydrogen will.

Persons with asthma or other breathing difficulties must sometimes inhale a mixture of helium and oxygen. The mixture enters the lungs more easily than air because the helium atoms are lighter than the nitrogen molecules of the air. Divers sometimes breathe a mix-

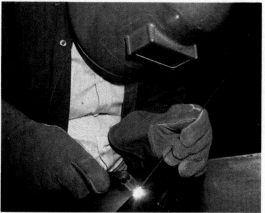

Larry Day

U.S. Navy

Helium has several uses. In heliarc welding, *above,* a blanket of helium is blown over certain metals to protect them from oxygen in the air. A diver, *left,* sometimes breathes a mixture of helium and oxygen to prevent an illness called *nitrogen narcosis.*

ture of helium and oxygen to avoid a painful illness called *nitrogen narcosis.* Nitrogen narcosis usually occurs at depths below 100 feet (30 meters). The pressure of the water on divers' bodies forces bubbles of nitrogen gas from the air into their blood when they breathe. The blood carries the nitrogen to the brain. This illness causes the divers to lose the ability to think clearly, and they may do dangerous things or pass out.

Production. Most of the world's helium comes from five natural-gas fields in the United States: (1) the Cliffside field in the Texas Panhandle, (2) the Greenwood field in Kansas and Colorado, (3) the Hugoton field in Kansas, Oklahoma, and Texas, (4) the Keyes field in Oklahoma, and (5) the Panhandle field in Texas. These fields contain an estimated 180 billion cubic feet (5 billion cubic meters) of helium. Helium plants in the United States produce about 2 billion cubic feet (57 million cubic meters) of helium each year.

Natural gas from some wells contains up to 8 per cent helium. Helium is purified by cooling the natural gas until all gases except helium, argon, hydrogen, and nitrogen change to liquid. Hydrogen is then burned out of the remaining mixture, and argon is absorbed by charcoal at low temperatures. Nitrogen often remains in helium as an impurity. Helium that is 99.995 per cent pure is called *grade A* helium. *Crude* helium contains about half helium and half nitrogen.

Properties. Helium is a colorless, odorless, and tasteless gas. Its chemical symbol is He. Its atomic number is 2 and its atomic weight is 4.00260. Helium has a density of .0001664 grams per cubic centimeter at 20° C. It changes to liquid when it is cooled to −268.9° C, about 4° C above absolute zero. Because helium can be

cooled to such a low temperature without freezing, it is used as a liquid refrigerant in low temperature devices and in cryogenics research (see **Cryogenics**). In addition, helium is the only chemical element that cannot be changed to a solid by cooling alone under ordinary pressures. It must be cooled and compressed. Helium freezes solid at −272.2° C under a pressure of 26 times atmospheric pressure.

Liquid helium is one of the strangest of all liquids. Unlike most liquids, it conducts heat extremely well, it flows toward relatively warm places, and it expands instead of contracting when it cools. Liquid helium forms a film over everything it touches. This film can act as a siphon, carrying helium over the side of a container to a lower level.   Frank C. Andrews

See also **Airship; Balloon; Element, Chemical** (Periodic table); **Ramsay, Sir William.**

Hell, according to many religions, is a place or state inhabited by demons, where wicked people are punished after death. Hell also is a symbol of the most powerful opposition to goodness and justice.

In Old Testament times, the Jews believed that all the dead, both good and evil, went to a dark, unhappy place called *Sheol.* By the time of Christ, some Jews thought that the wicked were separated from the righteous and then cast into a foul, burning valley called *Gehenna.*

Hell is no longer prominent in the teachings of Judaism, but Gehenna became the hell of Christianity and Islam. According to traditional Christian belief, hell is a place of unending anguish and pain caused by the loss of happiness. Through the centuries, however, some Christian theologians have questioned whether a just and loving God would have created such a hell. According to these scholars, hell is not a real place but a symbol of the anguish caused by the loss of God or goodness. Islam, the religion of the Muslims, regards hell as a vast, fiery crater that the souls of the dead cross on a narrow bridge. The wicked fall off the bridge into everlasting torment.

In Hinduism and Buddhism, a soul may descend into one of many hells as a result of wicked *karma* (thoughts, words, and deeds). The stay in hell is not eternal. It lasts only until the effects of the evil karma have been removed.   Robert S. Ellwood, Jr.

See also **Religion** (A doctrine of salvation); **Divine Comedy; Gehenna; Hades; Limbo; Purgatory.**

Hell-diver. See Grebe.

Hell Gate is a channel in the East River between Long Island and Manhattan Island. Early Dutch settlers of New York may have so named it because of its swift current and rough, dangerous reefs. Some people believe that the name Hell Gate came from the Dutch word *Hellegat,* a name once used for the whole of the East River. The channel was made deeper and wider in 1885. It is now 200 feet (61 meters) wide and 26 feet (8 meters) deep, and can be used by large ocean vessels. Hell Gate Bridge and the Triborough Bridge span the East River at this point.   William E. Young

Hellebore, *HEHL uh bawr,* is the common name of a genus of plants in the crowfoot family. They are found in Europe and Asia. Hellebores are perennials. They have thick, fibrous roots and large flowers. The *Christmas rose,* or *black hellebore,* blooms from late fall to early spring. Its white or pale purple flowers look like single roses. Its roots and leaves contain a powerful poison.

False hellebores, which are not related to the true hellebores, are found in Europe, Asia, and North America. The *American white hellebore,* or *Indian poke,* grows in damp places from Canada to Georgia. It is 2 to 8 feet (0.6 to 2.4 meters) high and has small green or greenish-yellow flowers. Its roots are dried and ground to powder for use as an insecticide.

Scientific classification. Hellebores belong to the crowfoot family, Ranunculaceae. They make up the genus *Helleborus.* The Christmas rose is *H. niger.* False hellebores are in the lily family, Liliaceae. American white hellebore is *Veratrum viride.*

Harold Norman Moldenke

Hellenes. See Greece, Ancient.

Hellenistic Age was a period in ancient history when Greek culture dominated much of what was then the civilized world. It began after the death of Alexander the Great in 323 B.C., and lasted nearly 200 years in Greece and almost 300 years in the Near East. The term *Hellenistic* is used to distinguish this period from the earlier Greek classical or *Hellenic* period.

The Hellenistic Age was a period of great achievement in scholarship, science, and the arts. For example, the mathematician Euclid developed the principles of geometry, and the inventor Archimedes discovered many basic laws of physics. The astronomer Aristarchus of Samos suggested that all the planets, including the earth, revolve around the sun. The mathematician Eratosthenes made a nearly correct calculation of the earth's circumference.

Paintings and sculpture became more realistic. Hellenistic sculptors created such masterpieces as the *Laocoön* and the *Winged Victory of Samothrace.*

Philosophers of the period were concerned with how people could achieve peace of mind. The major groups of Hellenistic philosophers were (1) the Stoics, (2) the Epicureans, and (3) the Cynics. *Stoics* believed that happiness resulted when people learned to accept events beyond their control and did their duty. *Epicureans* sought pleasure in moderation and avoidance of pain. *Cynics* tried to disregard all desires and pleasures, and pursued virtue. For religion, many people worshiped such Egyptian divinities as Isis and Serapis.

Earlier, Greece had been divided into independent *city-states,* each of which consisted of a city and its surrounding territory. During the Hellenistic Age, the city-states lost their independence. They came under the control of monarchies that governed large kingdoms. Some monarchs claimed to rule by divine right.

The major dynasties of the age were the Ptolemies of Egypt, Antigonids of Macedonia, Seleucids of Syria, and Attalids of Pergamum (now western Turkey). They fought against each other and among themselves. This disunity helped the Romans conquer most of the Hellenistic world in the 100's B.C. Donald Kagan

See also **Greece, Ancient** (The Hellenistic Age); **Sculpture** (Hellenistic sculpture).

Heller, Joseph (1923-), is an American novelist who established his reputation with the comic novel *Catch-22* (1961). The title describes the accumulated absurdities that characterize some complex organizations. The organization in *Catch-22* is the military. The novel is set during World War II and describes the misadventures of Yossarian, a U.S. officer. His ways of retaining

his identity depend on his ability to maneuver within an absurd and illogical system. In *Something Happened* (1974), Heller described the psychological pressures faced by an American business executive. *Good as Gold* (1979) describes the personal and professional problems of an American college professor. *God Knows* (1984) is a comic novel written in the form of an autobiography of the Biblical leader King David. With Speed Vogel, Heller wrote *No Laughing Matter* (1986), an autobiographical account of Heller's battle against a paralyzing illness.

Heller was born in Brooklyn, N.Y. He has been a teacher, an advertising writer, and a magazine promotion manager. Joseph N. Riddel

Heller, Walter Wolfgang (1915-1987), was an American economist who served as chairman of the Council of Economic Advisers from 1961 to 1964 under Presidents John F. Kennedy and Lyndon B. Johnson. Heller helped persuade both Presidents to rely heavily on economists in forming national policies. He played a major role in developing the "new economics"—the concept that the government should strive to control economic growth. During the early 1960's, he worked for fiscal and monetary actions to stimulate the economy. He was largely responsible for the tax cut passed by Congress in 1964.

Heller was born in Buffalo, N.Y. He received his Ph.D. from the University of Wisconsin in 1941 and taught economics at the University of Minnesota from 1946 to 1986. Heller's books include *State Income Tax Administration* (1959) and *New Dimensions of Political Economy* (1966). Leonard S. Silk

Hellespont, *HEHL ih SPAHNT,* is the former name of the strait between the Sea of Marmara and the Aegean Sea. Today, this strait is called the Dardanelles. The Hellespont was named for the mythical Helle, daughter of Athamas, king of Thessaly. Helle and her brother Phrixus ran away from their stepmother. They were flying across the sea on the ram of the Golden Fleece, when Helle fell and drowned. According to legend, Leander swam the Hellespont each night to see Hero, with whom he was in love. Padraic Colum

See also **Dardanelles; Hero and Leander.**

Hellgrammite, *HEHL gruh myt,* is the larva of a four-winged insect known as the dobsonfly. Hellgram-

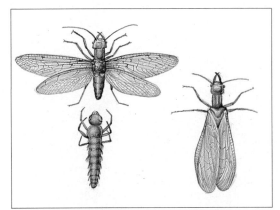

WORLD BOOK illustration by Shirley Hooper, Oxford Illustrators, Limited

Hellgrammite is the large black larva of an insect called the dobsonfly. Hellgrammites live in swift streams in North America.

mites live under stones in swift streams of North America. They have strong jaws and prey upon small water animals. They are a popular bait for bass fishing because they wriggle about. When hellgrammites are fully grown they leave the water, pupate for about two weeks, and emerge as dobsonflies.

Scientific classification. Dobsonflies belong to the order Neuroptera. They are *Corydalus cornutus.*   Carl L. Hubbs

Hellman, Lillian (1905-1984), was an American playwright whose work combines skillful construction with insight into psychological weakness and a deep concern with the social issues of her time. Her tightly woven plots reach strong dramatic climaxes, but maintain serious purpose and honest characterizations.

Hellman's plays of the 1930's and 1940's stress various forms of destructive selfishness and greed in individuals and in society. In *The Children's Hour* (1934), a resentful child ruins the lives of two female teachers by accusing them of an abnormal relationship. *The Little Foxes* (1939) is generally considered her best play. In it, material greed and lust for power release vicious passions within a Southern family. The family is a symbol of modern society. *Another Part of the Forest* (1946) shows similar corrupting forces in the preceding generation of the family. In *Watch on the Rhine* (1941), a passive, gentle man reluctantly chooses to act against the destructive evil of a Nazi.

Hellman's later plays also deal with human weakness, but do not place the same emphasis on social problems. The best of these plays include *The Autumn Garden* (1951) and *Toys in the Attic* (1960). Her autobiography, *An Unfinished Woman* (1969), won the National Book Award for arts and letters in 1970. Her first 12 plays were published as *The Collected Plays* (1972). She also wrote *Pentimento* (1973), a series of portraits of people she has known. She was born in New Orleans.   Alan Casty

Helmet is a dome-shaped hat of metal, leather, cork, or some other sturdy material. Its primary purpose is to protect the head. Helmets are shaped to fit well down over the head to protect the ears, neck, and eyes. Helmets are worn by soldiers, aviators, fire fighters, some police officers, some athletes, and some industrial workers. In tropical climates, people may wear *pith helmets* or *cork helmets* to protect their heads from the sun.

The steel helmet of infantry soldiers during World War II was worn over a light helmet liner that fitted

© Don Eaton, Higgins Armory Museum

A gladiator's helmet shielded a warrior who fought battles staged as entertainment for the ancient Romans.

Bequest of George C. Stone, 1936, The Metropolitan Museum of Art

Chinese helmet

Rogers Fund, 1904, The Metropolitan Museum of Art

Turkish helmet

© Michael T. J. Kulik

Modern combat helmet

AP/Wide World

Football helmet

© Mine Safety Appliances Company

Miner's helmet

NASA

Astronaut's helmet

Fletcher Fund, 1935, The Metropolitan Museum of Art

Greek helmet

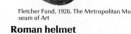
Fletcher Fund, 1926, The Metropolitan Museum of Art

Roman helmet

snugly into the steel helmet. The sweatband of the helmet liner was the only part which rested on the head. The steel helmet could not stop a bullet coming head-on, but acted as a shield against glancing bullets, falling earth and shot, and blows. In the field, a soldier often used his helmet as a cooking pot, dish, or wash basin.

The first helmets were worn by Ethiopian soldiers, who placed the skulls of horses, complete with ears and mane, on their heads. Ancient Assyrians, Persians, Greeks, and Romans used helmets. In the Middle Ages, knights usually wore helmets.   Theodore Ropp

See also **Armor; Bronze** (picture: Chalcidian helmet).

Helmholtz, *HEHLM hohlts,* **Hermann Ludwig Ferdinand von** *HEHR mahn LOOT vihk FEHR dih nahnt fuhn* (1821-1894), a German physicist, helped prove the law of the conservation of energy (see **Energy** [The conservation of energy]). His research on sound ranked as the outstanding work of his time in acoustics. He was the first to apply physical methods to the study of the nervous system by measuring the speed of nerve impulses. Helmholtz also invented the ophthalmoscope, used by doctors to examine eyes. He was born in Potsdam. See also **Color** (The three-component theory); **Ophthalmoscope; Heat** (Learning about heat).

R. T. Ellickson

Helminthology, *HEHL mihn THAL uh jee,* is the study of worms. Specialists in this field are *helminthologists.* See also **Worm.**

Helmont, Jan Baptista van. See **Gas** (History).

Helms, Jesse Alexander (1921-   ), has been a United States senator from North Carolina since 1973. He was the first Republican elected to the Senate from his state since 1895. Helms attracted a wide following among conservatives and became one of the most influential senators in the 1980's, during the Administration of President Ronald Reagan.

In 1981, Helms introduced a controversial bill in the Senate that would outlaw abortion at any time during a pregnancy. The bill declared that human life, as protected by the United States Constitution, begins at the time of *conception,* when a sperm fertilizes an egg. Helms also sponsored bills that would permit prayer in public schools, prohibit the busing of students solely to achieve racial integration, and require a balanced federal budget. From 1981 to 1987, Helms was chairman of the Senate Committee on Agriculture, Nutrition, and Forestry.

Helms was born in Monroe, N.C. He served on the Raleigh (N.C.) City Council from 1957 to 1961. From 1960 until his election to the U.S. Senate in 1972, Helms was an executive and commentator for the Capitol Broadcasting Company in Raleigh.   Lee Thornton

Héloïse. See **Abelard, Peter.**

Helsinki, *HEHL sihng kee* (pop. 484,471; met. area pop. 932,376), is the capital and largest city of Finland. It is also one of the nation's chief ports and the heart of its commercial and cultural life. Nearly 20 per cent of the Finnish people live in Helsinki or its suburbs. The city lies on the southern coast of the country, on the Gulf of Finland, and occupies a peninsula and several islands. For location, see **Finland** (political map).

Helsinki is a city of scenic bays and broad, treelined streets. The contrast of old and new architecture adds to its charm. The center of the city's old section is Senate

J. Messerschmidt, Bruce Coleman Inc.

The main cathedral of Helsinki towers over the city's harbor. Helsinki is famous for its many beautiful buildings.

Square, which has many buildings designed in the neoclassical style of the 1800's. They include the Government Palace and a towering Lutheran cathedral. The main business districts of Helsinki are west of Senate Square. These newer sections of the city include buildings designed by some of the finest modern architects. Most of Helsinki's people live in apartments. Since the mid-1900's, many apartment buildings have been converted to office buildings. Large numbers of people have moved to various suburbs, which include outstanding examples of city planning.

Universities in Helsinki include the Technical University and the University of Helsinki, which is Finland's principal university. The city has many theaters and several art galleries and museums. Its islands and parks have facilities for boating, skiing, swimming, and other sports.

Most of the city's people work for the government or in commerce, communications, and service occupations. Industrial employment has declined because some manufacturers have moved from the city to the suburbs. However, Helsinki remains the main Finnish industrial area. Its chief products include ceramics, clothing, machinery, paper, plywood, refined sugar, and ships.

Helsinki was founded in 1550 by King Gustavus I of Sweden, which then ruled Finland. Russia and Sweden fought numerous wars in Finland from the 1500's through the 1700's, and Helsinki twice was nearly destroyed in the fighting. The city passed from Swedish to Russian rule in 1809. In 1812, Czar Alexander I made Helsinki the capital of Finland and ordered a large-scale program of city planning and construction. Many of the impressive buildings around Senate Square were erected at that time. By 1900, Helsinki had become an industrial city with a population of more than 100,000.

Finland gained independence from Russia in 1917, and the Helsinki region's population and commercial importance have increased steadily since then. Today, Helsinki is the site of many international conferences. A striking convention center, built in the shape of a grand piano, opened in 1975. Pekka Kalevi Hamalainen

See also **Finland** (Climate; pictures).

Helsinki Agreement, *HEHL sihng kee,* is an agreement that pledged increased cooperation between the nations of Eastern and Western Europe. Its primary goal was to reduce international tensions that remained from World War II and the Cold War. Leaders of every European country except Albania and Andorra, along with those of the United States, Canada, and Cyprus, signed the agreement in Helsinki, Finland, on Aug. 1, 1975. The signing ended the Conference on Security and Cooperation in Europe, which was held from 1973 to 1975.

The agreement called for economic cooperation and the freer exchange of people and ideas across international borders. It also provided for the formal recognition of European borders as established after World War II ended in 1945, as well as better conditions for journalists working abroad, cooperation in education, and expanded cultural exchanges.

One section of the agreement dealt with such fundamental human rights as freedom of thought, religion, and conscience. Referring to this point, several writers and educators in the Soviet Union and other Communist countries publicly protested what they considered human rights violations by their government. Jimmy Carter, who became U.S. President in 1977, strongly supported the human rights. As a result, some Communist governments accused the United States of violating a provision of the agreement restricting interference by a country in the internal affairs of another nation.

Representatives of all the nations that participated in the original talks agreed to meet regularly to review the agreement. Further meetings took place during the late 1970's and early 1980's. Herbert J. Ellison

Helvetia. See **Switzerland.**

Helvetians, *hehl VEE shuhnz,* were members of a tribe that lived in what is now northwestern Switzerland. Germanic tribes threatened the Helvetians, and about 263,000 Helvetians tried to move to the Roman province of Gaul in 58 B.C. Julius Caesar's troops killed many Helvetians, and the survivors were forced to return home. Under Augustus, emperor from 27 B.C. to A.D. 14, Rome conquered all of Switzerland. The Helvetians adopted Rome's customs and its Latin language. The French-speaking people of western Switzerland sometimes refer to their area as *Helvetia.* Chester G. Starr

Hemangioma. See **Birthmark.**

Hemapheresis. See **Blood transfusion** (How blood is collected and stored).

Hematite, *HEHM uh tyt,* is an ore that supplies most of the world's iron. It is a *ferric oxide* (a compound of iron and oxygen) and has the chemical formula Fe_2O_3. In its purest form, hematite consists of about 70 per cent iron. The ore occurs in a variety of forms, including shiny crystals; grainy rock; and loose, earthy material. Hematite is black, brownish-red, or dark red, but a fresh scratch on hematite rock is blood-red. The word *hematite* means *bloodlike. Red ocher,* an earthy form of hematite, is used to color paint.

About 20 per cent of the iron produced in North America comes from hematite. Deposits of the ore lie near Lake Superior in Michigan, Minnesota, and Wisconsin; and in Alabama and Tennessee. Large amounts of hematite also occur near the border of Labrador and Quebec, and in Ontario. Other sources include Australia, Brazil, and South Africa. Donald F. Eschman

See also **Taconite.**

Hematology. See **Blood** (Medical uses of blood).

Hemingway, Ernest (1899-1961), was one of the most famous and influential American writers of the 1900's. He received the Nobel Prize for literature in 1954. He had won a Pulitzer Prize the previous year for his novel *The Old Man and the Sea* (1952).

Hemingway developed a plain, forceful prose style characterized by simple sentences and few adjectives or adverbs. He wrote crisp, vivid dialogue and exact descriptions of places and things. His style has been imitated by many writers.

Hemingway also created a type of male character, sometimes called the *Hemingway hero,* who faces violence and destruction with courage. The trait of "grace under pressure"—that is, unemotional behavior even in highly dangerous situations—is part of what became known as the *Hemingway code.*

Look Magazine from UPI
Ernest Hemingway

Early life. Ernest Miller Hemingway was born in Oak Park, Ill. After graduating from high school, he worked briefly as a reporter for the *Kansas City Star.* During World War I (1914-1918), he served as a volunteer ambulance driver in Italy and then as an infantryman in the Italian Army. He was seriously wounded in 1918. Hemingway's wartime experiences help explain why his writing emphasizes physical and psychological violence and the need for courage.

In 1921, Hemingway went to Paris, where he met a number of American authors, including F. Scott Fitzgerald, Ezra Pound, and Gertrude Stein. Hemingway became the principal spokesman for a group of disillusioned younger writers whom Stein named the "lost generation."

Hemingway's first published work, *Three Stories and Ten Poems,* appeared in 1923. It was followed by *In Our Time* (1924), a collection of short stories about his boyhood experiences in northern Michigan.

Rise to fame. Hemingway's most famous novels are two of his early works, *The Sun Also Rises* (1926) and *A Farewell to Arms* (1929). *The Sun Also Rises* portrays a group of Americans who, like the members of the "lost generation," were disillusioned by the war. *A Farewell to Arms,* set in Italy in World War I, is a tragic love story.

Hemingway returned to the United States in 1927. Two collections of his short stories were published during the 1930's. They contain some of his best writing, including "A Clean, Well-Lighted Place," "The Short Happy Life of Francis Macomber," and "The Snows of Kilimanjaro." He also wrote some nonfiction. *Death in the Afternoon* (1932) deals with bullfighting, which fascinated him. In *Green Hills of Africa* (1935), Hemingway described his experiences on an African safari.

In 1936, Hemingway went to Spain and covered the

Eastern and Western hemispheres

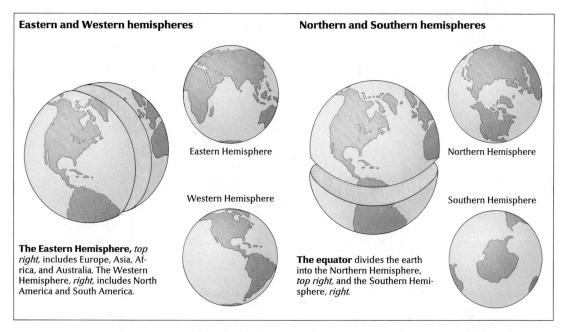

Eastern Hemisphere

Western Hemisphere

The Eastern Hemisphere, *top right,* includes Europe, Asia, Africa, and Australia. The Western Hemisphere, *right,* includes North America and South America.

Northern and Southern hemispheres

Northern Hemisphere

Southern Hemisphere

The equator divides the earth into the Northern Hemisphere, *top right,* and the Southern Hemisphere, *right.*

Spanish Civil War as a war correspondent. He used the war as the setting of *For Whom the Bell Tolls* (1940). This novel describes the adventures of an idealistic American fighting the fascist forces in Spain. It is one of Hemingway's finest books.

Later years. By the 1940's, Hemingway had become an international celebrity. He was famous for his colorful life style and his extreme concern with presenting a tough, masculine image.

Hemingway's first published work after 1940 was *Across the River and Into the Trees* (1950). This novel reflects his growing bitterness toward life. It is largely regarded as inferior because of its sentimentality. In *The Old Man and the Sea* (1952), Hemingway revived his theme of a strong man courageously accepting fate. The hero, an old fisherman, catches a giant marlin after a long, brutal struggle—only to have it eaten by sharks.

Hemingway suffered physical and mental illnesses during the 1950's, and he committed suicide in 1961. *A Moveable Feast* was published in 1964, after his death. It is an autobiographical book based on notebooks he kept in Paris in the 1920's. Two novels were also published after his death—*Islands in the Stream* (1970) and the unfinished *The Garden of Eden* (1986). Dean Doner

Additional resources

Baker, Carlos H. *Ernest Hemingway: A Life Story.* Scribner, 1969.
Young, Philip. *Ernest Hemingway: A Reconsideration.* Rev. ed. Pennsylvania State Univ. Press, 1966.

Hemiptera. See Bug and its list of *Related articles.*

Hemisphere, *HEHM uh sfihr,* is the name given to any half of the globe. It comes from the Greek word *hemisphairion,* which means *half a sphere.* The earth may be divided into six hemispheres. The Eastern Hemisphere, or Old World, includes the continents of Europe, Asia, Africa, and Australia. North America and South America make up the Western Hemisphere, or New World. Geographers have not definitely established boundaries

between the Eastern and Western hemispheres. But they usually draw them along the meridians of 20° West Longitude and 160° East Longitude.

Geographers also divide the earth into hemispheres by using the equator as a boundary line. All areas lying north of the equator make up the Northern Hemisphere, and all areas to the south make up the Southern Hemisphere.

The earth may also be divided into a land hemisphere and a water hemisphere. The land hemisphere includes the half of the earth with the most land. Its center lies near London, England. The other half of the earth, mostly water, makes up the water hemisphere. Its center lies near New Zealand. Samuel N. Dicken

Hemlock is a poisonous biennial herb sometimes called *poison hemlock.* It has many branches, purple-spotted hollow stems, and numerous clusters of small, white flowers. It grows from 2 to 6 feet (61 to 180 centimeters) high. Its egg-shaped fruit grows about $\frac{1}{8}$ inch (3 millimeters) long and ripens in August or September. Its leaves look like those of parsley, for which it is often mistaken. But the hemlock can be quickly recognized. It has a disagreeable odor that becomes quite strong

Poison hemlock has spreading flower stalks that resemble tiny umbrellas. The leaves contain a deadly poison.

when its leaves or stems are bruised. The plant is native to Europe and some parts of Asia. But it has been brought to North America.

Persons mistaking hemlock for parsley may be poisoned. Children are sometimes poisoned by hemlock when they make whistles or peashooters from its hollow stems. The plant can be killed by using 2,4-D and 2,4,5-T spray. The ancient Greeks made a brew from hemlock and gave it to criminals condemned to death. The philosopher Socrates died by drinking this brew.

Scientific classification. Poison hemlock belongs to the parsley family, Umbelliferae. It is classified as *Conium maculatum.*   Louis Pyenson

Hemlock is the common name of stately evergreen trees belonging to the pine family. They grow in the forests of North America, Japan, China, and India.

Hemlocks have blunt, soft needles. These are joined to the twig by small woody stalks that remain on the twig when the needles fall off. These small, peglike projections are a distinctive feature.

Eastern, or *Canadian, hemlock* ranges from southern Canada to the mountains of Georgia. It may live up to 800 years. It is a medium-to-large tree with a dense, pyramid-shaped crown. Its short, dark-green needles grow in two rows. Each needle has two whitish bands on its lower surface. The bark of this hemlock is an important source of tannin for the leather industry. The wood is soft, and splinters easily. It is used for building frames and clapboards. This kind of hemlock is the state tree of Pennsylvania.

Carolina hemlock is a handsome but rare tree found high in the Appalachian Mountains from Virginia to northern Georgia. The dark green needles extend from all sides of the twig instead of appearing in two rows. *Western hemlock* is an important tree of the Pacific Northwest and is the state tree of Washington. It resembles the Canadian hemlock, but is larger. It can grow to a height of 200 feet (60 meters) with a trunk diameter of 8 feet (2.4 meters). Its wood is valued both for lumber and for pulp. *Mountain hemlock* is found in the mountains from Alaska to California. It grows on ridges exposed to severe weather.

Scientific classification. Hemlocks belong to the pine family, Pinaceae. The Eastern hemlock is *Tsuga canadensis.* Carolina hemlock is *T. caroliniana.* Western hemlock is *T. heterophylla,* and mountain hemlock is *T. mertensiana.*   Ross W. Wein

See also **Cone-bearing plant; Tree** (Familiar broadleaf and needleleaf trees of North America [picture]).

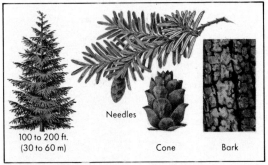

100 to 200 ft.
(30 to 60 m)

Needles

Cone

Bark

WORLD BOOK illustration by Chris Skilton

The western hemlock is a valuable timber tree.

Hemodialysis. See **Kidney** (Kidney diseases).

Hemoglobin, *HEE muh* GLOH *buhn,* is the pigment that transports oxygen in the blood. It is located in the red blood cells, and it gives blood its red color. When the red cells file through the *alveoli,* or air sacs, of the lungs, they take up oxygen. The hemoglobin combines with the oxygen to form a compound called *oxyhemoglobin.* When the red cells travel through the rest of the body, they give up the oxygen to the tissues. In the tissues, the hemoglobin takes up carbon dioxide, and releases it in the alveoli of the lungs. The carbon dioxide is then exhaled.

Hemoglobin is a complex molecule that includes iron and a protein called *globin.* Anemia may result from a shortage of hemoglobin or from hereditary abnormalities in the hemoglobin (see **Anemia**). Some kinds of poisons combine with hemoglobin in such a way that it can no longer combine with oxygen. Thus, aniline dyes and other chemicals cause the formation of *methemoglobin,* which cannot take up oxygen. The blood then becomes bluish-brown. Carbon monoxide, a poisonous gas, combines readily with hemoglobin, making the blood bright-red. But carbon monoxide prevents blood from taking up oxygen.

Scientists have identified many different kinds of hemoglobin. A person's hemoglobin type is inherited. *Hemoglobin A* ranks as the most common type. One abnormal type, called *hemoglobin S* or *sickle hemoglobin,* causes the disease sickle cell anemia. Red blood cells that contain mostly hemoglobin S may become stiff and misshapen. These cells may then plug blood vessels. See **Sickle cell anemia.**   Joseph V. Simone

See also **Blood; Hemolysis; Iron; Perutz, Max F.**

Hemolysis, *hih MAHL uh sihs,* is the breakdown of red blood cells. In the final stages of breakdown, *hemoglobin* (red pigment) is released from the red cells. Hemolysis in small amounts is a normal body process. About .8 of 1 per cent of all red cells in the body are *hemolyzed* (broken down) each day. Hemolysis is usually balanced by red cell production in the *marrow* (center part) of the bones. But, sometimes so many cells break down that marrow production is insufficient, and anemia may result. Chemical poisons may cause excessive hemolysis. Or hemolysis may occur when the body produces *autoantibodies* which cause red cells to break down.   Edward E. Morse

Hémon, *ay MAWN,* **Louis,** *lwee* (1880-1913), was a French author best known for his novel *Maria Chapdelaine.* This book describes the hardships of *habitants* (French-Canadian farmers) in the harsh climate of the Lac Saint-Jean region of southern Quebec. It is a classic portrait of the spirit and traditions of the habitants.

Hémon was born in Brest. In 1902, he moved to London, where he wrote for a newspaper. Hémon emigrated to Canada in 1911 and worked on a farm near Roberval, Que., for several months. He based *Maria Chapdelaine* on his experiences on the farm. Hémon died in a train accident shortly after completing the novel and mailing it to a French magazine. The magazine published the work in 1914. It appeared in book form in 1916.   Rosemary Sullivan

Hemophilia, *HEE muh FIHL ee uh,* is a hereditary disease in which the blood does not clot normally. People with hemophilia, called *hemophiliacs,* bleed excessively when injured because their blood clots extremely slowly. Almost all hemophiliacs are males.

Blood must contain a number of substances called *clotting factors* for clotting to take place. A hemophiliac's blood lacks the active form of one of these factors. Hemophiliacs suffer most when internal blood vessels break, causing bleeding into such areas as the head or joints. Leaking blood accumulates in these areas, putting pressure on the surrounding tissues and causing pain, swelling, and loss of function. Many hemophiliacs become crippled from repeated bleeding into joints. Some people believe that hemophiliacs can bleed to death from even a small external cut. However, such deaths do not occur because blood contains clotting factors that halt bleeding from the skin.

How hemophilia is inherited. Hemophilia is caused by a defective gene on the *X chromosome,* one of the two chromosomes that determine a person's sex (see **Heredity** [Patterns of heredity]). The *Y chromosome,* which has no genes for clotting factors, is the other. Males have one X chromosome and one Y chromosome. Females have two X chromosomes.

A boy who inherits the hemophilia defect on his X chromosome will be a hemophiliac. A girl who inherits the defective gene on one of her X chromosomes will be a *carrier.* She may transmit the defective gene to her children. But she will not be a hemophiliac because the normal gene on her other X chromosome provides enough of the essential clotting factor. In extremely rare cases, a girl inherits the defective gene on both X chromosomes and will be a hemophiliac.

Major types of hemophilia include classical hemophilia and Christmas disease. The name of Christmas disease comes from the last name of one of the first patients to be treated for it. About 85 per cent of all hemophiliacs have classical hemophilia. Their blood lacks a protein called *clotting factor number 8.* Nearly all other victims have Christmas disease, which involves the lack of *clotting factor number 9.* An extremely small number of hemophiliacs lack another kind of clotting factor.

Hemophilia

Hemophilia is a hereditary disease in which the blood does not clot normally. It results from a defective gene on the X chromosome, one of two sex chromosomes. Males have one X and one Y chromosome. Females have two X chromosomes.

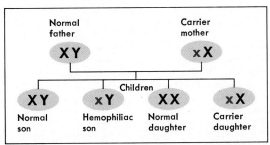

WORLD BOOK diagram

In the chart above, the small red x indicates the chromosome with the defect. A male who inherits the defective gene has hemophilia. A female who inherits it on only one X chromosome is a *carrier.* She does not have the disease, but she can pass the defective gene on to her children. Each son of a normal father and a carrier mother has one chance in two of being a hemophiliac. Each daughter has one chance in two of being a carrier.

A blood disorder called *von Willebrand's disease* is sometimes confused with hemophilia. Unlike hemophilia, von Willebrand's disease causes prolonged external bleeding and affects both sexes. However, few people with this disorder suffer bleeding into the joints.

Treatment for hemophilia consists of injections of the clotting factor that victims lack in their blood. The injections temporarily cause normal clotting. Treatment should be given soon after an injury, so that blood does not accumulate and thus damage body tissues. Many hemophiliacs keep a supply of clotting factor and inject themselves.   David Green

See also **Bleeding; Blood** (Blood clotting).

Hemorrhage, *HEHM uh rihj,* is bleeding, either within the body tissues or from the body surface. Severe hemorrhage may bring on dizziness or a sick feeling. Patients become pale, and their pulse and breathing are weak and rapid. They may go into a condition of shock. Loss of too much blood will result in death. See also **Bleeding; Cerebral hemorrhage; First aid; Tourniquet.**   James N. Davis

Hemorrhoids, *HEHM uh roydz,* are enlargements of the veins of the rectum. This condition is often called *piles.* There are two sets of veins in the rectum. The *internal* veins line the lower rectum and extend upward. The *external* veins lie beneath the skin at the bowel outlet. When any of these veins *dilate* (enlarge), they become hemorrhoids.

Many people seem to inherit a tendency toward developing hemorrhoids. However, any condition that causes prolonged or repeated increases in the blood pressure in the rectal veins may contribute to the development of hemorrhoids. Such conditions include constipation, pregnancy, and long periods of standing.

Hemorrhoids of the external veins usually cause little discomfort unless a blood clot forms in the affected vein and results in inflammation. Hemorrhoids of the internal veins may bleed or descend through the *anus* (rectal opening) as a result of bowel movements. Such hemorrhoids may cause pain or itching. Mild cases can be treated with medicated ointments or *suppositories* (inserted capsules), or by soaking in warm water. In cases where the victim repeatedly suffers painful attacks or bleeding, a physician may remove the hemorrhoids surgically.   James D. Whiffen

Hemp is a tall plant that provides useful fibers for making rope and cloth. It is raised in Asia, where it originated, as well as in Europe and North America.

Growing hemp. Hemp is an annual plant. Some kinds are grown for their seeds, and some are raised for their fiber. Both seed and fiber hemp have their pollen, or *staminate,* flowers on different plants from those that produce the seed, or *pistillate,* flowers. The pollen flowers are yellowish-green and grow in large clusters. The smaller, less colorful pistillate flowers bloom later.

Fiber hemp can be sown simply by scattering the seed on the ground. Each seed grows to a single slender stem 4 to 12 feet (1 to 4 meters) high. Fiber hemp is harvested when the pollen flowers have fully blossomed.

Seed hemp is planted in furrows, or drills, with earth covering them. The stalk reaches a height of 10 to 20 feet (3 to 6 meters). It is thicker than the fiber-hemp stalk, and has many branches.

E. R. Degginger

Hemp provides fibers that are used to make rope and cloth. Two drugs, marijuana and hashish, are obtained from hemp.

Hemp grows best in a moist, mild climate. The soil must be kept well drained, fertile, and free of acidity. The rich loamy soil of the Kentucky bluegrass region is well suited to it. In California, hemp thrives best in the fertile soils of low-lying lands along the rivers.

Hemp is harvested in the United States by reapers or harvesting machines that mow the stalks and spread them in even layers at the same time. After the long stalks are gathered, the hemp fibers must be removed. The fibers consist of many strings of long cells knitted together. They lie in the inner bark along the stem and must be separated from the bark, vegetable gums, and woody stem around them.

To free the fibers, the stalks are either soaked in soft water or hung up in the open, where they are exposed to the weather, especially to the action of dew. This process is called *retting,* or *rotting*. The water or the dew makes the matter around the fiber become rotten, so it can be removed easily. Italian hemp makers use the water-retting method and produce the finest hemp in the world. Their fibers are fine, lustrous, soft, and creamy white. American hemp growers use dew retting, which produces grayish fibers. It is cheaper than water retting.

When the material around the fibers rots enough, the stalks are beaten and crushed with a heavy wooden club. The fiber is freed from the stem and cleaned roughly. The rough fiber is tied into bales and sold.

Uses. Hemp fiber has great strength, and makes good rope and cordage. Twines, carpet thread, carpet yarns, sailcloth, and coarse sheeting and toweling are also made from hemp fiber. The waste fiber, called *oakum,* is often used as caulking. Some hemp is used in paper-making. Hempseeds are used as bird food as well as a source of marijuana and oil for soaps and paints (see **Marijuana**). A cordage fiber called *manila* hemp is made from the *abacá* plant.

Scientific classification. Hemp belongs to the mulberry family, Moraceae. It is *Cannabis sativa*. American hemp belongs to the mallow family, Malvaceae. It is *Abutilon theophrastii*.

Harold Norman Moldenke

See also **Abacá; Jute; Rope; Sisal.**

Hen. See Chicken.

Henbane, *HEHN bayn,* is a poisonous herb that is especially fatal to fowls. It is also called *black henbane.* Henbane is native to the Eastern Hemisphere, but also grows in North America. The plant has a bad odor. It grows from 1 to $2\frac{1}{2}$ feet (30 to 76 centimeters) high, and has sticky, hairy leaves and greenish-yellow flowers veined with purple. A drug made from henbane, called hyoscyamine, is used to dilate the pupils of the eyes.

Scientific classification. Henbane belongs to the night-shade family, Solanaceae. It is *Hyoscyamus niger.*

Harold Norman Moldenke

Henday, Anthony (? - ?), an English explorer and fur trader in Canada, was the first white man to visit the Blackfoot Indians and to report on their customs and habits. He left Hudson Bay in 1754 to travel to the Saskatchewan River. He made important explorations in what is now the province of Alberta. He was born on the Isle of Wight. James G. Allen

Henderson, Fletcher (1898-1952), was the first jazz artist to introduce the concept of the "big band" divided into brass, reed, and rhythm sections. Henderson's band was prominent from 1923 until 1938, but never achieved the fame critics believe it deserved. It included such jazz stars as Louis Armstrong, Buster Bailey, Coleman Hawkins, and Don Redman. Beginning in 1935, during the "swing era," Henderson gained fame as the writer of many successful arrangements for the Benny Goodman band.

Henderson was born in Cuthbert, Ga. He studied science in college, but drifted into music after moving to New York City in 1920. He played piano for Ethel Waters and other singers, and later wrote arrangements for several bands, including those led by Isham Jones and the Dorsey brothers. Leonard Feather

Hendricks, Thomas Andrews (1819-1885), was Vice President of the United States under President Grover Cleveland. Hendricks served as Vice President for only eight months before he died in office. He had sought the Democratic presidential nomination in 1868, 1876, 1880, and 1884. Although he was not a nominee in 1872, he received 42 of the 66 Democratic electoral votes won in that election. This happened because Horace Greeley, the Democratic nominee, died before the Electoral College met.

Hendricks was the unsuccessful Democratic nominee for Vice President in 1876 before winning with Cleveland in 1884. He served in the U.S. House of Representatives from 1851 to 1855 and in the Senate from 1863 to 1869. He was elected governor of Indiana in 1872.

Hendricks was born near Zanesville, Ohio. He was graduated from South Hanover (now Hanover) College in Indiana in 1841. Hendricks served in both houses of the Indiana state legislature. Irving G. Williams

Hendrix, Jimi (1942-1970), was a famous American rock music guitarist. He extended the range of the electric guitar chiefly by experimenting with the electronic elements of the instrument. For example, he manipulated switches on the guitar and pedals on the guitar amplifier to create sounds that were new to rock. Hendrix' music emphasized loud volume, a strong beat, and long solo passages that achieved great emotional impact.

James Marshall Hendrix was born in Seattle. During

the early 1960's, he toured as a guitarist with many famous rhythm and blues performers. He moved to New York City in the mid-1960's and formed his own band. In late 1966, Hendrix went to England and organized a new band called the Jimi Hendrix Experience. He gained international fame with the band, and continued to perform in concerts in Europe and the United States. Hendrix

Joel Axelrad, Retna Ltd.

Jimi Hendrix

died in London at the age of 27 of complications arising from a drug overdose.   Jerry M. Grigadean

Henequen, *HEHN uh kihn,* is a yellow rope fiber made from the leaves of an agave plant of Yucatán. The henequen plant is related to the century plant and to sisal hemp. The shiny-tipped leaves of henequen grow from a trunk, and are sometimes $7\frac{1}{2}$ feet (2.3 meters) long and 4 inches (10 centimeters) wide. Bundles of the tough fibers run through the leaves. Machines separate the henequen fibers from the softer portions. The fibers are then dried. Henequen is a source of twine.

Scientific classification. Henequen belongs to the agave family, Agavaceae. It is classified as *Agave fourcroydes.*

Harold Norman Moldenke

See also **Sisal; Yucatán Peninsula.**

Henna, *HEHN uh,* is an orange-red dye that varies in color with the article on which it is used. It comes from the leaves of a small shrub that grows in Arabia, Iran, the East Indies, and North Africa. The shrub is also known as *Egyptian privet* and *Jamaica mignonette.* The henna plant is also raised for its fragrant blossoms. Women in Asia use henna to color their nails, fingertips, and parts of their feet. It has been used to dye men's beards, as well as the manes and hoofs of horses. People have also colored wool, silk, and animal skins with henna. Henna is used in the United States as a hair dye.

Scientific classification. Henna is in the loosestrife family, Lythraceae. It is *Lawsonia inermis.*   Howard L. Needles

Hennepin, Louis, *HEHN uh pihn* (1626?-1705?), was a Belgian missionary and explorer who became famous for his journey to the Mississippi River Valley in North America. He accompanied the French explorer Sieur de La Salle across the Great Lakes and then explored the upper part of the Mississippi River.

Hennepin was born in Ath, in what is now Belgium. He joined the Franciscans, a Roman Catholic order. In 1675, King Louis XIV of France sent him to what is now Canada, where France had established a colony. In 1676, Hennepin went to Fort Frontenac, on the site of the present city of Kingston, Ont. There, he founded a mission among Iroquois Indians.

In 1679, Hennepin set out with La Salle's expedition near Niagara Falls. The explorers crossed Lakes Erie, Huron, and Michigan in the *Griffon,* the first ship to sail these waters. The expedition in time reached the Illinois River and constructed Fort Crèvecoeur (Fort Heartbreak) near present-day Peoria, Ill. The fort was the first European settlement in what is now Illinois.

Early in 1680, Hennepin and two associates explored

the upper Mississippi River Valley. Sioux Indians captured them and held them for several months. During this time, Hennepin saw and named the Falls of St. Anthony, later the site of Minneapolis, Minn. He returned to Canada in the spring of 1681 and then sailed to France.

During the 1690's, Hennepin wrote two books in which he took credit for being the first European to track the Mississippi River to its mouth at the Gulf of Mexico. He said he reached the gulf before being captured by the Indians. But historians credit La Salle as the first to track the river to the gulf.   J. E. Rea

Henri, *HEHN ry* or *HEHN ree,* **Robert** (1865-1929), was an American painter and art teacher. He taught his students to record life directly and spontaneously, an approach that clashed with the "art for art's sake" doctrine of his time.

Henri became the guiding spirit of *The Eight,* an informal association of painters. The painters specialized in realistic scenes from everyday life, but differed considerably from each other in style and often in subject matter. Henri's own work has a dark yet sparkling quality. Formed in New York City in 1907, the group included Henri and Arthur B. Davies, William J. Glackens, Ernest Lawson, George B. Luks, Maurice B. Prendergast, Everett Shinn, and John Sloan. Each has an article in *World Book.* The group was scorned as the *Revolutionary Black Gang,* the *Apostles of Ugliness,* and finally the *Ashcan School.*

Henri was born Robert Henry Cozad in Cincinnati. He taught in New York City from 1903 to his death. His book *The Art Spirit* (1923) is a valuable guide to his thoughts on art.   E. Maurice Bloch

Henry is the unit used to measure *inductance,* the reaction of an electric current against the magnetic field that surrounds it. If the flow of current in a circuit changes or alternates, the magnetic field around the circuit also changes. This changing magnetic field *induces* (creates) a voltage in the circuit that opposes any additional increase or decrease in the flow of current. A circuit has 1 henry of inductance if a current change of 1 ampere per second induces an opposing voltage of 1 volt. The henry was named after the American physicist Joseph Henry. Its symbol is H.   Gregory Benford

See also **Inductance.**

Henry was the name of eight kings of England.

Henry I (1068-1135) was the youngest son of William the Conqueror and third of the Norman line of kings. He succeeded his brother, William II, in 1100. Henry helped unite the Saxons and Normans in England. To gain the favor of his Saxon subjects, Henry married Matilda, daughter of Malcolm III of Scotland and his Saxon wife Margaret.

During his reign, Henry worked to restrain the growing power of the barons. He promoted the Norman system of centralized rule and gave the royal courts greater authority. His wars against rebellious nobles in France helped start a feeling of English nationalism.

See **William (I) of England.**

Henry II (1133-1189) was the son of Geoffrey Plantagenet, Count of Anjou, and a grandson of Henry I. He became king in 1154, the first English ruler of the Plantagenet family (see **Plantagenet**).

At the height of his power, Henry ruled England and

Detail of an illuminated manuscript (1200's) by an unknown English artist; reproduced by permission of the British Library Board

Henry I

Detail of an illuminated manuscript (1300's) by an unknown English artist; reproduced by permission of the British Library Board

Henry II

Detail of a bronze statue (1291) by William Torel; by courtesy of the Dean and Chapter of Westminster, Westminster Abbey, London

Henry III

Detail of an alabaster statue (early 1400's); Dean and Chapter of Canterbury, Canterbury Cathedral, Canterbury, England

Henry IV

almost all western France. His marriage to Eleanor of Aquitaine, the most famous woman of the age, brought the duchy of Aquitaine under his control (see **Eleanor of Aquitaine**). Henry also claimed to rule Scotland, Wales, and eastern Ireland.

Henry II carried on his grandfather's policy of limiting the power of the nobles. He also tried to make the Roman Catholic Church in England submit to his authority. This policy brought him into conflict with Thomas à Becket, Archbishop of Canterbury. Four of the king's knights murdered Becket while he was at vespers in his cathedral (see **Becket, Saint Thomas à**).

Henry made Anglo-Saxon common law, rather than the revised Roman law, the supreme law of the land (see **Common law**). He introduced trial by jury and circuit courts. In his later years, Henry's sons often rebelled against him. Two of them, Richard the LionHearted and John, became the next two kings of England.

Henry III (1207-1272) was the eldest son of King John, and a grandson of Henry II. He came to the throne in 1216 when he was only 9 years old, but did not rule until he came of age in 1227. Henry was a fickle tyrant who surrounded himself with favorites from other countries. The English nobles revolted against his rule and the foreign influences in his court. They forced Henry to grant the Provisions of Oxford, which transferred governing powers to a committee of barons. Later, Henry broke the agreement and raised an army. But he was defeated and captured at the battle of Lewes in 1264.

Simon de Montfort, leader of the reform party, then governed England until he was killed at the battle of Evesham in 1265 by Henry's son, Edward (see **Montfort, Simon de**). Edward ruled the country during the rest of Henry's lifetime (see **Edward** [I] **of England**).

Henry IV (1367-1413), son of John of Gaunt, Duke of Lancaster, was the first king of the House of Lancaster (see **John of Gaunt; Lancaster**). He was often called Henry of Bolingbroke. He defeated his cousin, King Richard II, in 1399, and parliament elected him king. Henry admitted that parliament had the right to choose the king. This admission formed an important increase in parliamentary power.

Revolts and conspiracies marred Henry's reign, but he put them down with great effort. He encouraged towns to develop, and helped England's growing trade. But he was intolerant of religious differences, and persecuted the Lollards (see **Lollards**).

Henry V (1387-1422), the eldest son of Henry IV, was crowned in 1413. Henry V followed his father's policy toward the Lollards. Many of them were put to death.

Henry renewed the Hundred Years' War with France, which had begun during the reign of Edward III. He was determined to make good Edward's old claim to the French throne. In 1415, Henry won one of the most famous victories in English history. His small army crushed a host of French lords and knights at Agincourt (see **Agincourt, Battle of**). Five years later, Henry married the daughter of Charles VI, King of France. By the Treaty of Troyes, Henry forced Charles to declare him heir to the French crown. When Henry died two years later, he had won the entire northern half of France. He appears as Prince Hal in Shakespeare's *Henry IV,* Part I and Part II.

Henry VI (1421-1471), the last English king of the House of Lancaster, held the thrones of both England and France when he was less than a year old. He was heir to both his father, Henry V, and to Charles VI of France, who died within two months of each other.

Henry VI was pious and gentle, but he was a weak ruler, and had occasional attacks of insanity. The English nobles took advantage of his weakness to misgovern the kingdom in their own selfish interests. In France, the great conquests of Henry V were gradually lost. By 1453, the French had retaken all their land except the port of Calais (see **Joan of Arc, Saint; Hundred Years' War**). In 1450, a popular uprising, known as Jack Cade's rebellion, shook England, and the supporters of the House of York challenged King Henry and the House of Lancaster (see **York**).

In 1461, the Yorkists drove Henry from the throne, and made Edward IV king. Henry ruled again briefly in 1470 and 1471, but Edward defeated his forces at the battles of Barnet and Tewkesbury. Henry was imprisoned in the Tower of London, where he died. See **Wars of the Roses.**

Henry VII (1457-1509), the first king of the House of Tudor, came to the throne in 1485 as a descendant of the House of Lancaster. He had killed Richard III at Bosworth Field, the last battle of the Wars of the Roses. To strengthen his claim to the throne, Henry married Elizabeth, daughter of Edward IV, uniting the houses of Lancaster and York.

Henry was tough, cold, shrewd, and sly. He kept the nobles in fear by increasing the political power of the

Oil painting on wood by an
unknown artist; National
Portrait Gallery, London

Henry V

Oil painting on wood (about 1520)
by an unknown artist; National
Portrait Gallery, London

Henry VI

Oil painting on wood (1505) by
M. Sittow; National Portrait
Gallery, London

Henry VII

Oil painting on canvas (about 1537)
by Hans Holbein the Younger;
National Gallery, Rome (Royal
Academy of the Fine Arts, London)

Henry VIII

wealthy middle classes, and he taxed the common people heavily. He eliminated pretenders to the throne, and managed to survive several revolts and conspiracies. See **Warbeck, Perkin.**

Henry VII increased England's influence in European affairs by making important alliances. He arranged a marriage between his son Arthur and Catherine of Aragon, daughter of Ferdinand and Isabella of Spain. After Arthur died, the king succeeded in securing the young widow, and her dowry, for his younger son, Henry. He also negotiated a marriage between his daughter Margaret and James IV of Scotland. He kept England out of European wars, however, and by severe economy accumulated an immense fortune.

During Henry VII's reign, England first turned its eyes toward America. In 1497, Henry sent John and Sebastian Cabot to explore North America (see **Cabot**).

See **Tudor, House of.**

Henry VIII (1491-1547) separated the Church of England from the Roman Catholic Church and established the Reformation in England. He helped England become one of the world's greatest naval powers, but spent his father's fortune on foreign wars. Henry is also famous for his six wives. His private life greatly influenced English political history. He was sometimes autocratic and sometimes cruel. But he understood his people and knew how to hold their confidence.

When Henry came to the throne in 1509, his first act was to marry his brother's widow, Catherine of Aragon. Catherine bore five children, but only one lived—Mary, who later became queen (see **Mary** [I]). Henry wanted a son. He turned his attentions to a maid of honor at court, Anne Boleyn. Thomas Cardinal Wolsey, Henry's able and ambitious chief minister, asked Pope Clement VII to annul the king's marriage. He argued that it was wrong for Henry to have married his brother's widow. But the pope refused, and Henry dismissed Wolsey in 1529 (see **Wolsey, Thomas Cardinal**).

The king was determined to have his divorce. He denied that the pope had authority over England, and secretly married Anne Boleyn early in 1533. Henry's choice for Archbishop of Canterbury, Thomas Cranmer, declared the marriage of Henry and Catherine null and void (see **Catherine of Aragon**). Anne was then crowned queen.

At Henry's insistence, parliament passed two acts in 1534 that made the break with the Roman Catholic Church complete. One declared that the pope had no authority in England. The other, the famous Act of Supremacy, made the Church of England a separate institution, and it also established the king as its supreme head.

The two acts officially established the Reformation in England (see **Reformation**). But the divorce did not produce a stable married life for Henry. Anne bore Henry a second daughter, Elizabeth (see **Elizabeth I**). Then in 1536, the king had his wife beheaded on a charge of infidelity (see **Boleyn, Anne**). His third wife, Jane Seymour, died shortly after the birth of a son (see **Edward** [VI]).

At the urging of his chief minister, Thomas Cromwell, Henry married a German princess, Anne of Cleves. But Cromwell was disgraced and executed, and Henry divorced Anne. The king later married Catherine Howard, who, in 1542, was convicted of misconduct and executed. Henry's sixth and last wife, Catherine Parr (1512-1548), outlived him.   Paul M. Kendall

See also **England** (History); **Shakespeare, William** (Shakespeare's plays); **Cranmer, Thomas.**

Additional resources

Erickson, Carolly. *Great Harry*. Summit Books, 1984. First published in 1980.
Lacey, Robert. *The Life and Times of Henry VIII*. Praeger, 1972.
Ridley, Jasper G. *Henry VIII*. Viking, 1985.
Scarisbrick, J. J. *Henry VIII*. Univ. of California Press, 1968.

Henry was the name of four French kings.

Henry I (1008?-1060) was the grandson of Hugh Capet, founder of the Capetian dynasty. During his reign, feudal power in France reached its height (see **Capetian dynasty**).

Henry II (1519-1559) succeeded his father, Francis I, in 1547. He was ambitious and persistent, but he differed from his father in most respects (see **Francis** [I] of France). He tormented Huguenots (French Protestants) and took away their lands. These actions helped start the destructive French religious wars (see **Huguenots**). Henry contested Spain's dominance over Italy, but he never could defeat the Spaniards. In 1559, he signed the Treaty of Cateau-Cambrésis, which formally recognized Spanish control in Italy. Elsewhere, Henry was more successful. He took Calais, England's last possession in France, and the cities of Metz, Toul, and Verdun from the Holy Roman Empire. Henry's wife was Catherine de Médicis (see **Catherine de Médicis**). His sons, Francis II, Charles IX, and Henry III, succeeded him.

Henry III (1551-1589), third son of Henry II, succeeded his brother Charles IX in 1574. He had received the Polish crown earlier the same year, but he left Poland when he heard of Charles' death. Henry was a weakling who divided his time between scheming and immorality. His mother, Catherine de Médicis, held great authority during the earlier part of his reign. Then influence passed to his favorites among the young nobles. Finally, a contest for power took place between two strong rival leaders, the Roman Catholic Henry, Duke of Guise, and the Protestant Henry of Navarre. The contest continued throughout the reign. Alarmed at concessions that were made to the Huguenots, the Catholics organized the Catholic League. This led to open war. In the War of the Three Henrys, the real contest was between Henry of Guise and Henry of Navarre. Henry III was jealous of the Duke of Guise, and arranged the duke's assassination. He then had to flee to Navarre for protection. Henry III was the last Valois king of France (see **Valois**).

Henry IV (1553-1610), who succeeded Henry III in 1589, was Henry of Navarre, the Protestant leader in the War of the Three Henrys. He was the first Bourbon king, and was a man of courage, vigor, and intelligence (see **Bourbon**). Religious conflict continued after the death of Henry III, and Henry IV realized that he could restore peace only if he himself became Catholic. In 1593, he gave up Protestantism and was accepted into the Roman Catholic Church. This brought recognition of his right to the kingship, and French cities welcomed him on his triumphal march to Paris.

Another of Henry's great successes was victory over Spain. Spain had repeatedly interfered in French affairs, plotting with rivals for the French throne and supporting the Catholic League. Henry decided to stop this interference, and joined the English and Dutch in their war against King Philip II. The Spanish ruler yielded and recognized Henry as king of France.

In 1598, Henry issued the Edict of Nantes, which granted considerable rights and privileges to the Huguenots (see **Nantes, Edict of**). The edict made remarkable concessions to the Huguenot minority in a country as strongly Catholic as France. Before he was murdered, Henry also reformed France's finances, strengthened its agriculture and commerce, and worked to maintain a balance of power in Europe that helped protect France.

William C. Bark

See also **France** (History); **Huguenots.**

Henry was the name of seven German rulers. All except Henry I were elected emperors of the Holy Roman Empire (see **Holy Roman Empire**).

Henry I (876?-936), called the Fowler, and **Henry II** (973-1024) were of the Saxon dynasty.

Henry III (1017-1056), of the Salian dynasty, became king of Germany in 1039. He was crowned emperor in 1046. Henry enforced German authority throughout the territories of the Holy Roman Empire. He supported reforms in the Roman Catholic Church by denouncing the marriages of priests and the buying of church offices. In 1046, he invaded Italy and had his own candidate for the papal throne recognized over three rivals. Later, he claimed control of nominations for pope.

Henry IV (1050-1106), son and successor of Henry III, became king of Germany at the age of six. The nobles revolted while his mother served as regent. When he took control of the kingdom in 1069, he tried to establish his authority throughout Germany. But he came into conflict with Pope Gregory VII. In 1075, Gregory denied civil rulers the authority to make appointments to church offices. In response, Henry called a council that met at Worms in 1076 and declared the pope deposed. Gregory in turn expelled Henry from the church and released his subjects from allegiance to him.

After a long struggle, Henry had to yield. Pope Gregory had retired to a stronghold at Canossa in the Apennines. It is said that Henry had to stand barefoot in the snow for three days before he was permitted to kneel at the pope's feet and be pardoned. But after his return to Germany, Henry renewed the struggle. For years his country was torn by civil war. In 1084, he captured Rome and replaced Gregory with a pope he had chosen. Gregory died in exile soon afterward, but his successors took up the contest. One of them again expelled Henry from the church. Finally, in 1105, Henry was forced to abdicate after one of his sons had been persuaded to rebel against him. Henry died while preparing for war. His son, **Henry V** (1081-1125), succeeded him and ruled Germany from 1106 to 1125.

Henry VI (1165-1197), a member of the Hohenstaufen family, succeeded his father, Frederick Barbarossa, in 1190 (see **Hohenstaufen**). His marriage to Constance of Sicily gave him a claim to her kingdom. He also collected a large ransom from King Richard the Lion-Hearted of England, who was a prisoner of the duke of Austria. Henry strengthened his position in Italy through

Detail of a drawing (mid-1000's) by an unknown French artist; Bibliothèque Nationale, Paris (Giraudon)

Henry I

Detail of a drawing (about 1550) by François Clouet; Bibliothèque Nationale, Paris

Henry II

Detail of a drawing (about 1588) by François Quesnel; Bibliothèque Nationale, Paris

Henry III

Detail of a painting (1610) by Frans Pourbus the Younger; the Louvre, Paris (Clichés des Musées Nationaux, Paris)

Henry IV

the aged Pope Celestine III. He also laid plans to keep the imperial throne in the Hohenstaufen family and to take Jerusalem as the start of a new crusade. But these projects ended suddenly when Henry died at 32.

Henry VII (1269-1313) was a member of the Luxembourg dynasty. Henry was emperor of the Holy Roman Empire from 1308 to 1313.   Franklin D. Scott

Henry, of Portugal. See **Henry the Navigator.**

Henry, Alexander (1739-1824), won fame as a fur trader in Canada after Great Britain gained control of the area from France in the 1760's. He helped open western Canada and the area north of Lake Superior to trade with the British.

Henry was born in New Jersey. He became a trader as a young man and was one of the first traders to reach Mackinac Island in the Straits of Mackinac. The island served as the center of the western fur trade. In 1763, an Indian friend saved Henry's life after Indians organized by Pontiac captured Mackinac Island (see **Pontiac**).

In 1781, Henry became a merchant in Montreal and sold his trading interests to the North West Company, a famous fur-trading firm. Henry described his experiences as a fur trader in his book *Travels and Adventures in Canada and the Indian Territories between the Years 1760 and 1776* (1809).   Hartwell Bowsfield

Henry, Duke of Guise. See **Henry (III) of France.**

Henry, John, a black laborer, is an American folk hero. He is the subject of perhaps the most famous American folk ballad and of many stories and songs.

The original story about John Henry is based on an actual event involving a man of that name. In the early 1870's, laborers were building the Big Bend Tunnel on the Chesapeake and Ohio Railroad in West Virginia. They used long-handled hammers to pound a steel drill into rock when making holes to hold blasting explosives. One day, a man brought an experimental steam drill to the site. He claimed it could dig a hole faster than 20 workers using hammers.

According to the ballad, John Henry raced the steam drill to prove that a man could dig faster than a machine:

> They placed John Henry on the right-hand side,
> The steam drill on the left;
> He said, "Before I let that steam drill beat me down
> I'll die with my hammer in my hand, O Lord,
> And send my soul to rest."

In the ballad, John Henry won the race but died from exhaustion at the moment of his victory. The real John Henry, after winning the race, is said to have been crushed by rock that fell from the tunnel ceiling.

The legend of John Henry developed from ballads, songs, and stories about him. He symbolized the workers' fight against being replaced by machines. The earliest known written version of the ballad appeared about 1900.   Harry Oster

Henry, Joseph (1797-1878), an American physicist, became famous for his discoveries in electromagnetism. He anticipated both Samuel F. B. Morse's invention of the telegraph and Michael Faraday's discovery of electromagnetic induction. Henry received no credit for his work at the time, but the unit of electrical inductance is now called the *henry* (see **Henry**).

Henry was born in Albany, N.Y. He was educated at Albany Academy, where he later taught mathematics and physics. He began experimenting in electromagnet-

ism while teaching there. His first major work was improving the electromagnet, which William Sturgeon had discovered. From 1832 to 1846, Henry was a professor at Princeton University. He later became the first secretary and director of the Smithsonian Institution. In 1867, he became president of the National Academy of Sciences, which was established in 1863.   Sidney Rosen

See also **Electromagnetism; Faraday, Michael; Morse, Samuel Finley Breese.**

Henry, O. (1862-1910), was the pen name of an American story writer, William Sydney Porter. In nearly all his 250 works of fiction, O. Henry showed his mastery of mechanical plots, which build up to sharp, unexpected endings, as in "The Gift of the Magi" (1905). Most of his stories are sentimental rather than psychologically deep. Yet his sympathy for human weaknesses and the naturalness of his characters make his stories appealing. He wrote in the language of the common people.

His works. O. Henry published about 14 volumes of stories, reflecting his own colorful experiences and those of his associates. The models of some of his best-known characters were criminals and soldiers of fortune, whom he met during two years in Central America and later in New York. His stories usually tell about victims of coincidence or fate. An example is "The Furnished Room" (1904). In this story, a lover seeks his sweetheart, who came to New York for a singing career. He rents a room where he commits suicide after being unable to find the girl. The lover never learns that his sweetheart had earlier killed herself in that same room. *The Voice of the City* (1908) deals with the loneliness and tragic predicaments of innocent country folk who come to the impersonal and evil city to seek their fortune.

O. Henry's other works include *Cabbages and Kings* (1904), *The Trimmed Lamp* (1907), *Heart of the West* (1907), *The Gentle Grafter* (1908), *Roads of Destiny* and *Options* (1909), *Strictly Business* and *Whirligigs* (1910), *Sixes and Sevens* (1911), and *Waifs and Strays* (1917). The complete works of O. Henry were published in 14 volumes in 1917.

His life. William Sydney Porter was born in Greensboro, N.C., on Sept. 11, 1862. He left public school when he was 15 and worked in his uncle's drugstore. Then he went to Texas and worked for two years on a ranch. Later he moved to Austin, Tex., where he was a bank clerk for a while. He began to write short sketches, some of which appeared in the Detroit *Free Press*. In 1894, he bought a paper called the *Iconoclast*, and renamed it *The Rolling Stone*. A year later, he moved to Houston, Tex., where he wrote for a newspaper.

In 1896, Porter was called back to Austin to stand trial on a charge of stealing funds from the bank. He might have been pardoned, because his errors were caused by loose bookkeeping rather than criminal intent. But he fled to Honduras. When he returned to Austin to the deathbed of his wife, he was arrested and impris-

Brown Bros.

O. Henry

oned for three years. Using various pen names, he wrote and published several short stories while he was in prison. After he was released, he went to New York City, where he worked first as a newspaper columnist and then a short-story writer.   Harry H. Clark

See also **Short story.**

Additional resources

Current-García, Eugene. *O. Henry.* Twayne, 1972. First published in 1965.
Harris, Richard C. *William Sydney Porter (O. Henry): A Reference Guide.* G. K. Hall, 1980.
Langford, Gerald. *Alias O. Henry: A Biography of William Sydney Porter.* Greenwood, 1983. First published in 1957.
Long, E. Hudson. *O. Henry: The Man and His Work.* Russell & Russell, 1969. First published in 1949.

Henry, Patrick (1736-1799), was a distinguished statesman, lawyer, and orator at the time of the Revolutionary War in America. He is remembered most for the words, "Give me liberty or give me death," which, according to tradition, he spoke in 1775 before the Virginia Provincial Convention. Henry was urging that the Virginia militia be armed for defense of the colony against England. A man who heard many of Henry's speeches once said of the orator: "He is by far the most powerful speaker I ever heard. Every word he says not only engages but commands the attention." Henry was also an excellent politician and administrator. He served as the governor of Virginia during the Revolutionary War.

Early life. Henry was born in Hanover County, Virginia. He attended public school for only a short time, but was taught by his father, who had a good education. As a young man, Henry was a storekeeper for a time. But he was a poor businessman and, as a result, he was soon hopelessly in debt. He then studied law and received his license to practice in 1760. Three years later, Henry's talent as an orator won him fame in Virginia in a noted lawsuit called the Parson's Cause.

In 1764, Henry was elected to the Virginia House of Burgesses. He soon became a leader, supporting frontier interests against the old aristocracy. He upheld the rights which the colonies were guaranteed by their charters. His speech against the Stamp Act in 1765 is one of his greatest orations (see **Stamp Act**). In it, according to tradition, appear the often-quoted words: "Caesar had his Brutus—Charles the First, his Cromwell —and George the Third—*may profit by their example.* If *this* be treason, make the most of it."

In August 1774, the colony of Virginia elected Henry a delegate to the First Continental Congress (see **Continental Congress**). He was also a member of the Second Continental Congress for a short time in 1775. After that, he became commander in chief of Virginia's military forces. He resigned this post in February 1776. A few months later, he was chosen a member of the

Portrait by Thomas Sully—Colonial Williamsburg

Patrick Henry

Detail of *Patrick Henry Before the Virginia House of Burgesses* (1851), an oil painting on canvas by Peter Frederick Rothermel (Patrick Henry Memorial Foundation)

Patrick Henry lashed out at English tyranny in a great speech before the Virginia House of Burgesses in 1765.

committee to draw up the first constitution of the commonwealth of Virginia.

Career as governor. Henry became governor of the new commonwealth of Virginia as soon as it was established in 1776. He moved into the palace at Williamsburg, where the English colonial governors had lived. He was a hard-working administrator. He showed his feeling of democracy when he became the first American politician to call the voters "fellow citizens."

The Revolutionary War brought many problems to Virginia, and Henry worked hard to solve them. He recruited the state's quota of about 6,000 men for the Continental Army, plus the state militia of nearly 5,000 soldiers. The state supplied its soldiers with clothing and shoes, and sent cattle to feed the men at Valley Forge. Henry encouraged mining lead to provide ammunition, and imported and manufactured gunpowder. He set up shipyards and dockyards to protect the Virginia coast, and he arranged for loans.

Henry was criticized in spite of his hard work, especially when the forces under the British General Banastre Tarleton overran Virginia. But he was elected governor again in 1777, 1778, 1784, and 1785. During his second term, Henry provided supplies for the George Rogers Clark expedition, which conquered the Northwest Territory (see **Northwest Territory**).

In 1788, Henry served in the Virginia state convention, that was called to ratify the United States Constitution. He opposed ratification because he believed that the Constitution endangered the rights of individuals and states. After he lost, however, he accepted the Constitution and joined the Federalist Party. Henry was largely responsible for the adoption of the first 10 amendments to the Constitution, known as the Bill of Rights (see **Bill of rights**).

Return to private life. Public service left Henry badly in debt, and in 1788 he returned to his law practice. His fame as a brilliant speaker gained him many clients, and he soon became a successful criminal lawyer.

Henry's famous speech

Patrick Henry delivered his best-known speech before the Virginia Provincial Convention on March 23, 1775. No written records of the speech exist. The speech was printed in an early biography of Henry by William Wirt, who relied chiefly on accounts given to him by people who heard the speech. The conclusion of the speech follows:

"Three millions of people, armed in the holy cause of liberty, and in such a country as that which we possess, are invincible by any force which our enemy can send against us. Besides, sir, we shall not fight our battles alone. There is a just God who presides over the destinies of nations, and who will raise up friends to fight our battles for us. The battle, sir, is not to the strong alone; it is to the vigilant, the active, the brave.

"Besides, sir, we have no election. If we were base enough to desire it, it is now too late to retire from the contest. There is no retreat, but in submission and slavery. Our chains are forged. Their clanking may be heard on the plains of Boston! The war is inevitable—and let it come! I repeat it, sir, let it come!

"It is in vain, sir, to extenuate the matter. Gentlemen may cry, peace, peace—but there is no peace. The war is actually begun! The next gale that sweeps from the north will bring to our ears the clash of resounding arms! Our brethren are already in the field! Why stand we here idle? What is it that gentlemen wish? What would they have? Is life so dear, or peace so sweet, as to be purchased at the price of chains and slavery? Forbid it, Almighty God! I know not what course others may take; but as for me, give me liberty, or give me death!"

His law fees helped him to buy land, and in 1794, he retired to his Red Hill estate, near Appomattox, Va.

During the next five years, Henry refused many requests to return to public life. He was offered a seat in the U.S. Senate, posts as minister to Spain and to France, a place in George Washington's Cabinet as Secretary of State, and the position of Chief Justice of the United States. In 1796, Henry was elected governor of Virginia for the sixth time, but he refused the office.

Finally George Washington persuaded him to become a candidate for representative in the Virginia state legislature. Henry made his last great speech during this campaign. The speech was a denial of a state's right to decide the constitutionality of federal laws. Henry told the voters: "United we stand, divided we fall. Let us not split into factions which must destroy that union upon which our existence hangs." Henry won the election, but he died before he could take office. Henry was buried at Red Hill.   William Morgan Fowler, Jr.

Additional resources

Beeman, Richard R. *Patrick Henry: A Biography.* McGraw, 1974.
Fritz, Jean. *Where Was Patrick Henry on the 29th of May?* Coward, 1975. For younger readers.
Mayer, Henry. *A Son of Thunder: Patrick Henry and the American Republic.* Watts, 1986.
Meade, Robert D. *Patrick Henry.* 2 vols. Lippincott, 1957-1969.

Henry of Navarre. See Henry (IV) of France.

Henry the Navigator (1394-1460) was a Portuguese prince who promoted explorations of the west African coast during the 1400's. These explorations helped advance the study of geography and made Portugal a leader in navigation among European nations of that time. Henry sent out more than 50 expeditions but went on none of these voyages himself.

Detail of an oil painting (mid-1400's); Museu Nacional de Arte Antiga, Lisbon, Portugal
Henry the Navigator

Henry was the son of King John I and Queen Philippa. He was a serious, studious youth with a special interest in mathematics and astronomy. Henry and two older brothers, Duarte and Pedro, wanted to prove they were worthy to be knighted. With their father's approval, they organized a Portuguese army and captured Ceuta, an important commercial town in Morocco.The three brothers were knighted, and Henry was made governor of Ceuta.

The commercial routes between Ceuta and inner Africa stirred Henry's interest in the geography of Africa. His skill in mathematics and astronomy helped him organize expeditions along the northwest African coast. In 1419, two Portuguese explorers sent by Henry reached Porto Santo, one of the Madeira Islands. These explorers, João Gonçalves and Tristão Vaz, sailed to the island of Madeira itself in the early 1420's. Portugal colonized both islands.

One of Henry's goals was to send explorers beyond Cape Bojador, in what is now Western Sahara. The cape was the southernmost point known to Europeans at that time. After several unsuccessful attempts, an expedition led by Gil Eanes finally passed the cape in 1434. Eanes reached Rio de Oro, also in Western Sahara, in 1436. One of Henry's explorers, Antão Gonçalves, returned to Portugal with some Africans he had captured on an expedition in 1441. These people were the first slaves brought from west Africa to Europe. One of the captives was a chieftain named Adahu, who told Henry about lands farther south and inland. In 1441, Nuño Tristão sailed as far south as Cape Blanc, on the border of Western Sahara and Mauritania. Diniz Diaz reached Cape Verde, in present-day Senegal, in 1445. By the time of Henry's death in 1460, Portuguese ships had reached the coast of Sierra Leone.

Henry planned and raised the money for the expeditions. He was aided by mapmakers, astronomers, and mathematicians of many nationalities, whom he gathered together at Sagres, near Cape St. Vincent, Portugal. The navigational knowledge gained under Henry's direction led to several historic voyages within 50 years after his death. They included the voyages of the Portuguese explorers Vasco da Gama and Bartolomeu Dias around the southern tip of Africa.   John Parker

Additional resources

Bradford, Ernle D. *A Wind from the North: The Life of Henry the Navigator.* Harcourt, 1960.
Chubb, Thomas C. *Prince Henry the Navigator and the Highways of the Sea.* Viking, 1970. For younger readers.
Ure, John. *Prince Henry the Navigator.* Constable, 1977.

Henson, Matthew Alexander (1867-1955), was the only American who accompanied Robert E. Peary when the explorer reached the North Pole in 1909. Henson, a black, was born on a farm in Maryland. Henson traveled on various expeditions with Peary for more than 20

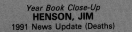
Year Book Close-Up
HENSON, JIM
1991 News Update (Deaths)

years as personal assistant and dog driver.

Henson received many honors for his part in the 1908-1909 expedition. He wrote the book *A Negro Explorer at the North Pole*. His biography, *Dark Companion*, written by Bradley Robinson, was published in 1947.

John Edwards Caswell

Bettmann Archive

Matthew A. Henson

Henze, *HEHN tsuh,* **Hans Werner,** *hahns VEHR nuhr* (1926-   ), is a German composer best known for his operas and ballets. His works combine the modern atonal style with more traditional musical forms. His music is harsh and unharmonious, but it is also known for its expressiveness and colorful orchestral sounds. Henze's radical political views, as well as his bold musical ideas, have made him controversial.

Henze's most famous opera is *Der junge Lord* (*The Young Lord*, 1965). His other operas include *Boulevard Solitude* (1952), *King Stag* (1956), and *Elegy for Young Lovers* (1961). His ballets include *Jack Pudding* (1949), *The Idiot* (1952), and *Ondine* (1958). Beginning in the late 1960's, Henze composed several theater pieces with revolutionary political themes. These works include *El Cimarrón* (1970) and *La Cubana* (1973). Henze has also composed instrumental works. His essays were collected in *Music and Politics* (1982).

Henze was born in Gütersloh. His early works show the influence of the composers Arnold Schönberg and Igor Stravinsky.   Miloš Velimirović

Hepatica, *hih PAT uh kuh,* is a sturdy but dainty woodland plant that grows in almost all countries of the Northern Hemisphere. It is related to the anemone. The name *hepatica* comes from a Greek word that means *liver*. The hepatica's dark green, leathery leaves have three scallops, or *lobes,* and are shaped somewhat like livers. For this reason, the plant is often called *liverleaf,* or *liverwort.* Six petallike sepals form the plant's buttercup-shaped blossoms. Each year, the blossoms appear before the new green leaves do.

Except for the ill-smelling skunk cabbage, the hepatica is the first flower that blooms in spring from Canada to northern Florida and west to Minnesota. Its pink, white, or lavender blossoms appear in profusion. Each flower grows on a stem 3 to 6 inches (8 to 15 centimeters) high. One hepatica has rounded leaf lobes and grows mostly in the eastern United States. Another has pointed leaf lobes and grows in the central states.

Scientific classification. Hepaticas belong to the crowfoot family, Ranunculaceae. Those with rounded lobes are *Hepatica americana.* The sharp-lobed plant is *H. acutiloba.*

George H. M. Lawrence

See also **Flower** (picture: Flowers of woodlands and forests).

Hepatitis, *HEHP uh TY tihs,* is a disease that involves inflammation of the liver. Its symptoms include weakness, loss of appetite, nausea, vomiting, and *jaundice,* a yellowish discoloration of the skin and tissues. There are two major types of hepatitis, *viral* and *toxic.*

Viral hepatitis. Scientists have identified two main forms of viral hepatitis. These forms are: (1) hepatitis A, or infectious hepatitis; and (2) hepatitis B, or serum hepatitis. They are caused by two different viruses. Hepatitis also may result from other viruses or from a combination of two different viruses.

Most cases of hepatitis A result from eating contaminated food or drinking contaminated water. Symptoms of the disease appear about four weeks later. Most cases of hepatitis A last from two to six weeks. The symptoms may be lessened—or even prevented—if injections of gamma globulin are administered within a week after the patient has been exposed to the virus (see **Gamma globulin**).

The virus of hepatitis B was once most commonly transmitted through the transfusion of contaminated blood. Since the 1970's, tests that detect the virus in blood donations have largely eliminated transmission through blood transfusions. Today, hepatitis B is spread mainly by the use of improperly sterilized medical instruments, by hypodermic needles shared by drug abusers, and through sexual contact with infected persons. During the 1980's, vaccines that protect against hepatitis B became available.

Symptoms of hepatitis B appear from 6 to 12 weeks after infection, and many patients do not know they have the disease until jaundice occurs. People who have had hepatitis B may carry the virus in their blood for years after recovery. Such carriers can spread the hepatitis B virus. Also, carriers have a moderate risk of developing cirrhosis of the liver and occasionally may develop liver cancer. About 1 per cent of all hepatitis B cases end in death.

In 1977, scientists discovered a new hepatitis virus. This virus, called the *delta agent,* cannot cause infection by itself. It is infectious only when it combines with the hepatitis B virus. Together, these two viruses cause an acute form of hepatitis known as *delta hepatitis.* People immune to hepatitis B are also immune to delta hepatitis.

One or more other viruses also cause hepatitis. This variety of the disease is called *non-A, non-B hepatitis.* It accounts for thousands of cases of post-transfusion hepatitis each year. It also occurs in many people who have not received a blood transfusion. Scientists do not know how the disease is transmitted in such patients.

Toxic hepatitis results from exposure to alcohol, a variety of medications, and certain chemicals, including carbon tetrachloride. Such chemicals can enter the body by being swallowed, inhaled, absorbed through the skin, or received in injections. The development and treatment of toxic hepatitis varies, depending on the substance that causes it.   Charles S. Lieber

See also **Disease** (graph: Main contagious diseases in the United States); **Liver** (Hepatitis).

Hepburn, Katharine (1909-   ), is an American motion-picture actress. She has been nominated for 12 Academy Awards—more than any other performer. She won awards for best actress in *Morning Glory* (1933), *Guess Who's Coming to Dinner* (1967), *The Lion in Winter* (1968), and *On Golden Pond* (1981). She became famous for her distinctive voice and manner.

Hepburn was born in Hartford, Conn. She made her film debut in 1932 in the melodrama *A Bill of Divorce-*

Special Report
HEPBURN, KATHARINE
2004 Year Book, p. 286

ment. Her performances include comic portrayals in *Adam's Rib* (1949) and *Pat and Mike* (1952)—both co-starring Spencer Tracy—and *The African Queen* (1952). She played serious dramatic roles in *Little Women* (1933), *Summertime* (1955), *The Rainmaker* (1956), and *Long Day's Journey into Night* (1962). Hepburn has made about 40 films and has also appeared on the stage in comedies and Shakespearean roles. She also starred in the musical *Coco* (1969). Alan Casty

United Press Int.

Katharine Hepburn

Hephaestus, *hih FEHS tuhs,* was the Greek god of fire and the forge. He was the blacksmith of the gods and the patron of metalworkers. Hephaestus resembled the Roman god Vulcan in many ways.

Most Greek gods became known for their beauty, but Hephaestus was lame and deformed. Greek artists showed him as a powerful, bearded workman wearing a short tunic and a cone-shaped hat and holding a hammer and tongs. Hephaestus created many masterpieces in metal, including the armor of the warrior Achilles and the golden throne of Zeus, the king of the gods. The marriage of Hephaestus and Aphrodite, the goddess of love, symbolized the union of art and beauty.

The Greeks associated Hephaestus with volcanic regions. In early times, he was worshiped on the volcanic island of Límnos (or Lemnos). Robert J. Lenardon

See also **Vulcan; Pandora; Zeus.**

Hepplewhite, George (? -1786), was an English furniture maker and designer. No documented examples of his furniture survive. Hepplewhite's reputation rests on his book of furniture designs, *The Cabinet-Maker and Upholsterer's Guide* (published in 1788, after his death). The *Guide* contains engravings of nearly 300 designs that Hepplewhite and other English furniture designers made popular between about 1770 and 1790. Furniture made according to these designs is known as Hepplewhite.

Hepplewhite furniture has graceful contours and features delicate ornamentation with painted *moldings* (wooden strips) and inlays of contrasting woods. Hepplewhite chairs have backs shaped like hearts, ovals, or shields and straight tapered legs.

Little is known about Hepplewhite's life. After 1760, he owned a workshop in London. Nancy E. Richards

See also **Furniture** (English neoclassical furniture).

Heptagon, *HEHP tuh gahn,* is a plane figure with seven sides. It is a type of polygon. The sides of a heptagon meet at points called *vertices,* forming seven *interior angles* within the heptagon. The sum of the interior angles of a heptagon is always 900°. A heptagon is *regular* if it has equal sides and equal interior angles. The *apothem* of a regular heptagon is the distance from the center of the figure to the midpoint of one of its sides. The area of a regular heptagon with side *s* and apothem *a* is found by the formula $\frac{7}{2}sa$. Arthur F. Coxford, Jr.

Heptarchy, *HEHP tahr kee,* was the name given to the seven most important English kingdoms that were es-

tablished after the Anglo-Saxon conquest of Roman Britain. These kingdoms were founded by the Angles, Saxons, and Jutes. They were Kent, Essex, Sussex, Wessex, Northumbria (now Northumberland), East Anglia, and Mercia. They battled among themselves from about A.D. 600 to 829, when Egbert of Wessex established the supremacy of his kingdom. He thus became the first king of all England, but had little power to enforce his rule. The word *heptarchy* comes from the Greek, and means *rule of seven.* Robert S. Hoyt

See also **Anglo-Saxons; Egbert.**

Heptathlon. See Pentathlon.

Hera, *HIHR uh,* was the sister and wife of Zeus, the king of the gods in Greek mythology. She was the queen of both the gods and humans. Hera was a protector of women, especially in marriage and childbirth. Greek artists portrayed her as beautiful, dignified, and matronly. The Roman goddess Juno resembled Hera in many ways.

A number of myths describe Hera's ruthless hostility toward her husband's many mistresses. Zeus changed one of his mistresses, the beautiful princess Io, into a cow to hide her from Hera. But Hera found Io and sent the monster Argus, who had 100 eyes, to guard her. On Zeus's orders, the god Hermes beheaded Argus. Hera honored Argus by putting his eyes on the tail of the peacock, her favorite bird. Hera also tormented Io by sending a gadfly to sting her. Robert J. Lenardon

See also **Juno; Io.**

Heracles. See Hercules.

Heraclitus, *HEHR uh KLY tuhs,* was a Greek philosopher who was active about 500 B.C. He said that everything is made of fire. This makes him sound like the other early Greek philosophers, who looked for one material they thought must be common to all that exists. But Heraclitus' view was more sophisticated.

Heraclitus believed that strife is the basic condition of the natural world and that everything is in continuous motion and change. He made the famous statement that a person cannot step into the same river twice. Heraclitus believed that the unity of things lies not in a material substance, but rather in a delicate balance or tension of opposing forces. Fire—because it is always in motion—is a good symbol of Heraclitus' view of the universe.

Heraclitus was born in Ephesus of an aristocratic family. He was scornful of people and lived in isolation. In ancient times, he was called *the Obscure* because his philosophy was hard to understand. Josiah B. Gould

See also **Pre-Socratic philosophy.**

Herald. In ancient times, direct communication between a ruler and the people was often impossible. The rulers used special officials, called *heralds,* to deliver messages and orders, and to announce important decisions and events to the people. During the Middle Ages, heralds became personal agents for the king and enjoyed great honor. It was a crime to interfere with their work or to harm them.

Medieval heralds became authorities on *coats of arms,* the emblems and designs used on the shields and clothing of nobles in battle. They supervised the selection of new designs to prevent duplication and to make sure that people did not claim ancestry to which they were not entitled. Joel T. Rosenthal

See also **Heraldry.**

Heraldry is the study of a system of symbols used to represent individuals, families, countries, and such institutions as churches and universities. The basic heraldic symbol is an emblem called a *coat of arms,* often known simply as *arms.* Coats of arms were originally used on the shields of knights.

Heraldry is related to similar systems of symbolism, such as seals and flags. It also is connected with *genealogy,* the study of family history.

The development of heraldry

Beginnings. The first coats of arms appeared during the early 1100's. They were used by Christian knights from western Europe who fought in a series of military campaigns called the *Crusades.* The Europeans wanted to regain control of Palestine from the Muslims. The knights wore heavy metal armor during battle, and helmets covered their faces. They displayed coats of arms on their shields and flags so their followers could recognize them on the battlefield.

Heraldry also served as a means of identification in civilian life. European societies were governed by a political and military system known as *feudalism.* Under feudalism, landowning nobles gave other nobles possession but not ownership of land in exchange for their military and other services. The upper classes consisted of royalty, nobility, and clergy. Members of these classes identified their possessions and official documents by marking them with their coats of arms. The common people did not have coats of arms.

Expansion. By the 1200's, heraldry had become firmly established as a system of identification. Upper-class families passed their coats of arms down from one generation to the next. By custom, and eventually by heraldic law, no two families could use the same coat of arms. The many heraldic designs, plus the possible confusion among them, led to the development of a group of men who regulated such matters. This class consisted of official messengers called *heralds.*

At first, the heralds carried messages between princes and armies, announced and directed tournaments, and conducted certain ceremonies. The heralds had to know one knight from another to perform their duties, and heraldic symbols provided the necessary identification.

The duties of the heralds increased as heraldry expanded to include more and more families. For example, the heralds became responsible for keeping track of families and their coats of arms. In addition, heralds made books called *armorials,* in which they recorded the designs of coats of arms. They also developed a special language known as *blazonry* for describing the arms. In blazonry, the *dexter side* of a shield is the right side from the wearer's viewpoint, and the *sinister side* is the left side. The colors and the representations of metals or furs used on a coat of arms are called *tinctures.* They include *argent* (silver or white), *azure* (blue), *gules* (red), *or* (gold), and *sable* (black).

After feudalism. During the 1200's and 1300's, feudalism began to decline in most European nations. At about the same time, armies developed new methods of warfare that did not require the use of coats of arms. However, heraldic symbols remained important in tournaments and in some ceremonies. The emblems served as decorations at such events and showed the importance of those who used them.

Heraldry today. Most nations have abolished heraldry and other social privileges that once belonged to the upper classes. However, some people in such countries as Great Britain and South Africa still use heraldic symbols to show their ancestry. In England, the College of Arms, also known as the Heralds' College, decides who has the right to use a coat of arms. The college, established in 1484 by King Richard III, also chooses the elements that must appear on the emblem.

The governments of many nations, states, provinces, cities, and towns have coats of arms. The use of the emblems by governments is called *civil heraldry.* Some international organizations also have coats of arms.

In the United States, anyone may create and use a coat of arms. Such a self-created emblem is called *arms of assumption.* Many coats of arms for common family names are sold in the United States and Canada, but few are authentic.

Elements of a coat of arms

By the late 1400's, heralds had established certain rules that affected the design of a coat of arms. These rules later came to be known as the *laws of heraldry.* The rules discussed in this article are those of England.

The basic element of any coat of arms is the *shield,* also known as the *escutcheon.* A coat of arms, sometimes called a *heraldic achievement,* may include certain *accessories* to the shield. For example, there may be a helmet above the shield and, on top of that, a crest. A cape, known as a *mantling,* may be attached to the helmet or draped around the shield. Many coats of arms have an accessory called a *supporter* on each side of the shield. Most supporters are animals or human beings.

Most coats of arms include an object or figure called a *charge* on the shield. Animals and plants are the most common charges, but they may not look as they do in nature. For example, a lion may be shown *couped* (with the tips of its head or limbs cut off). Gods, people, monsters, and certain lifeless objects are also used as charges. The shield and all accessories stand on a base, known as the *compartment,* or above a motto, which is called the *device.*

A family's coat of arms may indicate the *cadency* (status) of individual members or of different branches of the family. Symbols called *marks of cadency* designate these family relationships. For example, each son in a family uses a different, personal symbol to show his order of birth.   Whitney Smith

See also **Cartouche; Chevron; Herald.**

Additional resources

Buehr, Walter. *Heraldry: The Story of Armorial Bearings.* Putnam, 1964. For younger readers.
Dennys, Rodney. *Heraldry and the Heralds.* Merrimack Book Service, 1982.
Franklyn, Julian. *Shield and Crest: An Account of the Art and Science of Heraldry.* 3rd ed. Genealogical Publishing, 1969.
Neubecker, Ottfried. *A Guide to Heraldry.* McGraw, 1979.

Herb, *urb* or *hurb,* is a low-growing plant that has a fleshy or juicy stem when it is young. The stems of some herbs develop hard, woody tissue when they grow old. Most herbs are perennials. The tops of the plants die each growing season, but the roots remain alive and

Parts of a coat of arms

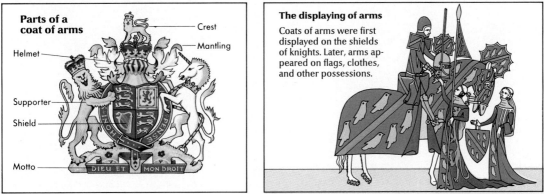

- Crest
- Mantling
- Helmet
- Supporter
- Shield
- Motto

DIEU ET MON DROIT

The displaying of arms

Coats of arms were first displayed on the shields of knights. Later, arms appeared on flags, clothes, and other possessions.

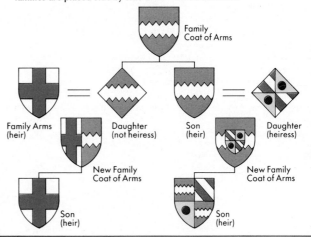

WORLD BOOK illustrations by Oxford Illustrators Limited

Symbols used on a coat of arms

Coats of arms were developed during the 1100's as a way to help a knight's followers recognize him on the battlefield. The colors, designs, lines, and *cadency* (status) symbols shown below became standard and were used in different combinations according to specific rules.

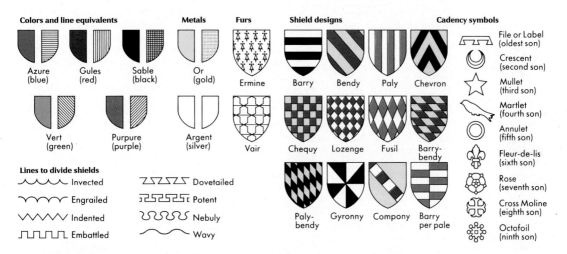

Colors and line equivalents

- Azure (blue)
- Gules (red)
- Sable (black)
- Vert (green)
- Purpure (purple)

Metals

- Or (gold)
- Argent (silver)

Furs

- Ermine
- Vair

Shield designs

- Barry
- Bendy
- Paly
- Chevron
- Chequy
- Lozenge
- Fusil
- Barry-bendy
- Paly-bendy
- Gyronny
- Company
- Barry per pale

Cadency symbols

- File or Label (oldest son)
- Crescent (second son)
- Mullet (third son)
- Martlet (fourth son)
- Annulet (fifth son)
- Fleur-de-lis (sixth son)
- Rose (seventh son)
- Cross Moline (eighth son)
- Octofoil (ninth son)

Lines to divide shields

- Invected
- Engrailed
- Indented
- Embattled
- Dovetailed
- Potent
- Nebuly
- Wavy

Kinds of charges

A charge is a symbol of an object or figure that appears on a shield. Animals are among the most popular charges.

- Swords
- Ship
- Tower
- Unicorn
- Lion
- Dragon
- Arms
- Wolf's head
- Tortoise

Patterns of family relationships

Two or more arms were sometimes combined on one shield in order to show family relationships. The earliest methods of *marshalling,* as this procedure is called, are shown below. The arms of two families are placed side by side or one within the other.

- Family Coat of Arms
- Family Arms (heir)
- Daughter (not heiress)
- Son (heir)
- Daughter (heiress)
- New Family Coat of Arms
- New Family Coat of Arms
- Son (heir)
- Son (heir)

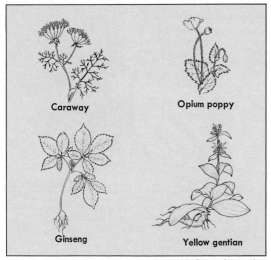

Caraway

Opium poppy

Ginseng

Yellow gentian

WORLD BOOK illustration by Jean Helmer

Herbs have many uses. Caraway seeds, *top left,* add flavor to various foods. Several drugs are made from the juice of the opium poppy, *top right.* Ginseng roots, *bottom left,* are prized as a stimulant and as a cure for some ailments. Gentian roots, *bottom right,* serve as a flavoring and as a stomach medicine.

produce new plants year after year. Some herbs are annuals. They live for only one growing season and must be raised from seed each year. The word *herb* comes from the Latin word *herba,* meaning *grass, green stalks,* or *blades.* Botanists use the word to mean any plant with soft, succulent tissues. But many people use the word to mean only herbs with some economic value.

Some herbs are used in cooking to flavor foods. Others give scents to perfumes. Still others are used for medicines. Some herbs, such as balm and sage, are valued for their leaves. Saffron is picked for its buds and flowers. Fennel seeds are valuable in relishes and seasoning. Vanilla fruit pods yield vanilla flavoring. Ginseng is valued for its aromatic roots.

People often grow herbs in their gardens. Many kinds of herbs can also be raised indoors. The plants grow well with little care. Gardeners plant herbs in good soil that has been well-cultivated. They choose a sunny spot that is easily accessible. When the herbs begin to grow, the gardener keeps the soil loose and free from weeds. The leaves, stems, or seeds of herbs can be used fresh, or they can be dried for later use. Dried herbs can be pounded to a fine powder, placed in airtight containers, and then stored. See **Gardening** (Food gardens).

Although herbs have little food value, they make food tasty and more flavorful. Cooking with herbs has become a culinary art, and it adds great variety to any menu.   Richard C. Keating

Related articles in *World Book* include:

Balm	Cicely	Horseradish
Basil	Cineraria	Lavender
Bitters	Coriander	Marjoram
Boneset	Elecampane	Mint
Calendula	Fennel	Parsley
Calla	Figwort family	Pennyroyal
Caraway	Geranium	Peppermint
Catnip	Ginseng	Portulaca
Celandine	Horehound	Rosemary

Saffron	Spikenard	Thyme
Sage	Tansy	Valerian
Spearmint	Telegraph plant	Vanilla

Herbarium, *hur BAIR ee uhm,* is an organized collection of dried plants. Herbariums serve an important function in the study of plants. They offer an easy way to examine many kinds of plants or many examples of one particular kind. Herbariums provide a valuable, permanent record of plant life.

Most specimens in a herbarium are glued to sheets of stiff paper. Some specimens, such as mosses, lichens, and fungi, are placed in folded paper packets. Each specimen is labeled with its name, the place and date of collection, the name of the collector, and other information. A good specimen shows all parts of the plant, such as the root, leaf, flower, and fruit. If they are protected from pests and moisture, specimens will last for hundreds of years.

The most valuable specimens in a herbarium are those from which the first descriptions of their kind were made. This is because the most common use of a herbarium is for naming unidentified plant specimens. By making comparisons with original specimens, botanists determine the best name to use for an unidentified specimen. Herbarium collections are also used in studies of plants of a particular kind or of a particular area. A good herbarium has many specimens of each kind of plant from the area in which it is located.

The oldest herbarium in the United States is in the Academy of Natural Sciences of Philadelphia. This herbarium was founded in 1812. The largest herbarium in the United States, and the third largest in the world, is the National Herbarium in Washington, D.C. It has more than 5 million specimens. Only the herbarium of the Royal Botanic Gardens in Kew, England, and the herbarium of the Komarov Botanic Institute in Leningrad, the Soviet Union, are larger.   David H. Wagner

Herbart, *HEHR bahrt,* **Johann Friedrich,** *YOH hahn FREE drihkh* (1776-1841), was a German philosopher and educator who greatly influenced educational theory of the late 1800's. He believed that education is closely related to *ethics* (the study of standards of right and wrong) and to psychology. Ethics provides the overall goal of education—to build strong moral character. Psychology furnishes the means of achieving this goal.

Herbart stressed the importance of developing and maintaining students' interest in learning. He called for four steps in teaching. First, the teacher presents information to students. Second, the instructor helps students analyze the new material and compare or contrast it with ideas they have already learned. Third, the teacher and the class use the new information to develop a general rule or principle. Fourth, the teacher helps students apply the new information in other situations or use the rule to solve other problems. Many educators in Europe and North America adopted Herbart's four steps, which his followers later expanded into five.

Herbart was born in Oldenburg, in what is now West Germany. He studied philosophy at the University of Jena. In 1797, he went to Switzerland as a private tutor. There he met the Swiss educator Johann H. Pestalozzi, who inspired many of his theories. Herbart taught education and philosophy at the University of Göttingen from 1802 to 1809 and at the University of Königsberg from 1809 to 1833. He then returned to Göttingen, where he taught until his death. Douglas Sloan

Herbert, Frank (1920-1986), was an American author of science fiction. He was best known for his *Dune* trilogy, which consists of *Dune* (1965), *Dune Messiah* (1969), and *Children of Dune* (1976). These three novels trace the struggle for survival and power among the inhabitants of a desert planet. Herbert continued the story in *God Emperor of Dune* (1981), *Heretics of Dune* (1984), and *Chapterhouse: Dune* (1985). The *Dune* novels, like Herbert's other works, have complex plots and strong philosophical and psychological themes. Herbert told in great detail the history and background of events in his stories.

Herbert's first novel, *Under Pressure* (1956), which is also known as *The Dragon in the Sea,* describes submarine warfare in the 2000's and predicts a worldwide oil shortage. His other novels include *The Heaven Makers* (1968), *Whipping Star* (1970), *Hellstrom's Hive* (1973), and *The White Plague* (1982). He was born in Tacoma, Wash., and attended the University of Washington. He worked as a newspaper reporter, photographer, and oyster diver. Judy-Lynn del Rey

Herbert, George (1593-1633), was a leading English poet of the 1600's. His collected poems were published shortly after his death as *The Temple.* In this volume, Herbert gracefully and lovingly built his short lyrics into a grand hymn of praise to God. His metrical variety and his intimate, homely, at times almost quaint tone gave a special quality to his verse. As one poet of Herbert's day wrote: Herbert "speaks to God like one who really believeth a God. . . . Heart-work and heaven-work make up his book." His poems include "The Collar," "Vertue," and "The Pulley."

Herbert was born into a noble Welsh family. Ordained about 1626, he gave up a career at court and at Cambridge University to become a devoted parish priest, from 1630 to his death. Richard S. Sylvester

See also **Metaphysical poets.**

Herbert, Victor (1859-1924), an American composer and conductor, is often called "the prince of operetta." One of his most famous operettas is *Babes in Toyland* (1903), which was based on Mother Goose and fairyland characters. "March of the Toys" and "Toyland" are well-loved numbers in this operetta. He also wrote *Mlle. Modiste* (1905), which includes the popular song "Kiss Me Again." *Naughty Marietta* (1910), one of the most tuneful of his operettas, includes such songs as "Ah! Sweet Mystery of Life," "I'm Falling in Love with Someone," "Italian Street Song," and "'Neath the Southern Moon."

Herbert was born in Dublin, Ireland. He studied the cello in Germany, and played in leading European orchestras. In 1886, he settled in New York City, where he played cello in the Metropolitan Opera Company Orchestra. In 1893, Herbert followed Patrick S. Gilmore as bandmaster of the Twenty-

Bettmann Archive
Victor Herbert

second Regiment Band. He wrote *Prince Ananias,* his first operetta to be staged, in 1894. It was not a great success, but *The Wizard of the Nile,* a year later, proved popular.

Herbert was appointed conductor of the Pittsburgh Symphony Orchestra in 1898, but resigned in 1904 to devote his time to composition. He was the first American composer to write an original score for a movie. His other works include the operettas *The Fortune Teller* (1898), with the song "Gypsy Love Song"; *The Red Mill* (1906); *Sweethearts* (1913); *Princess Pat* (1915); *Eileen* (1917), with the song "Thine Alone"; and *The Dream Girl* (1924). He composed two grand operas, *Natoma* (1911) and *Madeleine* (1914). Gerald Bordman

Herbicide, *HUR buh syd,* is a chemical compound used to control or destroy unwanted plants. Herbicides are sometimes called *weedkillers.* Farmers and ranchers use herbicides to control weeds among crops. People also use herbicides to eliminate weeds from lawns, parks, industrial sites, and other areas. More than 250 million acres (101 million hectares) of land in the United States are treated with herbicides yearly.

There are two types of herbicides, *selective* and *nonselective.* Most herbicides are selective—that is, they kill weeds but do not harm crops. Nonselective herbicides, sometimes called *soil sterilants,* destroy all plants and may prevent anything from growing in the soil. Soil sterilants are used along driveways, railroads, and other places where people do not want plants to grow.

Herbicides have been used since the early 1850's, when salt was spread to control unwanted plants. Salt, copper sulfate, and other early herbicides were nonselective. Selective herbicides came into use in 1944 with the development of *2,4-D.* This herbicide is still used to kill such broadleaf weeds as cocklebur and pigweed.

How herbicides work. Herbicides are manufactured in the form of tiny particles or a liquid. They are sprayed on growing weeds or mixed into the soil. Many herbicides control weeds by preventing weed seeds from sprouting. They are mixed into the soil before or at the same time that crops are planted, or applied to the soil surface before crops and weeds start to grow. Some herbicides kill plants by hindering photosynthesis, the process by which plants convert carbon dioxide into food. Others, called *growth regulator herbicides,* cause plants to die prematurely by altering their growth patterns. Most growth regulator herbicides are applied after the crop or weed appears above the soil surface.

Hazards of herbicides. In the United States, the Environmental Protection Agency (EPA) regulates the use of herbicides and registers their safe uses. The EPA has approved more than 180 herbicides. Most of them do not endanger human beings, animals, or the environment if used as directed by the manufacturer. However, some herbicides are extremely poisonous and must be used with extreme care. All herbicides should be stored where children and animals cannot get to them.

In the 1960's and 1970's, a mixture of the herbicides 2,4-D and 2,4,5-T was widely used to *defoliate* (cause leaves to fall off) trees and brush. During the Vietnam War, this mixture became known by the military code name *Agent Orange.* United States forces sprayed it on the trees of jungles in South Vietnam to expose enemy snipers. During the early 1970's, researchers found that

Agent Orange and all other 2,4,5-T products contained a highly poisonous substance called *dioxin*. Dioxin contamination was a possible health hazard to people and animals. In 1979, the Environmental Protection Agency banned most uses of 2,4,5-T.   Harold D. Coble

See also **Agent Orange; Dioxin; Pesticide; Weed** (Weed control).

Herbivore, *HUR buh vawr,* is any animal that eats chiefly plants. Herbivores are also called *herbivorous animals*. Animals that primarily eat flesh are called *carnivores*. Those that eat both flesh and plants are called *omnivores*.

There are many kinds of herbivores. Some, such as cattle, deer, and horses, eat grasses. Others, including many birds, eat seeds. Earthworms are among the herbivores that eat dead plant material.   William V. Mayer

See also **Carnivore; Mammal** (illustration: The teeth of mammals); **Omnivore.**

Herblock. See Block, Herbert Lawrence.

Herbs. See Herb.

Hercegovina. See Bosnia and Hercegovina.

Herculaneum, *HUR kyuh LAY nee uhm,* was an ancient Roman city in Italy. Like Pompeii and Stabiae, it was buried when Mount Vesuvius erupted in A.D. 79. However, the mud and lava that buried Herculaneum also preserved the city as a record of life in ancient times. Fifteen hundred years later, archaeologists dug through the hardened layers of mud and lava and discovered priceless manuscripts, works of art, and tools of daily life.

Herculaneum was a small, pleasant city with a good harbor. It stood at the foot of Mount Vesuvius, 6 miles

SCALA/Art Resource

A street in Herculaneum looks much as it did in ancient times. Archaeologists have excavated many parts of the Roman city, which was buried when Mount Vesuvius erupted in A.D. 79.

(10 kilometers) from Naples. The city had strong fortifications and was the home of many artistic treasures. Herculaneum was badly shaken by an earthquake in A.D. 63, but the damage was repaired.

Sixteen years later came the volcanic eruption that buried Herculaneum, Pompeii, and Stabiae, killing thousands of people. Pompeii and Stabiae were covered by ashes and lava. These cities were not as well preserved as Herculaneum, which was buried under a flow of lava and mud that was 100 feet (30 meters) deep in some places.

A village later grew up near the site of Herculaneum. In the early 1700's, a farmer sank a shaft for a well, and found marble statues far below the surface. Soon afterward, someone sank another shaft, and discovered a theater. The government of Naples took up the task of excavation in 1738. The deposits were much deeper at Herculaneum than at Pompeii, so digging was more difficult. Excavation was stopped in the 1800's but resumed in 1926 by the Italian government.

The site is now honeycombed by tunnels which robbers dug. It is believed that thieves have carried off many priceless works of art. But the excavators found wonderful marble and bronze statues, paintings, and papyrus rolls. Most of these precious works are now housed in an exhibit at the National Museum in Naples.
        Mary Francis Gyles

See also **Pliny; Pompeii; Vesuvius.**

Hercules, *HUR kyuh leez,* was one of the greatest heroes of Greek mythology. The Greeks called him *Heracles,* but he is usually known as *Hercules,* the name used by the Romans.

Early life. Hercules was born in Thebes. He was the son of the princess Alcmene, a mortal, and Zeus, the king of the gods. Hera, the wife of Zeus, was jealous of Alcmene and hated Hercules. She persecuted Hercules throughout his life.

When Hercules was an infant, Hera sent two serpents to kill him. However, Hercules strangled the snakes. As a young man, Hercules had a vision. In it, he was offered a choice of a life of ease, pleasure, and vice, or one of hardship, danger, glory, and virtue. He chose the more difficult—but virtuous—life.

The twelve labors. Hera caused Hercules to have a fit of madness, during which he killed his wife, Megara, and their children. The oracle at Delphi told Hercules that he had to serve King Eurystheus of Tiryns for 12 years to purify himself of the murders.

Eurystheus commanded Hercules to perform 12 labors, which are described, with many variations, by a number of ancient authors. This section deals with the most generally accepted versions of the labors.

The first six labors took place near Thebes. First, Hercules killed the fierce lion of Nemea, whose skin he then wore as a trophy. Next, with the help of his nephew Iolaus, Hercules slew the deadly Hydra of Lerna. This serpent had several heads that grew back as soon as they were cut off. Hercules cut off the heads, and Iolaus sealed each neck with fire to prevent them from growing back. The hydra also had one head that was immortal, which Hercules buried under a rock. He then used the hydra's blood to poison his arrows.

For the third and fourth labors, Hercules captured the huge boar of Erymanthus and the golden-horned Arcadian stag. For his fifth labor, he drove a flock of ferocious birds away from the woods near Lake Stymphalus. These birds had arrowlike feathers that they shot at people. Next, Hercules cleaned the stables of King Augeas, which had not been washed out for many years, by making two rivers flow through them.

The second six labors took Hercules increasingly farther from his home. For the seventh labor, he traveled to Crete to capture the bull of King Minos. For the eighth, Hercules brought the horses of King Diomedes of Thrace to Eurystheus. These horses ate human beings, but Hercules tamed them by feeding them Diomedes. For the ninth labor, Hercules obtained the *girdle* (belt) of Hippolyta, the queen of the Amazons, by defeating her in battle (see **Amazons**).

To perform the 10th and 11th labors, Hercules journeyed to the western edge of the ancient world. First, he captured the cattle of the fearful monster Geryon. Then he stole the Golden Apples of the Hesperides from the Tree of Life (see **Hesperides**). For his 12th labor, Hercules descended into the world of the dead, captured the three-headed watchdog Cerberus, and brought him back to the upper world (see **Cerberus**). The last three labors represented the conquest of death, and Hercules achieved immortality by carrying them out.

Other adventures of Hercules included accompanying the Argonauts on part of their voyage in search of the Golden Fleece. He also restored Alcestis, the wife of King Admetus, to life by outwrestling Death. Hercules released Prometheus from the punishment to which Zeus had condemned him. Also, Hercules overcame the giant Antaeus, whose strength was renewed by contact with his mother, Earth, by holding him off the ground until he weakened. See **Argonauts; Prometheus.**

The death of Hercules. Some time after completing the 12 labors, Hercules married the princess Deianira. The centaur Nessus tried to rape Deianira, and Hercules shot him with a poisoned arrow. The dying centaur told Deianira to smear some of his blood on Hercules' robe if she ever needed to win back his love. After Hercules fell in love with another princess, Iole, Deianira followed Nessus' advice. But the centaur's blood had been poisoned by Hercules' arrow. When Hercules put on the robe, it burned him so terribly he pleaded to be placed on a funeral pyre. His body was consumed by flames, and he was taken to Olympus, home of the gods. There, he became a god.   Paul Pascal

See also **Atlas** (god); **Cornucopia; Hebe; Renaissance** (picture: Mythological subjects).

Hercules is a constellation of the Northern Hemisphere between Corona Borealis and Lyra. It is best seen high overhead in summer. The red star marking the head of Hercules lies toward the south. It is a giant, hundreds of times larger than the sun. In the northwest side of Hercules, a cluster numbering more than 100,000 stars appears. It is so far away that light requires more than 30,000 years to reach the earth. Even under good conditions, the cluster is barely visible to the naked eye. In 1934, a star in Hercules suddenly began to grow brighter. It increased until it looked brighter than the North Star. Such a star is called a *nova.* Novas have appeared in other constellations during this century, but all have now faded and telescopes are needed to see them (see **Nova**).   I. M. Levitt

E. R. Degginger

Hercules beetles live in the United States, Central America, and the West Indies. Male hercules beetles have long, curved horns that project from the head and upper body. In some species, the horns make up more than half the beetle's length.

Hercules beetle is the name of several large, strong beetles that live in North America. Male Hercules beetles have long horns that project from the head and front underpart of the body. The horns are curved to meet each other and look like pincers. Males of one species found in the West Indies grow 5 to 6 inches (13 to 15 centimeters) long. The horns may make up more than half of the beetle's length. The rhinoceros beetle that is found in the southern and western United States is related to Hercules beetles. It is similar in appearance but smaller.

Scientific classification. Hercules beetles belong to the family Scarabaeidae. They are genus *Dynastes,* and they belong to the order Coleoptera.   H. H. Ross

Herd. See **Animal** (Flocks, herds, and schools).

Herder, Johann Gottfried von (1744-1803), was one of the most original and versatile German writers, critics, and philosophers. His deep influence on the humanities can be felt today. He inspired Goethe and the other writers of the *Sturm und Drang* (Storm and Stress) movement with new ideas in poetry, art, language, religion, and history. See **German literature** (The Storm and Stress movement).

Herder continued Gotthold Lessing's work in trying to free German writers from imitating French classicism, based on the ancient Greeks. He argued that Shakespeare, Ossian, the Hebrew poets, and folk songs equaled the works of the Greeks.

His admirable translations of Shakespeare and the songs of many nations formed models for translations by the German romanticists who followed him. His *Ideas to a Philosophy of History* (1784-1791), in four volumes, contributed important theories on the development of civilization. He explained cultural evolution as part of the evolution of nature, rather than a manifestation of the rational free will of human beings.

Herder was born in Mohrungen, East Prussia, the son of a poor schoolteacher. He worked to finance his education. At the University of Königsberg, he studied theology and philosophy. Immanuel Kant was one of his teachers there. After four successful years as a teacher and preacher in Riga, Russia, Herder traveled through Europe. In Strasbourg, he met Goethe, and they became friends. Through Goethe's influence, Herder was appointed general superintendent of churches and court preacher at Weimar in 1776.   Gottfried F. Merkel

Tom Stack
© William H. Amos, Bruce Coleman Inc.
© Jen & Des Bartlett, Bruce Coleman Inc.
© K. Gunnar, Bruce Coleman Inc.

Heredity affects all living things. The little girl, *top left,* has inherited her mother's freckles and red hair. The baby kangaroo also resembles its mother, *bottom left.* The young fir trees will grow up just like their huge parents, *bottom right.* The process of heredity occurs even among one-celled organisms like the protozoan splitting and forming two identical offspring, *top right.*

Heredity

Heredity is the passing on of characteristics from parents to their offspring. The process of heredity occurs among all living things—human beings, animals, plants, and even bacteria and other microscopic organisms. Heredity is the reason offspring resemble their parents. It explains why a mother cat always has kittens and why a human mother always has a human baby.

All human beings bear a basic resemblance to one another because of their shared human heredity. But people differ greatly in such features as height and the color of their eyes, hair, and skin. These variations are also due to heredity. Each individual inherits a different combination of traits. Even brothers and sisters may differ in many ways because they received different characteristics from their parents.

Some characteristics are caused entirely by heredity. Your heredity determined whether you would be a boy or a girl at the time you began life inside your mother's body. Certain other characteristics are determined by environmental factors instead of by heredity. For example, whether you can play a violin depends on whether you had lessons, not on heredity. Most characteristics are influenced by both heredity and environment. For example, your heredity determines the general shape of your body, but your actual weight depends largely on what kinds of food you eat and how much you eat.

Terms used in the study of heredity

Alleles are different forms of the same gene. For example, one allele of the gene for eye color produces blue eyes, and another allele produces brown eyes.

Chromosomes are tiny threadlike structures inside the nucleus of each cell. Chromosomes carry the genes.

DNA stands for *deoxyribonucleic acid.* It is the substance within the chromosomes that carries the hereditary instructions for producing proteins.

Genes are units of heredity that determine particular traits, such as eye color and blood type. Each gene is a segment of DNA that carries instructions for making all or part of a specific protein.

Genetic variation refers to the differences in inherited traits that exist among the members of a species.

Genetics is the scientific study of heredity.

Hybrid is a plant or animal produced by parents that have different hereditary characteristics.

Mutation is a chemical change in a gene. It may produce a new trait that can be inherited.

Nucleus is the structure within a cell that contains the chromosomes.

RNA stands for *ribonucleic acid.* It is a substance similar to DNA. RNA transmits DNA's instructions for making proteins from the nucleus to the cytoplasm of a cell.

Daniel L. Hartl, the contributor of this article, is Professor of Biology at Purdue University and the author of Our Uncertain Heritage: Genetics and Human Diversity.

Inherited traits are passed on by chemical instructions called *genes*. Genes are located on tiny threadlike structures called *chromosomes* within cells. Each person begins life as a single cell called a *fertilized egg.* This fertilized egg comes from the joining of a tiny *egg* cell from the mother with an even tinier *sperm* cell from the father. Both the egg and the sperm contain genes. These genes control the development of the fertilized egg and determine many of the characteristics the baby will have.

Except for identical twins, no two persons have exactly the same genes. Identical twins occur when a fertilized egg splits into two pieces during an early stage in its development. Each piece forms an individual baby. Although identical twins have exactly the same genes, they may differ in many ways because of differences in environment.

The scientific study of heredity is called *genetics.* Within genetics, there are several major areas of study. *Molecular genetics* is the study of the chemical basis of heredity. Specialists in *cytogenetics* study cell structure and cell behavior in relation to heredity. *Developmental genetics* is the study of how genes control the development of a fertilized egg. *Population genetics* deals with the effects of the laws of heredity on entire groups of organisms.

Human heredity

Physical traits. Almost all our physical characteristics are determined to some degree by heredity. Genes completely determine such characteristics as the color and texture of the hair and the color, size, and shape of the eyes. Heredity also greatly influences the general shape of the body and the size and shape of the ears, hands, and feet. In some of these physical characteristics, an individual may closely resemble one parent or even a grandparent.

Heredity influences much more than physical appearance. Genes also determine many chemical characteristics of the body, the best known of which is blood type. Each person inherits one of four blood types: A, B, AB, or O. Each blood type corresponds to the presence of certain chemicals on the surface of the *red blood cells,* one of the major types of cells in the blood. A person's genes also determine whether the red blood cells have another chemical characteristic called the *Rh factor.*

Many physical traits are influenced by environment as well as by heredity. For example, genes determine a person's skin color, but the skin also darkens when exposed to sunlight. Similarly, heredity determines the general shape of the body—whether it will be short and stocky or tall and thin. However, a person's eating and exercising habits also affect the shape of the body.

Mental traits. Every person inherits certain basic mental traits, such as the ability to learn and remember. But to develop such abilities, an individual must have a suitable environment. A baby's brain can develop normally only if the baby has the proper kind and amount of food. Babies who do not receive enough to eat may suffer a reduced ability to learn throughout life.

Mental abilities vary, even among members of the same family. One brother may learn mathematics more easily than another, but the other brother may find it easier to learn to read. Some people inherit special *apti-*

tudes (talents) in such fields as music, painting, or mathematics. However, environment plays an important role in the development of these aptitudes. Identical twins may inherit an equal talent for playing the piano, but the twin who studies and practices more will become the better musician.

Hereditary disorders. A wide range of diseases and defects can be passed on from parents to their children. Some children inherit a defect that causes them to have extra fingers or toes. Others are color blind because of an inherited defect in part of the eye. Neither of these defects is especially serious, but some inherited diseases have severe consequences. In *hemophilia,* for example, the blood does not clot normally. *Muscular dystrophy* causes the muscles to waste away. Another inherited defect produces a type of skin cancer, and still another results in cancer of the retina of the eye. Most forms of cancer are not inherited, however.

Some hereditary disorders can cause mental retardation. For example, children with *phenylketonuria* (PKU) cannot properly use a certain substance in food. This substance, called *phenylalanine,* accumulates in the blood and severely damages the brain. However, PKU victims do not suffer brain damage if they follow a special diet low in phenylalanine.

Serious diseases that result entirely from heredity occur only rarely. More often, people inherit a tendency to develop a particular disease, such as diabetes or *hypertension* (high blood pressure). Environmental factors also play an important role in the development of these diseases. For example, people with a tendency toward hypertension may increase their chances of getting the

Grant Heilman

The effects of environment can be seen in these corn plants. All were grown from identical seeds and so have indentical *genes* (units of heredity). However, the plants on the right grew in soil that lacked some nutrients needed for proper growth.

How chromosomes are inherited

WORLD BOOK diagrams

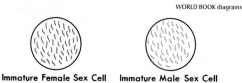

Immature Female Sex Cell   Immature Male Sex Cell

Early in their development, sex cells have matching pairs of *chromosomes* (structures that carry genes). The diagrams above show an immature human female and male sex cell. Each cell has 23 pairs of chromosomes, or 46 chromosomes altogether.

Egg   Sperm

Sex cells undergo a special type of cell division that forms cells with only one chromosome from each pair. This process, called *meiosis,* produces egg cells in females and sperm cells in males. Each human egg or sperm thus has 23 chromosomes.

Fertilized Egg

When a sperm unites with an egg, the resulting *fertilized egg* has the 23 matching pairs of chromosomes of a normal body cell. One chromosome in each pair came from the mother, and the other came from the father.

disease by eating too much salt or by smoking.

A person may also inherit a tendency toward certain types of emotional or mental illness. However, environmental conditions generally determine whether an individual with such an inherited tendency will actually become mentally ill.

A couple who fear that they may pass on a serious hereditary disorder to their children may consult a *genetic counselor.* A genetic counselor will carefully study the family history and perform medical tests to detect potentially harmful genes in one or both parents. The counselor can then advise the couple about their chances of having an abnormal child.

The physical basis of heredity

Genes and chromosomes. Each cell in the human body contains units of heredity called genes. The genes are located on chromosomes, tiny threadlike structures in the nucleus of the cell. A human chromosome is only about $\frac{1}{50,000}$ inch (0.0005 millimeter) long, and genes are far tinier still. Each chromosome carries about 1,000 genes. The genes are arranged in a line along the chromosome much like words in a sentence.

Chromosomes consist chiefly of proteins and a substance called *deoxyribonucleic acid,* commonly known as *DNA.* Each gene is a segment of DNA. The segments of DNA in a single chromosome form a long chain that is highly twisted and coiled. If this chain could be uncoiled and completely stretched out, it would measure almost 2 inches (5 centimeters) long.

The cells of different kinds of animals and plants have

a different number of chromosomes. In human beings, *body cells* (all cells except the egg and sperm cells) contain 46 chromosomes each. Body cells of gorillas and chimpanzees have 48 chromosomes, those of mice have 40, and those of most corn varieties have 20.

Chromosomes in body cells occur in pairs. Every human body cell contains two sets of 23 chromosomes. Each chromosome in one set has a matching chromosome in the other set. A chromosome and its matching partner carry genes for the same traits, and these genes are arranged in the same order.

How traits are inherited. Egg cells and sperm cells are formed in a special way and have only one set of 23 chromosomes. Thus, when an egg and a sperm unite, they produce a fertilized egg that has the 46 chromosomes of a normal body cell. Half the chromosomes come from the mother, and half from the father.

A fertilized egg grows and develops into a human baby by a process of cell division called *mitosis.* The fertilized egg first divides into two cells. Each of these cells then divides, producing four cells. The four cells divide, resulting in eight cells, and so forth. This process eventually produces the more than 1 trillion cells that make up a baby's body.

Just before a cell divides, each chromosome in the cell's nucleus makes an exact duplicate of itself. The two identical copies of each chromosome lie side by side and are attached to each other. When the cell divides, the attachment breaks, and the copies move apart. One of the new cells produced by the division receives one copy of each chromosome. The other new cell receives

How sex is determined

WORLD BOOK diagrams

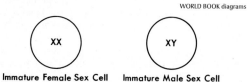

Immature Female Sex Cell   Immature Male Sex Cell

A pair of *sex chromosomes* determines whether a fertilized egg will become a girl or a boy. An immature female sex cell has two matching sex chromosomes called *X chromosomes.* An immature male sex cell has an X chromosome and a *Y chromosome.*

Egg   Sperm

When an immature female sex cell divides, each resulting egg cell receives a single X chromosome. When an immature male sex cell divides, half the resulting sperm cells receive an X chromosome, and the other half receive a Y chromosome.

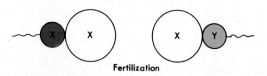

Fertilization

An egg fertilized by a sperm cell containing an X chromosome has two X chromosomes, *left.* It will develop into a girl. An egg fertilized by a sperm with a Y chromosome has one X and one Y chromosome, *right.* Such an egg will develop into a boy.

the other copy. In this manner, each new cell receives an exact duplicate of every chromosome present in the fertilized egg.

Like other cells, sex cells are first produced by mitosis. But before sex cells mature into eggs or sperm, they undergo another type of cell division called *meiosis*. In this process, the chromosomes duplicate, and then cell division occurs twice. The result is four cells with 23 chromosomes each, instead of two cells with 46 chromosomes each.

How sex is determined. A special pair of chromosomes called *sex chromosomes* determines whether a fertilized egg will develop into a girl or a boy. The two sex chromosomes in the body cells of a girl match exactly in shape and size. Geneticists call these sex chromosomes *X chromosomes.* A boy's body cells have the X chromosome and one smaller sex chromosome called a *Y chromosome.* The X chromosome carries about as many genes as other chromosomes do, but the Y chromosome carries fewer genes.

When an immature sex cell in a woman goes through meiosis, the X chromosomes pair with each other and separate just like the other chromosomes. Each egg cell thus receives a single X chromosome. When an immature sex cell in a man undergoes meiosis, the X and Y chromosomes pair with each other and separate. As a result, half the sperm cells have an X chromosome, and the other half have a Y chromosome.

If a sperm cell containing an X chromosome fertilizes an egg cell, the fertilized egg will have two X chromosomes and so will develop into a girl. If a sperm cell containing a Y chromosome fertilizes the egg cell, the fertilized egg will have one X chromosome and one Y chromosome. In this case, the fertilized egg will develop into a boy.

Patterns of heredity. Except for genes on the sex chromosomes in males, genes occur in pairs. Some hereditary traits are determined by a single pair of genes. For example, a chemical called *phenylthiocarbimide,* or *PTC,* tastes extremely bitter to some people. Other people cannot taste PTC at all. The difference between tasters and nontasters is due to a single pair of genes. Other traits are determined by several pairs of genes. For example, about six pairs of genes influence skin color. Each skin-color gene causes a slight darkening of the skin, and people with extremely dark skin may have up to six pairs of skin-darkening genes. Tens or even hundreds of gene pairs influence such traits as height, weight, and intelligence.

The two genes in a pair may differ in the effects they produce. Different forms of the same gene are called *alleles.* In some cases, one allele has such a strong effect that it overpowers the action of the other. For example, people who have one allele for tasting PTC and one allele for nontasting can taste the chemical. Geneticists say that the allele for tasting is *dominant* and the allele for nontasting is *recessive.* Other human traits due to dominant alleles include brown eyes and the presence of the Rh factor on red blood cells. Characteristics that result from recessive alleles include blue eyes, blond hair, and *albinism* (the absence of pigment in the skin). A recessive trait occurs only in an individual who has two recessive alleles for that trait.

Each person has no more than two alleles of any

Albinism

Albinism is a hereditary condition in which an organism cannot produce pigment. Albinism occurs in human beings and in many species of plants and animals.

WORLD BOOK diagram

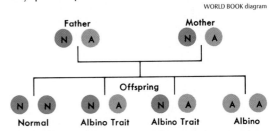

Albinism is a *recessive* trait, which means that only individuals with two albinism genes have the disorder. In the chart above, each parent carries one normal (N) gene and one albinism (A) gene. Each offspring of such parents has one chance in four of inheriting albinism from both parents. Individuals who inherit the albinism gene from only one parent are not albinos, but they may transmit the gene to their offspring. The albino rabbit below has pink eyes, which are characteristic of albino animals.

© Michael P. Gadomski, Bruce Coleman Inc.

gene, but some genes exist in more than two forms. Such genes are said to have *multiple alleles.* Three alleles are involved in determining ABO blood types: (1) an A allele, (2) a B allele, and (3) an O allele. A person who has two of the same allele has the corresponding blood type—A, B or O. A person with one A allele and one B allele has type AB blood. Both A and B are dominant over O. Thus, a person who inherits one A allele and one O allele will have type A, and one who inherits one B allele and one O allele will have type B.

Genes that lie on the same chromosome are called *linked genes* because they tend to be inherited together. Genes on the sex chromosomes are called *sex-linked genes.* Genes on the X chromosome are X-linked, and those on the Y chromosome are Y-linked. Color blindness, hemophilia, and one type of muscular dystrophy are all due to X-linked genes. These disorders generally occur only in males because males have only one X chromosome. Most females have a dominant allele on one X chromosome that prevents the harmful gene on the other X chromosome from producing its effects.

Linked genes are not always inherited together. Just before sex cells divide to form sperm or eggs, each chromosome lines up side by side with its partner chromosome. Through a process called *crossing over,*

A *World Book* science project

Studying heredity

The purpose of this project is to learn some of the principles of heredity by breeding common fruit flies. Geneticists have discovered many of the most important principles of heredity by conducting experiments similar to these.

Characteristics of fruit flies make these insects helpful in studying heredity. Fruit flies complete their life cycle in two weeks. This means that an experimenter can trace hereditary traits through several generations in a short time. Although the insects are small, you can see traits such as wing shape and eye color with a magnifying glass.

Normal female fruit fly has a thick abdomen that ends in a sharp point. Five black bands form stripes across the abdomen. Both the normal female and the normal male have red eyes and long, thin wings.

Normal male fruit fly has a narrow abdomen that is rounded at the end. Three black bands mark the abdomen. The last band extends over the end. Only males have comblike bristles that grow on the front legs.

Special traits such as vestigial wings and white eyes develop as the result of mutations. You can buy both male and female fruit flies with such special traits from a company that sells biological supplies.

Experiments in heredity

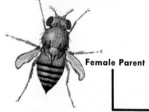

Female Parent

You can conduct experiments in breeding and demonstrate the results as shown, *upper right.* The experimenter traced the inheritance of eye color and wing type in fruit flies. He bred a female parent with red eyes and vestigial wings with a male parent with white eyes and normal wings. The inheritance of these traits in the first generation (hybrid) offspring is shown, *below.*

Male Parent

Offspring

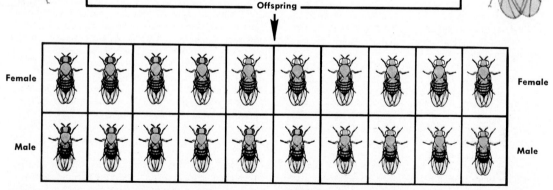

Female

Male

Female

Male

To show segregation. Select ten adult flies from a hybrid culture, such as the offspring in the above experiment, and breed a new generation. Take the new flies out of the jar. Examine the wings. What is the ratio of flies with normal wings to flies with vestigial wings? It should be about 3 to 1. Why?

To breed pure lines. Breed flies with vestigial wings from a second generation culture. Examine the wings of the offspring. Repeat the process for several generations. Try the same experiment using normal-winged flies from the second generation. Compare and explain the results of the two experiments.

Materials

You can get materials for the experiments from local stores. Capture fruit flies near ripe fruit, or buy them from a company that sells biological supplies.

Let them grow in a culture medium of fruit and liquid yeast, which is made by melting a yeast cake in warm water.

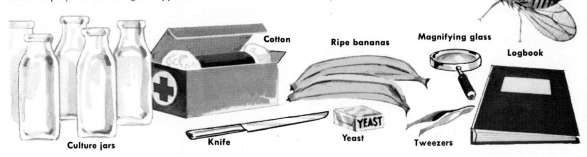

Culture jars — Knife — Cotton — Ripe bananas — YEAST Yeast — Magnifying glass — Tweezers — Logbook

Procedure

To sterilize the equipment, plug the culture jars with wads of cotton fitted snugly into the mouths. Place the jars and a knife in a cold oven and heat them slowly at about 250° F. (121° C) for a half hour or longer. Turn off the heat and let them cool. Do not take the plugs out until you are ready to put food in the jars.

To prepare the culture medium, peel a banana about halfway. Keep the fruit from touching anything. With the sterile knife, cut about 2 inches (5 centimeters) of the fruit into small pieces and drop them into the jar. Mash the fruit, add three drops of liquid yeast, and replace the plug.

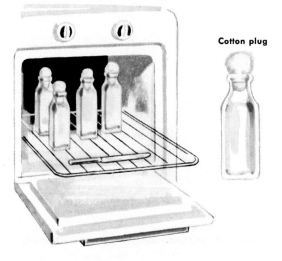

Cotton plug

To stock the culture jar, put a male and a female fruit fly into a prepared jar. The female must be less than 6 hours old if it is from one of your own cultures. When the pupae appear, remove the parents. To do this, put a jar over your culture jar, and point the bottom of this jar toward the light as shown, *below.*

To examine the fruit flies, use a magnifying glass. After the pupae become adults, place the culture jar in a refrigerator for a few minutes. The flies will drop to the bottom and stop moving. Remove the cotton and shake the flies onto clean paper. After examining the flies, record your findings in a logbook.

Illustrated by Bart Jerner for WORLD BOOK

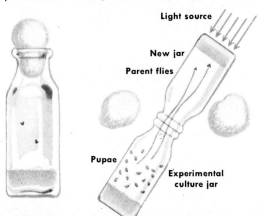

Light source — New jar — Parent flies — Pupae — Experimental culture jar

groups of genes from one chromosome may change places with groups of genes from its partner. As a result, different sperm or eggs may carry different combinations of linked genes. However, the X and Y chromosomes do not exchange genes.

Scientists measure the distance between genes by determining how often they become separated through crossing over. The farther apart two genes are on a chromosome, the more often they will be separated. Geneticists use this information to draw *chromosome maps,* which show the exact position of genes along a chromosome. By the early 1980's, scientists had mapped about 300 human genes, including more than 100 X-linked genes.

The chemical basis of heredity

All living things consist of many types of complex chemicals. A clear understanding of heredity depends on a basic knowledge of two types of these chemicals—*nucleic acids* and *proteins.* Nucleic acids store and transmit the genetic information passed on from cell to cell and from an organism to its offspring. This information consists of instructions for making proteins. Certain proteins make up most of the structural material in living things. Other proteins regulate the chemical processes that occur within the cells. Thus, the messages carried by nucleic acids control the structure and the activities of the cells by determining which proteins will be present.

The structure of nucleic acids. Every cell contains two main types of nucleic acids. One type is DNA. The other is *ribonucleic acid,* commonly called *RNA.*

DNA makes up the genetic substance of the chromosomes. DNA is a threadlike molecule about $\frac{1}{10,000,000}$ inch (0.0000025 millimeter) in diameter. Its structure resembles an extremely long, twisted ladder. The sidepieces of the ladder are composed of alternating units of chemical compounds called *phosphates* and a sugar called *deoxyribose.* Nitrogen compounds called *bases* form the rungs of the ladder. The bases are attached to the sugar units of the sidepieces. Four kinds of bases are found in DNA: *adenine, cytosine, guanine,* and *thymine.* These bases are commonly represented by the letters *A, C, G,* and *T* in the order named.

Each rung of a DNA ladder consists of two bases. One is attached to each sidepiece, and the two meet in the middle. A vital feature of DNA is that only two combinations of bases are possible. An A on one sidepiece always pairs with a T on the other sidepiece, and a G always pairs with a C. No other combinations of bases will fit. Thus, the sequence of bases attached to one *strand* (lengthwise half) of the DNA ladder determines the sequence of bases on the other strand. For example, if the sequence on one strand is ACGTGA, that on the other strand must be TGCACT. Each gene is a sequence of a thousand or more bases along a strand of DNA.

DNA never leaves the nucleus of a cell. But proteins are produced in the *cytoplasm,* the part of the cell outside the nucleus. Transmitting DNA's instructions to the cytoplasm is the task of RNA. RNA exists as single strands. It differs from DNA in two other ways—RNA has *ribose* sugar instead of deoxyribose, and it contains the base *uracil* (U) instead of thymine (T). However, U pairs with A to form complete rungs in the same way T does.

How DNA duplicates. Each body cell in an organism must have a complete set of genes. For this reason, every DNA molecule in a cell duplicates just before the cell divides. This duplication occurs in a remarkable manner. First, the DNA molecule splits down the middle betwen the bases and so forms two strands. Each strand consists of one sidepiece of the ladder along with its attached bases. Each strand then builds a new opposite half by linking with spare parts present in the cell nucleus. A spare part consists of a base and an attached sugar and phosphate.

Each spare part completes one rung of the DNA lad-

A model of a DNA molecule shows that DNA is shaped like a twisted ladder. The colored spheres represent the various types of chemical units that make up DNA. This model was proposed in 1953 by biologists Francis H. C. Crick and James D. Watson.

der. If a strand has an A half-rung, a spare part with a T completes the rung. Likewise, a spare part with a G completes a C half-rung. In this manner, each half-ladder builds a new opposite half with exactly the same sequence of bases as the half that split off. The cell now contains two DNA ladders exactly alike and identical to the original one. When the cell divides, each new cell receives one of the duplicated DNA ladders.

How proteins are made. The sequence of bases in DNA is actually a code that instructs the cell to make proteins. A protein consists of one or more long chains called *polypeptides*. The polypeptides, in turn, are made up of small chemical units called *amino acids*. A gene is a sequence of bases that tells the cell which amino acids to combine, and in what order to combine them, to form a particular polypeptide.

Making a protein involves two steps called *transcription* and *translation*. In transcription, a strand of DNA splits away from its opposite strand. It then builds a strand of RNA in the same manner that DNA produces a new strand of itself just before cell division. The strand of RNA then travels to the cytoplasm, where the process of translation occurs.

Translation takes place on tiny particles in the cytoplasm called *ribosomes*. A ribosome attaches to one end of a strand of RNA and moves along the strand, "translating" its coded instructions one "word" at a time. Each "word" is actually a group of three bases called a *codon*. Each codon instructs the ribosome to attach one particular amino acid. By linking amino acids, the ribosome builds a polypeptide. After the last amino acid has been attached, the ribosome releases the polypeptide. For a more detailed discussion of this process, see **Cell** (Producing proteins).

The genetic code is the set of correspondences between codons in RNA and amino acids in protein. For example, the genetic code for the amino acid *methionine* is the codon AUG, and the code for *tryptophan* is UGG. A total of 64 codons can be formed from the 4 bases of RNA. However, only 20 kinds of amino acids make up proteins. Thus, there is more than one codon for most amino acids. For example, CGA, CGC, CGG, and CGU all code for *arginine*. Three codons—UAA, UAG, and UGA—do not code for any amino acid. Instead, they signal that the polypeptide is complete and should be released from the ribosome.

One remarkable feature of the genetic code is that it is exactly the same in all living things. The same codons code for the same amino acids in viruses, bacteria, plants, animals, and human beings. This fact suggests that the genetic code must be as old as life itself.

Mutations are changes in the sequence of bases in genes. Mutations can occur through rare accidents during the duplication of DNA. The wrong base may mistakenly become attached to a DNA half-ladder. Mutations can also occur in DNA that has been damaged by X rays or certain chemicals. Once a gene has mutated, the new form duplicates just as faithfully as the original gene. A mutation that occurs in a body cell affects only the person who carries it. However, a mutation in a sex cell can be transmitted from generation to generation.

An incorrect base at a certain spot in a mutated DNA molecule causes the gene to produce RNA with an incorrect base at the corresponding position. The codon that contains the incorrect base may then cause the wrong amino acid to be added to the protein being produced. As a result, the protein may be unable to function normally. For example, a mutation in the gene for *hemoglobin* (an oxygen-carrying protein in the blood) can produce hemoglobin with a reduced ability to transport oxygen. Such defective hemoglobin can cause a disease called *sickle cell anemia.*

Heredity and change

According to the theory of evolution, every species of living things changes gradually over the course of time. This process of change occurs because of two basic facts about living things. (1) The individuals that make up a species differ from one another in their inherited characteristics. Biologists call these differences *genetic variation.* (2) The members of a species that are best suited to their environment are most likely to survive and reproduce. This principle is called *natural selection.*

Genetic variation results chiefly from three processes. They are (1) random assortment, (2) mutation, and (3) recombination.

Random assortment refers to the way in which chromosomes are distributed when a sex cell divides and forms eggs or sperm. An immature sex cell contains two of each chromosome—one from the individual's father and one from the mother. During cell division, each pair of chromosomes separates, and each egg or sperm receives one chromosome from each pair. Because the chromosomes separate in a random manner, each egg or sperm receives some chromosomes from the individual's mother and some from the father. This random assortment produces eggs and sperm with many new combinations of chromosomes. Random assortment reshuffles the existing chromosomes but does not introduce any new traits.

Mutation produces all new hereditary characteristics. Most mutations are harmful—that is, they reduce an organism's chances for survial and reproduction. Very few mutations are favorable, but these few allow evolution to take place. As a result of natural selection, organisms that have favorable mutations tend to survive and reproduce, and the others tend to die off before they have a chance to reproduce.

Recombination can result in new combinations of favorable mutations. Recombination results from crossing over, the exchange of genes that occurs between partner chromosomes just before sex cells divide. This process can bring together a mutation on one chromosome with another mutation on its partner chromosome. Recombination thus creates combinations of mutations.

Natural selection is the guiding force of evolution. Because of genetic variation, the members of a species differ from one another in many of their inherited characteristics. Some of these differences make certain individuals better able to survive in their environment. Because they survive longer, these individuals tend to produce more offspring than average. Many of their offspring inherit their favorable characteristics. As this process repeats itself generation after generation, the favorable characteristics become more and more common in the species as a whole.

Evolution by means of natural selection generally occurs so slowly that no change in a species is noticeable during a human lifetime. However, extreme changes in the environment sometimes cause rapid evolution. An example of such rapid change occurred in England during the 1800's among a species of moth called the *peppered moth.*

Peppered moths rest on the trunks of certain trees that are normally a light color. During the early 1800's, nearly all peppered moths were light-colored, and only a very few moths carried a mutation that made them black. In the mid-1800's, however, factories burned so much coal that soot settled over the countryside, blackening the trunks of trees. Light-colored moths on dark-colored trees were easily seen and so eaten by birds. But the birds could not see the black moths. As a result, most of the black moths survived and produced offspring. Within 50 years, most moths in heavily polluted areas were black.

Studying heredity and evolution. Evolution occurs within a group of individuals of the same species that live in a certain area and mate largely within their own group. Biologists call such a group a *population.* The evolution of any population takes place over a long period of time during which many generations of individuals are born and die. To learn about evolution, biologists study the genetic makeup of the entire population. This field of study is called *population genetics.*

The fundamental concept of population genetics is that each population has a *gene pool.* The gene pool is the total collection of all the genes present in the members of the population. The extent to which a certain gene is present in the gene pool is called its *gene frequency.* Natural selection increases the gene frequencies of favorable genes and decreases the frequencies of unfavorable genes. Thus, in an evolving population, the gene frequencies are changing from generation to generation.

The study of heredity

Early ideas about heredity. Ancient peoples knew the most important principle of heredity—offspring tend to resemble their parents. They even used this principle to improve the characteristics of some plants and animals. A 6,000-year-old engraved stone tablet found near the Persian Gulf traces various traits through five generations of horses. However, early peoples did not understand how or why heredity occurred.

The oldest known theory of inheritance was proposed by the Greek philosopher Aristotle, who lived during the 300's B.C. Aristotle taught that traits are inherited through the blood. This theory was wrong, but it was generally accepted for more than 1,000 years. The belief even became part of our language in such terms as *bloodline, blue blood,* and *blood relatives.*

A correct theory of inheritance could not be formulated until after eggs and sperm had been discovered and their functions determined. The discovery of eggs and sperm occurred during the late 1600's, soon after the development of the microscope by Anton van Leeuwenhoek of the Netherlands. At that time, many biologists thought that either the egg or the sperm contained a tiny but fully formed embryo that merely increased in size inside the mother. During the late 1700's, a German scientist named Caspar Friedrich Wolff proved embryos are not preformed. Wolff showed that the embryo de-

Mendel's experiments on heredity

In the mid-1800's, Gregor Mendel, developed his theory of heredity on the basis of experiments with pea plants. In the experiments below, he studied the inheritance of seed color.

WORLD BOOK diagrams by Zorica Dabich

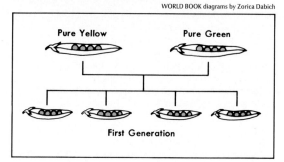

Mendel first experimented with purebred strains of pea plants— one with yellow seeds and one with green seeds. He crossed these strains, and all the resulting hybrid seeds were yellow. He concluded that yellow seed color was a dominant trait.

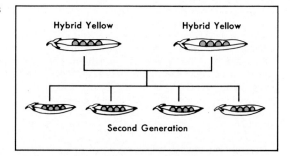

Plants grown from the hybrid yellow seeds produced yellow and green seeds in a ratio of about 3 to 1. The results of this and similar experiments helped Mendel develop the *law of segregation,* which describes the basic mechanism of heredity.

velops from the fertilized egg, and he argued that the sperm and the egg contribute equally to the embryo.

By the 1800's, biologists took great interest in heredity and in how inherited traits could change from generation to generation. A French biologist named Jean Baptiste de Lamarck suggested that traits acquired during the lifetime of an individual could be passed on to the offspring. Lamarck thought giraffes that stretched their necks to reach leaves high up in tall trees would have baby giraffes with longer necks.

Lamarck's theory was basically accepted by the British biologist Charles Darwin, who proposed the theory of natural selection in 1859. Darwin believed each part of the body produced tiny particles that moved through the bloodstream into the eggs or sperm. These particles supposedly influenced hereditary traits in offspring. Darwin's cousin, the British scientist Francis Galton, disproved this idea. Galton transfused blood from black rabbits into white rabbits to see if the white ones would have black offspring. But the white rabbits still produced white offspring.

Mendel's experiments. The greatest single contributor to the study of heredity was Gregor Johann Mendel, an Austrian monk. During the mid-1800's, Mendel conducted a series of experiments to study the inheritance of seven pairs of traits in garden pea plants. Through careful experimentation and mathematical analysis of his results, Mendel formulated the first correct theory of heredity. This theory consisted of two principles called *Mendel's laws of heredity.*

Mendel first studied the inheritance of each of the seven pairs of traits individually. He began his experiments with purebred strains of pea plants. One of the traits he studied was seed color. For example, one of his purebred strains had green seeds, and another had yellow seeds. Mendel crossed these two strains by transferring pollen from one to the other, and all the resulting hybrid seeds were yellow. He thus concluded yellow seed color was a dominant trait.

Mendel next grew plants from the hybrid yellow seeds. About three-fourths of the seeds produced by these plants were yellow, and about one-fourth were green. All the green seeds produced purebred plants. However, only about one-third of the yellow seeds produced purebreds, and the rest produced hybrids.

The results of these experiments formed the basis of Mendel's first law, the *law of segregation.* The law has three parts. (1) Hereditary units (now called genes) occur in pairs. (2) The genes in a pair *segregate* (separate) during the division of sex cells, and each sperm or egg receives only one member of the pair. (3) Each gene in a pair will be present in half the sperm or eggs.

Mendel also crossed pea plants that differed from one another in two or more characteristics. From the results of these experiments, he formulated his second law, the *law of independent assortment.* This law states that each pair of genes is inherited independently of all other pairs. Geneticists now know that independent assortment applies only to genes that are on different chromosomes. Genes that are linked, or on the same chromosome, tend to be inherited together.

The birth of genetics. Mendel published a report of his work in 1866, but it went unnoticed for nearly 34 years. Then, in 1900, three European biologists working independently rediscovered Mendel's report and immediately brought it to the attention of other scientists. These three scientists were Hugo de Vries of the Netherlands, Carl Correns of Germany, and Erich Tschermak of Austria.

The rediscovery of Mendel's work marked the beginning of genetics, the science of heredity. By 1900, biologists had discovered chromosomes and studied their behavior during cell division. It soon became clear to a number of scientists that the genes must be located on the chromosomes.

Rapid progress occurred in genetics during the early 1900's. The chief contributors to this progress were a group of biologists working under the direction of Thomas Hunt Morgan at Columbia University in New York City. Other members of the group included Calvin B. Bridges, Hermann J. Muller, and Alfred H. Sturtevant. Morgan and his co-workers studied the inheritance of such traits as eye color and wing shape in fruit flies. They discovered many important aspects of heredity, including sex-linked genes, crossing over, and multiple alleles.

Morgan and his co-workers used a type of fruit fly called *Drosophila melanogaster* in their studies. These insects proved to be an extremely useful tool in genetic research because they are subject to a large number of easily detectable genetic variations. In addition, they complete their life cycle in approximately two weeks. Researchers can therefore trace hereditary characteristics through many generations in a short period. Much of our modern knowledge of genetics comes from experiments on *Drosophila melanogaster.*

As early as 1900, Hugo de Vries had emphasized the importance of mutations in evolution. However, mutations were difficult to study because they normally occur so rarely. In 1927, Hermann J. Muller demonstrated that X rays could cause artificial mutations that resemble the natural ones. Other geneticists later discovered that mustard gas and many other chemicals could also cause mutations.

The study of the chemistry of genes became the focus of much research in genetics after 1940. In 1941, two American geneticists—George W. Beadle and Edward L. Tatum—discovered the chemical function of genes. Beadle and Tatum studied a type of mold called *Neurospora.* They discovered that mutations in any one gene always caused abnormalities in just one protein—a different protein for each gene. Beadle and Tatum therefore proposed that each gene controls the formation of a single protein.

In 1944, an American geneticist named Oswald T. Avery provided the first convincing proof that genes consist of DNA. Avery and his co-workers purified DNA from one type of bacteria and introduced it into cells of a different type of bacteria. Certain hereditary traits passed on by these cells were identical to those of the bacteria from which the DNA had come. Avery reasoned that genes must have been transferred from one type of bacteria to the other. Thus, genes must consist of DNA because only DNA had been transferred.

Two biologists, James D. Watson of the United States and Francis H. C. Crick of Great Britain, proposed a model of the ladderlike chemical structure of DNA in 1953. Watson and Crick suggested that DNA duplicates by splitting down the middle and building a complete ladder from each resulting half-ladder. They also proposed that mutations result from a change in the sequence of bases along the ladder.

By the late 1950's, biologists had discovered that RNA serves as the messenger in protein manufacture. They also knew that each codon in RNA consists of three bases. But the genetic code itself was not completely understood. During the early 1960's, scientists developed a method of manufacturing proteins from cellular materials in a test tube. Researchers added artificial RNA with simple base sequences to the test tube to see what sequence of amino acids the resulting protein would have. Comparisons of the sequence of bases in the RNA with the sequence of amino acids in the protein soon revealed the entire genetic code.

Current research is rapidly expanding our knowledge of heredity. Much of this study involves the use of a technique called *recombinant DNA research* or *gene splicing.* Scientists produce recombinant DNA by chemically attaching a gene from an animal or plant to bacterial DNA. They then transplant the recombinant DNA into a bacterium. By allowing the bacterium to reproduce researchers can obtain a huge number of bacterial cells that contain the artificially attached gene. Experiments with recombinant DNA have revealed much about the structure and function of genes.

Recombinant DNA research also has important medical applications. For example, certain proteins used in medical treatment are in short supply. Bacteria with recombinant DNA that contains the human gene for one of these proteins can produce an almost limitless amount of the protein. By the early 1980's, scientists had created such bacterial "factories" to produce human insulin for use in the treatment of diabetes. See **Genetic engineering.**

Many questions about heredity remain unanswered. One of the most important questions is "How does a gene know when it should become active and produce its protein?" Each body cell has a copy of every gene in the body. However, many genes are active only in certain cells. The gene for insulin, for example, is active only in specific cells in the pancreas. Other genes are active only during certain stages of life. For example, human embryos produce a different form of hemoglobin than adults do. But embryos have inactive genes for adult hemoglobin, and adults have inactive genes for embryonic hemoglobin.

No one knows what determines when and in which cells a gene becomes active. Geneticists think they have a clue, however. Only a small fraction of the DNA in an organism codes for proteins. The function of the rest of the DNA is unknown, but most geneticists believe some of it may help regulate the activity of genes.

A new and unexpected question about genes is the subject of much current research. Until the late 1970's, geneticists had assumed that each gene consists of a continuous strand of DNA that codes for a protein. However, several studies then revealed that some genes in higher organisms have one or more sequences of DNA that do not code for a protein. Discovering the function of these *intervening sequences* is one of the major challenges geneticists face in the 1980's.   Daniel L. Hartl

Related articles in *World Book* include:

Biographies

Beadle, George	Lamarck, Chevalier	Muller, Hermann J.
Burbank, Luther	de	Tatum, Edward L.
Crick, Francis H. C.	Lysenko, Trofim D.	Watson, James D.
Darwin, Charles R.	Mendel, Gregor Johann	Weisman, August
De Vries, Hugo	hann	Wilkins, Maurice
Galton, Sir Francis	Morgan, Thomas Hunt	H. F.

Other related articles

Abnormal psychology (Theories)	Genetic engineering
Albino	Genetics
Atavism	Hemophilia
Baldness	Hybrid
Breeding	Muscular dystrophy
Cell	Mutation
Chromosome	Natural selection
Clone	Neurofibromatosis
Color blindness	Nucleic acid
Environment	Races, Human
Eugenics	Reproduction
Evolution	Sickle cell anemia
Gaucher's disease	Sociobiology
Gene	Sport
Genetic counseling	Tay-Sachs disease

Outline

I. Human heredity
   A. Physical traits   C. Hereditary disorders
   B. Mental traits
II. The physical basis of heredity
   A. Genes and chromosomes   C. How sex is determined
      somes   D. Patterns of heredity
   B. How traits are inherited
III. The chemical basis of heredity
   A. The structure of nucleic   D. The genetic code
      acids   E. Mutations
   B. How DNA duplicates
   C. How proteins are made
IV. Heredity and change
   A. Genetic variation   C. Studying heredity and evo-
   B. Natural selection   lution
V. The study of heredity

Questions

What is the *genetic code*?

How many chromosomes does each human body cell contain?

What are some human physical traits that are determined completely by genes?

What are X-linked genes? Why do disorders caused by X-linked genes generally occur only in males?

Who was the greatest single contributor to the study of heredity?

What is *genetic variation*? What three processes are chiefly responsible for it?

How do scientists map the positions of genes along a chromosome?

What characteristics make fruit flies extremely useful in genetic research?

What are the major areas of study within genetics?

What are *mutations*?

Reading and Study Guide

See *Heredity* in the Research Guide/Index, Volume 22, for a *Reading and Study Guide.*

Additional resources

Level I

Asimov, Isaac. *How Did We Find Out About Genes?* Walker, 1983.

Bendick, Jeanne. *How Heredity Works: Why Living Things Are as They Are.* Parents' Magazine Press, 1975.

Dunbar, Robert E. *Heredity.* Watts, 1978.

Engdahl, Sylvia L., and Roberson, R. J. *Tool for Tomorrow: New Knowledge About Genes.* Atheneum, 1979.

Facklam, Margery and Howard. *From Cell to Clone: The Story of Genetic Engineering.* Harcourt, 1979.

Morrison, Velma F. *There's Only One You: The Story of Heredity.* Simon & Schuster, 1978.

Silverstein, Alvin and V. B. *The Code of Life.* Atheneum, 1972. *The Genetics Explosion.* Four Winds, 1980.

Level II

Bornstein, Jerry and Sandy. *What Is Genetics?* Simon & Schuster, 1979.

Frankel, Edward. *DNA: The Ladder of Life.* 2nd ed. McGraw, 1979.

Gardner, Eldon J. *Human Heredity.* Wiley, 1983.

Greenblatt, Augusta. *Heredity and You: How You Can Protect Your Family's Future.* Coward, McCann & Geoghegan, 1974.

Hoagland, Mahlon B. *Discovery: The Search for DNA's Secrets.* Houghton, 1981.

Judson, Horace F. *The Eighth Day of Creation: Makers of the Revolution in Biology.* Simon & Schuster, 1979.

Nyhan, William L., and Edelson, Edward. *The Heredity Factor: Genes, Chromosomes, and You.* Grosset, 1976.

Watson, James D. *The Double Helix: A Personal Account of the Discovery of the Structure of DNA.* Atheneum, 1968.

Hereford cattle. See Cattle (Hereford).

Heresy, *HEHR uh see,* is an opinion or idea that contradicts the beliefs of a religious group or closely knit organization. A person guilty of heresy is called a *heretic.* The Christian church once punished heretics with exile, torture, or even death. Churches today sometimes expel heretics. See also **Albigenses; Arianism; Eckhardt, Johannes; Inquisition; Roman Catholic Church** (The early church; Jansenism).

Herman, Woody (1913-1987), was an American bandleader and musician. He ranks with Duke Ellington and Count Basie as one of the three most durable figures in the history of big-band jazz. Herman's bands made several musicians and composers famous, including saxophonists Stan Getz, Flip Phillips, Zoot Sims, and Al Cohn; trumpet players Sonny Berman and Pete Condoli; trombonist Bill Harris; and composers Neal Hefti and Ralph Burns. Herman also won praise playing alto saxophone and clarinet with his bands.

Herman's two most influential bands were known as the First Herd (1944-1946) and the Second Herd (1947-1948). Herman was one of the first bandleaders to use elements of a jazz movement of the 1940's called *bebop,* or *bop,* as well as classical music. The Soviet composer Igor Stravinsky composed his *Ebony Concerto* (1946) for Herman's band. Herman developed an unusual reed section for the Second Herd consisting of three tenor saxophones and a baritone saxophone. The section was known for its bright, lyrical phrasing in such numbers as "Four Brothers."

Woodrow Charles Herman was born in Milwaukee. He formed his first big band, known as "The Band That Plays the Blues," in 1936. It became famous in 1939 with its recording of "Woodchoppers' Ball."   Gary Giddins

See also **Jazz** (picture: Woody Herman).

Hermaphrodite, *hur MAF ruh dyt,* is an animal with both male and female organs of reproduction. Some flatworms and segmented worms are normally hermaphrodites, as are some echinoderms and mollusks.

Although some hermaphrodites fertilize their own eggs, most do not. Some show *successive hermaphroditism,* in which the two sets of organs produce egg and sperm at different times. In others, the positions of the sex organs keep the animals from fertilizing themselves. For example, the common earthworm has active male and female organs located in different parts of the body. This allows two worms to fertilize each other, but prevents them from fertilizing themselves.

In the higher animals and human beings, hermaphroditism is not normal. The organs and functions of one or both sexes usually develop imperfectly in such rare individuals. Few human cases of hermaphroditism have been reported.   Lawrence C. Wit

Hermes, *HUR meez,* was the messenger of the gods in Greek mythology. He protected travelers, and the Greeks believed he brought good luck, especially in business. Hermes sometimes acted in a deceitful or mischievous way, and so the Greeks also considered him a protector of thieves. Under the name of Hermes Psychopompos, he guided the souls of the dead to the lower world. Hermes resembled the Roman god Mercury.

One famous Greek myth tells how Hermes, on the day of his birth, stole the cattle of the god Apollo. But Hermes and Apollo became close friends after Hermes invented the seven-stringed lyre and gave it to Apollo, who loved music.

Greek art showed Hermes as a handsome youth, often wearing winged shoes and a winged hat. He carried a winged staff entwined with snakes.   Robert J. Lenardon

See also **Hermes of Praxiteles; Mercury.**

Hermes of Praxiteles, *HUR meez, prak SIHT uh leez,* is an ancient Greek statue of Hermes, the messenger of the gods in Greek mythology. The Athenian sculptor Praxiteles created the masterpiece, probably in the 330's B.C. (see **Praxiteles**). Although the original statue was lost, a copy exists that was created about 100 B.C., probably by the Greek sculptor Pasiteles. The copy has beauty and charm and possesses the dreamy expression and the graceful "S" curve of the body that are characteristic of Praxiteles' style. The statue portrays Hermes holding his infant brother, Dionysus, on one arm. In the other arm, which is now missing, Hermes held a bunch of grapes that he offered to the infant.   Warren G. Moon

Hermione, *hur MY uh nee,* was the daughter of Menelaus and Helen of Troy. She was promised as wife to Orestes, the son of Agamemnon. But Menelaus gave her to Neoptolemus, son of Achilles. Neoptolemus was murdered at Delphi, probably by Orestes. Hermione then married Orestes. See also **Menelaus; Orestes.**   Justin M. Glenn

Hermit is a person who lives a solitary life, apart from social contact with others. Men and women become hermits for many reasons. They may want to avoid the evils or temptations they see in society. They may believe they can purify themselves by living alone. Or they may simply want nothing to do with other people.

Hermits give up comfort, family, marriage, property, and pleasure for chastity, fasting, meditation, and silence. They train themselves to eat simply, infrequently, and in small amounts. Hermits do not like to see or talk to visitors. But curious people or people who want spiritual guidance or physical healing seek them out. This attention sometimes drives hermits to even more secluded places.

Religious hermits are commonly regarded as holy persons. They have played important roles in forming the religious disciplines of Buddhism, Christianity, Hinduism, Islam, and Taoism. Religious hermits have withdrawn to caves, cells, holes, pillars, and tombs. They may live in deserts, forests, mountain ravines, or even in cities.

In some religions, particularly Buddhism and Christianity, there were hermits who came to regard solitude as selfish. They joined others in forming hermitages. In a hermitage, a number of hermits live in separate cells or rooms and follow religious disciplines. They have few social contacts. Monasteries developed from hermitages. In monastic communities, monks form self-sufficient social groups and set aside certain times for solitary meditation and prayer.

Anyone may want to be alone and silent for a time to think seriously, work, or prepare for some special event. Hermits find this experience so rewarding that it becomes a way of life for them.   William A. Clebsch

See also **Asceticism; Monasticism.**

Hermit crab lives alone in the shell of a sea snail. It uses the empty shell after the snail has died. But it may pull out the live snail, getting a new house and a feast as well. Sometimes one crab pulls another crab from the shell it wants.

WORLD BOOK illustration by James Teason

The hermit crab lives in a sea snail shell to protect the soft parts of its body. As it grows, the crab moves to larger shells.

Unlike other crabs, the hermit has soft, unprotected rear parts. It can thus twist its body into the spiral of an empty seashell. Only its claws remain outside, and it uses them as a tightly fitting door. As the crab grows, it changes its shell for a larger one.

Each hermit crab lives alone in its adopted shell. But large groups of hermit crabs often crowd areas of the ocean floor where seashells are abundant. They can be gathered from pools left after high tide, and make amusing pets. One kind of hermit crab grows 2 feet (61 centimeters) long. It is called the *robber crab* and *coconut crab* because it is said to climb coconut trees and pick the nuts. This crab lives in burrows which it digs beneath the coconut palms of tropical islands. It uses no adopted shell, but has plates of armor on the rear part of its body. It tears coconuts open for food.

Scientific classification. The hermit crab belongs to the hermit crab family, Paguridae. A common kind of hermit crab on the Atlantic Coast is classified as *Pagurus pollicaris.*

J. Laurens Barnard

Hermitage. See Leningrad (Education and cultural life).

Hermitage, The. See Jackson, Andrew (Business and politics; Later years; picture); Tennessee (Places to visit).

Herndon, William Henry (1818-1891), an American lawyer, was the law partner of Abraham Lincoln. He is known chiefly for his collection of letters to and from Lincoln and his contemporaries. These letters give valuable information on Lincoln's life and times.

Herndon was born in Greensburg, Ky. He was educated at Illinois College in Jacksonville. He became a crusading abolitionist and, at 25, Lincoln's law partner. Herndon published *Life of Lincoln* in 1889.

H. G. Reuschlein

Herne, *hurn,* **James A.** (1839-1901), was an American playwright, actor, and stage manager. He is best known for two plays that were well in advance of their time in their realistic treatment of serious social problems. *Drifting Apart* (1888) probes the consequences of man's slavery to drink. *Margaret Fleming* (1890) is an outspoken treatment of an unfaithful husband and his forgiving wife. The plays were praised by such literary figures as

William Dean Howells and Hamlin Garland, but they shocked the theater public of the day.

Herne's *Hearts of Oak* (1879), *Shore Acres* (1892), and *Sag Harbor* (1899) were warm-hearted and realistically detailed plays tailored to the American tastes of the time. Herne was born in Cohoes, N.Y. His real name was James Ahern. Richard Moody

Hernia, *HUR nee uh,* also called *rupture,* results from a break in cavity walls within the body. Many organs of the body, like the lungs, heart, or intestines, are inside hollow places called *body cavities.* Sometimes the wall of a cavity breaks, or ruptures, and part of the organ pushes through. Then the person has a hernia. When used alone, the word generally means an *abdominal hernia.* In this type of hernia, a loop of the bowel sticks out through the muscular wall of the abdomen. The hernia often occurs at a weak point of the muscular wall. It usually pushes out a part of the inner lining of the abdomen, the *peritoneum,* and forms a *hernial sac.* This sac may be felt or seen underneath the skin of the abdomen.

The danger of abdominal hernia is that the abdominal muscles may contract, *strangulating* (choking off) the part of the bowel that protrudes. Doctors usually operate immediately on persons with this condition. Supports such as trusses may relieve abdominal hernias by keeping the bowel inside the abdominal wall. But the only cure for a hernia is an operation.

In *hernia cerebri,* a portion of the brain protrudes through an opening in the skull. Hernia may also occur in various other internal organs, such as the bladder.

Hernia results from many causes. An abdominal hernia sometimes results from lifting a heavy object, or from a strain or other injury. Bruce Reider

Hero. See Invention (Ancient Greece); **Steam engine** (History).

Hero and Leander, *lee AN duhr,* were legendary Greek lovers. Hero was a priestess of the goddess Aphrodite at Sestos in Thrace. Leander lived at Abydos across the Hellespont, or Dardanelles. Every night, Hero put a light in her tower, and Leander swam across the water to visit her. He returned to Abydos at dawn. One stormy night, the wind put out Hero's light, and Leander was overwhelmed and drowned. At dawn, Hero saw his body floating beneath her tower, and in her grief she leaped into the sea and drowned herself.

William F. Hansen

Herod, *HEHR uhd,* was the name of a family from Edom (in Greek, Idumaea) that ruled in Palestine from 46 B.C. to about A.D. 100. They had been forcibly converted to Judaism about 125 B.C. The Herods founded a number of cities and improved existing ones.

Herod the Great (73?-4 or 1 B.C.) ruled all Palestine from 37 to 4 or 1 B.C. He maintained his rule by keeping friendly with the Roman emperors. He had 10 wives and many children. His cruelty is illustrated by the story of the massacre of the children of Bethlehem. The massacre caused Mary and Joseph to flee from Herod's soldiers to Egypt with the infant Jesus (see **Jesus Christ** [The Nativity]).

Herod Antipas, *AN tih PAS* (? -A.D. 40), a son of Herod the Great, was the sly, crafty ruler who beheaded John the Baptist and opposed Jesus (see **John the Baptist**). He ruled as *tetrarch,* or governor, of Galilee and Peraea. His wife, Herodias, persuaded him to ask the

Roman emperor Caligula to make him king of Palestine. But his nephew, Herod Agrippa, made false charges against him, and, in A.D. 39, Caligula banished Herod Antipas to Gaul. Soon afterward, Antipas died. His half brother, Herod Philip II, was the tetrarch of Ituraea in northeast Palestine.

Herod Agrippa I, *uh GRIHP uh* (10? B.C.-A.D. 44), a grandson of Herod the Great, became a friend of the nobles in Rome, where he was educated. When Caligula became emperor of Rome in A.D. 37, he gave Herod Agrippa the northeast territories that Herod Philip and Lysanias had ruled. In A.D. 39, when Herod Antipas was banished, Caligula gave Galilee and Peraea to Herod Agrippa, and added Judea and Samaria in A.D. 41. Herod Agrippa then ruled the same amount of territory as had Herod the Great.

Herod Agrippa is the king who killed the Apostle James and imprisoned Peter. He was one of the cruelest members of his family. The story of the death of Herod Agrippa is told in the New Testament in the Acts of the Apostles 12: 20-23.

Herod Agrippa II (A.D. 27?-100?), the son of Herod Agrippa I, was only 17 years old when his father died. Because Herod Agrippa II was so young, the Roman emperor Claudius refused to make him king of Palestine. However, after Herod Agrippa's uncle died in A.D. 50, he was made king of Chalcis, an area in Lebanon.

Herod Agrippa II was a friend of the Romans. On a visit to Festus, the Roman governor of Judea, he was asked to listen to Saint Paul's defense and appeal to the emperor (Acts 25-26). Herod Agrippa tried to persuade the Jews not to revolt in A.D. 66, but he failed. During the war that followed, he fought against the Jews on the side of the Romans.   Frederick C. Grant

Herodias. See Herod (Antipas); **John the Baptist.**

Herodotus, *hih RAHD uh tuhs* (484?-425? B.C.), was the first Greek historian. He undertook to write the history of the world up to his own time. The Roman orator Cicero called him the father of history.

Herodotus is famous for the nine books he wrote on the rise of the Persian Empire, the Persian invasions of Greece in 490 and 480 B.C., the heroic fight of the Greeks against the invaders, and the final Greek victory. Herodotus wrote his history in a lively manner. He even included many stories which he did not believe because they made his account more interesting. His natural style has made his books enjoyable from his own time down to the present.

Herodotus was born at Halicarnassus, in Asia Minor. During his youth, he traveled widely in Greece, the Middle East, and North Africa. Everywhere he went, he studied the manners, customs, and religions of the people, and learned as much as he could of their history. The things Herodotus learned in his travels formed the materials of his histories. In about 447 B.C., he visited Athens, and three years later settled in the colony of Thurii which Pericles was then founding in southern Italy. Nothing is known of the rest of the life of Herodotus, but it has been said that he died and was buried at Thurii. For a quotation from Herodotus, see **Post office** (Ancient times).   C. Bradford Welles

Heroic Age. See Age (Golden Age).

Heroic couplet. See English literature (Restoration drama); **Pope, Alexander.**

Heroic drama. See Drama (European drama); **English literature** (Restoration drama).

Heroin, *HEHR oh ihn,* is a drug made from morphine, an active chemical in opium. Like morphine, heroin relieves pain and brings sleep. But because it is stronger and more habit-forming than morphine, it is not used for medical purposes. The government of the United States forbids the manufacture, importation, and use of heroin, but many people obtain it illegally. Heroin has several nicknames, including "H," "horse," and "smack."

Drug addicts use heroin by *snorting* (sniffing it), by *skin popping* (injecting it under the skin), or by *mainlining* (injecting it into a vein). To addicts, heroin offers escape from a seemingly intolerable existence by providing a feeling of joy and relief. In time, the repeated use results in physical and psychological dependence on the drug. If an addict stops taking heroin, he or she suffers such withdrawal symptoms as body aches, diarrhea, muscle cramps, or nausea. The intensity of these symptoms peaks in 2 to 3 days and then gradually decreases over 7 to 10 days. Addicts who suddenly resume taking heroin in the same amounts they took previously risk having a fatal overdose. The addict's chief goal is getting more heroin. Many addicts turn to crime—particularly theft or prostitution—to get the large amounts of money needed to buy the drug.

Many addicts do not eat nourishing foods or maintain personal cleanliness. Also, the needle used to inject the drug is often unsterile. Such neglect can result in hepatitis, malnutrition, pneumonia, or skin infections. Babies born to mothers addicted to an opium-based drug are physically dependent on the drug and have to undergo withdrawal treatment.

Most addicts have severe personality problems. Programs offering treatment and rehabilitation for addicts have been developed throughout the United States.
      Donald J. Wolk

See also **Drug addiction; Morphine.**

Heron, *HEHR uhn,* is any of about 60 species of wading birds, including egrets and bitterns. Herons are graceful birds with long, pointed bills that seem to extend right into their eyes. They have narrow heads, long slender necks, and sticklike legs that are similar to the legs of cranes and storks. Some herons have long crests and plumes on their throats and bodies. Herons live on all continents except Antarctica..

Habits. In flight, herons stretch their long legs straight out behind them and curl their heads between their shoulders. Cranes, storks, and ibises fly with their necks extended. Herons usually nest and roost in flocks, but they hunt food alone. Their nesting places are called *heronries.* The nests consist of loose, crude masses of sticks built in treetops or in bushes. The female lays three to six eggs. Young herons are helpless for a few weeks after they hatch. Their parents carry food to the young birds until they can fly.

In search of food, the heron wades along the shores of streams with a stately stride, silent and alone. Sometimes the bird may stand for a long time with its head drawn between its shoulders. It appears to be asleep, but it is patiently waiting for fish, frogs, crayfish, and other small animals. As soon as it sees its prey, the heron makes a lightning dart and catches the victim in its spearlike bill.

Hal Harrison from Grant Heilman

The great blue heron, *above,* is the largest American heron. It uses its long, pointed bill to catch fish.

Ron Austing, Bruce Coleman Inc.

Green herons, *above,* build nests of sticks in trees or tall shrubs. Most of these birds live near water.

American herons. The largest American heron is the *great blue heron.* It lives throughout much of North America. Some species of herons have two color forms, one of which is white. The *great white heron* is actually the white color form of the great blue heron. The *green-backed heron* and the *Louisiana heron* are colorful species that lack white forms.

Scientific classification. Herons belong to the heron family, Ardeidae. The great blue heron is *Ardea herodias.* The green-backed heron is *Butorides striatus* and the Louisiana heron is *Egretta tricolor.*   Eric G. Bolen

See also **Bird** (picture: Birds of inland waters and marshes); **Bittern; Crane; Egret.**

Herpes, *HUR peez,* is any of a group of closely related viruses that cause various diseases. The most common of these diseases—*herpes simplex, herpes zoster,* and *chicken pox*—produce blisters on the skin and mucous membranes. Other herpes viruses cause various infectious diseases and birth defects. Some scientists believe that certain herpes viruses may cause some types of cancer.

There are two types of herpes simplex viruses—type 1 and type 2. Type 1 produces small blisters—commonly called *cold sores* or *fever blisters*—that usually appear on or near the mouth. Type 1 also causes an eye infection called *herpes keratitis* and some cases of *encephalitis* (brain inflammation). Type 2 causes *genital herpes,* a venereal disease that produces painful sores on the sex organs. For more information, see **Venereal disease** (Genital herpes). Type 2 also sometimes causes *meningi-*

tis (inflammation of the coverings of the spinal cord and brain).

The sores caused by herpes simplex viruses usually dry up and disappear in about two weeks. But the virus remains *latent* (present, but inactive) in the nerve cells, and symptoms may recur during times of physical or emotional stress. Such recurrence of symptoms is called *reactivation.*

A herpes virus called *varicella-zoster* causes both herpes zoster—commonly called *shingles*—and chicken pox. Chicken pox is usually a childhood illness, whereas shingles generally strikes people over the age of 50.

Other herpes viruses include the *Epstein-Barr,* or *EB, virus* and *cytomegalovirus.* EB virus causes most cases of *mononucleosis,* a disease that occurs mainly in young adults. EB virus is also associated with certain cancers, including Burkitt's lymphoma and nasopharyngeal carcinoma. Cytomegalovirus can cause severe birth defects, including deafness and mental retardation. This herpes virus also causes some cases of mononucleosis and other diseases.   John J. Holland

See also **Chicken pox; Cold sore; Mononucleosis; Shingles.**

Herpetology, *HUR puh TAHL uh jee,* is a branch of the science of zoology. Herpetology is the study of reptiles and amphibians, such as frogs and salamanders. Many herpetologists specialize in the study of snakes. The name comes from the Greek word *herpeton,* meaning *reptile.* See also **Amphibian** and **Reptile** and their lists of *Related articles.*   William C. Beaver

Herrera, *eh RAY rah,* **Tomás,** *toh MAHS* (1804-1854), was a soldier and statesman of Panama. He led the movement in 1840 to make Panama independent of Colombia. He was president of the Free State of Panama for the year that it existed, and later held high office in Colombia. Herrera was born in Panama City. In 1854, he put down a revolt in Colombia, and was killed leading his army into Bogotá.   Donald E. Worcester

Herrick, Robert (1591-1674), was one of England's finest lyric poets. He is best known for his love lyrics to imaginary ladies and graceful poems about nature and English country life. Herrick celebrated the earthy joys of rural life in such poems as "Corinna's Going A-Maying," "The Argument of His Book," and "To Daffodils." His playful poem about the importance of spending one's youth wisely, "To the Virgins, to Make Much of Time," contains the famous line, "Gather ye rosebuds while ye may." Herrick's lyric poetry reflects the influence of Roman poets and the English poet and playwright Ben Jonson.

Herrick was born in London. He was ordained in the Church of England in 1623 and served as a *vicar* (minister of a parish) in the rural county of Devonshire (now Devon). Only one collection of Herrick's poetry, *Hesperides* (1648), was published during his lifetime. The volume includes a section of religious poetry called *Noble Numbers.*   Thomas H. Fujimura

Herring is one of the most important food fish in the world. Europeans use it more widely than Americans. It belongs to the herring family, which also includes the shad, menhaden, sardine, and alewife. Herring abound along the sea coasts of the temperate and colder parts of the North Pacific and North Atlantic oceans, and in inland lakes. The Atlantic herring is one of the most numerous of all backboned animals. Overfishing of herring in the North Sea made breeding stock begin to decline greatly in the 1970's. To reverse the decline, several countries took steps to restrict herring fishing in North Sea waters. By the mid-1980's, herring stock began to increase.

Appearance and habits. Herring are well-formed fish. They have thin scales colored blue-green to blackish above, brilliant silver on the sides, and white below. Both jaws have small teeth. Small crustaceans are the herring's chief source of food. Millions of herring swim close together near the surface of the water, in areas ranging from 6 to 20 square miles (16 to 52 square kilometers).

Herring spend part of the time in deep water, then migrate to shallower coastal waters where they lay their eggs. A female deposits from 20,000 to 185,000 eggs, depending on her size. The eggs settle to the bottom, where they cover seaweed and rocks. Within a few weeks, the eggs hatch. Herring have many enemies. In spite of the number of eggs which are laid, few develop into adult herring. Crabs and such fish as haddock eat many of the eggs and young. The adult herring are eaten by other creatures of the sea, such as whales and seals, and by gulls and other birds.

Commercial fishing. Fishing crews find the great schools of herring, called shoals, by watching for the many sea birds that hover over the schools, and by the light, or luminescence, caused in the sea water by the swimming herring. Some boats now detect the schools

E. R. Degginger

Herring fishermen bring in a large catch of the fish from the Atlantic Ocean, near Cape Cod. Herring is one of the most important food fishes in the world.

by devices similar to those used for detecting submarines during wartime.

Herring are usually caught in large nets. A fishing crew goes to a spot where a large number of herring are seen, and lets an immense net out. The crew then rows along the edges of the net in small boats, and forces the mass of fish nearer the center. Then, the fishing boat approaches and many thousands of herring are raised in the net and thrown into the boat.

About $2\frac{1}{2}$ million short tons (2.3 million metric tons) of herring are caught each year. The Soviet Union leads all countries in the number of fish caught. In the United States, most herring is caught in the Atlantic between Cape Cod and the Bay of Fundy.

Uses. Many herring are frozen and used for bait in the halibut and cod fisheries. Industry makes millions into fertilizer, and uses the oil extracted from them to lubricate machinery and for other purposes.

In many parts of the world, herring are a favorite food, either pickled, smoked, or eaten fresh. Herring which have been smoked but not salted are known in England as *Yarmouth bloaters.* Those similarly prepared, but also split and cleaned, are called *kippered herring.* They are canned in Scotland and Norway and sent to America, where they are one of the most popular forms

WORLD BOOK illustration by Colin Newman, Linden Artists Ltd.

Pacific herring inhabit the ocean's northern waters.

The food value of herring

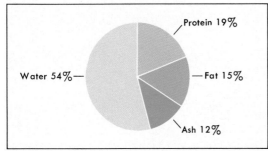

Protein 19%

Water 54%

Fat 15%

Ash 12%

Source: U.S. Agricultural Research Service.

of herring. Small herring are often put into tins and sold as *whitebait.* Pickled herring are put into brine, sometimes with onions and spices. They are sold either *round* or *split.* Round herring are salted whole. Split herring have the gills, heart, and other parts removed.

Scientific classification. Herring are members of the herring family, Clupeidae. The Atlantic herring is *Clupea harengus.* The Pacific herring is *C. pallasii.* Robert R. Rofen

See also **Alewife; Fish** (picture: Fish of coastal waters and the open ocean); **Menhaden; Sardine; Shad.**

Herrmann, Adelaide. See Magician (Illusions).

Herschel, *HUR shuhl,* is the family name of three British astronomers.

Sir William Herschel (1738-1822) founded the present-day system of star astronomy. In 1781, he discovered Uranus, the first planet discovered since prehistoric times. He found that Uranus rotated in a backward direction. He also found two of its satellites, and saw that they revolved around Uranus in the backward direction. Herschel discovered two satellites of Saturn. He also discovered infrared radiation. He became the first astronomer to undertake a thorough review of the heavens, and contributed pioneering ideas of the stellar system's structure. Herschel was born in Hannover, Germany. He moved to England in 1757.

Caroline Lucretia Herschel (1750-1848), the sister of Sir William, was the first woman to discover a comet. She found at least five of them, as well as several nebulae and star clusters (see **Nebula**). Herschel was born in Hannover, Germany. She later joined her brother in England, where he trained her in astronomy.

Sir John Frederick William Herschel (1792-1871), the son of Sir William, surveyed the southern skies as systematically as his father had studied the northern heavens. His discovery that *sodium thiosulfate* (hypo)

dissolves silver salts gave photography an improved fixing agent. He was born in Slough, England.
Edward Rosen

Hersey, *HUR see,* **John** (1914-   ), an American novelist and journalist, became famous for his works about World War II. He won a 1945 Pulitzer Prize for *A Bell for Adano.* This novel describes the impact of American soldiers occupying an Italian village. Hersey's best-known nonfiction work, *Hiroshima* (1946), portrays the destruction of the Japanese city of Hiroshima by an atomic bomb.

Alison Shaw, Knopf

John Hersey

Hersey was born in Tianjin, China, where his parents were missionaries. He became a war correspondent during World War II. Hersey's first book, *Men on Bataan* (1942), tells his observations of the war. His other works include *The Wall* (1950), *The Child Buyer* (1960), *The Algiers Motel Incident* (1968), *The Conspiracy* (1972), and *The Call* (1985). Harry R. Warfel

Hershey, *HUR shee,* Pa. (pop. 13,249), is the home of the Hershey Foods Corporation, which is famous for its manufacture of chocolate candy. The town is named for the company. Hershey lies about 12 miles (19 kilometers) east of Harrisburg (see **Pennsylvania** [political map]). It has an amusement park, sports arena, stadium, and rose garden. It is the home of the Milton S. Hershey Medical Center, a campus of Pennsylvania State University. Milton S. Hershey founded the community in 1905 as the home of the chocolate company. Dale A. Davenport

Hertz, *hurts,* is the unit used to measure the *frequency* (rate of occurrence) of waves and vibrations. Its symbol is Hz. Waves exist in many forms. For example, human vocal cords vibrate, making sound waves, and radio transmitters send electromagnetic waves. One important fact about each wave is the number of complete *cycles* (vibrations) that occur each second. This number is the frequency of the wave. The musical note "A" has a frequency of 440 Hz or 440 cycles per second. Radio waves may have frequencies of many million hertz.

The hertz was adopted in 1960 by an international group of scientists at the General Conference on Weights and Measures. It was named for Heinrich R. Hertz, a German physicist. Richard G. Fowler

See also **Hertz, Heinrich R.; Sound** (Frequency and pitch); **Waves.**

Hertz, *hurts* or *hehrts,* **Gustav,** *GUS tahf* (1887-1975), a German physicist, shared the 1925 Nobel Prize for physics for proving the validity of Niels Bohr's theory of the atom (see **Bohr, Niels**). In 1932, Hertz developed a way of separating isotopes (see **Isotope**). The United States government uses his process in its uranium separation plants. Hertz was born in Hamburg. He worked in the Soviet Union from 1945 to 1954, and won the Stalin Prize in 1951. Ralph E. Lapp

Hertz, *hurts* or *hehrts,* **Heinrich Rudolph,** *HYN rihkh* (1857-1894), was a German physicist. He opened the way for the development of radio, television, and radar with his discovery of electromagnetic waves between 1886 and 1888. James Clerk Maxwell had predicted such waves in 1864 (see **Maxwell, James Clerk**). Hertz used a rapidly oscillating electric spark to produce waves of ultrahigh frequency. He showed that these waves caused similar electrical oscillations in a distant wire loop. He also showed that light waves and electromagnetic waves were identical (see **Electromagnetism**). Hertz was born in Hamburg.   Richard G. Olson

Herzberg, Gerhard (1904-   ), is a Canadian physicist who won the 1971 Nobel Prize in chemistry. He received the award for determining the electronic structure of molecules. Herzberg's studies play an important part in such fields of science as astrophysics, physical chemistry, and quantum mechanics.

Herzberg has devoted his career to the *spectroscopy* of atoms and molecules—that is, the observation of radiation that atoms and molecules emit when excited. Such study reveals the structure of atoms and molecules. Herzberg has determined the structures of the molecules of many substances.

Herzberg was born in Hamburg, Germany, and graduated from the Darmstadt Institute of Technology in 1928. He moved to Canada in 1935 and became a Canadian citizen in 1945. In 1955, Herzberg became the director of the Division of Pure Physics of the National Research Council of Canada.   Richard L. Hilt

Herzen, *HEHRT suhl,* **Alexander Ivanovich** (1812-1870), was a Russian journalist and one of the best-known revolutionaries of his day. He published the newspaper *Kolokol* (*The Bell*) in London from 1857 to 1867. The newspaper criticized the Russian government, and Herzen's writings influenced such reforms as freeing the serfs. Although officially banned in Russia, *Kolokol* was very popular there. Even Russian officials read it to learn about conditions in their own country.

Herzen was born in Moscow and graduated from Moscow State University. He was exiled to Siberia in 1834 for antigovernment activities. Herzen left Russia in 1847 and never returned. He settled in London in 1852. His works include *From the Other Shore* (1850), a collection of articles; and *My Past and Thoughts* (1852-1855), a six-volume autobiography.   Alfred Erich Senn

Herzl, *HEHR tsuhl,* **Theodor,** *TAY aw DOHR* (1860-1904), was an Austrian journalist and playwright who founded the Zionist movement. The movement's aim was to set up a Jewish national home in Palestine (see **Zionism**). Herzl was born in Budapest, Hungary.

The growing problem of anti-Jewish feeling in Europe, increased by the Dreyfus case in France, attracted Herzl's attention (see **Dreyfus, Alfred**). He saw that European Jews had failed to gain social equality even when they had become politically free. So Herzl got the idea of gathering the scattered Jews into a country and a nation of their own. His motives were economic and social, rather than religious. Herzl's *Jewish State,* published in 1896, attracted many persons to the Zionist cause, including Max Nordau and Israel Zangwill.

Herzl kept up contact with the leaders of many nations. In 1897, he presided over the first Zionist congress in Basel, Switzerland. In 1901, Great Britain offered the Jewish people land in British East Africa. Worry about the dispute over this offer injured Herzl's health and hastened his death.   Gottfried F. Merkel

Herzog, Émile. See Maurois, André.

Hesburgh, *HEHS burg,* **Theodore Martin** (1917-   ), a Roman Catholic priest, served as president of the University of Notre Dame from 1952 until he retired in 1987. In addition to his university duties, Hesburgh gave much time to government and foundation service. Hesburgh was a member of the United States Commission on Civil Rights from 1958 to 1972 and served as chairman of the group from 1969 to 1972.

During the 1960's, Hesburgh greatly reduced his own powers and gave more authority to the Notre Dame faculty. He also started the practice of appointing lay persons to the university's board of trustees.

Hesburgh was born in Syracuse, N.Y. He became a priest in 1943 and is a member of the Holy Cross order. Hesburgh earned degrees at Gregorian University and Catholic University of America.   Richard E. Gross

Hesiod, *HEE see uhd* or *HEHS ee uhd,* was a Greek epic poet who probably lived during the 700's B.C. Scholars attribute two major poems, the *Theogony* and the *Works and Days,* to Hesiod. The *Theogony* combines traditional tales and Hesiod's ideas about the creation of the world, the succession of divine rulers, and the genealogy of the Greek gods. This poem is one of the earliest sources of information about Greek religion. For a discussion of the *Theogony,* see **Mythology** (Comparing myths; Greek mythology).

In the *Works and Days,* Hesiod examined human life and set forth his moral values. He addressed the poem to his brother, Perses. The *Works and Days* explains that life is difficult and people must work hard in spite of the just rule of Zeus, the king of the gods. The poem then tells the story of Pandora (see **Pandora**). The *Works and Days* also contains agricultural and moral advice to help people maintain a harmonious relationship with the gods. According to tradition, Hesiod was a farmer in Boeotia, a district of ancient Greece.   Joseph R. Tebben

Hesperia, *hehs PIHR ee uh,* was the name Greek poets gave to Italy. The name means *The Western Land.* Roman poets sometimes called Spain *Hesperia.*

Hesperides, *hehs PEHR uh deez,* in Greek mythology, were the daughters of Hesperis (Evening) and Atlas, a member of a race of gods called *Titans.* The Hesperides were nymphs who lived at the western end of the world. There they guarded the golden apples that Gaea (Earth) had given to the goddess Hera when Hera married Zeus, king of the gods. A sleepless dragon helped the Hesperides guard the apples. As one of his 12 labors, the hero Hercules had to steal these apples (see **Hercules**).   William F. Hansen

Hesperornis, *HEHS puh RAWR nihs,* was a bird that lived during the Upper Cretaceous period. It was about 6 feet (1.8 meters) tall. It had a long body and neck, a long bill with teeth, and webbed feet. It could not fly. It was an excellent diver and swimmer and caught fish to eat. Skeletons of these birds have been found in England and in the United States, especially in Kansas. See also **Bird** (The first known birds).   Samuel Paul Welles

Hess, Dame Myra (1890-1965), an English pianist, won fame for her playing of works by Scarlatti, Bach, and Mozart. In 1941, King George VI honored her for the noontime concerts she performed at London's National Gallery during the German air raids of World War II (1939-1945). She made her debut in 1907 in London. She made her American debut in New York City in 1922. Dame Myra was born in Hampstead, near London.

Robert U. Nelson

Hess, Rudolf (1894-1987), served as secretary and deputy to Adolf Hitler. In May 1941, he piloted a plane to Scotland to persuade Great Britain to get out of World War II. Hitler denied knowledge of Hess's plan. Hess was imprisoned in Great Britain during the war. In 1945, he was returned to Germany and, at Nuremberg, was sentenced to life imprisonment for war crimes. Hess was born in Alexandria, Egypt.   Lester B. Mason

Hesse, *hehs,* officially Hessen, *HEHS uhn,* became a state of the German Federal Republic (West Germany) in 1949. Hesse lies in west-central Germany. It was formed in 1945, during the American military occupation after World War II, by combining the former state of Hesse, also called Hesse-Darmstadt, and parts of the former Prussian provinces of Hesse-Kassel and Hesse-Nassau. Hesse covers 8,152 square miles (21,113 square kilometers), and has a population of 5,553,500.

Potatoes and grapes are the chief farm products of the state. The chief minerals are coal and iron. The principal towns in Hesse are Darmstadt, Frankfurt, Kassel, and Wiesbaden, which is the state capital.

The name of Hesse has been known in history throughout the Christian Era. The British hired troops from Hesse-Kassel, called *Hessians,* to fight the colonists during the American Revolution. In 1871, Hesse became part of the German Empire.   James K. Pollock

See also **Frankfurt; Wiesbaden; Hessians.**

Hesse, *HEHS uh,* **Hermann** (1877-1962), a German novelist and poet, won the 1946 Nobel Prize for literature. Hesse's view of life was influenced by the German romantic writers and the Hindu philosophy of India. His novels concern the spiritual loneliness of people in a mechanized urban society, the conflict between intellect and sensuality, and the problems of people outside society, such as some artists and vagabonds. The stories express a yearning for a synthesis between human sensual and intellectual capacities.

Hesse's best-known fiction includes *Knulp* (1915), *Demian* (1919), *Siddhartha* (1922), *Steppenwolf* (1927), *Narcissus and Goldmund* (1930, also called *Death and the Lover*), and *Magister Ludi* (1943, also called *The Glass Bead Game*). Hesse's simple, melodious poetry shows his love of nature. Like some of his novels, his poems tend to be self-conscious and overly sentimental.

Hesse was born in Calw in the Black Forest. He settled in Switzerland in 1919, and became a Swiss citizen in 1923.   Werner Hoffmeister

Hessian fly, *HEHSH uhn,* is a tiny, two-winged insect. It is called *Hessian fly* because people once believed that it was brought to America in the bedding of Hessian troops during the Revolutionary War (1775-1783). It probably came from southern Russia. It is now common in the United States and Canada. The *larva* (maggot) attacks wheat crops. In some years, it has destroyed 10 per cent of the U.S. and Canadian wheat crop. For methods of controlling the fly, see **Wheat** (Insects).

The adult Hessian fly is about $\frac{1}{8}$ inch (3.2 millimeters) long, with a dark brown body and dusky gray wings. Twice a year, the female lays from 250 to 300 tiny, pale-red eggs. She deposits them on a wheat leaf or stalk. In about five days, whitish maggots hatch and crawl down between the leaf sheath and the stem. They suck juice from the stem.

Scientific classification. The Hessian fly belongs to the gall gnat family, Cecidomyiidae. It is *Phytophaga destructor.*

Robert L. Usinger

Hessians, *HEH shuhnz,* were German soldiers hired by the British to fight the colonists during the Revolutionary War in America. About 30,000 Hessians fought

Detail from *Capture of the Hessians at Trenton* (about 1790), an oil painting by John Trumbull; Yale University Art Gallery

The surrender of the Hessians after the Battle of Trenton on Dec. 26, 1776, raised the spirits of the American troops during the Revolutionary War. About 1,000 Hessians were captured.

in the war. They were called *Hessians* because many came from Hesse-Kassel (now Hesse, West Germany). The Hessians were victims of a European system by which governments sold men into military service. They were paid about 25 cents a day. Princes who sold their services pocketed a large bonus from the British government.

The Hessians were not particularly interested in the war, but they were well trained and fought well. Their performance in the battles of Long Island, Fort Washington, Brandywine, Newport, and Charleston caused the American troops to know and respect their fighting ability. The defeat of the Hessians at Trenton on December 26, 1776, boosted American morale. Some Hessians were won over to the American cause and deserted the British army. Many remained in the United States after the war.　　　John R. Alden

Hestia, *HEHS tee uh,* was the Greek goddess of the hearth and its fire. The hearth served as the center of family life, and fire also had a vital role in ancient Greece. As a result, Hestia ranked as one of the most important goddesses. The Greeks worshiped her as a protector not only of the home, but also of the city and state.

According to Greek mythology, Hestia was the first child of Cronus and Rhea. Thus, she was one of the most beloved of the goddesses who lived on Mount Olympus. The Greeks called on her first in their prayers and offered her the richest share of their sacrifices. They believed that Zeus, king of the gods, granted her these honors after she vowed to remain a virgin. Hestia resembled the Roman goddess Vesta, who was served by priestesses called Vestal Virgins.　　　Robert J. Lenardon

See also **Vesta.**

Heteronym, *HEHT uhr uh nihm,* is a word having the same spelling as another word or words but different pronunciation and meaning. For example, the word *tear,* when pronounced *tair,* means to pull apart. But when it is pronounced *tihr,* it means a drop of salty liquid that comes out of the eye. See also **Homonym.**

William F. Irmscher

Hevesy, *HEH veh shee,* **Georg von,** *geh AWRG vawn* (1885-1966), won the 1943 Nobel Prize for chemistry. He received the award primarily for his research work on the use of isotopes as indicators in the study of chemical processes (see **Isotope**). In addition, Hevesy helped discover the element hafnium, which is found in zircon ore (see **Hafnium**).

Hevesy was born in Budapest, Hungary, but he later moved to Denmark. Hevesy conducted his research work at the Institute for Theoretical Physics in Copenhagen.　　　K. L. Kaufman

Hewes, Joseph (1730-1779), was a North Carolina signer of the Declaration of Independence. He served in the Continental Congress from 1774 to 1777, and again in 1779. While in Congress, Hewes became the first executive head of the United States Navy, although he did not have this official title at that time. He appointed John Paul Jones a navy officer, and provided him with a ship. Joseph Hewes was born in Kingston, N.J.

Richard B. Morris

Hexagon, *HEHK suh gahn,* is a plane figure that has six sides. It is a type of polygon. The sides of a hexagon meet at points called *vertices,* forming six interior angles. The sum of a hexagon's interior angles is always 720°. A hexagon is said to be *regular* if all its sides and angles are equal. Each angle of a regular hexagon measures 120°. The area of a regular hexagon equals one-half the product of its perimeter and its *apothem,* which is the distance from the center of a regular polygon to the midpoint of one of its sides.　　　Arthur F. Coxford, Jr.

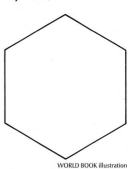

WORLD BOOK illustration

A regular hexagon, *above,* has six sides of equal length.

Hexahedron, *HEHK suh HEE druhn,* in geometry, is a solid figure that has six faces. It is a kind of *polyhedron,* which is a solid whose faces are polygons (see **Polygon**). A familiar hexahedron is the cube. See also **Cube.**　　　Philip S. Marcus

Hexameter. See **Meter** (poetry).

Hexapod, *HEHK suh pahd,* is an arthropod with six legs. The class *Hexapoda* is a synonym for *Insecta.* See also **Arthropod.**

Heydrich, *HY drihk,* **Reinhard,** *RYN hahrt* (1904-1942), called the *Hangman,* was one of the most feared men in Nazi Germany. As chief of the security police, he was responsible for killing hundreds of hostages. He was killed by a bomb in Czechoslovakia in 1942. In revenge, the Nazis killed more than 300 Czechs and destroyed the town of Lidice. Heydrich was born in Halle, Germany.　　　O. W. Wilson

Heyerdahl, *HY ehr dahl,* **Thor,** *thawr* (1914-　), is a Norwegian ethnologist and author. He won fame in 1947 by sailing a balsa-wood raft named *Kon-Tiki* from Peru to the Tuamotu Islands in eastern Polynesia. He and five companions made the trip to test his theory that the islands of Polynesia could have been settled by Indians from South America. His book, *Kon-Tiki* (1950), tells the story of the voyage. In 1958, he wrote *Aku-Aku,* a book about Easter Island. In 1970, Heyerdahl and a crew of seven sailed a papyrus reed boat named *Ra-2* from Morocco to Barbados in the West Indies. He claimed that this voyage proved that the ancient Egyptians could have sailed similar boats to the New World. Heyerdahl was born in Larvik, Norway. See also **Rafting** (picture: Rafts).　　　Ben Finney

Wide World

Thor Heyerdahl

Heyrovský, *HAY rawf skee,* **Jaroslav,** *YAH raw SLAHF* (1890-1967), a Czechoslovak scientist, won the Nobel Prize in chemistry in 1959. He won the award for the invention of *polarography,* an electrochemical method of analyzing complicated chemical solutions. This method became valuable in the field of metallurgy after it was developed by Heyrovský in 1922.

Heyward, *HAY wuhrd,* **Du Bose,** *duh BOHZ* (1885-1940), an American author, wrote poems and novels about the area around Charleston, S.C., his birth-place. He wrote mainly about the blacks of Charleston and the South Carolina sea islands. His most famous book is the novel *Porgy* (1925). Heyward and his wife, Dorothy Hartzell, adapted it for the stage, and George Gershwin used it later as the basis for his opera *Porgy and Bess.*

Heyward wrote the books of verse *Skylines and Horizons* (1924) and *Jasbo Brown and Selected Poems* (1931). His other novels include *Mamba's Daughters* (1929), *Peter Ashley* (1932), *Lost Morning* (1936), and *Star-Spangled Virgin* (1939). Heyward and his friend, Hervey Allen, published a book of verse, *Carolina Chansons,* in 1922.

John O. Eidson

Heyward, *HAY wuhrd,* **Thomas, Jr.** (1746-1809), an American patriot, statesman, soldier, and judge, was a South Carolina signer of the Declaration of Independence. He served as a delegate to the Continental Congress from 1776 to 1778. Heyward was born on his father's plantation in what is now Saint Luke's Parish, South Carolina. He studied law in England. Heyward served in the provincial congresses of South Carolina in 1774 and 1775. He fought with the South Carolina state militia.   Clarence L. Ver Steeg

Heywood, *HAY wud,* **Thomas** (1574?-1641), was a popular and productive English playwright of the Elizabethan Age. He claimed he wrote all or part of 220 plays, of which about 20 survive. His most enduring drama is *A Woman Killed with Kindness* (1603). This tragedy is almost unique in Elizabethan drama because the characters in the play are not of high rank, and its central situation is wholly domestic and free from political overtones. The play thus anticipates the direction that serious drama took almost 300 years later in the works of Henrik Ibsen.

Heywood's other plays include *Edward IV* (1599), *The Fair Maid of the West* (1610?), and adaptations of classical myths. He also produced translations and pamphlets. His most important pamphlet was *An Apology for Actors* (1612), a reply to Puritan attacks on the theater. Heywood was born in Lincolnshire.   Alan S. Downer

Hezekiah, *HEHZ uh KY uh,* was the king of Judah from about 727 to 698 B.C. His name means "God strengthens" in Hebrew.

During Hezekiah's reign, Judah was caught between the two major powers of Assyria and Egypt. Encouraged by the prophet Isaiah, Hezekiah resisted the mighty Assyrian army led by Sennacherib (see **Isaiah, Book of**). As a result, the Assyrians besieged Jerusalem in 701 B.C., but a plague struck them and forced them to withdraw. This story is told in the Bible in II Kings 18-19 and Isaiah 36-37.

Hezekiah is said to have "trusted in the Lord the god of Israel; so that there was none like him among all the kings of Judah . . ." (II Kings 18:5). This passage praised Hezekiah's attempts to reform religion in Jerusalem, and to rid Judah of idolatry. In the New Testament, Hezekiah is listed in the genealogy of Jesus Christ (Matt. 1:9-10).

Carole R. Fontaine

Hi-fi. See **High fidelity system.**

Hialeah, *HY uh LEE uh,* Fla. (pop. 145,254), in the Miami metropolitan area, is famous as the site of Hialeah Park Race Course. For location, see **Florida** (political map). The city grew rapidly after small industry developed in

the 1950's. It had more than seven times as many people in 1980 as it had in 1950. Hialeah's population is 85 per cent Hispanic. Hialeah was settled in 1910 and incorporated in 1917. It has a mayor-council government.

John S. Pancake, Jr.

Hialeah Park, *HY uh LEE uh,* is the home of Hialeah Race Course, about 12 miles (19 kilometers) from downtown Miami, Fla. About 1½ million persons visit there each year, most of them during the winter racing season. Such great horses as *Seabiscuit, Citation,* and *Nashua* have won at Hialeah. The park is open all year. The only flock of pink flamingos ever to propagate in captivity lives on the 32-acre (13-hectare) infield lake.

Hiawatha. See **Song of Hiawatha.**

Hibbing, Minn. (pop. 21,193), is often called the Iron-Ore Capital of the World. It is the chief community on the rich Mesabi iron range, which is about 60 miles (97 kilometers) northwest of Duluth (see **Minnesota** [map]). The village was founded in 1893. Expansion of the Hull-Rust open-pit iron mine in 1918 caused Hibbing to be moved about 2 miles (3 kilometers) south of its original location. The pit is referred to as "the world's largest man-made hole." It covers about 2,300 acres (930 hectares). Hibbing is also a tourist center. The city hosts the annual St. Louis County Fair. The Greyhound Bus Lines had its origin in Hibbing in 1914.   Alan T. Zdon

Hibernation is an inactive, sleeplike state that some animals enter during the winter. Animals that hibernate protect themselves against the cold and reduce their need for food. A hibernating animal's body temperature is lower than normal, and its heartbeat and breathing slow down greatly. An animal in this state needs little energy to stay alive and can live off fat stored in its body. Thus, hibernating animals can more easily survive cold winters when food is scarce.

Warm-blooded hibernators include such birds as nighthawks and swifts; and such mammals as chipmunks, ground squirrels, hedgehogs, fat-tailed lemurs, hamsters, marmots, bats, and bears. Most of these animals eat large amounts of food in the fall. The food is stored in the animals' bodies as fat, which provides energy during hibernation. Hibernating birds and mammals do not sleep straight through the winter. Instead, these animals experience several *bouts*—periods of deep hibernation—that alternate with periods of wakefulness. They are able to arouse themselves from hibernation at any time, and may also be aroused by heat. A few hibernators store food in their caves or burrows. They eat this food between bouts.

For many years, scientists did not classify bears as hibernators, because a bear's body temperature falls only slightly during winter sleep. Scientists now know that bears have a high body temperature during hibernation because their large bodies do not lose as much heat as the small bodies of other hibernators.

Scientists have discovered a chemical, called *hibernating inducing trigger* (HT), that is present in the blood of hibernating mammals. If this chemical is injected into hibernators during the summer, when the animals are active, it will *induce* (cause) them to hibernate out of season.

Cold-blooded hibernators include such amphibians as frogs and toads; and such reptiles as lizards, snakes, and turtles. The body temperature of these animals rises

Animals that sleep through the winter

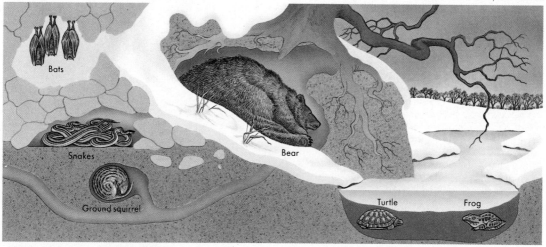

Bats

Snakes

Ground squirrel

Bear

Turtle   Frog

and falls with the temperature of the environment. When cold weather causes their body temperature to drop, the animals enter hibernation. An amphibian or reptile can only be aroused from hibernation when its environment warms up enough to heat its body.

Other kinds of hibernation. Some species of bats hibernate each day and become active each night. Some birds, such as hummingbirds, are active during the day and hibernate at night. These daily types of hibernation are known as *diurnal hibernation.* Some kinds of animals become *dormant* (inactive) during the summer, to protect themselves from heat and drought. This type of dormancy is called *estivation.* Many insects experience *diapause,* a period of inactivity and lack of growth. Diapause can occur in any season. When it occurs during the winter, it is sometimes called hibernation.

Albert R. Dawe

Related articles in *World Book* include:

Bat (Hibernation and migration)
Bear (Hibernation)
Butterfly (Hibernation)
Estivation
Insect (Hibernation and migration)
Snake (Regulation of body temperature)
Turtle (Hibernation)

Hibernia is an old name for Ireland. It comes from the Latin *Juverna,* which scholars believe to be the name Julius Caesar gave the country. Many uses of the name can be found in the Latin classics, especially in the writings of the Greek geographer Ptolemy, who described Ireland in detail.

Hibernians in America, Ancient Order of, is a fraternal benefit society that was founded in 1836 to promote the welfare of persons of Irish birth or descent in the United States. The order assists various charities. A women's auxiliary of the Ancient Order of Hibernians in America was founded in 1894. The order and its auxiliary have about 197,000 members in 648 local organizations. The headquarters of the Ancient Order of Hibernians in America are located at 31 Logan Street, Auburn, NY 13021.

Critically reviewed by the Ancient Order of Hibernians in America

Hibiscus, *huh BIHS kuhs* or *hy BIHS kuhs,* is the name of a group of plants that belong to the mallow family.

The *swamp rose mallow* grows wild in marshes in the eastern United States, sometimes growing 7 feet (2 meters) high. It has white or pink flowers 4 to 7 inches (10 to 18 centimeters) across. The *rose of Sharon,* or *shrubby althea,* is native to Asia. But United States gardeners often cultivate it as a small tree or shrub for borders and background. Its flowers resemble those of the hollyhock. The tropical *Chinese hibiscus* has striking blossoms that the Chinese sometimes use to stain their eyebrows and teeth. Both the rose of Sharon and the Chinese hibiscus can have single or double flowers that vary in color from white, pink, and red to lavender. *Okra* is a summer annual hibiscus of the vegetable garden. Its sticky pods are used in soups and stews. Other kinds of hibiscus are grown for their fiber.

Scientific classification. Hibiscus belong to the mallow family, Malvaceae. They make up the genus *Hibiscus.* The swamp rose mallow is *Hibiscus moscheutos.* The rose of

The Chinese hibiscus, *above,* makes a colorful garden flower. Hibiscus plants also have other uses. For example, people cook the pods of *okra,* another kind of hibiscus, as vegetables.

Sharon is *H. syriacus* and the Chinese hibiscus, *H. rosasinensis.* Okra is *H. esculentus.*   Michael A. Dirr

See also **Flower** (picture: The structure of a hibiscus); **Hawaii** (picture: The state flower); **Mallow; Okra; Rose of Sharon.**

Hiccup, also called *hiccough,* is an abrupt, involuntary intake of air caused by a spasm of the diaphragm. The *diaphragm* is a large, powerful, dome-shaped muscle that lies at the base of the chest cavity. It contracts and relaxes like a bellows to aid breathing. Normally, these contractions are rhythmic and gentle. But irritation of organs near the diaphragm, or, sometimes, certain diseases, may cause the diaphragm to contract suddenly. This spasm pulls air into the lungs through the *larynx* (voice box). The larynx is flanked by the vocal cords and topped by the *epiglottis,* a movable cap that keeps food from getting into the air passages. The epiglottis closes over the larynx when the diaphragm suddenly contracts. When the spasm of the diaphragm pulls air into the larynx, the air forcibly strikes the closed epiglottis and causes a movement of the vocal cords. These actions result in the *hic* sound that we hear.

The *hiccup* (spasm) may occur several times in a minute. The attack itself may last for several hours, or, rarely, for several days.

People can sometimes stop ordinary hiccups by breathing deeply or by holding their breath. Some people prefer to stop their hiccups by breathing into a paper bag.   Charles W. Cummings

See also **Diaphragm; Larynx.**

Hickam Air Force Base, Hawaii, is the headquarters of the U. S. Air Force Pacific Air Forces. It covers 2,259 acres (914 hectares) and lies southwest of the chief urban area of Honolulu. The base was a major headquarters during World War II and remains a vital air supply center, serving much of the Pacific. It was heavily damaged during the Japanese air attack on nearby Pearl Harbor on Dec. 7, 1941. Hickam Air Force Base was dedicated in 1935 in memory of Lieutenant Colonel Horace M. Hickam, who died in an airplane crash in 1934.

      Richard M. Skinner

Hickok, Wild Bill (1837-1876), was an American frontier scout and peace officer in the West. He was a tall man with a droopy mustache and brown hair that came to his shoulders. He won fame as a marksman. Hickok had a reputation for great courage and skill and controlled frontier outlaws single-handedly. But he never killed a man except in self-defense or in the line of official duty.

James Butler Hickok was born in Troy Grove, Ill. In 1855, he went to Kansas. There he did farm work, joined the Free State Army, and in 1858 became constable in Monticello. In 1859, he left as a teamster in a freight caravan for Santa Fe. He later worked as a stagecoach driver on the Santa Fe Trail and the Oregon Trail. In 1861, he went to Rock Creek, Nebr., to recover from an attack by a bear. He quarreled with settlers in Rock Creek, and killed three of them. But he was freed on grounds of self-defense.

Later in 1861, Hickok took charge of a government wagon train carrying supplies from Fort Leavenworth, Kans., to Sedalia, Mo. During the remainder of the Civil War, he served as a scout in the Union Army and as a guerrilla fighter. After he returned to Kansas, he fought

Kansas State Historical Society

Wild Bill Hickok was an American frontier scout and peace officer in the West. He served as a scout for the Union Army during the Civil War (1861-1865) and later was a marshal in Kansas.

against the Indians and scouted for Lieutenant Colonel George A. Custer (see **Custer, George A.**).

In 1869, Hickok was marshal of the rowdy frontier Kansas town of Hays City, later called Hays. For most of 1871, he served as marshal of the cattle town of Abilene, Kans. There he killed a gambler, and, by mistake, a special policeman. Hickok later had a term as marshal at Hays City. In 1872, he toured the East with the troupe of Buffalo Bill (see **Buffalo Bill**). He was shot to death in a saloon in Deadwood in the Dakota Territory. He was buried in a cemetery there.   Wayne Gard

Additional resources

Connelley, William E. *Wild Bill and His Era: The Life and Adventures of James Butler Hickok.* Cooper Square, 1972. Reprint of 1933 ed.
O'Connor, Richard. *Wild Bill Hickok.* Doubleday, 1959.
Rosa, Joseph G. *They Called Him Wild Bill: The Life and Adventures of James Butler Hickok.* 2nd ed. Univ. of Oklahoma Press, 1974. *The West of Wild Bill Hickok.* 1982.

Hickory is any one of a group of about 15 tree species. All are confined to eastern and central North America and Mexico except two, which grow in eastern Asia. Hickories are related to walnuts and some species are known for their edible nuts. They are also valuable for their hard wood and as shade trees. The name hickory comes from *pocohicora,* an Indian word for a drink prepared from the crushed nuts.

Hickories are medium to large trees common in the forests of the eastern and central United States. They grow very slowly. Their leaves are made up of 5 to 17 pointed and finely toothed leaflets. Their fruit is the

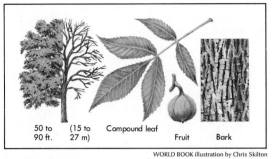

50 to (15 to Compound leaf
90 ft. 27 m)
Fruit Bark

WORLD BOOK illustration by Chris Skilton

The pignut hickory is one of the most common hickory trees in central and eastern North America. Its tough, hard wood is used to make handles for hammers, axes, picks, and other tools.

round, hard-shelled hickory nut. It grows in a husk that splits into four parts. *Pecans* are the most important hickory nuts. Improved varieties of pecan trees are planted for their large, oblong, thin-shelled nuts. *Bitternut hickory* and *water hickory* have bitter nuts. *Shagbark hickory* has rough, shaggy bark that splits off into long, curved strips. *Shellbark hickory* has rough bark that separates into long, straight plates. Both trees bear large, thick-shelled nuts that are sold in stores.

Mockernut hickory is the most abundant of the hickories in the southern states and is the only one that grows in the southern coastal pine belt. The closegrained, light brown to creamy white wood of the *pignut hickory* is hard and tough. This tree is the heaviest commercial hickory, weighing about 53 pounds per cubic foot (849 kilograms per cubic meter) when air-dried.

Manufacturers value hickory wood because it combines strength, toughness, hardness, and stiffness. It is the world's foremost wood for tool handles. Manufacturers use hickory wood especially for hammers, axes, hatchets, picks, and sledges. At one time vehicle makers used hickory wood to make wooden spokes for wagon wheels.

Hickory is also an excellent fuel wood because it produces much heat. It also yields a high quality of charcoal. It is often used for smoking meats. Bacon and ham have a fine flavor when they are cured in hickory smoke.

Scientific classification. The hickories belong to the walnut family, Juglandaceae. Shagbark hickory is *Carya ovata.* Shellbark hickory is *C. laciniosa.* Mockernut hickory is *C. tomentosa.* Pignut hickory is *C. glabra.* Water hickory is *C. aquatica.*

Elbert L. Little, Jr.

See also **Bitternut; Pecan; Tree** (Familiar broadleaf and needleleaf trees [picture]); **Walnut; Wood** (picture: Some types of wood).

Hicks, Edward (1780-1849), was an untrained American folk painter whose works reflect his Quaker religious beliefs. Hicks is best known for more than 60 versions of a subject called *The Peaceable Kingdom* he painted beginning in 1820. Hicks based these works on an Old Testament prophecy. In God's peaceable kingdom, the lion would lie down with the lamb and a little child would lead all creatures. Quakers believed that salvation lay in the "peaceable kingdom" of a serene and well-ordered heart. Hicks visualized this belief in spiritual landscapes crowded with animals that symbolize human vices and virtues. Hicks also painted patriotic historical themes and rural scenes.

Hicks was born in Attleborough (now Langhorne), Pa.

Oil painting on canvas (about 1840-1845); New York State Historical Association, Cooperstown, N.Y.

A Hicks painting called *The Peaceable Kingdom, left,* is based on an Old Testament prophecy. The prophecy proclaims that in God's kingdom, the lion would lie down with the lamb and a little child would lead all creatures. The background shows the American colonial leader William Penn signing a treaty with the Indians. Hicks painted dozens of versions of this subject.

He became an unpaid, wandering Quaker minister at the age of about 22. Hicks developed his extraordinary sense of design while apprenticed to a carriage maker. He learned to decorate carriages and paint tavern signs in bold, flat colors with strong outlines, characteristics that dominated his painting style.   Bess L. Hormats

See also **Folk art** (picture: A folk painting).

Hidalgo y Costilla, *ee DAHL goh ee kohs TEE yah,* **Miguel,** *mee GEHL* (1753-1811), a Mexican priest, is called "The Father of Mexican Independence." He led his Indian followers in a revolt against their Spanish rulers. He did not live to see Mexico free from Spain, but his country still honors him.

On Sept. 15, 1810, Hidalgo rang the bells of his church in the little village of Dolores. The church bells were still ringing as Hidalgo shouted the famous *Grito de Dolores* (cry of Dolores), in which he demanded independence.

Hidalgo called on his people to drive out the foreign rulers, and led his untrained soldiers against Spanish troops. For a short time, Hidalgo's forces were successful, but they could not stand up against the well-trained and well-equipped Spaniards. A year later, the Spaniards captured Hidalgo and put him to death.

Mexico now celebrates September 16 as Independence Day. Each year on September 15, the president of Mexico rings a bell in Mexico City and repeats the *Grito de Dolores.* Most towns have a Hidalgo monument or a Sixteenth of September street.

Hidalgo was born in Guanajuato, and was educated in Valladolid (now Morelia) and Mexico City. In 1803, he went to the parish of Dolores. There, he introduced silk manufacturing, brick-making, vineyards, and other industries to help the Mexican *peons* (laborers).

Harvey L. Johnson

See also **Mexico** (Revolt against the Spaniards).

Additional resources

Bazant, Jan. *A Concise History of Mexico from Hidalgo to Cárdenas, 1805-1940.* Cambrige, 1977.
Caruso, John A. *The Liberators of Mexico.* Pageant Press, 1954.
Hamill, Hugh M., Jr. *The Hidalgo Revolt: Prelude to Mexican Independence.* Greenwood, 1981. First published in 1966.
Noll, Arthur H., and McMahon, A. P. *The Life and Time of Miguel Hidalgo y Costilla.* Russell & Russell, 1973. First published in 1910.

Hidatsa Indians. See Gros Ventre Indians.
Hide. See Leather.
Hideyoshi, *hee deh yoh shee* (1536-1598), was a Japanese military and political leader. He ruled Japan from 1585 until his death and helped unite the country after civil war had divided it. Many Japanese regard him as a folk hero because he was a peasant who became a great leader.

Hideyoshi was born in what is now Aichi Prefecture. His full name was Toyotomi Hideyoshi. He joined the army and gained fame and power through his remarkable military achievements. As ruler, he helped unite Japan by forming alliances with his powerful enemies and by defeating his weak enemies in battle. To prevent rebellions, he reduced the number of armed family forts, allowed only soldiers to carry weapons, and kept close check on the people. Hideyoshi tried to conquer Korea in 1592 and 1597 in unsuccessful attempts to expand Japan's territory.   Tetsuo Najita

Hieratic writing. See Hieroglyphics.
Hieroglyphics, *HY uhr uh GLIHF ihks,* is a form of writing in which picture symbols represent ideas and sounds. The word *hieroglyphics* comes from two Greek words that mean *sacred carving.* Hieroglyphics most often refers to the writing of ancient Egypt. However, forms of picture writing were also used in other ancient cultures, notably by the Hittites, who lived in what is now Turkey, and by the Maya and Aztec Indians of Central America.

The ancient Egyptians used hieroglyphic writing for more than 3,000 years. They used such writing mainly for religious inscriptions on temples and stone monuments and to record the words and deeds of royalty. In fact, the Egyptians sometimes called their writing *the words of God.* The inscriptions were written or carved by highly trained men called *scribes.* After the A.D. 300's, the Egyptians replaced hieroglyphic writing with a simpler alphabet, and knowledge of these symbols was soon lost. The meaning of hieroglyphics remained a mystery until the early 1800's, when scholars deciphered the writing.

Development of hieroglyphic writing. The ancient Egyptians borrowed the idea of hieroglyphic writing from Mesopotamia about 3000 B.C. Egyptian hieroglyphics eventually included about 700 symbols. The symbols have the elegant, stiff quality typical of ancient Egyptian art.

The earliest *hieroglyphs* (symbols) consisted of pictorial characters known as *pictographs* or *ideograms.* These characters were literal representations of ideas. For example, Egyptians who wished to express the idea of a woman drew a picture of a woman.

Egyptian hieroglyphs included *determinatives.* Determinatives indicated the class of object to which the preceding hieroglyphs belonged. An example of a determinative might be the symbol for water placed after the name of a specific lake or river. Such determinatives helped explain and emphasize the meaning of other hieroglyphs.

Some hieroglyphic texts are read from right to left and others from left to right, depending on the direction the hieroglyphs face. Scribes also wrote in columns, which were read from top to bottom. Hieroglyphs often served as decoration. Sometimes, the symbols were painted with brilliant colors or covered with gold.

As writing became more common, the need developed for a material that was easier than stone to write on, store, and transport. For this purpose, the Egyptians invented *papyrus,* a paperlike material made from a reed plant. Scribes wrote on papyrus with pens made of sharpened reeds. Soot mixed with water served as ink.

The Egyptians also developed *phonetic hieroglyphs,* also called *phonograms.* Such hieroglyphs, like the characters of modern alphabets, represented the sounds of the language. Some represented only one sound. Others represented combinations of two or three sounds that formed syllables. But the phonetic symbols represented only the sounds of consonants. The Egyptians did not write the vowels. Thus, scholars remain unsure of how the ancient Egyptian language was pronounced.

The Egyptians developed a simplified *cursive* (flowing) script called *hieratic* writing suitable for writing

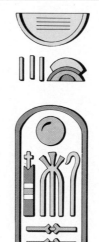

The symbols at the left mean *Lord of Crowns.* The top symbol is a basket, which stands for *Lord.* Beneath the basket is a crown. The three lines to the left of the crown represent a plural.

The illustration at the left is a *cartouche* of the pharaoh Ramses III. A cartouche is an oval frame that contains the name of a ruler. The translation of this cartouche is *Ramses, Ruler of Heliopolis.* The circle at the top represents the sun god Ra. Beneath the circle at the left is a pillar that stands for the city of Heliopolis. In the center is the symbol of three fox skins, which represents the letters *m s.* The shepherd's staff at the right stands for ruler. The two door bolts at the bottom represent forms of the letter *s.*

© Brian Brake, Photo Researchers

WORLD BOOK illustration by Bill and Judie Anderson

Egyptian hieroglyphics, *left,* were painted inside the tomb of the son of the pharaoh Ramses III during the 1100's B.C. The pharaoh is shown with the Egyptian goddess Isis. The illustration at the right interprets the hieroglyphics painted nearest the head of Ramses.

quickly on papyrus. Hieratic writing resembled hieroglyphic writing in much the same way that modern longhand resembles printing. Scribes used hieratic script for both religious and nonreligious purposes.

Later, about 700 B.C., the Egyptians developed a script called *demotic* that was simpler and could be written faster than hieratic writing. Most Egyptians used this form of writing. Scribes also used demotic script for correspondence and record-keeping.

Deciphering hieroglyphic writing. The Egyptians replaced hieroglyphic writing with a phonetic alphabet sometime after the A.D. 300's. Soon the meaning of the hieroglyphs was forgotten. People came to believe that the hieroglyphics really represented a secret and magical sacred code used by Egyptian priests.

In 1799, a French officer in the army of Napoleon I discovered a stone tablet near the mouth of the Nile River near Rosetta, Egypt. The tablet, named the Rosetta

Stone, carried an inscription in three scripts—Egyptian hieroglyphic, Egyptian demotic, and Greek. By reading the Greek portion of the stone, scholars learned that the text consisted of a decree, issued in 196 B.C., honoring King Ptolemy V.

Scholars tried to translate the Egyptian script using methods similar to modern cryptography. In 1814, Thomas Young, an English physician and scholar, found that some of the hieroglyphics were phonetic signs. Scholars also learned that hieroglyphs enclosed in an oval ring, called a *cartouche,* represented the names of individuals.

In 1822, a French scholar named Jean François Champollion achieved a breakthrough in deciphering the hieroglyphs of the Rosetta Stone. By studying the position and repetition of proper names in the Greek text, he picked out the same names in the Egyptian text. In addition, Champollion's knowledge of Coptic, a modern

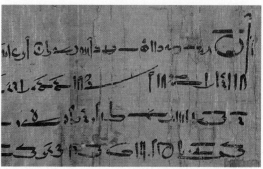

Oriental Institute, University of Chicago

Hieratic writing is a simplified script form of Egyptian hieroglyphics. The text shown above, from the 1100's B.C., is part of a creditor's plea for justice concerning repayment of a loan.

Oriental Institute, University of Chicago

Demotic writing was a form of hieroglyphic script that was used by most Egyptians after about 700 B.C. The example shown above is a portion of a marriage contract written about 365 B.C.

© Ronald Sheridan

Hittite hieroglyphics represented words or phonetic syllables. The Hittites developed their writing system about 1500 B.C., while they were a leading power in the Middle East.

Peabody Museum, Harvard University

Maya hieroglyphics consisted largely of pictorial characters representing ideas or things. The Maya carved hieroglyphics on stone in Mexico and Central America from about A.D. 300 to 900.

Egyptian language, enabled him to recognize many ancient Egyptian words in the hieroglyphic part of the text. Eventually, Champollion deciphered the entire text.

Today, complete grammars and dictionaries enable scholars to read Egyptian hieroglyphic writing easily. Knowledge of ancient Egyptian history would be nearly impossible to obtain without the ability to read hieroglyphics.

Other hieroglyphic writing. In Central America, the earliest examples of Maya hieroglyphs date from about A.D. 300. They consisted chiefly of ideograms, though some scholars believe a number of the signs represent sounds. Most Maya hieroglyphs have not been deciphered. The texts scholars have deciphered deal with religion, astronomy, and the recording of time. Aztec hieroglyphs consisted of pictographs, which also had a phonetic value. The Aztec combined the symbols of several objects to form the sound or name of an object or abstract idea not represented by a pictograph. These symbols resemble modern *rebus* writing (see **Rebus**).

The Hittites developed a hieroglyphic writing system about 1500 B.C. Some Hittite symbols represented words. Others represented phonetic syllables.

John Snyder

Related articles in *World Book.* For examples of hieroglyphics, see:

Alphabet
Aztec (picture: Aztec writing)
Cartouche
Hittites

Maya (picture: Maya writing)
Numeration systems (The
    Egyptian numeral system)
Rosetta Stone

Additional resources

Cleator, Philip E. *Lost Languages.* Day, 1960.
Katan, Norma J. *Hieroglyphs: The Writing of Ancient Egypt.* Antheneum, 1981. For younger readers.
Mertz, Barbara. *Temples, Tombs and Hieroglyphs: The Story of Egyptology.* Putnam, 1964.
Pope, Maurice. *The Story of Archeological Decipherment: From Egyptian Hieroglyphs to Linear B.* Scribner, 1975.

Higgins, Andrew Jackson (1886-1952), an American shipbuilder, was one of the largest builders of small craft during World War II. His firm, the Higgins Aircraft Company and Higgins Engine Company, Inc., also made plywood cargo planes for the Army. After the war, the firm made prefabricated houses. He organized his business in 1930.

Higgins was born in Columbus, Nebr. He began building boats when he was 12 years old. Later, Higgins worked as a lumberman and organized his own lumber company.   V. E. Cangelosi and R. E. Westmeyer

High blood pressure. See Hypertension.

High Church. See Anglicans (Episcopalians).

High Desert is located in central Oregon between the Blue Mountains and the Basin and Range region. It occupies the Malheur Basin, which ranges in elevation from 4,000 to 5,000 feet (1,200 to 1,500 meters). Volcanic ash blankets much of the area. Cinder cones are features of the western section. Localized interior drainage and temporary lakes are common. The High Desert area is a very thinly populated region. The area is used for seasonal grazing.   John Edwin Coffman

High-fidelity system is electronic equipment that reproduces sound with a high degree of accuracy. High-fidelity systems are designed to maintain the greatest possible *fidelity,* or faithfulness, to a sound source without producing distortion or background noise. High-fidelity systems are informally called *hi-fi systems.* They are often called *stereophonic sound systems,* or *stereos,* because they deliver *stereophonic sound.* Stereophonic sound involves the distribution of sound signals through two or more separate channels. In this way, stereo systems enable sounds to be reproduced from their proper directions.

There are two basic types of high-fidelity systems—*console systems* and *component systems.* Consoles consist of parts that a manufacturer has wired and assembled into a frame or cabinet. Component systems are made up of individual *components* (parts) that are purchased separately and connected by the consumer.

Component systems have several advantages over consoles. For example, consumers can easily combine different models and types of components to suit their individual needs, budget, and taste. A component can also be added, exchanged, or repaired without replacing the entire system. This article deals mainly with component systems.

Parts of a hi-fi system

A component hi-fi system consists of three general types of parts—*program source, amplifier,* and *reproducer.* Sounds travel in the form of electric signals from the program source to the amplifier to the reproducers. Program sources include tuners, record players, tape recorders, and compact disk players. Speakers and headphones serve as reproducers.

The tuner receives broadcast radio signals and converts them into weak electric signals. A tuner can be adjusted to receive signals of only a certain frequency—that is, the signals from a selected radio station. Some tuners pick up frequency modulation (FM) waves only, but others can receive amplitude modulation (AM) signals as well (see **Radio** [Kinds of broadcast waves]). In many high-fidelity systems, the tuner is combined with the amplifier into a single unit called a *receiver.*

The record player reproduces sound from a groove on a vinyl phonograph record. Record players are also called phonographs. The record player of a component hi-fi system is made up of three main parts: (1) the turntable, (2) the cartridge, and (3) the tone arm.

The turntable. Many people use the word *turntable* to refer to the entire record player. However, a turntable is technically the flat metal plate on which a record sits. The plate is covered with a rubber or felt pad to prevent it from scratching the record. Most turntables are run by either a *belt drive* or a *direct drive.*

A belt drive consists of a flexible rubber belt stretched from a wheel below the turntable to a *stepped* pulley—that is, a pulley with two separate diameters. The pulley is attached to the shaft of a motor. The speed of the turntable's rotation is changed by raising or lowering a forklike mechanism. In this way, the belt becomes engaged with the different diameters of the pulley. The speed of the motor remains the same, whether the turntable spins at $33\frac{1}{3}$ revolutions per minute (rpm) or 45 rpm.

With a direct drive system, the turntable is mounted directly on the motor shaft. The speed of the motor is controlled by a device called a *quartz crystal oscillator.* This speed varies, and it directly determines the speed of the turntable's rotation.

The cartridge picks up vibrations from the *stylus* (phonograph needle), which moves from side to side and up and down in the groove of a record. It then uses magnets and coils to convert these vibrations into weak electric signals.

The tone arm, also called the *pickup arm,* holds the stylus, the cartridge, and the wires that carry electric signals to the amplifier. Some record players are equipped with a *linear tracking* tone arm, which moves in a straight line across a record. However, in most record players, the tone arm is mounted on a pivot. The pivot enables the cartridge and stylus to move toward the center of the turntable without causing too much wear to the record. A weight at the pivot end of the tone arm balances the pressure of the stylus in the record groove. Too much pressure on the stylus causes poor sound quality and increased record wear. If there is too little pressure, the stylus will skip across the record.

The tape recorder records and reproduces sounds on magnetic tape. During recording, electromagnetic *heads* on the tape recorder convert electric signals into varying magnetic patterns on the tape. In reproducing or playing back sounds, the heads change the magnetic patterns into electric signals. There are two types of tape recorders used in component high-fidelity systems—cassette and reel-to-reel.

Some parts of a high-fidelity system High-fidelity systems reproduce sound with a great degree of accuracy. The parts pictured in the top level of the diagram below produce weak electric signals, which are strengthened by the parts shown in the middle section. Loudspeakers and headphones then convert the signals into sound.

WORLD BOOK illustrations by Burton Uhr

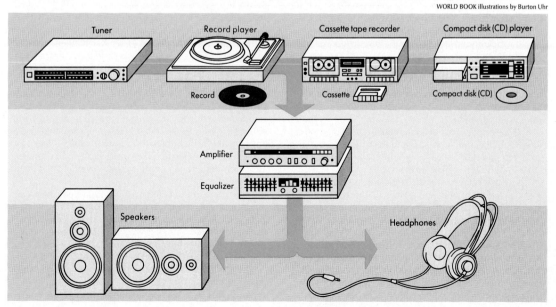

The compact disk (CD) player reproduces sound that has been recorded on a small, plastic-coated disk in *digital,* or numerical, code. The word *disk* is also spelled *disc.* CD players use a *laser* to read the code on the disk. The laser produces a concentrated beam of light that is broken into pulses of light as the laser moves from the center to the edge of the disk during play. The CD player converts the pulses of light into weak electric signals.

Compact disks measure about 4.7 inches (11.9 centimeters) in diameter. CD players spin the disks at 500 rpm at the beginning of play, but slow to a rate of 200 rpm by the time the laser reaches the outer edge.

With a CD player, a listener can skip forward or backward to any point on the disk. Most models can also be programmed for selections to be played in a certain order. CD players are an excellent program source because they produce no background noise.

The amplifier strengthens the weak electric signals that it receives from the tuner, record player, tape recorder, and compact disk player. An amplifier's power is rated by the number of watts in each stereo channel. Good high-fidelity systems require amplifiers with at least 50 watts per channel. Many amplifiers feature 100 watts or more per channel. In general, amplifiers with greater power provide better sound. However, speakers are designed to accommodate only a certain range of power, so the amplifier in a system must be coordinated with the speakers. Too much power from an amplifier can damage the speakers.

Amplifiers or receivers serve as the control center of stereo systems. They have a switch to turn the power of the hi-fi system on and off. They may also have switches to adjust loudness, tone, and the balance of stereophonic sound between the two channels. Some amplifiers are equipped with such additional controls as a *filter control* and a *microphone input.* A filter control helps reduce noise from record scratch and tape hiss. A microphone may be plugged into the system by means of a microphone input.

An *equalizer* and a *time delay* may also be added to a hi-fi system to improve stereo balance and general sound quality. An equalizer alters the pitch and frequency of sounds. Pitch falls into three groups—*bass, midrange,* and *treble.* The tone control of a regular amplifier adjusts only bass and treble, but an equalizer includes an adjustment for midrange as well. An equalizer therefore allows more precise tone control, because it can be used to increase or decrease the loudness of any range of frequencies.

The time delay puts off a sound signal for a certain length of time. In this way, a time delay may help to represent sound more accurately, especially in rooms where sound is not distributed evenly.

Speakers receive electric signals from the amplifier and convert them into sound waves. Stereophonic hi-fi systems require two speakers for reproducing sound—one speaker for the left stereo channel and one for the right.

Headphones, like speakers, change electric signals into sound waves. Most headphones consist of two cushioned earpieces connected by a headband to fit comfortably over the head and ears. Headphones are plugged into the amplifier, and each earpiece carries one stereo channel. Headphones are sometimes called earphones.

History

The term *high fidelity,* in relation to sound, was used at least as early as the 1930's. However, early radios and record players had poor sound quality by today's standards, and the 78 rpm records of the time produced excessive background noise. In 1948, $33\frac{1}{3}$ rpm records, also called long-playing (LP) records, began to replace 78 rpm records. LP's reproduced sound with greater fidelity than did previous records.

Several developments of the 1950's and 1960's eventually led to a demand on the part of consumers for equipment that could produce both better quality sound and greater volume. For example, rock 'n' roll music became popular in the mid-1950's, and stereophonic records appeared on the market in 1958. Also, radio stations began broadcasting in stereo during the 1950's and 1960's.

As manufacturers designed higher-performance equipment, they found that components produced separately provided sound quality superior to that of consoles. By the late 1960's, engineers had developed *quadraphonic sound* systems, which use four channels and four speakers. Digital recording techniques and CD players were developed in the late 1970's and early 1980's. Also in the 1980's, manufacturers introduced hi-fi components that could be connected to television sets and video cassette recorders (VCR's).   Stanley R. Alten

See also **Headphones; Phonograph; Radio; Speaker; Tape recorder.**

Additional resources

Berger, Melvin. *The Stereo-Hi Fi Handbook.* Morrow, 1979. Suitable for younger readers.
Fantel, Hans. *Better Listening: A Practical Guide to Buying and Enjoying Stereo Equipment for the Home.* Scribner, 1982.
Institute of High Fidelity. *Official Guide to High Fidelity.* 2nd ed. Sams, 1978.
Rosenthal, Murray P. *How to Select and Use Hi-Fi and Stereo Equipment.* Hayden, 1979.

High jump is a track and field event in which an athlete tries to jump over a bar supported by two posts at least 12 feet (3.66 meters) apart. The jumper lands in a pit of sawdust or foam rubber, or on an air-inflated pad.

A jumper takes a running start and may approach the bar from any angle. Almost all high-jumpers use one of two styles, the *straddle* or the *Fosbury flop.*

In the straddle, jumpers take off on their inside foot—the foot nearer the bar. They approach at a slow run and, when ready to jump, plant their take-off foot about an arm's length from the bar. As they spring, their outside leg and both arms swing upward. The jumpers have their abdomen and face toward the bar when they kick their outside leg over. They roll over so their inside leg comes over last.

Jumpers using the Fosbury flop begin their approach straight toward the bar but swing to one side just before jumping. They take off on their outside foot and turn their back to the bar. Then they arch their back over the bar and kick their legs out to clear it. They land on their shoulders and back.

The straddle was by far the most popular high-jump style until the late 1960's, when the Fosbury flop became famous. This style was originated by Dick Fosbury, a stu-

Tom Pantages

A high jumper can use one of several techniques to clear the bar. In the Fosbury flop, *above,* the jumper goes over the bar backwards and lands on his shoulders and back in the pit.

dent at Oregon State University. Using this new jumping style, Fosbury set an Olympic high-jump record of 7 feet 4¼ inches (2.24 meters) at the 1968 Summer Games.

In a track and field meet, the bar is placed at successively higher levels. Jumpers remain in the competition until they miss three consecutive times. They get credit for the highest height they clear. In most major meets, an athlete in men's competition must leap at least 7 feet (2.13 meters) to finish among the top three. Women must leap about 6 feet (1.83 meters).   Bert Nelson

For world championship figures in the high jump, see the tables with the articles **Track and field** and **Olympic Games.**

High-lift devices. See Aerodynamics.

High priest was the head of the Jewish priesthood in later Biblical times. He represented the Jewish people before God. His duties were to take care of the Temple and sanctuary and all its services. He was also the chief of the *Sanhedrin,* the highest governing council of the Jews. When he became high priest, he was anointed with holy oil as a symbol of authority.

There were special rules for a high priest's conduct (Lev. 21). For example, he was permitted to marry only a virgin of Israel. His official costume included a blue robe, partly covered with an embroidered garment called an *ephod.* On his head he wore a linen turban called a *miter.* He had a golden breastplate set with 12 precious stones that bore the names of the Hebrew tribes. Only the high priest was permitted to enter the Holy of Holies (see **Tabernacle**). He then wore a white linen robe.

Aaron, the brother of Moses, is believed to have been the first high priest of Israel (see **Aaron**). At first, a high priest served for life. Later, Herod and the Romans appointed and dismissed high priests as they wished.

Carole R. Fontaine

High school is a school that provides several years of education for young people beyond the elementary level. High schools also are called *secondary schools.* In the United States, a majority of high schools begin with ninth grade and offer four-year programs. High schools provide a general education and prepare students for

college or for a vocation. Canadian high schools are similar to those in the United States.

The United States has one of the world's highest high school enrollment rates. Almost all U.S. girls and boys enter high school, and about 75 per cent graduate. The United States has about 25,000 high schools, and about 6,800 combination elementary and high schools. About a million teachers provide instruction to about 14 million high school students.

High schools in the United States offer *college preparatory programs* and *vocational programs.* College preparatory programs give students the necessary background for admission to a college or university. Vocational programs prepare students for jobs immediately following high school. All high schools offer *required* courses—that is, classes in such subjects as English, mathematics, science, and social studies. Students also may choose from a wide variety of *elective* courses, such as music, foreign languages, or industrial arts. *Extracurricular* high school activities, which occur outside of classroom time, include sports, clubs, and plays.

Most U.S. high schools are free public schools supported chiefly by state and local taxes. Each local school district has a governing body, usually a school board, that makes school policies and monitors the quality of education students receive. A superintendent administers the district policies. Each high school is headed by an experienced educator, usually called the principal. About 90 per cent of U.S. students attend public high schools. The United States also has several types of secondary schools outside the public-school system. Most of these *private schools* charge tuition. They include *parochial schools,* which are operated by the Catholic Church or other religious groups. Each state has laws and rules that its high schools must follow.

High schools in other countries. The secondary school systems of Canada and many European countries resemble the U.S. systems. But some of these countries offer college-preparatory programs and vocational programs in separate schools. Most developed countries have well-established secondary school systems. For example, secondary school enrollment in Canada includes about 90 per cent of all youths of high-school age. In Japan and some European nations, the enrollment rate is even higher. But in some developing nations, only about 10 per cent of this group are enrolled.

Most non-Communist countries have both public and private high schools. In almost all these countries, the majority of high-school students attend a public school. In the Soviet Union and nearly every other Communist nation, the central government controls all education.

Development of U.S. high schools. Secondary education in North America began about 350 years ago, during colonial times. Early secondary schools included college-preparatory Latin grammar schools and vocational *academies.* The first free, public high school in the United States opened in Boston in 1821. Not until the 1900's did high schools become institutions designed to educate all young people.   Chris Buethe

Related articles in *World Book.* See the *Education* section of various country articles. For example, see **Union of Soviet Socialist Republics** (Education). See also **Education; Junior high school; Middle school; Parochial school; Private school; School.**

High seas are the areas of the oceans that lie outside the authority of any nation. They generally begin 200 nautical miles from the coasts of nations that border the oceans. A nautical mile is equal to about 1.2 statute miles and 1.9 kilometers. The high seas are also called *international waters.* Areas of the oceans over which nations exercise control include a nation's *territorial waters* (see **Territorial waters**).

All nations are expected to follow international rules regarding the high seas. Under international law, the high seas are open to every nation for fishing, travel, and research. All nations have equal rights on the high seas and must respect one another's rights.

During wartime, international law allows neutral nations to continue trading with other neutral nations and with nations at war. In such times, however, the ships of neutral nations are not supposed to carry *contraband of war* (illegal goods). The nations at war decide what materials they consider contraband of war.

Nations have long argued over the law of the sea. During the 1960's and 1970's, the United Nations (UN) worked to establish a set of sea laws that would satisfy all nations. This work led to the adoption of the Convention on the Law of the Sea in 1982. This treaty was signed by more than 100 UN members. In general, it would give countries exclusive rights to drill for oil and gas up to 350 nautical miles (648 kilometers) from shore and to fish within 200 nautical miles (370 kilometers) of their coasts. Within this 200 nautical miles, called the *exclusive economic zone,* all nations would have high seas rights of navigation and flight. But the coastal nations would control all the economic resources in this zone.

Most nations agree that mining is not a part of the freedom of the sea and can proceed only under the terms of the treaty. But the United States disagrees. It opposes the treaty because of disagreements with provisions on seabed mining, including the control of production and transfer of technology. The treaty will not become official until ratified by 60 nations, but most terms of the treaty are already being followed.

William T. Burke

See also **Contraband; International law; Neutrality; Pirate; Right of search.**

Highball is a railroad term that means *proceed.* In early railroading, a ball-shaped basket was raised over the track to indicate that the track was clear. A member of the train crew who sighted the object would shout "highball" to the rest of the crew. Later, large metallic balls were used to indicate a clear track. Even with modern signaling equipment, railroad workers continue to use the term.   Robert C. Post

Higher education. See Universities and colleges; Education.

Highlands. See Scotland (Land regions; Way of life).

Highway. See Road.

Highwayman robs passengers, or steals valuables, along rural thoroughfares. Highwaymen of the past have often been the subject of romantic fables. For example, such outlaws as Robin Hood, Pancho Villa, and Zorro were highwaymen. They won the reputation of taking from the rich and giving to the poor. But their charity was often a means of setting up a network of spies to warn them of danger. Historic American highwaymen included Jesse James and Sam Bass. They preferred to rob trains and stagecoaches rather than to steal from individuals.   Odie B. Faulk

Hijacking is the seizure of a commercial vehicle by force or the threat of force. For years, trucks have been hijacked and their cargo stolen. Today, hijacking involves chiefly airplanes and is also called *skyjacking* or *air piracy.* Since the late 1960's, skyjackers have seized several hundred planes. In most of these incidents, no one was killed. But several skyjackings resulted in the loss of lives and the destruction of aircraft. A number of governments, including those of the United States and Canada, impose severe penalties for skyjacking.

Most plane hijackers threaten to destroy an aircraft or kill the people aboard if their demands are not met. Some hijackers make political demands, such as certain policy changes by a nation's government or the release of imprisoned associates. Others demand a large sum of money in exchange for the safe return of the plane and the people aboard. Still other hijackers want to flee a country in order to escape punishment for a crime.

Gangsters frequently hijacked truckloads of liquor from one another in the 1920's and early 1930's, when alcoholic beverages were prohibited in the United States. One of the first skyjackings took place in 1930 in Peru. Skyjackings in the United States began in 1961, and a record total of 40 attempts occurred in 1969. In 1970, the airlines began a voluntary program of skyjack prevention. In 1973, the U.S. government began to require inspection of all passengers and other security action to prevent armed people from boarding planes. Since the early 1970's, the number of skyjackings has fallen sharply, particularly in the United States.

The Montreal Convention, a treaty providing punishment for international skyjackers, went into effect in 1973. More than 40 nations, including the United States and Canada, have agreed to support the terms of the treaty.   Thomas J. Andrews

See also **Airport** (Airport security; picture: Security checks at airports); **Aviation** (A new age of flight).

Additional resources

Arey, James A. *The Sky Pirates.* Scribner, 1972.
Blair, Ed, and Haas, W. R. *Odyssey of Terror.* Broadman, 1977. Pilot's account of a hijacking.

Hijra, another spelling for *Hegira.* See Hegira.

Hiking is a healthful, relaxing form of exercise. Millions of people of almost every age enjoy hiking the year around. A hike can last for a few hours or for several weeks. Many experienced hikers find special pleasure in wilderness areas in national parks and national forests. But numerous people prefer to hike in local parks or forest preserves—or even on city sidewalks.

For most hiking, people need only clothing suitable for the weather, including comfortable shoes or boots. Beginning hikers should start with walks that last no longer than a day. As their endurance increases, they may take overnight hikes. Eventually, they may go on camping trips that last several days or weeks.

A hiker can help provide for his or her safety by always having at least one companion. Hikers should be prepared for sudden changes in the weather. They also should know basic first-aid skills so they can treat such conditions as blisters and frostbite. Skill in using a map and a compass can be important in unfamiliar areas.

E. R. Degginger

Hikers on a camping trip carry backpacks containing food, cooking equipment, bedding, clothing, and other items.

In one of the most popular types of hiking, called *backpacking,* people carry food, clothing, a shelter, and other equipment on their backs. Backpackers can spend many days in remote areas where supplies cannot be obtained.

A hiking sport called *orienteering* involves map reading and using a compass. Hikers compete over an established cross-country course. With a map and a compass, they must locate checkpoints scattered throughout the course. The person who finds all the checkpoints first is the winner.

During the winter, many hikers enjoy two cross-country sports, *cross-country skiing* and *snowshoeing.* Cross-country skiing, for which a person should receive professional instruction, is hiking on skis over snow. In snowshoeing, which requires no special training, hikers wear snowshoes. See **Skiing** (Nordic skiing).

Mountain climbing, also called *mountaineering,* is a special type of hiking that can be both difficult and dangerous. Hikers should take a course in mountaineering before attempting a climb, and they should always be accompanied by an experienced climber.

Many organizations provide information for hikers. They include the Boy Scouts, Girl Scouts, and local hiking clubs. Rangers at national parks and national forests provide maps and other aids.   William R. Ruskin

See also **Camping; National Park System** (Visiting the parklands).

Additional resources

Fletcher, Colin. *The Complete Walker III: The Joys and Techniques of Hiking and Backpacking.* 3rd ed. Knopf, 1984.
Hart, John. *Walking Softly in the Wilderness: The Sierra Club Guide to Backpacking.* Rev. ed. Sierra Club, 1984.
Kuntzleman, Charles T., and Consumer Guide. *The Complete Book of Walking.* Simon & Schuster, 1980.
Manning, Harvey. *Backpacking: One Step at a Time.* 3rd ed. Random House, 1980.

Hill is an elevation of the earth's surface that has a distinct summit. It has much less surface area than a mountain and is lower in elevation. Hills rise less than 1,000 feet (305 meters) above the surrounding area. Mountains always exceed that height. However, a hill is not simply a small mountain. It is formed in a considerably different way.

Hills may be classified according to the way they were formed and the kinds of materials they are made of. There are two types, constructional and destructional. *Constructional hills* are created by a build-up of rock debris or sand deposited by glaciers and wind. Oval-shaped landforms called *drumlins* and sand dunes are examples of this type. *Destructional hills* are shaped by the deep erosion of areas that were raised by disturbances in the earth's crust. Such hills may consist of limestone overlying layers of more easily eroded rock.
      M. Dane Picard

See also **Butte.**

Hill, Graham (1929-1975), became a leading automobile racing driver. An Englishman, Hill won racing's world title in 1962 by earning the most points in the nine Grand Prix races that made up the championship circuit that year. He was runner-up for the world title from 1963 through 1966, and won the title again in 1968. Hill won the Indianapolis 500 in 1966, the first time he entered the event.

Hill was born in London. He began racing in 1957, for the Lotus car builders. In 1960, he started driving for the British Racing Motors. Known for his humor, Hill liked to claim he learned much about driving from his troubles with an old car. He said the brakes failed so often he became skilled at stopping the car by scraping the tires against the curb. In 1975, Hill was killed in an airplane crash.   Herman Weiskopf

Hill, James Jerome (1838-1916), was a famous businessman. He earned the name "Empire Builder" for his work in developing the area of the United States that lies between the Great Lakes and the Pacific Northwest. His energy and foresight in laying out a great transportation system played an important part in turning this unsettled region of the United States into a land of progress and prosperity.

Hill was born near Rockwood, Ontario. His father's death forced him to go to work at an early age. When he was 16, he went to St. Paul, Minn., and took a job with a steamboat company. At 25, he became an agent for the Northwestern Packet Company, and five years later organized the Red River Transportation Company. This was the first in a series of enterprises which led to completion of the Great Northern Railway. This railway, completed in 1893, combined existing lines and new construction. It ran from Lake Superior to Puget Sound, Washington. It was the first transcontinental railroad built without government aid. Hill later founded a steamship line offering the first direct transportation between the United States and the Orient.

In 1901, Hill and Edward Henry Harriman struggled for control of the Northern Pacific Railroad. The battle ended without a decisive victory for either man. Hill was also an outstanding financier and a great philanthropist. He was a fluent speaker and writer. His best-known work is *Highways of Progress* (1910).   R. E. Westmeyer

Hill, Joe (1879-1915), was a Swedish-born songwriter who popularized the goals of the American labor movement through his music. Hill's real name was Joel Hägglund. He was born in Gävle, Sweden. In 1902, he moved to the United States, where he roamed from place to place working at various jobs.

About 1910, Hill joined the Industrial Workers of the World (IWW), a labor organization that wanted to replace the American economic system with a society run by workers. Hill spread the IWW's beliefs by writing new lyrics for popular tunes. His best-known songs included "Casey Jones—The Union Scab" and "The Preacher and the Slave."

In 1914, a jury in Salt Lake City, Utah, convicted Hill of murdering two men and sentenced him to death. During his appeal, concerned people throughout the world protested the sentence. President Woodrow Wilson and the Swedish government tried to save his life, but Hill was executed by a firing squad. His casual lifestyle, his musical tributes to workers, and his dramatic death made him an American folk hero.　　Warren Van Tine

Hill, Octavia, *ahk TAY vih uh* (1838-1912), a British housing reformer, was equally interested in painting and social work when young. At the age of 14, she managed a workshop for poor girls, but it was through her painting that she became a pupil of the famous art critic, John Ruskin. Ruskin bought some slum property in 1864, and put her in charge. She improved the property, and gave the tenants cultural advantages. In time, she managed property for over 3,000 people.

Hill believed that housing conditions could be improved only if those living in them were helped to appreciate finer things. She served on the Central Council of the Charity Organization Society and the Royal Commission on the Poor Laws. But she distrusted organized charity, and emphasized personal relationships, businesslike practices, and self-help. A believer in beauty and recreation, she did much to establish and preserve London's "green belt" of parks and playgrounds. Hill was born in London.　　Alan Keith-Lucas

Hillary, *HIHL uh ree,* **Sir Edmund Percival** (1919-   ), a New Zealand mountain climber, became one of the first two men to reach the top of Mount Everest and return. On May 29, 1953, he and Tenzing Norgay, a Sherpa tribesman from Nepal, reached the 29,028-foot (8,848-meter) summit (see **Mount Everest**). Queen Elizabeth II knighted Hillary for the achievement.

Hillary made his first five expeditions on Himalayan peaks after World War II. He climbed part of the way up Everest in 1951 and 1952. He wrote *High Adventure* (1955), an account of the 1953 climb. In 1957 and 1958, he blazed a trail from McMurdo Sound to the South Pole for Sir Vivian Fuchs's transantarctic expedition (see **Antarctica** [picture]).

Wide World
Sir Edmund P. Hillary

In 1960, Hillary headed an expedition, which was sponsored by *The World Book Encyclopedia,* to climb 27,824-foot (8,481-meter) Mount Makalu I. The expedition tested the ability of human beings to live without oxygen at high altitudes. The climbers also searched for but did not find evidence of the *Abominable Snowman.* With Desmond Doig, Hillary wrote *High in the Thin Cold Air* (1962) about this climb (see **Abominable Snowman**).

Hillary was born in Auckland, New Zealand. His first job was beekeeping.　　Richard F. Dempewolff

Hillel I, *HIHL ehl* (70 B.C.?-A.D. 10?), was the most prominent spiritual leader among the Jews of Palestine from 30 B.C. until his death. He was called Hillel the Elder and was known for his humility and his love for others. Hillel described the meaning of Judaism in simple terms. He said: "What is hateful to thee, do not unto thy fellowman; this is the whole Law; the rest is mere commentary."

A descendant of the house of David, Hillel was born in Babylonia. He settled in Palestine and studied with two great scholars, Shemaiah and Abtalion. He became an authority on interpreting Biblical law.

Because of his great learning, Hillel was made a prince of the Sanhedrin, the highest court in the Jewish state. In 30 B.C., he became president of this court, and held office with distinction for 40 years. Hillel reorganized the extensive body of Jewish law. He made it easier to study by arranging the laws under six headings, where there had previously been 600. These six headings form the six major divisions of the *Talmud,* the book of Jewish laws. Hillel is also described as the first sage to have devised logical rules for interpreting the scriptures.

Hillel founded a school which was named for him. Thousands of students came to Jerusalem to study under him. Some of them became important enough to be mentioned in the Talmud, the Jewish book of civil, religious, and ethical laws. Hillel's chief rival was Shammai, who founded a more conservative school of interpretation. Some discussions on their differences in interpretation appear in the Talmud. Since 1923, the Hillel Foundation, a Jewish cultural youth movement, has set up branches at many universities in the United States.
Gary G. Porton

Hillman, Sidney (1887-1946), an American labor leader, was the guiding spirit of the Amalgamated Clothing Workers of America (now the Amalgamated Clothing and Textile Workers Union). He became the first president of the union in 1914. Under Hillman's leadership, the union pioneered in constructive union-management relations. The union also led in developing health and welfare programs and unemployment insurance, and it founded two banks and an insurance company.

Hillman helped found the Committee for Industrial Organization in 1935. When the committee became the Congress of Industrial Organizations (CIO) in 1938, he was one of the vice presidents. In 1943, he became chairman of the CIO Political Action Committee.

Hillman held posts on the National Industrial Recovery Board (1934), National Defense Advisory Council (1940), and in the Office of Production Management during World War II. He was born in Žagarė, Lithuania. He moved to the United States when he was 20 years old.
Jack Barbash

Hills, Carla Anderson (1934-   ), served as United States secretary of housing and urban development from 1975 to 1977. Hills, who served under President Gerald R. Ford, was the third woman Cabinet member in the nation's history. The others were Frances Perkins and Oveta Culp Hobby.

As secretary of housing and urban development, Hills worked to help the housing industry recover from an economic slump of the 1970's. She also directed programs to improve housing and living conditions in many communities.

Department of Housing and Urban Development

Carla Anderson Hills

Hills was born in Los Angeles. She graduated from Stanford University in 1955 and received a law degree from Yale University in 1958. From 1962 to 1974, she was a member of a Los Angeles law firm. Hills then served as an assistant United States attorney general and head of the civil division of the Department of Justice until Ford appointed her to the Cabinet post. Her husband, Roderick M. Hills, served as the chairman of the Securities and Exchange Commission from 1975 to 1977.   William J. Eaton

Hillyer, *HIHL yuhr,* **Robert Silliman,** *SIHL ih muhn* (1895-1961), an American poet, won the 1934 Pulitzer Prize for poetry for his *Collected Verse* (1933). He was an expert craftsman, writing in a wide variety of difficult poetic forms. His subjects include tributes to his friends and to poets he admired, lyric descriptions of the changing seasons in New England, and his experiences as an amateur yachtsman. Hillyer's poetry has a gentle, sophisticated tone that often reflects a sly sense of humor and self-mockery. He also wrote novels and literary criticism.

Hillyer was born in East Orange, N.J., and taught at Harvard University from 1919 to 1945. In the late 1940's, he aroused great controversy by attacking the poets T. S. Eliot and Ezra Pound. He wrote that these poets and their followers had rejected what was most important in American life and had adopted positions that were dangerously undemocratic.   Elmer Borklund

Hilo, *HEE loh* (pop. 35,269), is the largest city and chief port on the island of Hawaii. It lies on the shore of Hilo Bay, on the east side of the island. For location, see **Hawaii** (political map). For the monthly weather in Hilo, see **Hawaii** (Climate).

Hilo is the seat of Hawaii County and the home of a branch of the University of Hawaii. The city exports papaya, ginger, guava, macadamia nuts, and sugar. It is Hawaii's center of the orchid-growing and flower-packaging industries. Hilo lies near the Kilauea volcano district of Hawaii Volcanoes National Park. The district includes Kilauea, one of the world's most active volcanoes.

Polynesians settled in the Hilo area thousands of years ago. White missionaries settled there in 1824. After severe damage from tidal waves in 1946 and 1960, the city frontage was rebuilt farther inland.

Sherman R. Frederick

See also **Kilauea; Mauna Loa.**

Hilton, Conrad Nicholson (1887-1979), an American businessman, was sometimes called the *biggest hotel man in the world.* He organized the Hilton Hotel Systems in 1946. In 1948, he started to build hotels in such places as Istanbul, Madrid, Tokyo, and Berlin. By the mid-1960's, the Hilton Hotel System included more than 40 hotels in the United States and 40 hotels in 37 other countries. In 1967, the international operations of the Hilton Hotel Corporation became a subsidiary of Trans World Airlines.

Hilton was born in San Antonio, N.M. After World War I, he started his first hotel chain in Texas and New Mexico. He expanded to California in 1929, to New York in 1943, and to Chicago in 1945, where he bought the Stevens, then the world's largest hotel, and changed its name to the Conrad Hilton.   Donald L. Kemmerer

Hilton, James (1900-1954), an English novelist, sprang to fame with *Good-bye, Mr. Chips* (1934). This sentimental short novel tells of a teacher in an English boys' school. Alexander Woollcott helped make it a best seller in the United States when he praised it on his popular radio program. *Mr. Chips* brought attention to an earlier Hilton novel, *Lost Horizon* (1933). *Lost Horizon* is the story of a group of people who become stranded in *Shangri-La,* a peaceful Tibetan mountain retreat where no one grows old. Hilton never quite repeated these early successes.

Hilton was born in Leigh, Lancashire, and was graduated from Cambridge University. He lived in the United States from the mid-1930's until his death. He spent most of his time in Hollywood, where he worked on the motion picture versions of his novels.   John Espey

Himalaya, *HIH muh LAY uh* or *hih MAHL yuh,* also called Himalayas, is the highest mountain system in the world. The name *Himalaya* comes from the Sanskrit language and means the *House of Snow,* or the *Snowy Range.* The Himalaya consists of several parallel mountain ranges.

The mountains extend in a 1,500-mile (2,410-kilometer) curve across southern Asia from the Pamirs, west of the great bend of the Indus River, eastward to the great bend of the Brahmaputra River. They form a barrier that separates northern India from the plateau of Tibet, in China. Parts of the Himalayan range are as much as 200 miles (320 kilometers) wide. The Himalaya joins with other mountain ranges of Asia that stretch east and west. The Karakoram, or Mustagh, Range is the northwestern extension of the Himalaya.

Peaks. The Himalaya rises in steps from the plains of northern India, which have an elevation of about 1,000 feet (300 meters) above sea level. Mount Everest (29,028 feet, or 8,848 meters), which lies between Tibet and Nepal, is the highest mountain in the world. Mount Godwin Austen (28,250 feet, or 8,611 meters), in the Karakoram Range, is the world's second highest mountain.

One of the most famous peaks in the Himalaya is Mount Kailas (22,028 feet, or 6,714 meters), which lies in Tibet. The Tibetans call it Kang Rimpoche (the *Mountain of Precious Snow*). This mountain is holy to the Hindus and Buddhists and is said to contain the thrones of their gods. Pilgrims from all parts of central Asia and India climb the mountain. They usually climb on foot, and the journey takes them from tropical jungles to freezing heights. Lying below the peak is the holy Lake Manasarowar, where the pilgrims worship.

Kanchenjunga, or Kinchinjunga (28,208 feet, or 8,598 meters), the third highest mountain in the world, lies near Mount Everest. Other high peaks are Makalu I (27,824 feet, or 8,481 meters); Makalu II (25,130 feet, or 7,660 meters); Dhaulagiri (26,810 feet, or 8,172 meters); Nanga Parbat (26,660 feet, or 8,126 meters); and Mount Kamet (25,447 feet, or 7,756 meters).

Snow-capped Himalayan peaks in Nepal provide a dramatic view for these porters. Because of the rugged terrain, roads for vehicles have been impossible to build in many areas of the Himalaya, and goods must be transported on foot.

© G. Leroy, Pitch

Passes and glaciers. The passes that run through the Himalaya are among the highest in the world. Few of the passes are lower than 15,000 or 16,000 feet (4,570 or 4,880 meters) above sea level. Most are covered with snow from November to May and are then impossible to cross. Many glaciers form in the high passes.

Climate and plant life. Almost every kind of climate can be found in the Himalaya because of the great difference in altitude in various parts of the range. This wide range in climate makes possible a variety of plant life. On the steep southern slopes grow tropical plants, such as the fig and palm tree. These plants are found up to a height of 3,000 feet (910 meters). Oak, chestnut, and laurel trees are common up to 7,000 feet (2,100 meters). Deodar and pine trees begin to appear at 12,000 feet

(3,660 meters). Many shrubs and climbing plants are found in the forests. Rhododendrons grow on the mountain slopes. The tea plant is cultivated up to 5,000 feet (1,500 meters). On the southern slopes, rice, corn, and millet are grown up to 6,000 feet (1,800 meters). Wheat and barley are grown in slightly higher regions.

Animal life. The Himalaya has many animals that live in tropical, temperate, and cold regions. Tigers, leopards, rhinoceroses, elephants, yaks, and some kinds of monkeys are found there. J. E. Spencer

Related articles in *World Book* include:

Abominable Snow-	Mount Godwin	Nepal
man	Austen	Pamirs, The
Annapurna	Mount Kanchen-	Tibet
Kashmir	junga	Yak
Mount Everest	Mount Makalu	

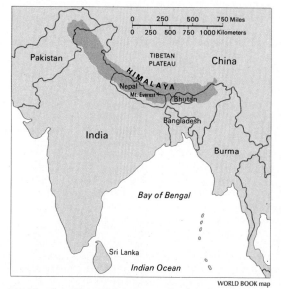

The Himalaya, the world's highest mountains, form a great natural barrier between India and the Tibetan plateau of China.

WORLD BOOK map

Himmler, Heinrich (1900-1945), was one of the most powerful leaders of Nazi Germany. As head of the German police, including the *Gestapo,* he ordered the deaths of millions of people. These killings began with the "blood purge" of 1934, and ended with systematic killings in World War II concentration camps.

Himmler was born in Munich. He was a follower of Adolf Hitler from the days of Hitler's unsuccessful attempt to gain power in 1923. He became chief of police for all Germany in 1936, minister of the interior in 1943, and minister of home defense in 1944. He committed suicide after Allied troops captured him. O. W. Wilson

Hinayana. See Buddhism (Buddhist schools).

Hinckley, John W., Jr. See Reagan, Ronald W. (Events at home).

Hincks, Sir Francis (1807-1885), was joint premier of the Province of Canada from 1851 to 1854. He and Augustin-N. Morin held office together. Their government promoted railroad construction during the early part of Canada's railway-building era. Hincks served as finance minister of the Dominion of Canada from 1869 to 1873. He played a key role in the passage of the Bank Act of 1871, which established government regulation of Canada's banking system.

Hincks was born in Cork, Ireland. He moved to York

(now Toronto), Canada, in 1830 and became manager of the People's Bank there in 1835. In 1838, he founded a newspaper, the *Examiner,* in Toronto. In 1841, Hincks was elected to the first Legislative Assembly of the Province of Canada. He also served as inspector-general in several administrations, including his own.

In 1855, the British government appointed Hincks governor of Barbados and the Windward Islands. In 1862, he became governor of British Guiana (now Guyana). Hincks was knighted in 1869. From 1873 to 1879, Hincks served as president of the City Bank of Montreal.

P. B. Waite

Hindemith, *HIHN duh muhth* or *HIHN duh mihth,* **Paul** (1895-1963), was a leading German composer and music theorist. Hindemith's compositions are noted for their use of music forms of the past and polyphonic melodies, as well as his own harmonic theories (see **Counterpoint**).

Hindemith wrote many sonatas for orchestral instruments, including such rarely featured instruments as the double bass, trombone, and tuba. He also wrote concertos for cello, clarinet, organ, piano, and violin, as well as concertos for such combinations of instruments as the trumpet and the bassoon. Hindemith's other orchestral works include seven pieces called *Kammermusik* (Chamber Music, 1922-1927) for various solo instruments and small orchestra. Hindemith's opera *Mathis der Maler* (1938) explores the role of the artist in society. The music was first performed as a symphony in 1934. Hindemith explained his system of music theory in *The Craft of Musical Composition* (1937, 1939, revised 1945).

Hindemith was born in Hanau in what is now West Germany. He taught at Yale University from 1940 to 1953 and became a United States citizen in 1946. While at Yale, he organized a *collegium musicum,* which is an association of musicians devoted to performing older music. This association made a significant impact on the revival of interest in early music. Mary Vinquist

Hindenburg. See **Airship** (The Hindenburg; picture).

Hindenburg, *HIHN duhn behrg* or *HIHN duhn burk,* **Paul von** (1847-1934), was a German soldier and statesman. He was military leader of Germany during World War I (1914-1918), and he served as president of Germany from 1925 until his death. Hindenburg appointed Adolf Hitler chancellor in 1933, and Hitler became ruler of Germany.

Hindenburg was born in Posen, East Prussia (now Poznań, Poland). He served as a junior officer in Prussian military victories over Austria in 1866 and France in 1870 and 1871. Hindenburg became a general in 1896, and he retired in 1911. When World War I began, Hindenburg came out of retirement to command the German Eighth Army. General Erich Ludendorff became his chief of staff. In the fall of 1914, Hindenburg and Ludendorff won important victories over Russian forces in East Prussia. Hindenburg was promoted to field marshal and became commander in chief on the eastern front. In 1916, he became supreme commander of all German forces, and one of the most powerful men in Germany. Ludendorff, whom many historians consider a better strategist, remained Hindenburg's second in command.

Early in 1917, Hindenburg and Ludendorff ordered the Siegfried Line built in northeastern France, to shorten the western front and to ease the strain on Ger-

many's troops. Germany held this line from March 1917 until the Allies broke through at the end of the war in September 1918. The Allies called it the Hindenburg Line. See **World War I** (The final stage).

Hindenburg was elected president of Germany in 1925, and was reelected in 1932. The Great Depression in 1929 caused unemployment and unrest in Germany and led to support for Hitler's Nazi Party. Hindenburg used his presidential power to keep Hitler out of power. But in the elections of 1932, the Nazi Party showed that it had become the strongest party in Germany. Hitler claimed the support of a majority of parliament. The aged and tiring Hinden-

Culver

Paul von Hindenburg

burg finally appointed Hitler chancellor on Jan. 30, 1933. After Hindenburg died in 1934, Hitler abolished the presidency and assumed its powers. George G. Windell

See also **Hitler, Adolf** (Rise of the Nazis; picture).

Hindenburg Line. See **Siegfried Line.**

Hindi, *HIHN dee,* is one of the official languages of India, though less than half the people speak it. In a broader sense, the word *Hindi* refers to a group of languages spoken in north central India. Modern Hindi developed from a dialect called Khari Boli but includes elements of Sanskrit, an ancient Indian language. During the 1800's, when the British controlled much of India, they encouraged the Indians to systematize Hindi. Today, the Indian government promotes Hindi as a national language. Frank E. Reynolds

See also **India** (Languages); **Alphabet** (picture: Some important alphabets).

Hindu-Arabic numerals. See **Arabic numerals; Numeration systems** (History).

Hindu Kush, *HIHN doo KUSH,* is a chain of mountains in Central Asia. For the location of the Hindu Kush, see **Afghanistan** (map). The name *kush,* which means death, was probably given to the mountains because of their dangerous passes. The Hindu Kush were called the Caucasus by historians of Alexander the Great. The mountains are a westward continuation of a region called the Pamirs. See **Pamirs, The.**

For 500 miles (800 kilometers), the Hindu Kush form a great *watershed,* or water divide, between the Indus and Amu Darya rivers. They are part of the boundary between eastern Afghanistan and northwestern Pakistan. The highest peak in the range is Tirich Mir (25,230 feet, or 7,690 meters). Tamerlane, a Mongol leader who lived in the 1300's, reportedly tried to cross these mountains.

J. E. Spencer

Hinduism, the major religion of India, is one of the oldest living religions in the world. The roots of Hinduism date to prehistoric times in India. Although most Hindus live in India, Hindu literature and philosophy have influenced people throughout the world.

Through the centuries, Hinduism has been the most important influence on the culture of India. For example, the caste system of India is a basic part of Hinduism. The

Edward S. Ross

© Alok Kavan, Photo Researchers

Hinduism has numerous sacred writings, and its believers worship many gods and goddesses. The priests shown at the left are reading from the Rig-Veda, the oldest sacred book in Hinduism. At the right, Hindus are praying before an image of the many-armed goddess known as Durga or Kali. This divinity is the wife of the god Shiva. She is worshiped as the feared goddess of destruction.

caste system determines the way of life of most Hindus, including what occupations they enter.

Beliefs of Hinduism

Unlike such religions as Buddhism, Christianity, and Islam, Hinduism was not founded on the teachings of one man. It developed gradually over thousands of years, and many cultures, races, and religions helped shape it. Many *sects* (groups) arose within Hinduism, and each developed its own philosophy and form of worship. Like most religions, Hinduism has basic beliefs about divinities, life after death, and how its followers should conduct their lives.

Sacred writings. Hinduism has no single book, such as the Bible, that serves as the source of its doctrines. But Hinduism has many sacred writings, all of which have contributed to its fundamental beliefs. The most important of these writings include the *Vedas,* the *Puranas,* the *Ramayana,* the *Mahabharata,* the *Bhagavad-Gita,* and the *Manu Smriti.*

The Vedas are the oldest Hindu scriptures and are older than the sacred writings of any other major religion. The teachings of the *Vedas* existed for centuries before they were finally written down. There are four *Vedas*—the *Rig-Veda,* the *Sama-Veda,* the *Yajur-Veda,* and the *Atharva-Veda.* Each has three parts—the *Samhitas,* the *Brahmanas,* and the *Upanishads.* The *Samhitas* contain prayers and hymns and are the most important part. The *Brahmanas* deal with ritual and theology and include explanations of the *Samhitas.* The *Upanishads* are works of philosophy written in the form of dialogues.

The Puranas are long verse stories that contain many important Hindu myths. The *Puranas* include stories about Hindu gods and goddesses and the lives of great Hindu heroes. They also describe the Hindu beliefs about how the world began and how it periodically ends and is reborn.

The Ramayana and the Mahabharata are long epics. The *Ramayana* tells the story of Prince Rama and his attempts to rescue Sita, his wife, who has been kidnapped by the demon king Ravana. The *Mahabharata* describes a battle between the Pandavas and the Kauravas, two families who are cousins.

The Bhagavad-Gita, a philosophical work, forms part of the *Mahabharata.* In it, the god Krishna and the Pandava warrior Arjuna discuss the meaning and nature of existence.

The Manu Smriti (Code of Manu) is a basic source of Hindu religious and social law. Part of it sets forth the basis of the caste system.

Divinities. Hinduism is *polytheistic.* That is, Hindus worship many gods. Early Hindus worshiped gods that represented powers in nature, such as rain and the sun. Gradually, some Hindus came to believe that, though divinities appear in separate forms, these forms are part of one universal spirit called *Brahman.* These Hindus believe that many divinities make up Brahman. The most important ones are Brahma, the creator of the universe; Vishnu, its preserver; and Shiva, its destroyer.

One of the most important Hindu divinities is Shiva's wife, who has several names. She is best known as Durga, Kali, Parvati, or Uma. As Parvati or Uma, she is the beloved goddess of motherhood. As Durga or Kali, she is the feared goddess of destruction. For many Hindus, these contrasting natures of the goddess represent the way in which time and matter constantly move from birth to death and from creation to destruction. Many Hindus find great religious truth in this symbolism and worship the goddess as their most important divinity.

According to Hindu doctrine, animals as well as human beings have souls. Hindus worship many animals as gods. Cows are the most sacred, but Hindus also worship monkeys, snakes, and other animals.

The six schools of philosophy. Many schools of Hindu thought have developed through the centuries.

Six of these schools have become especially prominent. In their traditional order, they are (1) *nyaya,* (2) *vaisheska,* (3) *sankhya,* (4) *yoga,* (5) *purva-mimamsa,* and (6) *vedanta.*

Nyaya deals with logic. Vaisheska concerns the nature of the world. Sankhya examines the origin and evolution of the universe. Yoga is a set of mental and physical exercises designed to free the soul from reliance on the body

The sacred word *om* is repeated many times by a Hindu while meditating. The written form of the word in the Sanskrit language of India, *above,* is a symbol of Hinduism.

so that the soul can unite with Brahman. Both purva-mimamsa and vedanta interpret the *Vedas.*

Caste is India's strict system of social classes. The caste system began about 1500 B.C., when Aryan invaders from central Asia attacked India. The Aryans gradually gained control of most of India. They developed the caste system to limit contact between themselves and the native Indian people. Later, the system became one of the teachings of Hinduism. Hinduism has four castes, called *varnas.* In order of rank, these hereditary groups are (1) *Brahmans,* the priests and scholars; (2) *Kshatriyas,* the rulers and warriors; (3) *Vaisyas,* the merchants and professionals; and (4) *Sudras,* the laborers and servants. The caste system includes thousands of subcastes, each of which has its own rules of behavior.

For centuries, one large group, the *untouchables,* existed outside the caste system and ranked below the lowest caste. The untouchables had such occupations as tanning, which Hindu law forbade for a member of any caste. The Indian Constitution of 1950 outlawed untouchability and gave the group full citizenship.

Through the years, the caste system has weakened. Some social distinctions have been abandoned, especially in the cities. Many educated Hindus of different castes mix freely with one another. Formerly, they would have mixed only with members of their own caste. But, the caste system is still a strong influence in Indian life.

Reincarnation and karma. Hinduism teaches that the soul never dies. When the body dies, the soul is reborn. This continuous process of rebirth is called *reincarnation.* The soul may be reborn in an animal or in a human, but Hindu doctrine is not clear on this point.

The law of *karma* is closely related to reincarnation. It states that every action of a person, no matter how small it is, influences how his or her soul will be born in the next reincarnation. If a person lives a good life, the soul will be born into a higher state, perhaps into the body of a brahman. If a person leads an evil life, the soul will be born into a lower state, perhaps into the body of a worm. Hindus believe that a person's reincarnation continues until he or she achieves spiritual perfection. The soul then enters a new level of existence, called *moksha,* from which it never returns.

Hindu worship

Worship in temples. Hinduism considers temples as buildings dedicated to divinities. Its followers worship

as individuals, not as congregations. Most Hindu temples have many shrines, each of which is devoted to a divinity. Each temple also has one principal shrine devoted to a single important god or goddess.

The shrines portray the divinities in sculptured images. Hindus treat these images as living human beings. Every day, for example, priests wash and dress the images and bring them food. Hindus do not consider this custom idol worship. They believe the divinities are actually present in the images.

Hindu temples hold annual festivals commemorating events in the lives of the divinities. Huge crowds gather for these festivals. They come to worship, to pray for assistance, and to enjoy the pageantry of the event. Millions of Hindus visit temples along the Ganges River, the most sacred river in India.

Worship in the home. Many observances of Hinduism take place in the home. Most homes have a shrine devoted to a divinity chosen by the family. The homes of some wealthy Hindus have a room used only for worship. In most homes, the husband or wife conducts the daily family worship. A number of important religious ceremonies are performed at home, including the one in which boys officially become members of the Hindu community. Others include marriage ceremonies and rituals connected with pregnancy and childbirth.

Worship of saints. Hindus worship both living and dead men as saints. Some saints may be *yogis* (men who practice yoga), and others may be *gurus* (spiritual teachers). Hinduism has many local and regional saints, rather than official saints for all its followers. A Hindu village, tribe, or religious order may elevate its own heroes or protectors to sainthood. Many Hindu monks and nuns have joined together in religious orders under the leadership of a saint.   Charles S. J. White

Related articles in *World Book* include:

Asia (Way of life in South Asia)	Karma	Sculpture (pictures: The Hindu goddess Durga; The Hindu god Shiva)
Bhagavad-Gita	Mahabharata	
Brahman	Manu	
Caste	Mythology (Hindu mythology)	
Culture (picture)	Ramayana	Shiva
Dharma	Religion (picture)	Upanishads
Ganges River	Religious life (Hinduism)	Vedas
India		Vishnu
Juggernaut		Yoga

See also *Hinduism* in the Research Guide/Index, Volume 22, for a *Reading and Study Guide.*

Additional resources

Bahree, Patricia. *Hinduism.* David & Charles, 1985. Suitable for younger readers.
Kinsley, David R. *Hinduism: A Cultural Perspective.* Simon & Schuster, 1982.
Patel, Satyavrata. *Hinduism: Religion and Way of Life.* Asia Book, 1980.

Hines, Earl (1905-1983), was an American jazz pianist. He became known for his inventive and witty piano style, featuring strong octaves and single "trumpet-style" notes played by the right hand.

Earl Kenneth Hines was born in Duquesne, Pa. He acquired the nickname of "Fatha" early in his career. During the late 1920's, he made a series of recordings with trumpeter Louis Armstrong that rank among the masterpieces of jazz. Hines led one of the most exciting jazz bands of the 1930's. In the 1940's, he led a famous band during the *bebop,* or *modern,* period of jazz. This band included trumpeter Dizzy Gillespie and alto saxophonist Charlie Parker. From the 1950's through the early 1960's, Hines remained active as a bandleader, but his work gained little national attention. He made a comeback during the mid-1960's and then led combos that featured him as soloist.   Nat Hentoff

Hinnom, Valley of. See Gehenna.

Hinny. See Donkey; Mule.

Hinton, S. E. (1948-   ), is an American writer of novels for young adults. She writes about teen-agers who face such problems as violence, poverty, and alcohol and drug abuse. Her young characters often reject authority while trying to cope with these problems.

Hinton was born and raised in Tulsa, Okla. The Tulsa area became the setting for her novels. Her full name is Susan Eloise Hinton. Hinton's first and probably best-known book is *The Outsiders,* written when she was 16 and published in 1967. It is a story about two rival gangs, one rich and one poor. The book is noted for its action-packed plot, believable characters, and realistic language.

Hinton's second novel, *That Was Then, This Is Now* (1971), focuses on teen-age boys and the problems of growing up, especially the problem of drug abuse. *Rumble Fish* (1975) tells the story of a 14-year-old boy who idolizes his older brother, a former gang leader. His efforts to be like his brother get him into serious trouble. *Tex* (1979) also deals with two brothers, ages 14 and 17. Their father abandons them, and tensions grow between them as the younger brother tries to become more independent.   Marilyn Fain Apseloff

Hip is the region of the body between the trunk and the thigh. The hip joint is formed by the hipbone (which consists of three united bones, the *ilium, ischium,* and *pubis*) and the head of the *femur* (thighbone). The head of the femur fits into the *acetabulum,* a socket in the hipbone. This arrangement forms a ball-and-socket joint, which provides great strength and allows a wide range of motion in all directions. Several powerful muscles surround the joint, including the large, round *gluteus maximus* at the back; the *gluteus medius* on the side; and the long, straplike *rectus femoris* in front. These muscles make the joint firm so a person can stand. They also move the leg for walking and running.

Many children are born with a hip socket that is too shallow. This condition is called *congenital dislocation* of the hip. In old age, the neck of the femur, located just below the head of the femur, becomes weak and breaks easily. The break can be repaired by fastening the head on the neck with a stainless steel nail. Many arthritis victims suffer disabling pain in the hip joint. In such cases, the joint can be replaced by a plastic socket and a metal ball.   Marshall R. Urist

See also **Human body** (Trans-vision picture).

Hipparchus, *hih PAHR kuhs* (? -514 B.C.), was a son of Pisistratus, a ruler of Athens in the 500's B.C. He came to power with his brother Hippias in 527 B.C., after the death of their father. But Hipparchus left government matters to his brother and concerned himself with cultural affairs. He brought such poets as Anacreon and Simonides to Athens. Hipparchus was killed by two young nobles, Harmodius and Aristogeiton. Another Athenian named Hipparchus was a relative of Pisistratus. He was elected archon in 496 B.C.   Donald Kagan

Hipparchus, *hih PAHR kuhs* (180 B.C.?-125 B.C.?), an ancient Greek astronomer, discovered the *precession* (movement) of the equinoxes. Excited by the appearance of a new star, he studied earlier observations and noticed that the stars had shifted eastward. He found that while their celestial longitude increased slightly, their latitude did not change. He explained these facts by a slow forward motion of the equinoxes. See **Equinox.**

Hipparchus drew up the first catalog of the stars, showing their brightness and position, and marked them on a celestial globe. He distinguished between two different lengths (tropical and sidereal) of the year. From his observations of the unequal length of the year's four seasons, he derived an improved description of the sun's movement. He used mathematics, especially plane trigonometry, in his work. See **Magnitude.**

Hipparchus was born in Nicaea. Only one of his writings, a commentary on an astronomical poem, still exists. His technical treatises have all been lost. Ptolemy, the foremost ancient authority on astronomy, absorbed everything of value in the treatises (see **Ptolemy** [Astronomer]).   Edward Rosen

Hippies were members of a youth protest movement of the 1960's. The hippie movement spread from the United States to Canada, England, and several other countries. It was mainly a protest against the customs and traditions of society. Most hippies came from white middle-class families and ranged in age from 17 to 25 years old.

Hippies believed in universal love and peace. They opposed the U.S. role in the Vietnam War (1957-1975).

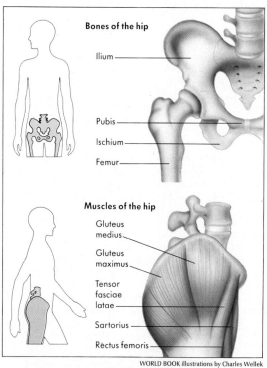

WORLD BOOK illustrations by Charles Wellek

The hip joint is a ball-and-socket arrangement that permits a wide range of movement in all directions. The illustration above depicts the bones of the hip joint and their attached muscles.

They did not think some people should be rich and others poor. They believed that most adults cared only about making money. Hippies also opposed what they considered society's unfair treatment of various minority groups.

Hippies believed in living together in small groups and sharing one another's belongings. They thought people should always say what they feel and should act naturally. Hippies wore odd-looking clothes, let their hair grow long, and walked around barefoot or in sandals. Many refused to work, and large numbers used drugs, such as marijuana and LSD.

Hippies were sometimes called "flower children" because they used flowers as a symbol of love. The movement also featured colorful posters with strange designs; whirling light shows; and rock music groups, such as the Grateful Dead and the Jefferson Airplane. The Beatles helped spread the hippie movement with their songs. Other hippie favorites included the psychologist Timothy Leary, who experimented with various drugs; the folk singers Joan Baez and Bob Dylan; the poet Allen Ginsberg; and the novelist Ken Kesey.

In time, most members of the hippie movement realized they could not reform society by "dropping out" of it. Many took up radical political and social causes. Others turned to a form of Gospel preaching in the streets.

Richard E. Gross

Hippocampus. See Seahorse.

Hippocrates, *hih PAHK ruh TEEZ* (460?-377? B.C.), was the father of modern medicine. His principles of medical

The oath of Hippocrates

I swear by Apollo, the physician, and Asclepius and Health and All-Heal and all the gods and goddesses that, according to my ability and judgment, I will keep this oath and stipulation:

To reckon him who taught me this art equally dear to me as my parents, to share my substance with him and relieve his necessities if required; to regard his offspring as on the same footing with my own brothers, and to teach them this art if they should wish to learn it, without fee or stipulation, and that by precept, lecture and every other mode of instruction, I will impart a knowledge of the art to my own sons and to those of my teachers, and to disciples bound by a stipulation and oath, according to the law of medicine, but to none others.

I will follow that method of treatment which, according to my ability and judgment, I consider for the benefit of my patients, and abstain from whatever is deleterious and mischievous. I will give no deadly medicine to anyone if asked, nor suggest any such counsel; furthermore, I will not give to a woman an instrument to produce abortion.

With purity and with holiness I will pass my life and practice my art. I will not cut a person who is suffering from a stone, but will leave this to be done by practitioners of this work. Into whatever houses I enter I will go into them for the benefit of the sick and will abstain from every voluntary act of mischief and corruption; and further from the seduction of females or males, bond or free.

Whatever, in connection with my professional practice, or not in connection with it, I may see or hear in the lives of men which ought not to be spoken abroad I will not divulge, as reckoning that all such should be kept secret.

While I continue to keep this oath unviolated may it be granted to me to enjoy life and the practice of the art, respected by all men at all times but should I trespass and violate this oath, may the reverse be my lot.

science were laid down 400 years before the birth of Christ, but they formed the basis for the medical theory developed in the 1800's. The Hippocratic oath, named for Hippocrates, gave the medical profession a sense of duty to humanity that it never lost. Many graduating medical students still take an oath modeled on that of Hippocrates. The oath includes rules for the relationship between doctors and patients.

In a time when superstition ruled people's minds, Hippocrates believed only in facts. He thought that people could find out the laws of nature by studying facts and reasoning from them. Hippocrates applied logic and reason to medicine. This made the practice of medicine workable.

His medical theories. Hippocrates showed that disease had only natural causes, and took treatment of disease out of the hands of religion. He insisted that, "Our natures are the physicians of our diseases." He treated his patients with proper diet, fresh air, change in climate, and attention to habits and living conditions. He objected to the use of strong drugs without careful tests of their curative values. His favorite diet for sick people was a barley gruel.

His favorite medicine was honey. He said, "The drink to be employed should there be any pain is vinegar and honey. If there be great thirst, give water and honey." Hippocrates also practiced surgery. He reduced dislocations of joints and set fractures. He bored holes in the skull to relieve pressure caused by brain tumors or other disorders. Long before antiseptic methods were introduced into surgery, he advised the use of tar for wounds. But he was primarily a medical doctor, and except for wounds, fractures, and dislocations, he used surgery only as a last resort. To him, the goal of the physician was the care and cure of the patient. As he put it, "For where there is the love of man, there is also love of the Art."

His life. Hippocrates was born on the Greek island of Kos. He had no connection with the temple hospitals of his time, which were controlled by the priests of Asclepius, the god of healing. His theories of medicine are summed up in *Corpus Hippocraticum,* which contains more than 70 treatises on medicine and scientific research. Hippocrates lived most of his life on Kos, but he also practiced in Athens and other Greek cities. He died in Larisa.   Caroline A. Chandler

Hippodrome, *HIHP uh drohm,* is a place for horse and chariot races. The ancient Greeks built hippodromes with seats in rows, or tiers, like bleachers. The seats surrounded a long race course, and curved around one end of it. A wall in the center divided the course. It was usually from 600 to 800 feet (180 to 240 meters) long.

The largest Greek hippodrome was in Constantinople (now Istanbul). The Roman Circus Maximus, like all Roman circuses, was a copy of the Greek hippodromes. The Circus Maximus was the largest of the ancient Roman hippodromes. It seated about 250,000 spectators.

In more recent times, race tracks, indoor circuses, and amusement places have been called hippodromes. The New York Hippodrome was the largest indoor playhouse in the world until it closed in 1928. It could seat about 5,200 persons at one time.   Alan K. Laing

Hippolyta. See Amazons.

A river hippopotamus has a stout, barrel-shaped body; short legs; and a huge head. It weighs as much as 5,800 pounds (2,630 kilograms) and ranks as one of the largest land animals. In spite of its clumsy appearance, the river hippopotamus is an excellent swimmer and can run as fast as a human being.

Mark Boulton, National Audubon Society

Hippopotamus, *HIHP uh PAHT uh muhs,* is the third largest animal that lives on land. Only the elephant and rhinoceros are larger. A large, wild river hippopotamus may weigh as much as 5,800 pounds (2,630 kilograms).

Hippopotamuses live in central, southern, and western Africa. They live close to water and spend much time in it. The word *hippopotamus* comes from two Greek words meaning *river horse.* However, the hippopotamus is more closely related to the hog than to the horse. There are two kinds of hippopotamuses: (1) the *river hippopotamus,* also called the *common hippopotamus,* and (2) the *pygmy hippopotamus.* The pygmy hippopotamus is much smaller than the river hippopotamus. It is also rarer.

The body of a river hippopotamus. The river hippopotamus has a large, barrel-shaped body; short legs; and a huge head. It weighs from 2,500 to 3,000 pounds (1,130 to 1,400 kilograms) and stands about 5 feet (1.5 meters) tall. It ranges from 12 to 15 feet (4 to 5 meters) long, not including the tail, which measures about 22 inches (56 centimeters) long. Each foot has four webbed toes.

The eyes of the river hippopotamus stick out from its head. The position of the ears, eyes, and nostrils enables the animal to hear, see, and breathe with most of its head underwater. The hippopotamus can also close its nostrils and ears when it swims or dives. Hippopotamuses have a good sense of smell, but their vision is only fair.

Where hippos live

The hippopotamus is found in central and southern Africa in rivers, lakes, and marshy ponds. The pygmy hippopotamus lives in Liberia, Sierra Leone, and south Nigeria.

 Hippopotamus

Pygmy hippopotamus

River hippopotamuses have thick, brownish-gray skin. They have no hair except for a few bristles on the head and tail. Special glands in the skin give off a clear, oily fluid that is either pink or red. This fluid keeps the animal's skin from getting too dry. The reddish color of the fluid led to the mistaken belief that hippopotamuses sweat blood.

A hippopotamus has long, curved front teeth. Its tusklike *canines* (side teeth) are even longer. All the teeth grow throughout the animal's life. But they seldom become too long, because the teeth of the upper and lower jaws grind together and wear each other away. The canines of a hippopotamus may grow more than 2 feet (61 centimeters) long, but only about half the tooth sticks out above the gum line.

The life of a river hippopotamus. River hippopotamuses are good swimmers and live in lakes, rivers, and streams near grasslands. They sometimes walk along the bottom of a body of water and can stay underwater for as long as six minutes. On land, they can run as fast as a human being—about 20 miles (32 kilometers) per hour.

River hippopotamuses live in herds of from 5 to 30 animals. They spend the day resting in the water, eating water plants, and sunning themselves on sandbanks. At night, the herd goes on land to feed. The animals eat fruit, grass, leaves, and vegetables. They sometimes wander for miles near the riverbank, grazing as they go. Each hippopotamus eats about 130 pounds (59 kilograms) of vegetable matter a day.

A female hippopotamus carries her young inside her body for about $7\frac{1}{2}$ months before it is born. She almost always has one baby at a time, but sometimes she bears twins. A baby hippopotamus, called a *calf,* weighs about 100 pounds (45 kilograms) at birth. It can swim almost immediately and usually nurses on its mother's milk underwater. It begins to eat grass at the age of 4 to 6 months. A young hippopotamus often climbs on its mother's back and suns itself as she floats on the water. On land, the mother hippopotamus keeps her calf close by. If the youngster wanders away, she butts it as punishment.

The skeleton of a river hippopotamus

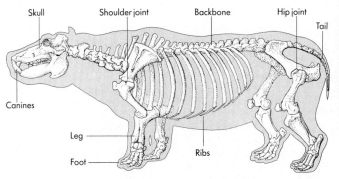

Skull   Shoulder joint   Backbone   Hip joint   Tail   Canines   Leg   Ribs   Foot

WORLD BOOK illustration by Marion Pahl

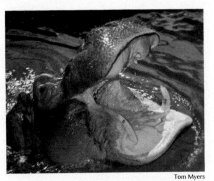

Tom Myers

A hippopotamus' tusklike canines can be seen when the animal opens its mouth. Hippopotamuses use their canines for fighting.

A female hippopotamus gives birth to her first baby when she is 5 or 6 years old. Hippopotamuses live about 30 years in their natural surroundings and 50 years in a zoo.

A hippopotamus has an enormous mouth and can open it to a width of 3 to 4 feet (91 to 120 centimeters). The animal often does so to show its powerful canines and challenge its enemies. When two hippopotamuses fight, they slash at each other with their canines. Many fights continue until one of the animals gets killed or suffers a broken leg. Almost no other kind of animal attacks adult hippopotamuses, but crocodiles, hyenas, and lions sometimes attack the young. If a hippopotamus feels threatened on land, it runs for the water.

The pygmy hippopotamus has a smaller head in proportion to its body than does the river hippopotamus. It weighs from 400 to 600 pounds (180 to 270 kilograms) and stands about 2½ feet (76 centimeters) tall. A pygmy hippopotamus ranges from 5 to 6 feet (1.5 to 1.8 meters) long, not including the tail, which measures 6 to 7 inches (15 to 18 centimeters) long. The animal has blackish skin.

Pygmy hippopotamuses live in thick forests near streams and spend less time in the water than do river hippopotamuses. They live alone or in pairs, rather than in herds. Although the law forbids killing pygmy hippopotamuses, Africans shoot many of them for food. As a

James Annan

A pygmy hippopotamus is much smaller than a river hippopotamus. The animal weighs from 400 to 600 pounds (180 to 270 kilograms). It has a rounded head and oily, blackish skin.

result, the animal faces the danger of becoming extinct.

Hippopotamuses and people. People have greatly reduced both the number of hippopotamuses and the size of the area in which they live. Hunters have killed large numbers of them, and farmers have made cropland out of many areas where hippopotamuses once made their home. At one time, the animals lived in rivers throughout Africa. Ancient Egyptian paintings show pharaohs hunting them on the Nile River.

African farmers shoot many hippopotamuses to keep the animals from eating or trampling their crops. They also kill hippopotamuses for the meat and use the hides in making soup. The canines of hippopotamuses provide valuable ivory. The ivory was once used for artificial teeth because it did not turn yellow.

Some food experts have urged that hippopotamuses be raised for their meat. The weight of the edible meat of a hippopotamus totals almost two-thirds the weight of the entire body. This proportion is much higher than with most other wild animals. In addition, hippopotamus flesh has an extremely high protein content.

Hippopotamuses have also benefited their environment in certain areas. Their solid wastes provide nourishment for many fish and water plants in the lakes and streams where hippopotamuses live.

Scientific classification. Hippopotamuses make up the hippopotamus family, Hippopotamidae. The river hippopotamus is *Hippopotamus amphibius.* The pygmy hippopotamus is *Choeropsis liberiensis.*   James M. Dolan, Jr.

See also **Animal** (picture: Animals of the grasslands).
Hiram. See **Phoenicia** (The spread of Phoenician influence).
Hirohito, *HEER oh HEE toh* (1901-   ), became emperor of Japan in 1926. According to tradition, he is the 124th ruler in a line which goes back to the origins of early Japan. He chose *Showa* as his reign name, and became known as the Showa Emperor.

Before World War II. Hirohito became regent for his father, Yoshihito, in 1921 and he became emperor in December 1926. His reign began during the days of parliamentary government. Universal manhood suffrage had just been introduced, and Japan seemed likely to become increasingly democratic and internationalist. Unfortunately, army circles, particularly those in Manchuria, wanted a stronger foreign policy. Within Japan, criticism of the political parties sharpened after economic crises struck. Military incidents abroad and assassinations in Tokyo soon reversed the democratic and internationalist trends of the 1920's.

Hirohito personally opposed the militarism of the 1930's. But his advisers kept him from making his wishes known, so that the radical militarists would not take direct action against the monarchy. As a result, Hirohito remained

Keystone

Hirohito

silent, and approved the decisions which led to World War II (see **Japan** [World War II]).

After the war. Hirohito took a personal part in the final surrender decision of 1945. His broadcasts to the Japanese people helped bring about the smooth transfer of control of Japan to the United States Army. For a time, it was thought he might have to abdicate or be tried as a war criminal. Although several of the emperor's advisers were tried and convicted of war crimes, Hirohito himself was not.

Hirohito did, however, take a new role. On Jan. 1, 1946, he renounced all claims to the divinity that had formerly been claimed for him. The constitution of 1947, which he approved, changed him from sovereign to "symbol of the state," and placed political control in the hands of elected representatives. As a democratic monarch, Hirohito toured the country, visiting scenes of disaster and inspecting Japan's postwar reconstruction. He permitted the imperial family to be photographed. American tutors began to teach his son, Crown Prince Akihito. In 1959, Akihito broke a centuries-old Japanese tradition by marrying a "commoner," a girl who did not belong to one of Japan's noble families (see **Akihito**). In 1971, Hirohito became the first Japanese emperor to travel outside Japan during his reign. He toured Europe for 18 days. He visited the United States in 1975. In private life, Hirohito carried on research in marine biology.

Marius B. Jansen

Hiroshige, HEER oh SHEE gay (1797-1858), was a master painter and designer of Japanese color prints. Many critics rank him second in importance only to Hokusai among Japanese artists. His paintings earned him the name of "the artist of the sweeping brush," because of his ability to suggest vast landscapes in a few lines. Bare paper is as important as color in showing great snowfields, the sea, and the sky in his paintings. His delicate color harmonies and his peculiar perspective influenced the work of the painter James Whistler.

Hiroshige was born in Edo (now Tokyo). His pupils imitated his work and often used his signature. His works include the sets of prints, *Eight Views of Biwa* and *The Hundred Views of Edo.*   S. W. Hayter

See also **Japanese print** (picture).

Hiroshima, HEER oh SHEE muh or hih ROH shih muh (pop. 1,044,129), is the Japanese city on which the first atomic bomb used in warfare was dropped. It lies on islands formed by a river delta on the north shore of the Inland Sea, in western Honshu. For location, see **Japan** (political map).

Hiroshima was originally a fishing village, but developed dramatically between 1600 and 1868 as a castle town of the Asano family. By the late 1600's, it had become one of Japan's largest cities. It served as a seat of local government, and as a trade center and a port of internal navigation. Its prosperity and population increased in the late 1800's and early 1900's with its industrial growth. By World War II, Hiroshima was an important military center.

During World War II, on Aug. 6, 1945, a United States Army plane dropped a single atomic bomb on the center of the city. Three days later, the Allies dropped a second atomic bomb on the city of Nagasaki. Japan surrendered to the Allied forces on Sept. 2, 1945.

The atomic bomb destroyed about 5 square miles (13 square kilometers) of the city. Between 70,000 and 100,000 people are estimated to have been killed. Others died later from the effects of atomic radiation.

Hiroshima was rebuilt after the war. It has developed

© Chuck Fishman, Woodfin Camp, Inc.

Hiroshima's Peace Park is a memorial to the victims of the first atomic bomb used in war. The domed ruin, the Prefectural Industrial Promotion Hall, *center*, marks the center of the blast.

major automobile, machinery, and shipbuilding industries and has regained its prewar population and importance. The Peace Memorial Park was built where the bomb exploded. A service is held there each year on the anniversary of the bombing, in memory of the victims. The Atomic Bomb Dome, a building left unreconstructed after the war, has become a symbol of the peace movement.   Kenneth B. Pyle

See also **Nuclear weapon** (picture).

Additional resources

Hersey, John. *Hiroshima.* Knopf, 1946. Account of the bombing of Hiroshima.

Knebel, Fletcher, and Bailey, C. W. *No High Ground.* Greenwood, 1983. The building and first military use of the atomic bomb, reprinted from the 1960 ed.

Lifton, Betty Jean. *Return to Hiroshima.* Atheneum, 1970. Looks at the effects of the bombing 25 years later, and is suitable for younger readers.

Lifton, Robert J. *Death in Life: Survivors of Hiroshima.* Basic Books, 1982. Reprint of 1967 ed.

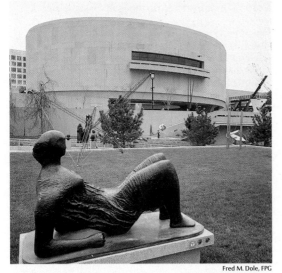

Fred M. Dole, FPG

The Hirshhorn Museum and Sculpture Garden features paintings and sculptures by American and European artists.

Hirshhorn Museum and Sculpture Garden, in
Washington, D.C., houses one of the world's largest collections of modern art. The Hirshhorn has more than 6,500 paintings and sculptures by leading American and European artists of the late 1800's and the 1900's. It is part of the Smithsonian Institution.

The Hirshhorn Museum is an unusual circular building. Most of the museum's paintings are by American masters, such as Willem de Kooning, Thomas Eakins, and Edward Hopper. The sculpture collection includes works by Alexander Calder, Edgar Degas, Alberto Giacometti, Henry Moore, Louise Nevelson, and Pablo Picasso. The sculpture garden and plaza alongside the museum feature massive works by some of these sculptors and others, including Auguste Rodin and Henri Matisse. The Hirshhorn's Moore sculptures make up the largest public collection in the United States of Moore's work.

The United States Congress established the museum in 1966 to house the huge art collection that had been donated to the nation by Joseph H. Hirshhorn, an American financier. The Hirshhorn Museum and Sculpture Garden opened in 1974.

Critically reviewed by the Hirshhorn Museum and Sculpture Garden

Hispanic Americans. See Latinos.

Hispaniola, *HIHS puhn YOH luh,* is the second largest island in the West Indies. It lies between Cuba and Puerto Rico in the Caribbean Sea, about 600 miles (970 kilometers) southeast of Florida. For the location of Hispaniola, see **West Indies** (map). The Republic of Haiti occupies the western third of Hispaniola, and the Dominican Republic covers the eastern two-thirds of the island. The island is about 400 miles (640 kilometers) long and 150 miles (240 kilometers) wide. Hispaniola has an area of about 29,418 square miles (76,192 square kilometers). Christopher Columbus arrived at Hispaniola in 1492 and called it *La Isla Española* (the Spanish Island).

Hispaniola has a population of about 12 million. Nearly all the people are blacks or have mixed black and white ancestry. More than half the people live in rural areas and make their living from agriculture. The chief crops are coffee and sugar cane.   Ivan A. Schulman

See also **Dominican Republic; Haiti.**

Hiss, Alger (1904-   ), became the center of a national controversy over Communist infiltration in the government during the Administration of President Harry S. Truman in the 1940's and 1950's. A number of Republican congressmen, including Representative Richard M. Nixon, had charged the government with unwittingly employing secret Communists who acted as agents for the Soviet Union.

The controversy reached a climax in 1948. At that time, Whittaker Chambers, a confessed former Communist spy, accused Hiss, a former high official in the U.S. Department of State, of having given him military secrets in the 1930's. Hiss denied the charge, but resigned from his position as head of the Carnegie Endowment for International Peace. Chambers then produced microfilms of confidential government papers that he had hidden in a pumpkin on his farm in Maryland. Chambers said Hiss had given him the secrets to send to the Soviet Union.

Hiss was brought to trial in 1949. He was charged with perjury for denying Chambers' accusations. Important government officials, including two associate justices

Wide World

Hiss and his accuser, Whittaker Chambers, were brought face to face during a session of the House Un-American Activities Committee in 1948. Hiss, *standing, left,* was convicted of perjury largely on evidence supplied to the government by Chambers, *standing, far right.*

of the Supreme Court of the United States, testified for Hiss. But the jury could not agree on a verdict.

Again, Hiss was brought to trial on the same perjury charges late in 1949. The government introduced new evidence in an attempt to prove that the personal typewriter of Hiss had been used to copy 42 confidential government documents. On Jan. 21, 1950, the jury found him guilty. Hiss was sentenced to five years in prison. He was paroled after serving 3 years and 8 months, and he continued to declare his innocence.

Hiss was born in Baltimore and graduated with honors from Johns Hopkins University and the Harvard Law School. He served in the Department of State from 1935 to 1947. He was executive secretary of the Dumbarton Oaks Conference, a technical adviser at the Yalta Conference, and secretary-general of the United Nations founding convention.   Carol L. Thompson

See also **Chambers, Whittaker; McCarthy, Joseph R.; Nixon, Richard M.; Truman, Harry S.** (Problems at home); **Yalta Conference.**

Additional resources

Cooke, Alistair. *A Generation on Trial: U.S.A. vs. Alger Hiss.* Greenwood, 1982. First published in 1950.
Weinstein, Allen. *Perjury: The Hiss-Chambers Case.* Knopf, 1978.

Histamine. See Allergy (How an allergy develops); Antihistamine.

Histology, *hihs TAHL uh jee,* is the biological science that studies the structure of the tissues of organisms. In the early 1600's, scientists began using simple microscopes to observe the structural features of various plants and animals. Histology developed as a science in the mid-1800's, when the use of compound microscopes made it possible to view features of cellular and subcellular tissues. Today, the electron microscope enables histologists to examine details of tissues magnified by hundreds of thousands of times. By using various chemical techniques, histologists can identify the precise location of various proteins, lipids, and carbohydrates in tissues.   Charlotte H. Greene

Related articles in *World Book* include:

Bichat, Marie F. X.	Cell	Microscope
Botany	Malpighi, Marcello	Tissue

Histoplasmosis, *HIHS tuh plaz MOH sihs,* is a fungal disease that attacks the lungs, mouth, throat, ears, spleen, liver, and lymphatic system. The infection in the lungs is usually mild. But the disease can be fatal if it spreads to other parts of the body.

Histoplasmosis occurs throughout the world. But it is most common in the Ohio and Mississippi river valleys of the United States. About 4,000,000 cases are reported throughout the world each year. The fungus, *Histoplasma capsulatum,* grows in moist soil. Its *spores* (cells) enter the body from the air.   E. Clinton Texter, Jr.

Historian. See History with its *Related articles.*
Historic age. See Age.
Historical Association, American, is an organization of about 15,000 historians, educators, and others interested in world history. It aids teachers through conferences and publications. The association publishes the *American Historical Review* five times a year. The American Historical Association was chartered in 1889. Its headquarters are at 400 A St. SE, Washington, DC 20003.

Critically reviewed by the American Historical Association

Historiography. See History (Interpreting historical events).

History is the study of the human past. Historians study records of past events and prepare new records based on their research. These records, as well as the events themselves, are also commonly called history. This article discusses history as a field of study. For information on events in history, see **World, History of the,** and the *History* sections of the various articles on continents, countries, states, and provinces.

The past has left many traces, including traditions, folk tales, works of art, archaeological objects, and books and other written records. Historians use all these sources, but they mainly study the past as it has been recorded in written documents. As a result, history is generally limited to human events that have taken place since the development of writing about 5,000 years ago.

Historians study all aspects of past human life—social and cultural conditions as well as political and economic events. Some historians study the past simply to understand better how people of other times acted and thought. Others seek to draw lessons from those actions and thoughts as a guide for decisions and policies today. However, historians disagree about the lessons of history, and so there are many different interpretations of the past.

History became a field of study in many schools during the 1800's. Today, students throughout the world study history in school. They learn about the past chiefly from textbooks, but also through such activities as field trips to historical sites and visits to museums. Most nations require schools to teach their country's heritage as a means of developing patriotism. History is thus used not only to tell students how their national way of life developed, but also to justify and support national ideals and institutions.

What historians study

The content of history. Until the 1900's, historians primarily studied political events. They wrote almost exclusively about diplomacy, wars, and affairs of state. Today, historians also study many other subjects. Some examine economic and social conditions. Others trace the development of religions, the arts, or other elements of culture.

History is often classified as one of the social sciences, along with such fields as economics, psychology, and sociology. However, historians differ from other social scientists in the way in which they study social processes. Other social scientists seek to develop general laws by examining patterns of behavior that recur throughout time. In contrast, historians study the conditions or events of a particular time. Historians may use theories from the other social sciences to help explain these conditions and events. But historians rarely attempt to develop general laws.

The divisions of history. The field of history is so vast that historians have traditionally split it into divisions. The three main divisions of history are based on *period, nation,* and *topic.*

Periods of time form the chief divisions in the study of history. Historians divide Western history into three periods: (1) ancient times, from about 3000 B.C. to the A.D. 400's; (2) medieval times, the 400's to the 1500's; and

A visit to a historical site helps people learn about the past and gain an understanding of life in earlier societies. Colonial Williamsburg, *left*, is a section of Williamsburg, Va., that has more than 80 buildings restored to appear as they did during the 1700's.

Virginia Division of Tourism

(3) modern times, the 1500's to the present. Scholars, in turn, may divide these periods into many shorter periods. For example, a historian may study a particular century or a certain period, such as the High Middle Ages (about the 1200's) or the Age of Reason (1700's).

The division of history into periods helps historians organize and focus their studies. However, this division may distort the evidence presented by history. For years, historians considered the medieval era as a period of superstition and disorganization that came between two supposedly better periods of history. This viewpoint prevented them from realizing that the Middle Ages had a vitality of its own and formed the basis of modern European civilization.

The division of history into ancient, medieval, and modern periods applies only to European societies. Historians who study Asian or African societies base their work on entirely different periods. Even the dating system differs because Western society uses the birth of Jesus Christ as a dividing line. The years before the birth of Christ are designated B.C. (before Christ), and those thereafter are considered A.D. (*anno Domini*—in the year of our Lord).

The division of history by nation involves, for example, the study of American, Chinese, or French history. The division by topic enables historians to deal with particular aspects of past human activity. Many historians study economic, social, and intellectual history in addition to studying traditional political history. Some historians focus on such specialized topics as the history of science, of an ethnic group, or of a city.

How historians work

The study of history involves many processes and techniques, but most historians follow a few basic steps in their work. First, they select for study an issue or person from some period of the past. Next, they try to read a variety of source materials—everything written by or

about the subject. Then they interpret the information obtained from these sources. Finally, they write a narrative history or a biography.

Choosing and evaluating sources. Historians use two main types of sources in their research, *primary sources* and *secondary sources*. Primary sources consist of documents and other records produced during the period being studied. They include books, diaries, letters, and government records. Motion pictures and tape recordings may serve as primary sources for events of the 1900's. Secondary sources are materials prepared later by people who studied the primary sources.

Historians choose documents that reveal most accurately the facts they wish to know. Therefore, they prefer primary sources to secondary ones, and confidential reports to public ones. Historians who study recent events use a special type of source. They go to participants in those events and record their oral testimony. Such *oral history* supplements documentary history.

The scarcity of sources is a great problem for historians, whose work sometimes resembles that of detectives. Many activities and thoughts of ordinary people, plus other useful data, were never recorded. Also, much that was written down has been lost or destroyed through the years. In addition, historians often must rely on the writings of only a few people. Such writings are mere fragments on which to base a reconstruction of the past.

Historians analyze the documents with which they work to determine the reliability of these sources. They compare documents with other sources and also check for such flaws as errors in the order of events or variations in writing style. In addition, the historian must determine whether the author's account of events can be trusted.

Interpreting historical events. Basic historical facts are data generally accepted by all historians because the evidence for them seems unquestionable. However, historians often disagree about the meaning and significance of such facts. These experts try to be as unbiased as possible, but their own beliefs and prejudices influence their interpretation. For example, a historian's social, economic, and religious views help determine what he or she accepts as "normal" in another person. This judgment, in turn, determines what the historian accepts as reliable testimony or as a likely sequence of events. Such interpretation explains why historians who use the same data may disagree about events and their significance.

Some historians rely heavily on information from other social sciences to form their interpretations. For example, the study of history that uses theories and insights from psychology is called *psychohistory.* Similarly, some historians use statistical methods to interpret data from such sources as old censuses and account books. This approach is called *cliometrics.*

As the last step in interpretation, a historian prepares a written account of events. The writing of history is part of a field called *historiography.* Some of the best historians use the techniques of the novelist and dramatist to entertain as well as inform.

Theories of history

Since ancient times, scholars have developed theories of history that attempt to explain the entire course of human events through some general principle. For example, the ancient Greeks regarded history as a cycle of events that repeated itself endlessly. In contrast, the traditional Christian theory considers history as a series of events with a beginning and an end. According to this theory, God directs human events toward the final goal of the redemption of humanity. This theory dominated nearly all the history written in Europe during the Middle Ages.

In modern times, scholars have proposed many other theories. During the late 1700's and the 1800's, philosophers developed the concept of history as a process of inevitable progress. They believed this progress would eventually lead to a thoroughly logical social order based on a scientific understanding of human events. The German historian Oswald Spengler argued in his book *The Decline of the West* (1918-1922) that civilizations, like organisms, go through a cycle of birth, development, and death. Arnold Toynbee, a British historian, also presented a cyclical theory in his 12-volume work, *A Study of History* (1934-1961). However, Toynbee disagreed with Spengler's belief that modern Western civilization is already doomed.

Nearly all theories of history assume that it has meaning and purpose, but there is no overwhelming evidence to support this concept. In fact, many scholars today question whether history has any meaning other than that which people read into it. As a result, most modern philosophers have turned away from such theories. Instead, they examine such issues as the nature of history as a field of knowledge and the method of explanation used by historians.

The development of historical writing

Ancient times. The world's oldest written history comes from China. Archaeologists have discovered records of Chinese history written before 1000 B.C. The first

great Chinese historian, Sima Qian (also spelled Sou-ma Ch'ien), wrote the earliest major history of China about 100 B.C.

Western historical writing began in ancient Greece. The first major Greek historian was Herodotus, who lived during the 400's B.C. He wrote a long account of the wars between the Greeks and the Persians. Herodotus, who is often called the "Father of History," had few Greek documents and could not read Persian. Therefore, he based his narrative primarily on tradition and oral testimony. He added fictitious details to make it more lively, but modern historians have confirmed the basic accuracy of his writing. Herodotus' most famous successor, Thucydides, strove to write critically and accurately. His *History of the Peloponnesian War* is an authentic account of the 27-year war in which Sparta finally defeated Athens in 404 B.C.

Several ancient Romans also became famous historians. Livy wrote a long, detailed narrative called *History from the Founding of the City.* It tells the story of Rome from the city's birth until 9 B.C. Cornelius Tacitus is known especially for his *Histories* and *Annals.* These works examine Roman history from the death of the emperor Augustus in A.D. 14 through the reign of Vitellius, which ended in A.D. 69.

Medieval times. Christian writers, including a number of monks, contributed almost all the historical accounts of medieval times that were written during that period. Some Christian historians attempted to write a *universal history* by combining Jewish and Christian history with the record of the Greek and Roman past. During the early 300's, Eusebius, the bishop of Caesarea in Palestine, produced the most important universal history of that type. In another work, *Ecclesiastical History,* Eusebius presented a history of Christianity to show that God controlled human events. During the 400's, Saint Augustine developed this idea fully into a philosophy of history in his book *The City of God.*

The greatest historian of the early Middle Ages was an English monk named Bede. His major work, *Ecclesiastical History of the English Nation* (731), is still the principal source for English history up to that time. Bede and the other medieval historians tried to show the hand of God in historical events. Today, their works are significant chiefly as records of the events of their times.

During the 1300's, a great Arab historian named Ibn Khaldun wrote his seven-volume *Universal History,* a study of world civilization. Also at this time in Europe, people other than members of the clergy started to write histories. European historians of the 1400's began to concentrate more on the human view of events·and less on the divine aspect.

Modern times. An important early modern historian was the British scholar Edward Gibbon. His masterpiece, *History of the Decline and Fall of the Roman Empire* (1776-1788), reveals Gibbon's accurate and thorough scholarship. This work also reflects the bias against Christianity of Gibbon and other great thinkers of his day. Gibbon's book blames Christianity for the fall of the Roman Empire.

The methods of modern historical study developed during the 1800's, and history became a recognized academic field. Leopold von Ranke, a German historian, had the most significant impact on the development of his-

Marble statue (A.D. 100's) by unknown Roman sculptor; Metropolitan Museum of Art, New York City, gift of George F. Baker, 1891

Detail of an oil portrait (1868) by Julius F. A. Schrader; National-galerie, Berlin (Bettmann Archive)

Herodotus, an ancient Greek historian, is often called the "Father of History."

Leopold von Ranke of Germany developed many basic historical research methods.

tory in the 1800's. Ranke, who is known as the "Father of Modern History," devised the basic methods used by modern historians to analyze and evaluate documents. He also introduced the use of seminars for training future historians in methods of research.

Ranke mainly studied political history. During the 1900's, however, European and American historians began to emphasize the importance of social and economic forces in history. Today, historians study these and all other aspects of the human past.

Genevieve Zito Berkhofer and Robert F. Berkhofer, Jr.

Related articles. See **World, History of the,** and the *History* sections of the various **World Book** articles on continents, countries, states, and provinces. See also the following articles:

American historians

Adams, Brooks	Freeman, Douglas Southall
Adams, Henry B.	Galarza, Ernesto
Bancroft, George	Morison, Samuel Eliot
Barzun, Jacques	Nevins, Allan
Beard, Charles and Mary	Parkman, Francis
Breasted, James H.	Parrington, Vernon L.
Catton, Bruce	Prescott, William H.
Commager, Henry Steele	Quarles, Benjamin A.
De Voto, Bernard	Robinson, James H.
Dodd, William E.	Schlesinger (family)
Du Bois, W. E. B.	Tuchman, Barbara W.
Durant, Will	Turner, Frederick Jackson
Fiske, John	Woodson, Carter G.
Franklin, John Hope	

British historians

Acton, Lord	Geoffrey of Monmouth
Bede	Gibbon, Edward
Bryce, James	Macaulay, Thomas B.
Carlyle, Thomas	Maitland, Frederic W.
Churchill, Sir Winston	Toynbee (Arnold Joseph)
Clarendon, Earl of	Trevelyan, Sir George M.

French historians

Froissart, Jean	Thiers, Louis A.
Montesquieu	Voltaire
Taine, Hippolyte A.	

German historians

Herder, Johann G. von	Spengler, Oswald
Ranke, Leopold von	

Other historians

Burpee, Lawrence J.	Herodotus
Caesar, Julius	Huizinga, Johan

Ibn Khaldun	Sallust
Josephus Flavius	Suetonius
Livy	Tacitus, Cornelius
Pirenne, Henri	Thucydides
Plutarch	Xenophon

Other related articles

See the following with their *Related articles:*

Ancient civilization	Mongol empire
Archaeology	Persia, Ancient
Byzantine Empire	Prehistoric people
Canada, History of	Pulitzer Prizes (History)
Culture	Reformation
Egypt, Ancient	Renaissance
Exploration	Rome, Ancient
Greece, Ancient	United Nations
Indian, American	United States, History of the
Industrial Revolution	War
Middle Ages	

Additional resources

Barker, John. *The Superhistorians: Makers of Our Past.* Scribner, 1982.

Davidson, James West, and Lytle, M. H. *After the Fact: The Art of Historical Detection.* Knopf, 1982.

Fitzsimmons, Matthew A. *The Past Recaptured: Great Historians and the History of History.* Notre Dame, 1983.

Gottschalk, Louis R. *Understanding History: A Primer of Historical Method.* 2nd ed. Knopf, 1969.

Kyvig, David E., and Marty, M. A. *Nearby History: Exploring the Past Around You.* American Assn. for State & Local History, 1982.

Lichtman, Allan J. *Your Family History: How to Use Oral History, Personal Family Archives, and Public Documents to Discover Your Heritage.* Random House, 1978.

Lichtman, Allan J., and French, Valerie. *Historians and the Living Past: The Theory and Practice of Historical Study.* Harlan Davidson, 1978.

Loewenberg, Peter. *Decoding the Past: The Psychohistorical Approach.* Random House, 1982.

Morgan, Edmund S. *So What About History?* Atheneum, 1969. For younger readers.

Sanderlin, David. *Writing the History Paper: How to Select, Collect, Interpret, Organize, and Write Your Term Paper.* Barrons, 1975.

Weitzman, David. *My Backyard History Book.* Little, Brown, 1975. For younger readers. *Underfoot: An Everyday Guide to Exploring the American Past.* Scribner, 1976.

Winks, Robin W., ed. *The Historian As Detective: Essays on Evidence.* Harper, 1969.

Hitchcock, Sir Alfred (1899-1980), won fame as a director and producer of suspense-filled motion pictures. Hitchcock made films in England during the 1920's and 1930's. His first successes were *The Lodger* (1926), based on the Jack the Ripper murders; and *Blackmail* (1929), the first British sound film. *The 39 Steps* (1935) and *The Lady Vanishes* (1938) brought Hitchcock to the attention of Hollywood. Both movies involve international intrigue.

Hitchcock moved to the United States in 1939, and became a U.S. citizen in 1955. His psychological thrillers are considered his best American films. They include *Shadow of a Doubt* (1942), *Strangers on a Train* (1951), and *Psycho* (1960). Hitchcock also directed motion pictures featuring exciting chases, including *The Man Who Knew Too Much* (1934, remade 1956), *North by Northwest* (1959), and *Frenzy* (1972). Alfred Joseph Hitchcock was born in London. He was knighted in January 1980.

Harvey R. Deneroff

Hitchcock, Tommy, Jr. See Polo (History).
Hitches. See Knots, hitches, and splices.

Pictorial Parade

Adolf Hitler was dictator of Germany from 1933 to 1945.

Adolf Hitler

Hitler's Signature

Hitler, Adolf (1889-1945), ruled Germany as dictator from 1933 to 1945. Hitler turned Germany into a powerful war machine and started World War II in 1939. He conquered most of Europe before he was defeated in 1945.

Hitler spread death as no person had ever done before. "Close your eyes to pity! Act brutally!" he told his soldiers. He ordered anyone who opposed him to be executed or thrown into prison. If even one person resisted his orders, his troops often shot an entire family, or sometimes hundreds of people in a town. Hitler hated Jewish people especially, and he ordered them wiped out in countries that he controlled. He set up numerous concentration camps where about 6 million Jews and millions of other people were murdered. Many of Hitler's victims in these death camps were tortured before they were killed. Others starved to death or died of disease.

As a boy, Hitler sang in a church choir and thought he would be a priest. But as an adult he hated Christianity, which he said was a religion for weaklings.

William A. Jenks, the contributor of this article, is Professor Emeritus of History at Washington and Lee University.

Adolf Hitler began his rise to power in 1919, the year after World War I ended. The old German Empire had been defeated in the war, and the economy of the country lay in ruins. Hitler became the leader of a small group of men who had organized the National Socialist German Workers' Party. The party's members were known as *Nazis*. Hitler and his followers believed that he could win back Germany's past glory. Hitler promised to rebuild Germany into a mighty empire that would last a thousand years.

Hitler's square black mustache and the lock of hair that hung down on his forehead made him look like a comic character to some people. But his fiery words and brilliant blue eyes seemed to hypnotize those who listened to him. Many Germans believed he was their friend and protector. His speeches, given in a high-pitched voice, made crowds cheer, *"Heil, Hitler!"* ("Hail, Hitler").

After Hitler became dictator of Germany, he threatened war and lied to gain territory in Europe. The leaders of Great Britain, France, and other countries tried to prevent war, and let Hitler have his way at first. But they joined to fight him when his hunger for power became too great.

Hitler was mentally unstable. But he had a clear vision

of what he wanted, and he had the daring to pursue it. Hitler had no respect for experts in any field. He repeatedly ignored the advice of his generals and followed his own judgment. Hitler continued to ignore his generals' advice even while Germany was being smashed into defeat in World War II. Finally, as American, British, and Soviet troops closed in on the heart of Germany, Hitler killed himself.

For a discussion of conditions in Germany during Hitler's time, see the *World Book* article on **Germany** (History).

Early life

Boyhood. Adolf Hitler was born on April 20, 1889, in Braunau, Austria, a small town just across the Inn River from Germany. He was the third child of the third marriage of his father, Alois, a customs official. Alois was 52 years old when Adolf was born. Hitler's mother, Klara Pölzl, was 28 years old. She had been a farm girl before her marriage.

Alois Hitler had been born to an unmarried woman named Anna Schicklgruber. A wandering miller later married her and signed papers saying he was Alois' father. The miller's name was Johann Georg Hiedler, but Alois spelled it Hitler. Years later, Adolf Hitler's political opponents called him Schicklgruber as an insult. Only four of Alois Hitler's seven children lived to adulthood. Adolf had a sister, Paula; a half brother, Alois; and a half sister, Angela.

Soon after Adolf's birth, Alois Hitler retired and the family moved near Linz, Austria. Adolf received good grades in elementary school, but he was a poor student in high school. His low grades angered his father, who was harsh and had a bad temper. Alois Hitler wanted his son to study and be a government worker, as he had been. But the boy wanted to be an artist.

Alois Hitler died in 1903, and Adolf quit school two years later at the age of 16. His mother was poor, but Adolf did not go to work. He spent his time daydreaming, drawing pictures, and reading books.

Years in Vienna. In 1907, Hitler went to Vienna, the capital of Austria, to be an art student. He took the entrance examination of the Academy of Fine Arts, but failed. A year later, Hitler again failed the examination. His mother died in 1907, and he decided to stay in Vienna.

Hitler avoided steady work. He took odd jobs shoveling snow, laboring on construction projects, or carrying suitcases at the railroad station. He earned a little money by painting scenes of Vienna and by making posters for storekeepers. His work was clumsy, but he considered himself an artist for the rest of his life. Hitler may have inherited some money following the death of his mother's aunt, but no one really knows. He lived in residences with furnished rooms, including a rooming house for men. At times, he lined up for soup at charity kitchens.

Men who knew Hitler in Vienna described him as odd, moody, and easily angered. He later wrote that "Vienna was the hardest, but also the most thorough, school of my life." As a boy, Hitler had learned to hate Jews, Slavs, and members of other ethnic groups. This hatred increased in Vienna. Like many German-speaking Austrians, Hitler considered himself German. He had fierce pride in his ancestry.

Hitler sneered at the Austrian parliament, which recognized eight languages as official. No form of government could last, he thought, if it treated people of different nationalities equally.

Corporal Hitler. In 1913, Hitler left Vienna and went to Munich, Germany. The Austrian Army later recalled him for a physical examination. Hitler failed the examination.

World War I began in 1914, and Hitler eagerly volunteered for service in the German Army. He served as a messenger on the western front for most of the war. He took part in some of the bloodiest battles, and twice was decorated for bravery. But he rose only to the rank of corporal. Hitler was wounded once in the leg. When Germany surrendered in 1918, he was in a military hospital recovering from temporary blindness caused by a poison gas attack. Hitler loved the army, and despised

Important dates in Hitler's life

1889	(April 20) Born in Braunau, Austria.
1914-1918	Fought in the German Army in World War I.
1923	Led the Beer Hall Putsch.
1924	Imprisoned for treason; began to write *Mein Kampf.*
1933	Named chancellor of Germany; began rearming Germany.
1936	Sent his troops into the Rhineland.
1939	Began World War II by invading Poland.
1945	Committed suicide in Berlin.

Folco, Sygma

Hitler's birthplace was an inn in Braunau, Austria, near the German border. As a boy, Hitler wanted to be an artist.

WORLD LEADERS OF HITLER'S TIME

Chiang
China

Churchill
Great Britain

Daladier
France

Mussolini
Italy

Roosevelt
United States

Stalin
Russia

soldiers who hated war. For the story of Germany in the war, see **World War I.**

Rise to power

Defeat in World War I shocked the German people. Despair increased as the army returned to a bankrupt country. Millions of Germans could find no jobs. A weak republic had replaced the defeated empire.

The German people blamed their troubles on the new government, which was attacked by many political parties. On one side were the Communists, who wanted a government like that of the Soviet Union. On the other side were many nationalist groups that wanted a strong, united Germany. The nationalists demanded punishment for the "criminals" who had made peace. They also kept up a constant attack on the Versailles Treaty, which had ended the war for Germany. This treaty stripped Germany of much territory, and forced the nation to disarm. It also ordered Germany to pay huge *reparations* (payments for war damages).

Birth of the Nazi Party. After the war, Hitler returned to Munich and joined a small nationalist group called the German Workers' Party. In 1920, this group changed its name to the National Socialist German Workers' Party, which became known as the Nazi Party. The Nazis called for the union into one nation of all Germans, including those in other countries. They also favored the creation of a strong central government and cancellation of the Versailles Treaty.

Hitler was a skillful schemer, politician, and organizer. He became leader of the Nazis and built up party membership quickly, partly by his ability to stir street crowds with his speeches. Hitler attacked the government, and declared that only the Nazi Party could assure jobs for the workers and greatness for Germany.

Hitler also organized a private army of hoodlums, who became known as *storm troopers.* They fought Communists and others who tried to break up Nazi rallies. By October 1923, the storm troops numbered 15,000 members, armed with machine guns and rifles. Hitler used brown-shirted uniforms and the swastika emblem to give his followers a sense of unity (see **Swastika**).

The Beer Hall Putsch. In 1923, Germany was deep in troubles. Its money had lost almost all value because of severe economic problems. France and Belgium had sent troops to occupy the Ruhr Valley of Germany. The Bavarian state government in Munich was in open conflict with the national government in Berlin. Hitler regarded this quarrel as a chance to overthrow both the Bavarian and the national German governments.

On Nov. 8, 1923, at a rally in a Munich beer hall, Hitler proclaimed a Nazi revolution. The next day he tried to seize the Bavarian government in what became known as the *Beer Hall Putsch* (revolution). Hitler led more than 2,000 storm troopers on a march against the government. The police opened fire and killed 16 Nazis. The plot failed. Hitler was arrested and sentenced to five years in prison for treason.

Mein Kampf. While he was in prison, Hitler began writing his book *Mein Kampf* (My Struggle). In it he stated his beliefs and his ideas for Germany's future, including his plan to conquer much of Europe. Territories lost in World War I would be retaken. Parts of Austria

and Czechoslovakia where Germans lived would be added to Germany. And the growing German nation would seize *lebensraum* (living space) from the Soviet Union and other countries to the east.

Hitler wrote that the Germans were the highest species of humanity on earth. They would stay "pure," he said, by avoiding marriage to Jews and Slavs. German children would be "images of the Lord and not monstrosities halfway between man and ape."

Hitler blamed the Jews for all the evils of the world. He wrote: "Was there any shady undertaking, any form of foulness . . . in which at least one Jew did not participate?" Democracy, said Hitler, could lead only to Communism. A dictatorship was the only way to save Germany from Communists and Jews.

Rise of the Nazis. Because many Germans agreed with his ideas, Hitler was freed after serving only nine months of his five-year sentence. He left prison in December 1924.

Great changes had taken place in Germany during Hitler's imprisonment. The nation at last showed signs of recovering from World War I. Most of the people had food, homes, jobs, and hope for the future.

The government had outlawed the Nazi Party after the Beer Hall Putsch. Party members had drifted into other political movements. After Hitler's release from prison, he convinced the government that his party would act legally. The government lifted the ban on the Nazis, and Hitler began to rebuild the party. He won friends in labor unions, business, industry, and agriculture. He also set up a private army of elite guards, the *Schutzstaffel,* known as the SS. Unlike the storm troopers, who were merely armed hoodlums, the SS was a battle-ready army. By 1929, the Nazis had become an important minority political party in Germany.

By this time also, Hitler had assembled the men who would help him rise to power. They included Joseph Goebbels, the chief Nazi propagandist; Hermann Goering, second in command to Hitler; Rudolf Hess, Hitler's secretary and deputy; Heinrich Himmler, who became the party's chief executioner; and Alfred Rosenberg, the party philosopher.

In 1925, Hitler's widowed half sister, Angela Raubal, became his housekeeper. Hitler, then 36, fell in love with her 17-year-old daughter, Geli. In 1931, the girl was found shot to death in Hitler's apartment in Munich. The official report said she had committed suicide. A year or two later, Eva Braun became Hitler's mistress. But for years he wept over Geli Raubal.

In 1930, a worldwide depression hit Germany. Workers again faced unemployment and hunger. That same year, Germany agreed to the Young Plan of 1929 to pay for the damage it had caused in World War I. Hitler's opposition to the plan made him known throughout the country. He led protest marches, organized mass meetings, and made many speeches.

Hitler added his old arguments to the question of the war debt payment plan. Jews and Communists, he charged, had caused Germany's defeat in World War I. Now they were plotting to cheat "true" Germans and to destroy the fruits of years of struggle. Hitler promised to rid Germany of Jews and Communists, and to reunite the parts of Europe in which German was spoken.

In 1932, five major elections were held in Germany as

its leaders struggled to give the nation political stability. In the July election, the Nazis became the strongest party in Germany. They received about 40 per cent of the vote—enough to keep any other party from forming an effective government. Hitler was offered cabinet posts in exchange for Nazi support. But he refused to accept any plan that did not give the Nazis control of the government. Hitler promised the aging president, Paul von Hindenburg, that he would act lawfully if he were named to head the government. On Jan. 30, 1933, Hindenburg named Hitler *chancellor* (prime minister) of Germany.

Dictator of Germany

Hitler moved steadily toward dictatorship. He had no place for freedom under his government, which he called the *Third Reich* (see **Reich**).

The New Order. On Feb. 27, 1933, the Nazis burned the *Reichstag* (parliament) building and accused the Communists of setting the fire. Hitler persuaded Hindenburg to sign a law "for the protection of the people and the state." This law wiped out individual rights in Germany and allowed the Nazis to jail anyone without a trial.

By July 1933, the government had outlawed freedom of the press, all labor unions, and all political parties except the Nazis. The Reichstag gave Hitler full law-making and financial powers. Hitler's secret police, the *Gestapo,* ruthlessly hunted down his enemies (see **Gestapo**). The Gestapo shot or jailed any person even suspected of opposing Hitler. By the time Hindenburg died in August 1934, Hitler ruled Germany completely. He gave himself the title of *Führer* (leader).

The Nazi-controlled press and radio flooded Germany with propaganda. Germans could read and hear only about the glories of the *New Order,* Hitler's term for his system of rule.

The Nazis forced employers in many industries and professions to fire Jews and political suspects. Hitler established strict controls over industry, labor, and agriculture. After 1938, the Nazis decided where a person could work and what he would earn.

Hitler set up the *Hitler Youth* organization to win the loyalty of future generations. All German boys and girls had to join it. They marched, exercised, learned Nazi beliefs, and worked on farms. The Nazis taught children to spy on anyone suspected of opposing Hitler, even their own parents. Concentration camps were built to imprison Hitler's enemies and suspected enemies.

A network of special police and spies kept watch on the German people and maintained an atmosphere of terror. The Reichstag met only to listen to Hitler. Judges and courts still existed, but Hitler or his lieutenants reversed any verdict they did not like.

The road to war. "Conquest," Hitler told the German people, "is not only a right, but a duty." From 1933 to 1939, he prepared Germany for war. He rearmed the nation, first secretly and then in open violation of the Versailles Treaty. Because of the fear of another world war, no nation did anything to stop Hitler. The German dictator had two main goals. First, he wanted Germany to get more territory to the east. Second, he was determined to avenge Germany's defeat in World War I.

In 1936, Hitler sent troops into Germany's Rhineland in violation of the Versailles Treaty. His generals had opposed this dangerous challenge to France. But Hitler guessed correctly that France would not stop him. The military occupation of the Rhineland was the first of the Nazi dictator's victories without war.

In March 1938, Hitler absorbed Austria into Germany. In September, with the consent of France and Great Britain, he took over the German areas of Czechoslovakia (see **Munich Agreement**). After each move, Hitler said he wanted no more territory. But after each success, he planned a new take-over. He grabbed the rest of Czechoslovakia in March 1939.

Poland came next on Hitler's list. Britain and France had promised to protect Poland against a Nazi attack, but Hitler did not believe they would do so. In August 1939, Hitler signed a treaty of friendship with Premier Joseph Stalin of the Soviet Union. The treaty assured him that the Soviet Union would not challenge a German attack against Poland. A few days later, on Sept. 1, 1939, German tanks rolled into Poland. Britain and France then declared war on Germany. This time, Hitler had guessed wrong. World War II had begun.

Pictorial Parade

Paul von Hindenburg, the president of Germany, named Hitler *chancellor* (prime minister) on Jan. 30, 1933. By the summer of 1933, Hitler had made himself dictator.

European Picture Service

Nazi rallies featured thousands of troops and deeply impressed the German people. Hitler used the rallies to persuade the nation to accept his plan of conquest for Germany.

Pictorial Parade

Hitler cheered the fall of France at his headquarters in Belgium on June 17, 1940.

World War II. Hitler's armies quickly overran Poland. In the spring of 1940, they easily conquered Denmark, Norway, Belgium, Luxembourg, and the Netherlands. Benito Mussolini, Italy's dictator, was impressed by Hitler's victories and declared war on Britain and France on June 10, 1940. The German war machine rolled through France, pushing the British and French forces to the sea. On June 22, 1940, France surrendered.

Now Britain stood alone. Hitler expected the British to surrender, but they fought on in spite of continual air raids by German bombers. Hitler kept delaying an invasion of Britain. Instead, he sent his armies rolling over Yugoslavia and Greece. In June 1941, he sent an army of 3 million men to invade the Soviet Union. That winter, Soviet resistance and the bitterly cold weather stopped the Germans outside Moscow.

In 1942, the war turned against Hitler. The United States had entered the war in December 1941 and was pouring huge amounts of supplies into Britain and the Soviet Union. Soon the Allies drove the Germans from Africa. In the Soviet Union, Hitler's wild desire to capture Stalingrad cost him 300,000 men. By 1944, Soviet forces were pushing Hitler's armies back toward Germany. In June 1944, a giant Allied force invaded Europe. Hitler became frantic. He ordered death for any soldier who retreated.

While his empire lasted, Hitler directed the Nazis in a campaign of mass slaughter. About 6 million Jews perished in Nazi

European Picture Service

Eva Braun was Hitler's mistress for many years. She and Hitler were married on April 29, 1945, about a week before Germany surrendered. The day after their wedding, they committed suicide.

death camps, where gas chambers, firing squads, torture, starvation, and disease killed thousands every day. The Nazis also killed millions of other prisoners by neglect or in tortures that they called "medical experiments."

On July 20, 1944, Hitler narrowly escaped death when a time bomb planted by a German officer exploded in the dictator's headquarters. Hitler's enemies in Germany had planned to overthrow or kill him as early as 1938, but all their plots failed. In revenge for the time bomb that almost killed him, Hitler had at least 4,980 persons executed. On his orders, some of them were strangled slowly with piano wire. Movies were taken of their suffering so Hitler could watch.

Early in 1945, the Allies raced on to the heart of Germany. Hitler's armies were retreating everywhere. For the story of Germany in the war, see **World War II.**

Death. At his headquarters in Berlin, Hitler had become a broken man. His head, hands, and feet trembled, and he was tortured by stomach cramps.

Eva Braun arrived in Berlin in April 1945. She and Hitler were married on April 29 in an underground bomb shelter of the Chancellery. The next day, Hitler swallowed poison and also shot himself, and his wife swallowed poison. Aides burned their bodies. Seven days later, Germany surrendered. William A. Jenks

Related articles in *World Book* include:

Auschwitz	Keitel, Wilhelm
Austria (picture)	Ludendorff, Erich F. W.
Belsen	Mein Kampf
Berchtesgaden	Mengele, Josef
Bonhoeffer, Dietrich	Munich Agreement
Buchenwald	Mussolini, Benito
Dachau	Nazism
Eichmann, Adolf	Nuremberg Trials
Facism (Fascism in Germany)	Papen, Franz von
Germany (History)	Propaganda (Simplicity and
Goebbels, Joseph	repetition; pictures)
Goering, Hermann W.	Ribbentrop, Joachim von
Hess, Rudolf	Rommel, Erwin
Himmler, Heinrich	Rosenberg, Alfred
Hindenburg, Paul von	Stalingrad, Battle of
Holocaust	Swastika
Jodl, Alfred	War crime
Jews (Beginnings of Nazi perse-	World War II
cution; The Holocaust)	

Outline

I. **Early life**
   A. Boyhood
   B. Years in Vienna
   C. Corporal Hitler
II. **Rise to power**
   A. Birth of the Nazi Party
   B. The Beer Hall Putsch
   C. *Mein Kampf*
   D. Rise of the Nazis
III. **Dictator of Germany**
   A. The New Order
   B. The road to war
   C. World War II
   D. Death

Questions

As a young man, what did Hitler want to study?
What was the *Beer Hall Putsch? Mein Kampf?*
Why was Hitler named chancellor of Germany?
How did Hitler touch off World War II?
How did Hitler win the support of the German people?
What were Hitler's two main goals as dictator?
What did Hitler mean by *Lebensraum?*
How did Hitler set young Germans against their parents?

As a boy, how did Hitler anger his father?
Why did no nation challenge Hitler before 1939?

Reading and Study Guide

See *Hitler, Adolf* in the Research Guide/Index, Volume 22, for a *Reading and Study Guide.*

Additional resources

Bullock, Alan. *Hitler: A Study in Tyranny.* Rev. ed. Harper, 1962.
Fest, Joachim C. *Hitler.* Harcourt, 1974.
Haffner, Sebastian. *The Meaning of Hitler.* Macmillan, 1979.
Staudinger, Hans. *The Inner Nazi: A Critical Analysis of* Mein Kampf. Louisiana State Univ. Press, 1981.
Stone, Norman. *Hitler.* Little, Brown, 1980.
Toland, John. *Adolf Hitler.* Doubleday, 1976.

Hittites, *HIH tyts,* were the earliest known inhabitants of what is now Turkey. They began to control the area about 1900 B.C. During the next several hundred years, they conquered parts of Mesopotamia and Syria. By 1500 B.C., the Hittites had become a leading power in the Middle East. The culture and language of the Hittites were Indo-European, but scholars do not know whether the Hittites came from Europe or from central Asia.

Way of life. Many elements of Hittite architecture, art, literature, and religion were influenced by neighboring peoples. The Hittites' system of government was more advanced than that of many of their neighbors. Their legal system was fair and humane, and their law code emphasized compensation for a wrong, rather than revengeful punishment. The Hittites established peaceful and profitable relations with the peoples they conquered. Their military superiority resulted from several innovations. The Hittites were among the first to

Odyssey Productions

A Hittite banquet appears in relief on this stone slab, which was carved during the 800's B.C.

smelt iron. They also built the lightest and fastest chariots of their time.

The Hittites used the Akkadian language written in cuneiform for their international correspondence. For their own royal and religious writings, they used the Hittite language recorded either in Hittite hieroglyphic writing or in cuneiform script borrowed from the Mesopotamians. Scholars deciphered the cuneiform in the early 1900's. But the scholars could not definitely decipher the hieroglyphs until 1947, when they found lengthy statements in both the Phoenician language and Hittite hieroglyphs. These bilingual documents provided scholars with the key for translating Hittite hieroglyphs.

History. The Hittites penetrated what is now central Turkey shortly after 2000 B.C. They conquered the local people and set up a number of city-states. The most important of these was Hattusas, located just east of the present Turkish capital, Ankara. When the city-states formed the Hittite empire, about 1650 B.C., Hattusas became the capital.

The Hittites conquered Babylon about 1595 B.C. They also gained control of northern Syria. The widow of an Egyptian pharaoh, probably Tutankhamen, asked the Hittite emperor to send one of his sons to be her husband and pharaoh of Egypt. But a group of Egyptians who did not like this arrangement murdered the son before the marriage.

One of the greatest battles of ancient times took place about 1285 B.C. at Kadesh on the Orontes River, north of Palestine. Mutwatallis, the Hittite leader, fought an indecisive battle against Egyptian forces under Ramses II, who barely escaped alive. The Hittites did not conquer Egyptian territory. They concluded a peace that was sealed by the marriage of a Hittite princess to Ramses. See **Ramses II.**

Shortly after this, allies of the Hittites in both east and west revolted. Tribes migrated from their homes around the Aegean Sea into the western part of the Hittite empire to escape the growing power of the Greeks. They burned Hattusas in about 1200 B.C. Hittite city-states continued to exist for another 500 years, but they were not very powerful. Carchemish came to be considered the eastern capital of the Hittites. But Sargon II of Assyria captured it in 717 B.C. This marked the end of a distinct Hittite government.

The Hittites are mentioned several times in the Old Testament. Abraham bought the field and cave of Machpelah from Ephron the Hittite as a burial place for his wife Sarah. Abraham's grandson, Esau, married two Hittite wives. As late as the time of David, certain people of Israel were called Hittites. David had Uriah the Hittite killed in battle so that he could marry Uriah's wife, Bathsheba.   Leonard H. Lesko

Hive. See **Bee.**

Hives are a form of skin rash that comes suddenly and disappears without leaving a trace. The rash consists of white or red *wheals* (raised patches) that itch. Hives may be caused by a food or drug to which the sufferer is hypersensitive. Patients may have an allergic reaction to some chemical they touch frequently, or to the fur of some animal. A person's skin can be tested to discover the substances to which his or her body is allergic. An outbreak of hives often may be treated with antihistamine drugs or by bathing the spots with lotions of baking soda and water, witch hazel, or some other cooling solution.

Hives are also known as *nettle rash.* The medical name for hives is *urticaria,* and comes from the Latin word for nettle.   Sidney Olansky

See also **Allergy; Itch.**

HI-Y club is the general name for special teen-age and youth clubs sponsored by the Young Men's Christian Association (YMCA). The clubs try to help young people develop their highest mental, physical, social, and spiritual potentials.

Boys of high school age may join HI-Y clubs and girls of high school age may join TRI-HI-Y. Many YMCA's sponsor CO-ED HI-Y clubs for teen-agers. There are over 3,000 teen-age HI-Y groups in the United States. These HI-Y groups have a total of over 80,000 participants. Other clubs include Jr. HI-Y, for junior high boys; Jr. TRI-HI-Y, for junior high girls; Gra-Y, for grade school boys; and Gra-TRI-Y, for grade school girls.

The HI-Y movement began in 1889. Through the various clubs, the YMCA tries to provide opportunities for educational growth and to encourage young people to accept responsibility. Each club determines its own activities and goals under the guidance of an adult adviser. HI-Y activities include recreational programs, service projects, and study and action programs on social problems and issues. The YMCA of the USA has national offices at 101 N. Wacker Drive, Chicago, IL 60606.

Critically reviewed by the YMCA of the USA

HMO. See **Health care plans.**

Ho Chi Minh, *hoh chee mihn* (1890-1969), a Vietnamese revolutionary leader, served as president of North Vietnam from 1954 until his death. Ho gained popularity when his forces defeated the French rulers of Vietnam in 1954. In the 1950's and 1960's, Ho's Communist government sent troops to aid rebels in South Vietnam who were trying to overthrow the anti-Communist government there. Ho's followers continued to aid the rebels after his death and, in 1975, the Communist forces won control of South Vietnam.

Tetlow, Pictorial Parade
Ho Chi Minh

Ho was born Nguyen Van Thanh in central Vietnam. He became a Communist in 1920, and helped found the French Communist Party. Near the end of World War II, Ho became head of a Vietnamese government that opposed France's rule. In 1946, fighting broke out between the French and Ho's troops, known as the Vietminh. After the Vietminh defeated the French in 1954, an international conference divided Vietnam into two nations. Ho then became president of North Vietnam.   Bernard B. Fall

See also **Indochina** (Independence); **Vietnam** (History); **Vietnam War.**

Additional resources

Archer, Jules. *Ho Chi Minh: Legend of Hanoi.* Macmillan, 1971. Suitable for younger readers.

Huyen, N. Khac. *Vision Accomplished? The Enigma of Ho Chi Minh.* Macmillan, 1971.
Lacouture, Jean. *Ho Chi Minh: A Political Biography.* Random House, 1968.

Ho Chi Minh City, *hoh chee mihn* (pop. 3,419,978), formerly called Saigon, is the largest city in Vietnam. It is also a leading Vietnamese industrial and commercial center. Ho Chi Minh City lies in southern Vietnam, between the Mekong River Delta and the South China Sea. For location, see **Vietnam** (map). The delta is a fertile agricultural region. Products from the delta are sent to Ho Chi Minh City for shipment.

Treelined boulevards beautify the center of Ho Chi Minh City and of Cholon, a largely Chinese section of the city. Ho Chi Minh City has much modern architecture, which contrasts with the city's many old Chinese and French-colonial buildings. The University of Ho Chi Minh City is the largest institution of higher learning in Vietnam.

In the 1700's, Vietnamese who had migrated from the north used the city, which was then called Saigon, as a port to ship back rice grown in the Mekong River Delta. The French took control of Saigon in 1861. They made it a military base and the administrative capital of their colony of Cochin China, a part of French Indochina (see **Indochina**). In 1954, Indochina gained independence from France. The Vietnamese parts of the colony were divided into two countries—South Vietnam and North Vietnam. Saigon became the capital of South Vietnam.

Saigon grew tremendously during the Vietnam War (1957-1975). Thousands of South Vietnamese and United States troops were stationed there, and many people moved there to escape fighting in the countryside. Communist North Vietnam defeated South Vietnam in the war. The Communists united the North and South into the single nation of Vietnam in 1976. They changed Saigon's name to Ho Chi Minh City, in honor of a former president of North Vietnam. Since the end of the war, the city's economy has declined somewhat and unemployment has increased. The government has forced large numbers of people to leave the city and to work in rural areas.   David P. Chandler

Hoarfrost. See **Frost.**

Hoarhound. See **Horehound.**

Hoatzin, *hoh AT sihn,* is a strange-looking bird that lives in marshy areas by waterways in northern South America. Hoatzins are born with claws on their wings. The young birds use the claws to climb on tree branches until they learn to fly. The claws fall off as the birds mature.

The hoatzin has short, rounded wings and a long tail. Loose yellow plumes on top of its head give it a ruffled look. Its upper body is dark brown, and its underparts are buff colored. The hoatzin grows a bit larger than a pigeon and usually eats leaves and fruit. It usually lives in tree branches that hang over marshy waters.

Hoatzins have no close relatives. However, they may be remotely related to domestic poultry.

Scientific classification. Hoatzins make up the hoatzin family, Opisthocomidae. They are classified as *Opisthocomus hoazin.*   George J. Wallace

Hobart, *HOH bahrt* (pop. 175,082), is the capital of the Australian island-state of Tasmania. The city lies on the Derwent River, about 12 miles (19 kilometers) from the sea. For location, see **Australia** (political map). Hobart's central city area has a population of 49,020. Most of Tasmania's trade and shipping go through the city.

The city was founded as Hobart Town in 1804 by David Collins. It was the capital when Tasmania became a separate colony in 1825. In its early days, Hobart was a major center for antarctic whalers. The city's name was changed to Hobart in 1881. Modern factories in the city produce cement, paper pulp, textiles, candy, and metal products. Two multi-lane bridges link the eastern and western shores of the Derwent River. Hobart is the home of the University of Tasmania and scientific research laboratories. Rod C. Boucher

Hobart, Garret Augustus (1844-1899), served as Vice President of the United States from 1897 until he died. He was a close friend of President William McKinley, and was often called "The Assistant President." He influenced the Senate to promote administration policy. Hobart's death made it necessary for the Republicans to find another running mate for McKinley in 1900. Their choice of Theodore Roosevelt was fateful, because McKinley was assassinated in 1901 and Roosevelt became President.

Hobart was born in Long Branch, N.J. He was graduated from Rutgers College, and studied law in Paterson, N.J. He served for many years in the state legislature, and became speaker of the state assembly in 1874. He was elected state senator in 1876 and became president of the state senate in 1881. Hobart served as a member of the Republican National Committee from 1884 to 1896. Irving G. Williams

See also **Vice President of the United States.**

Hobbes, Thomas (1588-1679), was an English philosopher. His most famous work, *Leviathan, or the Matter,*

Brown Bros.

Thomas Hobbes

Form, and Power of a Commonwealth, Ecclesiastical and Civil (1651), was concerned with political theory. In this work, he denied that people are naturally social beings. He argued instead that people's most basic motives are selfish considerations.

Hobbes was influenced by two developments of his time. One was the new system of physics that Galileo and others were working out (see **Galileo**). From their ideas, Hobbes concluded that only matter exists and that everything that happens can be predicted in accordance with exact, scientific laws. Many people of his time believed that his view denied the existence of both God and a free human soul that is immortal. But Hobbes himself denied this.

The second great influence on Hobbes's thought was the English Civil War. People, he concluded, are selfish. They are moved chiefly by desire for power and by fear of others. Thus, without an all-powerful sovereign to rule them, their lives would be "poor, nasty, brutish, and short." These views also shocked his contemporaries.

Hobbes's influence. Though modern physics is not so materialistic as it seemed to be in Hobbes's day and though human motives are more complex than he supposed, Hobbes's influence continues. He raised fundamental and challenging questions about the relationship between science and religion, the relationship between thought and the physiological processes on which it is based, and the nature and limitations of political power. The questions that Hobbes raised are ones that people still struggle to answer.

His life. Hobbes was born in Westport (now part of Malmesbury), England. He was educated at Oxford University, and served as secretary to Sir Francis Bacon and as tutor to William Cavendish, who later became Earl of Devonshire. Hobbes traveled widely with Cavendish and came into contact with many European philosophers and scientists.

During the English Civil War, Hobbes fled to the European continent. For a short time, he tutored the Prince of Wales, later Charles II, in mathematics. Though Hobbes returned to England while Oliver Cromwell's Protectorate was still in power, he was able to make peace with Charles II when Charles became king in 1660. Stephen A. Erickson

Additional resources

Peters, Richard S. *Hobbes.* Greenwood, 1979. First published in 1956.
Raphael, David D. *Hobbes: Morals and Politics.* Allen & Unwin, 1977.

Hobble skirt. See Clothing (The 1900's).

Hobby can be any type of activity people do during their leisure time. Most people take up a hobby for relaxation, pleasure, or friendships, or to develop new interests. Sometimes a hobby can lead to extra income.

People of almost any age can enjoy hobbies. A hobby offers a way to relax after periods of hard work. Hobbies

WORLD BOOK illustration by John Rignall, Linden Artists, Ltd.

The strange-looking hoatzin lives in South America. A young hoatzin has claws on its wings, which help the bird climb trees before it can fly. Adults have long, loose feathers on their head.

David R. Frazier

Painting is a popular hobby that provides opportunities for self-expression and creativity. The hobbyist shown above is using watercolor paints to depict an outdoor scene.

offer broadened areas of interest and ways to pass the time pleasantly. Hobbies can be important in helping patients recover from physical or mental illness because they provide distractions from the patients' problems. For people who are ill or bedridden, hobbies offer fascinating ways to pass the time. Hobbies can also be an important form of occupational therapy.

In the past, hobbies were largely limited to the wealthy. The average person was too busy earning a living to find time to pursue a hobby. People today generally have more leisure time because of higher incomes and improvements in working conditions. In addition, most people live longer and retire from their jobs at an earlier age. To fill their free time, they often develop interests in hobbies.

Kinds of hobbies

Almost any kind of leisure activity can become a hobby. Most hobbies fall into one of four general categories, which may overlap. They are (1) the arts, (2) collecting, (3) handicrafts, and (4) games and sports.

The arts provide outlets for hobbyists with a special interest in such art forms as dancing, drama, painting, graphic arts, and music. Each art form has many separate possibilities for a hobby. For example, music may include singing, playing an instrument, collecting records and tapes, learning ballet, or attending concerts and operas. Painting offers the hobbyist a wide choice of materials, such as oil paints or water colors.

Collecting is probably the most widespread kind of hobby because almost anything can be collected. Stamps and coins are probably the most popular collected items. Hobbyists also collect such things as autographs, comic books, costumes, baseball cards, buttons, dolls, hatpins, and matchbooks.

Handicrafts attract hobbyists who can work skillfully with their hands. Many hobbyists engage in needlework activities, notably crocheting, needlepoint, knitting, and sewing. Hobbyists use kits to make model airplanes, boats, and trains. Using woodworking tools, they can create carvings, furniture, and bowls. Other handicrafts include ceramics, metalworking, jewelry making, weaving, batik, and leatherworking.

Games and sports are popular with many hobbyists who enjoy competition, physical activity, and healthful exercise. Thousands of hobbyists take part in sports, such as bowling, fishing, mountain climbing, skiing, and tennis. These sports give hobbyists the opportunity to display their individual skills and sportsmanship. Popular indoor games include bridge and other card games, backgammon, chess, and Monopoly.

Other hobbies, Electronics-related hobbies are becoming increasingly popular. Many hobbyists enjoy flying model airplanes by remote control or assembling and operating ham radios. Both young people and adults have taken up computers as a hobby, frequently assembling computers from kits. Some people raise pets as a hobby. For many people, gardening and photography are rewarding hobbies.

Starting a hobby

People sometimes choose a hobby without realizing they are doing so. A casual interest grows into a fascination as the person learns more about the subject and devotes an increasing amount of time to it. After deciding on a hobby, individuals may gather as much information as they can from reference sources, especially books and magazines. They can also gain information by taking courses in school, attending hobby conventions,

Paul Robert Perry

Collecting is probably the most widespread kind of hobby. Almost anything can be collected. People who collect baseball cards often trade cards with other collectors.

David R. Frazier

Quilting is a popular handicraft throughout the world. Many people design and sew colorful quilts as a hobby. The woman shown above is stitching a patchwork quilt.

and joining hobby clubs. Hobbyists often can study exhibits relating to their hobby in museums and galleries. Clubs and other organizations sponsor tours that allow hobbyists to visit places where they can pursue their hobby and meet people with similar interests.

In most cases, beginning hobbyists should start with a few basic items. As they become more experienced and enthusiastic, they may buy more elaborate materials. Hobby dealers provide information about equipment, supplies, and techniques.   Dona Z. Meilach

Related articles in *World Book* include:

Arts hobbies

Art and the arts	Drawing	Music	Reading
Dancing	Finger paint-ing	Orchestra	Singing
Drama	Literature	Painting	Theater
		Poetry	

Collection hobbies

Antique	Coin collecting	Moth
Aquarium	Doll	Pet
Autograph	Flower	Rock
Automobile	Fossil	Shell
Book collecting	Furniture	Stamp collecting
Butterfly	Insect	Tropical fish
Button	Leaf	

Handicraft hobbies

Airplane, Model	Embroidery	Quilt
Appliqué	Handicraft	Railroad, Model
Astronomy	Jewelry	Rocket, Model
Automobile, Model	Kite	Rugs and carpets
Basket making	Knitting	Sampler
Beadwork	Leathercraft	Sewing
Bird (Bird study)	Macramé	Ship, Model
Block printing	Mosaic	Silk-screen printing
Bookbinding	Needlepoint	
Ceramics	Papier-mâché	Taxidermy
Cooking	Petit point	Ventriloquism
Crewel	Photography	Weaving
Crocheting	Pottery	Woodcarving
Decal	Puppet	Woodworking
Decoupage		

Games and sports

See the lists of *Related articles* with **Game; Play; Sports.**

Other hobbies

Bee	Gardening	Motion picture
Computer	High fidelity system	Radio, Amateur

Additional resources

Level I
Reader's Digest Crafts & Hobbies. Ed. by Daniel Weiss. Random House, 1979.
Schulz, Charles M. Charlie Brown's Super Book of Things to Do and Collect. Random House, 1975.

Level II
Brightbill, Charles K. Man and Leisure: A Philosophy of Recreation. Greenwood, 1973. First published in 1961.
Hobbies: How 37 Fascinating Hobbies Were Started. Ed. by James Sanders. Jonathan David, 1980.
Smaridge, Norah, and Hunter, Hilda. The Teen-ager's Guide to Collecting Practically Anything. Dodd, 1972. The Teen-ager's Guide to Hobbies for Here and Now. 1974.

Hobby, Oveta Culp (1905-   ), became the first United States secretary of health, education, and welfare. She served from 1953 to 1955.

During World War II (1939-1945), Hobby organized and directed the Women's Auxiliary Army Corps (later known as the WAC). She became the first woman to receive the Distinguished Service Medal.

In 1953, President Dwight D. Eisenhower appointed Hobby federal security administrator. That same year, she became secretary of health, education, and welfare. She was born in Killeen, Tex.   Harvey Wish

Hobson, Laura Zametkin (1900-1986), was an American novelist who wrote about controversial subjects. Her most famous novel is *Gentleman's Agreement* (1947). In the book, a young reporter pretends to be Jewish to gain material for a magazine article on anti-Semitism. He discovers that many well-meaning people hold prejudices and silently consent to religious intolerance.

In *The Trespassers* (1943), Hobson attacked the United States government for failing to sufficiently help European refugees before World War II (1939-1945). *The Tenth Month* (1971) concerns unwed mothers. *Consenting Adult* (1975) is about homosexuality. Hobson's other novels include *The Other Father* (1950), *The Celebrity* (1951), *First Papers* (1964), and *Over and Above* (1979).

Laura Keane Zametkin was born in New York City, the setting for most of her fiction. She married Thayer Hobson in 1930. Hobson's autobiography, *Laura Z.: A Life* (1983), describes her life up to the publication of *Gentleman's Agreement.*   Barbara M. Perkins

Hochhuth, HAHK hoot, **Rolf** (1931-   ), is a German playwright. His plays dramatize disputed moral decisions made by famous people of modern history. In *The Deputy* (1963), also known as *The Representative,* his most famous play, Hochhuth condemned Pope Pius XII for not protesting the Nazi extermination of Jews during World War II (1939-1945).

Hochhuth's second play, *Soldiers* (1967), was also set in World War II. In this drama, Hochhuth charged Prime Minister Winston Churchill of Great Britain with causing the death of General Władysław Sikorski, leader of Poland's government in exile. He asserted that Churchill had Sikorski killed for diplomatic reasons. He also portrayed Churchill as insensitive to the deaths of German civilians in cities bombed by the Allies.

In *Guerrillas* (1970), Hochhuth charged the United States with racial and political murders. This play portrays fictional public figures in the United States and Latin America. Hochhuth was born in Eschwege, Germany, near Kassel.   Malcolm Goldstein

Höchstädt, Battle of. See Blenheim, Battle of.

Focus on Sports

Hockey's fast, rough action makes it one of the most exciting sports. A high point in the action occurs when one team tries to shoot the puck into the opposing team's goal.

Hockey

Hockey, also called *ice hockey,* is a fast, exciting sport played by two teams on a sheet of ice called a rink. Each team has six players, and all the players wear skates. The players flash up and down the rink, slamming a hard rubber disk called a *puck* along the ice with long sticks. They try to score points by hitting the puck into a *goal cage,* or *net.* In many countries, the term *hockey* refers to field hockey. For information on this sport, see the **Field hockey** article in *World Book.*

Hockey has swifter action than almost any other sport. As the players streak across the ice, their powerful swings at the puck often send it traveling faster than 100 miles per hour (160 kilometers per hour). A goalkeeper on each team defends the team's net. Goalkeepers must often make lightning slides across the front of the net on their knees, stomach, or back to block shots of the puck. A puck that enters the goal cage or crosses the goal line scores a *goal* (point) for the other side. The side that scores the most goals wins the game. To keep the action fast, hockey has an unusual rule. It is the only major sport that allows players to be substituted while play is in progress. The game sometimes includes fights among players, though fighting is against the rules.

Hockey began in Canada in the mid-1800's. By the early 1900's, it had become Canada's national sport. Since then, hockey has become popular in many other countries, especially Czechoslovakia, the Soviet Union,

Gordie Howe, the contributor of this article, ranks among the greatest players in the history of professional hockey. He is the author of Hockey: Here's Howe *(paperback title,* Let's Play Hockey).

Sweden, and the United States. In Canada and the United States, thousands of amateur players take part in community, high school, and college contests.

How to play hockey

Hockey rules differ somewhat between professional and amateur groups. This section deals mainly with the rules followed by professional leagues in Canada and the United States. There is one major league—the National Hockey League (NHL)—plus several minor leagues. Most Canadian and U.S. amateur teams have nearly the same rules that professional leagues have. But U.S. high school and college teams follow a special set of amateur rules, as do most teams in international competition. This section notes the chief differences between the professional rules and various amateur rules.

The rink. The standard hockey rink measures 200 feet (61 meters) by 85 feet (26 meters). The corners are rounded. A low, white, solid wooden wall—called the *boards*—surrounds the rink. This wall, which in most cases is covered with fiberglass, stands 40 to 48 inches (102 to 122 centimeters) high. Most indoor rinks consist of a sheet of ice that is first painted white, with blue and red markings—and then covered with more clear ice.

A red *goal line* extends across each end of the rink, 10 feet (3 meters) from the boards. A goal cage stands in the middle of each goal line. The cage consists mainly of heavy netting supported by two metal *goal posts,* which are joined across the top by a metal crossbar. The opening at the front of the cage measures 4 feet (1.2 meters) high by 6 feet (1.8 meters) wide. Players aim the puck at this opening to score goals. An 8-foot (2.4-meter) by 4-foot (1.2-meter) area, called a *goal crease,* is outlined in red in front of each cage. A player may not enter the opposing team's crease unless that player is going after the puck. A goal does not count if an offensive player was in the crease when the puck crossed the goal line, unless an opponent forced the player into the crease.

Two blue lines divide the area between the goal lines into two 60-foot (18-meter) end zones and a center zone, which is also 60 feet long on most rinks. The end zone that a team defends is that team's *defending zone.* The opposite end zone is the team's *attacking zone.* Actually, one team's defending zone serves as the other team's attacking zone. The center zone is called the *neutral zone.* In all hockey games, except U.S. high school and college games, the rink also has a red *centerline.* It divides the neutral zone—and the rink—in half. Most outdoor rinks have the zone boundaries marked on the boards.

Hockey terms

Face-off occurs when an official drops the puck between the sticks of two opposing players, who try to hit it to a teammate or toward their opponents' goal.

Hat trick occurs when a player scores three goals in one game.

Icing the puck is a violation that occurs when a defending player shoots the puck from the team's half of the ice across the opponents' goal line. Icing is not called if, after the puck crosses the goal line, a member of the offending team is the first player to touch the puck. Icing is also not called if the offending team has fewer players on the ice than the other team or if the puck enters the goal cage. In games without a centerline, icing occurs when the puck is shot across both blue lines and the opposing team's goal line.

Offside is a violation that occurs (1) when any attacking player crosses the blue line into the opposing team's defending zone ahead of the puck; and (2) when a player passes the puck from the player's team's defending zone to a teammate beyond the centerline.

Power play occurs when a team sends all its players except the goalkeeper in a drive against the opposing team's goal while one or two of the opposing players are in the penalty box.

Colored *face-off spots* mark the places on the ice where officials hold *face-offs.* In a face-off, an official drops the puck between the sticks of two opposing players, who try to hit it to a teammate or in the direction of the opponents' goal. Face-offs are used to begin each game and to resume the game after play has been stopped. The neutral zone has four red face-off spots, and each end zone has two. Each end zone face-off spot is surrounded by a red circle. Only an official and two opposing players may stand inside a circle during a face-off. A blue face-off spot and circle are at the center of the rink.

Most hockey rinks have a *players' bench* for each team and a *penalty bench,* or *penalty box,* where players must stay temporarily if they break the rules. The benches are behind the sideboards. Every rink has two or more clocks to keep track of the playing time and the time players serve in the penalty box. Most indoor rinks also have a red light behind each goal that is flashed on when a puck enters the goal cage and scores.

Playing time. Most hockey games are played in three 20-minute periods separated by two 18-minute intermissions. The periods last less than 20 minutes in some amateur games. Only actual playing time is counted. The clock stops when play stops. An official's whistle stops play in most cases. In addition, each team is allowed one 30-second time out per game.

In the NHL, if a regular-season game ends in a tie after three periods of play, the teams play a 5-minute *sudden-death overtime.* The first team to score in the overtime wins. If neither team scores, the game ends in a tie. If an NHL play-off game ends in a tie, the teams play 20-minute overtime periods until one team scores.

The starting lineup consists of the goalkeeper, or *goalie;* three *forwards;* and two *defensemen.* The goalie

A standard hockey rink

Almost all professional and many amateur rinks are laid out like the one below. Other rinks differ in certain ways. In some amateur rinks, for example, the blue lines are less than 60 feet from the goal lines. But they still divide the area between the goals into three equal zones. In U.S. high school and college hockey, the rink does not have a centerline.

WORLD BOOK diagram

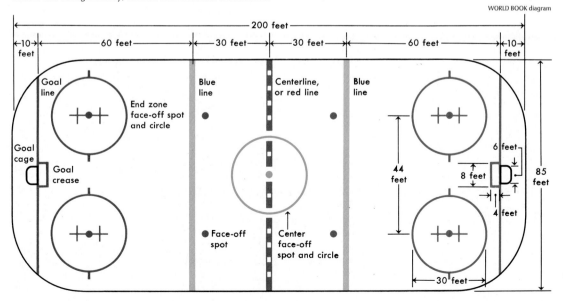

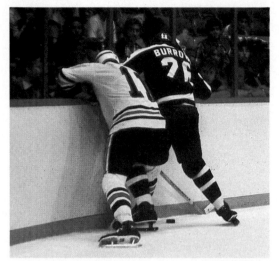

WORLD BOOK photo

Fighting for control of the puck often sends players slamming into the boards that surround a hockey rink. Fans seated close to the rink watch the game through shatterproof glass.

has the most demanding job on the team. The goalie is the last defense against a score by the opposing team, and the least mistake on the goalie's part may cost the team a goal. The goalie almost always remains in or near the goal crease. The goalie is the only player allowed to catch the puck or pick it up.

The main job of the forwards is to score goals. But they must also help defend their team's goal. Each forward has an assigned position—*center, left wing,* or *right wing*—which together make up the *forward line.* The center usually leads the team's attack and takes part in most face-offs. The center's starting position is in the middle of the forward line. But during play, the center chases the puck wherever it goes. The left wing generally patrols the left side of the rink. The right wing patrols the right side. But the wings skate into each other's territory when the play requires.

The defensemen's main job is to guard their team's defending zone and so keep the opposing team from scoring. But defensemen also sometimes lead the attack and score goals. They normally cover the part of the rink between their team's forward line and their goal. The *left defenseman* generally covers the left half of the rink, and the *right defenseman* covers the right half. But like the wings, they skate into each other's territory when necessary. The sections on *Offensive play* and *Defensive play* describe the players' duties in more detail.

Players may be substituted at any time, but play is never stopped to make substitutions. Coaches usually change the forward line and both defensemen about every 2 minutes during professional games. The starting goalie usually plays the entire game. A team often has to play *short-handed*—that is, with fewer players on the ice than the opposing team has. This situation occurs when one or two players on a team are in the penalty box.

Equipment. Hockey players need a puck, skates, and sticks. The puck is a hard, black rubber disk 1 inch (2.5 centimeters) thick and 3 inches (7.6 centimeters) in diameter. It weighs from $5\frac{1}{2}$ to 6 ounces (156 to 170 grams). Hockey skates have strong, heavy shoes designed for both support and protection. The blades are made of hard steel and are *rockered* (curved) along the bottom. A player can turn and make other maneuvers more easily with rockered blades than with flat ones. Each player uses an L-shaped stick. The *shaft* (handle) is made of wood or metal and may be no more than 55 inches (140 centimeters) long. The *blade* of the stick is wooden. Except on goalies' sticks, the blade must be no more than $12\frac{1}{2}$ inches (32 centimeters) long and 3 inches (8 centimeters) wide. The blade of a goalie's stick may be up to $15\frac{1}{2}$ inches (39 centimeters) long and $3\frac{1}{2}$ inches (9 centimeters) wide.

A player's uniform consists mainly of knee-length pants, a sweater, and long socks. Under the uniform, each player wears shoulder pads, elbow pads, a garter belt, and shin guards. Male players wear a special supporter. The pants of all players are padded to protect the kidneys and thighs. Each player also wears heavily padded gloves with long cuffs to protect the wrists. Nearly

Hockey equipment

Skates and a stick are part of every hockey player's equipment. Every player also wears special protective equipment, as shown in these drawings. The left-hand drawing shows a goalie's equipment. It is specially designed to protect the goalie against bulletlike shots of the puck. The right-hand drawing shows the equipment of the other players. In addition to this equipment, defensemen and some forwards wear ankle guards. Players may also wear protective face masks.

WORLD BOOK diagram by James Buckley

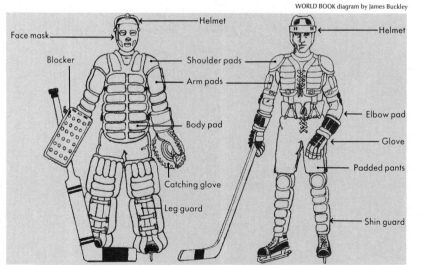

Helmet
Face mask
Blocker
Shoulder pads
Arm pads
Body pad
Catching glove
Leg guard
Helmet
Elbow pad
Glove
Padded pants
Shin guard

all amateur players must wear a protective helmet. Players in the NHL also must wear a helmet. Many players' helmets are equipped with a clear plastic shield that protects the upper part of the face.

A goalie wears extra-thick padding under the uniform, including pads to protect the arms and the front of the body. A leather pad 10 inches (25 centimeters) wide shields the front of each leg from above the knee to below the ankle. These pads help the goalie block shots at the net. One of a goalie's gloves, called a *blocker,* has a large pad on the back. The goalie uses this pad, along with the stick, to bat away lightning shots of the puck. The other glove resembles a first baseman's mitt with a long cuff. The goalie uses this glove to catch pucks and toss them away from the net. Goalies also wear a special protective face mask.

Hockey skills. Hockey requires a variety of skills. They include (1) skating, (2) stickhandling, (3) passing, (4) shooting, and (5) checking. Hockey has few standard plays, and so players must also have the skill to develop plays as the action progresses.

Skating is the most important hockey skill. Players must be able to turn sharply, skate backwards, and perform many other maneuvers—all at top speed. Their skating must be so automatic that they can make any maneuver without taking their attention from the game.

Stickhandling is the use of the stick to control the puck. In the most common form of stickhandling, a player moves the puck first with one side of the blade and then with the other while skating. The player makes some sweeps of the stick wide and some narrow. In this way, the player keeps the opponents guessing as to the next move and also makes it difficult for them to steal the puck.

Passing is the means by which a player who has possession of the puck transfers it to a teammate. In most cases, players use their sticks to propel the puck toward a receiver. Such passes are either *flat passes* or *flip passes.* To make a flat pass, the passer sends the puck traveling along the surface of the ice. To make a flip pass, the player causes it to rise off the ice to avoid interception by an opponent. Sometimes, a passer simply leaves the puck behind so that a teammate can get it. Such a pass is called a *drop pass.*

Shooting is the skill needed to drive the puck into the goal cage and so score goals. As in passing, a player propels the puck with the stick. Most shots are either *wrist shots* or *slap shots.* In a wrist shot, the blade does not leave the ice. The player uses strong wrist action to propel the puck. For a slap shot, the player raises the stick in a backswing and brings it down against the puck with great force. Slap shots are more powerful but less accurate than wrist shots.

Checking is the chief means a player uses to get the puck away from an opponent. There are two main types of checks: *stick checks* and *body checks.* For a stick check, a player uses the stick to hook or poke the puck away from an opponent's stick. In a body check, a player bumps against an opponent with a hip or shoulder to try to block the opponent's progress or throw the opponent off balance. Both stick checking and body checking are allowed only against a player in control of the puck or the last player to control it. In professional and most amateur play, body checks may be made anywhere on the

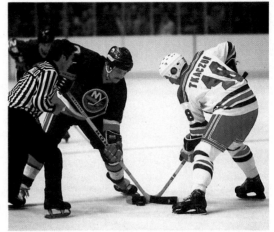

A face-off begins each period and starts play after a game has been stopped for any reason. An official drops the puck between two opposing players, who try to hit it to a teammate.

ice. In U.S. high school and college hockey, they are allowed only in the defending and neutral zones.

A goalie needs a special set of skills. To block shots at the net, the goalie must be able to move nearly every part of the body and all the equipment quickly, surely, and almost automatically.

Playing the game. Each period begins with a face-off at the center face-off spot. A face-off also starts play again after it has been stopped for any reason. These face-offs are held at various face-off spots, depending on the reason for stopping play. The team that gains control of the puck as a result of the face-off tries to move it into scoring position. During play, the puck must be kept moving. If it is hit over the boards, held by the goalie, out of the referee's sight, frozen between opposing players, or is otherwise temporarily out of play, an official blows a whistle for a face-off.

A player may *carry* (move) the puck along the ice, pass it to a teammate, or shoot it at the goal. But the rules limit these plays in certain ways. One extremely important rule states that no player of an attacking team may be in the attacking zone ahead of the puck. One member of the team must carry or shoot the puck across the attacking blue line before any other player on the team crosses the line. For violations of this rule, an official signals the offending team *offside* and conducts a face-off in the neutral zone.

A player may pass to a teammate anywhere in the same zone. The player may also pass from the defending zone to a teammate in their team's half of the neutral zone. If the pass is received beyond the centerline, an official signals the pass offside and conducts a face-off where the play began. In games played without a centerline, a player may pass from the defending zone to a teammate anywhere in the neutral zone.

Offensive play centers on the attack, or *rush,* against the opposing team's goal. An attacking team moves the puck down the ice until one player is in position to carry or shoot it across the defending team's blue line. If the player carries the puck across the blue line, teammates rush to an open area to receive a pass. If the player

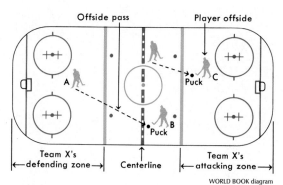

Offside pass   Player offside

Puck   C

A

Puck   B

Team X's   Team X's
←—defending zone—→ Centerline ←—attacking zone—→

WORLD BOOK diagram

Offside plays rank among the most common hockey violations. There are two types of offsides, illustrated above by players on Team X. An *offside pass* violation occurs when a player (A) hits the puck from the defending zone to a teammate (B) across the centerline. A *player offside* violation occurs when a player (C) enters his or her team's attacking zone ahead of the puck.

shoots the puck across the blue line, one or more teammates rush in to gain control of the puck. But a player remains back for defensive purposes in case the other team gets control of the puck.

Once the attackers control the puck in the opposing team's end zone, the attacking defensemen station themselves as *point men* at opposite ends of their opponents' blue line. Their main job is to keep the puck in the attacking zone. The center tries for shots at the goal or passes the puck to a wing in better scoring position. The center and one of the wings go after any shot that misses the goal or is batted away by the goalie and try to score it on the *rebound*. If the opposing team gets the puck, the attackers quickly begin checking to regain control. Checking an opponent who controls the puck in the opponent's defending zone is called *forechecking*. Throughout an attack, one wing must always play far enough back to go after an opponent who breaks into the neutral zone with the puck.

The most spectacular offensive play is the *power play*. This play occurs when one team is short-handed. The other team sends all its players except the goalie into the attacking zone in an all-out drive to score.

Defensive play is designed to break up attacks. At the start of an attack, both defensemen begin skating rapidly toward their defending zone. They skate backward to keep close watch on the attackers and use their sticks to prevent a pass or a shot at the goal. Each defending wing guards the attacking wing on the defending wing's side of the ice. After the puck crosses the defending team's blue line, one defenseman takes a position in front of the goalie. The other defenseman guards the puck carrier. The defending center goes after the puck. Each defending wing guards the attacking defenseman stationed on the wing's side of the ice as a point man. All the defending players must check strongly. Their chief aim is to get control of the puck and carry or pass it out of their end zone. Checking to break up an attack is called *back-checking*. To defend themselves against power plays, teams may send in substitutes called *penalty killers*. These players are expert at back-checking and keeping control of the puck.

An illegal defensive play called *icing the puck,* or

icing, occurs when a defending player shoots the puck from the defending team's half of the ice across the opponents' goal line. But for icing to occur, a player on the other team must be the first player to touch the puck after it crosses the goal line. In games played without a centerline, icing occurs when a player shoots the puck from the defending zone across both blue lines and the opponents' goal line. The penalty for icing is a face-off in the offending team's end zone. There are two major exceptions to the icing rule. If an iced puck enters the net, it counts as a score. In addition, a short-handed team may ice the puck as a defensive play.

Violations and penalties. Offside plays and icing account for most violations of the rules. For these violations, the offending team risks losing the puck in the resulting face-off. For more serious violations, players receive penalties ranging from 2 minutes in the penalty box to removal from the game. But a team must always have at least four players on the ice. If a third player is penalized while two teammates are in the penalty box, a substitute may replace the player on the ice. The third player's penalty time does not begin until one of the first two penalized players has served the penalty. But this player may not return to the ice until play is stopped for some reason. When the player returns, the substitute must leave the ice. A teammate may serve a goalie's penalties in most cases.

Hockey has five main kinds of penalties: (1) minor penalties, (2) major penalties, (3) misconduct penalties, (4) match penalties, and (5) penalty shots.

Minor penalties are given for such violations as holding or tripping an opponent or hooking an opponent with a stick. They bring 2 minutes in the penalty box. The team must play short-handed until the penalty is served or until the other side scores a goal. But if the same minor penalty is awarded against a player on each team at the same time, substitutes may replace both players.

Major penalties are given mainly for fighting and bring 5 minutes in the penalty box. The penalized team must play short-handed, and the entire penalty must be served. But if a player on each team receives a major penalty at the same time, substitutes may replace both players on the ice.

Misconduct penalties are given chiefly for improper behavior toward an official. A misconduct penalty brings 10 minutes in the penalty box, but a substitute may replace the penalized player. A *game misconduct penalty* is given chiefly for more serious offenses against officials. In the NHL, it is also awarded against the first player to join a fight between two other players. The offending player is removed for the rest of the game, but a substitute may replace him.

Match penalties are given for deliberately injuring or attempting to injure an opponent. The offending player is removed for the rest of the game. But a substitute may replace the player after 5 or 10 minutes, depending on the seriousness of the offense.

Penalty shots are free shots at the opposing team's goal defended only by the goalie. They are chiefly awarded against a defending team when an attacking player with a clear shot at the goal is pulled down from behind and so prevented from taking the shot.

The officials. The chief officials are the *referee* and two *linesmen*. They wear skates and are stationed on the ice. The referee supervises the entire game and decides nearly all penalties. The linesmen call offside and icing violations and conduct most face-offs.

All other officials work off the ice. The *game time-keeper* keeps track of actual playing time. The game timekeeper stops the official clock when a penalty or face-off is called and starts it again when play resumes. The *penalty timekeeper* keeps track of the time a player serves in the penalty box. The *official scorer* records the goals scored, the names of the scorers, and the players who score *assists*—that is, passes or other plays that contribute to goals. Two *goal judges,* one behind each goal cage off the ice, carefully watch shots at the goal. They turn on the red goal light to show that a puck has entered the net and scored. The *statistician* records team and individual performances.

Organized hockey

Professional leagues. There is one major professional hockey league in the United States and Canada—the National Hockey League. From 1972 to 1979, a second league, the World Hockey Association (WHA), also existed. In addition, there are several minor professional leagues. Most are associated with a particular NHL team to provide playing experience and training for that team's beginning players.

The regular hockey season lasts from October to April. In the NHL, the top four teams in each division qualify for post-season play-offs, which may last as late as June. The finalists play for the Stanley Cup. Finalists in the WHA play-offs had competed for the Avco World Trophy. The NHL also awards about 15 individual and team trophies annually, including the Art Ross Trophy to the leading scorer; the Hart Memorial Trophy to the player judged most valuable to his team; the Lady Byng Trophy for sportsmanship; and the William M. Jennings Trophy to the goalie or goalies on the team that had the fewest goals scored against it.

Amateur organization. There are four main types of amateur hockey competition: (1) U.S. and Canadian com-

Hockey penalty signals

Signals for penalties stop play at once. If the penalty is against the defending team, the official signals a *delayed call* and stops play when the other team loses possession of the puck.

WORLD BOOK photos by Dan Miller

Holding

Charging

Icing the puck

Slashing

Cross-checking

Boarding

Interference

High-sticking

Tripping

Hooking

Misconduct

Delayed call of penalty

petition, excluding U.S. high school, college, and women's play; (2) international competition; (3) U.S. high school and college competition; and (4) women's play. Each type has its own structure and set of rules.

The Amateur Hockey Association of the United States (AHAUS) regulates U.S. amateur play. In Canada, the Canadian Amateur Hockey Association (CAHA) is the controlling group. The rules of both resemble the professional rules. The AHAUS and the CAHA set up local organizations, hold tournaments, and establish amateur classifications by age groups. The main classifications are *mite* (age 9 and under); *squirt* (ages 10 and 11); *pee wee* (ages 12 and 13); *bantam* (ages 14 and 15); *midget* (ages 16 and 17); *junior* (ages 18 and 19); and *senior* (age 20 and above). Teams in each classification compete with one another.

International, or *world amateur,* hockey is regulated by the International Ice Hockey Federation (IIHF), which has its headquarters in London. Amateur hockey organizations from about 30 countries belong to the IIHF. They include the AHAUS and the CAHA. Players on teams registered with IIHF members are called *registered amateurs.* Canada has about 600,000 registered amateurs. The United States has about 250,000.

Each year, outstanding amateur teams from a number of countries compete for the world amateur championship. Until 1972, every fourth world competition was held as part of the Winter Olympics. Since 1972, the world and Olympic championships have been held separately (see **Olympic Games** [table: Ice hockey]). The IIHF establishes the rules for these contests. Most IIHF members have adopted IIHF rules.

The National Collegiate Athletic Association (NCAA) sets up the rules for U.S. college hockey and holds annual college championship matches. Most high school teams in the United States follow NCAA rules. Canadian

National Hockey League Stanley Cup Finals

Season	Winner	Loser	Games won-lost	Season	Winner	Loser	Games won-lost
1917-1918	Toronto Arenas	Vancouver Millionaires	3-2	1952-1953	Montreal Canadiens	Boston Bruins	4-1
1918-1919	No winner*			1953-1954	Detroit Red Wings	Montreal Canadiens	4-3
1919-1920	Ottawa Senators	Seattle Metropolitans	3-2	1954-1955	Detroit Red Wings	Montreal Canadiens	4-3
1920-1921	Ottawa Senators	Vancouver Millionaires	3-2	1955-1956	Montreal Canadiens	Detroit Red Wings	4-1
1921-1922	Toronto St. Pats	Vancouver Millionaires	3-2	1956-1957	Montreal Canadiens	Boston Bruins	4-1
1922-1923	Ottawa Senators	Edmonton Eskimos	2-0	1957-1958	Montreal Canadiens	Boston Bruins	4-2
1923-1924	Montreal Canadiens	Calgary Tigers	2-0	1958-1959	Montreal Canadiens	Toronto Maple Leafs	4-1
1924-1925	Victoria Cougars†	Montreal Canadiens	3-1	1959-1960	Montreal Canadiens	Toronto Maple Leafs	4-0
1925-1926	Montreal Maroons	Victoria Cougars	3-1	1960-1961	Chicago Black Hawks	Detroit Red Wings	4-2
1926-1927	Ottawa Senators	Boston Bruins	2-0	1961-1962	Toronto Maple Leafs	Chicago Black Hawks	4-2
1927-1928	New York Rangers	Montreal Maroons	3-2	1962-1963	Toronto Maple Leafs	Detroit Red Wings	4-1
1928-1929	Boston Bruins	New York Rangers	2-0	1963-1964	Toronto Maple Leafs	Detroit Red Wings	4-3
1929-1930	Montreal Canadiens	Boston Bruins	2-0	1964-1965	Montreal Canadiens	Chicago Black Hawks	4-3
1930-1931	Montreal Canadiens	Chicago Black Hawks	3-2	1965-1966	Montreal Canadiens	Detroit Red Wings	4-2
1931-1932	Toronto Maple Leafs	New York Rangers	3-0	1966-1967	Toronto Maple Leafs	Montreal Canadiens	4-2
1932-1933	New York Rangers	Toronto Maple Leafs	3-1	1967-1968	Montreal Canadiens	St. Louis Blues	4-0
1933-1934	Chicago Black Hawks	Detroit Red Wings	3-1	1968-1969	Montreal Canadiens	St. Louis Blues	4-0
1934-1935	Montreal Maroons	Toronto Maple Leafs	3-0	1969-1970	Boston Bruins	St. Louis Blues	4-0
1935-1936	Detroit Red Wings	Toronto Maple Leafs	3-1	1970-1971	Montreal Canadiens	Chicago Black Hawks	4-3
1936-1937	Detroit Red Wings	New York Rangers	3-2	1971-1972	Boston Bruins	New York Rangers	4-2
1937-1938	Chicago Black Hawks	Toronto Maple Leafs	3-1	1972-1973	Montreal Canadiens	Chicago Black Hawks	4-2
1938-1939	Boston Bruins	Toronto Maple Leafs	4-1	1973-1974	Philadelphia Flyers	Boston Bruins	4-2
1939-1940	New York Rangers	Toronto Maple Leafs	4-2	1974-1975	Philadelphia Flyers	Buffalo Sabres	4-2
1940-1941	Boston Bruins	Detroit Red Wings	4-0	1975-1976	Montreal Canadiens	Philadelphia Flyers	4-0
1941-1942	Toronto Maple Leafs	Detroit Red Wings	4-3	1976-1977	Montreal Canadiens	Boston Bruins	4-0
1942-1943	Detroit Red Wings	Boston Bruins	4-0	1977-1978	Montreal Canadiens	Boston Bruins	4-2
1943-1944	Montreal Canadiens	Chicago Black Hawks	4-0	1978-1979	Montreal Canadiens	New York Rangers	4-1
1944-1945	Toronto Maple Leafs	Detroit Red Wings	4-3	1979-1980	New York Islanders	Philadelphia Flyers	4-2
1945-1946	Montreal Canadiens	Boston Bruins	4-1	1980-1981	New York Islanders	Minnesota North Stars	4-1
1946-1947	Toronto Maple Leafs	Montreal Canadiens	4-2	1981-1982	New York Islanders	Vancouver Canucks	4-0
1947-1948	Toronto Maple Leafs	Detroit Red Wings	4-0	1982-1983	New York Islanders	Edmonton Oilers	4-0
1948-1949	Toronto Maple Leafs	Detroit Red Wings	4-0	1983-1984	Edmonton Oilers	New York Islanders	4-1
1949-1950	Detroit Red Wings	New York Rangers	4-3	1984-1985	Edmonton Oilers	Philadelphia Flyers	4-1
1950-1951	Toronto Maple Leafs	Montreal Canadiens	4-1	1985-1986	Montreal Canadiens	Calgary Flames	4-1
1951-1952	Detroit Red Wings	Montreal Canadiens	4-0	1986-1987	Edmonton Oilers	Philadelphia Flyers	4-3

*Play-off between Montreal Canadiens and Seattle Metropolitans not finished because of influenza epidemic in Seattle.
†Member, Pacific Coast League.

National Hockey League

Clarence Campbell Conference

James Norris Division
Chicago Black Hawks
Detroit Red Wings
Minnesota North Stars
St. Louis Blues
Toronto Maple Leafs

Conn Smythe Division
Calgary Flames
Edmonton Oilers
Los Angeles Kings
Vancouver Canucks
Winnipeg Jets

Prince of Wales Conference

Lester Patrick Division
New Jersey Devils
New York Islanders
New York Rangers
Philadelphia Flyers
Pittsburgh Penguins
Washington Capitals

Charles F. Adams Division
Boston Bruins
Buffalo Sabres
Hartford Whalers
Montreal Canadiens
Quebec Nordiques

Early hockey games, like this 1893 match in Montreal, featured unmarked rinks. The action was less rough than in today's games, and so the players needed little protective equipment.

high school and college teams follow CAHA rules.

Amateur hockey for women has gained increasing popularity in the United States and Canada. Women use the same rules that men use. But in most women's games, no checking is allowed and there is little body contact. In the United States, women's teams are divided into three classes. They are *open* (age 16 and older); *teen* (ages 13 to 15); and *junior* (ages 8 to 12).

History of hockey

Beginnings. Hockey developed in Canada. According to the CAHA, British soldiers in Kingston, Ont., and Halifax, N.S., played the first games, about 1855. The idea for ice hockey probably came from the older game of field hockey. In field hockey, the players use curved sticks to hit a rubber ball through a goal at each end of a playing field (see **Field hockey**).

In the 1870's, a group of students at McGill University in Montreal drew up the first formal ice hockey rules. The rules substituted a puck for the earlier rubber ball and set the number of players on a team at nine. The McGill rules were widely distributed during the 1880's. Hockey teams began to spring up in many parts of Canada. By 1893, the game was so popular that the governor general, Baron Stanley of Preston, donated a silver bowl to be awarded annually to Canada's champion hockey team. In 1894, a Montreal team won the first Stanley Cup match. The first hockey games in the United States were probably played about 1895 at Yale University and Johns Hopkins University.

Professional hockey. The first professional hockey team was organized at Houghton, Mich., in 1903. Most of the players were Canadians. Hockey's first professional league, the International Pro Hockey League, was started in 1904. It included teams from both Canada and the United States. Several other professional leagues were started soon after 1904.

The NHL was formed in Montreal in 1917 from an earlier professional league, the National Hockey Association. The original NHL teams were the Montreal Canadiens, Montreal Wanderers, Ottawa Senators, and Toronto Arenas. Six-man teams, first introduced in 1904, became the rule in the newly organized NHL.

In 1924, the Boston Bruins became the first U.S. team to join the NHL. A team each from Chicago, Detroit, and Pittsburgh and two teams from New York City joined in 1925 and 1926. The Pittsburgh team and one New York

City team later dropped out. By 1942, the NHL consisted of the Boston Bruins, Chicago Black Hawks, Detroit Red Wings, Montreal Canadiens, New York Rangers, and Toronto Maple Leafs. This membership remained unchanged until 1967.

Famous players and All-Star teams. The early hockey stars were almost all Canadians, as are most professional stars today. They included such colorful players as Newsy Lalonde, Joe Malone, Lester Patrick, and Cyclone Taylor. Hockey grew more popular after U.S. teams joined the NHL. Hockey fans of the late 1920's and early 1930's flocked to see such stars as forwards Bill Cook and Howie Morenz; defensemen King Clancy, Lionel Conacher, Ching Johnson, and Eddie Shore; and goalies Chuck Gardiner and George Hainsworth. Clancy, Cook, Gardiner, Johnson, Morenz, and Shore were named to the first annual NHL hockey All-Star teams. Hockey writers and broadcasters began the tradition of naming players to a first and second All-Star team just after the 1930-1931 season.

The NHL held its first annual All-Star Game in 1947. The All-Star team for this game was selected from the first and second All-Star teams of the preceding season. It included such players as forwards Doug Bentley and his brother Max, Ted Lindsay, Maurice Richard, and Milt Schmidt; defensemen Ken Reardon and Jack Stewart; and goalies Frank Brimsek and Bill Durnan. The All-Star team met the Toronto Maple Leafs, the 1947 Stanley Cup winners. The All-Stars won the game.

Today, first and second All-Star teams are chosen from both NHL divisions. A team of West All-Stars meets a team of East All-Stars for the All-Star Game. Since 1947, the games have featured such forwards as Jean Beliveau, Bobby Clarke, Marcel Dionne, Phil Esposito, Bernie Geoffrion, Wayne Gretzky, Gordie Howe, Bobby Hull, and Stan Mikita. Defensemen have included Doug Harvey, Guy Lapointe, Bobby Orr, Pierre Pilote, and Denis Potvin. Among the All-Star team goalies have been Ken Dryden, Tony Esposito, Ed Giacomin, Glenn Hall, Bernie Parent, Jacques Plante, and Terry Sawchuk. Since the 1985-1986 season, hockey fans have chosen the All-Star teams.

The Hockey Hall of Fame opened in Toronto in 1961.

It honors former players, referees, and other people who helped develop and promote the sport.

Amateur development. The IIHF was founded in 1908. The first amateur world championship was held in 1920 as part of the Olympic Games and marked the beginning of Olympic hockey competition. Canadian teams won most world and Olympic championships until the 1950's, when Soviet teams began a string of victories. The United States has won two amateur world titles—in 1933 and in 1960 as part of the Winter Olympics.

The CAHA was founded in 1914 and began organizing Canadian amateur hockey on a national basis. The AHAUS was founded in 1937 and by the early 1950's had organized U.S. amateur hockey nationally. The NCAA started its annual tournaments in 1948.

For many years, U.S. amateur hockey was limited largely to the northernmost states. Since the 1940's, many communities have built indoor rinks so that hockey can be played in any weather. Today, hockey is played in almost every state.

The World Ice Hockey Championships. Since 1924, various national teams have competed in the World Ice Hockey Championships. These championships take place annually, except during years when the Olympic Games are held. Professional hockey players may compete in the championships. But many of the best NHL players have been unable to play in them, because the championships take place while NHL teams are playing for the Stanley Cup.

Recent developments. During the 1960's, Canada tried to arrange a hockey match between the best Canadian and Soviet players. The Soviet Union rejected the offer because almost all of Canada's top players are professionals. The Soviets, on the other hand, take pride in their amateur standing. But in 1972, the Soviet Union let a Soviet team meet a team of Canada's top professionals for an eight-game tournament. Canada won four games, lost three, and tied one. In 1976, 1981, and 1984, six national teams, including teams from Canada and the Soviet Union, competed in the first Canada Cup tournaments. Canada won the tournament in 1976 and 1984. The Soviet Union won it in 1981. In 1979, a Soviet team won a three-game tournament, called the Challenge Cup, against an NHL all-star team. The Soviet team won two of the games and lost one.

During the late 1960's and the 1970's, professional hockey expanded to cities throughout the United States and Canada. The NHL began an expansion program in 1967, adding new divisions and enlarging the play-off structure to allow more professional hockey teams to compete.

The WHA was organized in 1971 and began its first season in 1972. It started with 12 teams, but by 1978 financial problems had reduced the number of teams to 6. After the 1978-1979 season, the WHA disbanded and four of its teams joined the NHL. These teams were the Edmonton Oilers, the New England (now Hartford) Whalers, the Quebec Nordiques, and the Winnipeg Jets.

Gordie Howe

Related articles in *World Book* include:

Esposito, Phil	Hull, Bobby	Richard, Maurice
Field hockey	Ice skating (picture:	Ringette
Gretzky, Wayne	Hockey skates)	Stanley Cup
Howe, Gordie	Orr, Bobby	

Outline

I. **How to play hockey**
  A. The rink
  B. Playing time
  C. The starting lineup
  D. Equipment
  E. Hockey skills
  F. Playing the game
  G. Offensive play
  H. Defensive play
  I. Violations and penalties
  J. The officials
II. **Organized hockey**
  A. Professional leagues
  B. Amateur organization
III. **History**

Questions

What are the only times that play is normally stopped during most hockey games?
Which player on a hockey team is the only one allowed to catch the puck?
What organizations regulate U.S., Canadian, and world amateur hockey?
What are the names of the three zones into which a hockey rink is divided?
What are the five main kinds of hockey penalties?
When was the NHL formed?
What are *stick checks? Body checks*?
When may players be substituted during a game?
What are *point men*? What is their main job?

Additional resources

Dryden, Ken. *The Game: A Thoughtful and Provocative Look at a Life in Hockey.* Times Books (New York City); Macmillan (Toronto), 1983.
Fischler, Stan and Shirley. *The Hockey Encyclopedia: The Complete Record of Professional Ice Hockey.* Macmillan, 1983. *Everybody's Hockey Book.* Scribner, 1984.
MacLean, Norman. *Hockey Basics.* Prentice-Hall, 1983. For younger readers.
Sporting News Hockey Guide. The Sporting News. An annual publication.

Hodgkin, Dorothy Crowfoot (1910-   ), a British chemist, won the 1964 Nobel Prize for determining the highly complex structure of the vitamin B_{12} molecule. She used X rays to make this important discovery. Knowledge of the molecular structure of vitamin B_{12} has enabled scientists to better understand how the body uses this substance to build red blood cells and prevent a disease called *pernicious anemia.*

Hodgkin has devoted her career to studying the structures of complex substances through a method called *X-ray crystallographic analysis* (see **X rays** [In scientific research]). During the 1940's, she determined the molecular structures of cholesterol iodide, penicillin, and other related organic compounds. In 1969, she revealed the three-dimensional structure of insulin, a protein used to treat diabetes.

Dorothy Crowfoot was born in Cairo, Egypt, and was educated in England. She graduated from Oxford University in 1931 and joined the faculty of the university in 1934. She conducted most of her research at Oxford. Crowfoot married Thomas L. Hodgkin, a historian, in 1937.   Marjorie C. Caserio

Hodgkin's disease is a type of cancer in which the lymph nodes become enlarged (see **Lymphatic system**). Other lymphoid tissues, such as the spleen, also may become swollen. Most victims of Hodgkin's disease are 20 to 40 years old. The disease, which strikes more men than women, may be fatal. Its cause is unknown.

Beginning in the 1960's, medical researchers discovered much about Hodgkin's disease and how to control or even conquer it. They learned that the disease

(1) spreads in a fairly predictable way from one group of lymph nodes to the next; (2) takes a relatively long time to spread to other areas of the body; (3) can usually be treated successfully with X rays in early stages; and (4) can often be treated successfully with drugs in advanced stages.

Hodgkin's disease resembles other diseases that also cause swelling of the lymph nodes. Physicians identify the condition by the presence in the swollen tissue of large cells called *Reed-Sternberg cells.* Most of these large cells have two nuclei. Hodgkin's disease was first described by Thomas Hodgkin, an English physician, in 1832.   Stanley Yachnin

Hoffa, *HAHF uh,* **James Riddle** (1913-1975?), an American labor leader, was international president of the Teamsters Union from 1958 to 1971. He disappeared in 1975. Police believe he may have been kidnapped and murdered. Hoffa helped increase the influence of the Teamsters, one of the strongest unions in the United States. In 1964, he signed the first national contract with trucking companies in Teamster history.

As a labor leader, Hoffa became a much-debated public figure. He was indicted by several grand juries on a variety of charges, including bribery and misusing union funds. He successfully defended himself several times. But in 1964, he was convicted of jury tampering and misusing union funds. In 1967, he began serving an eight-year prison term for the jury tampering conviction. In 1969, he was sentenced to an additional five years for the union funds conviction. He was released from prison in late 1971 after President Richard M. Nixon reduced his sentence and he received time off for good behavior.

Hoffa was born in Brazil, Ind. He joined the Teamsters in 1932 as a warehouseman.   James G. Scoville

Hoffer, *HAHF fur,* **Eric** (1902-1983), was a former longshoreman who became widely known as a political and social philosopher. His first book, *The True Believer* (1951), developed from his interest in the psychological makeup of the politically, socially, and economically disfranchised. In the book, Hoffer considered the nature and appeal of mass movements, and offered psychological observations on the nature of the people who join them. He believed that the zeal that characterizes these people is bred by frustration. Their fanaticism increases when the frustration increases.

Hoffer was born in New York City, and had little formal education. He was almost blind until he was 15. He was a migratory worker in California from 1920 to 1943, then became a longshoreman. Hoffer's other works include *The Ordeal of Change* (1963) and *The Temper of Our Time* (1967).   Stephen A. Erickson

Hoffman, Dustin (1937-   ), is an American actor. He is known for his skillful performances in unusual and demanding motion-picture and stage roles. Hoffman won the 1979 Academy Award as best actor for the film *Kramer vs. Kramer.*

Dustin Lee Hoffman was born in Los Angeles and studied acting at the Pasadena Playhouse. In 1958, he moved to New York City, where he appeared in several plays. Hoffman made his film debut in *The Tiger Makes Out* in 1967. He first won fame for his portrayal of a confused college graduate in *The Graduate* (1967).

Hoffman played an Indian scout in the Western *Little*

Big Man (1970). He starred as the controversial comedian Lenny Bruce in *Lenny* (1974) and appeared in the political thriller *All the President's Men* (1976). Hoffman played a man impersonating a woman in the comedy *Tootsie* (1982). Other films in which Hoffman appeared include *Midnight Cowboy* (1969), *Straw Dogs* (1971), *Papillon* (1973), *Marathon Man* (1976), *Straight Time* (1978),

The Howard Frank Archives

Dustin Hoffman

and *Ishtar* (1987). Hoffman returned to the stage in 1984 to star in a highly praised revival of the American drama *Death of a Salesman* (see **Drama** [picture: Willy Loman]).
          John F. Mariani

Hoffmann, *HAHF muhn,* **Ernst Theodor Amadeus,** *TAY aw DOHR AH mah DAY us* (1776-1822), was a German writer. He mingled weird and fantastic events with situations of everyday life. Hoffmann's imaginative blend of romanticism and realism influenced Edgar Allan Poe and Charles Baudelaire. Some of Hoffmann's stories were collected in *Fantastic Tales* (1813-1815) and *Night Pieces* (1817). His novels include *The Elixirs of the Devil* (1815-1816) and *Views on Life of the Tomcat Murr* (1820-1822). His *Mademoiselle de Scudéry* (1818) was a forerunner of the detective story.

Hoffmann was born in Königsberg, Germany (now Soviet Kaliningrad). He was an author, cartoonist, composer, musician, opera director, and orchestra conductor. His life and works inspired Jacques Offenbach's opera *The Tales of Hoffmann.*   Jeffrey L. Sammons

Hofmann, *HAHF muhn,* **Hans** (1880-1966), became famous for his abstract painting. His work as an artist and teacher greatly influenced the development of abstract art in the United States, especially after World War II (1939-1945). Many of his works are so thickly painted that the surface is rough. Hofmann often used such brilliant colors that his paintings seem to explode. There is a sense of action and space in his work. Hofmann's painting *The Golden Wall* appears in the **Painting** article.

Hofmann was born in Weissenburg, Bavaria, and studied art in Paris from 1904 to 1914. He worked with Henri Matisse there. In 1934, Hofmann opened an art school in New York City.   Allen S. Weller

See also **Drawing** (picture: A crayon drawing).

Hofmannsthal, *HOHF mahns tahl,* **Hugo von** (1874-1929), was an Austrian poet and playwright. He is best known for his *librettos* (words) for the operas of the German composer Richard Strauss. Hofmannsthal and Strauss began working together with *Elektra,* first staged in 1909. They continued with *Der Rosenkavalier* (1911), *Ariadne auf Naxos* (1912), *The Woman Without a Shadow* (1919), *The Egyptian Helen* (1928), and *Arabella,* produced in 1933 after Hofmannsthal's death.

Hofmannsthal was born and educated in Vienna. While still a young man, he created a literary sensation in Vienna with a series of symbolic verse dramas. Hofmannsthal's best-known play is *Everyman* (1911), an adaptation of an English medieval morality play.

See also **Strauss, Richard.**

Hogs are a major source of income for many farmers in the United States, especially in the Corn Belt of the Midwest. This photo shows a Yorkshire sow nursing her pigs.

Wendy Neefus, Animals Animals/Earth Scenes

Hog. About a fourth of the meat eaten in the United States comes from hogs. These animals provide pork, which is eaten as pork chops, ham, bacon, and sausage. The fat, skin, hair, glands, and other parts of hogs are used to make lard, leather, brushes, soap, fertilizer, glue, medicines, and many other products.

Farmers in almost every country raise hogs. Both young and adult hogs are also called *pigs* or *swine.* Young hogs are almost always called *pigs.* Farmers who raise hogs are sometimes called *pork producers.* Hogs are among the most intelligent of the *domesticated* (tamed) animals. Some people consider them dirty, yet hogs keep themselves cleaner than most other farm animals do. However, during warm weather, hogs often *wallow* (roll about) in mud to keep cool.

There are about 764 million hogs on farms throughout the world. China has the most hogs, about 40 per cent of the world total. The Soviet Union ranks second and the United States ranks third in hog production. About one-fifth of the farms in the United States raise hogs. Hogs rank with cattle, poultry, and dairy products as a chief source of farm income in the country.

Selective breeding, better housing, and more nutritious feeds have resulted in improved hogs. Hogs today grow faster on less food and produce more lean meat and less fat than did hogs raised in the past. Corn is one of the main ingredients in hog feed, and hogs eat about 20 per cent of the corn grown in the United States. For this reason, hog raising has become concentrated on "corn-hog farms" in the Corn Belt of the Midwest. Most of the hogs raised in the United States every year are raised in the Corn Belt states of Illinois, Indiana, Iowa, Minnesota, Missouri, Nebraska, and Ohio. Thousands of boys and girls raise hogs as part of their activities in 4-H Clubs and the Future Farmers of America.

Kinds of hogs

There are many kinds of hogs raised around the world. Because hogs have a short reproduction cycle, new breeds can be developed over a relatively short period of time. Often, such breeds reflect the climate and production methods of the region in which they are raised. In Europe, for example, each country has developed its own breeds of hogs. In the United States, re-

Main breeds of hogs

Breed	Place and date of origin	Identifying features
American Landrace	Indiana, 1930's	White; drooping ears; long body
Berkshire	England, 1700's	Black with white markings; erect ears; short snout
Chester White	Pennsylvania, early 1800's	White; drooping ears
Duroc	New York, early 1800's	Red; drooping ears
Hampshire	Kentucky, early 1800's	Black with white band around shoulders and front legs
Poland China	Ohio, late 1800's	Black with white markings; drooping ears
Spotted Swine	Ohio and Indiana, late 1800's	Black and white spotted
Yorkshire	England, early 1800's	White; erect ears

LaVern Weller & Sons (WORLD BOOK photo)

Durocs are a popular breed of hog in the United States because they produce large litters and gain weight rapidly.

gional differences among breeds of hogs are slight.

Farmers in the United States raise chiefly *crossbred* hogs. Crossbred hogs are produced by mating parents of different breeds. Crossbreds, also called *hybrids,* are more active at birth, grow more rapidly, and have higher reproduction rates than purebreds.

Hogs raised in the United States are classified as *meat-type* hogs. Meat-type hogs produce more lean meat in proportion to fat. Pork from such hogs is low in fat and is a good source of high-quality protein.

Main breeds. The eight commonly raised breeds of hogs in the United States are the American Landrace, Berkshire, Chester White, Duroc, Hampshire, Poland China, Spotted Swine, and Yorkshire. Farmers in the United States developed all these breeds except the Berkshire and Yorkshire, which were imported from England in the 1800's. The American Landrace breed includes hogs bred from Landrace stock from such countries as Denmark, England, Germany, and Sweden. No one breed is greatly superior to another in its ability to produce meat or to grow swiftly. However, pork producers are increasingly using Yorkshire and Landrace sows for crossbreeding because of their ability to produce large litters.

Other breeds. Common breeds of hogs in Europe include the Large White and the Landrace. Most European countries have their own Landrace breed. All such hogs are white and have droopy ears. The Large White is related to the Yorkshire breed raised in the United States. Pietrain is a muscular breed of hog found in Belgium, Luxembourg, and the Netherlands. There are about 40 breeds of hogs raised in China.

Garrett Beebe (WORLD BOOK photo)

Berkshires provide meat with little excess fat.

Hampshire Swine Registry

The Hampshire was developed in the United States.

American Landrace Association

The American Landrace is a long-bodied hog.

John W. Weber & Family (WORLD BOOK photo)

Spotted Swine may be mostly black or mostly white.

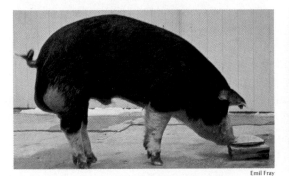

Emil Fray

Poland Chinas are often used for crossbreeding.

Lyle Bidner & Family (WORLD BOOK photo)

Chester Whites must have shade to avoid sunburn.

Hog terms

Barrow is a male hog whose reproductive organs have been removed by an operation.
Boar is a male hog of any age.
Farrow means to give birth to pigs.
Gilt is a female hog usually less than 1 year old that has not given birth to pigs.
Herd is a group of hogs.
Litter is the group of pigs a sow gives birth to at one time.
Pig is a young hog. The term is sometimes used for a hog of any age.
Pork is the flesh, or meat, of hogs.
Shote, or **shoat,** is a pig about 8 weeks old that has been *weaned* (taken off its mother's milk).
Sow is an adult female hog.
Swine is another name for hogs.

Wild hogs are strong, fierce animals that live in forests and jungles in many parts of the world. They include the babirussa, or babirusa, of the East Indies; the wart hog of Africa; and the wild boar that lives in some parts of Europe, Asia, and Africa. Wild hogs called *razorbacks* (because they have sharp, narrow backs) live in the Southeastern United States and in the West Indies. They are descended from tame hogs that escaped from farms and became wild again. Peccaries are wild, piglike animals that live in some parts of North and South America. They are not true hogs. See **Babirussa; Boar, Wild; Peccary; Wart hog.**

How we use hogs

Food. We eat the meat of hogs as pork chops, spareribs, loin roasts, ham, bacon, and sausage. Popular sausages made from pork include wieners, bologna, bratwurst, mettwurst, braunschweiger, and salami. Some hog meat, such as pig's feet and knuckles, is pickled. *Chitterlings* (fried hog intestines) and fried pig skin are popular foods in some regions of the United States. People also eat such hog parts as the stomach, kidneys, liver, ears, brain, snout, jowls, lips, tongue, and throat. Lard used for cooking is made from hog fat. Some religions, such as Islam and Judaism, forbid their followers to eat pork because they regard hogs as unclean.

Other uses. Tanneries process the skins of hogs into leather used for such products as belts, gloves, jackets, and shoes. The hair of the hog provides bristles for brushes. It is also used to stuff mattresses and baseball gloves, and to make insulating materials. Hog blood is used to make animal feeds, fertilizer, and medicines. Drug firms make insulin, ACTH, and other medicines from hog glands. Hog fat is made into lard, soap, candles, salves, shaving cream, explosives, and lubricating oils. The bones of the hog are ground for glue, fertilizer, animal feeds, and bone oil.

The bodies of hogs

The hog has a stout, strong body covered with coarse, bristly hair. The head and short, thick neck extend in a straight line from the body. The head ends in a snout. The hog's thick skin has no sweat glands to serve as a cooling system. Hogs like to wallow in mud because it helps them keep cool. Hogs have small eyes and poor eyesight. But a keen sense of smell helps them find food. They have short tails that are usually curled. Hogs grunt. They squeal when hurt or excited.

Size. Pigs weigh about $2\frac{1}{2}$ pounds (1.1 kilograms) at birth, and usually double their weight the first week. When fully grown, boars may weigh more than 500 pounds (230 kilograms) and sows more than 450 pounds (200 kilograms). The average adult boar weighs from 350 to 500 pounds (160 to 230 kilograms) and the average adult sow from 300 to 450 pounds (140 to 200 kilograms). Most hogs are sold when they are 6 to 7 months old and weigh from 210 to 250 pounds (95 to 115 kilograms). Hogs kept longer are usually used for breeding.

Snout. The hog's snout has a broad, leathery pad that includes the nostrils. The snout is very sensitive to touch. Hogs often use their snouts to root, or dig, for vegetable roots, one of their favorite foods.

Teeth. Hogs have a total of 34 or 44 teeth, depending on the species. Eight of these are *canine teeth* (pointed teeth) that often develop into sharp tusks, particularly in adult males. These tusks serve as tools for digging and as weapons. Farmers may clip the tusks off mature boars because they can cause injury. A hog protects itself by running away. But if cornered, it may charge and bite.

Feet. The hog has four toes on each foot. Each toe ends in a hoof. The two middle hoofs are divided on all hogs except the Mule-Foot breed. Mule-Foot hogs have a solid, or single-toed, hoof in the middle of each foot. The two other toes on each foot do not touch the ground when the hog stands.

Life history. Hogs reproduce rapidly and can be mated when about 8 months old. Sows carry their young about 114 days before *farrowing* (giving birth). Sows usually give birth to 8 to 12 pigs at a time, but the number may range up to 27 or more. Hogs reach full growth at $1\frac{1}{2}$ to 2 years of age and can live from 9 to 15 years. However, most hogs are marketed when they are 6 to 7 months old.

Raising hogs

Feeding. Farmers provide hogs with well-balanced diets. Carbohydrates from corn and such grains as sor-

Leading hog-raising states and provinces

Iowa	●●●●●●●●●●●●●●	14,800,000 hogs
Illinois	●●●●●	5,400,000 hogs
Minnesota	●●●●	4,270,000 hogs
Indiana	●●●●	4,200,000 hogs
Nebraska	●●●◖	3,900,000 hogs
Missouri	●●●◖	3,550,000 hogs
Ontario	●●●◖	3,545,000 hogs
Quebec	●●●◖	3,375,000 hogs
North Carolina	●●◖	2,300,000 hogs
Ohio	●●	2,100,000 hogs

Sources: U.S. Department of Agriculture; Statistics Canada. Figures are for 1983.

A hog farm has outdoor pens, called *feedlots,* where the animals eat and exercise. The hog farm in the photo at the left is located in South Dakota.

Phil Degginger, Bruce Coleman Inc.

ghum, barley, wheat, rye, and oats provide energy. Meals made from soybeans, linseed, cottonseed, peanuts, fish and meat scraps, skim milk, and *tankage* supply proteins. Tankage is a feed made from the bones, tendons, and other parts of animals. Hogs need several kinds of minerals, especially salt. Alfalfa and other pasture crops supply vitamins. However, such crops, also called *forages,* are difficult for hogs to digest. *Additives* are substances that are added to hog feeds to increase growth and improve health.

Shelter. There are two general methods of housing hogs. One method is to house them in buildings and in concrete yards. The other is to keep the hogs in such *open lots* as dirt yards or pastures. Such lots feature several small hog houses. Most young hogs spend their first few months in buildings, and later are moved to open lots. However, many pork producers keep all of their hogs in buildings.

Diseases. The most common diseases that attack hogs include respiratory infections, flu, and digestive disorders that cause diarrhea. *Mange* is a skin disease caused by tiny organisms called *mites* that burrow into the hog's skin. Hogs also may become infected with lice. Farmers kill mites and lice by spraying hogs with insecticides. Pork infected with *trichina worms* can cause trichinosis in people who eat the pork. Proper cooking of pork kills trichina worms.

Farrowing. A few days before a sow farrows, the farmer washes it and places it in a clean pen. The farmer must take special care to prevent the sow from crushing its young when it lies down. Many pork producers use farrowing stalls that confine each sow to a small space, but allow the pigs to move about. Farmers usually provide the pigs with a heated sleeping area. In addition to keeping them warm, the heat attracts the pigs and keeps them out of the sow's way.

Sows usually nurse their pigs for 3 to 5 weeks. After the pigs are *weaned* (taken off their mother's milk), they are fed a diet rich in protein. During this period, pigs are kept in houses called *nurseries.*

Marketing hogs. In the past, pigs were farrowed only during seasons with mild temperatures, generally spring and fall, and then marketed six to seven months later. Modern production methods now enable pork producers to farrow and market pigs throughout the year. This practice provides a consistent supply of pork products to consumers and makes better use of production facilities.

Some pork producers sell their hogs directly to a meat-processing plants. Others sell the animals through a broker or at a livestock auction. Still other farmers ship their hogs to a central market for sale at a later date.

History

Wild hogs roamed throughout Europe and other parts of the world as long as 6 million years ago. Scientists believe people began taming hogs about 8,000 years ago, during the Stone Age. Explorers and colonists from Spain, England, and other countries brought hogs to North and South America in the early 1500's.

Until the late 1940's, farmers in the United States classified hog breeds as *lard-type* or *bacon-type.* Lard-type hogs had more fat in proportion to lean meat. Meat-packing plants made the fat into lard that was used for cooking and other purposes. Shortenings made from vegetable oils largely replaced lard in the 1950's. In addition, petroleum products replaced lard as a lubricant and in the manufacture of soap. Farmers then began raising meat-type hogs.

Scientific classification. Hogs belong to the pig or hog family, Sudae. The European wild hog, from which domestic hogs are largely descended, is *Sus scrofa.*

William T. Ahlschwede

Related articles in *World Book* include:

Actinomycosis	Foot-and-mouth dis-	Peccary
Babirussa	ease	Pork
Bacon	Ham	Sausage
Bang's disease	Lard	Trichina
Boar, Wild	Meat	Undulant fever
Farm and farming	Meat packing	Wart hog
Fat		

Hogan is a house of the Navajo Indians of the American Southwest. Hogans may be round, square, or six-sided, and they may be constructed in many different ways. Most hogans are built of logs and earth, but some have stone walls. The most common hogan is probably a six-sided structure about 20 feet (6 meters) in diameter, with stacked log walls and a roof made of logs and dirt piled in a mound. Hogans have a single door, which almost always faces east. Michael D. Green

Hogan, Ben (1912-), an American golfer, was one of the greatest players in the history of the sport. Hogan won more than 60 tournaments, including the United States Open four times, the Professional Golfers' Association (PGA) tournament twice, the Masters twice, and the British Open once.

In 1949, a bus struck the car Hogan was driving. The collision fractured his left collarbone, left ankle, pelvis, and a rib. Hogan barely survived the injuries. Doctors feared he might not be able to walk again, much less play golf. Yet, just 17 months after the accident, Hogan won the 1950 U.S. Open. He played the tournament with his legs wrapped in bandages.

Hogan was born in Dublin, Tex. His full name is William Benjamin Hogan. He became famous for his determination to perfect his swing through hours of practice. Hogan was one of the smallest golf champions, weighing only 135 pounds (61.2 kilograms).

Marino A. Parascenzo

See also **Golf** (picture; tables).

Hogarth, *HOH gahrth,* **William** (1697-1764), was the leading English satirical painter of the 1700's. He was also a noted engraver and art critic. Hogarth became best known for paintings and engravings that humorously commented on the manners and morals of his time.

Hogarth created several series of paintings that told a story through a number of related scenes. These series include the eight paintings that make up *A Rake's Progress* (early 1730's) and the six paintings in *Marriage à la Mode* (1743). Hogarth made engravings of both series. The sale of these engravings made him wealthy.

Hogarth was born in London. He was trained to be a silversmith but decided to devote himself to fine art. Hogarth carefully studied the masters of Flemish, French, and Italian painting, but he was also inspired by the life he observed around him.

Hogarth first gained success as a painter with a picture based on *The Beggar's Opera* (1728), a musical play about criminals and corrupt public officials in London. This painting launched him on a career as a painter of comic scenes of everyday life. Hogarth also painted many realistic, often unflattering, portraits that reflected the artist's strong sense of color and his powers of observation.

Hogarth was a controversial and outspoken art critic whose opinions angered many of his fellow artists. He wrote one book, *The Analysis of Beauty* (1753), which combined practical advice on painting with his own theories of art. Douglas K. S. Hyland

See also **Fielding, Henry** (picture).

Hogg, Helen Sawyer (1905-), an American-born astronomer, became known for her research on *variable stars.* She discovered more than 250 of these stars, whose light varies in brightness. Hogg chiefly studied variable stars in *globular star clusters,* which are ball-like groups of stars in the Milky Way galaxy. Her work included measuring the *period* of many of these stars. A variable star's period is the time its light takes to change from bright to dim and back to bright. This information, in certain cases, helps astronomers determine the distance of the star from the earth.

Helen Battles Sawyer was born in Lowell, Mass. She and Frank S. Hogg, a Canadian astronomer, were married in 1930. She received a Ph.D. degree in astronomy

Oil painting on canvas (1743); the National Gallery, London

A Hogarth painting called *Signing the Marriage Contract* is part of a series of six paintings called *Marriage à la Mode.* The series provides a satirical commentary on upper-class marriage customs in England during Hogarth's time. The fathers of the bride and groom, seated at the right, arrange the bride's dowry with two lawyers. At the left, another lawyer explains financial details of the contract to the bride. The bored groom is at the far left.

from Radcliffe College in 1931. The first edition of her major work, *Catalogue of Variable Stars in Globular Clusters,* was published in 1939. In 1935, Hogg joined the faculty of the University of Toronto, where she conducted most of her research. In 1957, Hogg became the first woman to serve as president of the Royal Astronomical Society of Canada.   Raymond E. White

Hognose. See Adder.

Hogrogian, *HUH GROHG ih uhn,* **Nonny** (1932-   ), is an illustrator and designer of children's books. She won the Caldecott Medal in 1966 for her work in *Always Room for One More* by Sorche Nic Leodhas, and in 1972 for *One Fine Day,* which she also wrote. Many of Hogrogian's illustrations are *woodcuts* (pictures made from engraved wooden blocks). She illustrated *Gaelic Ghosts* (1964), also by Nic Leodhas; *Poems of Stephen Crane* (1964); and *The Fearsome Inn* (1967) by Isaac Bashevis Singer. Hogrogian was born in New York City.

Eloise Rue

Hogweed. See Ragweed.

Hohenstaufen, *HOH uhn SHTOW fuhn,* was the name of a princely family of medieval Germany which held the imperial throne from 1138 to 1254. The family took its name from the ancestral castle built at Staufen in southern Germany in the 1000's.

Frederick of Hohenstaufen received the duchy of Swabia from Emperor Henry IV as a reward for loyal service. He married Henry's daughter Agnes. Frederick's son, also called Frederick, claimed the hereditary right to the crown. But in 1125 the German princes reaffirmed their right of free election.

In 1138, a member of the Hohenstaufen family secured the German throne as Conrad III. Frederick I (Barbarossa), Henry VI, and Frederick II were also Hohenstaufen rulers.   Franklin D. Scott

See also **Frederick II** (Holy Roman emperor); **Germany** (History); **Henry** (VI), Germany.

Hohenzollern, *HOH uhn ZAHL uhrn,* is the name of the famous royal family that ruled Brandenburg, Prussia, and the German Empire. The name came from the family castle of Zollern in Swabia.

The Hohenzollerns started as counts. They became *electors* (rulers) of Brandenburg in 1417. In 1618, they began to add parts of Prussia to their holdings. Prussia was recognized as a kingdom in 1701 under Frederick I. After Germany was united in 1871, the Hohenzollerns were both kings of Prussia and German emperors. They established efficient governments and strong armies. The family lost its throne in World War I.

The best-known Hohenzollern rulers included Frederick William, the Great Elector; Frederick William I; Frederick II; and Wilhelm II. Wilhelm II was the German Kaiser during World War I.   Charles W. Ingrao

See also **Franco-Prussian War; Frederick II** (of Prussia); **Frederick III** (of Prussia); **Frederick William; Germany** (History); **Wilhelm.**

Hohokam. See Pima Indians.

Hohokam Pima National Monument, *huh HOH kuhm PEE muh,* is in south-central Arizona. It includes the remains of Hohokam Indian artwork, homes, irrigation canals, and tools dating from about 300 B.C. to A.D. 1200. Pima Indians, who believe the Hohokam were their ancestors, live in the area today. The United States government established the site as a national monument in 1972. The ruins are not yet on public display. For the area of the Hohokam Pima National Monument, see **National Park System** (table: National monuments).

Critically reviewed by the National Park Service

Hokkaido. See Japan (The land).

Hokusai, *HOH ku sy* or *HAW koo sy* (1760-1849), was a Japanese painter and designer of wood-block prints. Hokusai created an enormous number of paintings and prints using many styles and subjects, but he is best known for his landscape prints. Hokusai ranks with Hiroshige as the most famous Japanese landscape artist of the 1800's. Hokusai created several series of prints from 1823 to 1835. One famous set of prints consists of scenes of Mount Fuji as seen from various points, both near and far.

Katsushika Hokusai was born in Edo (now Tokyo). He studied under Katsukawa Shunshō, a leading Japanese artist. Hokusai had a long career, but he produced most of his important work after the age of 60. Although his works were popular, Hokusai spent much of his life in poverty. In the 1850's, after his death, some of his prints were displayed in the West. In the late 1800's, they influenced some Western artists, including James A. M. Whistler, Paul Gauguin, Vincent van Gogh, and Henri de Toulouse-Lautrec.   Robert A. Rorex

See also **Animal** (picture: People and animals).

Ono Waterfall (1827-1830), a color wood-block print; the British Museum, London

A Hokusai print shows the artist's skill in portraying landscapes. Hokusai's decorative style emphasizes the bold use of line. He generally limited his colors to blue, brown, and green.

Holbein, *HOHL byn,* **Hans, the Elder** (1465?-1534?), was a painter who worked in southern Germany and the region of Alsace in what is now France. Holbein was born in Augsburg, Germany, and maintained a workshop in the city during the late 1490's and early 1500's. His two sons, Ambrosius and Hans the Younger, received their first training as painters there.

Holbein's paintings include altarpieces for churches and convents. His best works, however, were his drawings, particularly portraits of his two sons done in a technique called *silverpoint.*   Jane Campbell Hutchison

Holbein, *HOHL byn,* **Hans, the Younger** (1497?-1543), ranks among the world's greatest portrait painters. Holbein was born in Augsburg, Germany. He received his earliest training there from his father and uncles, but moved to Switzerland when he was about 18 years old. Holbein worked in Basel, where he painted the portraits of many important people, notably the Dutch scholar Desiderius Erasmus. During this time, Holbein also designed a series of woodcuts called *The Dance of Death* (1523-1526) and painted several important religious works, such as *The Dead Christ* (1521).

Holbein spent the winter of 1526-1527 in London as the house guest of Erasmus' friend Saint Thomas More. Holbein painted and drew portraits of the More family and their friends. He settled permanently in England in 1532 and soon became court painter to King Henry VIII. His duties included designing jewelry and painting portraits of the king and other members of the royal court

Kunsthistorisches Museum, Vienna

A portrait by Hans Holbein the Younger shows how the artist realistically captured the character of his subjects. Holbein painted this picture of an unknown young merchant in 1541.

and household. Many of these portraits have a flat, patterned appearance, perhaps to emphasize that they represent royalty.   Jane Campbell Hutchison

For examples of Holbein's portraits, see **Clothing** (Puffs of fabric); **Edward (VI); Erasmus, Desiderius; Henry (VIII); More, Saint Thomas; Renaissance** (picture: Desiderius Erasmus).

Holberg, *HAHL barg,* **Ludvig,** *LOOTH vee* (1684-1754), was Scandinavia's first important playwright. Holberg, who wrote in Danish, modeled his comedies on the works of the Roman playwright Plautus. Like Plautus, Holberg used typical comic characters such as a talkative barber, an amateur politician, and a bragging soldier. He relied heavily on mistaken identities to add excitement to his plots. Among Holberg's best-known comedies are *The Political Thinker* (1722), *Jeppe of the Hill* (1722), and *Erasmus Montanus* (1731). Holberg also wrote *Peder Paars* (1719-1720), a satirical poem; and *Niels Klim* (1741), a prose satirical account of an imaginary underground journey. His *History of the Danish Kingdoms* (1732-1735) was the first cultural history of Denmark written in the Danish language.

Holberg was born in Bergen, Norway. He was educated in Copenhagen. Later he taught at the University of Copenhagen.   Richard B. Vowles

Holding company is any company which holds a majority or a large enough minority of the stock in another corporation to control its policies. The holding company may control the appointment of officers and may dictate business policies. Corporations controlled by holding companies are called *subsidiary* companies.

Corporation A might buy controlling interest in both Corporations 1 and 2. Corporation B might similarly buy control of Corporations 3 and 4. Corporations A and B have become holding companies, and Corporations 1, 2, 3, and 4 have become subsidiary companies. A third large corporation, C, might buy control of both Corporations A and B. This process, called *pyramiding,* has created financial empires, especially in public utilities, banking, and manufacturing.   Robert B. Carson

See also **Corporation; Antitrust laws.**

Holiday is any day on which people lay aside their ordinary duties and cares. The word comes from the Anglo-Saxon *halig daeg,* or *holy day.* At first, holidays honored some sacred event or holy person. People in Great Britain and other countries speak of holidays as Americans speak of vacations. For a discussion of religious holidays, see **Feasts and festivals.**

In the United States, Sunday is the only holiday recognized by common law. Congress has at different times set aside special holidays, such as the Day of Rejoicing after the end of the Civil War, or V-E and V-J days to celebrate the end of fighting in World War II. But there are no national holidays as such. Each state has the authority to specify the holidays it will observe. The governor of the state proclaims the holidays for the state. The President and Congress designate the holidays to be observed in the District of Columbia, and by federal employees throughout the country. Congress has declared the following as legal federal holidays: New Year's Day (January 1); Martin Luther King, Jr.,'s Birthday (January 15, but observed on the third Monday in January); Washington's Birthday (February 22, but observed on the third Monday in February); Memorial Day (the last Monday in May); Independence Day (July 4); Labor Day (the first Monday in September); Columbus Day (the second Monday in October); Veterans Day (November 11); Thanksgiving Day (the fourth Thursday in November); and Christmas Day (December 25).

Most states observe the last Monday in May as Memorial Day, sometimes called Decoration Day. Most Southern States also celebrate Confederate Memorial Day in April, May, or June. Several Southern States celebrate the birthdays of Jefferson Davis (June 3) and Robert E. Lee (January 19). Abraham Lincoln's birthday is a legal holiday in about 30 states. Most of these states celebrate it on February 12, but a few celebrate it on the first or third Monday of February. Some people in New England celebrate Forefathers' Day (December 21), and Maine and Massachusetts celebrate Patriots' Day (third Monday in April). In the year of a presidential election, Election Day (first Tuesday after the first Monday in November) is a legal holiday in many states. Some holidays are observed by one state only. For example, a state may observe a holiday to commemorate its admission into the Union.

Banks and schools usually close on a legal holiday. When such a holiday falls on Sunday, the following Monday is usually observed. Schools and organizations often observe days known as traditional holidays, although schools and businesses do not close then. These days are Valentine's Day (February 14); St. Patrick's Day (March 17); and Halloween (October 31). In some states, Arbor Day; Bird Day; and Flag Day are school holidays. Child Health Day (the first Monday in October) is widely observed in schools. Many schools and some businesses close on Good Friday.

In Canada, public holidays include: New Year's Day; Good Friday; Easter Monday; Queen's Birthday (also called Victoria Day, the Monday before May 25); Canada Day (July 1); Labour Day (the first Monday in September); Thanksgiving Day (the second Monday of October); Remembrance Day (November 11); and Christmas (December 25).

In other countries. Every country has its own special holidays. In Ireland, Saint Patrick's Day (March 17) is a legal holiday. The people of Scotland celebrate Saint Andrew's Day (November 30), though it is not an official holiday. Some outstanding French holidays include Bastille Day (July 14); Joan of Arc's Day (second Sunday of May); and Saint Catherine's Day (November 25). In Great Britain, Boxing Day (the first workday after Christmas) and May Day (May 1) are legal holidays. Some holidays commemorate special events in the development of a country. These holidays include Greece's Independence Day (March 25); Italy's Liberation Day (April 25); Japan's Constitution Day (May 3); West Germany's Day of German Unity (June 17); and India's Independence Day (August 15).   Sharron G. Uhler

Related articles in *World Book.* See the *Annual events* section of each state and province article, the *People* section of the country articles, and the articles on the months of the year. See also **Feasts and festivals** with its list of *Related articles.* Other related articles include:

April Fools' Day	Boxing Day	Easter
Arbor Day	Canada Day	Election Day
Armed Forces Day	Christmas	Fair
Bastille Day	Citizenship Day	Father's Day
Bill of Rights Day	Columbus Day	Flag Day

Freedom Day, National	Mardi Gras	United Nations Day
Ground-hog Day	May Day	V-E Day
Halloween	Memorial Day	V-J Day
Independence Day	Mother's Day	Valentine's Day
Kwanzaa	New Year's Day	Veterans Day
Labor Day	Remembrance Day	Victoria Day
Law Day U.S.A.	Saint Patrick's Day	Walpurgis Night
Lincoln's Birthday	Thanksgiving Day	Washington's Birthday

Additional resources

Level I
Burnett, Bernice. *Holidays.* Rev. ed. Watts, 1983.
Dobler, Lavinia G. *National Holidays Around the World.* Fleet Press, 1968.
Fenner, Phyllis R., comp. *Feasts and Frolics.* Knopf, 1948.
Manning-Sanders, Ruth, comp. *Festivals.* Dutton, 1973.
Marcus, Rebecca B. and Judith. *Fiesta Time in Mexico.* Garrard, 1974.
McSpadden, Joseph W. *Book of Holidays.* Rev. edition. Harper, 1958.

Level II
Gaer, Joseph. *Holidays Around the World.* Little, Brown, 1953.
Gregory, Ruth W. *Anniversaries and Holidays.* 4th ed. American Library Assn., 1983.
Hatch, Jane M., ed. *The American Book of Days.* 3rd ed. Wilson, 1978.
Ickis, Marguerite. *The Book of Festivals and Holidays the World Over.* Dodd, 1970.
Myers, Robert J., and others. *Celebrations: The Complete Book of American Holidays.* Doubleday, 1972.

Holiday, Billie (1915-1959), won recognition as the most moving jazz singer of her day. She was admired for the uniquely bittersweet quality of her voice, and for phrasing that had much in common with the solos of the great improvising jazz musicians. Although Holiday was often described as a blues singer, she was principally an interpreter of popular songs.

Billie Holiday was born in Baltimore and raised in a black ghetto. She described the hardships of her childhood in *Lady Sings the Blues* (1956), her autobiography. She made her first recordings with Benny Goodman in 1933. During the 1940's, Holiday was strikingly beautiful and known for the gardenia she usually wore in her hair. After 1950, drug addiction increasingly affected her health and her career.

Wide World
Billie Holiday

Leonard Feather

Holinshed's, *HAHL ihnz HEHDZ,* **Chronicles** is a book of English, Scottish, and Irish history and geography that was first published in 1578. The work is also known as the *Chronicles of England, Scotland, and Ireland.* William Shakespeare used it as source material for his tragedies *Macbeth* and *King Lear,* and for most of his history plays. The *Chronicles* is named for Raphael Holinshed, an English historian. Reginald Wolfe, a London printer, began the book. Holinshed worked with him on it until Wolfe's death in 1573. Holinshed then completed the work with the assistance of several other writers. He probably died in 1580. A revised version was published in 1587. For political reasons, the government of Queen Elizabeth I ordered the removal of certain parts from each version.　　Albert Wertheim

See also **Shakespeare, William** (picture: A belief in witches).

Holistic medicine, *hoh LIHS tihk,* also spelled *wholistic medicine,* is an approach to health care based on the belief that many factors may affect a person's health. Such factors include genetics, nutrition, physical activity, stress, family relationships, medical care, and living and working conditions. However, any single factor might be the most important one for a particular person. The term *holistic medicine* comes from the Greek word *holos,* which means *whole.*

The emphasis of holistic medicine differs from that of traditional medicine. Traditional medicine focuses chiefly on the treatment of disease. Holistic medicine emphasizes the prevention and treatment of disease. In addition, some of its methods of diagnosis and treatment are not usually used in traditional medical practice. For example, physicians who practice holistic medicine use many treatments in addition to drugs and surgery. These methods include acupuncture, herbs, hypnosis, and relaxation therapies. Holistic physicians try to reduce the excessive use of drugs.

Many physicians, psychologists, and other health care professionals practice holistic medicine. Holistic practitioners stress the responsibility of the patient in achieving and maintaining the best possible health. They help patients establish good eating and exercise habits. They also may teach patients various methods of medical self-care. For example, a patient might learn to control a normally involuntary body process, such as the rate of the heartbeat, by means of relaxation techniques, meditation, or *biofeedback* (see **Biofeedback**).

The idea of a holistic approach to health is as old as medicine itself. Good medical practice has always included elements of holistic medicine. After the early 1900's, holistic medicine gained increasing popularity in the United States. Its popularity grew because many Americans began to realize that the most common non-infectious diseases, including cancer and heart disease, were related to specific life styles and such personal habits as smoking and diet.　　Kenneth R. Pelletier

Holland. See Netherlands.

Holland (pop. 26,281) is a city in Michigan that was named for the homeland of its Dutch settlers. About 60 per cent of Holland's citizens are of Dutch descent. During its weeklong Tulip Festival, held every May, the city takes on the appearance of a village in the Netherlands, also called Holland. Thousands of bright tulips bloom along the streets. Many of the people dress in traditional Dutch costumes for the festival's parades and ceremonial street washing. One of Holland's chief attractions is Windmill Island, a city park that features the only authentic, operating Dutch windmill in the United States.

Holland lies at the head of Lake Macatawa, about 6 miles (10 kilometers) east of the point where the lake empties into Lake Michigan (see **Michigan** [political map]). Holland's industries produce boats, drugs, food products, furnaces, home and office furniture, and Dutch wooden shoes. Hope College is located in Holland.

A group of Dutch settlers who had fled from their homeland because of economic hardship and religious persecution founded Holland in 1847. Much of the city was destroyed by fire in 1871. During the early 1900's, Holland served as an important lake port, which shipped fruits and vegetables. The city has a council-manager form of government.　　Paul M. Van Kolken

Holland, John Philip (1841-1914), an Irish-American inventor, was mainly responsible for the development of the submarine. His vessel, the *Holland,* built in 1898, proved that the submarine was practical. It provided the model for later submarines.

Holland was born in County Clare, Ireland. He began work on the idea of a submarine while teaching school in Ireland from 1858 to 1872. By 1870, he had completed the first plans for his invention. In 1873, Holland came to the United States. He settled in Paterson, N.J., and taught school there. He submitted his submarine plans to the U.S. Navy in 1875, but they were rejected. But the Fenian Society, a group of Irish patriots in the United States who hoped to destroy England's naval power, became interested. They supported Holland's experiments and gave him money to build two submarines. His first boat was tested with mixed results in the Passaic River in 1878. His second boat, the *Fenian Ram,* was launched in 1881. Its success established many basic features of submarines.

In 1888, the U.S. Navy asked Holland to submit submarine plans. Seven years later, it awarded him a contract to build a ship. But this vessel failed, largely because the Navy forced Holland to drop many of his ideas. In order to prove that his ideas were correct, Holland privately built the *Holland* and launched it successfully in 1898. In 1900, the Navy bought the *Holland* and asked the inventor to build several more ships like it. Holland's firm, the Electric Boat Company (now the Electric Boat Division of General Dynamics Corporation), has continued to build most U.S. Navy submarines. It has also built many submarines for other countries.

Holland resigned from the Electric Boat Company in 1904 and attempted to establish a new firm. However, legal complications blocked the undertaking, and he died in obscurity.　　Jack Sweetman

See also **Submarine** (Early submarines).

Holland Tunnel. See Hudson River tunnels.

Holly is the common name for a group of shrubs and small trees. The two best-known hollies, the *American holly* and the *English holly,* are evergreen trees. These two hollies have glossy green leaves and red berries that are used to make attractive Christmas wreaths. In the past, holly was used in houses and churches at Christmastime, and was called *holy tree.* The word *holly* may have come from this name.

There are about 300 species of hollies. They grow in many temperate and tropical regions of the world. About 15 species are native to the United States and Canada. The American holly is usually 40 to 50 feet (12 to 15 meters) tall. Its dark green leaves have a leathery surface and spines along the edges. It grows throughout most of the eastern United States. The red fruits are not real berries, but *drupes,* which are fruits with stones. They appear only on the pistillate, or female, trees. Holly berries are poisonous.

The English holly is a favorite ornamental tree in Great Britain. Sometimes it is planted in hedges. The

Fred Whitehead, Earth Scenes

The holly tree has shiny green leaves and red berries.

WORLD BOOK illustration by Robert Hynes

The hollyhock has tall spires of colorful blossoms and large, heart-shaped leaves. The double hollyhock, *above,* has an extra clump of petals inside the wider outer petals.

white flowers of the holly bloom in May, the same month as those of another hedge plant, the hawthorn. Together, they make the English countryside white with blossoms.

Holly wood is very hard and has a close grain. It is valuable for musical instruments, furniture, and interior decoration. The inner bark yields the sticky material called *birdlime.* The leaves of a South American species are used to make a tealike drink called *maté.*

Scientific classification. The holly tree is in the family Aquifoliaceae. The different species make up the genus *Ilex.* The American holly is *I. opaca.* The English holly is *I. aquifolium.*

Jerry M. Baskin

See also **Tree** (Familiar broadleaf and needleleaf trees [picture]).

Holly, Buddy (1936-1959), was an American singer, composer, and electric guitarist. Holly became one of the first major performers of rock music. He gained fame in 1957 when his band, the Crickets, recorded "That'll Be the Day." That same year, he recorded his first solo hit, "Peggy Sue." He was co-composer of both songs. Holly and his band developed an energetic style that combined elements of country music with a strong background rhythm. This style influenced many American and British rock performers.

Howard Frank

Buddy Holly

Holly was born in Lubbock, Tex. His full name was Charles Hardin Holley. He began playing the piano when he was 11 years old but soon turned to playing the guitar. He performed as a country singer during the early 1950's. Holly died in a plane crash near Mason City, Iowa, at the age of 22.

Jerry M. Grigadean

Hollyhock is a tall, hardy plant grown for its large spires of colorful flowers. It is native to Asia, but is grown widely in the United States. Its large, fuzzy, heart-shaped leaves start as low rosettes. Tall, heavy stems rise to bear the flower spires. Hollyhocks bloom from

July to early September. They are used as background borders or along fences. The flowers are round and open wide. Their colors range from white, through yellow, salmon, and red, to purple.

Most hollyhocks are perennials that usually bloom the second year. They can be started outdoors. But some gardeners start hollyhocks in a frame in July and then transplant them to their garden the following spring. Annual hollyhocks bloom the same year that the seeds are planted.

Hollyhocks thrive in well-drained soil and full sunlight. When the flowers fade, the plant stalks lose their attractiveness, and can be cut down. A few stalks can be left standing if seed is desired. A fungal disease called *rust* sometimes attacks hollyhocks.

Scientific classification. Hollyhock belongs to the mallow family, Malvaceae. It is *Althea rosea.* Robert W. Schery

See also **Flower** (picture: Garden biennials); **Mallow.**

Hollywood, Calif., is generally considered the motion-picture capital of the world. It is not an incorporated city, but a district of Los Angeles. Hollywood extends from Griffith Park and Mulholland Drive on the north to Melrose Avenue on the south, and from about Hyperion Avenue on the east to about Crescent Heights Boulevard on the west. About 210,000 people live in this area. For location, see **Los Angeles** (map).

The Hollywood Bowl, a large open-air theater, is famous for its symphony programs, concerts, and Easter services. Restaurants, gift shops, theatrical agencies, and nightclubs line a section of Hollywood's Sunset Boulevard called "The Strip." The popular Walk of Fame consists of more than 1,800 bronze stars set in the sidewalks along Hollywood Boulevard and Vine Street. Each star has the name of a different Hollywood celebrity. The huge "Hollywood" sign, a landmark built in the hills above the district in 1922, was restored in 1978. Each letter of the sign is 45 feet (14 meters) tall.

One adobe hut stood on the site of Hollywood in 1853. By 1870, the area was a farming region. It was incorporated as Hollywood in 1903, but voted to join the city of Los Angeles in 1910 in order to gain access to the Los Angeles water supply.

The Nestor Company built the first motion-picture studio in Hollywood in 1911. Hollywood became a center of the motion-picture industry because it has a mild, dry climate, and because it lies in an area with a vast variety of natural scenery. Within 200 miles (320 kilometers), almost every kind of scenic background is available to moviemakers. The production of sound films began in Hollywood in the late 1920's and resulted in the building of huge sound stages, many now used for making television films.   Kenneth Reich

See also **Motion picture.**

Holm, Hanya (1894?-   ), is a dancer, *choreographer* (dance composer), and dance teacher. She is best known for her choreography in *Kiss Me, Kate* (1948); *The Golden Apple* (1954); *My Fair Lady* (1956); and other Broadway musicals. Her choreography has been praised for the way it fits with the dramatic action of the plays. Miss Holm also choreographed *Trend* (1937) and *Tragic Exodus* (1939) for the modern dance concert stage, and dances for operas, films, and television.

Hanya Holm was born in Worms, Germany. She was an original member of the dance group formed by Mary Wigman, a leader of modern dance in Germany. Miss Holm moved to New York City in 1931 to found a branch of the Wigman school. But she developed her own ideas about dance movement, and opened her own school in 1936.   Selma Jeanne Cohen

Holmes, David. See **Mississippi** (Statehood).

Holmes, Oliver Wendell (1809-1894), was an American writer who won fame for his essays and poems. He was also a physician and taught at the Harvard Medical School during the years of his greatest literary success. Holmes was known for his keen mind and charming, witty literary style. His enthusiasm and humor made him popular as a teacher and public speaker. His son, Oliver Wendell Holmes, Jr., became a famous associate justice of the Supreme Court of the United States.

His life. Holmes was born in Cambridge, Mass., where his father was a prominent Congregationalist minister. As a youth, Holmes rebelled against his father's strict religious beliefs. He later supported liberal religious views in many of his speeches and writings.

In 1829, Holmes graduated from Harvard College and entered law school. But law bored him and, in 1830, he began to study medicine. He studied at the Harvard Medical School and with private physicians in Boston and Paris. While a student, Holmes wrote many poems. They included "Old Ironsides" (1830), which protested the U.S. Navy's plan to destroy the *Constitution,* a historic but unseaworthy frigate. The poem helped save the ship. See **Constitution** (ship).

In 1836, Holmes received an M.D. degree from Harvard and became a Boston physician. He married Amelia Lee Jackson in 1840. They had two sons and a daughter.

Brown Bros.

Oliver Wendell Holmes

Holmes gained recognition by writing outstanding articles on medical subjects. His most important article was called "The Contagiousness of Puerperal Fever" (1843). Puerperal fever, which once killed many women, resulted from unsanitary conditions during childbirth. Medical workers of Holmes's time paid little attention to cleanliness. Holmes showed that physicians could help prevent the disease simply by washing their hands and putting on clean clothes before delivering babies. His publication helped save many lives. Holmes later considered it his greatest achievement.

In 1847, Holmes was appointed dean of the Harvard Medical School and professor of anatomy and physiology. He served as dean until 1853 and taught until 1882. Holmes was generally assigned the last period of the morning for his lectures, because his enthusiasm and humor kept tired, hungry students interested in their work.

Holmes also became popular as a public speaker. Through the years, he wrote and recited amusing poems for many special events and presented lively lectures on literature. His warmth and sense of fun won him many friends, including several leading authors.

In 1857, Holmes helped James Russell Lowell and other writers launch a new magazine. Holmes named it the *Atlantic Monthly* and joined the staff as a columnist. His wise, witty column made both Holmes and the *Atlantic Monthly* famous. Holmes continued to publish essays, fiction, and poetry until he was in his 80's.

His writings. Most of Holmes's poems are more like popular verse than serious poetry. But many are notable for their accurate descriptions of nature or their understanding of human character. His best-known poems, in addition to "Old Ironsides," include "The Last Leaf" (1831), "The Chambered Nautilus" (1858), "Contentment" (1858), and "The Deacon's Masterpiece: or, The Wonderful 'One-Hoss Shay' " (1858).

Holmes's best-known book, *The Autocrat of the Breakfast-Table* (1858), consists of his first 12 essays for the *Atlantic Monthly.* Each essay supposedly tells about a lively, witty conversation that takes place at the breakfast table of a boarding house. The talk actually expresses the author's own observations and opinions on many subjects, including human nature, manners, religion, and science.

Holmes also wrote three novels—*Elsie Venner* (1861); *The Guardian Angel* (1867); and *A Mortal Antipathy* (1885). All three promote Holmes's liberal religious views, but none ranks as outstanding fiction. In "Mechanism in Thought and Morals," a lecture given in 1870, Holmes explored the subconscious mind, which he called "the underground workshop of thought." He wrote this brilliant work more than 20 years before the great Austrian psychiatrist Sigmund Freud published his description of the subconscious.   Dean Doner

See also **American literature** (The Boston Brahmins); **Holmes, Oliver Wendell, Jr.**

Additional resources

Holmes, Oliver Wendell. *Writings of Oliver Wendell Holmes.* 13 vols. Scholarly, 1972. Reprint of 1891-1892 ed.

Hoyt, Edwin P. *The Improper Bostonian: Dr. Oliver Wendell Holmes.* Morrow, 1979.

Tilton, Eleanor M. *Amiable Autocrat: A Biography of Dr. Oliver Wendell Holmes.* Octagon, 1976. Reprint of 1947 ed.

Holmes, Oliver Wendell, Jr. (1841-1935), was one of the best-known American judges of the 1900's. He served as a member of the Supreme Court of the United States for nearly 30 years. During that period, he made great contributions to the changing concepts of law. His keen intellect, humor, and ability to express himself helped to direct American thought.

Early life. Holmes was born on March 8, 1841, in Boston, and was named for his famous father, the writer and doctor. He enlisted in the Union Army, fought through most of the Civil War, and was wounded three times. It is said that once when Holmes saw a tall civilian exposing himself to enemy fire, he yelled, "Get down, you fool." Later, he learned the civilian was President Lincoln. Holmes resigned as a lieutenant colonel after three years.

As a young man, Holmes was a close friend of William James, and thought of becoming a philosopher himself. Law, he said, was "a rag bag of details." Yet, at the end of his war service,

Bettmann Archive
Oliver Wendell Holmes, Jr.

he entered Harvard Law School at the urging of his father. Early in his career, he became coeditor of the *American Law Review* and wrote his great work, *The Common Law* (1881). In 1882, he became a professor of law at Harvard and was appointed to the Supreme Judicial Court of Massachusetts. He became chief justice of Massachusetts in 1899.

Supreme Court justice. President Theodore Roosevelt appointed Holmes an associate justice of the Supreme Court of the United States in 1902. At that time, the court was declaring many state laws unconstitutional because they did not conform to the judges' concept of "due process of law." Holmes insisted that this phrase in Amendment 14 had not been intended to deny the states a right to experiment with social legislation (see **Constitution of the United States** [Amendment 14]). He protested so frequently when the court seemed to write its economic theories into the Constitution, that he ultimately became known as the *Great Dissenter.* In later years, as new judges replaced some of the conservatives, the court accepted the ideas in many of his dissents.

Much of the legislation Holmes voted to save was designed to improve social conditions. But he was not primarily a reformer. He believed in bigness, and often expressed admiration for industrial tycoons. His dissents did not indicate that he approved the laws that the majority was striking down. Rather, he dissented because he believed that judges have no right to interfere with legislative policy unless that policy clearly violates the Constitution.

"The life of the law," Holmes wrote, "has not been logic; it has been experience." By insisting that the court look at facts in a changing society, instead of clinging to worn-out slogans and formulas, Holmes exercised a deep influence on the law. He influenced judges to keep from allowing their personal opinions to affect their de-

cisions. This doctrine, known as *judicial restraint,* has since come to dominate American judicial thinking.

Holmes's sharp phrases as well as his judicial philosophy caught the public imagination. People felt they understood him because he was "down to earth." In some respects, he is more famous as a philosopher than as a judge.

With all his brilliance, Holmes was a man of many contradictions. His inclination to let the states experiment led to some opinions now regarded as illiberal. His major contribution was in convincing people that the law should develop along with the society it serves.

Holmes is one of the few judges of his time who could truthfully say that he felt "the secret isolated joy of the thinker, who knows that, a hundred years after he is dead and forgotten, men who never heard of him will be moving to the measure of his thought."

Merlo J. Pusey

See also **Supreme Court of the United States.**

Additional resources

Bent, Silas. *Justice Oliver Wendell Holmes.* AMS, 1969. Reprint of 1932 ed.
Frankfurter, Felix. *Mr. Justice Holmes and the Supreme Court.* 2nd ed. Harvard, 1961.
Holmes, Oliver Wendell, Jr. *Touched with Fire: Civil War Letters and Diary.* DaCapo, 1967. Reprint of 1946 ed.
Howe, Mark DeWolfe. *Justice Oliver Wendell Holmes.* 2 vols. Harvard, 1957-1963.

Holmes, *hohmz,* **Sherlock,** is the most famous detective in fiction. He was created by Sir Arthur Conan Doyle, an English author, and appears in 56 short stories and 4 novels.

Holmes is known for his ability to solve baffling crimes through clever observation and deduction. He draws amazing conclusions from minute details. His remarkable powers of concentration and broad knowledge of science also help him solve many mysteries.

Holmes is assisted by his friend Dr. John Watson, who records most of Holmes's cases. The two men live in London at 221B Baker Street. Doyle described their quarters so realistically that many readers have visited Baker Street in order to search for the fictional address.

Holmes is a tall, thin man with a lean, narrow face. He is often pictured wearing a close-fitting cap and smoking a pipe. Holmes has many interests besides detective work. For example, he is an accomplished violinist and an expert on beekeeping.

Doyle introduced Holmes in the novel *A Study in Scarlet* (1887). He modeled him partly after Joseph Bell, a Scottish physician known for making brilliant diagnoses through observation. James Douglas Merritt

See also **Doyle, Sir Arthur Conan.**

Holmium, *HOHL mee uhm* (chemical symbol, Ho), is one of the rare-earth metals. Its atomic number is 67, and its atomic weight is 164.930. The Swiss scientist J. L. Soret first identified the element in 1878. In 1879, P. T. Cleve of Sweden independently discovered, and also named, the element. The name comes from *Holmia,* the Latin word for Stockholm, Sweden.

Holmium occurs in monazite and similar minerals that bear rare earths. It is best separated from other rare earths by ion exchange processes or by solvent extraction. The metal has a silver color. It melts at 1474° C, and boils at 2700° C. Its density is 8.78 grams per cubic centi-

282   Holocaust

meter at 25° C. The cream-colored oxide Ho_2O_3 is soluble in mineral acid.   Larry C. Thompson

See also **Element, Chemical; Rare earth.**

Holocaust, *HAHL uh kaust,* was the mass murder of European Jews by the Nazis during World War II. The Nazi dictator Adolf Hitler planned to wipe out the entire Jewish population as part of his plan to conquer the world. By the end of the war in 1945, the Nazis had killed about 6 million Jewish men, women, and children—over two-thirds of the Jews in Europe. They also killed many members of other ethnic groups, especially Gypsies and Poles. No one knows the exact number of civilians killed by the Nazis during the war. The word *holocaust* means *widespread destruction.* For detailed information on Hitler's hatred of Jews, see **Hitler, Adolf.**

The Nazi persecution of the Jews began after Hitler came to power in 1933. As Germany prepared for war, the government imposed many laws and restrictions that deprived Jews of their rights and possessions. For example, the Nazis prohibited Jews from attending universities and seized their property and businesses. In 1939, the Germans invaded Poland and gained control over that country's approximately 3 million Jews. The next year, the Nazis conquered Belgium, Denmark, France, Norway, and the Netherlands, and hundreds of thousands more Jews fell into their hands. Jews were forced to live in special areas called *ghettos* and to work as slave laborers.

The Nazis invaded the Soviet Union in 1941 and began a campaign of mass murder against all of the Jews of Europe. Special Nazi units followed the rapid advance of the German army and killed more than a million Jews in conquered areas.

Millions of Jews were also imprisoned in *concentration camps* (camps for political prisoners). These camps included gas chambers in which large numbers of victims were killed with poison gas. The camps also had factories in which prisoners were worked to death. The

captives lived under horrible conditions, and many died of starvation and disease. Doctors performed cruel experiments on some prisoners. Those unable to work—the aged, the sick, many women, and most children—were gassed.

During the Holocaust, the Germans kept their actions as secret as possible and deceived the victims in many ways to prevent resistance. After word of the slaughter leaked out, Jews fought back in Warsaw, Poland, and in other cities though they were outnumbered and mostly unarmed. Jews also staged uprisings in several concentration camps.   Leon A. Jick

Related articles in *World Book* include:

Anti-Semitism	Concentration camp
Auschwitz	Dachau
Babi Yar	Jews (The Holocaust)
Belsen	Wiesel, Elie
Buchenwald	

Additional resources

Bauer, Yehuda, and Keren, Nili. *A History of the Holocaust.* Watts, 1982.

Eisenberg, Azriel. *Witness to the Holocaust.* Pilgrim Press, 1981.

Gilbert, Martin. *The Final Journey: The Fate of the Jews in Nazi Europe.* Mayflower, 1979. *The Holocaust: A History of the Jews of Europe During the Second World War.* Holt, 1985.

Hausner, Gideon. *Justice in Jerusalem.* Herzl, 1978.

Jackson, Livia E. Bitton. *Elli: Coming of Age in the Holocaust.* Times Books, 1980.

Kren, George M., and Rappoport, Leon. *The Holocaust and the Crisis of Human Behavior.* Holmes & Meier, 1980.

Laqueur, Walter. *The Terrible Secret: The Suppression of the Truth About Hitler's Final Solution.* Little, Brown, 1981.

Holography, *hah LAWG ruh fee,* is a method of making three-dimensional images on a photographic plate or film. The depth in the scene makes its objects seem real. These types of images appear on some credit cards to prevent counterfeiting. Holographic images are also seen on pendants, fancy belt buckles, and advertising displays.

There are two basic steps in holography: (1) making a pattern called a *hologram* and (2) producing the three-dimensional image. In the first step, a special device splits a beam of light from a laser into two beams. One

Yad Vashem Archives

During the Holocaust, millions of Jews were forced to leave their homes and were imprisoned in concentration camps.

© Ronald R. Erickson

Some holograms, such as that of a bird on this credit card, are three-dimensional images used to prevent counterfeiting.

beam illuminates a scene and reflects its image on the film. The other beam, called a *reference beam,* shines directly on the film. The reflected image and the reference beam interfere with each other, forming a complex pattern on the film. The developed film is the hologram. In the second step, light that shines from the same direction as the reference beam illuminates the hologram. The hologram changes this light to reconstruct the light patterns from the original scene, making a three-dimensional image. In many cases, the light source is a laser.

Holography has a number of research and analytic applications. For example, it is used to check for flaws in aircraft wings, tires, lenses, and other objects. Holography is also used to measure velocities of moving particles and to produce three-dimensional images of objects viewed with a microscope.

Holography was invented in 1947 by Dennis Gabor, a Hungarian-born engineer. He received the 1971 Nobel Prize in physics for his invention.

George O. Reynolds and John B. DeVelis

Holst, Gustav (1874-1934), was an English composer and teacher. Holst composed many of his works for vocal soloists and chorus. These compositions show his sensitivity to the human voice and to language as well as his love for the English folk song tradition. However, Holst's best-known work is the orchestral suite *The Planets* (1914-1916). This suite consists of seven parts, each interpreting the astrological nature of a planet.

Holst composed two suites for military band (1909, 1911) based on English folk songs. *The Hymn of Jesus* (1917) is a work for orchestra and chorus based on the Apocrypha of the New Testament. The poetry of John Keats inspired Holst's *First Choral Symphony* (1925) for soprano, chorus, and orchestra. Holst also wrote a number of works that reflect his interest in Hindu literature. In 1908, for example, Holst composed nine hymns for vocal soloist and piano based on the ancient Hindu sacred book the *Rig-Veda.*

Holst was born in Cheltenham. From 1907 until his death, he served as musical director at Morley College. Holst also taught at the Royal College of Music from 1919 until his death.   Mary Vinquist

Holy Alliance was an agreement signed in Paris in September 1815, after the fall of Napoleon. Czar Alexander I of Russia originated the Alliance. The first two signers were Francis I, Emperor of Austria, and King Frederick William III of Prussia. All the other rulers in Europe except the pope, the king of Great Britain, and the sultan of Turkey, also signed it.

Supposedly, the purpose of the Alliance was to unite the monarchs of Europe in a holy brotherhood to advance Christian principles. The agreement said that, in accordance with the teachings of Christ, the principles of charity, justice, and peace should be the basis of each ruler's international relations.

The agreement contained many high-sounding phrases, but had no practical effect. People often confuse the Holy Alliance with the Quadruple Alliance, in which four nations—Austria, Prussia, Russia, and Great Britain—organized in 1815. The purpose of the Quadruple Alliance was to preserve peace in Europe. But soon the Austrian, Russian, and Prussian rulers became more interested in making Europe safe for autocracy. After Great Britain withdrew from the Quadruple Alliance, the autocratic rulers put down the democratic uprisings of 1820.

See also **Alexander** (I) of Russia; **Francis II** (Holy Roman emperor).

Holy Bible. See Bible.
Holy Communion. See Communion.
Holy Eucharist. See Communion.
Holy Ghost. See Trinity.
Holy Grail, in medieval legend, was the cup that Jesus Christ used at the Last Supper. According to some legends, the Grail was a dish or a stone.

The Holy Grail inspired some of the finest poetry of the Middle Ages. European poets established the basic parts of the Holy Grail story between about 1180 and 1240. These poets may have adapted the legend from a tale told much earlier by pagan Celtic people. The Celtic story described a magic cup or dish that provided food and drink for anyone who used it. Chrétien de Troyes, a French poet, wrote an unfinished poem about the Grail that later writers completed. Chrétien's poem became the best known of the Grail stories. Another poet, Wolfram von Eschenbach of Germany, wrote an important account of the legend that he based, at least partly, on Chrétien's work. The several versions of the Grail story written during the Middle Ages differ from one another on important points as well as in small details. But each version of the story describes a search for the Holy Grail by King Arthur's Knights of the Round Table.

Early history of the Grail. The Grail story begins with Joseph of Arimathea, a follower of Christ. Joseph used the cup to capture blood flowing from the wounds of Jesus as He hung from the cross. Later, the Romans imprisoned Joseph because he had been a follower of Jesus. While Joseph was in prison, the Grail mysteriously appeared to him. According to one version of the legend, the Grail fed Joseph in his cell for 42 years. After being freed from prison, Joseph led a group of Christians who carried the Grail throughout the Holy Land. They used it to hold the wine during the Communion service.

Joseph later took the Grail to Britain, where he built a castle called Corbenic. He kept the Grail in the castle. Joseph and his descendants served as rulers of Corbenic and guardians of the Grail. The legend tells how Pelles, one of the castle rulers, suffered a wound that did not heal. The wound made Pelles unable to father children. Also, as long as the wound remained unhealed, no vegetation could grow in the land around the castle. The countryside became a wasteland.

The search for the Grail. Much of the Grail legend describes the search for the cup by King Arthur's Knights of the Round Table. On the feast of Pentecost, the knights gathered in a hall in Arthur's castle. Suddenly, in a brief vision, they saw the Grail suspended in the air. About 150 knights decided to search throughout Britain for the Grail.

The knights underwent many dangerous adventures during their search. Their actions during these adventures revealed that only three knights—Bors, Galahad, and Perceval—were morally perfect and therefore fit to complete the quest. After searching for years, the three knights, with nine men from other lands, entered Castle Corbenic. There they saw a vision in which Joseph of Arimathea appeared as a priest. Angels brought in the

Grail and the bloody spear that had pierced Christ's side during the Crucifixion. A child appeared above the Grail and changed into bread. Then Christ emerged from the cup and gave Communion to the men. The vision was meant to prove that, in the Mass, the bread and wine are changed into the actual body and blood of Christ. This transformation became known as the miracle of the Grail.

Galahad healed Pelles, the wounded lord of the castle, with blood from the holy spear. As soon as the wound had healed, the land around the castle again became fertile.

After leaving the castle, the three knights sailed on a ship which, they discovered, carried the Grail. Guided by supernatural forces, the ship took the knights and the Grail to the distant city of Sarras. There, after Galahad died, Bors and Perceval saw the Grail rise into heaven. According to the legend, no one has seen the Holy Grail since that time.

Later versions of the legend. Through the centuries, the legend of the Grail has inspired many writers and composers. For example, the English poet Alfred, Lord Tennyson wrote the long poem "The Holy Grail" as part of his *Idylls of the King.* The German composer Richard Wagner based his opera *Parsifal* on parts of the Grail legend.   Robert W. Ackerman

See also **Chrétien de Troyes; Galahad, Sir; Wolfram von Eschenbach.**

Holy Land. See Palestine.

Holy Roman Empire is the name given to the territory that was ruled by German kings between 962 and 1806. The Holy Roman Empire was founded by Otto I of Germany, who was crowned Holy Roman emperor in A.D. 962. The essential feature of the Holy Roman Empire during the greatest phase of its history was the union of Germany and Italy (except the Kingdom of the Two Sicilies) under one ruler. By the end of the 1200's, however,

WORLD BOOK map

The Holy Roman Empire in 1250 extended from the North Sea to the Mediterranean Sea. The Kingdom of the Two Sicilies, a personal possession of the emperor, was geographically separated from the empire by the Papal States.

the empire had lost control over most of Italy and Burgundy, and even to a large extent over Germany. But German kings continued to use the title of Holy Roman emperor until 1806.

The empire of Otto was in some ways a revival of Charlemagne's empire, although Otto's empire did not include France and southern Italy. Charlemagne had been crowned Roman emperor in A.D. 800. Charlemagne died in 814, and his grandsons eventually divided his empire. During the 900's Otto succeeded in gaining control over several important duchies of Germany. He crossed the Alps in 951 and made himself king of Italy. In 961, he answered a call for help from the pope and crossed the Alps again. In return, in 962, the pope crowned Otto Holy Roman emperor.

For 200 years afterward, Otto's successors struggled to hold control of Italy. They had to fight not only the pope but the growing power of the cities of northern Italy. Because the emperors spent so much time trying to rule Italy, they granted far-reaching powers to their nobles in Germany. Instead of dominating the feudal lords, as the kings of England and France finally did, the emperors lost power to them. As a result, some states, such as Prussia, became almost independent. These developments delayed Germany's unification.

In the 1300's, a group of powerful German princes gained the right to elect the Holy Roman emperor. According to the Golden Bull of Charles IV, issued in 1356, there were to be seven German Imperial Electors, but the number was later increased to nine. In 1273, Rudolf of Habsburg became the first member of the Habsburg family to rule the empire. After Albert II of Habsburg was given the crown in 1438, the House of Habsburg controlled most of the votes. A Habsburg prince was almost always elected king of Germany and head of the empire.   William F. McDonald

Related articles in *World Book* include:

Austria (History)	Frederick II (Holy Roman emperor)
Charlemagne	
Charles (Holy Roman emperors)	Germany (History)
Crown (picture)	Habsburg, House of
Ferdinand II	Henry (of Germany)
Ferdinand III	Italy (History)
Flag (picture: Historical flags)	Maximilian I
Francis II (Holy Roman emperor)	Otto (I, the Great)
Frederick I (Holy Roman emperor)	Sicilies, Kingdom of the Two
	Sigismund
	Thirty Years' War

Additional resources

Barraclough, Geoffrey. *The Crucible of Europe: The Ninth and Tenth Centuries in European History.* Univ. of California Press, 1976.
Heer, Friedrich. *The Holy Roman Empire.* Praeger, 1968.
The Holy Roman Empire: A Dictionary Handbook. Ed. by Jonathan W. Zophy. Greenwood, 1980.
Lopez, Robert S. *The Birth of Europe.* Evans & Co., 1967.

Holy Scriptures. See Bible (introduction).

Holy Spirit. See Trinity.

Holy Thursday. See Holy Week; Maundy Thursday.

Holy Wars. See Crusades.

Holy Week is the period when Christians remember the final events in the life of Jesus Christ. It is the most solemn week of the Christian year, and a time of prayer and special services. Holy Week comes as the last week of Lent, just before Easter. It begins with Palm Sunday and ends with Easter Sunday. The Anglican, Roman

Catholic, Eastern Orthodox, and many Protestant churches observe Holy Week. Holy Week is called *Passion Week* in some Eastern Orthodox churches.

Palm Sunday, the first day of Holy Week, honors Christ's triumphal entry into Jerusalem, when the people spread palms and clothing before Him. Roman Catholics call this day the Second Sunday of the Passion. They observe it with a solemn procession of palms. Christians honor the Last Supper on Maundy Thursday, or Holy Thursday. They observe Good Friday, or Great Friday, in a somber manner in remembrance of the Crucifixion. Most Christian churches hold Good Friday services from noon to three o'clock to recall the last three hours of darkness while Christ suffered on the cross. The liturgy gives special attention to the words Jesus spoke from the cross. Some churches observe Holy Saturday as a time for baptism. Roman Catholic churches hold a special vigil service on Holy Saturday night, concluded with Mass. Holy Week ends on Easter Sunday with joyous ceremonies to celebrate the Resurrection of Jesus.

Bernard Ramm

Related articles in *World Book* include:
Easter / Lent / Palm Sunday
Good Friday / Maundy Thursday

Holyoake, Sir Keith Jacka. See New Zealand (New Zealand today).

Homage, *HAHM ihj,* during the Middle Ages, was a feudal ceremony by which one man became the vassal or follower of a lord. The ceremony set up a personal and honorable tie between the vassal and the lord, who promised faithfulness to each other. The knight who was to become a vassal knelt before the lord, placed his hands between those of the lord, and acknowledged himself to be the lord's man. The lord then recognized him as a vassal, raised him to his feet, and kissed him. After performing homage, the vassal usually took an oath of fealty, swearing on the Bible or on holy relics to keep the faith he had pledged. Bryce Lyon

See also **Feudalism** (The principles of feudalism).

Home. See Family; Home economics; House; Shelter.

Home, *hyoom,* **Lord** (1903-), served for a year as prime minister of Great Britain. A member of the Conservative Party, Home succeeded Harold Macmillan in October 1963. He was succeeded by Harold Wilson, leader of the Labour Party, in October 1964. Home served as foreign secretary from 1960 to 1963 and from 1970 to 1974.

Home served as a Conservative member of the House of Commons from 1931 to 1945. In 1945, he became joint parliamentary undersecretary of state for foreign affairs. After his father's death in 1951, Home became the 14th Earl of Home. He gave up his seat in the House of Commons and, as a member of the nobility, took his place in the House of Lords. He became secretary of state for Commonwealth relations in 1955 and leader of the House of Lords in 1957.

After Home was named prime minister, some members of the Conservative Party protested his being selected. Traditionally, the prime minister must be a member of the House of Commons, and Home was no longer a member. The protesters were also upset because party leaders had disregarded the wishes of other party members by choosing Home. But after Home became prime minister, he gave up his title and his seat in the

House of Lords and was again elected to the Commons. In 1975, Queen Elizabeth II gave him the title Baron Home of the Hirsel, and he returned to the House of Lords.

Home was born in London. His full name is Alexander Frederick Douglas-Home. He grew up at his ancestral home in Berwickshire in the Borders Region of Scotland. Richard Rose

Home computer. See Computer, Personal.
Home decoration. See Interior decoration.
Home economics is the field of study that deals with the management of a household. Home economics is a broad field that unifies knowledge from many other fields. It draws on the social sciences, the physical sciences, and the life sciences.

Home economics involves every area of home life, including cooking, clothing, home furnishings, and family relations. It teaches people how to eat better, dress well, care for their homes, and spend money wisely. It also teaches family members how to get along with one another and build a happy home life.

Home economics tries to improve the quality of life for all people. It promotes the well-being of individuals and families, and the values important in home life. The study of home economics provides homemakers with the knowledge and skills needed to manage a home effectively. Such factors as good nutrition and a pleasant home atmosphere contribute greatly to a person's health and happiness.

Elementary schools, high schools, and many colleges and universities in the United States offer courses in home economics. About 4 million students study home economics in junior and senior high school. At the college level, about 109,000 men and women study home economics. Elementary and high school students may study such subjects as cooking, sewing, nutrition, and consumer education. College students who major in home economics take such courses as chemistry and psychology for background knowledge. Many adults also study home economics in nonschool educational programs.

Major fields of home economics

Home economics has five major fields: (1) food and nutrition, (2) clothing and textiles, (3) home management and consumer education, (4) home furnishings and interior decoration, and (5) child development and family relations.

The study of the various fields of home economics helps prepare students for the wide range of responsibilities connected with managing a home. Students in elementary and high school may study in any or all of these areas. A person may also choose to study home economics at the college level and prepare for a career in home economics. Many home economics students in college specialize in only one field of the subject.

Food and nutrition involves the preparation of food and the basic elements of a good diet. The human body needs various nutrients to function properly. A well-balanced diet provides them. Foods must be stored and cooked carefully to keep their nutritional value.

Courses in food and nutrition teach people to plan and prepare nutritious meals. Students learn the nutritional needs of the body and which foods provide the essential nutrients. They also learn to prepare food in ways that conserve the food's nutritional value and make the food appetizing as well.

Good nutrition has an important effect on the mental and physical well-being of young and old. The quality of the meals also contributes to family relationships. Mealtimes may be the only time that the whole family gets together. Tasty and attractively served food makes the meal more pleasant for everyone.

Clothing and textiles deals with the skills and knowledge needed to design and sew clothes. It also involves knowledge of the different types of textiles and the principles of clothing selection.

Students in clothing and textiles learn the characteristics of various fabrics, such as strength and washability. They also learn about color combinations and what types of clothes look best on people of different sizes and figures. Fashion design requires knowledge of certain principles of art, including color combinations and the effects of line and texture.

Clothing primarily provides protection, but it also contributes to an individual's personal appearance. The study of clothing and textiles helps people select clothes that look attractive and wear well. In addition, the ability to sew clothes at home can save money for an individual or a family.

Home management and consumer education. The management of a home requires organization and planning. Meals, housework, and other shared family activities involve preplanning and preparation. Courses in home management teach people how to organize their work and run their homes more efficiently. Good organization gives members of the family more spare time. Home management also involves planning expenses and making a budget. Courses may offer information on insurance and credit plans.

Consumer education provides the knowledge necessary to make intelligent decisions when buying various products. The quantity and wide range of products make consumer education especially important. Many new products, including automatic washers and dryers, automatic dishwashers, and other appliances, save time and work. But homemakers need to know how to select, use, and care for such equipment.

Courses in consumer education teach people how to buy wisely and make the best use of various products. Intelligent shoppers read labels carefully and check a product's safety and reliability. They also may check a product's guarantee and compare its price at several stores before buying. In addition, consumer education informs people about misleading advertising.

Home furnishings and interior decoration involves the selection and arrangement of furniture and of lamps, pictures, and other accessories. Knowledge of interior decoration helps people make the best use of available space in the home. They learn to select furniture and decorations that go well together and fit in with different room arrangements.

The careful selection of home furnishings and interior decorations requires an understanding of basic principles of art. For example, an interior designer must know how to distribute colors throughout a room to create the desired effect. Home furnishings and accessories should be related to the needs and desires of various

David R. Frazier

Food and nutrition courses teach people to prepare tasty, nutritious meals and serve them attractively. These students in a home economics class are tasting food they cooked themselves.

members of the family. These furnishings and accessories contribute greatly to the overall atmosphere of a family's home.

Child development and family relations deals with the physical and emotional needs of children and the relationships among family members. Courses in this field may include the study of social and cultural influences on individuals and families.

Child development classes offer instruction in the care and guidance of young children through the various stages of growth. Students learn the needs and abilities of children at different ages. Parents and teachers need to know what to expect from a child at a certain age. Otherwise, a youngster may be pushed into various activities before he or she is ready for them. Parents may also fail to provide children with opportunities to develop certain skills.

Family relations involves the personal needs and problems of the members of a family. It teaches people how to get along with one another and how to solve problems within a family. A happy family life requires much cooperation and understanding among all the people in a household.

Careers in home economics

The field of home economics offers many career opportunities. The study of various subjects in home economics can lead to careers in such areas as personnel work, designing, journalism, research, selling, teaching, and television and radio broadcasting.

Except for homemaking, most careers in home economics require a bachelor's degree. Salaries and employment opportunities increase for persons with master's and doctor's degrees. Home economics can be studied in about 400 colleges and universities in the United States. To earn a bachelor's degree, a home economics student must take courses in such areas as the humanities and social sciences, as well as in home economics itself. Students may specialize in one area of the

Peter Gonzalez

Interior design involves planning and arranging furnishings for homes and other buildings. These high school students in an interior design class are learning how to coordinate colors.

field, such as clothing and textiles or home management and consumer education.

Most people who study home economics become homemakers. A large group of home economists work as teachers. Other home economists find employment in a variety of areas.

Homemaking. The term "homemaker" once referred only to the woman who managed a home. But homemaking actually involves both men and women. In many families, the members share the responsibilities and work of homemaking. Many homemakers put much time and energy into creating the type of home they desire. They get a great deal of satisfaction from their work and activities at home. Men and women may also combine homemaking with other careers outside the home.

Teaching. Many home economists teach in elementary schools, high schools, and colleges. They teach subjects in all fields of home economics. The largest number of home economics teachers have positions at the high school level.

Students who wish to prepare for a teaching career in home economics take courses in educational methods as well as home economics itself. A teaching career at most colleges requires a master's or doctor's degree.

Some home economists serve as *extension agents* for government agencies. Extension agents develop educational programs outside schools for men and women of all ages. Such programs may include courses in nutrition, child care, and home management. Extension agents also work with 4-H Clubs. They must have a bachelor's degree in home economics, and the college requirements are similar to those for teaching.

Other careers in home economics. Home economists in the field of food and nutrition find employment as dietitians, nutritionists, food service workers, and various other food specialists. They work in hospitals, schools, and restaurants. Other career areas include advertising, manufacturing, and selling.

Many people in the field of clothing and textiles work

in private industry. They design clothes and have jobs in the areas of production, distribution, and promotion. A career in production requires a thorough knowledge of clothing construction and pattern making. Distribution and promotion involve the selling and advertising of clothes. Some home economists in clothing and textiles become buyers of clothing and textiles for department stores. For a career in private industry, students may combine the study of home economics with business.

Home economists in child development and family relations serve as counselors and social workers in schools and social agencies. They also work as consultants to businesses that offer child care services. Home economists in home management and consumer education are financial counselors or consumer information specialists in businesses and social agencies.

Home economists with preparation in housing, home furnishings, and interior decoration work for the federal government and private industry. They help plan public housing projects and promote newly developed household equipment for various companies. Such home economists also have careers as interior designers in many businesses.

Government and private industry conduct research in every major area of home economics. Home economics researchers study child development, economics, education, family relations, foods, housing, and textiles.

Some home economists combine the professions of home economics and journalism. They work as writers and editors for newspapers, magazines, television, and radio. Most newspapers have a foods section, and many have a clothing section. Home economists may also write for journals in their field or for magazines that deal with homemaking. In addition, home economists work in advertising and photography.

History

Home economics has long been taught in schools in the United States under such names as cooking and sewing, homemaking, and domestic science. One of the first-known courses, a needlework class for girls, was taught in the Boston public schools about 1798.

Various other courses related to home economics were started during the 1800's. In 1871, Iowa State College offered the first college courses in home economics. Some adult education classes in the subject began at about the same time. In 1874, cooking instruction was started by the Training School for Women in New York City. Only girls and women studied home economics at first. Few men entered the field until the late 1960's.

In 1899, 10 women and one man held a home economics conference in Lake Placid, N.Y. The meeting led to the creation of the American Home Economics Association (AHEA), a professional organization of home economists.

Today, the AHEA has more than 50,000 members. The organization works to improve the quality of individual and family life through educational, research, and public information programs. It provides funds for scholarships, supports home economics workshops, and provides educational materials. The AHEA has committees on aging, consumer interests, family life, the status of women, and other subjects.

The field of home economics has expanded greatly

during the 1900's, when the government began to provide funds for vocational education. After World War II ended in 1945, many labor-saving household appliances became widespread in American homes. These appliances freed homemakers from many household tasks and, as a result, changed the teaching of home economics. New methods of cooking began to be taught, and other subjects, such as child development and household equipment, became more important.

The consumer-protection movement of the 1960's and the 1970's brought public attention to the need for consumer education (see **Consumerism**). Home economists started to teach consumer education in more high schools and supported legislation related to consumer interests.

Also during the 1960's and 1970's, some women's rights leaders began to criticize the home economics curriculum. They claimed that home economics classes taught girls to aim only for a job as a housewife. They also accused home economists of contributing to the impression that most women are happy and satisfied as homemakers. Criticism by the women's rights movement caused home economists to work toward changing the image of home economics.   Jean O. Cooper

Related articles in *World Book* include:

Adolescent	Dry cleaning	Health
Baby	Etiquette	House
Budget	Family	Interior decoration
Canning	First aid	Marriage
Careers (Home eco-	Food	Nutrition
nomics)	Food, Frozen	Parent education
Child	Food preservation	Safety
Consumerism	Furniture	Sewing
Cooking		

Additional resources

East, Marjorie. *Home Economics: Past, Present, and Future.* Allyn & Bacon, 1980.
Hatton, Hap, and Torbet, Laura. *Helpful Hints for Better Living: How to Live Better for Less.* Facts on File, 1984.
McCullough, Bonnie R. *Bonnie's Household Organizer: The Essential Guide for Getting Control of Your Home.* St. Martin's, 1980.
Weinstein, Grace W. *The Lifetime Book of Money Management.* New American Library, 1984.

D. C. Lowe, Shostal

Some home economists specialize in nutrition and become professional nutritionists or dietitians. This nutritionist is evaluating her patient's nutritional needs.

Home rule, in the United States, refers to the self-government that a state government gives cities and counties. The degree and kind of self-government permitted by the states may differ among various communities. State legislatures, unless restricted by their state constitutions, have the right to exercise complete control over local governments. But supporters of home rule argue that locally elected officials are more qualified to deal with local matters than are state legislators.

Since the late 1800's, the idea of home rule has gained wide acceptance in the United States. Today, over half the states allow local governments to decide their own form of organization and to have considerable freedom in local matters. But the growing interdependence of society has made it difficult to determine whether the federal, state, or local government has the most responsibility in such matters as finance, control of crime, welfare, transportation, and education.

In Great Britain, home rule refers to political movements in Ireland, Scotland, and Wales. The Irish home-rule movement began in the late 1800's. It aimed to gain a measure of independence for Ireland from British rule. The Republic of Ireland, which consisted of Ireland's southern counties, cut all ties with Britain in 1949. Home-rule movements gained strength in Scotland and Wales in the 1970's. Some people want complete independence from Britain. But most Scots and Welsh who favor home rule call for increased regional control over government affairs.   Holbert N. Carroll

See also **Local government; Ireland** (History); **Scotland** (Government).

Homelessness is the condition of someone who has no permanent address. Homeless people often live in abandoned buildings, areas under bridges, bus stations, cheap hotels, emergency shelters, subways, and the streets. Some sociologists use the word *homeless* to describe anyone who leads an isolated life, without the usual social ties to family, work, and community life. The United Nations reports that there are over 100 million homeless people worldwide. The problem is especially severe in developing countries.

In the United States, homelessness has become a serious problem. Estimates of the number of homeless Americans vary greatly, ranging from 250,000 to 3 million. Some homeless people are stranded only for a short time. Others may be homeless a number of times in their lives. Still others are permanently homeless. The main causes of homelessness in the United States are unemployment, severe shortages of low-income housing, widespread poverty, and untreated mental illness. Divorce, drug abuse, and other personal and family difficulties may also lead to homelessness.

During the 1950's, many Americans came to associate homelessness with run-down sections of cities called *skid rows.* Many people in such areas were elderly, poor white men. Large numbers of them suffered from alcoholism. Since the mid-1970's, however, the homeless population in the United States has been changing as well as growing. Today, many homeless people are young, minority men without jobs or the skills needed to get them. Large numbers of poor women also live in the streets, unable to afford housing. Some of the homeless are former psychiatric patients released into the community without adequate support. Cuts in federal

Special Report
HOMELESSNESS
1990 Year Book, p. 96

programs for the poor and weaknesses in the U.S. economy during the 1980's contributed to a rapid increase in the number of homeless families.

State and city governments across the nation are recognizing the need to deal with the homeless. Many are considering and adopting plans to provide more low-income housing and emergency shelters for the homeless. Other programs include job training and counseling, and medical and psychiatric care.   Kim Hopper

Homeopathy, *HOH mee AHP uh thee,* is a system of medical practice based on the attempt to "let like cure like." According to homeopathic physicians, a substance that produces certain symptoms in a healthy individual will cure those symptoms in a sick individual. Poison ivy, for example, causes rashes. Homeopathic physicians thus treat rashes with poison ivy. Onions cause crying and a watery discharge from the nose. Therefore, onions are used to treat colds. Samuel Hahnemann, a German physician, developed homeopathy in the late 1700's (see **Hahnemann, Samuel**).

Homeopathic remedies are discovered through a process called *proving.* In proving, various substances are administered to healthy people and their effects carefully observed. Homeopathic physicians give patients only one remedy at a time. They believe that using combinations of remedies interferes with the effectiveness of each particular remedy. Remedies are diluted so that the patient receives the minimum effective dose. This procedure is thought to maximize the benefits of the treatment. It also helps prevent harmful side effects.

Many homeopathic remedies contain substances that could be toxic or hazardous to people if given in larger doses. In addition, the medical effectiveness of homeopathic treatments has not been scientifically proven. For these reasons, homeopathy has been criticized by many physicians.   Thomas H. Maugh II

Homeostasis, *HOH mee uh STAY sihs,* is a term that refers to the ability of a living organism to maintain a stable set of conditions inside its body. In an animal, for example, such internal conditions as body temperature, blood pressure, and the composition of body fluids must remain relatively stable. A change in these internal conditions could result in disease or death.

In order to maintain homeostasis, an organism must react to its external environment by making internal adjustments. Such adjustments are triggered by *homeostatic reflexes.* An example of homeostatic reflexes occurs when a person steps outside on a hot day. If the body did not adjust to high outside temperatures, body temperature would go up so high that cells, especially brain cells, would be killed off at a massive rate. However, homeostatic reflexes help maintain a constant internal body temperature. When the heat from the sun strikes the skin, nerve endings sense that heat and send a message to the brain. The brain then sends nerve impulses that cause the blood vessels in the skin to expand. The resulting increase in blood flow to the skin produces greater heat loss from the skin surface. The brain also instructs the sweat glands to increase production, because the evaporation of sweat cools the skin. In addition, the brain initiates behavioral responses that make the person want to decrease physical activity and seek a cool place.   Matthew J. Kluger

See also **Motivation** (Kinds of motives).

Homer is traditionally considered the ancient Greek poet who composed the great epics the *Iliad* and the *Odyssey.* Scholars know almost nothing about Homer. Some believe that he may have lived in a Greek-speaking city on the eastern shore of the Aegean Sea or on the island of Khíos. Other scholars deny that he ever existed. According to tradition, Homer was blind.

Homer's poems. The events in the *Iliad* and the *Odyssey* occur during and after the Trojan War. This war was fought between Greece and the city of Troy, perhaps in the mid-1200's B.C. Many scholars believe the poems were composed between 800 and 700 B.C. They base these dates on references in the poems to social conditions at that time.

Archaeologists have discovered evidence in the ruins of Troy and ancient Greece that confirms the historical basis for some things described in the poems. But the poems' characters and events—even if partly based on real people and historical incidents—were altered over the centuries in the retelling of folk tales and in the poems of singing poets called *bards.* The bards created a series of poems called the *Trojan cycle,* which told the entire story of the Trojan War. The *Iliad* and the *Odyssey* are the only surviving parts of the cycle.

After Homer's time, the two poems were recited as part of great religious festivals in Greece. Copies of the poems became the basic textbooks that Greek children used to learn to read and to study the legends and myths of ancient Greece. As a result, the Greeks formed their religious views from Homer's portrayals of the gods and goddesses. His poems also furnished characters and plots for the great tragic dramatists of the 400's B.C. —Aeschylus, Euripides, and Sophocles.

Early scholarship. The Greek people came to know Homer's poems by hearing them recited or by reading handwritten copies of them. In making copies, writers sometimes made mistakes or deliberate changes in the text. By 300 B.C., many slightly different versions of the *Iliad* and the *Odyssey* existed in Greece.

From about 300 B.C. to about 100 B.C., scholars at the great Alexandrian Library in Egypt tried to correct the changes in the two poems and restore them to their original form. A few of the scholars came to believe that the poems were the work of two different poets. These scholars, called *separatists,* felt that the language, point of view, and subject matter of the two poems differed so greatly that they could not have been created by one person.

Analysts and unitarians. For many centuries, the question of who composed the *Iliad* and the *Odyssey* was almost forgotten. Then, in 1795, a German scholar named Friedrich August Wolf revived the issue. Wolf noted that archaeologists could find no evidence that the Greeks knew how to write when Homer was supposed to have lived. He argued that such long poems as the *Iliad* and the *Odyssey* could not have been composed without the knowledge of writing. Wolf led a school of critics called *analysts,* who developed a theory that Homer never existed. They believed the *Iliad* and the *Odyssey* were collections of short songs by several poets. The analysts insisted that inconsistencies in the stories and variations in language indicated many authors were involved.

A second group of scholars, called *unitarians,* opposed the analysts. The unitarians insisted that both poems were the work of one poetic genius or, at most, of two great poets. They stressed the unified overall plan of the poems and the consistent character portrayals. The dispute between the analysts and the unitarians became known as the *Homeric question.*

The Homeric question today has been greatly influenced by our increased knowledge of how oral poetry is created. During the 1930's, an American scholar named Milman Parry began studying the bards of modern Yugoslavia. These bards were *illiterate* (unable to read or write), but they composed long poems orally. They did not memorize their poems, but re-created them in slightly different form at each recitation. In creating their plots, the Yugoslav bards used and reused many traditional phrases, lines, and scenes. Parry pointed out that the *Iliad* and the *Odyssey* share these characteristics, though on a much larger scale.

Parry's studies have been developed by other scholars into a theory that Homer was an illiterate bard of exceptional ability. According to this theory, Homer sang the stories of the *Iliad* and the *Odyssey* on many occasions. Toward the end of his life, writing was introduced into Greece. Homer then dictated the *Iliad* and the *Odyssey* to someone. The poems were written in a form of Greek that does not belong to any one city or historical period. This fact has complicated attempts to trace Homer's life.

Most scholars today agree that the *Iliad* and the *Odyssey* reflect an oral tradition. But they still disagree over details of how the poems were composed or preserved.

George Kennedy

See also **Iliad; Odyssey.**

Additional resources

Camps, William A. *An Introduction to Homer.* Oxford, 1980.
Finley, Moses I. *The World of Odysseus.* Rev. ed. Viking, 1978.
Griffin, Jasper. *Homer.* Hill & Wang, 1981.
Schein, Seth L. *The Mortal Hero: An Introduction to Homer's 'Iliad.'* Univ. of California Press, 1984.

Homer, Winslow (1836-1910), was an American artist. He became famous for paintings of the sea that are remarkable for their intensity of feeling and stirring gran-

deur. He never painted fishermen and sea captains as individuals, but as symbols of the rugged quality of all people who follow the sea. In the same way, his vision of the sea is not local, but universal. Homer took American art out of the romanticism of the mid-1800's and carried it to the most powerful heights of realism. His painting *The Gulf Stream* is reproduced in the **Painting** article.

Homer was born in Boston. He was apprenticed to a lithographer in 1854 and became a free-lance illustrator in 1857. By 1859, he was living in New York City. There he worked for *Harper's Weekly,* which employed him during the Civil War to illustrate battlefield scenes. Homer did many war illustrations. At the same time, he painted his first oils and water colors, which are scenes of farm and country life.

Homer spent 10 months in Paris during 1867. He was not deeply influenced by his Paris stay, but the lightening of his colors reflected some influence of the early aspects of French impressionism. A trip to the coastal town of Tynemouth, England, in 1881 and 1882 centered Homer's interest on the sea.

Returning to America, Homer settled permanently at Prout's Neck on the coast of Maine. Most of his sea paintings were done at Prout's Neck. Homer often traveled to the Adirondack Mountains and to Florida, Bermuda, and Nassau. He developed his water color technique on these trips. He skillfully applied transparent *washes* (liquids) to instill a dramatic quality and fine feeling for light.   Frederick A. Sweet

Homestake Mine. See **Lead** (S. Dak.).

Homestead Act was passed by Congress in May 1862. It provided that any person over 21, who was the head of a family, and either a citizen or an alien who intended to become a citizen, could obtain the title to 160 acres (65 hectares) of public land if he or she lived on the land for five years and improved it. Or, the settler could pay $1.25 per acre (0.4 hectare) in place of the residence requirement.

The sponsors of this law believed that land was worthless before it was improved, and that people who converted unoccupied land into farms should not have

Oil painting on canvas (1872); The Butler Art Institute of American Art, Youngstown, Ohio

Winslow Homer painted many scenes of rural American life early in his career. *Snap the Whip, left,* pictures New England farm children in the naturalistic style characteristic of Homer's works.

to pay for the land. They also hoped that the law would help workers obtain *homesteads* (small farms) of their own.

Background. The demand that the government grant free land to settlers began during colonial times. After the Revolutionary War, the United States government regarded its public lands simply as a way of gaining money. This policy met with considerable opposition from farmers. They wanted the government at least to sell the land at a low price. In the 1840's and 1850's, the homestead movement became a national political issue. Proposals for a homestead law were often introduced in Congress. But questions of land policy became involved with the slavery issue, and most Southerners opposed the bills. When the Southern States seceded from the Union, passage of a homestead law became inevitable.

Effects of the law. The Homestead Act attracted thousands of settlers to the West. From 1862 until 1900, it provided farms and new homes for between 400,000 and 600,000 families. The opportunities offered by the act were widely advertised in America and Europe. On the whole, however, the act proved a disappointment to its friends. Through a series of other laws, Congress granted much of the best land in the West to railroad builders or to the states for the support of agricultural colleges. Workers were not attracted to the West.

Those who tried to develop homesteads in the West faced unexpected problems. They were not used to farming conditions on the plains. Farmers often had to use irrigation because rainfall was scarce. The development of farm machinery made a farm of only 160 acres (65 hectares) uneconomical. Some homesteaders sold their land to speculators because of the many problems.

Beginning in 1873, Congress passed a series of new measures that modified the act of 1862. These measures allowed the people to acquire larger tracts of land. But the chief beneficiaries were speculators and others who sought control of the natural resources of the West. Some historians question the value of the act because of the widespread abuses. Of the public lands that passed into private hands from 1862 to 1900, not more than 11 to 17 per cent was settled by homesteaders.

Much of the homesteading during the 1900's took place in Alaska. Many homesteaders acquired free land in the Anchorage area. The U.S. government ended the homesteading program in 1976 for all states except Alaska. The Homestead Act will expire in Alaska in 1986, but homesteading has been suspended there until all land claims by Alaska's native Eskimos, Indians, and Aleuts have been satisfied.   Harold W. Bradley

See also **Pre-emption; Public lands; Western frontier life; Westward movement.**

Homestead National Monument is in southeastern Nebraska. It is the site of one of the first claims in the United States under the Homestead Act of 1862. The monument was established in 1936. For its area, see **National Park System** (table).

Homestead strike of 1892 showed the power of American big business, and was a major defeat for the union movement. The strike involved the Amalgamated Association of Iron and Steel and the Carnegie Steel Company. The union called the strike on June 29, 1892, at Homestead, Pa., because of a wage cut. The company hired private detectives as guards. A battle between

workers and guards resulted in several deaths and many injuries. After peace was restored, most of the workers quit the union and went back to work. See also **Carnegie, Andrew** (The Homestead strike); **Goldman, Emma.**   David Brody

Homicide is the killing of one person by another. Homicide includes an excusable or justifiable killing, as well as murder and manslaughter. A person who finds a burglar attempting to force a way into his or her home sometimes has a legal right to shoot the burglar in self-defense, or to prevent the crime. But the killing is still a homicide. If a child dashes in front of a truck and gets killed, the truck driver may be entirely blameless, but the driver has nevertheless committed a homicide. When a person who kills another is found to have acted within his or her rights, the killing is considered a *justifiable homicide.* Justifiable homicide includes killing a person to prevent the commission of a felony by force or surprise, or to prevent escape after a felony has been committed. Courts also consider homicide in self-defense justifiable. All other homicides are punishable as murder or manslaughter.   Fred E. Inbau

See also **Manslaughter; Murder.**

Homing pigeon is a special breed of pigeon developed for racing and carrying messages. These pigeons are sometimes called *homers.* They can be trained to return to their home loft when released from a distant place. This homing ability has been greatly increased by selective breeding. Like all domestic pigeons, homers are descended from the rock pigeon that lives wild in Europe, Asia, and Africa.

The homing ability. No one knows exactly how pigeons and other birds find their way across strange territory to reach home. Homing pigeons have been known to fly more than 1,000 miles (1,600 kilometers) in two days. This would not allow much time for random searching, so they somehow know the proper direction to take. Some people believe these birds have a mysterious ability to orient themselves with the earth's magnetic field. But there is no real proof of this. Others think the birds are guided by the position of the sun. Just how

Hans Reinhard, Bruce Coleman Ltd.
Homing pigeons carry messages in a holder attached to the leg or back. They can fly up to 60 miles (97 kilometers) an hour.

they do this is not clear, but birds may lose their way in cloudy or foggy weather. Homing pigeons have a highly developed ability to recall visible landmarks. But this does not explain their homing over unfamiliar country.

Pigeon racing. Many people enjoy racing homing pigeons, and often organize races that cover as much as 600 miles (970 kilometers). Although homing pigeons have been bred for their homing ability, additional training of individual birds is important. Trainers first allow the young pigeons to become familiar with the area near the home loft. Then they take the birds 5 to 10 miles (8 to 16 kilometers) away and release them. They gradually increase the distance the bird must fly to reach its home loft.

If the birds are to be raced, the owner trains them over the area in which the race is to be held. Only the most successful homers are entered in competitions. The trainer chooses birds that are in the finest physical condition and have perfect, unbroken flight feathers. Some birds have flown 600 miles (970 kilometers) in one day, without stopping to eat or drink. Pigeons two or three years old make the speediest racers. But older birds perform better in bad weather. Birds with young in the nest are especially dependable homers. Their concern for the young makes them anxious to return.

In official races, clocking devices record the time at which the birds reach their home loft. Upon reaching home, the bird must enter the loft at once so that the owner can remove its band and record the time.

History. Homing pigeons carried messages for the ancient Egyptians and Persians 3,000 years ago. In Greece, pigeons carried news of Olympic games victories to the different cities. The Romans used them to send military messages. During the Franco-Prussian War, the French used homing pigeons, and the Germans trained hawks to catch them. Homing pigeons served the U.S. Signal Corps in World Wars I and II and in the Korean War. During World War I, amazing stories of pigeons delivering messages during combat were recorded. One bird carried a message about 24 miles (39 kilometers) in 25 minutes. It arrived with one leg shot off and its breast injured by a bullet. In 1956, the Army sold the last of its homing pigeons. They have been replaced by electronic devices.   Donald F. Bruning

See also **Pigeon** (picture).

Hominy, *HAHM uh nee,* is a food made from hulled corn. The corn is soaked in a weak lye solution. This causes the kernels to puff up. The skins come free and float to the top. After the kernels are washed, they are ready to be cooked. Hominy has been a favorite dish in the South since pioneer days. It may be boiled or fried, and is usually served with meat. Ground hominy is called *grits.*   Donald J. Reid

Homo erectus, *HOH moh ih REHK tuhs,* is regarded by most anthropologists as a species of human being that lived from about $1\frac{1}{2}$ million to 300,000 years ago. *Homo erectus* resembled people of today but had a slightly smaller brain and slightly larger teeth. *Homo erectus* stood over 5 feet (150 centimeters) tall and walked upright. The Latin word *homo* means *human being. Erectus* means *upright* and refers to the creature's erect posture.

Homo erectus made stone tools, including axes. These early people were probably the first human be-

ings to master the use of fire. They originated in Africa and became the first people to migrate from that continent, eventually reaching northern Asia and Europe.

Fossils of *Homo erectus* were first found in 1891 in Java (now Indonesia) by Eugène Dubois, a Dutch physician (see **Java man**). Other famous *Homo erectus* fossils were found near Heidelberg, Germany; and near Peking, China (see **Heidelberg man; Peking man**).

In 1984, two almost complete *Homo erectus* skeletons were found. One was uncovered at Lake Turkana in Kenya by the paleontologists Richard E. Leakey of Kenya and Alan Walker of Great Britain. The bones were about $1\frac{1}{2}$ million years old, one of the oldest *Homo erectus* specimens ever found. The lack of adult teeth indicated that the person died at about the age of 12. The size of the thighbone suggested that the person was already about $5\frac{1}{2}$ feet (168 centimeters) tall. This skeleton, which lacked some bones from the arms and feet, is the most complete skeleton of an early ancestor ever found. The other skeleton found in 1984 was uncovered in northeastern China. It lacked arm and leg bones and was about 300,000 years old. These discoveries gave scientists their first opportunity to study bones from a young person of the species, as well as bones from all parts of the skeleton instead of just teeth and the skull.

Many scientists believe that *Homo erectus* developed from a type of prehistoric human being known as *Homo habilis* (skillful human being). In turn, *Homo erectus* was an ancestor of our own species, called *Homo sapiens* (wise human being).   Adrienne L. Zihlman

Homo habilis, *HOH moh HAB uh luhs,* is considered by most anthropologists to be the oldest type of human being. Fossil evidence indicates that these prehistoric people lived in Africa about 2 million years ago. The Latin word *homo* means *human being. Habilis* means *skillful* or *handy.* Scientists gave *Homo habilis* this name because its fossils have been found along with some of the earliest known stone tools. The findings suggest that *Homo habilis* made the first such tools.

The first *Homo habilis* fossils were found at Olduvai Gorge in Tanzania in 1960 by Mary Leakey, wife of the anthropologist Louis Leakey, and one of their sons, Jonathan. Other *Homo habilis* fossils have been discovered at Lake Turkana in Kenya and at other sites in eastern Africa. The oldest known *Homo habilis* fossil is part of the skull of a person who lived about 1,900,000 years ago. Richard E. Leakey, another son of Louis and Mary Leakey, found this fossil at Lake Turkana in 1972. Scientists refer to the skull as ER-1470.

Many anthropologists believe that *Homo habilis* developed from humanlike creatures called *australopithecines. Homo habilis* had a brain larger than that of an australopithecine but only a little more than half the size of a modern human brain. Many scientists believe that *Homo habilis,* in turn, developed into a more advanced type of prehistoric human being known as *Homo erectus* (erect human being). *Homo erectus* appeared in eastern Africa about $1\frac{1}{2}$ million years ago.   Andrew Hill

See also **Australopithecus; Homo erectus; Leakey family; Prehistoric people** (Primitive human beings).

Homo sapiens. See **Prehistoric people** (Primitive human beings).

Homogenization, *huh MAHJ uh nuh ZAY shuhn,* is the breaking up of particles in an emulsion so that they are small enough not to separate. An *emulsion* is a mixture in which one liquid is scattered in the form of tiny globules throughout another liquid. Milk is an emulsion of butterfat in water. The butterfat separates to form a layer of cream. To prevent separation, milk is forced through a narrow opening at high pressure. This breaks the large globules into small ones. See also **Milk** (At a processing plant); **Emulsion.**   Walter J. Moore

Homologous structures, *hoh MAHL uh guhs,* are structures that have an essential similarity and develop in the same general way. For example, the flipper of a seal and the foreleg of a dog have the same basic structure. The legs of a turtle and the wings of a bird are also homologous, but they have different uses. Organs that have similar uses but are not similar in structure are said to be *analogous.* The wings of birds and the wings of insects are analogous structures.

Homonym, *HAHM uh nihm* or *HOH muh nihm,* is a word having the same spelling and pronunciation as another word or words, but a different meaning. Examples are *bark* (of a dog) and *bark* (of a tree); and *rest* (relief from activity) and *rest* (remainder).

Some linguists include *homophones* in their definition of homonyms. Homophones are words with the same pronunciation but different spellings and meanings (*site, cite, sight; ate, eight*). In addition, some linguists include *heteronyms* in their definition of homonyms (see **Heteronym**).   William F. Irmscher

Homoptera. See **Insect** (table).

Homosexuality is sexual activity between persons of the same sex. Both men and women may be homosexuals. Female homosexuals are often called *lesbians.* Both male and female homosexuals are sometimes referred to as *gay.* Scientists estimate that 10 per cent of the men in the United States feel sexually attracted primarily to members of their own sex. About 5 per cent of the women are believed to prefer their own sex.

Some persons are not entirely homosexual or entirely *heterosexual* (sexually attracted to the opposite sex). Some homosexuals marry persons of the opposite sex and have children. Many heterosexuals have participated in some kind of homosexual activity at some time in their lives. Persons who are regularly attracted to members of both sexes are called *bisexuals.*

It is fairly common for young boys—and, less frequently, for young girls—to *masturbate* (handle or rub their sex organs). Boys may stimulate each other in this way, and so may girls. Such activity rarely indicates a homosexual preference. In almost every case, the young people are simply exploring their own sexual development. See **Sex** (Puberty).

Some homosexual behavior results from the unavailability of partners of the opposite sex and does not reflect a true homosexual preference. For example, a person who spends long periods separated from the opposite sex may turn to members of his or her own sex for sexual partners. Such situations may occur in prisons, the armed forces, and some boarding schools.

Most homosexuals appear no different from other members of their own sex. But some behave, dress, and talk like members of the opposite sex. Many homosexuals hide their sexual preference. Others join gay groups. Sometimes two homosexuals establish a long-term relationship that is similar to marriage.

Causes of homosexuality are not fully understood. According to the most widely accepted theory, children can learn to be attracted to either of the sexes or to both sexes. They are taught heterosexuality as they learn the role of their sex in society. But some have experiences that lead to mistrust or fear of the opposite sex. Others find it hard to identify with their sex's role in society.

A second theory says that every boy and girl goes through a stage of attraction to members of his or her own sex. This stage occurs between the ages of 6 and 12 in most cases. Because of various emotional problems, some people never pass beyond this stage. Some psychiatrists support this view, but most do not. Still another theory says that homosexuality results from some combination of body chemicals. The evidence for each of these theories is contradictory and confusing. Many experts feel that a number of different factors can lead to homosexuality in different people.

Homosexuality may be more comfortable than heterosexuality for many men and women. Others may try to change their homosexual preference through psychiatric treatment. The younger the person—and the stronger the motives for changing—the more likely it is that the change will occur. A person with heterosexual friends who provide emotional support will probably find the change less difficult than one who lives mostly among homosexuals.

Throughout history, homosexuality has existed in most societies. Various cultures have differed in their attitudes toward it. For example, some ancient Greeks not only accepted homosexuality but considered it to be an ideal relationship—perhaps because ancient Greek men were taught to consider women inferior. Such men believed that only men could fulfill the role of true friend and lover. Other cultures have permitted homosexuality but have not encouraged it. Still others have forbidden it, and some have punished homosexuals.

Today, many people in most Western countries consider homosexuality immoral or unnatural. Many states of the United States prohibit homosexual acts.

Many social scientists oppose laws that prohibit homosexuality and provide punishment for it. These scientists believe that homosexuals are treated unfairly for ways of life that do not directly affect others. Many nations, including Canada, England, France, the Netherlands, and Sweden, have no laws against homosexual actions between consenting adults. In 1961, Illinois became the first U.S. state to abolish its laws against homosexual acts. Since the 1960's, homosexual organizations—sometimes called Gay Liberation groups—have urged society to adopt more tolerant attitudes. In the 1970's, several U.S. and Canadian cities passed laws banning discrimination against homosexuals in employment, housing, and other fields. In 1986, the U.S. Supreme Court ruled that private acts of homosexuality are not protected under the Constitution. This ruling gave states the right to prohibit private homosexual acts. See also **AIDS.**   Carlfred B. Broderick

Additional resources

Bullough, Vern L. *Homosexuality: A History.* Garland, 1979.
Fairchild, Betty, and Hayward, Nancy. *Now That You Know: What Every Parent Should Know About Homosexuality.* Harcourt, 1979.

Carl Frank, Photo Researchers

United Brands Co.

Tegucigalpa, the capital of Honduras, lies high among the country's central mountains. Spanish colonists built the Church of the Virgin of Sorrows.

Bananas, the country's leading product, are grown along the northern coast of Honduras.

Honduras

Honduras, *hahn DOO ruhs,* is a small Central American country that is known for the production of bananas. Honduras is a poor country. Its people have a low average income.

Large numbers of Hondurans grow bananas, the nation's leading source of income, in the northern lowlands along the Caribbean Sea. In the inland mountains, many people raise beans, cattle, coffee, and corn. Tegucigalpa, the capital and largest city of Honduras, is in this region. The country has limited transportation, and Tegucigalpa is one of the few capitals in the world with no railroad. Many Hondurans raise cattle and cotton on the plains bordering the Pacific Ocean in the southern part of the country.

Christopher Columbus arrived at Honduras in 1502. He or a later explorer called the land *Honduras,* the Spanish word for *depths,* because of the deep waters off the northern coast.

Government

The Constitution of Honduras was adopted in 1965. Under the Constitution, the people elect a president to head the government and a legislature to make the country's laws. The president appoints a Cabinet, and

Richard N. Adams, the contributor of this article, is Rapaport Centennial Professor of Social Sciences at the University of Texas at Austin and the author of The Second Sowing: Power and Secondary Development in Latin America.

the Cabinet members head departments that carry out the operations of the government.

The military has much influence in the government of Honduras. For example, the country's military leaders are completely responsible for its national security policies and they can veto any of the president's appointments to the Cabinet. Military leaders in Honduras have often taken complete control of the government. See

Facts in brief

Capital: Tegucigalpa.
Official language: Spanish.
Area: 43,277 sq. mi. (112,088 km²). *Greatest distances—*
   east-west, 405 mi. (652 km); north-south, 240 mi. (386 km).
   *Coastlines—*Caribbean, 382 mi. (615 km); Pacific, 48 mi. (77 km).
Elevation: *Highest—*Cerros de Celaque, 9,400 ft. (2,870 m) above
   sea level. *Lowest—*sea level along the coasts.
Population: *Estimated 1988 population—*4,801,000; distribution,
   60 per cent rural, 40 per cent urban; density, 111 persons per
   sq. mi. (43 per km²). *1974 Census—*2,656,948. *Estimated 1993
   population—*5,590,000.
Chief products: *Agriculture—*bananas, beans, beef and dairy
   cattle, coffee, corn, cotton, milk, sugar cane, tobacco. *Manufacturing—*clothing and textiles, processed foods and beverages, lumber. *Mining—*silver.
National holiday: Independence Day, September 15.
National anthem: "Himno Nacional de Honduras" ("National
   Hymn of Honduras").
Money: *Basic unit—*lempira. One hundred centavos equal one
   lempira. For the price of the lempira in U.S. dollars, see
   Money (table: Exchange rates).

the *History* section of this article for details of the military's role in the Honduran government.

People

More than 95 per cent of all Hondurans are *mestizos* (people with both Spanish and Indian ancestors). Almost all mestizos speak Spanish and are Roman Catholics. In the northern banana-growing areas and port cities, many people can speak English. They learned English because United States fruit companies have long done business there.

About 20,000 Miskito Indians live in thinly populated northeastern Honduras. This group is a mixture of native Indians, freed black slaves, and other groups. They speak the Miskito language. All are Christians, and many belong to the Moravian Church, a Protestant sect.

Garifuna, or Black Caribs, dwell along the northwestern coast of Honduras. These people are descended from black slaves and Arawak Indians on the Caribbean island of St. Vincent. In 1797, the British rulers of St. Vincent transported ancestors of the people to Honduras because they were considered rebellious. The Garifuna speak an Arawak language, but most also speak Spanish, English, or both.

The people of the Bay Islands, which lie off the northern coast, are mostly English-speaking Protestants. These people include descendants of Garifuna, of English planters, and of freed black slaves who emigrated from the Cayman Islands in the Caribbean in the 1800's.

About 60 per cent of the people of Honduras live in rural areas. Among all the countries in the Western Hemisphere, Honduras has one of the highest percentages of rural dwellers. Most rural Hondurans are poor peasants who own or rent small farms. These people have poor transportation and communication, and are cut off from the life of the cities. Modernizing changes are taking place in the cities because of expanding industry and education. But such changes are only slowly reaching the farm communities. Most rural Hondurans live in small houses made of adobe, boards, or poles, or of dirt and stones packed into a wooden frame.

Education. Honduran law requires children to go to school from the age of 7 through 12, but many do not do so. Honduras does not have enough schools, especially in the rural areas, and about 43 per cent of all adult Hondurans cannot read and write.

The country's only university, the National Autonomous University of Honduras, was founded in Tegucigalpa in 1847. It has about 27,000 students. The Pan American Agricultural School, financed by the United Brands Company of the United States, is near the capital.

Population. About 5 million people live in Honduras. The country's population is increasing at the rapid rate of about 3 per cent annually. In 1930, there were only about 850,000 people in Honduras.

Tegucigalpa, which has a population of about 300,000, is the capital and largest city. Other large cities include El Progreso, La Ceiba, and San Pedro Sula. See **Tegucigalpa; San Pedro Sula.**

The land

Honduras has four main land regions: (1) the Mountainous Interior, (2) the Northern Coast, (3) the Northeastern Plain, and (4) the Southern Coast.

The Mountainous Interior covers over 60 per cent of Honduras. The country's highest point is 9,400 feet (2,870 meters) above sea level in the Cerros de Celaque, a mountain range, but most Honduran mountains are much lower. Forests of oaks and pines cover slopes below 7,000 feet (2,100 meters). Above the height of the oak and pine forests are forests of broadleaf evergreens or, where these *cloud forests* have been cut down, patches of scrub pines.

Honduras has no live volcanoes, though neighboring countries do. As a result, Honduras lacks soils made especially fertile by volcanic ash. But a number of small upland valleys in the Mountainous Interior have rich soils that support many farmers, particularly in the western and central parts of the region.

The Northern Coast is the banana-producing region of Honduras. The most important banana areas are the fertile Ulua-Chamelecón River Basin and the coastal plain near the port of Tela. San Pedro Sula, the second largest city in Honduras, is the region's major commercial center. Nearby Puerto Cortés is the country's leading port. The Northern Coast has the only railroads in Honduras. The railroads, built chiefly to carry bananas from plantations to the ports, extend only about 65 miles (105 kilometers) inland.

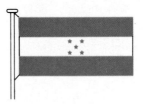 

The flag of Honduras was adopted in 1866. The stars represent five Central American republics that formed a union in the early 1800's.

The coat of arms describes Honduras as *Free, Sovereign, and Independent,* and shows the date of the nation's independence—Sept. 15, 1821.

Honduras, a Central American country, is about 1½ per cent as large as the United States, not counting Alaska and Hawaii.

WORLD BOOK map

East of Tela, the region is largely undeveloped and sparsely populated. It consists of grasslands, swamps, and palm and pine forests. There is some farming in the Aguán valley and other river valleys.

The Northeastern Plain is the least developed and most thinly populated region of Honduras. It has some small Indian communities and a few little towns. Tropical rain forests cover much of the region. They make up a hot, wet area called the Mosquito Coast, or Mosquitia. The plain also has grasslands and some forests of pine and palm trees.

The country's border with Nicaragua was disputed until 1960. The International Court of Justice in the Netherlands decided in favor of the Honduran claim, and the border was established at the Coco, or Wanks, River. Honduras also owns the Swan Islands, two small islands about 125 miles (201 kilometers) to the north in the Caribbean Sea.

The Southern Coast, on the Gulf of Fonseca, is Honduras' only outlet to the Pacific Ocean. Mangrove trees grow along the shoreline, behind which lie narrow plains. The largest plain, that of the Choluteca River in the Choluteca department, has rich soils that support many farms and cattle ranches. The waters off the southern coast of Honduras are too shallow for oceangoing ships, so the country's Pacific Ocean port, Amapala, is on an island in the Gulf of Fonseca.

Climate

Honduras has a tropical climate that becomes cooler in the mountains with the increase of altitude. The coastal lowlands have an average yearly temperature of 88° F. (31° C), with little seasonal change. Tegucigalpa,

3,070 feet (936 meters) above sea level, has an average of 74° F. (23° C). The capital's temperature rarely rises above 90° F. (32° C) in May, the warmest month, and seldom falls below 50° F. (10° C) in December, the coolest month. The highland areas are mild.

The rainy season begins in May. It ends by November or December in the southern and central highlands, which receive a yearly average of 30 to 60 inches (76 to 152 centimeters) of rain. The rain falls until February in the north, and almost throughout the year in the northeast. That region of tropical rain forests, the wettest part of Honduras, has more than 100 inches (250 centimeters) of rain a year. Hurricanes sometimes hit the Northern Coast and damage crops.

Economy

Honduras has few resources, and its economy is one of the most underdeveloped in Latin America. Agricul-

Land regions of Honduras

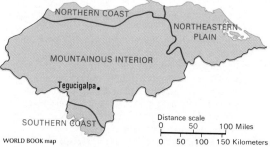

WORLD BOOK map

Honduras map index

Departments

Atlántida	148,440..B	3
Choluteca	192,145..D	3
Colón	77,239..B	4
Comayagua	135,450..C	3
Copán	151,331..C	2
Cortés	370,794..B	2
El Paraíso	140,840..C	4
Francisco Morazán	448,582..C	3
Gracias a Dios	21,221..B	6
Intibucá	80,763..C	2
Islas de la Bahía	13,227..A	4
La Paz	67,415..C	3
Lempira	127,584..C	2
Ocotepeque	50,812..C	1
Olancho	151,768..C	4
Santa Bárbara	184,517..B	2
Valle	90,954..D	3
Yoro	194,631..B	3

Cities and towns

Ajuterique	2,782..C	3
Amapala	1,908..D	3
Arada	1,914..C	2
Atima*	1,498..C	2
Azacualpa	3,350..B	2
Campamento	2,274..C	4
Cane	1,087..C	3
Catacamas	9,081..C	5
Choluteca	25,120..D	3
Comayagua	13,396..C	3
Copán	2,306..C	1
Corquín	2,629..C	2
Danlí	11,369..C	4
Dulce Nombre	2,328..C	2
El Negrito	2,686..B	3
El Níspero	1,636..C	2
El Paraíso (Copán)	2,654..B	2
El Paraíso (Cortés)	9,601..B	3
El Paraíso (El Paraíso)	6,717..D	4

El Porvenir*	2,343..C	4
El Progreso	27,911..B	3
El Triunfo	2,913..D	3
Florida	2,803..B	2
Gracias	2,332..C	2
Guaimaca	3,920..C	4
Gualaco*	3,001..B	4
Guanaja	1,938..A	5
Güinope	1,641..D	4
Intibucá	2,484..C	2
Jacaleapa	1,609..C	4
Jesús de Otoro	2,855..C	3
Jutiapa	1,347..B	4
Juticalpa	1,095..C	4
La Ceiba	38,582..B	4
La Esperanza	2,204..C	2
La Libertad	2,250..C	3
La Masica	1,753..B	3
Langue	2,456..D	3
La Paz	6,674..C	3
La Pimienta	1,708..B	3
La Unión	1,560..C	2
Lejamaní	1,913..C	3
Limón	1,697..B	5
Macuelizo	1,379..B	2
Marcala	3,237..C	2
Minas de Oro	2,716..C	3
Morazán	4,370..B	3
Moroceli	1,447..C	4
Nacaome	5,894..D	3
Naranjito	2,766..C	2
Nueva Arcadia*	5,853..B	2
Nueva Ocotepeque	4,618..C	1
Olanchito	7,297..B	4
Orica	1,479..C	4
Pespire	2,010..D	3
Potrerillos	5,365..B	3
Puerto Cortés	25,661..B	3
Quimistán	1,586..B	2
Roatán	1,952..A	4
Sabana Grande	1,408..D	3
Salamá	1,584..C	4
San Andrés*	2,451..C	2
San Antonio de Cortés	2,338..B	2
San Francisco*	1,783..B	3

San Francisco de Becerra*	1,432..C	4
San Francisco de la Paz	2,288..C	4
San Ignacio	2,204..C	3
San José	1,186..C	2
San José de Colinas	2,754..B	2
San Juan de Flores	1,205..C	3
San Lorenzo	9,261..D	3
San Luis	2,244..B	2
San Manuel	2,205..B	3
San Marcos (Ocotepeque)	2,008..C	2
San Marcos (Santa Bárbara)	2,519..B	2
San Marcos de Colón	4,397..D	4
San Matías*	1,749..D	4
San Nicolás (Copán)	1,886..C	2
San Nicolás (Santa Bárbara)	1,931..C	2
San Pedro Sula	146,842..B	2
San Vincente Centenario*	1,549..C	2
Santa Bárbara	5,910..C	2
Santa Cruz de Yojoa	1,832..C	3
Santa María del Real	1,531..C	5
Santa Rita (Santa Bárbara)	1,618..C	2
Santa Rita (Yoro)	4,417..B	3
Santa Rosa de Aguán	1,885..B	5
Santa Rosa de Copán	12,103..C	2
Savá*	2,809..B	4
Siguatepeque	12,005..C	3
Sonaguera	2,262..B	4
Talanga	4,805..G	3
Tegucigalpa	267,754..C	3
Tela	19,268..B	3
Teupasenti*	1,558..C	4

Tocoa	2,840..B	5
Trinidad (Copán)	1,408..C	2
Trinidad (Santa Bárbara)	2,491..B	2
Trujillo	4,019..B	5
Victoria	1,514..C	3
Villa de San Antonio	1,833..C	3
Villa de San Francisco	2,517..C	4
Villanueva	4,896..B	2
Yoro	4,429..B	3
Yuscarán	1,831..D	4
Zacapa*	3,382..C	2

Physical features

Aguán, Río (River)	..B	4
Bahía, Islas de la (Islands)	..A	4
Bahía de Omoa (Bay)	..B	2
Bahía de Tela	..B	3
Bay Islands, see Bahía, Islas de la		
Cabo Camarón (Cape)	..A	6
Cabo de Honduras (Cape)	..A	4
Cabo Falso (Cape)	..B	7
Caribbean Sea	..A	5
Cerros de Azacualpa (Mountains)	..C	4
Cerros de Celaque (Mountains)	..C	2
Cerros de Opalaca (Mountains)	..C	2
Cerros de Sulaco (Mountains)	..B	3
Cerros de Villaguaire (Mountains)	..D	3
Cerros del Ocote (Mountains)	..B	4
Chamelecón, Río (River)	..B	2
Coco (Wanks), Río (River)	..C	6

Cordillera de Agalta (Mountains)	..B	5
Golfo de Fonseca (Gulf)	..D	3
Guanaja, Isla (Island)	..A	5
Guayape, Río (River)	..C	4
Gulf of Honduras	..A	3
Jalán, Río (River)	..C	4
Lago de Yojoa (Lake)	..C	3
Laguna de Brus (Lagoon)	..B	6
Laguna de Caratasca (Lagoon)	..B	7
Laguna de Tilbalaca (Lagoon)	..B	6
Laguna Micos (Lagoon)	..B	3
Montaña de la Esperanza (Mountains)	..B	5
Montañas de Colón (Mountains)	..C	5
Montañas del Zapotillo (Mountains)	..C	4
Mosquito Coast	..C	7
Negro, Río (River)	..D	3
Patuca, Río (River)	..B	6
Punta Obispo (Point)	..B	3
Punta Patuca (Point)	..B	6
Punta Sal (Point)	..B	3
Roatán, Isla (Island)	..A	4
Santa Bárbara (Mountain)	..C	2
Sico, Río (River)	..B	5
Sierra de Comayagua (Mountains)	..C	3
Sierra de Montecillos (Mountains)	..C	3
Sierra de Omoa (Mountains)	..B	2
Ulua, Río (River)	..B	3
Utila, Isla (Island)	..A	4

*Does not appear on map; key shows general location.
Source: 1974 census.

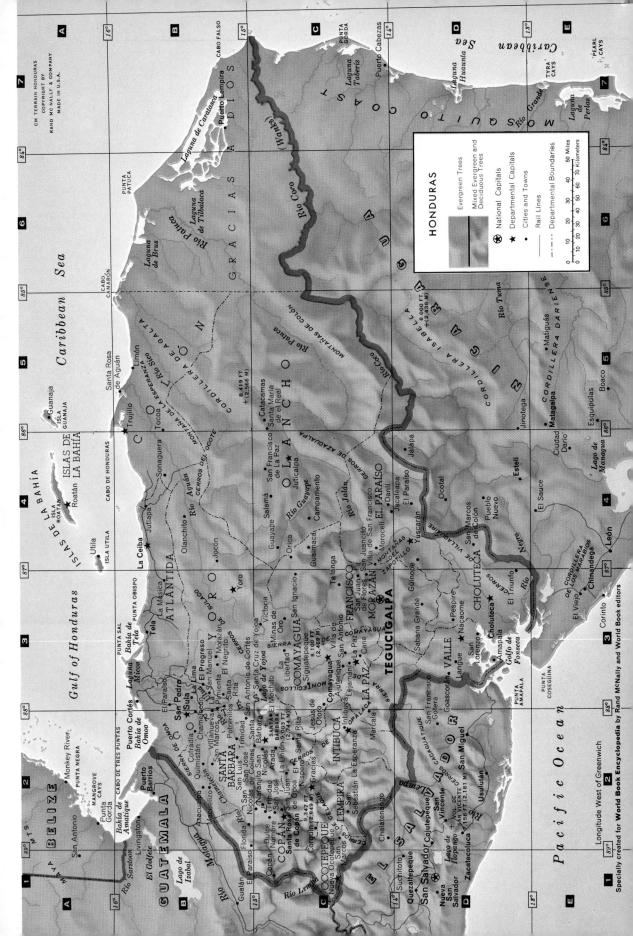

HONDURAS

Evergreen Trees

Mixed Evergreen and
Deciduous Trees

✪ National Capitals
★ Departmental Capitals
• Cities and Towns
— Rail Lines
-·- Departmental Boundaries

0 10 20 30 40 50 Miles
0 10 20 30 40 50 60 70 Kilometers

CM TERRAIN HONDURAS
COPYRIGHT BY
RAND MC NALLY & COMPANY
MADE IN U.S.A.

Specially created for **World Book Encyclopedia** by Rand McNally and World Book editors

Longitude West of Greenwich

ture is by far the most important economic activity in Honduras. Much of the country's income is from banana and coffee exports. The banana industry in Honduras was developed by U.S. companies in the early 1900's. Today, most of the banana plantations are owned by Honduran companies. But the firms that ship the bananas to foreign markets are mostly foreign-owned.

Agriculture employs more than half of all Honduran workers. Bananas account for about a third of the nation's exports, and coffee accounts for about a fourth. Corn is the people's main food. The corn crop covers more land than any other crop in Honduras. Farmers also grow beans, cotton, sugar cane, and tobacco. Beef and dairy cattle are raised in the highland valleys and southern grasslands.

Honduras exports shrimp, which are caught near the Bay Islands. It exports timber from pines and tropical hardwood trees. Beef is also an important export.

Service industries employ about a third of all Honduran workers. Wholesale and retail trade is the

most important service industry. Much of the country's trade industry is based on the distribution of agricultural products. Community, social, and personal services form the second most important category of service industry. This industry includes services such as education and health care. These services are most important in the country's largest cities, especially Tegucigalpa. Other service industries include housing; finance, insurance, and real estate; government; and utilities.

Manufacturing plays only a small part in the Honduran economy. Honduras imports most of its machinery and other manufactured goods from the United States, its major trading partner, and from other countries. Manufactured products consist largely of processed foods and beverages, clothing, and textiles—all produced mainly for use in Honduras. Sawmills provide much lumber for the furniture, paper, and wood products industries. Tegucigalpa and San Pedro Sula are the major manufacturing centers. Pottery articles, used widely in Honduran households, are made in rural homes as a craft industry.

Transportation. Roads in Honduras are scarce and few are paved, especially in the rural areas. There, the people travel mainly by buses, mules, or horses. Less than 2 per cent of the people own an automobile. Honduran railways—operated mostly by the fruit companies—serve only the Northern Coast region. The country has two international airports, at Tegucigalpa and San Pedro Sula.

Communication. Honduras has six daily newspapers. The largest is *La Tribuna* of Tegucigalpa. Most of the radio and television stations are privately owned. Honduras has an average of about one radio for every three people. Less than 3 per cent of the people own a television set. Almost all the telephone lines are owned by the government, and are in Tegucigalpa and San Pedro Sula. The fruit companies operate telephones in the banana-producing areas.

Honduras' gross national product

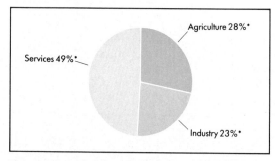

Agriculture 28%*

Services 49%*

Industry 23%*

The gross national product (GNP) is the total value of goods and services produced by a country in a year. The GNP measures a nation's total annual economic performance and can also be used to compare the economic output and growth of countries. Honduras' GNP was $2,839,500,000 in 1983.

Production and workers by economic activities

Economic activities	Per cent of GDP* produced	Employed workers Number of persons	Employed workers Per cent of total
Agriculture, forestry, & fishing	28	556,106	53
Manufacturing	15	142,444	14
Wholesale & retail trade	13	100,772	10
Community, social, & personal services	9	144,245	14
Transportation & communication	8	45,461	4
Housing	7	(†)	(†)
Construction	6	45,270	4
Finance, insurance, & real estate	5	9,504	1
Government	5	(†)	(†)
Mining	2	(‡)	(‡)
Utilities	2	(§)	(§)
Total	100	1,043,802	100

*Based on gross domestic product (GDP). GDP is gross national product adjusted for net income sent or received from abroad.
†Included in Community, social, & personal services.
‡Included in Manufacturing.
§Included in Transportation & communication.
Sources: Central Bank of Honduras; International Monetary Fund.

History

The Indian period. Little is known of what is now Honduras before the Spaniards arrived in the early 1500's. An eastern center of the famous Maya Indian civilization had thrived at Copán until the 800's. Copán had beautiful stone palaces, pyramids, and temples, and its people were advanced in science and learning. But by the time the Spaniards arrived, Copán lay in ruins, and the Indians of the region had forgotten the city.

The colonial period. In 1502, Christopher Columbus landed at Cabo de Honduras (Cape Honduras). He claimed the land for Spain. A number of Spanish explorers soon visited the region and founded settlements. The Spaniards gradually conquered the Indians. Many Indians were killed, died of disease, or were shipped as slaves to plantations in the West Indies.

The Spaniards developed gold and silver mines in Honduras. They brought many black slaves from Africa to work in the mines along with the Indians. The Spaniards also developed cattle ranches to supply food to the mining centers. But the mines were not profitable enough to attract many colonists.

Independence. On Sept. 15, 1821, Honduras and four other Central American states declared their independence from Spain. They became part of the Mexican empire, but broke away from it in 1823 and formed the United Provinces of Central America. This union generally followed liberal policies. It established some civil rights, and ended the special privileges of the powerful nobility and the Roman Catholic Church. Honduras left the union in 1838 after the union began to fall apart under various pressures, including efforts by landowners and the clergy to regain their privileges.

Honduras was the weakest country in Central America. It soon came under the influence of its more powerful neighbors, especially Guatemala. During the 1800's, Guatemala started or aided several revolts in Honduras. It supported Honduran conservatives or liberals, depending on which group was in power in Guatemala.

United States fruit companies began arriving during the 1890's to grow bananas in Honduras. They cleared forests and drained swamps for plantations in the Northern Coast region, and built railroads and ports. They also established towns, hospitals, and schools for the workers. During the early 1900's, bananas became Honduras' leading source of income. Export taxes paid by the U.S. fruit companies took care of most of the Honduran government's expenses. The government gave the companies special privileges to increase this income, and the firms developed a strong influence over the government. The term *banana republic,* referring to several Latin-American countries, was first used for Honduras.

Recent developments. Until 1933, most Honduran presidents did not serve long because of frequent revolutions. General Tiburcio Carías Andino became president in 1933 and held office for 16 years, the longest period. Carías ruled as a dictator. Several revolts failed to overthrow him, and he retired in 1948.

More political violence during the 1950's led to the election of Ramón Villeda Morales, a physician, who became president in 1957. Villeda established a land re-

form program, and built hospitals, roads, and schools.

In 1963, a military revolt led by Colonel Osvaldo López Arellano overthrew the government. An elected assembly wrote a new constitution that provided for López to become president. In 1971, the voters elected Ramón Ernesto Cruz, a lawyer, to the presidency. But in 1972, the armed forces overthrew the Cruz government and López again became president.

In 1969, a Honduran land reform law forced many families from El Salvador living in Honduras to give up their land. Salvadoran troops entered Honduras in July 1969, but left in August. In 1970, the Organization of American States helped the two nations set up a neutral zone along their border. In 1980, the countries signed an agreement to end their border dispute.

In 1975, the armed forces removed López from office and replaced him with Colonel Juan Alberto Melgar Castro. López' government had been involved in a scandal over a bribe from a United States company to reduce the export tax on bananas. In 1978, three leaders of the armed forces removed Melgar from office and took over the government. In 1981, elections for a civilian government were held. The people elected Roberto Suazo Córdova president and also chose a new legislature. In 1985, José Ancona Hoyo was elected to succeed Suazo as president.

In the 1980's, Honduras became a site of clashes between troops of the Sandinista government of Nicaragua and Nicaraguan rebels who were trying to overthrow the Sandinistas. The rebels, called *contras,* established guerrilla bases in Honduras and raided Nicaragua from the bases. Sandinista troops sometimes entered Honduras to attack the contras. The United States government opposed the Sandinistas. U. S. and Honduran forces staged military maneuvers in Honduras.

Richard N. Adams

Related articles in *World Book* include:

Banana	Mosquito Coast	Valle, José
Central America	San Pedro Sula	Cecilio del
Latin America	Tegucigalpa	Walker, William
Maya		

Outline

I. **Government**
II. **People**
    A. Education
    B. Population
III. **The land**
    A. The Mountainous Interior
    B. The Northern Coast
    C. The Northeastern Plain
    D. The Southern Coast
IV. **Climate**
V. **Economy**
    A. Agriculture   D. Transportation
    B. Service industries   E. Communication
    C. Manufacturing
VI. **History**

Questions

How did Honduras get its name?
What is Honduras' leading source of income?
How did U.S. fruit companies influence Honduras?
What ancient civilization thrived in Honduras?
What is the main food of the Hondurans?
What country is Honduras' major trading partner?
Where do Honduras' *cloud forests* grow?
Why is the Pacific port of Honduras on an island?
What are Honduras' chief manufactured products?

George Holton, Photo Researchers

A Maya ball court can still be seen at Copán, an ancient center of civilization. The Maya played a game like soccer.

Honecker, *HOHN uhk uhr,* **Erich,** *AY rihk* (1912-   ), became the leader of East Germany in 1971. He succeeded Walter Ulbricht as first secretary of the ruling Socialist Unity (Communist) Party.

Honecker was born in Neunkirchen, Saar, in what is now West Germany. He joined the Communist Party in 1929. From 1935 to 1945, he was held in prison by the Nazis. From 1946 to 1955, Honecker served as chairman of an East German Communist youth group called Free German Youth. He was elected to the Volkskammer, the East German legislature, in 1949. During the mid-1950's, he studied Communist theory and practice in the Soviet Union. In 1958, he became a member of the Political Bureau, the governing body of the Socialist Unity Party. He served as East German secretary for military and security affairs from 1958 to 1971.   Melvin Croan

Honegger, *HOH nehg uhr,* **Arthur** (1892-1955), was a French composer. In the early 1920's, he became a member of *Les Six,* a famous group of six French composers who rejected the prevailing taste for romanticism and impressionism in music. Honegger developed a highly personal style that featured energetic rhythms. He often wrote *polytonal* harmonies and even wrote *atonal* melodies. Polytonal melodies use two or more keys at the same time, and atonal melodies have no key center. Honegger's most popular composition is the tone poem *Pacific 231* (1924), which portrays in rhythm the motion of a locomotive. Honegger also wrote many works for the theater, notably *King David* (1921) and *Joan of Arc at the Stake* (1938). In addition he composed symphonies, concertos, chamber music, pieces for the piano, and works for chorus and solo voice. Honegger was born in Le Havre.   Mary Vinquist

Honey is the sweet, thick fluid made by bees from flower nectar. Nectar is a thin, watery liquid. Bees sip it from the blossoms and carry it to their hives. Each worker bee has a pouch in its body, called a honey stomach, where the nectar is stored. In the pouch, the sugar and nectar are broken down by a process called *inversion* into two simple sugars, *fructose* and *glucose.* After bees deposit the nectar in the hive, they allow most of the water to evaporate and the liquid thickens. They also add enzymes that enhance the flavor.

Kinds of honey. The flavor and color of honey are influenced by the kinds of flowers from which the nectar comes. Honey ranges in color from white through dark amber. Usually the light-colored honeys have the mildest flavor. The most common honey plants are alfalfa, alsike clover, sweet clover, and white clover. But many regional plants produce excellent honey. The clovers are common in the north. In the east, buckwheat flowers are used. In the south, tupelo, mesquite, sourwood, and gallberry supply nectar for honey. Among the white honeys, that of California white sage ranks first, followed by orange blossom honey. Fall flowers such as goldenrod and asters give a dark honey.

Most pure honeys *granulate* (develop sugary crystals). An exception is tupelo honey, which, because it contains more fructose than glucose, seldom granulates. Industrial users heat the honey to prevent granulation.

Food value. Honey is an excellent energy food because it contains simple sugars that can be used quickly by the body. It differs chemically from cane sugar, which is also an energy food. Honey contains mineral salts and other materials needed by the body. It is the only form of sugar food that does not need to be refined. Bakers often use it in place of sugar for their products. Many cough medicines and laxatives contain honey.

The honey industry. About 200 million pounds (90 million kilograms) of honey are produced in the United States each year. North Dakota, California, and South Dakota are the leading honey-producing states. In Canada, Alberta leads the provinces in honey production.

Honey was once sold only in the comb. That is, the little waxy cells that contain the honey were sold along with the liquid. Today, suppliers usually remove the comb and seal the honey in airtight containers. This keeps the honey fresh for many months. Commercial producers place the honeycombs in a *honey extractor.*

A. J. Deane, Bruce Coleman Ltd.

Bees store nectar in their hives in tiny, six-sided containers called cells, *above.* After it is stored in the cells, the water in the nectar evaporates, and the nectar changes into honey.

Leading honey-producing states and provinces

Annual honey production	
North Dakota	●●●●●●●●●●●●●●●●●●●●●●
	31,030,000 pounds (14,075,000 kilograms)
California	●●●●●●●●●●●●●●●●●●●(
	27,040,000 pounds (12,265,000 kilograms)
Alberta	●●●●●●●●●●●●●●●(
	22,800,000 pounds (10,342,000 kilograms)
South Dakota	●●●●●●●●●●●●●●●(
	22,713,000 pounds (10,302,000 kilograms)
Florida	●●●●●●●●●●●●●●(
	21,750,000 pounds (9,866,000 kilograms)
Manitoba	●●●●●●●●●●●●
	17,600,000 pounds (7,983,000 kilograms)
Saskatchewan	●●●●●●●●●●(
	14,400,000 pounds (6,532,000 kilograms)
Minnesota	●●●●●●●(
	10,608,000 pounds (4,812,000 kilograms)
Nebraska	●●●●●(
	7,600,000 pounds (3,447,000 kilograms)
Texas	●●●●●
	7,254,000 pounds (3,290,000 kilograms)

Figures are for 1986.
Sources: U.S. Department of Argriculture; Statistics Canada.

This machine whirls the honeycombs around, forcing the honey out. The honey is then bottled and sold.

When honey stands for a long time, the liquid may separate to form hard particles, called *crystals.* Many people prefer this crystal form, which is sold as *creamed honey. Honey butter,* made by beating honey and butter together, is also a popular spread.

History. Honey was an important sweet in ancient times. A jar of honey on the table was once considered a mark of great wealth. In the Bible, the Israelites were promised a "land flowing with milk and honey." The ancient Egyptians are believed to have used honey in embalming. Richard A. Havens

See also **Bee; Beeswax.**

Honey ant. See Ant (Honey ants; picture).

Honey badger. See Ratel.

Honey bee. See Bee.

Honey bear. See Sloth bear.

Honey locust is a medium-sized tree with spreading branches and handsome, finely divided leaves. Most

honey locust trees are native to Asia, Africa, and South America. The bark of the honey locust is furrowed. In some kinds, stout spines grow on the trunk and branches. The fruits of the honey locust look like long, somewhat flattened and twisted pea pods. They contain a sweetish pulp used as cattle feed. The wood of the honey locust is hard, heavy, and durable. It is used for posts and railroad ties. Honey locust trees are grown in the United States and are used as shade trees and ornamentals.

Scientific classification. Honey locusts belong to the pea family, Leguminosae. They make up the genus *Gleditsia.* The common honey locust is *G. triacanthos.* T. Ewald Maki

See also **Locust** (tree); **Tree** (Familiar broadleaf and needleleaf trees [picture]).

Honeybee. See Bee.

Honeybloom. See Dogbane.

Honeycomb. See Bee, with pictures.

Honeydew melon. See Muskmelon.

Honeyeater is the name of a family of about 170 species of land birds. Most honeyeaters live in Australia and New Guinea, but some are found in Hawaii and on other islands in the Pacific Ocean. Two kinds of honeyeaters, called *sugarbirds,* live in South Africa.

Honeyeaters have a long, tube-shaped tongue with brushlike edges. This tongue is especially suited for eating nectar from flowers. When honeyeaters are looking for nectar, they sometimes carry pollen from one plant to another (see **Pollen**). The birds also eat berries, fruits, and insects, but they digest nectar faster. They may get intoxicated and cannot fly if the nectar has been *fermented* (turned into alcohol) by rain and sunlight.

The honey locust, *below,* has a slender trunk and spreading branches. The wood of the honey locust is hard, heavy, and durable. The tree's fruit, *right,* resembles flat and somewhat twisted pea pods.

© D. Lecourt, Jacana

© Leonard Lee Rue III, Earth Scenes

WORLD BOOK illustration by James Teason

The honeyeater gets its name from its habit of eating nectar from the blossoms of trees and shrubs. These birds also eat caterpillars, spiders, and berries and other fruits.

302 **Honeysuckle**

Most honeyeaters are greenish- or grayish-brown with yellow or white marks on their heads. They range from about 3 to 20 inches (7 to 50 centimeters) long. Most honeyeaters live in forests and build cup-shaped nests in trees and bushes. They lay one to four eggs at a time. Some species can sing well, but most honeyeaters make only harsh, unpleasant noises.

Honeyeaters have become almost extinct on the Hawaiian Islands since white people settled there. American and English settlers brought animals that killed these birds. The destruction of forest areas has also reduced the number of honeyeaters. Five species once lived in Hawaii. But in the mid-1980's, only one bird of one species, the Kauai oo, was known to have survived. A Molokai oo, a bird last reported in Hawaii in 1904, was believed to have been seen there in 1981.

Scientific classification. Honeyeaters make up the family Meliphagidae.   James J. Dinsmore

Honeysuckle is any one of a family of ornamental shrubs and vines. Most honeysuckles are evergreens, or nearly so. They live in temperate regions throughout the world. All have dark green, oval leaves that are usually quite smooth and grow opposite each other in pairs. Sometimes the bases of the leaves are united around the stem. In other plants, the woody stem seems to grow through the leaves.

Honeysuckles usually produce a profusion of trumpet-shaped flowers. The blossoms of some are small, but all are quite beautiful. Many are fragrant. The colors vary from white, yellow, pink, and purple to bright scarlet. When the petals drop off, red, yellow, white, black, or blue berries form. Many birds eat these berries and carry the seeds away, distributing the plants widely.

Honeysuckles are easy to grow. Most are hardy and propagate easily, either from cuttings or from seeds. The plants grow compactly and seldom need pruning. They live a long time. Bush honeysuckles are grown as shrubs, and some types grow well in rock gardens.

WORLD BOOK illustration by Robert Hynes
Coral honeysuckle

Vine honeysuckles are often trained to twine over walls or fences.

Various insects bring pollen to the honeysuckles. The white-flowered kinds lure sphinx moths at night. The *bush honeysuckle,* with its small yellow blossoms, attracts bees. The *coral,* or *trumpet, honeysuckle* has blossoms that are red outside and orange-yellow inside. Hummingbirds like the sweet nectar of these flowers. Some honeysuckles are also called *woodbine.*

Scientific classification. Honeysuckles belong to the honeysuckle family, Caprifoliaceae. The bush honeysuckle is *Diervilla lonicera.* The coral honeysuckle is *Lonicera sempervirens.* Woodbine is *L. periclymenum.* Two species widely used in landscaping are *L. tatarica* and the fragrant *L. fragrantissima.*

J. J. Levison

See also **Black haw; Elder; Snowball; Viburnum.**

Hong Kong (pop. 5,930,000) is a British dependency on the southern coast of China. For many years, Great Britain considered Hong Kong a crown colony. Britain reclassified all its colonies as dependencies in the 1970's, but Hong Kong is still often called a colony. It lies near the mouth of the Zhu Jiang (Pearl River), about 90 miles (140 kilometers) southeast of Guangzhou (also called Canton), China.

Hong Kong is a bustling center of economic activity and one of the world's most crowded places. It ranks among Asia's major ports, and as a center of trade, finance, manufacturing, and tourism. Hong Kong has a land area of only about 410 square miles (1,061 square kilometers), but about 6 million people live there. On the average, about 14,500 people live on each square mile (5,600 per square kilometer).

Hong Kong consists of a peninsula attached to the mainland of China, and over 235 islands. The mainland area has two sections—the New Territories in the north and the Kowloon Peninsula in the south. The main island, Hong Kong Island, lies south of the peninsula.

Most of Hong Kong's economic activity takes place in the urban areas of Victoria and Kowloon, where a majority of the people live. Victoria is the capital of Hong Kong, and Kowloon is the largest urban settlement. Victoria is on the north shore of Hong Kong Island, and Kowloon is on the Kowloon Peninsula. The two communities are separated by Victoria Harbor. The Chinese call this large, beautiful area *hong kong* (fragrant harbor).

All of present-day Hong Kong was part of China from ancient times until the 1800's. Great Britain gained control of Hong Kong Island in 1842 and the Kowloon Peninsula in 1860 through treaty agreements with China. In 1898, China leased the New Territories to Britain for 99 years. The lease expires in 1997. During the late 1800's and early 1900's, Hong Kong served as a port for British trade with China. Since the mid-1900's, Hong Kong has grown into a center of international trade and finance and has also developed many of its own industries.

The Chinese Communists, who have governed China since 1949, never formally recognized Britain's control of Hong Kong. But China has not actively opposed British rule, probably because Hong Kong has great value for the Chinese economy. China earns much income by selling food, water, raw materials, and manufactured products to Hong Kong. The Chinese government also owns many banks, department stores, and hotels in Hong Kong.

Almost all the residents of Hong Kong are Chinese. Through the years, millions of people have moved from China to Hong Kong to find jobs. Since the Communist conquest of China, large numbers of Chinese have fled to Hong Kong to escape Communist rule.

Government

A governor heads the government of Hong Kong. The British monarch appoints the governor to a term of unspecified length. A 15-member Executive Council helps the governor carry out government operations. A Legislative Council, which has up to 50 members, makes Hong Kong's laws. All members of the two councils are nominated by the governor and appointed by the British monarch. Members of the Executive Council serve five-year terms, and Legislative Council members serve four

Victoria, the capital of Hong Kong, lies across a harbor from the larger urban area of Kowloon, *background.* Commuters cross the harbor on ferries that leave every few minutes.

years. British officials hold the governorship and most other top posts in the government. Chinese citizens of Hong Kong serve in many of the lower offices.

Although Britain controls the government, Hong Kong is basically Chinese in character. The British try to limit their role in the dependency. The government's functions include maintaining law and order and providing roads and sanitation facilities. The government works to provide housing for the needy, free education for all children, and care for the elderly. It also promotes Hong Kong's economy but tries as much as possible to avoid interfering in business activities and the lives of the people.

People

Population and ancestry. Hong Kong has about 5,930,000 people, of whom more than 98 per cent are Chinese. Most are immigrants from southern China or descendants of immigrants from that region. The relatively few non-Chinese residents of Hong Kong include people from Australia, Great Britain, India, Japan, the United States, and Vietnam.

Languages. Hong Kong has two official languages, English and Chinese. English was the only official language until 1974, but most of Hong Kong's Chinese people do not speak or understand it well, if at all. The majority of them speak the Cantonese dialect of Chinese. As a result, the government made Chinese an official language.

Way of life. About 90 per cent of Hong Kong's people live in urban areas. Many work in factories, and oth-

ers are employed by the government or the shipping industry. Most of the urban people live in Victoria and Kowloon. Hong Kong's other urban settlements include Tsuen Wan, Tuen Mun, and Sha Tin.

People in rural areas of Hong Kong live in small farming villages and raise crops and livestock. Some farmers still plant and harvest crops by hand or with hand tools. But new farming methods and machinery have enabled many to increase their production.

The people of Hong Kong eat large amounts of fresh vegetables, fish, and rice, and some poultry and pork. Many of them wear the same type of clothing worn in Western countries. Others wear Chinese-style clothing, such as dark-colored pants and shirts, and long robes. The major religions in Hong Kong are Buddhism and Taoism. Small groups of Christians, Hindus, Jews, and Muslims also live there.

Housing in Hong Kong's urban areas varies sharply. Most wealthy people live in luxury apartment buildings, and some live in beautiful houses with gardens. Large numbers of middle- and low-income people occupy crowded high-rise apartment buildings, which stand close together. In many cases, several poor families share one or two small rooms. Large numbers of refugees from China once lived in wood and tin shacks, which stood on hillsides, under bridges, and even on the roofs of buildings. Thousands of families also made their homes on boats in harbors. Some such dwellings still exist, but there are far fewer than in the past.

Hong Kong's government began a public housing program in the mid-1950's to improve housing. Since then, the government has erected low-rent apartment buildings for more than 2 million people. Most of these buildings are in huge housing complexes called *resettlement estates.*

The majority of Hong Kong's rural people live in one- or two-story houses made of brick or stone. Most of the homes have tile or tin roofs. Some rural villages in Hong Kong were settled more than 1,000 years ago.

Education. All children in Hong Kong are required by law to go to school for nine years—six years of elementary school and three of high school. The government supports the public school system, in which classes are taught in Chinese. A few private schools conduct classes in English. About 75 per cent of the people can read and write.

Hong Kong has two universities, four teachers colleges, and many technical schools. The largest university is the University of Hong Kong, which was founded in 1911 and has about 5,000 students. The Chinese University, founded in 1963, has about 4,700 students.

Victoria and Kowloon

Victoria and Kowloon are the main centers of trade, finance, industry, and tourism in Hong Kong. Many small shops, open markets, and high-rise buildings line the narrow streets of these crowded urban areas.

Victoria and Kowloon lie on opposite sides of Victoria Harbor. Every day, thousands of people cross the harbor on ferries to go to work or to shop. About 85,000 motor vehicles travel daily between the Kowloon Peninsula and Hong Kong Island by means of a tunnel under the harbor. An underwater subway links Victoria and Kowloon.

Victoria is the seat of government and the financial center of Hong Kong. The Victoria urban area has a population of about 1 million. Government buildings and banks and other financial establishments are in central Victoria. Local residents own some of the banks. Others are branches of large banks of China, Great Britain,

Japan, the United States, and other countries. High-rise commercial buildings and fashionable shops and hotels stand along Victoria's waterfront.

A beautiful mountain called Victoria Peak rises west of the central district of Victoria. Luxury apartment buildings and attractive houses line the steep sides of the mountain. A railway transports passengers between the central district and the top of the mountain. Many people live in crowded tenements in the Wanchai district, east of central Victoria.

Kowloon is larger and more crowded than Victoria. About 2,400,000 persons live in this urban area. It includes an old section and a newer area, called New Kowloon. The old section of Kowloon, which lies along Victoria Harbor, has a population of about 750,000. New Kowloon lies north of the old section and has a population of about $1\frac{1}{2}$ million.

The old section has many shops, hotels, and restaurants. Tourists flock to stores along Nathan Road in the center of Kowloon to buy cameras, jewelry, custom clothing, and other products. Many merchants sell their goods in the streets or at open-air market places. The market places offer such items as fresh vegetables, fish and poultry, and household goods. Many resettlement estates and factories are in New Kowloon.

Most visitors to Hong Kong arrive first at Kai Tak International Airport in Kowloon. Passenger ships dock at Kowloon's Ocean Terminal, one of the largest piers in Asia. A railroad runs through the New Territories and connects Kowloon with Canton, China. Ferries also provide transportation between Kowloon and Canton.

Land and climate

Hong Kong covers a total area of 1,126 square miles (2,916 square kilometers). But only 410 square miles (1,061 square kilometers) of the total area is land.

The land. Rugged mountains and rolling hills cover much of Hong Kong. Some mountains in the New Territories rise more than 3,000 feet (910 meters) above

Hong Kong

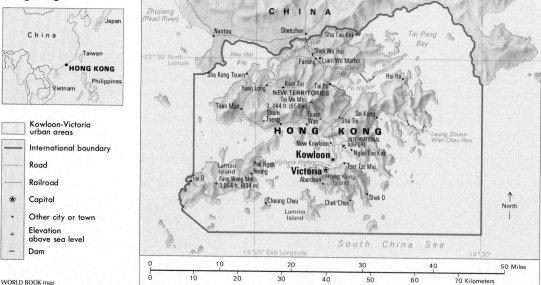

Kowloon-Victoria urban areas

International boundary

Road

Railroad

⊛ Capital

• Other city or town

+ Elevation above sea level

— Dam

WORLD BOOK map

Street markets in Hong Kong sell clothing, jewelry, textiles, and a wide variety of other items. They serve both Hong Kong residents and tourists. Over 2 million tourists visit Hong Kong each year.

sea level. Victoria Peak, on Hong Kong Island, is 1,818 feet (554 meters) high.

The rocky, indented coastlines of Hong Kong's islands and mainland provide many small harbors for fishing villages. Parts of Victoria Harbor have been filled in with earth to create new land. Kai Tak International Airport and many buildings are on land reclaimed from the harbor.

Barren mountains separate the business districts of the Kowloon Peninsula from farmland in the New Territories. Only about 10 per cent of the land in Hong Kong is suitable for farming. Throughout the New Territories, rice paddies and vegetable and flower fields lie crowded between areas of poor vegetation and rocky hillsides. A small river called the Sham Chun forms the border between Hong Kong and China.

Climate. Hong Kong has a semitropical climate. Summers are hot and humid, with temperatures reaching 95° F. (35° C) or higher. Hong Kong receives about 88 inches (224 centimeters) of rainfall yearly. More than 75 per cent of the rain falls in summer and causes flooding and mudslides.

Winters in Hong Kong are cool and dry, and the temperature seldom falls below 40° F. (4° C). Insufficient rainfall during the winter and other factors cause water shortages, and so Hong Kong buys millions of gallons of water from China every year.

Economy

Hong Kong has one of the strongest and most varied economies in Asia. It is a center of international trade, finance, and tourism. About half the people of Hong Kong work for manufacturing firms, and about 40 per cent have jobs in commerce or in the government. Less than 3 per cent of Hong Kong's people make their living by farming or fishing.

Hong Kong is a *free port*—that is, it collects no import duties on goods brought in from elsewhere. As a result, many products can be bought and sold more cheaply in Hong Kong than in most other parts of the world. Business firms of many countries operate in Hong Kong.

More than 100 banks and 4 stock exchanges are in Hong Kong. The banks finance housing, manufacturing, and trade there and in other parts of the world. Over 2 million tourists visit Hong Kong annually. The money they spend greatly aids the economy.

Since the early 1950's, Hong Kong has become an important industrial center. It has more than 38,000 factories, which make a wide variety of products. Almost all the manufactured products are exported, and textiles and clothing account for about half the exports. Hong Kong also exports large quantities of electronic equipment, metal goods, and plastic products. Hong Kong exports its products chiefly to, in order of importance, the United States, West Germany, Great Britain, and Japan. Hong Kong imports large quantities of food, machinery, steel, and iron and other raw materials. It imports these products mainly from Japan, China, the United States, and Taiwan.

Agriculture is a minor economic activity in Hong Kong, and the dependency must import large amounts of food to meet its needs. Farm products include vegetables, poultry, and rice. Fishing fleets from Hong Kong catch eels, sardines, and other seafood.

History

Early days. Since ancient times, people have lived in what is now Hong Kong. The area came under Chinese control about 220 B.C. Until the A.D. 1800's, it consisted of a few small fishing and farming villages. Pirates used Hong Kong as a land base.

British control. During the 1800's, the Chinese government tried to stop British merchants from smuggling opium into China. In 1839, this issue led to the Opium War between China and Great Britain. Britain won the war and received the island of Hong Kong as part of the Treaty of Nanjing in 1842. In 1860, Britain gained control of the Kowloon Peninsula as part of a settlement of further trade disputes with China. In 1898, China leased the New Territories to Britain for 99 years.

Population growth. In 1842, Hong Kong had only about 5,000 people. Its dramatic population growth resulted largely from five major waves of immigration. The first immigration wave began in 1911, during a movement by Chinese revolutionaries that overthrew China's Manchu dynasty and established the Republic of China. Many Chinese fled to Hong Kong and, by 1915, the population had increased to about 500,000.

The second wave of immigration began in 1937, after Japan invaded China. Large numbers of Chinese again fled to Hong Kong. By 1939, Hong Kong's population had reached 1,600,000. Japanese troops occupied Hong Kong from 1941 to 1945, during World War II. The population dropped to 600,000 in that period, mainly because many Chinese returned to China.

The third wave of immigration began in 1949, when Communists took control of China. This immigration soon pushed Hong Kong's population up to about 2 million. In 1962, a threat of widespread starvation in China set off a fourth wave of immigration into Hong Kong. By 1965, the number of people in Hong Kong had soared to more than 3 million.

Hong Kong's population grew steadily during the 1960's and 1970's. In addition, a fifth wave of immigration occurred in the late 1970's, when thousands of Vietnamese fled to Hong Kong (see **Vietnam** [Recent developments]). Today, the population of Hong Kong is about 6 million.

Relations with China. The government of China claims that Hong Kong is Chinese territory. In the late 1960's, some of Hong Kong's Chinese residents held violent demonstrations against British control of Hong Kong. However, the Chinese government did not try to take control of Hong Kong, and the riots ended.

In the late 1970's, China began to invest large sums of money in Hong Kong to help strengthen the Chinese economy. In 1984, after two years of negotiations, China and Great Britain worked out an agreement regarding the transfer of Hong Kong from British control to Chinese rule when Britain's lease expires in 1997. Under the agreement, Hong Kong will become a special administrative region of China with a high degree of control over its government affairs except in foreign policy and defense. Hong Kong will also be allowed to keep its capitalistic economy within the socialist system of China. These arrangements are to be in effect for 50 years after 1997.   Richard H. Solomon

Related articles in *World Book* include:

Asia (Way of life in East Asia
  (picture: Floating homes))
Flag (picture: Flags of Asia and
  the Pacific)
Kowloon
Money (table: Exchange rates)
Victoria (Hong Kong)

Honiara, *HOH nee AHR uh* (pop. 15,000), is the capital and largest community of Solomon Islands, an island country in the southwestern Pacific Ocean. Honiara, a small town, is on the north coast of Guadalcanal Island. For location, see **Solomon Islands** (map).

The town lies on two sides of Point Cruz, a harbor that serves both small and seagoing ships. Honiara has several prominent buildings, including Government House and an Anglican church. Many of the people live in houses on ridges near the center of the town. Honiara was built after World War II ended in 1945. The town stands on the site of a coconut plantation that Japan, and later the United States, used as a military base during the war.   Robert Langdon

Honolulu, *HAHN uh LOO loo,* is the capital, largest city, and chief port of Hawaii. The city's official name is the City and County of Honolulu. Technically, Honolulu covers the entire island of Oahu. However, only the large urban area on Oahu's southeastern coast is commonly called Honolulu. Other communities on Oahu are known by their own names. About 80 per cent of Hawaii's people live in Honolulu.

Honolulu, often called the *Crossroads of the Pacific,* is a stopping point for ships and planes crossing the Pacific Ocean. It is about 2,400 miles (3,860 kilometers) from San Francisco and 3,800 miles (6,120 kilometers) from Tokyo.

In 1794, Captain William Brown of England sailed into what is now Honolulu Harbor. The harbor provided shelter, and other ships began to stop there. Honolulu soon became an important trading center. *Honolulu* is a Hawaiian word meaning *sheltered bay.*

During the early 1900's, the United States built several military bases on Oahu. On Dec. 7, 1941, Japanese planes bombed Pearl Harbor, a U.S. naval base on the island. The United States entered World War II the next day. Jet air travel and lower plane fares have helped Honolulu become a popular tourist spot and one of the nation's fastest growing cities.

The city. The City and County of Honolulu consists of Oahu and several offshore islands and covers 621 square miles (1,608 square kilometers). The City and County of Honolulu and the Honolulu metropolitan area have the same boundaries.

The main urban area of Honolulu covers 86 square miles (223 square kilometers) on Oahu's southeastern coast. It has a population of about 365,000. This area includes downtown Honolulu and extends about 20 miles (32 kilometers) along the Oahu shore from Pearl Harbor on the west to Koko Head, an extinct volcano, on the east.

Diamond Head, Honolulu's most famous extinct volcano, is west of Koko Head. The Koolau Mountains rise north of the main urban area of Honolulu, and the Waianae Mountains are west of this area.

Downtown Honolulu, which lies next to Honolulu Harbor, has many office and apartment buildings. Government buildings in the downtown area include City Hall and the Hawaii State Capitol, completed in 1969. Iolani Palace, the former capitol and once the royal palace of Hawaiian monarchs, stands across a walkway from the new capitol. The governor of Hawaii lives in Washington Place, a home of Queen Liliuokalani, Hawaii's last monarch.

Factories occupy districts west of downtown Honolulu. The Ala Moana Center, a shopping area with more

Facts in brief

Population: *City and County of Honolulu and metropolitan area* —762,565. *City of Honolulu*—365,048.
Area: *City and County of Honolulu and metropolitan area*— 621 sq. mi. (1,608 km²); *City of Honolulu*—86 sq. mi. (223 km²).
Government: Mayor-Council. *Terms*—4 years for the mayor and the 9 council members.
Founded: 1794. Incorporated as a city and county in 1907.

than 150 stores, and Waikiki, a famous coastal resort section, lie east of the downtown district.

Residential communities have grown up throughout Honolulu. The largest communities include Aiea, Kailua, Kaneohe, Pearl City, and Waipahu.

The people. About a fourth of Honolulu's people have Japanese ancestry, and about another fourth of the people are white. About a sixth of the people in Honolulu are Hawaiian or part Hawaiian. Other groups include those of Chinese, Filipino, Korean, Puerto Rican, or Samoan descent. More than a fourth of the people have mixed ancestry. American military personnel and their families make up about 15 per cent of Honolulu's population.

Economy. Tourism is Honolulu's largest source of income. About 4 million tourists visit the city annually. Visitors enjoy the beautiful scenery, recreation areas, and mild climate. Honolulu's temperature varies little, averaging 72° F. (22° C) in February, the coldest month, and 78° F. (26° C) in August and September, the warmest months. For the monthly weather in Honolulu, see **Hawaii** (Climate). Most tourists stay in the Waikiki Beach area. As a result, this section is overcrowded and has severe traffic jams.

Honolulu's economy also depends on military activities. The city is the center of United States military operations in the Pacific region. The Air Force, Army, Marine Corps, and Navy have bases on Oahu. The second largest source of income in Honolulu is the money spent by the U.S. government in salaries for military personnel and civilian workers.

Honolulu has approximately 500 manufacturing companies. The city's leading industry is food processing, which includes the processing of Hawaii's chief agricultural products, pineapples and sugar cane. Other manufacturing industries in Honolulu produce cement, clothing, furniture, glass products, lumber, oil products, and plastics.

Honolulu's location makes it the center of air and sea travel in the Pacific. The Honolulu International Airport handles millions of passengers each year. Passenger and cargo steamship routes connect Honolulu with the U.S. mainland, Australia, Canada, China, Japan, and other Pacific islands. A steamship terminal operates at Honolulu Harbor.

Two newspapers, the *Advertiser* and the *Star-Bulletin,* have the largest daily readerships in Honolulu. The city also has daily newspapers printed in Japanese and Chinese. About 25 radio stations and 6 television stations serve Honolulu.

Education. Honolulu's public schools form part of the state school system controlled by the Hawaii State Board of Education. Honolulu has more than 230 elementary and high schools, with a total of approximately 160,000 students. About 40,000 students attend nearly 110 private schools.

The University of Hawaii at Manoa is in Honolulu. Its Hamilton Library is the largest library in Hawaii. The East-West Center, also located on the Manoa campus, serves as a meeting place for people of Eastern and Western nations to get together and exchange ideas. Chaminade University of Honolulu and Hawaii Pacific College are also in Honolulu.

Cultural life. The Honolulu Symphony Orchestra performs in concerts and operas. The Honolulu Community Theater and the Kennedy Theater at the East-West Cen-

Jack Zehrt, FPG

Waikiki Beach and Diamond Head Crater are landmarks of Honolulu. Waikiki, *foreground,* is a popular resort area, and Diamond Head, *background,* is an extinct volcano.

Honolulu

Honolulu is Hawaii's capital, largest city, and major port. It occupies the entire island of Oahu, which is shown on the map at the right. The map below shows the chief points of interest and main built-up area of Honolulu.

Park or forest reserve

Military area

Major highway

Other road

■ Point of interest

WORLD BOOK map

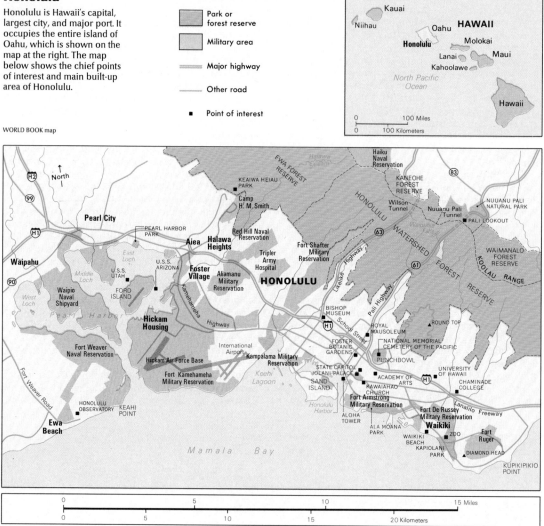

ter present plays and other stage productions. Leading ballet and opera companies appear at the Neal S. Blaisdell Center, which includes an arena, an auditorium, and an exhibition hall.

The Bernice P. Bishop Museum, which opened in 1889, is the oldest museum in Hawaii. It has exhibits of natural history and Pacific Island culture. The Honolulu Academy of Arts displays Western and Oriental art. People from Samoa, Tahiti, and other Pacific Islands live in six authentic Polynesian villages at the Polynesian Cultural Center. Many tourists visit Queen Emma's Summer Palace, a home of the wife of King Kamehameha IV.

Honolulu has many beautiful parks. Ala Moana and Kapiolani parks offer a variety of recreational facilities. Trained dolphins and other marine animals perform at Sea Life Park. The Foster Botanical Gardens feature 9 acres (4 hectares) of rare flowers and trees.

Government. The City and County of Honolulu has a mayor-council form of government. The voters elect the

mayor and the nine members of the council to four-year terms. Property taxes provide about half of the government's revenue.

History. Honolulu was a small Polynesian village when an English seaman, Captain William Brown, sailed into its harbor in 1794. Other ships started to use the harbor, and Honolulu became an important port.

During the 1800's, Honolulu flourished first as a center for the sandalwood trade and later as the major Pacific whaling base. In 1820, Protestant missionaries from New England came to Honolulu. They built schools and churches and converted many Hawaiians to Christianity. During the late 1800's, farmers began to raise large crops of pineapples and sugar cane. The processing of these products became the city's most important manufacturing activity. Thousands of laborers from China, Japan, and other countries came to work in the pineapple and sugar fields and the food-processing factories. By 1896, Honolulu had about 30,000 people.

Camera Hawaii

King Kamehameha I founded the Kingdom of Hawaii in the late 1700's. A bronze statue of the great ruler stands in front of the Judiciary Building in Honolulu's civic center.

King Kamehameha I, the first ruler of the Kingdom of Hawaii, lived in Honolulu from 1803 to 1811. The city became the permanent capital of Hawaii in 1845, and it remained the capital when Hawaii became a territory of the United States in 1900. The City and County of Honolulu, established in 1907, remained the capital when Hawaii became a state in 1959.

The United States built a naval base at Pearl Harbor in the early 1900's and established several Army camps on Oahu. The increased military activity helped raise Honolulu's population to about 95,000 in 1920 and 137,000 in 1930. The Japanese attack on Pearl Harbor on Dec. 7, 1941, forced the United States into World War II. Honolulu became a chief base for the Allied campaign against the Japanese.

The late 1940's and 1950's brought important social and economic changes to Honolulu. People from China, Japan, and other Oriental countries had long been kept out of politics and big business in the city. But after World War II ended in 1945, many Americans of Oriental descent became leaders in Honolulu's government and industry.

During the 1960's, the tourism industry boomed in Honolulu and high-rise apartment buildings and hotels went up in the city's main urban area. The start of jet air travel reduced the flying time between cities on the mainland of the United States and Honolulu. Airlines lowered their fares and scheduled more and more flights between many cities and Honolulu.

Honolulu's rapid growth has created several problems. The most serious one is a housing shortage, accompanied by high building costs and limited space.

The government has given financial aid to many home builders, but the shortage remains. Many residents fear that the hotel construction boom threatens Honolulu's scenic beauty. To help solve this problem, Honolulu's government has limited hotel construction in certain areas. City leaders are also studying improvements in mass transportation to relieve the growing traffic problem. George Chaplin

See also **Hawaii; Kamehameha I.**

Honorius, *hoh NOHR ee uhs,* was the name of four popes of the Roman Catholic Church. The dates of their reigns were:

Honorius I	(625-638)
Honorius II	(1124-1130)
Honorius III	(1216-1227)
Honorius IV	(1285-1287)

Honorius I (? -638) was involved with Patriarch Sergius of Constantinople in the attempt to settle heresies about Jesus Christ in the East. Honorius was condemned 40 years after his death for holding the heresy that there is only one will or principle of operation in Christ. Since this was a private teaching in a letter from Honorius to Sergius, it did not involve papal infallibility.

Honorius III (? -1227) promoted moral and educational reform, especially by aiding the development of the universities of Paris and Bologna. Honorius III launched a crusade, but it failed.

Thomas P. Neill and Fulton J. Sheen

Honshu. See **Japan** (The land).

Hooch, Pieter de. See **De Hooch, Pieter.**

Hood, a ship. See **Bismarck.**

Hood, John Bell (1831-1879), was a Confederate general who gained fame as a brigade and division commander in General Robert E. Lee's army. He fought gallantly at Gaines' Mill, the second Battle of Bull Run (also called Manassas), Antietam (Sharpsburg), Gettysburg, and Chickamauga.

General Hood commanded a corps in the Army of Tennessee and took command of that army with the rank of general in 1864. He fought General William T. Sherman at Atlanta, but had to abandon the city. Hood then began a campaign in Tennessee, but was beaten at Nashville.

Hood was born in Kentucky. He graduated from the U.S. Military Academy. After the war, he lived in Texas and Louisiana. Frank E. Vandiver

See also **Civil War** (The Atlanta campaign; North to Nashville).

Hood, Robin. See **Robin Hood.**

Hoof is a hard growth on the feet of mammals called *ungulates.* Ungulates include pigs, zebras, horses, and the horned animals. A hoof is made of horn, a substance developed from the *epidermis* (outer layer of skin). The hoof differs from a nail or claw because it is blunt and it encases the toe or foot. Hoofs developed from the animals' toes. The ungulates are divided into those with even and odd numbers of toes.

The horse's hoof developed from a single toe. It almost completely circles the bottom of the foot. Asses and zebras also have single toes. The even-toed animals never have more than four toes. Usually, the two middle toes form a *cleft* (divided) hoof. This group includes deer, antelope, sheep, goats, cattle, pigs, and the hippopotamus. Hoofs give the animal a firm footing and protect its feet. Some animals, such as the deer, can use their hoofs to defend themselves.   L. B. Arey

See also **Animal** (picture: Kinds of feet); **Horn; Ungulate.**

Hoof-and-mouth disease. See Foot-and-mouth disease.

Hooghly River, *HOOG lee,* in Bengal, India, is one of the channels through which the Ganges River flows into the Bay of Bengal. The Hooghly is a dying distributary, because the main flow of water has shifted to more easterly channels. The Hooghly flows southward for about 150 miles (241 kilometers). Large ships can sail up the river as far as Calcutta, 86 miles (138 kilometers) from the sea.   J. E. Spencer

Hook. See Fishing (Hooks).

Hookah. See Pipe (tobacco).

Hooke, Robert (1635-1703), an English experimental scientist, stated the currently accepted theory of elasticity in *Hooke's law.* This law states that the amount an elastic body bends or stretches out of shape (strain) is in direct proportion to the force (stress) acting on it. The law applies as long as the body is still elastic. Increased stress beyond this elastic limit will change the shape of the body permanently. Hooke also constructed the first Gregorian telescope, an early reflecting telescope. He was the first to use a spiral spring to regulate watches, and he discovered plant cells.

Hooke had varied interests. He abandoned many successful but slow-moving experiments without finishing them. Others profited from his findings. He stated the law of inverse squares (see **Light** [Measuring light]). He also recognized some aspects of the principle of the law of gravitation before Sir Isaac Newton. Hooke was born on the Isle of Wight.   Carl T. Chase

See also **Cell** (Cell research).

Hooked rug. See Rugs and carpets (Other methods).

Hooker, Joseph (1814-1879), was a Union general during the Civil War. At the beginning of the war, he became a brigadier general of volunteers. Later, he rose to the rank of major general and commanded a corps. In the eastern theater he fought in the Battles of the Seven Days, Antietam (Sharpsburg), and Fredericksburg. The newspapers called him "Fighting Joe." President Abraham Lincoln appointed him commander of the Army of the Potomac in 1863, but he was defeated at Chancellorsville. Relieved of command at his own request and transferred to the West, Hooker commanded a corps in the Chattanooga and Atlanta campaigns. He retired in 1868 because of paralysis

Brown Bros.

General Joseph Hooker

resulting from a wartime injury. Hooker was born in Hadley, Mass., and graduated from the U.S. Military Academy. He also served in Florida, on the Canadian border, and in the Mexican War.   T. Harry Williams

See also **Civil War** (Battle of Chancellorsville).

Hooker, Richard (1554?-1600), was an English scholar, theologian, and clergyman. His most famous and influential book was *Of the Laws of Ecclesiastical Polity,* which appeared in eight volumes. The first four were published in 1594, the fifth in 1597, and the last three in the mid-1600's, after his death.

In his book, Hooker defended the Church of England as a "middle way" between Roman Catholicism and Puritanism. Hooker denied the Puritan argument that the Bible should be used as a strict rulebook for church government, or *polity.* Instead, he argued that God had provided a "natural law" to guide the church in addition to the Bible. Hooker's ideas influenced such later political thinkers as the English philosopher John Locke. Hooker was born in Heavitree, near Exeter.
      Peter W. Williams

Hooker, Thomas (1586-1647), was a Congregational preacher and a founder of Connecticut. Hooker exerted strong influence in the drafting of the *Fundamental Orders,* under which Connecticut was governed for a long time.

Born in Leicestershire, England, Hooker was educated at Cambridge University and became famous as a preacher. Because of his Puritan beliefs, he fled to the Netherlands in 1630. He went to Newtowne (now Cambridge), Mass., in 1633, and settled as pastor in a house where Harvard University now stands. But his liberal beliefs clashed with Massachusetts conservatism. He thought each church should be independent, and that the people had a right to choose their magistrates and decide what powers they should have. So Hooker moved with his church members to Connecticut in 1636.
      Bradford Smith

See also **Connecticut** (English settlement).

Hooker process. See Extrusion.

Hooks, Benjamin Lawson (1925-   ), became executive director of the National Association for the Advancement of Colored People (NAACP) in 1977. He succeeded Roy Wilkins, who had served as executive director of the civil rights organization since 1955.

Hooks, a lawyer, banker, and minister, resigned as a member of the Federal Communications Commission (FCC) to head the NAACP. In 1972, President Richard M. Nixon had appointed him to the commission. Hooks was the first black member of the FCC, and he worked for equal opportunities for minorities in the communications industry.

NAACP

Benjamin L. Hooks

Hooks was born in Memphis. He graduated from LeMoyne-Owen College and received a law degree in 1948 from DePaul University. Hooks was appointed assistant public defender in Memphis in 1961. In 1965, he became the first black judge of the Shelby County Criminal Court in Tennessee. Hooks helped found and served as vice president of a savings and loan association in Memphis. He became a minister in 1955 and preached at churches in Memphis and Detroit.   Charles V. Hamilton

Hookworm is a small roundworm that enters the bodies of human beings and some animals through the skin.

Hookworms live as *parasites* in the intestines, sucking up blood and tissue fluids.

Hookworms can cause *anemia* (a shortage of red blood cells). They harm children more than adults. An infected child becomes weak and pale. The child's abdomen and legs may swell, and the child may become dull and listless. Certain hookworms attack animals, including cats and dogs. These hookworms can cause an itchy, red patch on human skin called *creeping eruption.*

Hookworm eggs pass out of the *host* (body in which the worm lives) with the body waste and hatch in moist, warm soil. The *larvae* (young worms) come to the surface of the soil. They burrow into the bare skin of animals that touch them. A person walking barefoot may pick up the worm in this way. A person may also become infected with the worms by swallowing impure food or water.

Once in the body, a hookworm enters the bloodstream and is carried to the lungs. It burrows into air channels there, passes into the throat, and is swallowed into the intestine. When hookworms reach the intestine, they become adults. Serious infections occur when more than 100 adult hookworms are in the intestine.

Hookworm eggs and larvae can live outside of the host's body only in warm, moist places. For this reason, hookworm disease is commonly found in tropical and subtropical countries.

Improving conditions of sanitation has reduced the amount of infection by hookworms. Medical treatment with drugs is also used today. Recovery is speeded by eating foods high in protein, vitamins, and iron.

Scientific classification. Hookworms belong to the family Ancylostomidae of the roundworm class Nematoda of the phylum Aschelminthes. The two kinds of hookworms that attack people are *Necator americanus* and *Ancylostoma duodenale.*

David F. Oetinger

See also **Roundworm.**

The path of a hookworm

A hookworm usually enters the body through the skin. In the body, it enters the bloodstream and is carried into the lungs. It then passes into the throat and is swallowed into the intestines.

WORLD BOOK illustration by Charles Wellek

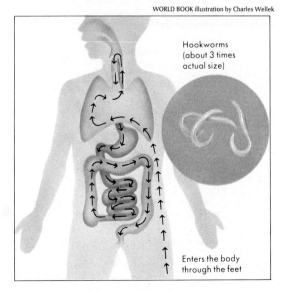

Hookworms (about 3 times actual size)

Enters the body through the feet

Hooper, William (1742-1790), was a signer of the Declaration of Independence. He served in the Continental Congress from 1774 to 1777 and in all five North Carolina provincial congresses. He favored a mild policy toward the Americans who sided with the British during the Revolutionary War even though the British destroyed his property. Hooper was born in Boston, and graduated from Harvard College. He studied law under James Otis, the radical lawyer, who probably influenced his political opinions. Hooper settled in Wilmington, N.C.   Robert J. Taylor

Hoopoe, *HOO poo,* is the name given to several birds related to hornbills. They live in the warmer parts of Europe, Asia, and Africa. The best known is the *European hoopoe.* This bird has a soft rose-buff color, with a handsome crest of feathers that it raises and lowers when alarmed.

WORLD BOOK illustration by John Rignall, Linden Artists Ltd.

Hoopoe

Hoopoes build their nests in holes in trees, walls, and rocks. The female lays five to seven white eggs. While the eggs hatch, the male feeds the female so she does not have to leave the nest. Hoopoes eat insects, and spend much time on the ground searching for food. When frightened, they flatten themselves to the ground and play dead. Their flesh is a favorite food in southern Europe.

Scientific classification.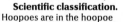
Hoopoes are in the hoopoe and wood hoopoe family, Upupidae. The European hoopoe is *Upupa epops.*   Rodolphe Meyer de Schauensee

Hoosac Mountains. See Green Mountains.

Hoosac tunnel, *HOO suhk,* is a 25,081-foot (7,645-meter) tunnel through the Berkshire Hills in western Massachusetts. It is on the main line of the Boston and Maine Railroad. The tunnel was begun in 1851 and completed in 1876, at a cost of 136 lives and about $14 million. The difficulty of the task forced private companies to give up the project. The state of Massachusetts completed the Hoosac tunnel. It marked the first American use of the power drill and of nitroglycerin for blasting. The state sold the tunnel to the railroad in 1884. The tunnel was enlarged in 1927.   William J. Reid

Hoosier Poet. See Riley, James Whitcomb.

Hoosier State. See Indiana.

Hooton, Earnest Albert (1887-1954), was an American physical anthropologist. His classification of the human races was at one time influential. Hooton worked chiefly on the fossil forms of early people, on the comparison of people with the other primates, and on physical types among criminals. Hooton was born in Clemansville, Wis. He studied at the University of Wisconsin, and as a Rhodes Scholar at Oxford. He taught at Harvard University from 1913 until his death. Among his principal books are *Up from the Ape* (1931) and *Man's Poor Relations* (1942).   David B. Stout

**31st President of
the United States 1929-1933**

Coolidge
30th President
1923-1929
Republican

Hoover
31st President
1929-1933
Republican

F.D. Roosevelt
32nd President
1933-1945
Democrat

Charles Curtis
·Vice President
1929-1933

Detail of an oil painting on canvas (1931) by Douglas Chandor; National Portrait Gallery, Smithsonian Institution, Washington, D.C.

Hoover, Herbert Clark (1874-1964), was President when the United States was swept by the Great Depression. Hoover had been a millionaire businessman and a successful public official before he became President. He entered the White House at a time of great prosperity in the United States. Americans expected him to lead them on to even better days. Then seven months after he took office, the stock market crashed and the Great Depression began.

President Hoover and many business leaders believed that prosperity would soon return to the United States. He appeared to act slowly in the emergency. But Hoover, a member of the Republican Party, was the first President to use the power of the federal government to fight a depression.

Hoover entered public life in 1914, after World War I began. He happened to be in London, and accepted the task of distributing food to the hungry Belgian people. President Woodrow Wilson then made him food administrator in the United States. For 19 months, Hoover supervised the production and distribution of food for American soldiers and civilians, and for the nation's allies.

In 1921, President Warren G. Harding appointed Hoover secretary of commerce. Hoover held this post until he ran for President in 1928. Hoover defeated Alfred E. Smith, the Democratic candidate, by the largest majority of electoral votes ever received by a candidate up to that time. Four years later, however, Franklin D. Roosevelt beat Hoover by an even larger majority of electoral votes.

Most people found Hoover shy and reserved. He had a quiet sense of humor and rarely laughed heartily. Hoo-

ver enjoyed fishing, hiking, and reading biographies and detective stories.

Early life

Boyhood. Herbert Hoover was the first President born west of the Mississippi River. He was born in West Branch, Iowa, on Aug. 10, 1874. One of his ancestors, Andrew Huber (or Hoover), had come to Pennsylvania from Germany in 1738. Huber moved to North Carolina, where his son John became a Quaker. John's descendants settled in Ohio, and moved to Iowa in 1853.

Herbert's parents, Jesse Clark Hoover and Hulda Randall Minthorn Hoover, had two sons and a daughter—Theodore, Herbert, and May. Jesse Hoover was a blacksmith and a dealer in farm equipment. Hulda Hoover, who was born in Canada, became a religious leader among the Quakers.

Hoover's father died in 1880 of heart trouble and other complications. He left a $1,000 life insurance policy and a little property. Hulda Hoover supported the family by preaching and sewing. She died of pneumonia and typhoid fever when Herbert was 9, and relatives reared the children. Most of the time, Herbert did not live with his brother and sister. He stayed with his uncle Allan Hoover near West Branch for about two years of his childhood.

Although an orphan, Herbert had a pleasant boyhood. He played in the woods and fished and swam in the streams. He picked potato bugs to earn money to buy fireworks and received a penny for every hundred bugs that he picked.

Education. In 1885, Hoover went to Newberg, Ore., to live with another uncle, Henry J. Minthorn. Hoover re-

Investors flocked to Wall Street after the crash.

The needy waited in bread lines to receive food.

The world of President Hoover

The stock market crash of Oct. 29, 1929, wiped out the savings of thousands of investors and helped cause the Great Depression.

The Great Depression, a worldwide economic slump, caused thousands of businesses to fail. Millions of workers lost their jobs.

Naturalism, a literary movement featuring realistic settings and characters, became an important force in American drama. Leading naturalistic plays included Elmer Rice's *Street Scene* (1929) and Eugene O'Neill's *Mourning Becomes Electra* (1931).

New inventions included the first practical all-electronic television system, demonstrated in 1929, and the first reliable analog computer, built in 1930.

The Smoot-Hawley Tariff Act of 1930 raised United States tariffs to an all-time high.

The Statute of Westminster, passed by the British Parliament in 1931, recognized Canada as an independent nation.

Japan invaded Manchuria on Sept. 18, 1931. The Japanese attack helped bring on World War II.

The "Bonus Army," a group of unemployed World War I veterans, marched on Washington, D.C., in June 1932. They demanded payment of a bonus for their military service.

The Nazi Party, led by Adolf Hitler, steadily gained power in Germany during the early 1930's.

The Norris-La Guardia Act of 1932 was one of the first laws in the United States that encouraged labor union activity. The act forbade an employer to sue a worker for breaking a promise not to join a union.

Wide World

ceived his secondary school education at Newberg College, a small Quaker academy of which his uncle was principal. Hoover worked to earn money whenever he could. One summer, he weeded onions at 50 cents a day. In 1888, Minthorn opened a real estate office in Salem, Ore. Hoover worked there as an office boy. He also studied algebra and geometry at a business college.

In 1890, Hoover became interested in engineering after talking with an engineer who visited his uncle's office. He decided to become a mining engineer. At the age of 17, Hoover enrolled in the first class of the newly founded Stanford University in Palo Alto, Calif. While in college, he managed a laundry agency and delivered newspapers to pay his expenses. He also worked as a part-time secretary for John Branner, head of the university's geology department. Hoover spent his summer va-

cations doing geological work in Arkansas, California, and Nevada. After graduation in 1895, he worked briefly as a miner in California.

Hoover's family. In the geology laboratory at Stanford, Hoover had met Lou Henry (March 29, 1874-Jan. 7, 1944), the daughter of a wealthy banker. They were married on Feb. 10, 1899, in Monterey, Calif.

Mrs. Hoover was a brilliant woman. She spoke several languages and had a deep interest in science, literature, and art. For about five years, the Hoovers spent their lei-

Important dates in Hoover's life

1874	(Aug. 10) Born in West Branch, Iowa.
1898	Became chief engineer of the Chinese Imperial Bureau of Mines.
1899	(Feb. 10) Married Lou Henry.
1908	Established his own engineering firm.
1914	Headed the Commission for Relief in Belgium.
1917	Named United States food administrator.
1921	Appointed secretary of commerce.
1928	Elected President of the United States.
1932	Defeated for reelection as President.
1944	Mrs. Lou Henry Hoover died.
1947	Named chairman of the Hoover Commission.
1954	The Herbert Hoover Foundation was established.
1964	(Oct. 20) Died in New York City.

Herbert Hoover Library

Hoover's birthplace stands in West Branch, Iowa. His grandparents were among the Quakers who settled the town in the 1840's. Hoover is buried on a rise overlooking the small house.

White House Historical Association

Lou Henry Hoover, Hoover's wife, was a brilliant woman who wrote articles for many scholarly publications. This portrait was painted by Lydia Field Emmett, an American artist.

sure time translating a famous old book on mining from Latin into English. They received special degrees from Stanford in recognition of their work. After her husband became President, Mrs. Hoover wrote articles for scientific and historical publications.

The Hoovers had two sons. Herbert, Jr. (1903-1969), also became a mining engineer. He served as undersecretary of state during President Dwight D. Eisenhower's first term. Allan (1907-   ) became a director of a lead- and zinc-mining company and of other businesses.

Engineer and businessman. In 1896, Hoover began his career in the San Francisco office of Louis Janin, a well-known mining engineer. The next year, a London company wanted an engineer to manage its gold mines in Australia. Hoover, then 23, got the job on Janin's recommendation. Late in 1898, after less than two years in Australia, Hoover accepted the post of chief engineer for the Chinese Imperial Bureau of Mines.

The Hoovers spent their honeymoon sailing from California to China. While her husband made prospecting trips and directed engineering projects, Mrs. Hoover learned to speak Chinese. The Boxer Rebellion began in 1900, and Hoover supervised the construction of defenses for the foreign settlement in Tianjin. During the two-month Boxer siege of the settlement, he directed the distribution of food and other supplies. See **Boxer Rebellion.**

The Chinese government discontinued its Bureau of Mines after the rebellion. Hoover went to London and helped organize a private company to develop the Chinese mines. In 1901, he returned to China as the company's general manager. He resigned after a few months

and went to London as a partner in the mining company with which he had been associated since 1897. In 1908, Hoover established his own engineering firm. Hoover reorganized mines in many parts of the world. By 1914, he had become a millionaire.

Political and public activities

Food administrator. Hoover was in London in 1914. The start of World War I had stranded thousands of Americans in Europe. United States officials in London asked Hoover to aid these people. He organized a committee that helped about 120,000 Americans get home. In August 1914, the U.S. ambassador in London asked Hoover to organize food relief for Belgium. German troops had conquered the country, and many Belgians were not getting enough food. Hoover set up the Commission for Relief in Belgium. From October 1914 to April 1917, he gathered and distributed food, and helped raise relief funds. His commission saved many thousands of lives.

The United States entered the war in April 1917. President Wilson asked Hoover to head the United States Food Administration. Hoover was given broad powers over the prices, production, and distribution of food. Americans responded eagerly to his campaign to save food for people in war-torn Europe. The term "Hooverize" came to mean saving and doing without various foods. Meatless and wheatless days were observed. After the war ended in 1918, Hoover returned to Europe to direct the feeding of millions of people. He had become internationally famous.

Secretary of commerce. As early as 1919, many Americans thought Hoover should be President. Both Republican and Democratic political leaders wanted him as a candidate in 1920. Hoover announced that he was a Republican but did not do well in the primary

United Press Int.

As head of the U.S. Food Administration during World War I, Hoover, *right,* directed efforts to save food for hungry Europeans. The term *Hooverize* came to mean *economize.*

elections. In 1921, President Warren G. Harding named Hoover secretary of commerce. Hoover held this office under Harding and President Calvin Coolidge.

As secretary of commerce, Hoover again showed his great skill as an administrator and planner. He reorganized the Department of Commerce and rapidly expanded its work. He became interested in so many activities that one official called him "Secretary of Commerce and Under Secretary of everything else." Hoover set up many conferences to consider such problems as industrial production, labor relations, child welfare, foreign trade, and housing. He also brought order into radiobroadcasting, promoted commercial aviation, and helped end the 12-hour workday in the steel industry.

Election of 1928. President Coolidge announced in August 1927 that he did not "choose to run" for reelection. In February 1928, Hoover became a candidate for the Republican presidential nomination. The party's national convention nominated him on the first ballot, and chose Senator Charles Curtis of Kansas for Vice President. The Democrats nominated Governor Alfred E. Smith of New York for President and Senator Joseph T. Robinson of Arkansas for Vice President.

In the election campaign, Hoover spoke hopefully about increasing prosperity. He observed, "The slogan of progress is changing from the full dinner pail to the full garage." Prohibition became a major issue of the campaign. Smith wanted to repeal Amendment 18 of the Constitution, which prohibited the sale of alcoholic drinks. Hoover called Prohibition an "experiment noble in motive." Millions of Americans felt that the Republicans would keep the nation prosperous. In addition, many voters opposed Smith because he was a Roman Catholic. Hoover carried 40 of the 48 states and received 444 electoral votes to only 87 for Smith.

After the election, President-elect Hoover made a good-will tour of Latin America. His trip helped lay the foundation for the "Good Neighbor Policy" of the Franklin D. Roosevelt era.

Hoover's Administration (1929-1933)

Champion of prosperity. President Hoover expected prosperity to continue. "Ours is a land rich in resources . . .," he said in his inaugural address. "In no nation are the fruits of accomplishment more secure."

During his campaign, Hoover had promised to help the farmers, who had not shared in the general prosperity. To fulfill his promise, he called a special session of Congress in April 1929. In June, Congress passed the Agricultural Marketing Act. This law established the Federal Farm Board, which promoted farm cooperatives and purchased farm surpluses. Hoover also wanted to raise tariffs on farm products to reduce foreign competition. But the Smoot-Hawley bill, which Congress passed in 1930 and Hoover signed, went too far and raised the tariff on many nonfarm products as well. The increased tariffs seriously damaged America's foreign trade and contributed to the depression.

The Great Depression. The United States had been building up to a crash for a long time. Other groups besides farmers had not shared in the prosperity of the 1920's. In the coal-mining and textile-manufacturing industries, for example, working conditions were poor and wages low. The economy was also weakened by widespread buying on credit. Thousands of people had borrowed money to pay for stocks. Stock prices soared to record heights. Then, in October 1929, the stock market crashed. The Great Depression had begun.

At first, few people believed that the depression would affect the entire nation. Many thought the stock market would recover in a few weeks or months. But by the end of 1929 the crash had caused losses estimated at $40 billion. The values of stocks listed on the New York Stock Exchange had dropped 40 per cent. Fortunes had been wiped out. Thousands of workers had lost their jobs.

Hoover told the people they had no reason for fear. He called business leaders, industrialists, and labor leaders together for conferences. All these groups promised to cooperate in an effort to keep wages stable and to avoid strikes. But economic conditions grew worse. By 1932, more than 12 million Americans were out of work. Factories closed and many banks failed. Thousands of people lost their homes because they could not keep up their mortgage payments. Many families lived in clumps of shacks that became known as *Hoovervilles.*

The Great Depression affected other nations, too. Germany could not pay the 1931 installment on its World War I reparations. Other countries also had difficulty paying their war debts. At Hoover's suggestion, a one-year postponement of international debt payments was negotiated.

Anti-depression action. Hoover was reluctant to interfere with the American economy. He called the depression "a temporary halt in the prosperity of a great people." At first, he depended on business companies and industries to solve their own problems and to take part in national stabilization efforts. But in 1932, at Hoover's request, Congress passed several laws enabling the government to help business. One of these laws set up the Reconstruction Finance Corporation (RFC). The RFC loaned money to banks and other firms to keep them from going bankrupt.

Hoover had believed that the states and local communities should provide relief for jobless workers. But it became clear that the unemployed needed much more assistance. Congress authorized the RFC to lend up to $300 million to the states for relief. Other laws provided credit for homeowners and farmers, and improved court practices and bankruptcy procedures.

Hoover supported many public works and conservation programs. In part, they were designed to help provide jobs. During his Administration, the Bureau of Reclamation started to build Boulder (now Hoover) Dam on the Colorado River. The government worked to develop

Hoover's election

Place of nominating convention	Kansas City
Ballot on which nominated	1st
Democratic opponent	Alfred E. Smith
Electoral vote*	444 (Hoover) to 87 (Smith)
Popular vote	21,411,991 (Hoover) to 15,000,185 (Smith)
Age at inauguration	54

*For votes by states, see **Electoral College** (table).

Vice President and Cabinet

Vice President	* Charles Curtis
Secretary of state	* Henry L. Stimson
Secretary of the treasury	* Andrew W. Mellon
	Ogden L. Mills (1932)
Secretary of war	Dwight F. Davis
	James W. Good (1929)
	Patrick J. Hurley (1929)
Attorney general	John G. Sargent
	William D. Mitchell (1929)
Postmaster general	Harry S. New
	Walter F. Brown(1929)
Secretary of the Navy	Curtis D. Wilbur
	Charles F. Adams (1929)
Secretary of the interior	Roy O. West
	Ray L. Wilbur (1929)
Secretary of agriculture	William M. Jardine
	Arthur M. Hyde (1929)
Secretary of commerce	William F. Whiting
	Robert P. Lamont (1929)
	Roy D. Chapin (1932)
Secretary of labor	James J. Davis
	William N. Doak (1930)

*Has a separate biography in WORLD BOOK.

inland waterways for navigation and flood control. It added about 3 million acres (1,200,000 hectares) to national parks and monuments and enlarged the national forests. It built more than 800 public buildings and helped states build about 37,000 miles (59,500 kilometers) of major highways.

The "Bonus Army." Unemployed workers staged hunger marches and demonstrations in several cities during the early 1930's. The most famous was that of the Bonus Expeditionary Force, an "army" of World War I veterans. The bonus law of 1924 had given every veteran a certificate that was payable in 1945. But now the veterans wanted the bonus paid immediately. The House of Representatives passed a bill to meet their demand. In June 1932, about 15,000 veterans from many states marched on Washington, D.C., to bring pressure on the Senate to pass the bill. Crowds of veterans stood on the Capitol steps, marched around the building, and visited senators. But the Senate defeated the bonus bill. Efforts to clear the veterans from public buildings led to a riot, and Hoover used troops to drive the veterans out of Washington. He opposed the bonus because he did not believe it was financially sound.

Foreign policy. Under Hoover, the United States moved toward cooperation with other nations on such problems as disarmament. In the London Naval Treaty of 1930, the United States, Great Britain, and Japan agreed to limit the number of their fighting ships. Hoover proposed a reduction in land weapons in 1932, but other countries refused to cooperate.

Hoover worked to improve relations with Latin America. He brought home the marines who had been helping to maintain peace in Nicaragua since 1912. The United States did "not wish to be represented abroad in such a manner," Hoover said. He made an agreement with Haiti under which U.S. troops would be withdrawn from that country in 1934. The troops had been sent to Haiti in 1915 to end a series of revolutions.

In 1931, Japanese forces invaded Manchuria. China protested to the League of Nations, and a League commission condemned Japan as an aggressor. Hoover declared that the United States would not recognize territorial gains made in violation of the Kellogg-Briand Peace Pact (see **Kellogg-Briand Peace Pact**).

Life in the White House. President and Mrs. Hoover gave the Executive Mansion a "new look." They decorated it with souvenirs and art objects that they had collected during years of world travel. A large cage of canaries was placed in the second-floor corridor. Around the cage, Mrs. Hoover put bamboo furniture and grass rugs from South America.

The Hoovers entertained frequently but avoided personal publicity as much as possible. Mrs. Hoover, a gracious hostess, hired three secretaries to help her prepare invitations. Once she invited 200 guests for dinner. Something went wrong, and 500 people arrived. The White House staff had to hurry out to neighborhood stores and buy more food.

In summer, President and Mrs. Hoover often escaped from the heat by vacationing in the Blue Ridge Mountains of Virginia. The President enjoyed fishing for trout in the Rapidan River. He built a summer home in the mountains and later gave it to the Shenandoah National Park. Hoover also exercised by playing a daily medicine ball game with a group of friends. The game usually began on the White House lawn at 7 a.m. The players included newsmen and government officials, and were called the "medicine ball cabinet."

Election of 1932. The Republicans had little hope of winning the 1932 presidential election. They renominated Hoover and Vice President Curtis but did not support the candidates vigorously. The Democrats nominated Governor Franklin D. Roosevelt of New York for President. They nominated Speaker of the House John N. Garner of Texas for Vice President.

The Democrats attacked Hoover's leadership in the depression. Roosevelt called for a "new deal" for the American people. He promised to balance the budget, bring relief to the unemployed, help the farmers, and end Prohibition. Hoover defended his record, promised economy in government, and opposed inflation. In the election, Roosevelt carried 42 of the 48 states. He won by an electoral vote margin of 472 to 59.

During Hoover's last four months in office, bank failures and unemployment increased. Congress paid little attention to his recommendations, and President-elect Roosevelt refused to promise support for Hoover's policies. Amendment 20 to the Constitution, known as the "lame duck amendment," became law in January 1933. It provided that a President's term of office should end on January 20 instead of March 4, but this provision did not go into effect until October 1933.

Elder statesman

After leaving the presidency, Hoover spent much time traveling, reading, speaking, and writing. He continued to develop the Hoover Institution on War, Revolution, and Peace that he had founded at Stanford in 1919. He and his wife moved from Palo Alto, Calif., to New York City. Mrs. Hoover died there on Jan. 7, 1944.

Hoover published *The Challenge to Liberty* in 1934. It was an attack on President Roosevelt's New Deal program. In 1940, during the first Russo-Finnish War, Hoover headed a committee that collected relief funds for Finland. He published *The Problems of Lasting Peace* (1942) and *The Basis of Lasting Peace* (1945). After

United Press Int.

As chairman of the Hoover Commission, Hoover recommended ways to improve the administration of the United States government. He submitted his final report, *above,* at age 81.

Roosevelt, Franklin Delano (Return to politics)

War debt (The Hoover Moratorium)

Outline

I. Early life
- A. Boyhood
- B. Education
- C. Hoover's family
- D. Engineer and businessman

II. Political and public activities
- A. Food administrator
- B. Secretary of commerce
- C. Election of 1928

III. Hoover's Administration (1929-1933)
- A. Champion of prosperity
- B. The Great Depression
- C. Anti-depression action
- D. The "Bonus Army"
- E. Foreign policy
- F. Life in the White House
- G. Election of 1932

IV. Elder statesman

Questions

How did Hoover become interested in engineering?

Why was Hoover in London when World War I began?

How did Hoover serve America during World War I?

What did the term "Hooverize" mean?

How did Hoover describe Prohibition?

How did the Reconstruction Finance Corporation try to help business during the Great Depression?

Why did Hoover oppose the veterans' bonus?

What was the "medicine ball cabinet"?

What did the Hoover Commission do?

Additional resources

Burner, David. *Herbert Hoover: A Public Life.* Knopf, 1978.

Hoover, Herbert C. *Memoirs.* 3 vols. Macmillan, 1951-1952.

Nash, George H. *The Life of Herbert Hoover: The Engineer, 1874-1914.* Norton, 1983.

Warren, Harris G. *Herbert Hoover and the Great Depression.* Greenwood, 1980. Reprint of 1959 edition.

Wilson, Joan Hoff. *Herbert Hoover: Forgotten Progressive.* Little, Brown, 1975.

World War II, Democratic President Harry S. Truman named Hoover chairman of the Famine Emergency Commission. In this post, Hoover surveyed the food needs of many nations. He went to Europe in 1947 to report to President Truman on relief needs.

Also in 1947, Hoover became chairman of the Commission on Organization of the Executive Branch of the Government (called the *Hoover Commission*). Commission proposals that were adopted streamlined the government and cut costs (see **Hoover Commission**). By 1961, Hoover was a director or trustee of nine private educational, scientific, and charitable institutions. The Herbert Hoover Library, which houses most of Hoover's official papers, was dedicated in West Branch in 1962.

Hoover published his *Memoirs* in three volumes (1951-1952) and *The Ordeal of Woodrow Wilson* (1958). He completed his four-volume work, *An American Epic,* in 1964.

Hoover gave all his income from government employment, including his pension, to charity and to public service projects. His services to government and society restored Hoover to popular favor. He lived longer after leaving the White House than any other former President. He died Oct. 20, 1964, at the age of 90 in New York City. The country mourned him as a truly great American. Hoover was buried near his birthplace in West Branch.   Ellis W. Hawley

Related articles in *World Book* include:

Great Depression

Iowa (Places to visit)

President of the United States

Prohibition

Hoover, J. Edgar (1895-1972), served as director of the Federal Bureau of Investigation (FBI) for 48 years. He held the office from 1924 until his death. Hoover built the FBI into one of the world's outstanding law-enforcement agencies. However, a congressional investigation after his death raised questions about some of his actions.

The Bureau of Investigation, which received its present name in 1935, was corrupt and disorganized when Hoover became director. Hoover reformed the agency, largely by appointing people for their ability and promoting them for good performance. He established the world's largest fingerprint file, a crime laboratory, and a training academy. Hoover became famous in the 1930's, when the FBI tracked down many well-known criminals. During and after World War II (1939-1945), the bureau smashed several foreign spy rings.

In 1975, congressional investigators disclosed that Hoover had abused his power a number of times. For example, he tried to win favor with several Presidents by gathering scandal about some of their opponents. Under Hoover, the FBI also violated the civil rights of many critics of government policies.

John Edgar Hoover

Wide World

J. Edgar Hoover

was born in Washington, D.C. He graduated from the George Washington University law school in 1917 and joined the United States Department of Justice that same year.   George T. Felkenes

See also **Federal Bureau of Investigation.**

Additional resources

Demaris, Ovid. *The Director: An Oral Biography of J. Edgar Hoover.* Harpers Mag. Press, 1975.
De Toledano, Ralph. *J. Edgar Hoover: The Man in His Time.* Arlington House, 1973.
Nash, Jay R. *Citizen Hoover: A Critical Study of the Life and Times of J. Edgar Hoover and His FBI.* Nelson-Hall, 1972.
O'Reilly, Kenneth. *Hoover and the Un-Americans: The FBI, HUAC, and the Red Menace.* Temple Univ. Press, 1983.

Hoover Commission was the popular name of two commissions that recommended ways to improve the administration of the United States government. Their official name was *Commission on Organization of the Executive Branch of the Government.* Former President Herbert C. Hoover headed the two commissions. The first commission, created by Congress in 1947, completed its report in 1949. The second commission, set up in 1953, made its recommendations in 1955.

The federal government adopted about 74 per cent of the first commission's 273 proposals. It accepted about 64 per cent of the second commission's 314 recommendations. The proposals of the two commissions were estimated to have saved the government $7 billion and $3 billion, respectively. They led to setting up the Department of Defense and the Department of Health, Education, and Welfare (now the Department of Health and Human Services).   Ellis W. Hawley

Hoover Dam is one of the highest concrete dams in the world. It stands in the Black Canyon of the Colorado River. The dam is part of the Boulder Canyon Project. The project consists of a dam, a hydroelectric power plant, and a reservoir. It controls floods of the Colorado River and supplies domestic and irrigation water and electric power for a large area of the Pacific Southwest. The project is on the Arizona-Nevada border, about 25 miles (40 kilometers) southeast of Las Vegas, Nev. (see **Arizona** [physical map]).

Hoover Dam is 725 feet (221 meters) high and 1,244 feet (379 meters) long. Elevators descend the equivalent of 44 stories into the dam and still do not reach its base. The concrete base is 660 feet (200 meters) thick. It contains over 4,400,000 cubic yards (3,360,000 cubic meters) of concrete, enough to pave a two-lane highway from New York to San Francisco.

Lake Mead, the dam reservoir, is one of the world's largest artificially created bodies of water. It is about 115 miles (185 kilometers) long and 589 feet (180 meters) deep. The reservoir can store about 29,755,000 acre-feet (36,702,300,000 cubic meters) of water. Lake Mead is also a major recreation area of the Southwest.

Water falling through the huge turbines of the dam generates electric power, which is sold to industries and to cities in the Pacific Southwest. The power plant has a capacity of 1,344,800 kilowatts. Several power lines lead from the Boulder Canyon Project to the Los Angeles area of California. Generators at the dam supply much of the power consumed in Arizona, Nevada, and southern California. Water from Lake Mead can irrigate about 1 million acres (0.4 million hectares) of farmland in the three-state area. The reservoir also supplies water for cities in southern California through an aqueduct that is 240 miles (386 kilometers) long.

The need for a dam on the Colorado River was apparent in the early 1900's. Floods were causing much damage in the Palo Verde Valley and in the Imperial Valley. Extensive levees were built, but crops withered and died when the river ran too low to meet the area's irrigation needs.

In 1928, Congress authorized the Boulder Canyon Project. The project's purpose is to control floods; improve navigation and river regulation; provide for storage and delivery of water; and generate electrical energy to help make the project self-supporting.

The Bureau of Reclamation designed the dam and supervised its construction. The entire project cost about $385 million. The dam itself cost more than $175 million. Hoover Dam was completed in 1936.

In 1931, the dam was named *Hoover Dam* to honor President Herbert Hoover. After Hoover left office in 1933, the Department of the Interior began to call the dam *Boulder Dam* or *Boulder Canyon Dam.* Congress officially named it *Hoover Dam* in 1947.   T. W. Mermel

See also **Dam; Lake Mead; Nevada** (picture).

Hop is a vine grown for its papery, yellowish-green flowers, which are used in brewing beer. The flowers, also called *hops,* grow in conelike clusters that measure from 1 to 4 inches (2.5 to 10 centimeters) in length. The petals have tiny glands that contain various oils and *resins* (sticky substances). These materials prevent the growth of bacteria in beer and give the beverage its bitter taste.

Hopvines may grow as long as 25 feet (8 meters) in a single growing season. The vines die in the fall. But the *rhizomes* (underground stems) of the plants continue to live, and they produce new vines the next spring.

Hops produce male and female flowers on different plants. The female flowers in the lower illustration are used to brew beer.

Hops grow in a wide range of climates and soils. The leading hop-growing state in the United States is Washington. Oregon ranks second, followed by Idaho and California. The plant is also grown in Australia, Germany, Great Britain, Japan, New Zealand, South Africa, and South America.

Growers plant hop rhizomes in mounds 6 to 8 feet (1.8 to 2.4 meters) apart. The vines are supported with poles or trellises to prevent them from spreading on the ground. Such supports allow the plants to be placed closer together, thus increasing the yield of each unit of land.

Hops are harvested in late summer or early autumn. Workers cut the vines by hand and place them in picking machines that separate the hops from the vines. The hops are then cleaned, dried in ovens, and pressed into bales for shipment or storage.

Scientific classification. Hops belong to the mulberry family, Moraceae. The European hop is *Humulus lupulus.* The American hop is *H. americanus.* The Japanese hop is *H. scandens.*

Max E. Austin

See also **Brewing** (Boiling).

Hope, Bob (1903-   ), is a popular American comedian and actor. He won fame for his fast-paced wisecracks in movies, on radio and television, and on the stage.

Hope was born in London. His given and family name was Leslie Townes Hope. He moved to Cleveland with his family at the age of 4. Hope became a vaudeville performer in the early 1920's and made his Broadway debut in 1927. He became a star in the musical comedy *Roberta* (1933). During the 1930's and 1940's, Hope starred in a popular radio show.

Hope has appeared in more than 50 motion pictures. His first feature film was *The Big Broadcast of 1938,* in which he first sang "Thanks for the Memory."

NBC

Bob Hope

This song became Hope's theme song. He co-starred with Bing Crosby and Dorothy Lamour in *Road to Singapore* (1940) and six later "Road" comedies. Hope has given many performances for charity and traveled throughout the world to entertain the armed forces. He received five special Academy Awards for his humanitarian activities and for his services to the film industry. He has also written several humorous books and an autobiography, *The Road to Hollywood* (1977).

Rachel Gallagher

Hope, John (1868-1936), was a black American educator. In 1906, he became the first black president of what is now Morehouse College in Atlanta. The four previous presidents of this black college had been white.

Hope headed Morehouse until 1929, when he became president of Atlanta University. That same year, he helped found the Atlanta University Center, which consisted of three schools—Atlanta, Morehouse, and Spelman College. Throughout his career, Hope encouraged blacks to attend college rather than vocational school.

His policy opposed that of the leading black educator Booker T. Washington, who believed blacks could benefit as much from job training as from a college education.

Hope was born in Augusta, Ga., and received his B.A. degree from Brown University. In 1898, he became a professor of classics at Atlanta Baptist College, whose name was changed to Morehouse College in 1913. After Hope's death, the National Association for the Advancement of Colored People (NAACP) awarded him the Spingarn Medal. Alton Hornsby, Jr.

HOPE, Project, is a program that teaches modern medical techniques to the physicians, dentists, nurses, and other health personnel of developing nations. The letters in its name stand for *Health Opportunity for People Everywhere.* The project is administered by The People-to-People Health Foundation, Inc., an independent, nonprofit corporation.

Project HOPE sponsors health care training programs in many countries, including Brazil, Colombia, Ethiopia, Peru, Tunisia, and certain Caribbean nations. It also operates medical training facilities for Navajo Indians in Arizona and for Mexican Americans in Texas. From 1960 to 1973, it sponsored a hospital ship, the S.S. *Hope,* that conducted medical training missions in Africa, Asia, South America, and the West Indies.

William B. Walsh, a Washington, D.C., physician, established Project HOPE in 1958. The program is supported primarily by private contributions. Project HOPE has headquarters at 2233 Wisconsin Avenue NW, Washington, D.C. 20007.

Critically reviewed by The People-to-People Health Foundation, Inc.

Hopewell Indians. See Mound Builders.

Hopi Indians, *HOH pee,* are one of the Pueblo Indian tribes. About 3,500 Hopi live on the Hopi reservation in northeastern Arizona. They live in 11 villages on or near three high *mesas* (tablelands). One village, Oraibi, is one of the oldest continuously inhabited villages in the United States. It was founded about 800 years ago.

Like their early ancestors, many Hopi raise small herds of sheep and grow crops on plots of valley land. Some Hopi earn additional income by making and selling baskets, pottery, silver jewelry, and *kachina* dolls. The carved wooden dolls represent messengers sent by the gods.

Religious ceremonies play an important part in the life of the Hopi Indians. At certain times of the year, Hopi men dress as kachinas and perform dances in the village square or in underground structures called *kivas.*

LaVerne Masayesva-Jeanne

Related articles in *World Book* include:

Arizona (Places to visit)	Indian, American (illustration: Indian ways of life)	Kachina
Family (Traditional families)		Pueblo Indians
		Snake dance

Hopkins, Esek (1718-1802), an American sea captain, commanded the tiny Continental Navy from 1775 to 1778. In 1776, his fleet captured the British fort at New Providence in the Bahamas, and took several British warships at Block Island. But Hopkins found it impossible to equip his ships properly. The Continental Congress condemned him for his failures and dismissed him from the naval service in 1778. Hopkins was born in Scituate, R.I.

Richard S. West, Jr.

Hopkins, Gerard Manley (1844-1889), ranks as a major poet of Victorian England, though his work remained almost unknown until 1918, when it was first published. Hopkins wrote most of his poetry in *sprung rhythm,* which emphasizes the natural rhythms and sounds of words as heard by the ear. He filled his verse with alliteration and unusual word combinations. His poems, which are especially effective when read aloud, include the long and complex "The Wreck of the *Deutschland."*

Hopkins was born in Essex. In 1863, he entered Oxford University. There, he experienced a spiritual crisis that led him to join the Roman Catholic Church in 1866. Hopkins entered the Jesuit order in 1868 (see **Jesuits**). He then stopped writing and burned the manuscripts of the poems he had written up to that time. Hopkins returned to writing in 1875 after being encouraged by his Jesuit superiors. He was ordained a priest in 1877.

James Douglas Merritt

See also **Poetry** (Sounds).

Hopkins, Harry Lloyd (1890-1946), an American public administrator, was a close friend and assistant to President Franklin D. Roosevelt. During the early 1930's, he served as a welfare worker in New York City. Later, he headed the state relief agency. Roosevelt appointed him head of the Works Progress Administration (WPA) in 1935. Opponents accused Hopkins of using the WPA to strengthen the Democratic Party.

From 1938 to 1940, Hopkins served as secretary of commerce. He directed the Lend-Lease program in 1941, and advised the President on important issues until Roosevelt's death. In 1945, President Truman sent Hopkins on a special mission to Russia. Hopkins was born in Sioux City, Iowa.   Harvey Wish

Hopkins, Johns (1795-1873), was an American merchant, financier, and philanthropist. He left $7 million to establish Johns Hopkins University and Johns Hopkins Hospital. He was born in Anne Arundel County, Maryland, and made a fortune as a wholesale grocer in Baltimore. Later, he helped organize the Baltimore and Ohio Railroad. He also helped Baltimore with large loans during the Civil War and the financial panic of 1873. Hopkins was a Quaker and an abolitionist.

Robert H. Bremner

Hopkins, Stephen (1707-1785), a signer of the Declaration of Independence, was one of the most prominent colonial leaders in Rhode Island. Although Hopkins was best known for his influence in politics, he showed keen interest in the colony's cultural life.

Hopkins was born in Providence, and became chief justice of the Superior Court of Rhode Island in 1751. In 1755, he was elected governor. He headed the major committee that opposed British measures, and was selected as a delegate to the Continental Congresses of 1774 and 1775.   Clarence L. Ver Steeg

Hopkinson, Francis (1737-1791), was a New Jersey signer of the Declaration of Independence. The talented and versatile Hopkinson was an artist, musician, and writer, as well as a lawyer, political leader, and judge. He also claimed credit for designing the American flag, although the evidence for his claim is not clear. Hopkinson's most important writings included political satires.

Hopkinson was born in Philadelphia. He was the first student to enroll in the Philadelphia Academy, and the first to be given a diploma by the College of Philadelphia. He practiced law in Philadelphia and in Bordentown, N.J. In 1776, he was elected to the Continental Congress. He was judge of admiralty for Pennsylvania from 1779 to 1789 and judge of the United States Court of the Eastern District of Pennsylvania from 1789 until his death.   Clarence L. Ver Steeg

Hopper. See **Railroad** (pictures: Kinds of railroad cars; A unit train).

Hopper, Edward (1882-1967), was an American painter whose pictures of New York City scenes and life in small New England towns rank among the finest realistic works of his time. Hopper painted in both oil and water color, and preferred such subjects as street scenes, highways, gas stations, bridges, theaters, railroads, lunch stands, and lighthouses. Most of his works are strangely empty of people, but are still full of emotion. Many express a sense of loneliness and finality and convey a feeling of great space and warm sunlight. The omission of distracting detail and the geometric arrangement of Hopper's compositions give his paintings an abstract power. A good example is *Nighthawks,* which is reproduced in the **Painting** article.

Hopper was born in Nyack, N.Y., and lived in New York City. He worked as a commercial artist and illustrator for many years. He was not able to concentrate fully on painting until he was past 40.   Allen S. Weller

See also **Drawing** (picture: A charcoal drawing).

Horace, *HAWR ihs* (65-8 B.C.), was one of the greatest poets of ancient Rome. He became famous for the beautiful songlike verses in his *Odes.* Horace wrote on many subjects, including friendship, heroism, politics, and religion. Some of Horace's poems reflect such moral values as respect for the gods and obedience to the law and the state.

Horace's short lyrics are collected in *Epodes* and in *Odes.* His collection called *Satires* includes some warm and human poems, among them a famous one about a bore. Horace wrote poems to his friends in the form of letters, which make up the collection called *Epistles.*

Quintus Horatius Flaccus was born in the province of Apulia in southern Italy. His father, though a former slave, gave him an excellent education in Rome and Athens. Horace left his studies in Athens to join the army of Marcus Junius Brutus, a Roman revolutionary general. In 42 B.C., Brutus was defeated in battle at Philippi and Horace returned to Rome. He became a clerk in the government of Emperor Augustus and began to write poetry. He devoted himself to writing after gaining the financial support of Gaius Maecenas, a wealthy patron of the arts.   Herbert Musurillo

Horatius, *huh RAY shuhs,* was a legendary Roman hero. Thomas Macaulay's *Lays of Ancient Rome* relates the story of Horatius' defense of the bridge over the Tiber River. When the last king of Rome was overthrown, he went to the Etruscans for help. The Etruscan army advanced to the bank of the Tiber River across from Rome. With two companions, Lartius and Herminius, Horatius held back the Etruscans while the Romans chopped down the bridge behind them. His friends ran back just in time, but Horatius remained alone until the bridge fell. Then, he jumped into the rushing Tiber and swam to safety. The people gave

Horatius many gifts and erected a statue in his honor for his bravery in saving the city.   Herbert M. Howe

Horehound is the name given to several plants in the mint family. The *common,* or *white, horehound* grows in the countryside and along the roads throughout Europe and northern Asia. It has been brought to America and grows in both continents. The plant grows from 1 to 3 feet (30 to 91 centimeters) high. Many cottony white hairs cover it and give it a whitish appearance. The flowers are small and almost white. The leaves and stems have a pleasant odor and a bitter taste. Cough medicines and candy are made from the leaves and stems. The *black,* or *fetid,* horehound, also used to make medicine, is an English flower that looks like the white horehound.

Scientific classification. Horehound belongs to the mint family, Labiatae. White horehound is genus *Marrubium,* species *vulgare.* Black horehound is classified as *Ballota nigra.*

Harold Norman Moldenke

Horizon is the distant, curved line where the earth and sky seem to meet. Most people near the ground on land cannot see to the horizon because buildings, trees, or mountains block their view. But a person on-board a ship can see all the way to the horizon on a clear day.

The horizon seems nearer to a person standing at sea level than to a person in an airplane or on a mountain peak. This is because the person up high can see farther over the curvature of the earth than the person at sea level. The horizon is about $2\frac{1}{2}$ miles (4 kilometers) away to someone at sea level. But it is 98 miles (158 kilome-

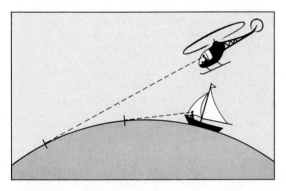

The distance to the horizon depends upon the position of the observer. The horizon the pilot sees is farther away than the horizon seen by the sailor, who is directly below the pilot.

ters) from someone in an airplane or on a mountain 1 mile (1.6 kilometers) above sea level.

Astronomers and navigators have several technical meanings for horizon. The *visible* horizon is the imaginary line where the earth and sky seem to meet. The *astronomical,* or *sensible,* horizon refers to the imaginary line where the *celestial sphere* (curved dome of the sky) meets the imaginary level plane through a person's eye. Because the earth is curved, the visible horizon is slightly below the astronomical horizon. The angle between an observer and the two horizons is called the *dip.*   Elizabeth Roemer

Hormone, *HAWR mohn,* is any of a number of chemical substances produced within an animal or a plant. A hormone is produced in one part of an organism, but it

causes an effect in a different part. Thus, hormones serve as a means of communication among various parts of an organism. They act as "chemical messengers" that help these parts function in a coordinated way.

The word *hormone* comes from a Greek word that means *to set in motion.* In human beings and other animals, hormones control such body activities as growth, development, and reproduction. In plants, hormones regulate many aspects of growth. If an organism fails to produce the proper kind or amount of hormones, serious disturbances—or even death—may result. For example, giants and dwarfs—among both animals and plants—can result from faulty hormone production.

In 1902, scientists found the first definite evidence of the existence of hormones. That year, British researchers discovered that a chemical substance controlled certain activities involved in digestion. Since then, scientists have identified more than 30 hormones produced by the human body. They also have developed ways of extracting hormones from living tissue and techniques for manufacturing them in the laboratory.

Human hormones

Most hormones in the human body are produced by organs called *endocrine,* or *ductless, glands.* The major endocrine glands include the two adrenal glands, the pituitary gland, the four parathyroid glands, the sex glands, and the thyroid gland. A few hormones are produced by endocrine tissue present in organs that are not primarily endocrine glands. Such organs include the stomach and pancreas. See **Gland.**

The endocrine glands secrete hormones into the blood, which carries them throughout the body. After a hormone arrives at its *target,* the organ or tissue it affects, it causes certain actions to occur.

Hormones regulate a variety of body functions. They may be grouped according to the functions they control. These functions include the way the body uses food; growth; sex and reproduction; the regulation of the composition of the blood; the reaction of the body to emergencies; and the control of hormones themselves.

Metabolic hormones regulate the various steps in *metabolism,* the process by which the body converts food into energy and living tissue. For example, the endocrine tissue of the stomach and small intestine secretes a number of *digestive hormones.* These hormones control the secretion of digestive juices, which break down food into simple substances that can be used by the body.

After molecules of digested food enter the bloodstream, other hormones control their use by the cells of the body. For example, the hormones *insulin* and *glucagon,* both secreted by the pancreas, regulate the amount of sugar available to the cells. Insulin enables cells to use sugar from the blood. If the pancreas secretes too little insulin, a serious disease called diabetes mellitus results. Glucagon causes the liver to release additional sugar into the blood.

Two hormones produced by the thyroid gland—*thyroxine* and *triiodothyronine*—control the rate at which the cells use food to release energy. Overproduction of these hormones results in many physical and emotional disturbances, including excitability, muscular weakness, rapid pulse and respiration, and weight loss. Underproduction causes such symptoms as low body temperature, mental and physical sluggishness, and weight gain. By controlling the production of energy, these hormones regulate the way in which the body uses food in building new tissue. Thus, they play a major role in the creation of new proteins by the body cells.

Other hormones also control the way cells use food to build new tissue. The *glucocorticoids* are a group of hormones that function primarily in regulating the metabolism of *carbohydrates* (sugars and starches), fats, and proteins. They control the processes by which the body converts digested proteins into carbohydrates and fats. These hormones include *corticosterone, cortisol,* and *cortisone.* The glucocorticoids are secreted by the *cortex* (outer part) of each adrenal gland. Insulin and *growth hormone* (GH), a hormone secreted by the *anterior lobe* (front part) of the pituitary gland, also regulate the creation of new tissue.

GH also controls the use of food in other ways. For example, it stimulates cells to use fat, rather than sugar, as an energy source, and so helps maintain a fairly high level of sugar in the blood. Such a level is necessary for the brain to function properly.

Growth and sex hormones. The body's development from infancy to adulthood involves a complex process of physical changes. Hormones play a key role in regulating these changes.

GH controls overall growth during childhood. Faulty production of this hormone during childhood can cause a person to become a dwarf or a giant. In adults, GH enables certain tissues to maintain their proper size and structure. Insulin, glucocorticoids, and thyroxine also play major roles in tissue growth and maintenance.

Beginning at the age of about 11 to 15, young people go through a period of rapid growth and physical change. Hormones control the development that occurs during this period, called *puberty.* At the start of puberty, the *hypothalamus,* the portion of the brain nearest the pituitary gland, greatly increases its secretion of *gonadotropin-releasing hormone.* This hormone acts on the anterior lobe of the pituitary. It stimulates the gland to secrete the *gonadotropic hormones—follicle-stimulating hormone* (FSH) and *luteinizing hormone* (LH). These hormones, in turn, act on the *gonads* (sex glands)—the testicles in males and the ovaries in females.

Under the influence of FSH and LH, the gonads grow and begin to secrete large amounts of *sex hormones.* The male sex hormones, including *testosterone* and *androsterone,* are called *androgens.* The female sex hormones include *progesterone* and the *estrogens.* The most important estrogens are *estradiol, estriol,* and *estrone.* The cortex of adrenal glands in men and women also secretes some sex hormones, especially androgens.

The sex hormones regulate the remarkable changes that occur during puberty. They help trigger a person's rapid growth in height and weight and, at the end of puberty, they stop this growth. Androgens cause the male sex organs to mature, and they stimulate male sexual behavior. Androgens also stimulate the development of such secondary male characteristics as a deep voice and a beard. Estrogens cause the female sex organs to develop fully, and they establish female sexual behavior. They also stimulate the development of secondary female characteristics, such as full breasts and wide hips.

In a woman's body, FSH, LH, estrogens, and progesterone work together to control the menstrual cycle (see **Menstruation**). Progesterone also regulates processes necessary for pregnancy.

Blood composition hormones. Healthy blood contains fairly exact levels of several chemical substances. If the level of these chemicals becomes too high or too low, the body can be harmed.

A number of hormones work together to ensure that the composition of the blood remains within normal ranges. *Parathormone,* secreted by the parathyroid glands, and *calcitonin,* from the thyroid, regulate the level of calcium in the blood. Parathormone also controls the amount of phosphate in the blood. The *mineralocorticoids,* a group of hormones secreted by the adrenal cortex, control the balance between salts and water in the blood. *Aldosterone* is the most important mineralocorticoid. *Vasopressin,* also called *antidiuretic hormone,* regulates the water level of the blood. It is produced by the hypothalamus, but it is stored in and released by the *posterior lobe* (rear part) of the pituitary.

Stress hormones are secreted in case of anger, fright, or injury. The *medulla* (inner portion) of the adrenal glands secretes *epinephrine* and *norepinephrine,* also known as *adrenalin* and *noradrenalin.* These substances, particularly epinephrine, prepare the body for stress. For example, epinephrine increases the pulse and speeds the conversion of food to energy in the muscles. The glucocorticoids also help the body adjust to stress.

Endocrine control hormones affect the production of other hormones. They include FSH and LH, the anterior pituitary hormones that regulate the secretions of the gonads. The anterior pituitary also secretes *thyroid-stimulating hormone* (TSH) and *adrenocorticotropic hormone* (ACTH). TSH stimulates the thyroid to secrete thyroxine. ACTH stimulates the adrenal cortex, causing increased secretions of glucocorticoids, mineralocorticoids, and adrenal sex hormones.

The anterior pituitary itself is regulated by hormones released by the hypothalamus. These substances are called *releasing hormones.* The gonadotropin-releasing hormone triggers the secretion of FSH and LH. Other releasing hormones stimulate the pituitary's production of ACTH, GH, and TSH. *Prolactin,* another hormone of the anterior pituitary, is also controlled by a hypothalamic hormone. One of the effects of prolactin is the stimulation of milk production in nursing mothers.

The hypothalamus, which forms part of the brain, consists of nerve tissue. Thus, the releasing hormones link the body's nervous and endocrine systems into one coordinated control unit. The sense organs gather information on changes in the environment, which they relay to the brain through the nervous system. If these changes call for a hormonal response, the hypothalamus triggers the appropriate pituitary secretions.

Other hormones in human beings include *oxytocin* and *relaxin,* both of which affect the process of birth. Oxytocin, like vasopressin, is produced by the hypothalamus and is stored in and secreted by the posterior pituitary. The ovaries produce relaxin. Relaxin widens the birth canal, the passageway through which a baby leaves its mother's body. Oxytocin causes the muscles of the uterus to contract during labor. Oxytocin also stimulates the release of milk from the mother's breasts when the infant nurses.

Melanocyte-stimulating hormone (MSH) is a hormone secreted by the anterior lobe of the pituitary. Among certain amphibians, fish, and reptiles, MSH regulates the amount of *pigment* (coloring matter) in the skin. Its function in the human body is not yet understood.

Hormones of other animals

Other vertebrates, especially other mammals, have most of the same hormones people have. These chemicals are nearly identical in structure and effect to human hormones. Thus, scientists can learn about human hormones by studying those of other vertebrates. Doctors use hormones secreted by these animals to treat patients whose body does not produce sufficient amounts of certain hormones. For example, millions of diabetics use insulin obtained from cattle, hogs, and sheep.

Invertebrates also have hormones, some of which play an important role in growth and development. For example, hormones control the series of changes through which such insects as bees and butterflies pass while growing. Scientists do not know so much about invertebrate hormones as they do about those of vertebrates.

Plant hormones

Plant hormones are produced mainly in actively growing parts, such as the tips of roots and stems. These hormones influence growth and are often called *growth regulators.* There are three main types of plant hormones: (1) *auxins,* (2) *cytokinins,* and (3) *gibberellins.*

Auxins cause various effects on different parts of a plant. In stems and roots, auxins regulate the *elongation* (lengthening) of cells. By stimulating cell elongation, auxins affect the manner in which stems bend toward light and away from gravity. Auxins also control the process by which roots bend toward gravity, but they do so by preventing the elongation of cells.

In many plants, auxins secreted by the bud at the tip of a stem prevent lower buds on the stem from growing. Thus, they slow the growth of side branches. Such branches could use up energy a plant needs to grow tall and sturdy. Auxins also stimulate the growth of fruit and prevent fruit and leaves from falling off a plant.

Cytokinins control cell division in plants. They apparently work together with other growth regulators, especially auxins. Cytokinins play an important role in determining which cells of a young plant will become root cells, which cells will become leaf cells, and so on.

Gibberellins stimulate many plants to grow larger. When used in experiments, they have made the stems of dwarf plants lengthen rapidly. Gibberellins also help regulate blossoming in certain plants. They cause the seeds and buds of many species to begin growing after *dormancy* (long periods of inactivity).

Other growth regulators include *abscisic acid* and *ethylene.* Abscisic acid blocks plant growth, thus stimulating dormancy. Ethylene regulates, among other things, the ripening of fruit.

How hormones work

Most human hormones can be divided into two groups according to their chemical structure. One group, called *steroids,* consists of the sex hormones and the hormones of the adrenal cortex. Most other human hormones contain some form of *amino acids,* the building blocks of proteins.

Scientists believe the chemical structure of a hormone enables it to combine with a *receptor* in the cells of its target. The union of the hormone with the receptor triggers a change in the chemical processes of the cell. This change, in turn, probably modifies many, if not all, of the hundreds of chemical activities of the cell. These changes cause the target to behave in a certain way.

Many *endocrinologists* (scientists who study hormones) think steroid hormones become attached to receptors and then enter the nucleus of the target cell. In the nucleus, the hormone affects the activity of the *genes,* the tiny units that contain hereditary information. The endocrinologists believe amino acid based hormones probably unite with receptors on the outer membrane of the target cell. This union may change the structure of the cell membrane, allowing certain substances to enter or leave the cell. These substances alter the chemical activities of the cell. In other cases, the union seems to influence the activity of enzymes located on the membrane. The enzymes react by causing the formation of a substance called *cyclic AMP.* This substance, in turn, alters the cell's chemical activities.

Synthetic hormones

Since the 1940's, biochemists have learned to *synthesize* (create artificially) many hormones in the laboratory. Until that time, almost all hormones had to be extracted from animals or plants. Only tiny quantities of hormones occur in living tissue. Synthesis has greatly increased the availability of hormones for human use.

Some synthetic hormones, including synthetic human hormones, are exact duplicates of the natural secretions. But scientists have altered the chemical structure of many synthetic hormones to provide more powerful action. The most common synthetic hormones include auxins; glucocorticoids, particularly cortisone; sex hormones; growth hormone; and insulin.

Not all hormones can be synthesized. Scientists do not know the exact chemical structure of some. The structure of other hormones is too complex for practical large-scale synthesis.

Uses of hormones

Medical uses. Physicians use hormones to treat people with *hormone deficiencies.* The body of a patient with such a condition cannot produce an adequate supply of one or more hormones. Hormone therapy enables a person to overcome many of the symptoms of various diseases. Such therapy cannot cure these diseases. It merely controls them. Hormone deficiency diseases include Addison's disease, diabetes mellitus, diabetes insipidus, and myxedema. See **Addison's disease; Diabetes; Thyroid gland** (Underactive thyroid).

Certain other conditions, which are not directly related to hormone deficiencies, may also be treated with hormones. These conditions include arthritis and asthma, for which many physicians prescribe cortisone.

In addition, hormones may be given to alter a function of the body in some way. Birth control pills, for example, contain synthetic female sex hormones. By taking these hormones, a woman alters the endocrine balance that controls the menstrual cycle. This alteration blocks *ovulation* (the release of eggs), thus making it almost impossible for pregnancy to occur.

Agricultural uses. Farmers use synthetic plant hormones, especially auxins, to achieve a variety of results in crop production. When treated with auxins, certain plants—including cucumbers and tomatoes—produce seedless fruit. Farmers also use auxin sprays on apples to prevent the fruit from falling off the tree before harvest. In addition, auxins serve as weedkillers. When sprayed in large concentrations, auxins cause broadleaf weeds to grow in an uncontrolled manner so that they soon die.

Much research has been done on the use of hormones in livestock production. In the United States, certain synthetic estrogens are used to stimulate the fattening of cattle. In 1979, the Food and Drug Administration, an agency of the federal government, took steps to ban the use of one such growth stimulant. This hormone, known as *diethylstilbestrol* or *DES,* had been linked to the development of cancer in human beings. Traces of DES had been found in the meat of slaughtered animals. See DES.   B. E. Frye

Related articles in *World Book* include:

ACTH	Epinephrine	Parathyroid gland
Adrenal gland	Estrogen	Pituitary gland
Auxin	Giant	Progesterone
Biochemistry	Gibberellin	Prostaglandin
Cortisone	Goiter	Steroid
Disease (Hormonal	Growth	Testicle
diseases)	Hypothalamus	Testosterone
Drug (Hormones;	Insulin	Thyroid gland
Animals)	Ovary	
Dwarf	Pancreas	

Additional resources

Goldsworthy, Graham J., and others. *Endocrinology.* Wiley, 1981.
Riedman, Sarah R. *Hormones: How They Work.* Rev. ed. Abelard-Schuman, 1973. Suitable for younger readers.
Silverstein, Alvin and Virginia B. *The Endocrine System: Hor-*

mones in the Living World. Prentice-Hall, 1971. For younger readers.

Hormuz, Strait of. See Persian Gulf.

Horn is a pointed, bony structure on the heads of many mammals. Most horned animals have a pair of horns. Such animals as cattle, sheep, goats, and antelope have true horns. Deer have hornlike growths that are not true horns. These growths are called *antlers.*

Horns have a bony core. The core is an extension of one of the skull bones. A layer of skin covers the core. This skin contains a large amount of a protein called *keratin.* Keratin makes the horn extremely tough and durable. See **Keratin.**

Among many horned animals, both the male and the female grow horns. The horns may be elaborately curved, but—except in the pronghorn antelope—they do not form branches as do antlers. Horned animals keep their horns for life. The pronghorn sheds the coverings of its horns and grows new coverings each year.

Among most antlered animals, only the male grows antlers. The animal sheds its antlers every year. Like horns, antlers grow out of bones in the skull. At first, antlers have a velvetlike covering of skin over the bone. But instead of becoming hard, this covering dies and is rubbed off by the animal. See **Deer** (Antlers; picture: How a deer's antlers grow); **Moose** (picture).

Horns and antlers have a number of functions. They serve as weapons to protect the animals from attack. Male animals sometimes use their horns or antlers to fight other males in the group. Such fighting establishes which male is the most important. More often, a male avoids a fight and establishes his superiority through gestures that may include displaying and threatening to use his horns or antlers.   Lawrence C. Wit

See also **Animal** (Ways of life [picture: Animal defenses and weapons]).

Horn is the general name for musical instruments of the brass family. The most popular horns include the bugle, cornet, flugelhorn, French horn, trombone, trum-

The structure of horns and antlers Both horns and antlers grow from the bones in an animal's skull. Horns are permanently covered by a hard layer of keratin-rich skin. Antlers at first have a velvetlike skin covering that is eventually rubbed off by the animal. Cross sections of a bull's horn and a deer's antler are shown below.

WORLD BOOK illustrations by John D. Dawson

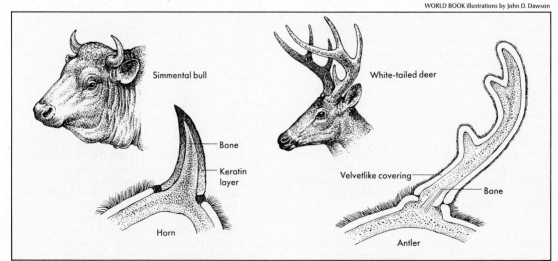

pet, and tuba. The term *horn* is often used to refer only to the French horn.

Most horns are made of brass, though a few are made of plastic or silver. Horns consist largely of tubing in many shapes and lengths. The differences in tubing produce a great variety of tone colors, ranging from the brilliant sound of the trumpet to the warm, mellow sound of the French horn. The pitches of all horns are determined by the tension of the player's lips in the instrument's mouthpiece. Horns also have valves or slides that permit additional changes in pitch.

The earliest horns were made from natural materials, such as animal horns, tusks, shells, or hollow lengths of wood. People originally used horns to send signals over distances too great to be covered by the human voice. As sophisticated instruments developed, various types of horns became popular in military bands and orchestras. However, in many parts of the world, primitive horns made of natural materials are used today for signaling or to accompany dances or ceremonies. The oldest horn in continual use is the ancient Hebrew *shofar,* made from a curved ram's horn. This instrument dates back about 6,000 years and is still used in Jewish religious services.　John Keil Richards

Related articles in *World Book* include:

Alpenhorn	Music (Wind
Bugle	instruments)
Cornet	Trombone
Flügelhorn	Trumpet
French horn	Tuba
Mellophone	

Horn of plenty. See Cornucopia.

Hornbill is an awkward-looking bird with an immense horny bill. It lives in tropical Africa and Asia. Its bill, filled with air cells, has a large base, a pointed end, and saw-toothed edges. The *rhinoceros hornbill* gets its name from a red and yellow growth that rises from its forehead like a horn.

Hornbills live in the tops of trees. They eat berries, fruits, and insects, chiefly, but also like reptiles and small mammals. The female lays her eggs in a hollow tree and remains there until they hatch.

Scientific classification. The hornbill is in the hornbill family, Bucerotidae. The rhinoceros hornbill is *Buceros rhinoceros.*

Rodolphe Meyer de Schauensee

See also **Bird** (picture: Birds of Europe and Asia).

Hornblende is any of a group of fairly hard rock-forming minerals. It is the most common type of *amphibole.* An amphibole is a *silicate,* a mineral composed chiefly of silicon and oxygen that is found throughout the earth's crust. Hornblendes occur in many *igneous* and *metamorphic* rocks (see **Rock**).

Hornblendes range in color from dark green to dark brown or black. Most hornblendes occur as shiny, crystals that are shaped like a prism. But some are small, irregularly shaped grains. All hornblendes contain aluminum, calcium, iron, and magnesium in addition to silicon and oxygen. Many also have potassium, sodium, and titanium. Hornblendes vary widely in chemical composition. For example, one variety called *hastingsite* is rich in sodium and iron. Another known as *tschermakite* has much aluminum.　Mary Emma Wagner

Hornbook. Paper was scarce and expensive during the Middle Ages and until the early 1800's. It had to be used sparingly. The hornbook was invented to protect the paper on which the first lessons of young children were printed. It was used as early as 1442. By the end of the 1500's, the hornbook was standard equipment in English schools. Its use continued in England and America until about 1800, when books became cheaper. Today, hornbooks are rare collector's items.

Granger Collection

Hornbook

The hornbook was a flat board with a handle. On the board was pasted a sheet of paper with the simple lesson of the beginning student. On the paper were usually the alphabet, the Benediction, the Lord's Prayer, and the Roman numerals. The alphabet often was given, with the vowels heading the list, followed by combinations of vowels and consonants, such as *ab, eb, ib, ob,* and *ub.* The whole board was covered with a thin, flat piece of clear horn, through which a person could read the paper. The flattened horn was made transparent by boiling and scraping.

The handles of many hornbooks had holes so that the hornbooks could be worn around the neck or fastened to a belt. In some wealthy English families, the backs of the boards were of leather ornamented with pictures or designs inlaid with silver or gold filigree. American settlers had simpler hornbooks.

In the 1700's, gingerbread "hornbooks" were often made. Students were allowed to eat a letter of the alphabet that they had learned. Hornbooks were used only in England and America.　Gerald L. Gutek

Horne, Lena (1917-　　), is an American singer and actress. She became famous for her beauty and as a popular singer of the blues. She developed a distinctive vocal style that ranged from a growl to a soft croon.

Horne was born in New York City. At the age of 16, she became a chorus dancer at the Cotton Club in Harlem. She then sang with dance bands and appeared in the musical revue *Blackbirds of 1939.* In 1942, Horne became the first black performer to sign a long-term contract with a major Hollywood film studio. She had made her movie debut in *The Duke Is Tops* (1938), but did not gain attention until her rendition of the song "Stormy Weather" from the 1943 movie of the same name.

After the end of World War II in 1945, Horne became a major nightclub attraction in the United States and Europe. She made a number of movie musicals in the 1940's and 1950's and starred in the Broadway musical *Jamaica* (1957). She also wrote an autobiography, *Lena* (1963). She toured in a popular one-woman show, *Lena Horne: The Lady and Her Music,* in the early 1980's.

© Yvonne Gunner, Sygma

Lena Horne

In 1983, Horne received the Spingarn Medal in recognition of her achievements. Rachel Gallagher

Horne, Marilyn (1934-), is an American opera star known for her singing as both a mezzo-soprano and a soprano. Her broad vocal range, which includes both soprano and contralto notes, has allowed her to sing an unusual variety of roles. Horne has also won fame for the rich quality of her lower voice.

Horne became famous for her performances in operas composed in the Italian *bel canto* style, which emphasizes beautiful tones and technical skill. She has sung roles in bel canto operas written by such composers as Vincenzo Bellini, Gaetano Donizetti, and Gioacchino Rossini.

Horne was born in Bradford, Pa. She made her operatic debut in 1954 with the Los Angeles Guild Opera in *The Bartered Bride*. Horne first sang with the Metropolitan Opera in 1970 in *Norma*. Ellen Pfeifer

Horned lizard is the name of 14 species of North American lizards. They are often called *horned toads* or *horny toads* because their body has a flattened, toadlike shape. Horned lizards grow $2\frac{1}{2}$ to $6\frac{1}{2}$ inches (6.4 to 16.5 centimeters) long. Their bodies are covered with sharp spines. Large hornlike spines project from the back of their head. Their spiny armor protects them from attacking animals. When attacked, horned lizards sometimes squirt little streams of blood from their eyes. This ability may help them ward off such enemies as coyotes.

J. Shaw, Bruce Coleman Inc.

Hornets construct large paper nests from chewed-up wood and plant fiber. They frequently build their nests in trees.

© John Gerlach, Tom Stack & Assoc.

A horned lizard has sharp spines on its head and its back. It feeds on ants and other insects.

Horned lizards live in deserts and other dry regions of the United States, Canada, and Mexico. Their colors resemble the colors of their surroundings and make them difficult to find. These lizards move slowly and feed chiefly on insects, especially ants. Most species lay eggs. In a few species, the young are born living.

Scientific classification. Horned lizards belong to the New World lizard family, Iguanidae. All species are members of the genus *Phrynosoma*. Raymond B. Huey

See also **Lizard** (Defenses).

Hornet is the name of any one of several large social wasps. One of the most common hornets in North America is the *baldfaced hornet*. Its stout, black body is covered with white markings and it has a white face. The nest of the baldfaced hornet is found hanging in shrubs and trees and occasionally on buildings. By late sum-

mer, it may be larger than a basketball and contain hundreds of adult hornets.

Hornets were the first papermakers. They make large paper nests from chewed up wood and plant fiber. A mated female called the *queen* starts to

WORLD BOOK illustration by James Teason

Giant hornet

make the nest in the spring. She constructs several hexagonal cells, lays a few eggs, and feeds the larvae. All the young of this first brood are females. When they mature, they become *workers* who help the queen enlarge the nest, gather food, and rear additional broods. Hornets use their nest for only one season. In the fall, new queens and males are born. After mating, the queens leave the nest to hibernate in a protected location. The workers and males die after the first frosts.

Hornets are nervous insects that will readily sting if disturbed. Stinging injects a *venom* (poison) that causes a painful swelling that may last for some time. Nevertheless, hornets are helpful insects. Workers capture flies, caterpillars, and other pests for the queen's young.

A species called the *giant hornet* is common along the east coast of the United States. It often flies during the evening and is sometimes attracted to porch lights. It was introduced from Europe into the United States during the mid-1800's. It nests mainly in hollow trees and occasionally in the walls of buildings.

Scientific classification. Hornets are members of the family Vespidae. The baldfaced hornet is *Dolichovespula maculata*. The giant hornet is *Vespa crabro*. Robert W. Matthews

See also **Wasp; Yellow jacket; Insect** (picture: Order Hymenoptera).

Horney, *HAWR ny,* **Karen** (1885-1952), was a German-born psychoanalyst. She became known chiefly for challenging the Austrian psychiatrist Sigmund Freud over the stress he put on biology in explaining human psychology. Horney believed that people often behave as they do for social reasons, not biological ones.

Horney particularly criticized Freud's views on the

psychology of women. Freud said that all women feel inferior to men by instinct. Horney agreed that many women do feel that way—but not because of instinct. She argued that society teaches women to feel inferior.

Horney was born Karen Danielsen in Hamburg. She married Oscar Horney, a Berlin attorney, in 1909. She received her M.D. degree from the University of Berlin in 1913. In 1932, Horney moved to the United States. She helped form the American Institute for Psychoanalysis in 1941 and served as its dean until her death. Her major works include *The Neurotic Personality of Our Time* (1937), *Self-Analysis* (1942), and *Our Inner Conflicts* (1945).   George H. Pollock

Hornsby, *HAWRNZ bee,* **Rogers** (1896-1963), an American baseball player, is often called the greatest right-handed hitter of all time. Nicknamed *Rajah,* he won seven National League batting titles, six in succession, and had a .358 lifetime batting average. Only Ty Cobb, with a .367, had a higher average. Hornsby batted .424 in 1924, a single season record.

A second baseman, Hornsby played for the St. Louis Cardinals from 1915 through 1926 and again in 1933; the New York Giants in 1927; the Boston Braves in 1928; the Chicago Cubs from 1929 through 1932; and the St. Louis Browns from 1933 through 1937. He also managed the Cardinals, Braves, Cubs, Browns, and Cincinnati Reds. Born in Winters, Tex., he was elected to the National Baseball Hall of Fame in 1942.   Dave Nightingale

Horology, *haw RAHL uh jee,* is the science of measuring time. It includes the design and construction of measuring devices, such as clocks and watches. Time was divided into years, months, weeks, and days long before any accurate measure was found for dividing the day. The hourglass was probably the first invention for marking the hours. See also **Time** (Measuring time); **Clock** and its *Related articles.*   Arthur B. Sinkler

Horoscope is a chart that supposedly reveals a person's character or future. The chart shows the position of the earth, planets, and stars at a certain time, such as the time of a person's birth. *Astrologers* (persons who tell fortunes by studying the stars) believe that the position of these bodies influences a person's life. An astrologer *casts* (draws) a person's horoscope and explains its supposed meaning.

Most scientists would say that there is no scientific basis for a belief in horoscopes. Yet, many persons believe in horoscopes and base important decisions on advice they receive from astrologers. Others find it amusing just to read general advice published in newspaper "horoscope" columns.

Parts of a horoscope. A horoscope has three main parts that represent three supposed influences on a person's life. The three parts are: (1) the zodiac, (2) the houses, and (3) the planets.

The zodiac is a band of stars that appears to encircle the earth (see **Zodiac**). The zodiac consists of 12 divisions called *signs.* Astrologers believe that a person comes under the special influence of a particular sign, depending on the date of the person's birth. For example, a person born from July 23 to August 23 has Leo as a zodiac sign and is often called "a Leo." Each zodiac sign has certain characteristics. For example, a Leo supposedly displays cheerfulness and pride.

The houses represent imaginary divisions of the surface of the earth. Astrologers believe there are 12 houses, which are represented by 12 divisions of a person's horoscope. Each house supposedly influences a certain part of a person's life. The first house, for example, is associated with an individual's appearance and personality. Other houses affect a person's career, health, marriage, or some other interest.

The planets, according to astrologers, include the moon and sun as well as Jupiter, Mars, Mercury, Neptune, Pluto, Saturn, Uranus, and Venus. The planets supposedly have an important influence on the houses and signs. A particular planet *rules* (most influences) each sign. This planet has certain characteristics that affect the sign it rules. For example, Mercury, which is associated with talkativeness and wittiness, rules Gemini. Therefore, persons born under the sign of Gemini are supposedly talkative and witty.

Astrologers also believe that the planets influence the activities or interests associated with individual houses. For example, if Venus (associated with beauty) were located in the first house (associated with appearance), an astrologer would conclude that the person had an attractive physical appearance. The various planets in a person's chart lie at particular angles to one another. These angles, called *aspects,* also have meaning. Astrologers think that certain angles represent signs of good fortune. Others supposedly reveal approaching evil.

Explaining a horoscope. A horoscope enables an astrologer to develop several kinds of character readings. Some horoscopes, for example, give only a general idea of an individual's character or future. Most of the horoscopes published in newspapers are of this type. They make predictions based only on the characteristics of the zodiac signs. Such a horoscope might tell persons born under the sign of Taurus simply that they face an important test in their career.

Astrologers may also cast a complete horoscope and study the complicated relationships formed by the houses, planets, and zodiac signs. For example, suppose that Saturn was located in the first house in the horoscope and in the sign of Virgo. An astrologer would probably conclude that the person was extremely neat both in manner of dress and habits. The astrologer would reach this conclusion because Saturn, a disciplined planet, is in the house of physical appearance and personality, under the sign of Virgo, which is associated with tidiness.   Christopher McIntosh

See also **Astrology; House** (in astrology); and the articles on signs of the zodiac, such as **Aries.**

Horowitz, *HAWR uh wihts,* **Vladimir,** *VLAD ih MEER* (1904-   ), a Russian-born pianist, is one of the world's greatest musicians. He won fame for his magnificent technique, which combines outstanding power and attention to detail. His performances feature the works of composers of the 1800's and 1900's.

Horowitz was born in Kiev, Russia, and received his early training there. In 1925, he began to play in leading European cities with the most famous conductors. Horowitz first performed in the United States in 1928. He settled in the United States in 1940 and became a U.S. citizen in 1944.

Horowitz did not perform from 1953 to 1965. Since 1965, he has given a number of recitals, which have been highly praised by critics.   F. E. Kirby

The beauty of horses contributes to their great popularity. The powerful bodies and flowing manes and tails of the Arabian horses shown above give the animals a noble appearance.

Horse

Horse has been one of the most useful animals for thousands of years. Horses once provided the fastest and surest way to travel on land. Hunters on horseback chased animals and killed them for food or for sport. Soldiers charged into battle on sturdy war horses. The pioneers used horses when they settled the American West in the days of stagecoaches, covered wagons, and the pony express.

The horse is not as important as a means of transportation as it once was. In most countries, the *iron horse* (train) and *horseless carriage* (automobile) have replaced the horse almost entirely. But people still use horses for recreation, sport, and work. Children and adults ride horses for fun and exercise. Large crowds thrill to the excitement of horse races. Horses perform in circuses, rodeos, carnivals, parades, and horse shows. They help ranchers round up great herds of cattle, and they may

be used to pull plows and do other farm work.

The horse is well-suited for working and running. For example, its wide nostrils help it breathe easily. Horses have a good sense of smell, sharp ears, and keen eyes. They have strong teeth, but they eat only grain and plants, never meat. Long, muscular legs give horses the strength to pull heavy loads or to run at fast speeds. Horses also use their legs as their chief weapons. The kick of a horse can seriously injure a human being or an animal.

Horses are eager to please their owners or trainers. Most horses have good memories and can easily be trained to obey commands. A horse may learn to come when its owner whistles. A circus horse takes "bows" when its trainer touches its front legs with a whip. Horses can learn to respond to even the slightest signals. People who watch an expert rider on a well-trained horse often cannot see these signs. For example, the horse moves forward when the rider's legs are pressed lightly against the horse's side. It turns at a touch of the reins against its neck. The quick obedience of the horse has helped make it one of our most valuable animals.

People have improved the natural qualities of the horse by breeding various kinds of horses. For example, horse raisers can breed a fast horse with a strong horse to produce an animal that has both speed and power.

The contributors of this article are Steven D. Price, author of Panorama of American Horses *and other books about horses; and Bill Landsman, president of Bill Landsman Associates, Inc.*

There are more than 150 breeds and types of horses and ponies. The breeds vary greatly in size, strength, speed, and other characteristics. The smallest breed is the Falabella, which grows only 30 inches (76 centimeters) high. Falabellas were originally bred in Argentina and are kept as pets. The largest breed of horse is the shire, which was originally developed in England. Shires may measure more than 68 inches (173 centimeters) high. They may weigh more than 2,000 pounds (910 kilograms).

Shires and other large breeds, such as the Belgian, Clydesdale, and Percheron, are the strongest horses. They can pull loads that weigh more than a short ton (0.9 metric ton). The two fastest breeds are the quarter horse and the thoroughbred, which are often bred and trained for racing. The quarter horse can run $\frac{1}{4}$ mile (0.4 kilometer) in about 20 seconds. But the thoroughbred can run longer distances faster. It can cover a mile (1.6 kilometers) in about $1\frac{1}{2}$ minutes.

The various breeds of horses are commonly divided into three main groups: (1) light horses, (2) heavy horses, and (3) ponies. Light horses have small bones and thin legs. Most weigh less than 1,300 pounds (590 kilograms). Heavy horses have large bones and thick, sturdy legs. Some weigh more than 2,000 pounds (910 kilograms). Ponies are small horses that stand less than 58 inches (147 centimeters) high. Most ponies weigh less than 800 pounds (360 kilograms).

Each of the three main groups of horses has many breeds. However, a single breed may include horses of more than one type. For example, certain kinds of Hack-

Some types and breeds of horses

Type or breed	Place of origin	Weight In lbs.	In kg	Height in hands*
Saddle horses				
American saddle horse	United States	900 to 1,200	410 to 540	14.3 to 16.1
American quarter horse	United States	900 to 1,200	410 to 540	14.2 to 15.3
Appaloosa	United States	950 to 1,175	430 to 530	14.2 to 15.2
Arabian	Arabia	850 to 1,000	390 to 450	14.2 to 15.3
Morgan	United States	800 to 1,100	360 to 500	14.2 to 15.2
Palomino	United States	900 to 1,300	410 to 590	14.1 to 16
Tennessee walking horse	United States	900 to 1,200	410 to 540	15 to 16
Thoroughbred	England	1,000 to 1,300	450 to 590	15 to 17
Light harness or roadster horses				
Hackney	England	900 to 1,200	410 to 540	14.3 to 16.2
Standardbred or American trotter	United States	800 to 1,200	360 to 540	15 to 16
Draft horses				
Belgian	Belgium	1,700 to 2,200	770 to 1,000	16 to 19
Clydesdale	Scotland	1,500 to 2,000	680 to 910	16 to 17.1
Percheron	France	1,600 to 2,100	730 to 950	15 to 17
Shire	England	1,800 to 2,300	820 to 1,040	16 to 17
Suffolk	England	1,500 to 1,900	680 to 860	15.2 to 16.2
Heavy harness or coach horses				
Cleveland bay	England	1,250 to 1,550	570 to 700	15.3 to 16.3
French coach	France	1,100 to 1,400	500 to 640	15.1 to 16.3
German coach	Germany	1,200 to 1,500	540 to 680	15.2 to 16.3
Ponies				
Hackney pony	England	600 to 850	270 to 390	12 to 14.2
Pony of the Americas	United States	500 to 900	230 to 410	11.2 to 13.2
Shetland pony	Shetland Islands	300 to 500	140 to 230	9 to 11.2

*One hand equals 4 inches (10 centimeters)

Horse terms

Bronco, or **Bronc,** is an untamed Western horse.
Colt, technically, is a male horse less than 4 years old. However, the word *colt* is often used for any young horse.
Crossbred means bred from a sire of one breed and a dam of another.
Dam is the mother of a foal.
Filly is a female horse less than 4 years old.
Foal is either a newborn male or a newborn female horse.
Frog is the elastic, horny, middle part of the sole of a horse's foot.
Gait is any forward movement of the horse, such as walking or galloping.
Gelding is a male horse that cannot be used for breeding because it has had some of its reproductive organs removed.
Grade is a horse or pony of mixed breed.
Hand is a unit used to measure the height of a horse, from the ground to the highest point of the withers. A hand equals 4 inches (10 centimeters).
Mare is a female horse more than 4 years old.
Mustang is the wild horse of the Western plains, descended from Spanish horses.
Pony is any small horse, but the word *pony* usually refers to a horse less than 58 inches (147 centimeters) tall when full-grown.
Purebred means bred from horses that are of the same breed.
Sire is the father of a foal.
Stallion is a male horse that can be used for breeding.
Yearling is a horse that is more than 1 and less than 2 years old. A race horse is considered a yearling from the first January 1 after its birth until the following January 1.
Withers is the ridge between a horse's shoulder bones.

neys are classified as light horses, and other kinds are considered ponies. In addition to light horses, heavy horses, and ponies, there are also a few kinds of wild horses.

Light horses

Saddle horses for riding make up an important group of breeds. Many people ride horses for pleasure or raise them as a hobby. Some riders achieve great skill and compete with other riders in horse shows and sports involving horses.

The most popular breeds used for pleasure riding in the United States include the American saddle horse, Tennessee walking horse, Morgan, quarter horse, and Arabian. Southern plantation owners developed the American saddle horse and the Tennessee walking horse. The owners wanted mounts that were comfortable to ride. Tennessee walking horses are especially noted for their comfortable running walk and smooth canter. All Morgan horses can be traced back to a New England stallion named Justin Morgan (see **Morgan, Justin**). Morgans were originally used as harness horses for pulling carriages and for harness racing. After auto-

American saddle horse

Tennessee walking horse

Morgan

Arabian

Quarter horse

mobiles became popular, breeders developed Morgans into excellent saddle horses.

Cowhands use quarter horses for *cutting* (sorting out) cattle from a herd and for other ranch work. Quarter horses can start, stop, and turn quickly. They respond instantly to the slightest shift of the cowhand's weight or movement of reins. These sure-footed horses have great endurance. They can scramble up and down steep mountain trails and ford swift streams.

Quarter horses were developed in America during the early 1700's. Breeders crossed thoroughbreds from England with horses from the Spanish colonies of North America. The new breed could start quickly and run at high speed for short distances. Owners used these horses for the sport of *quarter racing,* a $\frac{1}{4}$-mile (0.4-kilometer) race along a straight path.

The strong Arabian horse is noted for its endurance. Arabs developed this breed for use in the desert. For hundreds of years, breeders in many countries have brought these horses from Arabia and used them to develop new breeds.

One breed that developed from Arabian horses is the thoroughbred. All thoroughbreds can be traced back to three stallions named Darley Arabian, Godolphin Barb (sometimes called Godolphin Arabian), and Byerly Turk.

Alix Coleman

Thoroughbred

Ira Haas, Photo Researchers

Standardbred

In the late 1600's and early 1700's, European breeders crossed these stallions with their own horses to produce the first thoroughbreds. Thoroughbreds are high-spirited, sensitive horses. They have powerful lungs and strong legs, which makes them especially well-suited for racing. Thoroughbreds are also used for jumping and hunting. In addition, many polo ponies are part thoroughbred.

The Lipizzan horses, or Lipizzaners, come from horses imported into Austria from Spain and Italy during the middle 1500's. These beautiful show horses have strong bones, short legs, and thick, arched necks. They can make difficult jumps because of their powerful hindquarters. The best-known Lipizzan horses are those trained at the Spanish Riding School of Vienna in Austria. These horses perform graceful jumping and dancing feats.

Light harness horses, sometimes called *roadsters,* include the Morgan, the Hackney, and the standardbred. The standardbred, also called the American trotting horse, is considered the best horse for harness racing. Owners train standardbred horses to race at either a trot or a pace. Breeders developed the standardbred by crossing thoroughbreds with Morgans and other breeds.

Color types. Light horses are sometimes grouped according to color types instead of by breed. Such groups include palominos and albinos. Some people consider Appaloosas a color type, but these horses actually form a breed.

Palominos have a golden coat and a light blond or silvery mane and tail. Most of them have white only on the face and on the legs below the hocks and knees. Palominos belong to almost every breed except the thoroughbred. A palomino mare and stallion often produce a *foal* (baby horse) of another color. Breeders in the United

Jerry Cooke, Photo Researchers

Lipizzaner

Robert Shiflet, Palomino Horse Breeders of America

Palomino

Albino

Appaloosa

States and Mexico developed the Palomino line.

Albinos. Some breeders use the word *albino* to describe any horse with a white or pale-colored coat. However, a true albino is an animal that, because of heredity, has no color in its eyes, hair, or skin. Its offspring also lack color.

All albino horses have some color that their offspring can inherit. One kind of albino has a pink skin, ivory coat, white mane, and blue eyes. Another kind has pink skin, a white coat, and brown eyes. Horses that are born black and turn white as they grow older are not usually called albinos.

Appaloosas vary greatly in color. But the vast majority have a white area on the loin and hips with small, round or oval dark spots. Appaloosas are sometimes called *raindrop horses* because of their spots. They also have white-rimmed, humanlike eyes. Black and white stripes cover the hoofs of most Appaloosas.

Spanish adventurers first brought Appaloosas to North America. The Nez Percé Indians of what are now Idaho and Washington bred these horses in the Palouse River region. The name *Appaloosa* comes from the word *Palouse*.

Heavy horses

Draft horses are the tallest, heaviest, and strongest group of horses. They are descended from the great war horses that heavily armored knights rode into battle. *Draft* (work) horses once supplied much of the power needed for jobs that heavy trucks and tractors do today. They pulled plows on farms and hauled freight wagons from town to town. Draft breeds include the shire, Clydesdale, Belgian, Percheron, and Suffolk.

The shire is the largest horse. This breed developed in England after King Henry VIII had all horses less than 5 feet (1.5 meters) high destroyed as useless.

The Clydesdale, one of the handsomest draft breeds, has long, flowing hair below the knee and the *hock* (joint on the hind legs). This hair, called "feathers," gives the animals a smart and unusual look. Clydesdales are popular horses for pulling wagons in parades.

The Belgian ranks among the gentlest and strongest

Shire

Clydesdale

Belgian

WORLD BOOK photo

Suffolk

Walter Chandoha

Percherons

horses. Heavy muscles give the Belgian a stout appearance, and the head may seem too small for the huge body. Most Belgians have chestnut or bay-colored coats. Percherons look much like Belgians but have gray or black coats. These horses are lively for their size and may be used as a general-purpose horse. The Suffolk, a smaller, chestnut-colored horse, makes an ideal draft horse. It was a favorite for pulling milk wagons.

Heavy harness horses, also called *coach horses,* weigh less than draft horses and are not as strong. These horses can do light farm work and make good mounts for pleasure riding. European breeders developed heavy harness horses to pull coaches, wagons, and artillery. Breeds include the Cleveland bay, French coach (Normand), and German coach (Oldenburger).

Cleveland bays look like compact, rugged thoroughbreds. They make excellent general-purpose horses for driving, riding, and hunting. The French coach and German coach breeds were popular in North America until the early 1900's but are seldom seen now.

Ponies

Well-trained ponies make good pets for children. Ponies learn quickly and are usually gentle. They are used for pleasure riding and can pull small carts. Most ponies live longer than other horses. They need only grass and hay as food. Breeds include the Shetland, Welsh, Hackney, Connemara, and pony of the Americas.

A full-grown Shetland pony stands from 32 to 46 inches (81 to 117 centimeters) high. This favorite children's horse once pulled plows and wagons in its native Shetland Islands, north of Scotland. Miners in Wales developed the Welsh pony to work in the cramped tunnels

WORLD BOOK photo

Welsh pony

WORLD BOOK photo

Shetland pony

Hackney pony

WORLD BOOK photo

Chicago Zoological Society

Przewalski's horse

States are often called "wild horses." But they are actually descendants of tame horses that were ridden by Spanish explorers, American Indians, and cowhands of the Old West. The horses escaped from their owners and eventually formed bands. In the early 1900's, more than 2 million of these horses, also called *mustangs,* roamed the West. But people rounded up many of them to clear land for farms and ranches. Many were slaughtered and sold for use in pet food. Today, about 20,000 mustangs roam the West. Federal laws prohibit killing these horses, but some people hunt them illegally.

The body of a horse

Size. Horse owners measure the height of a horse in *hands,* from the ground to the highest point of the *withers* (ridge between the shoulder bones). A hand equals 4 inches (10 centimeters), the average width of a man's hand. A horse that stands 14.2 hands (14 hands and 2 inches) is 58 inches (147 centimeters) high.

Coat and skin. The horse's body is covered by a coat of hair. A healthy, glowing coat gives a splendid appearance. A thick winter coat grows every autumn and is shed every spring. Horses never shed the hair of the mane or the tail. If the mane and tail become too thick, the horse's owner may pull out some hair to make the horse look better. Pulling the hair does not hurt because the animal has no nerves at the roots of its hair. A horse uses its tail to brush off insects. A horse also has special muscles for twitching the skin to get rid of insects.

Sweat glands on the surface of the horse's body help

of coal mines. The Hackney is one of the largest pony breeds. The Irish Connemara ponies make good jumpers. The pony of the Americas looks like a miniature Appaloosa. This breed is popular in young people's riding competitions.

Wild horses

Two kinds of wild horses—*Przewalski's horse* and the *tarpan*—probably have the same ancestors that tame horses have. Some Przewalski's horses live in Mongolia, but most live in zoos. Tarpans, also called *forest horses,* once lived in parts of Europe, but they became extinct in the late 1800's. See **Przewalski's horse; Tarpan.**

Horses that roam freely in parts of the western United

Pinto

WORLD BOOK photo

The sizes of horses Horses range in height from less than 3 feet (0.9 meter) to more than 5 feet (1.5 meters) at the withers. These illustrations show how various breeds compare in height to an average-sized man.

WORLD BOOK illustration

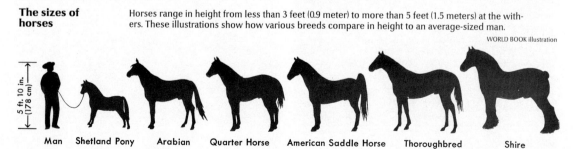

5 ft. 10 in. (178 cm)

Man   Shetland Pony   Arabian   Quarter Horse   American Saddle Horse   Thoroughbred   Shire

The body of a horse

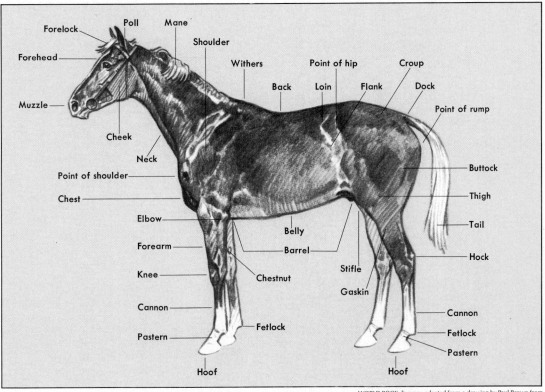

Forelock
Poll
Mane
Shoulder
Forehead
Withers
Point of hip
Croup
Muzzle
Back
Loin
Flank
Dock
Cheek
Point of rump
Neck
Buttock
Point of shoulder
Thigh
Chest
Tail
Elbow
Belly
Hock
Forearm
Barrel
Knee
Stifle
Cannon
Chestnut
Gaskin
Cannon
Pastern
Fetlock
Fetlock
Hoof
Pastern
Hoof

WORLD BOOK diagram; adapted from a drawing by Paul Brown from *The Horse,* © 1943, used with permission of Charles Scribner's Sons

the animal stay cool. The heavy coats of horses used for fast work, such as racing or polo, should be clipped in winter. The horses can then cool off more easily when they sweat. When the animals are resting, they should be covered with a blanket to keep them warm.

Horses have many colors, including various shades of black, brown, *chestnut* (reddish-brown), *dun* (yellowish-gray), gold, gray, *sorrel* (yellowish-brown), and white. *Bay* horses have a reddish-brown coat and black *points* (legs, mane, and tail). Many dark bays have brown hair on the back and reddish-brown hair on the flanks, underparts, and face. Chestnut horses may have *flaxen* (pale-yellow) or sorrel manes and tails, but not black points. Many gray horses are born a dark color and turn lighter as they grow older. Lipizzans and some other gray horses turn white by the time they are fully grown. *Roan* horses have a yellowish-brown or reddish-brown coat sprinkled with gray or white hairs. *Pintos,* also called *paints,* have a black or dark-colored coat with large white areas that vary in pattern.

Horse raisers often use special terms to describe the markings on a horse's face or legs. These terms include:
Baldface—a mostly white face.
Blaze—a large white patch on the face.
Race—a narrow strip down the center of the face.
Star—any small white patch on the forehead.
Snip—any small white patch near the muzzle.
Sock—a white patch above the foot.

Legs and hoofs. A horse's legs are suited for fast running. Large muscles in the upper part of the legs provide great speed with a minimum of effort. The long, thin lower legs give the horse a long stride. The front legs carry most of the horse's weight. They absorb the jolts when the animal runs or jumps. The rear legs provide power for running or jumping.

Thousands of years of evolution have given the horse feet ideally suited for running. Each foot is really a strong toe. Only the tip of the toe, protected by the strong, curved hoof, touches the ground. The remains of what were once two other toes grow as bony strips on the *cannon* bone of the horse's legs. The *frog* (an elastic

The bottom of a horse's hoof

WORLD BOOK illustration by Noel Sickles

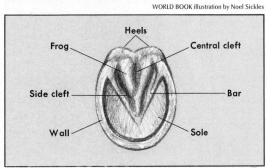

Heels
Frog
Central cleft
Side cleft
Bar
Wall
Sole

The skeleton of a horse

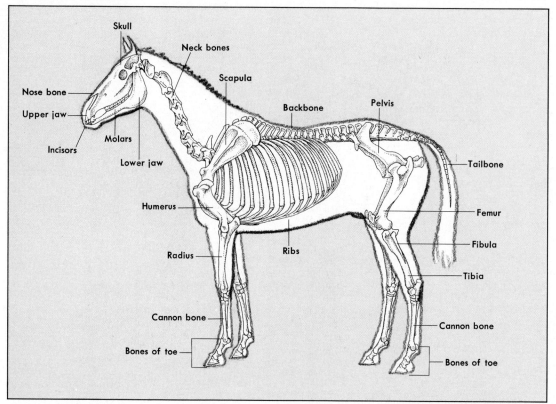

WORLD BOOK illustration by Noel Sickles and Patricia J. Wynne

The foot of a horse

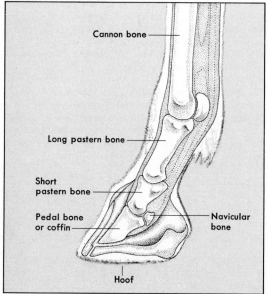

WORLD BOOK illustration by Noel Sickles and Patricia J. Wynne

A horse's foot has a single toe, which is formed by the pastern bones and the pedal bone. A horse walks on the tips of its toes, each of which is covered by a strong, hard hoof.

mass on the sole of the foot) acts like a rubber heel. It helps absorb the jolt when the hoof strikes the ground. The horse's real heel bone is the *hock,* located about halfway up the leg. The hock never touches the ground.

A horse with a bad fracture is usually killed because the break causes shock and extreme pain. But certain kinds of broken bones do not cause much pain and may heal. Veterinarians treat such breaks with slings and casts.

Teeth. Most male horses have 40 teeth, and most females have 36. The *molars* (back teeth) grind food as the horse chews. These teeth have no nerves, and they never stop growing. Sometimes the molars grow unevenly and must be filed down so the horse can chew properly.

An expert on horses can tell a horse's age by counting the number of teeth and checking their condition. Most foals are born toothless but soon get two upper and two lower front teeth. When 4 months old, the horse has four upper and four lower teeth. At the age of 1 year, it has six pairs of upper and lower *incisors* (cutting teeth). At 5 years, a horse has 12 pairs of incisors and is said to have a full mouth. Adult horses have six pairs of molars. Males grow four extra teeth at the age of 5. By the time a horse is 8 years old, the rough grinding surfaces of the bottom incisors have been worn down. The horse has a smooth mouth and is said to be *aged.* Sometimes tiny wolf teeth grow in front of the molars. These teeth interfere with the *bit,* which is the part of a bridle that goes into the horse's mouth. Wolf teeth are usually removed. The bit rests in spaces between the horse's incisors and molars.

Senses. Horses have larger eyes than any other land animals except ostriches. A horse's eyes are oval, and they are set on the sides of the head. The two eyes can be moved independently, each in a half circle. Thus, a horse can look forward with one eye and backward with the other. Because of the position of its eyes, a horse has a blind spot a short distance in front of it. A horse must turn its head to see a nearby object that lies directly ahead. The shape of a horse's eyes makes objects far to the side or back appear to move faster than they actually do. For this reason, a horse may *shy* (move suddenly) at the slightest movement of an object to the side or back. Horses' eyes require a fairly long time to adjust to changes of light. When a horse is moved from a dark stall into bright sunlight, it may appear nervous until its eyes adjust.

Horses have keen hearing. They have short, pointed ears that they can move around to pick up sounds from almost any direction. Certain positions of the ears may indicate a horse's attitude. For example, when a horse points its ears forward, it is curious about an object in front of it. When a horse twitches its ears or lays them back against the head, it is angry and may kick.

Horses have a well-developed sense of smell. Their nostrils are very large and can pick up scents from long distances. A strong wind and heavy rain interfere with the sense of smell and cause horses to become nervous.

The sense of touch varies among different breeds of horses. The thin skin of most breeds of light horses is sensitive to insects and rough objects. Most breeds of heavy horses are less sensitive to such irritations.

Intelligence. Horses can learn to follow signals, but they must be taught through constant repetition. They also must be encouraged to overcome their fear of unfamiliar objects and situations. Horses have excellent memories and can recall pleasant or unpleasant experiences many years after they occur. See **Animal** (Intelligence of animals).

Life history. A mare carries her foal for about 11 months before giving birth. This period may vary from 10 to 14 months. Foals can stand shortly after birth, and within a few hours they are able to run about. The legs of newborn horses seem much too long for their bodies. As the horse matures, the legs grow more slowly than the rest of the body.

A year-old colt is about half grown. Most horses reach full height and weight by the age of 5. Most horse raisers breed mares at the age of 3 or 4, and stallions at the age of 2. Most mares have five or six foals during their life, but some have as many as 19.

Race horses have their official birthday on January 1, except in the Southern Hemisphere, where it is on August 1. Regardless of their actual birth date, race horses become a year older on their official birthday. This system is used to qualify horses for races that are limited to certain age groups. For example, only 3-year-olds race in the Kentucky Derby. Most horses live from 20 to 30 years.

Equipment for horseback riding includes the rider's clothing, spurs, and whip. It also includes *tack* (gear) for the horse, such as the saddle and bridle.

Clothes for riding. Riders wear comfortable clothing suitable for their type of riding. Their clothes also must protect their legs from irritation while rubbing against the saddle. Blue jeans and a comfortable shirt are probably best for open-country riding. Cowhands often wear *chaps* (seatless leather trousers) that fit over their regular trousers. Chaps protect the rider's legs from being scratched by brush.

For English riding, *jodhpurs* (long, tight-fitting breeches) or regular riding breeches are usually worn. They provide both comfort and protection. Boots, or any shoes with heels, keep the feet from slipping out of the stirrups. Some riders wear hard caps to protect their head in case of a fall.

Spurs. Skilled riders use spurs to signal the horse without moving their legs or heels vigorously. Some riders in horse shows use spurs to give commands or to urge their mounts to run faster. Spurs should be worn only by expert riders.

Spurs called *dummy spurs* have either blunt *rowels* (little wheels) or no rowels. Some spurs have sharp points instead of rowels. *Racing spurs* have rowels on the inside to make it easy to touch the horse. Rowels on racing spurs and dummy spurs point downward. Most *dressage spurs* have sharp rowels. They curve upward so that riders need not shift their feet to touch the horse.

The whip. An expert rider uses a whip to give the horse special signals or to train the animal. Horse whips are lightweight and flexible and cause no pain if properly used. Horses learn to respond to signals from a trainer's whip when performing different steps and difficult movements in horse shows. Race horses increase their speed at a touch of the jockey's whip. A *riding crop* may be used like a whip. Crops have stiff handles. The tip is a large loop of rawhide. In fox hunting, riders use a *hunting whip,* which has a curved, wooden or bone handle at one end and a long leather lash at the other end. The lash is used to control the hounds.

Experienced riders apply whips as punishment only if the horse kicks or bites at another horse or stubbornly disobeys a command. The rider immediately strikes the horse sharply on the flanks.

The saddle. Riders in the United States generally use an *English saddle* or a *Western saddle*. A person should use the kind of saddle that feels most comfortable or that suits a particular type of riding.

Riders who prefer the English saddle like it because it

Riding equipment

Bit is the metal part of the bridle that fits in a horse's mouth.
Bridle is the headgear used to control a horse. It includes the bit.
Girth is a leather or canvas strap that fits under the horse's belly and holds a saddle in place.
Hackamore is a bitless bridle that controls the horse by pressure on its nose and jaw.
Reins are long, narrow leather strips attached at one end to the bit. The rider holds the other end.
Tack is riding equipment, such as the bridle and saddle.

English riding equipment

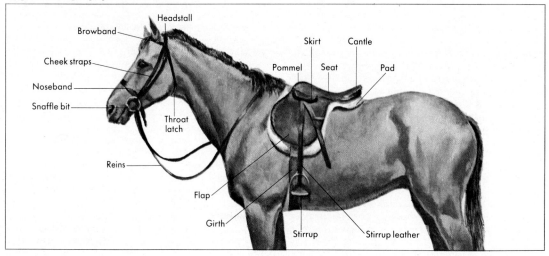

Western riding equipment

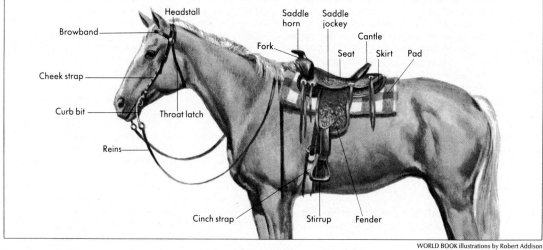

WORLD BOOK illustrations by Robert Addison

is padded and more comfortable. It is also flatter and weighs less than the Western saddle. Jockeys, jumpers, exhibition riders, and others who need extra speed from their horses use the English saddle because it interferes with the horse's movements less than a Western saddle does.

The Western saddle has wide stirrups and a *horn,* to which a rope may be fastened. Cowhands and rodeo riders use Western saddles. Cowhands may tie their ropes to the horn when roping cattle. They usually use a *double girth* (two saddle straps) on the Western saddle to hold it securely against the pull of roped cattle. A blanket under the saddle keeps the horse's back and sides from becoming sore. Most Western saddles have fleece padding that also helps to protect the horse's back.

The bridle is used to control the horse. It consists of straps and metal pieces that fit on the horse's head and in its mouth.

The simplest bridle is the *snaffle bridle.* This bridle has a jointed bit that is gentle on the horse. The bit of the snaffle bridle pulls on the corners of the horse's lips. The bridle's single set of reins can be handled easily by the rider.

The *double,* or *full, bridle* is used by advanced riders. This type of bridle has a double set of reins, a snaffle bit, and a *curb bit.* The curb bit fits between the horse's teeth on sensitive spaces called *bars.* This bit puts pressure on the horse's lower jaw. A separate set of reins controls each of the bits. The upper reins move the snaffle bit, and the lower reins operate the curb bit. Pressure on the snaffle bit causes the horse to raise its head. Pressure on the curb bit pulls the horse's head down and brings the animal to an abrupt halt. Cowhands and polo players use the curb bit to stop their horses quickly. Another kind of bridle, called the *Pelham bridle,* combines the snaffle and curb bits into one bit with a double set of reins.

The art of riding and managing horses is called *horse-manship.* Many people enjoy riding horseback for fun and sport. The basic techniques of English and Western riding are similar.

Selecting a horse. The selection of a horse depends partly on the skill of the rider. Experienced riders may prefer responsive, high-spirited horses. But most beginners feel at ease on a gentle, reliable horse. Youngsters may be more comfortable on a pony than on a large horse. *Geldings,* which are male horses that have had their sex organs removed, are easier to control than stallions or mares. In choosing a horse to buy, a person should also consider such factors as the animal's age, training, and physical condition. A well-trained horse over 10 years old is best for a beginning rider. An expert should ride the horse to determine how trained it is. In addition, a veterinarian should examine the animal and check for possible health problems.

Mounting a horse. The first things a rider learns are how to *mount* (get on) a horse and sit in the saddle.

The rider mounts on the horse's left side. Most horses become used to being mounted from the left side during training. Someone mounting from the right side might startle or confuse them. The custom of mounting from the left probably started when men wore long swords that hung down along the left leg. It was easier to throw the right leg across the horse's back than to throw the left leg and the heavy sword. Many horses trained to travel on mountain trails can be mounted from either side. Riders mount from the side that is least likely to cause the horse to lose its balance.

After mounting, the rider sits in a relaxed position. The weight should be settled firmly in the *dip* (middle of the saddle). The back is held erect but not stiff.

To start a horse, the rider squeezes both legs against its sides. As the horse moves forward, the rider lets the reins follow the movement of the horse's head. Riders should look where they are going, not at the horse.

To control a horse, riders use their hands, legs, and body weight. English riders call these skills the *aids.*

Western riders refer to them as *cues.* Skilled riders can put their mounts through difficult performances and tricks with only slight movements of their hands or legs. Riders in horse shows change gaits time after time with no apparent signals. Cowhand horses and polo ponies respond quickly to signs. They start, stop, or turn at a touch of the rider's hand or leg, or at the shifting of weight.

Trainers teach horses to move *away from the leg.* The horse moves to the right when the rider's left leg presses against its side, and to the left when it feels the rider's right leg.

In English riding, horses are taught to move *toward the hand.* The reins in the rider's hands lead to the bit in the horse's mouth. When the rider pulls the right rein, the bit pulls on the right side of the horse's mouth. The horse then turns in that direction. Horses trained for Western riding learn to respond to the touch of the reins against the neck. The horse turns away from this signal. At a touch of the rein on the right side of the neck, the horse turns left.

Skilled riders shift their weight in the direction of the horse's movement. They move forward when the horse goes forward, and to the right or left when turning. They also shift their body back a little in the saddle when slowing up or stopping. A good rider does all these things so smoothly that only the horse knows that the rider has changed balance.

To stop a horse, riders shift their balance back a little in the saddle. Then they squeeze their fingers to increase the pressure on the reins slightly without tugging on them. When the horse stops, the rider eases the pressure on the reins.

To move a horse backwards, the rider squeezes both reins equally, preventing the horse from moving forward, and presses both legs against the girth of the saddle. A well-trained horse will then step backwards.

Gaits are the ways a horse moves. Horses have three natural gaits: (1) walk, (2) trot, and (3) canter. A fast canter is often called a gallop. Many horses are trained for three speeds at each of the three natural gaits. Train-

WORLD BOOK illustrations by Robert Keys

How to mount a horse. Always mount a horse from the left side. Grip the reins and the horse's mane with your left hand, put your left foot in the stirrup, and grab the cantle with your right hand, *left.* Spring up, lift your right leg over the horse's rump, and move your right hand to the pommel, *center.* Sit down gently and put your right foot in the stirrup, *right.*

Holding the reins. The illustration at the left shows how to hold the reins. Keep your hands about 2 inches (5 centimeters) apart and slightly above the horse's withers.

WORLD BOOK illustrations by Robert Keys

How to dismount from a horse. Grip the reins and the horse's mane with your left hand and put your right hand on the pommel, *left.* Swing your right leg over the horse's rump and bring it next to your left leg, moving your right hand to the cantle, *right.* Balancing your body with your hands, remove your left foot from the stirrup and drop down.

ers also develop artificial gaits in some horses. Horses so trained compete in horse shows and perform in circuses, fairs, and rodeos. Artificial gaits include the pace, slow gait, and rack.

Walk is the slowest gait. The horse moves at a speed of about 4 miles (6 kilometers) an hour. It raises one foot after another and puts them down in the same order. The horse keeps its balance by altering its front and back feet, and its right and left feet. For example, the order may be (1) right forefoot, (2) left hind foot, (3) left forefoot, and (4) right hind foot.

Trot is a two-beat gait at a speed of about 9 miles (14 kilometers) an hour. The front leg on one side of the body and the hind leg on the other side hit the ground together. The horse bends its legs more when it is trotting than when it is walking. Harness-race horses trot around the track while pulling a driver in a *sulky* (two-wheeled cart).

When beginners first ride at a trot, they should hold onto the horse's mane or the saddle until they get used to the motion. On the first beat of a trot, riders raise their body slightly by pushing their feet down on the stirrups. They come down in the saddle on the second beat and then go right up again. This method of riding is called *posting.* A beginner should practice the movements of posting while the horse is walking.

Canter is a comfortable, three-beat rhythmic riding gait. A horse canters at a speed of 10 to 12 miles (16 to 19 kilometers) an hour. On the first beat, one forefoot strikes the ground. Then the other forefoot and opposite hind leg hit the ground together. On the third beat, the other hind foot strikes the ground.

Gallop is a horse's fastest natural gait. Horses gallop in a leaping and bounding motion. On the first beat, a hind foot strikes the ground. The other hind foot and opposite forefoot hit the ground together. On the third beat, the other forefoot strikes the ground. Then the horse leaps forward, and all its feet leave the ground. A racing horse runs at an extended gallop.

Pace, like the trot, is a gait used in harness racing. When a horse paces, it moves the legs on the same side of the body at the same time. The pace is an uncomfortable riding gait.

Slow gait is a slow, four-beat gait. Four beats of the hoofs can be heard as the horse moves forward.

Rack is a fast, smooth, four-beat gait. It resembles the slow gait but is faster. Five-gaited saddle horses are trained to slow gait and rack.

The three natural gaits of a horse

WORLD BOOK illustrations by H. Charles McBarron

The walk is a four-beat gait. The feet hit the ground as follows: (1) right forefoot, (2) left hind foot, (3) left forefoot, and (4) right hind foot.

The trot is a two-beat gait. The feet hit in the following order: (1) right forefoot and left hind foot and (2) left forefoot and right hind foot.

The gallop is a three-beat gait. The feet hit as follows: (1) left hind foot, (2) left forefoot and right hind foot, and (3) right forefoot.

The stall. A horse should live in a clean, comfortable stall that measures at least 10 feet by 10 feet (3 meters by 3 meters). The stable should be light, dry, and well ventilated. Clay or finely ground cinders make the best floor, but cement or wooden floors can be used. Bedding spread at least 1 foot (30 centimeters) thick over the floor gives the horse a comfortable resting place. Wood shavings, sawdust, straw, or peat moss make good bedding materials. Horses can sleep standing up and often doze while standing with their eyes wide open.

Food. A horse needs food at least three times a day. The horse's stomach is small for the size of its body and holds about 18 quarts (17 liters) of food. In comparison, a man's stomach holds little more than 1 quart (0.95 liter) of food.

Horses eat grass, grain, and hay. When a horse eats grain or hay, it gathers the food with its lips. When a horse eats grass, it bites off the blades close to the ground. Horses chew their food slowly and thoroughly. They do not chew a cud as do cows and deer.

Hay for horses should be placed in a net or on a *rack* (wooden frame). A *manger* (open box) holds the grain. A 1,000-pound (450-kilogram) horse that works three or four hours a day needs about 14 pounds (6.4 kilograms) of hay—5 pounds (2.3 kilograms) in the morning and the rest at night. A horse should never eat moldy or dusty hay or hay that contains coarse sticks, thorns, or rubbish. Timothy, or timothy mixed with clover or alfalfa, makes the best hay.

Horses like oats more than any other grain or hay. But they will eat oats too quickly unless they have some hay first. Working horses eat from 4 to 12 quarts (3.8 to 11.4 liters) of oats, or a mixture of oats and bran, every day. The exact amount depends on the animal's size, condition, and the amount of exercise it gets. A third of the feed should be given in the morning, a third at noon, and the rest at night.

Most horses require from 10 to 12 gallons (38 to 45 liters) of fresh, clean water daily. A horse should not be permitted to drink large amounts of water when the animal is hot or before it begins hard exercise.

Horses need salt for good health because their bodies lose salt when they sweat. A horse eats about 2 ounces (57 grams) of salt daily. A box of salt or a solid salt block in the stable and in the pasture provides this important part of the diet.

Grooming helps keep a horse healthy and improves its appearance. Horses kept in a stable should be groomed daily with a rubber currycomb, body brush, hoof pick, and mane and tail comb. Long, sweeping brush strokes in the direction of the growth of the hair help give the coat a healthy glow. Brushing removes dirt and dandruff. Areas touched by the saddle and girth, and the regions behind the heels and in the hock depressions, need special brushing. A thorough wiping with a soft cloth should follow the brushing. The hoof pick removes dirt and stones and other objects from the feet.

Cleaning a horse's hoofs is part of the daily care that the animal should receive. A hoof pick should be used to remove dirt and stones and other objects from the hoofs, *above.*

WORLD BOOK photos

Daily grooming of a horse's coat and mane helps maintain the animal's health and improves its appearance. The coat should be brushed thoroughly and then wiped with a soft cloth, *above.* The mane should be combed to untangle the hairs, *right.*

Horse shows and sports

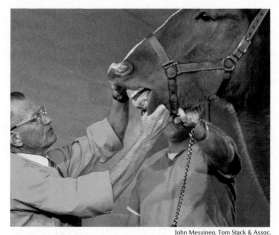

John Messineo, Tom Stack & Assoc.

Medical care of a horse includes periodic examinations by a veterinarian. As part of an examination, the doctor checks the condition of the animal's teeth and mouth, *above.*

Shoes protect the feet of horses that run or work on roads and other hard surfaces such as race tracks. Light shoes, weighing about 8 ounces (230 grams) and having only a few nails, make the best shoes for most horses. Some riding horses wear shoes weighted in the toes to help them raise their feet high. Race horses wear light shoes that may wear out after a few races. Shoes for wear in winter or for high mountain trails have cleats that help keep the horse from slipping on ice or snow.

Medical care. Horses should be examined by a veterinarian at least once or twice a year. They should be vaccinated against tetanus, influenza, and other diseases. When necessary, they should receive medicine to expel worms. Sometimes, a horse's teeth must be *floated* (filed down to remove sharp edges).

Horse owners can prevent many medical problems by feeding and bedding the animals properly, keeping them and their living quarters clean, and exercising the horses daily. Owners should watch for any changes in the condition or behavior of their horses and call a veterinarian if a horse appears ill. Signs of illness include loss of appetite, lack of vigor, mucous or bloody discharges from the eyes or nose, swellings or sores on the body, and hot legs or feet. A fast or slow breathing rate or pulse rate may also be a sign of illness. Normally, a resting horse breathes from 8 to 16 times per minute and has a pulse rate of from 30 to 40 beats per minute.

A horse's legs and feet easily become diseased if not cared for properly. Some common diseases of the legs and feet include *thrush, navicular,* and *laminitis.* Thrush is an infection of the frog. It can be prevented by providing clean, dry bedding for a horse. To treat thrush, veterinarians apply medication to the affected frog. Navicular is a disease of the foot bone that causes a horse's legs to become stiff and sore. It is treated with corrective shoeing and drugs. Laminitis, also called *founder,* is an inflammation of the foot. Its symptoms include lameness, hot feet, and increased pulse rate. Laminitis is treated by applying medication and soaking the foot in warm water.

Horse shows and sports involving horses include a variety of events that test the speed, strength, and other abilities of the animals. Success in these events also depends on the skill of the riders or drivers. Horse shows and sports have increased greatly in popularity during the 1900's. They are enjoyed by millions of people throughout the world and include local, national, and international competitions.

The Olympic Games have three kinds of *equestrian* (horseback riding) sports: (1) jumping, (2) dressage, and (3) eventing. The International Equestrian Federation regulates the Olympic equestrian events. It also regulates the world championships in *driving,* an event for harness horses and drivers. More than 60 nations belong to the federation.

This section describes horse shows, jumping, dressage, and eventing. *World Book* has separate articles on the sports of fox hunting, harness racing, horse racing, polo, rodeo, and steeplechasing.

Horse shows have three main types of competitions: (1) performance, (2) breeding, and (3) *equitation* (horsemanship). In performance competition, the horses and riders demonstrate various skills. For example, a show may include jumping, five-gaited riding, or driving events. In breeding competition, all the horses in the event must be of the same breed. They are displayed without saddles. The judges rank the horses on *conformation* (physical qualities) and decide which ones best represent the breed. In equitation competition, the contestants ride their horses around a ring. They are judged on their riding style and control of the horse.

Some horse shows are restricted to only one breed of horses. Others include events for many breeds. Shows may be held indoors or outdoors and may last from a few hours to a week or more.

Robert Frerck

A jumping course consists of different types of obstacles that the contestants must clear. The course shown above includes such standard obstacles as a stone wall and parallel bars.

Karl Leck

A well-performed jump requires harmony between the rider and horse. For example, the rider must adapt to the horse's movements and, as shown above, lean forward for the jump.

Many organizations sponsor horse shows in the United States. The American Horse Shows Association (AHSA) approves about 1,600 shows a year, including the trials for the United States Equestrian Team. The U.S. Equestrian Team represents the United States in the Olympic Games and other international competitions. The most important horse shows in the United States include the National Horse Show in New York City; the American Royal Horse Show in Kansas City, Kans.; and the Grand National Horse Show in San Francisco, Calif.

Jumping. In jumping competitions, the contestants ride across a specially designed course that has obstacles for the horses to leap over. The course may include high jumps, wide jumps, and two or more jumps set close together. The courses vary in difficulty, depending on the level of the competition. The contestants in jumping competitions receive *faults* (penalties) for falls, knocking down part of an obstacle, *refusals,* and other errors. A refusal occurs when the horse will not jump over an obstacle. After three refusals, the horse and rider are eliminated from the competition. The contestant with the fewest faults wins the event. In some jumping events, the contestants are timed. In case of a tie for first place, the contestant who completes the course in the shortest time wins.

The main kinds of jumping competitions include (1) Nations' Cup, (2) puissance, and (3) Grand Prix. In Nations' Cups, teams from different countries compete. In most cases, each team consists of four riders and their horses. The three best scores of each team are added to determine the winning team. Puissance events consist mainly of high jumps. The contestants who complete the course without any faults or with equal faults participate in a jump-off. In the jump-off, the number of obstacles is reduced, but the remaining obstacles are raised or widened. The contestants may have several jump-offs, until all except the winner fail to clear the obstacles. Grand Prix competitions are part of the Olympic Games. All contestants complete the course once, and then the top two or more riders participate in a jump-off. In case of a tie for first, the contestant who completes the course in the shortest time wins.

Dressage. In dressage competitions, the riders guide their horses through a series of movements at the walk, trot, and canter, using mainly leg and seat signals. The horse's movements should be smooth, precise, and graceful, and the rider's signals should not be visible to the spectators.

Special dressage movements include the *passage, piaffer,* and *pirouette.* A passage is a rhythmic, elevated trot in which the horse slowly moves forward. A piaffer resembles a trot, but it is performed without any forward, backward, or sideward movement. A pirouette is a circle that the hourse makes by pivoting its forelegs and one hind leg around the other hind leg.

In dressage competitions, the series of movements

Alix Coleman

The cross-country event is the most strenuous part of a type of equestrian competition called *eventing.* The contestants must ride over rough terrain, crossing streams and other obstacles, *left.*

Raising horses

Alix Coleman

Dressage competition consists of a series of smooth, graceful movements performed by the horse in response to signals by the rider. These signals should not be seen by the spectators.

must be performed in a specific order. In most cases, the contestants are judged by two or more officials who sit in various places around the ring. Each judge gives a contestant points for the performance of each movement and penalties for errors. The scores of all the judges are added, and the contestant with the most points wins.

Dressage techniques were originated by military officers who rode horseback. They had to use their hands to hold weapons, and so they gave signals to their horses with their legs and by shifting their body weight.

Eventing is often called the *Three-Day Event* because most major competitions take place during a three-day period. The contestants first compete in a dressage event. They then participate in a cross-country event. They ride over a course that may be more than 10 miles (16 kilometers) long and includes rough terrain and such obstacles as brush hedges, rail fences, and streams. The contestants receive penalties for falls, refusals, and failure to complete the course in the allotted time. Lastly, a stadium jumping competition is held. The results from the events of the three days are added, and the contestant with the fewest penalties wins.

Eventing is probably the most challenging equestrian event. It tests the endurance, obedience, jumping ability, and other qualities of the horse and the skill and daring of the rider. The cross-country event is extremely strenuous.

Raising horses for racing, driving, and other sports involves careful breeding and training. It is an important industry in the United States. California, Illinois, Kentucky, and Texas, and many other states have large breeding farms that raise horses.

Breeding horses. On breeding farms, stallions and mares are carefully selected for mating on the basis of their ancestry and physical qualities. Breeders of race horses also consider the racing records of the animals. An owner of a champion racing stallion may earn millions of dollars in *stud fees* by using the horse for breeding purposes. A stud fee is a sum of money paid to a stallion's owner for the use of the stallion to sire a foal. Breeding horses is not an exact science, and breeders can never be completely certain of producing a colt or filly of champion quality.

Most breeders mate their mares to a stallion in spring. The mares give birth about springtime the following year. People who raise race horses want their foals to be born as soon as possible after January 1 because the foals will be considered yearlings the following January. A foal that is born early in the year has more time to grow and develop before it races as a 2-year-old.

A foal stays with its mother for the first six months after birth. The owner then *weans* (separates) the foal from its mother and puts it out to pasture with other foals.

People who raise purebred horses enter their foals in the *registry* of the association for the particular breed. A registry is an official record that lists a horse's sire and dam and other information. Horses that appear in a

Leading horse-raising countries

Number of horses in each country

China	10,978,000 horses
United States	10,580,000 horses
Mexico	6,135,000 horses
Soviet Union	5,750,000 horses
Brazil	5,200,000 horses
Argentina	3,100,000 horses
Mongolia	1,961,000 horses
Colombia	1,906,000 horses
Ethiopia	1,580,000 horses
Poland	1,404,000 horses

Figures are for 1985.
Source: *FAO Production Yearbook 1985*, Food and Agriculture Organization of the United Nations.

A newborn foal is cared for by its mother. The mare nurses the foal for the first six months after birth. The owner then *weans* the foal by separating it from the mother and putting it out to pasture with other foals.

William Strode, Woodfin Camp, Inc.

breed registry are called *registered horses*. In the United States, there are about 70 breed associations that keep registries. The two largest ones are the Jockey Club, which registers thoroughbreds, and the American Quarter Horse Association. Many other countries also have breed associations and registries. Nations that are well known for breeding horses include Argentina, Canada, France, Great Britain, and New Zealand.

Leading horse-raising states

Number of horses in each state

California ●●●●●●●●●●●●●●●●●●●
858,000 horses

Texas ●●●●●●●●●●●●●●●●◖
784,000 horses

Oklahoma ●●●●●●◖
308,000 horses

Illinois ●●●●●◖
282,000 horses

Ohio ●●●●◖
251,000 horses

Missouri ●●●●◖
246,000 horses

Montana ●●●●◖
244,000 horses

Michigan ●●●●◖
226,000 horses

Kentucky ●●●●◖
225,000 horses

Colorado ●●●●
221,000 horses

Figures are 1985 estimates.
Source: American Horse Council, Inc.

Training horses requires great skill and patience. Expert trainers handle horses gently but firmly and teach them slowly. Soon after birth, a foal learns to accept handling by human beings. Some trainers begin to accustom a foal to a halter almost immediately. Others do not halter-break foals until they are several months old. After a horse is 1 year old, the trainer gradually accustoms it to having a saddle on its back. Then the horse is mounted and ridden a few steps. Most horses that are trained slowly and patiently do not buck when they are mounted for the first time.

A harness horse is also trained in gradual steps. The horse is first taught to respond to signals from long reins, which are held by a person who walks behind the animal. Later, the horse is taught how to pull a light buggy or carriage.

After a horse has learned to follow the signals of a rider or driver, it is trained for a certain sport. For example, Thoroughbred race horses learn to run when a starting gate swings open. Harness racing horses learn to trot or pace behind a moving starting gate that is attached to a car.

WORLD BOOK photo

Training a colt to lead. A colt learns to *lead*—that is, to follow a person who guides it with a strap—by being led around a ring behind its mother. The colt follows naturally.

Horses in history

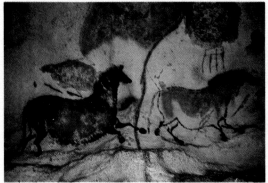

Prehistoric cave painting (about 15,000 B.C.) by
an unknown artist; Lascaux Cave, Dordogne, France (Jean Vertut)

Prehistoric paintings of horses have been found in many
caves in Europe. The painting shown above, from the Lascaux
Cave in southwestern France, is about 17,000 years old.

Origins of the horse. Scientists believe that the earliest ancestor of the horse was a small animal about 10 to
20 inches (25 to 50 centimeters) high. They call this animal *Eohippus* (dawn horse) or *Hyracotherium*. It lived
about 55 million years ago in what is now North America and Europe.

These prehistoric horses had arched backs and
snoutlike noses. They looked more like racing dogs,
such as greyhounds or whippets, than like the straight-
backed, long-faced modern horse. They had four toes
on their front feet and three toes on their hind feet. Each
toe ended in a separate small hoof. Large, tough pads
similar to those on a dog's foot kept the toes off the
ground. These pads bore the animal's weight.

The next important ancestor of the modern horse was
Mesohippus (middle horse). It lived about 35 million
years ago. It averaged about 20 inches (51 centimeters)
in height and had long, slender legs. Each foot had three
toes, of which the middle toe was longest. About 30 mil-

lion years ago, it gave way to a new horselike creature,
Miohippus. This animal stood from 24 to 28 inches (61 to
71 centimeters) tall, and its middle toe was longer and
stronger than that of its ancestors.

Horselike animals continued to develop, and *Mery-
chippus* (ruminant or cud-chewing horse) appeared
about 26 million years ago. It grew about 40 inches (100
centimeters) high. Like Miohippus, it had three toes on
each foot. The side toes were almost useless, but the
center toe grew long and strong. It ended in a large,
curved hoof and bore all the animal's weight.

By about 3 million years ago, horses probably looked
somewhat like modern horses. They grew larger than
their ancestors. The side toes on their feet became short
bones along the legs, leaving the strong center toe with
its hoof to support the animals. The teeth also changed,
becoming better fitted for eating grass. Scientists group
these horses, along with the modern domestic horse,
under the name *Equus.*

No one knows where horses originated. Fossils show
that during the Ice Age horses lived on every continent
except Australia. Great herds wandered throughout
North and South America. Then, for some unknown reason, they disappeared from the Western Hemisphere.

People tame the horse. Primitive people hunted
horses and ate their meat. No one knows who first
tamed horses and trained them for riding. Scientific discoveries at the ancient city of Susa in southwestern Asia
show that people rode horses over 5,000 years ago.

Stone tablets show that the Hittites trained horses for
sport and war about 1400 B.C. The Assyrians, about 800
B.C., hunted lions in two-wheeled chariots drawn by a
pair of horses. Tapestries show early Persians playing a
kind of polo. The early Greeks and Romans were expert
riders and used horses for racing and other sports.
Greek and Roman soldiers rode horses in battle. The
Greeks wrote about horsemanship as early as 400 B.C.
We still follow their principles of riding.

In 1066, William the Conqueror used mounted

**The development
of the horse**

The illustrations below show some of the ancestors of the modern horse. The earliest ancestor,
Eohippus, lived about 55 million years ago. Various horselike creatures gradually developed over
millions of years, changing in size and other body features. For example, the many-toed feet of
early horses developed into the single-toed hoofs of today's horses.

WORLD BOOK illustrations by Jean Helmer and Patricia J. Wynne

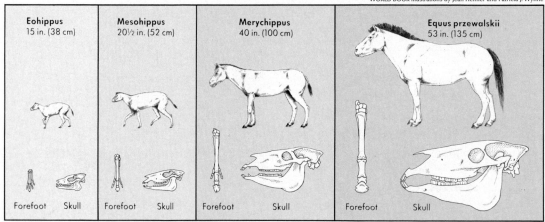

Eohippus 15 in. (38 cm)	Mesohippus 20½ in. (52 cm)	Merychippus 40 in. (100 cm)	Equus przewalskii 53 in. (135 cm)
Forefoot Skull	Forefoot Skull	Forefoot Skull	Forefoot Skull

The Metropolitan Museum of Art, Gift of John D. Rockefeller, Jr., 1933

Ornamented horses are led by a man paying tribute to his king. This piece of wall relief of the 700's B.C. comes from the palace of the ancient Assyrian ruler Sargon II, near Mosul, Iraq.

Famous horses in history and legend

Al Borak carried Muhammad from earth to the seventh heaven, according to Muslim legend.

Aristides won the first Kentucky Derby in 1875.

Black Horse, from the Bible (*Revelation*), is the horse of Famine.

Bucephalus could be ridden only by Alexander the Great, who founded the city of Bucephala about 326 B.C. in honor of his beloved horse.

Bulle Rock was the first thoroughbred imported from England to America, in 1730.

Cincinnati, a great black charger, carried General Ulysses S. Grant during the Civil War.

Clever Hans, who lived in the early 1900's, was a famous "talking" horse that solved arithmetic problems.

Comanche, a cavalry horse, was the only survivor of Lieutenant Colonel George A. Custer's "last stand" in 1876. **Vic,** Custer's horse, died in the battle.

Copenhagen carried the Duke of Wellington to victory in the Battle of Waterloo in 1815.

Diomed won the first English Derby at Epsom Downs, in 1780.

Eclipse, an English thoroughbred foaled in 1764, was the ancestor of many modern thoroughbreds.

Incitatus was made a priest and consul by the Roman Emperor Caligula about A.D. 40. This horse had an ivory manger and drank wine from a golden pail.

Iroquois, in 1881, became the first American-bred horse to win the English Derby.

Marengo, a white stallion, was ridden by Napoleon in his defeat at Waterloo in 1815.

Pegasus was the great winged horse of the Muses (nine goddesses in Greek mythology). See **Pegasus.**

Reckless, a small Korean racing mare, served as ammunition carrier for a U.S. Marine platoon during the Korean War (1950-1953). The mare was made a sergeant and received a medal for bravery under fire.

Sleipnir, the gray horse of Odin, chief god in Norse mythology, was said to have eight legs and be able to travel on land or sea.

Traveller, a spirited gray gelding, carried General Robert E. Lee during the Civil War. See **Lee, Robert E.** (picture).

Trojan Horse, a legendary wooden horse built by the Greeks, helped them capture the city of Troy during the Trojan War.

Xanthus was the horse of Achilles. He was supposed to have predicted his master's death, after being scolded by the mighty Greek warrior.

knights to invade England. The English then began to breed large, powerful war horses that could carry a man wearing a heavy suit of armor. During the 1300's, after armies began using gunpowder, swift, light steeds replaced the large mounts of the knights as war horses.

Horses in early America. The first European colonists found no horses in North America. Christopher Columbus had brought horses with him on his second voyage to the New World. But most American Indians did not know about horses until Spanish conquerors brought them to Mexico in 1519. Horses that the Spanish explorers left behind probably became the ancestors of the American wild horses.

The Indians, especially the tribes of the western plains, began to use horses about 1600. Indians rode horses to hunt buffalo and used them in battle.

Horses played an important part in the development and exploration of North America. The pioneers who settled the West rode horses and used them to pull their covered wagons. Mounted soldiers fought in the Revolutionary War and in the Civil War.

Horses pulled trains on several short railroads until the steam locomotive replaced them about 1830. They also pulled *horsecars* (streetcars) in cities before electricity was used. Stagecoaches and the pony express served as the fastest means of communication until the telegraph linked the East and West coasts in 1861.

Horses in the 1900's. With the development of railroads, tractors, trucks, and automobiles, horses became

The Metropolitan Museum of Art, New York, Fletcher Fund, 1919

A European war horse was large and strong enough to carry a heavily armored knight into battle. This print by Albrecht Dürer, a German artist, dates from the early A.D. 1500's.

Bettmann Archive

Automobiles began to replace horse-drawn carriages during the early 1900's. Horses lost importance in transportation as the use of motor-driven vehicles became widespread.

less useful. Horse-drawn milk wagons and garbage wagons were replaced by trucks. During World War II (1939-1945), the U.S. Army gave up cavalry horses.

The number of horses on United States farms declined steadily as more and more farmers began to use machinery. American farmers owned about 20 million farm horses in 1910. By the mid-1970's, there were only about 9 million horses in the United States. But, though the use of horses for heavy work declined, their importance in sports and recreation increased.

Several million wild horses roamed parts of the American West during the 1800's. The number declined to less than 20,000 by the early 1970's. Many people feared that the wild horses were becoming extinct, especially because the horses were being hunted for their meat. Manufacturers used the meat in making pet food. In 1971, the United States Congress passed a law that protects American wild horses.

Scientific classification. Horses belong to the horse family, Equidae. They are classified as genus *Equus,* species *E. caballus.*

Steven D. Price and Bill Landsman

Study aids

Related articles in *World Book* include:

Kinds of horses

Bronco	Przewalski's horse	Tarpan
Mustang	Shetland pony	

Members of the horse family

Donkey	Mule	Onager	Zebra

Diseases of horses

Distemper	Heaves	Spavin
Glanders	Mange	

Sports

Fox hunt	Olympic Games (table: Equestrian)
Harness racing	
Horse racing	Polo
Kentucky Derby	Rodeo
	Steeplechasing

Other related articles

Animal (Intelligence of animals)	Hoof
Bonheur, Rosa (picture)	Horse fly
Bot fly	Kentucky (pictures)
Centaur	Pegasus
Cowboy	Saddle
Harness	Ungulate
	Wyoming (pictures)

Outline

I. Kinds of horses
A. Light horses	C. Ponies
B. Heavy horses	D. Wild horses

II. The body of a horse
A. Size	E. Senses
B. Coat and skin	F. Intelligence
C. Legs and hoofs	G. Life history
D. Teeth	

III. Riding equipment
A. Clothes for riding	D. The saddle
B. Spurs	E. The bridle
C. The whip	

IV. How to ride
A. Selecting a horse	E. To stop a horse
B. Mounting a horse	F. To move a horse backwards
C. To start a horse	G. Gaits
D. To control a horse	

V. Care of a horse
A. The stall	D. Shoes
B. Food	E. Medical care
C. Grooming	

VI. Horse shows and sports
A. Horse shows	C. Dressage
B. Jumping	D. Eventing

VII. Raising horses
A. Breeding horses
B. Training horses

VIII. Horses in history

Questions

What does a *hand* mean in measuring a horse?
What are the three kinds of equestrian sports in the Olympic Games?
What are the horse's three natural gaits?
Why do horses need salt in their diet?
What did the earliest known ancestor of the horse look like?
How do you start and stop a horse when riding?
Why do owners sometimes cover horses with blankets?
How many teeth does a full-grown horse have?
What are the *aids* or *cues*? How are they used?
Which are the strongest horses?

Additional resources

Level I
Cole, Joanna. *A Horse's Body.* Morrow, 1981.
Edwards, Elwyn H. *The Larousse Guide to Horses and Ponies of the World.* Larousse, 1979.
May, Julian. *Horses: How They Came to Be.* Holiday House, 1968.
Paust, Gil. *The Complete Beginner's Guide to Horseback Riding.* Doubleday, 1977.

Level II
Condax, Kate Delano. *Riding: An Illustrated Guide.* Arco, 1983.
Copper, Marcia S. *Take Care of Your Horse: A Guide to the Essentials for Everyone Who Rides, Owns, or Hopes to Own a Horse.* Scribner, 1974.
Dent, Anthony. *The Horse: Through Fifty Centuries of Civilization.* Holt, 1974.
Edwards, Elwyn H., and Geddes, Candida, eds. *The Complete Book of the Horse.* Larousse, 1982.
Kauffman, Sandra. *Kauffman's Manual of Riding Safety.* Crown, 1978.
Kays, John M. *The Horse.* 3rd ed. Arco, 1982.
Price, Steven D., and others, eds. *The Whole Horse Catalog.* Simon & Schuster, 1977.
Ryden, Hope. *America's Last Wild Horses.* Rev. ed. Dutton, 1978.

Horse bean is a hardy annual plant that may grow 6 feet (1.8 meters) high. It is an important food crop in Latin America. It is sometimes called the *bean of history* because it was an important food to the early civilizations of northern Africa and southwestern Asia, where it grows wild.

The horse bean is also called the *windsor bean* and the *broad bean.* Its white flowers are spotted with purple. Its pods may be 1 foot (30 centimeters) long. They contain thick beans, or seeds, that sometimes are 1 inch (2.5 centimeters) wide.

Scientific classification. The horse bean belongs to the pea family, Leguminosae. It is classified as *Vicia faba.*

S. H. Wittwer

See also **Bean.**

Horse brier. See Greenbrier.

Horse chestnut is any one of a group of trees and shrubs that are often planted for their showy flowers and handsome leaves, and for shade. There are about 25 species in North America, Europe, and Asia, including seven that are native to the United States. They are not related to chestnuts (see **Chestnut**). The large, shiny brown seeds resemble chestnuts, but are bitter and poisonous. A spiny covering, or *capsule,* encloses one or two seeds. The trees have paired leaves. Each leaf has five or seven pointed and toothed leaflets that spread like fingers from the end of the long leafstalk.

The common horse chestnut of Europe is a favorite tree for streets and parks. Its large seeds have a scar that resembles a horse's hoof.

The native American trees are called *buckeyes,* because their seeds have a light brown scar that resembles the partly opened eye of a buck, or deer. *Ohio buckeye,*

© Irvin L. Oakes, Photo Researchers

The European horse chestnut, *above,* bears spikes of tiny flowers in May. The thick branches make it a good shade tree. The native American horse chestnut trees are called *buckeyes.*

or *fetid buckeye,* which grows in the Ohio and Mississippi valleys, gave Ohio the name *Buckeye State,* and is the state tree (see **Ohio** [picture: The state tree]). The *yellow buckeye* grows in the Ohio Valley and the Appalachian Mountains. Its soft, light, whitish wood is used for furniture, boxes and crates, and artificial limbs.

American Indians prepared the starchy buckeye seeds for food by roasting and washing them thoroughly to remove the poison. The Indians made a powder of the raw seeds and threw it into water to stupefy fish.

Scientific classification. Horse chestnuts belong to the horse chestnut family, Hippocastanaceae. They make up the genus *Aesculus.* The European horse chestnut is species *hippocastanum.* Ohio buckeye is *A. glabra.* Yellow buckeye is *A. octandra.* Elbert L. Little, Jr.

See also **Tree** (Familiar broadleaf and needleleaf trees [picture]).

Horse farms. See Kentucky (Places to visit).

Horse fly is a name for certain types of stout-bodied flies that live near water in pastures, fields, and forests. The adult male horse fly feeds on flower pollen and nectar. The female bites and sucks the blood of horses and other livestock, as well as people.

The female horse fly lays eggs in bunches on plants that grow in wet soil or hang over water. The wormlike *larvae* (young) develop in the mud and eat worms and other small animals. The eyes of the male

© Leonard Lee Rue III, Earth Scenes
© L. L. T. Rhodes, Earth Scenes

The horse chestnut has dark green leaves and beautiful white flowers, making it a favorite for ornamental planting in parks and along streets. Horse chestnut seeds are large and brown. They are enclosed by spiny coverings, *right.*

WORLD BOOK illustration
by Oxford Illustrators Limited

Horse fly

© Jerry Wachter, Focus on Sports Inc.

Race horses gallop into the first turn of the track as the crouching jockeys maneuver for position. Thousands of excited racing fans cheer for their favorite horses.

horsefly are large and touch at the top of the head. The female's eyes are smaller and do not touch.

Certain female horse flies carry diseases, such as tularemia and anthrax. They transmit the infection from one animal to another when they bite. Horse flies are difficult to control. Oil sprays and pyrethrum sprays have been used successfully to kill the adult flies.

Scientific classification. Horse flies are members of the order Diptera and belong to the horse fly and deer fly family, Tabanidae.   Sandra J. Glover

See also **Fly** (with picture: A horse fly's eyes).

Horse latitudes are regions noted for their lack of winds. Two belts of calm air extend around the earth at about 30° north and south latitude. The regions may have received their name because many horses died on ships delayed there by the lack of wind. Or the name may have come from a Spanish sailing term that called the winds there unpredictable, supposedly like a female horse. The horse latitudes lie between the belts of the trade winds and the prevailing westerlies. The name also is given to belts of light rainfall at about 25° north and 30° south latitude.   Sigismond deR. Diettrich

Horse nettle. See **Solanum.**

Horse racing is a popular sport based on the speed of horses and the skill of jockeys. Horse races have been held since ancient times, and millions of people throughout the world enjoy them today. Racing fans thrill to the sight of colorfully dressed jockeys on sleek horses galloping around a track toward the finish line. In the United States, more people attend horse races than any other type of sports event.

One of the features of horse racing is the chance to win money by betting on horses to finish first, second, or third in a race. People wager billions of dollars on horse races yearly.

Races in which jockeys ride horses around a flat track are called *flat races.* There are two other kinds of horse races—*harness races* and *steeplechases.* In a harness race, each horse pulls a driver in a two-wheeled carriage called a *sulky.* In a steeplechase, horses ridden by jockeys race over obstacles. This article discusses flat races. For information on harness races and steeplechases, see the *World Book* articles on **Harness racing** and **Steeplechasing.**

Race horses

Most race horses are *thoroughbreds*—that is, horses whose ancestry can be traced back to any of three Arabian stallions. One of these stallions, named the Byerly Turk, was taken to England in the late 1600's. The other two, called the Darley Arabian and the Godolphin Barb, were taken there in the early 1700's. Arabian horses are known for their speed, and these three stallions were carefully bred with English mares to produce swift, strong race horses.

Thoroughbreds weigh from 1,000 to 1,200 pounds (450 to 544 kilograms). They stand from 62 to 65 inches (157 to 165 centimeters) tall from the ground to the *withers,* the highest part of a horse's back.

Thoroughbreds are not allowed to race until they are 2 years old. In the Northern Hemisphere, the age of a thoroughbred is automatically figured from January 1 of the year in which it is born. Thus, all thoroughbreds born during the same year have the same birthday. This method of determining age simplifies the basic grouping of race horses according to age. Most thoroughbreds that race are 2, 3, 4, or 5 years old. Breeding programs are planned so that the horses are born in the first few months of the year. In the Southern Hemisphere, a thoroughbred's age is figured from August 1.

Various terms are used to classify thoroughbreds according to age and sex. A newborn thoroughbred is called a *foal* until its first birthday, when it becomes a *yearling.* A male is a *colt* from its second birthday until it reaches the age of 5. It is then called a *horse.* A female is a *filly* from the age of 2 until the age of 5, when it becomes a *mare.* A male parent is a *sire,* and a female parent is a *dam.* A male horse that has been castrated is called a *gelding.*

Jockeys

Jockeys control the horses in a race. The skill of a jockey in handling a horse can determine whether the horse wins the race.

Horses are required to carry a certain weight in races. A jockey must be light in weight because the weight the horses are assigned to carry includes that of the rider. Most jockeys weigh about 110 pounds (50 kilograms).

A jockey's equipment includes a saddle, a whip, boots, a safety helmet, and a special jacket and cap. The jacket and cap, which are called *silks,* are provided by the owner of the horse. The colors and the arrangement of the colors of silks identify the owner. Each owner's silks differ from those of other owners. Silks are also called *colors.*

In the United States, all jockeys are licensed by state racing commissions. Jockeys begin their careers as apprentices. Apprentice jockeys receive weight *allowances* in races. The usual allowance is five pounds, though the amount varies among states. For example, a horse assigned to carry 115 pounds would carry only 110 pounds if ridden by an apprentice.

At the races

Types of horse races. Most horse races are run over distances ranging from $\frac{5}{8}$ mile to $1\frac{1}{2}$ miles (1.2 to 2.4 kilometers). The distances of horse races are also expressed in units called *furlongs.* A furlong equals $\frac{1}{8}$ mile (201 meters).

The owners of the horses that finish first, second, third, and fourth in a race receive prize money. This money, called the *purse,* is put up by the race track. In the case of *stakes races,* also called *sweepstakes races,*

fees paid by horse owners are added to the purse. The owner of the winning horse gets most of the purse. But the owners of at least the next three finishers also receive shares. Most famous horse races are stakes races. For example, the best-known horse races in the United States—the Kentucky Derby, the Preakness, and the Belmont Stakes—are stakes races. These three annual events form the *Triple Crown* of horse racing. Other famous races include the Epsom Derby in Great Britain, the Irish Sweeps Derby in Ireland, and the Melbourne Cup in Australia. All are stakes races.

There are several classes of horse races. Some races are restricted to horses of a certain ability. Others are open only to horses of the same age or sex. Most races in the United States are *claiming races,* in which horses of about the same value run against one another. Each horse that competes can be bought for a specific price by any owner who runs a horse at the *meeting.* A meeting is a session of racing that extends over a certain number of days at a track. In some states, any licensed owner is eligible to buy a horse at a claiming race. Claiming races assure that thoroughbreds run against horses of similar ability. If the owner of a fast, high-priced horse enters it in a race against slower, lower-priced ones, another owner will claim the animal.

In a *handicap race,* the amount of weight the horses are assigned to carry depends on their speed. Faster horses are required to carry more weight than slower ones to provide better competition. Weight is added by inserting flat lead weights into pockets in a piece of cloth called a *lead pad.* The pad is placed on the back of the horse, under the saddle. An *allowance race* is a special kind of handicap race. Allowance races are open only to horses that have won a certain number of races or a certain amount of money. A *maiden race* features horses that have never won a race.

The race track. Major race tracks have both dirt and *turf* (grass) courses. Most U.S. horse races are run on dirt courses. These courses are flat and oval and consist

WORLD BOOK diagram by Tak Murakami

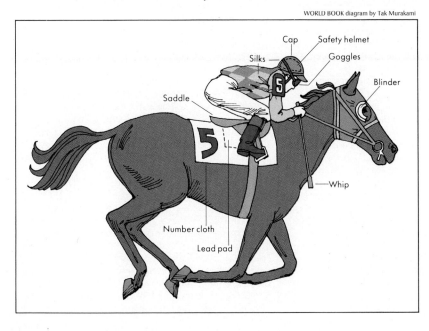

Cap   Safety helmet

Silks   Goggles

Blinder

Saddle

Whip

Number cloth

Lead pad

A jockey's equipment includes a saddle, whip, boots, goggles, a safety helmet, and a jacket and cap. The jacket and cap, which are called *silks,* identify the horse's owner by their colors and by the arrangement of the colors. The horse wears blinders and an identification number.

of several layers of crushed rock, sand, and dirt. They are designed to provide a fast racing surface.

At most major race tracks, the dirt course surrounds the turf course and is 1 mile (1.6 kilometers) long. A fence called the *rail* separates the two courses. An area known as the *infield* lies within the turf course. An electronic *totalizator board,* or *tote board,* stands in the infield. This device displays such information as the odds on the horses and the official results of the races.

Many racing fans watch horse races from the grandstand. This structure extends along the *home stretch,* the part of the track that ends with the finish line.

Betting. The major race tracks in the United States use the *pari-mutuel* system of betting. In this system, all the money wagered on horses to win a race is combined in a fund called a *pool.* The odds are based on the proportion of the amount of money in the pool to the amount bet on each horse. The horse on which the most money is wagered is the *favorite.* Horses with little backing are called *long shots.* The odds on a favorite may be 3 to 1, but the odds on a long shot may be 20 to 1. Such odds mean that if the favorite wins, people receive $3 for every $1 that they bet on it to win. If the long shot wins, they receive $20 for every $1.

Most of the money in the pool is divided among the people who bet on the winning horse. The race track, the state, and the owners of the top-finishing horses also receive a certain percentage of the pool.

The minimum wager is $2. A person wagers on a horse to *win, place* (finish second), or *show* (finish third) by purchasing one of three major types of tickets. The owner of a win ticket collects only if the horse wins the race. A person with a place ticket wins if the horse finishes first or second. People who purchase show tickets collect if the horse runs first, second, or third. Usually, a win ticket pays the most money, and a show ticket pays the least. Special types of bets include the *daily double* and the *trifecta.* In the daily double, a person tries to select the winners of two specified consecutive races. In the trifecta, a bettor tries to pick the first-, second-, and third-place horses in a specified race.

Betting on horse races at places other than race tracks is legal in only three states—Connecticut, Nevada, and New York. In those states, such *off-track betting* is closely supervised by the state government.

A system of betting called *bookmaking* is legal in Nevada and in Australia, Great Britain, and Ireland. People called *bookmakers* set the odds and accept bets. Bookmakers try to set odds that enable them to make a profit after paying the winning bettors.

"They're off!" Before a race, the jockeys are weighed with their equipment. This *weighing out* procedure is supervised by a track official called the *clerk of the scales.* The weight of each rider and the equipment must match the weight that is assigned to the jockey's horse.

About 30 minutes before a race, the horses are taken to the *paddock,* a fenced-in area where they are saddled. The jockeys then go to the paddock and, on a signal from an official called the *paddock judge,* they mount their horses. The horses parade past the grandstand and enter their assigned stalls in the starting gate. Another official, the *starter,* presses a button. A bell rings and all the stall doors open at the same instant.

The horses lunge from the gate, and the track announcer shouts, "They're off!" Several times during a race, the announcer tells the position of each horse.

Officials called *stewards* may disqualify a horse and change the results of a race if they spot any rule violations. Immediately after a race, to make sure the horses have not been drugged or received illegal medication, urine and blood tests are performed on the winner and others chosen at random. In addition, the jockeys and their equipment are weighed again to confirm that the horses carried the correct weight.

History

Early horse racing. Horse racing probably began about the time that horses were first domesticated. The earliest records of horse races date back to about 1500 B.C., when chariot races were held in eastern Europe and northern Africa. The Olympic Games in ancient Greece first featured chariot races in 680 B.C. Races between horses with riders were added to the games in 648 B.C. Horse racing later spread to what became Asia Minor, France, Germany, India, and Italy.

The Romans, who controlled what is now Great Britain from the A.D. 40's to the early 400's, introduced horse racing there. Through the centuries, English monarchs and members of the nobility owned race horses. As a result, horse racing is sometimes called the *sport of kings.* King James I established a racing center at Newmarket, England, near Haverhill, and races began to be held there about 1619. Newmarket is still a center of horse racing today.

Many people who came to America from Europe during the 1600's brought horses with them. They raced the animals on flat, straight courses. The first American race track, called New Market, was established in 1665. It lay near what is now Elmont, N.Y., the site of the Belmont Park race track.

The growth of racing. Pari-mutuel betting was developed during the late 1800's by Pierre Oller, the owner of a French perfume shop. In the 1890's, the American jockey Tod Sloan introduced the crouch position for riding. American jockeys still use this position, in which the rider leans forward over the horse's neck. Previously, jockeys had sat upright, which is the European style of riding.

Most of the famous stakes races were established from the late 1700's to the late 1800's. In England, the St. Leger Stakes was first held in 1776. It is one of the five "classics" of English racing. The others, and the year they were first run, are the Oaks, 1779; the Epsom Derby, 1780; the 2,000 Guineas, 1809; and the 1,000 Guineas, 1814. The most famous Australian race, the Melbourne Cup, was established in 1861. The Grand Prix de Paris was first held in 1863 in France, and the Irish Sweeps Derby in Ireland in 1866.

The top Canadian horse race, the Queen's Plate, began in 1860. This race is the oldest continually run stakes race in North America. In the United States, the Belmont Stakes was first held in 1867, followed by the Preakness in 1873 and the Kentucky Derby in 1875.

In 1894, American racing leaders formed the Jockey Club to regulate the sport in the United States and supervise the registration of thoroughbreds. The Jockey Club works with the state racing commissions and is considered by many people to be thoroughbred racing's principal authority.

Perhaps the most famous American race horse was Man o' War. In 1919 and 1920, Man o' War won 20 of 21 races. In 1919, Sir Barton became the first horse to win the Triple Crown. Citation, a Triple Crown winner in 1948, was the first horse to win $1 million.

Leading American jockeys of the 1900's include Eddie Arcaro, Bill Hartack, Johnny Longden, and Willie Shoemaker. Arcaro and Hartack were the only jockeys to ride five winners in the Kentucky Derby. Shoemaker won more than 8,000 races, and Longden won more than 6,000. Sir Gordon Richards of Great Britain won 4,970 races and became the first jockey to be knighted. Lester Piggott was the top British jockey of the 1960's and the 1970's.

Racing today. On Feb. 7, 1969, Diane Crump became the first woman jockey to ride in a race on a major American track. Other women jockeys, including Mary Bacon and Robyn Smith, soon began to compete in horse races.

Many racing fans consider Secretariat the greatest horse in American racing history. Secretariat raced in 1972 and 1973 only, but he won $860,404 in 1973, a one-year record that was broken by Affirmed in 1978 and Spectacular Bid in 1979. Secretariat also won the Triple Crown in 1973.

In 1977, a 17-year-old apprentice jockey named Steve Cauthen rode 488 winners and won $6,151,750 in purses. Cauthen was the first jockey to earn more than $5 million in one year. In 1978, Affirmed, ridden by Cauthen, won the Triple Crown. Affirmed was the first horse to win more than $2 million. By the time John Henry was retired in 1985, he had won $6,597,947—a career record.

Billy Reed

Related articles in *World Book* include:

Arcaro, Eddie
Grand National
Hippodrome
Horse
Kentucky Derby
Sande, Earl
Shoemaker, Willie

Horse show. See Horse (Horse shows).
Horseback riding. See Horse (How to ride).
Horsecar. See Streetcar.
Horsefly. See Horse fly.
Horsehair worm is a long, thin worm that looks like a coiled hair from the mane or tail of a horse. It is sometimes called a *hair snake* or *hairworm.* There are about 200 kinds of horsehair worms. Most of them live in damp soil and in the shallow water of lakes, ponds, and streams. They may grow as long as 28 inches (70 centimeters), but most are shorter. The majority of horsehair worms are black, brown, or cream colored.

Female horsehair worms lay thousands of eggs. A larva hatched from an egg forms a small, round structure called a *cyst.* The cyst may be eaten by a beetle, cricket, or grasshopper. The larva may then emerge from the cyst and penetrate beyond the insect's intestine. The young worm lives there as a parasite. The larva may also use a special organ to bore its way into the body of an insect. After the worm reaches maturity, it leaves the insect and lives freely in the water.

Scientific classification. Horsehair worms make up the phylum Nematomorpha. Robert D. Barnes

Horseheal. See Elecampane.

Horsemanship. See Horse (How to ride).
Horsepower is a unit used to express the *power* (rate of doing work) of an engine in the customary system of measurements. The term *horsepower* was first used by the Scottish engineer James Watt. He used it to compare the power of steam engines to the power of horses (see Watt, James). Today, this term is used to express the power of such devices as automobile engines, jet engines, electric motors, and atomic reactors. One horsepower is defined as 550 foot-pounds of work per second, or 33,000 foot-pounds of work per minute. One *foot-pound* is the work needed to lift one pound one foot. The metric unit of power is the *watt.* One horsepower equals 745.7 watts. See Foot-pound; Watt.

If an engine lifts a 550-pound object to a height of 2 feet in 1 second, it is working at a rate of 1,100 foot-pounds per second ($550 \times 2 \div 1 = 1,100$). This engine is delivering 2 horsepower ($1,100 \div 550 = 2$). If a 150-pound man climbs to a height of 88 feet, he does 13,200 foot-pounds of work ($150 \times 88 = 13,200$). If the man makes this climb in 1 minute (60 seconds), he is working at a rate of $\frac{4}{10}$ horsepower ($13,200 \div 60 = 220$; $220 \div 550 = \frac{4}{10}$). A person who is accustomed to hard work can work at a rate between $\frac{1}{10}$ and $\frac{1}{8}$ horsepower continuously during an 8-hour day.

The power of an engine can be measured in various ways. These are (1) indicated horsepower, (2) brake horsepower, and (3) S.A.E. horsepower.

Indicated horsepower is a measurement of the power produced inside the cylinders of an engine. The power in foot-pounds per minute is first calculated by multiplying together the average pressure on the pistons, the area of each piston, the length of the piston's stroke, the number of power strokes per minute, and the number of cylinders in the engine. This power must be divided by 33,000 to give the engine's indicated horsepower.

Brake horsepower is sometimes called *effective horsepower,* because it is the amount of power available at the engine's shaft. Brake horsepower is measured by an instrument called a *dynamometer.* This instrument measures the engine's speed and the *torque* (amount of twist) exerted by its shaft. Brake horsepower is the rating most widely used by engineers. It is lower than indicated horsepower because friction in the engine wastes part of the power produced in the cylinders.

S.A.E. horsepower is a calculated rating approved by the Society of Automotive Engineers (S.A.E.). Its most important use is in determining the licensing fees for automobiles in some states. The formula used to calculate S.A.E. horsepower is not exact, and it is rarely used by engineers. Robert L. Weber

See also Air conditioning (Capacity of air conditioners); Automobile (table: Interesting facts about automobiles); Power (In physics).

Horseradish is an herb whose root is used to make a pungent food relish. The plant is native to Europe. It has many long leaves and a large root. People grate the root to prepare it for use. They preserve the grated pieces in vinegar to prevent loss of the pungent, volatile compound that gives horseradish its biting taste. The root retains its pungency until it is ground. Whole roots will remain pungent for long periods.

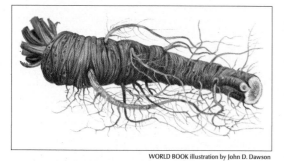

The root of the horseradish has a biting taste.

When workers harvest horseradish, they remove the side roots. These roots are used for the following year's crop. Farmers cut the side roots for planting in the spring.

Scientific classification. Horseradish belongs to the mustard family, Cruciferae. It is *Armoracia rusticana*.

John H. MacGillivray

Horseshoe. See Horse (Shoes); **Superstition** (Kinds of superstitions).

Horseshoe Bend, Battle of. See Indian wars (In the South); **Jackson, Andrew** (The Battle of Horseshoe Bend).

Horseshoe crab is a large marine animal with a shell shaped something like a horse's hoof. The horseshoe crab is sometimes called the *king crab*. However, it is not related to the commercially important *Alaskan king crab* or the giant *Japanese king crab,* both of which are actually crabs. Horseshoe crabs are the only surviving members of a large group of animals that appeared on

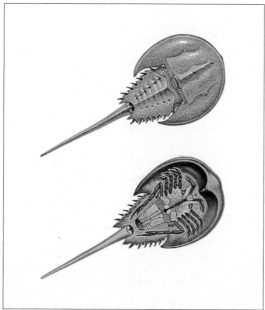

The horseshoe crab has a shell that resembles a horse's hoof. The bottom illustration shows the underside of the animal. The crab has six pairs of legs. The front pair have pincers used to capture prey. The other legs are used for walking.

earth millions of years ago. The closest living relatives of horseshoe crabs are scorpions and spiders.

There are four species of horseshoe crabs. The largest grows to about 24 inches (61 centimeters) long and lives along the eastern coast of North America from Nova Scotia to the Yucatán Peninsula. The other three species inhabit the coastal waters of southeast Asia and the Philippines.

The horseshoe crab's body consists of two "hinged" parts, the *prosoma* and the abdomen. The prosoma is the part of the body covered by the shell and includes the head. The shell has openings for the animal's eyes. The mouth and legs are located beneath the shell on the lower surface of the prosoma. Horseshoe crabs have six pairs of legs. The front pair have pincers and are used to capture prey. The other five pairs of legs are used for walking.

The horseshoe crab's abdomen has six pairs of flattened, platelike structures. The reproductive organs are in the front pair of these plates. The remaining plates each carry approximately 150 soft gills by which the animal breathes. A jointed spine sticks out from the end of the abdomen. The horseshoe crab uses this "tail" as a lever for digging.

The horseshoe crab lives in marine coastal waters. It feeds at night on worms and small mollusks, such as clams, that it digs up from sand and mud. Horseshoe crabs mate in the spring. The female carries the male on her back to shore, where she digs several holes in the sand. The female lays from 200 to 1,000 eggs in each of the holes, and the male then fertilizes the eggs.

Scientific classification. Horseshoe crabs belong to the family Limulidae in the order Xiphosura. They are included in three genera: *Limulus, Tachypleus,* and *Carcinoscorpius.* The largest and most common species is *L. polyphemus.*

P. A. McLaughlin

Horseshoe Falls. See Niagara Falls; **Ontario** (picture: Niagara Falls).

Horseshoe pitching is a game played by throwing horseshoes at a stake. Two, three, or four persons can play at a time. Players score points by getting the horseshoes close to or around the stake.

Rules. Regulation horseshoes are flat, U-shaped pieces of iron with a *calk* (small toe) at the closed end and at each tip. A shoe may not be more than $7\frac{1}{4}$ inches (18.4 centimeters) wide and $7\frac{5}{8}$ inches (19.4 centimeters) long. It must not weigh over 2 pounds 10 ounces (1.2 kilograms), and it must have no more than $3\frac{1}{2}$ inches (8.9 centimeters) of space between the calks at the open end.

A *pitching court* is about 10 feet (3 meters) wide and about 50 feet (15 meters) long. Within this area, two steel or iron stakes 1 inch (2.5 centimeters) in diameter are driven or anchored into the ground 40 feet (12 meters) apart. Each stake stands 14 inches (36 centimeters) high in a *pitching box* that is 6 feet (1.8 meters) square. Each pitching box has an area of clay, soil, or sand, in which the horseshoes land.

If two or three people play a game, they compete individually. If four play, two people make up each team. Players take turns throwing the horseshoes. A player throws two shoes each turn. Men pitch from a distance of 40 feet from the stake. Women and juniors (players under age 17) throw from a distance of 30 feet (9 me-

Horseshoe pitching   Horseshoe pitching is played on a rectangular court that has a stake set in a pitching box at each end. Players stand behind a foul line at one end of the court and pitch two horseshoes at the stake at the other end. The diagram below shows the dimensions of a regulation court and a horseshoe.

WORLD BOOK diagram by Steven Liska

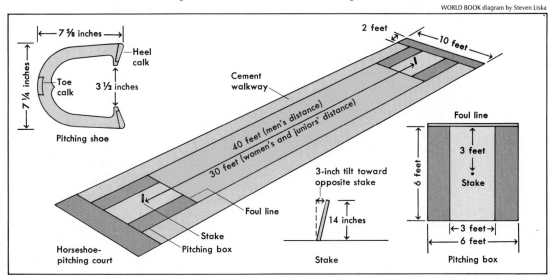

- 7 ⅝ inches
- Heel calk
- 7 ¼ inches
- Toe calk
- 3 ½ inches
- Pitching shoe
- Cement walkway
- 2 feet
- 10 feet
- 40 feet (men's distance)
- 30 feet (women's and juniors' distance)
- 3-inch tilt toward opposite stake
- Foul line
- 14 inches
- Stake
- Foul line
- 3 feet
- Stake
- 6 feet
- 3 feet
- 6 feet
- Pitching box
- Stake
- Horseshoe-pitching court
- Pitching box

ters). Players pitch horseshoes with an underhand motion. Fingertip control gives the shoe a flip or turn so the open end faces the stake as the shoe lands.

Scoring. A *ringer* is a shoe that encircles the stake so that a straight edge can touch both tips of the shoe without touching the stake. A ringer scores 3 points. A shoe that comes to rest within 6 inches (15 centimeters) of the stake scores 1 point. A *leaner* (a shoe that leans against the stake) is also worth 1 point. There are two main systems of scoring horseshoe pitching contests, *cancellation* and *count-all*. In cancellation, a game usually consists of 50 points. If opposing players throw ringers or shoes that land equally close to the stake, the shoes cancel each other. Points are scored by counting the ringer or shoe closest to the stake that is not tied by the opposing player. A count-all game normally consists of *25 innings* (50 shoes thrown by each player). In a count-all game, all ringers and horseshoes within 6 inches of the stake are scored according to their point values.

History. Horseshoe pitching originated in Roman army camps about A.D. 100. The game has long been popular in the United States and Canada, but for many years it had no set rules. In 1914, a group of men set up standards of play and equipment, and the popularity of the game increased. The National Horseshoe Pitchers' Association of America, incorporated in 1920, developed from this group. The association has headquarters at Route 5, Lucasville, Ohio, 45648. The Canadian Horseshoe Pitching Association, incorporated in 1929, has headquarters at 35 O'Neil Crescent, Saskatoon, Saskatchewan, S7N 1W7.   Jack Adams

Horsetail is a plant with a hollow, jointed, and usually grooved stem. All parts of the plant contain silica, an abrasive material (see **Silica**). The horsetail is sometimes called *scouring rush* because it was once used to polish metal.

Most horsetails are small plants. The stalks of some species resemble tiny trees. In prehistoric times, some

plants of this family grew to be large trees. The plant grows from perennial creeping rootstocks. It bears no flowers, and it is more closely related to ferns than to flowering plants. Horsetails reproduce by means of both spores and sex cells. The spores are contained in small cones at the tips of the stem or its branches, or sometimes on a separate stalk. The plant releases the spores, which germinate in damp places and grow into tiny plants. These plants produce male and female sex cells that unite and develop into mature horsetails.

WORLD BOOK illustration by Robert Hynes

Shoots of horsetail

Scientific classification. Horsetails make up the family Equisetaceae. They are genus *Equisetum*.   Roy E. Gereau

See also **Plant** (Club mosses and horsetails).

Horticulture, *HAWR tuh кинь chuhr,* is a branch of agriculture that specializes in fruits, vegetables, flowers, and ornamental shrubs and trees. Horticulture includes the production, distribution, and processing of fruits and vegetables for food. It also involves the use of plants in landscaping and in such decorations as corsages and floral arrangements.

The word *horticulture* comes from the Latin word *hortus,* which means *garden,* and horticulture includes the art and science of gardening. Most horticultural crops were originally grown in gardens. Today, they are raised commercially on farms and in greenhouses, nurseries, and orchards.

Horticulture is widely practiced as an industry and as a hobby. The horticulture industry is the main source of fruits and vegetables, and an important supplier of plants raised for their beauty. Horticulturists in the floral, landscaping, and nursery industries raise ornamental plants for use in creating attractive surroundings. Horticultural hobbies include flower arranging and gardening.

Much horticultural research is conducted at agricultural experiment stations, arboretums, botanical gardens, and colleges and universities. Some of this research involves developing methods to improve the cultivation of plants. For example, horticultural scientists experiment to determine the kind of environment and nutrition necessary for good plant growth. They also work to develop ways to control plant diseases and pests. Other research involves breeding plants to produce new varieties that are especially beautiful, hardy, or productive.

Horticulture is generally divided into four main specialties: (1) pomology, (2) olericulture, (3) floriculture, and (4) ornamental horticulture.

Pomology is the cultivation of shrubs, trees, vines, and other plants for their nuts or their sweet or tart fruits. Crops in this group include almonds, apples, coconuts, dates, grapes, oranges, peaches, pecans, and raspberries.

Olericulture deals with *herbaceous* (nonwoody) plants raised for use as vegetables. Any part of a herbaceous plant may be the edible part. For example, asparagus is grown for its stem, cauliflower for its flower, lettuce for its leaves, peas for their seeds, and tomatoes for their fruit.

Floriculture is the production and use of flowers and foliage plants. Floriculturists work mainly with house plants and with flowers and greenery for floral arrangements.

Ornamental horticulture is concerned with plants grown outdoors for landscaping. Such plants include shrubs; grasses for lawns; and maples, pines, and other ornamental trees. Ornamental horticulture also involves landscape design for homes, office buildings, highways, and recreational areas.   Jules Janick

Related articles in *World Book* include:

Agricultural experiment station	Greenhouse
Arboretum	Herb
Botanical garden	Hotbed
Botany	Landscape architecture
Burbank, Luther	Nursery
Espalier	Nut
Floriculture	Plant
Flower	Tree
Fruit	Truck farming
Gardening	Vegetable

Horus, *HAWR uhs,* was the ancient Egyptian god of the sky. Egyptians thought the king was Horus in living form. He was the first Egyptian god recognized as a national god, and he was worshiped in both Lower and Upper Egypt.

Horus was the son of Isis and Osiris. He was called "the great king of gods, king of the land, and king of the world, who spans the sky with his wings, and covers the land with his pinions." His sacred bird was the falcon. He was pictured either as a falcon or a human body with a falcon's head, capped by the double crown of Upper

and Lower Egypt. As the life-giving god, he held the *ankh,* the symbol of life, in his right hand.   I. J. Gelb

See also **Isis; Mythology** (The Great Ennead; picture); **Osiris; Set.**

Hosea, *hoh ZEE uh* or *hoh ZAYuh,* **Book of,** is a book of the Hebrew Bible, or Old Testament, named for an Israelite prophet. It deals with the prophet Hosea's ministry in the northern kingdom of Israel from about 745 to the 730's or 720's B.C., a period of great turmoil and uncertainty. The prophet witnessed the repeated killings and successions of kings. Many people worshiped pagan gods. Hosea regarded such worship as unfaithfulness to God and warned that evil would result.

Many scholars divide the Book of Hosea into two parts. The first describes Hosea's marriage as a symbol of God's relation with Israel. The second part tells the details and consequences of Israel's unfaithfulness to God, and promises God's love and blessings if it repents. Although Hosea shares many themes and ideas with other prophets, his use of symbolic names and the theme of marriage is unusual. His prophecy is also remarkable for its description of God as a loving father.
          Eric M. Meyers

Hosiery. See Stockings.

Hospice, *HAHS pihs,* is a family-centered concept of health care for people dying of an incurable illness. The hospice concept aims at easing the physical and psychological pain of the patient's illness, so that the person can appreciate his or her remaining life. It relies on a team approach to achieve this aim. The team includes the patient and his or her family, as well as physicians, nurses, social workers, members of the clergy, and volunteers. The modern system of hospice care began with the founding of St. Christopher's Hospice in London in 1967 by Cicely Saunders, an English physician.

The hospice concept emphasizes home care. Family members are encouraged to participate in caring for the patient when they desire to do so. The hospice staff works with the family and with community agencies to help the patient remain at home. Staff members visit the family regularly and are available at all times for emergencies. They try to provide what the patient and family need. Such services may include nursing care and pain control, meal preparation, laundry, or shopping. Hospice staff members are also available to sit with the patient while family members rest. After the patient's death, emotional support is provided for the family.

Hospice care is also available to *inpatients*—that is, patients who cannot remain at home. This care may be provided in a separate hospice medical center or in a hospice unit of a hospital. In some cases, a hospice team cares for patients throughout the wards of a general hospital. Inpatient hospice programs provide health care with a friendly attitude in a relaxed setting.

Patients are admitted to a hospice program on the basis of health needs, not according to their ability to pay. In the United States, Medicare—a government health insurance program—pays part of the cost of hospice care for elderly patients.

The word *hospice* also refers to a shelter for travelers, especially a refuge maintained by a monastery. The hospice of the Great St. Bernard is famous for rescuing people lost in the Swiss Alps (see **Saint Bernard passes**).   Sylvia A. Lack

Hospital is an institution that provides medical services for a community. The doctors, nurses, and other personnel of a hospital work to restore health to sick and injured people. They also try to prevent disease and maintain health throughout the community. In addition, a hospital serves as a center for medical education and research.

Every year, about 15 per cent of the people of the United States spend some time as hospital patients. Millions of others visit hospitals as *outpatients.* They receive treatment but do not stay in the hospital.

The United States has about 7,000 hospitals and over 1,400,000 hospital beds. Canada has about 1,400 hospitals and about 210,000 beds. Most hospitals have fewer than 200 beds. About 2,000 hospitals in the United States have from 200 to 500 beds. About 600 have over 500 beds.

Each state has laws that a hospital must follow to receive a license to operate. Most hospitals in the United States are also approved by the Joint Commission on Accreditation of Hospitals. Accredited hospitals must meet basic national standards established by the commission. They must also undergo periodic inspections.

In the mid-1970's, the United States government established *professional standards review organizations* (PSRO's). These groups review the quality of hospital care that is given to patients who are covered by federal medical assistance programs.

Some form of institution for the care of the sick has existed longer than recorded history. The first centers for the ill were probably operated together with religious temples. The priests of these temples served as healers.

How hospitals are classified

Every hospital is classified according to (1) how long patients stay, (2) kinds of services provided, and (3) type of ownership.

Length of stay. Most hospitals are *short-term* institutions in which the majority of patients stay less than 30 days. Patients spend an average of 6 to 10 days in a short-term hospital. In *long-term* hospitals, most patients stay more than 30 days. People having their tonsils removed would go to a short-term hospital. Those with tuberculosis or a mental illness would stay in a long-term institution because of the time needed to treat such conditions.

Kinds of services. A *general* hospital provides services for most people and for most types of illness. A *special* hospital cares for certain persons or certain illnesses. For example, *pediatric* hospitals treat only children. *Rehabilitation* hospitals care for persons who are handicapped.

A hospital may perform other services besides treating the sick. For example, *research* hospitals conduct various kinds of medical research. *Teaching* hospitals educate future physicians, nurses, laboratory specialists, and others planning a career in the medical field. A teaching hospital may form part of a university medical center, or it may be a general hospital associated with a medical school.

Type of ownership. Most hospitals are owned by their community. A board of trustees consisting of local residents manages such *community* hospitals in the

public interest. A *nonprofit voluntary* hospital is owned by such organizations as charitable or religious groups. Community and nonprofit voluntary hospitals do not try to make a profit. They almost always spend more money for patient care than they receive in fees. Such hospitals must depend on donations. Any money that remains after all expenses have been paid is used to improve the hospital.

A *private,* or *proprietary,* hospital is operated like a business to make a profit for the owners. Several corporations own chains of short-term general hospitals.

A *government* hospital is owned by the federal, state, or county or local government. The federal government operates hospitals that serve members of the armed forces and their dependents, veterans, American Indians, and certain other groups. Many state hospitals care for the mentally ill or for tuberculosis patients. Some county and local hospitals operate like general community institutions and serve all the people in the area, especially the poor. Others offer special services, such as treatment of contagious diseases.

Hospital departments and personnel

The professional services staff consists of the people directly concerned with the care of patients. The *medical staff,* made up of physicians, directs all other members of this team. Most physicians have an office practice and send their patients to the hospital when necessary. They then supervise the hospital treatment.

In many hospitals, some physicians work directly for the institution and do not have a private practice. These doctors include such specialists as the *radiologist,* who directs a hospital's X-ray services. In some hospitals, many or all members of the medical staff work directly for the hospital. This arrangement occurs chiefly in government and university hospitals and in hospitals operated by labor unions or other groups for the benefit of their members.

The medical staff also includes physicians in training. These *interns* and *residents* have graduated from medical school and work in a hospital for additional required experience (see **Medicine** [Internship and residency]).

The *nursing staff* forms the largest group on the patient care team. Professional nurses, generally called *registered nurses,* have graduated from a school of nursing operated by a hospital or a university. They carry out much of the patients' care under the direction of physicians. Registered nurses also direct other members of the nursing staff, including *practical nurses, nurse's aides,* and *nurse attendants.* These men and women do many routine necessary tasks and free the registered nurses for work requiring their special skills.

Professional services departments work with the physicians and nurses. The hospital *pharmacy* provides medicines that physicians order for patients. The *central service* department maintains supplies of other medical supplies. The *food service* department prepares meals for patients and staff members. A dietitian directs this department and plans the menus. The dietitian also develops special diets for patients with certain illnesses when ordered by a physician.

The hospital *laboratories* conduct tests that help doctors diagnose and treat illnesses. The *radiology* department makes X rays to help physicians diagnose diseases and injuries. Doctors also use X rays to treat cancer.

Many hospitals have a *rehabilitation* department that works with disabled patients to help them return to normal life. There are two basic types of rehabilitation therapy, *physical* and *occupational*. Physical therapy treats diseases or injuries. Occupational therapy helps overcome or reduce physical handicaps by teaching the patient various skills. See **Occupational therapy; Physical therapy.**

The *medical records* department keeps a record on every patient. If former patients return to the hospital, their medical record helps the physician diagnose and treat their illness.

Administrative departments. Most hospitals have an administrator who is responsible for the operation of the entire institution. The board of trustees or the owner appoints this official. In some cases, a private management firm provides the overall administration of the hospital.

Various departments handle a hospital's business affairs. The *admitting office* schedules patients for admission at the request of their physician and assigns them to a room. The *business office* lists each patient's charges, prepares a bill at the time of discharge, and records payments received. The *purchasing department* manages a hospital's stockroom and buys supplies and equipment.

A hospital maintains a *personnel department* to hire employees and handle employee relations. A large institution may have a *public relations office* to inform employees, patients, and the public about the hospital's operation. Some hospitals employ *patient representatives* to deal with patients' complaints.

The *volunteer services department* organizes the activities of a hospital's volunteers. These unpaid workers operate the coffee and gift shops in most hospitals. They also sew and help raise funds for the institution.

Other employees also help a hospital run smoothly around the clock. Cooks prepare nutritious meals in the hospital kitchen. Housekeepers and janitors keep the institution clean to help prevent the spread of infection. Workers in the laundry department clean, sort, press, and mark the hundreds of pounds of linens used daily. Such experts as carpenters, electricians, engineers, plumbers, and air-conditioning technicians make repairs and adjustments to keep a hospital's complicated machinery in top condition at all times. Hospitals also employ security personnel to protect patients and property.

Hospital care

Hospital units. Most hospitals are divided into various units, each of which cares for certain groups of patients. The number of units varies according to the size and type of a hospital.

Most general hospitals have several basic units. For example, the *maternity* unit helps protect mothers and newborn babies from infection by keeping them apart from other patients. Except in extremely small hospitals, children stay in a *pediatric* unit designed especially for their needs. Some hospitals also have a *teen-age* unit. Men and women who do not require surgery stay in the *adult* unit.

The *surgical* unit cares for patients awaiting surgery or recovering from an operation. Most hospitals also have a *recovery* unit in which a patient who has received a general anesthetic can be watched closely after surgery. Some hospitals have a *psychiatric* unit for mentally ill patients. A few have separate units for burn victims, heart patients, premature babies, and others who require special care.

Most hospital units are *intermediate care* units, in which the professional staff gives patients constant care and observation. *Intensive care* units serve critically ill patients. Some hospitals have *minimal care* units for patients who are well enough so that they or their families can provide much of the nursing care needed. A few institutions have *parent care* units for children.

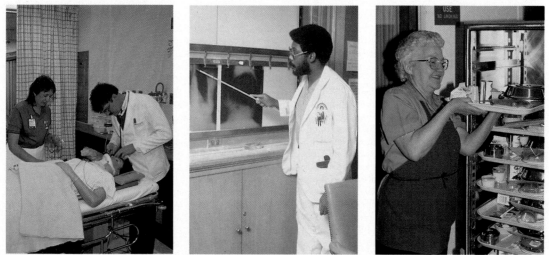

David R. Frazier   Joan Menschenfreund, Taurus   David R. Frazier

A hospital provides many services to patients. In the emergency unit, *left,* accident victims receive immediate care. A radiologist, *center,* studies *radiographs* (X-ray pictures) to help diagnose illness. At mealtime, hospital workers bring trays of food to patients, *right.*

There, a parent stays with the child and provides all nursing care except technical treatments.

A hospital also has an *emergency* unit that provides care for accident victims and persons who have suddenly become ill. Since the early 1960's, services for outpatients have become a major function of the emergency unit. As a result, the use of emergency units has increased about 80 per cent. Less than a fifth of the patients treated in emergency units actually have an urgent problem. They go to a hospital rather than a physician's office because the hospital provides medical care at any hour.

Nonmedical services. Hospitals provide many services not directly connected with a patient's medical needs. Relatives and friends may visit patients or talk with them by telephone. Many hospitals have lounges and sunrooms for patients who do not have to stay in bed. Hospitals furnish radios and television sets for patients, and many have lending libraries. Social workers and chaplains on the hospital staff try to help patients and their families solve personal problems.

Children have many special needs while hospitalized. Hospitals try to make pediatric units as pleasant as possible. These units provide playrooms and special activities for children. *Child life workers* give youngsters special attention and help them adjust to the hospital. Some hospitals arrange for children to visit the institution before being admitted so they can see what it is like. Some hospitals also let parents stay with their children and sleep in their room.

History

Early hospitals. The word *hospital* comes from the Latin word *hospitalis,* which means a *house* or *institution for guests.* As early as the 200's B.C., Buddhists had set up hospitals in India. Early in the Christian Era, hospitals were established for sick or weary travelers, and for the poor, the blind, and the crippled. Religious orders operated most of these early hospitals. For hundreds of years, hospitals served chiefly as institutions to care for people who were too poor or too sick to be treated at home. Doctors did not work in the hospitals. They treated most patients in the patients' homes or in their own offices.

The oldest hospital still in existence is the Hôtel Dieu in Paris, founded during the A.D. 600's. The Spanish governor of Hispaniola built the first hospital in the Western Hemisphere in 1503. Its ruins still stand in Santo Domingo, Dominican Republic. The Spanish explorer Hernando Cortés founded a hospital in Mexico City that has existed since 1524. The first Canadian hospital opened in Quebec in 1639. The first incorporated hospital in the United States was the Pennsylvania Hospital, established in Philadelphia with the assistance and support of Benjamin Franklin. The Pennsylvania Hospital, still in existence today, received its charter in 1751.

In the early 1700's, European cities and towns began to build hospitals. These hospitals served mainly the poor or the victims of contagious diseases. They operated as charity hospitals. The wealthy did not go to hospitals. They usually received medical care at home.

Early hospitals were dirty, crowded, and dark. The principles of sanitation were unknown. Diseases spread rapidly throughout hospitals because of lack of knowledge about the importance of cleanliness.

The 1800's. Medical discoveries in the 1800's helped begin the improvement of hospitals. In 1842, Crawford W. Long, a Georgia physician, became the first doctor to use ether as an anesthetic. Four years later, William T. G. Morton, a Boston dentist, arranged the first hospital operation using ether as an anesthetic. This operation was performed at the Massachusetts General Hospital in Boston.

During the late 1800's, doctors began to observe the principle of *antisepsis* (cleanliness to reduce infections). This principle made surgery much safer. It started the continuing trend of caring for patients in hospitals instead of at home. Doctors could not establish the neces-

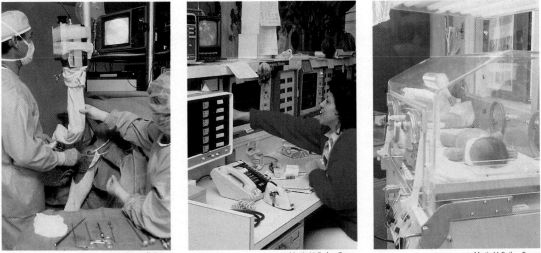

Eric Kroll, Taurus   Martin M. Rotker, Taurus   Martin M. Rotker, Taurus

Special equipment helps hospitals care for patients. In an operating room, *left,* surgeons use laser beams to perform complicated procedures. Electronic equipment, *center,* lets nurses monitor patients' bodily functions. Incubators, *right,* help premature or sick babies survive.

sary cleanliness at home. The use of X-ray equipment in hospitals began in the late 1890's.

Another feature of the late 1800's was the growth of hospital schools of nursing. Nursing schools in the United States were patterned after one founded in London by the famous English nurse Florence Nightingale (see **Nightingale, Florence**). Three hospitals established the first American nursing schools in 1873. These were the Massachusetts General Hospital, Bellevue Hospital in New York City, and the New Haven (Conn.) Hospital. With trained nurses caring for the patients, standards of hospital care improved rapidly and the number of patients increased.

Also in the 1800's, hospitals began to establish rooms for private patients. The idea of the charity hospital started to diminish. Patients began to pay for part of the cost of their hospitalization.

The 1900's. Many hospitals were built in the United States during the early 1900's. As the number of patients increased, the cost of hospital care rose because of the need for more equipment and personnel. Many people could not afford the cost of hospital care, especially during the Great Depression of the 1930's. Hospitals often faced financial problems.

The Blue Cross plan, developed in 1929, offered a form of prepayment insurance to help patients pay their hospital bills. During the 1930's and 1940's, more and more people purchased such insurance to protect themselves against the expense of hospitalization. Insurance helped put hospitals on a sounder financial basis because they could be sure of immediate payment.

Hospitals became overcrowded during the 1940's. To assist them, Congress passed the Hill-Burton Act in 1946. This law authorized government grants to help the states pay the cost of building new hospitals and enlarging and modernizing existing ones.

Recent developments. During the 1960's, hospitals became increasingly interested in serving the community. Many institutions set up outpatient clinics that offered general family or pediatric care. A number of hospitals began to provide laboratory tests, X rays, and various kinds of therapy for outpatients. Some established neighborhood health clinics, and a few started home care programs in which staff members visit patients at home. Hospitals also sponsored programs to help people with such problems as alcoholism or narcotics addiction.

Many scientific advances helped improve patient care. For example, surgical and intensive care units now use electronic equipment to keep a continuous record of a patient's blood pressure, heart rate, respiration, and temperature. Computers help hospitals keep laboratory, medical, and pharmacy records. In addition, hospitals use many disposable items for convenience and safety. Such items include plastic thermometers and hypodermic syringes and steel needles. They are used only once, so they cannot spread infection.

During the 1970's, the services of many hospitals became available over a wide area as a result of regional planning. Under the direction of regional or community councils, several hospitals may cooperate with one another to avoid duplication of expensive equipment and skilled personnel. Small or rural hospitals without certain facilities may transfer some patients to regional hospital centers for special care. In some areas, for example, premature or sick infants are transferred to regional *newborn centers.* Specially equipped vehicles transport patients to regional hospital centers.

Some states have regional hospital centers that treat serious *trauma* (injury). Emergency vehicles, including helicopters, quickly transport injured persons to the nearest trauma center. These hospitals have specialized equipment and their personnel are skilled in emergency lifesaving techniques.

Career opportunities

A hospital offers a large variety of careers for people interested in helping the sick. Large institutions have more than 200 kinds of jobs. Many of these jobs may also be found in small hospitals.

The training necessary for various hospital jobs differs widely. Many technical positions require a college degree, but other hospital careers involve on-the-job training.   Morris Green

Related articles in *World Book* include:

Ambulance	Hospice	Sanitarium
Biomedical	Mayo Clinic	Surgery
engineering	Medicine	Trauma center
Blue Cross and	Nurse's aide	Walter Reed Army
Blue Shield	Nursing	Medical Center

Additional resources

Howe, James. *The Hospital Book.* Crown, 1981. For younger readers.
Huttman, Barbara. *The Patient's Advocate.* Viking, 1981.
Nierenberg, Judith, and Janovic, Florence. *The Hospital Experience: A Guide to Understanding and Participating in Your Own Care.* Bobbs, 1978.
Richter, Elizabeth. *The Teenage Hospital Experience: You Can Handle It!* Coward, 1982.

Hospitalization insurance. See Health insurance, National; Insurance (Basic types of health insurance); Medicare; Medicine (Financing medical care); Social security.

Host, in biology. See Parasite.

Hostage is a person held prisoner to force fulfillment of an agreement or demand. If the agreement or demand is not met, the hostage will probably be killed.

Most hostages are taken in connection with crimes or political struggles. A bank robber or other criminal may seize hostages and threaten to kill them unless the police allow him or her to escape. Airplane hijackers may hold a plane's passengers and crew as hostages to obtain a ransom payment or transportation to a safe destination. Some kidnappers also hold their victims for ransom. Terrorists often take hostages to demand a certain action by a government. In 1979, for example, Iranian revolutionaries seized the U.S. Embassy in Teheran, Iran, and held a group of Americans as hostages. The revolutionaries demanded that the deposed shah of Iran be returned to the country for trial in exchange for the hostages. The shah died in 1980, but the Americans were not released until 1981.

In 1983, a United Nations treaty that outlaws the taking of hostages took effect. The treaty calls for the nations that have ratified it either to prosecute hostage takers or to send them back to their countries for trial.

Invading armies take hostages to discourage resistance. During World War II (1939-1945), Germany punished underground resistance forces by killing hostages taken in France, Poland, and other occupied countries.

During ancient and medieval times, nations often exchanged hostages to guarantee that both sides would carry out the terms of a treaty. The hostages, who were nobles or other important people, were treated as honored guests. But they could be executed if the treaty was broken. E. V. Walter

See also **Hijacking; Kidnapping; Terrorism.**

Hostel. See Youth hostel.

Hot dog. See Sausage.

Hot line is a two-way telegraph-teleprinter system that links Washington, D.C., and Moscow. The hotline is officially known as the Direct Communications Link. It allows the President of the United States and Soviet leaders to communicate directly and instantly when an international crisis arises. Its purpose is to reduce the risk of war caused by misunderstanding.

The hot line was set up in 1963. It was first used when fighting broke out between Israel and Arab nations in 1967. Hot-line messages originally were carried through undersea and underground cables. In 1978, the United States and the Soviet Union began to operate the line via communications satellites. It was expanded in 1986 to include the ability to transmit graphic material.

Hot rod is usually an older automobile with an improved engine or body design. Hot rodders build their cars for either racing or normal driving. Hot rods built for driving often are called *street rods.* Popular hot rod models include Ford Model T's and Model A's and Chevrolets of the 1930's and 1940's. Hot rodders seek to achieve the latest technology in brakes, steering, engines, and other parts to make the car run perfectly.

Hot rodding was started as an automotive hobby by the National Hot Rod Association in the late 1940's. Hot rods were originally stripped-down cars with fenders and hoods removed for streamlining. They were raced in supervised hot rod competitions in southern California. The sport soon spread to the rest of the United States. Hot rods run in types of races called *drag races* (see **Automobile racing** [Drag racing]).

Critically reviewed by the National Hot Rod Association

Hot Springs, Ark. (pop. 35,781); is the only city in the United States that has almost all of a national park within its city limits. The park is called Hot Springs National Park (see **Hot Springs National Park**). The city was named for the hot mineral springs located there. For location, see **Arkansas** (political map).

More than 5 million people visit Hot Springs each year. The city has numerous hotels, motels, resorts, and other types of lodging to accommodate the visitors. Most of the city's people work in the lodging facilities, or in bathhouses or other tourist attractions.

A trapper, Manuel Prudhomme, founded the first permanent settlement at Hot Springs in 1807. In 1832, President Andrew Jackson signed a special act of Congress that named the town. The city grew rapidly after the Diamond Joe Railroad was completed in 1874, connecting Hot Springs with St. Louis. Hot Springs has a mayor-council form of government and is the seat of Garland County. Walter L. Brown

Hot springs are springs that discharge water heated by natural processes within the earth. Most hot springs are steadily flowing streams or calm pools of water. But many are *fumaroles, geysers,* or bubbling pools of mud

called *mudpots* or *mud volcanoes* (see **Fumarole; Geyser**). Hot springs are also called *thermal springs.*

Hot springs originate when *surface water,* which results from rain and snow, seeps into the ground. Many springs occur in volcanic regions where hot molten rock called *magma* lies near the surface of the earth. Surface water trickles down through layers of rock until it is heated by the magma. Then the water rises to the surface through channels in the rock.

Hot springs also occur in regions that have *faults* (breaks) or *folds* (bends) in the layers of rock beneath the earth's surface. The temperature of the interior of the earth increases with depth. Faults and folds enable surface water to penetrate to depths where it is heated.

Many people believe that certain minerals found in some hot springs can relieve various ailments. Since ancient times, this belief has led people to bathe in the springs and to drink the water. Famous resort communities center around the hot springs in such places as Hot Springs National Park in Arkansas and Aachen, Baden-Baden, and Wiesbaden in West Germany.

Hot springs are a source of *geothermal energy,* which is energy produced by underground steam or hot water. Several countries, including New Zealand, the Soviet Union, and the United States, have power plants that use geothermal energy to generate electricity.

Roy M. Breckenridge

See also **Baden-Baden; Hot Springs National Park; Mineral water; Wiesbaden; Yellowstone National Park.**

Hot Springs National Park is a health and pleasure resort in the Ouachita Mountains of Arkansas. It is nearly surrounded by the city of Hot Springs. For the park's location, see **Arkansas** (physical map).

Hot Springs National Park is built around the famous hot mineral springs at the base of Hot Springs Mountain. These mineral waters are said to give relief to persons suffering from many painful diseases, such as arthritis, neuritis, and rheumatism. The water has an average temperature of about 143° F. (62° C).

Bathhouses in Hot Springs National Park operate under rules set up by the United States Department of the Interior. Eight of the bathhouses form what is called Bathhouse Row at the base of Hot Springs Mountain. The National Park Service maintains a water collection and distribution system that supplies purified spring water to the bathhouses in the park. The system also supplies water to four bathhouses and a national arthritis hospital in the city of Hot Springs.

Indians were the first to use the beneficial spring waters. Explorer Hernando de Soto was probably the first white person to see the springs. He passed through the area in 1541. The region, containing 47 hot springs, was set aside as a federal reservation in 1832. It was the first national health and recreation center in the United States. It became a national park in 1921. For its area, see **National Park System** (table: National parks).

Critically reviewed by the National Park Service

See also **Arkansas** (Springs); **Mineral water.**

Hotbed is a low, heated enclosure in which plants are grown during cold weather. Gardeners use hotbeds in spring to sprout seeds before the growing season. Hotbeds also protect plants from cold in fall and winter.

A hotbed consists of a four-sided wood or concrete frame built on the ground and covered by glass or

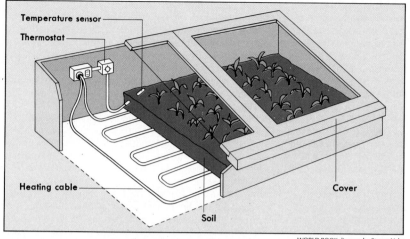

A hotbed protects plants grown during cold weather. The electric hotbed shown at the left has heating cables buried in the soil and a thermostat that controls the temperature. The slanted, transparent cover lets in sunlight and also helps keep the enclosure warm.

Temperature sensor

Thermostat

Heating cable

Soil

Cover

WORLD BOOK diagram by Steven Liska

transparent plastic. The cover is slanted to allow the maximum amount of sunlight to enter and help warm the growing area. Most of the warmth comes from electric heating cables, which are located under the soil and controlled by thermostats. In large hotbeds, such as those used by professional gardeners, the heat comes from pipes that surround the growing area or are buried in the soil. A furnace sends steam, hot water, or hot air through the pipes to heat the frame.

Gardeners once heated hotbeds by burying a thick layer of manure under the soil. As the manure decayed, it produced heat and fertilized the soil. A structure similar to a hotbed but heated only by sunlight is called a *cold frame* (see **Cold frame**).   William H. Carlson

See also **Greenhouse.**

Hotbox. See **Railroad** (Passenger and freight cars).

Hotchkiss gun is a type of automatic machine gun. It is air-cooled and gas-operated.

Hotel is an establishment that provides overnight lodging for the public. Hotels have clean, comfortable rooms for their guests, and most include at least one restaurant. Some hotels also furnish such services as shops and entertainment. The United States has more than 17,000 hotels, and Canada has about 5,000.

Hotels range in size from large buildings with more than 3,000 rooms to small inns that have as few as 8 or 10 rooms. Most large hotels maintain a staff of two employees for every three guests. The majority of small hotels do not offer the range of services provided by the large establishments. However, the prices for rooms and meals are lower at most small inns. Many small hotels are owned and operated by members of one family.

The rates of some hotels include both lodging and meals. This method of payment is called the *American plan.* Other hotels operate by the *European plan,* which covers only the price of a room. Still others offer the *continental plan,* which includes a small breakfast in the price of the room.

The hotel staff works around the clock to make the guests comfortable. The housekeeping staff cleans each room daily. Bellhops carry luggage and packages to the guests' rooms. The engineering department keeps the hotel's electricity, plumbing, heat, and air conditioning in good working order. The hotel security department

works to prevent fire and theft, and other disturbances.

Most hotel restaurants provide *room service,* by which guests can have food and beverages brought to their rooms. Guests also can have clothing cleaned and laundered by the hotel's *valet service.*

Motels differ from hotels chiefly in their building design. Most hotels occupy one multistory building that has a central lobby on the main floor. Restaurants and shops are located off the lobby, and most of the guest rooms are upstairs. Most motels consist of one building or a group of buildings. They serve automobile travelers primarily, and so they have a parking lot from which the rooms can easily be reached.

During the mid-1900's, motels became increasingly popular because they charge lower rates and have a more casual atmosphere than most hotels. The increase in automobile travel also stimulated motel development because many motels are near major highways. The growth of motels caused a decline in the use of hotels.

Kinds of hotels. There are three chief kinds of hotels: (1) commercial hotels, (2) resort hotels, and (3) residential hotels.

© Mike Yamashita, Woodfin Camp, Inc.

Resort hotels are often located near oceans. Vacationers at this resort hotel on the island of Maui enjoy swimming, surfing, golfing, and other outdoor activities.

Commercial hotels. Most commercial hotels are near the airport or the downtown area of large or medium-sized cities. These hotels serve mainly business travelers and other people on short trips. Many provide luxurious surroundings and a wide range of services.

The guests in most commercial hotels have a choice of several restaurants, ranging from inexpensive coffee shops to elegant dining rooms. Some of these hotel restaurants offer music, dancing, and other entertainment. Shops in commercial hotels include clothing stores, gift shops, and newsstands. Most commercial hotels have barber shops and beauty salons, and some have gymnasiums and swimming pools. The majority of commercial hotels in the United States and Canada operate under the European plan of payment.

Many commercial hotels have large rooms that their guests and other groups can use for banquets, conventions, and meetings. The hotel's catering department provides meals and snacks for such events.

Resort hotels feature golf, skiing, swimming, and other outdoor activities that attract vacationers. The guests at these establishments stay for periods ranging from a weekend to several weeks. Most resort hotels are near lakes, mountains, or oceans. But some are in the area of large cities and serve as vacation spots for nearby residents.

Business is seasonal at most resort hotels. During the winter months, for example, large numbers of people travel to seaside and mountain resorts in tropical areas or to ski lodges. Most of the resort hotels in the United States and Canada use the American plan of payment.

Resort hotels also provide indoor activities for their guests. Many have bowling alleys, game rooms, and indoor swimming pools and tennis courts. Some feature dancing, music, and other forms of entertainment.

Residential hotels rent one or more rooms to guests for long periods of time. These hotels resemble apartment buildings but also offer meals and maid and valet service. Some residential hotels have small apartments with kitchenettes.

Residential hotels called *retirement hotels* specialize in accommodations for senior citizens. They offer medical care in addition to regular hotel services.

History. The earliest inns were established about 3000 B.C. Most of them were private homes whose owners provided rooms for travelers. Many early innkeepers did not keep the rooms clean, and they provided only crude meals for their guests. The quality of inns, especially of those in England, improved during the A.D. 1700's, when more people began to travel for pleasure.

The first building in the United States constructed specifically as a hotel was the City Hotel, which opened in New York City in 1794. During the 1800's, American innkeepers became the leaders in hotel development. At that time, only the wealthy could afford to stay at European hotels. In the United States, however, there were many hotels that offered comfortable, inexpensive accommodations.

The rooms in early hotels had many beds and no locks on the doors. In 1829, the Tremont Hotel in Boston became the first hotel to provide private rooms with locks. The Tremont also introduced the practice of supplying soap and a pitcher of water in each hotel room.

Hotels expanded their services in the early 1900's.

National Monuments Record

Some hotels of the 1800's were connected to railway terminals to provide convenient lodging for passengers. The St. Pancras Station and Hotel, *above,* in London was designed in 1865.

During that period, Ellsworth M. Statler, an American hotel operator, opened hotels that included many new features. For example, Statler's hotels provided private baths and full-length mirrors in each room.

During the mid-1900's, many hotels owned by one person or company were built in cities throughout the United States. These hotels make up *hotel chains,* which can operate more efficiently and at less expense than most independent hotels. Some chains operate hotels in many countries.

Severe economic conditions in a number of countries caused a decline in travel during the 1970's. Many hotels tried to attract business by making lodging less expensive. For example, some hotels offered "package" rates that included the cost of travel, lodging, meals, and entertainment. Many hotels that serve primarily business travelers during the week lowered their weekend rates.

Robert A. Beck

See also **Hilton, Conrad N.; Motel; Youth hostel.**

Hotel Employees and Restaurant Employees International Union represents men and women employed in the public feeding and lodging industry. Members work at construction, logging, and mining camps; in factory cafeterias; in airport flight kitchens; on railroad dining cars; and in motels, hotels, restaurants, and bars. The union has locals in all parts of the United States and Canada. It is affiliated with the American Federation of Labor-Congress of Industrial Organizations. For the union's membership, see **Labor movement** (table).

Delegates from cooks' and waiters' unions organized the union in 1891. Membership in the union declined sharply during the 1920's, but grew rapidly with the later organization of unskilled hotel workers. The union has headquarters at 1219 28th Street NW, Washington, DC 20007.   Critically reviewed by the

Hotel Employees and Restaurant Employees International Union

Hothouse. See Greenhouse; Hotbed.

Hottentot, *HAHT uhn taht,* is a word sometimes used to refer to a yellow-skinned people of southern Africa. However, *Hottentot* has become an insulting term meaning *savage* or *barbarian.* Anthropologists prefer to use the people's own name for themselves, *Khoikhoi,* which means *men of men.*

There are no Khoikhoi in South Africa today. The only remaining Khoikhoi group, the Nama, live in Namibia (South West Africa). The Nama's way of life differs greatly from that of their ancestors. Less than 20 per cent of the Nama live in rural reserves. The rest work for whites on farms or in towns.

Anthropologists believe there were once at least 18 Khoikhoi tribes. The Khoikhoi were nomads who lived by herding sheep and cattle. The women did all the milking. The men tended the herds and also hunted. The Khoikhoi had a number of distinctive physical characteristics that set them apart from other African peoples. These features included tightly-coiled hair, plus inner eyefolds that gave their eyes a slanting appearance. The language of the Khoikhoi included clicking sounds and was unrelated to other African languages. The Khoikhoi in South Africa gradually disappeared as a separate people through warfare and intermarriage with other African groups and with the Dutch settlers called *Boers.*

Wade C. Pendleton

See also **Africa** (Racial groups).

Houdini, *hoo DEE nee,* **Harry** (1874-1926), was an American magician who won world fame as an escape artist. Houdini could quickly free himself from appar-

Brown Bros.

Harry Houdini, one of America's greatest magicians, became world famous for his ability to escape from almost any form of restraint, from chains and handcuffs to federal prison cells.

ently escapeproof devices, including leg irons, 10 pairs of handcuffs, jail cells, and nailed crates. His most sensational feat consisted of escaping from an airtight tank that was filled with water.

Houdini performed many publicity stunts to stimulate interest in his act. For example, he let himself be tied in a straitjacket and hung upside down from the eaves of a tall building. He struggled free in a few minutes. Houdini also became known for criticizing spiritualist mediums, who claimed they could communicate with the spirits of the dead. He believed that mediums deceived the public, and he duplicated their feats in an effort to show they were frauds. Houdini starred in several motion pictures.

Houdini was born in Budapest, Hungary. His family moved to Appleton, Wis., when he was a child, and Houdini later claimed he was born in Appleton. Houdini's given and family name was Ehrich Weiss. He took his stage name from Jean Eugène Robert-Houdin, a great French magician of the 1800's. He later made it his legal name.

Houdini began his career at the age of 17 as a magician in New York City. After developing his escape act, Houdini starred in many of the leading theaters in the world. Houdini's shows featured magic tricks, escapes, and demonstrations of what he regarded as spiritualist fraud.   Milbourne Christopher

See also **Magician** (picture).

Additional resources

Christopher, Milbourne. *Houdini: The Untold Story.* Crowell, 1969. *Houdini: A Pictorial Life.* 1976.
Fitzsimons, Raymond. *Death and the Magician: The Mystery of Houdini.* Atheneum, 1980.
Henning, Doug, and Reynolds, Charles. *Houdini: His Legend and His Magic.* Times Books, 1977.

Houdon, *oo DAWN,* **Jean Antoine** (1741-1828), was probably the greatest French sculptor of the 1700's. Most critics now rate him as the leading European sculptor of his time.

Houdon was primarily a portrait sculptor, but he also occasionally did mythological and religious figures. He worked in plaster, clay, stone, and metal. He made many popular works in each of the four media. Houdon created works of classical grandeur and dignity, as well as works of a much more informal and intimate character. He could suggest endless variety and shades of meaning in the personalities of his subjects. Houdon also had a control in working his materials that has seldom been equaled in sculpture.

Houdon was the first major European artist to visit North America. He arrived in 1785 to model a portrait of George Washington. Houdon made several portraits of Washington, including the full-length statue that stands in Richmond, Va. He also made portrait busts of Thomas Jefferson, Benjamin Franklin, John Paul Jones, and Robert Fulton. These portraits are among the most impressive artistic documents left from the early years of the American republic.

Houdon was born in Versailles. From 1764 to 1768 he studied at the French Academy in Rome. He returned to Paris in 1768 and settled down to a long, productive career lasting until 1814.   Robert R. Wark

Hound is the name of a group of dogs. Hounds are of two types: those that hunt by following the scent of their quarry, and those that hunt by sight. Scent hounds include the foxhound, black and tan coonhound, beagle, bloodhound, basset hound, and dachshund. Among sight hounds are the greyhound, Afghan, borzoi, Scottish deerhound, Saluki, and Irish wolfhound. The typical hound has long ears, strong legs, and a long tail. Hounds are alert, love the outdoors, and have great endurance. They are among the oldest known dogs. For additional information on hounds, see **Dog** (Hounds; picture: Hounds; table).

Critically reviewed by the American Kennel Club

Related articles in *World Book* include:

Afghan hound	Dachshund	Otter hound
American foxhound	English foxhound	Pharoah
Basenji	Foxhound	hound
Basset hound	Greyhound	Rhodesian ridge-
Beagle	Harrier	back
Black and tan coon-	Ibizan hound	Saluki
hound	Irish wolfhound	Scottish deer-
Bloodhound	Norwegian elk-	hound
Borzoi	hound	Whippet

Houphouët-Boigny, *oo FWAY bwah NYEE,* **Félix,** *fay LEEKS* (1905-), has served as president of Ivory Coast since that nation gained independence from France in 1960. As president, Houphouët-Boigny has helped unite the country's many ethnic groups. He has maintained close relations with France and other Western European nations. Ivory Coast receives much economic support from those nations. Under Houphouët-Boigny, Ivory Coast has achieved political stability and much economic progress.

Houphouët-Boigny was born in Yamoussoukro, near Dimbokro, Ivory Coast. He practiced medicine for many years before entering politics in the mid-1940's. He served in the French government from 1945 to 1959. He helped bring independence to Ivory Coast and other French-controlled African areas.   W. A. E. Skurnik

Hour is an interval of time. It consists of 60 minutes. A day, from midnight to midnight, has 24 hours. Every nation regulates its activities according to the hour. But people did not begin to use hours to mark uniform periods of a day until the 1300's, when the mechanical clock was invented.

The ancient Romans used the hour to note a point of time, such as sunrise and sunset. They later added the hour of noon. At the beginning of the Christian era, the Romans divided the hours of daylight into five periods, which they marked on their sundials. In A.D. 605, the Christian church named the *seven canonical hours,* or hours of prayer. They were (1) *matins* (morning) and *lauds* (praise), (2) *prime* (first), (3) *tierce* (third), (4) *sext* (sixth), (5) *nones* (ninth), (6) *vespers* (evening), and (7) *complin* (complete). These hours marked only periods of daylight, beginning at 6 a.m. The nights were sometimes divided into *watches,* which marked the times when guards reported for duty or were changed. The length of the hour varied with the season. The winter hours were shorter than the summer hours, because there was less daylight during the winter.

By the 1500's, many churches and palaces in Europe had installed mechanical clocks with 12-hour dials. These clocks did not keep good time, and had to be set every sunshiny day at noon, when the sun was at its highest point, or *on the meridian.* From this we get the letters a.m., meaning *ante* (before) *meridiem,* or before

noon. p.m. means *post* (after) *meridiem,* or after noon. When people first began to tell time by the clock, they substituted the word *o'clock,* meaning by the clock, for the word *hour.*

Confusion can result if the letters a.m. and p.m. are not used. European railroads and airplane timetables use a single 24-hour system. To avoid confusion, four figures are used. Thus, 1:00 a.m. is written 01:00. 1:00 p.m. is written as 13:00, and 12:00 midnight is 24:00. The United States armed forces also use this system, but without the colon. In conversation, all four figures are used, such as "O one hundred" for 1:00 a.m., "twelve hundred" for 12:00 noon, and "twenty-four hundred" for 12:00 midnight.   James Jespersen

See also **Clock; Day; Time.**

Hour circle. See **Astronomy** (Locating objects in the sky).

Hourglass is a device that measures time. It has two glass bulbs joined together by a small opening. One of the bulbs contains grains of fine, dry sand. The sand takes exactly one hour to drain from the top bulb to the bottom bulb. When all the sand has run from the top bulb, the hourglass is turned over, and the sand begins to run into the empty bulb as before. Some earlier hourglasses contained mercury, but sand works better because it flows at an even rate, regardless of the amount the bulb contains. An hourglass that contains sand may be called a *sandglass.*

Smaller glasses, such as the *half-hour glass,* measure shorter periods of time. Even smaller glasses measure the time needed to boil eggs. These are called *egg glasses.* For many years, hourglasses were used to limit the amount of time a speaker could talk. Until the 1900's, sailors used a device like an hourglass that measured less than a minute while the log line was allowed to run out. In this way, they could determine how fast the ship was traveling. Hourglasses were widely used before the invention of mechanical timepieces. However, they have been replaced by watches and clocks. Many writers have mentioned the hourglass to express the passage of time.

Arthur B. Sinkler

David R. Frazier

The hourglass was used to measure time before clocks were invented.

Housatonic River, *HOO suh TAHN ihk,* is of great importance in supplying water power to New England factories. The river is 148 miles (238 kilometers) long. It starts in the Berkshire Hills in Massachusetts, flows southward through Connecticut, and enters Long Island Sound about 4 miles (6 kilometers) east of Bridgeport. The tide rises in the Housatonic as far as the town of Derby, 14 miles (23 kilometers) from the Sound. The wooded shores of the Housatonic are noted for their great scenic beauty.   George Macinko

Eric Carle, Shostal

A Georgian house has a rectangular shape. Georgians developed from English architecture of the 1700's and 1800's.

David Forbert, Shostal

A ranch house has all its rooms on one level. Ranch houses are among the most popular types of homes in the United States.

George Goodman, Shostal

A split-level house has a level half a floor above the main level and, in some cases, another level half a floor below.

L&M Photo from FPG

Row houses, or town houses, line the streets of many cities. Such houses share a common wall with a neighboring unit.

House is a building that provides shelter, comfort, and protection. Houses stand along city streets, in suburban developments, and on quiet country roads. They range in size from small cottages to huge mansions. Their styles vary from graceful colonial-style houses to modern ranch-style and tri-level houses with long, low lines and large "picture" windows.

House building is a major industry in the United States, Canada, and other industrial nations. Every year, banks, insurance companies, mortgage companies, and savings and loan associations lend millions of dollars to help people buy used and new houses. Real-estate companies make house buying and selling easier, because they keep a record of houses for sale. Designers and architects plan houses to fit the needs of growing families. Carpenters, plasterers, bricklayers, plumbers, electricians, and other construction workers make these plans come to life. Interior decorators and furniture designers make rooms attractive.

Kinds of houses

Styles of houses vary widely. Many designs can be traced to particular regions or periods. *Colonial-style* houses, for instance, date back to the American colonial period of the 1600's and 1700's. The Spanish settlers in Florida and the southwestern United States built *Spanish colonial* houses, usually of whitewashed stucco or adobe. Square wood posts support a *veranda,* or outside corridor, that provides shade. These houses often have one or two wings, and feature a *patio,* or small courtyard. *French colonial* houses developed along the lower Mississippi Valley, especially around New Orle-

ans, where the French settled. On the outside, heavy upright posts were placed close together, and the spaces between were filled with clay or stone. French colonial houses have high-pitched, slanting tile roofs. Graceful *southern colonial* homes have tall columns across the front, with windows perfectly balanced on each side of the entrance. The *New England colonial* or Cape Cod house is the smallest colonial house. This simple, compact house has one story at ground level, and another half story beneath the steeply slanted roof.

Other styles include the red-brick *Georgian* house, with thin columns alongside the doors, and windows with small panes on each side and above the doorway. *Victorian* houses have fancy trimming, and large rooms with high ceilings. Georgian and Victorian houses developed from styles originated in Great Britain during the 1700's and 1800's.

The *ranch* house, which developed from early homes built in the West and Southwest, became one of the most popular styles during the mid-1900's. These low houses have all the rooms on one level. Architects design them with many windows, including picture windows, in an attempt to blend the indoors with the outdoors. Many ranch houses have no basements. *Split-level* houses have one living level about half a floor above the other. When this type of house is built on three living levels, it is called a *tri-level*. These houses usually have very large window areas. *Row* houses, often called *town* houses, are usually two floors high. A common wall separates each house from another.

Building materials. Houses are often classified according to the chief type of building material used. For example, we speak of *frame,* or wood, houses, brick houses, and stone houses. *Prefabricated* houses are built with factory-made sections assembled at the building site. *Manufactured* houses are built completely in factories and moved to the home site. The kind of building materials used in the construction of a house depends mainly on the size of the house, its location, its design, and the climate.

Wood has long been a popular building material because it is usually more plentiful and cheaper than other materials. About 80 of every 100 houses built in the United States have wood frame walls.

Wood can be cut and shaped to provide a variety of house styles. Wood is also popular because so many different types are available. Houses are often made of fir, pine, hemlock, redwood, and spruce. Other woods, including oak, cypress, maple, walnut, and birch, are used for such interior features as stairways, cabinets, floors, and doors. Wood can be made to blend with almost any setting or design. It can be natural, stained, painted, or carved. See **Lumber.**

Brick is one of the oldest and most common building materials. Brick wears well and, like wood, is usually easy to obtain. Bricks are available in a number of colors and finishes. They make attractive, substantial houses. See **Brick.**

Concrete block and stone make strong, attractive houses. Concrete blocks are made by pouring a mixture of cement into a mold. They make durable houses that are relatively cheap to maintain. Builders also make houses of stone that has been taken from quarries and split into usable sizes. Because stone is an expensive building material, it is usually applied in a *veneer,* or coating, over an inner wall of brick or concrete block. See **Building stone; Cement and concrete.**

Other materials in today's houses differ greatly from those of 100 or even 50 years ago. Industries have developed new materials that help architects design better, longer-lasting houses. For example, builders once used nails that rusted. The rust from these nails eventually rotted the wood in the beams and shingles. Today, manufacturers coat nails with zinc, copper, or aluminum to make them rustproof. Aluminum formerly was very expensive, and engineers seldom used it. Today, aluminum costs less, and it may replace steel and wood for such uses as window frames and siding.

Builders once did not have metal and composition siding, now often used to cover wood. This type of siding provides insulation, prevents rotting, and saves much repainting and repairs. Older houses usually had small windows that let in only a small amount of light. Their window frames were loosely constructed and were not always airtight. Houses today have airtight, metal window frames or improved wood frames. Many houses have large "picture" windows that may cover the entire side of a room. Others use glass bricks to let in light.

Building a house

Planning the house. If a person decides to build a house, he or she must first select a *lot,* or piece of land. The next step is to consult an architect or builder. This expert will check local zoning laws and electrical, building, and plumbing codes (see **Housing** [Local housing

controls]). Knowledge of these codes protects the buyer in both the present and the future. For example, the zoning law in the area may permit industrial construction, and therefore a factory could be built near the new house.

The architect then designs the house according to the buyer's ideas. He or she makes specifications and blueprints that become the basis for the contract between the builder and the buyer. They provide information on size, materials, and how the house is to be built. The architect also superintends the actual construction of the house.

The following sections describe the steps involved in building a typical frame house.

The foundation supports the house. First, construction workers begin *excavating,* or digging, holes or trenches for the *footings,* the lowest part of the foundation. The footings support each wall load. They are made by pouring concrete into wood or steel forms that workers place below the *frost line,* or the depth to which the ground freezes. This is done so that the footings will not be raised by freezing. Footings usually extend from 1 to 6 feet (30 to 180 centimeters) beneath ground level. Builders generally use concrete or concrete block for the house's foundation, which may extend from 8 inches to 3 feet (20 to 91 centimeters) above the ground.

The area within the foundation below the first story is the *basement.* Basements add to the cost of building a house, but they provide extra room. Many basements are partitioned into separate areas that are used for the heating unit, a playroom, laundry equipment, and general storage.

Only about two-fifths of the houses built today have basements. In many low or damp regions, houses are raised above the ground on concrete *piers,* or supports. Sometimes a *slab* foundation is laid directly on the

House-building terms

Attic is the space directly below the roof and above the ceiling of a house.
Ceiling joists are beams that rest on the top plate of the studs and support the ceiling.
Conduit is a tube that protects electrical wires.
Dry wall is an interior wall finish made in panels of dry material, usually gypsum. Dry wall is covered with paper on both sides.
Duct is a metal pipe for distributing air from the heating and cooling equipment to the rooms of a house.
Eaves are the part of the roof that hangs over the outside wall.
Girder is a heavy piece of timber or steel used for support.
Header is a beam perpendicular to the joists. It is nailed to the joists to make a frame for a chimney, stairway, window, door, or other opening.
Joists are beams that support floors and ceilings. They are supported at the ends by walls, girders, or larger beams.
Lath is a narrow strip, usually of wood, nailed to the inside of the frame. Laths provide support for plaster and tile walls.
Rafter is a sloping piece of lumber that extends from the *ridge* (top edge) of the roof to the eaves, and supports the roof covering.
Sash is the framework that holds glass in a window or door.
Sheathing refers to boards or other materials that cover the wall or roof before the finished siding or roofing is added.
Siding is the outer covering of a frame house. It may be made of wood, metal, or various composition materials.
Stud is a vertical part of the frame.

How a house is built   The construction of a house requires the services of many skilled workers, including carpenters, plumbers, and electricians. These specialists build the home according to plans prepared by an architect in consultation with the buyer or land developer.

Photographs by J. D. Barnell, Shostal

Preparing the foundation is the first step in building a house. Concrete blocks form the upper part of this foundation. They are laid on poured concrete that forms the base of the foundation.

Putting up the walls and roof. After the frame of the house has been constructed, workers nail on the *sheathing,* which is the first layer of the walls and the roof.

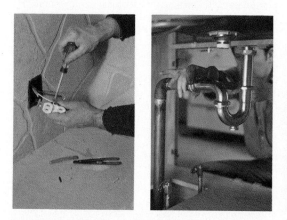

Installing the wiring and plumbing must be done carefully to prevent poor electrical connections and leaking pipes. Such problems are costly to repair after a house has been completed.

Finishing the exterior involves attaching *siding* to the sheathing to form the outer layer of the house. The siding is made of such materials as aluminum, brick, stone, or wood.

Interior construction involves such tasks as installing wall paneling, *left,* and putting in a door frame, *right.* Workers must also complete the floors and windows of the structure.

The completed house may have such features as landscaping and a paved driveway and front walk. They give the home an attractive appearance and increase the value of the property.

ground, especially if the earth beneath the house is hard. The ground must first be *graded,* or leveled. Workers then spread a *filler,* usually stone, and cover it with a moistureproof paper. The filler and the paper prevent moisture from coming through the slab that is made by pouring concrete, about 4 inches (10 centimeters) thick, directly on top of the paper.

The frame is the skeleton around which the rest of the house is built. After the footings and foundation have been formed, workers bolt wooden *sills,* or base plates, to the foundation. The sills support the outside walls. *Floor joists,* or support beams, are attached to the sills about 16 inches (41 centimeters) apart. A joist runs from one sill and joins with another joist from the opposite sill. They meet at a girder or basement wall about midway between the house's sides. Floor boards or plywood nailed on top of the joists make the bottom layer of the floor. The structure is then solid enough to hold the *wall frames* of the house.

Wall frames include vertical pieces of lumber called *studs* and horizontal pieces called *plates.* Carpenters as-

semble and nail together each wall frame separately before attaching it to the sill. Then they lift each frame into place and brace it temporarily. When all the outside walls have been raised, they are nailed together and braced permanently.

The *sheathing,* or inner layer of the outside walls, may be wood, fiberboard, or plasterboard nailed to the studs. Sometimes builders tack tar paper to the sheathing before adding the *siding,* or outer layer. Siding may be wood, asbestos shingles, brick, masonry, or aluminum placed directly over the sheathing or tar paper.

The roof seals the top of the house. Some roofs are flat, but most are slanted. Slanted roofs are often formed by pieces of lumber called *rafters.* Carpenters nail the bottom ends of the rafters to the plates at the top of the outside walls. The rafters slant from the plates and meet at the *ridgeboard,* a board placed at the *ridge,* or top edge, of the roof. Rafters support the weight of the roof just as joists support the weight of the floor.

After carpenters nail sheathing to the tops of the rafters, they add heavy building paper or building felt to it.

Some parts of a house

WORLD BOOK diagram by Richard Fickle

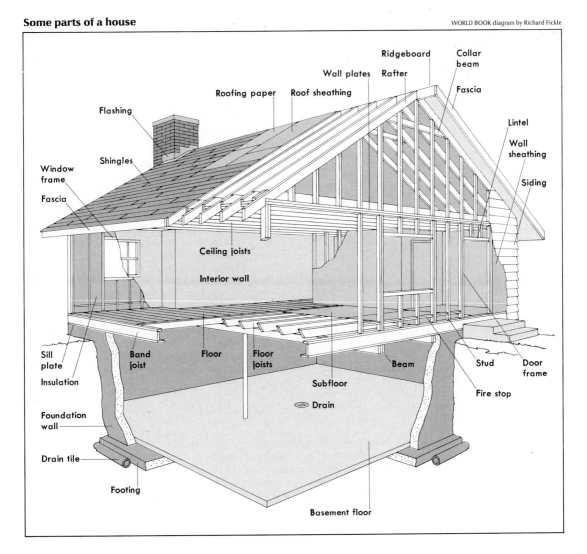

Then they add the final layer of slate or asphalt shingles, or roofing asphalt. *Flashing,* or strips of sheet metal, placed around the chimney and other roof openings, insulates the roof from the chimney and also prevents water from leaking into the house. See **Roof.**

Interior construction includes (1) floors, (2) walls, (3) windows, and (4) doors.

Floors have two layers. The lower layer lies at an angle across the floor joists. The upper, finished layer is made from *tongue and groove boards.* One side of each board has a *tongue,* or lip, and the other side has a *groove,* or slot. The tongue of one board fits snugly into the groove of another board. Carpenters drive nails through the groove side so that the nailheads do not show on the finished floor. Most finished floors are made of hardwoods such as maple or oak that have been finely sanded and later sealed with a wood filler. The wood may then be finished with wax, shellac, or varnish. Other floors have coverings such as linoleum or rubber, vinyl, or asphalt tile. See **Flooring.**

Walls. Rooms are made by building inside walls after the outside walls have been attached to the foundation. Inside walls, also called *partitions,* are really small-sized frames like the outside walls. They have studs and must be supported by plates, joists, and girders.

If plaster is to be applied, the interior walls must first be covered with *lath,* or strips of wood, metal, or plasterboard. The lath is set horizontally about 3 inches (8 centimeters) apart. Wallboard, plasterboard, or plywood may be used in place of plaster (see **Wallboard**).

Windows. Most parts of a window come from a lumber mill, already cut in the proper sizes. Carpenters leave space in the frame for windows and window pulleys, weights, and sashes. Window sashes are made of wood or metal, usually either aluminum or a lightweight steel. See **Window.**

Doors. Both doors and door frames may usually be bought ready-made. Carpenters attach the doors high enough to swing over rugs or carpets. A *threshold* fills in the space under an outside door.

Electrical wiring provides lighting and furnishes outlets for lamps, washing machines, and other appliances. In some houses, electricity also provides heat. Before construction starts, the builder determines the location and type of wiring. Wires vary in size, depending on the equipment in the house and how far the current must travel. Standard wiring is designed for 110-volt current. But builders often specify heavy-duty, 220-volt wiring if large electrical appliances such as a stove and an air conditioner will be used at the same time.

Electricians install wiring while carpenters build the frame. Wiring is done in a series of circuits. Each set of wires has several outlets. Electricians often place the wiring for a furnace on a separate circuit. This keeps the furnace running in case another circuit breaks down.

Wires become hot and can cause fires if they are overloaded, so electricians install a fuse for each electrical circuit (see **Fuse** [Electric]). A *fuse box* usually holds all the fuses. If too much current passes through a circuit, the wire in the fuse melts, or "blows." Electricians often install another protective device called a *circuit breaker,* instead of a fuse box (see **Circuit breaker**). If the circuit becomes overloaded, the circuit breaker automatically cuts off the current (See **Electric circuit**).

Plumbing. During construction, plumbers install the pipes that will supply gas and water, and carry away waste. They install bathroom fixtures and sinks just before other workers add the finishing touches to the house. Plumbers also install *traps* to keep out sewage gas. The trap used for bathroom wash basins, for example, is a P-shaped pipe directly below the drain. Water settles in the lower part of the pipe and prevents sewage gas from backing up and leaking into the room. To function properly, traps must have outside ventilation. The small pipe that projects from the roof of a house is a ventilating pipe for sewage gas.

A cast-iron waste-disposal pipe runs from inside the house to about 5 feet (1.5 meters) outside, where it connects with a pipe of another material, usually clay. This pipe connects the home-disposal pipe with the city sewerage system. In areas without a city sewerage system, a *septic tank* near the house holds sewage until it dissolves. Water from the sewage flows through pipes into the ground. The sludge remaining in the tank must be removed at intervals. See **Plumbing; Sewage.**

Insulation reduces the amount of heat or cold that passes through walls, floors, and ceilings. When the air around the house is warmer or colder than the air inside, heat passes from the warm air to the cold air. This means that in winter, the heat will pass to the outside, and the house will become cold. In summer, the heat outside passes into the house. Insulation fills the air spaces in walls, floors, and ceilings, and creates *dead-air space.* This helps prevent heat from passing through. Insulation can save fuel costs in heating a house.

Insulation is made from many fireproofed materials, including mineral wool, cotton, animal hair, and wood or composition fibers. These materials are formed into blankets, boards, paper, and sheathing. They also come in a loose, crumblike form. The type of insulation used depends on the climate and on whether it insulates floors, ceilings, or walls. See **Insulation.**

Heating and air conditioning. Most houses have *central heating* systems. One furnace, or heating unit, supplies heat for the entire house (see **Furnace**). Such houses are heated by warm air, steam, or hot water. In hot-air heating, a fan connected to the furnace blows warm air through *ducts,* or pipes, into the rooms. In steam or hot-water heating, the steam or hot water passes through radiators that stand throughout the house. In *radiant* heating, hot-water pipes run under the floors or in the ceilings or walls. See **Heating.**

Air-conditioning units may be used to cool and heat houses. An air conditioner takes warm air from the house, cools it, removes moisture, and recirculates cool air. It also may warm cold air, add moisture, and recirculate warm air. See **Air conditioning; Heat pump.**

Interior decoration. In a new house, the builder usually paints the rooms and finishes the floors as part of the contract with the homeowner. The owner generally selects, buys, and arranges the furnishings. But sometimes the owner hires a professional interior decorator to do this job. See **Interior decoration.**

Landscaping is the last step in building a house. Most builders try to keep the natural outline of the land and to preserve the trees. Of course, some grading and some excavating of land must be done. After the house is finished, the builder may plant seed or lay rolls of grass turf for a lawn around the house. The builder may also plant trees and shrubs. See **Gardening; Landscape architecture.**   Jack M. Landers

Related articles in *World Book* include:

Air conditioning	Flooring	Nail
Architecture	Furniture	Plaster
Brick	Heating	Plastics
Building construc-	Housing	Real estate
tion	Insulation	Roof
Building permit	Insulator, Electric	Shelter
Building stone	Interior decoration	Shingle
Building trade	Lighting	Smoke detector
Cement and con-	Lumber	Ventilation
crete	Mobile home	Wallboard
Electric circuit	Mortgage	Window

Additional resources

Carson, Alan, and Dunlop, Robert. *Inspecting a House: A Guide for Buyers, Owners, and Renovators.* Beaufort Books, 1982.
Connolly, William G. *The New York Times Guide to Buying or Building a Home.* Rev. ed. Times Books, 1984.
Hutchins, Nigel. *Restoring Old Houses.* Van Nostrand, 1980.
Jackson, Frank W. *Practical Housebuilding for Practically Everyone.* McGraw, 1985.
McAlester, Virginia S. and Lee. *A Field Guide to American Houses.* Knopf, 1984.
Robbins, Ken. *Building a House.* Four Winds, 1984. For younger readers.

House, in astrology, is a division of a chart that supposedly reveals a person's character or future. The chart, called a *horoscope,* is divided into 12 houses. The houses represent 12 departments of a person's life: (1) appearance and personality, (2) possessions, (3) family relations, (4) parents, (5) children, (6) health, (7) friends and marriage, (8) death, (9) travel, (10) career, (11) ideals, and (12) illness and sorrow. The houses also are related to 12 imaginary divisions of the earth's surface. Astrologers supposedly tell fortunes by explaining the influence of the planets and stars on each house (see **Horoscope** [Parts of a horoscope]).   Christopher McIntosh

See also **Astrology; Zodiac.**

House, Edward Mandell (1858-1938), was a statesman who made secret missions to Europe during World War I as the representative of President Woodrow Wilson. He helped Wilson draft the Fourteen Points, a set of principles intended to serve as the basis for a peace treaty to end the war. House also helped convince the Allies to accept the Fourteen Points. He served on the American commission at the Versailles Peace Conference, where he helped plan the League of Nations.

House was born in Houston, Tex., and attended Cornell University. He became known as "Colonel" House after a period of service on the staff of the governor of Texas. House became a leader in Texas state politics. He gained national influence in 1912 when he worked to obtain the presidential nomination for Wilson. He continued as Wilson's most trusted adviser until 1919, when he retired from public life.   Nelson M. Blake

House Committee on Un-American Activities.
See Un-American Activities Committee.

House of Burgesses, *BUR jehs ehs,* was the first representative legislative body in America, and the first in any English colony. It first met at Jamestown, then the capital of Virginia, on July 30, 1619. Governor Sir George Yeardley called the meeting. The session included two citizens, or *burgesses,* from each of the 11 *boroughs* (subdivisions) of Virginia.

The first act of the body was to approve an official great seal for the colony. The House also claimed the right to act on all tax laws. In 1621, the House received the authority to make all legislation, but the governor and his council had the right of veto. The House conformed to English law and used the same procedure as the English Parliament.

After the death of King James I in 1625, the English government became occupied with its internal affairs. England neither approved nor disapproved of the House. From then on, the House managed the affairs of the colony. The failure of Governor Sir William Berkeley to call a new election to the House was one of the many grievances that led to Bacon's Rebellion in 1676 (see **Bacon's Rebellion**).

The House of Burgesses was not completely democratic. But it was the first appearance of republican government. When it was temporarily dissolved in 1774, its members met in the first revolutionary convention of Virginia. There they elected delegates to the First Continental Congress. Some of the burgesses became leaders of the Revolutionary War.   Marshall Smelser

See also **Virginia** (History [The course toward independence]).

House of Commons is one of the two houses of Parliament, the lawmaking body of Great Britain. The House of Lords is the other. The House of Commons is the more powerful house.

A majority of the members of the House of Commons must approve all bills before they can become law. Money bills passed by the House of Commons become law one month after being sent to the House of Lords, whether that House approves them or not. Nonmoney bills passed by the House of Commons in two consecutive sessions automatically become law, regardless of the vote in the House of Lords.

Members of the House of Commons are elected from each of the four countries of Great Britain. The House has 650 members—523 from England, 72 from Scotland, 38 from Wales, and 17 from Northern Ireland. Each member represents a voting district called a *constituency.* The members do not have to live in the constituency they represent. Officials of the Church of England, the Church of Scotland, the Church of Ireland, and the Roman Catholic Church cannot be elected to the House of Commons. Members of the nobility—except peers of Ireland—and certain government employees are also ineligible for election.

Members of the House of Commons do not serve a fixed term. They are chosen in a *general election,* in which the entire nation votes. General elections must be held at least every five years. If a member dies or resigns, a *by-election* is held in the constituency.   Robert E. Dowse

See also **Great Britain** (Parliament); **Parliament** (The House of Commons).

House of Lords is one of the two houses of Parliament, the lawmaking body of Great Britain. The House of Commons is the other house and is more powerful than the House of Lords.

The main function of the House of Lords is to examine bills passed by the House of Commons. The House of Lords often amends bills but rarely challenges their basic principles. After the House of Commons has approved a bill, the House of Lords may delay the measure but cannot defeat it.

The House of Lords has about 1,170 members. About 800 members are *hereditary peers,* nobles who inherit their titles. About 320 members are *life peers,* persons given the rank of baron or baroness to honor their achievements in business, civil service, or other fields. Twenty *law lords* are selected from the nation's highest-ranking judges. These members hear final legal appeals. The *lords spiritual* are 26 senior officials of the Church of England. Only about 20 per cent of the members attend most debates.

Parliament was divided into the House of Lords and the House of Commons during the 1300's. The houses had nearly equal power until 1832, when a reform act took away much of the power of the House of Lords. The Parliamentary Acts of 1911 and 1949 further limited the actions of the House of Lords.   Robert E. Dowse

See also **Great Britain** (Parliament); **Parliament** (The House of Lords).

House of Representatives is one of the two law-making bodies of many legislatures. In many of these legislatures, the other chamber is called a *senate,* and the house of representatives is the larger of the two.

The national legislatures of such countries as the United States, Australia, Colombia, and Japan have a house of representatives. Most of the 49 two-chamber state legislatures in the United States also have a house of representatives. Nebraska has a one-house legislature. A number of states and many nations use a different name for a lower chamber. This article deals primarily with the U.S. House of Representatives.

The U.S. House of Representatives, usually called simply the *House,* is one of the two chambers of Congress. The other chamber is the Senate. The two houses of Congress have about the same amount of power. However, the Senate is frequently called the *upper house,* and the House is known as the *lower house.* Members of the House are generally called *representatives.* The House and Senate must approve identical versions of any legislation before it can become law.

The Constitutional Convention established the form of national government in 1787. But the convention reached a standstill on the problem of representation in

Number of representatives by state

This table shows the number of representatives each state sends to the U.S. House of Representatives. The number is based on the state's population, but each state must have at least one representative. The House has 435 members.

State	Representatives	State	Representatives
Alabama	7	Montana	2
Alaska	1	Nebraska	3
Arizona	5	Nevada	2
Arkansas	4	New Hampshire	2
California	45	New Jersey	14
Colorado	6	New Mexico	3
Connecticut	6	New York	34
Delaware	1	North Carolina	11
Florida	19	North Dakota	1
Georgia	10	Ohio	21
Hawaii	2	Oklahoma	6
Idaho	2	Oregon	5
Illinois	22	Pennsylvania	23
Indiana	10	Rhode Island	2
Iowa	6	South Carolina	6
Kansas	5	South Dakota	1
Kentucky	7	Tennessee	9
Louisiana	8	Texas	27
Maine	2	Utah	3
Maryland	8	Vermont	1
Massachusetts	11	Virginia	10
Michigan	18	Washington	8
Minnesota	8	West Virginia	4
Mississippi	5	Wisconsin	9
Missouri	9	Wyoming	1

Congress. Delegates from states with large populations favored representation according to population. Those from states that had small populations argued for equal representation for every state. Under a compromise, a state's representation in the House was based on population. Each state was given two senators, regardless of population.

Membership of the U.S. House of Representatives

Size. The Constitution gives Congress the power to determine the size of the House and to distribute representatives among the states. According to the Constitution, each member of the House must represent at least 30,000 persons, but every state must have at least one representative. The Constitution also requires a census

K. Jewell, U.S. House of Representatives

The House chamber, where the entire House of Representatives meets, has galleries for the public. Visitors may watch the legislators debate important bills. But most of the actual work of the House is done by committees.

Speakers of the House of Representatives

Speaker	Party	Years served	Speaker	Party	Years served
* Frederick A. C. Muhlenberg	Federalist	1789-1791	* Schuyler Colfax	Republican	1863-1869
Jonathan Trumbull	Federalist	1791-1793	Theodore M. Pomeroy	Republican	1869
* Frederick A. C. Muhlenberg	Federalist	1793-1795	* James G. Blaine	Republican	1869-1875
* Jonathan Dayton	Federalist	1795-1799	Michael C. Kerr	Democratic	1875-1876
Theodore Sedgwick	Federalist	1799-1801	Samuel J. Randall	Democratic	1876-1881
Nathaniel Macon	Dem.-Rep.†	1801-1807	J. Warren Keifer	Republican	1881-1883
Joseph B. Varnum	Dem.-Rep.†	1807-1811	John G. Carlisle	Democratic	1883-1889
* Henry Clay	Nat. Rep.**	1811-1814	* Thomas B. Reed	Republican	1889-1891
Langdon Cheves	Dem.-Rep.†	1814-1815	Charles F. Crisp	Democratic	1891-1895
* Henry Clay	Nat. Rep.**	1815-1820	* Thomas B. Reed	Republican	1895-1899
John W. Taylor	Dem.-Rep.†	1820-1821	David B. Henderson	Republican	1899-1903
Philip P. Barbour	Dem.-Rep.†	1821-1823	Joseph G. Cannon	Republican	1903-1911
* Henry Clay	Nat. Rep.**	1823-1825	James B. Clark	Democratic	1911-1919
John W. Taylor	Dem.-Rep.†	1825-1827	Frederick H. Gillett	Republican	1919-1925
Andrew Stevenson	Dem.-Rep.†	1827-1834	Nicholas Longworth	Republican	1925-1931
* John Bell	Whig	1834-1835	* John N. Garner	Democratic	1931-1933
* James K. Polk	Democratic	1835-1839	Henry T. Rainey	Democratic	1933-1935
Robert M. T. Hunter	Democratic	1839-1841	Joseph W. Byrns	Democratic	1935-1936
John White	Whig	1841-1843	William B. Bankhead	Democratic	1936-1940
John W. Jones	Democratic	1843-1845	* Sam Rayburn	Democratic	1940-1947
John W. Davis	Democratic	1845-1847	Joseph W. Martin, Jr.	Republican	1947-1949
Robert C. Winthrop	Whig	1847-1849	* Sam Rayburn	Democratic	1949-1953
Howell Cobb	Democratic	1849-1851	Joseph W. Martin, Jr.	Republican	1953-1955
Linn Boyd	Democratic	1851-1855	* Sam Rayburn	Democratic	1955-1961
Nathaniel P. Banks	American	1855-1857	* John W. McCormack	Democratic	1962-1971
James L. Orr	Democratic	1857-1859	* Carl B. Albert	Democratic	1971-1977
William Pennington	Whig	1859-1861	* Thomas P. O'Neill	Democratic	1977-1987
Galusha A. Grow	Republican	1861-1863	* James C. Wright, Jr.	Democratic	1987-

*Has a separate biography in *World Book.*
†Democratic-Republican
**National Republican

of the nation every 10 years to determine how many representatives each state should have. In 1976, Congress passed legislation providing that a census be conducted every 5 years instead of every 10. Congress uses only the census taken in years that end in zero to *apportion* (distribute) House seats among the states.

The first House, which was formed before the initial census, had 59 members when it originally met and 65 members by the end of the first Congress. The House grew as new states joined the Union and as the nation's population increased. In 1929, Congress passed legislation that limited the House to 435 members. In 1959, when Alaska and Hawaii became states, the House gained two additional members. However, reapportionment took place after the 1960 census, and the House returned to 435 members in 1962. Today, the House has one member per about 519,000 people.

Originally, Congress let each state decide how to choose its representatives. Some states established congressional districts, each of which elected one representative. Other states chose all their representatives *at large,* with an entire state serving as one congressional district. In 1842, Congress passed legislation that required every state to create a congressional district for each of its House seats. Under certain conditions, however, one or more of a state's representatives may be chosen at large.

At first, Congress required the congressional districts of each state to have a compact shape and nearly equal populations. However, these rules were largely ignored, and Congress omitted them from the 1929 law that limited the size of the House. In many cases, the most powerful party in a state legislature created oddly shaped districts that differed greatly in population. This practice, called *gerrymandering,* concentrated the supporters of

other parties into only a few districts. The opposition parties could win congressional elections in those districts. But the dominant party gained an unfair share of seats in the House of Representatives by winning in all the other districts.

The growth of cities widened the differences in population among congressional districts. For example, a state might have had an urban district of 900,000 persons and a rural district of 150,000. Since each district elected one representative, many urban voters were underrepresented in the House.

During the 1960's, the Supreme Court of the United States largely ended unfair apportionment of House seats. In 1962, the Supreme Court ruled in *Baker v. Carr* that citizens could ask federal courts to decide cases involving charges of unfair apportionment. In 1964, the court ruled in *Wesberry v. Sanders* that the congressional districts of a state must be as equal in population as possible. Gerrymandering declined as federal courts began to decide apportionment cases. But some gerrymandering persists because districts of equal populations can be created to favor one party.

Qualifications and election. The Constitution requires a representative to be at least 25 years old and to have been a citizen for at least seven years. Members of the House must be legal residents of the state from which they are elected. They are not legally required to live in the district they represent, but nearly all voters insist that they do so. Representatives serve two-year terms and are elected in the even-numbered years. They may be reelected to any number of terms.

Salary and privileges. The basic annual salary of House members is $89,500. The *Speaker,* who is the leader of the House, receives $115,000. Each representative also gets about $410,000 in allowances to pay assistants. Allowances for telephone and travel expenses vary according to the distance to the home district. An allowance for home district office rent depends on average local rents. Representatives also receive free office space in Washington, D.C.

Representatives have legal *immunity* (protection) for anything they write or say as members of Congress. With this immunity, a representative can make critical statements about people without fear of being sued.

Organization of the U.S. House

In January after a congressional election, House members meet to choose their party leaders for the next two years. The meeting of the House Democrats is called the Democratic *caucus,* and that of the Republicans is the Republican *conference.* The representatives deal mainly with organizational matters at these meetings, but they also may adopt party positions on bills.

The Speaker and other leaders. The Speaker of the House presides over House sessions and gives representatives permission to debate. The Speaker also appoints most House members of *joint committees,* which consist of members of both houses of Congress. The Speaker is officially elected by the full House but actually has already been chosen at the meeting of the majority party. The House election simply confirms the majority party's choice because representatives support their party's candidates for leadership positions.

The members of the majority party also select the *majority leader* of the House at their meeting. The candidate for speaker chosen by the minority party becomes the *minority leader.* Each party also elects an assistant leader called a *whip.* The whips work to persuade representatives of their party to support party policies.

Committees do most of the actual work of the House. Each party has members on these committees. Representatives serve on four types of committees: (1) *standing* (permanent), (2) select, (3) conference, and (4) joint.

Standing committees are the most important type. They consider bills that have been introduced in the House. The House has about 20 standing committees, each of which handles a particular field of legislation. The most powerful of these committees include Appropriations, Judiciary, Rules, and Ways and Means, which deals with tax bills.

Each standing committee is divided into several subcommittees. The House has about 140 subcommittees. The heads of committees and subcommittees are members of the majority party. They are chosen at the party meetings, largely by means of the *seniority principle.* According to this policy, a committee is headed by the majority party representative who has the longest continuous service with the group.

The proportion of Democrats and Republicans on the standing committees reflects that of each party's membership in the House. The Democratic caucus and the Republican conference make the committee assignments, which are then confirmed by the entire House. The Speaker nominates the majority party's members of the Rules Committee. Any bill opposed by the Rules Committee has little chance of reaching the entire House for consideration.

Select committees, also called *special committees,* are temporary groups formed for investigations or other special purposes. Conference and joint committees have senators and representatives. Conference committees resolve differences between versions of certain bills that have passed in both chambers. A joint committee deals with topics that concern both chambers, such as energy problems or economic matters.

The work of the House

Considering legislation is the principal activity of the House. Representatives introduce thousands of bills during each session of Congress, and the House passes hundreds of them. All legislation that deals with taxes or spending must originate in the House.

After a bill has been introduced in the House, the Speaker assigns it to a standing committee. Most bills die because the committee *tables* them—that is, lays them aside. Other bills are studied, released by the standing committee, and placed on a *legislative calendar* for consideration by the entire House. House leaders and the Rules Committee bring some bills out of calendar order to give them immediate consideration. A bill dies if Congress does not pass it before adjourning.

Most bills approved by the House are passed without debate. The House approves them under a *unanimous consent agreement,* a method of speeding legislative action. A bill that arouses disagreement among many representatives is likely to be debated. Under House rules, a representative may speak about a bill for one hour. However, representatives seldom get that much time. In most cases, the Rules Committee sets the amount of time for debate and divides it between the supporters and opponents of the legislation.

Both houses of Congress must pass a bill in identical form for it to become law. A conference committee works out any differences between the House and Senate versions of many major bills. This committee then submits its version to each house for approval.

Bills passed by Congress are sent to the President. The President may sign a bill—and thus make it law—or veto it. If the President fails to act on a bill for 10 days—not including Sundays—while Congress is in session, it becomes law. A bill that reaches the President fewer than 10 days—not including Sundays—before Congress adjourns must be signed to become law. A vetoed bill is returned to Congress. If at least two-thirds of the members present in each house vote to *override* (reverse) the veto, the bill becomes law.

Other powers and duties of the House include *impeaching* U.S. government officials and, under extraordinary conditions, electing the President. Impeachment is a charge of misconduct in office. The Senate conducts a trial to decide if the impeached official is guilty. The House elects the President if no candidate receives a majority of the votes in the *Electoral College.* The Electoral College is a group of officials chosen by the voters to elect the President and Vice President.

Lower houses in other countries

About half of all nations have a two-house legislature. The names of the lower houses include *Chamber of Deputies, House of Commons,* and *National Assembly.* Most lower houses have representation according to population. France, Great Britain, Italy, and West Germany have fewer people than the United States but have larger lower chambers. The lower chamber of most legislatures has more power than the upper chamber.

Members of lower chambers serve terms that range from two to six years. The members of the U.S. House of Representatives receive a higher salary and more benefits than those of any other lower chamber.

Kenneth Janda

Related articles in *World Book.* See the *Government* section of the articles on each country mentioned, such as **Australia** (Government). See also the *Legislature* section of each state article, such as **Ohio** (Legislature). Other related articles include:

Apportionment	Impeachment	Un-American
Congress of the	Senate	Activities
United States	Speaker	Committee
Constitution of the	State government	United States,
United States	(Legislative	Government
Gerrymander	branch)	of the
House of Commons		

Additional resources

Fenno, Richard F., Jr. *Home Style: House Members in Their Districts.* Little, Brown, 1978.
Galloway, George B. *History of the House of Representatives.* 2nd ed. Harper, 1976.
Porter, David L. *The Seventy-Sixth Congress and World War II, 1939-1940.* Univ. of Missouri Press, 1979. Case-study approach for a view of how the House operates.

House plant. See Gardening (Kinds of indoor gardens; Cultivating an indoor garden).

House sparrow. See Sparrow.

Houseboat is any kind of floating home. In the United States and Canada, houseboats are used mainly for pleasure, although some people use them as homes. People may own or rent houseboats on lakes and rivers.

Houseboats vary in length from 24 to 32 feet (7.3 to 9.8 meters), but some are more than 50 feet (15 meters) long. The hull can be made of several materials, including plywood, fiber-glassed plywood, aluminum, steel, or

© Tom Myers

Modern houseboats enable families to live on the water permanently or while vacationing on lakes and rivers.

a combination of aluminum and steel. Most houseboats are small and simply furnished. But some have several rooms, with all the conveniences of the modern home, including a stove, refrigerator, running water, hot-water heater, and electric lights.

Most houseboats must be towed from place to place.

But many modern houseboats are designed to remain in the water all year. A houseboat may have retractable wheels, and also serve as a house trailer. Many houseboats have engines. They have a maximum speed of about 12 miles (19 kilometers) an hour.

In other regions of the world, houseboats provide homes for many persons. In parts of China, thousands of people live on river boats all their lives. They buy their supplies from floating stores. During World War II, houseboats were used at navy bases in the Pacific Islands.   Robert H. Burgess

See also **Asia** (picture: Floating homes); **Sampan.**

Housefly. See Fly.

Houseleek, also called *live-forever,* is a group of succulent plants related to the sedums. Their fleshy leaves tend to form thick rosettes. Their star-shaped flowers grow on stems up to 1 foot (30 centimeters) tall and are greenish-white, rose, yellow, or purple. The *common houseleek* grows wild on Alpine rocks. This plant also thrives around houses throughout Europe, where it is used as a cover for walls and roofs.

The cut or bruised leaves of the houseleek are said to relieve the pain of burns and bee stings. People once thought that the houseleek protected against lightning, and called it *thunder plant.*

WORLD BOOK illustration by Christabel King
Houseleek

Scientific classification.
Houseleeks belong to the orpine family, Crassulaceae. The common plant is *Sempervivum tectorum.*

Harold Norman Moldenke

Housing includes any kind of building that provides shelter for people. In a broader sense, it includes problems of city planning, and community services that provide good living conditions.

Safe, sanitary, comfortable dwellings are called *standard housing.* Housing that has proper heating and ventilation helps people stay in good health. Good housing provides enough space for every member of the family to have some privacy and freedom. Standard housing includes hot and cold running water and a well-planned sewage disposal system. It also provides electric light at night and lets in plenty of sunlight by day.

Poorly constructed, run-down, unsanitary, or overcrowded dwellings are called *substandard housing.* Using this definition, most of the world's people live in substandard housing. Many people in Europe's less industrialized countries are badly housed. Throughout Asia, Africa, and Latin America, millions live in crude dwellings that barely provide shelter. The quality of housing in the United States has been improving steadily. Yet, numerous U.S. households today have substandard dwellings. A *household* is made up of all the people living in one housing unit.

A neighborhood with many substandard buildings is called a slum. The older, central areas of cities often

© Brent Jones

Substandard housing. Millions of people throughout the world live in run-down, unsanitary, or overcrowded dwellings.

deteriorate and become slums. Most occupants of slums have low incomes, and several families may live in one dwelling unit. As a neighborhood begins to decline, many of its residents who can afford to move to better areas do so. Their old homes may be taken over by persons moving into the city who cannot afford better housing. Most slums have high rates of illness, disease, and crime. Slums also have inferior community services, including poor schools, inadequate police and fire protection, infrequent garbage collection, and too few parks and playgrounds. Some financial institutions refuse to make mortgage or home-improvement loans in neighborhoods they consider to be declining. This practice is called *redlining.* The term comes from the practice of some financial institutions of outlining such areas in red on maps. Redlining may speed the development of slums by preventing the purchase or repair of houses in such neighborhoods. During the 1970's, several cities and states passed laws designed to discourage redlining.

Prejudice and discrimination prevent many members of minority groups from having adequate housing. In many Western countries, nonwhites, Jews, and immigrants have been forced to live in slums or segregated areas known as *ghettos.* Increasingly, legislation has been used to try to eliminate such conditions and to make good housing available to all.

Kinds of housing

The people of the United States live in more than 80 million housing units. These include houses, apartment buildings, hotels, motels, and *mobile homes* (trailers). An average of three persons live in each unit. Permanent housing lasts 50 to 75 years, or even longer. Most dwellings in the United States are permanent buildings made of lumber, brick, or concrete. Mobile homes can be

moved from place to place, but they are now usually designed for year-round living at one location.

About 70 per cent of the households in the United States live in *single-family homes.* About 15 per cent live in buildings of two to four apartments, or in commercial buildings that include apartments. About 15 per cent of America's households also live in *apartment buildings* with five or more apartments. Cities have more apartment buildings than do small towns and suburban areas, which have mostly single-family homes.

Baltimore, Philadelphia, and some other cities have many *row houses.* Most row houses, sometimes called *town houses,* are a series of single-family houses. At least one common wall connects each house with the houses next to it. A *duplex* is a building with two apartments, either side by side or one above the other.

Private housing

Home ownership is the goal of many Americans. In the early 1980's, about two-thirds of the nation's households owned their own homes. Most home buyers make a down payment on part of the purchase price and borrow the rest of the money.

Unlike most other countries, the United States provides an important incentive to encourage people to become the owners of their homes. It does this by allowing homeowners to deduct the interest they pay on their mortgage when determining their taxable income. This allowance is a significant form of government subsidy to homeowners. In fact, this subsidy is significantly greater than the U.S. government's combined subsidy to all public and assisted housing for lower income groups. There has been a great need for housing since World War II ended in 1945. Large-scale *speculative builders* have constructed many huge housing developments on a "mass-production" basis. These builders buy land and then build and sell homes on it. Most of these homes are built to suit what is regarded as the average family's desires. *Custom-built* homes (homes built according to the owner's plan) are built by *contract builders* on the owner's land.

Private housing projects are groups of buildings erected at the same time for several hundred or several

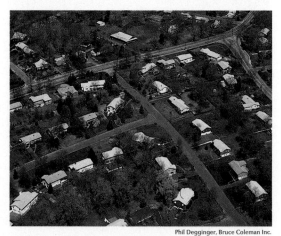

Phil Degginger, Bruce Coleman Inc.

Single-family homes like these provide housing for about 70 per cent of the households of the United States.

© Carl Purcell

Row houses, also called *town houses,* provide comfortable housing for many urban families. A number of such developments have common areas that may be used by all residents.

thousand families. A housing project may have a group of small houses built much alike to save costs, a group of row houses or apartment buildings, or a mix of all three.

Local governments often encourage large insurance companies or other institutions to build communities of homes and apartments. Some cities and states grant such companies special tax reductions on the property. Or they may clear the land to rid it of slums and then sell it to a private developer.

Fresh Meadows in New York City, built by the New York Life Insurance Company, is an example of a private housing project. Fresh Meadows covers 174 acres (70 hectares) and houses 11,000 persons in more than 3,000 apartments. The apartments range in size from three to six rooms. Two 13-story buildings have a total of 600 apartments, and the other units are in 137 garden-apartment buildings. These units are two or three stories high, grouped around grassy lawns, with trees, flowers, and shrubbery, and a recreation area.

Suburban developments. Most housing erected by individuals or private contractors is built on vacant land on the outskirts of cities and towns. Vacant land generally costs less in outlying areas, and there are no buildings that must be destroyed before construction can begin. Most of these new dwellings are one-family houses on lots of up to $\frac{1}{2}$ acre (0.2 hectare), and are bought by the families who move into them.

Every year, thousands of families move into newly built suburban homes. Entire new communities have been built with shops, motion-picture theaters, schools, churches, and parks. Many big city stores have branches in shopping centers in these communities.

New towns. In some cases, the growth of cities has taken the form of developments called *new towns.* Such planned communities are more complex than are suburban developments. Unlike most residential suburbs, new towns include factories and industries, and many of the residents both work and live in the community.

Cooperative housing. People sometimes form nonprofit corporations to plan, finance, build, and manage the apartment buildings or houses in which they live.

When a cooperative builds or buys an apartment building, individuals buy shares in the corporation. The shares entitle them to occupy apartments, but not to own the units. They share the expense of maintenance, repair, and improvement for the entire building.

Condominium housing resembles cooperative housing, with one important difference. In condominium housing, the occupants each own their own dwelling units, and each has a share in the parts of the building used by all occupants. They share expenses only for those parts and services of the building that all of them use. If one or more occupants fail to meet their financial obligations toward their own units, the other occupants are not affected. In cooperative housing, all shareholders are responsible if some occupants fail to meet their financial obligations.

Farm housing. There are about 3 million farm homes in the United States, and more than half are owned by the families who live in them. Before the 1930's, most farm homes lacked electricity and indoor plumbing. The Rural Electrification Act of 1936 provided for federal loans to private companies, cities, and other groups for building rural power lines (see **Rural Electrification Administration**). By the late 1960's, almost all U.S. farms

E. R. Degginger

Apartment buildings like these high-rises in the Brooklyn borough of New York City are the homes of millions of people. Most tall apartment buildings are located in heavily populated areas, where land is scarce and expensive.

had electricity and telephones, and the majority had indoor plumbing.

Low-income and assisted housing

Many people in the United States cannot afford the rents or mortgage payments for standard housing. Federal, state, and city governments have established programs to provide assistance for low-income families. Most federal housing aid is administered by the Department of Housing and Urban Development (HUD).

Public housing for low-income families has traditionally been provided by city housing *authorities* (organizations). These authorities are established under state laws that also permit their participation in federally aided programs. Most local housing authorities are composed of commissioners appointed by the mayor or the local governing body. The authority determines the need for public housing and then plans, develops, and manages the projects. In many cities, the demand for public housing exceeds the supply.

Public housing may be provided in several ways. The authority may build new housing or buy it from a developer. It may buy existing housing and restore it to good condition. Or it may lease existing housing.

The federal government, through HUD, provides funds for local housing authorities to build and operate public housing. It pays the difference between the cost of the housing and the rents that low-income families can afford. A family pays no more than 30 per cent of its income for rent. The low-rent public housing program was established by the U.S. Housing Act of 1937. Since then, all the states have approved projects under the program. Today, there are about $2\frac{1}{4}$ million public housing units in the United States.

Other housing programs encourage the development of private housing for low-income families. Under one of these programs, HUD provides cash allowances to enable low-income families to rent housing on the private market. Families receive an allowance to make up the difference between what they can afford and the actual cost of housing in their area. There are about $1\frac{1}{4}$ million private housing units receiving rent subsidies from the government.

Under another program, the Federal Housing Administration (FHA) provides mortgage insurance to a nonprofit organization that develops a project. The FHA also insures loans to private groups to provide housing for low- and moderate-income families.

Several federal programs make special provisions for elderly persons with low incomes. These programs include public housing, FHA mortgage insurance, and direct loans for nonprofit rental housing. Some states also have housing programs for the elderly.

Local housing controls

Building codes control the construction of new dwellings. They require that new structures be sturdily built, provide reasonable room sizes, and receive ample light and air. In most U.S. cities, the local government must approve the plans of a new building. The city then issues a building permit.

Housing codes have been adopted by many cities to insure that older housing is maintained in good condition. These codes require housing to have adequate lighting, ventilation, exits, heating, water, toilets, and garbage and waste disposal. The codes require owners to keep housing sanitary, to remove fire hazards, and to keep the building in good repair. Many housing codes limit the number of people that may sleep in one room.

Zoning laws. Many city and other local governments control the types of buildings that can be erected in a given place. The city is divided into residential, commercial, institutional, and industrial areas. Zoning laws assure owners of residential property that nearby vacant land will not be used for industrial or commercial purposes. These laws also prevent housing that may be constructed nearby from being built at a higher density than existing housing. See **Zoning.**

History

During colonial times, most people in the United States lived on farms or in small towns. As late as 1840, only about 8 per cent of the people lived in cities or towns with populations of more than 8,000. Today, about 80 per cent live in urban areas.

The Industrial Revolution, which began in the 1700's, produced much unplanned city development. Thousands of people moved to cities to find work, and builders put up almost any kind of housing to meet the demand. Many businesses, factories, and houses stood side by side on narrow streets. Blocks of tenement houses appeared in large cities of the United States, France, Great Britain, and other industrial countries. The first housing law in the United States was passed by New York City in 1867. The law set minimum ventilation, sanitation, and safety requirements for tenements.

By the 1900's, a world housing shortage existed, chiefly because of the population increase and the concentration of the population in urban areas. The expansion of industry, a shortage of construction workers, and a lack of money for new housing also helped cause the housing shortage.

Housing since 1900. New housing construction fell to inadequate levels during World Wars I and II because builders lacked materials. During the Great Depression of the 1930's, people had little money for building. During the 1960's, more and more families moved from rural areas to cities, causing serious housing shortages in spite of stepped-up housing construction.

The United States had a prosperous period and a building boom in the 1920's. The depression of the 1930's led the government to take an active part in housing. The Public Works Administration (PWA) built 59 projects in 36 cities. The FHA, created under the National Housing Act of 1934, established the *amortized mortgage.* This type of mortgage can be repaid in monthly installments, rather than in a lump sum. The United States Housing Act of 1937 set up a U.S. Housing Authority to help build public housing for low-income families. Federal housing activities were unified under the National Housing Agency in 1942 and, after 1947, under the Housing and Home Finance Agency. The Farmers Home Administration was established in 1946 to provide loans for rural housing.

Housing construction increased rapidly after World War II. Since 1949, private builders have constructed more than a million housing units yearly. The high point came in 1950, when they built almost 2 million new units. In the late 1960's, over half of all the homes in the United States had been built since 1945.

In 1965, the Department of Housing and Urban Development was created as an executive department of the U.S. government. The department seeks to improve urban housing. In April 1968, Congress passed a civil rights bill aimed at eliminating discrimination on the basis of race, color, or religion in the sale or rental of most housing. In June 1968, the Supreme Court of the United States went beyond the 1968 open housing law. The court ruled that a federal law passed in 1866 prohibits all housing discrimination. During the 1960's, many states and cities passed fair housing laws. In spite of these laws, however, most U.S. communities are still largely racially segregated by custom.

Condominiums became increasingly popular in the United States during the 1970's. Many rental apartment buildings were purchased by developers and turned into condominiums. This trend reduced the number of available rental units and led to an increased demand for such units, resulting in higher rents.

During the early 1980's, HUD ordered a stop to construction of new public housing. This action, designed to reduce federal spending and future obligations, worsened the existing shortage of housing for poor people. In the mid-1980's, a lowering of interest rates revived a housing industry troubled by previous high rates of interest. But the lack of government subsidy programs has placed about a third of Americans out of the housing market. Many housing experts believe affordable housing has become a major national need.

Canada. Private citizens build most housing in Canada. The Canada Mortgage and Housing Corporation, a government agency similar to the FHA, insures mortgage loans. Canada built about 3 million new housing units from the mid-1940's to the late 1960's. Since 1960, Canadians have spent from $1\frac{1}{2}$ billion to almost $3 billion a year on new housing.

Other countries. Millions of homes were damaged or destroyed throughout Europe during World War II (1939-1945). Since then, most of the housing built in Europe consists of government-owned, multifamily apartment housing that is rented at low cost. The apartments are generally small by U.S. standards. But they provide all the basics, including hot and cold running water, heat, electricity, and separate rooms for parents and children of each sex. Large numbers of people in almost every class of citizen, from unskilled worker to professional, live in government housing in Europe.

China has about a billion people, most of whom live in eastern China. The soil is fertile there, and so housing competes for space with valuable farm land. Thus, China can provide its people with only the most minimal housing. The typical Chinese family lives in one room the size of a modest American living room. If running water is available, it is most often a single tap providing cold water. Toilets and bathing facilities are shared by many people. In the mid-1980's, the Chinese government began massive new housing programs. But the new housing is still well below American and Western European standards.   Oscar Newman

Related articles in *World Book* include:

Architecture	Building construction	City planning Condominium

Federal Housing Administration	Houseboat	Quonset hut
Federal National Mortgage Association	Housing and Urban Development, Department of	Sanitation Segregation Shelter
Hill, Octavia	Levitt, William J.	Tenement
Homelessness	London (pictures)	Urban renewal
Hotel	Mortgage	Veterans Administration
House	Motel	
	Open housing	

Additional resources

Krissdottir, Morine, and Simon, Joan. *Shielding: People and Shelter.* Oxford, 1977. Focuses on housing in Canada.
McFarland, M. Carter. *Federal Government and Urban Problems: HUD—Successes, Failures, and the Fate of Our Cities.* Westview, 1978.
Newman, Oscar. *Community of Interest.* Doubleday, 1980.
Salins, Peter D. *The Ecology of Housing Destruction: Economic Effects of Public Intervention in the Housing Market.* New York Univ. Press, 1980.
Wright, Gwendolyn. *Building the Dream: A Social History of Housing in America.* Pantheon, 1981.

Housing and Urban Development, Department of (HUD),

is an executive department of the United States government. The department has responsibility for housing and community development programs throughout the nation. The secretary of housing and urban development, a member of the President's Cabinet, heads the department.

Functions. HUD makes grants to state and local governments to help finance community-development and housing programs. These governments determine their communities' needs and plan programs to meet them.

HUD insures home and rental mortgages and loans for home improvement. It directs government programs to help low-income families get decent housing. Under one such program, HUD provides federal funds for local housing authorities to provide public housing. HUD also pays the difference between the cost of maintaining the housing and the rents that low-income families can afford. A family pays no more than 30 per cent of its income for rent. The department makes loans to private sponsors of nonprofit housing for the elderly or handicapped. HUD also makes grants to help troubled cities and urban counties revive their economies and restore deteriorated neighborhoods. The Department of Housing and Urban Development includes the Government National Mortgage Association, which guarantees securities issued by financial institutions and backed by mortgage loans.

Organization. The secretary of housing and urban development is appointed by the President, subject to the approval of the Senate. The secretary directs and supervises all departmental activities. The undersecretary

Secretaries of Housing and Urban Development

Name	Took office	Under President
* Robert C. Weaver	1966	Johnson
* George W. Romney	1969	Nixon
* James T. Lynn	1973	Nixon, Ford
* Carla A. Hills	1975	Ford
* Patricia R. Harris	1977	Carter
Moon Landrieu	1979	Carter
* Samuel R. Pierce, Jr.	1981	Reagan

*Has a separate biography in *World Book.*

Mid Hunt

The Department of Housing and Urban Development directs programs to improve housing and other conditions in communities throughout the United States. The department's headquarters, *right,* are at 451 Seventh Street SW, Washington, DC 20410.

The President

Secretary of housing and urban development

Undersecretary of housing and urban development

Office of International Affairs

Office of Indian and Alaska Native Programs

Office of Small and Disadvantaged Business Utilization

Office of Labor Relations

Deputy undersecretary for field coordination

Deputy undersecretary for intergovernmental relations

Inspector general

Government National Mortgage Association

General counsel

Field office manager

Regional administrator-Regional housing commissioner

Assistant secretary for fair housing and equal opportunity

Assistant secretary for administration

Assistant secretary for community planning and development

Assistant secretary for legislation and congressional relations

Assistant secretary for housing-Federal housing commissioner

Assistant secretary for policy development and research

Assistant secretary for public and Indian housing

Assistant secretary for public affairs

of housing and urban development is the secretary's chief assistant. The undersecretary is assisted by the deputy undersecretary for field coordination and the deputy undersecretary for intergovernmental relations.

The secretary's staff has eight assistant secretaries:

(1) The assistant secretary for housing-federal housing commissioner directs the department's housing functions. He or she oversees aid to the construction and financing of new and substantially rehabilitated housing, and the preservation of existing housing.

(2) The assistant secretary for community planning and development administers the grant programs that help communities plan and finance their growth and development and increase their capacity to govern.

(3) The assistant secretary for policy development and research supervises the department's research activities and the development of its policies and is responsible for experimental housing and technical studies.

(4) The assistant secretary for administration directs the department's budget and administrative affairs.

(5) The assistant secretary for fair housing and equal opportunity supervises HUD's housing and community development activities to promote equal opportunity for all, regardless of race, religion, sex, or national origin.

(6) The assistant secretary for legislation and congressional relations maintains cooperation between the department and Congress and the state legislatures.

(7) The assistant secretary for public and Indian housing directs the department's low-income public housing program. This program provides funds for the development, operation, and modernization of public housing, including such housing for American Indians.

(8) The assistant secretary for public affairs is the main adviser to the secretary and department staff members on matters relating to public information.

History. The federal government took an active part in housing long before the department was created in 1965. The Great Depression of the 1930's caused widespread financial hardship. In 1934, Congress established the Federal Housing Administration to provide mortgage insurance programs. Congress founded the United States Housing Authority in 1937 to help finance public housing for the poor. The two agencies were joined under the National Housing Agency in 1942 and became part of the Housing and Home Finance Agency (HHFA) in 1947. The HHFA eventually included the Federal Housing Administration, the Federal National Mortgage Association, and other agencies.

Urban areas grew at a record rate during the 1950's and 1960's. The growth caused many housing and community problems. Presidents John F. Kennedy and Lyndon B. Johnson urged Congress to create a Cabinet-level department designed to solve such problems. Congress created the Department of Housing and Urban Development in 1965. The HHFA and all of its programs were transferred to HUD, and became the core of the new department. Critically reviewed by the Department of Housing and Urban Development

See also **Federal Housing Administration; Open housing; Urban renewal; Flag** (picture: Flags of the U.S. government); **Government National Mortgage Association.**

Housman, HOWS muhn, **A. E.** (1859-1936), a British poet and scholar, wrote melancholy lyrics about human suffering. His outlook on life was pessimistic, and his poems express the fleeting quality of love and beauty. Housman's verse is simple and direct. He published only two books of verse: *A Shropshire Lad* (1896) and *Last Poems* (1922). After his death, his brother Laurence published *More Poems* (1936), *Collected Poems* (1939), and *Manuscript Poems* (1955).

Alfred Edward Housman was born in Fockbury, England. He was a classical scholar, and he taught Latin at London and Cambridge universities.

William Van O'Connor

Houston, HYOO stuhn, is the largest city in Texas and one of the fastest-growing major cities in the United States. In 1940, Houston ranked 21st in population among U.S. cities. By 1980, it had jumped to 5th.

Houston lies in southeast Texas, about 50 miles (80 kilometers) from the Gulf of Mexico. In spite of its inland location, Houston is one of the world's major seaports. The Houston Ship Channel links it to the Gulf of Mexico and permits ships to sail to and from Houston. Among U.S. port cities, only New York City and New Orleans handle more cargo than does Houston.

Houston is a major industrial city. The region contains rich oil deposits, and the Houston area is the nation's top oil-refining center.

Houston also serves as a center of the United States space program. Space flights are directed from the National Aeronautics and Space Administration's Lyndon B. Johnson Space Center at Houston.

Two real estate promoters, the brothers Augustus C. and John K. Allen, founded Houston in 1836. They named the town for General Samuel Houston, commander of the army that won Texas' independence from Mexico in 1836. Development of the oil and shipping industries in the early 1900's helped bring about Houston's rapid population growth.

Metropolitan Houston

Houston covers 556 square miles (1,440 square kilometers). Most of the city is in Harris County, but parts of it extend into Fort Bend and Montgomery counties. The Houston metropolitan area covers 5,436 square miles (14,079 square kilometers). It includes all of Harris County and four other counties—Fort Bend, Liberty, Montgomery, and Waller. About a fifth of all Texans live in this metropolitan area.

The city. Downtown Houston lies near the center of the city. This busy area includes Houston's biggest office buildings and stores. Texas Commerce Tower, a 75-story skyscraper, is the tallest building in the Southwest.

Facts in brief

Population: *City*—1,595,138. *Metropolitan area*—2,735,766. *Consolidated metropolitan area*—3,101,293.
Area: *City*—556 sq. mi. (1,440 km²). *Metropolitan area*— 5,436 sq. mi. (14,079 km²). *Consolidated metropolitan area*—7,422 sq. mi. (19,223 km²).
Altitude: 41 ft. (12 m) above sea level.
Climate: *Average temperature*—January, 55° F. (13° C); July, 83° F. (28° C). *Average annual precipitation* (rainfall, melted snow, and other forms of moisture)—45 in. (114 cm).
Government: Mayor-council. *Terms*—2 years for the mayor and the 14 council members.
Founded: 1836. Incorporated as a city in 1839.

Houston Chamber of Commerce

The Albert Thomas Convention and Exhibit Center is in Houston's civic center, which also has sports facilities.

Peter W. Gonzalez

The Port of Houston has helped make Houston the largest city in Texas. Houston's skyline rises in the background.

About a dozen downtown buildings make up the Houston Civic Center. They include City Hall and buildings used for conventions, exhibits, and cultural events.

A stream called Buffalo Bayou cuts through Houston from west to east. The stream flows past the northern end of downtown Houston and becomes the Houston Ship Channel about 4 miles (6 kilometers) farther east. The Turning Basin is at the western end of the ship channel. Large ships can turn around in the Turning Basin.

Several universities and the Texas Medical Center are located south of the downtown area. The Astrodomain complex lies farther south. The complex includes the famous Astrodome—the world's first baseball and football stadium with a roof—the Astrohall convention center, and Astroworld and Waterworld amusement parks. The Lyndon B. Johnson Space Center is at the southeastern end of Houston.

Residential areas spread out in all directions from downtown Houston. Most of the residential units in Houston are single-family homes. However, since the mid-1900's, a large number of town houses and high-rise apartment buildings have been built in several parts of the city. Houston, like other cities, has slums. These run-down areas present a sharp contrast to the many clean, modern residential areas of Houston and its suburbs.

The metropolitan area of Houston includes dozens of communities, each with its own government. Ten of these communities lie entirely within the city. They are Bellaire, Bunker Hill, Hedwig Village, Hilshire Village, Humble, Hunters Creek Village, Piney Point Village, Southside Place, Spring Valley, and West University Place. Large suburban communities outside Houston include Baytown, Deer Park, La Porte, Missouri City, and Pasadena. The metropolitan areas of Houston, Brazoria,

and Galveston-Texas City, Tex., form the Houston-Galveston-Brazoria Consolidated Metropolitan Area.

People

About 60 per cent of Houston's people are white, and about 30 per cent are black. Hispanics make up 16 per cent of the city's population. Most of these people of Latin-American descent are whites. Others are blacks or people of mixed ancestry. Houston's population also includes people of English, German, Irish, French, or Italian ancestry.

In Houston, as elsewhere, poverty is widespread among members of minority groups. Many of the city's blacks and Hispanics face such problems as unemployment and poor housing. Many of them live in slums near the east end of downtown Houston.

Economy

Industry. More than 4,800 manufacturing firms operate in the Houston metropolitan area. These manufacturing firms employ about 12 per cent of all the nonagricultural workers in the area.

Symbols of Houston. The white star on the blue flag of Houston, *left,* represents the state of Texas. Both the flag and the city seal, *right,* bear the city and state names, a locomotive that stands for progress, and a plow that represents agriculture.

The production of chemicals—especially *petrochemicals*—and oil refining rank as Houston's chief industries. Petrochemicals are chemicals made from crude oil or from natural gas. Petrochemicals produced in the Houston area include benzene, ethylene, and propylene. The Houston area leads the United States in petrochemical production. About 30 major oil companies have headquarters in Houston. The Houston and Southeast Texas Gulf Coast area is the largest oil-refining center in the United States. The area is also an important source of natural gas.

Houston is also the nation's leading manufacturer of fertilizers, insecticides, and oil field equipment. Other important industries in the Houston area process food and manufacture electrical machinery, paper and paper products, scientific instruments, and transportation equipment.

Trade and shipping. Houston is the Southwest's leading trade center. Wholesale and retail trade employ about a fourth of all the nonagricultural workers in the Houston area. The Port of Houston handles about 80 million short tons (73 million metric tons) of cargo a year. It employs hundreds of dockworkers and helps make Houston an industrial center. Many firms built factories in this area because the port provides easy, and relatively inexpensive, transportation for raw materials and finished products.

Transportation. Houston Intercontinental Airport, in the northern part of the city, handles flights to about 100 U.S. and foreign cities. A smaller field, the William P. Hobby Airport, lies about 10 miles (16 kilometers) southeast of downtown Houston. Passenger trains, 5 rail freight lines, and about 50 truck lines serve Houston. Freeways form loops around downtown Houston and link the city with its suburbs.

Communication. Eight television stations and more than 40 radio stations serve Houston and its surrounding area. The city has two general daily newspapers, the *Chronicle* and the *Post.*

Education

Houston's public school system has about 230 schools with a total of more than 187,000 students. Approximately 30,000 students attend about 100 private and church-supported schools in Houston.

Universities in the city include Houston Baptist University, Rice University, Texas Southern University, the University of Houston, and the University of St. Thomas. Houston's Texas Medical Center includes the Baylor College of Medicine, the Texas Woman's University College of Nursing, and the University of Texas Health Science Center. The Health Science Center has dental, medical, public health, and other units.

The Houston Public Library system consists of the

Houston

Houston lies in southeastern Texas. The map at the right shows the city (outlined in red) and points of interest in the area. The map below shows Houston and its surrounding area.

Park | Major road
City boundary | Other road
County boundary | Point of interest

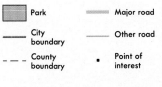

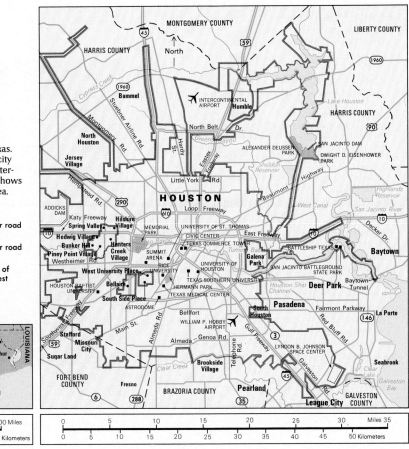

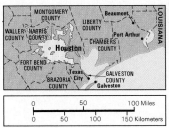

WORLD BOOK map

main library and about 30 branch libraries. The system owns about 3 million volumes.

Cultural life

The arts. The Houston Symphony performs in the Civic Center's Jesse H. Jones Hall for the Performing Arts. During the summer, the symphony gives concerts at the Miller Outdoor Theatre in Hermann Park. The Houston Grand Opera and the Houston Ballet perform in the Wortham Center. A professional acting company performs in Alley Theatre at the Civic Center. This acting company is nationally famous.

Museums. The Houston Museum of Fine Arts owns a large collection that includes works from ancient Egypt and Greece, as well as American and European paintings and sculpture. Houston's Contemporary Arts Museum exhibits works by modern artists. The city's Museum of Natural Science includes the Burke Baker Planetarium.

Recreation

Parks. Houston has about 300 parks. Hermann Park includes the Houston Zoological Gardens and the Municipal Rose Garden. Sam Houston Park features restored and reconstructed buildings from the mid-1800's to the early 1900's. Memorial Park has nature trails, bridle paths, picnic areas, and an arboretum.

Sports. The Houston Astros of the National League play baseball indoors in the Astrodome. The Houston Oilers of the National Football League also play their home games there. The Houston Rockets of the National Basketball Association play their home games in the Summit, a sports arena near downtown Houston.

Other interesting places to visit include:

Lyndon B. Johnson Space Center is the headquarters of all manned U.S. space flights. Workers there design spacecraft, train astronauts, and direct flights. Visitors can see exhibits and films on United States space programs.

San Jacinto Battleground State Park, about 22 miles (35 kilometers) east of downtown Houston, recalls the historic battle in which Texas won independence from Mexico. It includes the San Jacinto Museum of History and the San Jacinto Monument.

Houston Livestock Show and Rodeo attracts many visitors to the Astrodome and Astrohall. It is held every February.

Government

Houston has a mayor-council government. The voters elect the mayor and 14 council members to two-year terms. The mayor appoints all city department heads except the city controller. The city controller is elected. The mayor presides over city council meetings. The city gets most of its revenue from property and sales taxes. Houston is the seat of Harris County.

A Texas annexation law has helped Houston keep taxes relatively low for a city of its size. This law allows large cities to annex nearby communities that are not municipalities. Such annexations have given Houston new sources of property tax revenue.

History

Early settlement. Before white settlers arrived, Karankawa Indians lived along the Gulf Coast near what is now Houston. Two brothers, Augustus C. and John K. Allen, founded Houston in 1836. Houston served as the

capital of the Republic of Texas from 1837 to 1839. It was incorporated as a city in 1839.

Commercial growth. Houston's role as the capital of Texas helped the city grow. But in 1839, Austin became the capital of Texas. That same year, a yellow fever epidemic killed about 10 per cent of Houston's population.

Citizens working to revive Houston's growth established the Port of Houston on Buffalo Bayou in 1841. Buffalo Bayou was too narrow and shallow for oceangoing ships. But barges and small steamboats carried cargo on the stream between Houston and the ocean port of Galveston. Cotton and other products from nearby farmland came to Houston for shipment. By 1850, Houston had 2,396 people. Railroads built during the 1850's linked it with other parts of Texas.

A fire destroyed much of Houston in 1859. The Civil War (1861-1865) slowed trade activity, and another yellow fever epidemic struck the city in 1867. In spite of these difficulties, Houston's population rose to 9,332 by 1870. During the late 1800's, workers began building the Houston Ship Channel by widening and deepening Buffalo Bayou. The expansion of rail and water transportation brought more trade to Houston and helped the population reach 44,633 by 1900.

The 1900's. During the early 1900's, the federal government helped finance projects to further enlarge the Houston Ship Channel. Houston became an ocean port in 1914, when workers completed a deepwater harbor and the Turning Basin within the city. At about the same time, major oil discoveries in southeast Texas led sev-

William Plaster

Houston Sports Association

The Houston Astrodome was the first baseball and football stadium to be completely enclosed by a roof. At its highest point, the dome is 208 feet (63 meters) above the stadium floor. Spectators watch games in air-conditioned comfort.

eral oil companies to build refineries in the Houston area. World War I (1914-1918) created a large market for Houston's petroleum products. The industrial and shipping boom caused by the war helped Houston's population jump to 138,276 by 1920. By 1930, Houston—with 292,352 people—had become the largest city in Texas.

World War II (1939-1945) increased the demand for Houston's petroleum products. Rapid industrial expansion after the war, especially of the petrochemical industry, produced many jobs and brought thousands of new residents to Houston. The city's population soared from 384,514 in 1940 to 938,219 in 1960. During this period, Houston jumped from 21st to 7th in population among U.S. cities.

The Manned Spacecraft Center set up temporary offices in and near Houston in 1962. The center established its permanent quarters in the Clear Lake City area near Houston in 1964. In 1969, scientists and engineers at the center directed the first landing of astronauts on the moon. The center was renamed the Lyndon B. Johnson Space Center in 1973 following the former President's death.

Recent developments. During the 1970's, Houston continued its growth in industry, trade, and population. More than 200 corporations moved their headquarters to the city or established divisions or subdivisions there. Between 1970 and 1980, the city's population increased from 1,233,535 to 1,595,138. Its growth rate of 29 per cent was one of the highest in the nation. In 1977, Houston annexed Clear Lake City, which lies next to the Lyndon B. Johnson Space Center. The 1980 U.S. Census reported that Houston had become the nation's fifth largest city in population.

Growth brought problems, as well as prosperity, to Houston. Like many big cities, Houston has slums, traffic jams, and poor roads. The city also lacks sewage treatment facilities. Houston's rapid growth led to increased air and water pollution, particularly from industries along the Houston Ship Channel. But during the late 1960's and early 1970's, city officials introduced programs that significantly reduced the pollution, especially water pollution. Until the late 1970's, Houston did not have adequate public transportation. In 1979, the Metropolitan Transit Authority was created to provide public transportation throughout the area.

Between 1970 and 1980, the number of housing units in the Houston area increased by about 70 per cent. Most of the residential growth occurred in Houston's suburbs. Also, a construction boom took place in downtown Houston, and the office space in the downtown area nearly tripled.   Kuyk Logan

See also **Johnson Space Center; Texas** (pictures).

Houston, HYOO stuhn, **Samuel** (1793-1863), played a leading part in Texas' fight for independence from Mexico. He later served as president of the Republic of Texas and, after Texas joined the Union, as United States senator and governor of the state.

Houston was born in Virginia. His family took him to Tennessee when he was 13. They lived in a frontier settlement, and Houston worked as a clerk in a trader's store. When he was about 15, he ran away from home. He lived with the Cherokee Indians in eastern Tennessee, and was adopted into the tribe.

After nearly three years with the Indians, Houston re-

turned to the white settlements and opened a country school. He enlisted to serve in Andrew Jackson's army in the war against the Creek Indians, and was severely wounded in battle.

Houston resigned from the United States Army in 1818. He then studied law, and began to practice in Lebanon, Tenn. Shortly after beginning his law practice, he was elected district attorney for the Nashville district. In 1823, he was elected to Congress. He was well liked there, though he made few speeches. Four years later, he became governor of Tennessee.

Visual Instr. Bur., Univ. of Tex.

Samuel Houston

In 1829, Houston's wife left him, and he resigned as governor. He moved west to Texas to become an Indian trader. Texas was then a part of Mexico, but the Americans who settled there did not get along with the Mexican government. Houston became one of their leaders. In 1836, he organized a Texas army and became its commander in chief.

Houston led his troops in a series of battles against the forces of the Mexican general Antonio de Santa Anna. Houston won his greatest victory in the Battle of San Jacinto in April 1836. He captured Santa Anna, and the Mexican commander recognized the independence of Texas. In October, Houston was elected the first president of the new Republic of Texas. He served as president until 1838, and served again from 1841 to 1844.

Houston worked to have Texas admitted to the United States. He succeeded in 1845, and from 1846 to 1859 he served as United States senator from Texas. He disagreed with the other Southern statesmen in the disputes leading to the Civil War. Houston firmly opposed a break in the Union. In 1859, he ran for governor of Texas on an antisecession platform, and won. But, in 1861, Texas voted to secede. Houston refused to take Texas out of the Union, and Confederates removed him from the governorship. Houston then retired to private life. He died in Huntsville, Tex. Houston represents Texas in Statuary Hall in Washington, D.C. The city of Houston is named in his honor. A fort in San Antonio, Tex., also bears his name.   W. B. Hesseltine

See also **San Jacinto, Battle of.**

Additional resources

Braider, Donald. *Solitary Star: A Biography of Sam Houston.* Putnam, 1974.
Friend, Llerena B. *Sam Houston: The Great Designer.* Univ. of Texas Press, 1969. First published in 1954.
Fritz, Jean. *Make Way for Sam Houston.* Putnam, 1986. For younger readers.

Hovenweep National Monument, in Utah and Colorado, preserves the ruins of six Anasazi Indian villages. The ruins are noted for their square, oval, circular, and D-shaped towers. The monument was established in 1923. *Hovenweep* is a Ute Indian word that means "deserted valley." For area, see **National Park System** (table: National monuments).

Critically reviewed by the National Park Service

Hovercraft. See Air cushion vehicle.

Hovhaness, *HOHV uh nehs,* **Alan** (1911-   ), is an American composer. He became known for works that reflect his Armenian ancestry and his interest in Oriental music. Hovhaness has composed more than 200 works. Most of them are short, lasting less than 20 minutes. He has written about 35 symphonies and more than 15 concertos. He also has composed chamber music, vocal music, and music for solo piano. Hovhaness' music is noted for its harmonic richness, rhythmic delicacy, and skillful use of instrumental color.

Hovhaness incorporated traditional Armenian songs and dance music in *Armenian Rhapsody No. 1* (1944) and other compositions. He gave several of his symphonies Armenian names, such as *Etchmiadzin* for Symphony No. 21 (1970). His interest in the music of India appears in *Varuna* (1973), a string trio; and *Shambala* (1967), a concerto for violin, sitar, and orchestra. The influence of Japanese music can be heard in *Fantasy on Japanese Woodprints* (1965) for xylophone and orchestra. He used taped sounds of the humpback whale in *And God Created Great Whales* (1970) for orchestra. Hovhaness was born in Somerville, Mass. His full name is Alan Hovhaness Chakmakjian.   Mary Vinquist

Howard, Bronson Crocker (1842-1908), was sometimes called the dean of the American drama. He was the first professional playwright who was neither a theater manager nor an actor. He was also the first American dramatist to make a fortune from his plays.

Most of Howard's 18 plays deal with life in America and social problems of the day. Howard's best-known works include *Saratoga* (1870), *The Banker's Daughter* (1878), *Young Mrs. Winthrop* (1882), *The Henrietta* (1887), and *Shenandoah* (1889). His *The Autobiography of a Play* (1914) explains his principles of dramatic construction. Howard was born in Detroit. He worked as a journalist in Detroit and New York City before becoming a playwright.   Richard Moody

Howard, Catherine. See Henry (VIII) of England.

Howard, Henry. See Surrey, Earl of.

Howard, John (1726?-1790), a British prison reformer, was apprenticed to a London grocer as a young man and inherited a fortune at the age of 25. He built model cottages for his workers, but did not begin his major work until his appointment as High Sheriff of Bedfordshire in 1773. In this job, shocked by what he found in prisons, he began a monumental study called *The State of the Prisons in England and Wales* (1777). It led Parliament to correct many abuses.

To keep his study up-to-date, Howard visited every prison in the country four times. He also traveled throughout Europe visiting prisons and plague hospitals, measuring rooms, inspecting kitchens, and talking with inmates. He died while on a tour of military hospitals in Russia.

Howard spent his entire fortune on his remarkably thorough work. He refused to be sidetracked, and forced reforms by the objectivity of his evidence. He refused personal glory for his work. He was born in London.

The John Howard Association, a U.S. prison-reform group founded in 1901, was named after him. It works to improve prison conditions and help prisoners and ex-convicts. A similar prison-reform group in Great Britain is called the Howard League for Penal Reform.   Alan Keith-Lucas

See also **John Howard Association.**

Howard, Sidney (1891-1939), was a playwright who helped bring social drama to maturity in the United States. He was a master of play construction and characterization. His works show tolerance, a zest for life, and the need for freedom through responsibility.

Howard won fame for *They Knew What They Wanted* (1924), a Pulitzer prizewinning story of how an elderly husband and his young wife come to terms with life. His strongest play, *The Silver Cord* (1926), is a Freudian drama about a mother's excessive love for her son. *Alien Corn* (1933) is the story of an artist in a hostile community. *Yellow Jack* (1934) describes the battle against yellow fever. *Dodsworth* (1934) is based on Sinclair Lewis' satiric novel of American business. Howard was born in Oakland, Calif.   Thomas A. Erhard

Howard University, in Washington, D.C., is the largest predominantly black university in the United States. It is a private, coeducational institution. The university is made up of 17 schools and colleges and 12 research centers and institutes. It grants bachelor's, master's, and doctor's degrees, and offers professional degrees in such areas as law, medicine, dentistry, religion, engineering, architecture, and social work.

The Howard University library holds the finest collection of materials on Afro-American life and history in the United States. The university publishes the *Journal of Negro Education* and the *Journal of Religious Thought.* Special facilities include a commercial radio station, a public television station, and the Howard University Press, all of which are involved in training students. Howard also has one of the few laser chemistry laboratories in the eastern United States. The university was founded in 1867 to educate newly freed slaves and their descendants. For enrollment, see **Universities and colleges** (table).   Critically reviewed by Howard University

Howe is the family name of two brothers who fought for Great Britain in the American Revolutionary War.

Richard Howe (1726-1799), Earl Howe, was a famous naval officer. He joined the British Navy at the age of 14 and rose steadily in rank. At the start of the Revolutionary War, he was made vice admiral. In 1776, he took command of the British fleet in America.

At the end of the war, Howe became First Lord of the Admiralty. When England and France went to war in 1793, he took command of the Channel Fleet. The next year, he won the victory known as "the glorious first of June," and King George III made him a Knight of the Garter. Howe was promoted to the rank of Admiral of the Fleet in 1796. He was born in London.

William Howe (1729-1814), Viscount Howe, the younger brother of Richard Howe, saw his first military service in Flanders at the age of 17. During the French and Indian War, he fought at the siege and capture of Louisbourg, and was one of General James Wolfe's officers in the attack on Quebec (see **Quebec, Battle of**). Three years before the Revolutionary War began, he was promoted to the rank of major general. In May 1775, Howe joined General Thomas Gage in Boston. He led the British in the Battle of Bunker Hill, and in October 1775, succeeded Gage as commander of the British army in America. He won the battles of Long Island,

White Plains, and Brandywine, and occupied Philadelphia. But he did not accomplish the defeat of the American cause, and in 1778 was succeeded by Sir Henry Clinton. Howe was knighted in 1776. He was promoted to general in 1793.   W. B. Willcox

See also **Revolutionary War in America.**

Howe is the family name of two American social reformers, husband and wife.

Samuel Gridley Howe (1801-1876) worked in many areas of reform. In 1824, he went to Greece to help that country in its war against the Turks. He served there as a soldier and surgeon, and helped give relief to the wartorn people. He then returned to Boston, and in 1832 became the first director of the New England School for the Education of the Blind (now Perkins School for the Blind), the first such institution in the United States. Howe directed the school until his death on Jan. 9, 1876.

Howe also helped Horace Mann in his work on education, and Dorothea Dix in her work with the mentally ill. He and his wife, Julia Ward Howe, edited *The Commonwealth,* a Free Soil paper. Howe helped rescue fugitive slaves and raised money to keep Kansas a Free Soil state. He served in the federal government both during and after the Civil War. He was born in Boston. See **Abolition movement; Free Soil Party.**

Julia Ward Howe

(1819-1910), a writer, lecturer, and reformer, wrote the words of "The Battle Hymn of the Republic." She introduced the idea of Mother's Day (see **Mother's Day**). She was one of the most famous American women of her time.

Mrs. Howe was born into a prominent New York City family. She married Dr. Samuel Gridley Howe in 1843 and moved to Boston. She wrote poems, plays, and helped Howe edit *The Commonwealth.*

Brown Bros.
Julia Ward Howe

In 1861, after the Civil War started, she visited military camps near Washington, D.C. There she was inspired to write "The Battle Hymn of the Republic" to the tune of "John Brown's Body." It was published in the *Atlantic Monthly* the next spring and became the major war song of the Union forces.

After the war, Mrs. Howe became increasingly interested in reforms. In 1868, she helped organize the New England Woman's Club, and served for many years as its president. She also served as the first president of the New England Woman Suffrage Association. She was interested in world peace and led the American section of the Woman's International Peace Association.

Mrs. Howe became noted as a lecturer and writer on literary and other cultural topics as well as on woman's rights. Her writings include *A Trip to Cuba* (1860), *Sex and Education* (1874), *Modern Society* (1881), *Margaret Fuller* (1883), and *Reminiscences* (1899).   Louis Filler

Additional resources

Clifford, Deborah P. *Mine Eyes Have Seen the Glory: A Biography of Julia Ward Howe.* Little, Brown, 1979.

Richards, Laura E., and Elliott, M. H. *Julia Ward Howe, 1819-1910.* 2 vols. Larlin Corp., 1970. Reprint of 1915 biography by Howe's daughters.

Howe, Elias (1819-1867), an American inventor, constructed a practical sewing machine. He patented it in 1846. After a difficult but successful defense of his patent, he made a fortune.

Howe was born in Spencer, Mass. As a young man, he went to Boston to learn the machinist trade. While apprenticed to a scientific-instrument maker in Cambridge, he overheard a remark that the person who produced a workable sewing machine would make a fortune. In 1845, he finished a machine that sewed 250 stitches a minute, but he failed to find a market for it.

He went to England, and sold British rights to the machine. But he was disillusioned with the treatment he received, and he returned to the United States in 1849. While Howe was in England, others, including Isaac Singer, started manufacturing sewing machines. After a long and determined campaign, Howe established in 1854 his right to collect royalties on all machines manufactured.   Richard D. Humphrey

See also **Sewing machine** (History).

Howe, Gordie (1928-   ), scored more goals and more points than any other player in National Hockey League (NHL) history. In 26 seasons in the NHL, he made a total of 801 goals and 1,850 *points* (goals plus assists) in regular-season play. Howe also holds the NHL records for total assists, games played, seasons played, single-season point-scoring championships, and most valuable player awards.

Howe, a right wing, played for the Detroit Red Wings from 1946 to 1971. He helped lead the Red Wings to a record seven straight first-place finishes from the 1948-1949 season through the 1954-1955 season. Howe won the NHL point-scoring title in 1951, 1952, 1953, 1954, 1957, and 1963. He was named the most valuable player in 1952, 1953, 1957, 1958, 1960, and 1963. From 1973 to 1977, Howe played with the Houston Aeros of the World Hockey Association (WHA). He was named the association's most valuable player in 1974. In 1977, Howe signed a contract with the New England Whalers of the WHA. He remained with the team when it entered the NHL in 1979 as the Hartford Whalers. He retired after the 1979-1980 season. Gordon Howe was born in Floral, Sask.   Herman Weiskopf

Howe, Joseph (1804-1873), was a political leader and newspaper editor in the Canadian colony of Nova Scotia. Largely because of Howe's efforts, Nova Scotia became the first completely self-governing colony in the British Empire.

Howe was born in Halifax, N.S. From 1828 to 1841, he owned and edited the *Novascotian,* a Halifax newspaper that supported economic development and political reform. Howe was a member of the Legislative Assembly of Nova Scotia from 1836 to 1851. In the assembly, he promoted self-government for Nova Scotia. Nova Scotia became self-governing in 1848, and Howe served as premier of the colony from 1860 to 1863.

Howe led an unsuccessful effort to block Nova Scotia's entry into the Dominion of Canada, a union of Canadian colonies formed in 1867. He objected chiefly because the colony's membership was approved by the Nova Scotia legislature without a vote by Nova Scotians.

In 1869, Howe joined the Cabinet of Sir John A. Macdonald, Canada's first prime minister, as president of the Privy Council. Macdonald made him secretary of state for the Canadian provinces later that year. Howe became lieutenant governor of Nova Scotia in 1873.

Judith Fingard

Howells, William Dean (1837-1920), was an American novelist, editor, and critic. He attacked sentimentality and romanticism in American fiction and played an important part in the rise of the realism movement in the United States (see **Realism**).

Howells was born in Martins Ferry, Ohio. In 1861, President Abraham Lincoln appointed him U.S. consul in Venice, Italy. The appointment was a reward for writing the biography *Life of Lincoln* (1860). Howells lived in Venice until 1865 and described his experiences there in his first important work, *Venetian Life* (1866). This book of sketches brought Howells immediate recognition. In 1866, he became a member of the staff of the *Atlantic Monthly* magazine. Howells served as editor of the *Atlantic* from 1871 until he resigned in 1881.

Howells wrote his best novels after he left the *Atlantic*. Each of these novels deals with various issues of the day in an increasingly realistic manner. *A Modern Instance* (1882) concerns the then daring subject of divorce. *The Rise of Silas Lapham* (1885) is generally considered Howells' finest work. It describes the rise of a businessman in a society controlled by families who inherited positions of influence and power. *A Hazard of New Fortunes* (1890) portrays the problems of industrialization and the growth of labor unions.

Howells' influence as an editor and critic was perhaps even greater than as a novelist. As editor of the *Atlantic,* he helped introduce European writers—especially new realists—to American readers. He challenged American writers to choose American subjects, to portray them honestly, and to create characters who used native American speech.

Howells also wrote columns in *Harper's Monthly* called the "Editor's Study" (1886-1892) and the "Editor's Easy Chair" (1900-1920). In these columns, he campaigned for literary realism that examined life with scientific detachment. He helped introduce and support such realistic writers as Stephen Crane, Bret Harte, and Mark Twain. His essays describing his literary standards and ideas were collected in *Criticism and Fiction* (1891) and *My Literary Passions* (1895).   Dean Doner

Additional resources

Alexander, William R. H. *William Dean Howells: The Realist as Humanist.* Burt Franklin, 1981.
Cady, Edwin H. *Road to Realism: The Early Years, 1837-1885, of William Dean Howells.* Syracuse Univ. Press, 1956. *Realist at War: The Mature Years, 1885-1920, of William Dean Howells.* 1958.
Kirk, Clara M. and Rudolf. *William Dean Howells.* Twayne, 1962.
Lynn, Kenneth S. *William Dean Howells: An American Life.* Harcourt, 1971.

Howitzer. See **Artillery** (Kinds of artillery; pictures).
Howler is a large monkey that makes a loud, howling roar. It roars mostly at dawn, and also when two groups of howlers meet or when disturbed by noise or approaching rain. Its roar can be heard as far as 2 miles (3.2 kilometers) away. Howlers live in groups that generally have 15 to 20 members, but a group may have as few as 2 or as many as 45 monkeys. Howlers live in tropical forests from Mexico to Brazil.

Howlers weigh from 12 to 20 pounds (5.4 to 9 kilograms) and grow about 2 feet (61 centimeters) long. Their long, powerful tails may also measure 2 feet. Various species of howlers have black, brown, or reddish fur.

Howlers move slowly through the trees, feeding as they go. They eat leaves, flowers, fruits, and nuts, using their hands to grasp the branches or stems from which they nibble. Howlers often swing by their tails while feeding. They seldom leave the trees. See **Animal** (picture: Animals of the tropical forests).

Scientific classification: Howlers are members of the New World monkey family, Cebidae. They make up the genus *Alouatta.* One common species of howler is *A. palliata.*

John H. Kaufmann and Arleen Kaufmann

Hoxha, *HAW jah,* **Enver** (1908-1985), established a Communist government in Albania in 1944 and ruled the country until his death. He became known for his strong opposition to non-Communist countries. During the 1960's, his government criticized the Soviet Union for its policy of coexistence with non-Communist countries. Albania ended its relations with the Soviet Union and became a political partner of China. In 1978, relations between Albania and China became badly strained after Hoxha's government criticized China for improving its relations with non-Communist countries.

Hoxha was born in Gjirokastër, Albania. He founded the Albanian Communist Party in 1941. During World War II, he fought Italian and German forces in Albania. He led the Communist National Liberation Army, which fought non-Communist forces for control of Albania.

Walter C. Clemens, Jr.

Hoyle, Edmond (1672-1769), was an English teacher of whist, a card game somewhat like bridge. In 1742, he published *A Short Treatise on the Game of Whist, containing the Laws of the Game.* Later, he added rules on other card games and on backgammon and chess. Hoyle's book became so famous that the expression *according to Hoyle* came to mean *according to the rules of the game,* or *in the proper way.*

R. Wayne Schmittberger

Hsi Chiang. See **Xi Jiang.**
Hsi-Ling-Shi. See **Silk** (History).
Hsun-tzu. See **Xunzi**
Hu Yaobang, *hoo yow bahng* (1915-   ), also spelled *Hu Yao-pang,* served as general secretary of the Chinese Communist Party from 1981 to 1987. (The general secretary was called chairman before 1982.) As general secretary, Hu held the highest post in the Communist Party, which controls the government of China. However, Deng Xiaoping was the country's most powerful leader (see **Deng Xiaoping**).

Hu Yaobang was born in Hunan province. He joined the Communist Party in 1933. During the 1940's, Hu served in the political de-

Wide World

Hu Yaobang

partment of China's rebel Communist army and became a friend of Deng. He became head of the Communist Youth League in 1952. He was removed from office during China's Cultural Revolution (1966-1969). In 1973, Hu became an aide to Deng, who had become one of China's top leaders. In 1976, Deng and his associates, including Hu, were stripped of their power. Deng returned to power in 1977 and soon became China's top leader. Deng used his influence to help Hu become chairman of the Communist Party. Hu was removed from office in January 1987, and since then his involvement in the Communist Party has diminished. Demonstrations by Chinese university students for greater freedom of expression had taken place in a number of cities. Conservative Chinese leaders had criticized Hu for his liberal views on freedom of expression. Donald W. Klein

Hua Guofeng, *hwah gwoh fehng* (1918?-   ), also spelled *Hua Kuo-feng,* was chairman of the Chinese Communist Party from 1976 to 1981. He also served as premier, China's top government post, from 1976 to 1980. Hua was one of the country's most powerful leaders until the late 1970's. Then, he lost most of his power and Deng Xiaoping became the most powerful leader in China (see **Deng Xiaoping**). Hua resigned as premier in September 1980. In June 1981, he resigned as Communist Party chairman and became a vice chairman of the Communist Party. In 1982, the post of vice chairman was abolished. Also in 1982, Hua was dropped from the party's Politburo, China's main policymaking body. He then remained only a member of the party's Central Committee.

During the late 1970's, when Hua held power, China continued an earlier trend of improving relations with the United States. In 1979, the two countries established diplomatic ties for the first time.

Hua was born in Shanxi (or Shansi) province. Little is known about his early life. In 1955, he became the Communist Party secretary in the district of Hunan province. From 1958 to 1966, Hua served as one of the vice governors of Hunan. He remained a Hunan official during the Cultural Revolution (1966-1969), in which many Chinese leaders were *purged* (removed from office). In 1975, he became a vice premier of the State Council, the government's top administrative branch, and minister of public security. Donald W. Klein

Hua Kuo-feng. See Hua Guofeng.

Huang He, *hwahng hu,* also spelled *Huang Ho,* is a long river in China. It is sometimes called *China's Sorrow* because of the many floods which brought death and hunger to the people living along its banks. The river is called *Huang He* (Yellow River) because it carries large amounts of soft yellow earth.

The Huang He is China's second longest river. Only the Yangtze is longer. The Huang He runs a course of 2,903 miles (4,672 kilometers) and drains an area of about 400,000 square miles (1,036,000 square kilometers). It rises in Qinghai Province and flows eastward until it empties into the Yellow Sea. The earth carried by the river is deposited in such large amounts at the river's bottom that it raises the bed and causes the river to change its course often. The Huang He cannot be used by ships because the upper part is too swift, while the middle and lower parts are too shallow.

The worst Huang He flood occurred in 1887, when the river overflowed an area of about 50,000 square miles (130,000 square kilometers). Nearly a million people died in this flood. Dikes have been kept up for hundreds of years to lessen the danger, but the river has never been completely controlled. J. E. Spencer

See also **Flood; China** (terrain map).

Huang Ho. See Huang He.

Huaraches. See Mexico (Clothing).

Huascarán. See Andes Mountains (with picture).

Hubble, Edwin Powell (1889-1953), was an American astronomer. His studies of galaxies helped explain the structure, size, and evolution of the universe.

Hubble was the first to demonstrate that the universe contains star systems other than our galaxy, the Milky Way. He identified certain stars in the Andromeda Nebula as being of the same type as some stars in the Milky Way. However, Hubble showed that the stars in Andromeda were beyond the calculated boundaries of our galaxy and that Andromeda was therefore a separate galaxy.

Hubble later determined that all galaxies beyond the Milky Way are moving away from the earth. From this observation, he concluded that the universe is expanding. He also discovered that the galaxies that are farther from the earth recede faster than those that are nearer.

Hubble was born in Marshfield, Mo. He earned a Ph.D. degree from the University of Chicago in 1917. In 1919, he joined the staff of the Mount Wilson Observatory in California, where he did most of his work as an astronomer. C. R. O'Dell

See also **Astronomy** (Measuring distances in space; picture: Edwin Hubble).

Huckleberry is a small, round fruit that grows on a shrub. Huckleberries are black or blue and contain 10 hard seeds. They ripen in late summer and are used in pies and jams. Huckleberry plants grow 2 to 6 feet (0.6 to 1.8 meters) tall and sprout white, red, or reddish-green flowers.

The most common huckleberries are black huckleberries, which grow wild throughout eastern North America. They thrive in partially shaded areas in peaty or sandy soil. Blue huckleberries, the sweet-

WORLD BOOK illustration by Stuart Lafford, Linden Artists Ltd.

Black huckleberry

est type, are found chiefly along the Atlantic Coastal Plain of the United States. They grow in moist, peaty soil. Blue huckleberries are nicknamed tangleberries or dangleberries because of their long, arching stalks. Bear huckleberries, a black variety, grow in wooded areas from North Carolina to Georgia and west to Kentucky. They are eaten by bears and are sometimes called buckberries because deer also feed on them.

Scientific classification. Huckleberries belong to the heath family, Ericaceae. The black huckleberry is *Gaylussacia baccata;* the blue huckleberry, *G. frondosa;* and the bear huckleberry, *G. ursina.* Max E. Austin

Hudson, Henry (? -1611), was an English explorer and sea captain. He made four voyages in an attempt to discover a northern route between Europe and Asia. Hudson never found such a sea passage, but he sailed farther north than any previous explorer. He explored three North American waterways that were later named for him— the Hudson River, Hudson Bay, and Hudson Strait.

Northern voyages. Historians know nothing about Hudson's life except for the period of 1607 to 1611, when he made his four voyages. In 1607, the Muscovy Company, an English trading firm, hired Hudson to find a northern sea route to Asia. European merchants and geographers believed that a ship could reach the Orient by sailing north, northeast, or northwest. They thought such a route would be shorter than any other. The Arctic had not been explored, and people did not know that ice blocked the area around the North Pole.

Hudson set out from England in a ship called the *Hopewell* with his young son, John, and a crew of 10 men. He sailed northeast along the coast of Greenland and reached Spitsbergen. These islands lie only about 700 miles (1,100 kilometers) from the North Pole, and no explorer had sailed so far north before. Huge ice floes forced Hudson to return to England. He told of seeing many whales in the northern waters, and his report led to English and Dutch whaling near Spitsbergen. In 1608, Hudson again tried to find a northern route, but ice again blocked the *Hopewell*.

North American voyages. The Muscovy Company lost interest in further northern exploration, but in 1609, the Dutch East India Company hired Hudson to lead an

New York City Art Commission

Henry Hudson

expedition. The company gave him a ship, the *Half Moon,* and a crew of about 20 men. Hudson again headed northeast, but his crew became unruly because of the cold weather. Hudson changed the ship's course for North America, crossed the Atlantic Ocean, and sailed down the east coast.

Hudson sailed as far south as what is now North Carolina. He then turned north and briefly explored Chesapeake Bay and Delaware Bay. Hudson traveled up what became known as the Hudson River to the site of present-day Albany, N.Y. Holland based its claims to land in North America on Hudson's third voyage.

In 1610, a group of English merchants formed a company that provided Hudson with a ship called the *Discovery.* He crossed the Atlantic and arrived just off the northern coast of Labrador. The *Discovery* then reached a body of rough water, later named Hudson Strait, that led into Hudson Bay. Hudson thought he had at last come to the Pacific Ocean, and he sailed south into what is now James Bay. But he failed to find an outlet at the south end of this bay. Ice forced the men to spend the winter there, and Hudson and his crew suffered severely from cold, hunger, and disease.

In the spring of 1611, Hudson intended to search for a western outlet from James Bay. But the crew mutinied and set Hudson adrift in a small boat with his son, John, and seven loyal crewmen. Hudson and his party were never seen again. The mutineers sailed back to England, and their report gave continued hope that a passage existed between Hudson Bay and the Pacific. England based its claim to the vast Hudson Bay region on Hudson's last voyage. Exploration of the region led to the establishment in 1670 of the Hudson's Bay Company, a fur-trading firm.   John Parker

Additional resources

Asher, George M., ed. *Henry Hudson the Navigator: The Original Documents in Which His Career is Recorded.* Franklin, 1964. Reprint of 1860 ed.
Vail, Philip. *The Magnificent Adventures of Henry Hudson.* Dodd, 1965.

Colored engraving, 1800's (Granger Collection)

Henry Hudson explored North America during the early 1600's. He explored the Chesapeake and Delaware bays in his ship, the *Half Moon.* Then he traveled up what became known as the Hudson River, *above,* to the site of present-day Albany, N.Y.

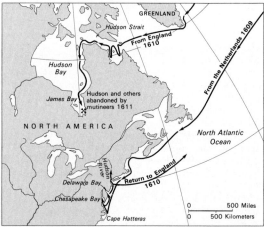

WORLD BOOK map

Hudson's two North American voyages were organized in search of a passage to the Far East. On his last voyage, the crew mutinied and abandoned Hudson, his son, and others in James Bay. Hudson and his party were never found.

Hudson, William Henry (1841-1922), was an English author and naturalist. Hudson grew up in Argentina. Most of his books are reports of personal experiences in bird watching and nature study in the remote regions of South America. Hudson wrote these works in an intimate, semiautobiographical style. Hudson's best-known book is *Green Mansions* (1904), a romantic novel about a mysterious girl who lives in the jungles of South America.

Hudson was born to American parents in Quilmes, Argentina, near Buenos Aires. He settled in England about 1869, and became a British citizen in 1900. Hudson's first book, the novel *The Purple Land* (1885), and his autobiography, *Far Away and Long Ago* (1918), are vivid accounts of life in Argentina. Both helped familiarize European and North American readers with the landscape and history of South America. Avrom Fleishman

Hudson Bay is a vast inland sea in northeast Canada. It covers about 316,500 square miles (819,731 square kilometers), more than three times the combined area of the Great Lakes.

The bay, together with its southern arm, James Bay, is about 1,050 miles (1,690 kilometers) long and 695 miles (1,118 kilometers) wide. It has an average depth of 330 feet (100 meters). Hudson Bay connects with the Atlantic Ocean through the Hudson Strait and with the Arctic Ocean through the Foxe Channel.

The land around the northern shore of the bay is part of a cold, flat, treeless area called a *tundra.* Forests grow to the south, and high, rocky bluffs rise on the east. In the west are flat, wet areas called *bogs.*

Shipping is the only important commercial activity, on Hudson Bay. In most years, the shipping season lasts from mid-July to mid-October. The bay is largely free of ice during this period. Vessels from many nations enter and leave the bay through the Hudson Strait. They carry a variety of cargoes, including beef products and grain. Churchill, Man., a grain-exporting center at the mouth of

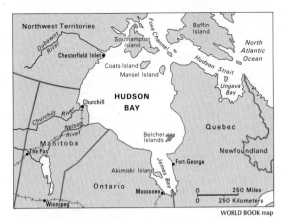
WORLD BOOK map

Location of Hudson Bay

the Churchill River, is the main port and largest community on the bay. The Hudson Bay Railway links Churchill with the cattle and grain regions of western Canada.

Eskimos and Indians were the first people who lived near Hudson Bay. Today, the Eskimos live chiefly in small, widely separated communities in the tundra. Most of the Indians make their homes on the southern end of the bay, near Churchill and James Bay. Many Eskimos and Indians who live in the bay area work in construction or retail trade. Others work for government agencies. Still other Eskimos and Indians fish and hunt for a living.

Hudson Bay was named for the English explorer Henry Hudson, who reached it in 1610. In 1670, one of the earliest and largest fur-trading posts in North America was established on the shores of the bay by the Hudson's Bay Company. This firm had been founded by English merchants, and Great Britain claimed the bay area. In 1811, settlers began to use the bay to reach farmlands in western Canada. In 1870, Britain gave Canada the bay area.

Little development occurred in the bay area until 1971. That year, the province of Quebec began to build a group of hydroelectric stations on La Grande River, which flows into James Bay. Two stations were completed in 1986. These hydroelectric stations were the first part of a long-term development project. Future construction of stations will depend on the demand for energy. J. Peter Johnson, Jr.

See also **Hudson, Henry; Hudson's Bay Company; James Bay.**

Hudson River is one of the most important trade waterways in the United States. At its mouth lies the harbor of New York City. In 1609, Henry Hudson became the first white person to explore the river, and it was named for him. The Hudson is sometimes called the *Rhine of America,* because some sections of its beautiful shores resemble the shores of the Rhine. The Hudson played an important part in U.S. history. For location, see **New York** (physical map).

The Hudson is 306 miles (492 kilometers) long and is the largest river that lies wholly in the state of New York. The river rises in a lake called Tear-of-the-Clouds, 4,322 feet (1,317 meters) above sea level in the Adirondack Mountains. The Hudson flows south near the eastern

R. Vroom, Miller Services
Shipping on the Hudson Bay is the Canadian waterway's only important commercial activity. The dock shown above is in Churchill, Manitoba's chief seaport.

boundary of New York and empties into the Atlantic Ocean at New York City. It passes through some of the state's most thickly settled areas.

In its upper course, the Hudson has many rapids, and the cities along its banks make use of the current for water power. Farther south, the Hudson passes through a farming and industrial area and then enters the colorful Highlands region, which is about 60 miles (97 kilometers) south of Albany. Here the Hudson winds for 16 miles (26 kilometers) through a narrow valley with high, rocky shores of great beauty. The rocks in this area look like the huge castles on the banks of the Rhine. Huge rock cliffs called the *Palisades* lie to the south of the Highlands. The Mohawk River, which ranks as the largest tributary of the Hudson, joins it just north of the city of Troy. South of this junction, the Hudson receives much water from the tides of the Atlantic Ocean.

Large ships can sail up the Hudson to Albany, which is 144 miles (232 kilometers) from the mouth of the river. Small boats can continue to Troy, 6 miles (10 kilometers) beyond Albany. Travelers from Europe come ashore at the huge docks in New York City on the east bank of the mouth of the Hudson. The George Washington Bridge spans the river near its mouth.

In 1524, the Italian sailor Giovanni da Verrazano became the first European to reach the river. The Dutch were the first Europeans to settle in the Hudson River Valley. The excellent harbor at the mouth of the Hudson determined the site of New York City. Many early explorers traveled up the Hudson on their way to Canada. During the Revolutionary War, a huge chain was hung across the river between Constitution Island and Gee's Point to keep the British ships from passing. Robert Fulton ran the first successful steamboat on the Hudson in 1807.   William E. Young

See also **Fulton, Robert; George Washington Bridge; Hudson, Henry; New York** (picture); **Palisades.**

Hudson River School was the name of the first group of American artists to develop a characteristic style of landscape painting. The school flourished from 1825 until the late 1800's. The early artists of this group painted many scenes of the Hudson River Valley in New York. Later artists of the school painted landscapes of various areas of North and South America.

Before the 1800's, most American artists had followed European styles of landscape painting. The Hudson River School paintings differed from the landscapes of peaceful countrysides painted by many Europeans. The American paintings showed the untamed beauty and the grandeur of canyons, rivers, and other natural features. These landscapes reflected the artists' pride in their country and their love of nature.

The Hudson River School first became known in 1825. That year, the landscapes of Thomas Cole gained popularity. The originality and directness of Cole's works impressed many artists, and he became a leader of the Hudson River group. Other artists who helped the school develop included Thomas Doughty and Asher B. Durand. Later artists included Albert Bierstadt, Frederick E. Church, Jasper F. Cropsey, John F. Kensett, and Thomas Moran.   Edward H. Dwight

See also **Bierstadt, Albert; Church, Frederick E.; Cole, Thomas; Painting** (The 1800's [United States painting]).

Hudson River tunnels provide links between Manhattan Island and New Jersey. Manhattan, the heart of New York City, is separated from New Jersey on the west by the broad Hudson River. The tunnels run under the Hudson.

As late as the year 1900, Manhattan was not connected with New Jersey by either bridge or tunnel. A few bridges crossed the narrow Harlem River on the north, connecting Manhattan with the Bronx. Brooklyn Bridge, across the East River, connected the lower end of Manhattan with Long Island. But the thousands of New Jersey people who worked in Manhattan had to cross the Hudson River every day by ferryboat. This was the same method that the Dutch had used nearly 300 years before when they bought Manhattan Island from the Indians. Today, seven tunnels under the Hudson River connect Manhattan with New Jersey. The tunnels are used for rail, automobile, truck, and bus traffic.

The PATH tunnels are four rapid transit tunnels. Two of the tunnels, called the uptown tunnels, run between Morton Street in Manhattan and Jersey City, N.J. They are each about 5,650 feet (1,750 meters) long. Two downtown tunnels extend between the World Trade Center in Manhattan and Jersey City. They are both nearly 5,280 feet (1,609 meters) long. The name *PATH* stands for the *P*ort *A*uthority *T*rans-*H*udson Corporation, which operates the tunnels. PATH is a subsidiary of the Port Authority of New York and New Jersey.

The uptown tunnels are the oldest of the Hudson River tunnels. The first attempt to dig one of them was made in 1874, but the work was stopped before it was finished. In 1902, a lawyer named William G. McAdoo

Oil painting on canvas (about 1840); the Metropolitan Museum of Art, New York City, Gift of Samuel P. Avery, 1895

The Hudson River School was a group of American landscape painters. Thomas Doughty, a leader of the school, painted *A River Glimpse, above,* which shows the Hudson River Valley.

raised money to complete the tunnel and to build a second one so two-way traffic could run under the river. At the time, McAdoo represented the Hudson and Manhattan Railroad Company. He later became secretary of the treasury under President Woodrow Wilson. McAdoo also raised money to build the downtown tunnels. The uptown tunnels were opened to traffic in 1908. The downtown tunnels opened in 1909.

Amtrak's Hudson River Tunnel, which opened in 1910, connects Pennsylvania Station in Manhattan with Newark, N.J. It is used by passenger trains traveling between New York and the South and West. It has two tubes and is 13,400 feet (4,100 meters) long. Amtrak operates the tunnel.

The Holland Tunnel provides a direct link from Canal Street in Manhattan to Jersey City. It has two tubes more than 8,000 feet (2,400 meters) long, with two traffic lanes in each for automobiles, trucks, and buses. The tunnel, which is operated by the Port Authority of New York and New Jersey, was opened to traffic in 1927. The method and principles used in the design and construction of the tunnel still form the basis for building vehicular tunnels throughout the world.

The Lincoln Tunnel, also used by motor vehicles, provides a link between 38th Street in midtown Manhattan and Weehawken, N.J. The Lincoln Tunnel, operated by the Port Authority of New York and New Jersey, is the only three-tube underwater vehicular tunnel in the world. Two of its tubes are over 8,000 feet (2,400 meters) long, and the third is about 7,500 feet (2,290 meters) long.

Each tube has two lanes for vehicular traffic. The center tube, used for eastbound, westbound, or two-way traffic as conditions require, opened in 1937. The north tube, for westbound traffic, opened in 1945. The south tube, used for eastbound traffic, opened in 1957.

Critically reviewed by the Port Authority of New York and New Jersey

See also **New York City** (map).

Hudson's Bay Company is a business firm that became famous for its role in western Canadian history. It was founded in London in 1670 to establish a fur trade in what is now the Hudson Bay region. Today, the Hudson's Bay Company ranks as one of Canada's largest corporations.

Beginnings. A group of English merchants and noblemen founded the Hudson's Bay Company with the help of two French fur traders, Sieur des Groseilliers and Pierre Esprit Radisson. The two traders knew that furs from North America could earn fortunes. After a quarrel with the French colonial government in Quebec over profits and taxes, they had offered their services to Charles II of England.

In 1668, Groseilliers helped direct a trading expedition to the Hudson Bay region. The expedition was so successful that the king gave the Hudson's Bay Company a charter in 1670. The firm received sole trading rights in all lands drained by the streams that flowed into Hudson Bay. Company agents built trading posts and forts along the bay. They traded with the Indians and exchanged such goods as guns, kettles, and knives for beaver pelts. In England, the pelts were made into expensive felt for garments and hats.

Growth and problems. For many years, the company struggled with the French, who also claimed the

Hudson's Bay Company

The Hudson's Bay Company contributed to Canada's settlement. This trading post in Ontario was photographed in 1886.

Hudson Bay region. French forces from Montreal and Quebec captured and destroyed many of the firm's trading posts. In addition, French fur traders began to threaten the company's trade monopoly with the Indians. But the British conquered Canada in 1763, and the company gained almost complete control of the fur trade in the region.

During the late 1770's and 1780's, the North West Company, a newly organized group of independent fur traders, began competing with the Hudson's Bay Company. Because of the growing competition, the Hudson's Bay Company sent expeditions far inland to find new sources of fur. Its explorers established a network of trading posts and transport routes. The Hudson's Bay Company thus helped open Canada to settlement all the way to the Pacific coast.

In 1821, the two rival companies combined under the name Hudson's Bay Company. This company was completely reorganized under the leadership of Sir George Simpson (see **Simpson, Sir George**). It held full land and trading rights in much of western British North America until 1870. That year, the company gave the British government much of the territory granted by its charter. The government, in turn, transferred the land to the newly formed Dominion of Canada. The company received about $1\frac{1}{2}$ million for the land from the Canadian government. It lost certain trading rights but kept large areas of the western plains. The Hudson's Bay Company later sold these lands to settlers.

Recent developments. Today, the Hudson's Bay Company ranks as the world's largest fur-trading firm. But its main business is retail trade. The company owns a chain of department stores in Canada. It also operates a large wholesale enterprise that distributes a variety of merchandise to stores throughout Canada and the United States. John Elgin Foster

See also **Groseilliers, Sieur des; Radisson, Pierre.**

Additional resources

MacKay, Douglas. *The Honourable Company.* Rev. ed. McClelland (Toronto), 1966.
Phillips, Paul C. *The Fur Trade.* Univ. of Oklahoma Press, 1961.
Rich, Edwin E. *Hudson's Bay Company: 1670-1870.* 3 vols. Macmillan, 1961.
Woodcock, George. *The Hudson's Bay Company.* Macmillan, 1970.

Hue. See **Color** (Characteristics of color).

Hue, *hway* (pop. 165,865), is a city in central Vietnam. For the location of Hue, see **Vietnam** (map). Sand dunes and shallow lagoons cut off Hue from the South China Sea. However, the land behind the dunes is flat and cultivated. The city is a center of student and religious life. The University of Hue was founded there in 1957.

Hue was the capital of Vietnam during the rule of the Nguyen dynasty in the 1800's. It continued as the royal capital until 1945. Palaces that were built in the Chinese style during the Nguyen period still stand in the city.

Hue became part of South Vietnam when that nation was formed in 1954. Communist forces seized Hue in 1968 in one of the largest attacks on South Vietnam of the Vietnam War. South Vietnamese and United States troops together recaptured the city less than a month later.

Hue and the rest of South Vietnam came under the control of Communist North Vietnam in 1975. The Communists unified North and South Vietnam into the single nation of Vietnam in 1976. David P. Chandler

Huemul. See **Deer** (Central and South American).

Hufstedler, Shirley Mount (1925-   ), served from 1979 to 1981 as the first United States secretary of education. President Jimmy Carter appointed her to head the United States Department of Education, which develops and coordinates national educational policies and programs. Congress had established the Department of Education in 1979, and it began operating in 1980.

Hufstedler was born in Denver, Colo. She graduated from the University of New Mexico and earned a law degree from the Stanford University School of Law. Hufstedler practiced law in Los Angeles until 1961, when she was appointed to the Superior Court of Los Angeles County. From 1966 to 1968, Hufstedler served as a justice of the California Court of Appeals. In 1968, President Lyndon B. Johnson appointed Hufstedler to the United States Court of Appeals in San Francisco. At that time, Hufstedler was the highest-ranking woman judge in the United States. William J. Eaton

Hugh Capet, *KAY peht* or *ka PEH* (940?-996), became king of France in 987. He founded the Capetian line, which ruled France from 987 to 1328. His election as king by the French nobles marked the end of the struggle between the nobility and the last feeble heirs of the Carolingian line. As king, Hugh had certain powers, but they were more theoretical than real. The only lands he actually ruled over were those he inherited as count of Paris. William C. Bark

See also **Capetian dynasty.**

Hughes, Charles Evans (1862-1948), won recognition as a judge, a statesman, a lawyer, and an investigator. He served as chief justice of the United States from 1930 to 1941. He is often called the greatest chief justice since John Marshall.

While Hughes presided over the Supreme Court, it held many of President Franklin D. Roosevelt's New Deal laws to be unconstitutional. Hughes resisted vigorously when the President tried to "pack"

Harris & Ewing

Charles Evans Hughes

the court, and he is considered the greatest influence in defeating the 1937 court reorganization bill (see **Roosevelt, Franklin Delano** [The Supreme Court]). Hughes also became noted for his opinions that upheld human liberties.

Hughes was born on Apr. 11, 1862, in Glens Falls, N.Y. He graduated from Brown University and from Columbia University Law School. He attracted attention in 1905 when he served as counsel for the New York legislative committees that investigated the gas industry and the insurance business. Hughes's fairness and thoroughness in exposing major scandals led to his election as governor of New York in 1906. He won a second term in 1908. Although political bosses thwarted many of his reforms, Hughes succeeded in establishing two Public Service Commissions and in starting a reorganization of the state government.

Hughes was appointed an associate justice of the Supreme Court of the United States in 1910. He resigned in 1916 to run for the presidency on the Republican ticket. He lost the election by a small margin to President Woodrow Wilson.

Hughes served as secretary of state from 1921 to 1925. He initiated the Dawes Plan to relieve Germany from its crushing war debts after World War I (see **Dawes Plan**). In 1928, he led the American delegation to the Pan American Conference and became a judge of the World Court. Merlo J. Pusey

Hughes, Howard Robard (1905-1976), an American businessman, became known as one of the world's richest people. During the 1930's and 1940's, he gained fame as a motion-picture producer and aviator. Then, in the mid-1950's, Hughes deliberately dropped out of sight. He became a mysterious figure who never appeared in public and even refused to have his photograph taken.

Hughes was born in

Wide World

Howard Hughes

Houston. His father died in 1924, leaving him the Hughes Tool Company, an oil-field equipment firm. The firm became the basis of Hughes's financial empire. He later owned the Hughes Aircraft Company, RKO Pictures Corporation, and a controlling interest in Trans World Airlines.

Hughes led a varied life. He became a Hollywood film producer after his father's death. His most successful movies included *Hell's Angels* (1930), *Scarface* (1932), and *The Outlaw* (1943). Hughes also designed and raced airplanes. He set several speed records, including an around-the-world mark of 3 days 19 hours 14 minutes. In the 1940's, he designed the plane that still holds the record for the largest wingspan of any plane ever built—319 feet 11 inches (97.57 meters). This eight-engine wooden flying boat, nicknamed *Spruce Goose,* had room for 700 passengers. In 1947, Hughes piloted the plane on its only flight. It flew 1 mile (1.6 kilometers) at a height of 70 feet (21 meters). Today, the *Spruce Goose* is on display in Long Beach, Calif.

At the time of Hughes's death, estimates of the value of his estate went as high as $2 billion. But in 1984, the United States Internal Revenue Service and the states of California and Texas valued the estate at $380 million for taxation purposes. California and Texas worked out an agreement to share the inheritance taxes from the Hughes estate. California received $44 million and trust control over land in Los Angeles, and Texas received $50 million. This action paved the way for further distribution of the Hughes fortune.

In 1971, the McGraw-Hill Book Company paid about $750,000 to a writer named Clifford Irving for a manuscript he presented as Hughes's autobiography. Irving claimed to have been working on the manuscript with Hughes, but Hughes denied even knowing Irving. In 1972, Irving and his wife admitted to misrepresenting the manuscript to the publisher. They were fined and given prison sentences.   Bobby H. Johnson

Additional resources

Barlett, Donald L., and Steele, J. B. *Empire: The Life, Legend, and Madness of Howard Hughes.* Norton, 1979.
Drosnin, Michael. *Citizen Hughes.* Holt, 1984.

Hughes, Langston (1902-1967), was an American poet and short-story writer. In his first collection of poetry, *The Weary Blues* (1926), Hughes expressed the despair of blacks over social and economic conditions under which they lived. This despair was relieved by what he then felt was the black's only defense—sharp humor and self-control.

Hughes's later volumes, from *The Dream Keeper* (1932) to *The Panther and the Lash* (1967), reflect the rapidly changing times. His work told of the black's growing demands for social justice, and warned the white: "You're the one/Yes, you're the one/Will have the blues." In spite of his increasing anger, Hughes avoided the violence that marks the work of such later black writers as James Baldwin and LeRoi Jones.

Hughes also wrote plays and autobiographical works. Many of his humorous sketches of black life were collected in *The Best of Simple* (1961).

Hughes was born in Joplin, Mo. He attended Columbia University for a year in 1921 and then held a variety of odd jobs before the publication of his first book. He

received the Spingarn Medal in 1960 (see **Spingarn Medal**).   Elmer W. Borklund

See also **Black Americans** (picture).

Additional resources

Barksdale, Richard K. *Langston Hughes: The Poet and His Critics.* American Library Assn., 1977.
Berry, Faith. *Langston Hughes: Before and Beyond Harlem.* Lawrence Hill, 1983.

Hughes, Ted (1930-   ), is an English poet known for his violent and symbolic nature poems. Hughes was appointed poet laureate of England in 1984.

Hughes's first collection of poetry, *The Hawk in the Rain* (1957), portrays in powerful and descriptive language the beauty and brutality he saw in nature. Hughes's reputation increased after he published a long cycle of lyrics dominated by a menacing bird called Crow. The bird is a composite symbol taken from several mythical and religious traditions. The Crow poems were published in five volumes in 1970 and 1971. The best-known work in the cycle is *Crow: From the Life and Songs of the Crow* (1970). Hughes continued his mythical themes in *Cave Birds* (1975). Hughes's later nature poems, beginning with *Moortown* (1980), carry a note of hope and affirmation absent from his previous work.

Edward James Hughes was born in Mytholmroyd in West Yorkshire. The birds and other animals Hughes observed on the moors near his home strongly influenced the content and imagery of his poetry. Hughes was married to the American poet Sylvia Plath from 1956 until her suicide in 1963.   Elmer W. Borklund

Hughes, Thomas (1822-1896), was an English author. He is best known for his novel *Tom Brown's School Days* (1857), the earliest story about life in a British public school. Hughes based the book on his experiences at Rugby School (see **Rugby School**). His next novel, *Tom Brown at Oxford* (1861), was less successful. He then devoted himself to religious and political writing.

Hughes was born in Berkshire and attended Oxford University. He became a lawyer and served in Parliament. He was active in the Christian Socialist movement and worked to improve conditions among the poor. Hughes sponsored a short-lived settlement for poor English boys in Rugby, Tenn.   Richard J. Dunn

Hugo, Victor Marie (1802-1885), a French author, led the romantic movement in French literature. His writings reveal his love of liberty, his sense of justice, and his sympathy with the suffering of ordinary people. Hugo's *The Hunchback of Notre Dame* and *Les Misérables* rank among the most popular fiction written.

Early life. Hugo was born in Besançon, the son of an officer in the army of Napoleon I. He spent his first 10 years in Corsica, Italy, and Spain, where his father was stationed. Hugo's experiences in those places influenced both him and his writings.

In 1822, Hugo married his childhood sweetheart, Adèle Foucher. About this

Chicago Historical Society
Victor Hugo

time, he decided to be a writer. In the preface to his play *Cromwell* (1827), Hugo demanded freedom for dramatists from the rigid literary rules that governed playwriting. This preface became the principal declaration of French romanticism. Many scholars consider Hugo's verse drama *Hernani* (1830) the beginning of the romantic movement in France because of its deliberate break with dramatic conventions.

Hugo wrote poetry and fiction during the same period that he wrote plays. He published a series of successful books of poetry, including *The Orientals* (1829), *Leaves of Autumn* (1831), *Songs of Twilight* (1835), and *Rays and Shadows* (1840). His best-known novel during this period was *The Hunchback of Notre Dame* (1831).

Political activity. In 1843, Hugo's play *The Burgraves* failed dismally. That same year, his eldest daughter, whom he idolized, drowned with her husband. These events, combined with Hugo's growing interest in politics, lessened his concern with literature. He published nothing for almost 10 years, but he continued to write.

Hugo was a political conservative as a young man, but he became increasingly liberal. After the Revolution of 1848 established the Second Republic in France, he was elected to the new National Assembly. There he fought for free education and an expansion of voting rights. At first, Hugo supported Louis Napoleon, president of the republic. But he soon opposed Louis because he felt the president was becoming a tyrant.

Exile and return. In December 1851, Louis Napoleon overthrew the republic. He established himself as dictator with the title Emperor Napoleon III. In protest, Hugo went into exile for almost 20 years. He lived first in Belgium and then on the island of Jersey in the English Channel. Then, from 1855 until his return to France in 1870, he lived on the channel island of Guernsey. In 1853, Hugo published *The Chastisements,* a collection of satirical poems that denounced Napoleon III for destroying the Second Republic. In 1859, Hugo rejected a government invitation to return to France. He declared that he would return only with the return of liberty.

During his exile, Hugo published many of his finest works. *The Contemplations* (1856) contains his best lyric poetry. These poems reveal the strong influence of Hugo's memories of his dead daughter and of his love for her. *The Legend of the Centuries* (1859, new sections added in 1877 and 1883) is Hugo's masterpiece in epic poetry. *Les Misérables* appeared in 1862.

Hugo became a symbol of freedom to Frenchmen during his years of exile. After the overthrow of Napoleon III in 1870 during the Franco-Prussian War, Hugo returned to France in triumph. He spent his final years honored by his fellow citizens as the champion of democracy and of the common people.

His works. Hugo wrote an enormous number of works during a career of more than 60 years. During his lifetime, he gained his greatest popularity for his plays. In Great Britain and the United States, he became known chiefly as a novelist. The French today consider him a giant of literature for his poetry.

Throughout his life, Hugo composed epic, lyric, and satirical poetry. He often combined these types into individual collections or even single poems. Hugo's finest poetry appeared after 1850. He wrote *The Chastisements* in a wide variety of poetic forms, including elegies, frag-

ments of epics, odes, and songs. *The Contemplations* expresses many of Hugo's philosophical and religious beliefs. These include his strong faith in God and his belief in immortality and the soul. *The Legend of the Centuries* traces humanity's historical and spiritual development from the Creation to the 1900's. At the end of this work, Hugo predicted that humanity faced a destiny of continual material and moral progress.

In his plays, Hugo used many devices of melodrama, including complicated and unrealistic plots, exaggerated emotions, and a flowery style. The plays rise above melodrama in their moral or political message and particularly in their superior use of poetry.

Hugo's novels endure because of their moral lessons and their vivid re-creations of history. *The Hunchback of Notre Dame* established Hugo as a master of the historical novel. The story takes place during the 1400's in Paris. The central characters of the novel are Quasimodo, a deformed bell ringer, and the Cathedral of Notre Dame itself. Another historical novel, *Ninety-Three* (1874), deals with events of the French Revolution.

Les Misérables is a novel set in the France of Hugo's day. The hero, Jean Valjean, is an escaped convict struggling to lead an honest, useful life despite the prejudices of a cruel society. This novel expresses Hugo's humanitarian feelings and his belief in democracy.

Hugo's reputation as a writer declined after his death. Many critics said that his ideas were shallow and his style often wordy and overly sentimental. Today, Hugo's works have found renewed interest because of his imaginative treatment of his subjects and his skillful use of literary forms.   Irving Putter

Huguenots, *HYOO guh nahts,* were a group of Protestants who became the center of political and religious quarrels in France in the 1500's and 1600's. They believed the teachings of John Calvin and belonged to the Reformed Church. The French Roman Catholics named them *Huguenots.* The name may have come from that of Besançon Hugues, a Swiss religious leader.

During the reign of Henry II (1547-1559), the Huguenots became a large and influential political group in France. As they grew strong, the Catholic government persecuted them more and more. Such important people as Anthony, King of Navarre; Louis I de Bourbon de Condé; and Admiral Gaspard de Coligny were Huguenots. The Guise family led the Catholic group. The Guises influenced Henry's son, King Francis II, against the Huguenots.

The massacre. After Francis II died and Charles IX became king, the queen mother, Catherine de Médicis, controlled France. For a time, she encouraged the Huguenots as a balance against the Guises. But feelings in both parties became so bitter that civil war broke out. Catherine feared that Coligny was influencing her son too much, so she allied herself with the Duke of Guise. Beginning on Aug. 24, 1572, they carried out the Massacre of Saint Bartholomew's Day. During the next several days, thousands of Huguenots were murdered.

But the political pendulum swung again in the other direction. Henry III feared the popularity of the Guise family and had the Duke of Guise and his brother, the cardinal, assassinated. These murders aroused public feeling against Henry, and he allied himself with Henry of Navarre and the Huguenots. Later, Henry III was as-

Detail of *Massacre of the Huguenots,* an oil painting by François Dubois (late 1500's); Musée Cantonal des Beaux-Arts, Lausanne, Switzerland

A massacre of Huguenots by pro-Catholic forces began in Paris on Saint Bartholomew's Day in 1572. The massacre spread through France and thousands of Huguenots were murdered.

sassinated, and Henry of Navarre became the new king.

Most of France was Catholic, and Henry decided he must become a Catholic to be a successful king. But he remembered the Huguenots and in 1598 issued the Edict of Nantes. This law gave the Huguenots freedom of worship in 100 communities. The edict also gave them political freedom. The Huguenots thus formed a sort of Protestant republic within the Catholic kingdom.

Flight from France. The Huguenots lost their political freedom during the reign of Louis XIII. His minister, Cardinal Richelieu, conquered their cities. But they were still allowed freedom of worship. They did not lose this until 1685, when Louis XIV repealed the Edict of Nantes. Thousands of Huguenots fled France to new homes in England, Prussia, the Netherlands, and America. Many settled and prospered in South Carolina, Virginia, Massachusetts, and New York. Among these resettled Huguenots were such families as the Legaré, Petigru, Maury, Revere, Jay, and DeLancey.

Some of the laws against the Huguenots were relaxed shortly before the French Revolution began in 1789. But Huguenots did not get religious and political freedom until the Constituent Assembly (1789-1791) gave equal rights to Roman Catholics, Protestants, and Jews.

Most of the Huguenots were craftworkers or textile workers. They played a large part in building up the English textile industry.   Edwin J. Westermann

Related articles in *World Book* include:

Catherine de Médicis
Charles (IX) of France
Henry (III, IV) of France
Nantes, Edict of

Richelieu, Cardinal
Saint Bartholomew's Day, Massacre of

Hui-tsung. See Huizong.
Huizinga, *HOY zihng ah,* **Johan,** *yoh HAHN* (1872-1945), was a noted Dutch historian. He was especially interested in portraying the spirit of an entire age or civili-

zation. His fame rests on the range and quality of his writings, and his ability to capture the very flavor of life. Huizinga's most famous work, *The Waning of the Middle Ages* (1919), is a study of life in the Netherlands during the 1300's and 1400's.

Huizinga was born in Groningen, the Netherlands, and studied at the University of Groningen. His major works include *In the Shadow of Tomorrow* (1935), a collection of essays on the cultural condition of people in modern society; and *Homo Ludens* (1938), a study of human culture as seen in play. Huizinga was jailed by Nazis during World War II, and died in February 1945, shortly after his release.   Roland N. Stromberg

Huizong, *hway dzawng* (reigned A.D. 1101-1126), also spelled *Hui-tsung,* the last emperor of the Northern Song dynasty of China, was the greatest imperial patron of art. A painter himself, he specialized in colorful, realistic bird and flower subjects. Huizong tried to keep court art at a high level of quality by supervising the training of candidates at the Imperial Academy. Huizong's art interests made him a careless and feeble ruler, and he was overthrown by the Tartars.

Robert A. Rorex

Hukbalahap, *huhk BAH lah hahp,* also called *Huk,* a Communist guerrilla movement, tried to overthrow the democratic government of the Philippines from 1945 to 1954. Its full name was *Hukbong Magpapalayang Bayan* (People's Liberation Army). The Huk movement failed because the Philippine government offered the people fair play and land reform, helped the Huks resettle on Mindanao Island, and defeated Communist guerrillas. Ramón Magsaysay, hero of the fight against the Huks, became president of the Philippines in 1953 and served until his death in 1957.   Stefan T. Possony

Hula. See **Hawaii** (Dancing and music).
Hull (pop. 262,000) has been one of England's leading industrial ports since it was founded by King Edward I in 1299. Hull, also called Kingston upon Hull, is the chief city of the county of Humberside. The city lies in northeastern England, at the point where the River Hull flows into the River Humber. For location, see **Great Britain** (political map).

Hull is an important manufacturing center. Its factories produce aircraft, beverages, chemicals, food products, and trailers. Hull's dock area extends about 7 miles (11 kilometers) along the Humber and serves as a headquarters for fishing fleets. The world's longest single-span suspension bridge crosses the River Humber near the city. Hull also has a university. The German Air Force caused extensive damage to Hull during World War II.

M. Trevor Wild

Hull, Que. (pop. 56,225; met. area pop. 717,978), is an industrial city in southern Quebec. It lies on the Ottawa River. Ottawa, Canada's capital, faces Hull across the river, and Hull is considered part of the Ottawa metropolitan area. Four bridges connect the cities. For location, see **Quebec** (political map).

Hull is primarily a paper and lumber producing center. But in the 1970's, the federal government moved some departments and agencies from Ottawa to Hull. Several government office buildings were constructed in Hull. About a fourth of the government employees in the Ottawa area work in Hull. The University of Quebec has a Hull campus.   Alje H. Kamminga

Hull, Bobby (1939-   ), ranks among the greatest goal scorers in the history of professional hockey. Hull, a left wing, was nicknamed the "Golden Jet" because of his blond hair and his skating speed. His powerful shots sometimes traveled 110 miles (177 kilometers) per hour.

Hull played for the Chicago Black Hawks of the National Hockey League (NHL) from 1957 to 1972. In 1972, he joined the Winnipeg (Man.) Jets of the World Hockey Association (WHA). Hull retired in 1978, but he returned to competition in 1979 after the WHA disbanded and Winnipeg became a member of the NHL. In 1980, Hull was traded to the Hartford Whalers. He retired in 1981.

During his NHL career, Hull scored 610 goals in regular-season play. This total ranks Hull third in the NHL, behind Gordie Howe and Phil Esposito. During his WHA career, Hull scored 303 regular-season goals. He set a WHA record by scoring 77 goals during the 1974-1975 season. Robert Marvin Hull was born in Pointe Anne, Ont.   Herman Weiskopf

Hull, Clark Leonard (1884-1952), was an American psychologist known for his research on the learning process and for his mathematical approach to the study of behavior. Hull believed that human behavior could be studied as a science. His major work was a mathematical theory of learning. This theory emphasized the interrelationship of learning, which Hull called *habit,* and motivation, which he called *drive.*

Hull was born near Akron, N.Y. He graduated from the University of Michigan in 1913 and received a Ph.D. from the University of Wisconsin in 1918. In 1929, he joined the faculty of Yale University.   Robert G. Weyant

Hull, Cordell (1871-1955), an American statesman, won the 1945 Nobel Peace Prize for his peace efforts while serving as U.S. secretary of state from 1933 to 1944. One of his greatest achievements was making the good-neighbor policy between the United States and Latin-American countries effective. He worked out the trade treaties that brought almost complete solidarity among all the American nations.

Hull also tried to avoid war in the Pacific. When Pearl Harbor was attacked in 1941, he denounced the Japanese ambassadors, Kichisaburo Nomura and Saburo Kurusu, for Japan's deceit. A leading figure in wartime diplomacy, Hull conceived the idea of the United Nations organization for peace. Before he resigned in 1944 because of poor health, he helped complete the first plans for the United Nations.

Hull was born in Overton County (now Pickett County), Tennessee. He graduated from Cumberland Law School. He served in the Tennessee legislature, fought as a captain in the Spanish-American War, and was a circuit court judge in Tennessee.

In 1907, Hull was elected to the United States House of Representatives. He wrote the income-tax law in 1913, and also the 1916 inheritance-tax law. A follower of Woodrow Wilson, Hull supported low tariffs as a basis for international economic cooperation.

Hull served as chairman of the Democratic National Committee in the 1920's. He was elected to the United States Senate in 1930. At the 1932 Democratic National Convention, he helped gain the presidential nomination for Franklin D. Roosevelt.   George M. Waller

Hull, Isaac (1773-1843), commanded the United States warship *Constitution* when it defeated the British

Guerrière in the War of 1812. This battle proved his ability as a naval officer, and made his ship famous as *Old Ironsides* (see **Constitution**). Hull was born in Derby, Conn. He went to sea at 14 and commanded a ship before he was 21.   Richard S. West, Jr.

Hull, William (1753-1825), was an American army officer who served in the Revolutionary War and the War of 1812. During the Revolutionary War (1775-1783), Hull fought bravely in many battles, including Princeton, Stony Point, and Trenton. During the War of 1812, he surrendered Detroit to the British, an action for which he was court-martialed.

In 1812, President James Madison ordered Hull to capture Upper Canada (now Ontario), which was British territory. The mission failed, and Hull's troops retreated to Detroit. The British army followed Hull, surrounded Detroit, and demanded surrender. Hull requested help from Fort Dearborn in the Illinois Territory, but Indians had captured or killed all the soldiers at the fort. Surrounded by the British and threatened by an Indian attack, Hull surrendered.

In 1814, a court-martial convicted Hull of cowardice and neglect of duty and sentenced him to death. However, President Madison canceled the sentence. Hull was born in Derby, Conn.   William Morgan Fowler, Jr.

See also **War of 1812** (Land campaign of 1812).

Hull House became the most famous settlement house in the United States. It was founded in Chicago in 1889 by two American social reformers, Jane Addams and Ellen Gates Starr. Hull House first occupied a dilapidated mansion that originally belonged to Charles J. Hull, a Chicago businessman. By 1907, the settlement included 12 new buildings and covered an entire block.

Many reform-minded people came to live in Hull House to help Chicago's poor. The residents organized the first public playground in Chicago in 1893 and the first juvenile court in the country in 1899. They also set up one of Chicago's first kindergartens, and promoted cleaner streets, better housing, and laws to regulate child labor. They also taught English, government, bookbinding, and other subjects to immigrants.

Addams served as head resident of Hull House until her death in 1935. She became one of the most famous women in the nation and a leader in many reform movements. Other Hull House residents who later became prominent included the social reformers Julia Lathrop and Florence Kelley and the physician Alice Hamilton.

In 1963, Hull House was torn down to make way for a campus of the University of Illinois. But the original Hull mansion and a dining hall were preserved and made into a museum. Today, the Hull House Association operates about 25 community centers in Chicago. The centers provide such services as child care, counseling, and housing. The association's headquarters are at 3179 N. Broadway, Chicago, IL 60657.   Allen F. Davis

See also **Addams, Jane; Kelley, Florence; Lathrop, Julia C.; Settlement house.**

Human being has the most highly developed brain of any animal. The human brain gives people many special abilities, the most outstanding of which is the ability to speak. Language has enabled human beings to develop *culture,* which consists of ways of behaving and thinking. These ways are passed on from generation to generation through learning. Culture also includes *technol-*

WORLD BOOK photo

Human beings, unlike any other creatures, use art and language to preserve a knowledge of history. The museum guide above is describing ancient Chinese buildings and ways of life.

ogy—that is, the tools and techniques invented by people to help satisfy their needs and desires. The richness and complexity of human culture distinguish human beings from all other animals.

The human brain helps make people the most adaptable of all creatures. They behave with the most flexibility and in the greatest variety of ways. The human body is highly adaptable because it has few specialized features that could limit its activities. In contrast, a seal has a body streamlined for swimming, but it has difficulty moving about on land. People cannot swim as well as a seal, but they can also walk, run, and climb. Human adaptability enables people to live in an extremely wide variety of environments—from the tropics to the Arctic.

People are inquisitive and have long sought to understand themselves and their place in the world. Throughout much of human existence, religion has helped provide such understanding. All societies have assumed one or more gods influence their lives and are responsible for their existence. Since ancient times, *philosophy* (the study of truth and knowledge) has also provided definitions of what it means to be human.

Today, religion and philosophy remain important parts of people's efforts to understand the nature of human existence. But many other fields of study also help human beings learn about themselves. For example, *anthropology* is the study of human cultures and of human physical and cultural development. *Linguistics* is the scientific study of language. Specialists in *psychology* study human and animal behavior and mental processes. *Sociology* deals with the groups and institutions that make up human societies, and *history* is the study of past human events. Each of these fields has a separate article in *World Book.*

This article describes the physical and cultural characteristics that distinguish human beings from other animals. It also traces human physical and cultural development. For more information on the life of early human beings, see **Prehistoric people.**

Characteristics of human beings

Scientific classification. Biologists classify all living things in groups, including *class, order, family, genus,* and *species.* Human beings belong to the class of animals called *mammals.* There are about 4,000 species of mammals, including such animals as cats, dogs, elephants, and otters. All mammals have a backbone, hair, four limbs, and a constant body temperature. Female mammals are the only animals with special glands that produce milk for feeding their young.

Human beings, along with apes, monkeys, lemurs, and tarsiers, make up the order of mammals called *primates.* Scientists classify human beings and apes in the superfamily *Hominoidea.* The family *Hominidae* consists of human beings and their closest prehuman ancestors. Human beings are the only living members of a genus called *Homo,* the Latin word for *human being.* This genus consists of one living species—*Homo sapiens*— and several extinct human species that are known only through fossil remains. The Latin words *Homo sapiens* mean *wise human being.* All existing peoples belong to the subspecies *Homo sapiens sapiens.*

Physical characteristics. Human beings and the other primates share many physical features. For example, both human beings and apes rely on their excellent vision for much of their information about the environment. They have large eyes, sensitive retinas, and *stereoscopic vision* (the ability to perceive depth). Human beings and apes also have a highly developed nervous system and a large brain. Human beings and many other primates have long, flexible fingers and *opposable thumbs,* which can be placed opposite the fingers for grasping. In addition, their fingers and toes have nails instead of claws.

Many of the physical characteristics that distinguish human beings from other primates are related to the ability of people to stand upright and walk on two legs. This ability chiefly requires long, powerful legs. The human rump has strong muscles that propel the body forward and balance the trunk alternately on each leg when a person walks. In contrast, apes spend most of their time climbing and swinging in trees or walking on all four limbs. Their rumps have relatively weak muscles, and their arms are longer and stronger than their legs.

The human spine, unlike the spine of any other animal, has a curve in the lower back. This curve helps make upright posture possible by placing the body's center of gravity directly over the pelvis. The human foot is also specially adapted for walking on two legs. Apes use all four limbs to support their weight, and they can grasp objects almost as well with their feet as with their hands. In human beings, however, the feet support the entire weight of the body, and the toes have little ability to grasp or to move independently.

The human brain is extremely well developed and at least twice as large as any ape's brain. Because of the brain's size, the human skull is rounder than any other primate's skull.

Physical differences between human beings and apes

The bodies of human beings are suited to walking on two feet. On the other hand, the bodies of apes are suited to walking on four limbs or climbing. Some of the resulting physical differences between people and apes are shown below.

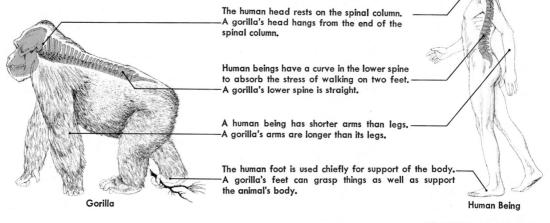

The human head rests on the spinal column. A gorilla's head hangs from the end of the spinal column.

Human beings have a curve in the lower spine to absorb the stress of walking on two feet. A gorilla's lower spine is straight.

A human being has shorter arms than legs. A gorilla's arms are longer than its legs.

The human foot is used chiefly for support of the body. A gorilla's feet can grasp things as well as support the animal's body.

Gorilla

Human Being

WORLD BOOK illustration by Anthony Saris

Human beings live longer and develop more slowly than other primates. The human life span varies from an average of about 40 years in many developing countries to more than 70 years in most industrial nations. A human infant is born completely helpless and depends on its parents for many years. Most human beings reach full maturity only between 18 and 25 years of age. Slow growth and development allow for a much longer period of learning and brain growth than exists in any other species.

Cultural characteristics. Some animals have simple aspects of culture. For example, young chimpanzees learn from older members of their group how to make some tools. They catch termites by peeling a twig and inserting it into a termite mound. They also chew leaves to make sponges for soaking up water to drink.

Certain animals, including apes and monkeys, com-municate by making a wide variety of sounds. These sounds express emotion and may communicate simple messages, but they apparently do not symbolize any object or idea. Language distinguishes human culture from all forms of animal culture. Through elaborate use of symbols, language enables people to express complex ideas and to communicate about objects and events that are distant in time and place. By using language, human beings have developed the ability to reason and to solve problems on a far higher level than any other animal. Language also enables human beings to pass on knowledge and skills from generation to generation.

Human physical development

The Bible describes how God created the world and all its living things, including the first human beings, in six days. Many people accept this description as fact.

Human cultural development

Human cultural development can be divided into three phases. The earliest societies, *left,* hunted wild animals and gathered wild plants for food. Agricultural societies, *center,* controlled their food sources by farming. Industrial societies, *right,* use advanced technology, resulting in both major achievements and complex problems.

WORLD BOOK illustration by George Suyeoka

Evidence from fossils has convinced most scientists that human beings developed over millions of years from ancestors that were not completely human. However, the fossil record does not yet provide enough information to trace human development in detail. As a result, not all experts agree on how human beings developed. This section describes human physical development as most anthropologists believe it occurred.

Prehuman ancestors. Anthropologists believe human beings, chimpanzees, and gorillas all developed from a common ancestor that lived from 14 to 18 million years ago. Many scientists once thought that the earliest direct ancestor of human beings was a creature called *Ramapithecus,* which lived from 8 to 14 million years ago. During the 1970's and early 1980's, however, discoveries of *Ramapithecus* fossils in China and Pakistan indicated that the creature was an ape.

More than 4 million years ago, a more advanced form of humanlike creature called *Australopithecus* appeared in Africa. Fossil remains of the australopithecine skeleton indicate that these creatures stood fully erect and walked on two legs. The australopithecines were about 4 to 5 feet (120 to 150 centimeters) tall and had a brain about a third the size of a modern human brain.

Early human beings. Most scientists regard the species *Homo habilis* (skillful human being) as the first type of human being. These primitive people appeared about 2 million years ago in Africa and are believed to have developed from the australopithecines. Archaeological evidence shows that *Homo habilis* used stone tools. *Homo habilis* fossils have been found at Lake Turkana, Kenya, and other areas in eastern Africa.

Most scientists believe that *Homo habilis* in turn developed into a more advanced type of prehistoric human being known as *Homo erectus* (erect human being). *Homo erectus* appeared about $1\frac{1}{2}$ million years ago in Africa and later spread to Asia and Europe. *Homo erectus* had a larger brain and a more humanlike skull than its ancestors. From the neck down, *Homo erectus* closely resembled the human beings of today. Like *Homo habilis* and the australopithecines, however, it had a low forehead and a large jaw. The culture of *Homo erectus* was more highly developed than that of *Homo habilis. Homo erectus* made and used a wider variety of stone tools than its ancestors. It learned how to make fire about $1\frac{1}{2}$ million years ago and was probably the first human species to do so. Fossils indicate that *Homo erectus* hunted large animals, and this sort of hunting required planning and cooperation.

Human beings of today. The first members of the species *Homo sapiens* appeared about 450,000 years ago. These people basically resembled *Homo erectus* but had a larger brain and smaller jaws and teeth. As time passed, *Homo sapiens* developed a rounded skull and long, straight limbs. By about 40,000 years ago, *Homo sapiens* looked like today's human beings. Most anthropologists classify all people who have lived since that time as *Homo sapiens sapiens.*

Human cultural development

Human culture has developed in three major phases. These phases have been based on (1) hunting and gathering societies, (2) agricultural societies, and (3) industrial societies.

Hunting and gathering societies. For almost the entire prehistoric period of human existence, people lived by hunting game and gathering fruit, nuts, roots, seeds, and other plant foods. Archaeological evidence suggests that the hunters and gatherers lived in widely separated groups of 25 to 50 persons. These primitive people wandered over large areas in search of food. They lived in harmony with their environment and used their natural resources efficiently.

The first inventions probably included weapons and cutting tools for butchering animals, plus containers for gathering plant foods. As people improved their hunting skills, they obtained large amounts of meat by killing huge mammals, including elephants.

Agricultural societies developed about 9000 B.C., as people began to domesticate wild animals and plants. These farming activities greatly increased the amount of food available in any area. Permanent villages started to appear, and then towns and cities developed. The larger and more dependable supply of food supported a continually increasing population.

Agriculture made it unnecessary for everyone to help in the production of food. Some people became specialists in other fields, such as manufacturing or trade. Governments were established and systems of writing were created. Thus, the invention of farming opened the way for the development of civilization.

Industrial societies appeared in their modern form during the A.D. 1700's, after people learned to run machinery with energy from coal and other fuels. Today, petroleum, coal, natural gas, and nuclear fuel furnish most of the energy used by industrial societies. These fuels have brought a great expansion of technology.

The processes and products developed by industrial technology have significantly improved the standard of living for countless people. These developments have also helped make possible many other advances, including tremendous increases in human knowledge and in the variety of artistic expression. But not all nations and economic classes have received the full benefits of industrial progress. Industrial technology also has produced many negative side effects. For example, its wastes pollute the environment, and its production methods have sometimes created monotonous, unfulfilling jobs.

Industrial societies today face many major challenges. New technologies must be developed to use the world's limited natural resources more efficiently. New, nonpolluting sources of energy are needed. In addition, people must find ways to control population growth and to extend the benefits of modern technology to all the world's people.   Bernard G. Campbell

Related articles. See **Prehistoric people** and its list of *Related articles.* See also the following articles:

Ape	Culture	Primate
Civilization	Human body	Races, Human

Additional resources

Bronowski, Jacob. *The Ascent of Man.* Little, Brown, 1973.
Dixon, Terence, and Lucas, Martin. *The Human Race.* McGraw, 1982.
Gowlett, John. *Ascent to Civilization: The Archaeology of Early Man.* Random House, 1984.
Van Loon, Hendrik W. *The Story of Mankind.* Norton, 1984. First published in 1921; updated by John Merriman. For younger readers.

Tony Duffy, Focus on Sports

The human body can perform amazing acts of strength and grace. A highly trained athlete can push the body to the limits of its powers.

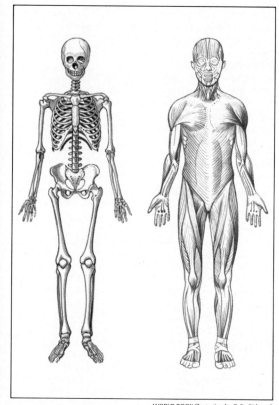

WORLD BOOK illustration by Colin Bidgood

The skeletal system in-cludes more than 200 bones and makes up about 18 per cent of the body's weight. It provides the body with a sturdy framework. Bone is strong, yet light and flexible.

The muscular system con-sists of more than 600 mus-cles and makes up about 40 per cent of the body's weight. Muscles can *contract* (short-en). By contracting, the mus-cles enable the body to move.

Human body

Human body. People sometimes call the human body a machine—the most wonderful one ever built. Of course, the human body is not a machine. But it can be compared to one in many ways. Like a machine, the body is made up of many parts. Each part of the body, like each part of a machine, does special jobs. But all the parts work together and so make the body or the ma-chine run smoothly. Also like a machine, the body needs energy to work. In such a machine as an automobile, the energy comes from gasoline. In the body, it comes from food and oxygen.

Although the human body can be compared to a ma-chine, it is far more amazing than any machine. It can do things that no machine can do. For example, the body can grow. The body starts out as one cell. In time, this tiny cell develops into a body consisting of trillions of

Robert S. Eisenberg, the contributor of this article, is Bard Professor of Physiology and Chairman of the Department of Physiology at Rush University Medical School.

cells. The human body can also replace certain worn-out parts. Each day, about 2 billion of the body's cells wear out and are replaced. Thus, the body is always rebuild-ing itself. Every 15 to 30 days, for instance, the human body replaces the outermost layer of skin.

The human body can defend itself against hundreds of diseases. The body can also repair itself after most small injuries. Many body parts, such as the heart and kidneys, work continuously. The heart of a 70-year-old person, for example, has pumped at least 46 million gal-lons (174 million liters) of blood during that person's life. In addition, the person's kidneys have removed wastes from more than 1 million gallons (3.8 million liters) of blood.

By using its senses, the body can detect changes in its surroundings, such as changes in temperature, light, or sounds. It can adjust to these changes immediately. The body's senses are truly incredible. For instance, people can learn to identify thousands of odors, yet smell is one of the least developed senses in human beings. The human body can also detect changes that occur within itself, such as changes in body temperature. The various parts of the body continuously adjust their activities to keep the "inside" environment normal. Such adjustments

Lennart Nilsson from *Behold Man*
© 1974 Little, Brown and Company

The human eye, like many parts of the body, rapidly adjusts to changes. In a darkened room, the pupil of the eye opens wide and so lets in more light, *left.* If the room lights are turned up, the pupil automatically shrinks within seconds, *right.*

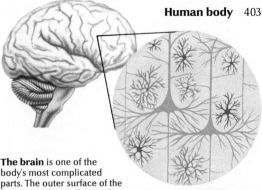

The brain is one of the body's most complicated parts. The outer surface of the brain is made up of more than 8 billion cells. A few of these cells are shown in the circle.

WORLD BOOK illustration by
Colin Bidgood

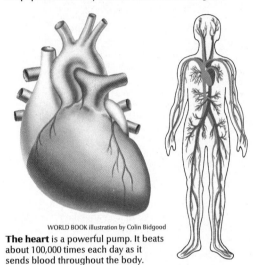

WORLD BOOK illustration by Colin Bidgood

The heart is a powerful pump. It beats about 100,000 times each day as it sends blood throughout the body.

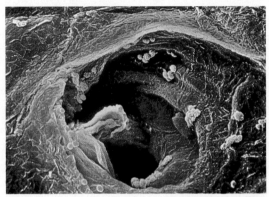

Lennart Nilsson from *Behold Man*
© 1974 Little, Brown and Company

A microscopic view of the skin shows bacteria as tiny green balls. Countless bacteria live on the skin. These bacteria are harmless unless they enter the body through a break in the skin.

rely on a system of nerves that carries messages from one part of the body to another. The messages travel at speeds of up to 100 yards (90 meters) per second.

The most remarkable part of the human body is the brain. The human brain is so highly developed that it makes people different from all other living things. Their magnificent brain makes people able to think. They can compose silly rhymes or beautiful poetry. They can imagine a dream world or study the mysteries of the atom. No animal—no matter how smart—and no computer—no matter how powerful—can think like a human being.

What the body is made of

The human body has many parts. This section of the article describes the organization of the body, from its smallest parts through its largest ones.

Chemical elements and molecules. Like all things—living and nonliving—the human body consists of atoms of chemical elements. The most common chemical elements in the body are carbon, hydrogen, nitrogen, and oxygen. The body also contains smaller amounts of many other elements, including calcium, iron, phosphorus, potassium, and sodium.

Atoms of chemical elements combine and form microscopic structures called *molecules.* The most com-

mon molecule in the human body is water. A molecule of water consists of two atoms of hydrogen and one atom of oxygen. Water makes up about 65 per cent of the body. Most of the chemical reactions that occur in the body require water.

Except for water, all of the chief molecules in the body contain the element carbon. The most important carbon-containing molecules are large, complicated structures called *macromolecules.* There are four main kinds of macromolecules in the body: *carbohydrates, lipids, proteins,* and *nucleic acids.* Carbohydrates provide energy that powers all the body's activities. Lipids have several jobs. Some lipids, particularly the fats, store extra fuel. Other lipids serve as one of the building materials for the cells that make up the body. Proteins also have various duties. Many proteins serve as building blocks for cells. Other proteins, called *enzymes,* speed up the chemical reactions within the body. Nucleic acids carry instructions that tell each cell how to perform its particular jobs. For more information on macromolecules, see the article **Life** (The chemical basis of life).

Cells and tissues. The cell is the basic unit of all living things. The cells of the human body consist chiefly of molecules of water, proteins, and nucleic acids. The molecules that make up the cells are not alive, but the cells themselves are living things. Each of the body's cells is able to take in food, get rid of wastes, and grow. Most of the cells can also reproduce. A thin covering consisting of lipid molecules encloses each cell. This lipid envelope permits only certain substances to enter or leave the cell.

Nearly all the cells in the body are too tiny to see without a microscope. Yet packed within each cell is the machinery that the cell needs to carry out its many activities. For a detailed discussion of a cell's machinery and how it works, see the article **Cell** (Inside a living cell; The work of a cell).

The body has many basic kinds of cells, such as blood cells, muscle cells, and nerve cells. Each kind of cell has special features and jobs. Cells of the same type form tissues. The body has four chief kinds of tissues. (1) *Connective tissue* helps support and join together various parts of the body. Most connective tissue is strong and elastic. (2) *Epithelial tissue* covers the body surface and so forms the skin. It also lines such body openings as the mouth and throat. Epithelial tissue prevents harmful substances from entering the body. (3) *Muscle tissue* consists of threadlike fibers that can *contract* (shorten). Muscle tissue makes it possible for the body to move. (4) *Nervous tissue* carries signals. It permits various parts of the body to communicate with one another.

Organs and organ systems. An organ consists of two or more kinds of tissues joined into one structure that has a certain task. The heart, for example, is an organ whose job is to pump blood throughout the body. Connective tissue, muscle tissue, and nervous tissue make up the heart.

Groups of organs form organ systems. Each organ system carries out a major activity in the body. For example, the digestive system consists of various organs that enable the body to use food. Similarly, the nervous system is made up of organs that carry messages from one part of the body to another. The remainder of this article discusses the main organ systems of the human body. For more detailed descriptions of the major organs and organ systems, see the articles listed in the *Related articles* at the end of this article.

The skin

The skin, which is sometimes called the *integumentary system,* is the largest organ of the body. If the skin of a 150-pound (68-kilogram) person were spread out flat, it would cover about 20 square feet (1.9 square meters). Skin has three layers: (1) the epidermis, (2) the dermis, and (3) subcutaneous tissues.

The epidermis forms the outermost layer of the skin. It serves as a barrier between the outside world and the inner tissues of the body. The outer portion of the epidermis consists of tough, dead cells that prevent bacteria, chemicals, and other harmful substances from entering the body. It also protects the body's inner tissues from the harsh rays of the sun and prevents the loss of water from these tissues.

The dermis is the middle layer of the skin. The dermis helps keep the temperature of the body within its normal range. The body produces tremendous amounts of heat as it uses food. Some of this heat escapes from the body through the blood vessels in the dermis. When the body needs to retain heat, these blood vessels nar-

row and so limit heat loss. When the body needs to give off heat, the blood vessels in the dermis expand and so increase heat loss. The sweat glands, which are part of the epidermis, also help control body temperature. These glands produce sweat, which is released through pores on the skin surface. As the sweat evaporates from the surface, it cools the body.

The dermis also serves as an important sense organ. Nerve endings within the dermis respond to cold, heat, pain, pressure, and touch.

Subcutaneous tissues form the innermost layer of the skin. This layer provides extra fuel for the body. The fuel is stored in fat cells. The subcutaneous layer also helps retain body heat, and it cushions the inner tissues against blows to the body.

The skeletal system

The skeleton of an adult consists of about 200 bones. The skeleton forms a strong framework that supports the body. It also helps protect the internal organs. For example, the brain is shielded by the skull, the spinal cord by the spinal column, and the heart and lungs by the ribs.

The skeleton works together with the muscles in enabling the body to move. The bones of the shoulders and arms, for instance, serve as levers against which the muscles that move the arm can pull. The place where bones meet is called a joint. There are two basic kinds of joints. (1) *Movable joints,* such as the elbow, knee, and shoulder joints, permit varying degrees of motion.The bones of a movable joint are held together by bundles of tough, flexible connective tissue called *ligaments.* (2) *Fixed joints* do not permit any movement of the bones. The bones of the skull, except for the jawbones, meet in fixed joints.

The skeleton serves as more than a framework for the body and a system of levers to help move the body. Bone tissue contains various kinds of cells that play a major role in keeping the blood healthy. The cells of bone *marrow*—the soft, fatty core of many bones—produce new blood cells and release them into the bloodstream. Two kinds of bone cells regulate the mineral content of the blood. One kind removes calcium, phosphorus, and other minerals from the blood and deposits them in the bone. The other kind dissolves old mineral deposits and releases the minerals back into the bloodstream as needed.

The muscular system

The muscular system moves the body. The body has more than 600 muscles, each of which consists of special fibers that can contract. When a muscle contracts, it pulls the tissue to which it is attached. This pulling results in movement.

The muscles of the human body can be divided into two main types: (1) skeletal muscles and (2) smooth muscles. A third kind of muscle, *cardiac muscle,* is found only in the heart. It has features of both skeletal muscle and smooth muscle.

Skeletal muscles are attached to the bones. They move the bones of the arms, legs, fingers, and other parts of the skeleton. We can consciously control the skeletal muscles, and so they are sometimes called *voluntary muscles.* The fibers that make up a skeletal mus-

Ligaments and tendons   Ligaments and tendons consist of tough, elastic connective tissue. Ligaments connect one bone to another. They hold the bones in place but still allow some movement. Tendons connect a muscle to a bone. When the muscle contracts, the strong, cablelike tendon pulls the bone to which it is attached. The large Achilles' tendon links the calf muscle to the heel bone.

WORLD BOOK illustration by Colin Bidgood

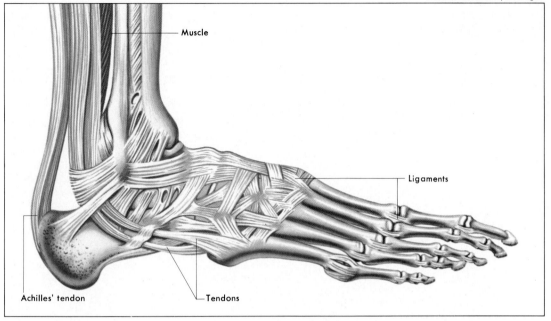

cle have alternate light and dark crossbands called *striations.*

One end of each skeletal muscle is attached to a bone that does not move when the muscle contracts. In most cases, the other end of the muscle is attached to another bone, either directly or by means of cordlike bundles of connective tissue called *tendons.* This second bone moves when the muscle contracts.

Muscles move the body only by pulling. They cannot push the tissues to which they are attached. Two sets of muscles therefore control most skeletal movements, such as the raising and then lowering of the forearm. One set of muscles pulls the bones in one direction, and the other set pulls the bones in the opposite direction. For example, one set of muscles pulls the forearm up, but it cannot push the forearm down. To lower the forearm, a second set of muscles must contract and pull it down.

Smooth muscles are found in most of the body's internal organs. Unlike skeletal muscles, smooth muscles do not have striations. Smooth muscles in the walls of the stomach and intestines move food through the digestive system. Smooth muscles also control the width of the blood vessels and the size of the breathing passages. In all these cases, the smooth muscles contract and relax automatically—that is, we do not consciously control them. For this reason, they are often called *involuntary muscles.*

Smooth muscles cannot contract as rapidly as skeletal muscles. However, smooth muscles can contract more completely than skeletal muscles, and they do not tire as quickly. Smooth muscles can thus produce powerful, rhythmic contractions over long periods.

Cardiac muscle has striations like skeletal muscle. But like smooth muscle, it contracts automatically and rhythmically without tiring. Cardiac muscle enables the heart to beat an average of 70 times a minute without rest throughout a person's lifetime.

The digestive system

The digestive system breaks down food into simple substances that the cells can use. It then absorbs these substances into the bloodstream and eliminates any leftover waste matter. The main part of the digestive system is a long tube called the *alimentary canal.* This tube consists of (1) the mouth, esophagus, and stomach; and (2) the small intestine and large intestine. Other parts of the digestive system include the gall bladder, liver, pancreas, salivary glands, and teeth.

The mouth, esophagus, and stomach. Digestion begins in the mouth, where the teeth tear and grind food into small pieces. Small pieces of food are more easily broken down during the digestive process than large ones. Therefore, thorough chewing is important. As food is chewed, three pair of large salivary glands pour saliva into the mouth. Saliva moistens the food, making it easier to swallow. Saliva also contains the first of the system's several digestive enzymes. The digestive enzymes break food down into chemicals the body can use.

After the food is swallowed, it enters the esophagus. The esophagus is a long, muscular tube that leads to the stomach. Contractions of smooth muscles move the food down the esophagus and into the stomach. The stomach is the widest part of the alimentary canal. It serves as a sort of "holding tank" in which food remains

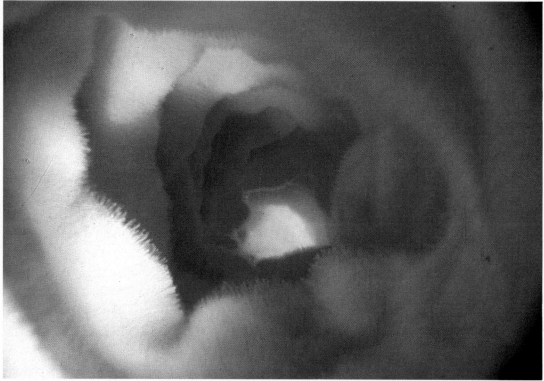

A magnified cross section of the small intestine shows the tiny, fingerlike structures that line this organ. These structures, called *villi,* increase the surface area of the small intestine. They enable the organ to absorb large amounts of useful substances from digested food.

for several hours. During this time, the stomach produces an acid and an enzyme that further break down much of the food. Muscle contractions mix the partly digested food into a thick liquid called *chyme.*

The small intestine and large intestine. Chyme passes from the stomach into the small intestine at a steady rate. Various digestive enzymes complete the breakdown of the food within the first section of the small intestine. The small intestine produces some of these enzymes. The rest are made by the pancreas. The pancreatic enzymes empty into the small intestine through a *duct* (tube). *Bile,* a liquid made by the liver and stored in the gall bladder, also enters the small intestine through a duct. Bile does not contain digestive enzymes, but it aids digestion by breaking up large molecules of fatty foods.

By the time the food leaves the first section of the small intestine, it has been completely digested. Special cells line the walls of the remainder of the small intestine. These cells absorb useful substances from the digested food. The absorbed substances enter the blood. Some of the substances are carried directly to cells throughout the body. The rest are transported to the liver. The liver stores some of the substances, releasing them as the body requires. It chemically alters the other substances, changing them into forms needed by the body.

The substances not absorbed by the small intestine pass to the large intestine. These substances consist of

water, minerals, and wastes. The large intestine absorbs most of the water and minerals, which then enter the bloodstream. The wastes move down toward the *rectum,* the end of the large intestine, and leave the body as bowel movements.

The respiratory system

The respiratory system consists of the organs of breathing. These organs include the nose, the *trachea* (windpipe), and a pair of lungs. The respiratory system has two main jobs. (1) It provides the body with oxygen. (2) It rids the body of carbon dioxide. The cells of the body need oxygen to break down and so release the energy in food. During this process, carbon dioxide forms as a waste product.

Breathing involves the acts of inhaling and exhaling. Inhaling occurs as the chest cavity expands. As the chest expands, so do the lungs. Air from the atmosphere rushes in and fills the enlarged lungs. Exhaling occurs as the chest cavity shrinks, which pushes air out of the lungs. Inhaling and exhaling result chiefly from contractions of the *diaphragm,* a large muscle that forms the floor of the chest cavity. As the diaphragm contracts, the cavity expands. As it relaxes, the cavity shrinks. The muscles that move the ribs also play a part in the breathing process.

The air passages. When we inhale, air enters the body through the nose. The air flows from the nostrils to the nasal passages. The nasal passages are lined with tiny hairlike structures and a sticky substance called *mucus.* These structures and the mucus filter dust and dirt from the air. In addition, cold air is warmed and moistened as it moves through the nasal passages. From the nose, the air passes through the *pharynx* (the cavity behind the nose and mouth) and the *larynx* (the voice box). The air then enters the trachea.

The trachea carries the air toward the lungs. Before reaching the lungs, the trachea splits into two tubes called the *primary bronchi.* Each tube enters one lung. Within the lungs, the primary bronchi divide into smaller and smaller tubes, finally branching into extremely tiny tubes called *bronchioles.* The bronchioles end in hundreds of millions of thin-walled structures called *alveoli* or *air sacs.* The alveoli give the lungs tremendous surface area. If the air sacs were flattened out, the lungs would cover from 600 to 1,000 square feet (56 to 93 square meters).

The exchange of carbon dioxide and oxygen occurs in the alveoli. Each alveolus is surrounded by a network of small blood vessels. Like the alveoli, these blood vessels have extremely thin walls. Blood that enters the vessels has a high level of carbon dioxide, which it picked up from the body tissues. It contains little oxygen. The carbon dioxide leaves the blood and moves through the walls of the blood vessels and alveoli into the lungs. Oxygen from the air in the lungs then passes through the walls of the alveoli and blood vessels and into the blood. The oxygen-rich blood leaves the lungs and travels to the heart, which pumps it to cells throughout the body. The carbon dioxide is expelled from the lungs when we exhale.

The circulatory system

The circulatory system moves blood throughout the body. Blood transports food and oxygen to the cells and carries away carbon dioxide and other wastes. The cells cannot live without a continuous supply of fresh blood. The circulatory system also carries disease-fighting substances that help protect the body. In addition, it transports chemical messengers called *hormones.* Hormones are discussed in the section of this article called *The endocrine system.*

The circulatory system consists chiefly of (1) the heart, (2) the blood vessels, (3) the blood, and (4) the lymphatic system.

The heart is a hollow muscle that pumps blood through the circulatory system by contracting and relaxing rhythmically. The heart actually consists of two pumps that lie side by side. The left side of the heart makes up the stronger pump. It receives oxygen-rich blood from the lungs and sends it to cells throughout the body. The blood, which picks up carbon dioxide and other wastes from the cells, returns to the right side of the heart. This weaker pump moves the blood to the lungs and then back to the left side of the heart. In the lungs, the carbon dioxide is removed from the blood, and oxygen is added.

The blood vessels form a branching network of about 60,000 miles (97,000 kilometers). They can be divided into three types (1) *Arteries* carry blood from the heart. (2) *Veins* carry blood to the heart. (3) *Capillaries* connect the arteries and veins.

Blood leaves the left side of the heart through the

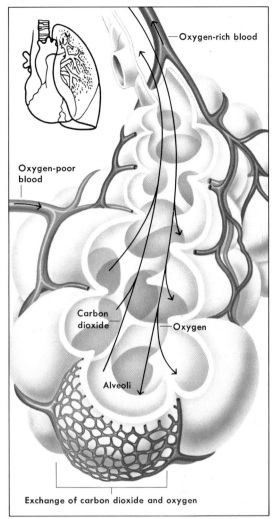

Carbon dioxide and oxygen are exchanged in the lungs, which lie close to the heart. One lung is shown with the heart at the upper left. Each lung contains millions of *alveoli,* or *air sacs.* Blood vessels, shown here only on the bottom sac, surround each alveolus. As blood flows through these vessels, it releases carbon dioxide, a waste picked up from the body tissues, into the alveoli. It then receives fresh oxygen from the alveoli.

aorta. This vessel is the largest artery in the body. Several major arteries branch off the aorta. These arteries, in turn, divide into smaller and smaller vessels. Finally, the smallest arteries empty into the tiny capillaries. Through the thin walls of the capillaries, food and oxygen in the blood are exchanged for carbon dioxide and other wastes from individual cells.

From the capillaries, the blood enters small veins, which join larger and larger veins. Finally, the blood enters the right side of the heart through the *superior vena cava* and *inferior vena cava,* the body's two largest veins. The right side of the heart then pumps the blood through the *pulmonary arteries* to the capillaries surrounding the air sacs in the lungs. The blood returns from the lungs to the left side of the heart through four

Anatomy of the human body

Each page in this series shows one or more of the human body's major systems. The index below keys the numbers found in the illustrations to an alphabetical list of each system's parts.

Skeletal system

Breastbone (sternum)	1
Calf bone (fibula)	2
Carpals (wrist bones)	3
Cheekbone (zygomatic bone)	4
Clavicle (collarbone)	5
Coccyx	6
Collarbone (clavicle)	5
Femur (thighbone)	7
Fibula (calf bone)	2
Finger bones (phalanges)	8
Frontal bone	9
Hipbone	11
Ilium	11a
Ischium	11b
Pubis	11c
Humerus	12
Ilium	11a
Ischium	11b
Jawbone, lower (mandible)	13
Jawbone, upper (maxilla)	14
Kneecap (patella)	15
Mandible (jawbone, lower)	13
Maxilla (jawbone, upper)	14
Metacarpals (hand bones)	10
Nasal bone	16
Occipital bone	17
Palm bones (metacarpals)	10
Parietal bone	18
Patella (kneecap)	15
Phalanges (finger bones)	8
Pubis	11c
Radius	19
Ribs	20
Sacrum	21
Scapula (shoulder blade)	22
Shinbone (tibia)	23
Shoulder blade (scapula)	22
Sphenoid bone	24
Spinal column (vertebrae)	25
Sternum (breastbone)	1
Teeth	26
Temporal bone	27
Thighbone (femur)	7
Tibia (shinbone)	23
Ulna	28
Vertebrae (spinal column)	25
Wrist bones (carpals)	3
Zygomatic bone (cheekbone)	4

Muscular system

Abdominal oblique, external	29
Abductor pollicis longus	30
Adductor longus	31
Biceps	32
Brachioradialis	33
Deltoid	34
Extensor pollicis brevis	35
Frontal muscle	36
Gastrocnemius	37
Gracilis	38
Masseter	39
Orbicularis oculi	40
Orbicularis oris	41
Pectineus	42
Pectoralis major	43
Rectus abdominis	44
Rectus femoris	45
Sartorius	46
Serratus anterior	47
Sternocleidomastoid	48
Sternohyoid	49
Temporal muscle	50
Tensor fasciae latae	51
Trapezius	52
Triceps	53
Vastus lateralis	54
Vastus medialis	55

Digestive system

Appendix, vermiform	56
Esophagus	57
Gall bladder	58
Intestine, large	59
Intestine, small	60
Liver	61
Mouth	62
Pharynx	63
Rectum	64
Salivary glands	65
Stomach	66

Respiratory system

Bronchus	67
Diaphragm	68
Larynx	69
Lung	70
Trachea (windpipe)	71
Windpipe (trachea)	71

Circulatory system

Heart	72
Spleen	*

Arteries

Aorta	73
Axillary	74
Brachial	75
Carotid, common	76
Carotid, external	77
Carotid, internal	78
Coronary	79
Femoral	80
Iliac, common	81
Iliac, external	82
Pulmonary	83
Radial	84
Renal	85
Subclavian	86
Temporal, superficial	87
Thyroid, superior	88
Ulnar	89

Veins

Brachial	90
Cephalic	91
Femoral	92
Iliac, common	93
Iliac, external	94
Jugular, external	95
Jugular, internal	96
Pulmonary	97
Renal	98
Saphenous, great	99
Subclavian	100
Vena cava, inferior	101
Vena cava, superior	102

Urinary system

Bladder	103
Kidney	104
Ureter	105
Urethra	106

Reproductive system

Male

Prostate gland	107
Seminal vesicle	108
Testicle	109
Vas deferens	110

Female

Fallopian tube	111
Ovary	112
Uterus	113
Vagina	114

Endocrine system

Adrenal gland	115
Ovary	112
Pancreas	116
Pineal gland	117
Pituitary gland	118
Testicle	109
Thymus	119
Thyroid gland	120

Nervous system

Brain	121
Cerebellum	121a
Cerebrum	121b
Pons	121c
Cerebellum	121a
Cerebrum	121b
Femoral nerve	122
Median nerve	123
Pons	121c
Radial nerve	124
Sciatic nerve	125
Spinal cord	126
Spinal nerves (31 pairs)	127
Ulnar nerve	128

*The spleen lies in front of and just above the left kidney (104). See the drawing with the Spleen article.

These illustrations were created for WORLD BOOK by Robert Demarest. Trans-Vision ® Milprint, Milwaukee, Wis.

Nervous system

Male

Female

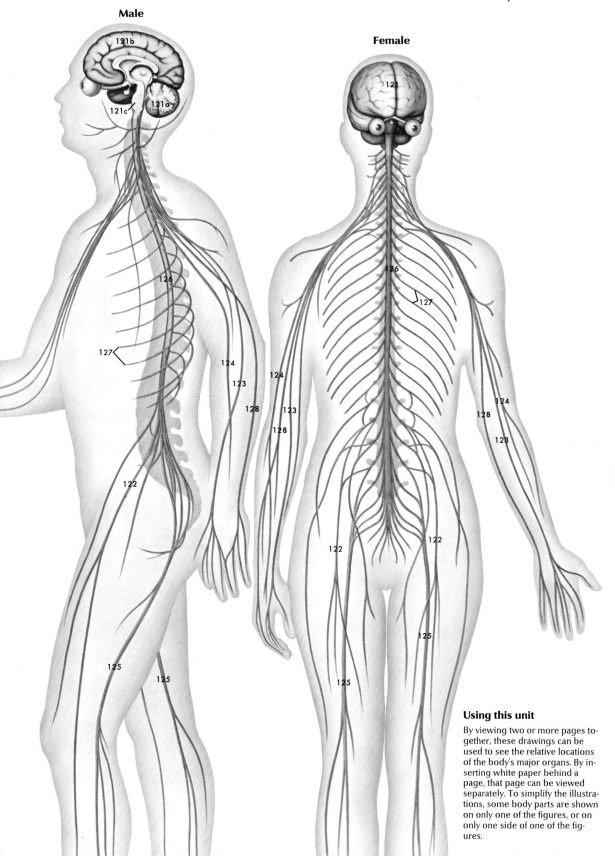

Using this unit

By viewing two or more pages together, these drawings can be used to see the relative locations of the body's major organs. By inserting white paper behind a page, that page can be viewed separately. To simplify the illustrations, some body parts are shown on only one of the figures, or on only one side of one of the figures.

pulmonary veins. The left side of the heart then pumps the blood out through the aorta, and the blood's journey begins once more.

The blood consists of a liquid and three kinds of solid particles called *formed elements.* The liquid, which makes up 55 to 65 per cent of the total volume of blood, is known as *plasma.* It carries many important substances. The food that enters the blood from the intestines and liver dissolves in the plasma, much as sugar dissolves in water. The plasma transports the dissolved food throughout the body. Many of the wastes that the blood picks up from the body tissues are carried in the plasma. These wastes include ammonia, urea, and much of the carbon dioxide.

The formed elements in blood consist of *red blood cells, white blood cells,* and *platelets.* Red blood cells carry oxygen from the lungs to the body tissues. They also carry some of the carbon dioxide from the tissues. White blood cells help protect the body from disease. These cells attack bacteria, viruses, poisons, and other harmful substances. Platelets are disklike structures that help prevent bleeding from damaged blood vessels. Together with various proteins in the plasma, platelets seal broken vessels by forming a clot.

The lymphatic system consists of a network of tubes that carries a clear, watery fluid called *lymph.* Lymph comes from the blood and eventually returns to it. Water, proteins, and dissolved food leave the blood through the capillary walls. This fluid, which is known as *interstitial fluid,* bathes and nourishes the cells of the body tissues. The fluid then drains into tiny, open-ended tubes called *lymphatic vessels.* At this point, the fluid is known as *lymph.*

The lymph flows through the small tubes into larger and larger lymphatic vessels. *Lymph nodes* occur at various points along the lymphatic vessels. These beadlike structures produce many white blood cells, which filter harmful substances out of the lymph. Eventually, all the lymph flows into either the *thoracic duct* or the *right lymphatic duct.* The lymph drains from these ducts into veins near the neck and so rejoins the blood.

The urinary system

The urinary system removes various wastes from the blood and flushes them from the body. The chief organs of this system are the two kidneys. Each kidney has about a million microscopic filtering units called *nephrons.* As blood passes through a nephron, a complicated network of capillaries and tubes filters out a small amount of water together with urea, sodium chloride, and certain other wastes. This filtered-out material forms a yellowish fluid called *urine.* Two tubes called *ureters* carry urine from the kidneys to the *urinary bladder,* a hollow storage organ. Urine eventually is squeezed

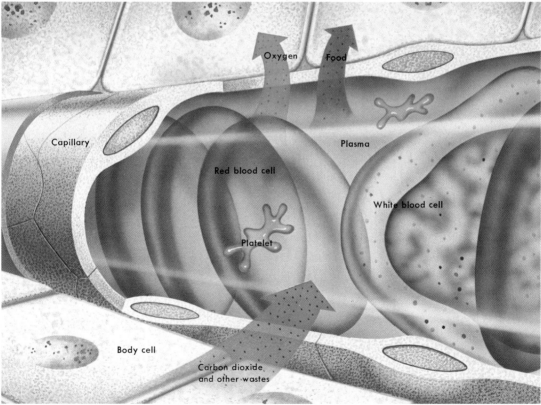

WORLD BOOK illustration by Colin Bidgood

Blood consists of a liquid and three kinds of solid particles. *Plasma,* the liquid portion, brings food to the body cells, and carries away wastes. *Red blood cells* transport oxygen, and *white blood cells* defend against disease. *Platelets* help prevent bleeding from damaged blood vessels.

out of the bladder by muscular contractions. It then leaves the body through a tube known as the *urethra.*

The reproductive system

The organs of the reproductive system enable men and women to have children. Human beings reproduce sexually. Sexual reproduction involves the union of sex cells. A new human being begins to develop after a sex cell produced by the father unites with a sex cell produced by the mother. The father's sex cells are called *sperm,* and the mother's are called *eggs.* The union of a sperm and an egg results in *fertilization.* The fertilized egg has all the information necessary for the development of a new human being.

The male reproductive system includes two *testicles,* which hang between the legs in a pouch called the *scrotum.* The testicles are glands that produce sperm. The sperm travel through tubes to the *penis,* an organ in front of the scrotum. Sperm leave a man's body through the penis.

Most of the female reproductive system lies within the woman's body. Deep within the body are two glands called *ovaries,* each of which contains hundreds of eggs. About once a month during a woman's childbearing years, one of the ovaries releases an egg. The egg travels down a narrow duct called the *Fallopian tube.* The female body has two Fallopian tubes, one leading from each ovary. The Fallopian tubes open into the top of the *uterus,* a hollow, muscular organ. The other end of the uterus leads to a canal called the *vagina.* The vagina extends to the outside of the body, opening between the legs.

During sexual intercourse, sperm from the penis enters the vagina. Each sperm has a tiny tail and can swim. The sperm swim from the vagina to the uterus and into the Fallopian tubes. If an egg is present in one of the tubes, a sperm may fertilize it.

The fertilized egg cell continues its journey to the uterus, where it becomes attached to the wall of the organ. The cell divides over and over, forming the beginning of a developing baby. Soon, a complex organ called the *placenta* forms. The placenta enables the developing baby to obtain food and oxygen from the mother's bloodstream.

After about nine months, the baby is ready to be born. Powerful contractions of the uterus push the baby out through the mother's vagina, which widens to allow the baby to pass through.

The endocrine system

The endocrine system consists of glands that regulate various body functions.The system plays a major role in regulating growth, the reproductive process, and the way the body uses food. It also helps prepare the body to deal with stress and emergencies.

The endocrine glands control body functions by producing hormones. These chemicals are released into the blood, which carries them throughout the body. Hormones act as chemical messengers. After a hormone reaches the organs or tissues it affects, it triggers certain actions. Many hormones have widespread effects. For example, the hormone *insulin* causes cells throughout the body to take in and use sugar from the bloodstream.

The chief endocrine glands include the adrenal

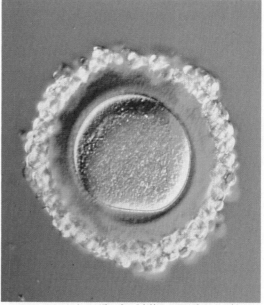

Lennart Nilsson from *Behold Man* © 1974 Little, Brown and Company

One egg cell is released from an ovary about every 28 days during a woman's childbearing years. The egg is surrounded by a covering, which appears as a ring in the photograph above. If a sex cell from a man penetrates the covering and unites with the egg, a new human being begins to develop.

glands, the pituitary gland, the parathyroid glands, the sex glands, and the thyroid gland. The brain, the kidneys, the stomach, and the pancreas also have endocrine tissues and produce hormones. The pituitary gland, which lies near the base of the brain, is often called the *master gland.* It releases a number of hormones, which, in turn, regulate other endocrine glands. However, the pituitary itself is controlled by hormones produced by the *hypothalamus,* a part of the brain. The hypothalamus links the nervous and endocrine control systems.

The body also has glands that do not produce hormones. These *exocrine glands* make chemicals that perform specific jobs in the area where they are released. Major exocrine products include the digestive juices, mucus, sweat, and tears.

The nervous system

The nervous system regulates and coordinates the activities of all the other systems of the body. It enables the body to adjust to changes that occur within itself and in its surroundings. The nervous system is made up of countless nerve cells, or *neurons.* The neurons form a communications network that extends to every part of the body. The nervous system has three main divisions. They are (1) the central nervous system; (2) the peripheral nervous system, which includes the eyes, ears, nose, and other sense organs; and (3) the autonomic nervous system.

The central nervous system consists of the brain and spinal cord. It functions as the control center of the nervous system. The central nervous system receives information from the senses. It analyzes this information and decides how the body should respond. It then sends instructions that trigger the required actions.

The central nervous system makes some simple decisions, such as directing the hand to pull away from a hot object, within the spinal cord. Such simple decisions are called *spinal reflexes.* Most decisions, however, involve the brain. The brain is an enormously complicated collection of billions of neurons. These neurons are linked together in precise patterns that enable the brain to think and remember. Much brain activity occurs at the conscious level. We are aware of decisions made at this level and can voluntarily control them. Other activity occurs at the subconscious level. This activity regulates the smooth muscles and is beyond voluntary control.

The peripheral nervous system is made up of the nerves that connect the central nervous system with every part of the body. These nerves include both *sensory neurons,* which carry information to the central nervous system, and *motor neurons,* which relay instructions from the central nervous system.

Sensory neurons run between the sense organs and the central nervous system. The sense organs have special sensory neurons called *receptors.* Receptors translate information about the internal or external environment into nerve impulses. These impulses are electrical signals that nerves can carry.

The body has many kinds of sense receptors. Vision receptors in the eyes change light waves into nerve impulses. Similarly, hearing receptors in the ears convert sound waves into nerve impulses. Smell receptors in the nose and taste receptors on the tongue convert chemical information into nerve impulses. Receptors in the skin respond to heat, cold, pressure, and pain. Sense receptors deep within the body provide information on the chemical and physical conditions of the inner body tissues.

Nerve impulses from the sense receptors travel along sensory neurons to the central nervous system. The central nervous system analyzes the information and decides what actions, if any, are necessary. If a response is needed, the central nervous system sends out instructions. The motor neurons of the peripheral nervous system carry the instructions from the central nervous system to the appropriate tissues.

The autonomic nervous system is a special part of the peripheral nervous system. It carries messages from the subconscious level of the brain to the internal organs. The autonomic nervous system regulates the automatic functions of the body, such as the beating of the heart and the movement of food through the digestive system.   Robert S. Eisenberg

Related articles in *World Book* include:

Muscular and skeletal systems

Achilles' tendon	Collarbone	Knee	Pelvis
Ankle	Elbow	Leg	Rib
Arm	Foot	Ligament	Shoulder
Back	Hand	Mandible	Skeleton
Bone	Head	Mastoid	Skull
Cartilage	Hip	Muscle	Spine
	Joint	Palate	Tendon

Digestive system

Alimentary canal	Bile	Digestive system
Assimilation	Colon	Enzyme

Esophagus	Mastication	Pharynx
Gall bladder	Mouth	Saliva
Hunger	Pancreas	Stomach
Intestine	Pepsin	Teeth
Liver		

Respiratory system

Chest	Lung	Respiration
Diaphragm	Nose	Windpipe
Larynx	Pleura	

Circulatory system

Aorta	Heart
Artery	Jugular vein
Blood	Lymphatic system
Capillary	Spleen
Circulatory system	Vein
Corpuscle	

Reproductive system

Baby	Pregnancy
Embryo	Reproduction
Embryology	Sex
Fertilization	Sterility
Menstruation	Testicle
Ovary	Umbilical cord
Penis	Uterus
Placenta	

Endocrine system

ACTH	Insulin
Adrenal gland	Pancreas
Epinephrine	Parathyroid gland
Estrogen	Pineal gland
Gland	Pituitary gland
Hormone	Thyroid gland

Nervous system

Brain	Perception
Cerebrospinal fluid	Reflex action
Ear	Senses
Eye	Smell
Funny bone	Solar plexus
Muscle sense	Taste
Nervous system	Touch
Pain	

Other related articles

Abdomen	Human being
Anatomy	Kidney
Appendix	Life
Biological clock	Medicine
Biology	Metabolism
Bladder	Nail
Connective tissue	Physical fitness
Disease	Physiology
Elimination	Posture
Growth	Prostaglandin
Hair	Skin
Health	Throat

Outline

I. **What the body is made of**
  A. Chemical elements and molecules
  B. Cells and tissues
  C. Organs and organ systems
II. **The skin**
  A. The epidermis
  B. The dermis
  C. Subcutaneous tissues
III. **The skeletal system**
IV. **The muscular system**
  A. Skeletal muscles
  B. Smooth muscles
  C. Cardiac muscle

V. **The digestive system**
   A. The mouth, esophagus, and stomach
   B. The small intestine and large intestine
VI. **The respiratory system**
   A. The air passages
   B. The exchange of carbon dioxide
      and oxygen
VII. **The circulatory system**
   A. The heart
   B. The blood vessels
   C. The blood
   D. The lymphatic system
VIII. **The urinary system**
IX. **The reproductive system**
X. **The endocrine system**
XI. **The nervous system**
   A. The central nervous system
   B. The peripheral nervous system
   C. The autonomic nervous system

Questions

How much of the human body consists of water?
What are the two main jobs of the respiratory system?
How do the salivary glands aid in digestion?
What are *receptors*? What role do they play in the nervous system?
In what ways can the human body be compared to a machine? How does it differ from one?
Why are capillaries important in the circulatory system?
How does the skin help keep the temperature of the body within its normal range?
Why is the pituitary gland called the *master gland*?
What are the four chief kinds of tissues in the human body?
What are the most common chemical elements in the human body?

Additional resources

Level I

Bruun, Ruth D. and Bertel. *The Human Body.* Random House, 1982.
Junior Body Machine: How the Human Body Works. Ed. by Christiaan Barnard. Crown, 1983.
Miller, Jonathan. *The Human Body: With Three-Dimensional, Movable Illustrations Showing the Workings of the Human Body.* Viking, 1983.
Your Wonderful Body! National Geographic Society, 1982.

Level II

The Body Machine: Your Health in Perspective. Ed. by Christiaan Barnard and John Illman. Crown, 1981.
Miller, Jonathan. *The Body in Question.* Random House, 1978.
Nilsson, Lennart, and Lindberg, Jan. *Behold Man: A Photographic Journey of Discovery Inside the Body.* Little, Brown, 1973.
Yokochi, Chihiro, and Rohen, J. W. *Photographic Anatomy of the Human Body.* 2nd ed. University Park Press, 1978.

Human Development Services, Office of, is a division of the United States Department of Health and Human Services. The office was established in 1973 to administer a variety of federal social and rehabilitation programs. These programs are designed to help American Indians, children, the elderly, the developmentally disabled, low-income families, and other groups with special needs.

The Office of Human Development Services has four main divisions. The *Administration on Aging* conducts programs to assist elderly people. The *Administration for Children, Youth, and Families* administers Head Start and other child development programs. It also administers programs for abused children and runaway youths. The *Administration for Native Americans* provides funds and other services to help American Indians, native Hawaiians, and Alaskan Eskimos. The *Administration on*

Developmental Disabilities supports and funds services that help people with birth defects or disabilities developed before the age of 22.

Critically reviewed by the Office of Human Development Services

See also **Children's Bureau.**

Human engineering is a technique that applies scientific knowledge of human behavior to build the various kinds of equipment used by people in their everyday life. It is also called *human factors engineering.* The purpose of human engineering is to make machines as suitable as possible for human use. Human factors engineers try to design machines that match the capabilities and limitations of human beings.

In the early 1900's, engineers discovered that the efficiency of a machine often depends on such human factors as the mood, comfort, and physical condition of the operator. At the same time, sociologists, psychologists, and other scientists studied human behavior to learn how it affects production. Human engineering grew from these various studies. Today, the technique is applied to the design of computer systems, automobiles, office equipment, farm and industrial machines, and household devices.   Thomas T. Liao

See also **Industrial psychology.**

Human relations is a field of study that deals with group behavior. Experts in human relations seek to discover the best means of achieving desired goals with a minimum of conflict. Human dignity and respect for the individual are considered basic. Knowledge gained from the social sciences is applied to situations ranging from family relations to international affairs.

Human relations assumes that each individual has certain needs, but that people differ in what they consider important. It also assumes that a person joins a group to get something from it, and that the group in turn expects a contribution from each member.

The basic elements in human relations

Individual needs. Individuals have two kinds of needs: inborn and acquired. *Inborn needs* include food, water, and rest. *Acquired needs* are learned from other people, and may be just as real as inborn needs. For example, a person may skimp on meals (inborn need) in order to meet the payments on a new automobile (acquired need).

Human relations experts must understand human needs. They must know why people act as they do, how they react to different situations, and what will make them change their minds. Experts study the economic, sociological, psychological, religious, and political motivations which cause various human actions.

Living together. Each individual lives in contact with others because people are social beings. A person's first group usually is his or her immediate family—parents, sisters, and brothers. In most societies, individuals also participate in a large group of other close relatives.

Children first learn to live with their family and playmates. As they grow, their activities may center around their church, neighborhood friends, age group at school, or special interests and hobbies. Adults may surround themselves with their own family or belong to a labor union, political party, or a lodge. Everyone joins temporary groups, such as concert audiences or shopping crowds.

Group conflicts. Every group situation provides opportunities for conflict between the needs of the various members of the group. For example, a building contractor may want to work overtime to finish a job. But the laborers may want to quit on time and go home to their families. In many cases of conflict, satisfying the wants of one person will automatically frustrate the wants of another. If the laborers go on strike, human relations have broken down. To prevent this, the people involved must find some way to maintain human relations by mutual accommodation.

Most groups have certain formal and informal regulations that minimize misunderstandings and conflicts. Each member of the group is expected to learn and follow these rules. People often learn the norms of the group so thoroughly that they are hardly aware of them. On the basis of accepted rules, group members can predict the behavior of their fellows. Without accepted norms, people are uncertain about what is expected of them, and the group may easily dissolve.

Conflict between individuals and groups is not always troublesome. Sometimes it increases the unity on each opposing side, reduces tensions, and clarifies the objectives of the individual and the organization.

Leadership is important in keeping the group working together and directing it to act in a certain way. Leadership skill is particularly important when conflicts arise. Leaders must use all their human relations skills to accommodate conflicting interests within their group. A group usually responds to its leader because it respects the leader's wisdom or experience or agrees with his or her opinion.

Human relations in action

Background information. Human relations depends on the contributions of the social sciences. Economists study the relationships of people as they produce and distribute goods and services. Political scientists compile knowledge about the behavior of people attempting to maintain order. Cultural anthropologists compare ways of living in various societies. Social psychologists concentrate on the ways in which group life molds the individual's attitudes and personality. Sociologists study the structure of social life and the ways in which groups are formed and function.

Programs in human relations vary according to the situation. But each program in human relations must take into account the basic goals of the group and other factors such as the organizational units and the system of control. The *organizational units* include the formal structure and the informal structure within the organization, and any outside influences that might have an effect on orderly group processes. The *system of control* includes all the elements (attitudes, motivations, and organizational units) guiding the actions of people in a certain situation.

Many school systems have introduced programs of intercultural education, an outstanding example of human relations in action. These programs try to reduce friction between people of varying backgrounds who live and work in close contact. Human relations programs also play an important role in many industrial firms. Since the 1940's, many employers have revised their attitudes about employees. They no longer regard an employee as just another pair of "hands," but as a personality with individual wants that the employer must take into account.   Raymond W. Mack

Related articles in *World Book* include:

Alienation	Minority group
Assimilation	Segregation
Group dynamics	Social psychology
Industrial relations	Social role

Human rights. See Bill of rights; Civil rights; Slavery (Views of slavery).

Human Rights, Universal Declaration of, was adopted by the United Nations General Assembly on Dec. 10, 1948. It sets forth the basic civil, economic, political, and social rights and freedoms of every person. The Universal Declaration of Human Rights states that all people are born free and equal in dignity and rights. Its preamble states that the declaration is meant to serve "as a common standard of achievement for all peoples and all nations."

See also **United Nations** (Human rights); **Civil rights** (Civil rights today).

Universal Declaration of Human Rights

Preamble

Whereas recognition of the inherent dignity and of the equal and inalienable rights of all members of the human family is the foundation of freedom, justice and peace in the world, Whereas disregard and contempt for human rights have resulted in barbarous acts which have outraged the conscience of mankind, and the advent of a world in which human beings shall enjoy freedom of speech and belief and freedom from fear and want has been proclaimed as the highest aspiration of the common people, Whereas it is essential, if man is not to be compelled to have recourse, as a last resort, to rebellion against tyranny and oppression, that human rights should be protected by the rule of law, Whereas it is essential to promote the development of friendly relations between nations, Whereas the peoples of the United Nations have in the Charter reaffirmed their faith in fundamental human rights, in the dignity and worth of the human person and in the equal rights of men and women and have determined to promote social progress and better standards of life in larger freedom, Whereas Member States have pledged themselves to achieve, in co-operation with the United Nations, the promotion of universal respect for and observance of human rights and fundamental freedoms, Whereas a common understanding of these rights and freedoms is of the greatest importance for the full realization of this pledge,
Now, therefore,
The General Assembly
proclaims this

Universal Declaration of Human Rights as a common standard of achievement for all peoples and all nations, to the end that every individual and every organ of society, keeping this Declaration constantly in mind, shall strive by teaching and education to promote respect for these rights and freedoms and by progressive measures, national and international, to secure their universal and effective recognition and observance, both among the peoples of Member States themselves and among the peoples of territories under their jurisdiction.

Article 1

All human beings are born free and equal in dignity and rights. They are endowed with reason and conscience and should act towards one another in a spirit of brotherhood.

Article 2

Everyone is entitled to all the rights and freedoms set forth in this Declaration, without distinction of any kind, such as race, colour, sex, language, religion, political or other opinion, national or social origin, property, birth or other status. Furthermore, no distinction shall be made on the basis of the political, jurisdictional or international status of the country or territory to which a person belongs, whether it be independent, trust, nonself-governing or under any other limitation of sovereignty.

Article 3

Everyone has the right to life, liberty and security of person.

Article 4

No one shall be held in slavery or servitude; slavery and the slave trade shall be prohibited in all their forms.

Article 5

No one shall be subjected to torture or to cruel, inhuman or degrading treatment or punishment.

Article 6

Everyone has the right to recognition everywhere as a person before the law.

Article 7

All are equal before the law and are entitled without any discrimination to equal protection of the law. All are entitled to equal protection against any discrimination in violation of this Declaration and against any incitement to such discrimination.

Article 8

Everyone has the right to an effective remedy by the competent national tribunals for acts violating the fundamental rights granted him by the constitution or by law.

Article 9

No one shall be subjected to arbitrary arrest, detention or exile.

Article 10

Everyone is entitled in full equality to a fair and public hearing by an independent and impartial tribunal, in the determination of his rights and obligations and of any criminal charge against him.

Article 11

1. Everyone charged with a penal offence has the right to be presumed innocent until proved guilty according to law in a public trial at which he has had all the guarantees necessary for his defence.

2. No one shall be held guilty of any penal offence on account of any act or omission which did not constitute a penal offence, under national or international law, at the time when it was committed. Nor shall a heavier penalty be imposed than the one that was applicable at the time the penal offence was committed.

Article 12

No one shall be subjected to arbitrary interference with his privacy, family, home or correspondence, nor to attacks upon his honour and reputation. Everyone has the right to the protection of the law against such interference or attacks.

Article 13

1. Everyone has the right to freedom of movement and residence within the borders of each state.

2. Everyone has the right to leave any country, including his own, and to return to his country.

Article 14

1. Everyone has the right to seek and to enjoy in other countries asylum from persecution.

2. This right may not be invoked in the case of prosecutions genuinely arising from non-political crimes or from acts contrary to the purposes and principles of the United Nations.

Article 15

1. Everyone has the right to a nationality.

2. No one shall be arbitrarily deprived of his nationality nor denied the right to change his nationality.

Article 16

1. Men and women of full age, without any limitation due to race, nationality or religion, have the right to marry and to found a family. They are entitled to equal rights as to marriage, during marriage and at its dissolution.

2. Marriage shall be entered into only with the free and full consent of the intending spouses.

3. The family is the natural and fundamental group unit of society and is entitled to protection by society and the State.

Article 17

1. Everyone has the right to own property alone as well as in association with others.

2. No one shall be arbitrarily deprived of his property.

Article 18

Everyone has the right to freedom of thought, conscience and religion; this right includes freedom to change his religion or belief, and freedom, either alone or in community with others and in public or private, to manifest his religion or belief in teaching, practice, worship and observance.

Article 19

Everyone has the right to freedom of opinion and expression; this right includes freedom to hold opinions without interference and to seek, receive and impart information and ideas through any media and regardless of frontiers.

Article 20

1. Everyone has the right to freedom of peaceful assembly and association.

2. No one may be compelled to belong to an association.

Article 21

1. Everyone has the right to take part in the government of his country, directly or through freely chosen representatives.

2. Everyone has the right of equal access to public service in his country.

3. The will of the people shall be the basis of the au-

thority of government; this will shall be expressed in periodic and genuine elections which shall be by universal and equal suffrage and shall be held by secret vote or by equivalent free voting procedures.

Article 22

Everyone, as a member of society, has the right to social security and is entitled to realization, through national effort and international co-operation and in accordance with the organization and resources of each State, of the economic, social and cultural rights indispensable for his dignity and the free development of his personality.

Article 23

1. Everyone has the right to work, to free choice of employment, to just and favourable conditions of work and to protection against unemployment.

2. Everyone, without any discrimination, has the right to equal pay for equal work.

3. Everyone who works has the right to just and favourable remuneration ensuring for himself and his family an existence worthy of human dignity, and supplemented, if necessary, by other means of social protection.

4. Everyone has the right to form and to join trade unions for the protection of his interests.

Article 24

Everyone has the right to rest and leisure, including reasonable limitation of working hours and periodic holidays with pay.

Article 25

1. Everyone has the right to a standard of living adequate for the health and well-being of himself and of his family, including food, clothing, housing and medical care and necessary social services, and the right to security in the event of unemployment, sickness, disability, widowhood, old age or other lack of livelihood in circumstances beyond his control.

2. Motherhood and childhood are entitled to special care and assistance. All children, whether born in or out of wedlock, shall enjoy the same social protection.

Article 26

1. Everyone has the right to education. Education shall be free, at least in the elementary and fundamental stages. Elementary education shall be compulsory. Technical and professional education shall be made generally available and higher education shall be equally accessible to all on the basis of merit.

2. Education shall be directed to the full development of the human personality and to the strengthening of respect for human rights and fundamental freedoms. It shall promote understanding, tolerance and friendship among all nations, racial or religious groups, and shall further the activities of the United Nations for the maintenance of peace.

3. Parents have a prior right to choose the kind of education that shall be given to their children.

Article 27

1. Everyone has the right freely to participate in the cultural life of the community, to enjoy the arts and to share in scientific advancement and its benefits.

2. Everyone has the right to the protection of the moral and material interests resulting from any scientific, literary or artistic production of which he is the author.

Article 28

Everyone is entitled to a social and international order in which the rights and freedoms set forth in this Declaration can be fully realized.

Article 29

1. Everyone has duties to the community in which alone the free and full development of his personality is possible.

2. In the exercise of his rights and freedoms, everyone shall be subject only to such limitations as are determined by law solely for the purpose of securing due recognition and respect for the rights and freedoms of others and of meeting the just requirements of morality, public order and the general welfare in a democratic society.

3. These rights and freedoms may in no case be exercised contrary to the purposes and principles of the United Nations.

Article 30

Nothing in this Declaration may be interpreted as implying for any State, group or person any right to engage in any activity or to perform any act aimed at the destruction of any of the rights and freedoms set forth herein.

Human sacrifice. See Aztec (Religion; picture: Human sacrifice); **Maya** (Religion).

Humane society is a group dedicated to protecting children and animals from human cruelty. Today, a person who sees an animal beaten or a child mistreated may notify the local humane society. The society takes legal action against the offender. The first humane societies were founded in the 1700's to teach people lifesaving methods and to prevent drownings. The first society to be established for the prevention of cruelty to animals was founded in England in 1824.

The first American Society for the Prevention of Cruelty to Animals was founded in New York in 1866. The New York Society for the Prevention of Cruelty to Children was organized in 1876. Philanthropist Henry Bergh took a leading part in organizing both of these societies. Similar societies were formed throughout the United States. In 1877, these local groups formed the American Humane Association. See also **Society for the Prevention of Cruelty to Animals.**

Critically reviewed by the American Humane Association

Humanism is a way of looking at our world which emphasizes the importance of human beings—their nature and their place in the universe. There have been many varieties of humanism, both religious and nonreligious. But all humanists agree that people are the center of their study. As the Latin writer Terence said more than 2,000 years ago: "I am a man, and nothing human is foreign to me." Humanism teaches that every person has dignity and worth and therefore should command the respect of every other person.

Although humanism had its roots in the life and thought of ancient Greece and Rome, it flourished as a historical movement in Europe from the 1300's to the

1500's. Its approach to the study of humanity formed the intellectual core of the cultural reawakening called the *Renaissance.* The humanistic attitude toward life has continued to the present day.

The development of humanism

The humanistic movement in the early Renaissance began with the exciting rediscovery of the writings of the classical Greeks and Romans. These writings had either been unknown in Europe since the decline of the Roman Empire, or they had been known in partial and inexact form. The humanists were interested in the ancient classics not only because they were models of literary style, but also because they were guides to the understanding of life.

This understanding was in contrast to the emphasis of many medieval scholars, who taught that life on earth should be despised. Such persons viewed human beings as sinful creatures who should devote their lives to trying to earn heaven. Humanists rejected this view of the sinful nature of humanity. Their fresh way of looking at life during this *revival of learning* began in Italy in the 1300's and spread to France, Germany, the Netherlands, and England. At its height in the 1500's, humanism was an international fellowship of scholars.

Leading humanists and their influence

Much of modern Western culture comes from humanistic achievements. The spirit and goals of humanism still influence the arts, education, and government.

The arts. Most early humanists were religious. But the main drift of their work led away from the ascetic teachings of the Middle Ages which urged the rejection of this world and its pleasures. Instead, the humanists urged a more robust recognition of the realities of human nature.

Humanistic literature is realistic, critical, and often humorous. The Italian humanist poet Petrarch portrayed the "Laura" of his sonnets as a real woman, not a medieval religious symbol. The brilliant Dutch humanist Erasmus was a priest who tried to find common elements in Greek philosophy and Christian thought. But his great work *The Praise of Folly* was a witty and satiric criticism of kings and churchmen, as well as a recognition of general human error.

England's Geoffrey Chaucer in his *Canterbury Tales* and Italy's Giovanni Boccaccio in his *Decameron* told humorous stories that show a keen understanding of human nature. François Rabelais of France satirized the church, universities, and other institutions in *Gargantua and Pantagruel.* Rabelais combined vast learning and wisdom with rollicking nonsense and earthiness. The English humanist Thomas More was a devout churchman who died a martyr. But *Utopia,* his best-known book, criticized the society of his time. Although all these humanists held high ideals for humanity, they looked at human nature candidly and honestly.

The humanistic attempt to view life both ideally and realistically is also seen in painting and sculpture. Renaissance painters and sculptors continued to create religious art to decorate churches. But they gradually abandoned the stiff, conventional style of medieval art, and developed techniques that emphasized individuality. Humanist painters also turned to nonreligious subjects,

such as battles, portraits, and classical themes. In the Netherlands, Pieter Bruegel the Elder painted accurate, vivid scenes of peasant life. Humanist sculptors, including Donatello and Michelangelo, created realistic, richly detailed, and highly individualized statues. All these artists showed men and women as they are, with their varieties of attitudes, gestures, and personalities. Their art also presented people as majestic and worthy of admiration.

Education to the Renaissance humanist meant the training of the "ideal gentleman" or "universal man." Such a person was skilled in many fields of knowledge, including art, science, sports, and politics.

Much later, in the 1800's, the English humanist Matthew Arnold set goals that are probably the best description of the modern humanistic ideal of education. Arnold wanted people to know "the best that has been thought and said in the world." His ideal was the person whose powers were all in balance—who had knowledge, who knew how to live in harmony with others, who appreciated beauty, and who had high standards of moral judgment.

Today, humanistic education centers around the *humanities,* which usually include religion, philosophy, languages, literature, history, and the arts. Together, these subjects have humanistic ideals at their center. They try to interpret the meaning of life, rather than just describing the physical world or society.

Government. Humanism's opposition to political tyranny in the late 1700's was an important influence in the American and French revolutions. Both the American Declaration of Independence and the French Declaration of the Rights of Man declare the dignity of humanity. They are, therefore, humanistic as well as political documents. Benjamin Franklin, Thomas Jefferson, and other American revolutionary leaders were among the leading humanists of their age.

Humanism today. Many educators and philosophers believe that the greatest challenge to humanism, and indeed a threat to the safety of society, comes from too great an emphasis on science and technology. They realize that scientific achievements have greatly increased our knowledge and power. But they also believe that humanism must teach us how to use this knowledge and power in a moral, human way.　John W. Dodds

See also **Renaissance** with its list of *Related articles.*

Additional resources

Braunthal, Alfred. *Salvation and the Perfect Society: The Eternal Quest.* Univ. of Massachusetts Press, 1979.
Brinton, Crane. *The Shaping of Modern Thought.* Prentice-Hall, 1963.
Bronowski, Jacob. *Science and Human Values.* Rev. ed. Harper, 1965.
Hadas, Moses. *Humanism: The Greek Ideal and Its Survival.* Harper, 1960.
Kristeller, Paul O. *Renaissance Thought and Its Sources.* Columbia, 1979.
Perry, Ralph Barton. *The Humanity of Man.* Braziller, 1956.

Humanities, The. See Humanism (Education); Careers (Fine arts and humanities).

Humber, River, in England, flows eastward through the county of Humberside and empties into the North Sea. The River Humber is about 40 miles (64 kilometers) long and from 1 to 7 miles (1.6 to 11 kilometers) wide. The Ouse and Trent rivers, two important trade routes, empty into the River Humber. Large steamers can sail up the Humber for a distance of about 20 miles (32 kilometers) from the river's outlet. Hull and Grimsby are important cities on the banks of the River Humber. When the Norsemen invaded England during the 800's and 900's, they sailed their boats up the River Humber.

The Humber Bridge, completed in 1981, crosses the river near Hull. It has the longest main span of any suspension bridge in the world. Its main span measures 4,626 feet (1,410 meters).   John W. Webb

Humboldt, *HUHM bohlt,* **Baron von** (1769-1859), was a German scientist and geographer. He helped found modern geography and pioneered in plant geography and climatology. Humboldt drew the first map with *isothermal* lines (lines connecting points of the same temperature). He traveled extensively in the Spanish territories of America. In his famous five-volume work, *Cosmos* (1845-1862), Humboldt tried to describe fully the physical universe.

Alexander von Humboldt was born in Berlin on Sept. 14, 1769. He studied geology, biology, and political science at the University of Göttingen, and mining and metallurgy at the School of Mines in Freiburg. From 1792 to 1797, he was a mine assessor in Prussia. Then he resigned to study nature, a strong interest since his childhood. Humboldt explored Mexico, Central America, and South America from 1799 to 1804. He lived for the next 20 years in Paris, which was then a center of geographical learning.

Humboldt spent most of his remaining years in Berlin. At the University of Berlin, he gave the lectures on which he based *Cosmos.* He made his most important later voyages for the Russian czar, who sent him to the Ural Mountains and Central Asia in 1829 to report on mineral resources.   J. Russell Whitaker

See also **Geology** (The rock dispute).

Humboldt Current. See Peru Current.

Humboldt River, *HUHM bohlt,* is the longest waterway in Nevada. The Humboldt flows southwestward through the state for 290 miles (467 kilometers). The river rises in Elko County in northeastern Nevada and empties into Humboldt Lake in the western part of the state. Alkali that the river picks up in its course makes Humboldt Lake salty. River water irrigates parts of the valley, making these parts suitable for farming. Two main-line railroads run through the river valley, which is the only pass going east and west through the mountains of Nevada.   E. R. Larson

Hume, *hyoom,* **David** (1711-1776), was a Scottish philosopher. He influenced the development of two modern philosophical schools, skepticism and empiricism.

His philosophy. Hume distrusted philosophical speculation. He believed that all knowledge came from experience and all experiences existed only in the mind as individual units of experience. Whatever a person directly experienced was nothing more than the contents of his or her own consciousness, or mind. Hume believed that a world existed outside of human consciousness, but he did not think this belief could be proved. See **Skepticism; Empiricism.**

Hume called lively and forceful units of experience *perceptions* and less lively and forceful units *beliefs* or *thoughts.* Words and concepts were meaningful for a person only if they related directly to these units of ex-

perience. Each unit of experience was separate and distinct from all other units, though the units were usually experienced as being connected.

According to Hume, three principles connected associated ideas with each other: (1) *resemblance,* (2) *contiguity,* and (3) *cause and effect.* In resemblance, if two units of experience resembled each other, thought of one led to thought of the other. In contiguity, if two units of experience adjoined each other, thought of one provoked thought of the other. In cause and effect, if one unit constantly preceded another, thought of the first resulted in thought of the second.

Hume was famous for his attack on the principle of *causality.* This principle states that nothing can happen or exist without a cause. Hume believed that although one *event* (set of impressions) always preceded another, this did not prove that the first event caused the second. The constant conjunction of two events, he said, built up the expectation that the second event would take place after the first. But this was nothing more than a strong belief or habit of mind taught by experience. One could never prove there were causal connections among impressions.

Hume, an agnostic, argued that the existence of God could not be proved. He said that even granting God's existence, nothing could be absolutely known about His nature. On the other hand, Hume believed that God's existence could not be disproved either.

Hume based his theory of morality on experience, rejecting the view that reason could distinguish virtue from vice. He examined the circumstances in which people spoke of morality. He concluded that virtuous characteristics in people were those that were agreeable or useful to them. Hume claimed that all people possessed the feeling of *benevolence* (good will) and that this feeling was the basis of moral judgments.

His life. Hume was born in Edinburgh and spent most of his life writing. Occasionally, he served on diplomatic missions in France and other countries. His major work, *A Treatise of Human Nature* (1739, 1740), attracted little attention when it was published. But Hume's fame grew, especially in France, after he published more works on philosophy, religion, and history. These works included *Philosophical Essays Concerning Human Understanding* (1748) and *An Enquiry Concerning the Principles of Morals* (1751). Hume's *History of Great Britain* (1754, 1756) and *History of England* (1759, 1762) rank among the first important histories of that country.   Stephen A. Erickson

See also **Philosophy** (Modern philosophy).

Humerus. See Arm.

Humidifier, *hyoo MIHD uh FY uhr,* is a device that increases the amount of moisture in indoor air or a stream of air. It operates by allowing water to evaporate from a pan or a wetted surface, or by circulating air through an air-washer compartment that contains moisture.

Humidifiers are used in industry to create an atmosphere suitable for testing or processing certain materials. In homes, humidifiers help reduce static electricity and prevent wood structures and furniture from becoming brittle. Many people use humidifiers in the winter to help them feel more comfortable. Heated air is very dry and can irritate nasal passages. Humidifiers help reduce such irritation. They also slow the evaporation of moisture from people's skin. The cooling effect of evaporation is thereby reduced, making people feel warmer at lower temperatures. Evan Powell

See also **Air conditioning** (Controlling the moisture); **Dehumidifier; Humidity.**

Humidity is a term that describes the amount of water vapor in the air. The humidity varies according to the temperature and pressure of the air. The warmer the air is, the more water vapor it can hold. When the air contains as much water vapor as it can hold at a certain temperature and pressure, the air is *saturated.*

The amount of water vapor in the air compared to the amount the air can hold at saturation is called *relative humidity.* If the air contains only half of the water vapor it can hold, the relative humidity is 50 per cent. In clouds and fog, the air is saturated and the relative humidity is 100 per cent. The lower air over oceans is almost saturated and the relative humidity is close to 100 per cent. In the Sahara and other subtropical deserts, the relative humidity may be as low as 10 per cent.

The relative humidity of an area may vary greatly during the day, even though the amount of water vapor in the air remains the same. In such cases, the relative humidity changes as the temperature rises and falls. For example, the relative humidity may be high in the morning, when the temperature is low and the air cannot hold a great deal more then its present water vapor. But as the temperature rises during the day, the air can hold more water vapor and the relative humidity therefore becomes lower.

As air at a fixed pressure and with a constant amount of water vapor is cooled, it will reach a temperature where it becomes saturated. This temperature is called the *dew point.* If the temperature is lowered further, water vapor will begin to condense and form clouds, fog, or dew. The closer the temperature of the air is to its dew point, the higher the relative humidity will be.

Humidity affects our comfort and health. When the temperature and the relative humidity are high, most people feel uncomfortable and "sticky" because their perspiration does not evaporate easily. Many people use air conditioners and dehumidifiers in the summer to take water vapor out of the air. In winter, the heated air in buildings is dry and the relative humidity indoors may be very low. These conditions can cause drying of nasal passages and other health problems. As a result, people often use humidifiers in winter to put water vapor into the air. Alexis B. Long

Related articles in *World Book* include:

Air conditioning	Evaporation	Rain
Cloud	Fog	Temperature-humidity index
Dehumidifier	Humidifier	
Dew	Hygrometer	Weather

Hummingbird is a family of birds that contains the smallest bird in the world. Hummingbirds live only in the Western Hemisphere. More than 300 species are known. Only 19 varieties live in the United States, and all but one of these are found in the western and southwestern states. Hummingbirds get their names from the humming sound made by their wings, which move 60 to 70 times a second in the smallest species.

Size. The smallest of the hummingbirds are no larger than bumble bees. Only a few are more than 6 inches (15 centimeters) long. The largest is the *giant hummingbird,* a native of the Andes Mountains of South America. It is about $8\frac{1}{4}$ inches (21 centimeters) long, including the bill. The smallest is the *bee hummingbird,* a native of Cuba. It is about 2 inches (5 centimeters) long. The smallest hummingbird in the United States is the *calliope hummingbird,* native to the western mountain regions. It is about 3 inches (8 centimeters) long.

Habits. Some members of the hummingbird family are among the most brightly colored birds in the world.

To make a hygrometer, cut a hole about $2\frac{1}{2}$ inches from the bottom of an empty milk carton and fill the carton with water up to the opening. Fasten two thermometers to the carton, one with the bulb just above the hole. Wrap cloth around this bulb and push it through the hole into the water.

To determine relative humidity, allow the hygrometer to stand for 15 minutes in a breeze away from direct sunlight. Read both thermometers and use the temperatures to find the humidity on the chart, *below.* Read across from the wet-bulb readings. Read downward from the dry-bulb readings. For example, if the dry-bulb thermometer reads 70° F. and the wet-bulb thermometer reads 60° F., the relative humidity is 55 per cent.

WORLD BOOK illustration by Sarah Woodward

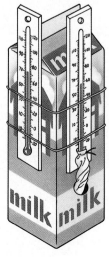

DRY-BULB TEMPERATURES °F.

WET-BULB °F.	56	58	60	62	64	66	68	70	71	72	73	74	75	76	77	78	79	80	82	84	86	88
38	7	2																				
40	15	11	7																			
42	25	19	14	9	7																	
44	34	29	22	17	13	8	4															
46	45	38	30	24	18	14	10	6	4	3	1											
48	55	47	40	33	26	21	16	12	10	9	7	5	4	3	1							
50	66	56	48	41	34	29	23	19	17	15	13	11	9	8	6	5	4	3				
52	77	67	57	50	43	36	31	25	23	21	19	17	15	13	12	10	9	7	5	3	1	
54	88	78	68	59	51	44	38	33	30	28	25	23	21	19	17	16	14	12	10	7	5	3
56		89	79	68	60	53	46	40	37	34	32	29	27	25	23	21	19	18	14	12	9	7
58			89	79	70	61	54	48	45	42	39	36	34	31	29	27	25	23	20	16	14	11
60				90	79	71	62	55	52	49	46	43	40	38	35	33	31	29	25	21	18	15
62					90	80	71	64	60	57	53	50	47	44	42	39	37	35	30	26	23	20
64						90	80	72	68	65	61	58	54	51	48	46	43	41	36	32	28	25
66							90	81	77	73	69	65	62	59	56	53	50	47	42	37	33	30
68								90	86	82	78	74	70	66	63	60	57	54	48	43	39	35
70									95	91	86	82	78	74	71	67	64	61	55	49	44	40
72											95	91	86	82	79	75	71	68	61	56	50	46
74													96	91	87	83	79	75	69	62	57	51
76															96	91	87	83	76	69	63	57
78																	96	91	84	76	70	64
80																			92	84	77	70
82																				92	84	77
84																					92	85
86																						92

Giant hummingbird
Patagona gigas
Found in the Andes, from Ecuador to Chile
Body length $8\frac{1}{4}$ inches (21 centimeters)

Bee hummingbird
Calypte helenae
Found in Cuba
Body length 2 inches (5 centimeters)

WORLD BOOK illustration by Walter Linsenmaier

The end of the hummingbird's tongue is forked. The edges of the two parts curl together and form a double trough through which nectar is taken into the mouth.

WORLD BOOK diagram adapted from "The Tongue Apparatus in Hummingbirds" by R. D. Weymouth in *ACTA Anatomica*, Vol. 58 (Karger, 1964).

Bob Smith

The rufous hummingbird covers the outside of its nest with lichens and holds the structure together with cobwebs.

How a hummingbird hovers

The diagram below shows how a hummingbird's wings move when the bird hovers in the air. The pictures represent one wingbeat. A hummingbird can beat its wings as fast as 70 times a second.

Illustrations adapted from *Hummingbirds* by Crawford H. Greenewalt. Copyright © 1960 by The American Museum of Natural History. Reprinted by permission of Doubleday & Company, Inc.

Direction of wings

Direction of air flow

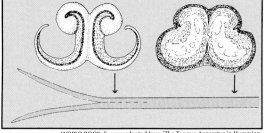

They have glittering patches of emerald green, deep violet, fiery red, and glowing orange. They fly quickly and can dart upward, downward, backward, or forward with remarkable speed. Their long, slender bills are especially suited for sucking nectar from flowers, even the deep-throated or trumpet-shaped flowers such as the honeysuckle and trumpet flower. The tongue of the hummingbird is also a useful tool for obtaining food from places difficult to reach. It is shaped like a long tube through which the birds suck the flower nectar.

Food. Insects form an important part of the hummingbird's diet. The bird often finds insects inside the flowers, or seizes them while it hovers. Sometimes it steals insects from spider webs. The hummingbird uses threads from the web to build its cottony nest.

The ruby-throated hummingbird, one of the smallest and daintiest birds in the United States, grows less than 4 inches (10 centimeters) long. It is the only hummingbird found east of the Mississippi River and north of Florida. Both male and female have a coat of metallic green feathers on the upper parts of their bodies. The male has a bright red throat. The female's throat is white.

The ruby-throated hummingbird's nest is as tiny and dainty as the bird itself. The female prefers a position high in the branches of a tree. There she builds her nest of shreds of bark, soft grass, and bits of plant or cattail fluff. Often she covers the outside with lichens or bits of bark. These blend so well with the background that a person hardly knows the little home is there. During the nesting season, the male becomes very bold. He will fight off enemies much larger than himself. The mother bird usually lays two tiny white eggs about the size of navy beans. The young hatch in about two weeks. They have no feathers when they are born, and they cannot see. But within three weeks they are fully feathered and strong enough to leave the nest.

Scientific classification. Hummingbirds make up the family Trochilidae. The ruby-throated hummingbird is *Archilochus colubris.* The giant hummingbird is *Patagona gigas;* the bee hummingbird, *Calypte helenae;* and the calliope, *Stellula calliope.*　Donald F. Bruning

See also **Bird** (picture: Birds of urban areas); **Photography** (picture).

Hummingbird moth. See Hawk moth.

Humor is any body fluid, such as the aqueous and vitreous humors in the eye. Humor also refers to chronic skin disease. In medieval medicine the four humors were blood, phlegm, yellow bile, and black bile. It was supposed that a person was healthy when the four humors were properly mixed in the body.

Humor. No one knows exactly why we laugh, or why anything that is funny should cause us to make such a peculiar noise. It would be just as logical to stick our thumbs in our ears and wiggle our fingers as it is to giggle or bellow or howl with laughter. But when something strikes our "funny bone," our diaphragm flutters up and down, and we laugh.

The urge to laugh appears very early. Babies smile, then coo, and finally chuckle when pleased. If certain parts of the body are tickled with the fingers, laughter is produced in babies as well as in many adults. But by the time children attend school, they also laugh at things they hear and see.

Stories are among the most popular forms of humor.

As a rule, a story is considered inferior if it makes some person blush with embarrassment, if it makes something sacred appear common, if it makes a person's weakness the cause for laughter, if it has to have profanity or vulgarity to be funny, or if everyone cannot join in the enjoyment of the joke.

The humor of situation

If a man meets a lady on the street, tips his hat to her, and a pigeon flies out from beneath it, most of the people who see it would roar with laughter. This is called the humor of the *unexpected happening.*

Another kind of situation humor is the *incongruous* (putting together unrelated things). Boys and girls see dogs every day and think nothing of them. But if a dog enters a classroom, everyone laughs. The dog does not belong there, and the situation is incongruous.

The humor of words

Situation humor need not be described in words. By far the greatest amount of humor is told rather than seen. Certain words are funny in their very sounds, like *bobble* and *squirt.* Sometimes people get mixed up in pronouncing their words, and instead of saying "people think" they might say "thinkle peep."

Puns, or double meanings, furnish us with much of our humor. Puns are *plays on words,* in which one word is said when another one is meant. For example, it is said that Ben Jonson was asked by a friend to make a pun. Ben replied, "Pun what subject?" for "Upon what subject?" The friend laughed at this pun, but said, "Oh, the king." Ben then said, "But the king is not a subject. He is the king."

Hyperbole is simply exaggeration. Sometimes it includes a twisting or distortion of the truth for the sake of humor. Common expressions of everyday life are often hyperboles. If a woman says "It's raining cats and dogs" she is using hyperbole. And if she is answered with "I know. I just stepped in a poodle," she hears a pun.

Repetition is also a popular way of gaining laughter, but it does not produce a very high grade of humor. In many of the jokes told, a thing happens twice in exactly the same way. But the third time it happens differently, and the point of the story is revealed.

A man's car stuck in the mud one rainy day. He walked to the nearest farmhouse to telephone for help. The farmer had no telephone, but said the farm some distance down the road had one. Muttering angrily, the man plodded on through the rain. The second farmer's telephone was out of order, but this farmer said another farm still farther down the road had one. The motorist was near the exploding point when he reached the third farm. As the farmer shuffled to the door, the motorist yelled, "You idiot! I wouldn't use your phone even if you had one!"

Comparison and contrast often give rise to humor. They are almost the same as the incongruous situation. "My head's as clear as a bell. In fact, I hear it ringing" shows comparison. Contrast is illustrated in such expressions as "not enough sense to varnish a walnut."

The types of humor

Humor of words takes many forms. It can be gentle and kindly, or it can be harsh and biting. There is no exact distinction between these various types of humor.

Wit differs from most humor in being purely intellectual, rather than relying on incongruities that come up naturally in many situations. Most humor produces a smile, but wit usually causes people to break out in sudden laughter.

Satire presents the weaknesses of humanity and makes fun of them. Usually, satire attempts to cure the foolishness by making people laugh at it.

Sarcasm is much more brutal than satire. It often takes the form of a biting speech. For example, if one woman says to another, "That's a lovely dress, dear. Too bad they didn't have your size," the woman is sarcastic.

Irony implies the opposite of what is apparently being stated. Irony may begin as a compliment or a simple statement, but it conceals a sting in the remark. It is usually expressed by a tone of voice, and is often an understatement. A sign on a freshly seeded plot of grass may say only "Please," but the sign probably means, "Have enough sense to stay on the sidewalk, where you belong!"

Farce, slapstick, and buffoonery involve such pranks as throwing custard pies or pushing unsuspecting persons into swimming pools.

Parody and burlesque change the wording of a well-known story or song to produce comic results.

Mimicry imitates another person's habits, gestures, or speech for comic effect.   Sarah Blacher Cohen

Related articles in *World Book* include:

American humorists

Ade, George	Nash, Ogden
Billings, Josh	Nye, Bill
Day, Clarence S., Jr.	Perelman, S. J.
Dunne, Finley P.	Rogers, Will
Lardner, Ring	Stockton, Frank R.
Marquis, Don	Thurber, James
Nasby, Petroleum	Twain, Mark
Vesuvius	Ward, Artemus

Other humorists

Beaumarchais, Pierre A.	Shaw, George Bernard
Leacock, Stephen B.	Wilde, Oscar
Munro, Hector H.	Wodehouse, P. G.
Rabelais, François	

Other related articles

Burlesque	Parody
Comedy	Pun
Hyperbole	Satire
Irony	

Humpback. See Hunchback.

Humperdinck, *HUM puhr* DIHNGK, **Engelbert** (1854-1921), a German composer, won great success with his opera *Hansel and Gretel* (1893). He wrote the music for a text his sister adapted from a Grimm's fairy tale. Humperdinck also wrote *The Royal Children* (1910), and music for Shakespeare's plays *The Winter's Tale* and *The Tempest.* He helped Richard Wagner score and cast *Parsifal* (1882). Humperdinck was born near Bonn, Germany.   Joyce Michell

Humphrey, Hubert Horatio (1911-1978), served as Vice President of the United States under President Lyndon B. Johnson, and was the Democratic presidential nominee in 1968. Humphrey lost to former Vice President Richard M. Nixon. Before his election as Vice President in 1964, Humphrey had been elected to the U.S.

Senate three times. He was the first Democrat ever elected to the Senate from Minnesota. In 1970, he was again elected to the Senate, and he was reelected in 1976. In 1977, the Senate made Humphrey the deputy president pro tempore of the Senate, a new post. The title will be given to all former Presidents and Vice Presidents who later become members of the Senate.

Early life. Humphrey was born on May 27, 1911, in Wallace, S. Dak. He graduated from the Denver College of Pharmacy in 1933, and worked for four years as a druggist in his father's drugstore. He later returned to college, and graduated from the University of Minnesota in 1939. Humphrey earned a master's degree at Louisiana State University. He then worked for the federal Works Progress Administration (WPA) and the War Manpower Commission in Minneapolis. He also taught political science at Macalester College in St. Paul, Minn.

In 1936, Humphrey married Muriel Fay Buck (1912-   ). They had four children, Nancy Faye (1939-   ), Hubert Horatio III (1942-   ), Robert Andrew (1944-   ), and Douglas Sannes (1948-   ).

Humphrey entered politics in 1943, when he ran unsuccessfully for mayor of Minneapolis. In 1944, he helped merge Minnesota's Democratic and Farmer-Labor parties into an organization known as the Democratic-Farmer-Labor Party. Humphrey was elected mayor of Minneapolis in 1945, and was reelected in 1947. He gained national fame at the Democratic National Convention in 1948, when he successfully led the fight for a strong party stand on civil rights.

Senator and Vice President. Humphrey was elected to the U.S. Senate in 1948, and was reelected in 1954 and 1960. In 1961, he became Senate Democratic *whip* (assistant leader). In the Senate, he was a leading spokesman for arms control, civil rights, medical aid to the needy, and aid to education. Humphrey suggested creation of the federal Food for Peace program, which makes U.S. farm products available to poor countries and needy people. He was also the first to prominently promote the establishment of a peace corps, an overseas volunteer work program. Humphrey campaigned for the presidential nomination in 1960, but withdrew after losing two primary elections to Senator John F. Kennedy of Massachusetts.

In the 1964 presidential election, President Johnson and Humphrey defeated their Republican opponents, Senator Barry M. Goldwater of Arizona and Representative William E. Miller of New York. Humphrey became one of the busiest Vice Presidents in U.S. history, serving as chairman of several government councils.

Presidential candidate. In 1968, the Democratic National Convention nominated Humphrey for President. He and his running mate, Senator Edmund S. Muskie of Maine, lost to their Republican opponents, Nixon and Governor Spiro T. Agnew of Maryland. For the electoral vote by states, see **Electoral College** (table).

Harris and Ewing

Hubert H. Humphrey

Humphrey campaigned for, but did not win, the 1972 Democratic presidential nomination. Finlay Lewis

See also **Johnson, Lyndon B.; Muskie, Edmund S.; Nixon, Richard M.; Vice President of the United States** (Growth of the vice presidency).

Humphreys, *HUHM freez,* **David** (1752-1818), served General George Washington as *aide-de-camp* (field secretary) during the Revolutionary War. His writings show a good understanding of military tactics. Historians find his battle descriptions valuable. After the war, Humphreys negotiated trade treaties in Europe for the United States. He was appointed minister to Spain in 1796. Humphreys brought Merino sheep to Connecticut from Europe in 1802. He helped establish the state's first important wool company in 1810. He was born in Ansonia (then Derby), Conn. Albert E. Van Dusen

Humus, *HYOO muhs,* is a dark brown substance found in soil. It is formed when roots, plants, and the dead bodies of small animals decay. The decay is caused by the action of microscopic living beings called *bacteria* and *fungi.* The amount of humus in soil affects the soil's texture and its ability to hold moisture and to supply necessary food. A good mixture of humus generally increases the size and quality of a crop.

Humus is soft and spongy. It fills the spaces between the mineral grains of the soil, and enables the plant roots to send out tiny hairs through which they absorb water and food. Humus also holds water and reduces the problem of water running off and *eroding* (wearing away) the soil. William Raymond Kays

See also **Sewage** (Rural sewerage systems).

Hun was a member of the wandering and warlike people that invaded the Roman Empire in the A.D. 400's. Under the direction of Attila, their greatest leader, the Huns nearly destroyed the Roman empires of the east and west.

The Huns moved westward across the Volga about A.D. 350 and defeated the Alani people. Then they conquered and drove out the Goths. With their subject peoples, the Huns invaded Gaul under Attila.

They were finally halted in 451, and they later failed in another attempt at invasion. After the death of Attila (453), the subject peoples revolted and defeated the Huns. The Huns were later absorbed into the various racial strains of Europe. William G. Sinnigen

See also **Attila; Goths.**

Hunchback is a severe rounded or sharp prominence of the upper part of the back. Because this part of the back sticks out like a big hump, the condition is sometimes called *humpback.* Hunchback is caused by any condition that deforms the bones of the upper part of the spine. The most common cause is tuberculosis of the spine, or Pott's disease. Hunchback involves the portion of the spine to which the ribs are connected. The hump results when the front part of the spinal bones collapses, spreading the back part. Irvin Stein

Hundred Years' War (1337-1453) extended over the reigns of five English and five French kings who fought for control of France. This struggle between England and France actually consisted of a succession of wars broken by truces and treaties. The English loss of Normandy in France in 1204 developed as the basic cause of the war. The war had several contributing causes. Efforts of French kings to control the English-held province of

Gascony in southwest France angered the English. The French supported the Scots against England, and the French attempted to control Flanders and the English wool trade there. English and French sailors and fishermen quarreled over rights in the English Channel. Edward III of England, whose mother was the sister of three French kings, formally claimed the throne of France in 1337 (see **Salic Law**). He landed an army in Normandy to begin the Hundred Years' War.

In the fighting that followed, the English won most of the battles. But the French won the war. English resources in manpower, supplies, and wealth were about a third as great as those of the French. Several events hindered the course of the war. These included peasant rebellions, pillaging in France by unemployed soldiers, the *Black Death,* or bubonic plague, in the two countries, and a peasants' revolt in England in 1381. The war weakened the powers of the nobility, and strengthened centralized government in both countries. It also marked the decline of feudalism, the rise of French unity, the development of new military tactics, and the growth of English sea power.

English archers and infantry won the war's greatest victory in the Battle of Crécy (1346). The English also won the Battle of Poitiers (1356). The Treaty of Brétigny in 1360 began a brief period of peace. But Henry V of England renewed the fighting, and emerged triumphant at the Battle of Agincourt (1415). The Treaty of Troyes in 1420 made Henry V heir to the French crown.

After Henry V died in 1422, the French disputed the English claim to the throne, and war flared again. By 1428 the English had swept through northern France and laid siege to Orléans. Joan of Arc led a French army in raising the siege in 1429. She became a prisoner of the English, who later burned her as a witch. The French continued to win battles. By the time the war ended in 1453, England had lost all its territory on the continent of Europe, except for Calais. The French gained possession of Calais in 1558. Robert S. Hoyt

Related articles in *World Book* include:

Agincourt, Battle of	Henry (V) of England
Crécy, Battle of	Joan of Arc, Saint (Joan sees
England (The Hundred Years'	the king)
War)	Poitiers, Battle of
Froissart, Jean	

Additional resources

Burne, Alfred H. *The Crecy War: A Military History of the Hundred Years War from 1337 to the Peace of Bretigny, 1360.* Greenwood, 1976. *The Agincourt War: A Military History of the Latter Part of the Hundred Years War, from 1369 to 1453.* 1976. First published in 1955 and 1956, respectively.
Perroy, Édouard M. J. *The Hundred Years War.* Capricorn, 1965. First published in 1951.
Seward, Desmond. *The Hundred Years War: The English in France, 1337-1453.* Atheneum, 1982. First published in 1978.
Society at War: The Experience of England and France During the Hundred Years War. Ed. by C. T. Allmand. Barnes & Noble, 1973.

Hundredweight is a unit of weight. In the United States it is equal to 100 pounds. This is called a *short hundredweight.* The English hundredweight of 112 pounds is called a *long hundredweight.* The *metric hundredweight* is equal to 50 kilograms. The long hundredweight contains 50.8 kilograms and the short hundredweight contains 45.36 kilograms. E. G. Straus

Hungarian pointer. See Vizsla.

C. M. Dixon from Carl Östman

E. Henriksson from Carl Östman

Hungary has changed greatly since the mid-1900's, when it was a largely agricultural nation. Today, many Hungarians work in industry, and over half the people live in urban areas, such as Budapest, *left,* the capital. Farmers, *right,* make up less than a fourth of the country's work force.

Hungary

Hungary is a small, landlocked country in central Europe. Great economic and social changes have occurred in Hungary since the late 1940's. Before that time, most of the country's income came from agriculture, and the majority of Hungarians lived in rural areas and worked on farms. But Hungary's economy has become increasingly industrialized. Today, manufacturing and other industries contribute more to the national income than does farming. More Hungarians now work in industry than on farms, and more than half of the Hungarian people live in cities and towns. Almost a fifth of Hungary's people live in Budapest, the country's capital and largest city.

As Hungary has become more industrialized, modern city ways of life have become popular. Many of the country's old rural customs are thus disappearing. But Hungarians still love the highly seasoned foods, excellent wines, and lively folk music for which they have long been famous.

Most of eastern Hungary is nearly flat, but the western part has hills and low mountains. The chief natural resources include fertile soil and a favorable climate for farming.

Hungary was a large, independent, and powerful kingdom until the late 1400's. From the early 1500's to the late 1600's, the Ottoman Turks ruled much of Hun-

gary. The country then became part of a huge empire ruled by the Austrian branch of the Habsburgs, a powerful European *dynasty* (line of rulers). The empire of the Habsburgs collapsed after World War I ended in 1918. Hungary then lost about two-thirds of its land but regained its independence.

In the late 1940's, Hungarian Communists gained control of the country's government. They adopted a constitution like the Soviet Union's and began to manage the entire economy. In 1956, the Hungarian people revolted against their Communist government. But Soviet troops quickly crushed the revolution. The Hungarian government then adopted economic, political, cultural, and social reforms to prevent future uprisings. By the 1960's, many previous restrictions on freedom were eased. As a

George Barany, the contributor of this article, is Professor of History at the University of Denver and the author of Stephen Széchenyi and the Awakening of Hungarian Nationalism, 1791-1841.

Facts in brief

Capital: Budapest.
Official language: Magyar (Hungarian).
Official name: Magyar Népköztársaság (Hungarian People's Republic).
Area: 35,919 sq. mi. (93,030 km²). *Greatest distances*—east-west, 312 mi. (502 km); north-south, 193 mi. (311 km).
Elevation: *Highest*—Mount Kékes, 3,330 ft. (1,015 m) above sea level. *Lowest*—near Szeged, 259 ft. (79 m) above sea level.
Population: *Estimated 1988 population*—10,827,000; distribution, 56 per cent urban, 44 per cent rural; density, 301 persons per sq. mi. (116 per km²). *1980 census*—10,709,463. *Estimated 1993 population*—10,831,000.
Chief products: *Agriculture*—corn, dairy products, livestock, potatoes, sugar beets, wheat, wine grapes. *Manufacturing*—alumina, chemicals, foods and beverages, machinery, steel, textiles, transportation equipment. *Mining*—bauxite.
National anthem: 'Himnusz" ("Hymn").
Money: *Basic unit*—forint. For its price in U.S. dollars, see **Money** (table: Exchange rates).

result, Hungarians now have more personal freedom and their living standards have improved.

Government

Hungary's Constitution, which was adopted in 1949 and revised in 1972, calls the country a *people's republic.* In theory, the people hold all political power. But in fact, the Communist Party—the only political party allowed in Hungary—controls the government.

All Hungarians 18 years of age and older may vote. Political activity centers on the People's Patriotic Front, an organization controlled by the Communist Party. Labor unions, women's associations, youth groups, and many other organizations participate in the Front. All candidates for political office must support the Front's program.

The Communist Party in Hungary is called the Hungarian Socialist Workers' Party. Only about 7 per cent of Hungary's people belong to the party. But party leaders hold important positions at all levels of government and in major nongovernmental organizations.

In theory, the Party Congress is the party's highest authority. It consists of about 935 delegates, who are elected by local party organizations throughout Hungary. The Congress meets every four years to establish policies and to elect a Central Committee of about 105 members. The Central Committee handles party affairs between sessions of the Congress. The Committee also elects the members of the Politburo and the Secretariat, the party's two most powerful organs. The number of members on each of these bodies varies from time to time. But the Politburo usually has about 15 members, and the Secretariat about 7. The Politburo makes major policy decisions, and the Secretariat then carries them out. The first secretary of the Central Committee heads both the Politburo and the Secretariat and is the most powerful person in Hungary.

National government. Hungary has a one-house legislature, called the National Assembly. Voters elect the legislature's 386 members to four-year terms. The Assembly formally enacts all laws previously approved by Communist Party leaders. The National Assembly elects 21 of its members to the Presidential Council, which serves as the legislature between Assembly sessions. The chairman of the Presidential Council is Hungary's head of state.

On the recommendation of the Presidential Council, the National Assembly appoints a Council of Ministers. Members of this group head the various government departments, which number about 15. The chairman of the Council of Ministers serves as Hungary's head of government, or premier.

Local government. Hungary is divided into 19 counties and 6 cities, including Budapest, that rank as counties. The counties and the cities of county rank are subdivided into districts. A council governs each county, city of county rank, and district, as well as each town and rural community. Members of county-level councils are elected by the district councils to four-year terms. Members of all councils below the county level are elected directly by the people to four-year terms.

Courts. The Supreme Court is Hungary's highest court. Other courts include county, district, labor affairs, and military courts.

Alexander M. Chabe

The Hungarian House of Parliament overlooks the Danube River in Budapest. The impressive building is the meeting place of the National Assembly, Hungary's legislature. It also houses a public library and various art treasures.

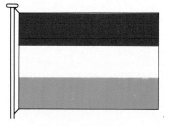

Hungary's flag has horizontal stripes of red, white, and green, the traditional national colors. It was adopted in 1957.

The coat of arms features the red star of Communism, a wreath of wheat, and a shield with the national colors.

WORLD BOOK map

Hungary is a landlocked country in central Europe. It is surrounded by five other countries.

Hungary political map

International boundary

Expressway

Road

Railroad

Canal

⊛ National capital

★ County seat

• Other city or town

WORLD BOOK map

| 0 | 50 | 100 | 150 | 200 | 250 | 300 Miles |

| 0 | 50 | 100 | 150 | 200 | 250 | 300 | 350 | 400 | 450 Kilometers |

Counties*

Bács-Kiskun ....558,645 ...D 4
Baranya ....431,919 ...D 3
Békés ....422,373 ...D 5
Borsod-Abaúj-Zemplén ....790,956 ...B 5
Csongrád ....456,168 ...D 5
Fejér ....425,697 ...C 3
Győr-Sopron ....428,057 ...B 2
Hajdú-Bihar ....550,850 ...C 6
Heves ....341,202 ...B 5
Komárom ....320,983 ...B 3
Nógrád ....233,184 ...B 4
Pest ....984,646 ...C 4
Somogy ....353,441 ...D 2
Szabolcs-Szatmár ....583,789 ...B 6
Szolnok ....435,761 ...C 5
Tolna ....265,938 ...D 3
Vas ....279,520 ...B 1
Veszprém ....387,856 ...C 2
Zala ....313,031 ...C 1

Cities and towns

Ajka ....34,068..C 2
Baja ....40,375..D 4
Balassagyar-
  mat ....19,582..B 4
Balaton-
  füred ....14,832..C 2
Barcs* ....12,155..E 2
Békés* ....22,202..D 6

Békéscsaba ......70,441..D 6
Berettyóúj-
  falu ....17,613..C 6
Bonyhád ....15,449..D 3
Budapest ......2,075,990..C 4
Cegléd ....40,114..C 4
Celldömölk ......12,321..C 2
Csongrád ....21,195..D 5

Csorna ....12,668..B 2
Debrecen .....211,823..B 6
Dombóvár ....21,356..D 3
Dunakeszi ....27,887..B 4
Dunaújvá-
  ros ....62,459..C 3
Eger ....65,156..B 5
Érd ....45,928..C 3
Esztergom ....32,204..B 3
Gödöllő ....29,536..B 4
Gyöngyös ....37,224..B 4
Győr ....129,116..B 2
Gyula ....35,599..D 6
Hajdúböször-
  mény ....31,232..B 6
Hajdúnánás .....18,448..B 6
Hajduszobos-
  zló ....24,208..C 6
Hatvan ....24,949..B 4
Hódmezővásár-
  hely ....54,510..D 5
Jászberény ......30,768..C 4
Kalocsa ....20,023..D 4
Kaposvár ....73,990..D 2
Kapuvár ....11,322..B 2
Karcag ....24,821..C 5
Kazincbar-
  cika ....39,136..A 5
Kecskemét .....102,889..C 4
Keszthely ....22,732..D 2
Kiskőrös ....15,342..D 4
Kiskunfélegy-
  háza ....35,650..D 4

Kiskunhalas ......31,494..D 4
Kisújszál-
  lás ....13,668..C 5
Kisvárda ....19,113..A 7
Komárom ....19,808..B 3
Komló* ....31,156..E 3
Körmend ....12,230..C 1
Kőszeg ....13,727..C 1
Lenin-
  város ....19,250..B 6
Makó ....29,161..D 5
Marcali ....12,971..D 2
Mátészalka ......19,773..B 7
Mezőkövesd .....18,403..B 5
Mezőtúr ....21,084..C 5
Miskolc ....211,660..B 5
Mohács ....21,491..E 3
Mosonmagyar-
  óvár ....29,833..B 2
Nagyatád ....14,779..D 2
Nagyka-
  nizsa ....55,336..D 2
Nagykőrös ....26,794..C 4
Nyír-
  bátor ....14,179..B 7
Nyíregy-
  háza ....116,782..B 6
Orosháza ....36,758..D 5
Oroszlány* ......21,374..C 3
Ózd ....47,167..A 5
Paks ....25,056..D 3
Pápa ....34,601..C 2
Pécs ....177,104..E 3

Salgótar-
  ján ....49,424..B 4
Sárospatak ......15,157..A 6
Sárvár ....15,778..C 1
Sátoral-
  jaújhely ....20,529..A 6
Siklós ....10,821..E 3
Siófok ....23,274..C 3
Sopron ....56,500..B 1
Szarvas ....19,396..C 5
Százhalom-
  batta* ....17,037..C 3
Szeged ....182,137..D 5
Székesfehér-
  vár ....111,478..C 3
Szekszárd ....38,364..D 3
Szentendre* .....19,012..B 4
Szentes ....35,664..D 5
Szigetvár ....12,764..E 2
Szolnok ....80,461..C 5
Szombath-
  ely ....86,013..C 1
Tapolca ....17,483..C 2
Tata ....25,631..B 3
Tatabánya ....76,465..B 3
Törökszent-
  miklós ....24,483..C 5
Túrkeve* ....11,209..C 5
Vác ....35,874..B 4
Várpalota ....28,665..C 3
Veszprém ....64,071..C 2
Zalaeger-
  szeg ....61,456..C 1

*County names and names of cities marked with an asterisk do not appear on map; key shows general location.

Source: 1986 official estimates.

Armed forces. About 103,000 people serve in Hungary's army and air force. A large number of men also serve in the country's internal security force. Men may be drafted for any of these services at age 18. Draftees serve in the armed forces for at least two years. Hungary belongs to the Warsaw Pact, a military alliance made up of the Soviet Union and most other Communist countries in Europe.

People

Ancestry and population. A number of ethnic groups live in Hungary. Magyars make up the largest group by far, with about 95 per cent of the country's people. Other groups, in order of size, include Germans, Slovaks, Croats, Serbs, Gypsies, and Romanians. Magyars are traditionally considered to be descendants of the Magyar tribes that migrated to Hungary from the east in the late 800's. The people of these tribes became the first Hungarians. Their language gradually developed into the language spoken in present-day Hungary. Today, Magyars also include people of other ethnic backgrounds who have adopted the Hungarian language and Hungarian customs. These people, in turn, have contributed much to Hungarian culture.

Hungary has a population of about 11 million. Since the late 1940's, many Hungarians have moved from rural areas to cities and towns to work in the country's growing industries. More than half the people now live in urban areas. More than 2 million people live in Budapest, the capital and largest city. Hungary has two other cities—Debrecen and Miskolc—with over 200,000 inhabitants. See **Budapest; Debrecen; Miskolc.**

Language. Magyar (also called Hungarian) is the official language and is spoken throughout the country. But members of minority groups use their own language among themselves. In parts of Hungary, the people speak various *dialects* (local forms) of Magyar. Magyar is a *Uralic-Altaic* language related to Estonian and Finnish. See **Language** (Language families).

Way of life. Most rural families in Hungary live in small houses. Many of these houses have *stucco* (rough plaster) outer walls and a tile roof. City dwellers live in apartments or one-family homes. In the cities, housing construction has not kept up with the rapid shift in population from rural to urban areas.

Most Hungarians, especially city dwellers, dress much as people do in the United States and other Western countries. Many rural Hungarians once wore colorfully embroidered costumes as everyday clothing. But today, they wear these costumes only on special occasions. The Hungarian way of life has also changed in many other respects. For example, countrypeople once made beautiful objects, such as carved wooden utensils and embroidered linens, for everyday use. Although Hungarian craftworkers still produce such items, rural Hungarians now use manufactured household items that are like those used by people in other industrialized countries.

Hungarians love good food in large quantities, especially on holidays and other festive occasions. They enjoy soup with special as well as everyday meals. The most famous Hungarian soup is a thick soup, or stew, called *goulash.* It consists of cubes of beef or other meat, gravy, onions, and potatoes. Other ingredients may also be added to the goulash, which is highly flavored with a seasoning called *paprika.* Hungarians use paprika in many of their dishes.

Hungarians eat more pork than any other kind of meat, but they also enjoy beef and poultry. Noodles, potatoes, and small dumplings are popular side dishes. Hungary is famous for its pastries. One of the most popular pastries is *rétes,* or *strudel.* It consists of a thin, flaky crust filled with fruit or cheese. The country is also famous for its many excellent wines.

E. Henriksson from Carl Östman

Budapest ranks as Hungary's largest city. It has nearly a fifth of the country's total population. In this scene, cars and pedestrians jam a busy street in one of the city's main shopping districts.

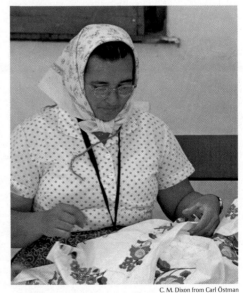

C. M. Dixon from Carl Östman

Colorful embroidery adds a traditional Hungarian touch to clothing and other items. Most such handcrafted items are used on special occasions or are exported.

E. Henriksson from Carl Östman

Hungary's medicinal baths attract Hungarians and foreigners who believe the warm, mineral-filled waters have healthful qualities. This picture shows the famous Gellert Baths in Budapest.

Recreation. Many Hungarians enjoy visiting coffee houses. There, they read or chat with friends over a cup of coffee or a glass of wine or beer. Hungarians also enjoy art exhibits and the theater. They love music, and going to concerts and operas is a popular pastime. Hungarians are famous for their lively folk music.

Soccer is the most popular sport in Hungary. Other favorite sports include basketball, fencing, and volleyball. Many Hungarians also enjoy swimming, boating, and fishing. In addition, the country has many health resorts called *spas,* which offer medicinal bathing in mineral waters.

Religion. About two-thirds of Hungary's people are Roman Catholics. Most of the rest are Protestants. The Reformed (Calvinist) Church and the Lutheran Church are the largest Protestant groups. Other religious groups include Catholics of the Byzantine Rite, Jews, and Unitarians. The government supervises the activities of all religious groups through the State Office of Church Affairs.

After the Communists gained control of the government in the late 1940's, they tried to discourage religious worship. They placed religious groups under strict control and imprisoned some religious leaders. But many Hungarians strongly opposed these practices. In the 1960's, the government began to relax its policies against religion to gain the people's support.

Education. Almost all adult Hungarians can read and write. All children must complete eight years of elementary school. They may then go on to a two-year *continuation* school or a four-year high school. Hungary has two main kinds of high schools—gymnasiums and vocational secondary schools. Gymnasiums, a traditional type of European high school, provide a general education. Vocational secondary schools offer training in agricultural,

commercial, or industrial skills in addition to providing a general education.

The Hungarian government controls all educational institutions. All elementary school and most high school students attend free public schools. The government allows religious groups to operate a limited number of secondary schools. These schools charge a fee.

Students who complete four years of high school may enter a school of higher learning. Hungary's many institutions of higher learning include five *academic* (general education) universities, four medical universities, and nine technical universities. The largest and most important universities are in Budapest.

The arts. Hungary's most outstanding contribution to the arts has been in music. The country has produced a number of world-famous composers. Franz Liszt was a prominent composer and pianist of the 1800's. The expressive and highly original works of Béla Bartók have established him as one of the greatest composers of the 1900's. His compositions and those of his friend Zoltán Kodály were strongly influenced by Hungarian folk music.

Hungary has also produced many fine writers. But few of them are known outside the country. Hungarians highly regard the works of the poet Sándor Petőfi and the novelist Mor Jókai, who wrote during the 1800's. The poets Endre Ady and Attila József rank among the most respected Hungarian writers of the 1900's. The most famous Hungarian author is Ferenc Molnár, who wrote many plays, novels, and short stories during the early 1900's.

Hungarian writers have traditionally been concerned with political and social problems. In the 1950's, for example, some writers expressed in their works the people's discontent with the Communist government. These authors thus spoke for the Hungarian people, whose desire for a better life led them to rebel in 1956. After the unsuccessful revolution, the writers who had criticized

Paul Quirico

Outdoor markets are a common sight in many Hungarian cities and towns. Sidewalk vendors offer live chickens and other food items for sale at a market in Budapest, *above.*

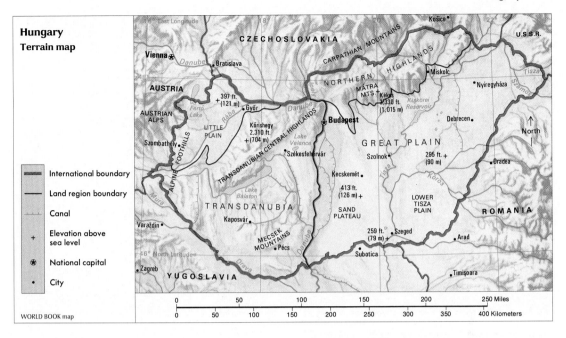

Hungary
Terrain map

International boundary

Land region boundary

Canal

+ Elevation above
sea level

National capital

• City

WORLD BOOK map

the government had to flee the country or were imprisoned. The government also clamped tight controls on literary and other artistic activities.

In the 1960's, the government began to relax its controls on cultural life to make its rule more acceptable to the people. Writers and other artists now have some freedom of expression, though they must follow guidelines set by the Communist Party.

The land and climate

Most of Hungary's land is low. About two-thirds of the country lies less than 650 feet (198 meters) above sea level. All of eastern Hungary is nearly flat, except for low mountains in the north. Mount Kékes, Hungary's highest point, rises 3,330 feet (1,015 meters) above sea level in these mountains. Western Hungary consists mainly of rolling hills and low mountains.

The country's longest river is the Tisza, which flows 360 miles (579 kilometers) from north to south through eastern Hungary. The Tisza is a branch of Hungary's most important river, the Danube. The Danube flows through seven European countries, including Hungary. It forms part of Hungary's northern border, then flows from north to south through the central part of the country. The Danube serves as the chief shipping route for trade between Hungary and its neighbors as well as for trade within the country. Lake Balaton in western Hungary is the largest lake in central Europe. It covers about 230 square miles (596 square kilometers) and is a popular recreation and vacation spot.

Land regions. Hungary has four main land regions: (1) the Great Plain; (2) Transdanubia; (3) the Little Plain; and (4) the Northern Highlands.

The Great Plain covers all of Hungary east of the Danube River, except for the mountains in the north. The region occupies about half the country's area. Its nearly flat surface is broken only by river valleys, sand dunes, and small hills. The Great Plain is mostly an agricultural

region. The far southeastern section has Hungary's richest soil.

Transdanubia covers all of Hungary west of the Danube, except for the northwest corner of the country. Transdanubia consists mostly of hills and mountains. A chain of low, rounded mountains called the Transdanubian Central Highlands stretches along the entire northern side of Lake Balaton. The chain extends to the bend of the Danube north of Budapest. Gently rolling hills lie south of Lake Balaton, and more low mountains lie still farther south. The foothills of the Austrian Alps rise in the west. The southeastern part of Transdanubia is a major farm region.

The Little Plain occupies the northwest corner of Hungary and is the smallest land region. It is flat except for the foothills of the Austrian Alps along the western boundary. Most of the area is good for farming.

The Northern Highlands rise northeast of the Danube River and north of the Great Plain. This mountainous region forms part of the great Carpathian mountain system of central Europe. Many of the mountain slopes are steep. Thick forests, small streams, and spectacular rock formations help make the Northern Highlands a region of scenic beauty. It is also an important manufacturing and mining area.

Climate. The climate varies little throughout Hungary because the country is small and has no great variety of natural features. In general, Hungary has cold winters and hot summers. January temperatures average about 29° F. (−2° C), and July temperatures average about 70° F. (21° C). Hungary receives an average of about 24 inches (60 centimeters) of *precipitation* (rain, snow, and other forms of moisture) yearly. May, June, and July are the wettest months.

Economy

Manufacturing and other industries employ more Hungarian workers and account for more of Hungary's

Oldrich Karasek from Peter Arnold

Hungary's Lake Balaton ranks as the largest lake in central Europe. It lies among the gently rolling hills and low mountains of Transdanubia, a land region in western Hungary. The lake and its scenic surroundings make the area one of the country's most popular recreation spots.

national income than does farming. But before World War II (1939-1945), Hungary was chiefly an agricultural country. After the Communists gained control of the government in the late 1940's, they began to manage the nation's economy. To carry out their program, they started a series of highly detailed plans that stressed industrial development. As a result, Hungary became increasingly industrialized.

The government's economic plans have required frequent readjustment, however. By the early 1950's, for example, the country's industries could not meet the government's extremely high production goals. Farm production lagged because the government did little to promote agriculture. Hungarians reacted strongly against these policies, and the government was forced to set more realistic industrial goals and place more emphasis on agriculture.

But in the 1960's, the country's economic growth rate and the people's standard of living remained low. In an attempt to solve these problems, the government introduced some features of a free market system into the economy through a program called the New Economic Mechanism (NEM). The NEM went into effect in 1968. Under it, the government still develops economic plans, but they are less detailed than earlier plans were. The NEM resulted in a higher economic growth rate for Hungary and an improved standard of living. But later, inflation, a worldwide rise in the price of oil and other energy sources, and other problems slowed down Hungary's economy.

Almost all Hungarian workers are employed in industries or on farms owned by the government or by cooperative groups. Only a small percentage of the people have their own business or farm. However, the government is now encouraging private ownership.

Natural resources. Hungary's chief resources include its fertile soil and its climate, which is generally favorable for agriculture. Farms cover about three-fourths of the land and produce most of the food the people need. About 15 per cent of Hungary's land is forested. These forests cannot supply all the timber the country needs. Thus, large amounts of timber are imported.

Hungary ranks as one of the world's leading producers of bauxite, the ore from which aluminum is made. The country also has coal, iron ore, manganese, natural gas, and oil. But the deposits of these minerals are small or of low quality. Hungary therefore imports additional supplies. Uranium, the main source of nuclear energy, was discovered in the Mecsek Mountains near Pécs in the 1950's. Uranium mines have been developed with the help of the Soviet Union, but production figures are kept secret.

Hungary's electric power production does not meet its needs, and so extra power has to be imported. During the 1980's, two nuclear reactors were constructed. These reactors use Hungary's uranium to produce electricity and help ease the power shortage. Two more reactors were scheduled for completion before 1990.

Manufacturing. The state owns almost all of Hungary's factories. Cooperative groups own the rest. Since the Communists came to power, the government has stressed the manufacture of machinery and other *capital goods*—that is, products that are used to make other products. Hungary's factories did not produce enough *consumer goods,* such as appliances and clothing, to satisfy the people's demands. One NEM goal has been to increase the output of consumer goods and so further improve the Hungarian standard of living.

Hungary's chief manufactured products include chemicals, foods and beverages, machinery, steel, textiles, and transportation equipment. Hungarian plants also process much of the country's bauxite into alumina, which is the first step in producing aluminum. However, the second step—processing alumina into aluminum—is mostly done in other countries, especially the Soviet Union. Hungary lacks the large amounts of cheap electricity needed to process alumina into aluminum economically.

The heaviest concentration of Hungary's factories is in the Budapest area. The government appoints managers to run its factories. Before the NEM went into effect, the government made all major business decisions, and the managers carried them out. But under the NEM, the managers have more freedom to make decisions in such matters as investment and production.

Agriculture. Crops account for about 60 per cent of the value of Hungary's farm output, and livestock accounts for about 40 per cent. The chief crops include corn, potatoes, sugar beets, wheat, and wine grapes. Farmers raise more chickens and hogs than any other kind of livestock. Other livestock include beef and dairy cattle, horses, and sheep.

Only about 5 per cent of Hungary's farmland is privately owned. The rest consists of collective farms and state farms.

The collective farms cover about 80 per cent of Hungary's farmland. Many families work together on these farms. The farms average about 5,440 acres (2,201 hectares), not including the small plots of land that the families may farm for themselves. The members of a collective farm own the farm equipment and land as a group, and each member receives a wage and a share of the farm's earnings. The government determines general

farm policies. But it allows members to make decisions on such matters as investment and production.

The state farms are owned by the state and cover about 15 per cent of Hungary's farmland. The farms average about 14,300 acres (5,787 hectares). Workers on a state farm receive a salary. The government appoints a director to manage each farm. Under the NEM, government control over the farms has been reduced, and the directors may now make policies.

Foreign trade. Hungary's economy depends heavily on foreign trade. The leading imports include advanced machinery, automobiles, coal, cotton, electric power, fertilizers, iron ore, livestock feed, and oil. The country's chief exports include alumina, livestock, machinery, medicines, processed foods and beverages, steel, and transportation equipment, especially buses.

Hungary belongs to the Council for Mutual Economic Assistance (COMECON), an economic union of several Communist countries, including the Soviet Union. Hungary does about a third of its trade with the Soviet Union and another third with the remaining COMECON members. Austria, Italy, the United Kingdom, and West Germany are Hungary's main non-Communist trading partners. In 1973, Hungary joined the General Agreement on Tariffs and Trade (GATT). About 80 countries belong to the GATT. All members have agreed to reduce trade barriers among themselves. In 1982, Hungary was admitted to the International Monetary Fund (IMF), which provides economic assistance to its members. See **General Agreement on Tariffs and Trade; International Monetary Fund.**

Transportation. The state owns and operates Hungary's railroad system, which is about 5,600 miles (9,000

Paul Quirico, Tom Stack & Assoc.

Fertile farmland covers about three-fourths of Hungary and is one of the country's most important natural resources. Nearly all the farmland consists of huge collective farms and government-owned state farms. This picture shows Nagyvázsony, a farm village in western Hungary.

Hungary's production

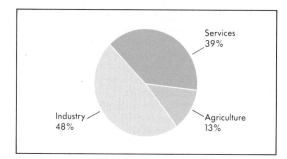

Services
39%

Industry
48%

Agriculture
13%

The net material product (NMP) is the total value of goods and services used in the production of goods by a country in a year. Such services include communication, trade, and transportation. NMP does not include financial services, government services, or community, social, and personal services. Hungary's NMP was $15,705,000,000 in 1984.

Production and workers by economic activities

Economic activities	Per cent of NMP produced	Employed workers	
		Number of persons	Per cent of total
Manufacturing, mining, & utilities	37	1,542,300	32
Agriculture, forestry, & fishing	13	1,139,800	23
Trade	12	504,400	10
Construction	11	356,600	7
Transportation & communication	7	398,500	8
Other	20	—	—
Community, social, & personal services	—	981,400	20
Total	100	4,930,000	100

Figures are for 1984. Sources: International Labor Organization; United Nations.

kilometers) long. Hungary has about 18,580 miles (29,900 kilometers) of roads, almost all of which are surfaced. Hungary has about one automobile for every eight people. Hungary's rivers and canals form a network of navigable waterways about 1,060 miles (1,700 kilometers) long. The country's one shipping line and one airline are owned and operated by the state. The airline operates only international flights. A number of foreign airlines also serve Hungary.

Communication. Hungary has about 30 daily newspapers, which have a total circulation of about $2\frac{1}{2}$ million copies. The largest daily newspaper, *Népszabadság* of Budapest, is published by the Communist Party. The country has three radio stations and two television stations. The state owns and operates the radio and television network, as well as the postal, telegraph, and telephone services. Most families own a radio, and many own a television set.

History

Early years. People have lived in what is now Hungary for thousands of years. But the history of the Hungarian state began in the late 800's. At that time, tribes of Magyars swept from the east into the middle Danube Basin—the great lowland region bordering the Danube

River that comprises most of present-day Hungary. The tribes were led by a chief named Árpád. As the Magyars advanced into the area, they began to establish settlements.

During the early 900's, Magyar armies looted towns throughout much of Europe. But in 955, the German king Otto I defeated the invading Magyars. The Magyars then ended their raids.

The Kingdom of Hungary. About 970, Árpád's great-grandson Géza became leader of the Magyars. Géza began to organize the various Magyar tribes into a united nation. After Géza died, his son, Stephen, carried on the work. Stephen, who was a Roman Catholic, asked Pope Sylvester II to give him the title king of Hungary. The pope agreed, and Stephen I, Hungary's first king, was crowned in 1000. As king, Stephen made Roman Catholicism the country's official religion. For this work, the Catholic Church declared him a saint in 1083, 45 years after his death. As a result of Stephen's reign, Hungary became closely identified with the culture and politics of Western Europe.

Árpád's descendants ruled Hungary until 1301, when the last Árpád king died without an heir. During the 300 years of the Árpáds' reign, Hungary became firmly established as a Christian state. The country also faced its first great challenge from the east during this period. In 1241, armies of the Mongol Empire invaded Hungary. The Mongols were a warlike people of central Asia who had gradually extended their rule westward into eastern Europe. Within a few months, the Mongol armies had overrun much of Hungary. The death of the Mongols' ruler forced the invaders to withdraw from Hungary in 1242. But they left much of the country in ruins. Under the leadership of the Árpád kings, Hungary gradually recovered from the disaster.

After the death of the last Árpád king in 1301, Hungary remained an independent kingdom for 225 more years. One of the greatest kings during this period was Charles Robert, a member of the Italian branch of the Anjou dynasty. He ruled Hungary from 1308 to 1342. Charles Robert restored order in the country, which had been troubled by civil conflict since the end of the Árpád rule. He also weakened the power of the nobles and strengthened the monarchy. Hungary gained much land through the conquests of Charles Robert's son, Louis I, called "the Great." But the land Louis gained was lost during his lifetime and shortly after his death in 1382.

John Hunyadi, a Hungarian nobleman of Romanian descent, led the Hungarians in defeating the Ottoman Turks in 1456. The Turks had been advancing into Europe since the mid-1300's. Hunyadi's son Matthias Corvinus became king of Hungary in 1458. Like Charles Robert, Matthias worked to strengthen royal power. Hungary prospered during his reign. It also became a center of the Italian Renaissance, the great artistic and cultural movement that spread across Europe during the 1400's and 1500's.

A period of conflict and disorder followed Matthias' death in 1490. The Hungarian *Diet,* an assembly of noblemen similar to a parliament, gained much power during this period, and the monarchy grew weak. At that time, most of Hungary's people were peasants who worked under wretched conditions for the nobles. As the nobles increased their power, they made the peasants' lives even more miserable. The peasants revolted in 1514, but the nobles soon put down the uprising. After the revolt, the peasants were condemned to *serfdom* (a condition similar to slavery) for all time.

Turkish and Habsburg rule. Hungary, weakened by internal problems, was defeated by the Turks in the Battle of Mohács in 1526. The defeat paved the way for the country's occupation by foreign troops. The Turks seized central Hungary soon after 1526. They made the eastern third of the country, a region called Transylvania, a *principality* (small state ruled by a prince) dependent on them. The Austrian Habsburgs, who had long wanted to make Hungary part of their empire, took the country's western and northern sections. In the late 1600's, Habsburg forces drove the Turks out of Hungary and gained control of the country.

The Habsburgs governed Hungary, especially the Protestant sections, harshly. The Protestant Reformation had begun in Germany in the 1500's and gained many followers in Hungary. Transylvania, in particular, had developed a tradition of religious freedom, which allowed Protestants and Unitarians as well as Catholics to establish churches. The harsh rule of the Habsburgs led to a nationwide uprising in 1703. It was headed by Francis Rákóczi II, a Catholic and the son of a prominent family that included princes of Transylvania. The Habsburgs finally put down the revolt in 1711. But it had persuaded them to relax their rule and improve economic and political conditions in Hungary. During the rest of the 1700's, most Hungarians accepted and benefited from this change of policy.

In the early 1800's, Count Stephen Széchenyi led a movement to revive Hungarian culture and national pride. He also promoted economic and social reforms. In the 1840's, Louis Kossuth became the most important leader of the reform movement and eventually turned it into a drive for Hungarian independence.

During the 1840's, democratic and liberal nationalist movements were sweeping over Europe. Revolution broke out in France in 1848 and heightened the unrest in other European countries (see **Revolution of 1848**). In Hungary, a government responsible to parliament was formed with Austrian consent in 1848. Other changes were also made, including the freeing of the serfs. But Hungary had not cut all ties with Austria, and disagreements between the two countries finally led Hungary to fight for its independence. Kossuth became head of a revolutionary Hungarian government, which declared the country's complete independence from Austria in April 1849. But the Austrians, aided by the Russians, defeated the Hungarian army in August of that year, and Hungary again came under Habsburg rule.

Austria-Hungary. Austria's power was soon shaken by two defeats. It lost a war with France and Italy in 1859 and with Prussia and Italy in 1866. In 1867, the Hungarians, led by Francis Deák, were thus able to force the emperor of Austria, Francis Joseph, to give Hungary equal status with Austria. Under this arrangement, called the *Dual Monarchy,* both countries had the same monarch and conducted foreign, military, and certain financial affairs jointly. But each country had its own constitutional government to handle all other matters. The creation of Austria-Hungary was followed by a period of prosperity

in the two countries. During the next 50 years, Hungary's economy, educational system, and cultural life developed rapidly.

Austria-Hungary included many Slavs, Romanians, and other national groups. These groups made up nearly half of Hungary's population. In the late 1800's and early 1900's, many of the national groups in Hungary began to demand the right of self-government. But most of the Hungarian politicians failed to heed these demands. In 1914, a Bosnian student killed the heir to the Austro-Hungarian throne. Austria-Hungary suspected that its southern neighbor Serbia was responsible for the killing. As a result, Austria-Hungary declared war on Serbia, marking the start of World War I (1914-1918). In the war, Germany, Bulgaria, and the Ottoman Empire supported Austria-Hungary, forming the Central Powers. They fought against Serbia, France, Russia, Great Britain, and other countries that made up the Allies. The United States entered the war on the Allied side in April 1917. See **World War I.**

Between world wars. A defeated Austria-Hungary signed an armistice on Nov. 3, 1918. On November 16, the Hungarian government declared Hungary a repub-

Important dates in Hungary

Late 800's The Magyars conquered Hungary.

1000 Stephen I became Hungary's first king and converted the country to Roman Catholic Christianity.

1458-1490 Matthias Hunyadi ruled Hungary and helped make it a center of Italian Renaissance culture.

1526 The Ottoman Turks defeated Hungary in the Battle of Mohács. Soon afterward, the Turks occupied central and eastern Hungary.

1600's Austrian Habsburg forces drove the Turks out of Hungary and took control of the country.

1703-1711 Francis Rákóczi II led an unsuccessful uprising to gain Hungarian independence.

1848 Louis Kossuth led an anti-Habsburg revolution, which was defeated the following year.

1867 The Dual Monarchy of Austria-Hungary was established.

1914-1918 Austria-Hungary was defeated in World War I.

1918 Hungary became a republic.

1919 Béla Kun established the first Hungarian Communist government. It lasted only a few months.

1919-1944 Admiral Nicholas Horthy, a conservative, ruled Hungary as a *regent* (in the place of a king).

1941 Hungary entered World War II on Germany's side.

1944 Germany, which mistrusted Hungary as an ally, occupied the country.

1945 Hungary and the Allies signed an armistice.

1946 Hungary again became a republic. The new government started political, economic, and social reforms.

1946-1949 Hungarian Communists gradually gained control of the government.

1947 The Allies signed a peace treaty with Hungary that confirmed the terms of the 1945 armistice.

1955 Hungary became a member of the United Nations.

1956 Soviet forces crushed an anti-Communist revolution in Hungary.

1968 The government adopted the New Economic Mechanism.

1973 Hungary joined the General Agreement on Tariffs and Trade.

1982 Hungary was admitted to the International Monetary Fund.

lic. Count Michael Károlyi became president. But Hungarian Communists and Socialists joined together to form a *coalition* government in March 1919. Károlyi resigned, and Béla Kun, leader of the Communists, took control of the new government as a dictator.

Kun's rule lasted only a few months. It collapsed largely because Kun could not defend Hungary against armed attacks by Romania, which sought Hungarian territory. Romanian troops occupied much of Hungary, including Budapest. In addition, most Hungarians did not support Kun's policies, which included taking over the country's factories and farms. Late in 1919, Admiral Nicholas Horthy came to power. His conservative government lasted 25 years. Under Horthy, Hungary again became a monarchy, though it had no king. Instead, Horthy ruled as *regent* (in the place of a monarch).

Hungary and the Allies signed the Treaty of Trianon in 1920. The treaty was part of the World War I peace settlements. It stripped Hungary of more than two-thirds of its territory. Parts of Hungary went to Czechoslovakia, Romania, Austria, and what is now Yugoslavia. Hungary's present boundaries are about the same as those set by the treaty. See **Trianon, Treaty of.**

World War II. The rise of Nazi Germany in the 1930's had far-reaching effects on Hungary. Adolf Hitler, the German dictator, promised the return of some territory that Hungary had lost under the Treaty of Trianon. Beginning in 1938, Hitler allowed Hungary to take parts of Czechoslovakia, Romania, and Yugoslavia. In April 1941, Hungary aided Hitler in an attack on Yugoslavia and so entered World War II. It joined Germany, Italy, and other Axis countries in fighting the Allies, which included Great Britain, France, and, by the end of 1941, China, the Soviet Union, and the United States. Japan entered the war on the Axis side in December 1941.

By 1943, Hitler no longer considered Hungary a reliable ally. He seized the country in March 1944. More than 500,000 Hungarian Jews were shipped to German concentration camps, where most of them were put to death in gas chambers. The Germans jailed Horthy in October and set up a Hungarian Nazi government.

The Soviet Union invaded Hungary late in 1944, and Hungary and the Allies signed an armistice in January 1945. Hungary agreed to give up all the territory it had gained since 1938. Hungary and the Allies signed a peace treaty in 1947. See **World War II.**

Communist Hungary. Elections were held in November 1945. Early the next year, Hungary was declared a republic. After the November elections, a coalition government was formed. It introduced many social and economic reforms, including land distribution among the peasants. The coalition consisted of the Smallholder, Social Democratic, Communist, and National Peasant parties. The Smallholders had won a clear majority of the votes in the elections. But Communists were gradually to gain control of the government. They were able to do so largely because of the continued presence of Soviet troops in Hungary.

Elections were held again in 1947, and the Communists again failed to win a majority of the votes. But by then, they held enough key government posts to extend their control over the country. They eliminated all opposition parties and, in 1949, gave Hungary a constitution patterned on that of the Soviet Union.

Matthias Rákosi, first secretary of the Communist Party and head of the Hungarian government, ruled as a dictator. By the early 1950's, his policies had nearly ruined the economy and produced widespread discontent among the people. In 1953, Imre Nagy replaced Rákosi as premier. But Rákosi remained head of the party. Nagy adopted policies that gave Hungarians more personal freedom and that aimed at improving their living conditions. But Rákosi and some other party members opposed these reforms. As party leader, Rákosi forced Nagy out of both the government and the party in 1955.

Rákosi's policies again caused unrest, especially among writers, young people, and others deeply concerned with human rights and freedom of expression. Rákosi was replaced as party leader in mid-1956, but the government's policies remained unchanged. In October, discontent with these policies erupted into street fighting in Budapest. The revolution spread swiftly throughout Hungary. Many political prisoners were freed, including Joseph Cardinal Mindszenty, head of the Roman Catholic Church in Hungary. The Communists had jailed Mindszenty in 1949. Nagy again became premier and declared Hungary to be a neutral country like its neighbor Austria. But the new government lasted only a few days. Soviet forces poured into the country and put down the uprising in November.

Many Hungarians were killed or imprisoned as a result of the 1956 revolution. About 200,000 fled the country. Mindszenty took refuge in the U.S. Legation (now the U.S. Embassy) in Budapest, where he lived until he was allowed to leave Hungary in 1971. Nagy was executed for his part in the revolt.

After the 1956 revolution, the Soviet Union kept Hungary under tight control. János Kádár, the new first secretary of the Communist Party, served as premier from 1956 to 1958 and from 1961 to 1965. At first, he followed stern policies designed to prevent further revolutionary acts. But in the 1960's, Kádár's government tried to win increased support from the people by easing some of its restrictions on cultural, economic, and social life. In 1968, the government adopted the New Economic Mechanism (NEM), a program that introduced features of a free market system into the socialized economy.

Hungary today. The policies begun by the government in the 1960's have produced many changes in Hungary. Today, Hungarians enjoy greater personal freedom than they did under Rákosi. In addition, the NEM has resulted in better living standards. Hungary's relations with Western countries have also improved. But Kádár, who continues to head the Hungarian Communist Party, keeps close ties with the Soviet Union, especially in foreign affairs. George Barany

Related articles in *World Book* include:

Biographies

Bartók, Béla	Lehár, Franz
Breuer, Marcel L.	Liszt, Franz
Gabor, Dennis	Mindszenty, Joseph Cardinal
Herzl, Theodor	Molnár, Ferenc
Hevesy, Georg von	Ormandy, Eugene
Houdini, Harry	Pulitzer, Joseph
Kádár, János	Reiner, Fritz
Kodály, Zoltán	Semmelweis, Ignaz P.
Koestler, Arthur	Seredy, Kate
Kossuth, Lajos	Solti, Sir Georg

Szell, George
Szilard, Leo
Teller, Edward

Von Neumann, John
Wallenberg, Raoul
Wigner, Eugene P.

Cities

Budapest
Debrecen
Györ

Miskolc
Pécs

Other related articles

Austria-Hungary
Clothing (picture: Traditional costumes)
Danube River
Habsburg, House of

Magyars
Radio Free Europe/Radio Liberty
Trianon, Treaty of
Warsaw Pact

Outline

I. Government
   A. The Communist Party
   B. National government
   C. Local government
   D. Courts
   E. Armed forces
II. People
   A. Ancestry and population
   B. Language
   C. Way of life
   D. Recreation
   E. Religion
   F. Education
   G. The arts
III. The land and climate
   A. Land regions   B. Climate
IV. Economy
   A. Natural resources
   B. Manufacturing
   C. Agriculture
   D. Foreign trade
   E. Transportation
   F. Communication
V. History

Questions

What role does the Hungarian Communist Party play in Hungary's government?
Who were the first Hungarians? When did they come to Hungary?
How do the surface features of the Great Plain differ from those of Transdanubia?
What are some popular recreational activities in Hungary?
How do collective farms differ from state farms in Hungary?
What Hungarian lake is the largest lake in central Europe?
Why were the Communists able to gain control of Hungary's government after World War II?
What is *goulash*?
What is the New Economic Mechanism?
What political role did some Hungarian writers play in the period before the 1956 revolution?

Additional resources

American University. *Area Handbook for Hungary.* U.S. Government Printing Office, 1973.
Berend, Ivan, and Ranki, György. *Hungary: A Century of Economic Development.* Harper, 1974.
Ferge, Zsuzsa. *A Society in the Making: Hungarian Social and Societal Policy, 1945-1975.* Sharpe, 1980.
Lengyel, Emil. *The Land and People of Hungary.* Rev. ed. Harper, 1972. For younger readers.
Macartney, Carlile A. *Hungary: A Short History.* Edinburgh Univ. Press, 1962.
Volgyes, Ivan. *Hungary: A Nation of Contradictions.* Westview, 1982. An introduction to present-day Hungary.

Hunger is an unpleasant, often painful sensation caused by the body's need for food. The most familiar hunger pains are stomach cramps, which are produced by strong contractions of the stomach muscles. Appetite is related to hunger, but it is merely a desire for food that we like.

In human beings and animals with backbones, chemicals in the fluid surrounding the brain and spinal cord probably play an important role in regulating the sensation of hunger. If some of this fluid is taken from a hungry animal and injected into an animal that has just finished eating, that animal will start to eat again. The amount of *glucose* (sugar) in the blood also affects hunger. People may become hungry if they have less than a normal amount of glucose in their blood.

People and animals need many substances besides glucose, including vitamins, minerals, and amino acids. Nerves called *internal chemoreceptors* in the brain, kidneys, digestive system, and elsewhere in the body detect the need for these substances when they are lacking. This action may lead to eating the needed foods.

In human beings, hunger and eating are also affected by social habits. We eat at certain times, and we usually eat only certain foods. Sometimes signals from internal receptor nerves that do not give information on hunger are interpreted as hunger. A person may then overeat and become overweight.   Bruce P. Halpern

See also **Nutrition; Senses; Weight control.**

Hunley. See Submarine (Early submarines).

Hunsaker, Jerome Clarke (1886-1984), was one of the pioneer aeronautical scientists in the United States. He set up the first formal course of instruction in aeronautics from 1912 to 1916 at the Massachusetts Institute of Technology. He then took charge of the aircraft program for the U.S. Navy, and designed the airship *Shenandoah* and the seaplane NC-4. In 1941, he became chairman of the National Advisory Committee for Aeronautics and served for about 15 years. He was born in Creston, Iowa, and was graduated from the United States Naval Academy.   Robert B. Hotz

Hunt, George Wylie Paul. See Arizona (Progress as a state).

Hunt, H. L. (1889-1974), an American oil producer, became one of the richest people in the world. He was noted both for his great wealth and for his extremely conservative political views.

Haroldson Lafayette Hunt was born in Vandalia, Ill. He had little formal schooling, but his mother, a former schoolteacher, taught him at home. Hunt made his fortune in the 1920's by *speculating* (buying and selling at great risk) in the newly discovered Arkansas oil fields. He founded the Hunt Oil Company and controlled many smaller firms.

In 1958, Hunt established a radio program called "Life Line" that broadcast his views to millions of people. Among other things, he believed that the wealthy should have greater voting power than the poor, and that Calvin Coolidge was the most recent successful President.   Leonard S. Silk

Hunt, Irene (1906-   ), an author of children's books, won the 1967 Newbery Medal for her novel *Up a Road Slowly* (1966). The book describes a girl's progress from self-centered childhood to independence and maturity. Irene Hunt was born in Newton, Ill. She spent her early years on a southern Illinois farm. The farm became the scene of her *Across Five Aprils* (1964), a runner-up for the 1965 Newbery award.

Hunt, Leigh (1784-1859), was an English journalist, essayist, and poet. He was a supporter of such English romantic poets as John Keats and Percy Bysshe Shelley when they were largely ignored or ridiculed. Hunt edited several periodicals and much of his best writing appeared as literary and informal essays in these publications. Only a few of Hunt's poems are still read, notably "The Story of Rimini" (1816) and "Abou Ben Adhem" (1834). Hunt described his friendships with major romantic and early Victorian writers in his *Autobiography* (1850).

James Henry Leigh Hunt was born in Southgate, a London suburb. With his brother John, Hunt founded a liberal weekly newspaper called the *Examiner* in 1808. Hunt was imprisoned from 1813 to 1815 for his attacks on the future King George IV in the *Examiner.*

Richard J. Dunn

Hunt, Richard Morris (1827-1895), an American architect, introduced the style of the French Gothic château to the United States. He is best known for the five houses he designed for the Vanderbilt family, and for other mansions built in New York City and Newport, R.I. He also designed the pedestal for the Statue of Liberty. He practiced from 1855 to 1895 and became unofficial "dean" of American architects. He was the first of many American architects to study at the École des Beaux-Arts in Paris. Hunt was born in Brattleboro, Vt.

Hugh Morrison

Hunting is the sport of capturing or killing wild animals. At one time, people could get their food only if they hunted for it. Today, however, most persons hunt because they enjoy it as a sport.

What makes hunting a sport. Many people do not like to hunt, because they dislike killing wild animals. But, for most hunters, the killing itself is not so important. They receive most of their satisfaction from outwitting the animals they are hunting. True hunting is a contest between the hunter and the hunted. Weapons give the hunter an advantage. But animals also have advantages. They can run faster than the hunter, they know the woods better, and they can smell and hear much better. If hunters depended only on their weapons, the animals would beat them at the game almost every time. Therefore, hunters must know the habits of the animal, so that they can come close enough to shoot. Many hunters enjoy the sport because it takes them outdoors and gives them a chance to study the habits of wild creatures. Some hunters enjoy the sport even if they do not always return home with a record catch.

Kinds of hunting depend on the game being hunted, the location, and the methods used to catch the animal. Upland hunting takes place in farm country. The hunter uses a shotgun to hunt pheasants, quail, grouse, and other similar birds. A bird dog may or may not be used. Trained hounds help the hunter chase and capture a variety of animals ranging from cottontail rabbits to mountain lions. Hunters also shoot waterfowl like ducks and geese from boats and from duck blinds. To deceive game, hunters often use decoys, such as wooden ducks for duck hunting. In big game hunting, the hunter uses a powerful rifle to shoot such animals as deer, brown bears, and moose. In the United States, the most popular big game animals are the mule deer, the white-tailed deer, the elk, and the antelope.

Some types of dogs are especially bred for hunting. Hound dogs follow the scent of game animals. Pointing dogs, like setters, pointers, and Brittany spaniels, discover game by scent and then show the hunter the game by *pointing* (standing in a rigid position). Retrievers swim out into the water for dead waterfowl.

For ducks and upland game, the shotgun cartridges are loaded with small shot. In some areas, larger shot, called *buckshot,* are used to kill deer. Hunters use an exceptionally powerful rifle to hunt elephants, tigers, and buffalo. Some hunters use a bow and arrow.

Game laws. All states in the United States and Mexico and all provinces in Canada have passed game laws that regulate the kind and amount of game that can be hunted. The laws carefully govern the methods used to take certain animals. They also specify the times during which animals may be hunted.

Local and national governments have established game reservations where animals and birds may not be hunted. Hunters must usually buy a hunting license, and some cities require that hunting guns be licensed. The money from the license fees is used to operate state game departments and to enforce game laws.

Jack O'Connor

Related articles in *World Book* include:

Ammunition	Prehistoric people (How pre-
Eskimo (Hunting and fishing)	historic hunters lived)
Fox hunt	Safari
Game	Shotgun
Indian, American (pictures)	Trapping
	Wildlife conservation

Additional resources

Elman, Robert. *The Hunter's Field Guide to the Game Birds and Animals of North America.* Rev. ed. Knopf, 1982.
Mitchell, John G. *The Hunt.* Knopf, 1980.
Strung, Norman. *The Art of Hunting.* Cy De Cosse, 1984.
Whisker, James B. *The Right to Hunt.* North River, 1981.

Hunting dog. See Dog (Sporting dogs; pictures).
Hunting leopard. See Cheetah.
Huntington is the family name of two businessmen who helped develop southern California.

Collis Potter Huntington (1821-1900), a Sacramento merchant, helped finance the Central Pacific Railroad during the 1860's. This railroad was linked with the Union Pacific in 1869 to become the first transcontinental railroad system. Huntington extended his railroad company throughout southern California and it became known as the Southern Pacific Company. He became its president in 1890. He was one of the "Big Four," a group of railroad executives that had great influence in politics in the late 1800's. He was also president of the Chesapeake & Ohio, the Mexican International Railway, and the Pacific Mail Steamship Company. He was born in Harwinton, Conn.

Henry Edwards Huntington (1850-1927), nephew of Collis P. Huntington, built extensive transportation systems in San Francisco and Los Angeles. Between 1900 and 1910, he built the Pacific Electric railroad that linked hundreds of towns in southern California. It operated more than 900 cars (called "big red cars") over 1,100 miles (1,770 kilometers) of track. In 1910, Huntington sold these lines and devoted himself to the development of electric power. He founded the Henry E. Huntington Library and Art Gallery in San Marino. He was born in Oneonta, N.Y.   Andrew F. Rolle

Huntington (pop. 63,684), is the largest city in West Virginia. Huntington dates back to 1871, when it was selected as the terminus of the Chesapeake and Ohio Railroad. Collis P. Huntington was president of the railroad at the time. Large railroad shops and the headquarters of the line are still there. Huntington stands at the junction of the Ohio and Guyandotte rivers, near the western border of West Virginia (see **West Virginia** [political map]). The metropolitan area of Huntington, which includes Ashland, Ky., has a population of 336,410.

The factories of Huntington produce chemicals, furniture, glass containers, nickel, and steel rails. Huntington is the center of a tobacco-growing region.

Railroad passenger trains, two rail freight lines, and an airport serve Huntington. West Virginia's first radio station, WSAZ, started broadcasting from Huntington in 1923. Its first television station, WSAZ-TV, began operations there in 1949. Huntington is the seat of Cabell County. The city has a mayor-council form of government.   Mack H. Gillenwater

Huntington, Samuel (1731-1796), was a Connecticut signer of the Declaration of Independence. He also represented Connecticut in the Continental Congress from 1776 to 1781, serving as president of the congress from 1779 to 1781. He also was a member of Connecticut's delegation to the Congress of the Confederation from 1781 to 1784. In 1784, he was appointed chief justice of the superior court of Connecticut. Huntington served as governor of Connecticut from 1786 to 1796. He was born in Windham, Conn.   Richard B. Morris

Huntington Beach, Calif. (pop. 170,505), is a suburb of Los Angeles. One of California's largest oil fields is located in Huntington Beach. The suburb has been one of the fastest-growing cities in the nation since 1960, when it had 11,492 persons. Its chief industries produce aircraft and missile and space systems. Huntington Beach was founded in 1901 as Pacific City. It became Huntington Beach in 1904, and was incorporated in 1909. It has a mayor-council government. For location, see **California** (political map).   Larry Allison

Huntington's disease is a severe hereditary disorder of the nervous system. It destroys brain cells and causes involuntary body movements, mental disturbances, and eventual death. The disorder afflicts people of either sex and of every race. It was named for George S. Huntington, an American physician, who first described it in 1871. The condition originally was called *Huntington's chorea* (see **Chorea**).

The symptoms in most cases of the disease begin when the person is from 35 to 50 years old. But some cases start in childhood or old age. Patients live an average of about 15 years after the first symptoms appear.

The first physical symptom of the disease may be slight clumsiness or restlessness. Later, muscles in the face and hands begin to twitch. As the disease progresses, the muscle spasms become stronger and eventually involve the whole body. The head, shoulders, arms, and legs jerk uncontrollably. When the patient walks, voluntary and involuntary movements combine and produce lurching, dancelike steps. Early mental symptoms include dullness and irritability, and carelessness about personal grooming. The disease gradually destroys the patient's intellect and memory. Severe mental illness may develop.

The patient may finally lose all muscle control and mental ability. Death results from pneumonia, heart failure, or other complications of the disease.

Huntington's disease is caused by an abnormal gene. Any person who inherits this gene will eventually be stricken by the disorder. Each child of a patient with Huntington's disease has a 50 per cent chance of inheriting the gene.

Physicians are not certain how widespread Huntington's disease is, because many patients may be misdiagnosed as suffering from schizophrenia or some other mental illness. Experts estimate that of every 100,000 persons, 4 to 7 have the gene for Huntington's disease. Researchers have developed a method of determining who may carry the gene. However, this technique is still in an experimental stage.

Huntington's disease has no cure. However, many of the symptoms may be eased by drugs and other forms of treatment.   Harold L. Klawans

Huntsman's-cup. See **Pitcher plant.**

Huntsville, Ala. (pop. 142,513; met. area pop. 196,966), is often called *Rocket City, U.S.A.* The Redstone Arsenal, the rocket and guided-missile center of the United States Army, lies just southwest of Huntsville. Wernher von Braun and other scientists developed the nation's first large guided missiles there during the 1950's. In the 1960's, von Braun's team designed the rockets that carried U.S. astronauts to the moon.

Huntsville covers 113 square miles (293 square kilometers) in northern Alabama. For location, see **Alabama** (political map).

The city is the home of Alabama Agricultural and Mechanical University, Oakwood College, and the University of Alabama at Huntsville. Huntsville has a symphony orchestra and several theatrical groups. The Alabama Space and Rocket Center in Huntsville exhibits the world's largest collection of space-related materials. The Huntsville area's leading private industries produce personal computers, computer software, and electronic equipment for automobiles.

Cherokee and Chickasaw Indians lived in the area before white settlers arrived. In 1805, John Hunt of Virginia set up the first permanent settlement there. He chose the site because of its fertile soil and a big spring. The settlement, called Hunt's Spring, was renamed Twickenham in 1809. In 1811, it was incorporated and renamed Huntsville for Hunt. The city was Alabama's first state capital, in 1819 and 1820.

Huntsville, with an economy based on cotton and textiles, grew steadily during the 1800's and early 1900's. The population of the city jumped from about 16,000 in 1950 to more than 72,000 in 1960. This dramatic increase resulted from guided-missile research at the arsenal and industrial growth in the area. In 1960, the National Aeronautics and Space Administration opened the George C. Marshall Space Flight Center at the arsenal. The city's population growth continued, reaching more than 142,000 by 1980.

Huntsville's Von Braun Civic Center opened in 1975, and a new public library was completed in 1987. Huntsville is the county seat of Madison County. The city has a mayor-council form of government.   John Ehinger

See also **Alabama** (picture: Exhibits at Space Flight Center in Huntsville).

Hunza, *HUN zuh,* is an area in the northern tip of Pakistan. It lies in the Pakistan-controlled part of Kashmir, near the borders of Afghanistan and China. Hunza covers about 3,900 square miles (10,101 square kilometers) and has a population of about 30,000. Karimabad is the largest city of Hunza.

Hunza consists of a long, narrow valley in the Karakoram mountain range. Most Hunzukuts are farmers who grow such crops as barley, grapes, plums, and wheat. The chief industries are the production of woolen cloth and fine handicrafts.

Many of Hunza's people live more than 90 years. They believe that mineral-rich mountain water and a simple diet contribute to their long life. Their diet consists chiefly of fruits, such as apricots and peaches, and grains, nuts, and vegetables. The majority of the people speak a language called *Burushaski.* They have no written language. Most Hunzukuts are Muslims, and Islamic religious holidays are important to them.

No one knows who first lived in what is now Hunza. According to legend, three soldiers from the army of Alexander the Great settled there with their Persian wives during the 300's B.C. For hundreds of years, Hunza was an isolated state ruled by a *Mir* (prince). Pakistan gained control of Hunza in 1949, as a result of a United Nations truce that ended fighting between Pakistan and India in Kashmir (see **Kashmir**). The Mir was allowed to rule over local matters until 1974, when Pakistan took over complete control.   Robert I. Crane

Hurdling is a track and field race in which runners jump over fencelike obstacles called *hurdles.* Most races have 10 hurdles that stand at equal intervals on the track.

There are two types of hurdle races: intermediate and high. Intermediate-hurdle races are 330 yards in high school and 400 meters or 440 yards elsewhere. The hurdles are 36 inches (91 centimeters) high for men and 30 inches (76 centimeters) high for women. Most high-hurdle races for men are 60 yards indoors and 120 yards or 110 meters outdoors. Women run a 100-meter high-hurdle race. In men's competition, the hurdles are 42 inches (106 centimeters) high. High hurdles are 39 inches (99 centimeters) high in high school. High hurdles in women's races are 33 inches (84 centimeters) high.

In men's high-hurdle races, the first hurdle is 15 yards from the starting line in the 120-yard race and 13.72 meters from the line in the 110-meter event. In the women's high hurdles, the first hurdle is 13 meters from the starting line. In all intermediate-hurdle races, the first hurdle is 45 meters from the starting line.

In a hurdle race, runners must adjust their stride so that they clear the hurdle without breaking stride. The race begins from a sprinting position. Runners jump over the hurdle straight on. The lead leg goes over the hurdle first, and the other leg is brought up behind so it also clears the hurdle. Runners keep their speed and gain momentum and balance by thrusting their arms toward the lead leg. Runners snap the lead leg down, then bring their trailing leg through so that they are in a running position.

Hurdlers must run in lanes. They are disqualified if they allow a foot or leg to trail along the side of a hurdle or if they clear a hurdle that is not in their lane. Runners are not penalized for knocking down hurdles in their own lane.   Bert Nelson

For hurdling championship figures, see the tables with **Track and field** and **Olympic Games.**

Hurdy-gurdy. See Hand organ.

Huron, Lake. See Lake Huron.

Huron Indians. See Ontario (History).

Hurricane is a powerful, whirling storm that measures 200 to 300 miles (320 to 480 kilometers) in diameter. The winds near the center of a hurricane blow at speeds of 74 miles (119 kilometers) per hour or more. Many hurricanes have caused widespread death and destruction.

Hurricanes develop from *easterly waves.* These long, narrow regions of low pressure occur in ocean winds called *trade winds.* Easterly waves may grow into a *tropical depression,* with winds of up to 31 miles (50 kilome-

Sygma

Huge waves caused by a hurricane produce floods that can destroy life and property. About 90 per cent of the deaths that occur during hurricanes result from drowning in floods.

Larry Day

High-hurdlers leap over the final hurdle in this exciting track event. Outstretched arms maintain balance and help the runners to "scissor" their legs over the 42-inch (106-centimeter) bars.

Regions of hurricane activity

Hurricanes develop over warm ocean water. They weaken after moving over land areas. This map shows the regions in which most hurricanes occur.

Average number of hurricanes per year

More than 5

Less than 5

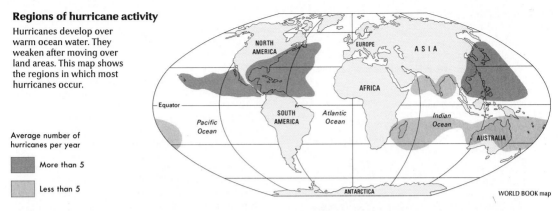

WORLD BOOK map

ters) per hour; then into a *tropical storm,* with winds of up to 74 miles (119 kilometers) per hour; and finally, into a hurricane.

Hurricane winds swirl around the *eye,* a calm area in the center of the storm. The eye of a hurricane measures about 20 miles (32 kilometers) in diameter and has few winds or clouds. Storm clouds called *wall clouds* surround the eye. The strongest winds and heaviest rain of a hurricane occur within its wall clouds.

A hurricane is an area of low air pressure that forms over oceans in tropical regions in either the North Atlantic Ocean or eastern North Pacific Ocean. Such a storm in the western Pacific Ocean is called a *typhoon,* and one in the Indian Ocean is called a *cyclone.*

In the United States, most hurricanes affect areas near the Atlantic Ocean or the Gulf of Mexico. Hurricanes occur in the North Atlantic and North Pacific oceans from June to November—most of them in September. On the average, about six to eight hurricanes form in the North Atlantic or North Pacific each year. However, as many as 15 have occurred in the Atlantic in a single year.

Movement. In the Northern Hemisphere, hurricane winds blow around the eye in a counterclockwise direction. They blow clockwise in the Southern Hemisphere. Hurricane eyes travel at speeds of 10 to 30 miles (16 to 48 kilometers) per hour. Most hurricanes move westward at first and become larger and stronger as they travel. Then they turn from the equator and pick up speed. Most hurricanes turn east after they reach temperate latitudes, where they are called *extra-tropical storms.* Many end as weak storm centers over cool oceans.

Destructive power. In many hurricanes, winds in the wall cloud area blow at speeds of 130 to 150 miles (209 to 241 kilometers) per hour. The winds and rain, combined with the force of the sea, produce huge waves. These waves, called a *storm surge,* rise several feet above normal and cause floods. A storm surge can be especially destructive if it occurs at high tide. Also, tornadoes are often present in hurricane clouds.

When a hurricane moves over land, strong winds and heavy rain hit the area for several hours. As the eye

NASA

Hurricane winds rotate around the *eye,* a calm area in the center of the storm. This photograph was taken from the space shuttle *Discovery* in 1985. It shows the wall clouds, which surround the eye, and the other whirling rain clouds. The arrow indicates the direction of the winds.

Famous hurricanes of the 1900's

1900 A hurricane and storm surge killed about 6,000 people in the Galveston, Tex., area.

1928 About 1,800 people died in a hurricane and floods in the Lake Okeechobee area of Florida. The storm also killed 300 people in Puerto Rico.

1935 The barometer fell to 26.35 inches (66.93 centimeters) during a hurricane that struck Tampa, Fla. This was the lowest reading ever recorded in the Western Hemisphere. Over 400 people were killed in the storm.

1955 Hurricane Diane caused about $1¼ billion in damage from North Carolina to New England. The storm killed 184 people.

1957 Hurricane Audrey struck Louisiana, Mississippi, and Texas, killing 550 people.

1960 Hurricane Donna became the first recorded storm to strike Florida, the Middle Atlantic States, and the New England States with hurricane-force winds.

1963 Hurricane Flora killed about 5,000 people in Haiti, over 1,700 in Cuba, and over 400 in the Dominican Republic.

1965 Hurricane Betsy killed 76 people and caused more than $1 billion in damage in the Bahamas, southern Florida, and Louisiana.

1967 Hurricane Beulah hit Caribbean islands, Mexico, and Texas, causing 58 deaths and over $1 billion in damage.

1969 Hurricane Camille killed more than 250 people in seven states from Louisiana to Virginia. It caused about $1½ billion in damage.

1970 Hurricane Celia battered the Texas coast near Corpus Christi, causing 11 deaths and $467 million in damage.

1972 Floods of Hurricane Agnes killed 122 people and caused $2 billion in damage from Florida to New York.

1974 Hurricane Fifi struck Honduras, killing about 8,000 people and causing $1 billion in damage.

1976 Hurricane Liza struck Baja California Sur, Mexico, causing over 400 deaths and $9¾ million in damage.

1979 Hurricane David battered the Dominican Republic, Puerto Rico, and the southeastern coast of the United States. It caused more than 2,000 deaths and nearly $2 billion in damage.

1980 Hurricane Allen struck several Caribbean islands, killing 272 people and causing extensive property damage.

1983 Hurricane Alicia struck near Galveston, Tex., killing 21 people and causing $2 billion in damage, the most in Texas history.

reaches the area, the rain stops and the air becomes calm. Less than an hour later, the eye passes and the rain and wind return. The hurricane weakens as it moves over land because it needs the warm sea to supply energy by evaporation. Friction caused by the rougher land surface also helps to slow the winds. Heavy rain continues even after the winds decrease.

Hurricane warnings. During the hurricane season in the United States, meteorologists of the National Weather Service keep a close watch on the Atlantic and Pacific oceans, particularly on the Caribbean Sea and the Gulf of Mexico. They also examine pictures of the area taken by weather satellites and collect such information as air pressure, temperature, and wind speeds. They use this information to forecast where a hurricane will hit and how strong it will be. They track the storm with satellites, airplanes, and radar. The National Hurricane Center issues warnings to communities in the storm's path.

Wayne M. Wendland

See also **Cyclone; Flag** (Flags that talk: Hurricane warning); **Tornado; Typhoon; Weather.**

Additional resources

Brown, Billye W. and W. R. *Historical Catastrophes: Hurricanes and Tornadoes.* Addison-Wesley, 1972. For younger readers.
Simpson, Robert H., and Riehl, Herbert. *The Hurricane and Its Impact.* Louisiana State Univ. Press, 1981.

Hurston, Zora Neale (1901?-1960), was a black American writer known for her novels and collections of folklore. Hurston's best-known novel is *Their Eyes Were Watching God* (1937). The story sensitively portrays a young black woman's rising consciousness of her own identity as a woman. Hurston wrote three other novels— *Jonah's Gourd Vine* (1934), *Moses, Man of the Mountain* (1939), and *Seraph on the Suwanee* (1948). All her novels display the author's gift for storytelling, her interest in Southern folk customs, her metaphorical language, and her robust sense of humor.

Hurston was born in Eatonville, Fla., a town founded by black Americans. In 1928, she graduated from Barnard College, where she studied anthropology. Hurston recognized the significance of the folklore of the Southern United States and the Caribbean countries. She collected Florida folk tales and descriptions of Louisiana folk customs in *Mules and Men* (1935). In *Tell My Horse* (1938), she described folk customs of Haiti and Jamaica. Hurston also wrote an autobiography, *Dust Tracks on a Road* (1942).   Darwin T. Turner

Hurtado, Miguel de la Madrid. See De la Madrid Hurtado, Miguel.

Hus, John (1369?-1415), was a Bohemian religious reformer. His name is also spelled *Huss.* Hus's teachings were forerunners of those of the Protestant Reformation. He was burned at the stake on a charge of heresy.

Hus was born in Husinec, a town in southwestern Bohemia, and took his last name from the first letters of the town. After he was ordained in 1401, he began preaching fiery sermons in Prague, and attracted many followers. Hus attacked the practices of bishops, cardinals, and popes, and called for reform in the church. He was influenced by the works of John Wycliffe, an English religious reformer of the 1300's. But unlike Wycliffe, Hus did not attack the sacrament of the Mass.

Hus vigorously attacked the papacy. Because of a confused papal election in 1378, two men claimed to be pope. After 1409, a third man claimed the papal throne. During this period, many devout people questioned papal authority. Hus went further, calling the papacy an "institution of Satan."

In 1409, the king of Bohemia turned the University of Prague over to the Czechs, and Hus became rector. This action angered the German teachers and students at the university. They left and established the University of Leipzig. The Germans spread the story that Hus was a notorious heretic. Because of this story, and his attack on the church practice of selling indulgences, Hus was excommunicated in 1412. In 1414, Hus was called before the Council of Constance, a meeting of church leaders at Constance, Germany. There he was condemned and burned at the stake, even though he had been promised safety if he attended the council to defend himself. Hus's reform movement was carried on for several years after his death by followers known as Hussites.

Richard Marius

See also **Czechoslovakia** (The rise of Bohemia); **Wycliffe, John.**

Additional resources

Betts, R. R. *Essays in Czech History.* Oxford, 1969. These essays deal with the Hussite period.

Spinka, Matthew. *John Hus' Concept of the Church.* Princeton, 1966. *John Hus: A Biography.* Greenwood, 1978. Reprint of 1969 edition.

Husking bee was a frontier custom of neighbors helping a family *husk* (shuck) corn and having fun while they worked. The corn was cut and piled ahead of time. People chose sides, and each side competed to shuck their half first. When a boy found a red ear of corn, he could kiss the girl of his choice. Singing, dancing, and refreshments added to the fun.   Walker D. Wyman

Husky. See Siberian husky.

Huss, John. See Hus, John.

Hussar, *hu ZAHR,* was a European light cavalryman armed with a carbine, sword, and sometimes a pistol. The term came from the Magyar words *husz,* or *twenty,* and *ar,* or *pay.* Every twentieth house in a village provided one mounted soldier. The hussars wore bright, colorful uniforms, including a high cylindrical hat called a *busby,* and a loose cape called a *dolman.* Hussars, first used by the Magyars in the 1400's, reached their peak of

A Cavalry Officer of the Imperial Guard (1812), an oil painting on canvas, by Theodore Géricault (Granger Collection)

Hussars were bold and reckless fighters.

efficiency under Napoleon. They won fame for their bold and reckless fighting. The hussar became obsolete soon after World War I (1914-1918).   Theodore Ropp

Hussein I, *hoo SAYN* (1935-   ), became king of Jordan in 1952. He succeeded his father, Talal, and developed Jordan's economy with aid from Western countries. With the support of his army, he prevented his

government's overthrow by agents of Egypt's Gamal Abdel Nasser. Hussein kept peace with Israel, until Israel destroyed the Jordanian village of As Samu in 1966. He took part in the 1967 and 1973 Arab-Israeli wars. During the 1967 war, Hussein's air force was destroyed, and Israel occupied west Jordan. His strong stand against Palestinian guerrillas in Jordan led to civil war in 1970. In 1972, he proposed making the Israeli-held part of Jordan a semi-independent Palestinian state. Hussein was born in Amman. See **Jordan** (History).   Sydney N. Fisher

Hussites, *HUH syts,* were followers of the Bohemian religious reformer John Hus. They were organized by about 450 nobles to avenge the killing of Hus in 1415 (see **Hus, John**). The most prominent Hussite conflict with the Roman Catholic Church concerned the administering of communion. But, because of political, social, and religious differences that existed before Hus's death, the Hussites broke into two main groups. The moderates, called Ultraquists, agreed to discuss religious issues with the church at the Council of Basel in 1433 and won a concession on communion. The more radical Taborites refused to negotiate with the church or to accept the nobles' political control. The Taborites fought the armies of Emperor Sigismund and the forces of the church and Ultraquists from 1419 until the Taborites were finally defeated in 1434.   Dale A. Johnson

Huston, *HYOO stuhn,* is the family name of two motion-picture personalities—Walter, an actor; and his son John, a screenwriter and director. They made one film together, *The Treasure of the Sierra Madre* (1948). The movie earned Walter an Academy Award as best supporting actor and John Academy Awards for screenplay and directing.

Walter Huston (1884-1950) was born in Toronto, Canada, and became a U.S. citizen in 1922. Huston toured in vaudeville, and starred in such Broadway plays as *Desire Under the Elms* (1924) and *Knickerbocker Holiday* (1938). His movies include *Rain* (1932), *Yankee Doodle Dandy* (1942), and *Duel in the Sun* (1946).

John Huston (1906-1987) won fame for directing movies that have a sense of brooding atmosphere. The first movie he directed was *The Maltese Falcon* (1941), a classic detective story. He also directed *Key Largo* (1948), *The Asphalt Jungle* (1950), *The Red Badge of Courage* (1951), *The African Queen* (1951), *Beat the Devil* (1953), *Moulin Rouge* (1953), *Moby Dick* (1956), *The Bible* (1965), *Fat City* (1972), *The Man Who Would Be King* (1975), *Under the Volcano* (1984), and *Prizzi's Honor* (1985). Huston was born in Nevada, Mo. He gave up his U.S. citizenship and became an Irish citizen in 1964. He wrote *An Open Book* (1980), his autobiography. Anjelica Huston, his daughter, is a motion-picture actress who won the 1985 Academy Award as best supporting actress for her performance in *Prizzi's Honor.*   Howard Thompson

Hutchins, Robert Maynard (1899-1977), an American educator, became well known for his unconventional theories about higher education. In 1929, he was appointed president of the University of Chicago. He became chancellor in 1945. At Chicago, he promoted intellectual rather than narrow moral considerations as the primary aim of higher education. He reduced the emphasis on athletics. He served as associate director of the Ford Foundation from 1951 to 1954. Hutchins served as president of the Fund for the Republic from 1954 to

1969 and as chairman from 1969 to 1974. He was chairman of the board for a new edition of the *Encyclopaedia Britannica,* which was published in 1974.

Hutchins was born in Brooklyn, N.Y., and graduated from Yale University. He served as secretary of Yale from 1923 to 1927. In 1928, he became dean of the Yale Law School.   Douglas Sloan

See also **Chicago, University of; Ford Foundation.**

Hutchinson, Anne Marbury (1591-1643), headed a group of Puritans whose religious beliefs were unacceptable to Puritan leaders of the Massachusetts Bay Colony. Her teachings caused deep divisions in the colony between 1636 and 1638.

Anne Marbury was born in Alford, Lincolnshire, England. She married William Hutchinson in 1612. In 1634, the Hutchinson family moved to the Massachusetts Bay Colony. There, Anne joined the congregation in Boston. She began holding religious meetings in her home, where she interpreted church teachings in ways that Puritan leaders considered dangerous. For example, Hutchinson preached that nothing people could do by choice, including obeying church and state law, could win God's love and favor. She also said that God communicated to people directly instead of through public and church officials. She and her followers were called *Antinomians,* meaning people who are against law.

Massachusetts officials ordered Hutchinson to leave the colony in 1637, and the church expelled her in 1638. She moved with her family to Rhode Island, and then to New York after her husband died in 1642. She and several members of her family were murdered there by Indians in 1643.   Pauline Maier

Hutchinson, Thomas (1711-1780), was one of the last royal governors of the Massachusetts Bay Colony. His refusal to let the tea ships leave Boston Harbor led to the Boston Tea Party in 1773 (see **Boston Tea Party**). He was just and able, but he became the symbol of royal power to colonists seeking independence.

Hutchinson, born in Boston, was the son of a wealthy merchant. He graduated from Harvard College in 1727, and entered his father's business. He was elected to the Boston board of selectmen and the general court of Massachusetts in 1737, and became chief justice of the colony in 1760. He issued the famous and unpopular writs of assistance (see **Writ of assistance**). He opposed the Stamp Act, but declared it legal and tried to enforce it. In 1765, angry colonists burned his house. He became acting governor in 1769 and governor in 1771.

After the Boston Tea Party, Hutchinson went to England. He advised King George III, and continued writing his important *History of the Colony and Province of Massachusetts Bay.*   Bradford Smith

Hutterites, *HUHT uh ryts,* also called Hutterian Brethren, are members of a religious sect who believe in the common ownership of goods. They follow the example of the early Christians who "had all things common" (Acts 2: 44). They do not believe in war or violence. They live in *Bruderhofs* (colonies) of about 85 persons. About 320 Bruderhofs are in South Dakota, Montana, and the prairie provinces of Canada.

The Hutterites are farmers who lead simple lives. They meet daily for worship. A preacher and a *Wirt* (boss), who is the financial manager, head each colony. The group maintains its own kindergarten and school.

The Hutterites originated in 1528 in Moravia as a branch of the Anabaptists. They were named for Jacob Hutter, who was their leader from 1533 until 1536 when he was burned at the stake. The Hutterites were severely persecuted. After 1564, they prospered in Moravia. But in 1595, they were driven to nearby countries and to the Ukraine in Russia. They settled in the United States in 1874. Many migrated to Canada in 1918. About 9,000 Hutterites live in the United States and 18,000 live in Canada.   John A. Hostetler

See also **Alberta** (People); **Anabaptists.**

Hutton, James (1726-1797), a Scottish geologist and physician, became famous for theories on the earth's origin. He is called the father of modern geology.

According to one of Hutton's theories, heat played an important part in the formation of the earth. He believed that rocks of basalt and granite were formed from a molten mass. Most other scientists thought that water had once covered the earth and that all rocks were formed when minerals settled at the bottom of the water. Hutton also theorized that the earth changed gradually by natural processes and would continue to change through the same processes. Other scientists believed that the earth was completely formed about 6,000 years ago and that only rare catastrophes could change its features.

See also **Geology** (History).   R. H. Dott, Jr.

Huxley, *HUHKS lee,* is the family name of three distinguished scientists and writers.

Thomas Henry Huxley (1825-1895) was a famous zoologist, lecturer, and writer. He was one of the first to be convinced by Charles Darwin's analysis of organic evolution, and he extended and defended it (see **Darwin, Charles R.**). Through his lectures, writings, and committees, Huxley helped advance scientific thought.

His writings include *Evidence as to Man's Place in Nature* (1863), *Critiques and Addresses* (1873), and *A Manual of the Anatomy of Invertebrated Animals* (1877). His essay "On a Piece of Chalk" (1868) and his essay about changes in the feet of fossil horses are outstanding.

Many of Huxley's expressions became famous. He introduced the word *agnostic* to describe one who believes that the existence of God or a spiritual world cannot be proved. He coined the word *biogenesis* to emphasize that life arises only from previous life (see **Biogenesis**).

Huxley was born near London, and studied by himself until he entered

Chicago Historical Society

Thomas Henry Huxley

medical school. He became a surgeon in the British navy and spent four years in the Indian Ocean and East Indies. He wrote a pioneering account of jellyfishes, and returned to England to find that he had become famous. From 1854 to 1885, he taught history at the Royal School of Mines. He served as president of the Royal Society from 1881 to 1885.   Lorus J. Milne and Margery Milne

Additional resources

Bibby, Cyril. *T. H. Huxley: Scientist, Humanist and Educator.* Hori-

zon, 1959. *Scientist Extraordinary: The Life and Scientific Work of Thomas Henry Huxley, 1825-1895.* St. Martin's, 1972.
Huxley, Leonard, ed. *Life and Letters of Thomas Henry Huxley.* 2 vols. West, 1979. Reprint of 1901 edition.
Paradis, James G. *T. H. Huxley: Man's Place in Nature.* Univ. of Nebraska Press, 1978.

Sir Julian Sorell Huxley (1887-1975), a grandson of Thomas Huxley, became a noted biologist. He did research in *ornithology* (the study of birds) and on the experimental analysis of development. He made a study of the relative rates of growth of bodily organs and developed a mathematical method to analyze body proportions. In 1946, Huxley helped establish the United Nations Educational, Scientific and Cultural Organization (UNESCO). He was elected its first director-general in 1946. In 1958, Huxley was knighted for his contributions to science.

Huxley's writings include *Essays of a Biologist* (1923); *The Science of Life* (with H. G. and G. P. Wells, 1929-1930); *Problems of Relative Growth* (1932); *Elements of Experimental Embryology* (with G. R. de Beer, 1934); *Evolution, the Modern Synthesis* (1942); *Man in the Modern World* (1947); *Essays of a Humanist* (with H. B. Kettlewell, 1964); and several poems.

Huxley was born in London. He taught at Rice Institute in Texas from 1912 to 1916. He later became a professor at King's College, London.   Mordecai L. Gabriel

Aldous Leonard Huxley (1894-1963), the brother of Julian Huxley, had one of the most varied literary careers of his time. He published three collections of poems and a book of short stories before beginning the series of witty, sophisticated novels that made him famous. The series includes *Crome Yellow* (1921), *Antic Hay* (1923), *Those Barren Leaves* (1925), and *Point Counter Point* (1928). The books satirize English society of the 1920's. The characters in *Point Counter Point* are based on Huxley and his friends.

Harper & Row, Publishers
Aldous L. Huxley

Huxley believed science was destroying human and political values. He expressed this concern in the satirical novel *Brave New World* (1932). This famous book describes a totalitarian society that disregards individual dignity and worships science and machines.

Huxley was born in Godalming, Surrey. He moved to the United States in the late 1930's, and spent most of the rest of his life there.   John Espey

Huygens, *HY guhnz,* **Christian** (1629-1695), a Dutch mathematician, physicist, and astronomer, was the first person to study the polarization of light. He also investigated and developed the wave theory of light. He coined the word *ether* for the medium in which light waves were then assumed to travel (see **Ether**). Huygens developed an improved method of grinding telescope lenses in 1655. He built the first powerful telescopes, which made possible his discovery of a satellite and ring of Saturn. He was the first to use a pendulum to regulate a clock. Huygens also invented the *micrometer,* a device

that is used to measure extremely small distances.

Huygens was born at The Hague, the Netherlands. He studied law and mathematics at Leiden. In 1663, he joined The Royal Society, England's oldest scientific society. From 1666 to 1681, he worked in Paris at the invitation of King Louis XIV of France.   Carl T. Chase

See also **Light** (People's understanding of light); **Polarized light; Saturn.**

Hwang Ho. See Huang He.

Hyacinth, *HY uh sihnth,* is a favorite spring flower of the lily family. It originated in the Mediterranean region and *Asia Minor* (now Turkey), and was brought to western Europe in the early 1500's. It is a popular plant in many parts of the world. The bell-shaped flowers of blue, pink, white, yellow, or purple, bloom from February to April on stalks which grow from 8 to 15 inches (20 to 38 centimeters) high.

Hyacinths grow from bulbs. They can be planted in open beds, greenhouses, and in the home. When raised in the open, they need rich, well-drained soil. The bulbs are planted from September to November, depending on the climate.

Early in the spring, the flowers appear. Gardeners sometimes tie the stems to slender stakes to protect them. After the plant flowers, gardeners remove the stalks and let the leaves die. This encourages new bulb growth. Florists pot specially treated bulbs early in September to force the plants to blossom by Christmas.

The soil and climate of the Netherlands provide an especially favorable place for growing the bulbs. The Dutch plant a large number of hyacinths every year near Haarlem. They ship the bulbs to many parts of the world for gardeners and florists to use.

Scientific Classification. Hyacinths belong to the lily family, Liliaceae. They are *Hyacinthus orientalis.*

August A. De Hertogh

See also **Bulb; Flower** (picture: Garden perennials [Bulbs]).

Hyaline membrane disease, *HY uh lihn,* or *respiratory distress syndrome,* is a lung condition that affects

WORLD BOOK illustration by Robert Hynes
The hyacinth is a spring flower that grows from a bulb. It produces small, fragrant, bell-shaped flowers on a slender stalk.

premature babies. Such babies are born before the end of a normal nine-month pregnancy. The disease is related to the underdevelopment of the lungs of these infants. The air sacs of the lungs collapse, causing rapid, difficult breathing and, in many cases, death by suffocation. Hyaline membrane disease ranks as a major cause of death among premature infants. It attacks few babies born after a nine-month pregnancy.

The term *hyaline membrane* refers to the clear, glassy membranes found in the lungs of babies that die of the disease. Many physicians believe these membranes are produced as a reaction to lung damage caused by the strain of breathing air in an immature lung.

A victim of the disease has difficulty breathing within minutes after birth. Underdeveloped lungs lack a substance called *pulmonary surfactant.* This substance prevents the air sacs from collapsing. The intensive care units in many hospitals include respirators and high-humidity incubators for treating hyaline membrane victims. Such treatment keeps many babies alive long enough for their lungs to become sufficiently developed to produce pulmonary surfactant. This development takes four to five days in most cases, but it may require several weeks. Most infants who recover have no permanent aftereffects. Scientists hope to develop artificial surfactants that could be given to infants soon after birth to prevent the disease.

In the early 1970's, doctors discovered a way to determine whether an unborn baby's lungs lack pulmonary surfactant. With this knowledge, a physician may try to delay a premature birth until the lungs have developed sufficiently. If a premature birth is not delayed, a physician can give the mother a synthetic hormone to accelerate the lung development of the fetus.

Mary Ellen Avery

Hybrid is the offspring of parents of different races, varieties, or species. Hybrids occur naturally and contribute to the great variety of living things. However, the term *hybrid* is used most often to refer to crops and ornamental plants bred by human beings.

Hybrid plants are extremely important in agriculture. Nearly all the corn and sorghum produced in the United States are grown from hybrid seed. Most commercial varieties of sugar beets and burley tobacco are hybrids, as are some varieties of alfalfa, barley, rice, and wheat. Vegetables produced from hybrid seed include broccoli, cabbage, carrots, cauliflower, melons, onions, peppers, pumpkins, squash, and tomatoes. Hybrids of such fruits as grapes, pears, and plums are also grown. Many marigolds, orchids, petunias, roses, and other flowers that beautify homes and parks are hybrids.

Some hybrid animals are also bred, but animal hybrids have been less commercially successful than plant hybrids. In most cases, the parents of animal hybrids are members of the same large hereditary group, called a *family,* but belong to a different *genus* (subgroup of a family) or *species* (subgroup of a genus). Animal hybrids include mules, which are bred from female horses and male donkeys; and cattaloes and beefaloes, the offspring of cattle and American buffaloes. The remainder of this article deals with plant hybrids.

Producing hybrids. People produce hybrids in order to improve the quality and productivity of cultivated plants. Plants selected for hybrid production have

Producing hybrid corn

Most hybrid corn results from *single-crossing.* In this process, selected corn plants are forced to breed with other plants of the same variety. This procedure produces *inbred seed.* Two inbred varieties are then bred, resulting in single-cross seed.

WORLD BOOK diagram by Zorica Dabich

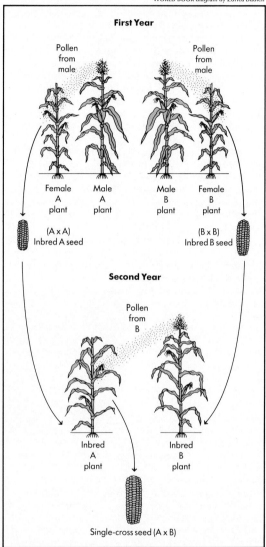

First Year

Pollen from male

Pollen from male

Female A plant   Male A plant

Male B plant   Female B plant

(A x A) Inbred A seed

(B x B) Inbred B seed

Second Year

Pollen from B

Inbred A plant

Inbred B plant

Single-cross seed (A x B)

hereditary characteristics that growers want to continue into future generations. For example, one variety of corn may resist disease better than another variety does. But the second variety may be hardier in cold weather than the first. By *crossing* (mating) the two varieties, growers can obtain hybrid seeds. These seeds develop into plants that have the traits of both parents. Seed from the hybrid offspring, however, produces plants of varying quality. Some hybrids may also be *sterile* (unable to reproduce). As a result, growers plant new hybrid seed each year to maintain the quality of their crops.

Most flowering plants have both male and female sex parts, contained either in separate flowers or in the same flower. To ensure that only certain plants cross, growers select some to serve as males and some as females. They generally remove the male sex parts, which produce pollen, from the plants that will act as females, thereby preventing the plants from pollinating themselves or other females. In some cases, they use female plants that have been specially bred to produce infertile pollen. The male plants are untouched.

The hybrid seed produced from the crossing of selected parents is often the result of a long and complicated process. Corn growers, for example, first cause selected corn plants of the same variety to breed. This procedure is called *inbreeding.* The seeds produced from the inbred plants are planted, and the plants that grow from them are in turn forced to inbreed. This process continues through several generations until plants having pure hereditary lines are established.

Growers then cross two inbred varieties. They remove the *tassels* (male corn flowers) from the plants chosen as females, leaving the *ears* (female corn flowers) for pollination by the inbred males. The seed resulting from this breeding produces *single-cross hybrids.* These plants combine the hereditary characteristics of two inbred varieties.

History. Many different kinds of hybrid plants were described by naturalists during the 1700's and 1800's. In 1922, hybrid seed corn was sold to farmers in the United States for the first time. By the mid-1940's, nearly all the corn planted in the major U.S. corn-growing areas was hybrid corn. During the 1960's, hybrids became important for other kinds of crops.   John W. Dudley

See also **Breeding** and its list of *Related articles.*

Hyderabad, *HY duhr uh BAD,* was an independent nation until it became a state of India in 1950. In 1956, India reorganized its states and divided Hyderabad among the states of Bombay (now Gujarat and Maharashtra), Mysore (now Karnataka), and Andhra Pradesh. Hyderabad covered 82,698 square miles (214,187 square kilometers) in southern India, and had a population of over 18 million.

Hyderabad was part of the Mogul Empire from 1687 to 1724. Then a Mogul *viceroy* (governor) made it independent. During the 1800's Britain gained control of Hyderabad's foreign affairs. The *Nizams* (rulers) of Hyderabad were famous for being among the richest persons in the world. Although the Nizams were Muslims, four-fifths of their subjects were Hindus.

When India was partitioned in 1947, the Nizam refused to join either Pakistan or India. Clashes followed between Muslims and Hindus. In 1948, India set up a military government in Hyderabad. When Hyderabad State was partitioned, Hyderabad City became the capital of the state of Andhra Pradesh.   Robert I. Crane

Hyderabad, *HY duhr uh BAD* (pop. 2,142,087; met. area pop. 2,545,836), is one of India's largest cities. Founded in 1589 as a royal capital, it became the capital of the state of Hyderabad in 1950 and the capital of Andhra Pradesh in 1956 (see **India** [political map]).

It has many palaces and the *Char Minar,* built in 1591. This building has four *minarets* (towers) and four arches through which the main streets of the city pass. Hyderabad is a trading center, and manufactures textiles, guns, glassware, paper, flour, and railway cars. It is the home of Osmania University.   Robert I. Crane

Hyderabad, *HY duhr uh BAD* (pop. 751,529), is a city in the Sind province of Pakistan. It lies on the banks of the Indus River. For location, see **Pakistan** (political map). Hyderabad is a rail and road junction and an important trade center. Its industries include cotton ginning, rice and oilseed milling, tanning, and the manufacture of agricultural machinery and cement. The city is famous for its hand embroideries and leatherwork. Sarfaraz Khan built the city in 1782 as a fort.   Robert I. Crane

Hyderabad, *HY duhr uh BAD,* **Nizam of,** *nih ZAHM* (1886-1967), Sir Usman Ali, ruled the nation of Hyderabad from 1911 to 1948. He was one of the world's wealthiest people. In 1950, Hyderabad became an Indian state, but the Nizam continued as *Rajpramukh,* the symbolic head of government. He retired in 1956 when Hyderabad was dissolved as a state.   Richard L. Park

Hydra, *HY druh,* was a many-headed serpent of Greek mythology. It is known as the *Lernaean Hydra* or the *Hydra of Lerna* because it lived in Lake Lerna in Argolis. One of the hydra's heads could not die, and the rest grew back as soon as they were cut off. However, Hercules and his nephew Iolaus killed the monster by first cutting off all the heads except the immortal one and sealing each neck with fire. Hercules then cut off the immortal head and buried it under a rock. See also **Hercules** (The twelve labors).   Mary R. Lefkowitz

Hydra, *HY druh,* is a tiny, slender animal that lives in ponds and lakes. Hydras are *coelenterates,* a group that also includes jellyfish, sea anemones, and corals.

The hydra has one of the simplest structures of the many-celled animals. It is shaped like a thin cylinder about as thick as heavy thread and is about $\frac{1}{4}$- to $\frac{1}{2}$-inch (6 to 13 millimeters) long. A hydra may be gray, tan, brown, or green. The green hydra gets its color from algae that live in certain cells of its body wall.

One end of a hydra's body attaches to sticks, stones, and water plants. The other end contains the mouth, which is surrounded by five to seven *tentacles* (tiny

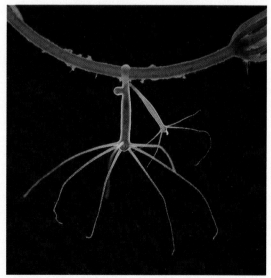

Kim Taylor, Bruce Coleman Ltd.

The hydra usually begins life as a bud that grows on the body of its parent, *above.* When fully developed, the young hydra detaches itself and lives independently.

arms). The hydra can stretch out or contract its entire body. Sometimes it stretches its tentacles until they look like long, delicate threads. At other times, it pulls in its tentacles. Then its body looks like a tiny egg with a group of knobs on the end. The hydra usually stays attached in one place for some time. But it can move about by slowly somersaulting on the bottom of the pond or lake, or by drifting upside down beneath the water's surface film.

A hydra eats other small water animals that it captures with its tentacles. Each tentacle has tiny cells that contain stinging threads. The hydra drives these threads into its prey, and they give off a poison that paralyzes the victim. Then the tentacles draw the victim into the mouth to be swallowed. The hydra's mouth is a small opening leading directly into a large digestive cavity inside the body. The undigested remains pass out through the mouth.

Hydras usually reproduce by *budding. Buds* are small, knoblike growths that appear on the body of the hydra from time to time. As the buds develop, they grow tentacles. When the buds are fully developed, they break off and live as independent hydras. Hydras also may produce eggs and sperm in the body wall. An egg unites with a sperm, grows larger, and eventually separates from the parent and drops into the water. A tough outer capsule protects the egg from damage, freezing, or drying out. After a while, a small hydra hatches.

Hydras can *regenerate* (regrow) parts of their bodies. It is estimated that in a period of several weeks a hydra replaces all the cells in its body. The hydra, therefore, never grows old.

Scientific classification. Hydras belong to the phylum Coelenterata and the class Hydrozoa.   L. Muscatine

Hydrangea, *hy DRAYN juh,* is a genus of handsome shrubs in the saxifrage family. Hydrangeas grow in North and South America and in China and Japan. One species grows 30 feet (9 meters) high. A dwarf variety grows to about 12 feet (3.7 meters). The flowers may be white, pink, or bluish. Each small flower grows with

The hydrangea is an attractive shrub that produces small flowers which grow in clusters. A species called the large bush hydrangea, *above,* may grow to a height of 30 feet (9 meters).

WORLD BOOK illustration by Robert Hynes

many others in large, showy clusters. Pink hydrangeas may produce blue flowers when grown in soils treated with aluminum sulfate, or alum. Lime added to the soil makes blue hydrangeas produce pink flowers. Hydrangeas need a rich and slightly moist soil. They grow well in partly shaded places. They flower more freely in the sun if they have sufficient moisture. Hydrangeas are grown by planting either cuttings or seeds. They bloom from late summer until fall.

Scientific classification. Hydrangeas belong to the saxifrage family, Saxifragaceae. The large bush is *Hydrangea paniculata.* The dwarf is *H. macrophylla.*   J. J. Levison

See also **Flower** (picture: Garden perennials [Flowering shrubs]).

Hydrate, *HY drayt,* is a chemical compound made of a definite amount of water and another substance. For example, the hydrate *blue vitriol* (copper sulfate pentahydrate) is formed by the combination of a copper atom, a sulfur atom, and four oxygen atoms with five water molecules. Its chemical formula is $CuSO_4 \cdot 5H_2O$. When the water in a solution of copper sulfate evaporates, the blue vitriol crystals that form are dry. But they retain a certain amount of water. This water is called *water of crystallization* or *water of hydration.*

In many cases, the water of hydration is driven off by heating the hydrate. The compound then becomes *dehydrated.* When all the water is gone, the compound becomes *anhydrous.* Anhydrous salts often differ from their hydrates in color and crystal form. The blue crystals of blue vitriol change into a white powder when the compound becomes anhydrous. Anhydrous copper sulfate has the formula $CuSO_4$.

Some hydrates, such as *washing soda* (sodium carbonate decahydrate, $Na_2CO_3 \cdot 10H_2O$), spontaneously lose their water of hydration when exposed to the air at room temperature. These compounds are called *efflorescent.* Their crystals slowly turn into a powder as they lose water. Efflorescence takes place faster when the humidity is low.   Peter A. Rock

Hydraulic brake. See Brake.

Hydraulic engine, *hy DRAW lihk,* or *fluidic engine,* is a machine that produces motion by means of pressure from water or other fluid. This type of engine can be used to drive machinery or move heavy loads. Examples of hydraulic engines include jacks, hoists, the power steering and brake mechanisms of automobiles, and the control systems of aircraft.

There are two basic types of hydraulic engines—*reciprocating engines,* such as hydraulic elevators and suction pumps; and *turbines,* such as those that turn electric generators. Reciprocating engines operate at fairly slow speeds. Turbines function at high speeds.

Early hydraulic engines used water to produce power. Today, engines that use water are rare except for water turbines in hydroelectric plants. Modern hydraulic engines use fluids that do not freeze at low temperatures. Such fluids include oil, certain silicones, and some gases. The fluid in some hydraulic engines is put under pressure mechanically. In other engines, the pressure comes from the weight of the fluid stored in a reservoir above the engine.   Richard G. Fowler

See also **Hydraulics; Locomotive** (Diesel locomotives); **Pump** (Reciprocating pumps); **Turbine** (Water turbines).

Hydraulics, *hy DRAW lihks,* is the branch of physics that studies the behavior of liquids at rest and in motion. Some laws of hydraulics apply to both gases and liquids. But they apply only under certain conditions, such as when gases flow at low velocity and are not compressed. Scientists sometimes divide the study of hydraulics into two categories—*hydrostatics* and *hydrodynamics.* Hydrostatics describes the behavior of liquids at rest. Hydrodynamics describes their behavior in motion.

Hydraulics is studied and applied in two of the specialty fields of engineering: civil engineering and mechanical engineering. Civil engineers use the principles of hydraulics mainly to study the flow of water in open or partially filled pipes. They design embankments and levees that provide flood control along rivers, as well as canals, irrigation systems, and sewage systems. They also plan water supply systems for cities and towns.

Mechanical engineers are usually more concerned with the flow of fluids in filled pipes under pressure. They use the principles of hydraulics to design *hydraulic machines.* These machines include hydraulic turbines, hydraulic brakes, power steering for cars, controls for airplanes and spacecraft, and construction equipment.

Pressure from water or some other fluid supplies the power that runs hydraulic machines. Some hydraulic machines, including turbines, operate by the force of a flowing fluid. Turbines are large wheels that change the potential energy of a fluid into work that can be used to power an electric generator or perform some other type of work. Steam or gas powers other kinds of turbines.

Other hydraulic machines, called *hydraulic presses,* increase and transfer force through a fluid from one piston to a larger piston. Industry uses hydraulic presses for such jobs as lifting heavy loads and pressing metal parts. One form of hydraulic press is called a *hydraulic jack.*

Liquids at rest

Use of hydrostatic principles is fundamental to the design of many machines and instruments. The design of hydraulic presses and the operation of such instruments as manometers and barometers depend on laws of hydrostatics.

A simple hydraulic press consists of a cylinder that contains two pistons, one smaller than the other. The cylinder is filled with a fluid. A force applied to the smaller piston is transferred through the fluid to the larger piston. The force increases in direct proportion to the ratio of the area of the larger piston to the area of the smaller piston. Automobile brakes operate on the principle of the hydraulic press. Pressure applied to the brake pedal is transmitted through a liquid to brake shoes, which press against the car's wheels.

A *manometer* measures the pressure exerted by a liquid or a gas. The simplest kind of manometer is a U-shaped tube with open ends. The tube contains a liquid, usually mercury or water, which fills the bottom of the U and rises a short distance in each arm. The liquid in the manometer must have a different weight per unit of volume than the substance whose pressure is to be measured. One arm is connected to the place where the pressure is to be measured. The other arm remains open to the atmosphere. The difference in liquid level in

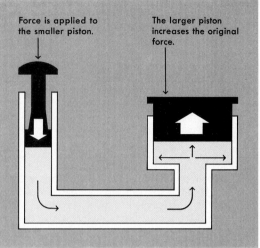

A hydraulic press increases and transfers the force applied to one piston through a liquid to a larger piston. The force increases in direct proportion to the ratio of the area of the larger piston to the area of the smaller piston. Industry uses hydraulic presses to lift heavy loads.

the arms indicates the pressure compared to atmospheric pressure. See **Manometer.**

A *barometer* measures atmospheric pressure. It is used primarily to forecast weather and to measure heights of mountains. One type of barometer consists basically of a tube containing mercury. At sea level, a column of mercury about 30 inches (76 centimeters) high equals in weight the force of atmospheric pressure on that column. The level of mercury in the tube rises or falls as the atmospheric pressure changes. See **Barometer.**

Laws of hydrostatics describe the behavior of liquids at rest.

One principle of hydrostatics states: *The pressure caused by the weight of a column of fluid is determined by the height of the column.* The shape of the column does not affect the pressure that is exerted by the fluid.

Suppose that a pipe extends in a zigzag pattern from the ceiling to the floor. Another pipe of equal diameter extends straight down from the ceiling to the floor. The second pipe is, of course, shorter than the first. If both pipes are filled with water, the longer one will hold more water. But the water pressure at the bottom of both pipes will be equal because the height of both columns of water is equal.

An illustration of the above principle is the buoyant force exerted by a fluid on an object submerged in it. The bottom of an object submerged in water is deeper than the top of the object. Therefore, the column of water pressing on the bottom of the object is taller than the column pressing on the top of the object. Thus, the water exerts an upward force on the object, called a *buoyant force.* Buoyant forces act to keep boats afloat.

Archimedes' principle comes from the principle discussed above. It states: *An object placed in a fluid seems to lose an amount of weight equal to the weight of the fluid it displaces.* A buoyant force exerted on the object by the fluid causes the apparent loss of weight. Archimedes, a Greek mathematician, developed this principle during the 200's B.C.

To illustrate this principle, imagine that a 1-liter metal can is placed in water. If the can weighs 3 kilograms, it will displace 1 liter of water, which weighs 1 kilogram. Thus, the buoyant force equals 1 kilogram. The can will then seem to weigh only 2 kilograms—that is, 1 kilogram less than its original weight.

Pascal's law states: *A fluid in a container transmits pressure equally in all directions.* Blaise Pascal, a French scientist and mathematician, developed this law during the A.D. 1600's.

To illustrate Pascal's law, take a bottle with a neck opening of 1 square inch and fill it with water. Put a plug in the neck so that the plug seals the top of the bottle and moves freely in the neck. Place a 1 pound weight on the plug. The pressure of the water will increase by 1 pound over each square inch (1 pound per square inch, or 1 *psi*) of the inside surface of the bottle.

Liquids in motion

Use of hydrodynamic principles is basic to hydraulic engineering and to the design of certain machines. Engineers use hydrodynamics when planning water supply systems, canals, and irrigation systems. They also apply hydrodynamic principles to the design of airplanes and to the construction of certain hydraulic machines, such as water turbines.

Engineers consider many factors to determine the proper pressure for a water supply system. For instance, the height of the reservoir or tank affects the pressure in water flow from the reservoir, and this pressure determines the flow rates that can be obtained. Most reservoirs have a long series of pipes that connects the source of water with its destination. Such factors as pipe size and the friction between the water and the pipes affect the flow of water.

Laws of hydrodynamics play a fundamental role in the design of water turbines. Some water turbines are submerged in rivers, and the normal flow of water provides power. Other water turbines are located at the bases of dams. Water pressure created by the dam is used to speed up the water when it enters the turbine. The turbines then change the kinetic energy of the moving water into rotational energy, which turns generators that produce electricity.

Laws of hydrodynamics describe the behavior of flowing fluids. Fluid flow may be steady or unsteady. An unsteady flow results from changes in the velocity, temperature, or pressure of a fluid. The movement of a fluid around obstructions may also cause an unsteady flow.

There are three basic laws of hydrodynamics. All of them apply only to steadily flowing liquids.

The principle of continuity in fluid flow states: *The velocity of a fluid flowing through a pipe increases as the area of the pipe decreases, and decreases as the pipe's area increases.*

The nozzle of a garden hose uses the principle of continuity. The nozzle decreases the size of the opening at the end of the hose. As a result, water flows faster through the nozzle than through the hose.

Bernoulli's principle, also called *Bernoulli's law,* states: *The pressure of a fluid increases as its velocity decreases, and decreases as the fluid's velocity increases.* Daniel Bernoulli, a Swiss mathematician, developed this principle during the 1700's.

Bernoulli's principle is used in the design of airplane wings. Engineers curve the upper surface of the wing so air will flow faster over the top than it does over the bottom of the wing. The faster-flowing air exerts less pressure on the top of the wing. As a result, the greater pressure under the wing lifts the airplane.

Torricelli's law states: *The velocity with which a liquid flows through an opening in a container equals the velocity of a body falling from the surface of the liquid to the opening.* Evangelista Torricelli, an Italian physicist, developed this law during the 1600's.

According to Torricelli's law, a stream of water flowing through a hole 10 feet (3 meters) below the water surface in a dam has the same velocity as a stone falling that 10-foot distance. Torricelli's law does not apply to gases because a gas has no surface. The velocity at which a gas flows from a container depends on the pressure under which the gas is confined in the container.   James D. Chalupnik

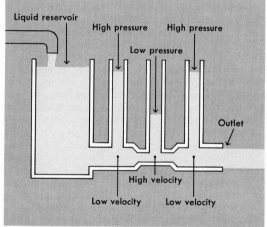

WORLD BOOK diagram

Bernoulli's principle describes both the flow of water through a pipe and the flow of air around an airplane wing. The velocity of flowing water, *above,* increases in the narrow section of pipe. The increased velocity produces less pressure, as indicated by the lower water level in the center vertical pipe. *Below,* air flows faster over the curved surface of a wing than over the flat surface. The increased velocity reduces the air pressure, and the greater pressure under the wing causes the airplane to rise.

WORLD BOOK diagram

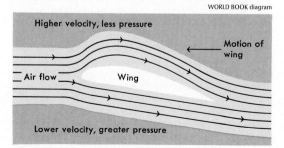

Related articles in *World Book* include:

Archimedes	Hydraulic engine	Turbine
Bernoulli's principle	Pascal, Blaise	Water power
Brake	Pump	

Hydraulus. See Organ (History).

Hydrazine, *HY druh zeen,* is an important chemical compound used in jet and rocket fuels. Industry also uses it to make agricultural and textile chemicals, explosives, photographic developers, and blowing agents used in the manufacture of foam rubber. Hydrazine derivatives are used to regulate the growth of plants, such as grass on parkways. These chemicals keep the grass from growing so fast that it needs constant attention.

Hydrazine occurs as a colorless, fuming, corrosive liquid. This is a nitrogen-containing base and a powerful reducing agent (see **Base**). It mixes readily with water and alcohol. Hydrazine boils at 114° C (237° F.) and its chemical formula is H_2NNH_2. It burns readily in air, giving off a great amount of heat, to form nitrogen gas and water. Industry prepares it by various methods from hydrazine hydrate, $H_2NNH_2 \cdot H_2O$.   James S. Fritz

Hydriodic acid. See Hydrogen iodide.

Hydrobromic acid. See Hydrogen bromide.

Hydrocarbon, *HY droh KAHR buhn,* refers to the most important class of organic compounds. Hydrocarbons contain only the elements hydrogen and carbon. They occur in petroleum and natural gas. Commercial petroleum products such as gasoline, kerosene, airplane fuel, lubricating oils, and paraffin, are mixtures of hydrocarbons. Some hydrocarbons are found in coal tar and coal gas. Many others are *synthesized* (made artificially) from hydrocarbons found in nature.

Hydrocarbons are starting materials for the petrochemical industry. Petrochemical companies use hydrocarbons from crude oil and natural gas to manufacture solvents, plastics, and synthetic fibers and rubbers.

Organic chemistry is sometimes called the "chemistry of hydrocarbons and their derivatives," because all organic compounds are essentially related to the hydrocarbons. Hydrocarbons can be divided into three large classes: (1) aliphatics, (2) alicyclics, and (3) aromatics.

Aliphatic hydrocarbons have the principal carbon atoms arranged in chains. They are further divided into the paraffin, olefin, and acetylenic series.

Paraffins or *alkanes* include the greatest number of hydrocarbon compounds. They have the general formula C_nH_{2n+2}. Methane, CH_4, is the first member of the series. Others are formed by adding CH_2 groups to methane. For example, ethane is C_2H_6, and propane is C_3H_8. Paraffins react by *substitution*. Hydrogen atoms are replaced by other atoms or groups of atoms, such as halogens or hydroxyls.

Olefins or *alkenes* have at least one double bond between two carbon atoms. They have the general formula C_nH_{2n}. Ethylene, C_2H_4, is the first member. Olefins react primarily by *addition* of molecules such as water, oxygen, and halogens. They can also react with themselves to form *polymers* (large chain molecules) such as polyethylene, which is used in plastics.

Acetylenes or *alkynes* have at least one triple bond between two carbon atoms. They have the general formula C_nH_{2n-2}. Acetylene, C_2H_2, is the first and most important member of the series. Acetylenic hydrocarbons have reactions similar to the olefins.

Alicyclics have their carbon atoms arranged in a ring. These atoms may have single or double bonds between them. Triple bonds in alicyclics are rare, but they can occur in sufficiently large rings. Many important natu-

rally occurring organic compounds fall into this class. The reactions of alicyclics are similar to those of the aliphatics.

Aromatics are a small but highly important class of hydrocarbons. They are characterized by a six-carbon ring. This ring differs from the alicyclics in that it contains three double bonds. *Benzene,* C_6H_6, is the most important aromatic. Others in the benzene series include toluene, $C_6H_5CH_3$, and the xylenes, $C_6H_4(CH_3)_2$. Other aromatic series include the *naphthalenes,* $C_{10}H_8$, and the *anthracenes,* $C_{14}H_{10}$.   Robert C. Gadwood

Related articles in *World Book* include:

Acetylene	Ethane	Petroleum
Benzene	Ethylene	Smog (Pho-
Carbon	Methane	tochemical
Coal tar	Natural gas	smog)
Coke oven gas	liquids	Toluene
Damp	Paraffin	

Hydrochloric acid is a dangerous chemical that has many important industrial uses. The acid is a colorless liquid with an irritating odor. It fumes when exposed to air. It is highly corrosive and can cause serious burns.

Hydrochloric acid is also called *muriatic acid.* Its chemical formula is HCl. The acid is made by dissolving hydrogen chloride gas in water. The hydrogen chloride gas itself is prepared by burning hydrogen and chlorine gases together or by treating common table salt, sodium chloride, with sulfuric acid. Hydrochloric acid is most commonly sold as a 30 per cent solution, called concentrated hydrochloric acid. Neutralization of the acid forms salts called *chlorides.*

Industry uses hydrochloric acid in preparing many chemical compounds. The acid is also used in metallurgy and food processing. The human stomach secretes small amounts of hydrochloric acid, which aids in digestion. However, excess production of the acid by the stomach contributes to the formation of stomach ulcers.   Carolyn J. Smith

See also **Acid; Aqua regia; Chloride.**

Hydrocyanic acid gas. See Gas chamber; Prussic acid.

Hydrodynamics. See Hydraulics.

Hydroelectric power. See Electric power; Water power.

Hydrofluoric acid, *HY droh flu AWR ihk,* is an *extremely* dangerous inorganic chemical. It is produced by dissolving hydrofluoric gas in water. The chemical formula of hydrofluoric acid is HF. Neutralization of the acid forms salts called *fluorides.*

Hydrofluoric acid is used in manufacturing aluminum and certain refrigerants. Industry also uses it to etch glass. In the laboratory, hydrofluoric acid is used in separating uranium isotopes (see **Uranium**).

Hydrofluoric acid is a colorless liquid with an irritating odor. The acid fumes when exposed to air. It is highly corrosive and can cause serious, painful burns to the skin, eyes, and mucous membranes. Burns from dilute hydrofluoric acid may not be immediately evident, but may appear later as deep ulcerations.

Because hydrofluoric acid corrodes glass, ceramic, and many metals, containers made from these materials are unsuitable for storing it. Instead, the acid is usually stored in polyethylene bottles and polyethylene-lined drums.   Carolyn J. Smith

Commercial hydrofoils typically serve as passenger ferries between islands, along seacoasts, and on rivers. The commercial hydrofoil shown at the left operates on a waterway in Hong Kong.

E. R. Degginger

Hydrofoil is a boat whose hull can lift above the surface of the water when traveling at high speeds. The craft has wings that are designed to move underwater. These wings, which are called *foils,* have a curved upper surface and work like airplane wings to lift the hull above the water.

The foils are attached to the hull of the boat by long, thin supports called *struts.* At low speeds, the hydrofoil moves through the water on its hull. When the craft reaches higher speeds, water rushes over the foils at a fast rate. This water action decreases the pressure on the top of the foils and causes them to rise in the water. The hull of the hydrofoil then "flies" above the water on its foils. The lift of the foils supports the hull on its struts.

Hydrofoils use less engine power than other kinds of vessels when traveling at high speeds, because their hulls do not have to be pushed through the water. They generally travel at speeds from 30 to 55 knots. One knot equals 1.15 miles (1.85 kilometers) per hour. Experimental craft have reached speeds of more than 80 knots.

An important feature of hydrofoils is their ability to ride smoothly in rough water at high speeds. The foils act to reduce the effects of waves on the craft, both when it is *foilborne* (traveling on its foils) and when it is *hullborne* (traveling on its hull).

Commercial hydrofoils carry hundreds of thousands of passengers and many tons of supplies and equipment each year. Passenger hydrofoils operate between the islands of Greece, across the English Channel, and in many other parts of the world. The Soviet Union operates the world's largest fleet of commercial hydrofoils.

Military hydrofoils perform such duties as carrying out patrol missions and tracking enemy vessels at high speeds. Some carry guided missiles. The Soviet Union has more military hydrofoils than any other country. Other countries that operate military hydrofoils include Great Britain, Italy, and the United States.

Kinds of hydrofoils

Hydrofoils range from about 15 to 200 feet (4.5 to 61 meters) in length. Most are powered by gas turbine or diesel engines, or both. Propellers or waterjets propel the craft.

When a hydrofoil is foilborne, its weight is generally distributed between two foils, one at the bow and one at the stern. In the *canard system,* the foil at the stern is larger than the one at the bow. In the *tandem system,* both of the foils are of equal size. The *airplane system* has a larger foil at the bow than it has at the stern.

In rough water, hydrofoils change their "flight" path to keep their hulls above the waves. When the waves are small in comparison to the hydrofoil, the craft easily

Boeing Marine Systems

Military hydrofoils, such as the United States Patrol Hydrofoil Missileship (PHM) shown at the left, are used primarily to patrol coastal waters and to track enemy vessels. PHM's carry guided missiles.

clears the tops of the waves while maintaining a fixed path. This method is called *platforming.* When the waves are large in comparison to the hydrofoil, the craft adjusts its path to follow the shape of the waves. This method is called *contouring. Intermediate response* combines features from both platforming and contouring for traveling over small and large waves. The hydrofoil maintains a fixed path when moving over the small waves, but it follows the shape of the waves when traveling over large ones.

Hydrofoils are classified according to the way their foil systems operate when they are foilborne. There are two basic types: (1) surface-piercing hydrofoils and (2) fully submerged hydrofoils.

Surface-piercing hydrofoils are most commonly used on rivers, lakes, and other areas where the water is relatively calm. Two popular types of surface-piercing

How hydrofoils travel over waves

Hydrofoils traveling in rough water keep their hulls above the waves in three basic ways. These methods are (1) platforming, (2) contouring, and (3) intermediate response.

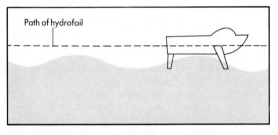

Platforming occurs when the waves a hydrofoil encounters are small in comparison to the size of the craft. The craft maintains a fixed path and the hull easily passes above the water.

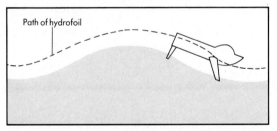

Contouring is used when the waves are large in comparison to the size of the hydrofoil. The craft adjusts its path to match the shape of the waves, and it rides up and down them.

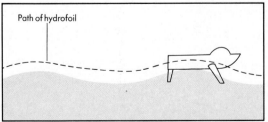

WORLD BOOK illustrations by Arthur Grebetz

Intermediate response combines both platforming and contouring. The craft maintains a fixed path over small waves, but it follows the shape of the waves when passing over large ones.

Two kinds of hydrofoils

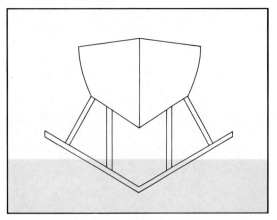

Surface-piercing hydrofoils ride on foils that are only partly submerged. The upper part of the foils rides above the surface of the water and helps to stabilize the craft.

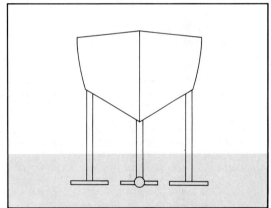

WORLD BOOK illustrations by Arthur Grebetz

Fully submerged hydrofoils travel with their foils completely underwater. Fully submerged hydrofoils perform well in rough water but need special stabilizing equipment to ride smoothly.

craft are the *V-foil hydrofoil* and the *trapeze-foil hydrofoil.* The V-foil hydrofoil has foils that form a "V" shape. The trapeze-foil hydrofoil has foils that form part of a trapezoid.

Surface-piercing hydrofoils use the surface area of the foils for stability and control. When a surface-piercing hydrofoil is in "flight," the upper parts of the foils stick out of the water. The speed of the craft determines the distance of the hull above the water. As the speed of the craft increases, the foil area required for lift decreases, and the upper part of the foil therefore rises out of the water. When the speed decreases more area is required to lift the craft, and the foils settle deeper into the water.

Fully submerged hydrofoils are used most often in oceans or other areas where exceptionally rough water might be encountered. The foils of a fully submerged hydrofoil stay completely underwater when the craft is in "flight." The craft is kept stable by changing the angle of the foils, called their *angle of attack,* to keep water flowing over them at an even rate. The angle of attack of

Shallow draft hydrofoils are a common means of water transportation in the Soviet Union. Soviet scientists developed the shallow draft hydrofoil during the 1940's, and such craft began regular commercial service in the Soviet Union in 1957.

Tass from Sovfoto

fully submerged hydrofoils is changed through the use of automatic stabilizing systems. These systems are either electrical or mechanical.

Electrical stabilizing systems use *sensors* (detecting devices) to pick up changes in the size of the waves. The sensors feed this information into a computer, which sends signals to the craft's stabilizing equipment to adjust the angle of attack. Some craft make such adjustments through the use of movable flaps on the foils. Others have air pumps that create an air cavity around the foils.

Mechanical stabilizing systems use floats attached to the foils by mechanical links to change the angle of attack. The floats ride along the surface of the water. As they travel up and down the waves, they move the mechanical links. This action then rotates the foils.

Fully submerged hydrofoils called *shallow draft hydrofoils* have the self-stabilizing ability of surface-piercing hydrofoils. The foils of these craft lose lift as they approach the water surface and do not rise higher than one *chord* (the distance from the front edge to the back edge of the foil) from the surface. They maintain this height as long as their speed is kept constant. These craft are used on calm, shallow waterways.

History

Early hydrofoil experiments began in Europe during the late 1800's. In 1906, an Italian engineer named Enrico Forlanini successfully tested the first full-sized, self-propelled hydrofoil. In 1907, the Scottish-born in-

ventor Alexander Graham Bell started work on a series of hydrofoils he called *Hydro-Dromes.* In 1918, one of these craft, the *HD-4,* set a world water speed record of 61.6 knots. This record remained the top speed for a hydrofoil until 1963, when an experimental hydrofoil developed in the United States, the *Fresh I,* set the new record of 84 knots.

Modern hydrofoil development. In 1927, Baron Hanns von Schertel, a German engineer, started work on designing a hydrofoil for commercial use. After nine years of trials, Schertel developed a surface-piercing V-foil that eventually became the first passenger hydrofoil to be put into regular service. During World War II (1939-1945), Schertel and his design team created 15 different types of hydrofoils for the German military.

In 1945, Rostislav Alexeyev, a Soviet scientist, began experiments that led to the development of the shallow draft hydrofoil. In 1957, Alexeyev's first shallow draft vessel, the *Raketa,* began passenger service on the Volga River in the western Soviet Union.

In 1947, the United States Navy began extensive research into hydrofoils and soon became the world's leader in the development of oceangoing hydrofoils. In 1958, it launched *Sea Legs,* the first fully submerged hydrofoil craft to meet with great success. During the 1960's, the U.S. Navy launched a number of fully submerged hydrofoil vessels, including the *Tucumcari* and the *Flagstaff,* both gunboats. During the late 1970's and early 1980's, the Navy commissioned six fully submerged hydrofoils called *Patrol Hydrofoil Missileships* (*PHMs*).

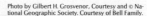

Photo by Gilbert H. Grosvenor, Courtesy and © National Geographic Society. Courtesy of Bell Family.

An early hydrofoil boat, built by Alexander Graham Bell, had foils arranged like rungs on a ladder. In 1918, Bell's boat set a world water speed record of 61.6 knots. This record remained the top speed for a hydrofoil until 1963, when an experimental hydrofoil reached a speed of 84 knots.

They were designed for tracking enemy vessels and launching missiles against them.   John D. Bogus

See also **Missile boat; Ship** (Other passenger vessels).
Hydrogen is a tasteless, odorless, colorless gas and one of the most important chemical elements. The hydrogen atom is the lightest and simplest atom known. This atom consists of only one proton, which has a positive charge, and one electron, which has a negative charge. Hydrogen has the chemical symbol H. Its atomic number is 1, and its atomic weight is 1.0079. The term *hydrogen* comes from two Greek words meaning *water-former.* A water molecule consists of two hydrogen atoms and one oxygen atom.

Occurrence. Hydrogen is the ninth most abundant element in the earth's crust. It makes up almost 1 per cent of the crust. Most of this hydrogen occurs in combination with other elements. However, pockets of uncombined hydrogen have caused violent explosions in underground coal mines. The sun and many other stars consist mostly of hydrogen.

Hydrogen is combined with other chemical elements in plant and animal tissues as well as in water. An important class of compounds called *hydrocarbons* contain only hydrogen and carbon. Petroleum and natural gas, for example, consist of various mixtures of hydrocarbons. The common acids, many bases, and other compounds also contain hydrogen.

Properties. Henry Cavendish, an English scientist, discovered the properties of hydrogen and identified it as an element in 1766. Hydrogen may be condensed to a liquid that boils at $-257.87°$ C and freezes at $-259.14°$ C. The gas is so light that it weighs about one-fourteenth as much as an equal volume of air. At 20° C, hydrogen has a density of 0.00008375 gram per cubic centimeter. The gas is only slightly soluble in water. Hydrogen cannot support life but is not poisonous.

Hydrogen, like most other elements, has more than one *isotope.* Isotopes are atoms of the same element that have different numbers of electrically neutral neutrons in the nucleus. Hydrogen has three isotopes. In the most common hydrogen isotope, *protium,* the nucleus consists of only a proton. In 1932, Harold C. Urey, an American chemist, discovered the second isotope, called *deuterium* or *heavy hydrogen.* For this discovery, Urey won the 1934 Nobel Prize in chemistry. The nucleus of a deuterium atom has one proton and one neutron. Deuterium atoms make up about 1 part in 4,000 to 6,000 parts of normal hydrogen. In 1934, scientists discovered the third isotope, *tritium.* Its nucleus has one proton and two neutrons. It is radioactive and has been used in the hydrogen bomb. See **Deuterium; Tritium.**

Preparation of hydrogen. In the laboratory, hydrogen can be produced by the electrolysis of water (see **Electrolysis**). In electrolysis, an electric current breaks down the water into its two elements, the gases hydrogen and oxygen. Commercially, large amounts of hydrogen are a by-product of the manufacture of sodium hydroxide by the electrolysis of brine. But most commercial hydrogen is produced either by passing steam over hot coke or iron or by causing steam and natural gas to react in the presence of a catalyst (see **Catalysis**).

Sodium and many other active metals react directly with water and release hydrogen from the water even at room temperature. Less chemically active metals, such as magnesium, will liberate hydrogen from steam (see **Electromotive series**). Zinc and numerous other metals react better with acids than with water. Sometimes, these metals are used to displace hydrogen from solutions of acids in water.

Hydrogen compounds. Hydrogen combines directly with several of the most active elements, but most hydrogen compounds are made by indirect methods. When two hydrogen atoms unite and form a molecule, they give off relatively large amounts of heat. Hydrogen's ability to ignite makes it useful in producing a number of compounds. For example, mixtures of hydrogen and oxygen explode violently when ignited by a spark. In the presence of air or oxygen, hydrogen burns with a hot flame and forms water. Chlorine burns in hydrogen and forms a colorless gas, *hydrogen chloride* (HCl). Solutions of hydrogen chloride in water are known as *hydrochloric acid.* In the Haber process, large quantities of *ammonia* (NH_3) are made by combining hydrogen and nitrogen (see **Haber process**). Other hydrogen compounds prepared indirectly include *hydrogen peroxide* (H_2O_2), *acetic acid* (CH_3COOH), and *ethyl alcohol* (C_2H_5OH).

Under suitable conditions, hydrogen combines directly with a variety of compounds. In the Patart process, it combines with carbon monoxide (CO) and forms *methanol,* or wood alcohol (CH_3OH). It also unites with liquid fats and forms solid fats. This process, called *hydrogenation,* is used to convert vegetable oils into semisolid shortenings used in cooking (see **Hydrogenation**).

Uses. Many hydrogen compounds, such as ammonia, ethyl alcohol, and hydrogen peroxide, have extensive industrial uses. Hydrogen is widely used to recover some metals from their compounds because it is a good *reducing agent.* In other words, hydrogen can withdraw oxygen and other nonmetallic elements from metallic compounds, leaving a pure metal. For example, pure metallic tungsten can be formed by passing a stream of hydrogen over heated tungsten trioxide. The hydrogen removes the oxygen and unites with it, forming water. In the same way, free metal and hydrogen chloride result when hydrogen passes over certain hot metallic chlorides. Water and iron result when iron rust, or ferric oxide, is heated with hydrogen. Hydrogen's low density also makes it useful for inflating balloons.

Hydrogen's ability to produce heat when united with oxygen makes it a good fuel. Scientists in such countries as Canada, Japan, the United States, and Russia have developed or are researching ways to use hydrogen as an energy source. For example, hydrogen fuel powers the main engine of the orbiter in the United States space shuttle system. In New York City, a power plant produces electricity using hydrogen fuel. By the mid-1980's, experimental hydrogen-powered automobiles may be used in Japan and the United States. Probably by the year 2000, some commercial aircraft will be powered by hydrogen.   Lawrence P. Verbit

Related articles in *World Book* include:

Ammonia	Hydrocarbon
Atom (diagrams: How atoms compare; The isotopes of hydrogen)	Hydrochloric acid
	Hydrogen bromide
	Hydrogen iodide
Cavendish, Henry	Hydrogen peroxide
Gas	Nuclear weapon
Heavy water	

Hydrogen bomb. See Nuclear weapon; Fallout.

Hydrogen bromide (chemical formula, HBr) is a colorless gas that fumes in moist air. It can be prepared by combining hydrogen (H) and bromine (Br) directly, or by treating a salt of HBr, such as sodium bromide (NaBr), with a strong nonvolatile acid. A solution of hydrogen bromide in water is called *hydrobromic acid.* Both HBr gas and the water solution are used in making various organic compounds. Walter J. Moore

Hydrogen chloride. See Hydrochloric acid.
Hydrogen fluoride. See Hydrofluoric acid.
Hydrogen iodide (chemical formula, HI) is a heavy, colorless gas with a strong odor. Chemists prepare it by combining hydrogen and iodine at 200° to 300° C, or by adding water to a mixture of iodine and red phosphorus.

Hydrogen iodide dissolves readily in water to form hydriodic acid, also called hydroiodic acid, a *strong* (extremely active) acid. Chemists use hydriodic acid in laboratory experiments as a powerful *reducing agent.* Such a substance gives some of its electrons to other substances during a chemical reaction. The acid is too expensive for large-scale industrial use.

Robert W. Medeiros

Hydrogen peroxide, is an important industrial chemical that consists of hydrogen and oxygen. Its chemical formula is H_2O_2.

Hydrogen peroxide, also called *hydrogen dioxide,* is a colorless, syrupy liquid that has a sharp odor. Chemists classify any solution of water and hydrogen peroxide that contains more than 8 per cent hydrogen peroxide as corrosive. Such solutions irritate the skin, eyes, and mucous membranes. Concentrations of hydrogen peroxide higher than 50 per cent can cause serious burns.

Pure hydrogen peroxide is stable if handled properly and kept free from contamination. Such factors as light, heat, chemical catalysts, dirt, and rust may cause hydrogen peroxide to decompose into water, oxygen, and heat. Decomposition of a sufficiently concentrated hydrogen peroxide solution yields enough heat for an explosion. Contact with combustible materials may result in fire. However, hydrogen peroxide's instability makes it a good oxidizing agent because the oxygen freed in decomposition readily combines with other substances.

Hydrogen peroxide is widely used in industry. Solutions containing 3 to 6 per cent hydrogen peroxide are used as antiseptics and germicides and as a skin cleanser. Higher concentrations are used in the manufacture of many chemical compounds. They also serve as bleaching agents for textiles and paper pulp, and as rocket propellants. Carolyn J. Smith

See also Antiseptic; Barium; Bleach; Oxidation.
Hydrogen sulfide is a colorless, extremely poisonous gas that smells like rotten eggs. Its chemical formula is H_2S. Eggs and many other substances contain organic compounds made up partly of sulfur. When such compounds decompose, they produce hydrogen sulfide. For this reason, the gas may be present in the air around cesspools and sewers. The decomposition of metal sulfides also produces hydrogen sulfide, resulting in the presence of the gas in mines and mineral springs.

Hydrogen sulfide is flammable. It dissolves slightly in water, forming a weak acid called *hydrosulfuric acid.* Small amounts of hydrogen sulfide in the air cause silver objects to tarnish. Chemists usually make hydrogen sulfide in the laboratory by combining hydrochloric acid and iron sulfide. They use the gas mainly in analyzing the composition of other substances. Hydrogen sulfide is also used in the production of high-pressure lubricants and oils. Lawrence P. Verbit

Hydrogenation, *HY druh juh NAY shuhn,* is a chemical process that adds hydrogen to a substance. Oils and liquid fats are often hydrogenated to improve their quality. For example, peanut oil is hydrogenated to change it to a solid and improve its odor and flavor. The hydrogenation process is important in the preparation of gasolines. Hydrogen is added to the ends of long petroleum molecules after they are cracked by heat and pressure to form shorter molecules of gasoline. Hydrogenation is used in making crude oil from coal. In this process, powdered coal is mixed with a little oil and hydrogenated under heat and pressure.

A substance whose molecules contain some hydrogen atoms, but can accept more, is said to be *unsaturated.* For example, the gas *ethylene* (C_2H_4) is an unsaturated compound. When ethylene is hydrogenated, the double *bond* (chemical connection) that links its two carbon atoms breaks. This leaves a single bond and adds two hydrogen atoms to the molecule. The resulting compound is a gas called *ethane* (C_2H_6). Ethane is called a *saturated* compound because its molecules contain as many hydrogen atoms as they can.

Catalysts (substances that speed up chemical reactions) are needed to make hydrogenation economical. In 1912, French chemist Paul Sabatier received the Nobel Prize in chemistry for discovering that nickel is a good hydrogenation catalyst. Other catalysts used today for hydrogenation include platinum and *Raney nickel* (an aluminum-nickel alloy treated with caustic soda). John P. Fackler, Jr.

See also **Coal** (Coal research).
Hydrography, *hy DRAHG ruh fee,* is the branch of physical geography that deals with the surface waters of the earth. Most countries of the world have developed well-organized hydrographic agencies. Hydrographers make studies of navigable water, including oceans, rivers, and lakes. They make and publish charts and maps which show the formation of the coasts, the depth of the waters, and the position of channels, reefs, shoals, rocks, and currents. Hydrographers also study tides and winds.

Hydrographic work in the United States is carried on by the National Ocean Survey, by the Office of the Oceanographer of the Navy, and by the Corps of Engineers of the United States Army. Canada maintains a hydrographic service in its Department of Energy, Mines, and Resources. Sigismond deR. Diettrich

See also **Geology** (picture: Hydrographers).
Hydrolite. See Geode.
Hydrologic cycle. See Water (Nature's water cycle).
Hydrology, *hy DRAHL uh jee,* is the study of the movement and distribution of the waters of the earth. People use billions of gallons of fresh water every day. *Hydrologists* (scientists who study water) help provide information needed to find adequate supplies of fresh water. They also study floods and water pollution. In addition, hydrologists study the chemical and physical properties of water.

In nature, water circulates through a system called the *water cycle* or *hydrologic cycle*. This cycle begins when heat from the sun causes ocean water to evaporate and become water vapor. The atmosphere holds the water vapor while the vapor gradually cools and forms clouds. The water eventually falls as rain or snow. Most rain and snow falls back into the oceans. But some falls on the land and flows back to the seas, completing the cycle. See **Water** (Nature's water cycle).

There are two main sources of fresh water: (1) surface water and (2) ground water. Surface water flows over the land in lakes, rivers, and streams. Ground water seeps through the soil or through tiny cracks in rock. Some ground water flows in underground rivers.

Hydrologists study the water cycle to locate sources of fresh water. They help choose the best sites to drill wells to find ground water in desert areas. Hydrologists also help plan dams and irrigation projects.

Hydrologists try to prevent or reduce water pollution. They study the effects of pollution as it moves through the water cycle.

Hydrology provides information needed to predict and control floods. Architects and civil engineers use this information to help plan towns and roads near waterways where floods often occur.   Douglas S. Cherkauer

Hydrolysis, *hi DRAHL uh sihs,* is a chemical reaction involving water as one of the reacting substances. Its name comes from the Greek prefix *hydro-,* meaning *water,* and the Greek word *lysis,* meaning a *loosening.* In industry hydrolysis is important in making soap, sugar, alcohols, hydroxides, and silicones.

Hydrolysis produces either of two chemical changes: (1) the acidity of the reacting system may change, or (2) molecules of both water and another substance may split and recombine to form new substances.

An example of hydrolysis that increases the acidity of a system is the reaction of antimony chloride ($SbCl_3$) with water. This hydrolysis produces antimony oxychloride (SbOCl) and hydrochloric acid. In the chemical equation, the presence of the acid is indicated by the *hydronium ion* (H_3O^+). This equation is written:

$$SbCl_3 + 3H_2O \rightleftarrows SbOCl + [2H_3O^+ + 2Cl^-]$$

An example of hydrolysis that decreases the acidity of a system is the reaction of sodium carbonate (Na_2CO_3) with water. This hydrolysis forms a mixture of sodium ions (Na^+), bicarbonate ions (HCO_3^-), and hydroxide ions (OH^-). The chemical equation is written:

$$Na_2CO_3 + H_2O \rightleftarrows 2Na^+ + HCO_3^- + OH^-$$

An example of hydrolysis in which molecules of both water and another substance split and recombine differently is the reaction of sucrose (cane sugar, $C_{12}H_{22}O_{11}$) with water in the presence of acid. This hydrolysis produces two simpler sugars, glucose and fructose. These simpler sugars have the same chemical formula ($C_6H_{12}O_6$), but they differ in molecular structure. The chemical equation for the hydrolysis of sucrose is:

$$\overset{\text{acid}}{C_{12}H_{22}O_{11} + H_2O \rightarrow \underset{\text{glucose}}{C_6H_{12}O_6} + \underset{\text{fructose}}{C_6H_{12}O_6}}$$

The hydrolysis of sucrose is an important part of digestion. Sucrose cannot be used by the body, but glucose and fructose can.   Stanley Kirschner

See also **Acid; Base; Neutralization.**

Hydrometallurgy. See Metallurgy (Leaching).

Hydrometer, *hy DRAHM uh tuhr,* is an instrument used to determine the density of liquids. The design is based on Archimedes' principle that a body in liquid seems to grow lighter, and that the loss of weight is equal to the weight of the displaced liquid.

The hydrometer is usually a glass tube with a weight in the bottom. It is placed in the fluid to be measured, and allowed to sink. The level to which the weight sinks is compared with a scale on the side of the hydrometer. Suppose the hydrometer sinks 6 centimeters when placed in water. Then it is placed in another liquid and sinks to a level of 8 centimeters. The second liquid is 6 divided by 8, or .75 times as dense as water.

By comparing known densities of the liquids to be measured, the amounts of the liquids mixed together can be determined.

One type of hydrometer, called a *lactometer,* is used to test the purity of milk. An *alcoholometer* is used to test alcohol. The strength of brine in the boilers of seagoing ships is tested with a *salinometer.*

One type of hydrometer is made especially to test storage batteries. It is called an *acidimeter,* and is used to determine the amount of acid in the batteries. The concentration of battery acid increases the density of the liquid in the battery.   Robert F. Paton

See also **Density.**

Hydrophobia. See Rabies.

Hydrophone is an instrument used to listen to sounds transmitted through water. For example, the position of a submarine may be detected by the noise of its en-

© Dan Hulburt

A hydrometer is an instrument frequently used by automobile mechanics to measure the amount of acid in a storage battery.

gines. The hydrophone employs the principle of a microphone. Max Mason, a staff member of the Naval Experimental Station in New London, Conn., invented the hydrophone during World War I. See also **Microphone.**

Edith Lillian Smith Webster

Hydrophyte. See **Plant** (Aquatic regions).

Hydroplane is a fast motorboat that skims over the water almost in the way a flat skipping stone does when thrown. The hydroplane's bottom is shaped to lift the hull as it speeds up, until the boat is "planing" over the surface. The shape of the bottom allows the pressure of the water to lift the boat and keep it on the surface as long as it keeps moving quickly. For this reason, the bottom must be flat, or only slightly curved. In some hydroplanes, the bottom is a single surface. Others have two or more separated bottom sections. Many racing hydroplanes are called "three-point" boats. The only parts of the boat that touch the water at high speed are a float, or *sponson,* on each side of the hull, and the propeller. See also **Motorboat racing.**

Robert H. Burgess

Hydroponics is the science of growing plants without soil. Developed during the mid-1800's, it is also called *soilless agriculture, nutriculture,* or *chemical culture.*

Land plants normally obtain nitrogen, phosphorus, potassium, and other *nutrients* from the soil. Plants need these chemical substances for proper growth and development. Hydroponics involves growing plants in containers filled with water or with coarse sand, gravel, or other materials, known as *substrate materials,* to which nutrients have been added. The containers should be made of metal or plastic. They range in size from small pots for individual plants to huge tanks for large-scale growing.

Plants growing without soil require the same amount of light and warmth that they would if they were growing in soil. Growers who use hydroponics indoors provide a source of light and heat.

Methods of hydroponics. There are two main methods of growing plants without soil. They are *water culture* and *aggregate culture.*

In water culture, plants are suspended with their roots submerged in water that contains plant nutrients. The roots absorb water and nutrients, but do not anchor the rest of the plant. Therefore, the plants must be mechanically supported from above. Because oxygen is also taken up by the roots, air must be regularly pumped or mixed into the nutrient solution.

There are many different kinds of nutrient solutions. A basic solution might contain 5 pounds 13 ounces (2.6 kilograms) of potassium nitrate, 1 pound (0.5 kilogram) of ammonium sulfate, $4\frac{1}{2}$ pounds (2 kilograms) of magnesium sulfate, $2\frac{1}{2}$ pounds (1.1 kilograms) of monocalcium phosphate, and 5 pounds (2.3 kilograms) of calcium sulfate. Mixed together, these materials will provide enough nutrients for 1,000 gallons (3,800 liters) of water.

Once the solution is in the tank, 1 gallon (3.8 liters) of water containing 1 ounce (28 grams) of manganous sulfate and 3 to 5 drops of concentrated sulfuric acid should be added to each 1,000 gallons of solution once a month. In addition, 4 ounces (113 grams) of ferrous sulfate in 1 gallon (3.8 liters) of water should be added once a week.

In aggregate culture, although plants are grown without soil, the roots not only absorb water and nutrients, but also anchor the plant. Instead of being placed directly in a water and nutrient solution, the roots are placed in a substrate material, such as coarse sand, gravel, peat, perlite, or vermiculite. A nutrient solution is then repeatedly applied to the substrate material. The solution is either pumped up from below the roots or trickled down from above them.

Importance of hydroponics. Scientists have not proved that hydroponics produces sturdier plants and better and larger crops. However, growing plants without soil is an effective way to study the needs of plants. By varying the amounts of nutrients, scientists can find the best ratio for successful growth.

Some scientists have suggested using hydroponics for commercial crop production. In places where soil is not available, such as on ships at sea and in ice-covered Arctic areas, hydroponics is an effective alternative.

Good soil has the nutrients necessary for plant growth. When plants are grown without soil, all plant nutrients must be added to allow for proper growth. The nutrients a plant receives in its early growth stages will largely determine how well the plant will grow and its later quality. During this early period, it is difficult to know what the plant lacks. Only a person specially skilled at studying a plant's *foliage* (leaves) is likely to recognize signs of poor nutrition at this stage. By the time poor growth is noticed, it may be too late to correct the nutrient deficiency that caused it.

William H. Carlson

Hydrosphere. When we think of the earth, we think mostly of areas of land. But the land, or *lithosphere,* makes up only a small part of the world. Water, or the *hydrosphere,* makes up most of the earth's surface. We

Growing plants by hydroponics

Hydroponics involves growing plants without soil by one of two chief methods. The plants may be suspended with their roots in a tank of water, *right,* or the roots can be placed in such material as coarse sand or gravel, *far right.*

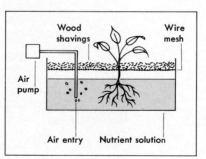

Growing plants in water

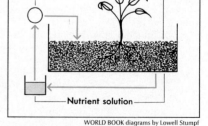

WORLD BOOK diagrams by Lowell Stumpf

Growing plants in gravel

see the hydrosphere mostly in the basins of lakes and oceans, where it has an average depth of about $2\frac{1}{3}$ miles (3.8 kilometers). In some parts of the Pacific Ocean, the hydrosphere is 6 miles (9.7 kilometers) deep.

The hydrosphere resembles another part of the earth, the *atmosphere,* because its pressure and temperature change at different depths. Oceanographers find that even in tropical oceans, the temperature at great depths is just a few degrees above freezing. The chemical content of the hydrosphere does not change with variations of temperature and pressure. But it does vary according to whether the body of water is fresh water or salt water. *Fresh water* is usually found in rivers and in lakes. It is composed of the chemical elements that make up water and of various other elements which depend upon the type of soil and rock surrounding the water. *Salt water* is found mostly in seas and oceans. In addition to the elements which make up water, it always has a high content of salt, or *sodium chloride.* Salt water also contains magnesium, sulfites, calcium, carbonates, bromides, and potassium. Small amounts of a number of other elements, such as gold, silver, and radium, are also found in salt water.   Henry Stommel

See also **Earth** (The earth's surface).

Hydrostatics. See Hydraulics; Mechanics.

Hydrotherapy, *HY droh THEHR uh pee,* is a method of treating muscle, joint, and skin disorders and injuries by using water. The water may be used in any of its forms, from ice to steam. Most modern hospitals and clinics have hydrotherapy facilities in their departments of physical therapy. Physical therapists use hydrotherapy to alter the temperature of the layers of tissue that make up the skin.

Physical therapists apply ice in cases of acute injury to muscles and joints. The ice causes the small blood vessels near the surface of the skin to *constrict* (narrow), reducing swelling and pain. The ice affects the central nervous system by stimulating nerve endings located in the skin.

Warm water can be used to promote relaxation, to relieve chronic muscle and joint discomfort, and to improve joint flexibility. Warm water causes the small

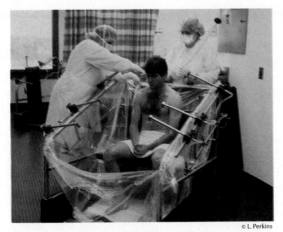

© L. Perkins

Hydrotherapy is used to treat the burn victim shown above. The plastic lining of the whirlpool tank is provided for sanitary purposes. The lining is replaced for each patient.

blood vessels near the skin's surface to *dilate* (widen), bringing more blood to the surface tissues to fight disease there. Warm water in a whirlpool bath is excellent for the removal of dressing and for cleaning wounds in the treatment of burn patients. Physical therapists generally use arm or leg whirlpools to treat small body parts, and whirlpool tanks to treat the whole body. The buoyant effect of water is important when a patient is trying to regain strength in weak or partly paralyzed muscles. In such cases, the patient may do exercises in a therapeutic pool. Doctors also use warm-water hydrotherapy to wash out the stomach, bowel, or other body cavities.

Health resorts called *spas* offer medicinal bathing in mineral waters, therapeutic steam baths, and other forms of hydrotherapy. In Europe, famous spas are located in Karlovy Vary, Czechoslovakia; Vichy, France; and Baden-Baden, West Germany. In the United States, popular spas include those in Hot Springs, Ark., and Saratoga Springs, N.Y.   Mary T. Moffroid

See also **Bath; Mineral water.**

Hydrotropism. See Tropism.

Hydroxide, *hy DRAHK syd,* is a chemical ion. An ion is one or a group of atoms with an electric charge that act together in chemical reactions. The hydroxide ion has a negative charge and is composed of a hydrogen atom and an oxygen atom. Its chemical formula is OH^-. Many compounds containing the hydroxide ion dissolve in water solutions, producing *ionic solutions.* For example, sodium hydroxide (NaOH) dissolves to form sodium ions (Na^+) and hydroxide ions (OH^-) in water. The hydroxide ion combines with metals and certain nonmetals to form compounds that are basic, acidic, *amphoteric* (basic or acidic), or neutral.

Basic hydroxides are the most familiar hydroxides. A dilute solution of ammonium hydroxide (NH_4OH) is household ammonia. Basic hydroxides in water solutions conduct electricity. They have a bitter taste and feel slimy or soapy. Strong basic solutions burn the skin. When a basic hydroxide combines with an acid, water and a salt are formed. Both the acid and the base are neutralized, thereby increasing the alkalinity of the resulting solution and reducing its acidity. Hydroxides are used to make such products as detergents, medicines, paper, and textiles.   Mark S. Wrighton

Hyena, *hy EE nuh,* is a mammal that is famous for its weird howl, which resembles a hysterical human laugh. The hyena hunts animals for its food. It also eats the remains of animals it finds dead. Hyenas have powerful jaws and strong teeth that enable them to crush and eat even large bones.

The most common hyena is the *spotted,* or *laughing, hyena.* Other species include the *striped hyena* and the *brown hyena.* The spotted hyena lives in Africa, south of the Sahara. Its coarse fur is yellowish-gray with black spots. Striped hyenas live in northern Africa and from Turkey to India in Asia. They are smaller than spotted hyenas. Their coats are grayish, with narrow black stripes across the body and legs.

The brown hyena is found in southern Africa, south of the Zambezi River. It has long hair on its back. It has a coarse blackish-gray coat and stripes only on its legs. Farmers who claim that brown hyenas prey on their livestock have poisoned or shot thousands of them. This species is now found in large numbers only in national

Michael C. T. Smith, Photo Researchers

The spotted hyena has massive, powerful jaws and strong teeth that can crack even large bones. Spotted hyenas hunt live prey and also feed on the remains of animals that they find dead.

parks and game reserves, where hunting is prohibited.

Scientific classification. Hyenas belong to the hyena family, Hyaenidae. The spotted hyena is *Crocuta crocuta.* The striped hyena is *Hyaena hyaena.* The brown is *H. brunnea.*

Duane A. Schlitter

See also **Aardwolf.**

Hygiene. See Health.

Hygiene, Mental. See Health (Elements of mental health).

Hygiene, Public. See Public health.

Hygrometer, *hy GRAHM uh tuhr,* is an instrument used to measure the amount of water vapor in the air. Scientists use hygrometers to determine the *relative humidity.* Relative humidity is the amount of water vapor in the air compared with the amount required for saturation of the air at the same temperature. The most common types of hygrometers are the *psychrometer* and the *hair hygrometer.*

The psychrometer consists of two thermometers mounted on the same frame. One type of psychrometer, called the *sling psychrometer* or the *whirled psychrometer,* has a frame that can be whirled in the air by hand. The bulb of one thermometer is covered with a tight-fitting muslin sack and wetted with water. This thermometer is known as the *wet-bulb thermometer.* The other is the *dry-bulb thermometer.* The psychrometer is whirled to provide ventilation for the bulbs. The dry bulb indicates the temperature of the air. The wet bulb helps determine the relative humidity.

When the sling psychrometer whirls through the air, water from the muslin evaporates. The evaporating water cools the wet bulb. The amount of cooling that occurs depends on the relative humidity. The lower the humidity, the faster the water in the muslin will evaporate, and the more the bulb will cool. High humidity will cause less evaporation, slowing the cooling process.

In air that has less than 100 per cent relative humidity, the wet bulb will record a lower temperature than the dry bulb. This difference in temperature is known as *wet-bulb depression.* A special chart is used to convert the wet-bulb depression to relative humidity.

The *Assman psychrometer,* an extremely accurate type of psychrometer, has a built-in fan. The fan draws the proper amount of air through two stationary metal tubes that hold wet-bulb and dry-bulb thermometers.

The hair hygrometer uses a bundle of human hairs to detect relative humidity. The length of the hair increases as it absorbs moisture from the air. One end of the bundle is anchored. The other end is attached to a lever that moves a pointer on a scale. As the humidity lengthens or shortens the hair, the lever moves the pointer on the scale, indicating the relative humidity.

Other hygrometers measure relative humidity by different methods. An *absorption hygrometer* uses a chemical that absorbs water vapor from the air. The chemical gets heavier as it absorbs the moisture, and the change in weight is measured to determine relative humidity. An *electrical hygrometer* uses carbon or some other substance whose electrical resistance responds to changes in humidity. A *dew-point hygrometer* measures *dew point,* the temperature at which the air has 100 per cent relative humidity (see **Dew point**). Its polished surface is chilled until dew appears. A device on the surface measures the temperature at which the dew forms.

David D. Houghton

See also **Humidity** (picture: To make a hygrometer).

Hyksos, *HIHK sahs,* were invaders from Palestine and nearby areas who settled in ancient Egypt in the 1700's B.C. They gradually seized control of Egypt from the *pharaohs* (kings). The Hyksos dominated Egypt until 1570 B.C. They introduced the horse, the horsedrawn chariot, new weapons, and perhaps a new type of fortification in Egypt. These changes later helped Egypt to build a vast empire. The Hyksos are sometimes called *shepherd kings,* but the Egyptian word *Hyksos* actually means *chieftains of foreign countries.* See also **Egypt, Ancient** (The Middle Kingdom). Leonard H. Lesko

Hymenoptera. See Insect (table).

Hymn is a song of praise. Most hymns glorify God, but some honor a country or a hero. This article discusses only religious hymns.

The ancient Greeks sang hymns to their gods. Since Biblical times, Jews have used the Psalms of the Old Testament as hymns. Today, both Jews and Christians sing hymns during their religious services. There are more than 400,000 hymns. The largest number were originally written in German.

Words and music. Most hymns were originally written as poems and were later set to music. The music of a hymn is called the *hymn tune.* Some hymns have become closely associated with a certain tune, though the words and music may have been written by different persons. For example, "O God, Our Help in Ages Past" was written by Isaac Watts, an English clergyman. But this hymn is almost always sung to a tune created by William Croft, an English composer. In other cases, a hymn is sung to several tunes, or one tune is used for several hymns.

Until the 1900's, many hymnals had only the words to songs and were commonly considered books of poetry. In many churches, the people memorized certain hymn tunes, and the minister announced the tune for each hymn. Today, hymnals have both the words and the music. Many hymnals include tunes by great composers. For example, "Hark, the Herald Angels Sing," written by Charles Wesley, an English hymnist, is sung to music by Felix Mendelssohn, a famous German composer.

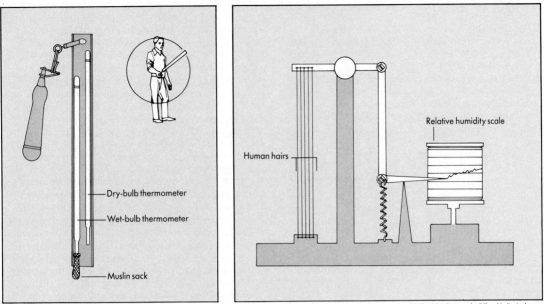

WORLD BOOK diagrams by Bill and Judie Anderson

Hygrometers measure the amount of moisture in the air. They include the *sling* or *whirled psychrometer, left,* and the *hair hygrometer, right.* The psychrometer has two thermometers. The bulb of one is covered with a wet muslin sack. When the psychrometer is whirled in nonsaturated air, the wet bulb records a lower temperature than the dry bulb. The difference in temperature is converted to relative humidity with a chart. A hair hygrometer uses a bundle of human hairs to measure relative humidity. One end of the bundle is connected to a lever that moves a pointer on a relative humidity scale. The humidity changes the length of the hair, moving the pointer.

History. Until the 1500's, most Christians sang hymns in Latin. During the Protestant Reformation, which began in Europe in 1517, many churches began to conduct religious services in their national language. Martin Luther, a German leader of the Reformation, wrote numerous hymns in German and translated a number of Latin hymns. In England, Switzerland, and other countries where many churches followed the teachings of John Calvin, a French religious reformer, most Christians sang only Biblical Psalms during religious services. As a result, verse translations of the Psalms became the chief hymns in those countries.

During the 1700's, Isaac Watts, known as the Father of English Hymnody, broke the tradition of basing hymns on the Psalms and wrote many original hymns. Charles Wesley, another great hymnist of the 1700's, wrote about 9,500 sacred poems, most of which were sung as hymns. Over 500 of Wesley's hymns are still sung.

In the 1800's, Fanny Crosby, an American hymnist, wrote more than 8,000 hymns. During the late 1800's, Dwight Lyman Moody, an American evangelist, and Ira D. Sankey, an American gospel singer, used many of Crosby's hymns in revival meetings throughout the United States. The tunes they sang became popular and are used in many churches today.   Leonard W. Van Camp

Related articles in *World Book* include:

Bay Psalm Book	Luther, Martin	Newman, John
Brooks, Phillips	Mason, Lowell	Henry Cardinal
Cowper, William	National anthem	Watts, Isaac
Howe (Julia W.)		Wesley, Charles

Hyperactive child is a youngster who is overactive in the classroom or in other situations in which such activity is inappropriate. Physicians call hyperactivity *hyperkinesis* or *hyperkinetic impulse disorder.*

Most hyperactive children can concentrate on a game or a work assignment for only a few minutes, and so they seldom carry out instructions. As a result, they tend to fall behind in school, even though most of them have normal or even superior intelligence. Other children and adults may regard them as disobedient, stubborn, or simply "bad." From 1 to 5 per cent of the elementary-school children in the United States suffer from hyperactivity. Most hyperactive children are boys.

Physicians believe many cases of hyperkinesis result from a physical disorder, such as a problem in the functioning of the brain. Hyperactivity also may result from social problems at home or at school, or from a combination of physical and social difficulties. Some evidence suggests that dyes and other additives in their food may aggravate hyperactive behavior in an extremely small number of children.

Many doctors treat hyperkinesis with stimulant drugs, such as amphetamines. These drugs calm from half to two-thirds of the children treated. Tranquilizers are prescribed for some hyperactive children, but many physicians oppose the use of stimulants or tranquilizers in treating hyperkinesis. These physicians believe too little is known about the drugs' long-term effects.

Some schools use special teaching methods to help hyperactive children increase their ability to concentrate and to complete assignments. A school may also provide counseling for both the children and their parents. Many hyperactive children become calmer as they grow older. But some never completely overcome their prob-

lems in learning and in getting along with others.
Frank M. Hewett

Hyperbola, *hy PUR buh luh,* is a curve with two branches formed by a plane that cuts through two right circular cones that are joined at their tips. Circles, ellipses, hyperbolas, and parabolas all intersect a cone-shaped surface and so are called *conic sections.*

The equation $y = \frac{1}{x}$, when graphed, shows a hyperbola. As *x* increases, the curve flattens out and approaches a straight line called an *asymptote.* The two points at which the axis of a hyperbola's plane intersects

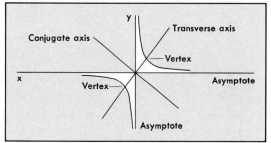

WORLD BOOK diagram

A hyperbola can be produced by graphing the mathematical equation $y = \frac{1}{x}$, as shown in the diagram above.

the two branches are called the *vertices.* The *transverse axis* connects the vertices. A line called the *conjugate axis* bisects the transverse axis and is perpendicular to it.
Philip S. Marcus

Hyperbole, *hy PUR buh lee,* is a figure of speech which is an exaggeration. People often use expressions such as "I nearly died laughing" and "I tried a thousand times." Such statements are not literally true, but people make them to sound impressive or to emphasize something, such as a feeling, effort, or reaction. Sometimes there is humor in such statements, and usually everybody knows they are not true. Hyperboles are common in everyday speech and in literature.   Paul B. Diehl

See also **Humor** (The humor of words); **Metaphor.**

Hypericum. See Saint-John's-wort.

Hyperkinesis. See Hyperactive child.

Hyperopia. See Farsightedness.

Hypertension is the medical term for the disease commonly called *high blood pressure.* There are many varieties of hypertension. They range from mild forms to an extremely severe—and often rapidly fatal—type called *malignant hypertension.* High blood pressure is not only a serious condition by itself, but it is also the leading cause of heart attacks, strokes, and kidney failure.

Many people of all ages suffer from hypertension. About 20 per cent of the people of the United States have the disease. The percentage of black Americans who suffer from hypertension is about twice as large as the percentage of white Americans who have it.

Measurements of blood pressure are written as a fraction. For example, the normal blood pressure for a young adult is 120/80. Most physicians believe that a reading greater than 140/95 for an adult indicates hypertension. For information about such figures and how doctors obtain them, see **Blood pressure.**

Causes. Some cases of hypertension result from other illnesses, such as kidney disease or overactive

adrenal glands. However, physicians cannot determine the cause of high blood pressure in about 90 per cent of the cases. They call such cases *essential hypertension.* People whose parents have hypertension are much more likely to develop the ailment than those whose parents have normal blood pressure. *Obesity* (fatness), stress, smoking, or eating too much salt may trigger hypertension in people who have inherited such a tendency. These conditions and habits may also make the disease worse in people who already have it.

Physicians know that an enzyme called *renin* plays an important role in regulating blood pressure. Renin is secreted by the kidneys under certain circumstances, such as a drop in the pressure of the blood flowing through the kidneys. Renin causes the formation of a chemical substance called *angiotensin,* which raises the blood pressure by causing the blood vessels to *constrict* (become narrower). Angiotensin also stimulates the adrenal glands to secrete the hormone *aldosterone.* Aldosterone causes the body to retain sodium, which, in turn, then causes the body to retain fluids. The extra fluid increases the volume of the blood, thereby further raising the blood pressure. After the blood pressure has risen to a certain level, the kidneys normally stop secreting renin. But in many people with essential hypertension, something interferes with this controlling system. In such cases, the blood pressure remains elevated. When the pressure is high inside the heart, the heart releases a hormone called *atrial natriuretic factor.* This hormone helps lower the blood pressure by inhibiting the secretion of renin and aldosterone.

Effects. In most cases, hypertension produces no symptoms until dangerous complications occur. For example, it can cause an artery in the brain to burst, producing a stroke. High blood pressure also forces the heart to work harder, and so it may cause a heart attack. The disease can cause kidney failure by reducing the flow of blood to the kidneys. In addition, high blood pressure is a major cause of *arteriosclerosis* (hardening of the arteries).

Treatment. People of all ages should have their blood pressure checked frequently. Many cases of mild hypertension can be controlled by weight reduction, avoidance of salty foods, and increased exercise. Physicians can control almost all other cases with drugs, including some medications that reduce the secretion of renin and aldosterone. The more serious consequences of hypertension, such as heart attacks and strokes, can be prevented by treating high blood pressure before it reaches dangerous levels.   John H. Laragh

See also **Reserpine.**

Additional resources

Kahn, Ada P. *High Blood Pressure.* Contemporary Books, 1983.
Rees, Michael K. *The Complete Family Guide to Living with High Blood Pressure.* Prentice-Hall, 1980.

Hyperthyroidism. See Thyroid gland.

Hyperventilation is abnormally rapid, deep breathing. It occurs most frequently if anxiety or emotional stress stimulates the part of the brain that regulates breathing. Certain illnesses, such as kidney failure and diabetes, may also trigger hyperventilation. However, the condition is rarely a serious medical problem.

During hyperventilation, a person exhales too much

carbon dioxide. As the level of carbon dioxide in the blood drops, the blood vessels narrow, allowing less blood to circulate. If too little blood reaches the brain, the person feels dizzy and may faint. The calcium in the blood also decreases, causing some muscles and nerves to twitch. The twitching may result in a tingling or stabbing sensation near the mouth or in the chest.

Some symptoms of hyperventilation resemble those of certain heart or lung ailments. These symptoms include a tight feeling in the chest, as though the lungs cannot receive enough air. This sensation leads to faster and deeper breathing. The heart may begin to pound, and the pulse rate may rise. Such symptoms increase a person's anxiety, which can make the condition worse.

An attack of hyperventilation may last 30 minutes or longer. People who hyperventilate can help control attacks by trying to slow their breathing rate when symptoms of the condition appear. They also can exhale into a paper bag and rebreathe the exhaled air to restore lost carbon dioxide to the body.　　Brian J. Sproule

Hyphen. See Punctuation.

Hypnos was the god of sleep in Greek mythology. The Romans called him Somnus. Hypnos was a kind and gentle youth, but he had the power to lull to sleep even the mightiest gods. His mother was Nyx, the goddess of night, but he had no father. Thanatos (Death) was his brother. Hypnos had hundreds of sons, called the Dreams. The most famous was Morpheus (see **Morpheus**). Hypnos lived in a large cave where he slept on a soft, dark bed. Everything in the cave helped bring about sleep. Lethe, the river of forgetfulness, flowed through the cave.　　Justin M. Glenn

Hypnotic. See Sedative.

Hypnotism, *HIHP nuh tihz uhm,* is the scientific and clinical use of *hypnosis*. Hypnosis, or a *hypnotic state,* is a temporary condition of altered attention in an individual. A hypnotist is a person who uses hypnotism. Scientific evidence suggests that hypnotism is useful when it is practiced by qualified professionals. For example, some professionals use hypnotism to treat patients who have certain medical or psychological problems.

People have used hypnotic techniques since ancient times. But the practice of hypnotism has been condemned at times because of its misuse or because of ignorance, mistaken beliefs, and overstated claims. Today, professional organizations accept hypnotism when it is used for valid medical or scientific purposes.

What hypnotism is

Scientists have shown that hypnosis is a natural part of human behavior that affects psychological, social, and physical experience. There is no magic connected with hypnotism, and the hypnotist has no special power. The effects of hypnotism depend on the ability, willingness, and motivation of the person being hypnotized. In hypnosis, a change in the quality and focus of a person's attention alters his or her internal and external experience.

Hypnosis has been compared to dreaming and sleepwalking. The term *hypnosis* comes from the Greek word *hypnos,* which means *sleep.* However, hypnosis is not actually related to sleep. It involves a more active and intense mental concentration. Hypnotized people can talk, write, and walk about. They are usually fully aware of what is said and done.

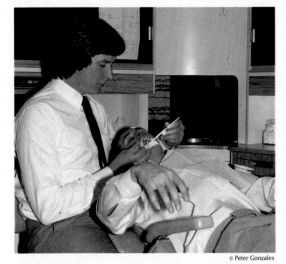

© Peter Gonzales

A hypnotized patient can undergo dental work with no pain or other discomfort. This patient has been told under hypnosis to keep his right arm raised. As long as his arm remains raised, the dentist knows he is still in a hypnotic trance.

A hypnotist uses certain methods to *induce* (guide) hypnosis in another person. As the person responds to the methods, the person's state of attention changes. This altered state often leads to various other changes or phenomena. For example, the person may experience different levels of awareness, consciousness, imagination, memory, and reasoning or become more responsive to suggestions. Additional phenomena may be produced or eliminated. Such phenomena may include sensations, blushing, blood flow, sweating, paralysis, tensing of muscles, and *anesthesia* (loss of pain sensation). Scientists have shown that changes in almost every body function and system may occur with hypnosis.

None of the experiences of hypnosis are unique. Some or all of the phenomena can occur without the use of hypnotic techniques. For example, people who are very responsive to hypnosis show an increased responsiveness to suggestions before they are hypnotized. This responsiveness increases during hypnotism.

People once believed that hypnotists could force their subjects to perform criminal acts or other actions against the subjects' will. There is no clear evidence to show that hypnosis causes such behavior. Hypnotized people can and do resist suggestions. They do not lose control of their actions and can distinguish between right and wrong.

Public performances of hypnotism are responsible for many popular misconceptions about hypnosis. Many people are first exposed to hypnotism through a magic show or a motion picture. Such presentations often make hypnotism appear simple. They may tempt untrained people to try to perform hypnotism on themselves or on other people. Because of these possible dangers, many governments have outlawed public performances of hypnotism.

The hypnotic experience

Some people can go into hypnosis within a few seconds or minutes. Others cannot be hypnotized easily.

There are various levels of hypnosis. For example, with light hypnosis, the person becomes rested and follows simple directions easily. In deep hypnosis, complete anesthesia may be experienced. The level of hypnosis is not usually related to the effectiveness of treatment.

Inducing hypnosis in another person can be achieved through several techniques. Perhaps the best-known techniques use direct commands. These commands consist of simple suggestions repeated continuously in much the same tone of voice. The hypnotist instructs the subject to focus his or her attention on an object or fixed point, such as a spot on the ceiling. Then the hypnotist tells the subject to relax, breathe deeply, and allow the eyelids to grow heavy and to close.

Many professionals use verbal and nonverbal techniques known as *indirect inductions.* Such procedures usually omit the use of a focal object. The subject responds to a story or a mental puzzle presented by the hypnotist. The hypnotist does not tell the patient to relax or to close the eyes. Instead, the hypnotist suggests these actions indirectly through the story or puzzle. The hypnosis treatment remains much the same.

Some hypnotists give their subjects a challenge suggestion to test for hypnosis. For example, the hypnotist may say, "You will have difficulty moving your right hand." The person may then find the movement difficult or impossible to perform. Such tests do not necessarily indicate a hypnotic state. They may merely demonstrate a person's response to suggestion.

Historically, various drugs occasionally have been used to help induce hypnosis. These drugs include thiopental ("truth serum"), alcohol, and other drugs. However, drugs and special tools or other gimmicks are rarely necessary for inducing hypnosis. Most professionals do not make use of them.

Hypnotic phenomena. There are many individual differences in what a person experiences with hypnosis. A hypnotized person may experience changes in awareness, creative imagination, reasoning, and wakefulness. Physical changes within the body also may be produced by suggestion. These phenomena include changes in blood flow, blood pressure, heart rate, and sensations of cold and heat.

Professionals sometimes concentrate on a certain phenomenon of hypnosis to help treat their patients. One useful phenomenon is the ability of some hypnotized people to remember forgotten experiences. After people have a shocking or painful experience, they often *repress* (block) memories associated with the experience from their conscious thoughts. Sometimes, the repressed memories influence the individual's normal behavior and may result in certain forms of mental illness. For example, during World War II (1939-1945), soldiers occasionally developed *amnesia* (loss of memory) as a result of some of their experiences. By hypnotizing these patients, doctors were able to help the patients remember their experiences and relieve the emotional tensions that had built up. This treatment helped the patients regain their health.

Another hypnotic phenomenon is called *age regression.* The doctor suggests that the hypnotized patient is a certain age. The patient may then recall or "relive" incidents in his or her life. If the doctor suggests that the patient is 7 years old, for example, the patient may appear to talk, act, and even think much as a 7-year-old. In this way, patients may remember events and feelings that may have had some bearing on their present illness. The patient can then reinterpret the situation with additional information and increased coping skills.

Sometimes, on the hypnotist's command, subjects may believe they are living in some past or future time. They may feel that they have traveled back to the Middle Ages or on to the next century. Untrained hypnotists may look upon such changes as proof that the individual was or will be reincarnated. Professionals consider these fantasies to be much the same as dreams.

Ending the hypnosis session is generally not difficult. A person usually remains in hypnosis until given a signal by the hypnotist. The hypnotist may count to five, make an indirect suggestion, or produce some type of sound. Sometimes the subject ends the experience even when no signal is given. Occasionally a hypnotist may have difficulty ending the hypnosis. This problem is one of the reasons why only trained professionals should practice hypnotism.

Uses of hypnotism

Modern methods of hypnotism have helped scientists increase their understanding of the human mind and body, and normal and abnormal behavior. Hypnotism is used in research; in medicine, particularly surgery and dentistry; and in psychotherapy (see **Psychotherapy**). Hypnosis has occasionally been used in legal cases.

Hypnotism has been the subject and a tool in many studies. Tests have been developed to measure a person's hypnosis experience. Research has shown that children can usually be hypnotized more easily than adults and that males and females can be hypnotized.

Some physicians use hypnosis as a sedative to soothe patients who are nervous or in pain. Some patients become less aware of pain with hypnosis, while others report no pain at all. Physicians may use deep hypnosis as a form of anesthesia, so that patients will feel no pain while undergoing surgery or childbirth. Hypnotism has also been used to lessen the discomfort of patients recovering from surgery or other medical procedures.

Physicians also have made use of the ability of a hypnotized person to remain in a given position for long periods of time. In one case, doctors had to graft skin onto a patient's badly damaged foot. First, skin from the person's abdomen was grafted onto his arm. Then the graft was transferred to his foot. With hypnosis, the patient held his arm tightly in position over his abdomen for three weeks, then over his foot for four weeks. Even though these positions were unusual, the patient at no time felt uncomfortable.

Some dentists may use hypnotism as an anesthetic. After the patient has been hypnotized, the dentist drills the tooth and fills the cavity. The patient remains relaxed and feels comfortable throughout the procedure.

Mental health professionals who may use hypnotism include psychiatrists, psychologists, and clinical social workers. Therapists may use hypnosis as the main focus or as a part of the treatment. Hypnotism may be used to calm disturbed patients. This treatment may help the patients to become more aware of their feelings, modify their behavior, and learn new ways of thinking and solving problems. Psychological conditions that have been

© Peter Gonzalez

Under hypnosis, people can sometimes be made to believe they are living in an earlier period of their lives. The woman in the photograph has been told under hypnosis that she is 7 years old. The top of the illustration at the left shows how she wrote her name and the date before hypnosis. The bottom portion shows these items as she wrote them while hypnotized.

treated through hypnosis include anxiety, depression, phobias, stress, and problem solving.

Hypnosis helps some people control or stop such problem habits as eating disorders and smoking. Hypnotism has been used to improve learning, reading, sleep, speech problems, sports performance, and behavioral problems.

Hypnotism can also be effective in controlling certain physical problems that are linked to psychological factors. These so-called *psychophysiological* problems include certain conditions in the nervous system, as well as some ailments of the heart, stomach, and lungs. Hypnotism occasionally has aided in the treatment of patients with chronic illnesses like arthritis, cancer, multiple sclerosis, pain, and stroke.

Hypnosis occasionally has been used with witnesses and victims of crime. In hypnosis, people may remember important clues, such as a criminal's physical appearance or another significant detail that might help in solving the crime. Care must be taken to also obtain independent information as people can lie and make mistakes while hypnotized. Hypnosis cannot make a person give away a secret.

Dangers of hypnotism

Hypnotism can only be dangerous if it is abused. Only a qualified professional should practice hypnotism. Although many people can learn to hypnotize, the skill is not a substitute for training in medicine and psychology. People who practice hypnotism need sufficient education and experience to be able to analyze a condition, determine that hypnosis is an appropriate treatment, and evaluate the results.

An untrained person cannot deal with the difficulties that might occur as the result of inappropriately hypnotizing an individual. For example, an unqualified hypnotist may give treatment for the wrong condition or may overlook significant details. An inappropriate suggestion may mask or cover an illness or symptom. If the hypnotist uses an incorrect method or approach, a symptom may be interpreted as a completely different problem. The symptom may remain undetected, and the

subject may not learn the proper skills for solving the real problem. In addition, appropriate nonhypnosis treatment techniques may be ignored or may not be used effectively.

The American Medical Association (AMA) requires all physicians who use hypnosis to do so only for purposes related to their special practice. Similar standards have been set for clinical psychologists and dentists. Ethical codes usually stop professionals from advertising themselves as hypnotists and from listing the problems they treat. Some physicians, dentists, and psychologists take specialty board examinations that certify that they have met advanced qualifications in the use of hypnotism.

Many scientists believe that the use of hypnotism in legal situations can cause serious problems. In 1985, the Council on Scientific Affairs of the AMA reported that memories refreshed through hypnosis may include inaccurate information, false memories, and *confabulation* (fact and fantasy combined). The report recommended guidelines for the legal use of hypnosis. In 1987, the U.S. Supreme Court ruled that in some instances recollections obtained through hypnosis could be used by defendants as testimony in criminal cases.

Some people learn self-hypnosis, also called *autohypnosis.* Self-hypnosis should be used only after an expert has determined that it is the appropriate treatment for the particular problem. A person learning self-hypnosis should have professional instruction. Complications may arise if self-hypnosis is practiced incorrectly.

History

Throughout history, various cultures and groups have used rituals and techniques that can best be described as hypnotism. Hypnotic experiences have been described by the ancient Egyptians and Greeks and by tribal cultures. References to deep sleep and anesthesia have been found in the Old Testament and in the Talmud, a collection of sacred writings of Judaism.

Mesmerism. The scientific development of hypnotism can be traced to the efforts of Franz Anton Mesmer, an Austrian physician who became prominent during the 1770's. Mesmer called his work *animal magnetism.*

Some people believed that disease developed when invisible magnetic fluids were cut off or improperly distributed. Mesmer used water tubs and magnetic wands to direct the supposed fluids to his patients. Many patients claimed that this treatment cured them.

In 1784, a French commission was formed to study the claims of Mesmer and his followers. The commission reported that the magnetic fluids did not exist. It explained the cures as a product of the patients' imagination.

Many of Mesmer's patients and students helped spread the belief in animal magnetism, which became known as *mesmerism.* Students of mesmerism continued to experiment with some of his methods. Some of these people soon found that magnets or fluids were unnecessary.

Scientific studies. The term *hypnotism* was used by James Braid, a British physician who studied suggestion and hypnosis in the mid-1800's. Braid pointed out that hypnosis differed from sleep and that hypnotism was a physiological response in the subject, not the result of secret powers. Perhaps Braid's most valuable contribution was his attempt to define hypnotism as a phenomenon that could be scientifically studied. During this same period, James Esdaile, a Scottish doctor working in India, began to use hypnotism as an anesthetic in major surgery, including leg amputations. He performed about 200 operations with the aid of hypnosis.

During the late 1800's, the French neurologist Jean Martin Charcot performed landmark experiments involving hypnosis. He found that hypnosis relieved many nervous conditions. His clinic for nervous disorders achieved a widespread reputation among scientists of the time, including the French psychologist Alfred Binet and the Austrian physician Sigmund Freud. Also in the late 1800's, the French physicians Hippolyte Bernheim and Ambroise Auguste Liébeault explored the role of suggestibility in hypnosis. These two scientists used hypnosis to treat more than 12,000 patients.

Freud was especially interested in the work of Charcot and Bernheim. He used hypnotized people in his early studies of the unconscious state. For various reasons, Freud abandoned the use of hypnosis in his clinical practice. However, he continued to view hypnosis as an important research phenomenon. Late in his life, Freud modified his once negative views on hypnotism. See **Freud, Sigmund.**

During the early 1900's, the Russian physiologist and psychologist Ivan Pavlov sought to discover a physiological basis of hypnosis. Pavlov maintained that hypnosis is based on *inhibition* (blockage) of certain nerve impulses in the brain.

Hypnotism became widely used by physicians and psychologists during World War I and World War II. Hypnosis was used to treat battle fatigue and mental disorders resulting from war. After the wars, scientists found additional uses of hypnotism in clinical treatment.

Various American scientists have made important advances in the study of hypnotism during the 1900's. Morton Prince showed that hypnotized people can maintain several mental activities at the same time. Clark L. Hull demonstrated that hypnosis is a form of heightened suggestibility. Milton H. Erickson developed new strategies of hypnotism by combining clinical and research

techniques. Harold Crasilneck showed that hypnotic strategies can be effective with stroke patients. Herbert Spiegel described the natural hypnotic talents of patients. The studies of Ernest and Josephine Hilgard helped increase understanding of pain mechanisms in the body. Research by Martin and Emily Orne showed the importance of social and psychological factors in hypnosis.   Ray William London

Related articles in *World Book* include:

Mental illness	Psychology
Mesmer, Franz	Psychotherapy
Psychiatry	Suggestion
Psychoanalysis	Trance

Additional resources

Buranelli, Vincent. *The Wizard from Vienna: Franz Anton Mesmer.* Coward, 1975.
Wallace, Benjamin. *Applied Hypnosis: An Overview.* Nelson, 1979.
Wolberg, Lewis R. *Hypnosis: Is It for You?* Dembner, 1982.

Hypochlorous acid, *hy puh KLAWR uhs,* is a weak, inorganic acid that forms when chlorine is added to water. It is unstable and decomposes rapidly when exposed to heat or light. Hypochlorous acid is used as a household bleach and disinfectant. Chemists believe that when chlorine is added to swimming pools and city water supplies, it is the hypochlorous acid that forms which kills the bacteria. Neutralizing hypochlorous acid produces salts called *hypochlorites.* Both the acid and its salts are powerful oxidizing agents.

Hypochlorous acid is the weakest chlorine acid. Its chemical formula is $HOCl$, but it is sometimes written $HClO$. Hypochlorous acid is relatively unstable and has never been isolated in pure form. It usually occurs as a dilute solution of $HOCl$ in water.   Carolyn J. Smith

Hypochondria, *HY puh KAHN dree uh,* is a state of mind in which people persistently and morbidly worry about their health, even though they have no disease. Such people, convinced that they are ill, complain of puzzling symptoms. They seek, and may receive, various medical treatments. But at best, they get only temporary relief. Vague symptoms of this kind are frequently seen in people with various types of mental illness, such as hysteria. In popular usage, any person complaining of vague or persistent symptoms may be called a *hypochondriac.* See also **Mental illness; Neurosis.**

Nancy C. Andreasen

Hypodermic injection is a method for administering drugs under the skin. The equipment for the injection includes a *syringe* and a hollow needle. A syringe is a tube with a plunger attached. The needle has a sharp point that permits it to easily slip into the skin. The doctor attaches the needle to the syringe barrel, puts the liquid medicine in the syringe, and inserts the needle into the patient's skin. Then, the doctor presses on the plunger to force the medicine through the needle. The hollow needle was invented in 1844 by Francis Rynd, an Irish physician. Charles Pravaz, a French physician, invented the first practical metal syringe in 1853. See **Syringe.**

Hypodermic injections are named for the tissue into which the injection is made. *Intradermal injections* are made between the layers of skin. For these, the doctor inserts a needle just under the top layer of skin. Injections made beneath the outer layers of skin are called subcutaneous injections. Intramuscular injections are given into deep muscle tissue. A hypodermic needle can be inserted into a vein to give medicine intravenously (see **Intravenous injection**).   Edwin S. Munson

Hypoglycemia, *HY poh glih SEE mee uh,* is a condition that occurs when the blood does not contain enough *glucose* (sugar). Glucose provides energy for the body's cells. Some cells require a continuous supply of glucose. The nerve cells, especially those of the brain, are most seriously affected by too little glucose.

The symptoms of hypoglycemia may include hunger, dilated pupils, headache, nervousness, rapidly pounding heartbeat, and sweating. People suffering from more severe hypoglycemia may show confusion, poor coordination, and slurred speech. In advanced cases, the patient may have convulsions and lose consciousness. In rare cases, brain damage or even death occurs.

Most cases of hypoglycemia occur among people who are taking medicine for diabetes. These people have too little *insulin,* a hormone that regulates the body's sugar. Their blood contains too much sugar, and so they take insulin or a hypoglycemic drug to lower the blood sugar. Hypoglycemia may occur if the dosage is too large or has a stronger effect than intended.

Physicians classify other cases of hypoglycemia into

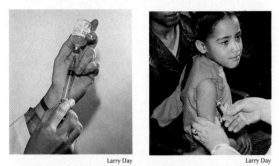

Larry Day   Larry Day

A typical hypodermic injection uses a *syringe,* a tube with a plunger, to inject drugs. A physician fills a syringe with typhoid vaccine, *left.* A child receives a vaccination, *right.*

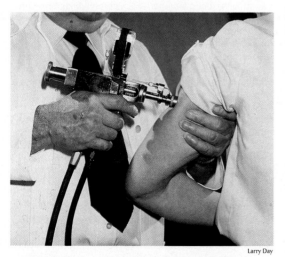

Larry Day

A jet injector gun, or *hypospray injector,* sprays vaccine through the skin at high pressure and requires no needle.

two groups—*organic* and *functional.* Organic hypoglycemia, which is much more severe than the functional condition, results from a physical abnormality. Various diseases of the liver may lead to organic hypoglycemia. The liver normally stores sugar as *glycogen* (animal starch). The liver reconverts glycogen to glucose and releases it into the blood as the cells need it. A diseased liver may fail to release the proper amounts of glucose. Disorders of the *endocrine* (hormone-producing) glands may also result in organic hypoglycemia. For example, some tumors of the pancreas, the organ that produces insulin, can release too much insulin. The treatment typically involves surgery to remove the tumor and thus correct the abnormality.

The major form of functional hypoglycemia is *reactive hypoglycemia,* which is simply an exaggeration of the body's normal reaction to eating. Normally, the amount of sugar in the blood increases for a few hours after a meal, especially one that includes many *carbohydrates* (starches and sugars). In many healthy people, the glucose level often may drop to a point clearly lower than that before the meal, and then rise back to the starting level. In most people, this drop in blood sugar is not noticed. In a person who has reactive hypoglycemia, the drop in blood sugar to below normal triggers symptoms of hypoglycemia. In most cases, without treatment, the symptoms disappear in a few minutes—or even sooner if the person eats something that contains sugar.

Functional hypoglycemia occurs far more frequently than organic hypoglycemia, but it is not a common condition. Some physicians once did not realize that a temporary fall in blood sugar often occurs normally in response to eating. This lack of knowledge led to widespread wrong diagnosis of functional hypoglycemia. Many common problems, such as fatigue, nervousness, and poor job performance, were blamed on the condition. Most doctors now agree that in most cases, these problems result from other causes. The treatment for functional hypoglycemia may include a diet that contains a planned balance of protein- and carbohydrate-containing foods.   Jesse Roth

Hypotenuse. See **Triangle.**

Hypothalamus, *hy puh THAL uh muhs,* is a small area at the base of the brain. It plays a key role in regulating the body's general level of activity. The hypothalamus helps control the *autonomic nervous system,* the part of the nervous system that regulates such automatic body processes as breathing and heart rate. The hypothalamus also controls the *pituitary gland,* the so-called "master gland" of the body's *endocrine* (hormone-producing) system.

Certain parts of the hypothalamus regulate body temperature, breathing, sleep, hunger, thirst, urination, sexual drives, and emotions. Other portions produce hormones called *releasing hormones* or *releasing factors.* The releasing hormones travel in the bloodstream directly to the *anterior lobe* (front part) of the pituitary gland and control the secretion of individual pituitary hormones. The pituitary hormones, in turn, affect many of the body's endocrine glands. These glands secrete hormones that influence growth, sexual development, and the rate at which the body changes food into energy and living tissue.

In addition to the releasing hormones, the hypothamus produces the hormones *vasopressin, oxytocin,* and *somatostatin.* These hormones are stored in, and released by, the *posterior lobe* (rear part) of the pituitary gland. Vasopressin, which is also known as *antidiuretic hormone,* reduces the amount of water lost from the body in urine. Oxytocin helps regulate the birth process and milk production in females. Somatostatin slows the secretion of growth hormone.   Don H. Nelson

See also **Brain; Gland; Pituitary gland; Stress.**

Hypothermia, *HY puh THUR mee uh,* is a condition in which the temperature of the human body is below the normal level of 98.6° F. (37° C). It generally results from accidental exposure to cold. But a physician may bring about hypothermia to perform various operations. During hypothermia, the activity of the organs and tissues slows down and their need for oxygen decreases.

Some cases of hypothermia occur among hunters, skiers, and others who get lost in cold weather. However, even exposure to indoor temperatures as high as 65° F. (18° C) can bring on hypothermia. Such cases occur most often among elderly people, many of whom lose the ability to sense cold. A victim of hypothermia may die if the body continues to lose heat. The body can be rewarmed by placing the victim in warm water and later wrapping him or her in warm blankets.

The heart rate and blood pressure decrease during mild to moderate hypothermia—95° to 82° F. (35° to 28° C). Breathing is slower and shallower. From 86° to 82° F. (30° to 28° C), the victim becomes unconscious. During deep hypothermia—64° to 59° F. (18° to 15° C)—the action of the heart, the flow of the blood, and the electrical activity of the brain stop completely.

Doctors may bring on hypothermia to perform brain or open heart surgery, or other operations for which they want to stop the circulation of blood. At the normal body temperature, many organs would be permanently damaged if they did not receive oxygen from the blood for more than a few minutes. The brain would be damaged beyond repair without oxygen for more than 3 to 5 minutes. But during deep hypothermia, the blood flow can be safely stopped for an hour or even longer.

Hypothermia may be produced by putting the patient into ice water. If the physician uses a heart-lung machine, the blood can be cooled before it reenters the patient's body (see **Heart** [Treatment of heart problems; picture]). Sometimes these methods are combined. The body temperature is returned to normal by heating the blood as it goes through the heart-lung machine, or by placing the patient in special blankets or warm water.

Milton Weinberg, Jr.

Hypothesis. See Science (Forming a hypothesis).

Hyrax. See Cony.

Hyssop, *HIHS uhp,* is a bushy evergreen shrub of the mint family. The plant comes from southern Europe and now grows in the warm parts of the United States. The hyssop has a square, coarse stem from 1 to 2 feet (30 to 61 centimeters) high. The seeds, flow-

© Giuseppe Mazza

Hyssop

ers, and green parts of the plant have a strong odor and taste. At one time, people used hyssop to season foods and as a medicine. Most people prefer milder flavors today, and they no longer use it as an herb. Gardeners sometimes plant hyssop as a shrub for the borders of lawns and gardens. The Bible mentions hyssop, but the plant may not be the same one that is known today.

Scientific classification. The hyssop belongs to the mint family, Labiatae. It is *Hyssopus officinalis.*   J. J. Levison

Hysterectomy, *HIHS tuh REHK tuh mee,* is the surgical removal of the *uterus,* the organ in which unborn babies develop. This surgery also includes the removal of the Fallopian tubes. If only the uterus and Fallopian tubes are taken out, the operation is called a *subtotal hysterectomy.* A total hysterectomy includes the additional removal of the *cervix,* the mouth of the uterus. In some cases, the surgeon also removes one or both ovaries while performing a hysterectomy. See the **Reproduction** article for an explanation and diagram of the female reproductive system.

Menstruation ends after a woman has a hysterectomy, and she no longer can become pregnant. The "hot flashes" or other symptoms of hormonal changes that sometimes accompany menopause do not occur unless both ovaries have been removed (see **Menopause**).

The most common reason for a hysterectomy is the growth of fibroid tumors on the uterus. Such tumors are not cancerous, but they may cause pain or bleeding. A hysterectomy may also be necessary if hormonal imbalances produce irregular or extremely heavy uterine bleeding. Other reasons for the operation include cancer, a long-term infection, or the shifting of the uterus from its normal position.   Gretajo Northrop

Hysteria, *hihs TIHR ee uh,* is a mental illness in which a person has physical complaints when no physical cause can be found. The ancient Greek physician Hippocrates was one of the first to identify this disorder. He noticed that hysteria was common in women and thought it was caused by a displaced uterus. The word *hysteria* comes from *hystera,* the Greek word for *uterus.*

A person with hysteria may have any sort of physical complaint. The person may complain of heart disease, paralysis, sexual problems, stomach pains, vomiting, or weakness of the arms or the legs. In this way, hysteria may imitate any of many physical illnesses. Sometimes, the complaints are so frequent or severe that a doctor may think the patient actually has a physical illness, such as appendicitis. In these cases, the diagnosis of hysteria might not be made until surgery indicates that no physical illness is present.

People are often called hysterical when they are upset, excited, and unable to control their feelings. We often hear of "hysterical weeping" or "hysterical rage." Such outbursts of feeling may have nothing to do with the disorder that psychiatrists call hysteria. In some cases, they occur in normal people. They may also occur in people who have mental illnesses other than hysteria, as well as in those with hysteria.

Psychiatrists usually treat hysteria by using some type of psychotherapy or behavior therapy. Treatment with drugs and hypnosis may also be used along with the psychotherapy. The causes of hysteria are still not known, but the disorder remains more common in women than in men.   Nancy C. Andreasen